BASIC CRIMINAL PROCEDURE

CASES, COMMENTS AND QUESTIONS

Ninth Edition

By

Yale Kamisar

Clarence Darrow Distinguished University Professor of Law,
University of Michigan

Wayne R. LaFave

Professor Emeritus in the College of Law
and Center for Advanced Study,
University of Illinois

Jerold H. Israel

Ed Rood Eminent Scholar in Trial Advocacy and Procedure,
University of Florida, College of Law
Alene and Allan F. Smith Professor of Law,
University of Michigan

Nancy J. King

Professor of Law and Associate Dean,
Vanderbilt University School of Law

AMERICAN CASEBOOK SERIES®

WEST GROUP

A THOMSON COMPANY

ST. PAUL, MINN., 1999

American Casebook Series, and the West Group
symbol are used herein under license.

COPYRIGHT © 1994 WEST PUBLISHING CO.
COPYRIGHT © 1999 By WEST GROUP
        610 Opperman Drive
        P.O. Box 64526
        St. Paul, MN 55164–0526
        1–800–328–9352

ISBN 0–314–23899–9

*TEXT IS PRINTED ON 10% POST
CONSUMER RECYCLED PAPER*

2nd Reprint — 2001

Preface to the Ninth Edition

In many schools the student first wrestles with problems of the administration of criminal justice or "criminal procedure" in a short course, increasingly offered in the first year, or even in a large segment of the basic criminal law course. This volume, based on our much larger *Modern Criminal Procedure* (9th ed. 1999), deals almost exclusively with "police practices" and other investigative alternatives (see Ch. 10, dealing with grand jury investigations), and is published on the premise that it may serve as a basis for a "first course" on criminal procedure.

The success of the previous edition of this short volume confirms our belief that when allocated 30 (or even 45) class hours for criminal procedure (or a third or half of the crowded first-year criminal law course for procedural problems), many teachers will find it more useful and meaningful to explore in depth a few fundamental and closely related areas (e.g., search and seizure, electronic surveillance and entrapment, right to counsel, confessions and line-ups) than to make a whirlwind tour through the investigatory process, joinder and severance, speedy trial, "trial by newspaper" (and TV), criminal discovery, appeals, post-conviction review and all of the other topics treated in the 29 chapters of our larger book. In preparing this shorter volume, therefore, rather than shrinking down each chapter in the larger book, we have kept the first eleven chapters intact and omitted all others.

Because we contemplate that these materials will mark the student's first real exposure to the subject—and quite possibly her or his first real exposure to the U.S. Supreme Court as an institution—we have resisted the temptation to edit further the leading cases set forth at considerable length in our larger book (and we have taken pains to set forth the views of *all* Justices at length). For the same reasons, and because we feel strongly that the student should see the subsequently overruled or distinguished opinion "in the original" rather than rely on the overruling or distinguishing case's version of the earlier opinion, we have retained older cases which contribute significantly to an understanding of new trends and developments, e.g., *Betts v. Brady, Rochin, Boyd,* and *Wolf;* as well as such "stepping stone" cases as *Escobedo.*

This volume includes significant developments up to January 1, 1999. Important developments thereafter will appear in annual supplements, which will also contain relevant federal court rules and statutory materials. The supplement accompanying this book and published simultaneously with it will contain all notable cases handed down by the Supreme Court during the 1998-1999 Term. It will also include the recently revised Federal Rules of Criminal Procedure and proposed amendments to the rules.

Case citations in the text and the footnotes of judicial opinions and in the writings of commentators have been omitted without so specifying. Numbered footnotes are from the original materials; lettered footnotes are ours.[1] Omissions from the text of the original are indicated by asterisks and brackets.

One or more of the authors has been fortunate enough to participate actively in four major criminal procedure projects: The American Bar Association's project on *Standards for Criminal Justice*; The American Law Institute's *Model Code of Pre-Arraignment Procedure*; The National Conference of Commissioners on Uniform State Laws' *Uniform Rules of Criminal Procedure*; and the ongoing revision of the *Federal Rules of Criminal Procedure*. We are indebted to the members of the various committees with whom we have worked for providing us with many leads and insights. We are also indebted to the many users of this book who have offered helpful suggests on content as to this edition and previous editions. That list, like the list of our student research assistants over the years, has now grown far too long to mention each person individually.

We are especially appreciate of the able secretarial assistance provided on this ninth edition, too often under great stress, by Carol Haley, Carolyn Lloyd, Mary Lebert, Myrtle Smith, and Janice Stewart.

Finally, one additional note from Yale Kamisar, Wayne LaFave, and Jerry Israel: We are delighted that Nancy King has agreed to join us in this venture. We greatly appreciate the important contributions she has made to this new edition.

YALE KAMISAR
WAYNE R. LaFAVE
JEROLD H. ISRAEL
NANCY J. KING

June, 1999

---

1. Standard abbreviations are used throughout. On occasion, a book or article is used so frequently in a chapter as to call for a shorter citation form. Here we have given the full citation to the book or article in the first footnote of the chapter and indicated there the shorter citation form. For our own books, we simply have used the shorter citation form through the book. These are:

LaFave, *Search and Seizure: A Treatise on the Fourth Amendment* (2d ed. 1987), cited as LaFave § ___.

LaFave & Israel, *Criminal Procedure Hornbook* (2d ed.1992), cited as LaFave & Israel, § ___.

LaFave, Israel, and King, *Criminal Procedure Treatise* (forthcoming 2d ed.), cited as LaFave, Israel, and King, § ___.

Articles collected in Kamisar, *Police Interrogation and Confessions: Essays in Law and Policy* (1980) are usually cited as Kamisar Essays.

Acknowledgments

Excerpts from the following books and articles appear with the kind permission of the copyright holders.

Beale, Sara Sun, Reconsidering Supervisory Power in Criminal Cases: Constitutional and Statutory Limits on the Authority of the Federal Courts, 84 Colum.L.Rev. 1433 (1984). Copyright © 1984 by the Columbia Law Review Association. Reprinted by permission.

Bloom, Robert M.., Inevitable Discovery: An Exception beyond the Fruits, 20 Am.J.Crim.law 79 (1992). Copyright © 1992 by the American Journal of Criminal Law. Reprinted by permission.

Bradley, Craig, Two Models of the Fourth Amendment, 83 Mich.L.Rev. 1468 (1985). Copyright © 1985 by the Michigan Law Review. Reprinted by permission.

Caplan, Gerald, Questioning *Miranda*, 38 Vand.L.Rev. 1417 (1985). Copyright © 1985 by the Vanderbilt Law Review. Reprinted by permission.

Cassell, Paul G., *Miranda*'s Social Costs: An Empirical Assessment, 90 Nw.U.L.Rev. 387 (1996). Copyright © 1996 by the Northwestern University Law Review. Reprinted by special permission of Northwestern University School of Law, *Law Review*, vol. 90, issue 2, 1996.

Dressler, Joshua, Understanding Criminal Procedure (2d ed. 1997). Copyright © 1997 by Matthew Bender & Co. Inc. Reprinted by permission.

Goldsmith, Michael, The Supreme Court and Title III: Rewriting the Law of Electronic Surveillance, 74 J.Crim.L. & Criminology 1 (1983). Copyright © 1983 by the Northwestern University School of Law. Reprinted by permission.

Goldwasser, Katherine, After Abscam: An Examination of Congressional Proposals to Limit Targeting Discretion in Federal Undercover Investigations, 36 Emory L.J. 75 (1987). Copyright © 1987 by the Emory University School of Law. Reprinted by permission.

Grano, Joseph, Confessions, Truth and the Law (1993). Copyright © 1993 by the University of Michigan. Reprinted by permission.

Inbau, Fred, Police Interrogation—A Practical Necessity, 52 J. Criminology & P.S. 16 (1961). Copyright © 1962 by the Northwestern University School of Law. Reprinted by permission.

Kainen, James, The Impeachment Exception to the Exclusionary Rules: Policies, Principles, and Politics, 44 Stan.L.Rev. 1301 (1992). Copyright © 1992 by the Board of Trustees of the Leland Stanford Junior University. Reprinted by permission of the Stanford Law Review and Fred B. Rothman & Co.

Kamisar, Yale, Equal Justice in the Gatehouse and Mansions of American Criminal Procedure, in Kamisar, Inbau & Arnold, Criminal Justice in Our Time (Howard ed. 1965). Copyright © 1965 by the Rector and Visitors of the University of Virginia. Reprinted by permission.

_____, Killing *Miranda* in Baltimore: Reflections on David Simon's Homicide, Jurist: Books-on-Law, Feb. 1999, vol. 2, no. 2. Copyright © 1999 by Jurist: Books-on-Law. Reprinted by permission.

Kennedy, Randall L., Race, Crime, and the Law (1997). Copyright © 1997 by Randall L. Kennedy. Reprinted by permission.

Whitebread, Charles, and Slobogin, Christopher, Criminal Procedure (3d ed. 1993). Copyright © 1993 by The Foundation Press, Inc. Reprinted by permission.

Wollin, David, Policing the Police: Should *Miranda* Violations Bear Fruit?, 53 Ohio State L.J. 805 (1992). Copyright © 1992 by the Ohio State Law Journal. Reprinted by permission.

*

Summary of Contents

*

Table of Contents

PART TWO

POLICE PRACTICES

Table of Cases

The principal cases are in bold type. Cases cited or discussed in the text are roman type. References are to pages. For Commonwealth v. ___, People v. ___, State v. ___, United States v. ___, see the name of the other party. For Ex parte ___, In re ___, Matter of ___, see the name of the party. For People ex rel. ___, State ex rel. ___, United States ex rel. ___, see the name of the first party. Where a case is discussed in another case, reference is made only to the first page at which it is cited. No reference is made to discussion of a principle case in the Notes and Questions that follow that case.

*

Table of Articles, Books, Proposed Standards and Reports

Bold type indicates major extracts

*

BASIC CRIMINAL PROCEDURE

CASES, COMMENTS AND QUESTIONS

Ninth Edition

*

Part One

INTRODUCTION

Chapter 1

AN OVERVIEW OF THE CRIMINAL JUSTICE PROCESS

The materials in this book describe and discuss what is commonly referred to as the "American criminal justice process." Succinctly defined, a criminal justice process is that series of procedures through which the substantive criminal law is enforced. Part One of this book describes some general features of the American criminal justice process and the law that governs that process. Parts Two to Five then consider each of the major steps in the process. They do so largely following the chronological sequence of the process. Part Two treats the major legal issues presented in the detection and investigation of crime (basically "police practices"); Part Three considers a variety of issues flowing out the commencement of formal proceedings through the filing of charges; Part Four examines various steps in the process of adjudicating those charges; and finally, Part Five considers appellate and collateral review of the judicial decisions rendered throughout the process.

This chapter presents a brief overview of the basic structure of the American criminal justice process.[a] In actuality, there is no single American criminal justice process, but many different processes, and with diversity being one of the hallmarks of those processes, no one set of procedures is truly representative of the process as applied throughout the country. The laws that shape the process vary from one jurisdiction to another, and they sometimes vary even within the same jurisdiction according to the offense and the officials involved. The diversity becomes even greater when one takes account of differences, from one community to another, in the administration of the same laws. Accordingly, both in the step-by-step tracing of the process presented in section two of this chapter, and in the analysis of specific process stages presented in later chapters, some degree of overgeneralization has been inevitable.

In the first section of this chapter, we seek to partially compensate for those overgeneralizations by calling the reader's attention to several structural elements that account for much of the diversity in the process. If those elements are kept in mind in the course of reading the materials that follow in this and other chapters, the potential for variations beyond those specifically noted should be readily

a. The data cited in this chapter is taken from the various sources cited in LaFave, Israel, and King, *Criminal Procedure Treatise* § 1.3 (forthcoming 2nd ed.), which relies on the same statistics. Among those sources, the Bureau of Justice Statistics' *Sourcebook of Criminal Justice Statistics*, published annually, contains the most complete collection of criminal justice statistics.

apparent by reference to the general character of the law and the administrative setting applicable to a particular procedure.

SECTION 1. ELEMENTS OF DIVERSITY

1. *Fifty-two lawmaking jurisdictions.* Under our federated governmental structure, the federal government and each of the individual states has the authority to create its own substantive criminal law and its own criminal justice process for enforcing that law. Moreover, the federal government has chosen to divide its jurisdictional authority by creating a separate criminal code and criminal justice process for the District of Columbia, which stands apart from the general federal criminal justice system. As a result, we have fifty-two separate jurisdictions (i.e., the 50 states, the District of Columbia, and the general federal system), each with its own criminal justice process and its own law of criminal procedure.

In other fields in which the federal government and the states share regulatory authority, the federal system dominates and its regulatory impact far outstrips that of all of the states combined. That certainly has not occurred in the criminal justice field. Of the roughly 1.75 million felony cases prosecuted in this country each year, only about 3% are brought in the federal system. Of the more than 13 million prosecutions for minor offenses, less than 1% are brought in the federal system. Of course, the federal system has far greater influence than its small proportion of the total caseload might suggest. Due to its concentration upon certain types of crimes (e.g., white collar offenses) that often attract considerable public attention, and the number of states that look to it in modeling their own criminal justice process, the federal system is often characterized as the "most important" of the fifty-two lawmaking jurisdictions. Nonetheless, it remains no more than a leader among the fifty-two, not the actor that dwarfs all others.

2. *The importance of "local" law.* As discussed in Ch. 2, § 1, the commands of various Bill of Rights guarantees in the federal constitution apply to both federal and state criminal justice systems. Those guarantees, as interpreted by the Supreme Court, have given to the federal constitution a critical role in providing a common grounding for the law of criminal procedure throughout the country. The reach of federal constitutional regulation is limited, however. As to many parts of the process (e.g., the preliminary hearing), the constitution says very little. As to others, such as searches and seizures, federal constitutional regulation is extremely extensive, rivaling the Internal Revenue Code in its detail and complexity. Yet even such comprehensive constitutional regulation of a particular procedure typically leaves some gaps to be filled by "local laws" (i.e., the separate laws of each of the 52 jurisdictions). Moreover, the federal constitution establishes only the minimal level of rights that *must* be recognized in a jurisdiction. Each jurisdiction may by local law impose additional safeguards, and in many areas of constitutional regulation, a substantial portion of the fifty-two jurisdictions have done exactly that (requiring, for example, a unanimous jury verdict where the constitution would allow a less-than-unanimous verdict). The end result is that while federal constitutional law may be the most important single body of law regulating the criminal justice processes of this country, the local laws of the individual jurisdictions, in their combined impact, play at least an equally significant role in that regulation.

Within each jurisdiction, the local law will come from a variety of sources. For the state systems, those sources typically will be: (1) the state's constitution, (2) state statutes, (3) the state's general court rules, and (4) rulings of state courts based on their common law authority. In the federal system, counterpart statutes, court rules, and judicial rulings (here frequently based on the court's supervisory power, see Ch. 2, § 4) will be the primary sources of local law. Jurisdictions will vary in their reliance upon the different sources. What is governed by statute in one jurisdiction may be governed by court rule or common law ruling in another.

3. *Diversity in local law.* Of course, the allocation of substantial lawmaking responsibility to individual jurisdictions does not necessarily have to result in substantial variations in the law from one jurisdiction to another. Though given broad autonomy, the states could seek on their own initiative to achieve uniformity. In many other fields, the states have done exactly that, usually by adopting proposed uniform acts or by modeling their individual state laws after a dominant federal provision. In the criminal justice field, however, the states have followed that path only to a limited extent. One does find a basic process framework that is common to the fifty-two jurisdictions, having been derived from the heritage of the English common law and preserved in part by the commands of those Bill of Rights guarantees applicable to the state and federal systems. But beyond that basic framework, the most that one can expect to find in the way of uniformity is the clustering of the majority of jurisdictions around two or three alternative models, with at least a few (and often more) jurisdictions adopting an approach of their own which differs in important respects from all of those models. Moreover, even within a group of states that may be characterized as following a particular model, one or more will vary from that model in certain refinements.

Of the various models available to the states, arguably the most influential has been the court rules and statutes of the federal system. Roughly half of the states have court rules or statutory codes that borrow heavily from the Federal Rules of Criminal Procedure (set forth in App. C of the Supplement). While only a handful of these states have adopted almost complete replications of the Federal Rules, most incorporate more of the Rules' provisions than they reject. Similarly, prominent federal legislative reforms, such as the Bail Reform Acts of 1966 and 1984 and the Jury Selection Act of 1968 (see App. B), have served as models for numerous state statutes (although those statutes typically will depart from one or more of the basic provisions of the federal model). One factor that obviously has limited state use of federal law as a model is the striking differences in the institutional setting of federal enforcement. The crimes investigated and prosecuted in the federal system have a somewhat different character (with greater emphasis on white collar crime and less emphasis on street crime); federal enforcement officers have different qualifications, different training, and different responsibilities (which do not include the general peacekeeping, traffic control, and social service functions of local police departments); federal prosecutors exercise considerably more control over the investigative process, are not elected officials, and are subject to a central authority (the Attorney General); and federal trial judges are totally insulated from the electorate and have a criminal caseload which is substantial, but still considerably lighter than that carried by state trial judges of urban courts.

In many other fields in which the state enforcement setting is considerably different from the federal, distinguished groups within the legal profession have proposed models for state enactments that have been quite successful in achieving uniformity in state law. Those same groups have also been at work in the field of criminal procedure, but with much more limited impact. The American Law Institute put forth a Code of Criminal Procedure in 1931 and a Model Code of Pre–Arraignment Procedure in 1975. The National Conference of Commissioners on Uniform State Laws in 1952 adopted its first version of the Uniform Rules of Criminal Procedure, in 1974 substituted a completely revised Uniform Rules of Criminal Procedure, and in 1987 adopted a redraft of the 1974 Rules that produced the current version of the Uniform Rules. The American Bar Association completed its original version of the ABA's Standards for Criminal Justice in 1973, issued a revised second edition in 1978–79, and has recently introduced parts of its third edition. Although not offering nearly as comprehensive coverage, various national commissions, dating back to the Wickersham Commission of 1929–31, have advanced models for reform on particular aspects of the process.

The influence of these models has varied. All included proposals that were adopted in at least a few states, and most advance at least one proposal that gained the support of a substantial body of states. Only the ABA Standards, however, have had a widespread influence on numerous aspects of the process. The Standards have been cited thousands of times by appellate courts and have been utilized by numerous states in formulating their court rules or statutes. Unlike the Federal Rules, however, the Standards have been incorporated into state law on a piecemeal basis, with the state reforms typically looking either to an individual standard or a grouping of standards dealing with a particular aspect of the process (e.g., pretrial discovery). Still, the majority of the Standards have been incorporated into state law in at least a few states, and many reflect the governing law in most states.

4. *Diversity in the applicable law within a single jurisdiction.* Even within a single jurisdiction, the law governing the process will not be the same for each and every case. All fifty-two jurisdictions utilize at least a few lines of division that produce "procedural subsets," with separate legal standards for different categories of offenses or different categories of officials performing a particular administrative function.

Initially, most jurisdictions have at least a few special rules for specific types of offenses. The substantive criminal law that is enforced through the criminal justice process reaches a tremendously broad range of offenses. These include crimes of violence against the person, property crimes, public-order crimes, regulatory offenses, vice offenses, and misuses of positions of trust. A criminal justice process that provides for the investigation, prosecution, adjudication, and sentencing on such a broad range of offenses must allow for variations in process to accommodate certain differences among those crimes and the proof they require. In particular, the investigative procedures needed for effective enforcement often will vary with the nature of the crime. Ordinarily, the criminal justice system accommodates the need for process diversity by creating a full range of process options and leaving to the discretion of the officials involved the choice of the options to be used. On occasion, however, the law will limit the use of a particular process to a particular offense, as where electronic surveillance is restricted to certain specified offenses, preventive detention is made available only for certain types of crimes, or special venue rules are applied to particular crimes.

Far more common procedural subsets are those tied to the level of the criminal offense. The two traditional distinctions drawn in this regard separate procedures for capital felonies from other felonies and for minor crimes from major crimes. With capital punishment now limited to certain classes of murder, and a substantial group of states no longer authorizing capital punishment, the separate procedures utilized for capital cases are now of concern in a minute portion of the total felony caseload. Most of those special procedures relate to the capital sentencing hearing, but special rules for capital cases also often apply to other parts of the process (e.g., bail and waiver of prosecution by indictment).

Undoubtedly the most frequently utilized procedural dividing line is that distinguishing the processes applicable to major and minor crimes. All jurisdictions provide for separate treatment of major and minor crimes for at least a few aspects of the process, and some recognize major distinctions at almost every stage in the process. At the investigatory stage, the most common distinctions are likely to be different standards for arrest, the availability of alternatives to arrest for minor crimes, and the unavailability of certain procedures in investigating many minor crimes. In the charging process, the major distinction is that the defendant accused of a minor offense is not entitled to either a preliminary hearing or grand jury review—the two procedures commonly utilized for major offenses to provide independent screening of the prosecutor's charging decision. The trial and pretrial stages probably present the broadest range of distinctions between major and minor crimes. For minor crimes, the jurisdiction may provide a smaller jury (or no jury at all for some minor offenses), may not require any form of pretrial discovery, and may even relax some aspects of the rules of evidence.

In many jurisdictions, a single line is used to distinguish between minor and major offenses for all stages at which different procedures apply. That line is the substantive law's designation of the offense as a misdemeanor or felony.[a] Other jurisdictions use different lines to distinguish between minor and major offenses at different stages of the process. At the investigatory stage, a misdemeanor/felony distinction is drawn, but once charges are filed, the major distinction is between lower-level misdemeanors, usually those punishable by not more than a certain term of imprisonment (commonly six months or ninety days) and all higher offenses (i.e., misdemeanors not within the lower-level category are treated in much the same manner as felonies). Ordinance violations that duplicate in substance and penalty lower-level misdemeanors commonly are subject to the same procedures as those misdemeanors, but this too varies from one jurisdiction to another.

In general, jurisdictions impose the same legal restraints on all types of officials performing the same function in the criminal justice process. Thus, a state's "peace officers" will include officers in a wide range of agencies (e.g., sheriff's departments, municipal police departments, and state highway patrols), and it will impose the same general limitations upon basic police investigative authority (e.g., searches and interrogations) as to all of those officials. Occasionally, special limits will be imposed upon peace officers of agencies that have law enforcement responsibilities limited to particular geographical enclaves (e.g., park police) or to enforcement of a limited group of offenses (e.g., conservation officers), but those special limitations tend to be minor in nature. As to prosecutors, the law similarly tends to treat all the same, whether they are county prosecutors, attorneys for a municipality enforcing criminal ordinances, or a state attorney general with prosecutorial authority. The same ordinarily is true of defense counsel, whether retained private practitioners, or court appointed private practi-

a. American jurisdictions commonly use one of two different standards in distinguishing between felonies and misdemeanors. Some classify as felonies all offenses punishable by a maximum term of imprisonment of more than one year; offenses punishable by imprisonment for one year or less are then misdemeanors. Others look to the location of the possible imprisonment. If the offense is punishable by imprisonment in a penitentiary, it is a felony; if punishable only by a jail term, it is a misdemeanor. As a matter of practice, both dividing lines frequently produce the same result since state correction codes commonly provide for imprisonment in the penitentiary if a sentence exceeds one year and for imprisonment in jail if the sentence is for one year or less.

tioners, public defenders, or contract attorneys representing indigents. In the regulation of the judiciary, however, while trial judges of different courts of general jurisdiction usually are given the same authority, many states draw distinctions among the different courts assigned the functions of a magistrate.

The magistrate courts (known by various titles, including "justice of the peace courts," "municipal courts," "police courts," and "magistrate courts") are the courts of first instance in the administration of the criminal justice process. Their jurisdiction traditionally extends to the preliminary steps in the processing of felonies (e.g., issuance of arrest and search warrants, and presiding at the first appearance and the preliminary hearing) and trial authority over some or all misdemeanors. Roughly half the states have two or more different types of magistrate courts with territorial jurisdiction divided among those courts (e.g., municipal courts in urban districts, and justices of the peace in rural districts). Here, there often will be major differences in applicable trial procedures for misdemeanor cases, with the states distinguishing between those magistrate courts that are "courts of record" and those courts "not of record."

Historically, courts not of record lacked the capacity to prepare a complete transcript of their trials. Without that record, their convictions in misdemeanor cases could not be submitted to the next highest court (the general trial court) for the traditional form of appellate review. Accordingly, on appeal, the higher court would simply give the case *de novo* consideration through a new trial before that court. Although the *trial de novo* was described as a form of appellate "review," it was actually a second proceeding starting from scratch. Today, magistrate courts typically have the mechanical equipment needed to provide a complete recording of their proceedings. Nonetheless, the states with different types of magistrate courts continue to designate some of those courts as "not of record" and continue to utilize a *trial de novo*. That system has been retained in large part because of the nature of the misdemeanor trial provided in those courts. Courts not of record typically are designed to be " 'courts of convenience, to provide speedy and inexpensive means of disposition of minor charges.' " *Colten v. Kentucky,* 407 U.S. 104, 92 S.Ct. 1953, 32 L.Ed.2d 584 (1972). Accordingly, they commonly are authorized to utilize simplified procedures. In many, no jury trial is allowed, motion practice is restricted, discovery is limited, and the rules of evidence may not be followed precisely. In most states, judges in such courts need not be lawyers, and in the rural areas, they tend not to be lawyers.

5. *Diversity in administration.* The American criminal justice system commonly is pictured as presenting a tremendous chasm between its day-to-day practice and its doctrine. That chasm is often attributed to deviance by the professional participants in the process—that is, the failure of police, prosecutors, magistrates, trial judges, and defense counsel to follow the dictates of the law in the performance of their roles. Indeed, some (see Ch. 4) would contend that, for the police, deviance is a pervasive feature of administrative practice due to various influences that encourage police to disregard certain legal limits placed upon the investigative portion of the process. Even if that contention is accepted, however, it clearly is discretion, rather than deviance, that explains by far the largest part of what is characterized as the "gap" between the "law in the books" and the "law in action."

The law authorizes procedures and imposes certain limits on their use, but at the same time, it commonly grants to administrators the discretion that allows them not to use those procedures or to bypass those limitations. So too, the law grants certain rights to individuals that are subjected to the process, but at the same time gives them the discretion not to exercise those rights. The end result is that the various grants of discretion often produce a practice that looks quite different from what one might expect from a reading of constitutional provisions, statutes, court rules or judicial decisions. Those sources set forth process standards which may appear on their face to be mandated requirements, but are often rendered no more than possible options as a result of the discretion also allowed under the law. They speak of rights and powers, but discretion may produce a system in which those rights and powers are not exercised in many or most instances.

Discretion not only allows the practice to depart from what one might expect if simply looking to the law's basic statement of procedures, but it also allows for considerable diversity in the shaping of that practice. The range of that diversity will depend both on the extent of the discretion granted and the extent to which the administrative structure encourages or discourages uniformity in the exercise of discretion. The notes that follow deal initially with the general character of the grants of discretion in the criminal justice process, and then with elements in the administrative structure that bear upon the exercise of that discretion.

6. *The range of discretion.* Although not always recognized as an element of the discretion authorized in the criminal justice process, the choices given to the individual who is the target of governmental action (depending upon the stage of the proceeding, the suspect, the accused, or the convicted defendant) play an important role in shaping the actual operation of the process. In general, the law allows the individual to voluntarily relinquish the various limitations on governmental authority and procedural rights that are established for his benefit. Through the exercise of that option, he may expand the power of government and allow it to do legally what would be illegal absent his consent. Moreover, as is evident in the practice of plea bargaining, the government often may be allowed, through the use of concessions as to the exercise of its powers, to induce the individual to choose that option. The end result can be a practice that is characterized by the individual's exercise of certain rights (e.g., the right to trial) being the exception rather than the general rule.

The other side of discretion—the leeway granted to the public administrator (i.e., the police, prosecutor, magistrate, and trial judge) is much more varied in structure and range. At every stage of the criminal justice process, the law allows those administrators some leeway to shape the process through their exercise of discretion in the performance of the functions assigned to them. This authority is established through a legal normlessness that creates a regulatory vacuum and thereby grants the administrator legal autonomy either in deciding whether to exercise power at all, or in choosing between alternative paths for exercising power. The leeway granted to the administrator will vary with the nature of the decision. It tends to be broadest where the decision is not to exercise governmental power adversely to the individual (sometimes described as "ameliorative discretion"). Yet, even here, there usually are some legal limits. A prosecutor has great latitude, for example, in deciding not to prosecute, but that decision cannot be based on a bribe. Where the official exercises governmental power and the choice is between alternative procedures (e.g., the police officer's choice between taking a detained misdemeanant into custody or releasing him on issuance of a summons), the governing law tends to offer somewhat less discretionary latitude. Here the law typically will specify some general prerequisites for taking action, but then give the administrator a choice, based upon open-ended objectives, between different alternatives. In still other areas, the law will provide for a single procedure that is available only under specific conditions, but then allow the administrator some degree of discretion as to the timing and precise form given to that procedure.

Administrative discretion starts with the investigatory process, where the police initially have broad discretion in deciding whether or not to investigate, and then somewhat narrower discretion in choosing a particular mode of investigation. For many modes of investigation, certain legal prerequisites will be demanded, but once those are met, the police will have various options open to them (e.g., where a person is lawfully arrested, whether to simply frisk or conduct a full search). Prosecutorial discretion arguably is even broader than police discretion. Initially, the prosecutor has discretion not to charge even though the available evidence supports a charge. Once deciding to charge, the prosecutor will have available, depending upon the jurisdiction, a range of options that will shape the further proceedings. These may include the joinder or separate charging of multiple counts and parties, determining by the mode of charge whether review will be by preliminary hearing or grand jury, accepting or rejecting the waiver of a jury trial, and the offering or refusal to offer concessions in return for a guilty plea.

Judicial discretion tends to be considerably narrower than the discretion granted to the police or prosecutor. Also, there tends to be more variation among the states as to where and how much discretion is granted. At the magistrate level, some jurisdictions grant considerable discretion on bail setting, both as to the procedure and the factors evaluated, while others confine the magistrate with reasonably specific standards. In felony sentencing, some states use guidelines or presumptive sentencing structures that sharply restrict judicial discretion, while others commonly give the judge extensive leeway, requiring only that the sentence fall within the wide range of statutory limits. So too, while most jurisdictions have a series of specific standards governing required pretrial discovery, several leave discovery to the discretion of the trial judge, utilizing only a very general "interests of justice" standard. On the other hand, as to other aspects of pretrial proceedings, such as the scope of *voir dire* and the granting of continuances, all jurisdictions grant to the trial judge considerable room for the exercise of personal judgment.

7. *Factors influencing the exercise of discretion.* To some extent, diversity in administrative practice is an inevitable consequence of the broad range of discretion found throughout the criminal justice process. Additional factors must be taken into account, however, to explain the tremendous degree of administrative variation that will be found even within a single jurisdiction.[b] Those factors include the number of different actors making discretionary decisions, the extent to which those actors differ in their personal value judgments, and the great diversity in the institutional framework that shapes their decisions.

The institutional framework is especially significant in determining the degree of variation. Although differences in the perceptions, values, and abilities of individual administrators will undoubtedly be reflected in their exercise of discretion, to a considerable extent those qualities are a product of, and subordinate to, the influence of the agencies of which the administrators are a part and the local community in which they operate. Initially, the organizations (in the case of appointed officials) and the community (in the case of elected officials) commonly play a substantial role in determining the type of people who will be placed in the various roles of criminal justice administrators. Even more significantly, they

---

b. The discussion that follows is based upon numerous studies of criminal justice administration in individual communities. See LaFave, Israel and King, *Criminal Procedure Treatise* § 1.9 (forthcoming 2nd ed).

combine to shape the administrative environment that heavily influences the individual official in her or his choice of action. Indeed, in some settings, they seek through administrative regulation to confine or guide various aspects of discretionary decisionmaking. Of course, considerable room will always remain for administrative decisionmaking based upon the idiosyncratic values of the individual, but as to the administrative practice as a whole, numerous studies suggest that the dominant influence in the long run is in the administrative environment shaped by agency bureaucracy and the local community. Among the various elements that contribute to the diversity in administrative environment, four have attracted the most attention. They are briefly described in Notes 8–11.

8. *Fragmentation of enforcement agencies.* As administrative responsibilities are divided among more and more agencies, the likelihood of complete likemindedness among those units decreases and the potential for diversity in administrative practice increases. Thus fragmentation of administrative responsibility and variation in administrative practice tend to go hand in hand. In the United States, fragmentation is greatest as to criminal justice enforcement agencies, where it far exceeds that found in any other industrialized country. Indeed, the decentralization or "balkanization" of state law enforcement agencies is probably the most prominent feature of the administrative structure of the criminal justice process in this country. Only in the federal system, where the Department of Justice has supervisory authority over most (but not all) of the major federal police agencies and all of the United States Attorneys, does a single governmental unit have the broad powers of supervision and coordination needed to obtain a system-wide uniformity as to major policy issues presented in the exercise of enforcement discretion.

The initial division in the fragmentation of state enforcement agencies lies in the separation of police and prosecutorial agencies. Although local prosecutors often are described as the "chief law enforcement officer" of the county, they have no direct regulatory authority over the various police departments operating within their jurisdiction. Prosecutorial and police agencies are not only legally autonomous, but most often are parts of different units of local government (i.e., county and municipality). Of course, the prosecutor does have control over any prosecutions that may be brought, and that power-base may be utilized to help convince police to adhere to policies adopted by the prosecutor's office, but it is hardly comparable to the authority of a supervisory official. Not all police actions exercising discretionary authority are aimed at obtaining a prosecution, and police agencies are aware that if they produce evidence adequate to gain a possible trial conviction or plea bargain as to a serious offender, the prosecutor will be under considerable pressure to go forward with the prosecution even though the police did not proceed as the prosecutor's office would have preferred.

The fragmentation of enforcement responsibility extends as well to the units charged with performing the separate roles of prosecutor and police. A few states make the attorney general responsible for all prosecutions under state law, but the dominant scheme is to divide such authority among local prosecutors who have territorial jurisdiction over a single county or a group of sparsely-populated counties combined to form a single prosecutorial district. There are roughly 2,350 such independent local prosecuting agencies in the United States. Moreover, in most states, there will be an additional layer or two of officials, besides the local prosecutors, who have some prosecutorial authority. The attorney general may be another autonomous prosecutor, with independent authority to initiate prosecutions under some or all state laws (although that authority tends to be used quite sparingly). City attorneys will be autonomous prosecutors as to ordinance violations, including those that largely duplicate state misdemeanor offenses, and that authority will be exercised quite frequently, with municipal police commonly bringing such offenses to the city attorney rather than the county prosecutor.

Even greater fragmentation exists among police agencies. Throughout the United States, there are over 17,000 agencies within the state criminal justice systems that can be characterized as police agencies. While a small percentage of these agencies are state-wide agencies, most are units of local governments (counties, cities, and townships). As a consequence, in a major metropolitan area, police agencies are likely to include a state police post, one or more Sheriff's departments, a large municipal department (with several thousand sworn officers) a few mid-sized municipal departments (over 100 officers) for larger suburbs, smaller departments for numerous other cities, townships, and villages in the metropolitan area, and several special district police agencies (e.g., park, campus, or transit)

9. *Organizational variations*. Various studies establish that administrators in the criminal justice process tend to be heavily influenced in their exercise of discretion by the "administrative ethos" of the organizations of which they are a part. Those studies also suggest that a wide range of factors contribute to the manner and direction of each organization's approach to the exercise of discretion. To some extent, that approach will be shaped by the character of the local community and the leadership of the organization. However, other factors, more structural in nature, often play a most important role in setting the administrative culture of the organization.

Commentators have pointed to a wide range of differences in the nature and resources of criminal justice organizations performing each of the basic administrative functions in the application of the criminal justice process. They suggest further that most of those differences will contribute, in varying degrees, to the character of the administrative ethos of the individual agency. The most frequently cited differences relate to the following factors: (1) the range of responsibilities of the organization (e.g., whether a police agency is a specialized agency, charged only with a law enforcement function, as in the case of the F.B.I., or a general agency that has such additional responsibilities as traffic control, providing basic social services, and maintenance of the public order, as in the case of a municipal police department); (2) the size of the organization (with the most striking differences found among local police agencies, where over one-third of all departments have less than five officers, while departments of medium-sized cities have several hundred officers, and departments of large cities have several thousand); (3) standards for selecting personnel (e.g., educational qualifications for police departments, and the choice between non-partisan, merit oriented or highly political selection standards for prosecutors' and defenders' offices); (4) allocation of responsibilities within the organization [e.g., in a prosecutor's office, whether the general assignment system is "horizontal," with different assistants assigned to each major stage in the process (e.g., intake, preliminary hearing, and trial), or "vertical," with the assistant starting with the case at intake and carrying it through to final disposition, and whether all cases come within the general assignment system or specialized units are charged with prosecuting certain types of crimes (e.g., sexual assaults) or selected offenders (e.g., "career" criminals)]; and (5) caseload pressures (which vary considerably, with courts and prosecutors' offices in smaller communities often having caseloads per judge or prosecutor only half of that found in larger communities). Quite obviously, with the great potential for variation as to such factors individually and in combination, criminal justice organizations can be expected to develop a broad range of differing perspectives as the exercise of most elements of their discretionary authority.

10. *Variations in administrative interactions.* As the commentators also have noted, analysis of administrative decisionmaking in the criminal justice process cannot be restricted to a "one-party" focus. Each participant in the process, whether police officer, prosecutor, defense counsel, or judge, is influenced not only by the institutional concerns of the organization of which he is a part, but also by concerns that flow from the necessity of interacting with representatives of those other organizations that share in the administration of the process. The criminal justice system is a blend of interdependent parts, thereby creating a functional interlocking among its key administrators. As a result, each must take account of the responses of the others in shaping his or her administrative decisions. In many instances, those decisions will be made in settings that require explicit interchange between different participants, as in the many courtroom actions that require participation of the judge, prosecutor, and defense counsel. In others, though the administrative action may appear to be taken unilaterally (as in the case of the police officer's exercise of arrest authority), the underlying decision nonetheless entails predictions of, and reactions to, the administrative decisions of other participants. The outputs of one participant will be the inputs of another, and the impact of the exercise of discretionary authority by one participant commonly is determined in good part by the responsive use of discretionary authority by others.

A commonplace consequence of recurring interactions of persons with interdependent administrative responsibility is the development of informal workgroups with their own distinctive norms, values, and social relationships, and the criminal justice process is no exception in this regard. Indeed, some commentators have suggested that the workgroup relationships developed through recurring interactions of criminal justice administrators may become more influential than any other element in the administrative setting, including the personal values of individual administrators, the administrative ethos of the "sponsoring organizations" of the workgroup members, and the character of the local community. Not surprisingly, the studies suggest that the workgroup influence tends to be at its highest where the group of interacting participants is small, stable, and homogeneous. Those qualities are most often found in courthouse workgroups in small communities, where there is likely to be only one or two judges, a prosecutor's office with no more than a few attorneys, a defense bar that is only slightly larger, and a social setting that produces ties beyond the courtroom. However, stability and smallness, if not homogeneity, can also be found even in courts of the largest cities. Under fairly common assignment systems that give trial judges long term assignments to the criminal division and prosecutors and public defenders fairly long term assignments to the courtroom of a particular judge, the same handful of persons will be interacting with each other on a daily basis month after month.

11. *Community variations.* Many elements of the administrative structure of the criminal justice process clearly are aimed at ensuring that the local community has a substantial input in shaping the enforcement of the criminal law to suit its needs and values. Primary administrative responsibility is placed in units of local government, and with respect to the police, fragmentation is carried to the point where even the smallest local units have their own police agency. The key administrative officials are either themselves elected (as in the case of sheriffs, judges, and prosecutors) or appointed by local elected officials (as in the case of the local police departments). Although the local officials are bound to follow state

law, broad grants of discretionary authority provide substantial leeway for administrative variations that reflected the differences in local communities.

The success of such structural arrangements in ensuring responsiveness to the local community is a matter of ongoing debate. Some commentators contend that the bearing of community values on discretionary decisionmaking is insubstantial, as compared to the influence of the internal values of agency bureaucracies and interacting workgroups. They acknowledge that in small insular communities, the dominant community values are likely to have a bearing upon discretionary decisionmaking at every stage in the process. However, in the larger communities, with a more divergent population, they see community values as having a significant impact only for those exceptional cases that touch a special nerve in the community as a whole or in a particular segment of the community that is politically potent. In the everyday administration of justice, a combination of developments—including, most notably, the removal of politics from the selection process for various officials, an increased tendency of the public to defer to claims of "professional expertise," and the decrease in the visibility of performance to the general public—are said to have largely insulated administrators from the will of the community. Other commentators contend that community values continue to exercise considerable influence over criminal justice administration even in mid-sized and large communities. They argue that responsiveness to the community is not keyed to political vulnerability, and that administrators, even when shielded by the low visibility of their actions and the protection of civil service, will nonetheless feel constrained to act in accord with the dominant values of the local community. Moreover, they conclude that those values will differ in many specifics even when the communities share the same general attitudes on crime control, and that those differences will be reflected in distinctive styles of administration that vary from one community to another.

SECTION 2. THE STEPS IN THE PROCESS

This section presents an overview of the procedural steps that carry the process from start to finish in an individual case. The basic objectives of the overview are to position each step within the typical progression of the process, to introduce the relevant terminology, and to briefly describe what occurs at each step. This information should provide a useful backdrop for the discussion in later chapters. An additional objective is to provide the reader with a general indication of the significance of each step as measured by its quantitative impact.[a] Though lawyers typically approach an issue from the perspective of its bearing upon the individual case, they also must keep in mind the systemic implications of the issue as it relates to the administration of the process in general, and those implications clearly include a quantitative element.

The overview looks primarily to the processing of the "typical felony" in the "typical jurisdiction." This approach ignores a host of variations. Initially, as to variations that exist from one state to another, the overview takes account only of

---

a. For each step in the process, the overview utilizes such statistics as are available regarding the use and outcome of the various procedures applicable to the particular stage. See LaFave, Israel, and King, *Criminal Procedure Treatise* § 1.3 (forthcoming 2d ed.). Very often, the available statistics are limited in coverage. Criminal justice statistics usually are collected by individual governmental agencies for the particular city, county, or state served by that agency, and rarely are parallel statistics available for all agencies of a particular type throughout the nation. Thus, some rough generalizations are involved even in accepting those statistics as typical of jurisdictions of a particular character (e.g., large urban communities).

those differences that are both fundamental and characteristic of a substantial number of states. Secondly, as to variations that exist in the administration of common procedures from one community to another, we again concentrate only on fundamental and widespread practices, with emphasis on mid-sized to large communities. Third, procedural variations that are tied to the type of felony (e.g., capital vs. non-capital) are almost entirely ignored and only the most basic of those variations that distinguish misdemeanor processing are noted. Finally, the overview does not consider many possible variations in chronology. It describes the chronology that is followed in the vast majority of all felony cases, and ignores the special situations that often produce a different chronology. For example, prosecutorial screening ordinarily comes after an arrest is made, and that is where it is placed in the overview (see step 6), although situations do arise in which the prosecutor will have reviewed the charge before an arrest is made. So too, the process of plea negotiation is discussed in connection with the original entry of the plea (see step 12), although plea negotiation may occur at much earlier steps (e.g., prior to the filing of the charge) or much later stages (e.g., during the trial).

Of course, the division of the process into separate steps in itself is somewhat misleading. It suggests a separation in timing which is not always present. While some steps have definite starting and ending points, others are continuing and overlap later steps. Investigatory procedures, for example, do not always stop with the filing of charges, but may continue through to the initiation (and sometimes the end) of the trial. So too, the decision on pretrial release, though it comes initially at the first appearance, is subject to possible reconsideration as the case progresses.

Step 1: The Reported Crime. Descriptions of the sequence of events in the criminal justice process commonly start with the commission of a crime. Our focus, however, is on the major steps taken in the *administration* of the process. From that perspective, the starting point ordinarily is the event that brings to the attention of the police the possible commission of a crime, for it is that event which commonly triggers the enforcement process. Quantitatively, there is a vast difference between the number of instances in which crimes are committed and the number in which the possible commission of a crime is brought to the attention of the police. Various studies suggest that substantially less than half of all committed felonies are brought to the attention of the police.

Police may learn about possible crimes from reports of citizens (usually victims), discovery in the field (usually observation on patrol), or from investigative and intelligence work. Where the police conclude that a crime may well have been committed, it will be recorded as a "reported crime" or "known offense."[b] This record-keeping function has no legal significance with respect to further police action; police are not required to investigate further because a crime is recorded as a "known offense" and they are not prevented from seeking to obtain information where they do not have knowledge of an offense. The long standing tradition of police departments, however, is to devote the vast bulk of their enforcement efforts to solving "known offenses." Accordingly, the distribution of "known offenses" provides a good general picture of the types of crimes that are the subject of the enforcement activities of police. The dominant offenses among the reported crimes (i.e., including both misdemeanors and felonies) are those

b. The leading source of known offenses, the F.B.I.'s Uniform Crime Reports, provides annual statistics for only eight offense categories, known as Index offenses—(1) murder and non-negligent manslaughter, (2) forcible rape, (3) robbery (personal and commercial), (4) aggravated assault, (5) burglary (household and commercial), (6) larceny/theft, (7) motor vehicle theft, and (8) arson.

involving the taking or destruction of property (likely to approximate 50%), offenses relating to the use of alcohol or drugs, and assaults of various types. The most serious violent offenses (e.g., robbery, rape, aggravated assault and homicide) are likely to constitute as a group no more than 7% of all reported crimes. Of course, as discussed below, enforcement efforts will vary with the type of crime.

Step 2: Prearrest Investigation. Various distinctions are used in grouping prearrest investigatory procedures, but the most common are the agency involved (distinguishing primarily between the investigative activities of the police and the prosecutor) and the focus of the procedure (distinguishing primarily between activities aimed at solving past crimes and activities aimed at anticipated crimes). Those distinctions create three basic groups of prearrest investigative procedures: (1) police procedures that are aimed at solving specific past crimes known to the police (commonly described as "reactive" procedures), (2) police procedures that are aimed at anticipated ongoing and future criminal activity (commonly described as "proactive" procedures), and (3) prosecutorial and other non-police investigations conducted primarily through the use of subpoena authority. Each of these groups is discussed below, but initially note should be taken of the large number of arrests made by police with little or no prearrest investigation.

"On–Scene Arrests." A substantial percentage of arrests for a wide range of crimes are of the "on-scene" variety. These are arrests made during the course of the crime or immediately thereafter, either at the place where the crime occurred or in its immediate vicinity. Ordinarily, on-scene arrests will be based on the officer's own observation (leading to the alternative description of such arrests as "on-view"), although they will sometimes be based on the direction of a witness who has just viewed the crime. For some offenses on-scene arrests typically are the product of prearrest investigative activities designed to place the police in a position where the officer will be able to view the crime as it is committed. That usually is the case, for example, with so-called "victimless" crimes (i.e., crimes which do not involve an interaction with a victim, such as possession of a weapon, and crimes which ordinarily involve willing participants, such as vice crimes or narcotics-transfer offenses).

For most offenses, on-scene arrests typically come about with basically no investigative activity beyond the immediate response to the event that calls the commission of the crime to the officer's attention. Thus, a prompt response to a victim's call for assistance or a burglar alarm may place the officer in a position to make an arrest while the crime is in progress or immediately following its completion. So too, the officer may simply come across a crime, open to view, in the course of regular patrol activities. Although such arrests are a rare consequence measured against all of the calls to which police must respond and all of the activities they engage in while on patrol, they constitute a substantial portion of all arrests made for some serious felonies that otherwise are very difficult to solve. Thus, one study indicated that 42% of all arrests for nonviolent property crimes (basically theft and burglary) were made within 5 minutes of the commission of the offense. Indeed, even as to robberies and other violent crimes involving interaction with a victim, where there is a better chance of later solving the offense because the victim has seen the offender (and may be able to provide a useful description), as many as a quarter of all arrests may be made within 5 minutes of the commission of the offense.

Reactive Investigations. Where the police learn of the possible commission of a crime, but are not in the position to make an "on-scene" arrest, their responsibility then is to "solve" that crime. This involves (1) determining whether there actually was a crime committed, (2) if so, determining who committed the crime, (3) collecting evidence of that person's guilt, and (4) locating the offender so that he can be taken into custody. Investigations directed at performing these crime-solving functions commonly are described as "reactive" or "retrospective" in nature because they focus on past criminal (or presumably criminal) activity. They reflect what is characterized as an "incident-driven" or "complaint-responsive" style of policing, which has long dominated the deployment of police investigative resources.

A wide variety of investigative activities may be utilized prearrest in the course of a reactive investigation. These include: (1) the interviewing of victims; (2) the interviewing of witnesses at the crime scene; (3) canvassing the neighborhood for (and interviewing) other witnesses; (4) the interviewing of suspects, which may require a physical stopping of the suspect on the street and a frisking of the suspect (i.e., pat-down of the outer clothing) for possible weapons; (5) the examination of the crime scene and the collection of physical evidence found there; (6) checking departmental records and computer files; (7) seeking information from informants; (8) searching for physical evidence of the crime (e.g., stolen property or weapons) in places accessible to the suspect (e.g., his home or automobile) and seizing any evidence found there; (9) surveillance of a suspect (including electronic surveillance) aimed at obtaining leads to evidence or accomplices; and (10) using undercover operatives to gain information from the suspect.

A variety of factors will determine which of the investigative practices noted above will be used in a particular investigation. One of the most important is the investigative direction suggested by those "traces" of the crime that are immediately available to the police. In some instances, the limitations of available traces foreclose the use of a particular investigative practice. Any attempt to interview suspects depends upon the presence of some trace (e.g., a witness who can describe the criminal or a unique modus operandi) that allows for the designation of a manageable group of persons who might be considered possible suspects. A search for physical evidence only makes sense if the traces indicate that the criminal activity was of a type which might produce such evidence. In other instances, though the available traces will not absolutely rule out the use of a particular investigative practice, they suggest that the likelihood of gaining useful information will be so remote that the time, energy, and financial costs involved simply do not make use of that practice worthwhile. There is almost always some possibility, for example, that canvassing the neighborhood will produce a witness who saw the offender, but police frequently will not canvass for witnesses unless there is a fairly substantial likelihood that such a person might be found.

In general, the strength and nature of the available leads will determine the scope of the investigation, but other factors may alter that natural correlation. A more serious offense may lead police to utilize a technique that would be rejected as to a less serious crime because it is not sufficiently likely to be successful. A technique less likely to be successful may be chosen over one more likely to be successful because the latter simply is not available under the law without stronger leads and the former presents no legal difficulties. In such a situation, the second-choice procedure hopefully will produce additional information that will enable the police legally to use their first choice, but that strategy may not be successful and the investigation may end without the police ever using the preferred procedure.[c]

---

c. The choice among possible investigative procedures also will be influenced by the poli-cies of the police agency involved and the assignment and work habits of the particular

Where the traces of the crime are very weak and the offense is not of an especially serious nature, the police are likely to terminate their investigation after having done little more than interview the victim and any other witnesses available at the scene. Police are aware that, for most crimes, the odds of arresting the offender are slim unless there are witnesses at the scene who can provide information that either specifically identifies the offender or makes that identification readily determinable. While the absence of such information from witnesses will not necessarily lead to an immediate termination of the investigation, it will certainly work against a substantial extension of the investigation (unless further steps are especially fruitful). The end result is that for a great many crimes, including even offenses as serious as burglary, very little is done besides interviewing the person reporting the crime.

While the variation among investigations is far too great to characterize any single combination of investigative procedures as "average," even for a particular type of offense, it is clear that prearrest investigations rarely take on the characteristics of popularized depictions of the crime solving process. In general, investigations do not involve the use of scientific methods of investigation, confrontations with crafty criminals, or reliance upon informants. A study of robbery and burglary investigations found, for example, that the interviewing of the victim and the examination of the crime scene were by far the most common steps in the prearrest process. Aside from the canvassing for and interviewing of additional witnesses, no other procedure was used in as many as a third of all cases. In burglary cases, two of the departments surveyed reported that evidence was collected at the scene of the crime in roughly 15% of all investigations. The frequency of interviews of suspects varied considerably, but even as to robberies (where victims were more likely to identify a specific suspect), such interviews occurred in less than 25% of all cases. Interviews of informants occurred in less than 5% of all investigations. Other sources indicate that prearrest searches of premises are even rarer. The most complete data on the use of an investigative procedure is for non-consensual electronic surveillance (primarily telephone wire-tapping). That procedure is used in less than a thousand instances annually throughout the United States.

Proactive Investigations. General purpose police agencies, who employ over 85% of all full-time police officers in this country, devote the vast majority of their investigative efforts to the solving of known crimes. However, those agencies also have a long tradition of engaging as well in proactive investigations, and in recent years, many local police agencies have sought to make greater use of proactive investigative procedures. Also, many special-function police agencies (such as the federal Drug Enforcement Administration) traditionally have devoted a substantial portion of their resources to proactive investigations.

Proactive investigations are aimed at uncovering criminal activity that is not specifically known to the police. The investigation may be aimed at placing the police in a position where they can observe ongoing criminal activity that otherwise would both be hidden from public view and not reported (as typically is the

officers conducting the investigation. Departmental guidelines may suggest limits on the use of investigative practices that are expensive or politically troublesome, low thresholds for the investigation of specific categories of crime, and the termination of efforts to obtain further corroborating evidence when particular types of evidence justify filing a criminal charge. Studies indicate that while patrol officers and detectives employ some of the same techniques, certain investigative practices are utilized primarily by detectives. Also individual officers vary in their pursuit of investigations, as evidenced by the District of Columbia study finding that over half of the felony arrests leading to a conviction were made by a group of 149 officers, representing less than 10% of the total number of officers making arrests.

case with the continuing possession of contraband). It may be aimed at inducing persons who have committed crimes of a certain type, including many unknown to the police, to reveal themselves (as in a "fencing sting"). Proactive investigations also often are aimed at anticipating future criminality and placing police in a position to intercept when the crime is attempted. Here, the investigative technique may be designed simply to gain information that will permit the police to predict when and where a crime is likely to be committed, or it may be designed to "instigate" or "induce" the criminal attempt at a particular time and place by creating a setting likely to spur into action those prone to criminality.

A variety of different procedures may be used in a proactive investigation, with the choice of procedure largely tied to the specific objective of the investigation. Deception is a common element of many proactive procedures. In traditional undercover operations, the police assume a false identity and present themselves as willing to participate in criminal activities (as where undercover agents "set up" fencing operations or narcotics transactions). So too, deception is the key to a "decoy tactic" of providing what appears to be an easy target for victimization (e.g., a drunk with an exposed wallet or a business of the type that is readily subject to extortion). Where police utilize as informants persons whose activities expose them to a criminal milieu, they are counting on the criminals associating with those persons believing that they will be discrete (usually because the persons are themselves engaged in criminal activity, gain their livelihood in part from criminals, or have social ties to the criminals). Surveillance through stake-outs, covert patrols, and electronic monitoring also rests on deception by hiding the surveillance.

Other proactive techniques rely on intrusive confrontations designed to place police in a position where they can observe what otherwise would be hidden or to elicit nervous or unthinking incriminatory responses that will provide a legal grounding for taking further investigative action (e.g., an arrest or stop). Thus, police following an aggressive motorized patrol strategy will fully utilize traffic laws to maximize stops of motorists, thereby gaining greater opportunity to peer into car windows, to ask questions, and to request consent to a search of the vehicle. Similarly, under a practice of heavy field interrogation, police will frequently approach pedestrians and initiate questions to determine who they are and what they are doing. Such intrusive confrontations are most often used on a selective basis, with police concentrating their efforts on those characteristics of the social environment that suggest to them possible criminality (e.g., high-crime neighborhood, suspicious class of persons, unusual behavior). In general, proactive procedures are more resource intensive, more intrusive, arguably more likely to foster community opposition, and clearly pose more legal problems than typical reactive procedures.

Prosecutorial Investigations. Not all prearrest investigations are conducted by police. For certain types of crimes, and for certain types of traces of crime, the best investigatory tool is the subpoena—a court order directing a person to appear in a particular proceeding for the purpose of testifying and presenting specified physical evidence (e.g., documents) within his possession. The subpoena authority generally is available for the investigation of crime only through the grand jury, although other agencies may be able to use it to investigate specific types of crimes in particular jurisdictions. The grand jury, though it tends to be known more for its screening function in reviewing the prosecution's decision to charge (see step 11), also has authority to conduct investigations into the possible commission of crimes within the judicial district in which it sits. In carrying out this function, the grand jurors, being a group of laypersons with no special expertise in investigation, quite naturally rely heavily on the direction provided by their legal advisor, who is the prosecutor. Thus, grand jury investigations become, for all practical purposes, investigations by the prosecutor.

Compared to police investigations, grand jury investigations are expensive, time consuming, and logistically cumbersome. Accordingly, they usually are reserved for special settings where a grand jury investigation has a distinctive advantage over a police investigation. Typically, those settings involving crimes of public corruption (e.g., bribery), misuse of economic power (e.g., price-fixing), and widespread distribution of illegal services or goods (e.g., organized crime operations). With the exception of the federal system, those offenses provide only a minute portion of all reported offenses or prosecutions, suggesting that grand jury investigations are used in a fraction of 1% of all criminal investigations.

Step 3: Arrest. Once a police officer has obtained sufficient information to justify arresting a suspect (i.e., probable cause to believe the person has committed a crime), the arrest ordinarily becomes the next step in the criminal justice process. The term "arrest" is defined differently for different purposes. We refer here only to the act of taking a person into custody for the purpose of charging that person with a crime (the standard commonly used in the reporting of arrest statistics). This involves the detention of the suspect (by force if necessary) for the purpose of first transporting him to a police facility and then requesting that charges be filed against him. As an alternative to such a "full custody" arrest, many jurisdictions authorize the officer in some situations to briefly detain the suspect and then release him upon issuance of an official document (commonly titled a "citation," "notice to appear" or "appearance ticket") which directs the suspect to appear in court on a set date to respond to the charge specified in the document. This release-on-citation alternative commonly is authorized only for minor offenses, with the choice between the release procedure and the custodial arrest then lying in the discretion of the individual officer.

Where there is no immediate need to arrest a suspect, an officer may seek to obtain an arrest warrant (a court order authorizing the arrest) prior to taking the person into custody. Arrest warrants in most jurisdictions are issued by magistrates. To obtain a warrant, the police must establish, to the satisfaction of the magistrate, that there exists probable cause to believe that the prospective arrestee committed the crime for which he will be arrested. The showing of probable cause may be made by affidavits or live testimony of either the investigating officer or a witness (usually the victim). Where a warrant is issued, it ordinarily will authorize the arrest to be made by any police officer in the state, not simply the officer seeking the warrant.

Arrests also can be made without a warrant, and that is the predominant practice in all localities. Of course, in a large percentage of all arrests (including, for example, "on-scene" arrests), the police officer will make the arrest immediately after he has obtained probable cause for believing the person committed a crime. Yet, even where the investigating officer, after establishing probable cause, expects a lapse of a day or more before making an arrest, the common practice in most jurisdictions is not to use that opportunity to obtain an arrest warrant. Officers will seek to obtain a warrant, rather than rely on a warrantless arrest, only in special settings which make a warrant legally necessary or otherwise advantageous. The most common of those settings are: (1) cases in which the offender is located in another jurisdiction (as a warrant is needed to utilize procedures for having the person arrested by officers of another state and later extradited); (2) cases in which the person cannot be found and his name therefore will be entered into the computerized state or local law enforcement information network as someone who is subject to an arrest on the basis of an outstanding warrant; (3) cases in which there will probably be a need to enter into a dwelling without consent in order to make the arrest (a situation that requires a warrant); (4) cases in which the offense was a misdemeanor not committed in the officer's presence (a situation requiring a warrant in some states); and (5) cases in which the police have sought the advice of the prosecutor before deciding to proceed (where the prosecutor responds affirmatively, a complaint typically will be filed immediately, with a warrant then obtained prior to the arrest).

As previously noted, many offenses that come to the attention of the police cannot be solved. Hence, the number of arrests made will be substantially less than the number of offenses recorded as a known offense. The proportion of known offenses that are "cleared" by an arrest varies substantially with the nature of the crime. For those offenses on which national data is collected by the F.B.I. (i.e., fn. b supra), the overall clearance rate is roughly 20%, ranging from a high of 67% for homicide to a low of 14% for burglary. The vast majority of arrests (60–80%) will be for misdemeanors, with more arrests made for driving-under-the-influence than for any other offense. Among felony arrests, property offenses will account for roughly a third, drug offenses for 25–30%, and crimes of violence for another 25%.[d]

Step 4: Booking. Immediately after making an arrest, the arresting officer usually will search the arrestee's person and remove any weapons, contraband, or evidence relating to a crime. If the arrested person was driving a vehicle, the officer may also search the passenger compartment of the vehicle for the same items. The arrestee will then be taken, either by the arresting officer or other officers called to the scene, to the police station, a centrally located jail, or some similar "holding" facility. It is at this facility that the arrestee will be taken through a process known as "booking." Initially, the arrestee's name, the time of his arrival, and the offense for which he was arrested are noted in the police "blotter" or "log." This is strictly a clerical procedure, and it does not control whether the arrestee will be charged or what charge might be brought. As part of the booking process, the arrestee also will be photographed and fingerprinted.

Following booking, a person arrested on a minor offense may be able to gain his release upon posting a cash security deposit ("stationhouse bail") with the police. Persons arrested for more serious offenses, and those eligible for stationhouse bail but lacking the resources, will remain at the holding facility until presented before a magistrate (see step 9). Ordinarily they will be placed in a "lockup," which usually is some kind of cell. Before entering the lockup, they will be subjected to another search, more thorough than that conducted at the point of arrest. This search is designed primarily to inventory the arrestee's personal belongs and to prevent the introduction of contraband into the lockup.

Step 5: Post–Arrest Investigation. The initial post-arrest investigation by the police consists of the search of the person (and possibly the interior of the automobile) as discussed above. The extent of any further post-arrest investigation will vary with the fact situation. In some cases, such as where the arrestee

---

d. A substantial percentage of all felony arrestees (e.g., 10–15%) will be subject to the juvenile justice system, with that percentage varying considerably with the offense. Ordinarily, juvenile arrestees will be separated from adult arrestees shortly after they are taken into custody, and will be processed through the juvenile justice system. However, where the juvenile court may waive its jurisdiction, a small percentage (e.g., 5%) will later be returned to the regular criminal justice process and be prosecuted as adults. From this point onward, we assume that the juveniles have been removed from the process.

was caught "red-handed," there will be little left to be done. In others, police will utilize many of the same kinds of investigative procedures as are used before arrest (e.g., interviewing witnesses, searching the suspect's home, and viewing the scene of the crime). Post-arrest investigation does offer one important investigative source, however, that ordinarily is not available prior to the arrest—the person of the arrestee. Thus, the police may seek to obtain an eyewitness identification of the arrestee by placing him in a lineup, having the witness view him individually (a "showup"), or taking his picture and showing it to the witness (usually with the photographs of several other persons in a "photographic line-up"). They may also require the arrestee to provide handwriting or hair samples that can be compared with evidence the police have found at the scene of the crime. The arrest similarly facilitates questioning the arrestee at length about either the crime for which he was arrested or other crimes thought to be related (although warnings must be given prior to the custodial interrogation).

Although we do not have precise data on the use of these post-arrest procedures involving the arrestee, the best available estimates indicate they are not utilized in the vast majority of cases. In most communities, they are used almost exclusively in the investigation of felony cases and even then their use is tied to need and likely success. Eyewitness identification, for example, is not sought where there were no eyewitnesses, where an eyewitness was well acquainted with the arrestee, or where the officer observed the crime and immediately thereafter made the arrest. Police more frequently seek to engage felony arrestees in sustained interrogation, but in many police departments, a substantial portion of these arrestees (e.g., 20–40%) are either never questioned or simply given warnings and asked if they desire to make a statement.

Step 6: The Decision to Charge. The initial decision to charge a suspect with the commission of a crime ordinarily comes with the decision of a police officer to arrest the suspect. That decision will subsequently be reviewed, first by the police and then by the prosecutor. As discussed in step 9, the arrestee must be brought before a magistrate within a relatively short period (typically 24 or 48 hours), and prior to that point, the charges against the arrestee must be filed with the magistrate. It is during this period that the police will review the arresting officer's initial decision to charge. The prosecutor's review of the decision to charge often occurs during this same period, but prosecutorial review is, in any event, an ongoing process. Whether or not the charges were initially reviewed before being filed, they remain subject to review (and possible rejection) by the prosecutor up to and through the trial. Thus, the decision to charge a person with a crime may be seen as having four components: (1) the decision of the investigating officer to arrest and charge; (2) the police review of that decision prior to filing charges; (3) possible prosecutorial review prior to filing; and (4) ongoing prosecutorial review after the filing. The first component has already been noted in step (3) (the arrest), and we consider here the remaining three.

Pre–Filing Police Screening. Sometime between the booking of the arrestee and the point at which the arrestee is to be taken before the magistrate, there will be an internal police review of a warrantless arrest. Ordinarily that occurs shortly after the booking, when the arresting officer prepares an arrest report to be given to his or her supervisor. The supervisor may approve the bringing of charges at the level recommended in the police report, raise or reduce the level of the recommended charges, or decide against bringing charges. A decision not to bring charges ordinarily will be based on the supervisor's conclusion either that the evidence is insufficient to charge or that the offense can more appropriately be handled by a "stationhouse adjustment" (e.g., in the case of a fight among acquaintances, a warning and lecture may be deemed sufficient). If the supervising officer decides against prosecution, the arrestee will be released from the lockup on that officer's direction (though some departments follow the practice of seeking prosecutor approval before releasing any felony arrestees). Studies that track the ultimate disposition of arrests have typically been limited to felony arrests. They indicate that police are likely to decide against proceeding in the range 4–10% of those arrests. Since police are more likely to utilize stationhouse adjustments for misdemeanor arrests, the percentage of misdemeanor arrestees released by the police without charging is likely to be somewhat higher.

Pre–Filing Prosecutor Screening. Prosecutors' offices vary substantially in their approach to pre-filing review of the decision to charge. In many jurisdictions, all arrests, both for misdemeanors and felonies, will be screened, and no charges will be filed except upon approval of the prosecutor. In urban districts, however, police often file charges on their own initiative for at least some types of offenses. Typically, prosecutors will screen the vast majority of the felony charges, but there are jurisdictions in which prosecutors review only the most serious felony charges before they are filed. In these jurisdictions, the primary prosecutorial screening of felony charges ordinarily occurs sometime between the first appearance and the preliminary hearing or grand jury review (see steps 9 and 10 infra). Where prosecutors permit police filing of misdemeanor charges without advance prosecutorial screening, prosecutors commonly will not review a misdemeanor charge until it is scheduled for trial (and thus may never screen those charges that result in an initial guilty plea).

Prosecutors' offices also vary as to the information that typically will be considered in pre-filing screening. Some will utilize only the police officer's arrest report. Others will regularly interview the arresting officer, at least in felony cases, and some will also insist upon interviewing the victim in certain types of felony cases. The screening prosecutor may accept the charge recommended by the police, raise or reduce that charge, request that the police obtain further evidence (which may require releasing the arrestee at this point and then rearresting him when and if that evidence is obtained), decide against prosecution if the arrestee will participate in a diversion program, or simply decide against prosecution without condition.

A prosecutorial decision not to proceed commonly is described as a "rejection," "declination" or "no-paper" decision. The leading statistical studies on pre-charge prosecutor review have sorted out 6 major grounds for that decision. These are: (1) insufficient evidence; (2) witness difficulties (e.g., where the victim was acquainted with the offender and does not desire to proceed, the witness fears reprisal and is reluctant to cooperate, or the witness no longer can be located); (3) due process problems (e.g., critical evidence was obtained illegally and will not be admissible at trial); (4) adequate disposition will be provided by other criminal proceedings (e.g., prosecution by another jurisdiction, probation revocation, or prosecution for another offense); (5) the "interests of justice" (a determination that prosecution is not appropriate even though proof of guilt is not troublesome); and (6) anticipated use of a diversion program.[e] The first two grounds are the

---

e. A diversion program offers the arrestee the opportunity to avoid conviction if he or she is willing to perform prescribed "rehabilitative steps" (e.g., making restitution to the victim, undertaking a treatment program). The diversion agreement operates, in effect, to place the arrestee on a probationary status without conviction. In many jurisdictions, this is achieved by the prosecutor promising not to file charges if the arrestee complies with the prescribed conditions. In others, charges initially are filed with the court, then held in abeyance for the period during which the arrestee is to meet the prescribed conditions, and dismissed with prejmost frequently cited. While rejections based on the "interests of justice" attract the greatest attention, they typically account for less than 10% of all rejections.

As one might expect from the differences among prosecutors' offices in the proportion of arrests reviewed pre-filing, the differences in the depth of such review, and the subjective nature of many of the grounds for declining prosecution, studies reveal considerable variation from one community to another in the impact of pre-filing prosecutorial screening. Thus, a study of 13 urban prosecutorial districts found that the percentage of felony arrests that did not result in charges ranged from a low of 0% (in a jurisdiction which apparently did no pre-filing screening) to a high of 38%. The most comprehensive study, covering six states, reported a pre-filing rejection rate of 11%.

Substantial variations are also found in the frequency with which pre-filing screening results in the reduction of charges. In one district, all felony arrests that result in charges may be filed as felony charges while in another district as many as 50% may be reduced prior to filing to misdemeanor charges. Prosecutors most often reduce the recommended charge because they believe that the evidence only supports a lower charge, but reductions also may be based on the prosecutor's determination that the penalty for the higher charges is too severe for the nature of the crime or that the additional process costs involved in proceeding on a felony (rather than a misdemeanor) are not justified. In some offices, certain felony offenses are viewed as so clearly overgraded legislatively as to necessitate almost automatic reductions on arrests for that offense (e.g., where shoplifting is a felony and all first offender cases are reduced to petty larceny charges).

Post–Filing Prosecutor Screening. Post-filing prosecutorial review of the charging decision is inherent in the many post-filing procedures that require the prosecutor to review the facts of the case. If the prosecutor should determine that the charge is not justified, a dismissal can be obtained through a *nolle prosequi* motion (noting the prosecutor's desire to relinquish prosecution), which ordinarily will be granted in a perfunctory fashion by the court. Similarly, if the prosecutor considers the charge to be too high, a motion can be entered to reduce the charges. In deciding whether to make such motions, the prosecutor will look to basically the same grounds that might justify a pre-filing rejection or reduction of the charge recommended by the police. Even where a charge was carefully screened and approved prior to filing, post-filing review can readily lead to a contrary conclusion as circumstances change (e.g., evidence becomes unavailable) or the prosecutor learns more about the facts of the case. Of course, where the charge was not previously screened or was screened only on a skimpy arrest report, post-filing review is even more likely to lead to a decision to drop or reduce the charges.

Although post-filing review is an ongoing process, the most critical point, particularly where there has been no pre-filing review, is the first instance at which the prosecutor must carefully review the facts of the case. In felony cases, that will usually come in the preparation of the case for the preliminary hearing or grand jury review (see steps 10 and 11), although it may even come before that.

udice once the arrestee meets those conditions. Pretrial diversion tends to be used mostly with first-offense, non-violent misdemeanor arrestees. Indeed, in a jurisdiction that makes heavy use of diversion programs, for some misdemeanors (e.g., passing worthless checks), the number of arrestees placed on diversion may come close to equaling the number convicted of the crime. Diversion tends to be used far more sparingly for felony offenses. A study of 13 urban prosecutorial districts found that all but two of the districts placed on diversion no more than 6% of their felony arrestees. Where diversion programs are entered after the filing of charges, they are measured against the total for felony dispositions, and here account for a higher portion (as high as 20% in some states), with property offenses and drug possession offenses having the highest percentage.

Accordingly, dismissals and reductions based on post-filing prosecutorial screening of the charging decision are most likely to come before the felony case reaches the general trial court, but even after that point, changed circumstances or additional information can lead the prosecutor to file a *nolle prosequi* motion or seek a charge reduction.

Available statistics make it difficult to measure the precise impact of post-filing prosecutorial screening. Dismissal rates for a particular jurisdiction commonly will include both dismissals based on a prosecutor's decision that the case does not merit prosecution and dismissals that are a part of a negotiated plea. The same is also true of statistics on charge reductions made on motion of the prosecution. Studies on the attrition of felony arrests do indicate, however, that the combination of pre-filing review and post-filing review is likely to produce a total rejection rate in the neighborhood of 30–45% for a "typical" urban jurisdiction. As would be expected, a higher rate of rejection by *nolle* motion is likely to be found where there is only limited pre-filing screening. Thus a jurisdiction which screens out less than 10% of its felony arrests prior to charging is likely to have a dismissal rate (exclusive of plea-bargaining dismissals) that approximates 30%. A similar pattern is indicated for charge reductions, as jurisdictions with limited pre-filing screening tend to have a somewhat higher percentage of post-filing reductions of felonies to misdemeanors.

Step 7: Filing the Complaint. Assuming that the pre-filing screening results in a decision to prosecute, the next step is the filing of charges with the magistrate court. Typically, the initial charging instrument will be called a "complaint." In misdemeanor cases, which are triable before the magistrate court, the complaint will serve as the charging instrument throughout the proceedings. In felony cases, on the other hand, the complaint serves to set forth the charges only before the magistrate court; an information or indictment will replace the complaint as the charging instrument when the case reaches the general trial court.

For most offenses, the complaint will be a fairly brief document. Its basic function is to set forth concisely the allegation that the accused, at a particular time and place, committed specified acts constituting a violation of a particular criminal statute. The complaint will be signed by a "complainant," a person who swears under oath that he or she believes the factual allegations of the complaint to be true. The complainant usually will be either the victim or the investigating officer. When an officer-complainant did not observe the offense being committed, but relied on information received from the victim or other witnesses, the officer ordinarily will note that the allegations in the complaint are based on "information and belief." With the filing of the complaint, the person accused in the complaint will have become a "defendant" in a criminal proceeding.[f]

Step 8: Magistrate Review of the Arrest. Following the filing of the complaint and prior to or at the start of the first appearance (see step 9), the magistrate must undertake what is often described as the "*Gerstein* review." As prescribed by

f. Just as the mix of offenses for which arrests were made differed from the mix of offenses known to police, the mix of offenses charged by complaint will differ from the mix of those arrest offenses. The pre-filing decisions by police and prosecutor–including juvenile arrestees transferred to juvenile court, arrestees not charged, arrestees placed in diversion programs, and the reduction of charges–reduces the portion of felonies (10–20% of all complaints as compared to 20–40% of all arrests). The percentages for felony charges within the categories property offenses (roughly 1/3), drug offenses (roughly 30%) and crimes of violence (roughly 25%) will be similar to that for arrests, but within those categories, the percentages for particular offenses (e.g., motor vehicle theft in the property category) are likely to decrease because they more frequently result in rejected charges or reduced charges.

the Supreme Court's decision in *Gerstein v. Pugh* (see § 3.5(a) infra), if a person was arrested without a warrant and remains in custody, the magistrate must determine that there exists probable cause for that person's continued detention. This ordinarily is an *ex parte* determination, similar to that made in the issuance of an arrest warrant and relying on the same sources of information. Where the arrest was made pursuant to a warrant, the judicial probable cause determination has already been made and a *Gerstein* review is not required. If the magistrate finds that probable cause has not been established, he will direct the prosecution to promptly produce more information or release the arrested person. Such instances are exceedingly rare, however.

Step 9: The First Appearance. Once the complaint is filed, the case is before the magistrate court, and the accused must appear before the court within a specified period. This appearance of the accused is usually described as the "first appearance," although the terminology varies, with jurisdictions also using "preliminary appearance," "initial presentment," "preliminary arraignment," "arraignment on the warrant," and "arraignment on the complaint." The timing of the first appearance varies with the custodial status of the accused. Where the accused is not in custody, having been released upon the issuance of a citation or the posting of stationhouse bail, there is likely to be an interval of at least several days. Where the accused was arrested and kept in custody (typically the case for the felony arrestee), he must be brought before the magistrate court "without unnecessary delay." Ordinarily, the time consumed in booking, transportation, limited post-arrest investigation, reviewing the decision to charge, and preparing and filing the complaint makes it unlikely that an arrestee will be presented before the magistrate until at least several hours after his arrest. Accordingly, if the magistrate court does not have an evening session, a person arrested in the afternoon or evening will not be presented before the magistrate until the next day. Many jurisdictions do not allow any longer detention than this, as they require that the first appearance be within 24 hours of the arrest. Others allow up to 48 hours for the first appearance, although that type of delay typically occurs only on weekends.

The first appearance often is a quite brief proceeding. Initially, the magistrate will make certain that the person before the court is the person named in the complaint. The magistrate then will inform the defendant of the charge in the complaint and will note various rights that the defendant may have in further proceedings. Commonly, the magistrate also will inform the defendant of his right to remain silent and warn him that anything he says in court or to the police may be used against him at trial. In felony cases, the magistrate will advise the defendant of the next step in the process, the preliminary hearing and will set a date for that hearing unless the defendant desires to waive it. If the defendant is charged with a misdemeanor, he is not entitled to a preliminary hearing or a subsequent grand jury review (see steps 10 and 11). Here the magistrate will ask the defendant to enter a plea and will set a trial date if the defendants pleads not guilty. If the defendant enters a guilty plea to the misdemeanor charge, the magistrate proceeds to the acceptance of that plea and imposing the sentence or setting a date for sentencing (see steps 13 and 16).

At least where the defendant is not accompanied by counsel, the magistrate will inform the defendant of his right to be represented by retained counsel, and, if indigent, his right to court appointed counsel. The latter right is applicable in all jurisdictions to all defendants charged with felonies or serious misdemeanors, but in some jurisdictions, it is not afforded to defendants charged with minor misdemeanors who will not be sentenced to incarceration if convicted. Where the right applies, the magistrate has the responsibility to determine whether the defendant is indigent, and if so, to initiate the appointment process (unless the defendant waives his right to counsel).

Appointed counsel will be required for a substantial percentage of all felony defendants. The most complete national survey estimated the overall felony indigency rate at 48%, but a later sampling of felony defendants in the 75 largest counties indicated that approximately 80% receive court appointed attorneys. Three basic systems are used to provide counsel for indigent defendants. In slightly over one-third of all counties in the United States, containing roughly 70% of the total population, counsel is provided primarily through a state or county public defender service. In slightly under 60% of the counties, containing 25% of the population, an assigned counsel system is used. Here private attorneys are selected from a list of available attorneys, either on an *ad hoc* basis (with individual judges choosing attorneys as they please) or through a coordinated selection system (with selection by a single administrator according to established guidelines). The remaining counties, with less than 10% of the population, have contract systems under which a private law firm, a group of private practitioners, or a nonprofit organization (such as a bar association) contracts to provide representation for the bulk of the indigent defendants for an extended period of time.

One of the most important first-appearance functions of the magistrate is to set bail (i.e., the conditions under which the defendant can obtain his release from custody pending the final disposition of the charges against him). In many misdemeanor cases, there will be no need to set bail. The defendant will already have been released on the police issuance of a citation or on the posting of stationhouse bail or the defendant will enter a guilty plea at the first appearance and be promptly sentenced. However, a bail determination ordinarily must be made in all felony and serious misdemeanor cases and in a substantial portion of the lesser misdemeanor cases.

At one time, bail was limited almost entirely to the posting of cash or a secured bond purchased from a professional bondsman. Today, those are only two of several alternatives available to the magistrate. Others are: (1) release upon a promise to appear (release on "personal recognizance"); (2) release on making a personal promise to forfeit a specified dollar amount upon a failure to appear (an "unsecured" personal bond); (3) release upon the imposition of one or more nonfinancial conditions (e.g., restrictions on defendant's associations or travel); and (4) the posting with the court of a percentage of the bail forfeiture amount (commonly 10%), which will be returned to the defendant if he appears as scheduled. In general, the magistrate is directed to impose such bail conditions as appear reasonably needed to assure that the defendant will make court appearances as scheduled throughout the proceedings. In making that determination, the magistrate looks to a variety of factors that might indicate a likelihood of flight (e.g., severity of possible punishment if convicted). Most jurisdictions also direct the magistrate to consider community safety, and roughly half allow for preventive detention—a procedure under which the magistrate orders that the accused be detained because no bail condition will provide satisfactory assurance against his commission of an offense posing danger to the community.

In misdemeanor cases, magistrates most commonly utilize release on personal recognizance or personal bonds, and even where a secured bond is required, the amount is sufficiently low so that only a small percentage of defendants fail to gain their release. As a result, studies that cover both misdemeanor and felony arrestees report overall release rates of 85% or higher, with the vast majority of defendants released on nonfinancial conditions. However, when felony defendants alone are considered, the picture changes dramatically, especially for the most serious felony offenses. Thus, a study of the nation's 75 largest counties found that 37% of all felony defendants were detained until the final disposition of their charges, and that percentage rose to 50% or above for those charged with murder, rape, or robbery. As for the felony defendants who were released, more were released on nonfinancial then on financial conditions alone. However, for the group released, a non-appearance rate of roughly 25% and a rearrest rate of 14% for new offenses led to revocation of bail for a significant number. Also, at the end of the year, 8% of those released were unapprehended fugitives.

Step 10: Preliminary Hearing. Following the first appearance, the next scheduled step in a felony case ordinarily is the preliminary hearing (sometimes called a preliminary "examination"). For various reasons, however, a preliminary hearing may not be held. Initially, in many jurisdictions, a substantial portion of the felony caseload will be disposed of during the period (usually one or two weeks) between the first appearance and the scheduled preliminary examination. Particularly, where the primary screening by the prosecutor occurs after the complaint is filed, a substantial number of felony charges are likely to be dismissed or reduced to a misdemeanor during this period. For those felony charges that remain, a substantial percentage of defendants (e.g., 30–50%) will waive their right to a preliminary hearing, usually because they intend to plead guilty. Finally, even though the defendant desires a preliminary hearing, state law commonly allows the prosecutor to bypass the hearing by immediately obtaining a grand jury indictment, and in some localities, prosecutors use that bypass authority with great frequency (see fn. g infra).

Where the preliminary hearing is held, it will provide, like grand jury review, a screening of the decision to charge by a neutral body. In the preliminary hearing, that neutral body is the magistrate, who must determine whether, on the evidence presented, there is probable cause to believe that defendant committed the crime charged. Ordinarily, the magistrate will already have determined that probable cause exists as part of the *ex parte* screening of the complaint (see step 8). The preliminary hearing, however, provides screening in an adversary proceeding in which both sides are represented by counsel. Jurisdictions vary in the evidentiary rules applicable to the preliminary hearing, but most require that the parties rely primarily on live witnesses rather than affidavits. Typically, the prosecution will present its key witnesses and the defense will limit its response to the cross-examination of those witnesses. The defendant has the right to present his own evidence at the hearing, but conventional defense strategy advises against possibly helping the prosecution prepare for trial by presenting its witnesses and subjecting them to cross-examination at this pretrial stage.

If the magistrate concludes that the evidence presented establishes probable cause, she will "bind the case over" to the next stage in the proceedings. In an indictment jurisdiction (see step 11), the case is boundover to the grand jury, and in an "information jurisdiction" (see step 12), the case is boundover directly to the general trial court. If the magistrate finds that the probable cause supports only a misdemeanor charge, she will reject the felony charge and allow the prosecutor to substitute the lower charge, which will then be set for trial in the magistrate court. If the magistrate finds that the prosecution's evidence does not support any charge, she will order that the defendant be released. The rate of dismissals at the preliminary hearing quite naturally varies with the degree of previous screening exercised by the prosecutor. In a jurisdiction with fairly extensive screening, the percentage of dismissals is likely to fall in the range of 5–10% of the hearings held. However, in jurisdictions in which the hearings are more sparingly utilized, the dismissal rules can readily be in the range of 20–30%.

Step 11: Grand Jury Review. Although almost all American jurisdictions have provisions authorizing grand jury screening of felony charges, such screening is mandatory only in those jurisdictions requiring felony prosecutions to be instituted by an indictment, a charging instrument issued by the grand jury. Eighteen states, the federal system, and the District of Columbia currently require grand jury indictments for all felony prosecutions (unless waived by the defendant). Four additional states require prosecution by indictment only for felonies subject to the most severe punishment (life imprisonment and capital punishment). In the remaining states, the prosecution is allowed to proceed at its option either by indictment or by information, a charging instrument issued on the authority of the prosecutor. Because prosecutors here most often choose to proceed by information, these states are commonly described as "information states".

The grand jury is composed of a group of private citizens who are selected to review cases presented over a term that may range from one to several months. Traditionally the grand jury consisted of 23 persons, with the favorable vote of a majority needed to indict. Today, many states use a somewhat smaller grand jury (e.g., 12) and some require more than a simple majority to indict. As in the case of the magistrate at the preliminary hearing, the primary function of the grand jury is to determine whether there is sufficient evidence to justify a trial on the charge sought by the prosecution.[g] The grand jury, however, participates in a screening process quite different from the preliminary hearing. It meets in a closed session and hears only the evidence presented by the prosecution. The defendant has no right to offer his own evidence or to be present during grand jury proceedings. If a majority of the grand jurors conclude that the prosecution's evidence is sufficient, the grand jury will issue the indictment requested by the prosecutor. If the grand jury majority refuses to approve a proposed indictment, the charges against the defendant will be dismissed. In most indictment jurisdictions, grand juries refuse to indict in only a small percentage (e.g., 3 to 5%) of the cases presented before them.

Step 12: The Filing of the Indictment or Information. If the prosecution was presented to the grand jury and an indictment was issued, it will be filed with the general trial court and will replace the complaint as the accusatory instrument in the case. If the prosecution is permitted by information (either because a grand jury indictment is not required or the defendant waived), that instrument will be filed with the trial court. In most "information states," the charge in the information must be supported by a preliminary hearing bindover (unless the preliminary hearing was waived), but several information states allow for "direct filing" by the prosecutor without either a bindover or a waiver.

g. The grand jury and the preliminary hearing are not necessarily alternative screening devices. In most information states, where the prosecution chooses the option of seeking a grand jury indictment, that selection is made to avoid a preliminary hearing. Thus, defendants will have either a preliminary hearing (the usual situation) or a grand jury review (the unusual). Similarly, in some indictment jurisdictions, prosecution policy is almost always to proceed directly to the grand jury, thereby cutting off the preliminary hearing. However, in other indictment states, felony cases usually are presented first to a magistrate at a preliminary hearing (unless the defendant waives) and then to the grand jury. The grand jury is in no way bound by any prior ruling at the preliminary hearing. It may indict even though the magistrate dismissed the charge at the preliminary hearing and may refuse to indict even though the magistrate found probable cause.

Step 13: Arraignment on the Information or Indictment. After the indictment or information has been filed, the defendant is arraigned—i.e., he is brought before the trial court, informed of the charges against him, and asked to enter a plea of guilty, not guilty, or, as is permitted under some circumstances, *nolo contendere.* In the end, most of those felony defendants whose cases reach the trial court will plead guilty. At the arraignment, however, they are likely to enter a plea of not guilty. Where there has not been a preliminary hearing, defense counsel probably will not be fully apprised of the strength of the prosecution's case at this point in the proceedings. Also, in most jurisdictions, guilty pleas in felony cases are the product of plea negotiations with the prosecution, and in many places, that process does not start until after the arraignment. When the defendant enters a plea of not guilty at the arraignment, the judge will set a trial date, but the general expectation is that the trial will not be held.

Between the arraignment and the scheduled trial date, three possible dispositions can result in the termination of the case without trial. Although there will have been extensive prosecutorial screening by this point, changed circumstances and new information typically will lead to dismissals on a prosecutor's *nolle prosequi* motion in roughly 5–15% of the cases. A smaller percentage of the informations or indictments will be dismissed on motion of the defense, as discussed in step 14. The vast majority of the dispositions without trial will be the product of guilty pleas.

Guilty pleas in felony cases commonly will be entered in response to a plea agreement under which the prosecution offers certain concessions in return for the defendant's entry of the plea. Those concessions may take the form of a reduction of the charges (sometimes to misdemeanor and sometimes to a lesser felony charge), a dismissal of related charges where the defendant faces multiple charges, a recommendation on sentence, or a specific sentence (when agreed to by the trial court). Prosecutors' offices vary in the concessions they offer and their willingness to bargain over concessions (as opposed to presenting a take-it-or-leave-it offer). Prosecutors also vary as to the types of cases in which they will offer concessions, with some generally refusing to do so on the most serious charges. Indeed, there are jurisdictions in which prosecutors will not plea bargain, although defendants here may still find an inducement to plead guilty in a general policy of trial judges to give favorable weight in sentencing to the defendant's willingness to plead guilty.

Although the guilty plea remains the primary mode of disposition for felony indictments and informations in all jurisdictions, considerable variation exists in the percentage of defendants who enter guilty pleas. Most jurisdictions appear to fall within the range of 60–85%. Of course, when dispositions by dismissals are excluded, and only guilty pleas and trials are compared, the rate of guilty pleas is much higher. Thus, a leading study of 14 communities found a median ratio of 11 pleas for every trial, with one jurisdiction having as many as 37 pleas for each trial.

The guilty plea rate also tends to be very high in the disposition of misdemeanor charges in the magistrate court. Although there tends to be less plea negotiation on charges originally filed as misdemeanors (particularly lower-level misdemeanors), the ratio of guilty pleas to trials is often as high or higher than that in felony courts. Indeed, there are jurisdictions in which the magistrate will receive more than a hundred guilty pleas for every trial held. On the other hand, other jurisdictions report ratios in magistrate courts that are lower than the typical ratio for felonies.

Step 14: Pretrial Motions. In most jurisdictions, a broad range of objections must be raised by a pretrial motion. Those motions commonly present challenges to the institution of the prosecution (e.g., claims regarding the grand jury indictment process), attacks upon the sufficiency of the charging instrument, requests for disclosure of evidence within the government's possession that has not been made available through discovery, and requests for the suppression of evidence allegedly acquired by the government through a constitutional violation. While some pretrial motions are made only by defendants who intend to go to trial, other motions (e.g., for further discovery) may benefit as well defendants who expect in the end to plead guilty. Nevertheless, pretrial motions are likely to be made in only a small portion of the felony cases that reach the trial court. Their use does vary considerably, however, with the nature of the case. In narcotics cases, for example, motions to suppress are quite common. In the typical forgery case, on the other, pretrial motions of any type are quite rare.

As a group, pretrial motions are likely to result in the dismissal of not more than 5% of all of the felony cases coming before the trial judge. The pretrial motion most likely to produce a dismissal is the motion to suppress. Quite frequently, if the defendant gains suppression of unconstitutionally obtained evidence, there will be insufficient remaining evidence to continue with the prosecution. In misdemeanor cases before the magistrate court, motions tend to be made only in cases slated for trial and even there, they are uncommon. Thus, the percentage of magistrate-court cases dismissed on the basis of a successful defense motion probably falls below one percent.

Step 15: The Trial. Assuming that there has not been a dismissal and the defendant has not entered a guilty plea (or a *nolle contendere* plea), the next step in the criminal process is the trial. In most respects, the criminal trial resembles the civil trial. There are, however, several distinguishing features that are either unique to criminal trials or of special importance in such trials. These include: (1) the presumption of defendant's innocence; (2) the requirement of proof beyond a reasonable doubt; (3) the right of the defendant not to take the stand; (4) the exclusion of evidence obtained by the state in an illegal manner; and (5) the more frequent use of incriminating statements of defendants. In most jurisdictions, the misdemeanor trial before a "court of record" will be almost indistinguishable from a felony trial. In some jurisdictions, however, even such misdemeanor trials tend to be less formal (as is typically the case for trials in magistrate courts "not of record").

As noted previously, most felony and misdemeanor cases are likely to be disposed of either by a guilty plea or by a dismissal. Quite commonly, only 5–15% of the felony cases that reach the trial court actually will go to trial. Before the magistrate court, the percentage of misdemeanor cases resolved by a trial tends to be even lower. The median time frame from the arrest of the defendant to the start of the trial will vary substantially from one community to another, but in congested urban districts, it is likely to fall within the range of 5–10 months. While most jurisdictions have speedy trials requirements that impose time limits of 6 months or less, there are various excludable time periods (for factors such as witness unavailability and the processing of motions) which commonly extend the time limit by at least a few months.

The trial itself tends to be relatively short. Misdemeanor trials typically last less than a day. Felony jury trials are somewhat longer, but most will be completed within 2–3 days. One variable will be the local practice governing *voir dire* (the questioning of prospective jurors, either by judge or counsel), as some jurisdictions tend to spend considerably more time on jury selection than others. Another will be the type of case, as certain types of offenses (e.g., complex white collar offenses and capital homicide cases) produce trials substantially longer than the typical felony. In general trials to the bench are considerably shorter, and unlikely to last more than a day.

In all jurisdictions, the defendant will have a right to a jury trial for all felony offenses and for misdemeanors punishable by more than 6 months imprisonment. Most states also provide a jury trial for lesser misdemeanors as well (although that right may exist only through the opportunity to seek a trial *de novo* in the general trial court after an initial bench trial before the magistrate court). Juries traditionally were composed of 12 persons, but many states now utilize 6 person juries in misdemeanor cases and several use the smaller juries in non-capital felony cases as well. Of course, the right to a jury trial can be waived, and in most jurisdictions, a significant number of defendants will waive the jury in favor of a bench trial. Over the country as a whole, however, roughly 70% of all felony trials are tried to a jury. In misdemeanor cases, in contrast, bench trials often predominate (sometimes by a substantial margin) even in jurisdictions that extend the defendant's jury trial right to all misdemeanors. In all but a few jurisdictions, the jury verdict in misdemeanor and felony cases, whether for acquittal or conviction, must be unanimous. Where the jurors cannot agree, no verdict is entered and the case may be retried. Such "hung juries" occur in only a very small percentage of the cases tried to a jury (e.g., 3–6%).

Whether a criminal case is tried to the bench or the jury, the odds favor conviction over acquittal. A fairly typical ratio for felony charges will be 3 convictions for every acquittal. That ratio may vary significantly, however, with the nature of the offense. In some jurisdictions, the rate of conviction at trial tends to be substantially lower (though still well above 50%) for some crimes (e.g., rape and murder) than for others (e.g., drug trafficking).

With the end of the trial stage, the criminal justice process will have produced a disposition as to all persons who originally entered the process through an arrest or the issuance of citation. As for those who were arrested on felony charges, only one out of a hundred is likely to have had the case against him carried through to a trial that resulted in an acquittal. A much larger portion of the felony arrestees, roughly anywhere from 30–50%, also will not have been convicted, but the dispositions in their favor will have come at the very outset, through pre-filing police and prosecutor screening, or before the trial, either through *nolle prosequi* motions or judicial and grand jury screening procedures.[h] Of the 50–70% of the felony arrestees who will have been convicted, many will not have been convicted of felonies. Depending upon the plea negotiation practices followed in the particular jurisdiction, anywhere from 10–30% of those felony arrestees convicted are likely to have been convicted of misdemeanors.

Step 16: Sentencing. Following conviction, the next step in the process is the determination of the sentence. In all but a few jurisdictions (which allow for jury sentencing, even apart from capital punishment), the sentence determination is the function of the court. Basically three different types of sentences may be used:

---

h. In some jurisdictions, another disposition—transfer to the "inactive docket" or "prosecution terminations"—will account for as many as 5–10% of all felony cases not resulting in convictions. These are cases in which the defendant is "unavailable"—usually because he has absconded, but sometimes because he is incarcerated elsewhere or is outside the jurisdiction. To avoid building a docket backlog, courts eventually require that these cases be removed from docket by some "disposition". In some instances, the prosecution will be renewed, but the cases then are listed as new prosecutions.

(1) financial sanctions (e.g., fines, restitution orders); (2) some form of release into the community (e.g., probation, unsupervised release, house arrest); and (3) incarceration in a jail (for lesser sentences) or prison (for longer sentences). The process applied in determining the sentence is shaped in considerable part by the sentencing options made available to the court by the legislature. For a particular offense, the court may have no choice. The legislature may have prescribed that conviction automatically carries with it a certain sentence and there is nothing left for the court to do except impose that sentence. Most frequently, however, legislative narrowing of options on a particular offense does not go beyond eliminating the community release option (by requiring incarceration) and setting some limits on the use of those sanctions that remain available.

The sentence of incarceration for a felony offense probably presents the widest diversity of approach to judicial sentencing authority. The sentence may be indeterminate (setting a maximum and minimum term of imprisonment, with the parole board determining the actual release date within the span set by those two terms) or determinate (a set term, with the defendant required to serve a high percentage of that term, less credits for good behavior). In some jurisdictions, the court has complete discretion in setting the term or terms within its control. In others, however, sentencing guidelines direct the judge in exercising her authority, although departures from the guidelines are allowed upon a judicial finding of specific justification.

The process utilized in felony sentencing varies to some extent according to whether judicial discretion is broad or is channeled or limited by guideline or legislative reference to specific sentencing circumstances. In all jurisdictions, the process is designed to obtain for the court information beyond that which will have come to its attention in the course of trial or in the acceptance of a guilty plea. The primary vehicle here is the presentence report prepared by the probation department, although the prosecution and defense commonly will be allowed to present additional information and to challenge the information contained in the presentence report. The presentation of this information is not subject to the rules governing the presentation of information at trial. The rules of evidence do not apply, and neither side is given an automatic right to call witnesses or to cross-examine the sources of adverse information presented in the presentence report or in any additional documentation presented by the opposing side. However, where the sentencing authority of the judge is restricted by guidelines or legislatively mandated sentencing controls that require findings of fact as to specific factors, the sentencing process tends to be more formal. Here, the court often will find it necessary to hold an evidentiary hearing and utilize trial-type procedures if the presence of a critical factor is controverted.

Although individual sentences vary with, such factors as aggravating and mitigating circumstances, past criminal convictions, criminal behavior that did not result in a conviction, and the defendant's acceptance of responsibility, some general patterns emerge in accordance with gravity of the crime for which the sentence is imposed. As for misdemeanor convictions, at least where they do not reflect a negotiated plea reduction from a felony charge, the vast majority of sentenced defendants will be sentenced to a fine and/or some form of community release. Lower-level felony convictions and plea-reduced misdemeanor convictions more commonly result in a sentence of incarceration (often to a short jail term), although a substantial proportion of such offenders (e.g., 30–40%) are likely to be sentenced only to probation (or another sentence not involving incarceration). Convictions for higher-level felonies typically produce sentences of incarceration in prison. For offenses such as burglary and drug trafficking, the proportion of offenders sentenced to prison is likely to approach or exceed 50%, with the remainder equally divided between jail sentences (often combined with probation) and straight probation. Serious violent crimes such as rape and robbery have the highest rate of prison sentences, ranging as high as 80%. While the terms will vary by offense and sentence structure, illustrative means for the offenses of robbery and rape, measured by time actually served, would be in the neighborhood of 29–41 months for robbery and 33–48 months for rape. Substantially longer terms will be imposed, however, where the defendant is proceeded against as a recidivist.

Turning back to the start of the process, with the report of a felony offense, the criminal justice process has taken the shape of a funnel. More crimes were reported than investigated, more investigated than arrests made, more persons arrested than charged, more charged than convicted, and more convicted than sentenced to incarceration. An extreme example of this "funnel effect" is illustrated by one author's analysis of the "statistics for New York City" in 1988. These statistics started with 550,000 felonies reported to police (evidencing, perhaps, one million felonies committed), 124,000 arrests on felony charges, 35,000 felony indictments, 27,800 felony convictions, and 16,755 persons "sent to jail or prison".

Step 17: Appeals. For criminal cases disposed of in the general trial court, the initial appeal is to the intermediate appellate court. If the state has no intermediate appellate court, then the initial and final appeal within the state system is to the state's court of last resort. Initial appeals in cases disposed of by the magistrate court will be to the general trial court. If the magistrate court is not of record, the appeal procedure is a trial *de novo* before the general trial court.

Although all convicted defendants are entitled to appeal their convictions, appeals are taken predominantly by convicted defendants who were sentenced to imprisonment on a felony conviction. Imprisoned defendants convicted pursuant to a guilty plea are included in this group, but they account for only a narrow slice of all appeals. Though the trial court's acceptance of a guilty plea may be challenged on appeal, such appellate challenges are limited to exceptional circumstances, so that appeals by guilty plea defendants tend to be sentencing challenges, which are limited in scope in most jurisdictions. Appeals challenging the conviction itself come primarily from imprisoned defendants who are seeking review of a trial conviction. Indeed, in some jurisdictions, as many as 90% of the defendants who were convicted after trial and sentenced to prison will appeal their convictions. Even with almost automatic appeal by this group, however, the total number of appeals to the intermediate appeals court is likely to amount to less than 10% of all convictions entered by the state's general trial court. Where the jurisdictions do provide for extensive appellate review of sentencing, that percentage may be somewhat higher. At the misdemeanor level, on the other hand, the appeals rate will be substantially lower.

Defense success on appeal varies with the particular appellate court. Among the federal Courts of Appeals, for example, for criminal appeals terminated on the merits in 1990, the percentage of reversals ranged from a high of 15% in the District of Columbia Circuit to a low of 7.4% in the First Circuit, with an overall rate of 10.4% for all circuits. State intermediate appellate courts commonly have a reversal rate on defense appeals of right in the 5–10% range, although some have higher rates when reversals in-part are included. Courts of last resort with discretionary jurisdiction are most likely to limit their review to close cases and therefore, may have a substantially higher rate of reversals.

Step 18: Postconviction Remedies. After the appellate process is exhausted, imprisoned defendants may be able to use postconviction remedies to challenge their convictions on limited grounds. In particular, federal postconviction remedies are available to state as well as federal prisoners to challenge their convictions in the federal courts on most constitutional grounds. The federal district courts currently receive annually roughly 18,000 state-prisoner postconviction applications. Relief is granted on less than 3% of these petitions, however, and the relief often is limited to requiring a further hearing. In the state system, annual postconviction challenges typically fall below 5% of all felony filings.

Chapter 2

THE NATURE AND SCOPE OF FOUR-TEENTH AMENDMENT DUE PROCESS; RETROACTIVITY; THE FEDERAL "SUPERVISORY POWER"; STATE RIGHTS PROTECTIONS

SECTION 1. THE "ORDERED LIBERTY"—"FUNDAMENTAL FAIRNESS," "TOTAL INCORPORATION" AND "SELECTIVE INCORPORATION" THEORIES

In *Twining v. New Jersey,* 211 U.S. 78, 29 S.Ct. 14, 53 L.Ed. 97 (1908); *Palko v. Connecticut,* 302 U.S. 319, 58 S.Ct. 149, 82 L.Ed. 288 (1937); and *Adamson v. California,* 332 U.S. 46, 67 S.Ct. 1672, 91 L.Ed. 1903 (1947), the Court rejected the "total incorporation" view of the history of the Fourteenth Amendment, the view—which has never commanded a majority—that the Fourteenth Amendment made all of the provisions of the federal Bill of Rights fully applicable to the states.[a] But *Twining* recognized that "it is possible that some of the personal rights safeguarded by the first eight Amendments against National action may also be safeguarded against state action, because a denial of them would be a denial of due process of law." And the Court early found among the procedural requirements of Fourteenth Amendment due process certain rules paralleling

---

a. *Palko,* which held that the Fourteenth Amendment did not encompass at least certain aspects of double jeopardy prohibition of the Fifth Amendment, was later overruled in *Benton v. Maryland,* 395 U.S. 784, 89 S.Ct. 2056, 23 L.Ed.2d 707 (1969). The position taken in *Twining* and *Adamson*—that the Fifth Amendment privilege against self-incrimination was not incorporated in the Fourteenth—was rejected in *Malloy v. Hogan* (1964), discussed below. *Griffin v. California,* Ch. 25, § 4, subsequently applied *Malloy* to overrule the specific holdings of *Twining* and *Adamson,* which had permitted comment on a state defendant's failure to take the stand. These later decisions, while overruling *Palko, Twining* and *Adamson,* were still consistent with the rejection of the "total incorporation" interpretation.

The total incorporation position had received its strongest support in the *Adamson* dissents. In the principal dissent, Justice Black, joined by Douglas, J., maintained that the history of the Fourteenth Amendment suggested its pur-

pose was to totally incorporate the federal Bill of Rights. Dissenting separately in *Adamson,* Justice Murphy, joined by Rutledge, J., "agree[d] that the specific guarantees of the Bill of Rights should be carried over intact into [the Fourteenth but was] not prepared to say that the latter is entirely and necessarily limited by the Bill of Rights. Occasions may arise where a proceeding falls so far short of conforming to fundamental standards of procedure as to warrant constitutional condemnation in terms of a lack of due process despite the absence of a specific provision of the Bill of Rights."

Responding to the dissents, Justice Frankfurter's concurring opinion in *Adamson* stressed the "independent potency" of the Fourteenth Amendment Due Process Clause, maintaining that that Amendment "neither comprehends the specific provisions by which the founders deemed it appropriate to restrict the federal government nor is confined to them."

provisions of the first eight amendments. For example, it held in *Powell v. Alabama* (1932) (discussed at pp. 64, 68) that defendants in a capital case were denied due process when a state refused them the aid of counsel. "The logically critical thing, however," pointed out Justice Harlan years later, "was not that the rights had been found in the Bill of Rights, but that they were deemed [to] be fundamental." *Duncan v. Louisiana,* Ch. 23, § 1. (dissenting opinion joined by Stewart, J.).

Particular procedural safeguards included in the Bill of Rights were said to be applicable to the states if they were "implicit in the concept of ordered liberty," Cardozo J., in *Palko;* "of the very essence of a scheme of ordered liberty," ibid.; "a fair and enlightened system of justice would be impossible without them," ibid.; required by "the 'immutable principles of justice' as conceived by a civilized society," Frankfurter, J., concurring in *Adamson;* or "fundamental to the American scheme of justice," White, J., in *Duncan v. Louisiana.*

As Justice WHITE noted (fn. 14) for the Court in DUNCAN v. LOUISIANA, 391 U.S. 145, 88 S.Ct. 1444, 20 L.Ed.2d 491 (1968) (holding the Sixth Amendment right to jury trial applicable to the states via the Fourteenth), the different phraseology is not without significance:

"Earlier the Court can be seen as having asked, when inquiring into whether some particular procedural safeguard was required of a State, if a civilized system could be imagined that would not accord the particular protection [quoting from *Palko*]. The recent cases, on the other hand, have proceeded upon the valid assumption that state criminal processes are not imaginary and theoretical schemes but actual systems bearing virtually every characteristic of the common-law system that has been developing contemporaneously in England and this country. The question thus is whether given this kind of system a particular procedure is fundamental—whether, that is, a procedure is necessary to an Anglo American regime of ordered liberty. It is this sort of inquiry that can justify the conclusions that state courts must exclude evidence seized in violation of the Fourth Amendment, *Mapp v. Ohio* [p. 124] [and] that state prosecutors may not comment on a defendant's failure to testify, *Griffin v. California* [Ch. 24, § 4]. [Of] each of these determinations that a constitutional provision originally written to bind the Federal Government should bind the States as well it might be said that the limitation in question is not necessarily fundamental to fairness in every criminal system that might be imagined but is fundamental in the context of the criminal processes maintained by the American States.

"When the inquiry is approached in this way the question whether the States can impose criminal punishment without granting a jury trial appears quite different from the way it appeared in the older cases opining that States might abolish jury trial. A criminal process which was fair and equitable but used no juries is easy to imagine. It would make use of alternative guarantees and protections which would serve the purposes that the jury serves in the English and American systems. Yet no American State has undertaken to construct such a system. Instead, every American State, including Louisiana, uses the jury extensively, and imposes very serious punishments only after a trial at which the defendant has a right to a jury's verdict. In every State, including Louisiana, the structure and style of the criminal process—the supporting framework and the subsidiary procedures—are of the sort that naturally complement jury trial, and have developed in connection with and in reliance upon jury trial."[b]

b. See also Justice Powell, concurring in the companion 1972 "jury unanimity" cases of

Although the Court has remained unwilling to accept the total incorporationists' reading of the Fourteenth Amendment, in the 1960's it "selectively" "incorporated" or "absorbed" more and more of the specifics of the Bill of Rights into the Fourteenth Amendment. As Justice White observed in *Duncan:*

"In resolving conflicting claims concerning the meaning of this spacious [Fourteenth Amendment] language, the Court has looked increasingly to the Bill of Rights for guidance; many of the rights guaranteed by the first eight Amendments to the Constitution have been held to be protected against state action by the Due Process Clause of the Fourteenth Amendment. That clause now protects [the] Fourth Amendment rights to be free from unreasonable searches and seizures and to have excluded from criminal trials any evidence illegally seized; the right guaranteed by the Fifth Amendment to be free of compelled self-incrimination; and the Sixth Amendment rights to counsel, to a speedy and public trial [*Klopfer v. North Carolina,* Ch. 19, § 1], to confrontation of opposing witnesses [*Pointer v. Texas,* Ch. 14, § 1] and to compulsory process for obtaining witnesses [*Washington v. Texas,* Ch. 25, § 3]."[c]

Moreover, the Court seemed to be "incorporating" not only the basic notion or general concept of the "selected" provision of the Bill of Rights, but applying the provision to the states *to the same extent* it applied to the federal government. As some Justices, especially Harlan, protested, the federal guarantees were being incorporated into the Fourteenth "freighted with their entire accompanying body of federal doctrine" (Harlan, J., joined by Clark, J., dissenting in *Malloy v. Hogan,* discussed below); "jot-for-jot and case-for-case" (Harlan, J., joined by Stewart, J., dissenting in *Duncan*); "bag and baggage, however securely or insecurely affixed they may be by law and precedent to federal proceedings" (Fortas, J., concurring in *Duncan*).

Thus, Justice Brennan observed for a majority of the Court in *Malloy v. Hogan,* 378 U.S. 1, 84 S.Ct. 1489, 12 L.Ed.2d 653 (1964):

Johnson v. Louisiana and *Apodaca v. Oregon* (discussed below) (fn. 9):

"I agree with Mr. Justice White's analysis in *Duncan* that the departure from earlier decisions was, in large measure, a product of a change in focus in the Court's approach to due process. No longer are questions regarding the constitutionality of particular criminal procedures resolved by focusing alone on the element in question and ascertaining whether a system of criminal justice might be imagined in which a fair trial could be afforded in the absence of that particular element. Rather, the focus is, as it should be, on the fundamentality of that element viewed in the context of the basic Anglo–American jurisprudential system common to the States. That approach to due process readily accounts both for the conclusion that jury trial *is* fundamental and that unanimity *is not.*"

c. See also Justice Black, joined by Douglas, J., concurring in *Duncan:* "[I] believe as strongly as ever that the Fourteenth Amendment was intended to make the Bill of Rights applicable to the States. I have been willing to support the selective incorporation doctrine, however, as an alternative, although perhaps less historically supportable than complete incorporation [because it] keeps judges from roaming at will in their own notions of what policies outside the Bill of Rights are desirable and what are not. And, most importantly for me, the selective incorporation process has the virtue of having already worked to make most of the Bill of Rights' protections applicable to the States."

In the area of criminal procedure, the Court has indeed come very close to incorporation of all of the relevant Bill of Rights guarantees. In addition to the provisions noted above, the double jeopardy prohibition has also been made applicable to the states in *Benton,* fn. a supra. The Court has refused, however, to apply to the states the Fifth Amendment requirement that prosecution be initiated by grand jury indictment. See Ch. 15. On the application of the prohibition against excessive bail, see Ch. 12. See also Israel, *Selective Incorporation Revisited,* 71 Geo. L.J. 253 (1982), for an overview of the development and application of the selective incorporation doctrine.

"We hold that the Fourteenth Amendment guaranteed the petitioner the protection of the Fifth Amendment's privilege against self-incrimination, and that *under the applicable federal standard,* the [state court] erred in holding that the privilege was not properly invoked. [The State urges] that the availability of the federal privilege to a witness in a state inquiry is to be determined according to a less stringent safeguard than is applicable in a federal proceeding. We disagree. We have held that the guarantees of the First Amendment, the prohibition of unreasonable searches and seizures of the Fourth Amendment, and the right to counsel guaranteed by the Sixth Amendment, *Gideon v. Wainwright* [p. 67], are all to be enforced against the States under the Fourteenth Amendment *according to the same standards that protect those personal rights against federal encroachment.* [The] Court thus has rejected the notion that the Fourteenth Amendment applies to the States only a 'watered-down, subjective version of the individual guarantees of the Bill of Rights.' "(Emphasis added.)

And Justice White put it for a majority of the Court in *Duncan:* "Because we believe that trial by jury in criminal cases is fundamental to the American scheme of justice, we hold that the Fourteenth Amendment guarantees a right of jury trial in all criminal cases which—*were they to be tried in a federal court*—would come within the Sixth Amendment's guarantee." (Emphasis added.)

Justice Harlan repeatedly voiced his opposition to the *Malloy-Duncan* approach to Fourteenth Amendment Due Process. "The consequence," he protested in his *Malloy* dissent, "is inevitably disregard of all relevant differences which may exist between state and federal criminal law and its enforcement. The ultimate result is compelled uniformity, which is inconsistent with the purpose of our federal system and which is achieved either by encroachment on the State's sovereign powers or by dilution in federal law enforcement of the specific protections found in the Bill of Rights." See also Justice Harlan's concurring opinion in *Pointer v. Texas,* 380 U.S. 400, 85 S.Ct. 1065, 13 L.Ed.2d 923 (1965) (holding that an accused's Sixth Amendment right to confront the witnesses against him applies in its entirety to the states via the Fourteenth Amendment) and his dissenting opinion in *Benton v. Maryland,* fn. a supra.

In the 1970's matters were brought to a head by the "right to jury trial" cases:[d] BALDWIN v. NEW YORK, 399 U.S. 117, 90 S.Ct. 1914, 26 L.Ed.2d 446 (1970) (no offense can be deemed "petty," thus dispensing with the Fourteenth and Sixth Amendment rights to jury trial, where more than six months incarceration is authorized); WILLIAMS v. FLORIDA, 399 U.S. 78, 90 S.Ct. 1893, 26 L.Ed.2d 446 (1970) ("that jury at common law was composed of precisely 12 is an historical accident, unnecessary to effect the purposes of the jury system"; thus 6–person jury in criminal cases does not violate Sixth Amendment, as applied to the states via Fourteenth);[e] and the 1972 *Apodaca* and *Johnson* cases, discussed below, dealing with whether unanimous jury verdicts are required in criminal cases.

Dissenting in *Baldwin* and concurring in *Williams,* Justice HARLAN maintained:

"[*Williams*] evinces [a] recognition that the" incorporationist's view of the Due Process Clause of the Fourteenth Amendment, which underlay *Duncan* and is

d. For a fuller discussion of these cases, see Ch. 23, § 1.

e. But the Court subsequently held, in *Ballew v. Georgia,* 435 U.S. 223, 98 S.Ct. 1029, 55 L.Ed.2d 234 (1978), that a state trial in a non-petty criminal case to a jury of only five persons did deprive a defendant of the right to trial by jury guaranteed him by the Sixth and Fourteenth Amendments.

now carried forward into *Baldwin,* must be tempered to allow the States more elbow room in ordering their own criminal systems. With that much I agree. But to accomplish this by diluting constitutional protections within the federal system itself is something to which I cannot possibly subscribe. Tempering the rigor of *Duncan* should be done forthrightly, by facing up to the fact that at least in this area the 'incorporation' doctrine does not fit well with our federal structure, and by the same token that *Duncan* was wrongly decided.

"[Rather] than bind the States by the hitherto undeviating and unquestioned federal practice of 12–member juries, the Court holds, based on a poll of state practice, that a six-man jury satisfies the guarantee of a trial by jury in a federal criminal system and consequently carries over to the States. This is a constitutional *renvoi.* With all respect, I consider that before today it would have been unthinkable to suggest that the Sixth Amendment's right to a trial by jury is satisfied by a jury of six, or less, as is left open by the Court's opinion in *Williams,* or by less than a unanimous verdict, a question also reserved in today's decision.[f]

"[These] decisions demonstrate that the difference between a 'due process' approach, that considers each particular case on its own bottom to see whether the right alleged is one 'implicit in the concept of ordered liberty,' and 'selective incorporation' is not an abstract one whereby different verbal formulae achieve the same results. The internal logic of the selective incorporation doctrine cannot be respected if the Court is both committed to interpreting faithfully the meaning of the federal Bill of Rights and recognizing the governmental diversity that exists in this country. The 'backlash' in *Williams* exposes the malaise, for there the Court dilutes a federal guarantee in order to reconcile the logic of 'incorporation,' the 'jot-for-jot and case-for-case' application of the federal right to the States, with the reality of federalism. Can one doubt that had Congress tried to undermine the common law right to trial by jury before *Duncan* came on the books the history today recited would have barred such action? Can we expect repeat performances when this Court is called upon to give definition and meaning to other federal guarantees that have been 'incorporated'? * * *

" 'Incorporation' in *Duncan* closed the door on debate, irrespective of local circumstances, such as the backlogs in urban courts like those of New York City, and has, without justification, clouded with uncertainty the constitutionality of these differing states modes of proceeding pending approval by this Court; it now promises to dilute in other ways the settled meaning of the federal right to a trial by jury. Flexibility for experimentation in the administration of justice should be returned to the States here and in other areas that now have swept into the rigid mold of 'incorporation.'

"[It] is time, I submit, for this Court to face up to the reality implicit in today's holdings and reconsider the 'incorporation' doctrine before its leveling tendencies further retard development in the field of criminal procedure by stifling flexibility in the States and by discarding the possibility of federal leadership by example."

In the companion cases of *Apodaca v. Oregon,* 406 U.S. 404, 92 S.Ct. 1628, 32 L.Ed.2d 184 (1972) and *Johnson v. Louisiana,* 406 U.S. 356, 92 S.Ct. 1620, 32 L.Ed.2d 152 (1972), upholding the constitutionality of less-than-unanimous jury

f. Cf. Frankfurter, J., for the Court in *Rochin v. California* (1952) (discussed in the next section): "Words being symbols do not speak without a gloss. [T]he gloss may be the deposit of history, whereby a term gains technical content. Thus the requirements of the Sixth and Seventh Amendments for trial by jury in the federal courts have a rigid meaning. No changes or chances can alter the content of the verbal symbol of 'jury'—a body of twelve men who must reach a unanimous conclusion if the verdict is to go against the defendant."

verdicts in state criminal cases, eight Justices adhered to the *Duncan* position that each element of the Sixth Amendment right to jury trial applies to the states to the same extent it applies to the federal government, but split 4?4 over whether the federal guarantee *did require* jury unanimity in criminal cases. State convictions by less than unanimous votes were sustained only because the ninth member of the Court, newly appointed Justice Powell read the Sixth Amendment as requiring jury unanimity, but—taking a Harlan-type approach—concluded that *this feature* of the federal right is not "so fundamental to the essentials of jury trial" as to require unanimity in state criminal cases as a matter of Fourteenth Amendment Due Process.[g]

Observed Powell: "[I]n holding that the Fourteenth Amendment has incorporated 'jot-for-jot and case-for-case' every element of the Sixth Amendment, the Court derogates principles of federalism that are basic to our system. In the name of uniform application of high standards of due process, the Court has embarked upon a course of constitutional interpretation that deprives the States of freedom to experiment with adjudicatory processes different from the federal model. At the same time, the Court's understandable unwillingness to impose requirements that it finds unnecessarily rigid (e.g., *Williams*), has culminated in the dilution of federal rights that were, until these decisions, never seriously questioned. The doubly undesirable consequence of this reasoning process, labeled by Mr. Justice Harlan as 'constitutional schizophrenia,' may well be detrimental both to the state and federal criminal justice systems. Although it is perhaps late in the day for an expression of my views, I [believe] that, at least in defining the elements of the right to jury trial, there is no sound basis for interpreting the Fourteenth Amendment to require blind adherence by the States to all details of the federal Sixth Amendment standards."[h]

Dissenting Justice Brennan, joined by Marshall, J., observed:"Readers of today's opinions may be understandably puzzled why convictions by 11–1 and 10–2 jury votes are affirmed [when] a majority of the Court agrees that the Sixth Amendment requires a unanimous verdict in federal criminal jury trials, and a majority also agrees that the right to jury trial guaranteed by the Sixth Amendment is to be enforced against the States according to the same standards that protect that right against federal encroachment. The reason is that while my Brother Powell agrees that a unanimous verdict is required in federal criminal trials, he does not agree that the Sixth Amendment right to a jury trial is to be applied in the same way to State and Federal Governments. In that circumstance, it is arguable that the affirmance of the convictions * * * is not inconsistent with a view that today's decision is a holding that only a unanimous verdict will afford the accused in a state criminal prosecution the jury trial guaranteed him by the Sixth Amendment. In any event, the affirmance must not obscure that the majority of the Court remains of the view that, as in the case of every specific of the Bill of Rights that extends to the States, the Sixth Amendment's jury trial

g. But the Court subsequently held, in *Burch v. Louisiana*, Ch. 22, § 1, per Rehnquist, J. (without a dissent on this issue), that conviction by a nonunanimous *six-person* jury in a state criminal trial for a non-petty offense did violate the Sixth and Fourteenth Amendment rights to trial by jury.

h. In his continued resistance to "jot-for-jot" or "bag and baggage" incorporation of a "selected" provision of the Bill of Rights, Justice Powell soon gained two allies. See Powell, J., joined by the Chief Justice and Rehnquist, J., dissenting in *Crist v. Bretz*, Ch. 26, § 1. In *Ballew*, fn. e supra, although he concurred in the judgment, Justice Powell, again joined by the Chief Justice and Rehnquist, J., did not join Justice Blackmun's opinion because it Assumes full incorporation of the Sixth Amendment, contrary to my view in *"podaca."*

guarantee, however it is to be construed, has identical application against both State and Federal Governments."[i]

SECTION 2. THE PROBLEM OF BODILY EXTRACTIONS: ANOTHER LOOK AT THE "DUE PROCESS" AND "SELECTIVE INCORPORATION" APPROACHES

As noted in the previous section, dissenting in *Baldwin* and concurring in *Williams,* Justice Harlan maintained that "the difference between a 'due process' approach [and] 'selective incorporation' is not an abstract one whereby different formulae achieve the same results." But he made this observation in the context of the applicability to the states of the Sixth Amendment right to trial by jury, which had, or was thought to have, a relatively rigid meaning. Most language in the Bill of Rights, however, is rather vague and general, at least when specific problems arise under a particular phrase. In such cases, does dwelling on the literal language simply *shift the focus of broad judicial inquiry* from "due process" to, e.g., "freedom of speech," "establishment of religion," "unreasonable searches and seizures," "excessive bail," "cruel and unusual punishments," and "the assistance of counsel"? See Henry J. Friendly, *The Bill of Rights as a Code of Criminal Procedure,* 53 Calif.L.Rev. 929, 937 (1965); Sanford H. Kadish, *Methodology and Criteria in Due Process Adjudication–A Survey and Criticism,* 66 Yale L.J. 319, (1957); John E. Nowak, *Due Process Methodology in the Postincorporation World,* 70 J.Crim.L. & C. 397, 400–01 (1979) (arguing that decisions based on specific guarantees tend to rely on definitional analysis and fail to explore the interests at stake.)

In considering whether the right to counsel "begins" at the time of arrest, preliminary hearing, arraignment, or not until the trial itself, or includes probation and parole revocation hearings or applies to juvenile delinquency proceedings, deportation hearings or civil commitments, or, where the defendant is indigent, includes the right to *assigned* counsel or an assigned psychiatrist at state expense, how helpful is the Sixth Amendment language entitling an accused to "the assistance of counsel for his defense"? Is the specificity or direction of this language significantly greater than the "due process" clause?

To turn to another cluster of problems—which form the basis for this section—in considering whether, and under what conditions, the police may direct the "pumping" of a person's stomach to uncover incriminating evidence, or the taking of a blood sample from him, without his consent, do the "specific guarantees" in the Bill of Rights against "unreasonable searches and seizures" and against compelling a person to be "a witness against himself" free the Court from the demands of appraising and judging involved in answering these questions by interpreting the "due process" clause?

ROCHIN v. CALIFORNIA, 342 U.S. 165, 72 S.Ct. 205, 96 L.Ed. 183 (1952), arose as follows: Having "some information" that Rochin was selling narcotics, three deputy sheriffs "forced open the door of [his] room and found him sitting partly dressed on the side of the bed, upon which his wife was lying. On a 'night stand' beside the bed the deputies spied two capsules. When asked 'Whose stuff is

---

i. In a separate dissent, Stewart, J., joined by Brennan Marshall, J.J., protested that "unless *Duncan* is to be overruled," "the only relevant question here is whether the Sixth Amendment [guarantees] that the verdict of the jury must be unanimous. The answer to that question is clearly 'yes,' as my Brother Powell has cogently demonstrated * * *."

this?' Rochin seized the capsules and put them in his mouth. A struggle ensued in the course of which the three officers 'jumped upon him' and [unsuccessfully] attempted to extract the capsules. [Rochin] was handcuffed and taken to a hospital. At the direction of one of the officers, a doctor forced an emetic solution through a tube into Rochin's stomach against his will. This 'stomach pumping' produced vomiting. In the vomited matter were found two capsules which proved to contain morphine. [Rochin was convicted of possessing morphine] and sentenced to sixty days' imprisonment. The chief evidence against him was the two capsules."

The Court, per FRANKFURTER, J., concluded that the police conduct violated fourteenth amendment due process: "This is conduct that shocks the conscience. Illegally breaking into the privacy of the petitioner, the struggle to open his mouth and remove what was there, the forcible extraction of his stomach's contents—this course of proceeding by agents of government to obtain evidence is bound to offend even hardened sensibilities. They are methods too close to the rack and the screw to permit of constitutional differentiation.

"It has long since ceased to be true that due process of law is heedless of the means by which otherwise relevant and credible evidence is obtained. [The confession] decisions [are] only instances of the general requirement that States in their prosecutions respect certain decencies of civilized conduct. Due process of law, as a historic and generative principle, precludes defining, and thereby confining, these standards of conduct more precisely than to say that convictions cannot be brought about by methods that offend 'a sense of justice.' It would be a stultification of the responsibility which the course of constitutional history has cast upon this Court to hold that in order to convict a man the police cannot extract by force what is in his mind but can extract what is in his stomach.

"[E]ven though statements contained in them may be independently established as true, [c]oerced confessions offend the community's sense of fair play and decency. So here, to sanction the brutal conduct which naturally enough was condemned by the court whose judgment is before us, would be to afford brutality the cloak of law. Nothing would be more calculated to discredit law and thereby to brutalize the temper of a society."

Concurring Justice BLACK reasoned that the Fifth Amendment's protection against compelled self-incrimination applied to the states and that "a person is compelled to be a witness against himself not only when he is compelled to testify, but also when as here, incriminating evidence is forcibly taken from him by a contrivance of modern science." He maintained that "faithful adherence to the specific guarantees in the Bill of Rights insures a more permanent protection of individual liberty than that which can be afforded by the nebulous [Fourteenth Amendment due process] standards stated by the majority."

In a separate concurring opinion, Justice DOUGLAS also criticized the majority's approach. He contended that the privilege against self-incrimination applied to the states as well as the federal government and because of the privilege "words taken from [an accused's] lips, capsules taken from his stomach, blood taken from his veins are all inadmissible provided they are taken from him without his consent. [This] is an unequivocal, definite and workable rule of evidence for state and federal courts. But we cannot in fairness free the state courts from the [restraints of the Fifth Amendment privilege against self-incrimination] and yet excoriate them for flouting the 'decencies of civilized conduct' when they admit the evidence. This is to make the rule turn not on the Constitution but on the idiosyncracies of the judges who sit here."

Irvine v. California, 347 U.S. 128, 74 S.Ct. 381, 98 L.Ed. 561 (1954), limited *Rochin* to situations involving coercion, violence or brutality to the person.[a] BREITHAUPT v. ABRAM, 352 U.S. 432, 77 S.Ct. 408, 1 L.Ed.2d 448 (1957), illustrated that under the *Rochin* test state police had considerable leeway even when the body of the accused was "invaded." In *Breithaupt,* the police took a blood sample from an unconscious person who had been involved in a fatal automobile collision. A majority, per CLARK, J., affirmed a manslaughter conviction based on the blood sample (which showed intoxication), stressing that the sample was "taken under the protective eye of a physician" and that "the blood test procedure has become routine in our everyday life." "[T]he interests of society in the scientific determination of intoxication, one of the great causes of the mortal hazards of the road," outweighed "so slight an intrusion" of a person's body.

Dissenting Chief Justice WARREN, joined by Black and Douglas, JJ., deemed *Rochin* controlling and argued that police efforts to curb the narcotics traffic, involved in *Rochin,* "is surely a state interest of at least as great magnitude as the interest in highway law enforcement. * * * Only personal reaction to the stomach pump and the blood test can distinguish the [two cases]."

Justice DOUGLAS, joined by Black, J., also wrote a separate dissent, maintaining that "if the decencies of a civilized state are the test, it is repulsive to me for the police to insert needles into an unconscious person in order to get the evidence necessary to convict him, whether they find the person unconscious, give him a pill which puts him to sleep, or use force to subdue him."

Nine years later, even though in the meantime the Court had held in *Mapp* that the federal exclusionary rule in search and seizure cases was binding on the states and in *Malloy v. Hogan,* supra, that the Fifth Amendment's protection against compelled self-incrimination was likewise applicable to the states, the Court still upheld the taking by a physician, at police direction, of a blood sample from an injured person, over his objection. SCHMERBER v. CALIFORNIA, 384

---

a. In *Irvine* the police made repeated illegal entries into petitioner's home, first to install a secret microphone and then to move it to the bedroom, in order to listen to the conversations of the occupants—for over a month.

Jackson, J., who announced the judgment of the Court and wrote the principal opinion, recognized that "few police measures have come to our attention that more flagrantly, deliberately, and persistently violated the fundamental principle declared by the Fourth Amendment as a restriction on the Federal Government," but adhered to the holding in *Wolf v. Colorado* (1949), p. 122, that the exclusionary rule in federal search and seizure cases is not binding on the states. (*Wolf* was overruled in *Mapp v. Ohio* (1961), p. 124.) Nor did Justice Jackson deem *Rochin* applicable: "However obnoxious are the facts in the case before us, they do not involve coercion, violence or brutality to the person [as did *Rochin*], but rather a trespass to property, plus eavesdropping."

Because of the "aggravating" and "repulsive" police misconduct in *Irvine,* Frankfurter, J., joined by Burton, J., dissented, maintaining

that *Rochin* was controlling, not *Wolf.* (He had written the majority opinions in both cases.) Black, J., joined by Douglas, J., dissented separately, arguing that petitioner had been convicted on the basis of evidence "extorted" from him in violation of the Fifth Amendment's privilege against compelled self-incrimination, which he considered applicable to the states. Douglas, J., dissenting separately, protested against the use in state prosecutions of evidence seized in violation of the Fourth Amendment.

Speaking for himself and Chief Justice Warren, Justice Jackson suggested that copies of the Court's opinion and the record in the case be sent to the U.S. Attorney General for possible federal prosecution. The FBI did conduct an investigation which revealed that the officers who placed the microphone in Irvine's home were acting under orders of the Chief of Police and with the full knowledge of the local prosecutor. Thus, concluded the Department of Justice, "it would be both useless and inadvisable to present [the] matter to the Federal grand jury." See Comment, 7 Stan.L.Rev. 76, 94, fn. 75 (1954).

U.S. 757, 86 S.Ct. 1826, 16 L.Ed.2d 908 (1966).[b] In affirming the conviction for operating a vehicle while under the influence of intoxicating liquor, a 5–4 majority, per BRENNAN, J., ruled: (1) that the extraction of blood from petitioner under the aforementioned circumstances "did not offend 'that "sense of justice" ' of which we spoke in *Rochin*," thus reaffirming *Breithaupt;* (2) that the privilege against self-incrimination, now binding on the states, "protects an accused only from being compelled to testify against himself, or otherwise provide the State with evidence of a testimonial or communicative nature and that the withdrawal of blood and use of the analysis in question did not involve compulsion to these ends";[c] and (3) that the protection against unreasonable search and seizure, now binding on the states, was satisfied because (a) "there was plainly probable cause" to arrest and charge petitioner and to suggest "the required relevance and likely success of a test of petitioner's blood for alcohol"; (b) the officer "might reasonably have believed that he was confronted with an emergency, in which the delay necessary to obtain a warrant, under the circumstances, threatened 'the destruction of evidence' "; and (c) "the test chosen to measure petitioner's blood-alcohol level was a reasonable one * * * performed in a reasonable manner."

Dissenting Justice BLACK, joined by Justice Douglas, expressed amazement at the majority's "conclusion that compelling a person to give his blood to help the State to convict him is not equivalent to compelling him to be a witness against himself." "It is a strange hierarchy of values that allows the State to extract a human being's blood to convict him of a crime because of the blood's content but proscribes compelled production of his lifeless papers."[d]

Notes and Questions

1. In light of *Rochin, Breithaupt* and *Schmerber,* when courts decide constitutional questions by "looking to" the Bill of Rights, to what extent do they proceed, as Justice Black expressed it in *Adamson*, "within clearly marked constitutional boundaries"? To what extent does resort to these "particular standards" enable courts to avoid substituting their "own concepts of decency and fundamental justice" for the language of the Constitution?

2. Did *Mapp* and *Malloy,* decided in the interim between *Breithaupt* and *Schmerber,* affect any Justice's vote? Did the applicability of the "particular standards" of the Fourth and Fifth Amendments inhibit Justices Black, Douglas or Brennan from employing their own concepts of "decency" and "justice" in *Schmerber?* After *Schmerber,* how much force is there in Justice Black's view, concurring in *Rochin,* that "faithful adherence to the specific guarantees in the Bill of Rights assures a more permanent protection of individual liberty than that which can be afforded by the nebulous standards stated by the majority"?

3. Applying the "shocks-the-conscience" test first articulated in the *Rochin* case, COUNTY OF SACRAMENTO v. LEWIS, 523 U.S. 833, ___, 118 S.Ct. 1708,

---

b. For other aspects of *Schmerber,* see p. 250.

c. In fn. 7 to its opinion, the Court compared "Wigmore's view, 'that the privilege is limited to testimonial disclosure. It was directed at the employment of legal process *to extract from the person's own lips* an admission of guilt, which would thus take the place of other evidence.' 8 Wigmore, *Evidence* § 2263 (McNaughton rev. 1961)." "Our holding today," noted the Court, "is not to be understood

as adopting the Wigmore formulation." But see *United States v. Wade,* p. 641.

d. Warren, C.J., and Douglas, J., dissented in separate opinions,, each adhering to his dissenting views in *Breithaupt*. In a third dissenting opinion, Fortas, J., maintained that "petitioner's privilege against self-incrimination applies" and, moreover, "under the Due Process Clause, the State, in its role as prosecutor, has no right to extract blood from an accused or anyone else, over his protest."

1711, 140 L.Ed.2d 1043 (1998) (also discussed at p. 317), held, per SOUTER, J., that a police officer did not violate substantive due process by causing death through "reckless indifference" to, or "reckless disregard" for, a person's life in a high-speed automobile chase of a speeding motorcyclist. (The chase resulted in the death of the motorcyclist's passenger when the police car skidded into the passenger after the cycle had tipped over). In such circumstances, concluded the Court, "only a purpose to cause harm unrelated to the legitimate object of arrest will satisfy the element of arbitrary conduct shocking to the conscience, necessary for a due process violation [and for police liability under 42 U.S.C. § 1983]."

The Court recalled that it had held in *Graham v. Connor*, 490 U.S. 386, 109 S.Ct. 1865, 104 L.Ed.2d 443 (1989), that "where a particular amendment provides an explicit textual source of constitutional protection against a particular sort of government behavior, that Amendment, not the more generalized notion of substantive due process, must be the guide for analyzing [claims of substantive due process violations]." But the "more-specific-provision" rule of *Graham* did not bar respondents' lawsuit because neither the high-speed chase of the motorcycle nor the accidental killing of the motorcycle passenger constituted a Fourth Amendment "seizure." The Court then addressed respondents' substantive due process claim:

"Our cases dealing with abusive executive action have repeatedly emphasized that only the most egregious official conduct can be said to be 'arbitrary in the constitutional sense.' [For] half a century now we have spoken of the cognizable level of executive abuse of power as that which shocks the conscience. We first put the test this way in *Rochin* [and] we have repeatedly adhered to *Rochin*'s benchmark."

The Court emphasized that much turns on the particular context in which the executive misconduct arises. Thus, in a prison custodial situation, when the state has rendered an individual unable to care for himself, and at the same time fails to provide for his basic needs, "the point of the conscience-shocking is reached" when injuries are produced by reckless or grossly negligent executive conduct. On the other hand, "deliberate indifference does not suffice for constitutional liability (albeit under the Eighth Amendment) even in prison circumstances when a prisoner's claim arises not from normal custody but from response to a violent disturbance." Continued the Court:

"[A] police officer deciding whether to give chase must balance on one hand the need to stop a suspect and show that flight from the law is no way to freedom, and, on the other, the high-speed threat to everyone within stopping range, be they suspects, their passengers, other drivers, or bystanders. To recognize a substantive due process violation in these circumstances when only mid-level fault has been shown [i.e., something more than simple negligence, but something less than intentional misconduct] would be to forget that liability for deliberate indifference to inmate welfare rests upon the luxury enjoyed by prison officials of having time to make unhurried judgments, upon the chance for repeated reflection, largely uncomplicated by the pulls of competing obligations. When such extended opportunities to do better are teamed with protracted failure even to care, indifference is truly shocking. But when unforeseen circumstances demand an officer's instant judgment, even precipitate recklessness fails to inch close enough to harmful purpose to spark the shock that implicates 'the large concerns of the governors and the governed.' Just as a purpose to cause harm is needed for Eighth Amendment liability in a riot case, so it ought to be needed for Due Process liability in a pursuit case. Accordingly, we hold that high-speed chases with no intent to harm suspects physically or to worsen their legal plight do not give rise to liability under the Fourteenth Amendment, redressible by an action under § 1983. [Regardless of whether the officer's] behavior offended the reasonableness held up by tort law or the balance struck in law enforcement's own codes of sound practice, it does not shock the conscience * * *."a

SECTION 3. THE RETROACTIVE EFFECT OF A HOLDING OF UNCONSTITUTIONALITYa

Rejecting what it called the Blackstonian theory that a new ruling merely sets forth the law as it always existed, *Linkletter v. Walker*, 381 U.S. 618, 85 S.Ct. 1731, 14 L.Ed.2d 601 (1965), declined to apply *Mapp v. Ohio* (p. 124) (overruling *Wolf v. Colorado*, and imposing the Fourth Amendment exclusionary rule on the states as a matter of Fourteenth Amendment Due Process) to cases which had become final (i.e., direct appellate review had been exhausted) prior to the overturning of *Wolf*. The *Linkletter* Court maintained that the retroactivity of *Mapp* should be determined by examining the purpose of the exclusionary rule, the reliance of the states on prior law, and the effect on the administration of justice of a retroactive application of the exclusionary rule.

The prime purpose of *Mapp*, emphasized the Court, was to deter future police misconduct and the purpose would not be advanced by applying the rule to "finalized" cases. The Court recognized that it had given full retroactive effect to some recent law-changing decisions—*Gideon* (p. 67), *Griffin v. Illinois* (p. 78), and the coerced confession cases—but, unlike *Mapp*, the principles established in those cases "went to the fairness of the trial—the very integrity of the fact-finding process. [Here] the fairness of the trial is not under attack."

Relying upon the *Linkletter* analysis, *Stovall v. Denno*, 388 U.S. 293, 87 S.Ct. 1967, 18 L.Ed.2d 1199 (1967), set forth a framework for determining whether a new ruling should be given retroactive effect. The "criteria guiding the resolution of the question," observed *Stovall*, "implicate (a) the purpose to be served by the new standards, (b) the extent of the reliance by law enforcement authorities on the old standards, (c) the effect on the administration of justice of a retroactive application of the new standards." These three criteria were later described as the *"Linkletter* standard," "the *Stovall* standard," or the *"Linkletter–Stovall"* standard.

a. Concurring in the judgment, Scalia, J., joined by Thomas J. would not have decided the case by applying the "shocks-the-conscience" test but "on the ground that respondents offer no textual or historical support for their alleged due process right." The concurring Justices maintained that in *Washington v. Glucksberg*, 521 U.S. 702, 117 S.Ct. 2258, 138 L.Ed.2d 772 (1997) (upholding a criminal prohibition against physician-assisted suicide), "the Court specifically rejected the method of substantive-due-process analysis employed by Justice Souter in that case, which is the very same method employed by Justice Souter in his opinion for the Court today."

Justice Kennedy, joined by O'Connor, J. joined the opinion of the Court, but also wrote separately. They "share[d] Justice Scalia's concerns about using the phrase 'shocks the conscience' in a manner suggesting that it is a self-defining test." The phrase, they observed, "has the unfortunate connotation of a standard laden with subjective assessments. In that respect, it must be viewed with considerable skepticism."

a. This cluster of problems has generated a vast literature, starting in the 1960's. See, e.g., Laurence H. Tribe, *American Constitutional Law* 29–32 (2d ed. 1988); Richard H. Fallon & Daniel J. Meltzer, *New Law, Non–Retroactivity, and Constitutional Remedies*, 104 Harv. L.Rev. 1733 (1991); James B. Haddad, *The Finality Distinction in Supreme Court Retroactivity Analysis: An Inadequate Surrogate for Modification of the Scope of Federal Habeas Corpus*, 79 Nw.U.L.Rev. 1066 (1985).

Prior to *Linkletter*, the *Mapp* case had already been applied to cases still pending on direct appeal, so the only issue considered by the *Linkletter* Court was whether *Mapp* should be applied to a collateral attack upon a conviction (there, habeas corpus challenge). In applying the *Linkletter* standard, however, *Stovall* and subsequent cases did not draw a distinction between final convictions attacked collaterally and convictions challenged at various stages of trial and direct review.

Moreover, in limiting the retroactive effect of new rulings, cases applying the *Linkletter* standard selected different "starting points." Because *Escobedo* (p. 462) and *Miranda* (p. 475) were not primarily designed to protect the innocent from wrongful conviction, *Johnson v. New Jersey*, 384 U.S. 719, 86 S.Ct. 1772, 16 L.Ed.2d 882 (1966) held that those landmark confession rulings affected only cases in which *the trial began* after the date of those decisions. Because the use of unfair lineups could still be challenged on due process grounds even if the law-changing decisions on lineups were not applied retroactively, *Stovall v. Denno*, supra, declined to give retroactive effect to *Wade* and *Gilbert* (p. 641), the 1967 cases establishing the right to counsel at certain pretrial lineups. But this time the Court selected a different starting point for application of the nonretroactive rulings: *Wade* and *Gilbert* "affect only those cases [involving] *confrontations for identification purposes* conducted in the absence of counsel *after* [the date of these decisions]." (Emphasis added).[b]

Selection of the date of the challenged *police conduct* as the starting point, rather than the date of the trial or some other point in the criminal process, indicated that *police reliance* on the overturned rule was a major factor in retroactivity disputes. In this respect, *Desist v. United States*, 394 U.S. 244, 89 S.Ct. 1030, 22 L.Ed.2d 248 (1969), followed *Johnson v. New Jersey*. The *Desist* Court held that *Katz v. United States* (p. 155) (overruling *Olmstead*, p. 360, and holding that electronic surveillance is subject to Fourth Amendment restraints) should be given what the Court called "wholly prospective application," i.e., applied only to *police activity* occurring *after* the date of the *Katz* decision.[c]

The *Desist* Court saw no significant distinction for retroactivity purposes between direct review and collateral attack: All of the reasons for making *Katz* prospective only "also undercut any distinction between final convictions and those still pending on review. Both the deterrent purpose of the exclusionary rule and the reliance of law enforcement officers focus upon *the time of the search*, not any subsequent point in the prosecution as the relevant date." (Emphasis added.)

Twenty years later, Justice Harlan's dissent in *Desist* seems a good deal more significant than the opinion of the Court in that case. Unable to accept a rationale

---

b. Although "at first glance the prospectivity rule appears to be an act of judicial self-abnegation," "in reality," observes Francis Allen, *The Judicial Quest for Penal Justice: The Warren Court and the Criminal Cases*, 1975 U.Ill.L.F. 518, 530, such a rule "encourages the making of new law by reducing some of the social costs." See also James Haddad, *Retroactivity Should be Rethought: A Call for the End of the Linkletter Doctrine*, 60 J.Crim.L.C. & P.S. 417, 439 (1969): "The alternative to the prospective-only technique is a more conservative approach to constitutional criminal procedure. * * * Detailed federal standards such as those laid down in *Miranda* would no longer be possible. Adoption of safeguards, such as the right to counsel at lineups, which not a single state anticipated, would also be impossible."

c. The Court recognized that "[o]f course, Katz himself benefitted from the new principle announced on [the date of the *Katz* decision], and [to] that extent the decision has not technically been given wholly prospective application. But [this] is an 'unavoidable consequence of the necessity that constitutional adjudications not stand as mere dictum.' Whatever inequity may arguably result from applying the new rule to those 'chance beneficiaries' is 'an insignificant cost for adherence to sound principles of decision-making.' "

that "permits this Court to apply a 'new' constitutional rule entirely prospectively, while making an exception only for the particular litigant whose case was chosen as the vehicle for establishing that rule," dissenting Justice Harlan maintained:

"[A]ll 'new' rules of constitutional law must, at a minimum, be applied to all those cases which are still subject to direct review by this Court at the time the 'new' decision is handed down.

"[We release a prisoner] only because the Government has offended constitutional principle in the conduct of his case. And when another similarly situated defendant comes before us, we must grant the same relief or give a principled reason for acting differently. We depart from this basic judicial tradition when we simply pick and choose from among similarly situated defendants those who alone will receive the benefit of a 'new' rule of constitutional law.

"* * * If a 'new' constitutional doctrine is truly right, we should not reverse lower courts which have accepted it; nor should we affirm those which have rejected the very arguments we have embraced. Anything else would belie the truism that it is the task of this Court, like that of any other, to do justice to each litigant on the merits of his own case. It is only if each of our decisions can be justified in terms of this fundamental premise that they may properly be considered the legitimate products of a court of law, rather than the commands of a super-legislature."

RETHINKING RETROACTIVITY: HARLAN'S
VIEWS COME TO THE FORE

More than a decade after the *Desist* Court had found no valid distinction for retroactivity purposes between final convictions and those still pending on direct review, the Court, relying heavily on Harlan, J.'s dissent in *Desist,* deemed such a distinction persuasive and applied it in *United States v. Johnson,* 457 U.S. 537, 102 S.Ct. 2579, 73 L.Ed.2d 202 (1982) (per Blackmun, J.). *Johnson* applied *Payton v. New York* (1980) (p. 266) (holding that police must obtain an arrest warrant when entering a suspect's home to make a routine felony arrest) to cases still pending on direct appeal at the time *Payton* was handed down. The Court pointed out that "*Payton* overturned no long-standing practice approved by a near-unanimous body of lower court authority [and thus] does not fall into that narrow class of decisions whose nonretroactivity is effectively preordained because they unmistakably signal 'a clean break with the past.' "

The *Johnson* Court "express[ed] no view on the retroactive application of decisions construing any constitutional provision other than the Fourth Amendment," but as *Shea v. Louisiana,* immediately below, soon made clear, the *Johnson* approach was not to be confined to the Fourth Amendment setting.

SHEA v. LOUSIANA, 470 U.S. 51, 105 S.Ct. 1065, 84 L.Ed.2d 38 (1985) arose as follows: Upon being read his *Miranda* rights, petitioner asserted his right to counsel and the interview was then terminated. But the next day, before petitioner had communicated with a lawyer and without any indication from him that he was willing to be questioned, the police again read petitioner the *Miranda* warnings. Petitioner agreed to talk and confessed. The confession was admitted into evidence and petitioner was convicted. While his appeal was pending, the U.S. Supreme Court ruled in *Edwards v. Arizona,* p. 548, that a suspect's rights were violated by the use of his confession obtained by police-instigated interrogation— without counsel present—after he had requested a lawyer. The state supreme court held *Edwards* inapplicable to a case pending on direct appeal at the time *Edwards* was decided. The Court, per BLACKMUN, J., disagreed:

"The primary difference between *United States v. Johnson,* on the one hand, and *Solem v. Stumes,* 465 U.S. 638, 104 S.Ct. 1338, 79 L.Ed.2d 579 (1984) [holding that *Edwards* does not apply retroactively to a state-court conviction finally affirmed by the state supreme court *before Edwards* was decided], on the other, is the difference between a pending and undecided direct review of a judgment of conviction and a federal collateral attack upon a state conviction which has become final. We must acknowledge [that] *Johnson* does not directly control the disposition of the present case.[a] [But] [w]e now conclude [that there] is nothing about a Fourth Amendment rule that suggests that in this context it should be given greater retroactive effect than a Fifth Amendment rule. Indeed, a Fifth Amendment violation may be more likely to affect the truthfinding process than a Fourth Amendment violation. And Justice Harlan's reasoning—that principled decisionmaking and fairness to similarly situated petitioners requires application of a new rule to all cases pending on direct review—is applicable with equal force to the situation presently before us.

"[It is argued] that drawing a distinction between a case pending on direct review and a case on collateral attack produces inequities and injustices that are not any different from those that *Johnson* purported to cure. The argument is that the litigant whose *Edwards* claim will not be considered because it is presented on collateral review will be just as unfairly treated as the direct-review litigant whose claim would be by-passed were *Edwards* not the law. The distinction, however, properly rests on considerations of finality in the judicial process. The one litigant already has taken his case through the primary system. The other has not. For the latter, the curtain of finality has not been drawn. Somewhere, the closing must come."

WHITE, J., joined by the Chief Justice, and Rehnquist and O'Connor, JJ., dissented:

"We concluded [in *Stumes*] that the prophylactic purpose of the *Edwards* rule, the justifiable failure of police and prosecutors to foresee the Court's decision in *Edwards,* and the substantial disruption of the criminal justice system that retroactive application of *Edwards* would entail all indicated the wisdom of holding *Edwards* nonretroactive. Today, however, the majority concludes that notwithstanding the substantial reasons for restricting the application of *Edwards* to cases involving interrogations that postdate the Court's opinion in [that case], the *Edwards* rule must be applied retroactively to all cases in which the process of direct appeal had not yet been completed when *Edwards* was decided.

"[The] futility of this latest attempt to use retroactivity doctrine to avoid the super-legislature difficulty is highlighted by the majority's unwillingness to commit itself to the logic of its position. For even as it maintains that retroactivity is essential to the judicial function, today's majority, like the majority in *Johnson,* continues to hold out the possibility that a 'really' new rule—one that marks a clear break with the past—may not have to be applied retroactively even to cases pending on direct review at the time the new decision is handed down. Of course,

a. The Court noted that *Johnson* specifically declined to address the implications of its approach to non-Fourth Amendment cases and "also declined to address situations clearly controlled by existing retroactivity precedents, such as where the new rule of law is so clean a break with the past that it has been considered nonretroactive almost automatically. Whatever the merits of a different retroactivity rule for cases of that kind may be, [*Stumes*] recognized that *Edwards* was 'not the kind of clean break with the past that is automatically nonretroactive.' "

if the majority were truly concerned with the super-legislature problem it would be 'clear break' decisions that would trouble it the most. Indeed, one might expect that a Court as disturbed about the problem as the majority purports to be would swear off such decisions altogether, not reserve the power both to issue them and to decline to apply them retroactively. In leaving open the possibility of an exception for 'clear break' decisions, the majority demonstrates the emptiness of its proposed solution to the super-legislature problem.

"[The] majority recognizes that the distinction between direct review and habeas is problematic, but justifies its differential treatment by appealing to the need to draw 'the curtain of finality' on those who were unfortunate enough to have exhausted their last direct appeal at the time *Edwards* was decided. Yet the majority offers no reasons for its conclusion that finality should be the decisive factor. When a conviction is overturned on direct appeal on the basis of an *Edwards* violation, the remedy offered the defendant is a new trial at which any inculpatory statements obtained in violation of *Edwards* will be excluded. It is not clear to me why the majority finds such a burdensome remedy more acceptable when it is imposed on the state on direct review than when it is the result of a collateral attack. The disruption attendant upon the remedy does not vary depending on whether it is imposed on direct review or habeas; accordingly, if the remedy must be granted to defendants on direct appeal, there is no strong reason to deny it to prisoners attacking their convictions collaterally. Conversely, if it serves no worthwhile purpose to grant the remedy to a defendant whose conviction was final before *Edwards*, it is hard to see why the remedy should be available on direct review.

"[The] principles of retroactivity set forth in *Linkletter* and most recently applied in *Stumes* provide a rational framework for thinking about the question whether retroactive application of any particular decision makes sense—that is, whether the benefits of retroactivity outweigh its costs. Because the Court has already determined that the relevant considerations set forth in *Linkletter* (the purpose of the new rule, the extent of law enforcement officials' justifiable reliance on the prior rule, and the effects on the criminal justice system of retroactivity) dictate nonretroactive application of the rule in *Edwards*, I cannot join in the majority's conclusion that that rule should be applied retroactively to cases pending on direct review at the time of our decision in *Edwards*."

Notes and Questions

1. *Rejection of the "clear break" exception.* Answering a question left open in the *Johnson* and *Shea* cases, *Griffith v. Kentucky,* 479 U.S. 314, 107 S.Ct. 708, 93 L.Ed.2d 649 (1987), applied *Batson v. Kentucky* (Ch. 23, § 2) (defendant may establish prima facie case of racial discrimination in selection of petit jury on basis of prosecution's use of peremptory challenges at defendant's trial) to all convictions not final at the time of the ruling even though *Batson* was "an explicit and substantial break with prior precedent." Observed a 6–3 majority, per Blackmun, J.: "[T]he 'clear break' exception * * * reintroduces precisely the type of case-specific analysis that Justice Harlan rejected as inappropriate for cases pending on direct review [and] creates the same problem of not treating similarly situated defendants the same. [The] fact that the new rule may constitute a clear break with the past has no bearing on the 'actual inequity that results' when only one of many similarly situated defendants receives the benefit of the new rule."

2. *Adoption of the other part of Harlan's approach to retroactivity.* Justice Harlan believed that new rulings should always be applied retroactively to cases on *direct* review (a view adopted in *Shea*), but that generally new rulings should

not be applied retroactively to cases on *collateral* review. In TEAGUE v. LANE, 489 U.S. 288, 109 S.Ct. 1060, 103 L.Ed.2d 334 (1989) (set forth in Ch. 28, § 1), seven Justices adopted Harlan's basic position with respect to retroactivity on collateral review. There was, however, no clear majority as to what the exceptions to this general approach should be.

A four-Justice plurality, per O'CONNOR, J. (joined by Rehnquist, C.J., and Scalia and Kennedy, JJ.), identified two exceptions: A new ruling should be applied retroactively to cases on collateral review only (1) if it "places 'certain kinds of primary, private individual conduct beyond the power of the criminal law-making authority to proscribe'" or (2) if it mandates "new procedures without which the likelihood of an accurate conviction is seriously diminished." The latter exception is "'best illustrated by recalling the classic grounds for the issuance of a writ of habeas corpus—that the proceeding was dominated by mob violence; that the prosecutor knowingly made use of perjured testimony; or that the conviction was based on a confession extorted from the defendant by brutal methods.'"

A fifth member of the Court, concurring Justice White, characterized the plurality's view as "an acceptable application in collateral proceedings of the theories embraced by the Court in dealing with direct review." Two other members of the Court, concurring Justice STEVENS, joined by Blackmun, J., agreed that "the Court should adopt Justice Harlan's analysis of retroactivity for habeas corpus cases as well as for cases still on direct review," but disagreed with the plurality about the exceptions to such a general approach.

3. *What constitutes a "new rule"?* The *Teague* plurality, per O'Connor, J., observed that "a case announces a new rule when it breaks new ground or imposes a new obligation on [the government]. To put it differently, a case announces a new rule if the result was not *dictated* by precedent existing at the time the defendant's conviction became final."

Consider *Butler v. McKellar* (1990), discussed more extensively in Ch. 28, § 1. At issue in *Butler* was the retroactive application on habeas of *Arizona v. Roberson* (1988) (p. 548). *Roberson* held that *Edwards v. Arizona* (1981), which prohibits the police from initiating further interrogation once a suspect has asserted his right to counsel, applies even when (unlike the facts in *Edwards*) the further interrogation relates to a different crime. Although the *Roberson* Court had characterized its ruling as "controlled" by *Edwards*, the *Butler* Court held that *Roberson* had announced a "new rule" under the *Teague* standard: Although the *Roberson* Court had said that its decision was within the "logical compass" of *Edwards*, "the outcome in *Roberson* was susceptible to debate among reasonable minds"—"it would not have been an illogical or even a grudging application of *Edwards* to decide that it did not extend to the facts of *Roberson*."

Is *Teague*'s definition of the claims that will be deemed to rest on new law— and thus barred from relitigation on habeas, unless they fall within an exception— far too expansive? Don't most cases, as Justice Brennan argued in his *Teague* dissent, "involve a question of law that is at least debatable, permitting a rational judge to resolve the case in more than one way"? By disabling federal habeas corpus from granting relief whenever reasonable disagreement is possible about the scope or application of an existing rule, does *Teague* "reduce the incentives for state courts, and state law enforcement officials, to take account of the evolving direction of the law"? Should a "new rule" be defined more narrowly, "to exclude rules and decisions that are clearly foreshadowed, not just those that are 'dictated by precedents'"? See Richard H. Fallon & Daniel J. Meltzer, *New Law, Non-Retroactivity, and Constitutional Remedies*, 104 Harv.L.Rev. 1731, 1816–17 (1991).

SECTION 4. THE FEDERAL COURTS' "SUPERVISORY POWER" OVER THE ADMINISTRATION OF FEDERAL CRIMINAL JUSTICE

As the Court, per FRANKFURTER, J., observed in McNABB v. UNITED STATES (1943) (more extensively discussed at p. 457), "while the power of this Court to undo convictions in *state* courts is limited to the enforcement of those 'fundamental principles of liberty and justice' secured by [fourteenth amendment due process]" (emphasis added), the standards of *federal* criminal justice "are not satisfied merely by observance of those minimal historic safeguards." Rather, "[i]n the exercise of its supervisory authority over the administration of criminal justice in the federal courts, [this Court has] formulated rules of evidence to be applied in federal criminal prosecutions." Thus, in *McNabb,* the Court held incriminating statements obtained during prolonged and hence unlawful detention (i.e., while the suspect was held in violation of federal statutory requirements that he be promptly taken before a committing magistrate) inadmissible in federal courts "[q]uite apart from the Constitution."

For a long, hard look at *McNabb* itself and the federal "supervisory power" generally, see Sara Sun Beale, *Reconsidering Supervisory Power in Criminal Cases: Constitutional and Statutory Limits on the Authority of the Federal Courts,* 84 Colum.L.Rev. 1433 (1984). Professor Beale maintains, inter alia, that "the supervisory power has blurred the constitutional and statutory limitations on the authority of the federal courts [and] fostered the erroneous view that the federal courts exercise general supervision over federal prosecutors and investigators"; and that "there is no statutory or constitutional source of authority broad enough to encompass all of the supervisory power decisions." Id. at 1434–35.

"In cases not involving questions of judicial procedure or a statutory violation," concludes Beale, id. at 1521–22, the federal courts lack the authority "to exclude evidence or to dismiss a prosecution unless the government's conduct violated the Constitution. This analysis requires the federal courts to decide some constitutional issues they are now able to avoid—or at least defer—by grounding their rulings on supervisory power. [Requiring the federal courts to ground decisions on a constitutional basis] would be likely to result in eliminating some restrictions on federal investigators and prosecutors that have been grounded solely on supervisory power. This is as it should be.

"But this approach need not straitjacket the courts. Where there has been a legislative grant of authority, such as the rules enabling legislation, the power of the courts is extensive. Amendments to the Federal Rules of Criminal Procedure may properly regulate some matters that have been the subject of highly questionable supervisory power rulings. * * * But the concept of separation of powers dictates that federal prosecutors and investigators, like their state counterparts, should perform their duties subject only to the requirements imposed by the federal Constitution and statutes, not subject to the federal judiciary's preference for particular policies and practices."

In *United States v. Russell* (1973) (discussed at p. 401), in the course of rejecting respondent's argument that he had been "entrapped" because there had been an intolerable degree of government involvement in the criminal enterprise, the Court, per Rehnquist, J., observed:

"[Several lower federal court decisions] have undoubtedly gone beyond this Court's [precedents] in order to bar prosecutions because of what they [considered] 'overzealous law enforcement.' But the [entrapment defense] was not intended to give the federal judiciary a 'chancellor's foot' veto over law enforcement practices of which it does not disapprove. The execution of the federal laws under our Constitution is confined primarily to the Executive Branch of the Government, subject to applicable constitutional and statutory limitations and to judicially fashioned rules to enforce those limitations."

When a three-justice plurality (Rehnquist, J., joined by the Chief Justice and White, J.,) quoted the "chancellor's foot" passage with approval in *Hampton v. United States* (1976) (discussed at p. 413), concurring Justice Powell, joined by Blackmun, J., observed:

"The plurality's use of the 'chancellor's foot' passage from *Russell* may suggest that it also would foreclose reliance on our supervisory power to bar conviction of [a defendant predisposed to commit the crime] because of outrageous police conduct. * * * I do not understand *Russell* to have gone so far. There we indicated only that we should be extremely reluctant to invoke the supervisory power in cases of this kind because that power does not give the 'federal judiciary a "chancellor's foot" veto over law enforcement practices of which it [does] not approve.' * * * I therefore am unwilling to join the plurality in concluding that, no matter what the circumstances, neither due process principles nor our supervisory power could support a bar to conviction in any case where the Government is able to prove predisposition [to commit the crime]."[a]

Whatever the implications of the "chancellor's foot" passage, both in *Payner,* infra, and in *Hasting,* infra, the Court left no doubt that it took a dim view of the federal courts' exercise of their "supervisory power."

UNITED STATES v. PAYNER, 447 U.S. 727, 100 S.Ct. 2439, 65 L.Ed.2d 468 (1980), arose as follows: An IRS investigation into the financial activities of American citizens in the Bahamas focused on a certain Bahamian bank. When an official of that bank visited the United States, IRS agents stole his briefcase for a time, removed hundreds of documents from the briefcase and photographed them. As a result of this "briefcase caper," defendant Payner was convicted of federal income tax violations. Because Payner lacked "standing" to challenge the "briefcase caper" under the Court's Fourth Amendment precedents (see Ch. 11, § 1), the federal district court invoked its supervisory power to exclude the tainted evidence. The district court found, and these findings were undisturbed by the higher courts, that "the Government counsels its agents that the Fourth Amendment standing limitation permits them to purposefully conduct an unconstitutional search and seizure of one individual in order to obtain evidence against third parties who are the real targets of the government intrusion" and that IRS agents "transacted the 'briefcase caper' with a purposeful, bad faith hostility toward the Fourth Amendment rights of [the bank official] in order to obtain evidence against persons like Payner." But a 6–3 majority, per POWELL, J., held that the supervisory power "does not authorize a federal court" to exclude evidence that did not violate the defendant's Fourth Amendment rights:

"[T]he interest in deterring illegal searches does not justify the exclusion of tainted evidence at the instance of a party who was not the victim of the challenged practices. The values assigned to the competing interests do not change

---

a. Dissenting Justice Brennan, joined by Stewart and Marshall, JJ., agreed with Justices Powell and Blackmun that *"Russell* does not foreclose imposition of a bar to conviction—based upon our supervisory power or due process principles—where the conduct of law enforcement authorities is sufficiently offensive, even though the individuals entitled to invoke such a defense might be 'predisposed.'"

because a court has elected to analyze the question under the supervisory power instead of the Fourth Amendment. In either case, the need to deter the underlying conduct and the detrimental impact of excluding the evidence remain precisely the same." [The] district court's reasoning, which the [Sixth Circuit] affirmed, amounts to a substitution of individual judgment for the controlling decisions of this Court. Were we to accept this use of the supervisory power, we would confer on the judiciary discretionary power to disregard the considered limitations of the law it is charged with enforcing."

Dissenting Justice MARSHALL, joined by Brennan and Blackmun, JJ., maintained that the Court's holding "effectively turns the standing rules created by this Court for assertions of Fourth Amendment violations into a sword to be used by the Government to permit it deliberately to invade one person's Fourth Amendment rights in order to obtain evidence against another person. Unlike the Court, I do not believe that the federal courts are unable to protect the integrity of the judicial system from such gross government misconduct." Continued the dissent:

"The Court's decision to engraft the standing limitations of the Fourth Amendment onto the exercise of supervisory powers is puzzling not only because it runs contrary to the major purpose behind the exercise of the supervisory powers—to protect the integrity of the court—but also because it appears to render the supervisory powers superfluous. In order to establish that suppression of evidence under the supervisory powers would be proper, the Court would also require Payner to establish a violation of his Fourth or Fifth Amendment rights, in which case suppression would flow directly from the Constitution. This approach is totally unfaithful to our prior supervisory power cases, which, contrary to the Court's suggestion, are not constitutional cases in disguise."

UNITED STATES v. HASTING, 461 U.S. 499, 103 S.Ct. 1974, 76 L.Ed.2d 96 (1983), arose as follows: Five defendants were convicted of kidnapping and transporting women across state lines for immoral purposes. Concluding that the prosecutor had violated *Griffin v. California* (p. 34, fn. a) by, in effect, commenting on the failure of any defendant to take the stand in his own defense, the U.S. Court of Appeals for the Seventh Circuit reversed. The Seventh Circuit was motivated at least in part by what it perceived to be continuing violations of *Griffin* by the prosecutors within its jurisdiction. Although impermissible comment on a defendant's failure to take the stand is subject to a "harmless error" doctrine (See Ch. 27, § 4), the Seventh Circuit declined to apply that doctrine, stating that its application "would impermissibly compromise the clear constitutional violation of the defendants' Fifth Amendment rights." The Court, per BURGER, C.J., reversed:

"[W]e proceed on the assumption that, without so stating, the court was exercising its supervisory powers to discipline the prosecutors of its jurisdiction. * * * We hold that the [harmless error doctrine] may not be avoided by an assertion of supervisory power, simply to justify a reversal of these criminal convictions.

"[I]n the exercise of supervisory powers, federal courts may, within limits, formulate procedural rules not specifically required by the Constitution or the Congress. The purposes underlying use of the supervisory powers are threefold: to implement a remedy for violation of recognized rights; to preserve judicial integrity by ensuring that a conviction rests on appropriate considerations validly before the jury; and finally, as a remedy designed to deter illegal conduct.

"[These goals] are not, however, significant in the context of this case if, as the Court of Appeals plainly implied, the errors alleged are harmless. Supervisory power to reverse a conviction is not needed as a remedy when the error to which it is addressed is harmless since by definition, the conviction would have been obtained notwithstanding the asserted error. Further, in this context, the integrity of the process carries less weight, for it is the essence of the harmless error doctrine that a judgment may stand only when there is no 'reasonable possibility that the [practice] complained of might have contributed to the conviction.' Finally, deterrence is an inappropriate basis for reversal where, as here, the prosecutor's remark is at most an attenuated violation of *Griffin* and where means more narrowly tailored to deter objectionable prosecutorial conduct are available.[5]

"To the extent that the values protected by supervisory authority are at issue here, these powers may not be exercised in a vacuum. Rather, reversals of convictions under the court's supervisory power must be approached 'with some caution,' *Payner,* and with a view toward balancing the interests involved. [T]he Court of Appeals failed in this case to give appropriate—if, indeed, any—weight to these relevant interests. It did not consider the trauma the victims of these particularly heinous crimes would experience in a new trial [or] the practical problems of retrying these sensitive issues more than four years after the events. The conclusion is inescapable that the Court of Appeals focused exclusively on its concern that the prosecutors within its jurisdiction were indifferent to the frequent admonitions of the court. The court appears to have decided to deter future similar comments by the drastic step of reversal of these convictions. But the interests preserved by the doctrine of harmless error cannot be so lightly and casually ignored in order to chastise what the court viewed as prosecutorial overreaching."[b]

Justice BRENNAN, joined by Marshall, J., concurred in part and dissented in part, observing:

"[Various cases] indicate that the policy considerations supporting the harmless error rule and those supporting the existence of an appellate court's supervisory powers are not in irreconcilable conflict. Both the harmless error rule and the exercise of supervisory powers advance the important judicial and public interest in the orderly and efficient administration of justice. [If] Government prosecutors have engaged in a pattern and practice of intentionally violating defendants' constitutional rights, a court of appeals certainly might be justified in reversing a conviction, even if the error at issue is harmless, in an effort to deter future violations. If effective as a deterrent, the reversal could avert further damage to judicial integrity. [It] is certainly arguable that the public's interests in preserving judicial integrity and in insuring that Government prosecutors, as its agents, refrain from intentionally violating defendants' rights are stronger than its

5. Here, for example, the court could have dealt with the offending argument by directing the District Court to order the prosecutor to show cause why he should not be disciplined, or by asking the Department of Justice to initiate a disciplinary proceeding against him. The Government informs us that in the last three years, the Department of Justice's Office of Professional Responsibility has investigated 28 complaints of unethical conduct and that one assistant United States attorney resigned in the face of an investigation that he made improper arguments to a grand jury. The Court also could have publicly chastised the prosecutor by identifying him in its opinion.

b. Stevens, J., concurred in the judgment, deeming the prosecutor's comments "free of constitutional error." Blackmun, J., would vacate the judgment and remand the case for consideration of whether the Fifth Amendment violation it perceived was "harmless."

interest in upholding the conviction of a particular criminal defendant. Convictions are important, but they should not be protected at any cost."

Notes and Questions

1.   Under the *Massiah* doctrine (p. 460), an indicted defendant has a Sixth Amendment right to counsel as well as his *Miranda* safeguards. Stressing that the "strict standard" governing waiver of counsel at trial should apply to an alleged waiver of the *Massiah* right to counsel as well, in *United States v. Mohabir*, 624 F.2d 1140 (2d Cir.1980), the court invoked its federal supervisory power to hold that a "valid waiver of the Sixth Amendment right to have counsel present during post-indictment interrogation must be preceded by a federal judicial officer's explanation of the content and significance of this right." However, in *Patterson v. Illinois* (1988) (p. 629), the Supreme Court specifically rejected *Mohabir*'s holding that warnings in addition to the *Miranda* warnings are required to effectuate a waiver of the *Massiah* right (see fn. 8 in *Patterson*), without mentioning that *Mohabir* was an exercise of the Second Circuit's federal supervisory power.

2.   The *Hasting* Court noted that, within limits, federal courts may exercise their "supervisory power [to] formulate procedural rules not specifically required by the Constitution or the Congress." After *Payner* and *Hasting, what* procedural rules? Consider Note 4, p. 686 (exercise of federal supervisory power over grand juries). After *Payner* and *Hasting,* may the federal courts still *exclude evidence* or reverse a conviction based in part on inadmissible evidence if such exclusion or reversal is not required by the Constitution or the Congress? Cf. *Bank of Nova Scotia v. United States*, 487 U.S. 250, 108 S.Ct. 2369, 101 L.Ed.2d 228 (1988) (set forth in Ch. 15, § 4).

3.   Why has the effort to impose "extraconstitutional" standards on federal law enforcement officials, best illustrated by *McNabb* and its progeny, fared so badly in recent decades? Consider Bennett Gershman, *The New Prosecutors,* 53 U.Pitt.L.Rev. 393, 432 (1992): "First, [the supervisory power] required judges to impose on government officials their own notions of 'good policy.' The judiciary has resisted this invitation. Second, supervisory power increasingly has been viewed as an unwarranted judicial intrusion into the exclusive domain of a coordinate branch of the government. Finally, once supervisory power became subservient to the harmless error rule, it became largely irrelevant."

SECTION 5. TRENDS AND COUNTERTRENDS: THE "NEW FEDERALISM IN CRIMINAL PROCEDURE" AND NEW LIMITATIONS ON STATE RIGHTS PROTECTIONS[a]

When the Warren Court's "criminal procedure revolution" came to a halt, a number of state courts "greeted the Burger Court's retreat from activism not with submission, but with a stubborn independence that displays a determination to keep alive the Warren Court's philosophical commitment to protection of the criminal suspect." Donald E. Wilkes, *More on the New Federalism in Criminal Procedure,* 63 Ky.L.J. 873 (1975). The most influential article on the subject of state constitutional rights is Justice William Brennan's *State Constitutions and*

---

a. The phrase "new federalism in criminal procedure" was coined by Professor Donald E. Wilkes, Jr., in his 1974 article, *The New Feder-* alism in Criminal Procedure: State Court Evasion of the Burger Court, 62 Ky.L.J. 421.

the Protection of Individual Rights, 90 Harv.L.Rev. 489 (1977), one of the most frequently cited law review articles of modern times. See, too, Justice Brennan's updated views in *The Bill of Rights and the States: The Revival of State Constitutions as Guardians of Individual Rights,* 61 N.Y.U.L.Rev. 535 (1986). See also e.g., Barry Latzer, *State Constitutional Criminal Procedure* (1995); Robert F. Williams, *State Constitutional Law: Cases & Materials* (2d ed. 1993) (especially Ch.3); Ronald Collins, Foreword: *The Once "New Judicial Federalism" and Its Critics,* 64 Wash.L.Rev. 5 (1989); Hans Linde, *First Things First: Rediscovering the States' Bill of Rights,* 9 U.Balt.L.Rev. 379 (1980).

A state supreme court bent on providing the accused with greater protection than that said to be required by the federal constitution may insulate its decision from U.S. Supreme Court review if, to quote the High Court in *Michigan v. Long* (p. 58), the state court "indicates clearly and expressly" that its decision rests on "adequate and independent state grounds." Typically, the state court construes a state constitutional provision more expansively than the U.S. Supreme Court has interpreted a *textually identical* or *parallel* provision of the Federal Bill of Rights. But sometimes, as in *People v. Jackson,* 391 Mich. 323, 217 N.W.2d 22 (1974) (rejecting the position taken by the U.S. Supreme Court in two pretrial identification cases, *Kirby v. Illinois* (p. 655), and *United States v. Ash* (p. 660), the state court may rest its decision on its authority to establish rules of evidence for its own courts.

Justice Brennan and Marshall, who often found themselves in a dissenting role in the 1970's, frequently pointed to–and approved and encouraged—the practice of some state courts (a distinct minority) to interpret state procedural rights more expansively than does the current U.S. Supreme Court. See especially Justice Brennan's dissenting opinion in *Michigan v. Mosley* (p. 547). Justice Brennan also forcefully stated his views on this matter in his 1977 law review article, supra, emphasizing that "the decisions of the [U.S. Supreme] Court are not, and should not be, dispositive of questions regarding rights guaranteed by counterpart provisions of state law. [A]lthough in the past it might have been safe for counsel to raise only federal constitutional issues in state courts, plainly it would be most unwise these days not also to raise the state constitutional questions."

Justice Brennan's advice has not gone unheeded. A dozen years after Brennan wrote his first article on state constitutional rights, Washington Supreme Court Justice Robert Utter, *State Constitutional Law, the United States Supreme Court, and Democratic Accountability,* 64 Wash.L.Rev. 19, 27 (1989), reported that "more than 450 published state court opinions [had interpreted] state constitutions as going beyond federal constitutional guarantees."

For example, a number of state courts have declined to adopt the U.S. Supreme Court's position in *United States v. Leon,* p. 129 (establishing a so-called "good faith" exception to the fourth amendment exclusionary rule at least in search warrant cases); *Illinois v. Gates* (p. 186) (establishing a new approach to "probable cause"); *Harris v. New York* (permitting use of statements obtained in violation of *Miranda* for impeachment purposes); and *Moran v. Burbine* (p. 571) (police need not inform a suspect that a lawyer retained by relatives or friends is trying to reach him). See generally Charles H. Whitebread & Christopher Slogbogin, *Criminal Procedure* 951–53 (3d ed. 1993).

The New Federalism has not escaped strong criticism. Some judges and commentators, for example, have charged that it generates uncertainty and confusion among state officials and that "state activism" not based on local factors is a result-oriented response to U.S. Supreme Court decisions and therefore unprincipled. See Whitebread & Slobogin, supra, at 956–63 and cases and authorities discussed therein.

Although the "new federalism in criminal procedure" became apparent in the early 1970's, "recent constitutional and statutory changes in state law * * * have imposed new restrictions on the new federalism." Donald E. Wilkes, *The New Federalism in Criminal Procedure in 1984: Death of the Phoenix?*, in Developments in State Constitutional Law 166, 169 (B. McGraw ed. 1985) (hereinafter referred to as "Wilkes").

"Many of the best and brightest of the new federalism decisions have come from the California Supreme Court," Wilkes at 171, but The California Victims' Bill of Rights, often called Proposition 8, an initiative approved by the voters in 1982, "represents a major victory for the opponents of the new federalism in California, who have become increasingly vocal in their attacks since the early 1970s." Id. Proposition 8 added a new Section 28 to Article I of the California Bill of Rights. A so-called "right to truth-in-evidence" provision of the new section reads: "Except as provided by statute hereafter enacted by a two thirds vote of the membership in each house of the Legislature, relevant evidence shall not be excluded in any criminal proceeding * * *." *In re Lance W.*, 694 P.2d 744 (Cal.1985), held that this provision abrogated the vicarious exclusionary rule that was established in *People v. Martin* (1955) (p. 770) and applied to both Fourth Amendment and state constitutional violations.

The New Federalism also suffered a setback in Florida. When the state supreme court held that the state guarantee against unreasonable search and seizure, Art. 1, § 12 of the Florida Constitution, furnished more protection against governmental intrusion than did the Fourth Amendment to the U.S. Constitution, Florida voters amended the state guarantee so that it now provides that "[t]his right shall be construed in conformity with the 4th Amendment to the United States Constitution, as interpreted by the United States Supreme Court." Unlike the California Amendment, which only affects the exclusionary remedy, the Florida amendment eliminates the power of its state courts to develop their own substantive law of search and seizure. See generally Christopher Slobogin, *State Adoption of Federal Law: Exploring the Limits of Florida's "Forced Linkage" Amendment*, 39 U.Fla.L.Rev. 653 (1987).

———

As might be expected, the state courts' interpretation of state constitutional provisions so that they provide greater protection than that required by the present Supreme Court's interpretation of analogous provisions of the Bill of Rights has received a chilly reception in some U.S. Supreme Court Justices' chambers. Thus, concurring in the dismissal of the writ of certiorari as improvidently granted in *Florida v. Casal,* 462 U.S. 637, 103 S.Ct. 3100, 77 L.Ed.2d 277 (1983), Chief Justice Burger expressed satisfaction with the 1982 amendment to the Florida Constitution. "As amended," he noted, Art. 1, § 12 "ensures that Florida courts will no longer be able to rely on the State Constitution to suppress evidence that would be admissible under the decisions of the Supreme Court of the United States. [W]hen state courts interpret state law to require *more* than the Federal Constitution requires, the citizens of the state must be aware that they have the power to amend state law to ensure rational law enforcement."

In MICHIGAN v. LONG, 463 U.S. 1032, 103 S.Ct. 3469, 77 L.Ed.2d 1201 (1983) (also discussed at p. 334), rejecting the argument that "the Michigan courts have provided greater protection from searches and seizures under the state constitution than is afforded under the Fourth Amendment, and the [state supreme court's] references to the state constitution therefore establishes an adequate and independent ground for the decision below," the Court, per O'CON-NOR, J., took the occasion to "reexamine our treatment of [the] jurisdictional issue in order to achieve the consistency that is necessary" when various forms of references to state law are said to constitute adequate and independent state grounds:

"[W]hen, as in this case, a state court decision fairly appears to rest primarily on federal law, or to be interwoven with the federal law, and when the adequacy and independence of any possible state law ground is not clear from the face of the opinion, we will accept as the most reasonable explanation that the state court decided the case the way it did because it believed that federal law required it to do so. If a state court chooses merely to rely on federal precedents as it would on the precedents of all other jurisdictions, then it need only make clear by a plain statement [that] the federal cases are being used only for the purpose of guidance, and do not themselves compel the result that the court has reached. In this way, both justice and judicial administration will be greatly improved. If the state court decision indicates clearly and expressly that it is alternatively based on bona fide separate, adequate, and independent grounds, we, of course, will not undertake to review the decision.

"The principle that we will not review judgments of state courts that rest on adequate and independent state grounds is based, in part, on 'the limitations of our own jurisdiction.' The jurisdictional concern is that we not 'render an advisory opinion, and if the same judgment would be rendered by the state court after we corrected its views of federal laws, our review could amount to nothing more than an advisory opinion.' Our requirement of a 'plain statement' that a decision rests upon adequate and independent state grounds does not in any way authorize the rendering of advisory opinions. Rather, in determining, as we must, whether we have jurisdiction to review a case that is alleged to rest on adequate and independent state grounds, we merely assume that there are no such grounds when it is not clear from the opinion itself that the state court relied upon an adequate and independent state ground and when it fairly appears that the state court rested its decision primarily on federal law."[a]

Dissenting Justice STEVENS could not accept the Court's decision "to presume that adequate state grounds are intended to be dependent on federal law unless the record plainly shows otherwise." He continued:

"I am confident that all members of this Court agree that there is a vital interest in the sound management of scarce federal judicial resources. All of those policies counsel against the exercise of federal jurisdiction. They are fortified by my belief that a policy of judicial restraint—one that allows other decisional bodies to have the last word in legal interpretation until it is truly necessary for this Court to intervene—enables this Court to make its most effective contribution to our federal system of government.

a. The Court then reviewed the decision below under this framework and came away "unconvinced that it rests upon an independent state ground."

"The nature of the case before us hardly compels a departure from tradition. These are not cases in which an American citizen has been deprived of a right secured by the United States Constitution or a federal statute. Rather, they are cases in which a state court has upheld a citizen's assertion of a right, finding the citizen to be protected under both federal and state law. The complaining party is an officer of the state itself, who asks us to rule that the state court interpreted federal rights too broadly and 'over-protected' the citizen. Such cases should not be of inherent concern to this Court. * * *

"In this case the State of Michigan has arrested one of its citizens and the Michigan Supreme Court has decided to turn him loose. The respondent is a United States citizen as well as a Michigan citizen, but since there is no claim that he has been mistreated by the State of Michigan, the final outcome of the state processes offended no federal interest whatever. Michigan simply provided greater protection to one of its citizens than some other State might provide or, indeed, than this Court might require throughout the country.

"[Until] recently we had virtually no interest in cases of this type. Some time during the past decade, * * * our priorities shifted. The result is a docket swollen with requests by states to reverse judgments that their courts have rendered in favor of their citizens. I am confident that a future Court will recognize the error of this allocation of resources. When that day comes, I think it likely that the Court will also reconsider the propriety of today's expansion of our jurisdiction."[b]

———

See also *Florida v. Meyers,* 466 U.S. 380, 104 S.Ct. 1852, 80 L.Ed.2d 381 (1984) (per curiam), summarily reversing a state intermediate appellate court because it "either misunderstood or ignored our prior rulings with respect to the constitutionality of the warrantless search of an impounded automobile." (The state supreme court had denied discretionary review.) Respondent argued that the Court should not review the search and seizure issue because the state court had reversed the conviction on two independent grounds, one of which (restricted cross-examination) the state did not contest. But the Court found no "clear indication that the cross-examination ruling provided an independent and adequate basis for reversal of the conviction. See *Michigan v. Long.*"

Dissenting Justice Stevens, joined by Brennan and Marshall, JJ., who saw "no reason why we cannot leave to the Florida Supreme Court the task of managing its own discretionary docket," took issue with the Court's reliance on *Long.* And he noted: "Since the beginning of the October 1981 Term, the Court has decided in summary fashion 19 cases, including this one, concerning the constitutional rights of persons accused or convicted of crimes. All 19 were decided on the petition of the warden or prosecutor, and in all he was successful in obtaining reversal of a decision upholding a claim of constitutional right. [T]his pattern of results, and in particular the fact that in its last two and one-half Terms the Court has been unwilling in even a single criminal case to employ its discretionary power of summary disposition in order to uphold a claim of constitutional right, is quite striking."

b. Although he was satisfied that the Court had jurisdiction in this particular case, concurring Justice Blackmun did not join the part of the Court's opinion "fashioning a new presumption of jurisdiction over cases coming here from state courts." Brennan, J., joined by Marshall, J., agreed that the Court had jurisdiction to decide the case, but dissented on the merits of the search and seizure issue. (See p. 335).

Chapter 3

THE RIGHT TO COUNSEL, TRANSCRIPTS AND OTHER AIDS; POVERTY, EQUALITY AND THE ADVERSARY SYSTEM

REPORT OF THE ATTORNEY GENERAL'S COMMITTEE
ON POVERTY AND THE ADMINISTRATION OF
FEDERAL CRIMINAL JUSTICE 5–11 (1963)[a]

POVERTY AND CRIMINAL JUSTICE: THE NATURE
OF GOVERNMENT'S OBLIGATION * * *

a. *The Concept of "Poverty."* [The] concept proved an elusive one and the difficulties of definition substantial.[b] It is apparent that a total absence in the accused of all means and resources cannot be adequate for these purposes. Even the constitutional rights to the appointment of counsel are not conditioned on a showing of total destitution. Rather, the criterion appears to be a lack of financial resources adequate to permit the accused to hire his own lawyer.[c] Reflection led the Committee to the conclusion that the poverty must be viewed as a relative concept with the consequence that the poverty of accused must be measured in each case by reference to the particular need or service under consideration.

Thus in the criminal process a problem of poverty may arise at each stage of the proceedings. There is a problem of poverty if the defendant is unable to obtain pre-trial release by reason of financial inability to meet the bail requirements or to retain a lawyer to represent him at the trial. There is also a problem of poverty if the accused is unable to finance a pretrial investigation of the case or to obtain the services of expert witnesses when such investigation or testimony is essential to an adequate defense.[d] So, too, in the appellate process, there is a problem of poverty if through lack of means the accused is inhibited or prevented from

---

a. The Report is often called *The Allen Report*, after the Chairman of the Committee, Professor Francis A. Allen.

b. "[F]ew statutory standards are available to guide the [trial court] in its determination of indigency sufficient to warrant court-appointed counsel; as a result, the courts have utilized various criteria for determining eligibility. While some courts have limited the scope of inquiry, for example, to whether the accused is working and has money to hire a lawyer, other courts have considered the accused's assets, debts, employment, ability to post bail, and responsibility for dependents. The confusion and lack of consistency that exist in federal indigency standards are mirrored in the state courts." Note, 12 U.S.F.L.Rev. 717, 720–21 (1978).

c. Should the test of eligibility for court-appointed counsel be whether a private attorney would be interested in representing the defendant in his present economic circumstances? Can this standard be applied with any uniformity?

d. On the indigent's right to investigatory, expert and other assistance in addition to counsel, see *Ake v. Oklahoma* (p. 90) and accompanying Notes.

presenting grounds of reversal to the appellate court or from making adequate presentation.

It follows that concern with poverty and the administration of criminal justice requires attention to be extended beyond those who are unable at the outset of the proceedings to obtain release on bail or to hire counsel.[e] It requires consideration, also, of those who, although possessing means to obtain some elements of an adequate defense (such as hiring a lawyer), lack means to secure other essential elements.[f] Indeed, it requires attention be given to the plight of the accused with substantial means rendered indigent by the levy of a jeopardy assessment and thus unable to hire the services of an accountant in defense of a net-worth tax prosecution.

[In] summary, the Committee believes that, for the purposes at hand, poverty must be conceived as a relative concept. An impoverished accused is not necessarily one totally devoid of means. A problem of poverty arises for the system of criminal justice when at any stage of the proceedings lack of means in the accused substantially inhibits or prevents the proper assertion of a right or a claim of right.

b.　*The obligation of "Equal Justice."*

[It] should be understood that governmental obligation to deal effectively with problems of poverty in the administration of criminal justice does not rest or depend upon some hypothetical obligation of government to indulge in acts of public charity. It does not presuppose a general commitment on the part of the federal government to relieve impoverished persons of the consequences of limited means, whenever or however manifested. It does not even presuppose that government is always required to take into account the means of the citizen when dealing directly with its citizens.

[The]　obligation of government in the criminal cases rests on wholly different considerations and reflects principles of much more limited application. The essential point is that the problems of poverty with which this Report is concerned arise in a process *initiated* by government for the achievement of basic governmental purposes. It is, moreover, a process that has as one of its consequences the imposition of severe disabilities on the persons proceeded against. Duties arise from action. When a course of conduct, however legitimate, entails the possibility of serious injury to persons, a duty on the actor to avoid the reasonably avoidable injuries is ordinarily recognized. When government chooses to exert its powers in the criminal area, its obligation is surely no less than that of taking reasonable measures to eliminate those factors that are irrelevant to just administration of the law but which, nevertheless, may occasionally affect determinations of the accused's liability or penalty. While government may not be required to relieve the accused of his poverty, it may properly be required to minimize the influence of poverty on its administration of justice.

The Committee, therefore, conceives the obligation of government less as an undertaking to eliminate "discrimination" against a class of accused persons and more as a broad commitment by government to rid its processes of all influences

e. I *A.B.A. Standards* § 5–6.1 provides that assigned counsel "should not be denied merely because friends or relatives have resources adequate to retain counsel or because bond has been or can be posted."

f. I *A.B.A. Standards* § 5–6.1 provides: "Supporting services necessary to an adequate defense should be available to all persons eligible for representation *and to the clients of retained counsel* who are financially unable to afford necessary supporting services." (Emphasis added.)

that tend to defeat the ends a system of justice is intended to serve. Such a concept of "equal justice" does not confuse equality of treatment with identity of treatment. We assume that government must be conceded flexibility in devising its measures and that reasonable classifications are permitted. The crucial question is, has government done all that can reasonably be required of it to eliminate those factors that inhibit the proper and effective assertion of grounds relevant to the criminal liability of the accused or to the imposition of sanctions and disabilities on the accused at all stages of the criminal process?

c. *Poverty and the Adversary System.*

[The] essence of the adversary system is challenge. The survival of our system of criminal justice and the values which it advances depend upon a constant, searching, and creative questioning of official decisions and assertions of authority at all stages of the process. The proper performance of the defense function is thus as vital to the health of the system as the performance of the prosecuting and adjudicatory functions. It follows that insofar as the financial status of the accused impedes vigorous and proper challenges, it constitutes a threat to the viability of the adversary system. We believe that the system is imperiled by the large numbers of accused persons unable to employ counsel or to meet even modest bail requirements and by the large, but indeterminate, numbers of persons, able to pay some part of the costs of defense, but unable to finance a full and proper defense.[g] Persons suffering such disabilities are incapable of providing the challenges that are indispensable to satisfactory operation of the system. The loss to the interests of accused individuals, occasioned by these failures, are great and apparent. It is also clear that a situation in which persons are required to contest a serious accusation but are denied access to the tools of contest is offensive to fairness and equity. Beyond these considerations, however, is the fact that the conditions produced by the financial incapacity of the accused are detrimental to the proper functioning of the system of justice and that the loss in vitality of the adversary system, thereby occasioned, significantly endangers the basic interests of a free community.

Notes and Questions

1. *The indigent defendant's "obligation" to repay the government for defense costs; reimbursement as a condition of probation.* Rinaldi v. Yeager, 384 U.S. 305, 86 S.Ct. 1497, 16 L.Ed.2d 577 (1966), invalidated a New Jersey statute which required only those indigent defendants who were sentenced to prison to reimburse the state for the cost of a transcript on appeal, finding an "invidious discrimination" between those convicted defendants and others sentenced only to pay fines or subject only to a suspended sentence or to probation. *James v. Strange,* 407 U.S. 128, 92 S.Ct. 2027, 32 L.Ed.2d 600 (1972), held that a Kansas recoupment statute (which applied whether or not the indigent defendant was convicted) violated equal protection because the indigent defendant could not avail himself of restrictions on wage garnishments and other protective exemptions afforded to other civil judgment debtors.

Fuller v. Oregon, 417 U.S. 40, 94 S.Ct. 2116, 40 L.Ed.2d 642 (1974), however, upheld an Oregon recoupment statute which, under certain circumstances, authorized repayment to the state of the costs of a free legal defense as a condition of

---

g. The percentage of state felony cases in which defendants were given appointed counsel rose from just under 50% in the late 1970s to about 80% by 1992. See William J. Stuntz, *The Uneasy Relationship Between Criminal Procedure and Criminal Justice,* 107 Yale L.J. 1, 9 (1997).

probation. A 7–2 majority, per Stewart, J., stressed that "the recoupment statute is quite clearly directed only at those convicted defendants who are indigent at the time of the criminal proceedings against them but who subsequently gain the ability to pay the expenses of legal representation. Defendants with no likelihood of having the means to repay are not put under even a conditional obligation to do so, and those upon whom a conditional obligation is imposed are not subjected to collection procedures until their indigency has ended and no 'manifest hardship' [to defendant or his immediate family] will result."

Distinguishing *James* and *Rinaldi,* the Court rejected petitioner's equal protection challenge. It pointed out that Oregon had not denied exemptions from execution afforded to other judgment debtors. Unlike the classification struck down in *Rinaldi,* it deemed a distinction between defendants who are convicted, on the one hand, and those acquitted or whose convictions are reversed, on the other hand, "wholly noninvidious": "Oregon could surely decide with objective rationality that when a defendant has been forced to submit to a criminal prosecution that does not end in conviction, he will be freed of any potential liability to reimburse the state for the costs of his defense."

Nor was the Court impressed with the argument that a defendant's knowledge that he may be obligated to reimburse the state for expenses incurred in providing him a legal defense might lead him to reject the services of appointed counsel and thus "chill" his constitutional right to counsel: "The fact that an indigent who accepts [appointed counsel] knows that he might someday be required to repay the costs of these services in no way affects his eligibility to obtain counsel. The Oregon statute is carefully designed to insure that only those who actually become capable of repaying the State will ever be obliged to do so."

Dissenting Justice Marshall, joined by Brennan, J., protested that "the important fact which the majority ignores" is that because the repayment of the indigent defendant's debt to the state can be made a condition of his probation, as it was in this case, "[p]etitioner's failure to pay his debt can result in his being sent to prison. In this respect the indigent defendant in Oregon, like [his counterpart in *James*], is treated quite differently from other civil judgment debtors."

2. Notwithstanding the *Fuller* case, I *A.B.A. Standards* § 5–6.2 (commentary) "recommends that defendants be ordered to [make reimbursement] for their defense only in instances where they have made fraudulent representations for purposes of being found eligible for counsel. [The] offer of free legal assistance is rendered hollow if defendants are required to make payments for counsel for several years following conviction. Reimbursement requirements also may serve to discourage defendants from exercising their right to counsel * * *."

SECTION 1. THE RIGHT TO APPOINTED COUNSEL AND RELATED PROBLEMS

A. THE RIGHT TO APPOINTED COUNSEL IN CRIMINAL PROCEEDINGS

BETTS v. BRADY
316 U.S. 455, 62 S.Ct. 1252, 86 L.Ed. 1595 (1942).

Justice ROBERTS delivered the opinion of the Court.

Petitioner, an indigent, was indicted for robbery. His request for counsel was denied because local practice permitted appointment only in rape and murder prosecutions. Petitioner then pled not guilty and elected to be tried without a jury. At the trial he chose not to take the stand. He was convicted and sentenced to eight years imprisonment.

[The] due process clause of the Fourteenth Amendment does not incorporate, as such, the specific guarantees found in the Sixth Amendment although a denial by a state of rights or privileges specifically embodied in that and others of the first eight amendments may, in certain circumstances, * * * deprive a litigant of due process of law in violation of the Fourteenth. [Due process] formulates a concept less rigid and more fluid than those envisaged in other specific and particular provisions of the Bill of Rights. Its application is less a matter of rule. Asserted denial is to be tested by an appraisal of the totality of facts in a given case.

[Petitioner] says the rule to be deduced from our former decisions is that, in every case, whatever the circumstances, one charged with crime, who is unable to obtain counsel, must be furnished counsel by the state. Expressions in the opinions of this court lend color to the argument, but, as the petitioner admits, none of our decisions squarely adjudicates the question now presented.

In *Powell v. Alabama,* 287 U.S. 45, 53 S.Ct. 55, 77 L.Ed. 158 [1932], ignorant and friendless negro youths, strangers in the community, without friends or means to obtain counsel, were hurried to trial for a capital offense without effective appointment of counsel on whom the burden of preparation and trial would rest, and without adequate opportunity to consult even the counsel casually appointed to represent them. This occurred in a State whose statute law required the appointment of counsel for indigent defendants prosecuted for the offense charged. Thus the trial was conducted in disregard of every principle of fairness and in disregard of that which was declared by the law of the State a requisite of a fair trial. This court held the resulting convictions were without due process of law. It said that, in the light of all the facts, the failure of the trial court to afford the defendants reasonable time and opportunity to secure counsel was a clear denial of due process. The court stated further that "under the circumstances [the] necessity of counsel was so vital and imperative that the failure of the trial court to make an effective appointment of counsel was likewise a denial of due process," but added: "whether this would be so in other criminal prosecutions, or under other circumstances, we need not determine. All that it is necessary now to decide, as we do decide, is that in a capital case, where the defendant is unable to employ counsel, and is incapable adequately of making his own defense because of ignorance, feeblemindedness, illiteracy, or the like, it is the duty of the court, whether requested or not, to assign counsel for him as a necessary requisite of due process of law * * *."

* * * We have construed the [Sixth Amendment] to require appointment of counsel in all [federal] cases where a defendant is unable to procure the services of an attorney, and where the right has not been intentionally and competently waived. [*Johnson v. Zerbst,* 304 U.S. 458, 58 S.Ct. 1019, 82 L.Ed. 1461 (1938)].[a]

a. In holding that the Sixth Amendment required appointment of counsel, the Court, per Black, J., had reasoned: "The Sixth Amendment stands as a constant admonition that if the constitutional safeguards it provides be lost, justice will not 'still be done.' Cf. *Palko.* It embodies a realistic recognition of the obvious truth that the average defendant does not have the professional legal skill to protect himself when brought before a tribunal with power to take his life or liberty, wherein the prosecution is presented by experienced and learned counsel. [The] Sixth Amendment withholds from federal courts, in all criminal proceedings, the power and authority to deprive an accused of his life or liberty unless he has or waives the assistance of counsel."

Though [the] amendment lays down no rule for the conduct of the states, the question recurs whether the constraint laid by the amendment upon the national courts expresses a rule so fundamental and essential to a fair trial, and so, to due process of law, that it is made obligatory upon the states by the Fourteenth Amendment. Relevant data on the subject are afforded by constitutional and statutory provisions subsisting in the colonies and the states prior to the inclusion of the Bill of Rights in the national Constitution, and in the constitutional, legislative, and judicial history of the states to the present date.

[I]n the great majority of the states, it has been the considered judgment of the people, their representatives and their courts that appointment of counsel is not a fundamental right, essential to a fair trial. On the contrary, the matter has generally been deemed one of legislative policy. In the light of this evidence we are unable to say that the concept of due process incorporated in the Fourteenth Amendment obligates the states, whatever may be their own views, to furnish counsel in every such case. Every court has power, if it deems proper, to appoint counsel where that course seems to be required in the interest of fairness.

The practice of the courts of Maryland gives point to the principle that the states should not be straight-jacketed in this respect, by a construction of the Fourteenth Amendment. Judge Bond's opinion states, and counsel at the bar confirmed the fact, that in Maryland the usual practice is for the defendant to waive a trial by jury. This the petitioner did in the present case. Such trials, as Judge Bond remarks, are much more informal than jury trials and it is obvious that the judge can much better control the course of the trial and is in a better position to see impartial justice done than when the formalities of a jury trial are involved.

In this case there was no question of the commission of a robbery. The State's case consisted of evidence identifying the petitioner as the perpetrator. The defense was an alibi. Petitioner called and examined witnesses to prove that he was at another place at the time of the commission of the offense. The simple issue was the veracity of the testimony for the State and that for the defendant. As Judge Bond says, the accused was not helpless, but was a man forty-three years old, of ordinary intelligence and ability to take care of his own interests on the trial of that narrow issue. He had once before been in a criminal court, pleaded guilty to larceny and served a sentence and was not wholly unfamiliar with criminal procedure. It is quite clear that in Maryland, if the situation had been otherwise and it had appeared that the petitioner was, for any reason, at a serious disadvantage by reason of the lack of counsel, a refusal to appoint would have resulted in the reversal of a judgment of conviction.

[To] deduce from the due process clause a rule binding upon the states in this matter would be to impose upon them, as Judge Bond points out, a requirement without distinction between criminal charges of different magnitude or in respect of courts of varying jurisdiction. As he says: "Charges of small crimes tried before justices of the peace and capital charges tried in the higher courts would equally require the appointment of counsel. Presumably it would be argued that trials in the Traffic Court would require it." * * *

[While] want of counsel in a particular case may result in a conviction lacking [in] such fundamental fairness, we cannot say that the [Fourteenth Amendment] embodies an inexorable command that no trial for any offense, or in any court, can be fairly conducted and justice accorded a defendant who is not represented by counsel.

The judgment is affirmed.

Justice BLACK, dissenting, with whom Justice DOUGLAS and Justice MURPHY concur.

To hold that the petitioner had a constitutional right to counsel in this case does not require us to say that "no trial for any offense, or in any court, can be fairly conducted and justice accorded a defendant who is not represented by counsel." This case can be determined by resolution of a narrower question: whether in view of the nature of the offense and the circumstances of his trial and conviction, this petitioner was denied the procedural protection which is his right under the federal constitution. I think he was.

The petitioner [was] a farm hand, out of a job and on relief. [The] court below found that [he] had "at least an ordinary amount of intelligence." It is clear from his examination of witnesses that he was a man of little education.

If this case had come to us from a federal court, it is clear we should have to reverse it, because the Sixth Amendment makes the right to counsel in criminal cases inviolable by the federal government. I believe that the Fourteenth Amendment made the sixth applicable to the states. But this view [has] never been accepted by a majority of this Court and is not accepted today. * * * I believe, however, that under the prevailing view of due process, as reflected in the opinion just announced, a view which gives this Court such vast supervisory powers that I am not prepared to accept it without grave doubts, the judgment below should be reversed.

[The] right to counsel in a criminal proceeding is "fundamental." *Powell v. Alabama.* [A] practice cannot be reconciled with "common and fundamental ideas of fairness and right" which subjects innocent men to increased dangers of conviction merely because of their poverty. Whether a man is innocent cannot be determined from a trial in which as here, denial of counsel has made it impossible to conclude, with any satisfactory degree of certainty, that the defendant's case was adequately presented.[b] * * *

Denial to the poor of the request for counsel in proceedings based on charges of serious crime has long been regarded as shocking to the "universal sense of justice" throughout this country. In 1854, for example, the Supreme Court of Indiana said: "It is not to be thought of, in a civilized community, for a moment, that any citizen put in jeopardy of life or liberty should be debarred of counsel because he was too poor to employ such aid. No Court could be respected, or respect itself, to sit and hear such a trial. The defense of the poor, in such cases, is a duty resting somewhere, which will be at once conceded as essential to the accused, to the Court, and to the public." *Webb v. Baird,* 6 Ind. 13, 18. And most of the other states have shown their agreement by constitutional provisions, statutes, or established practice judicially approved which assure that no man shall be deprived of counsel merely because of his poverty. Any other practice seems to me to defeat the promise of our democratic society to provide equal justice under the law.

THE AFTERMATH OF BETTS v. BRADY—
NOTES AND QUESTIONS

b. Consider William Beaney, *The Right to Counsel in American Courts* 163, 185 (1955): "Surely the [*Betts*] majority, in adopting [Judge] Bond's position that counsel could have done little or nothing for the defendant was pursuing a line of reasoning which would inevitably destroy all rights. Rights are agreed upon in order to insure that justice will be done prospectively, in the ordinary run of affairs. To hold that an individual can be deprived of rights except in those cases where a retrospective view of events reveals a shocking situation is to defeat the whole rationale of the rule of law." See also Note 1 infra.

1. *Was Betts "prejudiced"?* When the Court reviewed Betts' case, he had appellate counsel, but his lawyer was confident—too confident—that the Court would apply the full measure of the Sixth Amendment right to counsel to the states. Thus he did not make any analysis of the trial and present any specific examples of how Betts might have been prejudiced by the absence of counsel. For the view that a number of such examples could have been shown and that competent trial counsel could have raised many more issues than "the simple issue [of] the veracity of the testimony for the State and that for the defendant," see Kamisar, *The Right to Counsel and the Fourteenth Amendment,* 30 U.Chi. L.Rev. 1, 42–56 (1962).

2. *The "flat" requirement of counsel in capital cases.* In *Bute v. Illinois,* 333 U.S. 640, 676, 68 S.Ct. 763, 781, 92 L.Ed. 986, 1006 (1948), and subsequent noncapital cases, the Court suggested that there was a "flat" requirement of counsel in capital cases. In *Hamilton v. Alabama,* 368 U.S. 52, 55, 82 S.Ct. 157, 159, 7 L.Ed.2d 114, 117 (1961), holding that arraignment is so critical a stage in Alabama procedure that denial of counsel at that stage in a capital case violates due process, a unanimous Court declared, per Douglas, J., that "when one pleads to a capital charge without benefit of counsel, we do not stop to determine whether prejudice resulted. [T]he degree of prejudice can never be known." For an explanation and criticism of the Court's distinction between capital and noncapital cases, see Francis A. Allen, *The Supreme Court, Federalism, and State Systems of Criminal Justice,* 8 DePaul L.Rev. 213, 230–31 (1959).

3. *The absolute right to retained counsel.* During the *Betts* reign, the Court made it clear that denying a defendant the assistance of *his own lawyer* on *any* issue in the trial of *any* case, constituted a per se violation of "fundamental fairness." Thus, in *Chandler v. Fretag,* 348 U.S. 3, 75 S.Ct. 1, 99 L.Ed. 4 (1954), the Court stamped the right of petitioner "to be heard through his own counsel" as "unqualified." And *Ferguson v. Georgia,* 365 U.S. 570, 81 S.Ct. 756, 5 L.Ed.2d 783 (1961), held, in effect, that a state may not deny a criminal defendant the right to have his own counsel guide him on direct examination. Could these cases be reconciled with *Betts*? See Israel, *Gideon v. Wainwright: The "Art" of Overruling,* 1963 Sup.Ct.Rev. 211, 243, Kamisar, *Betts v. Brady Twenty Years Later,* 61 Mich.L.Rev. 219, 227?28, 256–60 (1962).

GIDEON v. WAINWRIGHT
372 U.S. 335, 83 S.Ct. 792, 9 L.Ed.2d 799 (1963).

Justice BLACK delivered the opinion of the Court.

Petitioner was charged in a Florida state court with having broken and entered a poolroom with intent to commit a misdemeanor. This offense is a felony under Florida law. Appearing in court without funds and without a lawyer, petitioner asked the court to appoint counsel for him, whereupon the following colloquy took place:

"The Court: Mr. Gideon, I am sorry, but I cannot appoint Counsel to represent you in this case. Under the laws of the State of Florida, the only time the Court can appoint Counsel to represent a Defendant is when that person is charged with a capital offense. * * *

"The Defendant: The United States Supreme Court says I am entitled to be represented by Counsel."

Put to trial before a jury, Gideon conducted his defense about as well as could be expected from a layman. He made an opening statement to the jury, cross-examined the State's witnesses, presented witnesses in his own defense, declined to testify himself, and made a short argument "emphasizing his innocence to the charge contained in the Information filed in this case." The jury returned a verdict of guilty, and petitioner was sentenced to serve five years in the state prison. Later, petitioner [unsuccessfully attacked his conviction and sentence in the state supreme court on the ground that the trial court's refusal to appoint counsel for him violated his constitutional rights]. Since 1942, when *Betts v. Brady* was decided by a divided Court, the problem of a defendant's federal constitutional right to counsel in a state court has been a continuing source of controversy and litigation in both state and federal courts. To give this problem another review here, we granted certiorari [and] appointed counsel to represent [petitioner].

We accept *Betts*'s assumption, based as it was on our prior cases, that a provision of the Bill of Rights which is "fundamental and essential to a fair trial" is made obligatory upon the States by the Fourteenth Amendment. We think the Court in *Betts* was wrong, however, in concluding that the Sixth Amendment's guarantee of counsel is not one of these fundamental rights. Ten years before *Betts,* this Court, after full consideration of all the historical data examined in *Betts,* had unequivocally declared that "the right to the aid of counsel is of this fundamental character." *Powell.* While the Court at the close of its *Powell* opinion did by its language, as this Court frequently does, limit its holding to the particular facts and circumstances of that case, its conclusions about the fundamental nature of the right to counsel are unmistakable. [The] fact is that in deciding as it did—that "appointment of counsel is not a fundamental right, essential to a fair trial"—the [*Betts* Court] made an abrupt break with its own well-considered precedents. In returning to these old precedents, sounder we believe than the new, we but restore constitutional principles established to achieve a fair system of justice. Not only these precedents but also reason and reflection require us to recognize that in our adversary system of criminal justice, any person haled into court, who is too poor to hire a lawyer, cannot be assured a fair trial unless counsel is provided for him. This seems to us to be an obvious truth. Governments, both state and federal, quite properly spend vast sums of money to establish machinery to try defendants accused of crime. Lawyers to prosecute are everywhere deemed essential to protect the public's interest in an orderly society. Similarly, there are few defendants charged with crime, few indeed, who fail to hire the best lawyers they can get to prepare and present their defenses. That government hires lawyers to prosecute and defendants who have the money hire lawyers to defend are the strongest indications of the widespread belief that lawyers in criminal courts are necessities, not luxuries. The right of one charged with crime to counsel may not be deemed fundamental and essential to fair trials in some countries, but it is in ours. From the very beginning, our state and national constitutions and laws have laid great emphasis on procedural and substantive safeguards designed to assure fair trials before impartial tribunals in which every defendant stands equal before the law. This noble ideal cannot be realized if the poor man charged with crime has to face his accusers without a lawyer to assist him. * * *

The Court in *Betts* departed from the sound wisdom upon which the Court's holding in *Powell* rested. Florida, supported by two other States, has asked that *Betts v. Brady* be left intact. Twenty-two States, as friends of the Court, argue that *Betts* was "an anachronism when handed down" and that it should now be overruled. We agree. * * *

Reversed.[a]

Justice CLARK, concurring in the result.

[T]he Constitution makes no distinction between capital and noncapital cases. The Fourteenth Amendment requires due process of law for the deprival of "liberty" just as for deprival of "life," and there cannot constitutionally be a difference in the quality of the process based merely upon a supposed difference in the sanction involved. How can the Fourteenth Amendment tolerate a procedure which it condemns in capital cases on the ground that deprival of liberty may be less onerous than deprival of life—a value judgment not universally accepted—or that only the latter deprival is irrevocable? * * *

Justice HARLAN, concurring.

I agree that *Betts* should be overruled, but consider it entitled to a more respectful burial than has been accorded, at least on the part of those of us who were not on the Court when that case was decided. I cannot subscribe to the view that *Betts* represented "an abrupt break with its own well-considered precedents." [In *Powell*] this Court declared that under the particular facts there presented— "the ignorance and illiteracy of the defendants, their youth, the circumstances of public hostility [and] above all that they stood in deadly peril of their lives"—the state court had a duty to assign counsel for the trial as a necessary requisite of due process of law. It is evident that these limiting facts were not added to the opinion as an afterthought; they were repeatedly emphasized [and] were clearly regarded as important to the result.

Thus when this Court, a decade later, decided *Betts,* it did no more than to admit of the possible existence of special circumstances in noncapital as well as capital trials, while at the same time to insist that such circumstances be shown in order to establish a denial of due process. The right to appointed counsel had been recognized as being considerably broader in federal prosecutions, see *Johnson v. Zerbst,* but to have imposed these requirements on the States would indeed have been "an abrupt break" with the almost immediate past. The declaration that the right to appointed counsel in state prosecutions, as established in *Powell,* was not limited to capital cases was in truth not a departure from, but an extension of, existing precedent.

The principles declared in *Powell* and in *Betts,* however, had a troubled journey throughout the years that have followed first the one case and then the other.

[In] noncapital cases, the "special circumstances" rule has continued to exist in form while its substance has been substantially and steadily eroded. In the first decade after *Betts,* there were cases in which the Court found special circumstances to be lacking, but usually by a sharply divided vote. However, no such decision has been cited to us, and I have found none, [after] 1950. At the same time, there have been not a few cases in which special circumstances were found in little or nothing more than the "complexity" of the legal questions presented, although those questions were often of only routine difficulty. The Court has come to recognize, in other words, that the mere existence of a serious criminal charge constituted in itself special circumstances requiring the services of counsel at trial. In truth the *Betts* rule is no longer a reality.

a. Gideon was retried, this time with appointed counsel, and acquitted. See Anthony Lewis, *Gideon's Trumpet* 223–38 (1964).

This evolution, however, appears not to have been fully recognized by many state courts, in this instance charged with the front-line responsibility for the enforcement of constitutional rights. To continue a rule which is honored by this Court only with lip service is not a healthy thing and in the long run will do disservice to the federal system.

The special circumstances rule has been formally abandoned in capital cases, and the time has now come when it should be similarly abandoned in noncapital cases, at least as to offenses which, as the one involved here, carry the possibility of a substantial prison sentence. (Whether the rule should extend to *all* criminal cases need not now be decided.) * * *

Notes and Questions

1. *The significance of Powell v. Alabama and Johnson v. Zerbst.* Did the Court in *Betts* make, as Justice Black asserts in *Gideon,* "an abrupt break with its own well-considered precedents"? Did *Powell* furnish a steppingstone to either a *Betts* or a *Gideon,* depending on how far and fast the Supreme Court was willing to use the opinion's potential for expansion? Did the *Palko* doctrine constitute a clear warning that the Court would not impose the same requirements for appointed counsel upon the states as it had upon the federal government in *Johnson v. Zerbst?* See Israel, *Gideon v. Wainwright: The "Art" of Overruling,* 1963 Supreme Court Rev. 211, 234–38, 240–41.

2. *Alternative techniques of overruling available in Gideon.* Among the traditional arts of overruling are the arguments that (a) the old precedent has not withstood the "lessons of experience" and (b) that its rejection is required by later "inconsistent precedents." See e.g., *Mapp v. Ohio,* p. 124. Were these arguments available in *Gideon?* As to (b) reconsider, for example, the *Chandler* and *Ferguson* cases, establishing the unqualified right to the assistance of counsel *one can hire;* and the post-*Betts* development of the "automatic right" to appointed counsel in capital cases and its implicit admission of the unsoundness of the "fair trial" rule. As to (a), consider how, in the two decades since *Betts,* the assumption that a lawyerless defendant would usually be able to defend himself had fared in light of the constant expansion of the "special circumstances" concept; and how the assumption that a "special circumstances" test was more consistent with the "obligations of federalism" than an "absolute rule" had stood up in the face of the proliferation of federal habeas corpus cases produced by the *Betts* rule and the resulting friction between state and federal courts. See generally Israel, supra at 242–69.

3. *Why did the Gideon opinion take the route it did?* If the foregoing techniques of overruling were available in *Gideon,* why did Justice Black fail to utilize them? Would it have been most desirable to emphasize that the overruling of *Betts* was not attributable to recent changes in personnel, but that it constituted the product of a long line of Justices who, over two decades, participated in various decisions undermining *Betts?* See Israel, supra at 225, 269. Is the failure to employ the usual overruling "arts" in *Gideon* attributable to Justice Black's personal interest in vindicating his own dissenting opinion in *Betts?* Or his reluctance to admit even the *original validity* of a decision that exemplifies the evils (to him) of the "fundamental rights" interpretation of the fourteenth amendment? See id. at 270–72.

4. *The unrealized dream of Gideon.* For the view, spelled out at considerable length, that more than thirty years after *Gideon,* the dream of that landmark case—the dream of a country "in which every person charged with a crime will be

capably defended, no matter what his economic circumstances"—remains largely unrealized, see Stephen B. Bright, *Counsel for the Poor: the Death Sentence not for the Worst Crime but for the Worst Lawyer*, 103 Yale L.J. 1835 (1994). According to Bright, id. at 1870, "a properly working adversary system will never be achieved unless defender organizations are established and properly funded to employ lawyers at wages and benefits equal to what is spent on the prosecution, to retain expert and investigative assistance, to assign lawyers to capital cases, to recruit and support local lawyers and to supervise the performance of counsel defending capital cases. Judges are not equipped to do this. Management of the defense is not a proper judicial function."

5. *"Our double standards of criminal defense."* In many jurisdictions, notes Deborah L. Rhode, *Simpson Sound Bites: What Is and Isn't News About Domestic Violence*, in Postmortem: The O.J. Simpson Case 83, 84 (Jeffrey Abramson ed. 1996), the average fee for a court-appointed defense lawyer in a felony case is under $400—a total "less than what one of [O.J.] Simpson's lawyers typically charges by the hour." As for public defenders, continues Professor Rhode, each generally handles hundreds of felony cases per year and usually lacks adequate time or resources for investigation and expert testimony. "By contrast, in the Simpson case, [the] complete defense bill, including legal fees, may have reached $10 million. That figure exceeds what some states spend on appointed counsel for thousands of indigent defendants."

In ARGERSINGER v. HAMLIN, 407 U.S. 25, 92 S.Ct. 2006, 32 L.Ed.2d 530 (1972), the Court, per DOUGLAS, J., struck down a Florida rule (following the line marked out in the jury trial cases) requiring that counsel be appointed only "for nonpetty offenses punishable by more than six months imprisonment," and held that "absent a knowing and intelligent waiver, no person may be *imprisoned* for any offense, whether classified as petty, misdemeanor, or felony unless he was represented by counsel" (emphasis added):

"While there is historical support for limiting the [right] to trial by jury [to] 'serious criminal cases,' there is no such support for a similar limitation on the right to assistance of counsel. [Thus,] we reject [the] premise that since prosecutions for crimes punishable by imprisonment for less than six months may be tried without a jury, they may always be tried without a lawyer. [The] requirement of counsel may well be necessary for a fair trial even in a petty offense prosecution. We are by no means convinced that legal and constitutional questions involved in a case that actually leads to imprisonment even for a brief period are any less complex than when a person can be sent off for six months or more. * * *

"Beyond the problem of trials and appeals is that of the guilty plea, a problem which looms large in misdemeanor as well as in felony cases. Counsel is needed so that the accused may know precisely what he is doing, so that he is fully aware of the prospect of going to jail or prison, and so that he is treated fairly by the prosecution.

"In addition, the volume of misdemeanor cases, far greater in number than felony prosecutions, may create an obsession for speedy dispositions, regardless of the fairness of the result. * * *

"We must conclude, therefore, that the problems associated with misdemeanor and petty offenses often require the presence of counsel to insure the accused a fair trial. [In his concurring opinion,] Mr. Justice Powell suggests that these problems are raised even in situations where there is no prospect of imprisonment. We need not consider the requirements of the Sixth Amendment as regards the right to counsel where loss of liberty is not involved, however, for here, petitioner was in fact sentenced to jail * * *.

"Under the rule we announce today, every judge will know when the trial of a misdemeanor starts that no imprisonment may be imposed, even though local law permits it, unless the accused is represented by counsel. He will have a measure of the seriousness and gravity of the offense and therefore know when to name a lawyer to represent the accused before the trial starts."[a]

Analyzing the problem in terms of general due process rather than the sixth amendment right to counsel, concurring Justice POWELL, joined by Rehnquist, J., concluded that "there is a middle course, between the extremes of Florida's six month rule and the Court's rule, which comports with the requirements of the Fourteenth Amendment"—"fundamental fairness" requires that a defendant have the assistance of counsel in petty cases when, but only when, "necessary to assure a fair trial":

"Due process, perhaps the most fundamental concept in our law, embodies principles of fairness rather than immutable line-drawing as to every aspect of a criminal trial. While counsel is often essential to a fair trial, this is by no means a universal fact. Some petty offense cases are complex; others are exceedingly simple. [The] government often does not hire lawyers to prosecute petty offenses; instead the arresting police officer presents the case. Nor does every defendant who can afford to do so hire lawyers to defend petty charges. Where the possibility of a jail sentence is remote and the probable fine seems small, or where the evidence of guilt is overwhelming, the costs of assistance of counsel may exceed the benefits. It is anomalous that the Court's opinion today will extend the right of appointed counsel to indigent defendants in cases where the right to counsel would rarely be exercised by nonindigent defendants.

"Indeed, one of the effects of this ruling will be to favor defendants classified as indigents over those not so classified yet who are in low income groups where engaging counsel in a minor petty offense case would be a luxury the family could not afford. The line between indigency and assumed capacity to pay for counsel is necessarily somewhat arbitrary, drawn differently from State to State and often resulting in serious inequities to accused persons. The Court's new rule will accent the disadvantage of being barely self-sufficient economically.

"[The] rule adopted today [is] limited to petty offense cases in which the sentence is some imprisonment. The thrust of the Court's position indicates, however, that when the decision must be made, the rule will be extended to all petty offense cases except perhaps the most minor traffic violations. If the Court rejects on constitutional grounds, as it has today, the exercise of any judicial discretion as to need for counsel if a jail sentence is imposed, one must assume a similar rejection of discretion in other petty offense cases. * * *

"I would hold that the right to counsel in petty offense cases is not absolute but is one to be determined by the trial courts exercising a judicial discretion on a case-by-case basis. * * * [T]hree general factors should be weighed. First, the

---

a. Burger, C.J., concurred in the result. Brennan, J., joined by Douglas and Stewart, JJ., joined the Court's opinion and, in a brief concurring opinion, added the observation that "law students as well as practicing attorneys may provide an important source of legal representation for the indigent. [M]ore than 125 of the country's 147 accredited law schools have established clinical programs in which faculty-supervised students aid clients in a variety of civil and criminal matters."

court should consider the complexity of the offense charged. Second, the court should consider the probable sentence that will follow if a conviction is obtained. The more serious the likely consequences, the greater is the probability that a lawyer should be appointed. Third, the court should consider the individual factors peculiar to each case. These, of course, would be the most difficult to anticipate. One relevant factor would be the competency of the individual defendant to present his own case. The attitude of the community toward a particular defendant or particular incident would be another consideration. * * *

"Such a rule is similar in certain respects to the special circumstances rule applied to felony cases in *Betts,* which this Court overruled in *Gideon.* One of the reasons for seeking a more definitive standard in felony cases was the failure of many state courts to live up to their responsibilities in determining on a case-by-case basis whether counsel should be appointed. But this Court should not assume that the past insensitivity of some state courts to the rights of defendants will continue. Certainly if the Court follows the course of reading rigid rules into the Constitution, so that the state courts will be unable to exercise judicial discretion within the limits of fundamental fairness, there is little reason to think that insensitivity will abate."

Petitioner, an indigent, was charged with shoplifting merchandise valued at less than $150, punishable by as much as a $500 fine, or one year in jail, or both. He was not provided counsel. After a bench trial he was convicted of the offense and fined $50. The Supreme Court of Illinois declined to "extend *Argersinger*" to a case where one is charged with an offense for which imprisonment upon conviction is authorized but not actually imposed. A 5–4 majority of the Supreme Court, per REHNQUIST, J., agreed, SCOTT v. ILLINOIS, 440 U.S. 367, 99 S.Ct. 1158, 59 L.Ed.2d 383 (1979):

"Although the intentions of the *Argersinger* Court are not unmistakably clear from its opinion, we conclude today that *Argersinger* did indeed delimit the constitutional right to appointed counsel in state criminal proceedings. Even were the matter *res nova,* we believe that the central premise of *Argersinger*—that actual imprisonment is a penalty different in kind from fines or the mere threat of imprisonment—is eminently sound and warrants adoption of actual imprisonment as the line defining the constitutional right to appointment of counsel. * * * We therefore hold that the Sixth and Fourteenth Amendments to the United States Constitution require only that no indigent criminal defendant be sentenced to a term of imprisonment unless the State has afforded him the right to assistance of appointed counsel in his defense."

Concurring Justice POWELL noted that "the drawing of a line based on whether there is imprisonment (even for overnight) can have the practical effect of precluding provision of counsel in other types of cases in which conviction can have more serious consequences." He also thought that an "actual imprisonment" rule "tends to impair the proper functioning of the criminal justice system in that trial judges, in advance of hearing any evidence and before knowing anything about the case except the charge, all too often will be compelled to forego the legislatively granted option to impose a sentence of imprisonment upon conviction." Nevertheless, Justice Powell joined the opinion of the Court because "[i]t is important that this Court provide clear guidance to the hundreds of courts across the country that confront this problem daily." He hoped, however, "that in due time a majority will recognize that a more flexible rule is consistent with due process and will better serve the cause of justice."

Justice BRENNAN, joined by Marshall and Stevens, JJ., dissented:

"[*Argersinger*] established a 'two dimensional' test for the right to counsel: the right attaches to any 'non-petty' offense punishable by more than six months in jail and in addition to any offense where actual incarceration is likely regardless of the maximum authorized penalty. See Steven B. Duke, *The Right to Appointed Counsel: Argersinger and Beyond,* 12 Am.Crim.L.Rev. 601 (1975).

"The offense of 'theft' with which Scott was charged is certainly not a 'petty' one. It is punishable by a sentence of up to one year in jail. Unlike many traffic or other 'regulatory' offenses, it carries the moral stigma associated with common-law crimes traditionally recognized as indicative of moral depravity. The State indicated at oral argument that the services of a professional prosecutor were considered essential to the prosecution of this offense. Likewise, nonindigent defendants charged with this offense would be well advised to hire the 'best lawyers they can get.' Scott's right to the assistance of appointed counsel is thus plainly mandated by the logic of the Court's prior cases, including *Argersinger* itself.

"Perhaps the strongest refutation of respondent's alarmist prophecies that an authorized imprisonment standard would wreak havoc on the States is that the standard has not produced that result in the substantial number of States that already provide counsel in all cases where imprisonment is authorized—States that include a large majority of the country's population and a great diversity of urban and rural environments. Moreover, of those States that do not yet provide counsel in all cases where *any* imprisonment is authorized, many provide counsel when periods of imprisonment longer than 30 days, 3 months, or 6 months are authorized. In fact, Scott would be entitled to appointed counsel under the current laws of at least 33 States.

"It may well be that adoption by this Court of an authorized imprisonment standard would lead state and local governments to re-examine their criminal statutes. A state legislature or local government might determine that it no longer desired to authorize incarceration for certain minor offenses in light of the expense of meeting the requirements of the Constitution. In my view this re-examination is long overdue. In any event, the Courts actual imprisonment standard must inevitably lead the courts to make this re-examination, which plainly should more properly be a legislative responsibility."

In a separate dissent, Justice Blackmun maintained that the right to counsel "extends at least as far as the right to jury trial" and thus that "an indigent defendant in a state criminal case must be afforded appointed counsel whenever the defendant is prosecuted for a nonpetty criminal offense, that is, one punishable by more than six months' imprisonment, *or* whenever the defendant is actually subjected to a term of imprisonment."

Notes and Questions

1. Were Justice Powell's reasons for switching from his position in *Argersinger* to the "actual confinement" approach in *Scott*—to "provide clear guidance" to lower courts and to reach a result consistent with *Argersinger*—persuasive? Did Justice Powell explain why the "actual confinement" test provides clearer guidance than the alternative to it? Did he explain why he declined to join Justice Blackmun's dissenting opinion? Of all the opinions in *Scott,* does the Blackmun opinion diverge least from the views Powell expressed in *Argersinger?* See Lau-

rence Herman & Charles A. Thompson, *Scott v. Illinois and the Right to Counsel: A Decision in Search of a Doctrine?* 17 Am.Crim.L.Rev. 71, 94 (1979).

2. Are unrepresented defendants likely to waive their right to a jury trial, hoping that a judge who sits as factfinder will be able to provide assistance? If so, how in a *non-jury* case, can a judge *properly* make an intelligent pre-trial determination as to whether the sentence is likely to include incarceration, at least where he will hear the case? Isn't a considerable amount of potentially prejudicial information likely to be injected into the factfinding process? If an indigent defendant charged with an offense usually punished only by a fine is appointed counsel, would a *different* judge hearing the case assume that a colleague had found that the defendant had a "bad record" or had committed the minor offense in an egregious manner? See Commentary to Unif.R.Crim.P. 321(b); Note, 1979 U.Ill.L.F. 739, 752.

3. May the problems raised in Note 2 never be reached because of judicial reluctance to conduct pretrial inquiries about the likely sentence? Consider Note, 93 Harv.L.Rev. 82, 87 (1979): "It seems far more likely that, due to the sheer volume of misdemeanor cases, judges simply will not appoint counsel, thereby relinquishing their discretion to impose the penalty of imprisonment." If so, would this constitute improper judicial interference with the legislature's judgment concerning the appropriate range of penalties? See id.

4. *Can a prior uncounseled misdemeanor conviction by used to enhance a defendant's prison sentence when, given counsel, he is convicted of a second crime?* At first, a 5–4 majority answered in the negative, *Baldasar v. Illinois*, 446 U.S. 222, 100 S.Ct. 1585, 64 L.Ed.2d 169 (1980) (a defendant may not be given an increased term of imprisonment only because he was convicted in a previous case "in which he had *not* had the assistance of counsel"). However, *Baldasar* was overruled in *Nichols v. United States*, 511 U.S. 738, 114 S.Ct. 1921, 128 L.Ed.2d 745 (1994), where the Court, per Rehnquist, C.J., expressed agreement with the *Baldasar* dissenters "that a logical consequence of [*Scott*] is that an uncounseled [misdemeanor] conviction valid under *Scott* [because no prison term was imposed] may be relied upon to enhance the sentence for a subsequent offense, even though that sentence entails imprisonment." In 1983 Nichols had pled *nolo contendere* to a state misdemeanor, driving under the influence of alcohol (DUI), and paid a $250 fine. He was not represented by counsel. Seven years later, when Nichols pled guilty to a federal drug charge, this uncounseled misdemeanor conviction was used to enhance his prison sentence.[a]

B. THE "BEGINNINGS" OF THE RIGHT TO COUNSEL: HEREIN OF "CRIMINAL PROSECUTIONS" AND "CRITICAL STAGES"

The point at which the right to the assistance of counsel "begins" or first "attaches" is a question that arises in a number of different contexts and one that is considered at various parts of the book. See, e.g., *Miranda* (p. 475) ("custodial interrogation"); *United States v. Wade* (p. 641) (pretrial lineups); *Coleman v. Alabama* (Ch. 14, § 2) (preliminary hearing).

Compelled self-incrimination considerations aside, one only has a right to counsel at (1) a "critical stage" of (2) the "prosecution." As Justice Stewart

a. Souter, J., concurred only in the judgment. Blackmun, J., joined by Stevens and Ginsburg, JJ., dissented, maintaining that "[i]t is more logical and more consistent with the reasoning in *Scott*, to hold that a conviction is invalid for imposing a sentence for the offense itself remains invalid for increasing the term of imprisonment imposed for a subsequent conviction."

observed, concurring in a pretrial identification case, *United States v. Ash* (p. 660):[a] "The requirement that there be a 'prosecution' means that [the] 'right to counsel attaches only at or after the time that the adversary judicial proceedings have been initiated against [an accused].' 'It is this point [that] marks the commencement of the 'criminal prosecutions' to which alone the explicit guarantees of the Sixth Amendment are applicable.' "[b]

Although at one time the *Escobedo* case (p. 462) indicated otherwise, it is now clear that the right to counsel does not come into play simply because a person is or becomes the "prime suspect" or "focal point," or even when he is arrested (absent "interrogation" or its equivalent). "[A] person is entitled to the help of a lawyer"—assuming the stage of the "prosecution" is a "critical" one[c]—"at or after the time that judicial proceedings have been initiated against him—'whether by way of formal charge, preliminary hearing, indictment, information, or arraignment [presumably as early as the first appearance before a judicial officer].' " *Brewer v. Williams* (p. 619) (the Court, per Stewart, J.)

As indicated by the cases dealing with the use of informants and other secret government agents to obtain incriminating statements (see, e.g., *Hoffa, Osborn* and *White,* all discussed in Ch. 6, § 4), when judicial proceedings have not been initiated against a person, the privilege against self-incrimination as interpreted in *Miranda*—and *Miranda* alone—strikes the appropriate balance. If and when the conditions surrounding or inherent in a "preformal charge" confrontation are sufficiently coercive, "interrogation" or its equivalent may bring the "*Miranda* right to counsel" into play. But the right to counsel as such, what might be called the "pure" right to counsel, is not brought into play. At the "pre-charge" stage, at least when the suspect neither has nor has expressed a desire for counsel, the right to counsel is triggered by, and dependent on, forces that "jeopardize" the privilege against compelled self-incrimination; it has no life it can call its own.

UNITED STATES v. GOUVEIA, 467 U.S. 180, 104 S.Ct. 2292, 81 L.Ed.2d 146 (1984), per REHNQUIST, J., reaffirmed that one does not become an "accused" for right to counsel purposes simply because he has been detained by government authorities who contemplate filing charges against him. During the investigation of murders of fellow inmates in a federal prison, defendants were

a. *Ash* held that the right to counsel did not apply to a post-indictment *photographic* identification proceeding, maintaining that the right has always been limited to "trial-like confrontations" between prosecuting authorities and the accused, where the lawyer acts as "a spokesman for, or advisor to the accused." Dissenting Justice Brennan, joined by Douglas and Marshall, JJ., insisted that, regardless of whether the accused is physically present, "a 'stage' of the prosecution must be deemed 'critical' for the purpose of the Sixth Amendment if it is one at which the presence of counsel is necessary 'to protect the fairness of *the trial itself.*' "

b. Justice Stewart quoted from his four-justice plurality opinion in *Kirby v. Illinois* (p. 655) (right to counsel inapplicable to identification procedures held prior to the start of adversary judicial proceedings). To the same effect is Justice Powell's opinion for the Court in *Moore v. Illinois* (p. 658), also quoting from Justice Stewart's plurality opinion in *Kirby.*

c. In *Ash,* fn. a supra, the photographic display was conducted after adversary proceedings had begun, but the photographic identification was not considered a "critical stage." Compare *Coleman v. Alabama* (1970) (Ch. 14, § 2): "The inability of the indigent accused on his own to realize [the] advantages of a lawyer's assistance [at the preliminary hearing, e.g., skilled examination and cross-examination of witnesses, effective discovery of the prosecution's case, and effective arguments for the accused for an early psychiatric examination or bail] compels the conclusion that the Alabama preliminary hearing is a 'critical stage' of the State's criminal process at which the accused is 'as much entitled to [counsel] as at the trial itself.' *Powell v. Alabama.*"

placed in administrative detention. A disciplinary hearing held shortly thereafter led prison officials to conclude that defendants had participated in the murders. But defendants remained in administrative detention without appointed counsel for periods ranging from eight to nineteen months until their indictment on federal criminal charges. The Ninth Circuit reasoned that the administrative detention of an inmate for more than 90 days because of a pending felony investigation constitutes an "accusation" for Sixth Amendment right to counsel purposes[a] and that, in order to ensure that a prisoner or his lawyer will be able to take pre-indictment investigatory steps to preserve his defense at trial, indigent prisoners isolated in administrative detention while the subject of a felony investigation must be afforded counsel after 90 days or be released back into the prison population. The Supreme Court disagreed:

"[O]ur cases have long recognized that the right to counsel attaches only at or after the initiation of adversary proceedings against the defendant [referring to *Kirby v. Illinois* and subsequent cases]. That interpretation of the Sixth Amendment right to counsel is consistent not only with the literal language of the Amendment, which requires the existence of both a 'criminal prosecution' and an 'accused,' but also with the purposes which we have recognized that the right to counsel serves. We have recognized that the 'core purpose' of the counsel guarantee is to assure aid at trial, 'when the accused [is] confronted with both the intricacies of the law and the advocacy of the public prosecutor.' *Ash.*

" * * * Although we have extended an accused's right to counsel to certain 'critical' pre-trial proceedings, *Wade,* we have done so recognizing that at those proceedings, 'the accused [is] confronted, just as at trial, by the procedural system, or by his expert adversary, or by both,' *Ash,* in a situation where the results of the confrontation 'might well settle the accused's fate and reduces the trial itself to a mere formality.' *Wade.*

"[Of] course, both inside and outside the prison, it may well be true that in some cases pre-indictment investigation could help a defendant prepare a better defense. [But] our cases have never suggested that the purpose of the right to counsel is to provide a defendant with a pre-indictment private investigator, and we see no reason to adopt that novel interpretation of the right to counsel in this case."

Concurring Justice STEVENS, joined by Brennan, J., maintained that "[i]f the authorities take a person into custody [to] interrogate him or to otherwise facilitate the process of making a case against him, then under the rationale of *Escobedo, Miranda,* and our other cases, [he] is sufficiently 'accused' to be entitled to the protections of the Sixth Amendment." He concurred in the result, however, because he agreed that defendants' administrative detention "did not serve an accusatorial function. [Under the circumstance] there can be no doubt that concern for the welfare of other inmates or respondents themselves fully justified administrative detention entirely apart from its relation to an ongoing criminal investigation. Indeed, there is no finding [that] respondents were placed in [administrative detention] at the behest of [or in order to aid] prosecutorial authorities [nor] is there a finding that their detention facilitated the investigation of the two murders at issue."

Dissenting Justice MARSHALL shared Justice Stevens' view that "the government treats an individual as an accused when that individual 'is deprived of liberty in order to aid the prosecution in its attempt to convict him, and when the

---

a. The Ninth Circuit arrived at the 90–day figure based on its reading of federal prison regulations as permitting detention for up to 90 days for disciplinary reasons.

deprivation is likely to have the extended effect,' "but his reading of the record led him to a different conclusion: "[The] District Court [was] justified in concluding that respondents' 'commitment to [administrative detention] was neither a form of prison discipline nor an attempt to ensure prison security,' [but] 'part and parcel of a sequence of prosecutive acts integrally related to the application of criminal sanctions.' "

SECTION 2. THE *GRIFFIN-DOUGLAS* "EQUALITY" PRINCIPLE

GRIFFIN v. ILLINOIS: "THERE CAN BE NO EQUAL JUSTICE WHERE THE KIND OF TRIAL A MAN GETS DEPENDS ON THE MONEY HE HAS"

Prior to GRIFFIN v. ILLINOIS, 351 U.S. 12, 76 S.Ct. 585, 100 L.Ed. 891 (1956), full direct appellate review could only be had in Illinois by furnishing the appellate court with a bill of exceptions or report of the trial proceedings, certified by the trial judge. Preparation of these documents was sometimes impossible without a stenographic transcript of the trial proceedings, but such a transcript was furnished free only to indigent defendants sentenced to death. *Griffin* upheld by a 5–4 vote the contention that the due process and equal protection clauses of the fourteenth amendment require that *all* indigent defendants be furnished a transcript, at least where allegations that manifest errors occurred at the trial are not denied. See generally Francis A. Allen, *Griffin v. Illinois: Antecedents and Aftermath,* 25 U.Chi.L.Rev. 151, 152 (1957).

There was no opinion of the Court in *Griffin.* Justice Black announced the Court's judgment in a four-justice opinion; Justice Frankfurter concurred specially. In the course of his opinion, Justice BLACK observed: "In criminal trials a State can no more discriminate on account of poverty than on account of religion, race, or color. Plainly the ability to pay costs in advance bears no rational relationship to a defendant's guilt or innocence and could not be used as an excuse to deprive a defendant of a fair trial. [It] is true that a State is not required by the federal constitution to provide appellate courts or a right to appellate review at all. [But] that is not to say that a State that does grant appellate review can do so in a way that discriminates against some convicted defendants on account of their poverty. * * *

"All of the States now provide some method of appeal from criminal convictions, recognizing the importance of appellate review to a correct adjudication of guilt or innocence. Statistics show that a substantial proportion of criminal convictions are reversed by state appellate courts. Thus to deny adequate review to the poor means that many of them may lose their life, liberty or property because of unjust convictions which appellate courts would set aside. Many States have recognized this and provided aid for convicted defendants who have a right to appeal and need a transcript but are unable to pay for it. A few have not. Such a denial is a misfit in a country dedicated to affording equal justice to all and special privileges to none in the administration of its criminal law. There can be no equal justice where the kind of trial a man gets depends on the amount of money he has. Destitute defendants must be afforded as adequate appellate review as defendants who have money enough to buy transcripts."

A. APPLICATION (OR EXTENSION) OF *GRIFFIN*

In the decade and a half following *Griffin,* its underlying principle was broadly applied. See *Burns v. Ohio,* 360 U.S. 252, 79 S.Ct. 1164, 3 L.Ed.2d 1209 (1959) (state cannot require indigent defendant to pay filing fee before permitting him to appeal); *Smith v. Bennett,* 365 U.S. 708, 81 S.Ct. 895, 6 L.Ed.2d 39 (1961) (extending ban on filing fees to state post-conviction proceedings); *Long v. District Court of Iowa,* 385 U.S. 192, 87 S.Ct. 362, 17 L.Ed.2d 290 (1966) (indigent must be furnished a free transcript of a state habeas corpus hearing for use on appeal from a denial of habeas corpus, although availability of transcript not a sine qua non to access to the appellate court); *Gardner v. California,* 393 U.S. 367, 89 S.Ct. 580, 21 L.Ed.2d 601 (1969) (indigent prisoner entitled to free transcript of lower court habeas proceeding for use in filing application for a new habeas proceeding before a higher state court, even though that application need contain only a "brief statement" of prior proceedings and need not assign errors or refer to testimony in the prior proceeding); *Roberts v. LaVallee,* 389 U.S. 40, 88 S.Ct. 194, 19 L.Ed.2d 41 (1967) (indigent defendant entitled to free transcript of preliminary hearing for use at trial, even though both defendant and his counsel attended preliminary hearing and no indication of use to which preliminary hearing transcript could be put—points stressed by dissenting Justice Harlan); *Williams v. Illinois,* 399 U.S. 235, 90 S.Ct. 2018, 26 L.Ed.2d 586 (1970) (defendant unable to pay fine could not be incarcerated beyond maximum term fixed by statute; equal protection requires that "statutory ceiling" on imprisonment be same for all "irrespective of their economic status"); *Tate v. Short,* 401 U.S. 395, 91 S.Ct. 668, 28 L.Ed.2d 130 (1971) (indigent convicted of offenses punishable by fine only cannot be incarcerated a sufficient time to satisfy fines);[a] *Britt v. North Carolina,* 404 U.S. 226, 92 S.Ct. 431, 30 L.Ed.2d 400 (1971) (recognition that under ordinary circumstances indigent would be entitled to free transcript of previous trial ending with a hung jury because such a transcript would be "valuable to the defendant" as a discovery device and "as a tool at the [second] trial itself for the impeachment of prosecution witnesses").

In MAYER v. CHICAGO, 404 U.S. 189, 92 S.Ct. 410, 30 L.Ed.2d 372 (1971), a unanimous Court, per BRENNAN, J., carried the *Griffin* principle further than it ever has the *Gideon* principle by holding that an indigent appellant "cannot be denied a 'record of sufficient completeness' to permit proper consideration of his claims" because he was convicted of ordinance violations punishable by fine only. "The size of the defendant's pocketbook bears no more relationship to his guilt or innocence in a non-felony than in a felony case." Nor was the Court impressed with the argument that appellant's interest in a transcript in a case where he is not subject to imprisonment is outweighed by the State's fiscal and other interests in not burdening the appellate process:

"*Griffin* does not represent a balance between the needs of the accused and the interests of society; its principle is a flat prohibition against pricing indigent defendants out of as effective an appeal as would be available to others able to pay their own way. The invidiousness of the discrimination that exists when criminal procedures are made available only to those who can pay is not erased by any

---

a. A decade later, the Court relied on *Williams* and *Tate* to hold that a sentencing court cannot "automatically revoke" probation because a defendant cannot pay his fine without determining that the defendant "had not made sufficient bona fide efforts to pay or that adequate alternative forms of punishment did not exist." *Bearden v. Georgia,* 461 U.S. 660, 103 S.Ct. 2064, 76 L.Ed.2d 221 (1983).

differences in the sentences that may be imposed. The State's fiscal interest is, therefore, irrelevant.

"We add that even approaching the problem in the terms the city suggests hardly yields the answer the city tenders. The practical effects of conviction of even petty offenses of the kind involved here are not to be minimized. A fine may bear as heavily on an indigent accused as forced confinement.[b] The collateral consequences of conviction may be even more serious, as when (as was apparently a possibility in this case) the impecunious medical student finds himself barred from the practice of medicine because of a conviction he is unable to appeal for lack of funds."[c]

B. THE IMPACT OF THE "EQUALITY" PRINCIPLE ON THOSE WHO CANNOT AFFORD COUNSEL OR OTHER FORMS OF ASSISTANCE

Prior to *Gideon,* the *Griffin* case posed a challenge to *Betts:* How could the *Betts* line of cases be reconciled with the language, if not the holding, of *Griffin?* Since there was an unqualified right to have one's own paid counsel of his choosing at state trial, capital or not, did *Griffin* not imply that an indigent also has this unqualified right? By requiring *special circumstances* to exist before the indigent was entitled to appointed counsel in non-capital state cases, was the indigent not denied equal protection of the law? When the Supreme Court finally overruled the *Betts* case, somewhat surprisingly, it did not rely on *Griffin* at all, but *Douglas v. California,* infra, decided the same day, is another story.

DOUGLAS v. CALIFORNIA
372 U.S. 353, 83 S.Ct. 814, 9 L.Ed.2d 811 (1963).

Justice DOUGLAS delivered the opinion of the Court.

* * * The record shows that petitioners requested, and were denied, the assistance of counsel on appeal, even though it plainly appeared they were indigents. In denying petitioners' requests, the California District Court of Appeal stated that it had "gone through" the record and had come to the conclusion that "no good whatever could be served by appointment of counsel." [The court] was acting in accordance with a California rule of criminal procedure which provides that state appellate courts, upon the request of an indigent for counsel, may make "an independent investigation of the record and determine whether it would be of advantage to the defendant or helpful to the appellate court to have counsel appointed. [After] such investigation, appellate courts should appoint counsel if in their opinion it would be helpful to the defendant or the court, and should deny the appointment of counsel only if in their judgment such appointment would be of no value to either the defendant or the court." * * *

We agree, however, with Justice Traynor of the California Supreme Court, who said that the "[d]enial of counsel on appeal [to an indigent] would seem to be a discrimination at least as invidious as that condemned in [*Griffin,*" where] we held that a State may not grant appellate review in such a way as to discriminate against some convicted defendants on account of their poverty. [Whether the issue is a transcript on appeal or the assistance of counsel on appeal] the evil is the

b. But cf. *Argersinger v. Hamlin,* p. 71; *Scott v. Illinois,* p. 73.

c. Chief Justice Burger joined the Court's opinion, but in a separate opinion emphasized

that "there are alternatives in the majority of cases to a full verbatim transcript of an entire trial."

same: discrimination against the indigent. For there can be no equal justice where the kind of an appeal a man enjoys "depends on the amount of money he has."

[Under California's] present practice the type of an appeal [one is afforded] hinges upon whether or not he can pay for the assistance of counsel. If he can the appellate court passes on the merits of his case only after having the full benefit of written briefs and oral argument by counsel. If he cannot the appellate court is forced to prejudge the merits before it can even determine whether counsel should be provided. At this stage in the proceedings only the barren record speaks for the indigent, and, unless the printed pages show that an injustice has been committed, he is forced to go without a champion on appeal. Any real chance he may have had of showing that his appeal has hidden merit is deprived him when the court decides on an *ex parte* examination of the record that the assistance of counsel is not required.

* * * We are dealing only with the first appeal, granted as a matter of right to rich and poor alike (Cal.Penal Code §§ 1235, 1237), from a criminal conviction. We need not now decide whether California would have to provide counsel for an indigent seeking [discretionary review or] whether counsel must be appointed for an indigent seeking review of an appellate affirmance of his conviction in this Court. [But] it is appropriate to observe that a State can, consistently with the Fourteenth Amendment, provide for differences so long as the result does not amount to a denial of due process or an "invidious discrimination." Absolute equality is not required; lines can be and are drawn and we often sustain them. [But] where the merits of the one and only appeal an indigent has as of right are decided without benefit of counsel, we think an unconstitutional line has been drawn between rich and poor.

When an indigent is forced to run this gantlet of a preliminary showing of merit, the right to appeal does not comport with fair procedure. [T]he discrimination is not between "possibly good and obviously bad cases," but between cases where the rich man can require the court to listen to argument of counsel before deciding on the merits, but a poor man cannot. There is lacking that equality demanded by the Fourteenth Amendment where the rich man, who appeals as of right, enjoys the benefit of counsel's examination into the record, research of the law, and marshalling of arguments on his behalf, while the indigent, already burdened by a preliminary determination that his case is without merit, is forced to shift for himself. The indigent, where the record is unclear or the errors are hidden, has only the right to a meaningless ritual, while the rich man has a meaningful appeal. * * *

Judgment of the District Court of Appeals vacated and case remanded.

Justice CLARK, dissenting.

* * * We all know that the overwhelming percentage of *in forma pauperis* appeals are frivolous. Statistics of this Court show that over 96% of the petitions filed here are of this variety. [California's courts] after examining the record certified that [an] appointment [of counsel] would be neither advantageous to the petitioners nor helpful to the court. It, therefore, refused to go through the useless gesture of appointing an attorney. In my view neither the Equal Protection Clause nor the Due Process Clause requires more. I cannot understand why the Court says that this procedure afforded petitioners "a meaningless ritual." To appoint an attorney would not only have been utter extravagance and a waste of the State's funds but as surely "meaningless" to petitioners.

Justice HARLAN, whom Justice STEWART joins, dissenting.

[T]he Court appears to rely both on the Equal Protection Clause and on the guarantees of fair procedure inherent in the Due Process Clause of the Fourteenth Amendment, with obvious emphasis on "equal protection." In my view the Equal Protection Clause is not apposite, and its application to cases like the present one can lead only to mischievous results. This case should be judged solely under the Due Process Clause, and I do not believe that the California procedure violates that provision.

EQUAL PROTECTION

To approach the present problem in terms of the Equal Protection Clause is, I submit, but to substitute resounding phrases for analysis. I dissented from this approach in [*Griffin*] and I am constrained to dissent from the implicit extension of the equal protection approach here—to a case in which the State denies no one an appeal, but seeks only to keep within reasonable bounds the instances in which appellate counsel will be assigned to indigents.

The States, of course, are prohibited by the Equal Protection Clause from discriminating between "rich" and "poor" *as such* in the formulation and application of their laws. But it is a far different thing to suggest that this provision prevents the State from adopting a law of general applicability that may affect the poor more harshly than it does the rich, or, on the other hand, from making some effort to redress economic imbalances while not eliminating them entirely.

Every financial exaction which the State imposes on a uniform basis is more easily satisfied by the well-to-do than by the indigent. Yet I take it that no one would dispute the constitutional power of the State to levy a uniform sales tax, to charge tuition at a state university, to fix rates for the purchase of water from a municipal corporation, to impose a standard fine for criminal violations, or to establish minimum bail for various categories of offenses. Nor could it be contended that the State may not classify as crimes acts which the poor are more likely to commit than are the rich. And surely, there would be no basis for attacking a state law which provided benefits for the needy simply because those benefits fell short of the goods or services that others could purchase for themselves.

Laws such as these do not deny equal protection to the less fortunate for one essential reason: the Equal Protection Clause does not impose on the States "an affirmative duty to lift the handicaps flowing from differences in economic circumstances." To so construe it would be to read into the Constitution a philosophy of leveling that would be foreign to many of our basic concepts of the proper relations between government and society. The State may have a moral obligation to eliminate the evils of poverty, but it is not required by the Equal Protection Clause to give to some whatever others can afford.

[I]t should be noted that if the present problem may be viewed as one of equal protection, so may the question of the right to appointed counsel at trial, and the Court's analysis of that right in *Gideon* [is] wholly unnecessary. The short way to dispose of *Gideon,* in other words, would be simply to say that the State deprives the indigent of equal protection whenever it fails to furnish him with legal services, and perhaps with other services as well, equivalent to those that the affluent defendant can obtain.[a]

a. One may ask, too, why the Court failed even to discuss the applicability of the *Griffin-Douglas* "equality" principle to the issue raised in *Scott v. Illinois* p. 73. Since it is plain that one charged with an offense *punishable* by incarceration may *retain* counsel for his de- fense, does not the "equality" principle—especially in light of its application in *Mayer*— suggest that the "actual imprisonment" standard, even if it defensibly defines the Sixth Amendment right to appointed counsel, is unsatisfactory under the equal protection clause?

The real question in this case, I submit, and the only one that permits of satisfactory analysis, is whether or not the state rule, as applied in this case, is consistent with the requirements of fair procedure guaranteed by the Due Process Clause. Of course, in considering this question, it must not be lost sight of that the State's responsibility under the Due Process Clause is to provide justice for all. Refusal to furnish criminal indigents with some things that others can afford may fall short of constitutional standards of fairness. The problem before us is whether this is such a case.

DUE PROCESS * * *

We have today held that in a case such as the one before us, there is an absolute right to the services of counsel at trial. *Gideon.* [But] the appellate procedures involved here stand on an entirely different constitutional footing. *First,* appellate review is in itself not required by the Fourteenth Amendment, *McKane v. Durston,* 153 U.S. 684, 14 S.Ct. 913, 38 L.Ed. 867 [1894]; see *Griffin,* and thus the question presented is the narrow one whether the State's rules with respect to the appointment of counsel are so arbitrary or unreasonable, *in the context of the particular appellate procedure that it has established,* as to require their invalidation. *Second,* the kinds of questions that may arise on appeal are circumscribed by the record of the proceedings that led to the conviction; they do not encompass the large variety of tactical and strategic problems that must be resolved at the trial. *Third,* as California applies its rule, the indigent appellant receives the benefit of expert and conscientious legal appraisal of the merits of his case on the basis of the trial record, and whether or not he is assigned counsel, is guaranteed full consideration of his appeal. It would be painting with too broad a brush to conclude that under these circumstances an appeal is just like a trial.

What the Court finds constitutionally offensive in California's procedure bears a striking resemblance to the rules of this Court and many state courts of last resort on petitions for certiorari or for leave to appeal filed by indigent defendants *pro se.* Under the practice of this Court, only if it appears from the petition for certiorari that a case merits review is leave to proceed *in forma pauperis* granted, the case transferred to the Appellate Docket, and counsel appointed. Since our review is generally discretionary, and since we are often not even given the benefit of a record in the proceedings below, the disadvantages to the indigent petitioner might be regarded as more substantial than in California. But as conscientiously committed as this Court is to the great principle of "Equal Justice Under Law," it has never deemed itself constitutionally required to appoint counsel to assist in the preparation of each of the more than 1,000 *pro se* petitions for certiorari currently being filed each Term. We should know from our own experience that appellate courts generally go out of their way to give fair consideration to those who are unrepresented.

The Court distinguishes our review from the present case on the grounds that the California rule relates to "the first appeal, granted as a matter of right." [But] I fail to see the significance of this difference. Surely, it cannot be contended that the requirements of fair procedure are exhausted once an indigent has been given one appellate review. Nor can it well be suggested that having appointed counsel is more necessary to the fair administration of justice in an initial appeal taken as a matter of right, which the reviewing court on the full record has already determined to be frivolous, than in a petition asking a higher appellate court to exercise its discretion to consider what may be a substantial constitutional claim.

I cannot agree that the Constitution prohibits a State in seeking to redress economic imbalances at its bar of justice and to provide indigents with full review, from taking reasonable steps to guard against needless expense. This is all that California has done. * * *

ROSS v. MOFFITT
417 U.S. 600, 94 S.Ct. 2437, 41 L.Ed.2d 341 (1974).

Justice REHNQUIST delivered the opinion of the Court.

[Like many other states, the North Carolina appellate system is multitiered, providing for both an intermediate Court of Appeals and a Supreme Court. North Carolina authorizes appointment of counsel for a convicted defendant appealing to the intermediate court of appeals, but not for a defendant who seeks either discretionary review in the state supreme court or a writ of certiorari in the U.S. Supreme Court. In one case, the Mecklenburg County forgery conviction, respondent sought appointed counsel for discretionary review in the state supreme court. In another case, the Guilford County forgery conviction, respondent was represented by the public defender in the state supreme court, but sought court-appointed counsel to prepare a writ of certiorari to the U.S. Supreme Court. On federal habeas corpus, a unanimous panel of the U.S. Court of Appeals for the Fourth Circuit, per Haynsworth, C.J., held that the *Douglas* rationale required appointment of counsel in both instances.

[In *Griffin,* the Court struck down] an Illinois rule allowing a convicted criminal defendant to present claims of trial error to the [state supreme court] only if he procured a transcript of the testimony adduced at his trial. No exception was made for the indigent defendant, and thus one who was unable to pay the cost of obtaining such a transcript was precluded from obtaining appellate review of asserted trial error.

[*Griffin* and succeeding cases, such as *Burns v. Ohio* and *Smith v. Bennett* (the filing fee cases summarized at p. 79),] stand for the proposition that a State cannot arbitrarily cut off appeal rights for indigents while leaving open avenues of appeal for more affluent persons. In *Douglas,* however, [the] Court departed somewhat from the limited doctrine of [these] cases and undertook an examination of whether an indigent's access to the appellate system was adequate. [The *Douglas* Court] concluded that a State does not fulfill its responsibility toward indigent defendants merely by waiving its own requirements that a convicted defendant procure a transcript or pay a fee in order to appeal, and held that the State must go further and provide counsel for the indigent on his first appeal as of right. It is this decision we are asked to extend today.

[The] precise rationale for the *Griffin* and *Douglas* lines of cases has never been explicitly stated, some support being derived from the Equal Protection Clause of the Fourteenth Amendment, and some from the Due Process Clause of that Amendment. Neither clause by itself provides an entirely satisfactory basis for the result reached, each depending on a different inquiry which emphasizes different factors. "Due process" emphasizes fairness between the State and the individual dealing with the State, regardless of how other individuals in the same situation may be treated. "Equal protection," on the other hand, emphasizes disparity in treatment by a State between classes of individuals whose situations are arguably indistinguishable. We will address these issues separately in the succeeding sections.

Recognition of the due process rationale in *Douglas* is found both in the Court's opinion and in the dissenting opinion of Mr. Justice Harlan. The Court in *Douglas* stated that "[w]hen an individual is forced to run this gauntlet of a preliminary showing of merit, the right to appeal does not comport with fair procedure." Mr. Justice Harlan thought that the due process issue in *Douglas* was the only one worthy of extended consideration. * * *

We do not believe that the Due Process Clause requires North Carolina to provide respondent with counsel on his discretionary appeal to the State Supreme Court. At the trial stage of a criminal proceeding, the right of an indigent defendant to counsel [is] fundamental and binding upon the States by virtue of the Sixth and Fourteenth Amendments. But there are significant differences between the trial and appellate stages of a criminal proceeding. The purpose of the trial stage from the State's point of view is to convert a criminal defendant from a person presumed innocent to one found guilty beyond a reasonable doubt. To accomplish this purpose, the State employs a prosecuting attorney who presents evidence to the court, challenges any witnesses offered by the defendant, argues rulings of the court, and makes direct arguments to the court or jury seeking to persuade them of the defendant's guilt. Under these circumstances " * * * reason and reflection require us to recognize that in our adversary system of criminal justice, any person haled into court, who is too poor to hire a lawyer, cannot be assured a fair trial unless counsel is provided for him." *Gideon.*

By contrast, it is ordinarily the defendant, rather than the State, who initiates the appellate process, seeking not to fend off the efforts of the State's prosecutor but rather to overturn a finding of guilt made by a judge or jury below. The defendant needs an attorney on appeal not as a shield to protect him against being "haled into court" by the State and stripped of his presumption of innocence, but rather as a sword to upset the prior determination of guilt. This difference is significant for, while no one would agree that the State may simply dispense with the trial stage of proceedings without a criminal defendant's consent, it is clear that the State need not provide any appeal at all. *McKane v. Durston.* The fact that an appeal *has* been provided does not automatically mean that a State then acts unfairly by refusing to provide counsel to indigent defendants at every stage of the way. Unfairness results only if indigents are singled out by the State and denied meaningful access to that system because of their poverty. That question is more profitably considered under an equal protection analysis.

Language invoking equal protection notions is prominent both in *Douglas* and in other cases treating the rights of indigents on appeal. * * * Despite the tendency of all rights "to declare themselves absolute to their logical extreme," there are obviously limits beyond which the equal protection analysis may not be pressed without doing violence to principles recognized in other decisions of this Court. The Fourteenth Amendment "does not require absolute equality or precisely equal advantages," nor does it require the State to "equalize economic conditions." *Griffin* (Frankfurter, J., concurring). It does require [that] indigents have an adequate opportunity to present their claims fairly within the adversarial system. The State cannot adopt procedures which leave an indigent defendant "entirely cut off from any appeal at all," by virtue of his indigency, *Lane,* or extend to such indigent defendants merely a "meaningless ritual" while others in better economic circumstances have a "meaningful appeal." *Douglas.* The question is not one of absolutes, but one of degrees. In this case we do not believe that the Equal Protection Clause when interpreted in the context of these cases, requires North Carolina to provide free counsel for indigent defendants seeking to take discretionary appeals to the North Carolina Supreme Court, or to file petitions for certiorari in this Court.

[The] facts show that respondent, in connection with his Mecklenburg County conviction, received the benefit of counsel in examining the record of his trial and in preparing an appellate brief on his behalf for the state Court of Appeals. Thus, prior to his seeking discretionary review in the State Supreme Court, his claims "had once been presented by a lawyer and passed upon by an appellate court." *Douglas.* We do not believe that it can be said, therefore, that a defendant in respondent's circumstances is denied meaningful access to the North Carolina Supreme Court simply because the State does not appoint counsel to aid him in seeking review in that court. At that stage he will have, at the very least, a transcript or other record of trial proceedings, a brief on his behalf in the Court of Appeals setting forth his claims of error, and in many cases an opinion by the Court of Appeals disposing of his case. These materials, supplemented by whatever submission respondent may make *pro se,* would appear to provide the Supreme Court of North Carolina with an adequate basis on which to base its decision to grant or deny review.

We are fortified in this conclusion by our understanding of the function served by discretionary review in the North Carolina Supreme Court. The critical issue in that court, as we perceive it, is not whether there has been "a correct adjudication of guilt" in every individual case, but rather whether "the subject matter of the appeal has significant public interest," whether "the cause involves legal principles of major significance to the jurisprudence of the state," or whether the decision below is in probable conflict with a decision of the Supreme Court. The Supreme Court may deny certiorari even though it believes that the decision of the Court of Appeals was incorrect, since a decision which appears incorrect may nevertheless fail to satisfy any of the criteria discussed above. Once a defendant's claims of error are organized and presented in a lawyer-like fashion to the Court of Appeals, the justices of the Supreme Court of North Carolina who make the decision to grant or deny discretionary review should be able to ascertain whether his case satisfies the standards established by the legislature for such review.

This is not to say, of course, that a skilled lawyer, particularly one trained in the somewhat arcane art of preparing petitions for discretionary review, would not prove helpful to any litigant able to employ him. An indigent defendant seeking review in the Supreme Court of North Carolina is therefore somewhat handicapped in comparison with a wealthy defendant who has counsel assisting him in every conceivable manner at every stage in the proceeding. But both the opportunity to have counsel prepare an initial brief in the Court of Appeals and the nature of discretionary review in the Supreme Court of North Carolina make this relative handicap far less than the handicap borne by the indigent defendant denied counsel on his initial appeal as of right in *Douglas.* And the fact that a particular service might be of benefit to an indigent defendant does not mean that the service is constitutionally required. The duty of the State under our cases is not to duplicate the legal arsenal that may be privately retained by a criminal defendant in a continuing effort to reverse his conviction, but only to assure the indigent defendant an adequate opportunity to present his claims fairly in the context of the State's appellate process. We think respondent was given that opportunity under the existing North Carolina system.

Much of the discussion in the preceding section is equally relevant to the question of whether a State must provide counsel for a defendant seeking review of his conviction in this Court. North Carolina will have provided counsel for a convicted defendant's only appeal as of right, and the brief prepared by that counsel together with one and perhaps two North Carolina appellate opinions will be available to this Court in order that it may decide whether or not to grant certiorari. This Court's review, much like that of the Supreme Court of North Carolina, is discretionary and depends on numerous factors other than the perceived correctness of the judgment we are asked to review.

There is also a significant difference between the source of the right to seek discretionary review in the Supreme Court of North Carolina and the source of the right to seek discretionary review in this Court. The former is conferred by the statutes of the State of North Carolina, but the latter is granted by statutes enacted by Congress. Thus the argument relied upon in the *Griffin* and *Douglas* cases, that the State having once created a right of appeal must give all persons an equal opportunity to enjoy the right, is by its terms inapplicable. The right to seek certiorari in this Court is not granted by any State, and exists by virtue of federal statute with or without the consent of the State whose judgment is sought to be reviewed.

The suggestion that a State is responsible for providing counsel to one petitioning this Court simply because it initiated the prosecution which led to the judgment sought to be reviewed is unsupported by either reason or authority. It would be quite as logical under the rationale of *Douglas* and *Griffin,* and indeed perhaps more so, to require that the Federal Government or this Court furnish and compensate counsel for petitioners who seek certiorari here to review state judgments of conviction. Yet this Court has followed a consistent policy of denying applications for appointment of counsel by persons seeking to file jurisdictional statements or petitions for certiorari in this Court. In the light of these authorities, it would be odd, indeed, to read the Fourteenth Amendment to impose such a requirement on the States, and we decline to do so.

We do not mean by this opinion to in any way discourage those States which have, as a matter of legislative choice, made counsel available to convicted defendants at all stages of judicial review. Some States which might well choose to do so as a matter of legislative policy may conceivably find that other claims for public funds within or without the criminal justice system preclude the implementation of such a policy at the present time. [T]he Fourteenth Amendment leaves these choices to the State * * *.

Reversed.

Justice DOUGLAS, with whom Justice BRENNAN and Justice MARSHALL concur, dissenting.

[In his opinion below] Chief Judge Haynsworth could find "no logical basis for differentiation between appeals of right and permissive review procedures in the context of the Constitution and the right to counsel." More familiar with the functioning of the North Carolina criminal justice system than are we, he concluded that "in the context of constitutional questions arising in criminal prosecutions, permissive review in the state's highest court may be predictably the most meaningful review the conviction will receive." The North Carolina Court of Appeals, for example, will be constrained in diverging from an earlier opinion of the State Supreme Court, even if subsequent developments have rendered the earlier Supreme Court decision suspect. "[T]he state's highest court remains the ultimate arbiter of the rights of its citizens."

Chief Judge Haynsworth also correctly observed that the indigent defendant proceeding without counsel is at a substantial disadvantage relative to wealthy defendants represented by counsel when he is forced to fend for himself in seeking discretionary review from the State Supreme Court or from this Court. It may well not be enough to allege error in the courts below in layman's terms; a more sophisticated approach may be demanded:

"An indigent defendant is as much in need of the assistance of a lawyer in preparing and filing a petition for certiorari as he is in the handling of an appeal as of right. In many appeals, an articulate defendant could file an effective brief by telling his story in simple language without legalisms, but the technical requirement for applications for writs of certiorari are hazards which one untrained in the law could hardly be expected to negotiate. * * *"

[The] right to discretionary review is a substantial one, and one where a lawyer can be of significant assistance to an indigent defendant. It was correctly perceived below that the "same concepts of fairness and equality which require counsel in a first appeal of right, require counsel in other and subsequent discretionary appeals."

ON THE MEANING OF *ROSS v. MOFFITT*

1. Is *Mayer v. Chicago* (p. 79) "good law" after *Ross*? Are *Long v. District Court, Gardner v. California, Roberts v. LaVallee,* and *Britt v. North Carolina* (all summarized at p. 79) "good law" after *Ross*? Does the *Long-Gardner* line of cases (never mentioned by the *Ross* Court) constitute a significant "departure" from what the *Ross* Court calls the "limited doctrine" of *Griffin* and succeeding cases?

2. Consider Laurence H. Tribe, *American Constitutional Law* 1647 (2d ed.1988): "[The *Ross* Court] disengaged *Griffin* from *Douglas*, deftly rewove the *Griffin* transcript and filing fee decisions together as minimal access cases rather than equal protection cases, and neatly severed *Douglas* from this newly created body of law." See also Kamisar, *Poverty, Equality, and Criminal Procedure*, in National College of District Attorneys, *Constitutional Law Deskbook* 1–97 to 1–100 (1977).

3. Does the *Ross* opinion's "equal protection analysis" closely resemble a "due process analysis"? Indeed, now that *Ross* is on the books, does the "equality" principle *add anything* to what the indigent defendant or prisoner already has in his arsenal? Consider Kamisar, supra, at 1–101 to 1–108:

"[The *Ross* 'equal protection analysis'] seems to put to one side the admitted fact that an indigent seeking discretionary review is 'somewhat handicapped in comparison with a wealthy defendant who has counsel assisting him' and focuses instead on whether an indigent seeking discretionary review without counsel has a '*meaningful* opportunity' (emphasis added) to present his claims in the state supreme court—to provide the court 'with an *adequate* basis for its decision to grant or deny review' (emphasis added)—*regardless* of whether a wealthy defendant who has counsel at this stage has a *significantly better* opportunity to present his claims.

"[What *Ross*] really seems to be asking, and deciding, is whether an indigent in respondent's circumstances has a *fair chance,* a *fighting chance* (or the requisite *minimum* chance), to get the attention of the state supreme court. [This] is 'due process,' not 'equal protection' reasoning. * * *

"So long as the indigent defendant's 'brand of justice' satisfies certain minimal standards—passes government inspection, one might say—[*Ross* tells us that] *it need not be* the same brand of justice or the same 'choice' or 'prime' grade of justice as the wealthy man's. [In some phases of the criminal process an indigent will not have 'meaningful access' to the hearing body or an 'adequate opportunity' to present his claim], but in [such] cases 'fundamental fairness'—'due process'—will require the state to furnish counsel. In those cases where due process *does not* impose a duty on the state to provide counsel, *neither,* it seems, *will 'equal protection.' "*[a]

4. What light, if any, is shed on the meaning of *Ross* by *United States* v. *MacCollom*, 426 U.S. 317, 96 S.Ct. 2086, 48 L.Ed.2d 666 (1976)? *MacCollom* upheld the constitutionality of 28 U.S.C. § 753 (f), which provides for a free transcript for indigent prisoners seeking relief under 28 U.S.C. § 2255 (the statutory counterpart to habeas corpus for federal prisoners) only if the trial judge certifies that (a) the claim is "not frivolous" and (b) the transcript is needed to decide the issues presented." The principal opinion was written by Rehnquist, J., joined by Burger, C.J., and Stewart and Powell, JJ.

After noting that respondent "chose to forgo his opportunity for direct appeal with its attendant unconditional free transcript," Justice Rehnquist emphasized that the adequacy of respondent's access to procedures for review of his conviction "must be decided in the light of avenues which respondent chose not to follow as well as those he now seeks to widen." It was "enough at the collateral-relief stage that Congress has provided that the transcript be paid for by public funds if one [satisfies the conditions imposed by § 753 (f)]. Under the circumstances, § 753 (f) afforded respondent "an adequate opportunity to attack his conviction."

Concurring Justice Blackmun, who provided the fifth vote for the Court's judgment, underscored the lack of any statement of "articulable facts" in respondent's claim indicating that "a transcript would assist him in his § 2255 proceeding." He thought it clear that "there is no constitutional requirement that the [government] provide an indigent with a transcript when that transcript is not necessary in order for him to prove his claim, or when his claim is frivolous on its face. Nor does the Constitution require that an indigent be furnished every possible legal tool, no matter how devoid of assistance it may be, merely because a person of unlimited means might choose to waste his resources in a quest of that kind."

Dissenting Justice Brennan, joined by Marshall, J., maintained, that the government's refusal to furnish a free transcript in a § 2255 proceeding "upon merely a showing of indigency" violated the "equal protection" element of fifth amendment due process: "The *Griffin* principle of equality was not limited to transcripts for purposes of direct appellate review [discussing, e.g., *Lane v. Brown, Long v. District Court, Gardner v. California*]. I reject as wholly fallacious the argument that adequacy of opportunity to present claims at trial and on direct appeal so far diminishes the importance of collateral review, that discrimination between indigent and nonindigent in post-conviction proceedings is constitutionally tolerable."[a]

5. What light, if any, is shed on the meaning of *Ross* by *Ake v. Oklahoma,* below. Note that while it held that, under the circumstances, the state must provide defendant free access to a psychiatrist's assistance, the *Ake* Court recognized that the *Griffin-Douglas* principle does not require a state to "purchase for the indigent defendant all the assistance that his wealthier counterpart might

---

a. But compare Israel, *Criminal Procedure, the Burger Court, and the Legacy of the Warren Court,* 75 Mich.L.Rev. 1319, 1334–36 (1977).

a. In a separate dissent, Stevens, J., joined by Brennan, White and Marshall, JJ., maintained that § 753(f) should be construed to make free transcripts available as a matter of course to § 2255 petitioners, as well as to convicted defendants pursuing direct appeals. The plurality's response was that Justice Stevens' construction of § 753(f) "would do violence to the intent of Congress."

buy." Note, too, that the *Ake* Court viewed its task in cases of this sort as one that has "focused on identifying the 'basic tools of an adequate defense or appeal.' "

C. The Indigent Defendant's Right to Expert Services in Addition to Counsel

In AKE v. OKLAHOMA, 470 U.S. 68, 105 S.Ct. 1087, 84 L.Ed.2d 53 (1985), the Court broke its thirty-year silence on the issue of an indigent defendant's right to a psychiatrist and other expert assistance and held that (1) at least when a defendant has made a preliminary showing that his sanity at the time of the offense is likely to be a significant factor at trial, the state must provide access to "the psychiatric examination and assistance necessary to prepare an effective defense based on [the defendant's] mental condition" and (2) when, at a capital sentencing proceeding, the state presents psychiatric evidence of the defendant's future dangerousness, due process requires access to psychiatric assistance.

The case arose as follows: Ake, an indigent, was charged with first-degree murder. At his arraignment, Ake's behavior was so bizarre that the trial judge ordered him to be examined by a psychiatrist. The examining psychiatrist found Ake incompetent to stand trial. Six weeks after being committed to the state mental hospital, Ake was found to be competent to stand trial on the condition that he continue to be sedated with an antipsychotic drug. Petitioner's attorney informed the court that he would raise an insanity defense, but his motion for a psychiatric evaluation at state expense was denied. The jury rejected the insanity defense and petitioner was convicted of first-degree murder. At the capital sentencing proceeding, the state asked for the death penalty, relying on the examining psychiatrist's testimony to establish the likelihood of petitioner's future dangerousness. Petitioner had no expert witness to rebut this testimony or to give evidence in mitigation of his punishment, and he was sentenced to death. In reversing, the Court observed, per MARSHALL, J:

"This Court has long recognized that when a State brings its judicial power to bear on an indigent defendant in a criminal proceeding, it must take steps to assure that the defendant has a fair opportunity to present his defense. This elementary principle, grounded in significant part on the Fourteenth Amendment's due process guarantee of fundamental fairness, derives from the belief that justice cannot be equal where, simply as a result of his poverty, a defendant is denied the opportunity to participate meaningfully in a judicial proceeding in which his liberty is at stake. [Thus,] this Court held almost 30 years ago that once a State offers to criminal defendants the opportunity to appeal their cases, it must provide a trial transcript to an indigent defendant if the transcript is necessary to a decision on the merits of the appeal. *Griffin v. Illinois*. Indeed, in *Little v. Streater*, 452 U.S. 1, 101 S.Ct. 2202, 68 L.Ed.2d 627 (1981), we extended this principle of meaningful participation to a 'quasi-criminal' proceeding and held that, in a paternity action, the State cannot deny the putative father blood grouping tests, if he cannot otherwise afford them.

"Meaningful access to justice has been the consistent theme of these cases. [A] criminal trial is fundamentally unfair if the State proceeds against an individual defendant without making certain that he has access to the raw materials integral to the building of an effective defense. Thus, while the Court has not held that a State must purchase for the indigent defendant all the assistance that his wealthier counterpart might buy, see *Ross v. Moffitt*, it has often reaffirmed that fundamental fairness entitles indigent defendants to 'an adequate opportunity to present their claims fairly within the adversary system,' id. To implement this principle, we have focused on identifying the 'basic tools of an adequate defense or appeal,' and we have required that such tools be provided to those defendants who cannot afford to pay for them.

"[W]ithout the assistance of a psychiatrist to conduct a professional examination on issues relevant to the defense, to help determine whether the insanity defense is viable to present testimony, and to assist in preparing the cross-examination of a State's psychiatric witnesses, the risk of an inaccurate resolution of sanity issues is extremely high. With such assistance, the defendant is fairly able to present at least enough information to the jury, in a meaningful manner, as to permit it to make a sensible determination.

"A defendant's mental condition is not necessarily at issue in every criminal proceeding, however, and it is unlikely that psychiatric assistance of the kind we have described would be of probable value in cases where it is not. The risk of error from denial of such assistance, as well as its probable value, are most predictably at their height when the defendant's mental condition is seriously in question. When the defendant is able to make an ex parte threshold showing to the trial court that his sanity is likely to be a significant factor in his defense, the need for the assistance of a psychiatrist is readily apparent. It is in such cases that a defense may be devastated by the absence of a psychiatric examination and testimony; with such assistance, the defendant might have a reasonable chance of success. In such a circumstance, where the potential accuracy of the jury's determination is so dramatically enhanced, and where the interests of the individual and the State in an accurate proceeding are substantial, the State's interest in its fisc must yield.

"We therefore hold that when a defendant demonstrates [that] his sanity at the time of the offense is to be a significant factor at trial, the State must, at a minimum, assure the defendant access to a competent psychiatrist who will conduct an appropriate examination and assist in evaluation, preparation, and presentation of the defense. This is not to say, of course, that the indigent defendant has a constitutional right to choose a psychiatrist of his personal liking or to receive funds to hire his own. Our concern is that the indigent defendant have access to a competent psychiatrist for the purpose we have discussed, and as in the case of provision of counsel we leave to the State the decision on how to implement this right.

"Ake also was denied the means of presenting evidence to rebut the State's evidence of his future dangerousness. The foregoing discussion compels a similar conclusion in the context of a capital sentencing proceeding, when the State presents psychiatric evidence of the defendants future dangerousness. * * *

"This Court has upheld the practice [in state capital sentencing proceedings] of placing before the jury psychiatric testimony on the question of future dangerousness, at least where the defendant has had access to an expert of his own. * * * Without a psychiatrist's assistance, the defendant cannot offer a well-informed expert's opposing view, and thereby loses a significant opportunity to raise in the jurors' minds questions about the State's proof of an aggravating factor. In such a circumstance, where the consequence of error is so great, the relevance of responsive psychiatric testimony so evident, and the burden on the State so slim, due process requires access to a psychiatric examination on relevant issues, to the testimony of the psychiatrist, and to assistance in preparation at the sentencing phase."[a]

---

a. Burger, C.J. concurred in the judgment, maintaining: "The facts of this case and the question presented confine the actual holding of the Court. In capital cases the finality of the

Notes and Questions

1. *The significance of Ake.* How much of an exaggeration, if any, is it to say, as one commentator has, that "*Ake* represents the final and complete collapse of the equality principle into due process analyses" and "the full ascendancy of Justice Harlan's position in *Griffin* and *Douglas*"? See David Harris, *The Constitution and Truth Seeking: A New Theory on Expert Services for Indigent Defendants,* 83 J.Crim.L. & C. 469, 482, 488 (1992).

2. *The breadth of the supporting services that may be needed.* "Quality legal representation," emphasizes I *A.B.A. Standards* § 5–1.4 (commentary), "cannot be rendered either by defenders or by assigned counsel unless the lawyers have available for their use adequate supporting services. These [include] expert witnesses * * *, personnel skilled in social work and related disciplines to provide assistance at pretrial release hearings and at sentencing, and trained investigators to interview witnesses and to assemble demonstrative evidence. The quality of representation at trial, for example, may be excellent and yet valueless to the defendant if the defense requires the assistance of a psychiatrist or handwriting expert and no such services are available. If the defense attorney must personally conduct factual investigations, the financial cost to the justice system is likely to be greater. Moreover, when an attorney personally interviews witnesses, [he] may be placed in the untenable position of either taking the stand to challenge their credibility if their testimony conflicts with statements previously given or withdrawing from the case."

3. *The meaning of "basic tools."* Under *Ake,* how basic does a tool have to be before a state is required to supply it to an indigent defendant? Consider Harris, Note 1 supra, at 486–87:

"As lower courts have struggled to define 'basic tools,' they have asked whether the particular resource requested by an indigent defendant is a 'virtual necessity' for the defense. Is the resource so important that the defense simply cannot do without it? Thus, 'basic tool' has come to mean not just something fundamental to a defendant's legal arsenal, but a resource without which the defense fails. Under this interpretation, most expert services remain luxuries for indigent defendants because the tasks experts perform and the issues with which they deal are not usually outcome determinative by themselves. Rather, the service any one expert or investigator provides is typically germane only to one or a few elements of the crime. If any one of the links in the evidentiary chain weakens, an acquittal may result, but this usually does not depend on the testimony of a single expert, such as the psychiatrist in *Ake.* Since lower courts have interpreted *Ake* to mean that the defense receives assistance only when the accused's case will fail without it, the basic tools standard does very little for most indigent defendants."

4. *A new approach.* Instead of trying to make indigent defendants "equal" or giving them "basic tools," Professor David Harris suggests, id. at 491–92, that

sentence imposed warrants protections that may or may not be required in other cases. Nothing in the Court's opinion reaches noncapital cases." Can (should) the Court's opinion be limited to capital cases? See Note, 84 Mich.L.Rev. 1326 (1986).

Rehnquist, J., dissented. He did not believe that "the facts of this case warrant" the estab-

lishment of the constitutional rule announced by the Court and, in any event, he thought the rule "far too broad." He would limit it to capital cases and "make clear that the entitlement is to an independent psychiatric evaluation, not to a defense consultant." Is it clear that the entitlement *is* to a "defense consultant?"

courts use a theory that "targets the implications of economic disparity in criminal justice by focusing on whether the defendant's poverty could prevent the jury from hearing all of the relevant evidence on contested issues. Based on the Sixth Amendment, this theory would have judges ask two questions in deciding whether to grant a request for expert services. First, is the issue to which the requested resource pertains in dispute? Second, is the information that could be brought to trial as a result of granting the defendant's request for expert services helpful to the factfinder's decision? In other words, could this information, either by itself or in combination with other information, be the basis for a finding of reasonable doubt?"

5. *The resource imbalance—a problem the Simpson case illustrated in reverse.* Consider Peter Arenella, *Foreword: O.J. Lessons,* 69 S.Cal.L.Rev. 1233, 1234–35 (1996):

"[The] resource factor usually favors the state because most criminal defendants are poor. The prosecutor can use law enforcement agencies, state and private forensic laboratories, an experts on the public payroll to develop, shape, and present her evidence. Crime victims and witnesses usually cooperate with the prosecution. If they do not, the prosecutor can command their appearance before a grand jury and compel their testimony.

"In contrast, a skilled and experienced public defender is lucky if she gets an investigator to spend a few hours investigating the 'facts.' Crime victims and civilian witnesses frequently refuse to answer the investigator's questions. If the public defender needs expert assistance, she must petition the court for funds to pay for the expert's time. The one or two state funded experts she may obtain won't be [the caliber of O.J. Simpson's experts] and they will rarely spend hundreds of hours looking for flaws in the state's case.

"This resource imbalance is particularly egregious in death penalty prosecutions. [Far] too often, underpaid defense lawyers in capital cases spend less time and effort on death penalty cases than the Simpson defense team expended prepping for his preliminary hearing.

"The 'trial of the century' illustrated this resource imbalance problem in reverse. One of Robert Shapiro's wisest decisions was to hire some of this country's leading medical, forensic, and legal experts before Simpson was even arrested. With the aid of [various experts], the defense's forensic attorney team * * * transformed incriminating hair, blood, DNA, and fiber data into evidence of police and criminalist incompetence and corruption. While defense counsel for the indigent can read the Simpson trial transcripts and learn new ways to attack forensic evidence, they lack the resources to buy the experts whose prestige and skills made the 'garbage in-garbage out' strategy so effective."

SECTION 3. THE RIGHT TO APPOINTED COUNSEL IN PROCEEDINGS OTHER THAN CRIMINAL PROSECUTIONS: THE CONTINUED VITALITY OF THE *BETTS v. BRADY* APPROACH

A. THE PENO-CORRECTIONAL PROCESS

GAGNON v. SCARPELLI
411 U.S. 778, 93 S.Ct. 1756, 36 L.Ed.2d 656 (1973).

Justice POWELL delivered the opinion of the Court.

[Respondent Scarpelli] pleaded guilty in July, 1965, to a charge of armed robbery. The trial judge sentenced him to 15 years' imprisonment, but suspended the sentence and placed him on probation for seven years. [A month later, Scarpelli and one Fred Kleckner were apprehended] in the course of the burglary of a house. After being apprised of his constitutional rights, respondent admitted that he and Kleckner had [unlawfully] broken into the house [but] he now asserts that his statement was made under duress and is false. [Probation was revoked without a hearing on the stated grounds that:]

"1. [Scarpelli] has associated with known criminals, in direct violation of his probation regulations and his supervising agent's instructions;

"2. [Scarpelli] while associating with a known criminal, namely Fred Kleckner, was involved in, and arrested for, a burglary * * *."

[A month after the burglary, Scarpelli began serving the 15 years to which he had been sentenced.]

In *Mempa v. Rhay*,[a] the Court held a probationer is entitled to be represented by appointed counsel at a combined revocation and sentencing hearing. Reasoning that counsel is required "at every stage of a criminal proceeding where substantial rights of a criminal accused may be affected," and that sentencing is one such stage, the Court concluded that counsel must be provided an indigent at sentencing even when it is accomplished as part of a subsequent, probation revocation proceeding. But this line of reasoning does not require a hearing or counsel at the time of probation revocation in a case such as the present one, where the probationer was sentenced at the time of that trial.[b]

Of greater relevance [is] *Morrissey v. Brewer,* 408 U.S. 471, 92 S.Ct. 2593, 33 L.Ed.2d 484 (1972), [holding that] even though the revocation of parole is not a part of the criminal prosecution, [the] loss of liberty entailed is a serious deprivation requiring that the parolee be accorded due process. * * * Probation revocation, like parole revocation, is not a stage of a criminal prosecution, but does result in a loss of liberty. Accordingly, we hold that a probationer, like a parolee, is entitled to a preliminary and a final revocation hearing, under the conditions specified in *Morrissey*.

The [more difficult question] is whether an indigent probationer or parolee has a due process right to be represented by appointed counsel at these hearings.[6]

a. In *Mempa,* 389 U.S. 128, 88 S.Ct. 254, 19 L.Ed.2d 336 (1967), petitioners' sentencing was deferred subject to probation. The prosecutor subsequently moved to have their probation revoked on the ground that petitioners had committed other crimes. At these hearings neither petitioner was represented by counsel or offered counsel. As a result of these hearings, each petitioner's probation was revoked and he was sentenced to a term of imprisonment. A unanimous Court, per Marshall, J., held that "a lawyer must be afforded at this [deferred sentencing] procedure whether it be labeled a revocation of probation or a deferred sentencing."

b. But see Fred Cohen, *Sentencing, Probation, and the Rehabilitative Ideal,* 47 Texas L.Rev. 1, 2–6 (1968), viewing *Mempa* as "the beginning of judicial activity in the sentencing-to-final discharge area of law, and not as a rear guard mopping-up operation in the natural evolution of right-to-counsel decisions," and stressing that "[t]here is no other area of law, except perhaps the civil commitment of the mentally ill, where the lives of so many people are so drastically affected by officials who exercise a virtually absolute, unreviewed discretion."

6. [Since] respondent did not attempt to retain counsel but asked only for appointed counsel, we have no occasion to decide in this case whether a probationer or parolee has a right to be represented at a revocation hearing by retained counsel in situations other than those where the State would be obliged to furnish counsel for an indigent.

[While a rule] that the State is under a constitutional duty to provide counsel for indigents in all probation or parole revocation cases [has] the appeal of simplicity, it would impose direct costs and serious collateral disadvantages without regard to the need or the likelihood in a particular case for a constructive contribution by counsel. In most cases, the probationer or parolee has been convicted of committing another crime or has admitted the charges against him. And while in some cases he may have a justifiable excuse for the violation or a convincing reason why revocation is not the appropriate disposition, mitigating evidence of this kind is often not susceptible of proof or is so simple as not to require either investigation or exposition by counsel.

The introduction of counsel into a revocation proceeding will alter significantly the nature of the proceeding. If counsel is provided for the probationer or parolee, the State in turn will normally provide its own counsel; lawyers, by training and disposition, are advocates and bound by professional duty to present all available evidence and arguments in support of their clients' positions and to contest with vigor all adverse evidence and views. The role of the hearing body itself, aptly described in *Morrissey* as being "predictive and discretionary" as well as fact-finding, may become more akin to that of a judge at a trial, and less attuned to the rehabilitative needs of the individual probationer or parolee. In the greater self-consciousness of its quasi-judicial role, the hearing body may be less tolerant of marginal deviant behavior and feel more pressure to reincarcerate rather than continue nonpunitive rehabilitation. Certainly, the decision-making process will be prolonged, and the financial cost to the State—for appointed counsel, counsel for the State, a longer record, and the possibility of judicial review—will not be insubstantial.[7]

In some cases, these modifications in the nature of the revocation hearing must be endured and the costs borne because [the] probationer's or parolee's version of a disputed issue can fairly be represented only by a trained advocate. But due process is not so rigid as to require that the significant interests in informality, flexibility, and economy must always be sacrificed.

In so concluding, we are of course aware that the case-by-case approach to the right to counsel in felony prosecutions adopted in *Betts* [was] later rejected in favor of a *per se* rule. [But we do not] draw from *Gideon* and *Argersinger* the conclusion that a case-by-case approach to furnishing counsel is necessarily inadequate to protect constitutional rights asserted in varying types of proceedings: there are critical differences between criminal trials and probation or parole revocation hearings, and both society and the probationer or parolee have stakes in preserving these differences.

In a criminal trial, the State is represented by a prosecutor; formal rules of evidence are in force; a defendant enjoys a number of procedural rights which may be lost if not timely raised; and, in a jury trial, a defendant must make a presentation understandable to untrained jurors. In short, a criminal trial under our system is an adversary proceeding with its own unique characteristics. In a revocation hearing, on the other hand, the State is represented not by a prosecutor but by a parole officer with the orientation described above; formal procedures and rules of evidence are not employed; and the members of the hearing body are familiar with the problems and practice of probation or parole. The need for

7. The scope of the practical problem which would be occasioned by a requirement of counsel in all revocation cases is suggested by the fact that in the mid–1960's there were an estimated average of 20,000 adult felony parole revocations and 108,000 adult probation revocations each year. President's Commission on Law Enforcement and Administration of Justice *Task Force Report: The Courts* 56, fn. 28 (1967).

counsel at revocation hearings derives not from the invariable attributes of those hearings but rather from the peculiarities of particular cases.

The differences between a criminal trial and revocation hearing do not dispose altogether of the argument that under a case-by-case approach there may be cases in which a lawyer would be useful but in which none would be appointed because an arguable defense would be uncovered only by a lawyer. [But] we think it a sufficient answer that we deal here not with the right of an accused to counsel in a criminal prosecution, but with the more limited due process right of one who is a probationer or parolee only because he has been convicted of a crime.

We thus find no justification for a new inflexible constitutional rule with respect to the requirement of counsel. We think, rather, that the decision as to the need for counsel must be made on a case-by-case basis in the exercise of a sound discretion by the state authority charged with responsibility for administering the probation and parole system. Although the presence and participation of counsel will probably be both undesirable and constitutionally unnecessary in most revocation hearings, there will remain certain cases in which fundamental fairness—the touchstone of due process—will require that the State provide at its expense counsel for indigent probationers or parolees.

* * * Presumptively, it may be said that counsel should be provided in cases where, after being informed of his right to request counsel, the probationer or parolee makes such a request, based on a timely and colorable claim (i) that he has not committed the alleged violation of the conditions upon which he is at liberty; or (ii) that, even if the violation is a matter of public record or is uncontested, there are substantial reasons which justified or mitigated the violation and make revocation inappropriate and that the reasons are complex or otherwise difficult to develop or present. In passing on a request for the appointment of counsel, the responsible agency also should consider, especially in doubtful cases, whether the probationer appears to be capable of speaking effectively for himself. In every case in which a request for counsel at a preliminary or final hearing is refused, the grounds for refusal should be stated succinctly in the record.

We return to the facts of the present case. Because respondent was not afforded either a preliminary hearing or a final hearing, the revocation of his probation did not meet the standards of due process prescribed in *Morrissey,* which we have here held applicable to probation revocations. Accordingly, respondent was entitled to a writ of habeas corpus. [His] admission to having committed another serious crime creates the very sort of situation in which counsel need not ordinarily be provided. But because of respondent's subsequent assertions regarding that admission, we conclude that the failure [to] provide respondent with the assistance of counsel should be reexamined in light of this opinion. The general guidelines outlined above should be applied in the first instance by those charged with conducting the revocation hearing.

Affirmed in part, reversed in part, and remanded.

Justice DOUGLAS, dissenting in part.

I believe that due process requires the appointment of counsel in this case because of the claim that respondent's confession of the burglary was made under coercion. See *Morrissey v. Brewer.*

Notes and Questions

1. Compare the *Gagnon* Court's views of the role and utility of counsel at revocation hearings with Sanford H. Kadish, *The Advocate and the Expert— Counsel in the Peno–Correctional Process,* 45 Minn.L.Rev. 803, 833–38 (1961):

"The central task of ascertaining whether the prisoner has committed the acts alleged, and measuring the acts proven against a standard to which he was obliged to conform is precisely the business of the criminal trial itself where the right to the assistance of counsel has been recognized as one of the 'immutable principles of justice.' Indeed, in many contested revocation proceedings, the conduct charged actually constitutes the commission of a criminal act. [The] issue is not whether the lawyer's paraphernalia of technicalities appropriate to other areas are proper in parole matters; no one has seriously suggested that rules of pleading and evidence should be imported into parole hearings. The issue is whether the attorney may speak for his client, given the areas of relevance of parole and revocation proceedings and always subject to the authority of the agency to draw the ground rules. A sensible and pragmatic adaptation of the nature of legal advocacy to the needs and purposes of the inquiry is as plausible in parole as it has proven to be in such 'non-legal' areas as labor arbitration and the regulatory and adjudicative work of administrative agencies."

2. *Betts, Gideon and Gagnon compared.* How likely is it that a probationer or parolee will be able to convince a court, *without* the benefit of counsel, on the basis of a record made *without* the assistance of counsel, that there are "substantial reasons which justified or mitigated the violation" or that "the reasons are complex or otherwise difficult to develop or present"? How many probationers or parolees will know *what* to point to or look for and *why?* How intelligent a decision can be made as to whether "the probationer appears to be capable of speaking effectively for himself" without knowing what justifications or mitigations a competent lawyer might have raised or developed? Can *Gagnon* escape the criticism of *Betts?* Consider, e.g., Kamisar, *The Right to Counsel and the Fourteenth Amendment: A Dialogue on "the Most Pervasive Right" of an Accused,* 30 U.Chi.L.Rev. 53, 65 (1962).

3. *The A.B.A. Standards approach.* "In common [with] numerous commentators," III *ABA Standards* § 18–7.5 (commentary) "rejects [the] vague and uncertain [*Gagnon*] standard." Continues the commentary:

"Few legal inquiries could be more inherently speculative and problematic than examining a record after the event seeking to determine whether the defendant would have fared better if counsel had been present. The problem is that records made by laypersons do not reflect what a trained advocate would have seen: lines of inquiry not followed, bases for impeachment of witnesses never explored, alternative dispositions that might have been proposed. No hint of these will appear when an inexperienced and probably scared layperson is forced to defend himself or herself and has a 'fool for a client.' * * * Given a context in which only a minority of offenders can be said not to have needed the assistance of counsel, it appears far more expeditious and efficient to establish a bright-line standard that grants counsel in all cases than to litigate the hazy and narrow contours of the constitutionally permissible case in which counsel need not be provided."

4. *Juvenile court proceedings.* The *Gagnon* Court talked about "the rehabilitative needs of the individual probationer or parolee" and viewed the probation or parole officer's function "not so much to compel conformance to a strict code of behavior as to supervise a course of rehabilitation." But compare *In re Gault,* 387 U.S. 1, 87 S.Ct. 1428, 18 L.Ed.2d 527 (1967), holding that, in respect to juvenile delinquency proceedings that may result in loss of the juvenile's freedom, fourteenth amendment due process requires that "the child and his parent [be] notified of the child's right to be represented by [retained counsel] or, if they are

unable to afford counsel that counsel will be appointed to represent the child." The Court stressed the need for counsel to assure a fair hearing in a proceeding "comparable in seriousness to a felony prosecution." It rejected the state's suggestion that the probation officers, parents, and judge might be relied on to "represent the child," finding "no material difference in this respect between adult and juvenile proceedings of the sort involved here."

Gault was hailed as demonstrating the Court's reluctance to be "hemmed in by such artificial labels as 'criminal,' 'civil', or 'quasi-administrative,' " and for taking the position that "a desire to help—the rehabilitation ideal—no longer will serve as the incantation before which procedural safeguards must succumb." Fred Cohen, *Sentencing, Probation, and the Rehabilitative Ideal,* 47 Texas L.Rev. 1, 2 (1968).

5. *Summary courts-martial; loss of liberty does not trigger the Sixth Amendment right to counsel.* In *Middendorf v. Henry,* 425 U.S. 25, 96 S.Ct. 1281, 47 L.Ed.2d 556 (1976), a 7–2 majority held there is no right to appointed counsel at summary courts-martial, even though the officer conducting these proceedings can impose a maximum punishment of 30 days confinement at hard labor. In rejecting even the view that counsel must be provided in "special circumstances," the Court, per Rehnquist J., observed:

"[E]ven were the Sixth Amendment to be held applicable to court-martial proceedings, the summary court-martial provided for in these cases was not a 'criminal prosecution' within the meaning of that Amendment. [T]he fact that the outcome of a proceeding may result in loss of liberty does not by itself, even in civilian life, mean that the Sixth Amendment's guarantee of counsel is applicable. In *Gagnon,* the respondent faced the prospect of being sent to prison as a result of the revocation of his probation, but we held that the revocation proceeding was nonetheless not a 'criminal proceeding.' [In *Gault*] the juvenile faced possible initial confinement as a result of the proceeding in question, but the Court nevertheless based its conclusion that counsel was required on [Fourteenth Amendment due process], rather than on any determination that the hearing was a 'criminal prosecution' within the meaning of the Sixth Amendment."

6. *Parental status termination proceedings; is potential loss of liberty a necessary, if not a sufficient, requirement, for the automatic right to appointed counsel?* Over the dissenters' protest that "the unique importance of a parent's interest in the care and custody of his or her child cannot constitutionally be extinguished through formal judicial proceedings without the benefit of counsel" and the dissenters' charge that the Court was "reviv[ing] an ad hoc approach thoroughly discredited nearly 20 years ago in *Gideon,*" in *Lassiter v. Department of Social Services,* 452 U.S. 18, 101 S.Ct. 2153, 68 L.Ed.2d 640 (1981), a 5–4 majority, per Stewart, J., rejected the view that due process requires the appointment of counsel in every parental status termination proceeding involving indigent parents. Thus, the Court left the appointment of counsel in such proceedings to be determined by the state courts on a case-by-case basis.

"The pre-eminent generalization that emerges from the Court's precedents on an indigent's right to appointed counsel," observed the Court, "is that such a right has been recognized to exist only where the litigant may lose his physical liberty if he loses the litigation. * * * Significantly, as a litigant's interest in personal liberty diminishes, so does his right to appointed counsel. [Thus, *Gagnon*] declined to hold that indigent probationers have, *per se,* a right to counsel at revocation hearings, and instead left the decision whether counsel should be appointed to be made on a case-by-case basis."

The Court then examined the termination hearing and found it to be fundamentally fair. "In light of the unpursued avenues of defense, and of the experiences petitioner underwent at this hearing," the dissenters found the Court's conclusion "virtually incredible." Consider Laurence Tribe, *American Constitutional Law* 1651?52 (2d ed. 1988): "[The *Lassiter* majority's conclusion]— after reading a cold record that had been compiled without the aid of counsel— that the case before the Court 'presented no specially troublesome points of law, either procedural or substantive' * * * parallels the infamous rule of *Betts v. Brady,* which the Court had denounced two decades earlier."

7. *Where to draw the line.* Was the *Lassiter* Court's greatest concern where to draw the line? If the state must provide indigents counsel in parental termination proceedings, why not in a child custody fight growing out of a divorce action when one parent is indigent? Why not in an eviction proceeding, when an indigent is about to lose his place of residence? Is there a stronger case for providing counsel in parental termination proceedings than in these other proceedings? Why (not)? See Kamisar, *Gideon v. Wainwright A Quarter–Century Later,* 10 Pace L.Rev. 343, 357–59 (1990).

B. COLLATERAL ATTACK PROCEEDINGS: Does the Right of "Meaningful Access" to the Courts Include A State Prisoner's Right to Appointed Counsel in State Postconviction Proceedings (At Least For Inmates Under Sentence of Death)?

1. *The duty to provide "meaningful access" to the courts.* BOUNDS v. SMITH, 430 U.S. 817, 97 S.Ct. 1491, 52 L.Ed.2d 72 (1977), per MARSHALL, J., rejected the contention that the constitutional duty to provide "meaningful access"[a] to the courts "merely obliges states to allow inmate 'writ writers' to function" and does not require the expenditure of state funds "to implement affirmatively the right of access." The state must do more than refrain from interfering with indigents seeking assistance from other prisoners; the right of access to the courts "requires prison authorities to assist inmates in the preparation and filing of meaningful legal papers by [furnishing] adequate law libraries or adequate assistance from persons trained in the law."

The Court noted that while adequate law libraries are "one constitutionally acceptable method" of assuring meaningful access to the courts, "our decision [today] does not foreclose alternative means to achieve that goal. Nearly half the States and the District of Columbia provide some degree of professional or quasi-professional legal assistance to prisoners. * * * Legal services plans not only result in more efficient and skillful handling of prisoner cases, but also avoid the disciplinary problems associated with writ writers. Independent legal advisors can mediate or resolve administratively many prisoner complaints that would otherwise burden the courts, and can convince inmates that other grievances against the prison or the legal system are ill-founded."

Dissenting Justice REHNQUIST, J., joined by Burger, C.J., protested that the Court was enunciating "a 'fundamental constitutional right of access to the courts,' which is found nowhere in the Constitution." In an opinion that foreshadowed his plurality opinion in *Murray v. Giarratano* (p. 101), Justice Rehnquist

---

a. In an earlier case, *Johnson v. Avery*, 393 U.S. 483, 89 S.Ct. 747, 21 L.Ed.2d 718 (1969) (sometimes called the "jailhouse lawyer" case), the Court had held that "unless and until the State provides some reasonable alternative to assist inmates in the preparation of petitions for post-conviction relief," it may not prohibit inmates from furnishing such assistance to fellow prisoners.

observed: "It would seem, *a fortiori,* to follow from [*Ross v. Moffitt*] that an incarcerated prisoner who has pursued all his avenues of direct review would have no constitutional right whatever to state appointed counsel [in] a collateral attack on his conviction. [Yet] this is the logical destination of the Court's reasoning today. If 'meaningful access' to the courts is to include law libraries, there is no convincing reason why it should not also include lawyers appointed at the expense of the State."[b]

2. *If a state establishes a right to appointed counsel in collateral postconviction proceedings, must it follow federal constitutional procedures governing appointed counsel?* No, answered the Court in PENNSYLVANIA v. FINLEY, 481 U.S. 551, 107 S.Ct. 1990, 95 L.Ed.2d 539 (1987). The case arose as follows: The state supreme court held that under state law respondent was entitled to appointed counsel in her postconviction proceedings.[a] On remand, the trial court appointed counsel. But counsel concluded there were no arguable grounds for collateral relief and asked permission to withdraw. The trial court agreed with appointed counsel that respondent's petition lacked any merit and dismissed the petition for postconviction relief. The Pennsylvania Superior Court held that by failing to comply with the federal constitutional procedures prescribed in *Anders v. California* (Ch. 20, § 5) for withdrawal of appointed counsel on direct appeal, the conduct of counsel had violated respondent's constitutional rights. The U.S. Supreme Court, per REHNQUIST, C.J., reversed:

"We have never held that prisoners have a constitutional right to counsel when mounting collateral attacks to their convictions and we decline to so hold today. Our cases establish that the right to appointed counsel extends to the first appeal of right and no further [referring, inter alia, to *Ross v. Moffitt*, p. 84].

"[The] procedures followed by respondent's habeas counsel fully comported with fundamental fairness. Postconviction relief is even further removed from the criminal trial than is discretionary direct review. It is not part of the criminal proceeding itself, and it is in fact considered to be civil in nature. It is a collateral attack that normally occurs only after the defendant has failed to secure relief through direct review of his conviction. States have no obligation to provide this avenue of relief, and when they do, the fundamental fairness mandated by the Due Process Clause does not require that the State supply a lawyer as well.

" * * * Since respondent has no underlying constitutional right to appointed counsel in state postconviction proceedings, she has no constitutional right to insist on the *Anders* procedures which were designed solely to protect that underlying constitutional right. [The] Constitution does not put the State to the difficult choice between affording no counsel whatsoever or following the strict procedural guidelines annunciated in *Anders.*"[b]

b. In a second dissent, Stewart, J., joined by Burger, C.J., expressed the conviction that " 'meaningful access' to the federal courts can seldom be realistically advanced by the device of making law libraries available to prison inmates untutored in their use." In a third dissent, Burger, C.J., maintained that there was "no basis on which a federal court may require States to fund costly law libraries for prison inmates."

a. Although a majority of states provide for the appointment of counsel in postconviction proceedings in the discretion of the court, and in some jurisdictions appointment appears to be mandatory once an evidentiary hearing has been granted, "[c]ourts have generally held that there is no constitutional grounding for requiring the appointment of counsel in what is basically a civil proceeding," LaFave & Israel, § 27.9(a).

b. Dissenting Justice Brennan, joined by Marshall, J., maintained that "the Federal Constitution requires that the *Anders* procedures must be followed when a State provides assistance of counsel in collateral proceedings" and that "[e]ven if the *Anders* requirements were not mandated by due process, the performance of Finley's counsel clearly violated minimal standards of fundamental fairness."

3. *The tension between Bounds and Finley; must death-row inmates who lack counsel to pursue postconviction proceedings be provided counsel at state expense?* No, answered the Court in MURRAY v. GIARRATANO, 492 U.S. 1, 109 S.Ct. 2765, 106 L.Ed.2d 1 (1989). The case arose as follows: Indigent Virginia death-row inmates brought a civil rights action against various state officials maintaining that they had to be provided counsel at state expense. The federal district court agreed. Three considerations led it to conclude that death-row inmates were incapable of using law books to raise their postconviction claims: (1) the limited time they had to prepare and present their petitions; (2) the complexity and difficulty of the legal work involved; and (3) the emotional instability of inmates preparing themselves for impending death. Persuaded by the opinion and findings of the district court, a 6–4 majority of the U.S. Court of Appeals for the Fourth Circuit, sitting en banc, affirmed. In light of the inability of death-row inmates to use law books effectively, the inadequacy of the assistance of seven part-time lawyers to meet the needs of over 2,000 prisoners, and the "scarcity of lawyers willing to assist death-row inmates seeking postconviction remedies," the court of appeals held that Virginia must provide death-row inmates trained legal assistance in preparing their state habeas corpus remedies. In resisting the inmates' law suit, the state relied heavily on *Finley*, but the court of appeals distinguished that case on various grounds: *Finley* was not a "meaningful access" case, it did not address the rule announced in *Bounds* and, "most significantly," it did not involve the death penalty.

The Supreme Court reversed. The principal opinion was written by Chief Justice REHNQUIST, joined by White, O'Connor and Scalia, JJ., who ruled that the decision below was "inconsistent" with *Finley* and based on "a misreading" of *Bounds*:

"[W]e held in *Ross v. Moffitt* that the right to counsel at [trial and on the first appeal] did not carry over to a discretionary appeal provided by [state] law from the intermediate appellate court to the [state supreme court]. We contrasted the trial stage of a criminal proceeding [with] the appellate stage of such a proceeding, where the defendant needs an attorney 'not as a shield to protect him against being "hauled into court" by the State and stripped of his presumption of innocence, but rather as a sword to upset the prior determination of guilt.'

"We held in *Finley* that the logic of *Ross* required the conclusion that there was no federal constitutional right to counsel for indigent prisoners seeking state postconviction relief. [The] rule of *Finley* should apply no differently in capital cases than in noncapital cases. State collateral proceedings are not constitutionally required as an adjunct to the state criminal proceedings and serve a different and more limited purpose than either the trial or appeal. The additional safeguards imposed by the Eighth Amendment at the trial stage of a capital case are, we think, sufficient to assure the reliability of the process by which the death penalty is imposed. We therefore decline to read either the Eighth Amendment or the Due Process Clause to require yet another distinction between the rights of capital case defendants and those in noncapital cases.

"The Court of Appeals, as an additional basis for its holding, relied on what it perceived as a tension between the rule in *Finley* and the implication of our decisions in *Bounds*; we find no such tension. Whether the right of access at issue in *Bounds* is primarily one of due process or equal protection, in either case it rests on a constitutional theory considered in *Finley*. The Court held in *Bounds* that a prisoner's 'right of access' to the courts required a state to furnish access to adequate law libraries in order that the prisoners might prepare petitions for judicial relief. But it would be a strange jurisprudence that permitted the extension of that holding to partially overrule a subsequently decided case such as *Finley* which held that prisoners seeking judicial relief from their sentence in state proceedings were not entitled to counsel.

"It would be an even stranger jurisprudence to allow, as the dissent would, the 'right of access' involved in *Bounds* to partially overrule *Finley*, based on 'factual' findings of a particular District Court regarding matters such as the perceived difficulty of capital sentencing law and the general psychology of death-row inmates. Treating such matters as 'factual findings,' presumably subject only to review under the 'clearly erroneous' standard, would permit a different constitutional rule to apply in a different State if the district judge hearing that claim reached different conclusions. Our cases involving the right of counsel have never taken this tack; they have been categorical holdings as to what the Constitution requires with respect to a particular stage of a criminal proceeding in general. Indeed, as the dissent itself points out, it was the Court's dissatisfaction with the case-by-case approach of *Betts v. Brady* that led to the adoption of the categorical rule requiring appointed counsel for indigent felony defendants in *Gideon*.

"There is no inconsistency whatever between the holding of *Bounds* and the holding in *Finley*; the holding of neither case squarely decides the question presented in this case. For the reasons previously stated * * * we now hold that *Finley* applies to those inmates under sentence of death as well as to other inmates, and that holding necessarily imposes limits on *Bounds*.[7]

"Petitioner and respondent disagree as to the practices currently in effect in Virginia state prisons with respect to death-row prisoners. Respondents contend that these prisoners are denied adequate and timely access to a law library during the final weeks before the date set for their execution. If respondents are correct, the District Court on remand may remedy this situation without any need to enlarge the holding of *Bounds*."[a]

Justice KENNEDY, joined by O'Connor, J., concurred in the judgment "on the facts and record of this case," observing:

"The complexity of our jurisprudence in this area * * * makes it unlikely that capital defendants will be able to file successful petitions for collateral relief without the assistance of persons learned in the law.

"The requirement of meaningful access can be satisfied in various ways, however. This was made explicit in *Bounds*. The intricacies and ranges of options are of sufficient complexity that state legislatures and prison administrators must be given 'wide discretion' to select appropriate solutions. * * *

"Unlike Congress, this Court lacks the capacity to undertake the searching and comprehensive review called for in this area, for we can decide only the case

---

7. Many States automatically provide counsel to death-row inmates in state habeas corpus proceedings, as a matter of state law. Under the Anti–Drug Abuse Act of 1988, attorneys will be appointed in federal habeas corpus actions involving a challenge to a death sentence. Respondents suggest that appointment of counsel might even benefit Virginia by speeding, or at least clarifying, the Virginia postconviction process. The situation of death-row inmates may well be the basis for state policy to provide them extra legal assistance or more lenient standards of *pro se* pleading.

a. Justice O'Connor joined the Chief Justice's opinion, but also wrote a separate concurring opinion, observing: "Beyond the requirements of *Bounds*, the matter is one of legislative choice based on difficult policy considerations and the allocation of scarce legal resources. Our decision today rightly leaves these issues to resolution by Congress and the state legislatures."

before us. While Virginia has not adopted procedures for securing representation that are as far reaching and effective as those available in other States, no prisoner on death row in Virginia has been unable to obtain counsel to represent him in postconviction proceedings, and Virginia's prison system is staffed with institutional lawyers to assist in preparing petitions for postconviction relief. I am not prepared to say that this scheme violates the Constitution."

Justice STEVENS, joined by Brennan, Marshall, and Blackmun, JJ., dissented:

" * * * Three critical differences between *Finley* and this case demonstrate that even if it is permissible to leave an ordinary prisoner to his own resources in collateral proceedings, it is fundamentally unfair to require an indigent death row inmate to initiate collateral review without counsel's guiding hand. I shall address each of these differences in turn.

"*First.* These respondents [have] been condemned to die. Legislatures conferred greater access to counsel on capital defendants than on persons facing lesser punishment even in colonial times. Our First Congress required assignment of up to two attorneys to a capital defendant at the same time it initiated capital punishment; nearly a century passed before Congress provided for appointment of counsel in other contexts. Similarly, Congress at first limited the federal right of appeal to capital cases. Just last year, it enacted a statute requiring provision of counsel for state and federal prisoners seeking federal postconviction relief—but only if they are under sentence of death.[7]

"This Court also expanded capital defendants' ability to secure counsel and other legal assistance long before bestowing similar privileges on persons accused of less serious crimes. * * *

"Ideally, 'direct appeal is the primary avenue for review of a conviction or sentence, and death penalty cases are no exception. * * * ' There is, however, significant evidence that in capital cases what is ordinarily considered direct review does not sufficiently safeguard against miscarriages of justice to warrant this presumption of finality.[12] Federal habeas courts granted relief in only 0.25% to 7% of noncapital cases in recent years; in striking contrast, the success rate in capital cases ranged from 60% to 70%.[13] Such a high incidence of uncorrected

---

7. The Anti–Drug Abuse Act of 1988 [21 U.S.C. § 848(q)(4)(B)] provides in pertinent part:

"(B) In any post conviction proceeding under section 2254 or 2255 of title 28, United States Code, seeking to vacate or set aside a death sentence, any defendant who is or becomes financially unable to obtain adequate representation or investigative, expert, or other reasonably necessary services shall be entitled to the appointment of one or more attorneys and the furnishing of such other services in accordance with [various paragraphs].

12. Nor can we overlook our experience that capital litigation proceeds apace after affirmance of a conviction. With the vigorous opposition of state legal departments, capital defendants seek not only review of state and federal judicial decisions, but also relief from state governors and parole boards. See Powell, *Capital Punishment*, 102 Harv.L.Rev. 1035, 1038–1041 (1989). Thus the conviction and

sentence in a capital case will not be "final," or undisturbed, until the sentence either is executed or set aside. With the cases of over half the Nation's more than 2,100 inmates yet to move into collateral proceedings, Wilson & Spangenberg, *State Post–Conviction Representation of Defendants Sentenced to Death*, 72 Judicature 331, 332 (1989), the need for an orderly sequence of review is pellucid. * * *

13. Mello, *Facing Death Alone: The Post–Conviction Attorney Crisis on Death Row*, 37 Am.U.L.Rev. 513, 520–521 (1988). The former Chief Judge of the Eleventh Circuit, which has the greatest volume of capital litigation, recently estimated that in his Circuit capital defendants' success rate in collateral proceedings may be as high as one-third to one-half of all such cases. Godbold, *Pro Bono Representation of Death Sentenced Inmates*, 42 Record of N.Y.C.B.A. 859, 873 (1987).

error demonstrates that the meaningful appellate review necessary in a capital case extends beyond the direct appellate process.

"*Second*. In contrast to the collateral process discussed in *Finley*, Virginia law contemplates that some claims ordinarily heard on direct review will be relegated to postconviction proceedings. Claims that trial or appellate counsel provided constitutionally ineffective assistance, for instance, usually cannot be raised until this stage. The postconviction procedure in Virginia may present the first opportunity for an attorney detached from past proceedings to examine the defense and to raise claims that were barred on direct review by prior counsel's ineffective assistance. A fresh look may reveal, for example, that a prior conviction used to enhance the defendant's sentence was invalid or that the defendant's mental illness, lack of a prior record, or abusive childhood should have been introduced as evidence in mitigation at his sentencing hearing. Defense counsel's failure to object to or assert such claims precludes direct appellate review of them. The postconviction proceeding gives inmates another chance to rectify defaults. In Virginia, therefore, postconviction proceedings are key to meaningful appellate review of capital cases. * * *

"*Third*. As the District Court's findings reflect, the plight of the death row inmate constrains his ability to wage collateral attacks far more than does the lot of the ordinary inmate considered in *Finley*. * * * Unlike the ordinary inmate, who presumably has ample time to use and reuse the prison library and to seek guidance from other prisoners experienced in preparing *pro se* petitions, a grim deadline imposes a finite limit on the condemned person's capacity for useful research.[20]

"Capital litigation, the District Court observed, is extremely complex. Without regard to the special characteristics of Virginia's statutory procedures, this Court's death penalty jurisprudence unquestionably is difficult even for a trained lawyer to master. A judgment that it is not unfair to require an ordinary inmate to rely on his own resources to prepare a petition for postconviction relief does not justify the same conclusion for the death row inmate who must acquire an understanding of this specialized area of the law and prepare an application for stay of execution as well as a petition for collateral relief. * * *

"These three critical factors demonstrate that there is a profound difference between capital postconviction litigation and ordinary postconviction litigation in Virginia. The District Court's findings unequivocally support the conclusion that to obtain an adequate opportunity to present their postconviction claims fairly, death row inmates need greater assistance of counsel than Virginia affords them.

"[The] basic question in this case is whether Virginia's procedure for collateral review of capital convictions and sentences assures its indigent death row inmates an adequate opportunity to present their claims fairly. The District Court and Court of Appeals en banc found that it did not, and neither the State nor this Court's majority provides any reasoned basis for disagreeing with their conclusion. Simple fairness requires that this judgment be affirmed."

Notes and Questions

1. *Epilogue*. Three days before his scheduled execution, Virginia Governor L. Douglas Wilder commuted Giarratano's death sentence to life imprisonment, with eligibility for parole in 25 years. See Note, 75 Iowa L.Rev. 1305, 1334 (1990).

---

20. An execution may be scheduled for any time 30 days after the date of sentencing. A 1988 study commissioned by the American Bar Association found that *attorneys* spent an average of 992 hours and $3,686 on each capital postconviction proceeding in Virginia.

2. *The need for quality postconviction representation.* Consider *ABA Guidelines for the Appointment and Performance of Counsel in Death Penalty Cases* 34 (1989) (commentary to Guideline 1.1) (published on the eve of *Giarratano*):

"While the Federal Constitutional right to counsel has not been extended to collateral postconviction proceedings, the need for quality postconviction representation is nonetheless vital. Death row inmates who have found counsel to represent them in postconviction proceedings in the federal courts have secured rulings that their constitutional rights have been violated in a much higher percentage of cases than is typical of criminal appeals generally.

"Collateral proceedings present yet another set of obstacles unique to capital cases. In addition to the general, often difficult procedural requirements common to all habeas corpus actions, death penalty cases may be subject to rules that provide less time for preparation then is available in non-capital cases. Substantive pleadings may have to be prepared simultaneously with, or even be delayed for, pleadings to stay the client's execution. Only quality legal representation can see a defendant fairly through the maze of post judgment proceedings."

3. *"Each step in the process from arrest to the cemetery is equally necessary."* Consider Michael Mello, *Is There a Federal Constitutional Right to Counsel in Capital Post–Conviction Proceedings?*, 79 J.Crim.L. & C. 1065, 1104 (1989) (written on the eve of the Supreme Court's decision in *Giarratano*):

"The risk of execution—final and irrevocable death—triggers a conclusive finding of emergency. No greater risk is available in our legal world. Nowhere is a mistake more profound. At the same time, the state, scenting blood and subject to a panoply of external pressures, deploys its finest to secure a death. To restate plainly. The state sends its lawyers to seek the death of a person. It does so through the avenue it has imposed on itself—the adversarial process. Trial is adversarial. So is direct appeal, so is state post-conviction, and so is federal habeas corpus. The *posture* changes, but posture is an intermural concrete of legalism, meaningless to laypeople, worthless to the person whose life is at risk.

"More compelling than this, however, is the fact that later stages of the process move the condemned person closer to death. Anthony Amsterdam's lambent metaphor of the assembly line is apt: The finished product is a dead person, but each step in the process from arrest to the cemetery is equally necessary to the final product. No stage is without its risk to the condemned. The state knows this; it sends its gladiators to fight in each round; one would like to see what would happen to state officials who neglected to do so. What point, then, can there be in treating the early stages of the assembly differently from the final touches?"

4. *Justice Kennedy's concurring opinion.* Recall that Chief Justice Rehnquist did not speak for a majority of the Court. The pivotal fifth vote was cast by Justice Kennedy, who concurred in the judgment "on the facts and record of this case." Moreover, he observed that "no prisoner on death row in Virginia has been unable to obtain counsel to represent him in postconviction proceedings" and that the state's prison system "is staffed with institutional lawyers to assist in preparing petitions for postconviction relief." Would Justice Kennedy allow the execution of a death row inmate who has *not* secured counsel for his state postconviction proceeding? Or would he consider it sufficient that lawyers were available to challenge death sentences in *federal* habeas corpus proceedings?

5. *Where a claim of ineffective assistance of counsel cannot be raised on appeal.* Where state law holds that a claim of ineffective assistance of counsel at

trial cannot be raised on an appeal from the conviction, but must be presented through state habeas corpus, is there a constitutional right to the assistance of counsel in presenting that claim in the habeas proceeding (as there would have been on first appeal if it could have been raised there)? Consider the treatment of this issue in *Coleman v. Thompson* (1991) (Ch. 28, § 2).

6. *A capital defendant's federal statutory right to counsel.* Consider *McFar-. land v. Scott*, 512 U.S. 849, 114 S.Ct. 2568, 129 L.Ed.2d 666 (1994), which arose as follows: Petitioner, who had been sentenced to death, requested the appointment of counsel under 21 U.S.C. § 848(q)(4)(B) (the 1988 statutory right to qualified legal representation for capital defendants in federal habeas corpus proceedings). He also sought a stay of execution to give that counsel time to prepare and file a habeas petition. The federal court denied the motion, concluding that because no "postconviction proceeding" had commenced, petitioner was not entitled to counsel and the court lacked jurisdiction to issue a stay. The Supreme Court, per Blackmun, J., reversed: A capital defendant need not file a formal habeas corpus petition in order to invoke his right to counsel under § 848(q)(4)(B) or to establish a federal court's jurisdiction to enter a stay of execution.

7. *Bounds v. Smith revisited.* Two decades after it had decided *Bounds v. Smith*, the Court read that case quite narrowly in LEWIS v. CASEY, 518 U.S. 343, 116 S.Ct. 2174, 135 L.Ed.2d 606 (1996), which arose as follows: Inmates of various prisons operated by the Arizona Department of Corrections brought a class action alleging that prison officials were furnishing them inadequate legal research facilities and thus depriving them of their right of access to the courts in violation of *Bounds*. After finding a variety of shortcomings in the Arizona prison system, the federal district court appointed a special master to investigate and report about the appropriate relief. Some months later the court adopted the special master's proposed permanent injunction, a 25–page order mandating sweeping changes designed to ensure that the prison system would "provide meaningful access to the courts for all present and future prisoners." The U.S. Court of Appeals for the Ninth Circuit affirmed both the finding of a *Bounds* violation and the injunction's major terms.

The Supreme Court, per SCALIA, J., reversed, holding that the success of the inmates' systemic challenge was dependent on their ability to show widespread "actual injury" and the district court's "failure to identify anything more than isolated instances of actual injury renders its findings of a systemic *Bounds* violation invalid." The Court emphasized that *Bounds* did *not* establish the right to a law library or to legal assistance:

"The right that *Bounds* acknowledged was the (already well-established) right of access to the courts. In the cases to which *Bounds* traced its roots, we had protected that right by prohibiting State prison officials from actively interfering with inmates' attempts to prepare legal documents or file them and by requiring state courts to waive filing fees or transcript fees for indigent inmates. *Bounds* focused on the same entitlement of access to the courts. [In] other words, prison law libraries and legal assistance programs are not ends in themselves, but only the means for ensuring 'a reasonably adequate opportunity to present claimed violations of fundamental constitutional rights to the courts' [quoting *Bounds*].

"Because *Bounds* did not create an abstract, free-standing right to a law library or legal assistance, an inmate cannot establish relevant actual injury simply by establishing that his prison's law library or legal assistance program is sub-par in some theoretical sense. [Insofar] as the right vindicated by *Bounds* is concerned, 'meaningful access to the courts is the touchstone' and the inmate must go one step further and demonstrate that the alleged shortcomings in the library or legal assistance program hindered his efforts to pursue a legal claim.

"* * * *Bounds* does not guarantee inmates the wherewithal to transform themselves into litigating engines capable of filing everything from shareholder derivative actions to slip-and-fall claims. The tools it requires to be provided are those that the inmates need in order to attack their sentences, directly or collaterally, and in order to challenge the conditions of their confinement. Impairment of any other litigating capacity is simply one of the incidental (and perfectly constitutional) consequences of conviction and incarceration."

Justice SOUTER, joined by Ginsburg and Breyer, JJ., concurred in the judgment and in portions of the Court's opinion, but dissented in part. "Given that adequately stocked libraries go far in satisfying the *Bounds* requirements," Justice Souter considered it "an abuse of discretion for the District Court to aggregate discrete, small-bore problems in individual prisons and to treat them as if each prevailed throughout the prison system, for the purpose of justifying a broad remedial order covering virtually every aspect of each prison library." He also thought that other elements of the injunction were unsupported by any factual finding. "It is this overreaching of the evidentiary record," he emphasized, "not the application of standing or even class action rules, that call for the judgment to be reversed."

Justice Souter "would go no further than to hold (in a case not involving substantial, systemic deprivation of access to court) that Article III requirements will normally be satisfied if a prisoner demonstrates that (1) he has a complaint or grievance, meritorious or not, about the prison system or the validity of his conviction that he would raise if his library research (or advice, or judicial review of a form complaint or other means of 'access' chosen by the State) were to indicate that he had an actionable claim; and (2) that the access scheme provided by the prison is so inadequate that he cannot research, consult about, file, or litigate the claim, as the case may be."

Part Two

POLICE PRACTICES

Chapter 4

SOME GENERAL REFLECTIONS ON THE POLICE, THE PROSECUTORS, THE LEGISLATURES, THE COURTS AND THE CRIMINAL PROCESS*

WILLIAM J. STUNTZ—THE UNEASY RELATIONSHIP BETWEEN CRIMINAL PROCEDURE AND CRIMINAL JUSTICE
107 Yale L.J. 1, 3–12, 72–76 (1997).

Most talk about the law of criminal procedure treats that law as a self-contained universe. The picture looks something like this: The Supreme Court says that suspects and defendants have a right to be free from certain types of police or prosecutorial behavior. Police and prosecutors, for the most part, then do

---

* In addition to the articles extracted in this chapter, see Francis A. Allen, *The Judicial Quest for Penal Justice: The Warren Court and the Criminal Cases*, 1975 U.Ill.L.F. 518; Albert Alschuler, *Failed Pragmatism: Reflections on the Burger Court*, 100 Harv.L.Rev. 1436 (1987); Akhil Reed Amar, *The Constitution and Criminal Procedure: First Principles* (1997); Anthony Amsterdam, *The Supreme Court and the Rights of Suspects in Criminal Cases*, 45 N.Y.U.L.Rev. 785 (1970); Peter Arenella, *Rethinking the Functions of Criminal Procedure: The Warren and Burger Courts' Competing Ideologies*, 72 Geo.L.J. 185 (1983); Susan Bandes, *"We the People" and Our Enduring Values*, 96 Mich.L.Rev. 1376 (1998) (Book Review); Craig Bradley, *The Failure of the Criminal Procedure Revolution* (1993); Donald Dripps, *Akhil Amar on Criminal Procedure and Constitutional Law: "Here I Go Down the Wrong Road Again,"* 74 N.C.L.Rev. 1559 (1996); Jerold Israel, *Criminal Procedure, the Burger Court, and the Legacy of the Warren Court*, 75 Mich.L.Rev. 1319 (1977); Yale Kamisar, *The Warren Court and Criminal Justice*, in The Warren Court: A Retrospective 116

(Bernard Schwartz ed. 1996); Herbert Packer, *The Courts, the Police and the Rest of Us*, 57 J.Crim.L.C. & P.S. (1966); William Pizzi, *Punishment and Procedure: A Different View of the American Criminal Justice System*, 13 Const. Comm. 55 (1996); Stephen Saltzburg, *Foreword: The Flow and Ebb of Constitutional Criminal Procedure in the Warren and Burger Courts*, 69 Geo.L.J. 1512 (1980); Stephen Schulhofer, *The Constitution and the Police: Individual Rights and Law Enforcement*, 66 Wash.U.L.Q. 11 (1988); Louis Michael Seidman, *Criminal Procedure as the Servant of Politics*, 12 Const.Comm. 207 (1995); Carol Steiker, *Counter-Revolution in Constitutional Criminal Procedure? Two Audiences, Two Answers*, 94 Mich.L.Rev. 2466 (1996); George Thomas III, *Remapping the Criminal Procedure Universe*, 83 Va.L.Rev. 1819 (1997) (Book Review); Robert Weisberg, *Criminal Procedure Doctrine: Some Versions of the Skeptical*, 76 J.Crim.L. & C. 832 (1985); Charles Whitebread, *The Burger Court's Counter–Revolution in Criminal Procedure*, 24 Washburn L.J. 471 (1985).

as they're told. When they don't, and when the misconduct is tied to criminal convictions, the courts reverse the convictions, thereby sending a message to misbehaving officials. Within the bounds of this picture there is room for a lot of debate about the wisdom or constitutional pedigree of particular doctrines, and the literature is filled with debate of that sort. There is also room for theorizing about the optimal specificity of the rules the Supreme Court creates; the literature contains some of that, though less than it should. Finally, there is room for arguing about remedies—about whether reversing criminal convictions is an appropriate means of getting the police, prosecutors, and trial judges to do what the law says they ought to do. At least in the sphere of Fourth and Fifth Amendment law, a lively debate along those lines exists. But for all their variety, these debates take for granted the same basic picture of the process, a process whose only variables are the rules themselves and the remedies for their violation.

The picture is, of course, wrong. Criminal procedure's rules and remedies are embedded in a larger system, a system that can adjust to those rules in ways other than obeying them. And the rules can in turn respond to the system in a variety of ways, not all of them pleasant. The more one focuses on that dynamic, the more problematic the law of criminal procedure seems.

The heart of the problem is the system's structure. The criminal justice system is dominated by a trio of forces: crime rates, the definition of crime (which of course partly determines crime rates), and funding decisions—how much money to spend on police, prosecutors, defense attorneys, judges, and prisons. These forces determine the ratio of crimes to prosecutors and the ratio of prosecutions to public defenders, and those ratios in turn go far toward determining what the system does and how the system does it. But the law that defines what the criminal process looks like, the law that defines defendants' rights, is made by judges and Justices who have little information about crime rates and funding decisions, and whose incentives to take account of those factors may be perverse. High crime rates make it easy for prosecutors to substitute cases without strong procedural claims for cases with such claims. Underfunding of criminal defense counsel limits the number of procedural claims that can be pressed. Both phenomena make criminal procedure doctrines seem inexpensive to the appellate judges who define those doctrines. Unsurprisingly, given that regulating the criminal justice system has seemed cheap, the courts have done a lot of regulating—more, one suspects, than they would have done in a world where defendants could afford to litigate more often and more aggressively, or where prosecutors could not so easily substitute some cases for others. Criminal procedure is thus distorted by forces its authors probably do not understand.

The distortion runs both ways. As courts have raised the cost of criminal investigation and prosecution, legislatures have sought out devices to reduce those costs. Severe limits on defense funding are the most obvious example, but not the only one. Expanded criminal liability makes it easier for the government to induce guilty pleas, as do high mandatory sentences that serve as useful threats against recalcitrant defendants. And guilty pleas avoid most of the potentially costly requirements that criminal procedure imposes. These strategies would no doubt be politically attractive anyway, but the law of criminal procedure makes them more so. Predictably, underfunding, overcriminalization, and oversentencing have increased as criminal procedure has expanded.

Nor are the law's perverse effects limited to courts and legislatures. Constitutional criminal procedure raises the cost of prosecuting wealthier defendants by giving those defendants more issues to litigate. The result, at the margin, is to steer prosecutors away from such defendants and toward poorer ones. By giving defendants other, cheaper claims to raise, constitutional criminal procedure also raises the cost to defense counsel of investigating and litigating factual claims, claims that bear directly on their clients' innocence or guilt. The result is to steer defense counsel, again at the margin, away from those sorts of claims and toward constitutional issues. More Fourth, Fifth, and Sixth Amendment claims probably mean fewer self-defense claims and mens rea arguments. This turns the standard conservative criticism of the law of criminal procedure on its head. Ever since the 1960s, the right has argued that criminal procedure frees too many of the guilty. The better criticism may be that it helps to imprison too many of the innocent.

It also does little about the concern that, more than anything else, prompted its creation. The post–1960 constitutionalization of criminal procedure arose, in large part, out of the sense that the system was treating black suspects and defendants much worse than white ones. Warren-era constitutional criminal procedure began as a kind of antidiscrimination law. But the criminal justice system is characterized by extraordinary discretion—over the definition of crimes (legislatures can criminalize as much as they wish), over enforcement (police and prosecutors can arrest and charge whom they wish), and over funding (legislatures can allocate resources as they wish). In a system so dominated by discretionary decisions, discrimination is easy, and constitutional law has surprisingly little to say about it. * * *

Interestingly, judicial intervention in other aspects of the criminal justice system—the definition of crimes and the funding of criminal defense—does not seem likely to have these sorts of perverse effects. Constitutionalizing procedure, in a world where substantive law and funding are the province of legislatures, may tend to encourage bad substantive law and underfunding. But constitutionalizing some aspects of substantive criminal law and defense funding would not tend to encourage bad procedure, or bad anything else. Yet substance and funding are the areas where courts have most deferred to legislatures, where passivity rather than activism has been the judicial norm. It may be that the broad structure of constitutional regulation of criminal justice has it backward, that courts have been not too activist, but activist in the wrong places. * * *

Criminal procedure is, basically, a subset of constitutional law. That is why the criminal procedure literature focuses so thoroughly on the latest Supreme Court cases—in this area, the Supreme Court makes the relevant policy judgments, albeit with some fleshing out by other federal and state appellate courts. And once made, those judgments stick.

Or do they? Consider the effects of two other variables, both of which legislatures control and both of which go far toward defining what the law of criminal procedure means on the ground. The first is the scope of criminal liability. Broader substantive criminal law allows the state to end-run much of criminal procedure. In a world where trivial crimes stay on the books, or one where routine traffic offenses count as crimes, the requirement of probable cause to arrest may mean almost nothing. Officers can arrest for a minor offense— everyone violates the traffic rules—in order to search or question a suspect on a major one.[6] This allows arrests and searches of suspected drug dealers without any ex ante support for the suspicion, the very thing the probable cause standard is supposed to forbid. In a world where sodomy laws remain valid long after their

---

6. See *Whren v. United States* (1996) [p. 240] (holding that police can detain motorists where there is a probable cause to believe that they have violated traffic laws, regardless of whether the stop is pretextual).

enforcement has ceased, prosecutors can induce guilty pleas in some problematic sexual assault cases—the need to prove nonconsent disappears, and with it (again, in some cases) the ability to mount a plausible defense. This amounts to convicting defendants of sexual assault without proving the crime, by pointing to another crime that serves as the excuse for punishment, but not the reason.

Notice that procedural constraints on police and prosecutors actually encourage the government to behave in this fashion. One of the government's biggest gains from overcriminalization is the ability to avoid costly criminal procedure doctrines. Traffic "crimes" reduce the cost of the probable cause requirement, just as no-longer-enforced sodomy laws reduce the cost of the beyond-a-reasonable-doubt standard of proof. Those criminal procedure doctrines thus raise the government's incentive to overcriminalize. Not only can the state get around inconvenient constitutional limits by expanding criminal law's scope; the limits themselves tend, at the margin, to induce the expansion. These effects do not cover the whole of criminal litigation. But the pair of examples offered above (and there are many others) shows how thoroughly a state's definition of its criminal law can undermine important parts of criminal procedure.

Which leads to the second variable legislatures control: They fund the system. Legislatures decide how many police officers, prosecutors, and judges to have, and how much to pay them. They also decide how generously to fund criminal defense counsel in those cases (the majority) in which the court appoints counsel.

Over the course of the past couple of decades, legislatures have exercised this funding power to expand substantially the resources devoted to law enforcement, though the budget increases appear less substantial in light of parallel increases in crime. * * * [N]otwithstanding nominal budget increases, spending on indigent defendants in constant dollars per case appears to have declined significantly between the late 1970s and the early 1990s.

The predictable result is public defenders' offices with very large ratios of cases to lawyers. One recent study found a jurisdiction in which some public defenders represented over four hundred felony defendants in an eight-month span, and the average representation was more than half that number. [Those familiar with the system agree:] Public defenders are terribly overburdened.

The story is essentially the same in jurisdictions that use separately appointed defense counsel rather than public defenders. * * * [A] typical appointed defense lawyer faces something like the following pay scale: $30 or $40 an hour for the first twenty to thirty hours, and zero thereafter. * * *

[There] are a great many constitutional rules, most of which are highly contestable. The rules are produced by a court system that acts quite independently of legislative preference, at least in this area. (*Mapp v. Ohio* and *Miranda v. Arizona* were hardly examples of majoritarian lawmaking.) Perhaps more so than anywhere else in constitutional law, in criminal procedure the broad exercise of judicial power tends to be justified precisely by legislators' unwillingness to protect constitutional interests. Yet these judge-made rules are enforced through the efforts of criminal defense counsel who, in most cases, are paid by the state— the same state whose preferences the rules purport to trump. By buying less criminal defense, the state can buy less enforcement of constitutional criminal procedure. It can, to some degree, trump the trump. Of course, if it does so it necessarily also buys less of whatever else criminal defense counsel do. * * *

* * * Why has constitutional law focused so heavily on criminal procedure, and why has it so strenuously avoided anything to do with substantive criminal

law and the funding of defense counsel? * * * Why the turn away from substance and toward process?

Part of the answer is historical. Constitutional criminal procedure has deep roots; constitutional criminal substance and constitutional funding requirements do not. There is something to this answer, but not much. The large majority of the law of criminal procedure is of very recent creation; the field basically did not exist until a few decades ago. It is hard to argue that our constitutional roots require a regime that no one imagined until almost two centuries after the Constitution was ratified, and one century after the Fourteenth Amendment redefined the federal-state relationship. Another part of the answer has to do with constitutional text: The Bill of Rights says a great deal about criminal process and nothing about substantive criminal law or spending for defense lawyers. This too is less of an explanation than first appears. The texts of the Fourth, Fifth, and Sixth Amendments do not dictate the large body of law that exists in their name. We could have a very small and unobtrusive law of criminal procedure—as we mostly did until a generation ago—with no violence to the text. Proof of that proposition lies in the extreme rarity of textual argument in this area.[247]

Meanwhile, substantive criminal law could be constrained quite easily under the authority of the Due Process Clause and the Eighth Amendment. The prohibition of cruel and unusual punishments could plausibly be read to imply a proportionality principle for sentencing, capital and noncapital alike. [And] due process already has been read to require notice, which in turn suggests that criminalizing conduct in which ordinary people might innocently engage should be impermissible. As for funding, a decent level of resources for criminal defense counsel is a natural extrapolation from the Sixth Amendment's requirement to appoint counsel for indigent defendants. None of these arguments requires a huge stretch in terms of text or structure. They perhaps require abandoning original intent as a baseline, but that bridge has already been crossed: No one thinks current Fourth, Fifth, and Sixth Amendment law is faithful to the Framers' wishes. In short, neither the Constitution nor history bars a very different relationship between constitutional law and criminal justice than the one we now see.

The real difficulty with regulating substantive criminal law and funding decisions may be more basic. There is no nonarbitrary way to arrive at the proper legal rules, no way to get to sensible bottom lines by something that looks and feels like legal analysis. Whether proportionality review is lodged in appellate or trial courts, the only way to do it is to do it, to decide that this sentence is too great but not that one. There is no metric for determining right answers, no set of analytic tools that defines what a given sentence ought to be. That, after all, was the problem with discretionary sentencing regimes, the problem that produced the current infatuation with guidelines. Similarly, heightened mens rea requirements for overbroad crimes beg the question of which crimes are overbroad. Special culpability rules for, say, mail fraud would inevitably rest on a judicial judgment that mail fraud is badly defined, that Congress criminalized more than it should have. Desuetude appears simpler, as it requires only that courts determine whether a given offense is regularly enforced. But regular enforcement is both hard to define and hard to determine; judges would likely retreat to asking whether they would have expected this behavior to be treated as a crime. All this amounts not just to open-ended judicial regulation—constitutional law has a lot of that, and courts do not seem terribly bothered by it—but also to arbitrary judicial

247. Akhil Amar's work is a notable exception to this tendency. * * *

regulation, regulation that produces outcomes untethered to any definable legal principle. * * *

Similarly, the only way to set funding floors is to set them—to say, states must spend this much on criminal defense, but need not spend more. There is no analytic structure that allows one to specify the right dollar amount. [A] good deal of constitutional law may consist of judicial policy preferences with a thin legal veneer, but here the veneer seems transparent.

That simple point may be the source of much of constitutional law's troubled relationship with criminal justice. Constitutional law has focused relentlessly on the sorts of issues that are susceptible to legal analysis—how to select juries, when to require warrants, which mistrials permit retrial and which ones mean the defendant must go free. These are classic lawyers' issues; they give rise to classic lawyers' arguments. But courts' decisions on those issues are embedded in a system shaped by more open-ended—and more flagrantly political—judgments: How bad should something be before we call it a crime? How much money should we spend on criminal defense? Perhaps courts would do a sufficiently poor job of making these open-ended political judgments that we are better off leaving them to other actors. That is the system's current premise, and the premise is entirely plausible. But if that premise is right, those other actors—chiefly legislators and prosecutors—are able to defeat courts' work on courts' own turf: All those judge-made procedural rules are likely not to work the way they are supposed to. In the criminal justice system's three-legged stool—procedure, substance, and money—procedure is the least stable leg, the one that most depends on the others for support.

So criminal procedure may be no more than an instance of courts properly recognizing the need to intervene in a system that imposes terrible costs on large numbers of people, and then doing what comes naturally, regulating the kinds of things courts are used to regulating. That includes avoiding a kind of decision-making that, for courts, seems unnatural. All of which might be fine if the judicially regulated sphere could be isolated from the rest of the system. Sadly, it cannot. * * *

[The law of criminal procedure prevents some serious wrongs and produces other benefits, some of which are quite familiar.] Yet there are substantial tradeoffs, and the tradeoffs are not so familiar. The criminal process is much harder to control than courts suppose; it is driven by forces the courts do not, and perhaps cannot, direct. When courts do act, their actions are shaped by those forces in ways the courts themselves may not understand, ways that are at best ambiguous and at worst bad. Some part of what the Fourth, Fifth, and Sixth Amendments protect has probably come at the cost of a criminal justice system that is less focused on the merits and hence more likely to convict innocents, a system that disproportionately targets the poor, and a system that convicts for "crimes" that cover vastly more than anyone would wish to punish. The merits of this bargain are at least open to question.

Does that mean constitutional criminal procedure should be scrapped? No: Limits on police violence are essential to a free society, just as *Gideon* and the reasonable doubt rule are essential to any adversarial system that takes accuracy seriously. Now ask the question differently: Should the law of criminal procedure be scaled back, perhaps dramatically? Maybe so—not because it is wrong in principle, but because it is at odds with the system in which it operates. * * * [That] evaluation should begin with a sense of the limits of the enterprise, the difficulty of doing what criminal procedure seeks to do without also doing other, much worse things. * * *

[For] the past thirty-five years, the legal system's discussion of criminal defendants' rights has suffered from an air of unreality, a sense that all goals can be satisfied and all values honored—that we can, for example, have the jury selection process we want at no cost to anything else we might want. A sense of rank ordering, of assigning priority to some constitutional norms rather than treating all as equally deserving of regulatory attention, is absent.

That should change. It is time to acknowledge the tradeoffs, to take seriously the nature of the system the law of criminal procedure regulates and the ways in which that system can evade or undermine the regulation. In a regime like ours, countermajoritarian restraints on the criminal process can succeed only at a cost, the cost is probably substantial, and it is disproportionately imposed on those who least deserve to bear it. Leaving more of the process to majoritarian institutions might be better, not least for some of the defendants the process is designed to protect.

That need not mean leaving defendants to the mercies of state legislatures and local prosecutors. If constitutional law's response to criminal justice has failed, it has failed not just from too much intervention but from too little as well. Making *Gideon* a formal right only, without any ancillary funding requirements, has produced a criminal process that is, for poor defendants, a scandal. Courts' reluctance to police legislatures' criminalization and sentencing decisions—coupled with the way those legislative decisions can be used in a system that gives prosecutors blanket authority to choose whom to go after and for what—has produced its own scandals. Defendants' interests might best be protected by less procedure, coupled with a much more activist judicial posture toward funding, the definition of crime, and sentencing—all areas where judges have been loath to take dramatic stands.

This judicial reticence seems to have been motivated by a desire not to trench on the prerogatives of the politicians, a desire to stick to the more law-like and presumably less contentious ground of process. That the 1960s produced a revolution in criminal *procedure* may testify to the underrated conservatism of Warren Court constitutional thought, to that radical Court's willingness to confine its intervention to conventional categories. If so, in this area these conservative instincts may have been misplaced—as, perhaps, was the Court's reformist (procedural) zeal. The system might be better off today had Warren and his colleagues worried less about criminal procedure, and more about criminal justice.

JEROME H. SKOLNICK & JAMES J. FYFE—ABOVE THE LAW: POLICE AND THE EXCESSIVE USE OF FORCE*
115–16, 119–20, 131–33, 194–95 (1993).

* * * The view of police officers as soldiers engaged in a war on crime not only diverts attention from more effective strategies for crime control but also is a major cause of police violence and the violation of citizens' rights. Those who hold and urge this view wrongly presume—or worse, *pretend*—that grand strategies

---

* For a thoughtful exploration of whether "community policing" offers a promising means of preventing the abuses discussed in *Above the Law*, see Debra Ann Livingston, *Brutality in Blue: Community, Authority, and the* *Elusive Promise of Police Reform*, 92 Mich. L.Rev. 1556 (1994). See also Professor Livingston's *Police Discretion and the Quality of Life in Public Places: Courts, Communities, and the New Policing*, 97 Colum.L.Rev. 551 (1997).

devised by police chiefs, no-nonsense prosecutors, drug czars, law-and-order politicians, and other would-be generals can banish crime, disorder, and the scourge of drugs. They have urged a *war model* of policing that aggrandizes these top cops, hardnosed prosecutors, and other assorted tough guys in suits, most of whom have never made a drug buy, never made an arrest, never faced physical danger, and never come face to face with a criminal on a dark street. Less obviously, it reduces the role of the cop on the street to that of unquestioning grunt in the trenches. * * *

[The] *war model* of policing encourages police violence of the type that victimized Rodney King. When any soldiers go to war, they must have enemies. When cops go to war against crime, their enemies are found in inner cities and among our minority populations. There, in a country as foreign to most officers as Vietnam was to GIs, cops have trouble distinguishing the good guys from the bad. In this environment, the more cynical officers give up and do nothing or, worse, occasionally become corrupt and share in the profits of the illegal underground markets that flourish around them. There, some of the more passionate officers, who are not so easily discouraged from fighting the battles to which they have been assigned, and who typically are incorruptible, become frustrated and angry. Soon, *everybody* becomes suspect in their eyes. The community and the police become alienated and distrustful of each other, and incidents like the King beating occur more frequently than we would like to think. * * *

* * * Every day, out of their supervisors' sight, police officers at the lowest levels of their departments make what law scholar Joseph Goldstein called "low visibility decisions" that have great effects on the lives and liberties of individual members of the public. At any moment, for example, police officers throughout the United States are deciding whether to ticket or merely to warn this motorist; whether or not to destroy the marijuana cigarette that kid was found holding and send him on his way without marking his life history with a record of arrest; whether or not to arrest this abusive husband; whether to back off a bit or stand firm and shoot the oncoming emotionally disturbed person wielding the knife.

These are momentous decisions that can be reviewed only after the fact and, often, only after their consequences have been realized. Before there is any opportunity to determine whether the officer has acted appropriately, the ticket has been issued, the arrest or release has occurred, the shot has struck flesh. Further, absent videotaping or other reasonably objective recording, reviews usually must rely solely upon the accounts of the officers and citizens involved. When citizens benefit from officers' exercise of discretion, as when they are given what police call *scares* rather than tickets, any opportunity officially to review the appropriateness of officers' decisions disappears with them as they leave the scenes of their encounters with police. When the wisdom or reasonableness of officers' actions is challenged, review frequently consists of trying to *eff the ineffable*—attempting to resolve irresolvable swearing contests between citizens and police officers. Conversely, whenever police chiefs make decisions, their discretion is recorded and subject to comment by myriad critics, both before and after the fact. As an old saw has it, police chiefs' decisions are put on paper in the form of orders and policy statements and are there for everybody to see; but cops' decisions quickly disappear into the ozone, where there is nobody to criticize the cops' version of what occurred. It is hard to think of any hierarchical organization in which the lowest-level employees routinely exercise such great discretion with such little opportunity for objective review. * * *

Over time [the] analogy between local police and the FBI has proved no more apt than that between the military and the police. Hoover was successful because the enemy in his war was not so much crime as a few sensational public enemies—the John Dillingers and Baby Face Nelsons—who were relatively easy to catch. This, we began to discover during the mid–1960s, is not the crime problem facing our local police.

Today the police work in inner cities, where poverty, unemployment, teenage pregnancy, and drug use have achieved nearly institutional status and where young men are steered by their peers to commit crimes before they have reached puberty. In such circumstances, cops' wars on crime are unwinnable. Police detectives—or FBI agents—can track down a few *individual criminals*. They do so with some success, considerable prestige, and the resulting sense of a job well done. But in the grand picture, all police administrators know that their investigators' best efforts and most spectacular arrests will never solve the *problem* of inner-city violence.

* * * Day after day, patrol officers—trained and socialized to think of themselves as soldiers—see around them the evidence that their enforcement efforts are in vain. One of us (Skolnick) was riding with an NYPD cop in Washington Heights, the main marketplace of New York City's drug scene. Youthful drug sellers were standing in threes and fours on virtually every corner.

Our police companion, an experienced narcotics officer, was asked, "How effective are the police in controlling the drug trade?" "We are," he answered, "like a gnat biting on a horse's ass." * * *

Frustration grows, and it should surprise no one that some patrol officers, those who operate directly in the streets, rather than detectives working out of offices and assigned the unambiguous task of investigating specific crimes, apparently account for most of police brutality against citizens. * * * Street cops exercise greater discretion than any police officials. They are society's first responders to an incredible array of human problems, some of which simply are beyond resolution. [They] should be encouraged to stay on the street and to develop their talents. The good ones—and most, but not all, are good ones— should be appropriately rewarded for their extraordinary work, both financially and in terms of prestige and influence within their occupation, agency, and community. Most important, street cops should not be encouraged to see themselves as soldiers locked in a war.

[The popular view] of the courts' influence on police activity is exaggerated. The exclusionary rule, for example, is no bar to the search practices of officers or police departments who engage in indiscriminate "street sweep" techniques with the goal of cleaning up the streets by causing embarrassment and harassment without regard to whether any arrests they happen to make will survive cross-examination.

[The] widespread belief that the Supreme Court's best-known decisions on search, seizure, and interrogation somehow have *handcuffed* the police or otherwise have made citizens less safe is not supported by any objective evidence. * * * Most offenders are caught redhanded in circumstances so rich in incriminating evidence that the police simply do not need to ask them for anything but their names and addresses. When police *buy* narcotics on the street and *bust* the seller, or search a crack house and seize the drugs, attempts to obtain confessions serve only to gild the lily of already invulnerable prosecution cases. * * *

Popular overestimation or exaggeration of the court's effects on police effectiveness is a matter of more than academic interest. Like the view of *cops-as-soldiers,* the charges that due process protections foil the war on crime not only distract us from more promising strategies of crime control but also increase the likelihood of police violence and violation of citizens' rights. Cops who feel that *their enemy* has been given unreasonable advantages by people who have not themselves experienced the battle may come to disrespect all the rules and to administer "street justice"—as in the case of Rodney King—to ensure that offenders are appropriately and severely punished. * * *

TRACEY MACLIN—"BLACK AND BLUE ENCOUNTERS"— SOME PRELIMINARY THOUGHTS ABOUT FOURTH AMENDMENT SEIZURES: SHOULD RACE MATTER?*
26 Valparaiso U.L.Rev. 243, 250, 252–61, 265–70 (1991).

* * * I submit that the dynamics surrounding an encounter between a police officer and a black male are quite different from those that surround an encounter between an officer and the so-called average, reasonable person. My tentative proposal is that the Court should disregard the notion that there is an average, hypothetical, reasonable person out there by which to judge the constitutionality of police encounters. When assessing the coercive nature of an encounter, the Court should consider the race of the person confronted by the police, and how that person's race might have influenced his attitude toward the encounter.

* * * [The] Supreme Court has said over and over that *all citizens*—not just rich, white men from the suburbs—are free to ignore a police officer who accosts them. In *Florida v. Royer,* Justice White explained that: "The person approached ... need not answer any question put to him; indeed, he may decline to listen to the questions at all and may go on his way. He may not be detained even momentarily without reasonable, objective grounds for doing so; and his refusal to listen or answer does not, without more, furnish those grounds."[43]

This is what the law is supposed to be; black men, however, know that a different "law" exists on the street. Black men know they are liable to be stopped at anytime, and that when they question the authority of the police, the response from the cops is often swift and violent. This applies to black men of all economic strata, regardless of their level of education, and whatever their job status or place in the community.

If the stories of black men in Boston are not convincing, consider what happened to Don Jackson, a former police officer from southern California. Mr. Jackson was trying to document that the police in Long Beach, California were discriminating against and harassing minority citizens who lived and visited Long Beach. [When he asked the officers why they had stopped him while driving] an

---

* See also Elizabeth A. Gaynes, *The Urban Criminal Justice System: Where Young + Black + Male = Probable Cause,* 20 Ford. Urb.L.J. 621 (1993); David A. Harris, *Factors for Reasonable Suspicion: When Black and Poor Means Stopped and Frisked,* 69 Ind.L.J. 659 (1994); David A. Harris, *Driving While Black and All Other Traffic Offenses: The Supreme Court and Pretextual Traffic Stops,* 87 J.Crim.L. & C. 554 (1997); Sheri Lynn Johnson, *Race and the Decision to Detain a Suspect,* 93 Yale L.J. 214 (1983); Sheri Lynn Johnson, *Unconscious Racism and the Criminal Law,* 73 Cornell L.Rev. 1016 (1988); Randall Kennedy, *The State, Criminal Law, and Racial Discrimination: A Comment,* 107 Harv.L.Rev. 1255 (1994); *Developments in the Law—Race and the Criminal Process,* 101 Harv.L.Rev. 1472 (1988).

43. Florida v. Royer [p. 326], (1983) (plurality opinion) * * *.

officer pushed Mr. Jackson through a plate glass store window. Unknown to the officers, an NBC camera crew filmed the entire incident.

In a *New York Times* op-ed article entitled, *Police Embody Racism To My People,* Mr. Jackson wrote: "Operating free of constitutional limitations, the police have long been the greatest nemesis of blacks, irrespective of whether we are complying with the law or not. We have learned that there are cars we are not supposed to drive, streets we are not supposed to walk. We may still be stopped and asked 'Where are you going, boy?' Whether we're in a Mercedes or a Volkswagen."

Mr. Jackson's remarks demonstrate the illusory quality of the Court's view that police encounters are not deserving of Fourth Amendment scrutiny because citizens will feel free to leave and *know* of their right to ignore a police officer who has accosted them. The Court's approach, as it is applied in the case of black men, is flawed not because black males have not been informed, as a technical matter, of their legal rights. I have spoken with a number of black lawyers and law students who know their constitutional rights but never feel free to ignore the police. The Court's view is wrong because it is out of touch with the reality on the streets of America. Most black men simply do not trust police officers to respect their rights.

* * * Black males learn at an early age that confrontations with the police should be avoided; black teenagers are advised never to challenge a police officer, even when the officer is wrong. Even if a police officer has arguable grounds for stopping a black male, such an encounter often engenders distinct feelings for the black man. Those feelings are fear of possible violence or humiliation.

To be sure, when whites are stopped by the police, they too feel uneasy and often experience fear. [But] I wonder whether the average white person worries that an otherwise routine police encounter may lead to a violent confrontation. When they are stopped by the police, do whites contemplate the possibility that they will be physically abused for questioning why an officer has stopped them? White teenagers who walk the streets or hang-out in the local mall, do they worry about being strip-searched by the police? Does the average white person ever see himself experiencing what Rodney King or Don Jackson went through during their encounters with the police?

Police officers have shown [that] they will not hesitate to "teach a lesson" to any black male who, even in the slightest way challenges his authority. For example, in Los Angeles, even before [the Rodney King beating], blacks knew not to argue with the police unless they wanted to risk death in a police choke-hold that seemed to be applied more frequently in the case of black males than other citizens.[56]

In addition to fear, distrust is another component that swirls around encounters between black males and the police. Over the years, black males have learned that police officers have little regard for their Fourth Amendment rights. Two years ago in Boston, for instance, a city learned what can happen when a police department is encouraged to ignore the constitutional rights of a targeted class of individuals—black males. In the aftermath of a tragic shooting of a white couple and the declaration of a "war" against teenage gangs and their associates, black

---

56. See City of Los Angeles v. Lyons, 461 U.S. 95, 116 n. 3 (1983) (Marshall, J., dissenting) ("[S]ince 1975 no less than sixteen persons have died following use of a chokehold by an LAPD police officer. Twelve have been Negro males. [Thus] in a city where Negro males constitute nine per cent of the population, they have accounted for seventy-five per cent of the deaths resulting from the use of chokehold."). * * *

males were subjected to what one state judge called "martial law"[57] tactics by a police department that offered no apologies for its disregard of constitutional liberties.[58] * * *

* * * [B]eing black constitutes a "double-brand" in the mind of the police. Black men are associated with "crimes against the person, with bodily harm to police officers, and with a general lack of support for the police."[67] Also, because of their race, black males "are bound to appear discordant to policemen in most of the environment of a middle-class white society. For this reason, black males doubly draw the attention of police officers."[68] In essence, the police officer "identif[ies] the black man with danger."[69]

From the perspective of the black man, however, these police attitudes only reinforce the view that " '[t]he police system is a dictatorship toward the black people.' "[70] * * * Black men are considered suspicious and targeted for questioning not because of any objective or empirical evidence that they are involved in criminality, but because of police bias and societal indifference to the plight of black males who are on the receiving-end of aggressive police tactics. In effect, black men are accorded "sub-citizen" status for Fourth Amendment purposes. * * *

[T]he use of deadly force by the police has always generated tension between the police and minority citizens. Before the Supreme Court pronounced Fourth Amendment restrictions on the use of deadly force in *Tennessee v. Garner* [p. 227], which involved a police shooting of a burglary suspect in Memphis, Tennessee, Professor James Fyfe found that black property crime suspects in Memphis were four times as likely to be wounded, and forty per cent more likely to be killed by the police than their white counterparts. Interestingly, the *Garner* Court never mentioned that Garner was black.

Perhaps the Court believed that Garner's race was irrelevant to the question of whether the use of deadly force to apprehend a fleeing felon was unreasonable police behavior under the Fourth Amendment. Maybe the Court believed race-based police decisions on whether to use deadly force were no longer a problem. Whatever the motivation, ignoring the impact of race does a disservice to blacks and the country as a whole.

* * * Currently, the Court assesses the coercive nature of a police encounter by considering the *totality of the circumstances* surrounding the confrontation. All I want the Court to do is to consider the role race might play, along with the other factors it considers, when judging the constitutionality of the encounter.

Some will no doubt object to the explicit use of race in deciding constitutional questions. Understandably, some will ask: If we really wish to live in a future non-

---

57. Commonwealth v. Phillips and Woody, No. 080275–6, Memorandum and Order, at 3 (Suffolk Sup.Ct. Sept. 17, 1989) (Judge Cortland Mathers found that a police order that all known gang members and their associates would be searched on sight was "a proclamation of martial law in Roxbury for a narrow class of people, young blacks, suspected of membership in a gang or perceived by the police to be in the company of someone thought to be a member."). * * *

58. Boston Police Deputy Superintendent William Celester had been quoted as saying: " 'People are going to say we're violating their [gang members'] constitutional rights, but we're not too concerned about that.... If we have to violate their rights, if that's what it takes, then that's what we're going to do." * * *

67. D. Bagley & H. Mendelsohn, *Minorities and the Police* 107 (1969).

68. Id.

69. J. Skolnick, *Justice Without Trial* 49 (1966).

70. B. Blauner, *Black Lives, White Lives* 110 (1989).

racial society, shouldn't we be moving away from procedures and decisions in which people are classified by their race?

I too would like to see a future in which decision-makers will not have to consider the race of individuals in deciding important legal and constitutional questions. But in *today's* world, where the anger and distrust between black males and the police is rising, not decreasing, we must recall Justice Blackmun's familiar stance in the affirmative action debate. "In order to get beyond racism, we must first take account of race. There is no other way."[108]

RANDALL L. KENNEDY—RACE, CRIME, AND THE LAW
158–60 (1997).

When a Mexican–American motorist is selected for questioning in part on the basis of his perceived ancestry, he is undoubtedly being burdened more heavily at that moment on account of his race than his white Anglo counterpart. He is being made to pay a type of racial tax for the campaign against illegal immigration that whites, blacks, and Asians escape. Similarly, a young black man selected for questioning by police as he alights from an airplane or drives a car is being made to pay a type of racial tax for the war against drugs that whites and other groups escape. That tax is the cost of being subjected to greater scrutiny than others. But is that tax illegitimate?

One defense of it is that, under the circumstances, people of other races are simply not in a position to pay the tax effectively. In contrast to apparent Mexican ancestry, neither apparent white nor black nor Asian ancestry appreciably raises the risk that a person near the Mexican border is illegally resident in the United States. Similarly, the argument would run that in contrast to the young black man, the young white man is not as likely to be a courier of illicit drugs. The defense could go on to say that, in this context, race is *not* being used invidiously. It is not being used as a marker to identify people to harm through enslavement, or exclusion, or segregation. Rather, race is being used merely as a signal that facilitates efficient law enforcement. In this context, apparent Mexican ancestry or blackness is being used for unobjectionable ends in the same way that whiteness is used in the affirmative action context: as a marker that has the effect, though not the purpose, of burdening a given racial group. Whereas whites are make to pay a racial tax for the purpose of opening up opportunities for people of color in education and employment, Mexican–Americans and blacks are made to pay a racial tax for the purpose of more efficient law enforcement.

We need to pause here to consider the tremendous controversy that has surrounded affirmative action policies aimed at helping racial minorities. Many of the same arguments against race-based affirmative action are applicable as well in the context of race-based police stops. With affirmative action, many whites claim that they are victims of racial discrimination. With race-based police stops, many people of color complain that they are victims of racial discrimination. With affirmative action, many adversely affected whites claim that they are *innocent* victims of a policy that penalizes them for the misconduct of others who also happened to have been white. With race-based police stops, many adversely affected people of color maintain that they are *innocent* victims of a policy that penalizes them for the misconduct of others who also happen to be colored. Many

---

108. Regents of Univ. of Cal. v. Bakke, 438   mun, J., dissenting).* * *
U.S. 265, 407, 438 U.S. 265, 407 (1978) (Black-

whites claim that a major drawback of affirmative action which makes it more costly than valuable is the fact of their intense resentment against such programs. Many people of color claim that one of the drawbacks of race-based police stops that makes it more costly than valuable is their resentment against such policies.

There, exist, however, a remarkable difference in reactions to these racial policies, both of which involve race-dependent decisionmaking. While affirmative action is under tremendous pressure politically and legally, racial policing is not.

* * *

Chapter 5

ARREST, SEARCH AND SEIZURE[a]

SECTION 1. THE EXCLUSIONARY RULE[b]

WOLF v. COLORADO
338 U.S. 25, 69 S.Ct. 1359, 93 L.Ed. 1782 (1949).

Justice FRANKFURTER delivered the opinion of the Court.

The precise question for consideration is this: Does a conviction by a State court for a State offense deny the "due process of law" required by the Fourteenth Amendment, solely because evidence that was admitted at the trial was obtained under circumstances which would have rendered it inadmissible in a prosecution for violation of a federal law in a court of the United States because there deemed to be an infraction of the Fourth Amendment as applied in *Weeks v. United States,* 232 U.S. 383, 34 S.Ct. 341, 58 L.Ed. 652 [1914]? * * *

The security of one's privacy against arbitrary intrusion by the police—which is at the core of the Fourth Amendment—is basic to a free society. It is therefore implicit in "the concept of ordered liberty" and as such enforceable against the States through the Due Process Clause. * * *

Accordingly, we have no hesitation in saying that were a State affirmatively to sanction such police incursion into privacy it would run counter to the guaranty of the Fourteenth Amendment. But the ways of enforcing such a basic right raise questions of a different order. How such arbitrary conduct should be checked, what remedies against it should be afforded, the means by which the right should be made effective, are all questions that are not to be so dogmatically answered as to preclude the varying solutions which spring from an allowable range of judgment on issues not susceptible of quantitative solution.

In *Weeks v. United States,* this Court held that in a federal prosecution the Fourth Amendment barred the use of evidence secured through an illegal search and seizure. This ruling * * * was not derived from the explicit requirements of the Fourth Amendment; it was not based on legislation expressing Congressional policy in the enforcement of the Constitution. The decision was a matter of

a. For detailed treatment of this subject and reference to other secondary sources, consult Wayne R. LaFave, *Search and Seizure: A Treatise on the Fourth Amendment* (3d ed.1996) [cited herein as LaFave].

b. Although the concern here is with the exclusion of evidence obtained in violation of the Fourth Amendment, it should be noted that an arrest or search which passes Fourth Amendment muster may nonetheless violate state law. The exclusionary sanction is also used when state constitutional provisions similar to the Fourth Amendment have been violated, but if a state chooses not to do so this does not violate federal due process. *California v. Greenwood,* p. 159. As for violations of statutes, court rules and administrative regulations, it is customary to require exclusion if the violation significantly affected the defendant's substantial rights.

judicial implication. Since then it has been frequently applied and we stoutly adhere to it. But the immediate question is whether the basic right to protection against arbitrary intrusion by the police demands the exclusion of logically relevant evidence obtained by an unreasonable search and seizure because, in a federal prosecution for a federal crime, it would be excluded. As a matter of inherent reason, one would suppose this to be an issue as to which men with complete devotion to the protection of the right of privacy might give different answers. When we find that in fact most of the English-speaking world does not regard as vital to such protection the exclusion of evidence thus obtained, we must hesitate to treat this remedy as an essential ingredient of the right. The contrariety of views of the States is particularly impressive in view of the careful reconsideration which they have given the problem in the light of the *Weeks* decision.

* * * As of today 30 States reject the *Weeks* doctrine, 17 States are in agreement with it. * * * Of 10 jurisdictions within the United Kingdom and the British Commonwealth of Nations which have passed on the question, none has held evidence obtained by illegal search and seizure inadmissible. * * *

The jurisdictions which have rejected the *Weeks* doctrine have not left the right to privacy without other means of protection. Indeed, the exclusion of evidence is a remedy which directly serves only to protect those upon whose person or premises something incriminating has been found. We cannot, therefore, regard it as a departure from basic standards to remand such persons, together with those who emerge scatheless from a search, to the remedies of private action and such protection as the internal discipline of the police, under the eyes of an alert public opinion, may afford. Granting that in practice the exclusion of evidence may be an effective way of deterring unreasonable searches, it is not for this Court to condemn as falling below the minimal standards assured by the Due Process Clause a State's reliance upon other methods which, if consistently enforced, would be equally effective. * * * There are, moreover, reasons for excluding evidence unreasonably obtained by the federal police which are less compelling in the case of police under State or local authority. The public opinion of a community can far more effectively be exerted against oppressive conduct on the part of police directly responsible to the community itself than can local opinion, sporadically aroused, be brought to bear upon remote authority pervasively exerted throughout the country.

We hold, therefore, that in a prosecution in a State court for a State crime the Fourteenth Amendment does not forbid the admission of evidence obtained by an unreasonable search and seizure. * * *

Justice BLACK, concurring.

* * * I agree with what appears to be a plain implication of the Court's opinion that the federal exclusionary rule is not a command of the Fourth Amendment but is a judicially created rule of evidence which Congress might negate. * * *

Justice MURPHY, with whom Justice RUTLEDGE joins, dissenting.

[T]here is but one alternative to the rule of exclusion. That is no sanction at all.

* * * Little need be said concerning the possibilities of criminal prosecution. Self-scrutiny is a lofty ideal, but its exaltation reaches new heights if we expect a District Attorney to prosecute himself or his associates for well-meaning violations of the search and seizure clause during a raid the District Attorney or his

associates have ordered. But there is an appealing ring in another alternative. A trespass action for damages is a venerable means of securing reparation for unauthorized invasion of the home. Why not put the old writ to a new use? When the Court cites cases permitting the action, the remedy seems complete.

But what an illusory remedy this is, if by "remedy" we mean a positive deterrent to police and prosecutors tempted to violate the Fourth Amendment. The appealing ring softens when we recall that in a trespass action the measure of damages is simply the extent of the injury to physical property. If the officer searches with care, he can avoid all but nominal damages—a penny, or a dollar. Are punitive damages possible? Perhaps. But a few states permit none, whatever the circumstances. In those that do, the plaintiff must show the real ill will or malice of the defendant, and surely it is not unreasonable to assume that one in honest pursuit of crime bears no malice toward the search victim. If that burden is carried, recovery may yet be defeated by the rule that there must be physical damages before punitive damages may be awarded. In addition, some states limit punitive damages to the actual expenses of litigation. * * * Even assuming the ill will of the officer, his reasonable grounds for belief that the home he searched harbored evidence of crime is admissible in mitigation of punitive damages. * * * The bad reputation of the plaintiff is likewise admissible. * * * If the evidence seized was actually used at a trial, that fact has been held a complete justification of the search, and a defense against the trespass action. * * * And even if the plaintiff hurdles all these obstacles, and gains a substantial verdict, the individual officer's finances may well make the judgment useless—for the municipality, of course, is not liable without its consent. Is it surprising that there is so little in the books concerning trespass actions for violation of the search and seizure clause? * * *

Justice DOUGLAS, dissenting.

* * * I agree with Justice Murphy that * * * in absence of [an exclusionary] rule of evidence the Amendment would have no effective sanction. * * *

MAPP v. OHIO
367 U.S. 643, 81 S.Ct. 1684, 6 L.Ed.2d 1081 (1961).

Justice CLARK delivered the opinion of the Court. * * *

On May 23, 1957, three Cleveland police officers arrived at appellant's residence in that city pursuant to information that "a person [was] hiding out in the home who was wanted for questioning in connection with a recent bombing, and that there was a large amount of policy paraphernalia being hidden in the home." Miss Mapp and her daughter by a former marriage lived on the top floor of the two-family dwelling. Upon their arrival at that house, the officers knocked on the door and demanded entrance but appellant, after telephoning her attorney, refused to admit them without a search warrant. * * *

The officers again sought entrance some three hours later when four or more additional officers arrived on the scene. When Miss Mapp did not come to the door immediately, at least one of the several doors to the house was forcibly opened and the policemen gained admittance. Meanwhile Miss Mapp's attorney arrived, but the officers, having secured their own entry, and continuing in their defiance of the law, would permit him neither to see Miss Mapp nor to enter the house. [When the officers broke into the hall, Miss Mapp] demanded to see the search warrant. A paper, claimed to be a warrant, was held up by one of the officers. She grabbed the "warrant" and placed it in her bosom. A struggle ensued in which the officers recovered the piece of paper and as a result of which they handcuffed appellant because she had been "belligerent" in resisting their official rescue of the "warrant" from her person. * * * Appellant, in handcuffs, was then forcibly taken upstairs to her bedroom where the officers searched a dresser, a chest of drawers, a closet and some suitcases. * * * The search spread to the rest of the second floor * * *. The basement of the building and a trunk found therein were also searched. The obscene materials for possession of which she was ultimately convicted were discovered in the course of that widespread search.

At the trial no search warrant was produced by the prosecution, nor was the failure to produce one explained or accounted for. At best [as the Ohio Supreme Court, which affirmed the conviction, expressed it], "there is, in the record, considerable doubt as to whether there ever was any warrant for the search of defendant's home." * * *

The State says that even if the search were made without authority, or otherwise unreasonably, it is not prevented from using the unconstitutionally seized evidence at trial, citing *Wolf v. Colorado,* * * *. On this appeal, * * * it is urged once again that we review that holding. * * *

The Court in *Wolf* first stated that "[t]he contrariety of views of the States" on the adoption of the exclusionary rule of *Weeks* was "particularly impressive" * * * While in 1949, prior to the *Wolf* case, almost two-thirds of the States were opposed to the use of the exclusionary rule, now, despite the *Wolf* case, more than half of those since passing upon it, by their own legislative or judicial decision, have wholly or partly adopted or adhered to the *Weeks* rule. * * * Significantly, among those now following the rule is California which, according to its highest court, was "compelled to reach that conclusion because other remedies have completely failed to secure compliance with the constitutional provisions * * *." In connection with this California case, we note that the second basis elaborated in *Wolf* in support of its failure to enforce the exclusionary doctrine against the States was that "other means of protection" have been afforded "the right to privacy." The experience of California that such other remedies have been worthless and futile is buttressed by the experience of other States. * * *

It, therefore, plainly appears that the factual considerations supporting the failure of the *Wolf* Court to include the *Weeks* exclusionary rule when it recognized the enforceability of the right to privacy against the States in 1949, while not basically relevant to the constitutional consideration, could not, in any analysis, now be deemed controlling.

* * * Today we once again examine *Wolf's* constitutional documentation of the right to privacy free from unreasonable state intrusion, and, after its dozen years on our books, are led by it to close the only courtroom door remaining open to evidence secured by official lawlessness in flagrant abuse of that basic right, reserved to all persons as a specific guarantee against that very same unlawful conduct. We hold that all evidence obtained by searches and seizures in violation of the Constitution is, by that same authority, inadmissible in a state court.

Since the Fourth Amendment's right of privacy has been declared enforceable against the States through the Due Process Clause of the Fourteenth, it is enforceable against them by the same sanction of exclusion as is used against the Federal Government. Were it otherwise then just as without the *Weeks* rule the assurance against unreasonable federal searches and seizures would be "a form of words," valueless and undeserving of mention in a perpetual charter of inestimable human liberties, so too, without that rule the freedom from state invasions of privacy would be so ephemeral and so neatly severed from its conceptual nexus with the freedom from all brutish means of coercing evidence as not to merit this Court's high regard as a freedom "implicit in 'the concept of ordered liberty.' "

* * * [I]n extending the substantive protections of due process to all constitutionally unreasonable searches—state or federal—it was logically and constitutionally necessary that the exclusion doctrine—an essential part of the right to privacy—be also insisted upon as an essential ingredient of the right newly recognized by the *Wolf* case. In short, the admission of the new constitutional right by *Wolf* could not consistently tolerate denial of its most important constitutional privilege, namely, the exclusion of the evidence which an accused had been forced to give by reason of the unlawful seizure. To hold otherwise is to grant the right but in reality to withhold its privilege and enjoyment. Only last year the Court itself recognized that the purpose of the exclusionary rule "is to deter—to compel respect for the constitutional guaranty in the only effectively available way—by removing the incentive to disregard it."

Indeed, we are aware of no restraint, similar to that rejected today, conditioning the enforcement of any other basic constitutional right. The right to privacy, no less important than any other right carefully and particularly reserved to the people, would stand in marked contrast to all other rights declared as "basic to a free society." * * * [N]othing could be more certain than that when a coerced confession is involved, "the relevant rules of evidence" are overridden without regard to "the incidence of such conduct by the police," slight or frequent. Why should not the same rule apply to what is tantamount to coerced testimony by way of unconstitutional seizure of goods, papers, effects, documents, etc.? We find that, as to the Federal Government the Fourth and Fifth Amendments and, as to the States, the freedom from unconscionable invasions of privacy and the freedom from convictions based upon coerced confessions do enjoy an "intimate relation" in their perpetuation of "principles of humanity and civil liberty * * *." They express "supplementing phases of the same constitutional purpose—to maintain inviolate large areas of personal privacy." The philosophy of each Amendment and of each freedom is complementary to, although not dependent upon, that of the other in its sphere of influence—the very least that together they assure in either sphere is that no man is to be convicted on unconstitutional evidence.

Moreover, our holding * * * is not only the logical dictate of prior cases, but it also makes very good sense. There is no war between the Constitution and common sense. Presently, a federal prosecutor may make no use of evidence illegally seized, but a State's attorney across the street may, although he supposedly is operating under the enforceable prohibitions of the same Amendment. Thus the State, by admitting evidence unlawfully seized, serves to encourage disobedience to the Federal Constitution which it is bound to uphold. * * *

There are those who say, as did Justice (then Judge) Cardozo, that under our constitutional exclusionary doctrine "[t]he criminal is to go free because the constable has blundered." *People v. Defore*, 150 N.E. 585 (N.Y.1926). In some cases this will undoubtedly be the result. But, "there is another consideration—the imperative of judicial integrity." The criminal goes free, if he must, but it is the law that sets him free. Nothing can destroy a government more quickly than its failure to observe its own laws, or worse, its disregard of the charter of its own existence. As Justice Brandeis, dissenting, said in *Olmstead v. United States* [p. 360]: "Our government is the potent, the omnipresent teacher. For good or for ill, it teaches the whole people by its example. * * * If the government becomes a lawbreaker, it breeds contempt for law; it invites every man to become a law unto himself; it invites anarchy." Nor can it lightly be assumed that, as a practical matter, adoption of the exclusionary rule fetters law enforcement. Only last year this Court expressly considered that contention and found that "pragmatic evidence of a sort" to the contrary was not wanting. *Elkins v. United States*, 364 U.S. 206, 80 S.Ct. 1437, 4 L.Ed.2d 1669 (1960). * * * The Court noted that:

"The federal courts themselves have operated under the exclusionary rule of *Weeks* for almost half a century; yet it has not been suggested either that the Federal Bureau of Investigation has thereby been rendered ineffective, or that the administration of criminal justice in the federal courts has thereby been disrupted. Moreover, the experience of the states is impressive * * *. The movement toward the rule of exclusion has been halting but seemingly inexorable."

The ignoble shortcut to conviction left open to the State tends to destroy the entire system of constitutional restraints on which the liberties of the people rest. Having once recognized that the right to privacy embodied in the Fourth Amendment is enforceable against the States, and that the right to be secure against rude invasions of privacy by state officers is, therefore, constitutional in origin, we can no longer permit that right to remain an empty promise. Because it is enforceable in the same manner and to like effect as other basic rights secured by the Due Process Clause, we can no longer permit it to be revocable at the whim of any police officer who, in the name of law enforcement itself, chooses to suspend its enjoyment. Our decision, founded on reason and truth, gives to the individual no more than that which the Constitution guarantees him, to the police officer no less than that to which honest law enforcement is entitled, and, to the courts, that judicial integrity so necessary in the true administration of justice. * * *

Reversed and remanded.[a]

Justice HARLAN, whom Justice FRANKFURTER and Justice WHITTAKER join, dissenting. * * *

I would not impose upon the States this federal exclusionary remedy. The reasons given by the majority for now suddenly turning its back on *Wolf* seem to me notably unconvincing.

First, it is said that "the factual grounds upon which *Wolf* was based" have since changed, in that more States now follow the *Weeks* exclusionary rule than was so at the time *Wolf* was decided. While that is true, a recent survey indicates that at present one half of the States still adhere to the common-law non-exclusionary rule, and one, Maryland, retains the rule as to felonies. * * * But in any case surely all this is beside the point, as the majority itself indeed seems to recognize. Our concern here, as it was in *Wolf*, is not with the desirability of that rule but only with the question whether the States are Constitutionally free to follow it or not as they may themselves determine, and the relevance of the disparity of views among the States on this point lies simply in the fact that the judgment involved is a debatable one. Moreover, the very fact on which the majority relies, instead of lending support to what is now being done, points away from the need of replacing voluntary state action with federal compulsion.

The preservation of a proper balance between state and federal responsibility in the administration of criminal justice demands patience on the part of those who might like to see things move faster among the States in this respect. Problems of criminal law enforcement vary widely from State to State. One State, in considering the totality of its legal picture, may conclude that the need for

a. Concurring opinions by Black and Douglas, JJ., and a memorandum by Stewart, J., are omitted.

embracing the *Weeks* rule is pressing because other remedies are unavailable or inadequate to secure compliance with the substantive Constitutional principle involved. Another, though equally solicitous of Constitutional rights, may choose to pursue one purpose at a time, allowing all evidence relevant to guilt to be brought into a criminal trial, and dealing with Constitutional infractions by other means. Still another may consider the exclusionary rule too rough and ready a remedy, in that it reaches only unconstitutional intrusions which eventuate in criminal prosecution of the victims. Further, a State after experimenting with the *Weeks* rule for a time may, because of unsatisfactory experience with it, decide to revert to a non-exclusionary rule. And so on. * * * For us the question remains, as it has always been, one of state power, not one of passing judgment on the wisdom of one state course or another. In my view this Court should continue to forbear from fettering the States with an adamant rule which may embarrass them in coping with their own peculiar problems in criminal law enforcement. * * *

* * * Our role in promulgating the *Weeks* rule and its extensions * * * was quite a different one than it is here. There, in implementing the Fourth Amendment, we occupied the position of a tribunal having the ultimate responsibility for developing the standards and procedures of judicial administration within the judicial system over which it presides. Here we review State procedures whose measure is to be taken not against the specific substantive commands of the Fourth Amendment but under the flexible contours of the Due Process Clause. I do not believe that the Fourteenth Amendment empowers this Court to mould state remedies effectuating the right to freedom from "arbitrary intrusion by the police" to suit its own notions of how things should be done * * *.

Finally, it is said that the overruling of *Wolf* is supported by the established doctrine that the admission in evidence of an involuntary confession renders a state conviction constitutionally invalid. Since such a confession may often be entirely reliable, and therefore of the greatest relevance to the issue of the trial, the argument continues, this doctrine is ample warrant in precedent that the way evidence was obtained and not just its relevance, is constitutionally significant to the fairness of a trial. I believe this analogy is not a true one. The "coerced confession" rule is certainly not a rule that any illegally obtained statements may not be used in evidence. I would suppose that a statement which is procured during a period of illegal detention is, as much as unlawfully seized evidence, illegally obtained, but this Court has consistently refused to reverse state convictions resting on the use of such statements. * * *

The point, then, must be that in requiring exclusion of an involuntary statement of an accused, we are concerned not with an appropriate remedy for what the police have done, but with something which is regarded as going to the heart of our concepts of fairness in judicial procedure. The operative assumption of our procedural system is that "ours is the accusatorial as opposed to the inquisitorial system. * * *." * * * The pressures brought to bear against an accused leading to a confession, unlike an unconstitutional violation of privacy, do not, apart from the use of the confession at trial, necessarily involve independent Constitutional violations. What is crucial is that the trial defense to which an accused is entitled should not be rendered an empty formality by reason of statements wrung from him, for then "a prisoner * * * [has been] made the deluded instrument of his own conviction." That this is a *procedural right,* and that its violation occurs at the time his improperly obtained statement is admitted at trial, is manifest. * * *

This, and not the disciplining of the police, as with illegally seized evidence, is surely the true basis for excluding a statement of the accused which was unconstitutionally obtained. In sum, I think the coerced confession analogy works strongly *against* what the Court does today. * * *

UNITED STATES v. LEON

468 U.S. 897, 104 S.Ct. 3405, 82 L.Ed.2d 677 (1984).

Justice WHITE delivered the opinion of the Court. * * *

This case presents the question whether the Fourth Amendment exclusionary rule should be modified so as not to bar the use in the prosecution's case-in-chief of evidence obtained by officers acting in reasonable reliance on a search warrant issued by a detached and neutral magistrate but ultimately found to be unsupported by probable cause. * * *

The Fourth Amendment contains no provision expressly precluding the use of evidence obtained in violation of its commands, and an examination of its origin and purposes makes clear that the use of fruits of a past unlawful search or seizure "work[s] no new Fourth Amendment wrong." The wrong condemned by the Amendment is "fully accomplished" by the unlawful search or seizure itself, and the exclusionary rule is neither intended nor able to "cure the invasion of the defendant's rights which he has already suffered." The rule thus operates as "a judicially created remedy designed to safeguard Fourth Amendment rights generally through its deterrent effect, rather than a personal constitutional right of the person aggrieved."

Whether the exclusionary sanction is appropriately imposed in a particular case, our decisions make clear, is "an issue separate from the question whether the Fourth Amendment rights of the party seeking to invoke the rule were violated by police conduct." Only the former question is currently before us,[a] and it must be resolved by weighing the costs and benefits of preventing the use in the prosecution's case-in-chief of inherently trustworthy tangible evidence obtained in reliance on a search warrant issued by a detached and neutral magistrate that ultimately is found to be defective.

The substantial social costs exacted by the exclusionary rule for the vindication of Fourth Amendment rights have long been a source of concern. "Our cases have consistently recognized that unbending application of the exclusionary sanction to enforce ideals of governmental rectitude would impede unacceptably the truth-finding functions of judge and jury." An objectionable collateral consequence of this interference with the criminal justice system's truth-finding function is that some guilty defendants may go free or receive reduced sentences as a result of favorable plea bargains.[6] Particularly when law enforcement officers have acted

a. A large quantities of drugs were suppressed on the ground the warrant had not issued on probable cause, in that the affidavit reported only the allegations of an untested informant and limited corroboration by police surveillance of events themselves "as consistent with innocence as * * * with guilt." The Court earlier noted that whether this warrant would pass muster under the intervening and less demanding test of *Illinois v. Gates*, p. 186, "has not been briefed or argued," and thus chose "to take the case as it comes to us."

6. Researchers have only recently begun to study extensively the effects of the exclusionary rule on the disposition of felony arrests. One study suggests that the rule results in the nonprosecution or nonconviction of between 0.6% and 2.35% of individuals arrested for felonies. Davies, *A Hard Look at What We Know (and Still Need to Learn) About the "Costs" of the Exclusionary Rule: The NIJ Study and Other Studies of "Lost" Arrests*, 1983 A.B.F.Res.J. 611, 621. The estimates are higher for particular crimes the prosecution of which depends heavily on physical evidence.

in objective good faith or their transgressions have been minor, the magnitude of the benefit conferred on such guilty defendants offends basic concepts of the criminal justice system. Indiscriminate application of the exclusionary rule, therefore, may well "generat[e] disrespect for the law and the administration of justice." Accordingly, "[a]s with any remedial device, the application of the rule has been restricted to those areas where its remedial objectives are thought most efficaciously served."

Close attention to those remedial objectives has characterized our recent decisions concerning the scope of the Fourth Amendment exclusionary rule. The Court has, to be sure, not seriously questioned, "in the absence of a more efficacious sanction, the continued application of the rule to suppress evidence from the [prosecution's] case where a Fourth Amendment violation has been substantial and deliberate * * *." Nevertheless, the balancing approach that has evolved in various contexts—including criminal trials—"forcefully suggest[s] that the exclusionary rule be more generally modified to permit the introduction of evidence obtained in the reasonable good-faith belief that a search or seizure was in accord with the Fourth Amendment."

In *Stone v. Powell*, 428 U.S. 465, 96 S.Ct. 3037, 49 L.Ed.2d 1067 (1976), the Court emphasized the costs of the exclusionary rule, expressed its view that limiting the circumstances under which Fourth Amendment claims could be raised in federal habeas corpus proceedings would not reduce the rule's deterrent effect, and held that a state prisoner who has been afforded a full and fair opportunity to litigate a Fourth Amendment claim may not obtain federal habeas relief on the ground that unlawfully obtained evidence had been introduced at his trial. Proposed extensions of the exclusionary rule to proceedings other than the criminal trial itself have been evaluated and rejected under the same analytic approach. In *United States v. Calandra* [p. 146], for example, we declined to allow grand jury witnesses to refuse to answer questions based on evidence obtained from an unlawful search or seizure since "[a]ny incremental deterrent effect which might be achieved by extending the rule to grand jury proceedings is uncertain at best." Similarly, in *United States v. Janis* [p. 148], we permitted the use in federal civil proceedings of evidence illegally seized by state officials since the likelihood of deterring police misconduct through such an extension of the exclusionary rule was insufficient to outweigh its substantial social costs. * * *

[C]ases considering the use of unlawfully obtained evidence in criminal trials themselves [also] make clear [that] it does not follow from the emphasis on the exclusionary rule's deterrent value that "anything which deters illegal searches is thereby commanded by the Fourth Amendment." *Alderman v. United States* [p. 771]. In determining whether persons aggrieved solely by the introduction of damaging evidence unlawfully obtained from their co-conspirators or codefendants could seek suppression, for example, we found that the additional benefits of such

Thus, the cumulative loss due to nonprosecution or nonconviction of individuals arrested on felony drug charges is probably in the range of 2.8% to 7.1%. Davies' analysis of California data suggests that screening by police and prosecutors results in the release because of illegal searches or seizures of as many as 1.4% of all felony arrestees, id., at 650, that 0.9% of felony arrestees are released because of illegal searches or seizures at the preliminary hearing or after trial, *id.*, at 653, and that roughly 0.5% of all felony arrestees benefit from reversals on appeal because of illegal searches. * * *

Many of these researchers have concluded that the impact of the exclusionary rule is insubstantial, but the small percentages with which they deal mask a large absolute number of felons who are released because the cases against them were based in part on illegal searches or seizures. * * * Because we find that the rule can have no substantial deterrent effect in the sorts of situations under consideration in this case, we conclude that it cannot pay its way in those situations.

an extension of the exclusionary rule would not outweigh its costs. *Alderman.* Standing to invoke the rule has thus been limited to cases in which the prosecution seeks to use the fruits of an illegal search or seizure against the victim of police misconduct. *Rakas v. Illinois* [p. 776]. Even defendants with standing to challenge the introduction in their criminal trials of unlawfully obtained evidence cannot prevent every conceivable use of such evidence. Evidence obtained in violation of the Fourth Amendment and inadmissible in the prosecution's case in chief may be used to impeach a defendant's direct testimony. *Walder v. United States* [p. 811]. A similar assessment of the "incremental furthering" of the ends of the exclusionary rule led us to conclude in *United States v. Havens* [p. 814] that evidence inadmissible in the prosecution's case in chief or otherwise as substantive evidence of guilt may be used to impeach statements made by a defendant in response to "proper cross-examination reasonably suggested by the defendant's direct examination."

When considering the use of evidence obtained in violation of the Fourth Amendment in the prosecution's case in chief, moreover, we have declined to adopt a *per se* or "but for" rule that would render inadmissible any evidence that came to light through a chain of causation that began with an illegal arrest. *Brown v. Illinois* [p. 787]; *Wong Sun v. United States* [p. 786]. We also have held that a witness' testimony may be admitted even when his identity was discovered in an unconstitutional search. *United States v. Ceccolini* [p. 796]. The perception underlying these decisions—that the connection between police misconduct and evidence of crime may be sufficiently attenuated to permit the use of that evidence at trial—is a product of considerations relating to the exclusionary rule and the constitutional principles it is designed to protect. * * * Not surprisingly in view of this purpose, an assessment of the flagrancy of the police misconduct constitutes an important step in the calculus. *Brown v. Illinois,* supra.

The same attention to the purposes underlying the exclusionary rule also has characterized decisions not involving the scope of the rule itself. We have not required suppression of the fruits of a search incident to an arrest made in good-faith reliance on a substantive criminal statute that subsequently is declared unconstitutional. *Michigan v. DeFillippo* [p. 144]. Similarly, although the Court has been unwilling to conclude that new Fourth Amendment principles are always to have only prospective effect, *United States v. Johnson* [p. 47], * * * [t]he propriety of retroactive application of a newly announced Fourth Amendment principle * * * has been assessed largely in terms of the contribution retroactivity might make to the deterrence of police misconduct. *Johnson.*

As yet, we have not recognized any form of good-faith exception to the Fourth Amendment exclusionary rule. But the balancing approach that has evolved during the years of experience with the rule provides strong support for the modification currently urged upon us. As we discuss below, our evaluation of the costs and benefits of suppressing reliable physical evidence seized by officers reasonably relying on a warrant issued by a detached and neutral magistrate leads to the conclusion that such evidence should be admissible in the prosecution's case in chief. * * *

Only [when a warrant is grounded upon an affidavit knowingly or recklessly false] has the Court set forth a rationale for suppressing evidence obtained pursuant to a search warrant;[b] in the other areas, it has simply excluded such

---

b. The reference is to the *Franks* case, p. 203, where the Court declared "it would be an unthinkable imposition upon [the magistrate's] authority if a warrant affidavit, revealed after the fact to contain a deliberately or recklessly evidence without considering whether Fourth Amendment interests will be advanced. To the extent that proponents of exclusion rely on its behavioral effects on judges and magistrates in these areas, their reliance is misplaced. First, the exclusionary rule is designed to deter police misconduct rather than to punish the errors of judges and magistrates. Second, there exists no evidence suggesting that judges and magistrates are inclined to ignore or subvert the Fourth Amendment or that lawlessness among these actors requires application of the extreme sanction of exclusion.[14]

Third, and most important, we discern no basis, and are offered none, for believing that exclusion of evidence seized pursuant to a warrant will have a significant deterrent effect on the issuing judge or magistrate. Many of the factors that indicate that the exclusionary rule cannot provide an effective "special" or "general" deterrent for individual offending law enforcement officers apply as well to judges or magistrates. And, to the extent that the rule is thought to operate as a "systemic" deterrent on a wider audience, it clearly can have no such effect on individuals empowered to issue warrants. Judges and magistrates are not adjuncts to the law enforcement team; as neutral judicial officers, they have no stake in the outcome of particular criminal prosecutions. The threat of exclusion thus cannot be expected significantly to deter them. Imposition of the exclusionary sanction is not necessary meaningfully to inform judicial officers of their errors, and we cannot conclude that admitting evidence obtained pursuant to a warrant while at the same time declaring that the warrant was somehow defective will in any way reduce judicial officers' professional incentives to comply with the Fourth Amendment, encourage them to repeat their mistakes, or lead to the granting of all colorable warrant requests.[18]

If exclusion of evidence obtained pursuant to a subsequently invalidated warrant is to have any deterrent effect, therefore, it must alter the behavior of individual law enforcement officers or the policies of their departments. One could argue that applying the exclusionary rule in cases where the police failed to demonstrate probable cause in the warrant application deters future inadequate presentations or "magistrate shopping" and thus promotes the ends of the Fourth Amendment. Suppressing evidence obtained pursuant to a technically defective warrant supported by probable cause also might encourage officers to scrutinize more closely the form of the warrant and to point out suspected judicial errors. We find such arguments speculative and conclude that suppression of evidence obtained pursuant to a warrant should be ordered only on a case-by-case basis and only in those unusual cases in which exclusion will further the purposes of the exclusionary rule.[19]

false statement, were to stand beyond impeachment."

14. Although there are assertions that some magistrates become rubber stamps for the police and others may be unable effectively to screen police conduct, we are not convinced that this is a problem of major proportions.

18. Limiting the application of the exclusionary sanction may well increase the care with which magistrates scrutinize warrant applications. We doubt that magistrates are more desirous of avoiding the exclusion of evidence obtained pursuant to warrants they have issued than of avoiding invasions of privacy.

Federal magistrates, moreover, are subject to the direct supervision of district courts. They may be removed for "incompetency, misconduct, neglect of duty, or physical or mental disability." 28 U.S.C. § 631(i). If a magistrate serves merely as a "rubber stamp" for the police or is unable to exercise mature judgment, closer supervision or removal provides a more effective remedy than the exclusionary rule.

19. Our discussion of the deterrent effect of excluding evidence obtained in reasonable reliance on a subsequently invalidated warrant assumes, of course, that the officers properly executed the warrant and searched only those places and for those objects that it was reasonable to believe were covered by the warrant. * * *

We have frequently questioned whether the exclusionary rule can have any deterrent effect when the offending officers acted in the objectively reasonable belief that their conduct did not violate the Fourth Amendment. "No empirical researcher, proponent or opponent of the rule, has yet been able to establish with any assurance whether the rule has a deterrent effect * * *." But even assuming that the rule effectively deters some police misconduct and provides incentives for the law enforcement profession as a whole to conduct itself in accord with the Fourth Amendment, it cannot be expected, and should not be applied, to deter objectively reasonable law enforcement activity. * * *[20]

This is particularly true, we believe, when an officer acting with objective good faith has obtained a search warrant from a judge or magistrate and acted within its scope. In most such cases, there is no police illegality and thus nothing to deter. It is the magistrate's responsibility to determine whether the officer's allegations establish probable cause and, if so, to issue a warrant comporting in form with the requirements of the Fourth Amendment. In the ordinary case, an officer cannot be expected to question the magistrate's probable-cause determination or his judgment that the form of the warrant is technically sufficient. "[O]nce the warrant issues, there is literally nothing more the policeman can do in seeking to comply with the law." Penalizing the officer for the magistrate's error, rather than his own, cannot logically contribute to the deterrence of Fourth Amendment violations.[22]

We conclude that the marginal or nonexistent benefits produced by suppressing evidence obtained in objectively reasonable reliance on a subsequently invalidated search warrant cannot justify the substantial costs of exclusion. We do not suggest, however, that exclusion is always inappropriate in cases where an officer has obtained a warrant and abided by its terms. [T]he officer's reliance on the magistrate's probable-cause determination and on the technical sufficiency of the warrant he issues must be objectively reasonable,[23] and it is clear that in some

---

20. We emphasize that the standard of reasonableness we adopt is an objective one. Many objections to a good-faith exception assume that the exception will turn on the subjective good faith of individual officers. "Grounding the modification in objective reasonableness, however, retains the value of the exclusionary rule as an incentive for the law enforcement profession as a whole to conduct themselves in accord with the Fourth Amendment." The objective standard, moreover, we adopt requires officers to have a reasonable knowledge of what the law prohibits. As Professor Jerold Israel has observed:

"The key to the [exclusionary] rule's effectiveness as a deterrent lies, I believe, in the impetus it has provided to police training programs that make officers aware of the limits imposed by the fourth amendment and emphasize the need to operate within those limits. [An objective good-faith exception] * * * is not likely to result in the elimination of such programs, which are now viewed as an important aspect of police professionalism. Neither is it likely to alter the tenor of those programs; the possibility that illegally obtained evidence may be admitted in borderline cases is unlikely to encourage police instructors to pay less attention to fourth amendment limitations. Finally,

[it] * * * should not encourage officers to pay less attention to what they are taught, as the requirement that the officer act in 'good faith' is inconsistent with closing one's mind to the possibility of illegality."

22. * * * Our cases establish that the question whether the use of illegally obtained evidence in judicial proceedings represents judicial participation in a Fourth Amendment violation and offends the integrity of the courts "is essentially the same as the inquiry into whether exclusion would serve a deterrent purpose." * * * Absent unusual circumstances, when a Fourth Amendment violation has occurred because the police have reasonably relied on a warrant issued by a detached and neutral magistrate but ultimately found to be defective, "the integrity of the courts is not implicated."

23. [O]ur good-faith inquiry is confined to the objectively ascertainable question whether a reasonably well-trained officer would have known that the search was illegal despite the magistrate's authorization. In making this determination, all of the circumstances—including whether the warrant application had previously been rejected by a different magistrate—may be considered.

circumstances the officer[24] will have no reasonable grounds for believing that the warrant was properly issued.

Suppression therefore remains an appropriate remedy if the magistrate or judge in issuing a warrant was misled by information in an affidavit that the affiant knew was false or would have known was false except for his reckless disregard of the truth. The exception we recognize today will also not apply in cases where the issuing magistrate wholly abandoned his judicial role in the manner condemned in *Lo-Ji Sales, Inc. v. New York,* [p. 209][c], in such circumstances, no reasonably well-trained officer should rely on the warrant. Nor would an officer manifest objective good faith in relying on a warrant based on an affidavit "so lacking in indicia of probable cause as to render official belief in its existence entirely unreasonable." Finally, depending on the circumstances of the particular case, a warrant may be so facially deficient—i.e., in failing to particularize the place to be searched or the things to be seized—that the executing officers cannot reasonably presume it to be valid.

* * * The good-faith exception for searches conducted pursuant to warrants is not intended to signal our unwillingness strictly to enforce the requirements of the Fourth Amendment, and we do not believe that it will have this effect. As we have already suggested, the good-faith exception, turning as it does on objective reasonableness, should not be difficult to apply in practice. When officers have acted pursuant to a warrant, the prosecution should ordinarily be able to establish objective good faith without a substantial expenditure of judicial time.

Nor are we persuaded that application of a good-faith exception to searches conducted pursuant to warrants will preclude review of the constitutionality of the search or seizure, deny needed guidance from the courts, or freeze Fourth Amendment law in its present state.[25] There is no need for courts to adopt the inflexible practice of always deciding whether the officers' conduct manifested objective good faith before turning to the question whether the Fourth Amendment has been violated. Defendants seeking suppression of the fruits of allegedly unconstitutional searches or seizures undoubtedly raise live controversies which Article III empowers federal courts to adjudicate. * * *

If the resolution of a particular Fourth Amendment question is necessary to guide future action by law enforcement officers and magistrates, nothing will prevent reviewing courts from deciding that question before turning to the good-faith issue.[26] Indeed, it frequently will be difficult to determine whether the

24. References to "officer" throughout this opinion should not be read too narrowly. It is necessary to consider the objective reasonableness, not only of the officers who eventually executed a warrant, but also of the officers who originally obtained it or who provided information material to the probable-cause determination. Nothing in our opinion suggests, for example, that an officer could obtain a warrant on the basis of a "bare bones" affidavit and then rely on colleagues who are ignorant of the circumstances under which the warrant was obtained to conduct the search.

c. There the magistrate was held not to have "manifest[ed] that neutrality and detachment demanded of a judicial officer when presented with a warrant application," where he went to the scene and made judgments there about what should be seized as obscene, as he

"allowed himself to become a member, if not the leader of the search party which was essentially a police operation."

25. The argument that defendants will lose their incentive to litigate meritorious Fourth Amendment claims as a result of the good-faith exception we adopt today is unpersuasive. Although the exception might discourage presentation of insubstantial suppression motions, the magnitude of the benefit conferred on defendants by a successful motion makes it unlikely that litigation of colorable claims will be substantially diminished.

26. It has been suggested, in fact, that "the recognition of a 'penumbral zone,' within which an inadvertent mistake would not call for exclusion, * * * will make it less tempting for judges to bend fourth amendment stan-officers acted reasonably without resolving the Fourth Amendment issue. Even if the Fourth Amendment question is not one of broad import, reviewing courts could decide in particular cases that magistrates under their supervision need to be informed of their errors and so evaluate the officers' good faith only after finding a violation. In other circumstances, those courts could reject suppression motions posing no important Fourth Amendment questions by turning immediately to a consideration of the officers' good faith. We have no reason to believe that our Fourth Amendment jurisprudence would suffer by allowing reviewing courts to exercise an informed discretion in making this choice. * * *

In the absence of an allegation that the magistrate abandoned his detached and neutral role, suppression is appropriate only if the officers were dishonest or reckless in preparing their affidavit or could not have harbored an objectively reasonable belief in the existence of probable cause. Only respondent Leon has contended that no reasonably well-trained police officer could have believed that there existed probable cause to search his house; significantly, the other respondents advance no comparable argument. Officer Rombach's application for a warrant clearly was supported by much more than a "bare bones" affidavit. The affidavit related the results of an extensive investigation and, as the opinions of the divided panel of the Court of Appeals make clear, provided evidence sufficient to create disagreement among thoughtful and competent judges as to the existence of probable cause. Under these circumstances, the officers' reliance on the magistrate's determination of probable cause was objectively reasonable, and application of the extreme sanction of exclusion is inappropriate.

Accordingly, the judgment of the Court of Appeals is *reversed.*

Justice BLACKMUN, concurring. * * *

What must be stressed * * * is that any empirical judgment about the effect of the exclusionary rule in a particular class of cases necessarily is a provisional one. * * * If it should emerge from experience that, contrary to our expectations, the good faith exception to the exclusionary rule results in a material change in police compliance with the Fourth Amendment, we shall have to reconsider what we have undertaken here. The logic of a decision that rests on untested predictions about police conduct demands no less. * * *

Justice BRENNAN, with whom Justice MARSHALL joins, dissenting. * * *

[The majority's reading of the Fourth Amendment] appears plausible, because, as critics of the exclusionary rule never tire of repeating, the Fourth Amendment makes no express provision for the exclusion of evidence secured in violation of its commands. A short answer to this claim, of course, is that many of the Constitution's most vital imperatives are stated in general terms and the task of giving meaning to these precepts is therefore left to subsequent judicial decision-making in the context of concrete cases. * * *

* * * Because seizures are executed principally to secure evidence, and because such evidence generally has utility in our legal system only in the context of a trial supervised by a judge, it is apparent that the admission of illegally obtained evidence implicates the same constitutional concerns as the initial seizure of that evidence. Indeed, by admitting unlawfully seized evidence, the judiciary becomes a part of what is in fact a single governmental action prohibited by the terms of the Amendment. Once that connection between the evidence-gathering role of the police and the evidence-admitting function of the courts is acknowledged, the plausibility of the Court's interpretation becomes more suspect.

dards to avoid releasing a possibly dangerous criminal because of a minor and unintentional miscalculation by the police."

Certainly nothing in the language or history of the Fourth Amendment suggests that a recognition of this evidentiary link between the police and the courts was meant to be foreclosed. It is difficult to give any meaning at all to the limitations imposed by the Amendment if they are read to proscribe only certain conduct by the police but to allow other agents of the same government to take advantage of evidence secured by the police in violation of its requirements. The Amendment therefore must be read to condemn not only the initial unconstitutional invasion of privacy—which is done, after all, for the purpose of securing evidence—but also the subsequent use of any evidence so obtained. * * *

[T]he question whether the exclusion of evidence would deter future police misconduct was never considered a relevant concern in the early cases from *Weeks* to *Olmstead*. In those formative decisions, the Court plainly understood that the exclusion of illegally obtained evidence was compelled not by judicially fashioned remedial purposes, but rather by a direct constitutional command. * * *

* * * Indeed, no other explanation suffices to account for the Court's holding in *Mapp*, since the only possible predicate for the Court's conclusion that the States were bound by the Fourteenth Amendment to honor the *Weeks* doctrine is that the exclusionary rule was "part and parcel of the Fourth Amendment's limitation upon [governmental] encroachment of individual privacy."

Despite this clear pronouncement, however, the Court * * * has gradually pressed the deterrence rationale for the rule back to center stage. The various arguments advanced by the Court in this campaign have only strengthened my conviction that the deterrence theory is both misguided and unworkable. First, the Court has frequently bewailed the "cost" of excluding reliable evidence. In large part, this criticism rests upon a refusal to acknowledge the function of the Fourth Amendment itself. If nothing else, the Amendment plainly operates to disable the government from gathering information and securing evidence in certain ways. In practical terms, of course, this restriction of official power means that some incriminating evidence inevitably will go undetected if the government obeys these constitutional restraints. It is the loss of that evidence that is the "price" our society pays for enjoying the freedom and privacy safeguarded by the Fourth Amendment. Thus, some criminals will go free *not*, in Justice (then Judge) Cardozo's misleading epigram, "because the constable has blundered," but rather because official compliance with Fourth Amendment requirements makes it more difficult to catch criminals. Understood in this way, the Amendment directly contemplates that some reliable and incriminating evidence will be lost to the government; therefore, it is not the exclusionary rule, but the Amendment itself that has imposed this cost.

In addition, the Court's decisions over the past decade have made plain that the entire enterprise of attempting to assess the benefits and costs of the exclusionary rule in various contexts is a virtually impossible task for the judiciary to perform honestly or accurately. Although the Court's language in those cases suggests that some specific empirical basis may support its analyses, the reality is that the Court's opinions represent inherently unstable compounds of intuition, hunches, and occasional pieces of partial and often inconclusive data. * * * To the extent empirical data is available regarding the general costs and benefits of the exclusionary rule, it has shown, on the one hand, as the Court acknowledges today, that the costs are not as substantial as critics have asserted in the past, and, on the other hand, that while the exclusionary rule may well have certain deterrent effects, it is extremely difficult to determine with any degree of precision whether the incidence of unlawful conduct by police is now lower than it was prior to *Mapp.* The Court has sought to turn this uncertainty to its advantage by casting the burden of proof upon proponents of the rule. "Obviously," however, "the assignment of the burden of proof on an issue where evidence does not exist and cannot be obtained is outcome determinative. [The] assignment of the burden is merely a way of announcing a predetermined conclusion."

By remaining within its redoubt of empiricism and by basing the rule solely on the deterrence rationale, the Court has robbed the rule of legitimacy. A doctrine that is explained as if it were an empirical proposition but for which there is only limited empirical support is both inherently unstable and an easy mark for critics. The extent of this Court's fidelity to Fourth Amendment requirements, however, should not turn on such statistical uncertainties. * * *

Even if I were to accept the Court's general approach to the exclusionary rule, I could not agree with today's result. * * *

At the outset, the Court suggests that society has been asked to pay a high price—in terms either of setting guilty persons free or of impeding the proper functioning of trials—as a result of excluding relevant physical evidence in cases where the police, in conducting searches and seizing evidence, have made only an "objectively reasonable" mistake concerning the constitutionality of their actions. But what evidence is there to support such a claim?

Significantly, the Court points to none, and, indeed, as the Court acknowledges, recent studies have demonstrated that the "costs" of the exclusionary rule—calculated in terms of dropped prosecutions and lost convictions—are quite low. Contrary to the claims of the rule's critics that exclusion leads to "the release of countless guilty criminals," these studies have demonstrated that federal and state prosecutors very rarely drop cases because of potential search and seizure problems. For example, a 1979 study prepared at the request of Congress by the General Accounting Office reported that only 0.4% of all cases actually declined for prosecution by federal prosecutors were declined primarily because of illegal search problems. If the GAO data are restated as a percentage of *all* arrests, the study shows that only 0.2% of all felony arrests are declined for prosecution because of potential exclusionary rule problems.[11] Of course, these data describe only the costs attributable to the exclusion of evidence in all cases; the costs due to the exclusion of evidence in the narrower category of cases where police have made objectively reasonable mistakes must necessarily be even smaller. The Court, however, ignores this distinction and mistakenly weighs the aggregated

---

11. In a series of recent studies, researchers have attempted to quantify the actual costs of the rule. A recent National Institute of Justice study based on data for the four year period 1976–1979 gathered by the California Bureau of Criminal Statistics showed that 4.8% of all cases that were declined for prosecution by California prosecutors were rejected because of illegally seized evidence. However, if these data are calculated as a percentage of all arrests that were declined for prosecution, they show that only 0.8% of all arrests were rejected for prosecution because of illegally seized evidence.

In another measure of the rule's impact—the number of prosecutions that are dismissed or result in acquittals in cases where evidence has been excluded—the available data again show that the Court's past assessment of the rule's costs has generally been exaggerated. For example, a study based on data from 9 mid-sized counties in Illinois, Michigan and Pennsylvania reveals that motions to suppress physical evidence were filed in approximately 5% of the 7,500 cases studied, but that such motions were successful in only 0.7% of all these cases. The study also shows that only 0.6% of all cases resulted in acquittals because evidence had been excluded. In the GAO study, suppression motions were filed in 10.5% of all federal criminal cases surveyed, but of the motions filed, approximately 80–90% were denied. Evidence was actually excluded in only 1.3% of the cases studied, and only 0.7% of all cases resulted in acquittals or dismissals after evidence was excluded. And in another study based on data from cases during 1978 and 1979 in San Diego and Jacksonville, it was shown that only 1% of all cases resulting in nonconviction were caused by illegal searches.

costs of exclusion in *all* cases, irrespective of the circumstances that led to exclusion, against the potential benefits associated with only those cases in which evidence is excluded because police reasonably but mistakenly believe that their conduct does not violate the Fourth Amendment. When such faulty scales are used, it is little wonder that the balance tips in favor of restricting the application of the rule.

What then supports the Court's insistence that this evidence be admitted? Apparently, the Court's only answer is that even though the costs of exclusion are not very substantial, the potential deterrent effect in these circumstances is so marginal that exclusion cannot be justified. The key to the Court's conclusion in this respect is its belief that the prospective deterrent effect of the exclusionary rule operates only in those situations in which police officers, when deciding whether to go forward with some particular search, have reason to know that their planned conduct will violate the requirements of the Fourth Amendment.

* * * But what the Court overlooks is that the deterrence rationale for the rule is not designed to be, nor should it be thought of as, a form of "punishment" of individual police officers for their failures to obey the restraints imposed by the Fourth Amendment. Instead, the chief deterrent function of the rule is its tendency to promote institutional compliance with Fourth Amendment requirements on the part of law enforcement agencies generally. Thus, as the Court has previously recognized, "over the long term, [the] demonstration [provided by the exclusionary rule] that our society attaches serious consequences to violation of constitutional rights is thought to encourage those who formulate law enforcement policies, and the officers who implement them, to incorporate Fourth Amendment ideals into their value system." It is only through such an institution-wide mechanism that information concerning Fourth Amendment standards can be effectively communicated to rank and file officers.[13]

If the overall educational effect of the exclusionary rule is considered, application of the rule to even those situations in which individual police officers have acted on the basis of a reasonable but mistaken belief that their conduct was authorized can still be expected to have a considerable long-term deterrent effect. If evidence is consistently excluded in these circumstances, police departments will surely be prompted to instruct their officers to devote greater care and attention to providing sufficient information to establish probable cause when applying for a warrant, and to review with some attention the form of the warrant that they have been issued, rather than automatically assuming that whatever document the magistrate has signed will necessarily comport with Fourth Amendment requirements.

After today's decision, however, that institutional incentive will be lost. Indeed, the Court's "reasonable mistake" exception to the exclusionary rule will tend to put a premium on police ignorance of the law. Armed with the assurance provided by today's decision that evidence will always be admissible whenever an officer has "reasonably" relied upon a warrant, police departments will be encouraged to train officers that if a warrant has simply been signed, it is reasonable, without more, to rely on it. Since in close cases there will no longer be any incentive to err on the side of constitutional behavior, police would have every

---

13. * * * A former United States Attorney and now Attorney General of Maryland, Stephen Sachs, has described the impact of the rule on police practices in similar terms: "I have watched the rule deter, routinely, throughout my years as a prosecutor * * *. [P]olice-prosecutor consultation is customary in all our cases when Fourth Amendment concerns arise * * *. In at least three Maryland jurisdictions, for example, prosecutors are on twenty-four hour call to field search and seizure questions presented by police officers."

reason to adopt a "let's-wait-until-its-decided" approach in situations in which there is a question about a warrant's validity or the basis for its issuance.[14]

Although the Court brushes these concerns aside, a host of grave consequences can be expected to result from its decision to carve this new exception out of the exclusionary rule. A chief consequence of today's decision will be to convey a clear and unambiguous message to magistrates that their decisions to issue warrants are now insulated from subsequent judicial review. Creation of this new exception for good faith reliance upon a warrant implicitly tells magistrates that they need not take much care in reviewing warrant applications, since their mistakes will from now on have virtually no consequence: If their decision to issue a warrant was correct, the evidence will be admitted; if their decision was incorrect but the police relied in good faith on the warrant, the evidence will also be admitted. Inevitably, the care and attention devoted to such an inconsequential chore will dwindle. Although the Court is correct to note that magistrates do not share the same stake in the outcome of a criminal case as the police, they nevertheless need to appreciate that their role is of some moment in order to continue performing the important task of carefully reviewing warrant applications. Today's decision effectively removes that incentive.

Moreover, the good faith exception will encourage police to provide only the bare minimum of information in future warrant applications. The police will now know that if they can secure a warrant, so long as the circumstances of its issuance are not "entirely unreasonable," all police conduct pursuant to that warrant will be protected from further judicial review. The clear incentive that operated in the past to establish probable cause adequately because reviewing courts would examine the magistrate's judgment carefully, has now been so completely vitiated that the police need only show that it was not "entirely unreasonable" under the circumstances of a particular case for them to believe that the warrant they were issued was valid. The long-run effect unquestionably will be to undermine the integrity of the warrant process.

Finally, even if one were to believe, as the Court apparently does, that police are hobbled by inflexible and hypertechnical warrant procedures, today's decision cannot be justified. This is because, given the relaxed standard for assessing probable cause established just last Term in *Illinois v. Gates*, the Court's newly fashioned good faith exception, when applied in the warrant context, will rarely, if ever, offer any greater flexibility for police than the *Gates* standard already supplies. In *Gates*, the Court held that "the task of an issuing magistrate is simply to make a practical, common-sense decision whether, given all the circumstances set forth in the affidavit before him, * * * there is a fair probability that contraband or evidence of a crime will be found in a particular place." The task of a reviewing court is confined to determining whether "the magistrate had a 'substantial basis' for concluding that probable cause existed." Given such a relaxed standard, it is virtually inconceivable that a reviewing court, when faced with a defendant's motion to suppress, could first find that a warrant was invalid under the new *Gates* standard, but then, at the same time, find that a police officer's reliance on such an invalid warrant was nevertheless "objectively reasonable" under the test announced today. * * *

Justice STEVENS, * * * dissenting * * *.

---

14. The authors of a recent study of the warrant process in seven cities concluded that application of a good faith exception where an officer relies upon a warrant "would further encourage police officers to seek out the less inquisitive magistrates and to rely on boiler-plate formulae, thereby lessening the value of search warrants overall. * * *

* * * It is probable, though admittedly not certain, that the Court of Appeals would now conclude that the warrant in *Leon* satisfied the Fourth Amendment if it were given the opportunity to reconsider the issue in the light of *Gates*. Adherence to our normal practice following the announcement of a new rule would therefore postpone, and probably obviate, the need for the promulgation of the broad new rule the Court announces today.

[W]hen the Court goes beyond what is necessary to decide the case before it, it can only encourage the perception that it is pursuing its own notions of wise social policy, rather than adhering to its judicial role. I do not believe the Court should reach out to decide what is undoubtedly a profound question concerning the administration of criminal justice before assuring itself that this question is actually and of necessity presented by the concrete facts before the Court. * * *[d]

Notes and Questions

1. Must (should) the Fourth Amendment be read, as dissenting Justice Brennan maintains, "to condemn not only the initial unconstitutional invasion of privacy" but "also the subsequent use of any evidence so obtained"? Consider Arnold H. Loewy, *Police-Obtained Evidence and the Constitution: Distinguishing Unconstitutionally Obtained Evidence from Unconstitutionally Used Evidence*, 87 Mich.L.Rev. 907, 909–11, 939 (1989):

"[F]reedom from unreasonable searches and seizures is a substantive protection available to all inhabitants of the United States, whether or not charged with crime. The right thus differs from protections under most of the fifth amendment and all of the sixth amendment, which refers to persons charged with crime or the 'accused.' * * * [Because] the fourth amendment, in language and origin, is clearly substantive [the] Court was correct in holding the exclusionary rule to be simply a remedial device designed to make the substantive right more meaningful, rather than an independent procedural right.

" * * * Procedural rights are supposed to exclude evidence. Substantive rights need not. Consequently, fourth amendment rights should be deemed different from, but not less important than, the procedural rights protected by the fifth, sixth and fourteenth amendments. By way of comparison, first and third amendment rights are substantive, but nobody would deem them second class. * * *

"Whether evidence is unconstitutionally obtained or unconstitutionally used makes a difference. If the only constitutional wrong inheres in using the evidence, the Court has no business considering concepts of deterrence. The Court should prohibit use of such evidence. Conversely, when obtaining evidence is the constitutional wrong, exclusion should be subjected to a cost/benefit analysis."

2. Which of the Supreme Court's express or implicit assumptions in *Mapp* and *Leon* regarding the behavior of police and judges are correct? Consider Myron W. Orfield, *Deterrence, Perjury, and the Heater Factor: An Exclusionary Rule in the Chicago Criminal Courts*, 63 U.Colo.L.Rev. 75, 82–83 (1992), summarizing the views of interviewed actors in the Chicago criminal justice system:

d. For commentary on *Leon* and related cases, see Craig M. Bradley, *The "Good Faith" Exception Cases: Reasonable Exercises in Futility*, 60 Ind.L.J. 287 (1985); Craig D. Uchida, Timothy S. Bynum, Dennis Rogan & Donna Murasky, *Acting in Good Faith: the Effects of United States v. Leon on the Police and Courts*, 30 Ariz.L.Rev. 467 (1988); and the spirited debate in Donald A. Dripps, *Living with Leon*, 95 Yale L.J. 906 (1986); Steven B. Duke, *Making Leon Worse*, 95 Yale L.J. 1405 (1986); and Donald A. Dripps, *More on Search Warrants, Good Faith and Probable Cause*, 95 Yale L.J. 1424 (1986).

"Respondents in the Courts Study[e] report the same perceptions of the deterrent effect of the rule as the officers in the Police Study.[f] First, respondents uniformly believe that officers care about convictions and experience adverse personal reactions when they lose evidence. Respondents report that police change their behavior in response to the suppression of evidence. They also believe that suppression effectively educates officers in the law of search and seizure and that the law is not too complicated for police officers to do their jobs effectively.

"The Courts Study respondents believe even more strongly than the Police Study respondents that the exclusionary rule's deterrent effect is greater when officers are working on big or important cases. They also believe the exclusionary rule has a greater deterrent effect on officers in specialized units like the Narcotics Section.

"Respondents also stated that the exclusionary rule fosters a closer working relationship between prosecutors and police. They note that prosecutors help police officers conduct proper searches and understand why evidence is suppressed. * * *

"Significantly, the Courts respondents outlined a pattern of pervasive police perjury intended to avoid the requirements of the Fourth Amendment. Dishonesty occurs in both the investigative process and the courtroom. The respondents report systematic fabrications in case reports and affidavits for search warrants, creating artificial probable cause which forms the basis of later testimony. Moreover, police keep dual sets of investigatory files; official files and 'street files.' Exculpatory material in the street files may be edited from the official record. Respondents, including prosecutors, estimate that police commit perjury between 20 and 50% of the time they testify on Fourth Amendment issues. This perjury may be tolerated, or even encouraged, by prosecutors at each step in the process in both direct and indirect ways.

"The Courts respondents, including judges, also believe that judges may purposefully ignore the law to prevent evidence from being suppressed, and even more often, knowingly accept police perjury as truthful. When the crime is serious, this judicial 'cheating' is more likely to occur due to three primary reasons; first, the judge's sense that it is unjust to suppress the evidence under the circumstances of a particular case, second, the judge's fear of adverse publicity, and third, the fear that the suppression will hurt their chances in judicial elections. In addition, serious cases in Chicago are diverted to judges who are more likely to convict the defendant.

"However, even in the face of persistent police perjury and judicial abdication of function, the Courts respondents, like the police respondents, believe that the exclusionary rule, although imperfect and often avoided, clearly leads to increased police professionalism and greater observance of the law of the Fourth Amendment. They do not believe that the rule causes significant harm to police work. Although the Courts respondents acknowledge that the rule can sometimes be unjust to crime victims, they believe that the rule's benefits to society equal or exceed its costs. Respondents report that there is no more effective remedy for Fourth Amendment violations, and that a tort remedy would be less effective. Finally, they believe the rule should be retained."

e. 14 public defenders, 14 prosecutors and 13 judges, all assigned to the felony trial courtrooms in the Criminal Division of the Circuit Court of Cook County.

f. 26 police officers in the Narcotics Section of the Organized Crime Division, Chicago Police Department.

3. Consider the proposal in Abraham S. Goldstein, *The Search Warrant, the Magistrate, and Judicial Review,* 62 N.Y.U.L.Rev. 1173, 1207, 1209–10 (1987), that *Leon* be interpreted as requiring resort to "a process-oriented standard" whereby if the reviewing judge finds "that the warrant hearing was too summary because the magistrate did not go behind the allegations contained in the police affidavit, either for lack of time or for lack of inclination," then the reviewing "judge should look into the issue of probable cause himself, and scrutinize more closely than usual the question whether reliance on the warrant was in good faith. On the other hand, he may find that the magistrate's hearing was not summary— that the magistrate probed the assertions in the affidavit, asked for additional evidence, and called witnesses when necessary. In that case, the magistrate's decision to issue a warrant deserves reliance from the police and deference from the court. The judge would then play an appellate role, reviewing the record before the magistrate simply to assure that the warrant decision meets the standard laid down in *Leon.*"

4. Does (should) *Leon* mean that "when the Court speaks of the good faith of the police, it is talking about their good faith *before going* to the magistrate and not about their good faith *after* they have received the warrant"? Craig M. Bradley, p. 140, fn. d, at 297. Consider *Malley v. Briggs,* p. 153, which the majority explained involved application of "the same standard of objective reasonableness that we applied in the context of a suppression hearing in *Leon.*"

5. Will (should) *Leon* be extended to warrantless arrests and searches? In *Lopez-Mendoza,* p. 149, involving a warrantless arrest, White, J., dissenting, asserted *Leon* was applicable, so that "if the agents neither knew nor should have known that they were acting contrary to the dictates of the Fourth Amendment, evidence will not be suppressed even if it is held that their conduct was illegal." If that is wrong, then does it follow, as concluded in *United States v. O'Neal,* 17 F.3d 239 (8th Cir.1994), that *Leon* cannot save a search warrant where it now appears that some of the facts essential to the probable cause showing in the affidavit were acquired in a prior illegal warrantless search?

6. In the companion case of MASSACHUSETTS v. SHEPPARD, 468 U.S. 981, 104 S.Ct. 3424, 82 L.Ed.2d 737 (1984), a detective prepared an affidavit for a search warrant to search for various specified items of evidence of a homicide but, because it was Sunday, could only find a warrant form for controlled substances. He presented his affidavit and that form to a judge at his home and pointed out the problem to him, and the judge, unable to locate a more suitable form, told the detective that he would make the necessary changes to make it a proper warrant. He made some changes, but failed to change that part of the warrant which authorized a search only for controlled substances and related paraphernalia. The detective took the two documents and he and other officers then executed the warrant, seizing evidence of the homicide. That evidence was suppressed in the state court because the warrant failed to particularly describe the items to be seized, as required by the Fourth Amendment. The Supreme Court, per WHITE, J., held this situation fell within *Leon* because "there was an objectively reasonable basis for the officers' mistaken belief" that "the warrant authorized the search that they conducted." As for defendant's objection that the detective knew when he went to the judge that the warrant was defective, the Court stated: "Whatever an officer may be required to do when he executes a warrant without knowing beforehand what items are to be seized,[6] we refuse to rule that an officer

6. Normally, when an officer who has not been involved in the application stage receives a warrant, he will read it in order to determine the object of the search. In this case, Detective is required to disbelieve a judge who has just advised him, by word and by action, that the warrant he possesses authorizes him to conduct the search he has requested."[g]

What if the detective who obtained the warrant had simply turned it over to another officer for execution and that officer, after a careful reading of the warrant, had made a search for and found drugs within an envelope, a place he would not have been entitled to look had he been aware that the warrant should have described certain larger items which could not be concealed in the envelope?

7.   What result under *Leon* and *Sheppard* on the following facts, essentially those in *People v. Deitchman,* 695 P.2d 1146 (Colo.1985)? Four teenage girls were sexually assaulted in the same area over a 10–day span, and they gave a similar general description of their assailant. One said he wore distinctively marked shoes; one said he had a red bandana; and two said his car license was CN–4714. Those facts were put into a search warrant affidavit, along with a statement that investigation "revealed that CN–4714 lists to Jerry M. Deitchman of 1755 South Pecos Street." The affidavit asserted, without explanation, that there was "reason to believe" that the shoes and bandana were at 3300 West Ohio Avenue; the magistrate issued a warrant to search that location for the shoes and bandana, which were found there in execution of the warrant. Police had earlier been unable to locate Deitchman until his employer said he had moved to 3300 West Ohio, and police arrested him there prior to obtaining the warrant, but those facts were not reported to the magistrate.

8.   Are there other "limitations" which might well be imposed upon the exclusionary rule? Consider the two proposals made in John Kaplan, *The Limits of the Exclusionary Rule,* 26 Stan.L.Rev. 1027 (1974). One is that "the rule not apply in the most serious cases—treason, espionage, murder, armed robbery, and kidnapping by organized groups," where exclusion would occur only under the *Rochin* [p. 40] test. In support, it is said that "the political costs of the rule, the possibility of releasing serious and dangerous offenders into the community, and the disproportion between the magnitude of the policeman's constitutional violation and the crime in which the evidence is to be suppressed are sufficient reasons to modify the rule."

The second proposal is "to hold the exclusionary rule inapplicable to cases where the police department in question has taken seriously its responsibility to adhere to the fourth amendment. Specifically, departmental compliance would require a set of published regulations giving guidance to police officers as to proper behavior in situations such as the one under litigation, a training program calculated to make violations of the fourth amendment rights isolated occurrences,

O'Malley, the officer who directed the search, knew what items were listed in the affidavit presented to the judge, and he had good reason to believe that the warrant authorized the seizure of those items. Whether an officer who is less familiar with the warrant application or who has unalleviated concerns about the proper scope of the search would be justified in failing to notice a defect like the one in the warrant in this case is an issue we need not decide. We hold only that it was not unreasonable for the police in this case to rely on the judge's assurances that the warrant authorized the search they had requested.

g. Brennan and Marshall, JJ., dissented for the same reasons as in *Leon*. Stevens, J., concurring, argued there had been no Fourth Amendment violation because the particularity requirement was intended to prohibit general searches, which had been accomplished here because "the judge who issued the warrant, the police officers who executed it, and the reviewing courts all were able easily to ascertain the precise scope of the authorization provided by the warrant."

and, perhaps most importantly, a history of taking disciplinary action where such violations are brought to its attention.''[h]

9. Should the Court instead abolish the exclusionary rule entirely on the ground that the deterrence function stressed in *Leon* is more generally not served by exclusion? Consider Burger, C.J., dissenting in *Bivens v. Six Unknown Named Agents,* p. 154, asserting a lack of deterrent efficacy because: (i) "The rule does not apply any direct sanction to the individual official whose illegal conduct results in the exclusion of evidence in a criminal trial." (ii) Police "have no * * * stake in successful prosecutions," and "the prosecutor who loses his case because of police misconduct is not an official in the police department; he can rarely set in motion any corrective action or administrative penalties." (iii) "Policemen do not have the time, inclination, or training to read and grasp the nuances of the appellate opinions that ultimately define the standards of conduct they are to follow." (iv) "[T]here are large areas of police activity which do not result in criminal prosecutions—hence the rule has virtually no applicability and no effect in such situations." Would such abolition be more palatable if, as the Chief Justice also suggested in *Bivens,* Congress were to "develop an administrative or quasi-judicial remedy against the government itself to afford compensation and restitution for persons whose Fourth Amendment rights have been violated"? Consider also Richard A. Posner, *Excessive Sanctions for Governmental Misconduct in Criminal Cases,* 57 Wash.L.Rev. 635 (1982), applying an economic analysis to the problem and concluding it should suffice if the government were required to compensate the victim of an illegal search for his "cleanup costs."

10. In *Michigan v. DeFillippo,* 443 U.S. 31, 99 S.Ct. 2627, 61 L.Ed.2d 343 (1979), the Court reaffirmed its earlier holdings "that the exclusionary rule required suppression of evidence obtained in searches carried out pursuant to statutes" subsequently held unconstitutional when the statutes, "by their own terms, authorized searches under circumstances which did not satisfy the traditional warrant and probable cause requirements of the Fourth Amendment." But after *Leon* the Court concluded otherwise in the 5–4 decision in ILLINOIS v. KRULL, 480 U.S. 340, 107 S.Ct. 1160, 94 L.Ed.2d 364 (1987), concerning an unconstitutional search made pursuant to a statute authorizing warrantless inspection of the records of licensed motor vehicle and vehicular parts sellers. The Court, per BLACKMUN, J., reasoned:

"The approach used in *Leon* is equally applicable to the present case. The application of the exclusionary rule to suppress evidence obtained by an officer acting in objectively reasonable reliance on a statute would have as little deterrent effect on the officer's actions as would the exclusion of evidence when an officer acts in objectively reasonable reliance on a warrant. Unless a statute is clearly unconstitutional, an officer cannot be expected to question the judgment of the legislature that passed the law. * * *

"Any difference between our holding in *Leon* and our holding in the instant case, therefore, must rest on a difference between the effect of the exclusion of evidence on judicial officers and the effect of the exclusion of evidence on legislators. Although these two groups clearly serve different functions in the

h. For strong criticism of Professor Kaplan's proposal that the exclusionary rule not apply in the most serious cases and of a similar proposal by James D. Cameron & Richard Lustiger, *The Exclusionary Rule: A Cost–Benefit Analysis,* 101 F.R.D. 109 (1984) that the rule apply neither in the most serious cases nor in any case where the reprehensibility of the defendant's crime is greater than the gravity of the officer's illegality, see Yale Kamisar, *"Comparative Reprehensibility" and the Fourth Amendment Exclusionary Rule,* 86 Mich.L.Rev. 1 (1987).

criminal justice system, those differences are not controlling for purposes of this case. We noted in *Leon* as an initial matter that the exclusionary rule was aimed at deterring police misconduct. Thus, legislators, like judicial officers, are not the focus of the rule. Moreover, to the extent we consider the rule's effect on legislators, our initial inquiry, as set out in *Leon,* is whether there is evidence to suggest that legislators 'are inclined to ignore or subvert the Fourth Amendment.' * * *

"There is no evidence suggesting that Congress or state legislatures have enacted a significant number of statutes permitting warrantless administrative searches violative of the Fourth Amendment. * * * Thus, we are given no basis for believing that legislators are inclined to subvert their oaths and the Fourth Amendment and that 'lawlessness among these actors requires application of the extreme sanction of exclusion.' *United States v. Leon.*

"Even if we were to conclude that legislators are different in certain relevant respects from magistrates, because legislators are not officers of the judicial system, the next inquiry necessitated by *Leon* is whether exclusion of evidence seized pursuant to a statute subsequently declared unconstitutional will 'have a significant deterrent effect' on legislators enacting such statutes. Respondents have offered us no reason to believe that applying the exclusionary rule will have such an effect. Legislators enact statutes for broad, programmatic purposes, not for the purpose of procuring evidence in particular criminal investigations. Thus, it is logical to assume that the greatest deterrent to the enactment of unconstitutional statutes by a legislature is the power of the courts to invalidate such statutes. Invalidating a statute informs the legislature of its constitutional error, affects the admissibility of all evidence obtained subsequent to the constitutional ruling, and often results in the legislature's enacting a modified and constitutional version of the statute, as happened in this very case. There is nothing to indicate that applying the exclusionary rule to evidence seized pursuant to the statute prior to the declaration of its invalidity will act as a significant, additional deterrent."

O'CONNOR, J., for the dissenters, emphasized: (1) "[B]oth the history of the Fourth Amendment and this Court's later interpretations of it, support application of the exclusionary rule to evidence gathered under the 20th century equivalent of the act authorizing the writ of assistance." (2) "The distinction drawn between the legislator and the judicial officer is sound" because "a legislature's unreasonable authorization of searches may affect thousands or millions" and thus "poses a greater threat to liberty." (3) "[L]egislators by virtue of their political role are more often subjected to the political pressures that may threaten Fourth Amendment values than are judicial officers." (4) "Providing legislatures a grace period during which the police may freely perform unreasonable searches in order to convict those who might have otherwise escaped creates a positive incentive to promulgate unconstitutional laws." (5) "The scope of the Court's good-faith exception is unclear," as "it is not apparent how much constitutional law the reasonable officer is expected to know. In contrast, *Leon* simply instructs courts that police officers may rely upon a facially valid search warrant. Each case is a fact-specific self-terminating episode. Courts need not inquire into the officer's probable understanding of the state of the law except in the extreme instance of a search warrant upon which no reasonable officer would rely. Under the decision today, however, courts are expected to determine at what point a reasonable officer should be held to know that a statute has, under evolving legal rules, become 'clearly' unconstitutional."

11. Should the fruits of constitutional but yet illegal arrests and searches be excluded? Reconsider fn. b, p. 122, and consider UNITED STATES v. CACERES, 440 U.S. 741, 99 S.Ct. 1465, 59 L.Ed.2d 733 (1979), holding that the failure of an IRS agent to follow IRS electronic surveillance regulations did not require suppression. STEVENS, J., for the majority, reasoned:

"Regulations governing the conduct of criminal investigations are generally considered desirable, and may well provide more valuable protection to the public at large than the deterrence flowing from the occasional exclusion of items of evidence in criminal trials. Although we do not suggest that a suppression order in this case would cause the Internal Revenue Service to abandon or modify its electronic surveillance regulations, we cannot ignore the possibility that a rigid application of an exclusionary rule to every regulatory violation could have a serious deterrent impact on the formulation of additional standards to govern prosecutorial and police procedures. Here, the Executive itself has provided for internal sanctions in cases of knowing violations of the electronic surveillance regulations. To go beyond that, and require exclusion in every case, would take away from the Executive Department the primary responsibility for fashioning the appropriate remedy for the violation of its regulations. But since the content, and indeed the existence, of the regulations would remain within the Executive's sole authority, the result might well be fewer and less protective regulations. In the long run, it is far better to have rules like those contained in the IRS Manual, and to tolerate occasional erroneous administration of the kind displayed by this record, than either to have no rules except those mandated by statute, or to have them framed in a mere precatory form."

NOTES ON THE "DIMENSIONS" OF
THE EXCLUSIONARY RULE

1. *Evidence obtained by government agents, used as basis for questions to grand jury witness.* In UNITED STATES v. CALANDRA, 414 U.S. 338, 94 S.Ct. 613, 38 L.Ed.2d 561 (1974), the Court, per POWELL, J., held that a grand jury witness may not refuse to answer questions on the ground that they are based on evidence obtained from him in an earlier unlawful search. After observing that a contrary holding would unduly interfere with the effective and expeditious discharge of the grand jury's duties [see p. 702], the Court asserted: "Whatever deterrence of police misconduct may result from the exclusion of illegally-seized evidence from criminal trials, it is unrealistic to assume that application of the rule to grand jury proceedings would significantly further that goal. Such an extension would deter only police investigation consciously directed toward the discovery of evidence solely for use in a grand jury investigation. The incentive to disregard the requirement of the Fourth Amendment solely to obtain an indictment from a grand jury is substantially negated by the inadmissibility of the illegally-seized evidence in a subsequent criminal prosecution of the search victim. For the most part, a prosecutor would be unlikely to request an indictment where a conviction could not be obtained. We therefore decline to embrace a view that would achieve a speculative and undoubtedly minimal advance in the deterrence of police misconduct at the expense of substantially impeding the role of the grand jury."

BRENNAN, J., joined by Douglas and Marshall, JJ., dissenting, quoted from *Weeks* to show that "the twin goals of enabling the judiciary to avoid the taint of partnerships in official lawlessness and of assuring the people * * * that the government would not profit from its lawless behavior, * * * not the rule's possible deterrent effect, were uppermost in the minds of the framers of the rule," and then argued:

"It is no answer, as the Court suggests, that the grand jury witnesses' Fourth Amendment rights will be sufficiently protected 'by the inadmissibility of the illegally-seized evidence in a subsequent criminal prosecution of the search victim.' This, of course, is no alternative for Calandra, since he was granted transactional immunity and cannot be criminally prosecuted. But the fundamental flaw of the alternative is that to compel Calandra to testify in the first place under penalty of contempt necessarily 'thwarts' his Fourth Amendment protection and 'entangle the courts in the illegal acts of Government agents' * * *."

2. *Evidence obtained by government agents, used in criminal case after conviction.* Should illegally seized evidence be admissible after conviction for consideration by the judge in determining the sentence to be imposed? *Verdugo v. United States,* 402 F.2d 599 (9th Cir.1968), holding no, was distinguished in *United States v. Schipani,* 315 F.Supp. 253 (E.D.N.Y.1970), aff'd, 435 F.2d 26 (2d Cir.1970), in that the decision in *Verdugo* was "predicated upon the fact that the search which had produced the improper evidence was conducted outside the course of the regular criminal investigation. It was undertaken, not to obtain evidence to support an indictment and conviction, but to recover contraband and thus to enhance the possibility of a heavier sentence after the basic investigation had been completed. [Under these circumstances,] law enforcement officials would have little to lose, but much to gain, in violating the Fourth Amendment." That situation was not present in *Schipani,* and thus the court concluded that "no appreciable increment in deterrence would result from applying a second exclusion at sentencing after the rule has been applied at the trial itself."

In PENNSYLVANIA BOARD OF PROBATION AND PAROLE v. SCOTT, 514 U.S. 357, 118 S.Ct. 2014, 141 L.Ed.2d 344 (1998), parole officers made an illegal search of parolee Scott's residence and found weapons there, which were later admitted at his parole revocation hearing, resulting in Scott being recommitted to serve 36 months. Thereafter, the state supreme court, although following the prevailing general rule against application of the exclusionary rule at parole revocation hearings, carved out an exception for cases in which the officer who conducted the search was aware of the person's parole status. The Supreme Court, in a 5–4 decision, disagreed. THOMAS, J., for the majority, relying upon *Calandra,* supra, and *Janis* and *Lopez-Mendoza,* infra, declined "to extend the operation of the exclusionary rule beyond the criminal trial context" because "application of the exclusionary rule would both hinder the functioning of state parole systems and alter the traditionally flexible, administrative nature of parole revocation proceedings," but at the same time "would provide only minimal deterrence benefits in this context." On the matter of deterrence, the majority declared it would be "minimal" even in the special situation which concerned the state court, for if the searcher was a police officer he would be deterred by the risk of exclusion of evidence at a criminal trial and would be unaffected by what happened at the parole proceeding, which, in the words of *Janis,* "falls outside the offending officer's zone of primary interest." If the searcher was a parole officer, he will likewise be deterred by the risk of evidence exclusion at a criminal trial, and, in any event, is not "engaged in the often competitive enterprise of ferreting out crime" and thus can be sufficiently deterred by "departmental training and discipline and the threat of damages actions." The dissenters, per SOUTER, J., noted "the police very likely do know a parolee's status when they go after him," which is significant because (1) police officers with such knowledge, "especially those employed by the same sovereign that runs the parole system, * * * have every incentive not to jeopardize a recommitment by rendering evidence inadmissible," and thus could be deterred by the threat of exclusion at a parole hearing; (2) "the actual likelihood of trial is often far less than the probability of a petition for parole revocation" because, as the Court itself noted on an earlier occasion, parole revocation "is often preferred to a new prosecution because of the procedural ease of recommitting the individual on the basis of a lesser showing by the State," and this means there will be "nothing 'marginal' about the deterrence provided by an exclusionary rule operating" in the parole revocation context, and (3) "the cooperation between parole and police officers * * * casts serious doubt upon the aptness of treating police officers differently from parole officers," who themselves "are considered police officers with respect to the offenders under their jurisdiction" and who, consequently, can no more than other police be thought to be adequately deterred by the risk of departmental discipline or the threat of damages actions.

3. *Evidence obtained by government agents, used in "quasi-criminal" or civil case.* In ONE 1958 PLYMOUTH SEDAN v. PENNSYLVANIA, 380 U.S. 693, 85 S.Ct. 1246, 14 L.Ed.2d 170 (1965), a unanimous Court held that the *Weeks-Mapp* exclusionary rule applies to forfeiture proceedings. *Boyd v. United States,* "the leading case on the subject of search and seizure * * * itself was not a criminal case," pointed out the majority, "but was a proceeding by the United States to forfeit 35 cases of plate glass which had allegedly been imported without payment of the customs duty * * *. [As] pointed out in *Boyd,* a forfeiture proceeding is quasi-criminal in character. Its object, like a criminal proceeding, is to penalize for the commission of an offense against the law. In this case * * * the driver and owner of the automobile was arrested and charged with a criminal offense against the Pennsylvania liquor laws. * * * In this forfeiture proceeding he was subject to the loss of his automobile, which at the time involved had an estimated value of approximately $1,000, a higher amount than the maximum fine in the criminal proceeding. It would be anomalous indeed, under these circumstances, to hold that in the criminal proceeding the illegally seized evidence is excludable, while in the forfeiture proceeding, requiring the determination that the criminal law has been violated, the same evidence would be admissible."

Los Angeles police seized wagering records and $4,940 in cash pursuant to a search warrant, and then notified the IRS, which made an assessment against Janis for wagering taxes and levied upon the seized cash in partial satisfaction. After Janis' motion to suppress was granted in the state criminal proceedings, he sued for refund of the money and to quash the assessment because it was based upon illegally seized evidence. The federal district court ruled for Janis, and the court of appeals affirmed. In UNITED STATES v. JANIS, 428 U.S. 433, 96 S.Ct. 3021, 49 L.Ed.2d 1046 (1976), the Court, per BLACKMUN, J., reversed: "Working, as we must, with the absence of convincing empirical data, common sense dictates that the deterrent effect of the exclusion of relevant evidence is highly attenuated when the 'punishment' imposed upon the offending criminal enforcement officer is the removal of that evidence from a civil suit by or against a different sovereign. In *Elkins* [p. 127] the Court indicated that the assumed interest of criminal law enforcement officers in the criminal proceedings of another sovereign counterbalanced this attenuation sufficiently to justify an exclusionary rule. Here, however, the attenuation is further augmented by the fact that the proceeding is one to enforce only the civil law of the other sovereign.

"This attenuation coupled with the existing deterrence effected by the denial of use of the evidence by either sovereign in the criminal trials with which the searching officer is concerned, creates a situation in which the imposition of the exclusionary rule sought in this case is unlikely to provide significant much less substantial, additional deterrence. It falls outside the offending officer's zone of primary interest."

BRENNAN and Marshall, JJ., dissented on the basis of their *Calandra* dissent. STEWART, J., dissenting, argued that the majority's deterrence theory compelled the opposite result in light of the fact that "federal and local law enforcement personnel regularly provide federal tax officials with information, obtained in criminal investigations, indicating liability under the wagering tax. The pattern is one of mutual cooperation and coordination, with the federal wagering tax provisions buttressing state and federal criminal sanctions." He noted that it was admitted by the local police officer in the instant case that he notified the IRS whenever he uncovered a gambling operation involving a substantial amount of cash.

Utilizing the *Janis* cost-benefit approach, the Court held 5–4 in I.N.S. v. LOPEZ–MENDOZA, 468 U.S. 1032, 104 S.Ct. 3479, 82 L.Ed.2d 778 (1984), that the exclusionary rule is inapplicable in a civil deportation hearing. O'CONNOR, J., explained that the deterrent value of the exclusionary rule in this context was reduced because (i) "deportation will still be possible when evidence not derived directly from the arrest is sufficient to support deportation," (ii) INS agents know "that it is highly unlikely that any particular arrestee will end up challenging the lawfulness of his arrest," (iii) "the INS has its own comprehensive scheme for deterring Fourth Amendment violations" by training and discipline, and (iv) "alternative remedies" including the "possibility of declaratory relief" are available for institutional practices violating the Fourth Amendment. On the cost side, the Court continued, are these factors: (i) that application of the exclusionary rule "in proceedings that are intended not to punish past transgressions but to prevent their continuance or renewal would require courts to close their eyes to ongoing violations of the law," (ii) that invocation of the exclusionary rule at deportation hearings, where "neither the hearing officers nor the attorneys * * * are likely to be well versed in the intricacies of Fourth Amendment law," "might significantly change and complicate the character of these proceedings," and (iii) that because many INS arrests "occur in crowded and confused circumstances," application of the exclusionary rule "might well result in the suppression of large amounts of information that had been obtained entirely lawfully." WHITE, J., dissenting, objected that "unlike the situation in *Janis,* the conduct challenged here falls within 'the offending officer's zone of primary interest,' "and concluded that "the costs and benefits of applying the exclusionary rule in civil deportation proceedings do not differ in any significant way from the costs and benefits of applying the rule in ordinary criminal proceedings."

4. *Evidence obtained by private persons, used in criminal proceedings.* In *Burdeau v. McDowell,* 256 U.S. 465, 41 S.Ct. 574, 65 L.Ed. 1048 (1921), the exclusionary rule was characterized "as a restraint upon the activities of sovereign authority and * * * not * * * a limitation upon other than governmental agencies," and on this basis courts have declined to exclude evidence in criminal cases when obtained by private persons. However, the Fourth Amendment *is* applicable "to private individuals who are acting as instruments or agents of the government. * * * Whether a private individual is an agent of the government is determined by a totality-of-the-circumstances test. Circumstances to be considered in this test include the motive of the private actor; any compensation or other benefit the private actor receives from the government; and the advice, direction, and level of participation given by the government. Using this test, if it is found that the private actor was sufficiently influenced and supported by the state, the

exclusionary rule will apply to any evidence obtained by the private actor." Comment, 65 U.Cin.L.Rev. 665, 672 (1997).

One issue which frequently arises with respect to private person searches is whether, if that person then summons the police, police activity with respect to the same object is a separate "search" subject to Fourth Amendment constraints. For example, in UNITED STATES v. JACOBSEN, 466 U.S. 109, 104 S.Ct. 1652, 80 L.Ed.2d 85 (1984), Federal Express employees opened a damaged box and found newspapers covering a tube which, when cut open, was found to contain plastic bags of white powder. Federal drug agents were summoned, but before their arrival the bags had been put back into the tube and the tube and newspapers back into the box, which was left open. A federal agent reopened the packaging to the extent necessary to expose the powder, which he field tested and found to be cocaine. The Court, per STEVENS, J., concluded the agent's actions were not a significant expansion of the earlier private search and that consequently no warrant was required. "Respondents could have no privacy interest in the contents of the package, since it remained unsealed and since the Federal Express employees had just examined the package and had, of their own accord, invited the federal agent to their offices for the express purpose of viewing its contents. The agent's viewing of what a private party had freely made available for his inspection did not violate the Fourth Amendment.

"Similarly, the removal of the plastic bags from the tube and the agent's visual inspection of their contents enabled the agent to learn nothing that had not previously been learned during the private search. It infringed no legitimate expectation of privacy and hence was not a 'search' within the meaning of the Fourth Amendment."[a]

Three members of the Court rejected that reasoning. WHITE, J., objected:

"The majority opinion is particularly troublesome when one considers its logical implications. I would be hard-pressed to distinguish this case, which involves a private search, from (1) one in which the private party's knowledge, later communicated to the government, that a particular container concealed contraband and nothing else arose from his presence at the time the container was sealed; (2) one in which the private party learned that a container concealed contraband and nothing else when it was previously opened in his presence; or (3) one in which the private party knew to a certainty that a container concealed contraband and nothing else as a result of conversations with its owner. In each of these cases, the approach adopted by the Court today would seem to suggest that the owner of the container has no legitimate expectation of privacy in its contents and that government agents opening that container without a warrant on the strength of information provided by the private party would not violate the Fourth Amendment."

5. *Evidence obtained by virtue of conduct of nonpolice government employee, used in criminal proceedings.* The *Burdeau* rule, grounded in the proposition that the Fourth Amendment is entirely inapplicable where there is no governmental action, must be distinguished from that recognized in ARIZONA v. EVANS, 514 U.S. 1, 115 S.Ct. 1185, 131 L.Ed.2d 34 (1995): that some government searches covered by the Fourth Amendment are nonetheless inappropriate occasions for use of the exclusionary rule, considering the kind of government official who was at fault. After Evans was stopped for a traffic violation, the patrol car's computer indicated he had an outstanding arrest warrant, so Evans was arrested; incident

a. As for the field test, see p. 169.

thereto, the officer found marijuana. It was later learned that this warrant (issued because of Evans' nonappearance on several traffic violations) had been quashed upon Evans' voluntary appearance in court a few weeks earlier, but that apparently the court clerk had not thereafter followed the usual procedure of notifying the sheriff's department so that the warrant could be removed from the computer records. The state supreme court held this amounted to a violation of the Fourth Amendment and that consequently the evidence must be suppressed, but the Supreme Court, per REHNQUIST, C.J., considering only the latter point, disagreed:

"This holding is contrary to the reasoning of *Leon,* [p. 142]; *Massachusetts v. Sheppard* [p. 144]; and *Krull* [p. 129]. If court employees were responsible for the erroneous computer record, the exclusion of evidence at trial would not sufficiently deter future errors so as to warrant such a severe sanction. First, as we noted in *Leon,* the exclusionary rule was historically designed as a means of deterring police misconduct, not mistakes by court employees. Second, respondent offers no evidence that court employees are inclined to ignore or subvert the Fourth Amendment or that lawlessness among these actors requires application of the extreme sanction of exclusion. To the contrary, the Chief Clerk of the Justice Court testified at the suppression hearing that this type of error occurred once every three or four years.

"Finally, and most important, there is no basis for believing that application of the exclusionary rule in these circumstances will have a significant effect on court employees responsible for informing the police that a warrant has been quashed. Because court clerks are not adjuncts to the law enforcement team engaged in the often competitive enterprise of ferreting out crime, they have no stake in the outcome of particular criminal prosecutions. The threat of exclusion of evidence could not be expected to deter such individuals from failing to inform police officials that a warrant had been quashed.

"If it were indeed a court clerk who was responsible for the erroneous entry on the police computer, application of the exclusionary rule also could not be expected to alter the behavior of the arresting officer. * * * There is no indication that the arresting officer was not acting objectively reasonably when he relied upon the police computer record. Application of the *Leon* framework supports a categorical exception to the exclusionary rule for clerical errors of court employees.[5]"

O'CONNOR, J., joined by Souter and Bryer, concurring, cautioned: "Surely it would not be reasonable for the police to rely, say, on a recordkeeping system, their own or some other agency's, that has no mechanism to ensure its accuracy over time and that routinely leads to false arrests, even years after the probable cause for any such arrest has ceased to exist (if it ever existed)."

STEVENS, J., dissenting, objected: "Taken on its own terms, *Leon*'s logic does not extend to the time after the warrant has issued; nor does it extend to court clerks and functionaries, some of whom work in the same building with police officers and may have more regular and direct contact with police than with judges or magistrates."

---

5. The Solicitor General, as amicus curiae, argues that an analysis similar to that we apply here to court personnel also would apply in order to determine whether the evidence should be suppressed if police personnel were responsible for the error. As the State has not made any such argument here, we agree that "[t]he record in this case ... does not adequately present that issue for the Court's consideration." Accordingly, we decline to address that question.

GINSBURG, J., joined by Stevens, while mainly disagreeing with the majority's invocation of "the *Long* presumption" [see p. 58] to assert jurisdiction, made these comments on the merits: "In the Court's view, exclusion of evidence, even if capable of deterring police officer errors, cannot deter the carelessness of other governmental actors.[5] Whatever federal precedents may indicate—an issue on which I voice no opinion—the Court's conclusion is not the lesson inevitably to be drawn from logic or experience.

"In this electronic age, particularly with respect to recordkeeping, court personnel and police officers are not neatly compartmentalized actors. Instead, they serve together to carry out the State's information-gathering objectives. Whether particular records are maintained by the police or the courts should not be dispositive where a single computer database can answer all calls. Not only is it artificial to distinguish between court clerk and police clerk slips; in practice, it may be difficult to pinpoint whether one official, e.g., a court employee, or another, e.g., a police officer, caused the error to exist or to persist."

In *New Jersey v. T.L.O.,* p. 341, involving search of a student by a high school administrator, the Court reaffirmed that "the Fourth Amendment [is] applicable to the activities of civil as well as criminal authorities." However, because the search was found to be reasonable, the Court avoided expressing any opinion about the question which prompted the original grant of certiorari: whether the exclusionary rule is also applicable to searches by school authorities. In light of *Evans,* what is the answer to that question?

6. *Evidence obtained by foreign officials, used in domestic criminal proceedings.* Would any purpose be served by applying the exclusionary rule in such circumstances? What if American authorities requested or participated in the actions of the foreign police?

Even if there has been direct U.S. involvement in the foreign search, the Fourth Amendment may be inapplicable for yet another reason. In *United States v. Verdugo–Urquidez,* 494 U.S. 259, 110 S.Ct. 1056, 108 L.Ed.2d 222 (1990), the opinion of the Court, per Rehnquist, C.J., declares that the phrase "the people" in the Fourth Amendment (and the First, Second, Ninth and Tenth Amendments) "refers to a class of persons who are part of a national community or who have otherwise developed sufficient connection with this community to be considered part of that community." The defendant in the instant case was deemed not to be such a person; he was a Mexican citizen and resident who, to be sure, just two days before the search of his residence in Mexico had been turned over to U.S. authorities by Mexican police, but "this sort of presence—lawful but involuntary—is not the sort to indicate any substantial connection with our country." (The Court added it was an open question whether even the illegal aliens in *Lopez–Mendoza,* p. 149, were such persons, though their situation was different from the defendant's here because they "were in the United States voluntarily and presumably had accepted some societal obligations.") The three dissenters

5. It has been suggested that an exclusionary rule cannot deter carelessness, but can affect only intentional or reckless misconduct. This suggestion runs counter to a premise underlying all of negligence law—that imposing liability for negligence, i.e., lack of due care, creates an incentive to act with greater care. That the mistake may have been made by a clerical worker does not alter the conclusion that application of the exclusionary rule has deterrent value. Just as the risk of respondeat superior liability encourages employers to supervise more closely their employees' conduct, so the risk of exclusion of evidence encourages policymakers and systems managers to monitor the performance of the systems they install and the personnel employed to operate those systems. In the words of the trial court, the mistake in Evans' case was "perhaps the negligence of the Justice Court, or the negligence of the Sheriff's office. But it is still the negligence of the State."

agreed, as Blackmun, J., put it, "that when a foreign national is held accountable for purported violations of United States criminal laws, he has effectively been treated as one of 'the governed' and therefore is entitled to Fourth Amendment protections." Because the two concurring Justices placed great emphasis upon the inapplicability of the Fourth Amendment's warrant clause to the search in the instant case (Kennedy, J., stressing this was not a case in which "the full protections of the Fourth Amendment would apply" because of the "absence of local judges or magistrates available to issue warrants"; Stevens, J., that "American magistrates have no power to authorize such searches"), the application of *Verdugo–Urquidez* to a foreign search of an alien's property made even without probable cause is not entirely clear.

NOTES ON OTHER REMEDIES

1. *The "constitutional tort" by state officers. Monroe v. Pape*, 365 U.S. 167, 81 S.Ct. 473, 5 L.Ed.2d 492 (1961), concerned an action for damages under 42 U.S.C. § 1983[b] against the City of Chicago and 13 Chicago police officers. The complaint alleged that the officers broke into petitioners' home in the early morning, routed them from bed, made them stand naked in the living room, and ransacked every room in the house, after which Mr. Monroe was taken to the station and interrogated incommunicado about a murder. The Court rejected the respondents' argument that the suit was barred because no "statute, ordinance, regulation, custom or usage" of Illinois made a state remedy unavailable: "It is no answer that the State has a law which if enforced would give relief. The federal remedy is supplementary to the state remedy, and the latter need not be first sought and refused before the federal one is invoked. Hence the fact that Illinois by its constitution and laws outlaws unreasonable searches and seizures is no barrier to the present suit in the federal court."

In *Pierson v. Ray*, 386 U.S. 547, 87 S.Ct. 1213, 18 L.Ed.2d 288 (1967), involving arrests under a breach of the peace statute thereafter found unconstitutional, the Court held that "if the jury found that the officers reasonably believed in good faith that the arrest was constitutional, then a verdict for the officers would follow even though the arrest was in fact unconstitutional." But on the ground that "substantial costs attend the litigation of the subjective good faith of government officials," this defense was later reformulated by the Court as a purely objective standard. *Harlow v. Fitzgerald*, 457 U.S. 800, 102 S.Ct. 2727, 73 L.Ed.2d 396 (1982).

The *Harlow* standard, not absolute immunity, is the rule with respect to a police officer's action in applying for an arrest warrant; notwithstanding the magistrate's issuance of the warrant, the question "is whether a reasonably well-trained officer in petitioner's position would have known that his affidavit failed to establish probable cause and that he should not have applied for the warrant." *Malley v. Briggs*, 475 U.S. 335, 106 S.Ct. 1092, 89 L.Ed.2d 271 (1986). Powell and Rehnquist, JJ., dissenting in part, objected that this means "less weight should be accorded the magistrate's decision in a § 1983 damages suit" than in a suppression hearing context where *Leon* would apply.

b. "Every person who, under color of any statute, ordinance, regulation, custom, or usage, of any State or Territory, subjects, or causes to be subjected, any citizen of the United States or other person within the jurisdiction thereof to the deprivation of any rights, privileges, or immunities secured by the Constitution and laws, shall be liable to the party injured in an action at law, suit in equity, or other proper proceeding for redress."

Although *Monroe* also held that the City of Chicago was properly dismissed as a party because "Congress did not undertake to bring municipal corporations within the ambit" of the statute, the Court took another look at the legislative history in *Monell v. New York City Dep't of Social Services*, 436 U.S. 658, 98 S.Ct. 2018, 56 L.Ed.2d 611 (1978), and ruled otherwise.[c] The Court in *Monell* cautioned that the statute did not "impose liability vicariously on governing bodies solely on the basis of the existence of an employer-employee relationship with a tortfeasor," and thus concluded "that a local government may not be sued for an injury inflicted solely by its employees or agents. Instead, it is when execution of a government's policy or custom, whether made by its lawmakers or by those whose edicts or acts may fairly be said to represent official policy, inflicts the injury that the government as an entity is responsible under § 1983." In *Owen v. City of Independence*, 445 U.S. 622, 100 S.Ct. 1398, 63 L.Ed.2d 673 (1980), the Court held, 5–4, that the statute did not confer upon municipalities the tort law immunities for "governmental" functions and "discretionary" activities, and also that a municipality may not assert as a defense the good faith of its officers.

2. *The "constitutional tort" by federal officers.* Section 1983 applies only to persons acting under color of state law, thus excluding federal officers acting under color of their authority. In BIVENS v. SIX UNKNOWN NAMED AGENTS, 403 U.S. 388, 91 S.Ct. 1999, 29 L.Ed.2d 619 (1971), the Court held that, although Congress had not provided a tort remedy under such circumstances, a complaint alleging that the Fourth Amendment had been violated by federal agents acting under color of their authority gives rise to a federal cause of action for damages.[d] (The *Harlow* standard, Note 1 supra, whereunder personal liability turns on the "objective legal reasonableness" of the action, assessed in light of the legal rules that were "clearly established" at the time, applies also to a *Bivens* action against a federal officer. *Anderson v. Creighton*, 483 U.S. 635, 107 S.Ct. 3034, 97 L.Ed.2d 523 (1987).)

As for liability of the federal government, the Court in *Bivens* stated this issue was better left to Congress because "the federal purse was involved." In 1974 Congress amended the Federal Tort Claims Act to make it applicable "to acts or omissions of investigative or law enforcement officers of the United States Government" on any subsequent claim arising "out of assault, battery, false imprisonment, false arrest, abuse of process, or malicious prosecution. For the purpose of this subsection, 'investigative or law enforcement officer' means any officer of the United States who is empowered by law to execute searches, to seize evidence, or to make arrests for violations of Federal law." 28 U.S.C. § 2680(h). The "effect of this provision is to deprive the Federal Government of the defense of sovereign immunity in cases * * * [involving] the same kind of conduct that is alleged to have occurred in *Bivens*." S.Rep.No. 93–588, 93d Cong., 2d Sess., 1974 *U.S.Code Cong. & Ad.News* 2789, 2791 (1974). The availability of a FTCA remedy against the government does not bar a *Bivens* suit against the offending officer, as

c. Because "by the time of the enactment of § 1983, municipalities no longer retained the sovereign immunity they had previously shared with the States," *Monell* is "fully consistent" with the holding in *Will v. Michigan Dep't of State Police*, 491 U.S. 58, 109 S.Ct. 2304, 105 L.Ed.2d 45 (1989), that a state is not a "person" within the meaning of § 1983.

d. On remand, 456 F.2d 1339 (2d Cir.1972), it was held that federal police officers "have no immunity to protect them from damage suits charging violations of constitutional rights," but "that it is a valid defense to such charges to allege and prove that the federal agent or other federal police officer acted in the matter complained of in good faith and with a reasonable belief in the validity of the arrest and search and in the necessity for carrying out the arrest and search in the way the arrest was made and the search was conducted."

the latter is "a more effective deterrent." *Carlson v. Green,* 446 U.S. 14, 100 S.Ct. 1468, 64 L.Ed.2d 15 (1980).

3. *Dismissal of criminal charges.* Although an illegal arrest or other unreasonable seizure of the person is itself a violation of the Fourth and Fourteenth Amendments, the exclusionary sanction comes into play only when the police have obtained evidence as a result of the unconstitutional seizure. It is no defense to a state or federal criminal prosecution that the defendant was illegally arrested or forcibly brought within the jurisdiction of the court. The trial of such a defendant violates neither Fifth nor Fourteenth Amendment Due Process nor any federal legislation. *Frisbie v. Collins,* 342 U.S. 519, 72 S.Ct. 509, 96 L.Ed. 541 (1952); *Ker v. Illinois,* 119 U.S. 436, 7 S.Ct. 225, 30 L.Ed. 421 (1886). In *Gerstein v. Pugh,* p. 228, the Court declined to "retreat from the established rule that illegal arrest or detention does not void a subsequent conviction." See also *United States v. Crews,* p. 790, holding an illegally arrested defendant "is not himself a suppressible 'fruit' and the illegality of his detention cannot deprive the Government of the opportunity to prove his guilt through the introduction of evidence wholly untainted by the police misconduct."

In *United States v. Alvarez–Machain,* 504 U.S. 655, 112 S.Ct. 2188, 119 L.Ed.2d 441 (1992), the Court held that *Ker,* involving forcible abduction from a foreign country, was "fully applicable to this case" despite the fact that here the abduction was from Mexico, with whom the U.S. has an extradition treaty. "The Treaty says nothing about the obligations of the [parties] to refrain from forcible abductions of people from the territory of the other nation, or the consequences under the Treaty if such an abduction occurs."

4. *Self-help.* "At least twenty-one jurisdictions have followed the example of the Model Penal Code, providing by statute no justification for forceful resistance to an unlawful arrest by a known officer. At least six jurisdictions have, by judicial decision, abandoned the common law resistance right." Penn Lerblance, *Resisting Unlawful Arrest: A Due Process Perspective,* 35 Clev.St.L.Rev. 261, 269 (1987). Compare the view of Justice Douglas, dissenting from the dismissal of the writ of certiorari in *Wainwright v. New Orleans,* 392 U.S. 598, 88 S.Ct. 2243, 20 L.Ed.2d 1322 (1968), that one has "the right to offer some resistance to an unconstitutional 'seizure' or 'search' " under "the principle that a citizen can defy an unconstitutional act," and consider Paul Chevigny, *The Right to Resist an Unlawful Arrest,* 78 Yale L.J. 1128, 1141 (1969): "The impairment of fourth amendment rights, however, is not enough to justify resistance to an unlawful arrest. The problem is to determine the circumstances under which such a seizure becomes so provocative as to make unfair the imposition of a criminal penalty for resisting it."

SECTION 2. PROTECTED AREAS AND INTERESTS

KATZ v. UNITED STATES
389 U.S. 347, 88 S.Ct. 507, 19 L.Ed.2d 576 (1967).

Justice STEWART delivered the opinion of the Court.

The petitioner was convicted [of] transmitting wagering information by telephone from Los Angeles to Miami and Boston in violation of a federal statute. At trial the Government was permitted, over the petitioner's objection, to introduce evidence of the petitioner's end of telephone conversations, overheard by FBI agents who had attached an electronic listening and recording device to the outside of the public telephone booth from which he had placed his calls. In affirming his conviction, the Court of Appeals rejected the contention that the recordings had been obtained in violation of the Fourth Amendment, because "[t]here was no physical entrance into the area occupied by [the petitioner]." We granted certiorari in order to consider the constitutional questions thus presented.

The petitioner has phrased those questions as follows:

"A. Whether a public telephone booth is a constitutionally protected area so that evidence obtained by attaching an electronic listening recording device to the top of such a booth is obtained in violation of the right to privacy of the user of the booth.

"B. Whether physical penetration of a constitutionally protected area is necessary before a search and seizure can be said to be violative of the Fourth Amendment to the United States Constitution."

We decline to adopt this formulation of the issues. In the first place the correct solution of Fourth Amendment problems is not necessarily promoted by incantation of the phrase "constitutionally protected area." Secondly, the Fourth Amendment cannot be translated into a general constitutional "right to privacy." That Amendment protects individual privacy against certain kinds of governmental intrusion, but its protections go further, and often have nothing to do with privacy at all. Other provisions of the Constitution protect personal privacy from other forms of governmental invasion. But the protection of a person's *general* right to privacy—his right to be let alone by other people—is, like the protection of his property and of his very life, left largely to the law of the individual States.

Because of the misleading way the issues have been formulated, the parties have attached great significance to the characterization of the telephone booth from which the petitioner placed his calls. The petitioner has strenuously argued that the booth was a "constitutionally protected area." The Government has maintained with equal vigor that it was not. But this effort to decide whether or not a given "area," viewed in the abstract, is "constitutionally protected" deflects attention from the problem presented by this case. For the Fourth Amendment protects people, not places. What a person knowingly exposes to the public, even in his own home or office, is not a subject of Fourth Amendment protection. * * * But what he seeks to preserve as private, even in an area accessible to the public, may be constitutionally protected. * * *

The Government stresses the fact that the telephone booth from which the petitioner made his calls was constructed partly of glass, so that he was as visible after he entered it as he would have been if he had remained outside. But what he sought to exclude when he entered the booth was not the intruding eye—it was the uninvited ear. He did not shed his right to do so simply because he made his calls from a place where he might be seen. No less than an individual in a business office, in a friend's apartment, or in a taxicab, a person in a telephone booth may rely upon the protection of the Fourth Amendment. One who occupies it, shuts the door behind him, and pays the toll that permits him to place a call, is surely entitled to assume that the words he utters into the mouthpiece will not be broadcast to the world. To read the Constitution more narrowly is to ignore the vital role that the public telephone has come to play in private communication.

The Government contends, however, that the activities of its agents in this case should not be tested by Fourth Amendment requirements, for the surveillance technique they employed involved no physical penetration of the telephone booth from which the petitioner placed his calls.

* * * [A]lthough a closely divided Court supposed in *Olmstead* [p. 360] that surveillance without any trespass and without the seizure of any material object fell outside the ambit of the Constitution, we have since departed from the narrow view on which that decision rested. Indeed, we have expressly held that the Fourth Amendment governs not only the seizure of tangible items, but extends as well to the recording of oral statements overheard without any "technical trespass under * * * local property law." *Silverman v. United States*. Once this much is acknowledged, and once it is recognized that the Fourth Amendment protects people—and not simply "areas"—against unreasonable searches and seizures it becomes clear that the reach of that Amendment cannot turn upon the presence or absence of a physical intrusion into any given enclosure.

We conclude that the underpinnings of *Olmstead* and *Goldman* [p. 364] have been so eroded by our subsequent decisions that the "trespass" doctrine there enunciated can no longer be regarded as controlling. The Government's activities in electronically listening to and recording the petitioner's words violated the privacy upon which he justifiably relied while using the telephone booth and thus constituted a "search and seizure" within the meaning of the Fourth Amendment. The fact that the electronic device employed to achieve that end did not happen to penetrate the wall of the booth can have no constitutional significance.

The question remaining for decision, then, is whether the search and seizure conducted in this case complied with constitutional standards. In that regard, the Government's position is that its agents acted in an entirely defensible manner: They did not begin their electronic surveillance until investigation of the petitioner's activities had established a strong probability that he was using the telephone in question to transmit gambling information to persons in other States, in violation of federal law. Moreover, the surveillance was limited, both in scope and in duration to the specific purpose of establishing the contents of the petitioner's unlawful telephonic communications. The agents confined their surveillance to the brief periods during which he used the telephone booth, and they took great care to overhear only the conversations of the petitioner himself.

Accepting this account of the Government's actions as accurate, it is clear that this surveillance was so narrowly circumscribed that a duly authorized magistrate, properly notified of the need for such investigation, specifically informed of the basis on which it was to proceed, and clearly apprised of the precise intrusion it would entail, could constitutionally have authorized, with appropriate safeguards, the very limited search and seizure that the Government asserts in fact took place. * * *

The Government * * * urges the creation of a new exception to cover this case. It argues that surveillance of a telephone booth should be exempted from the usual requirement of advance authorization by a magistrate upon a showing of probable cause. We cannot agree. Omission of such authorization "bypasses the safeguards provided by an objective predetermination of probable cause, and substitutes instead the far less reliable procedure of an after-the-event justification for the * * * search, too likely to be subtly influenced by the familiar shortcomings of hindsight judgment." And bypassing a neutral predetermination of the *scope* of a search leaves individuals secure from Fourth Amendment violations "only in the discretion of the police."

These considerations do not vanish when the search in question is transferred from the setting of a home, an office, or a hotel room, to that of a telephone booth. Wherever a man may be, he is entitled to know that he will remain free from unreasonable searches and seizures. The government agents here ignored "the procedure of antecedent justification * * * that is central to the Fourth Amendment," procedure that we hold to be a constitutional precondition of the kind of electronic surveillance involved in this case. * * *

Judgment reversed.[a]

Justice HARLAN, concurring. * * *

As the Court's opinion states, "The Fourth Amendment protects people, not places." The question, however, is what protection it affords to those people. Generally, as here, the answer to that question requires reference to a "place." My understanding of the rule that has emerged from prior decisions is that there is a twofold requirement, first that a person have exhibited an actual (subjective) expectation of privacy and, second, that the expectation be one that society is prepared to recognize as "reasonable."[b] Thus a man's home is, for most purposes, a place where he expects privacy, but objects, activities, or statements that he exposes to the "plain view" of outsiders are not "protected" because no intention to keep them to himself has been exhibited. On the other hand, conversations in the open would not be protected against being overheard, for the expectation of privacy under the circumstances would be unreasonable. * * *

The critical fact in this case is that "[o]ne who occupies it, [a telephone booth] shuts the door behind him, and pays the toll that permits him to place a call, is surely entitled to assume" that his conversation is not being intercepted. The point is not that the booth is "accessible to the public" at other times, but that it is a temporarily private place whose momentary occupants' expectations of freedom from intrusion are recognized as reasonable. * * *

Justice BLACK, dissenting. * * *

Tapping telephone wires, of course, was an unknown possibility at the time the Fourth Amendment was adopted. But eavesdropping (and wiretapping is nothing more than eavesdropping by telephone) was * * * "an ancient practice which at common law was condemned as a nuisance. In those days the eavesdropper listened by naked ear under the eaves of houses or their windows, or beyond their walls seeking out private discourse." There can be no doubt that the Framers were aware of this practice, and if they had desired to outlaw or restrict the use of evidence obtained by eavesdropping, I believe that they would have used the appropriate language to do so in the Fourth Amendment. They certainly would not have left such a task to the ingenuity of language-stretching judges. * * *

* * * By clever word juggling the Court finds it plausible to argue that language aimed specifically at searches and seizures of things that can be searched and seized may, to protect privacy, be applied to eavesdropped evidence of conversations that can neither be searched nor seized. Few things happen to an individual that do not affect his privacy in one way or another. Thus, by arbitrarily substituting the Court's language, designed to protect privacy, for the

a. Justice Marshall took no part in the case. Concurring opinions by Douglas, J., joined by Brennan, J., and by White, J., are omitted.

b. Consider Anthony Amsterdam, *Perspectives on the Fourth Amendment,* 58 Minn. L.Rev. 349, 384 (1974): "But Justice Harlan himself [dissenting in *United States v. White,* p. 391] later expressed second thoughts about this conception, and rightly so. An actual, subjective expectation of privacy obviously has no place in a statement of what *Katz* held or in a theory of what the fourth amendment protects. It can neither add to, nor can its absence detract from, an individual's claim to fourth amendment protection. If it could, the government could diminish each person's subjective expectation of privacy merely by announcing half-hourly on television * * * that we were all forthwith being placed under comprehensive electronic surveillance."

Constitution's language, designed to protect against unreasonable searches and seizures, the Court has made the Fourth Amendment its vehicle for holding all laws violative of the Constitution which offend the Court's broadest concept of privacy. * * *

The Fourth Amendment protects privacy only to the extent that it prohibits unreasonable searches and seizures of "persons, houses, papers and effects." No general right is created by the Amendment so as to give this Court the unlimited power to hold unconstitutional everything which affects privacy. Certainly the Framers, well acquainted as they were with the excesses of governmental power, did not intend to grant this Court such omnipotent lawmaking authority as that. The history of governments proves that it is dangerous to freedom to repose such powers in courts. * * *

Notes and Questions

1. In *Katz,* the Court held that the police conduct "constituted a 'search and seizure' within the meaning of the Fourth Amendment" because of the intrusion upon the defendant's privacy interest. But this does not mean that privacy is the *only* interest protected by the Fourth Amendment. The Fourth Amendment also protects the interests in possession of property and liberty of person, as in *United States v. Place,* p. 331 (detention of traveler's luggage 90 minutes was an unreasonable seizure in two respects, as it constituted a deprivation of defendant's "possessory interest in his luggage" and his "liberty interest in proceeding with his itinerary").

2. In *Soldal v. Cook County,* 506 U.S. 56, 113 S.Ct. 538, 121 L.Ed.2d 450 (1992), a § 1983 action was commenced against sheriff's deputies who knowingly participated in an unlawful eviction which involved disconnecting the plaintiff's trailer home from its utilities and hauling it off the landlord's property, in the process of which the trailer was badly damaged. The court of appeals affirmed the officers motion for summary judgment on the ground that the Fourth Amendment offered no protection where, as here, the intrusion upon a possessory interest was unaccompanied by an intrusion upon a privacy interest or, for that matter, upon a liberty interest. A unanimous Supreme Court reversed, holding "that seizures of property are subject to Fourth Amendment scrutiny even though no search within the meaning of the Amendment has taken place."

CALIFORNIA v. GREENWOOD
486 U.S. 35, 108 S.Ct. 1625, 100 L.Ed.2d 30 (1988).

Justice WHITE delivered the opinion of the Court. * * *

In early 1984, Investigator Jenny Stracner of the Laguna Beach Police Department received information indicating that respondent Greenwood might be engaged in narcotics trafficking. * * *

On April 6, 1984, Stracner asked the neighborhood's regular trash collector to pick up the plastic garbage bags that Greenwood had left on the curb in front of his house and to turn the bags over to her without mixing their contents with garbage from other houses. The trash collector cleaned his truck bin of other refuse, collected the garbage bags from the street in front of Greenwood's house, and turned the bags over to Stracner. The officer searched through the rubbish and found items indicative of narcotics use. She recited the information that she had gleaned from the trash search in an affidavit in support of a warrant to search Greenwood's home.

Police officers encountered both respondents at the house later that day when they arrived to execute the warrant. The police discovered quantities of cocaine and hashish during their search of the house. Respondents were arrested on felony narcotics charges. They subsequently posted bail.

The police continued to receive reports of many late-night visitors to the Greenwood house. On May 4, Investigator Robert Rahaeuser obtained Greenwood's garbage from the regular trash collector in the same manner as had Stracner. The garbage again contained evidence of narcotics use.

Rahaeuser secured another search warrant for Greenwood's home based on the information from the second trash search. The police found more narcotics and evidence of narcotics trafficking when they executed the warrant. Greenwood was again arrested.

The Superior Court dismissed the charges against respondents on the authority of *People v. Krivda,* 486 P.2d 1262 (Cal.1971), which held that warrantless trash searches violate the Fourth Amendment and the California Constitution. The court found that the police would not have had probable cause to search the Greenwood home without the evidence obtained from the trash searches.

The Court of Appeal affirmed [on Fourth Amendment grounds only]. * * *

The California Supreme Court denied the State's petition for review of the Court of Appeal's decision. We granted certiorari, and now reverse.

The warrantless search and seizure of the garbage bags left at the curb outside the Greenwood house would violate the Fourth Amendment only if respondents manifested a subjective expectation of privacy in their garbage that society accepts as objectively reasonable. Respondents do not disagree with this standard.

They assert, however, that they had, and exhibited, an expectation of privacy with respect to the trash that was searched by the police: The trash, which was placed on the street for collection at a fixed time, was contained in opaque plastic bags, which the garbage collector was expected to pick up, mingle with the trash of others, and deposit at the garbage dump. The trash was only temporarily on the street, and there was little likelihood that it would be inspected by anyone.

It may well be that respondents did not expect that the contents of their garbage bags would become known to the police or other members of the public. An expectation of privacy does not give rise to Fourth Amendment protection, however, unless society is prepared to accept that expectation as objectively reasonable.

Here, we conclude that respondents exposed their garbage to the public sufficiently to defeat their claim to Fourth Amendment protection. It is common knowledge that plastic garbage bags left on or at the side of a public street are readily accessible to animals, children, scavengers, snoops,[4] and other members of the public. Moreover, respondents placed their refuse at the curb for the express purpose of conveying it to a third party, the trash collector, who might himself have sorted through respondents' trash or permitted others, such as the police, to

---

4. Even the refuse of prominent Americans has not been invulnerable. In 1975, for example, a reporter for a weekly tabloid seized five bags of garbage from the sidewalk outside the home of Secretary of State Henry Kissinger. Washington Post, July 9, 1975, p. A1, col. 8. A newspaper editorial criticizing this journalistic "trash-picking" observed that "[e]vidently . . . 'everybody does it.'" Washington Post, July 10, 1975, p. A18, col. 1. We of course do not, as the dissent implies, "bas[e] [our] conclusion" that individuals have no reasonable expectation of privacy in their garbage on this "sole incident."

do so. Accordingly, having deposited their garbage "in an area particularly suited for public inspection and, in a manner of speaking, public consumption, for the express purpose of having strangers take it," respondents could have had no reasonable expectation of privacy in the inculpatory items that they discarded.

Furthermore, as we have held, the police cannot reasonably be expected to avert their eyes from evidence of criminal activity that could have been observed by any member of the public. Hence, "[w]hat a person knowingly exposes to the public, even in his own home or office, is not a subject of Fourth Amendment protection." *Katz v. United States.* We held in *Smith v. Maryland,* 442 U.S. 735, 99 S.Ct. 2577, 61 L.Ed.2d 220 (1979), for example, that the police did not violate the Fourth Amendment by causing a pen register to be installed at the telephone company's offices to record the telephone numbers dialed by a criminal suspect. An individual has no legitimate expectation of privacy in the numbers dialed on his telephone, we reasoned, because he voluntarily conveys those numbers to the telephone company when he uses the telephone. Again, we observed that "a person has no legitimate expectation of privacy in information he voluntarily turns over to third parties."

Similarly, we held in *California v. Ciraolo,* 476 U.S. 207, 106 S.Ct. 1809, 90 L.Ed.2d 210 (1986) that the police were not required by the Fourth Amendment to obtain a warrant before conducting surveillance of the respondent's fenced backyard from a private plane flying at an altitude of 1,000 feet. We concluded that the respondent's expectation that his yard was protected from such surveillance was unreasonable because "[a]ny member of the public flying in this airspace who glanced down could have seen everything that these officers observed."[a] * * *

[Greenwood] urges that the state-law right of Californians to privacy in their garbage, announced by the California Supreme Court in *Krivda,* survived the subsequent state constitutional amendment eliminating the suppression remedy as a means of enforcing that right. Hence, he argues that the Fourth Amendment should itself vindicate that right.

Individual States may surely construe their own constitutions as imposing more stringent constraints on police conduct than does the Federal Constitution. We have never intimated, however, that whether or not a search is reasonable within the meaning of the Fourth Amendment depends on the law of the particular State in which the search occurs. We have emphasized instead that the Fourth Amendment analysis must turn on such factors as "our *societal* understanding that certain areas deserve the most scrupulous protection from government invasion." We have already concluded that society as a whole possesses no such understanding with regard to garbage left for collection at the side of a public street. Respondent's argument is no less than a suggestion that concepts of privacy under the laws of each State are to determine the reach of the Fourth Amendment. We do not accept this submission.[b] * * *

Justice BRENNAN, with whom Justice MARSHALL joins, dissenting. * * *

a. *Ciraolo* was a 5–4 decision. The dissenters objected that "the actual risk to privacy from commercial or pleasure aircraft is virtually nonexistent. Travelers on commercial flights, as well as private planes used for business or personal reasons, normally obtain at most a fleeting, anonymous, and nondiscriminating glimpse of the landscape and buildings over which they pass. The risk that a passenger on such a plane might observe private activities, and might connect those activities with particular people, is simply too trivial to protect against."

b. Justice Kennedy took no part in the consideration or decision of this case.

A trash bag, like any of the above-mentioned containers, "is a common repository for one's personal effects" and, even more than many of them, is "therefore . . . inevitably associated with the expectation of privacy." A single bag of trash testifies eloquently to the eating, reading, and recreational habits of the person who produced it. A search of trash, like a search of the bedroom, can relate intimate details about sexual practices, health, and personal hygiene. Like rifling through desk drawers or intercepting phone calls, rummaging through trash can divulge the target's financial and professional status, political affiliations and inclinations, private thoughts, personal relationships, and romantic interests. It cannot be doubted that a sealed trash bag harbors telling evidence of the "intimate activity associated with the 'sanctity of a man's home and the privacies of life,' " which the Fourth Amendment is designed to protect.

The Court properly rejects the State's attempt to distinguish trash searches from other searches on the theory that trash is abandoned and therefore not entitled to an expectation of privacy. As the author of the Court's opinion observed last Term, a defendant's "property interest [in trash] does not settle the matter for Fourth Amendment purposes, for the reach of the Fourth Amendment is not determined by state property law." In evaluating the reasonableness of Greenwood's expectation that his sealed trash bags would not be invaded, the Court has held that we must look to "understandings that are recognized and permitted by society." Most of us, I believe, would be incensed to discover a meddler—whether a neighbor, a reporter, or a detective—scrutinizing our sealed trash containers to discover some detail of our personal lives. That was, quite naturally, the reaction to the sole incident on which the Court bases its conclusion that "snoops" and the like defeat the expectation of privacy in trash. When a tabloid reporter examined then-Secretary of State Henry Kissinger's trash and published his findings, Kissinger was "really revolted" by the intrusion and his wife suffered "grave anguish." N.Y. Times, July 9, 1975, p. A1, col. 8. The public response roundly condemning the reporter demonstrates that society not only recognized those reactions as reasonable, but shared them as well. Commentators variously characterized his conduct as "a disgusting invasion of personal privacy," Flieger, Investigative Trash, U.S. News & World Report, July 28, 1975, p. 72 (editor's page); "indefensible . . . as civilized behavior," Washington Post, July 10, 1975, p. A18, col. 1 (editorial); and contrary to "the way decent people behave in relation to each other," *ibid*.

Beyond a generalized expectation of privacy, many municipalities, whether for reasons of privacy, sanitation, or both, reinforce confidence in the integrity of sealed trash containers by "prohibit[ing] anyone, except authorized employees of the Town . . ., to rummage into, pick up, collect, move or otherwise interfere with articles or materials placed on . . . any public street for collection." In fact, the California Constitution, as interpreted by the State's highest court, guarantees a right of privacy in trash vis-à-vis government officials.

That is not to deny that isolated intrusions into opaque, sealed trash containers occur. When, acting on their own, "animals, children, scavengers, snoops, [or] other members of the general public," *actually* rummage through a bag of trash and expose its contents to plain view, "police cannot reasonably be expected to avert their eyes from evidence of criminal activity that could have been observed by any member of the public." * * *

Had Greenwood flaunted his intimate activity by strewing his trash all over the curb for all to see, or had some nongovernmental intruder invaded his privacy and done the same, I could accept the Court's conclusion that an expectation of privacy would have been unreasonable. Similarly, had police searching the city dump run across incriminating evidence that, despite commingling with the trash of others, still retained its identity as Greenwood's, we would have a different case. But all that Greenwood "exposed . . . to the public," were the exteriors of several opaque, sealed containers. * * *

The mere *possibility* that unwelcome meddlers *might* open and rummage through the containers does not negate the expectation of privacy in its contents any more than the possibility of a burglary negates an expectation of privacy in the home; or the possibility of a private intrusion negates an expectation of privacy in an unopened package; or the possibility that an operator will listen in on a telephone conversation negates an expectation of privacy in the words spoken on the telephone. "What a person . . . seeks to preserve as private, *even in an area accessible to the public,* may be constitutionally protected." *Katz.* We have therefore repeatedly rejected attempts to justify a State's invasion of privacy on the ground that the privacy is not absolute. See *Chapman v. United States,* [p. 357] (search of a house invaded tenant's Fourth Amendment rights even though landlord had authority to enter house for some purposes); *Stoner v. California,* [p. 357] (implicit consent to janitorial personnel to enter motel room does not amount to consent to police search of room); *O'Connor v. Ortega,* 480 U.S. 709, 107 S.Ct. 1492, 94 L.Ed.2d 714 (1987) (a government employee has a reasonable expectation of privacy in his office, even though "it is the nature of government offices that others—such as fellow employees, supervisors, consensual visitors, and the general public—may have frequent access to an individual's office"). * * *

Nor is it dispositive that "respondents placed their refuse at the curb for the express purpose of conveying it to a third party, . . . who might himself have sorted through respondents' trash or permitted others, such as police, to do so." In the first place, Greenwood can hardly be faulted for leaving trash on his curb when a county ordinance commanded him to do so, and prohibited him from disposing of it in any other way. More importantly, even the voluntary relinquishment of possession or control over an effect does not necessarily amount to a relinquishment of a privacy expectation in it. Were it otherwise, a letter or package would lose all Fourth Amendment protection when placed in a mail box or other depository with the "express purpose" of entrusting it to the postal officer or a private carrier; those bailees are just as likely as trash collectors (and certainly have greater incentive) to "sor[t] through" the personal effects entrusted to them, "or permi[t] others, such as police to do so." Yet, it has been clear for at least 110 years that the possibility of such an intrusion does not justify a warrantless search by police in the first instance. See *Ex parte Jackson,* 96 U.S. (6 Otto) 727, 24 L.Ed. 877 (1878). * * *

Notes and Questions

1. Should *Greenwood* apply even when the defendant has resorted to rather extraordinary means to ensure that the incriminating character of his garbage is not perceived by others? Yes is the answer given in *United States v. Scott,* 975 F.2d 927 (1st Cir.1992), where IRS agents painstakingly reassembled documents which defendant shredded into ⁵⁄₃₂–inch strips before putting them in the garbage later placed outside his curtilage. The court offered this analogy: "A person who prepares incriminating documents in a secret code (or for that matter in some obscure foreign language), and thereafter blithely discards them as trash, relying on the premise or hope that they will not be deciphered [or translated] by the authorities could well be in for an unpleasant surprise if his code is 'broken' by the police [or a translator is found for the abstruse language], but he cannot make

a valid claim that his subjective expectation in keeping the contents private by use of the secret code [or language] was reasonable in a constitutional sense."

2. *"Open fields" and other lands.* (a) After *Greenwood,* what result as to garbage left for pickup in a can well within the curtilage, if (i) the police merely enter and take the garbage, or (ii) the police have the garbage collector pick up and segregate the garbage from that can? More generally, what lands are protected by the Fourth Amendment from what kinds of police intrusions?

(b) In OLIVER v. UNITED STATES, 466 U.S. 170, 104 S.Ct. 1735, 80 L.Ed.2d 214 (1984), the Court, per POWELL, J., held that the "open fields" doctrine of *Hester v. United States,* 265 U.S. 57, 44 S.Ct. 445, 68 L.Ed. 898 (1924), by which police entry and examination of a field is free of any Fourth Amendment restraints, had not been implicitly overruled by *Katz.* This was because the *Hester* rule "was founded upon the explicit language of the Fourth Amendment. That Amendment indicates with some precision the places and things encompassed by its protections. As Justice Holmes explained for the Court in his characteristically laconic style: '[T]he special protection accorded by the Fourth Amendment to the people in their "persons, houses, papers, and effects," is not extended to the open fields. The distinction between the latter and the house is as old as the common law.' "

The Court in *Oliver* reasoned that this interpretation of the Amendment was consistent with *Katz,* as "open fields do not provide the setting for those intimate activities that the Amendment is intended to shelter from government interference or surveillance. There is no societal interest in protecting the privacy of those activities, such as the cultivation of crops, that occur in open fields. Moreover, as a practical matter these lands usually are accessible to the public and the police in ways that a home, an office or commercial structure would not be. It is not generally true that fences or no trespassing signs effectively bar the public from viewing open fields in rural areas. And both petitioner Oliver and respondent Thornton concede that the public and police lawfully may survey lands from the air. For these reasons, the asserted expectation of privacy in open fields is not an expectation that 'society recognizes as reasonable.'

"The historical underpinnings of the 'open fields' doctrine also demonstrate that the doctrine is consistent with respect for 'reasonable expectations of privacy.' As Justice Holmes, writing for the Court, observed in *Hester,* the common law distinguished 'open fields' from the 'curtilage,' the land immediately surrounding and associated with the home. The distinction implies that only the curtilage, not the neighboring open fields, warrants the Fourth Amendment protections that attach to the home. At common law, the curtilage is the area to which extends the intimate activity associated with the 'sanctity of a man's home and the privacies of life,' and therefore has been considered part of home itself for Fourth Amendment purposes. Thus, courts have extended Fourth Amendment protection to the curtilage; and they have defined the curtilage, as did the common law, by reference to the factors that determine whether an individual reasonably may expect that an area immediately adjacent to the home will remain private.[a]

---

a. As the Court explained in *United States v. Dunn,* 480 U.S. 294, 107 S.Ct. 1134, 94 L.Ed.2d 326 (1987), "curtilage questions should be resolved with particular reference to four factors: the proximity of the area claimed to be curtilage to the home, whether the area is included within an enclosure surrounding the home, the nature of the uses to which the area is put, and the steps taken by the resident to protect the area from observation by people passing by." Applying these factors, the Court then concluded the barn into which the police looked was not within the curtilage, as it was 60 yards from the house, was outside the area surrounding the house enclosed by a fence, did not appear to the police to be "used for inti-

Conversely, the common law implies, as we reaffirm today, that no expectation of privacy legitimately attaches to open fields."

As for the contention of Oliver and Thornton that the circumstances may sometimes show the existence of a reasonable expectation of privacy, the Court said it was answered by the "language of the Fourth Amendment," but added that such a case-by-case approach would in any event be unworkable because "police officers would have to guess before every search whether landowners had erected fences sufficiently high, posted a sufficient number of warning signs, or located contraband in an area sufficiently secluded to establish a right of privacy." The *Oliver* majority also asserted that it rejected "the suggestion that steps taken to protect privacy establish that expectations of privacy in an open field are legitimate. It is true, of course, that petitioner Oliver and respondent Thornton, in order to conceal their criminal activities, planted the marijuana upon secluded land and erected fences and no trespassing signs around the property. And it may be that because of such precautions, few members of the public stumbled upon the marijuana crops seized by the police. Neither of these suppositions demonstrates, however, that the expectation of privacy was *legitimate* in the sense required by the Fourth Amendment. The test of legitimacy is not whether the individual chooses to conceal assertedly 'private' activity. Rather, the correct inquiry is whether the government's intrusion infringes upon the personal and societal values protected by the Fourth Amendment. As we have explained, we find no basis for concluding that a police inspection of open fields accomplishes such an infringement."

MARSHALL, J., joined by Brennan and Stevens, JJ., dissenting, argued (1) that the Court's first ground could not be squared with earlier decisions, including *Katz* itself, for "neither a public telephone booth nor a conversation conducted therein can fairly be described as a person, house, paper, or effect"; and (2) that society *is* prepared to recognize as reasonable the expectations of Oliver and Thornton, which were supported by the law of criminal trespass, the private uses to which privately owned lands could be put, and the precautions which they had taken to manifest their privacy interest to others. From this the dissenters posited this "clear, easily administrable rule": "Private land marked in a fashion sufficient to render entry thereon a criminal trespass under the law of the state in which the land lies is protected by the Fourth Amendment's proscription of unreasonable searches and seizures."[b]

(c) FLORIDA v. RILEY, 488 U.S. 445, 109 S.Ct. 693, 102 L.Ed.2d 835 (1989), presented the question: "Whether surveillance of the interior of a partially covered greenhouse in a residential backyard from the vantage point of a helicopter located 400 feet above the greenhouse constitutes a 'search' for which a warrant is required under the Fourth Amendment." WHITE, J., for the 4–Justice plurality, concluded it did not "make a difference for Fourth Amendment purposes that the helicopter was flying at 400 feet when the officer saw what was growing in the greenhouse through the partially open roof and sides of the structure. We would have a different case if flying at that altitude had been contrary to law or regulation. But helicopters are not bound by the lower limits of

mate activities of the home," and the fences outside the barn were not of a kind "to prevent persons from observing what lay inside the enclosed area." The Court added that even assuming the barn was protected business premises, it still was no search to look into the open barn from an open fields vantage point.

b. See Stephen A. Saltzburg, *Another Victim of Illegal Narcotics: The Fourth Amendment (As Illustrated by the Open Fields Doctrine)*, 48 U.Pitt.L.Rev. 1 (1986).

the navigable airspace allowed to other aircraft. Any member of the public could legally have been flying over Riley's property in a helicopter at the altitude of 400 feet and could have observed Riley's greenhouse. The police officer did no more. This is not to say that an inspection of the curtilage of a house from an aircraft will always pass muster under the Fourth Amendment simply because the plane is within the navigable airspace specified by law. But it is of obvious importance that the helicopter in this case was *not* violating the law, and there is nothing in the record or before us to suggest that helicopters flying at 400 feet are sufficiently rare in this country to lend substance to respondent's claim that he reasonably anticipated that his greenhouse would not be subject to observation from that altitude. Neither is there any intimation here that the helicopter interfered with respondent's normal use of the greenhouse or of other parts of the curtilage. As far as this record reveals, no intimate details connected with the use of the home or curtilage were observed, and there was no undue noise, no wind, dust, or threat of injury. In these circumstances, there was no violation of the Fourth Amendment.''

O'CONNOR, J., concurring only in the judgment because ''the plurality's approach rests the scope of Fourth Amendment protection too heavily on compliance with FAA regulations whose purpose is to promote air safety not to protect'' Fourth Amendment rights, concluded: ''Because there is reason to believe that there is considerable public use of airspace at altitudes of 400 feet and above, and because Riley introduced no evidence to the contrary before the Florida courts, I conclude that Riley's expectation that his curtilage was protected from naked-eye aerial observation from that altitude was not a reasonable one. However, public use of altitudes lower than that—particularly public observations from helicopters circling over the curtilage of a home—may be sufficiently rare that police surveillance from such altitudes would violate reasonable expectations of privacy, despite compliance with FAA air safety regulations.''

BRENNAN, J., joined by Marshall and Stevens, JJ., dissenting, objected: ''Under the plurality's exceedingly grudging Fourth Amendment theory, the expectation of privacy is defeated if a single member of the public could conceivably position herself to see into the area in question without doing anything illegal. It is defeated whatever the difficulty a person would have in so positioning herself, and however infrequently anyone would in fact do so. In taking this view the plurality ignores the very essence of *Katz.* * * * Finding determinative the fact that the officer was where he had a right to be, at bottom, an attempt to analogize surveillance from a helicopter to surveillance by a police officer standing on a public road and viewing evidence of crime through an open window or a gap in a fence. In such a situation, the occupant of the home may be said to lack any reasonable expectation of privacy in what can be seen from that road—even if, in fact, people rarely pass that way.

''The police officer positioned 400 feet above Riley's backyard was not, however, standing on a public road. The vantage point he enjoyed was not one any citizen could readily share. His ability to see over Riley's fence depended on his use of a very expensive and sophisticated piece of machinery to which few ordinary citizens have access. In such circumstances it makes no more sense to rely on the legality of the officer's position in the skies than it would to judge the constitutionality of the wiretap in *Katz* by the legality of the officer's position outside the telephone booth. The simply inquiry whether the police officer had the legal right to be in the position from which he made his observations cannot suffice, for we cannot assume that Riley's curtilage was so open to the observations of passersby in the skies that he retained little privacy or personal security to be lost to police surveillance. The question before us must be not whether the police were where they had a right to be, but whether public observation of Riley's curtilage was so commonplace that Riley's expectation of privacy in his backyard could not be considered reasonable."

BLACKMUN, J., dissenting, first concluded that "a majority of this Court" (himself, the other three dissenters and O'Connor, J.) agreed "that the reasonableness of Riley's expectation depends, in large measure, on the frequency of nonpolice helicopter flights at an altitude of 400 feet." As for how this factual issue should be decided, he noted Brennan "suggests that we may resolve it ourselves without any evidence in the record on this point," while O'Connor "would impose the burden of proof on Riley" but would not now "allow Riley an opportunity to meet this burden." Blackmun, on the other hand, would impose upon the prosecution the burden of proving those "facts necessary to show that Riley lacked a reasonable expectation of privacy" and, "because our prior cases gave the parties little guidance on the burden of proof issue," would "remand this case to allow the prosecution an opportunity to meet this burden."

3.　*Other premises.* (a) *Business and commercial premises* are covered by the Fourth Amendment. As stated in *See v. City of Seattle,* 387 U.S. 541, 87 S.Ct. 1737, 18 L.Ed.2d 943 (1967), "[t]he businessman, like the occupant of a residence, has a constitutional right to go about his business free from unreasonable official entries upon his private commercial property."

(b) *Private areas in public places.* What if a police officer, positioned at an overhead vent above a rest room, looks down into an individual closed stall and observes criminal conduct? See *State v. Bryant,* 177 N.W.2d 800 (Minn.1970) (is a search). What, however, if the stalls had no doors? What if the observed conduct had not occurred within a stall?

(c) *Detention facilities.* In *Hudson v. Palmer,* 468 U.S. 517, 104 S.Ct. 3194, 82 L.Ed.2d 393 (1984), involving a § 1983 action brought by a state prison inmate who alleged a prison guard had conducted a "shakedown" search of his cell and had destroyed his noncontraband property for purposes of harassment, the Court held, 5–4, "that the Fourth Amendment has no applicability to a prison cell." The Chief Justice reasoned: "The two interests here are the interest of society in the security of its penal institutions and the interest of the prisoner in privacy within his cell. The latter interest, of course, is already limited by the exigencies of the circumstances: A prison 'shares none of the attributes of privacy of a home, an automobile, an office, or a hotel room.' We strike the balance in favor of institutional security, which we have noted is 'central to all other correctional goals.' A right of privacy in traditional Fourth Amendment terms is fundamentally incompatible with the close and continual surveillance of inmates and their cells required to ensure institutional security and internal order. We are satisfied that society would insist that the prisoner's expectation of privacy always yield to what must be considered the paramount interest in institutional security. We believe that it is accepted by our society that '[l]oss of freedom of choice and privacy are inherent incidents of confinement.'" The Court added that for "the same reasons" the seizure and destruction of a prisoner's effects did not fall within the protections of the Fourth Amendment. It is unclear whether *Hudson* applies to the search of the person of a prisoner[c] or, in any event, to a pretrial detention

c. As the dissenters noted, the majority "appears to limit its holding to a prisoner's 'papers and effects' located in his cell" and apparently "believes that at least a prisoner's 'person' is secure from unreasonable search and seizure." In *Bell v. Wolfish,* 441 U.S. 520, 99 S.Ct. 1861, 60 L.Ed.2d 447 (1979), where the Court declared that at best prisoners have facility.[d]

4. *Vehicles.* (a) In *Cardwell v. Lewis,* 417 U.S. 583, 94 S.Ct. 2464, 41 L.Ed.2d 325 (1974), police seized a car from a public parking lot and later took a small paint sample off the car and matched the tire tread with tracks at a crime scene. The Court divided on the propriety of the seizure of the car, but the plurality opinion seemed to view the later activity as no search: "With the 'search' limited to the examination of the tire on the wheel and the taking of paint scraping from the exterior of the vehicle left in the public parking lot, we fail to comprehend what expectation of privacy was infringed."

(b) In *New York v. Class,* 475 U.S. 106, 106 S.Ct. 960, 89 L.Ed.2d 81 (1986), an officer stopped a car for traffic violations and then, after the driver exited the car, opened the door and reached in to move papers obscuring the dashboard Vehicle Identification Number, at which time he saw a gun inside the car. Noting that "federal law requires that the VIN be placed in the plain view of someone *outside* the automobile," the Court concluded "there was no reasonable expectation of privacy in the VIN," so that the "mere viewing of the formerly obscured VIN was not" a search. But the Court then concluded that because "a car's interior [is] subject to Fourth Amendment protection," the officer's action in reaching inside the car "constituted a 'search'" (albeit a reasonable one in the circumstances).[e]

5. *Enhancing the senses.* Generally speaking, it is fair to say that it is not a search for an officer, lawfully present at a certain place, to detect something by one of his natural senses. *United States v. Mankani,* 738 F.2d 538 (2d Cir.1984) (no search where conversations in adjoining motel room "were overheard by the naked human ear"). The result ordinarily is the same when common means of enhancing the senses, such as a flashlight or binoculars, are used.[f] But what if more sophisticated or less common means are used?[g]

(a) *The canine nose.* In UNITED STATES v. PLACE, dealing with a temporary seizure of luggage (see p. 331) at an airport so that it could be brought into contact with a drug detection dog, the majority declared "that a person possesses a privacy interest in the contents of personal luggage that is protected by the Fourth Amendment. A 'canine sniff' by a well-trained narcotics detection dog, however, does not require opening the luggage. It does not expose noncontraband items that otherwise would remain hidden from public view, as does, for example, an officer's rummaging through the contents of the luggage. Thus, the manner in which information is obtained through this investigative technique is much less

---

a "reasonable expectation of privacy * * * of a diminished scope," it was held that neither strip searches nor body cavity inspections of pretrial detainees after contact visits with outsiders were unreasonable.

d. Much, but certainly not all, of the Court's analysis in *Hudson* has to do with circumstances existing in facilities housing those convicted of crime. But O'Connor, J., concurring, stated the broader proposition that the "fact of arrest and incarceration abates all legitimate Fourth Amendment privacy and possessory interests in personal effects."

e. See Tracey Maclin, *New York v. Class: A Little–Noticed Case With Disturbing Implications,* 78 J.Crim.L. & C. 1 (1987).

f. But consider *Raettig v. State,* 406 So.2d 1273 (Fla.App.1981) (use of flashlight to look

into camper through half-inch wide crack a search, as "a minute crack on the surface of such area can hardly be regarded as an implied invitation to any curious passerby to take a look"); *State v. Ward,* 617 P.2d 568 (Hawaii 1980) (use of binoculars to see crap game in 7th story apartment from closest vantage point an eighth of a mile away a search, as "the constitution does not require that in all cases a person, in order to protect his privacy, must shut himself off from fresh air, sunlight and scenery").

g. See Melvin Gutterman, *A Formulation of the Value and Means Models of the Fourth Amendment in the Age of Technologically Enhanced Surveillance,* 39 Syrac.L.Rev. 647 (1988).

intrusive than a typical search. Moreover, the sniff discloses only the presence or absence of narcotics, a contraband item. Thus, despite the fact that the sniff tells the authorities something about the contents of the luggage, the information obtained is limited. This limited disclosure also ensures that the owner of the property is not subjected to the embarrassment and inconvenience entailed in less discriminate and more intrusive investigative methods.

"In these respects, the canine sniff is *sui generis*. We are aware of no other investigative procedure that is so limited both in the manner in which the information is obtained and in the content of the information revealed by the procedure. Therefore, we conclude that the particular course of investigation that the agents intended to pursue here—exposure of respondent's luggage, which was located in a public place, to a trained canine—did not constitute a 'search' within the meaning of the Fourth Amendment."[h]

Is the notion that "the fourth amendment exists to protect the innocent and may normally be invoked by the guilty only when necessary to protect the innocent," so that "if a device could be invented that accurately detected weapons and did not disrupt the normal movement of people, there could be no fourth amendment objection to its use"? Arnold H. Loewy, *The Fourth Amendment as a Device for Protecting the Innocent*, 81 Mich.L.Rev. 1229, 1246, 1248 (1983). Is the use of these dogs nonetheless objectionable because people have a right to be free of unwanted suspicion, Martin R. Gardner, *Sniffing for Drugs in the Classroom*, 74 Nw.U.L.Rev. 803, 844–47 (1980), or is the answer that the innocent are benefited by "the dog that freed them from the unwarranted suspicion which otherwise would have continued"? Loewy, supra, at 1247. What then of other concerns about the use of such dogs: "To the extent that the dog is less than perfectly accurate, innocent people run the risk of being searched. Additionally, the very act of being subjected to a body sniff by a German Shepherd may be offensive at best or harrowing at worst to the innocent sniffee." Id. at 1246–47. Finally, what if a dog were utilized to ascertain that there were drugs inside a particular dwelling?[i]

Place was relied upon in *United States v. Jacobsen*, p. 150, holding that where police lawfully came upon a white powder in a package originally opened by private parties, an on-the-spot chemical test of a trace of the powder which would reveal only whether or not it was cocaine was not a search. "Here, as in *Place*, the likelihood that official conduct of the kind disclosed by the record will actually compromise any legitimate interest in privacy seems much too remote to characterize the testing as a search subject to the Fourth Amendment." Brennan and Marshall, JJ., dissenting, objected that "under the Court's analysis in these cases, law enforcement officers could release a trained cocaine-sensitive dog * * * to roam the streets at random, alerting the officers to people carrying cocaine. Or, if a device were developed that, when aimed at a person, would detect instantaneously whether the person is carrying cocaine, there would be no Fourth Amend-

---

h. Brennan and Marshall, JJ., concurring in the result, objected that this issue, neither reached by the court of appeals nor briefed and argued in the Supreme Court, should not be decided in "a discussion unnecessary to the judgment." Blackmun, J., concurring separately, expressed the same concern and added: "While the Court has adopted one plausible analysis of the issue, there are others. For example, a dog sniff may be a search, but a minimally intrusive one that could be justified

in this situation under *Terry* upon mere reasonable suspicion."

i. See *United States v. Thomas*, 757 F.2d 1359 (2d Cir.1985), reading *Place* with *United States v. Karo*, p. 171, and concluding such use of those dogs is a search. *Thomas* was questioned and distinguished in *United States v. Colyer*, 878 F.2d 469 (D.C.Cir.1989), holding there was no search where a drug dog in the public corridor of a train "alerted" to a particular sleeper compartment.

ment bar, under the Court's approach, to the police setting up such a device on a street corner and scanning all passersby. In fact, the Court's analysis is so unbounded that if a device were developed that could detect, from the outside of a building, the presence of cocaine inside, there would be no constitutional obstacle to the police cruising through a residential neighborhood and using the device to identify all homes in which the drug is present.''

(b) *Weapons detector.* The device imagined by Prof. Loewy back in 1983 may soon become a reality. As a result of Department of Justice funding, several organizations have undertaken to develop concealed weapons detection technology in order to produce a commercially and technologically viable device that could do an "electronic frisk" of a suspect from a distance of ten to twenty feet. Two of the detectors under development use magnetic fields, albeit in quite different ways. Raytheon's device would illuminate the subject with a low intensity electromagnetic pulse and then measure the time decay of the radiated energy from metal objects carried by the person. The device detects only metal objects, but produces no images. Rather, by measurement of the intensity and the time decay of the secondary radiation, there are produced "signatures" which can be identified as indicating whether the detected metal object is or is not a gun. By comparison, the INEL system uses magnetic gradiometers to measure fluctuations produced when anything made of ferromagnetic material moves through the earth's magnetic field. No electronic energy is directed at the subject, as these instruments merely measure what certain objects do to the earth's magnetic field. By use of target recognition software, the readings would be compared with known "signatures" of weapons of similar mass, shape and density to determine the likelihood that the device has focused upon a weapon. The third device, the Millitech system, uses passive millimeter wave imaging technology. The amplitude of radiation at which the waves are emitted varies with the object's temperature and other properties, and thus the Millitech detector scans the waves emitted by the human body and any objects concealed on the person and produces a small image on the back of the device in which the outlines of concealed objects, usually dark, are clearly visible against the much brighter image of the body.

Would the use of any or all of these systems constitute a Fourth Amendment search? Would the answer be the same in those twenty-five jurisdictions which have enacted some variety of a concealed weapon permit statute? See David Harris, *Superman's X–Ray Vision and the Fourth Amendment: The New Gun Detection Technology*, 69 Temple L.Rev. 1 (1996).

(c) *Electronic tracking.* With the consent of a chemical company, police installed a "beeper," a battery operated radio transmitter, into a container of chloroform, a chemical used to manufacture illicit drugs, prior to its purchase by suspect Armstrong. By a combination of visual surveillance and monitoring of the beeper signal the police tracked the container as it was carried in Petschen's automobile to a cabin in a rural area. On that evidence and other information obtained during surveillance of those premises, a search warrant for the cabin was issued, and an illicit drug lab was discovered within. Knotts, the owner of the cabin, was one of those convicted of conspiracy to manufacture controlled substances. In *United States v. Knotts,* 460 U.S. 276, 103 S.Ct. 1081, 75 L.Ed.2d 55 (1983), the Court, per Rehnquist, J., held that the use of the "beeper" did not constitute a Fourth Amendment search:

"Visual surveillance from public places along Petschen's route or adjoining Knotts' premises would have sufficed to reveal all of these facts to the police. The fact that the officers in this case relied not only on visual surveillance, but on the use of the beeper to signal the presence of Petschen's automobile to the police receiver, does not alter the situation. Nothing in the Fourth Amendment prohibited the police from augmenting the sensory faculties bestowed upon them at birth with such enhancement as science and technology afforded them in this case."

To Knotts' objection that under such a view "twenty-four hour surveillance of any citizen of this country will be possible, without judicial knowledge or supervision," the Court responded that "if such dragnet type law enforcement practices as respondent envisions should eventually occur, there will be time enough then to determine whether different constitutional principles may be applicable."

In UNITED STATES v. KARO, 468 U.S. 705, 104 S.Ct. 3296, 82 L.Ed.2d 530 (1984), the Court was "called upon to address two questions left unresolved in *Knotts:* (1) whether installation of a beeper in a container of chemicals with the consent of the original owner constitutes a search or seizure within the meaning of the Fourth Amendment when the container is delivered to a buyer having no knowledge of the presence of the beeper, and (2) whether monitoring of a beeper falls within the ambit of the Fourth Amendment when it reveals information that could not have been obtained through visual surveillance." The Court, per WHITE, J., answered the first question in the negative, reasoning that the mere transfer of the can containing an unmonitored beeper "infringed no privacy interest" because it "conveyed no information that [the recipient] wished to keep private, for it conveyed no information at all," and thus was no search, and that "it cannot be said that anyone's possessory interest was interfered with in a meaningful way," and thus there was no seizure. (STEVENS, Brennan and Marshall, JJ., dissenting on this branch of the case, argued that by "attaching the beeper and using the container to conceal it, the Government in the most fundamental sense was asserting 'dominion and control' over the property," which "is a 'seizure' in the most basic sense of the term.")

The Court answered the second question in the affirmative, first noting that unquestionably it would be an unreasonable search to surreptitiously enter a residence without a warrant to verify that the container was there. "For purpose of the Amendment, the result is the same where, without a warrant, the Government surreptitiously employs an electronic device to obtain information that it could not have obtained by observation from outside the curtilage of the house. The beeper tells the agent that a particular article is actually located at a particular time in the private residence and is in the possession of the person or persons whose residence is being surveilled. Even if visual surveillance has revealed that the article to which the beeper is attached has entered the house, the later monitoring not only verifies the officers' observations but also establishes that the article remains on the premises." The Court next concluded that absent "truly exigent circumstances" such use of the beeper was governed by "the general rule that a search of a house should be conducted pursuant to a warrant."[j] Such monitoring was characterized by the Court as "less intrusive than a full-scale search," but the Court did not have occasion to decide whether as a consequence such a warrant could issue upon reasonable suspicion rather than probable cause.[k]

j. In response to the government's claim that a warrant should not be required because of the difficulty in satisfying the particularity requirement of the Fourth Amendment, in that it is usually not known in advance to what place the container with the beeper in it will be taken, the Court concluded that it would suffice if the warrant were "to describe the object into which the beeper is to be placed, the circumstances that led agents to wish to install the beeper, and the length of time for which beeper surveillance is requested."

k. See Clifford Fishman, *Electronic Tracking Devices and the Fourth Amendment:*

(d) *Photographic magnification.* In DOW CHEMICAL CO. v. UNITED STATES, 476 U.S. 227, 106 S.Ct. 1819, 90 L.Ed.2d 226 (1986), the Court, per BURGER, C.J., held that aerial photography of a chemical company's industrial complex was not a Fourth Amendment "search": "It may well be, as the Government concedes, that surveillance of private property by using highly sophisticated surveillance equipment not generally available to the public, such as satellite technology, might be constitutionally proscribed absent a warrant. But the photographs here are not so revealing of intimate details as to raise constitutional concerns. Although they undoubtedly give EPA more detailed information than naked-eye views, they remain limited to an outline of the facility's buildings and equipment. The mere fact that human vision is enhanced somewhat, at least to the degree here, does not give rise to constitutional problems.[5] An electronic device to penetrate walls or windows so as to hear and record confidential discussions of chemical formulae or other trade secrets would raise very different and far more serious questions; other protections such as trade secret laws are available to protect commercial activities from private surveillance by competitors.[6]

"We conclude that the open areas of an industrial plant complex with numerous plant structures spread over an area of 2,000 acres are not analogous to the 'curtilage' of a dwelling for purposes of aerial surveillance; such an industrial complex is more comparable to an open field and as such it is open to the view and observation of persons in aircraft lawfully in the public airspace immediately above or sufficiently near the area for the reach of cameras."

POWELL, J., for the dissenters, objected that "Dow has taken every feasible step to protect information claimed to constitute trade secrets from the public and particularly from its competitors," and accordingly "has a reasonable expectation of privacy in its commercial facility in the sense required by the Fourth Amendment." Moreover, the rationale of *Ciraolo,* discussed below, is inapplicable here, for "the camera used in this case was highly sophisticated in terms of its capability to reveal minute details of Dow's confidential technology and equipment. The District Court found that the photographs revealed details as 'small as ½ inch in diameter.' Satellite photography hardly could have been more informative about Dow's technology. Nor are 'members of the public' likely to purchase $22,000.00 cameras."

Knotts, Karo, and the Questions Still Unanswered, 34 Cath.U.L.Rev. 277 (1985).

5. The partial dissent emphasizes Dow's claim that under magnification power lines as small as ½–inch diameter can be observed. But a glance at the photographs in issue shows that those power lines are observable only because of their stark contrast with the snow-white background. No objects as small as ½–inch diameter such as a class ring, for example, are recognizable, nor are there any identifiable human faces or secret documents captured in such a fashion as to implicate more serious privacy concerns. Fourth Amendment cases must be decided on the facts of each case, not by extravagant generalizations. "[W]e have never held that potential, as opposed to actual, invasions of privacy constitute searches for purposes of the Fourth Amendment." *United*

States v. Karo, [p. 171]. On these facts, nothing in these photographs suggests that any reasonable expectations of privacy have been infringed.

6. The partial dissent relies heavily on Dow's claim that aerial photography of its facility is proscribed by trade secret laws. While such laws may protect against use of photography by competitors in the same trade to advance their commercial interests, in no manner do "those laws constitute society's express determination" that *all* photography of Dow's facility violates reasonable expectations of privacy. No trade secret law cited to us by Dow proscribes the use of aerial photography of Dow's facilities for law enforcement purposes, let alone photography for private purposes unrelated to competition such as mapmaking or simple amateur snapshots.

(e) *Thermal imaging.* Police sometimes use an infrared thermal detection device, which detects differences in the surface temperature of targeted objects, to acquire evidence of marijuana growing activities inside of premises. Most appellate courts which have confronted the issue have held, often by analogy to *Greenwood*, p. 159, and *Place*, p. 168, that such use of these devices does not constitute a search. Those decisions, it was concluded in *United States v. Cusumano*, 67 F.3d 1497 (10th Cir.1995), "have reduced the Fourth Amendment inquiry to an analysis of the reasonable expectation of privacy residing in the 'waste heat' which is measured merely by 'a passive device, employed from beyond the curtilage, which emits no rays or beams and which does not intrude in any fashion upon the observed property.' "But this, the court continued, "is to ignore both the purpose of the device and the manner in which it operates," for the "imager measures not 'waste heat' but rather heat differentials" across "the exterior surface of a building" which in turn reveal "the amount of heat generated by heat sources in proximity to the interior of that wall"; in short, "the true worth of the device— the very reason that the government turned the imager on the home of the Defendants—is predicated upon the translation of these thermal records into intelligible (albeit speculative) information about the activities that generate the observed heat."

The court in *Cusumano* thus concluded the better analogy was to *Katz:* "It must be remembered that the bug at issue in *Katz* was fixed to the outside of a public phone booth. Reduced to its operational fundamentals, that bug did not monitor the interior of the phone booth at all; rather, it measured the molecular vibrations of the glass that encompassed that interior. Alternatively, it might fairly be said that the bug passively recorded the propagation of waste vibrational energy into the public sphere. Drawing upon the logic embraced by our fellow circuits, one could reason that the translation of the vibrational record into an account of that which transpired within the phone booth was simply a useful interpretation of abandoned energy—an analysis which would, we note, approve the search condemned in *Katz.* * * *

" * * * *Katz* looked not to the tools employed by the government nor to the phenomena measured by those tools but to the object of the government's efforts; we see no reason to do otherwise here. We acknowledge that the thermal imager monitors and records the heat signatures of the activities ongoing inside a structure. The pertinent inquiry is not, therefore, whether the Defendants retain an expectation of privacy in the 'waste heat' radiated from their home but, rather, whether they possess an expectation of privacy in the heat signatures of the activities, intimate or otherwise, that they pursue within their home."[l]

(f) *Gas Chromatography* involves using an extremely sensitive filtering machine to break down a gas sample or a liquid mixture into its molecular subcomponents. The sample to be tested is forced through a column, which is a glass tube filled with special filtration material, and a detector attached at the outgoing end of the column records the quantity and concentration of each particular molecular compound contained in the sample. Government-funded product development in recent years has turned GC from simply "a scientific laboratory technique" to one that is also used "on the streets." A law enforcement agent can use an eight-pound sampling unit, which resembles a large flashlight and works like a vacuum, to suck in vapors and particles from the immediate vicinity of a suspected

---

l. This opinion, vacated on rehearing en banc, 83 F.3d 1247 (10th Cir.1996), on the ground it was not necessary to reach the issue, was followed in *United States v. Kyllo*, 140 F.3d 1249 (9th Cir.1998).

container or individual. The analytical unit, also at the scene, then takes this sample and produces a chemical sketch of it, which is then compared to the make-up of known explosives (under one version of the equipment) or drugs (under another). The assumption is that a positive GC report establishes the presence of explosives or drugs, as the case may be, upon the object person or within the object container. Is such use of a portable unit, sometimes characterized as an "electronic canine," governed by the *Place* decision, p. 168? See Bober, *The "Chemical Signature" of the Fourth Amendment: Gas Chromatography/Mass Spectometry and the War on Drugs*, 8 Seton Hall Const.L.J. 75 (1997).

————

In *Gouled v. United States*, 255 U.S. 298, 41 S.Ct. 261, 65 L.Ed. 647 (1921), the Court held that search warrants "may not be used as a means of gaining access to a man's house or office and papers solely for the purpose of making search to secure evidence to be used against him in a criminal or penal proceeding." The Court derived from *Boyd v. United States*, p. 687, the proposition that warrants may be resorted to "only when a primary right to such search and seizure may be found in the interest which the public or the complainant may have in the property to be seized, or in the right to the possession of it, or when a valid exercise of the police power renders possession of the property by the accused unlawful and provides that it may be taken," that is, when the property is an instrumentality or fruit of crime or contraband. This "mere evidence" rule, as it came to be called, was finally repudiated in *Warden v. Hayden*, 387 U.S. 294, 87 S.Ct. 1642, 18 L.Ed.2d 782 (1967). Stressing that "the principal object of the Fourth Amendment is the protection of privacy rather than property," the Court noted that "privacy 'would be just as well served by a restriction on search to the even-numbered days of the month. * * * And it would have the extra advantage of avoiding hair-splitting questions.'" The government need not have a property interest in the property to be seized, as "government has an interest in solving crime," and that interest and the protection of privacy are best accommodated, the Court reasoned, by merely requiring probable cause that "the evidence sought will aid in a particular apprehension or conviction." But the Court cautioned:

"The items of clothing involved in this case are not 'testimonial' or communicative' in nature, and their introduction therefore did not compel respondent to become a witness against himself in violation of the Fifth Amendment. This case thus does not require that we consider whether there are items of evidential value whose very nature precludes them from being the object of a reasonable search and seizure."

ANDRESEN v. MARYLAND
427 U.S. 463, 96 S.Ct. 2737, 49 L.Ed.2d 627 (1976).

Justice BLACKMUN delivered the opinion of the Court.

[State authorities obtained search warrants to search petitioner's law office and also corporate offices for specified documents pertaining to a fraudulent sale of land. The papers found in the execution of the warrants were admitted against the petitioner at his trial, and he was convicted.]

The Fifth Amendment * * * provides that "[n]o person * * * shall be compelled in any criminal case to be a witness against himself." * * * The "historic function" of the privilege has been to protect a " 'natural individual from compulsory incrimination through his own testimony or personal records.' " There is no question that the records seized from petitioner's offices and introduced against him were incriminating. Moreover, it is undisputed that some of these business records contain statements made by petitioner. The question, therefore, is whether the seizure of these business records, and their admission into evidence at his trial, compelled petitioner to testify against himself in violation of the Fifth Amendment. This question may be said to have been reserved in *Warden v. Hayden.*

Petitioner contends that "the Fifth Amendment prohibition against compulsory self-incrimination applies as well to personal business papers seized from his offices as it does to the same papers being required to be produced under a subpoena." He bases his argument, naturally, on dicta in a number of cases which imply, or state, that the search for and seizure of a person's private papers violate the privilege against self-incrimination. Thus, in *Boyd v. United States* the Court said: "[W]e have been unable to perceive that the seizure of a man's private books and papers to be used in evidence against him is substantially different from compelling him to be a witness against himself." And in *Hale v. Henkel* [p. 692], it was observed that "the substance of the offense is the compulsory production of private papers, whether under a search warrant or a *subpoena duces tecum,* against which the person * * * is entitled to protection."

We do not agree, however, that these broad statements compel suppression of this petitioner's business records as a violation of the Fifth Amendment. In the very recent case of *Fisher v. United States* [p. 743], the Court held that an attorney's production, pursuant to a lawful summons, of his client's tax records in his hands did not violate the Fifth Amendment privilege of the taxpayer "because enforcement against a taxpayer's lawyer would not 'compel' the taxpayer to do anything—and certainly would not compel him to be a 'witness' against himself." We recognized that the continued validity of the broad statements contained in some of the Court's earlier cases had been discredited by later opinions. In those earlier cases, the legal predicate for the inadmissibility of the evidence seized was a violation of the Fourth Amendment; the unlawfulness of the search and seizure was thought to supply the compulsion of the accused necessary to invoke the Fifth Amendment. Compulsion of the accused was also absent in *Couch v. United States,* 409 U.S. 322, 93 S.Ct. 611, 34 L.Ed.2d 548 (1973), where the Court held that a summons served on a taxpayer's accountant requiring him to produce the taxpayer's personal business records in his possession did not violate the taxpayer's Fifth Amendment rights.

Similarly, in this case, petitioner was not asked to say or to do anything. The records seized contained statements that petitioner had voluntarily committed to writing. The search for and seizure of these records were conducted by law enforcement personnel. Finally, when these records were introduced at trial, they were authenticated by a handwriting expert, not by petitioner. Any compulsion of petitioner to speak, other than the inherent psychological pressure to respond at trial to unfavorable evidence, was not present.

This case thus falls within the principle stated by Mr. Justice Holmes: "A party is privileged from producing the evidence but not from its production." * * * Thus, although the Fifth Amendment may protect an individual from complying with a subpoena for the production of his personal records in his possession because the very act of production may constitute a compulsory authentication of incriminating information, a seizure of the same materials by law enforcement officers differs in a crucial respect—the individual against whom the search is directed is not required to aid in the discovery, production, or authentication of incriminating evidence.

A contrary determination that the seizure of a person's business records and their introduction into evidence at a criminal trial violates the Fifth Amendment, would undermine the principles announced in earlier cases. * * * These cases recognize a general rule: "There is no special sanctity in papers, as distinguished from other forms of property, to render them immune from search and seizure, if only they fall within the scope of the principles of the cases in which other property may be seized, and if they be adequately described in the affidavit and warrant."

Moreover, a contrary determination would prohibit the admission of evidence traditionally used in criminal cases and traditionally admissible despite the Fifth Amendment. For example, it would bar the admission of an accused's gambling records in a prosecution for gambling; a note given temporarily to a bank teller during a robbery and subsequently seized in the accused's automobile or home in a prosecution for bank robbery; and incriminating notes prepared, but not sent, by an accused in a kidnapping or blackmail prosecution. * * *

Finally we do not believe that permitting the introduction into evidence of a person's business records seized during an otherwise lawful search would offend or undermine any of the policies undergirding the privilege.

In this case, petitioner, at the time he recorded his communication, at the time of the search, and at the time the records were admitted at trial, was not subjected to "the cruel trilemma of self-accusation, perjury or contempt." Indeed, he was never required to say or to do anything under penalty of sanction. Similarly, permitting the admission of the records in question does not convert our accusatorial system of justice into an inquisitorial system. * * * Further, the search for and seizure of business records pose no danger greater than that inherent in every search that evidence will be "elicited by inhumane treatment and abuses." In this case, the statements seized were voluntarily committed to paper before the police arrived to search for them, and petitioner was not treated discourteously during the search. Also, the "good cause" to "disturb," petitioner was independently determined by the judge who issued the warrants; and the State bore the burden of executing them. Finally, there is no chance in this case, of petitioner's statements being self-deprecatory and untrustworthy because they were extracted from him—they were already in existence and had been made voluntarily. * * *

Justice BRENNAN, dissenting. * * *

The matter cannot be resolved on any simplistic notion of compulsion. Search and seizure is as rife with elements of compulsion as subpoena. The intrusion occurs under the lawful process of the State. The individual is not free to resist that authority. * * *

And compulsion does not disappear merely because the individual is absent at the time of search and seizure. The door to one's house, for example, is as much the individual's resistance to the intrusion of outsiders as his personal physical efforts to prevent the same. To refuse recognition to the sanctity of that door and, more generally, to confine the dominion of privacy to the mind compels an unconstitutional disclosure by denying to the individual a zone of physical freedom necessary for conducting one's affairs. * * *

Until today, no decision by this Court had held that the seizure of testimonial evidence by legal process did not violate the Fifth Amendment. Indeed, with few exceptions, the indications were strongly to the contrary. * * * These cases all reflect the root understanding of *Boyd v. United States:* "It is not the breaking of his doors, and the rummaging of his drawers, that constitutes the essence of the offence [to the Fifth Amendment]; but it is the invasion of his indefeasible right of personal security, personal liberty and private property. * * * [A]ny forcible and compulsory extortion of a man's own testimony or his private papers to be used as evidence to convict him of crime * * *, is within the condemnation of [the Amendment]. In this regard the fourth and fifth amendments run almost into each other."[a]

Notes and Questions

1. If the item to be seized was a diary instead of the business records in *Andresen*, would there be a stronger Fourth Amendment[b] or Fifth Amendment[c] argument against permitting the seizure? Consider *Model Pre–Arraignment Code* § SS 210.3(2): "With the exception of handwriting samples, and other writings or recordings of evidentiary value for reasons other than their testimonial content, things subject to seizure * * * shall not include personal diaries, letters, or other writings or recordings, made solely for private use or communication to an individual occupying a family, personal, or other confidential relation, other than a relation in criminal enterprise, unless such things have served or are serving a substantial purpose in furtherance of a criminal enterprise."

ZURCHER v. STANFORD DAILY
436 U.S. 547, 98 S.Ct. 1970, 56 L.Ed.2d 525 (1978).

Justice WHITE delivered the opinion of the Court.

[Nine policemen were injured by demonstrators at Stanford University Hospital. Two days later the Stanford Daily carried articles and photos devoted to the demonstration and attack; the photos by a staff member indicated he had been located where he could have photographed the assailants. A warrant was obtained to search the Daily's offices for negatives, film and pictures relevant to identification of the assailants. Executing officers searched photo labs, filing cabinets and desks, but found no evidence. The Daily later brought a civil action in district court, where declaratory relief was granted. That court held (i) that the Fourth Amendment forbade the issuance of a warrant to search for materials in the possession of one not suspected of crime except upon a showing of probable cause a subpoena *duces tecum* would be impracticable; and (ii) that the First Amendment bars search of newspaper offices except upon a clear showing that important materials would otherwise be destroyed or removed and that a restraining order would be futile.]

It is an understatement to say that there is no direct authority in this or any other federal court for the District Court's sweeping revision of the Fourth Amendment. Under existing law, valid warrants may be issued to search *any*

---

a. Marshall, J., dissented on other grounds and thus found it unnecessary to reach the Fifth Amendment issue.

b. In *Fisher,* relied upon in *Andresen,* the Court, after stating that the taxpayers "have not raised arguments of a Fourth Amendment nature * * * and could not be successful if they had," cautioned that the "[s]pecial problems of privacy which might be presented by

subpoena of a personal diary * * * are not involved here." See also n. 7 on p. 745.

c. "[I]t has been thought that a diary in which its author has recited his criminal conduct, seized in an otherwise lawful search, should not be used against him, just as any other kind of involuntary confession is unusable under the Fifth Amendment." *United States v. Boyette,* 299 F.2d 92 (4th Cir.1962).

property, whether or not occupied by a third party, at which there is probable cause to believe that fruits, instrumentalities, or evidence of a crime will be found. Nothing on the face of the Amendment suggests that a third-party search warrant should not normally issue. * * *

Against this background, it is untenable to conclude that property may not be searched unless its occupant is reasonably suspected of crime and is subject to arrest. * * * The Fourth Amendment has itself struck the balance between privacy and public need, and there is no occasion or justification for a court to revise the Amendment and strike a new balance by denying the search warrant in the circumstances present here and by insisting that the investigation proceed by subpoena *duces tecum,* whether on the theory that the latter is a less intrusive alternative, or otherwise. * * *

In any event, the reasons presented by the District Court and adopted by the Court of Appeals for arriving at its remarkable conclusion do not withstand analysis. First, as we have said, it is apparent that whether the third-party occupant is suspect or not, the State's interest in enforcing the criminal law and recovering the evidence remains the same; and it is the seeming innocence of the property owner that the District Court relied on to foreclose the warrant to search. But as respondents themselves now concede, if the third party knows that contraband or other illegal materials are on his property, he is sufficiently culpable to justify the issuance of a search warrant. Similarly, if his ethical stance is the determining factor, it seems to us that whether or not he knows that the sought-after articles are secreted on his property and whether or not he knows that the articles are in fact the fruits, instrumentalities, or evidence of crime, he will be so informed when the search warrant is served, and it is doubtful that he should then be permitted to object to the search, to withhold, if it is there, the evidence of crime reasonably believed to be possessed by him or secreted on his property, and to forbid the search and insist that the officers serve him with a subpoena *duces tecum*.

Second, we are unpersuaded that the District Court's new rule denying search warrants against third parties and insisting on subpoenas would substantially further privacy interests without seriously undermining law enforcement efforts. As the District Court understands it, denying third-party search warrants would not have substantial adverse effects on criminal investigations because the non-suspect third party, once served with a subpoena, will preserve the evidence and ultimately, lawfully respond. The difficulty with this assumption is that search warrants are often employed early in an investigation, perhaps before the identity of any likely criminal and certainly before all the perpetrators are or could be known. The seemingly blameless third party in possession of the fruits or evidence may not be innocent at all; and if he is, he may nevertheless be so related to or so sympathetic with the culpable that he cannot be relied upon to retain and preserve the articles that may implicate his friends, or at least not to notify those who would be damaged by the evidence that the authorities are aware of its location. In any event, it is likely that the real culprits will have access to the property, and the delay involved in employing the subpoena *duces tecum,* offering as it does the opportunity to litigate its validity, could easily result in the disappearance of the evidence, whatever the good faith of the third party. * * *[8]

8. It is also far from clear, even apart from the dangers of destruction and removal, whether the use of the subpoena *duces tecum* under circumstances where there is probable cause to believe that a crime has been committed and that the materials sought constitute evidence of its commission will result in the production of evidence with sufficient regularity to satisfy

We are also not convinced that the net gain to privacy interests by the District Court's new rule would be worth the candle.[9] In the normal course of events, search warrants are more difficult to obtain than subpoenas, since the latter do not involve the judiciary and do not require proof of probable cause. Where, in the real world, subpoenas would suffice, it can be expected that they will be employed by the rational prosecutor. On the other hand, when choice is available under local law and the prosecutor chooses to use the search warrant, it is unlikely that he has needlessly selected the more difficult course. His choice is more likely to be based on the solid belief, arrived at through experience but difficult, if not impossible, to sustain a specific case, that the warranted search is necessary to secure and to avoid the destruction of evidence.

[The Framers] did not forbid warrants where the press was involved, did not require special showings that subpoenas would be impractical, and did not insist that the owner of the place to be searched, if connected with the press, must be shown to be implicated in the offense being investigated. Further, the prior cases do no more than insist that the courts apply the warrant requirements with particular exactitude when First Amendment interests would be endangered by the search. As we see it, no more than this is required where the warrant requested is for the seizure of criminal evidence reasonably believed to be on the premises occupied by a newspaper. Properly administered, the pre-conditions for a warrant—probable cause, specificity with respect to the place to be searched and the things to be seized, and overall reasonableness—should afford sufficient protection against the harms that are assertedly threatened by warrants for searching newspaper offices.

There is no reason to believe, for example, that magistrates cannot guard against searches of the type, scope, and intrusiveness that would actually interfere with the timely publication of a newspaper. Nor, if the requirements of specificity and reasonableness are properly applied, policed, and observed, will there be any occasion or opportunity for officers to rummage at large in newspaper files or to intrude into or to deter normal editorial and publication decisions. The warrant issued in this case authorized nothing of this sort. Nor are we convinced, * * * that confidential sources will disappear and that the press will suppress news because of fears of warranted searches. Whatever incremental effect there may be in this regard if search warrants, as well as subpoenas, are permissible in proper circumstances, it does not make a constitutional difference in our judgment.

the public interest in law enforcement. Unlike the individual whose privacy is invaded by a search, the recipient of a subpoena may assert the Fifth Amendment privilege against self-incrimination in response to a summons to produce evidence or give testimony. See *Maness v. Meyers*, 419 U.S. 449, 95 S.Ct. 584, 42 L.Ed.2d 574 (1975). This privilege is not restricted to suspects. We have construed it broadly as covering any individual who might be incriminated by the evidence in connection with which the privilege is asserted. *Hoffman v. United States*, 341 U.S. 479, 71 S.Ct. 814, 95 L.Ed. 1118 (1951). The burden of overcoming an assertion of the Fifth Amendment privilege, even if prompted by a desire not to cooperate rather than any real fear of self-incrimination, is one which prosecutors would rarely be able to meet in the early stages of an investigation despite the fact they did not regard the witness as a suspect. Even time spent litigating such matters could seriously impede criminal investigations.

9. We reject totally the reasoning of the District Court that additional protections are required to assure that the Fourth Amendment rights of third parties are not violated because of the unavailability of the exclusionary rule as a deterrent to improper searches of premises in the control of nonsuspects. * * * It is probably seldom that police during the investigatory stage when most searches occur will be so convinced that no potential defendant will have standing to exclude evidence on Fourth Amendment grounds that they will feel free to ignore constitutional restraints. * * *

The fact is that respondents and *amici* have pointed to only a very few instances in the entire United States since 1971 involving the issuance of warrants for searching newspaper premises. This reality hardly suggests abuse; and if abuse occurs, there will be time enough to deal with it. Furthermore, the press is not only an important, critical, and valuable asset to society, but it is not easily intimidated—nor should it be. * * *

* * * Of course, the Fourth Amendment does not prevent or advise against legislative or executive efforts to establish nonconstitutional protections against possible abuses of the search warrant procedure,[a] but we decline to reinterpret the Amendment to impose a general constitutional barrier against warrants to search newspaper premises, to require resort to subpoenas as a general rule, or to demand prior notice and hearing in connection with the issuance of search warrants. * * *

Justice BRENNAN took no part in the consideration or decision of this case.

Justice POWELL, concurring.

* * * Even aside from the difficulties involved in deciding on a case-by-case basis whether a subpoena can serve as an adequate substitute,[1] I agree with the Court that there is no constitutional basis for such a reading. * * *

Justice STEWART, with whom Justice MARSHALL joins, dissenting. * * *

It seems to me self-evident that police searches of newspaper offices burden the freedom of the press. The most immediate and obvious First Amendment injury caused by such a visitation by the police is physical disruption of the operation of the newspaper. * * *

But there is another and more serious burden on a free press imposed by an unannounced police search of a newspaper office: the possibility of disclosure of information received from confidential sources, or of the identity of the sources themselves. Protection of those sources is necessary to ensure that the press can fulfill its constitutionally designated function of informing the public, because important information can often be obtained only by an assurance that the source will not be revealed. * * *

A search warrant allows police officers to ransack the files of a newspaper, reading each and every document until they have found the one named in the warrant,[7] while a subpoena would permit the newspaper itself to produce only the specific documents requested. A search, unlike a subpoena, will therefore lead to the needless exposure of confidential information completely unrelated to the purpose of the investigation. The knowledge that police officers can make an unannounced raid on a newsroom is thus bound to have a deterrent effect on the

a. Consider the Privacy Protection Act of 1980, Supp. App. B.

1. For example, respondent had announced a policy of destroying any photographs that might aid prosecution of protestors. While this policy probably reflected the deep feelings of the Vietnam era, and one may assume that under normal circumstances few, if any, press entities would adopt a policy so hostile to law enforcement, respondent's policy at least illustrates the possibility of such hostility. Use of a subpoena, as proposed by the dissent would be of no utility in face of a policy of destroying evidence. And unless the policy were publicly announced, it probably would be difficult to show the impracticality of a subpoena as opposed to a search warrant.

7. The Court says that "if the requirements of specificity and reasonableness are properly applied, policed, and observed" there will be no opportunity for the police to "rummage at large in newspaper files." But in order to find a particular document, no matter how specifically it is identified in the warrant, the police will have to search every place where it might be—including, presumably, every file in the office—and to examine each document they find to see if it is the correct one. I thus fail to see how the Fourth Amendment would provide an effective limit to these searches.

availability of confidential news sources. The end result, wholly inimical to the First Amendment, will be a diminishing flow of potentially important information to the public. * * *

Justice STEVENS, dissenting. * * *

In the pre-*Hayden* era warrants were used to search for contraband, weapons and plunder, but not for "mere evidence." The practical effect of the rule prohibiting the issuance of warrants to search for mere evidence was to narrowly limit not only the category of objects, but also the category of persons and the character of the privacy interests that might be affected by an unannounced police search.

Just as the witnesses who participate in an investigation or a trial far outnumber the defendants, the persons who possess evidence that may help to identify an offender, or explain an aspect of a criminal transaction, far outnumber those who have custody of weapons or plunder. Countless law abiding citizens— doctors, lawyers, merchants, customers, bystanders—may have documents in their possession that relate to an ongoing criminal investigation. The consequences of subjecting this large category of persons to unannounced police searches are extremely serious. The *ex parte* warrant procedure enables the prosecutor to obtain access to privileged documents that could not be examined if advance notice gave the custodian an opportunity to object. The search for the documents described in a warrant may involve the inspection of files containing other private matter. The dramatic character of a sudden search may cause an entirely unjustified injury to the reputation of the persons searched. * * *

A showing of probable cause that was adequate to justify the issuance of a warrant to search for stolen goods in the 18th century does not automatically satisfy the new dimensions of the Fourth Amendment in the post-*Hayden* era. * * * The only conceivable justification for an unannounced search of an innocent citizen is the fear that, if notice were given, he would conceal or destroy the object of the search. Probable cause to believe that the custodian is a criminal, or that he holds a criminal's weapons, spoils, or the like, justifies that fear, and therefore such a showing complies with the Clause. But if nothing said under oath in the warrant application demonstrates the need for an unannounced search by force, the probable cause requirement is not satisfied. In the absence of some other showing of reasonableness, the ensuing search violates the Fourth Amendment. * * *

Notes and Questions

1.   Compare *O'Connor v. Johnson*, 287 N.W.2d 400 (Minn.1979), involving a warrant issued for an attorney's office to search for and seize a certain client's business records:

"Even the most particular warrant cannot adequately safeguard client confidentiality, the attorney-client privilege, the attorney's work product, and the criminal defendant's constitutional right to counsel of all of the attorney's clients. It is unreasonable, in any case, to permit law enforcement officers to peruse miscellaneous documents in an attorney's office while attempting to locate documents listed in a search warrant. Even if it were possible to meet the particularity requirement regarding the place to be searched, the file would still contain some confidential information that is immune from seizure under the attorney-client privilege or the work product doctrine. Once that information is revealed to the police, the privileges are lost, and the information cannot be erased from the minds of the police. * * *

"It will not unreasonably burden prosecutors' offices and effective law enforcement to require officers to proceed by subpoena duces tecum in seeking documents held by an attorney. Attorneys are required by statute, the Code of Professional Responsibility, and the oath of admission to the bar to preserve and protect the judicial process. Thus, attorneys must respond faithfully and promptly, while still being allowed the opportunity to assert applicable privileges by a motion to quash."

2. It is noted in 67 A.B.A.J. 33 (1981) "that California's legislative response to the problem of surprise searches of offices of 'privilege-holders' may serve as a model for other states. The law calls for appointment of a special master to spearhead the search. * * *

"The California solution hasn't satisfied everyone, however. John Cleary, head of the federal public defender office in San Diego, said the law is 'unhealthy. There is an illusion of protection.' Robert Philibosian, chief assistant California attorney general, said: 'We vigorously opposed [the law].' He said it impairs law enforcement, especially in the white-collar crime area: 'We have to jump through hoops [to obtain evidence].' "[b]

3. Compare *Model Pre–Arraignment Code* §§ 220.5(2) & (3) providing that if the documents to be seized "cannot be searched for or identified without examining the contents of other documents, or if they constitute items or entries in account books, diaries, or other documents containing matter not specified in the warrant, the executing officer shall not examine the documents but shall either impound them under appropriate protection where found, or seal and remove them for safekeeping pending further proceedings." At a later adversary judicial hearing, a motion may be made for return of the documents or for "specification of such conditions and limitations on the further search for the documents to be seized as may be appropriate to prevent unnecessary or unreasonable invasion of privacy." If return is not ordered, "the search shall proceed under such conditions and limitations as the order shall prescribe."

4. The requirement (as stated in *Zurcher*) "that the courts apply the warrant requirement with particular exactitude when First Amendment interests would be endangered by the search" does *not* mean, the Court later held in *New York v. P.J. Video, Inc.*, 475 U.S. 868, 106 S.Ct. 1610, 89 L.Ed.2d 871 (1986), that a higher probable cause standard applies in such cases. The Court deemed sufficient "the longstanding special protections" established in its earlier cases, namely: (a) "that the police may not rely on the 'exigency' exception to the Fourth Amendment's warrant requirement in conducting a seizure of allegedly obscene materials, under circumstances where such a seizure would effectively constitute a 'prior restraint' "; (b) "that the large-scale seizure of books or films constituting a 'prior restraint' must be preceded by an adversary hearing on the question of obscenity"; (c) "that, even where a seizure of allegedly obscene materials would not constitute a 'prior restraint,' but instead would merely preserve evidence for trial, the seizure must be made pursuant to a warrant and there must be an opportunity for a prompt post-seizure judicial determination of obscenity"; and (d) "that a warrant authorizing the seizure of materials presumptively protected by the First Amendment may not issue based solely on the conclusory allegations of a police officer that the sought-after materials are obscene."

b. See Ronald Goldstock & Steven Chananie, *"Criminal" Lawyers: The Use of Electronic Surveillance and Search Warrants in the Inves-* *tigation and Prosecution of Attorneys Suspected of Criminal Wrongdoing,* 136 U.Pa.L.Rev. 1855 (1988).

SECTION 3. "PROBABLE CAUSE"

SPINELLI v. UNITED STATES
393 U.S. 410, 89 S.Ct. 584, 21 L.Ed.2d 637 (1969).

Justice HARLAN delivered the opinion of the Court.

William Spinelli was convicted * * of traveling to St. Louis, Missouri, from a nearby Illinois suburb with the intention of conducting gambling activities proscribed by Missouri law. At every appropriate stage in the proceedings in the lower courts, the petitioner challenged the constitutionality of the warrant which authorized the FBI search that uncovered the evidence necessary for his conviction. * * * Believing it desirable that the principles of [*Aguilar v. Texas*, 378 U.S. 108, 84 S.Ct. 1509, 12 L.Ed.2d 723 (1964)] should be further explicated, we granted certiorari * * *.

In *Aguilar*, a search warrant had issued upon an affidavit of police officers who swore only that they had "received reliable information from a credible person and do believe" that narcotics were being illegally stored on the described premises. While recognizing that the constitutional requirement of probable cause can be satisfied by hearsay information, this Court held the affidavit inadequate for two reasons. First, the application failed to set forth any of the "underlying circumstances" necessary to enable the magistrate independently to judge of the validity of the informant's conclusion that the narcotics were where he said they were. Second, the affiant-officers did not attempt to support their claim that their informant was " 'credible' or his information 'reliable.' "The Government is, however, quite right in saying that the FBI affidavit in the present case is more ample than that in *Aguilar*. Not only does it contain a report from an anonymous informant, but it also contains a report of an independent FBI investigation which is said to corroborate the informant's tip. We are, then, required to delineate the manner in which *Aguilar's* two-pronged test should be applied in these circumstances.

In essence, the affidavit * * * contained the following allegations:

1. The FBI had kept track of Spinelli's movements on five days during the month of August 1965. On four of these occasions, Spinelli was seen crossing one of two bridges leading from Illinois into St. Louis, Missouri, between 11 a.m. and 12:15 p.m. On four of the five days, Spinelli was also seen parking his car in a lot used by residents of an apartment house at 1108 Indian Circle Drive in St. Louis, between 3:30 p.m. and 4:45 p.m. On one day, Spinelli was followed further and seen to enter a particular apartment in the building.

2. An FBI check with the telephone company revealed that this apartment contained two telephones listed under the name of Grace P. Hagen, and carrying the numbers WYdown 4–0029 and WYdown 4–0136.

3. The application stated that "William Spinelli is known to this affiant and to federal law enforcement agents and local law enforcement agents as a bookmaker, an associate of bookmakers, a gambler, and an associate of gamblers."

4. Finally, it was stated that the FBI "has been informed by a confidential reliable informant that William Spinelli is operating a handbook and accepting wagers and disseminating wagering information by means of the telephones which have been assigned the numbers WYdown 4–0029 and WYdown 4–0136."

There can be no question that the last item mentioned, detailing the informant's tip, has a fundamental place in this warrant application. Without it, probable cause could not be established. The first two items reflect only innocent-seeming activity and data. Spinelli's travels to and from the apartment building and his entry into a particular apartment on one occasion could hardly be taken as bespeaking gambling activity; and there is surely nothing unusual about an apartment containing two separate telephones. Many a householder indulges himself in this petty luxury. Finally, the allegation that Spinelli was "known" to the affiant and to other federal and local law enforcement officers as a gambler and an associate of gamblers is but a bald and unilluminating assertion of suspicion that is entitled to no weight in appraising the magistrate's decision. *Nathanson v. United States,* 290 U.S. 41, 46, 54 S.Ct. 11, 12, 78 L.Ed. 159 (1933).

So much indeed the Government does not deny. Rather, following the reasoning of the Court of Appeals, the Government claims that the informant's tip gives a suspicious color to the FBI's reports detailing Spinelli's innocent-seeming conduct and that, conversely, the FBI's surveillance corroborates the informant's tip, thereby entitling it to more weight. * * * We believe, however, that the "totality of circumstances" approach taken by the Court of Appeals paints with too broad a brush. Where, as here, the informer's tip is a necessary element in a finding of probable cause, its proper weight must be determined by a more precise analysis.

The informer's report must first be measured against *Aguilar's* standards so that its probative value can be assessed. If the tip is found inadequate under *Aguilar,* the other allegations which corroborate the information contained in the hearsay report should then be considered. At this stage as well, however, the standards enunciated in *Aguilar* must inform the magistrate's decision. He must ask: Can it fairly be said that the tip, even when certain parts of it have been corroborated by independent sources, is as trustworthy as a tip which would pass *Aguilar's* tests without independent corroboration? * * *

Applying these principles to the present case, we first consider the weight to be given the informer's tip when it is considered apart from the rest of the affidavit. It is clear that a Commissioner could not credit it without abdicating his constitutional function. Though the affiant swore that his confidant was "reliable," he offered the magistrate no reason in support of this conclusion. Perhaps even more important is the fact that *Aguilar's* other test has not been satisfied. The tip does not contain a sufficient statement of the underlying circumstances from which the informer concluded that Spinelli was running a bookmaking operation. We are not told how the FBI's source received his information—it is not alleged that the informant personally observed Spinelli at work or that he had ever placed a bet with him. Moreover, if the informant came by the information indirectly, he did not explain why his sources were reliable. In the absence of a statement detailing the manner in which the information was gathered, it is especially important that the tip describe the accused's criminal activity in sufficient detail so that the magistrate may know that he is relying on something more substantial than a casual rumor circulating in the underworld or an accusation based merely on an individual's general reputation.

The detail provided by the informant in *Draper v. United States,* 358 U.S. 307, 79 S.Ct. 329, 3 L.Ed.2d 327 (1959), provides a suitable benchmark. While Hereford, the FBI's informer in that case, did not state the way in which he had obtained his information, he reported that Draper had gone to Chicago the day before by train and that he would return to Denver by train with three ounces of heroin on one of two specified mornings. Moreover, Hereford went on to describe, with minute particularity, the clothes that Draper would be wearing upon his arrival at the Denver station. A magistrate, when confronted with such detail, could reasonably infer that the informant had gained his information in a reliable way. Such an inference cannot be made in the present case. Here, the only facts supplied were that Spinelli was using two specified telephones and that these phones were being used in gambling operations. This meager report could easily have been obtained from an off-hand remark heard at a neighborhood bar.

Nor do we believe that the patent doubts *Aguilar* raises as to the report's reliability are adequately resolved by a consideration of the allegations detailing the FBI's independent investigative efforts. At most, these allegations indicated that Spinelli could have used the telephones specified by the informant for some purpose. This cannot by itself be said to support both the inference that the informer was generally trustworthy and that he had made his charge against Spinelli on the basis of information obtained in a reliable way. Once again, *Draper* provides a relevant comparison. Independent police work in that case corroborated much more than one small detail that had been provided by the informant. There, the police, upon greeting the inbound Denver train on the second morning specified by informer Hereford, saw a man whose dress corresponded precisely to Hereford's detailed description. It was then apparent that the informant had not been fabricating his report out of whole cloth; since the report was of the sort which in common experience may be recognized as having been obtained in a reliable way, it was perfectly clear that probable cause had been established.

We conclude, then, that in the present case the informant's tip—even when corroborated to the extent indicated—was not sufficient to provide the basis for a finding of probable cause. * * *

The judgment of the Court of Appeals is reversed * * *.

Justice WHITE, concurring.

* * *

The tension between *Draper* and the *Nathanson-Aguilar* line of cases is evident from the course followed by the majority opinion. * * * Since [the informant's] specific information about Spinelli using two phones with particular numbers had been verified, did not his allegation about gambling thereby become sufficiently more believable if the *Draper* principle is to be given any scope at all? I would think so, particularly since the information from the informant which was verified was not neutral, irrelevant information but was material to proving the gambling allegation: two phones with different numbers in an apartment used away from home indicates a business use in an operation, like bookmaking, where multiple phones are needed. The *Draper* approach would reasonably justify the issuance of a warrant in this case, particularly since the police had some awareness of Spinelli's past activities. The majority, however, while seemingly embracing *Draper*, confines that case to its own facts. Pending full scale reconsideration of that case, on the one hand, or of the *Nathanson-Aguilar* cases on the other, I join the opinion of the Court and the judgment of reversal especially since a vote to affirm would produce an equally divided Court.[a]

ILLINOIS v. GATES
462 U.S. 213, 103 S.Ct. 2317, 76 L.Ed.2d 527 (1983).

Justice REHNQUIST delivered the opinion of the Court.

* * * A chronological statement of events usefully introduces the issues at stake. Bloomingdale, Ill., is a suburb of Chicago located in DuPage County. On

---

a. Black, Fortas, and Stewart, JJ., dissented separately; Marshall, J., took no part in the case.

May 3, 1978, the Bloomingdale Police Department received by mail an anonymous handwritten letter which read as follows:

"This letter is to inform you that you have a couple in your town who strictly make their living on selling drugs. They are Sue and Lance Gates, they live on Greenway, off Bloomingdale Rd. in the condominiums. Most of their buys are done in Florida. Sue his wife drives their car to Florida, where she leaves it to be loaded up with drugs, then Lance flys down and drives it back. Sue flys back after she drops the car off in Florida. May 3 she is driving down there again and Lance will be flying down in a few days to drive it back. At the time Lance drives the car back he has the trunk loaded with over $100,000.00 in drugs. Presently they have over $100,000.00 worth of drugs in their basement.

They brag about the fact they never have to work, and make their entire living on pushers.

I guarantee if you watch them carefully you will make a big catch. They are friends with some big drugs dealers, who visit their house often.

  Lance & Susan Gates

Greenway
in Condominiums"

The letter was referred by the Chief of Police of the Bloomingdale Police Department to Detective Mader, who decided to pursue the tip. Mader learned, from the office of the Illinois Secretary of State, that an Illinois driver's license had been issued to one Lance Gates, residing at a stated address in Bloomingdale. He contacted a confidential informant, whose examination of certain financial records revealed a more recent address for the Gates, and he also learned from a police officer assigned to O'Hare Airport that "L. Gates" had made a reservation on Eastern Airlines flight 245 to West Palm Beach, Fla., scheduled to depart from Chicago on May 5 at 4:15 p.m.

Mader then made arrangements with an agent of the Drug Enforcement Administration for surveillance of the May 5 Eastern Airlines flight. The agent later reported to Mader that Gates had boarded the flight, and that federal agents in Florida had observed him arrive in West Palm Beach and take a taxi to the nearby Holiday Inn. They also reported that Gates went to a room registered to one Susan Gates and that, at 7:00 a.m. the next morning, Gates and an unidentified woman left the motel in a Mercury bearing Illinois license plates and drove northbound on an interstate frequently used by travelers to the Chicago area. In addition, the DEA agent informed Mader that the license plate number on the Mercury registered to a Hornet station wagon owned by Gates. The agent also advised Mader that the driving time between West Palm Beach and Bloomingdale was approximately 22 to 24 hours.

Mader signed an affidavit setting forth the foregoing facts, and submitted it to a judge of the Circuit Court of DuPage County, together with a copy of the anonymous letter. The judge of that court thereupon issued a search warrant for the Gates' residence and for their automobile. The judge, in deciding to issue the warrant, could have determined that the *modus operandi* of the Gates had been substantially corroborated. As the anonymous letter predicted, Lance Gates had flown from Chicago to West Palm Beach late in the afternoon of May 5th, had checked into a hotel room registered in the name of his wife, and, at 7:00 a.m. the following morning, had headed north, accompanied by an unidentified woman, out of West Palm Beach on an interstate highway used by travelers from South Florida to Chicago in an automobile bearing a license plate issued to him.

At 5:15 a.m. on May 7th, only 36 hours after he had flown out of Chicago, Lance Gates, and his wife, returned to their home in Bloomingdale, driving the car in which they had left West Palm Beach some 22 hours earlier. The Bloomingdale police were awaiting them, searched the trunk of the Mercury, and uncovered approximately 350 pounds of marijuana. A search of the Gates' home revealed marijuana, weapons, and other contraband. The Illinois Circuit Court ordered suppression of all these items, on the ground that the affidavit submitted to the Circuit Judge failed to support the necessary determination of probable cause to believe that the Gates' automobile and home contained the contraband in question. This decision was affirmed in turn by the Illinois Appellate Court and by a divided vote of the Supreme Court of Illinois.

The Illinois Supreme Court concluded—and we are inclined to agree—that, standing alone, the anonymous letter sent to the Bloomingdale Police Department would not provide the basis for a magistrate's determination that there was probable cause to believe contraband would be found in the Gates' car and home. The letter provides virtually nothing from which one might conclude that its author is either honest or his information reliable; likewise, the letter gives absolutely no indication of the basis for the writer's predictions regarding the Gates' criminal activities. Something more was required, then, before a magistrate could conclude that there was probable cause to believe that contraband would be found in the Gates' home and car.

The Illinois Supreme Court also properly recognized that Detective Mader's affidavit might be capable of supplementing the anonymous letter with information sufficient to permit a determination of probable cause. In holding that the affidavit in fact did not contain sufficient additional information to sustain a determination of probable cause, the Illinois court applied a "two-pronged test," derived from our decision in *Spinelli v. United States*. The Illinois Supreme Court, like some others, apparently understood *Spinelli* as requiring that the anonymous letter satisfy each of two independent requirements before it could be relied on. According to this view, the letter, as supplemented by Mader's affidavit, first had to adequately reveal the "basis of knowledge" of the letter writer—the particular means by which he came by the information given in his report. Second, it had to provide facts sufficiently establishing either the "veracity" of the affiant's informant, or, alternatively, the "reliability" of the informant's report in this particular case.

The Illinois court, alluding to an elaborate set of legal rules that have developed among various lower courts to enforce the "two-pronged test,"[4] found

4. In summary, these rules posit that the "veracity" prong of the *Spinelli* test has two "spurs"—the informant's "credibility" and the "reliability" of his information. Various interpretations are advanced for the meaning of the "reliability" spur of the "veracity" prong. Both the "basis of knowledge" prong and the "veracity" prong are treated as entirely separate requirements, which must be independently satisfied in every case in order to sustain a determination of probable cause. Some ancillary doctrines are relied on to satisfy certain of the foregoing requirements. For example, the "self-verifying detail" of a tip may satisfy the "basis of knowledge" requirement, although not the "credibility" spur of the "veracity" prong. Conversely, corroboration would seem not capable of supporting the "basis of knowlthat the test had not been satisfied. First, the "veracity" prong was not satisfied because, "there was simply no basis [for] * * * conclud[ing] that the anonymous person [who wrote the letter to the Bloomingdale Police Department] was credible." The court indicated that corroboration by police of details contained in the letter might never satisfy the "veracity" prong, and in any event, could not do so if, as in the present case, only "innocent" details are corroborated. In addition, the letter gave no indication of the basis of its writer's knowledge of the Gates' activities. The Illinois court understood *Spinelli* as permitting the detail contained in a tip to be used to infer that the informant had a reliable basis for his statements, but it thought that the anonymous letter failed to provide sufficient detail to permit such an inference. Thus, it concluded that no showing of probable cause had been made.

We agree with the Illinois Supreme Court that an informant's "veracity," "reliability" and "basis of knowledge" are all highly relevant in determining the value of his report. We do not agree, however, that these elements should be understood as entirely separate and independent requirements to be rigidly exacted in every case, which the opinion of the Supreme Court of Illinois would imply. Rather, as detailed below, they should be understood simply as closely intertwined issues that may usefully illuminate the common sense, practical question whether there is "probable cause" to believe that contraband or evidence is located in a particular place.

This totality of the circumstances approach is far more consistent with our prior treatment of probable cause than is any rigid demand that specific "tests" be satisfied by every informant's tip. Perhaps the central teaching of our decisions bearing on the probable cause standard is that it is a "practical, nontechnical conception." *Brinegar v. United States,* 338 U.S. 160, 69 S.Ct. 1302, 93 L.Ed. 1879 (1949). "In dealing with probable cause, * * * as the very name implies, we deal with probabilities. These are not technical; they are the factual and practical considerations of everyday life on which reasonable and prudent men, not legal technicians, act." Our observation in *United States v. Cortez,* [p. 319], regarding "particularized suspicion," is also applicable to the probable cause standard:

> The process does not deal with hard certainties, but with probabilities. Long before the law of probabilities was articulated as such, practical people formulated certain common-sense conclusions about human behavior; jurors as factfinders are permitted to do the same—and so are law enforcement officers. Finally, the evidence thus collected must be seen and weighed not in terms of library analysis by scholars, but as understood by those versed in the field of law enforcement.

As these comments illustrate, probable cause is a fluid concept—turning on the assessment of probabilities in particular factual contexts—not readily, or even usefully, reduced to a neat set of legal rules. Informants' tips doubtless come in many shapes and sizes from many different types of persons. * * * Rigid legal rules are ill-suited to an area of such diversity. "One simple rule will not cover every situation."[7]

---

edge" prong, but only the "veracity" prong. * * *

7. The diversity of informants' tips, as well as the usefulness of the totality of the circumstances approach to probable cause, is reflected in our prior decisions on the subject. In *Jones v. United States,* 362 U.S. 257, 80 S.Ct. 725, 4 L.Ed.2d 697 (1960), we held that probable cause to search petitioners' apartment was established by an affidavit based principally on an informant's tip. The unnamed informant claimed to have purchased narcotics from petitioners at their apartment; the affiant stated that he had been given correct information from the informant on a prior occasion. This, and the fact that petitioners had admitted to

Moreover, the "two-pronged test" directs analysis into two largely independent channels—the informant's "veracity" or "reliability" and his "basis of knowledge." There are persuasive arguments against according these two elements such independent status. Instead, they are better understood as relevant considerations in the totality of circumstances analysis that traditionally has guided probable cause determinations: a deficiency in one may be compensated for, in determining the overall reliability of a tip, by a strong showing as to the other, or by some other indicia of reliability.

If, for example, a particular informant is known for the unusual reliability of his predictions of certain types of criminal activities in a locality, his failure, in a particular case, to thoroughly set forth the basis of his knowledge surely should not serve as an absolute bar to a finding of probable cause based on his tip. Likewise, if an unquestionably honest citizen comes forward with a report of criminal activity—which if fabricated would subject him to criminal liability—we have found rigorous scrutiny of the basis of his knowledge unnecessary. Conversely, even if we entertain some doubt as to an informant's motives, his explicit and detailed description of alleged wrongdoing, along with a statement that the event was observed first-hand, entitles his tip to greater weight than might otherwise be the case. Unlike a totality of circumstances analysis, which permits a balanced assessment of the relative weights of all the various indicia of reliability (and unreliability) attending an informant's tip, the "two-pronged test" has encouraged an excessively technical dissection of informants' tips, with undue attention being focused on isolated issues that cannot sensibly be divorced from the other facts presented to the magistrate. * * *

We also have recognized that affidavits "are normally drafted by non-lawyers in the midst and haste of a criminal investigation. Technical requirements of elaborate specificity once exacted under common law pleading have no proper place in this area." Likewise, search and arrest warrants long have been issued by persons who are neither lawyers nor judges, and who certainly do not remain abreast of each judicial refinement of the nature of "probable cause." The rigorous inquiry into the *Spinelli* prongs and the complex superstructure of evidentiary and analytical rules that some have seen implicit in our *Spinelli* decision, cannot be reconciled with the fact that many warrants are—quite

police officers on another occasion that they were narcotics users, sufficed to support the magistrate's determination of probable cause.

Likewise, in *Rugendorf v. United States,* 376 U.S. 528, 84 S.Ct. 825, 11 L.Ed.2d 887 (1964), the Court upheld a magistrate's determination that there was probable cause to believe that certain stolen property would be found in petitioner's apartment. The affidavit submitted to the magistrate stated that certain furs had been stolen, and that a confidential informant, who previously had furnished confidential information, said that he saw the furs in petitioner's home. Moreover, another confidential informant, also claimed to be reliable, stated that one Schweihs had stolen the furs. Police reports indicated that petitioner had been seen in Schweihs' company and a third informant stated that petitioner was a fence for Schweihs.

Finally, in *Ker v. California,* 374 U.S. 23, 83 S.Ct. 1623, 10 L.Ed.2d 726 (1963), we held that information within the knowledge of officers who searched the Ker's apartment provided them with probable cause to believe drugs would be found there. The officers were aware that one Murphy had previously sold marijuana to a police officer; the transaction had occurred in an isolated area, to which Murphy had led the police. The night after this transaction, police observed Ker and Murphy meet in the same location. Murphy approached Ker's car, and, although police could see nothing change hands, Murphy's *modus operandi* was identical to what it had been the night before. Moreover, when police followed Ker from the scene of the meeting with Murphy he managed to lose them after performing an abrupt U-turn. Finally, the police had a statement from an informant who had provided reliable information previously, that Ker was engaged in selling marijuana, and that his source was Murphy. We concluded that "To say that this coincidence of information was sufficient to support a reasonable belief of the officers that Ker was illegally in possession of marijuana is to indulge in understatement."

properly—issued on the basis of nontechnical, common-sense judgments of laymen applying a standard less demanding than those used in more formal legal proceedings. Likewise, given the informal, often hurried context in which it must be applied, the "built-in subtleties" of the "two-pronged test" are particularly unlikely to assist magistrates in determining probable cause.

Similarly, we have repeatedly said that after-the-fact scrutiny by courts of the sufficiency of an affidavit should not take the form of *de novo* review. A magistrate's "determination of probable cause should be paid great deference by reviewing courts." "A grudging or negative attitude by reviewing courts toward warrants" is inconsistent with the Fourth Amendment's strong preference for searches conducted pursuant to a warrants; "courts should not invalidate * * * warrant[s] by interpreting affidavit[s] in a hypertechnical, rather than a common-sense, manner."

If the affidavits submitted by police officers are subjected to the type of scrutiny some courts have deemed appropriate, police might well resort to warrantless searches, with the hope of relying on consent or some other exception to the warrant clause that might develop at the time of the search. In addition, the possession of a warrant by officers conducting an arrest or search greatly reduces the perception of unlawful or intrusive police conduct, by assuring "the individual whose property is searched or seized of the lawful authority of the executing officer, his need to search, and the limits of his power to search." Reflecting this preference for the warrant process, the traditional standard for review of an issuing magistrate's probable cause determination has been that so long as the magistrate had a "substantial basis for * * * conclud[ing]" that a search would uncover evidence of wrongdoing, the Fourth Amendment requires no more. We think reaffirmation of this standard better serves the purpose of encouraging recourse to the warrant procedure and is more consistent with our traditional deference to the probable cause determinations of magistrates than is the "two-pronged test."

Finally, the direction taken by decisions following *Spinelli* poorly serves "the most basic function of any government": "to provide for the security of the individual and of his property". The strictures that inevitably accompany the "two-pronged test" cannot avoid seriously impeding the task of law enforcement. If, as the Illinois Supreme Court apparently thought, that test must be rigorously applied in every case, [anonymous tips would be] of greatly diminished value in police work. Ordinary citizens, like ordinary witnesses, generally do not provide extensive recitations of the basis of their everyday observations. Likewise, as the Illinois Supreme Court observed in this case, the veracity of persons supplying anonymous tips is by hypothesis largely unknown, and unknowable. As a result, anonymous tips seldom could survive a rigorous application of either of the *Spinelli* prongs. Yet, such tips, particularly when supplemented by independent police investigation, frequently contribute to the solution of otherwise "perfect crimes." While a conscientious assessment of the basis for crediting such tips is required by the Fourth Amendment, a standard that leaves virtually no place for anonymous citizen informants is not.

For all these reasons, we conclude that it is wiser to abandon the "two-pronged test" established by our decisions in *Aguilar* and *Spinelli*.[11] In its place

11. * * *

Whether the allegations submitted to the magistrate in *Spinelli* would, under the view we now take, have supported a finding of prob-
able cause, we think it would not be profitable to decide. There are so many variables in the probable cause equation that one determination will seldom be a useful "precedent" for

we reaffirm the totality of the circumstances analysis that traditionally has informed probable cause determinations. The task of the issuing magistrate is simply to make a practical, common-sense decision whether, given all the circumstances set forth in the affidavit before him, including the "veracity" and "basis of knowledge" of persons supplying hearsay information, there is a fair probability that contraband or evidence of a crime will be found in a particular place. And the duty of a reviewing court is simply to ensure that the magistrate had a "substantial basis for * * * conclud[ing]" that probable cause existed. We are convinced that this flexible, easily applied standard will better achieve the accommodation of public and private interests that the Fourth Amendment requires than does the approach that has developed from *Aguilar* and *Spinelli*.

Our earlier cases illustrate the limits beyond which a magistrate may not venture in issuing a warrant. A sworn statement of an affiant that "he has cause to suspect and does believe that" liquor illegally brought into the United States is located on certain premises will not do. *Nathanson v. United States.* An affidavit must provide the magistrate with a substantial basis for determining the existence of probable cause, and the wholly conclusory statement at issue in *Nathanson* failed to meet this requirement. An officer's statement that "affiants have received reliable information from a credible person and believe" that heroin is stored in a home, is likewise inadequate. *Aguilar v. Texas.* As in *Nathanson,* this is a mere conclusory statement that gives the magistrate virtually no basis at all for making a judgment regarding probable cause. Sufficient information must be presented to the magistrate to allow that official to determine probable cause; his action cannot be a mere ratification of the bare conclusions of others. In order to ensure that such an abdication of the magistrate's duty does not occur, courts must continue to conscientiously review the sufficiency of affidavits on which warrants are issued. But when we move beyond the "bare bones" affidavits present in cases such as *Nathanson* and *Aguilar,* this area simply does not lend itself to a prescribed set of rules, like that which had developed from *Spinelli.* Instead, the flexible, common-sense standard articulated in *Jones, Ventresca,* and *Brinegar* better served the purposes of the Fourth Amendment's probable cause requirement.

Justice Brennan's dissent suggests in several places that the approach we take today somehow downgrades the role of the neutral magistrate, because *Aguilar* and *Spinelli* "preserve the role of magistrates as independent arbiters of probable cause * * *." Quite the contrary, we believe, is the case. Nothing in our opinion in any way lessens the authority of the magistrate to draw such reasonable inferences as he will from the material supplied to him by applicants for a warrant; indeed, he is freer than under the regime of *Aguilar* and *Spinelli* to draw such inferences, or to refuse to draw them if he is so minded.

The real gist of Justice Brennan's criticism seems to be a second argument, somewhat at odds with the first, that magistrates should be restricted in their authority to make probable cause determinations by the standards laid down in *Aguilar* and *Spinelli* and that such findings "should not be authorized unless there is some assurance that the information on which they are based has been obtained in a reliable way by an honest or credible person." However, under our opinion magistrates remain perfectly free to exact such assurances as they deem necessary, as well as those required by this opinion, in making probable cause

another. Suffice it to say that while we in no way abandon *Spinelli's* concern for the trustworthiness of informers and for the principle that it is the magistrate who must ultimately make a finding of probable cause, we reject the rigid categorization suggested by some of its language.

determinations. Justice Brennan would apparently prefer that magistrates be restricted in their findings of probable cause by the development of an elaborate body of case law dealing with the "veracity" prong of the *Spinelli* test, which in turn is broken down into two "spurs"—the informant's "credibility" and the "reliability" of his information, together with the "basis of knowledge" prong of the *Spinelli* test. That such a labyrinthine body of judicial refinement bears any relationship to familiar definitions of probable cause is hard to imagine. * * *

Justice Brennan's dissent also suggests that "words such as 'practical,' 'nontechnical,' and 'common sense,' as used in the Court's opinion, are but code words for an overly permissive attitude towards police practices in derogation of the rights secured by the Fourth Amendment." * * * "Fidelity" to the commands of the Constitution suggests balanced judgment rather than exhortation. The highest "fidelity" is achieved neither by the judge who instinctively goes furthest in upholding even the most bizarre claim of individual constitutional rights, any more than it is achieved by a judge who instinctively goes furthest in accepting the most restrictive claims of governmental authorities. The task of this Court, as of other courts, is to "hold the balance true," and we think we have done that in this case.

Our decisions applying the totality of circumstances analysis outlined above have consistently recognized the value of corroboration of details of an informant's tip by independent police work.

Our decision in *Draper v. United States,* however, is the classic case on the value of corroborative efforts of police officials. There, an informant named Hereford reported that Draper would arrive in Denver on a train from Chicago on one of two days, and that he would be carrying a quantity of heroin. The informant also supplied a fairly detailed physical description of Draper, and predicted that he would be wearing a light colored raincoat, brown slacks and black shoes, and would be walking "real fast." Hereford gave no indication of the basis for his information.[12]

On one of the stated dates police officers observed a man matching this description exit a train arriving from Chicago; his attire and luggage matched Hereford's report and he was walking rapidly. We explained in *Draper* that, by this point in his investigation, the arresting officer "had personally verified every facet of the information given him by Hereford except whether petitioner had accomplished his mission and had the three ounces of heroin on his person or in his bag. And surely with every other bit of Hereford's information being thus personally verified, [the officer] had 'reasonable grounds' to believe that the remaining unverified bit of Hereford's information—that Draper would have the heroin with him—was likewise true."

The showing of probable cause in the present case was fully as compelling as that in *Draper.* Even standing alone, the facts obtained through the independent investigation of Mader and the DEA at least suggested that the Gates were involved in drug trafficking. In addition to being a popular vacation site, Florida is well-known as a source of narcotics and other illegal drugs. Lance Gates' flight to

12. The tip in *Draper* might well not have survived the rigid application of the "two-pronged test" that developed following *Spinelli.* The only reference to Hereford's reliability was that he had "been engaged as a 'special employee' of the Bureau of Narcotics at Denver for about six months, and from time to time gave information to [the police] for small sums of money, and that [the officer] had always found the information given by Hereford to be accurate and reliable." Likewise, the tip gave no indication of how Hereford came by his information. At most, the detailed and accurate predictions in the tip indicated that, however Hereford obtained his information, it was reliable.

Palm Beach, his brief, overnight stay in a motel, and apparent immediate return north to Chicago in the family car, conveniently awaiting him in West Palm Beach, is as suggestive of a prearranged drug run, as it is of an ordinary vacation trip.

In addition, the magistrate could rely on the anonymous letter, which had been corroborated in major part by Mader's efforts—just as had occurred in *Draper*.[13] The Supreme Court of Illinois reasoned that *Draper* involved an informant who had given reliable information on previous occasions, while the honesty and reliability of the anonymous informant in this case were unknown to the Bloomingdale police. While this distinction might be an apt one at the time the police department received the anonymous letter, it became far less significant after Mader's independent investigative work occurred. The corroboration of the letter's predictions that the Gates' car would be in Florida, that Lance Gates would fly to Florida in the next day or so, and that he would drive the car north toward Bloomingdale all indicated, albeit not with certainty, that the informant's other assertions also were true. "Because an informant is right about some things, he is more probably right about other facts," *Spinelli, supra* (White, J., concurring)—including the claim regarding the Gates' illegal activity. This may well not be the type of "reliability" or "veracity" necessary to satisfy some view of the "veracity prong" of *Spinelli,* but we think it suffices for the practical, common-sense judgment called for in making a probable cause determination. It is enough, for purposes of assessing probable cause, that "corroboration through other sources of information reduced the chances of a reckless or prevaricating tale," thus providing "a substantial basis for crediting the hearsay."

Finally, the anonymous letter contained a range of details relating not just to easily obtained facts and conditions existing at the time of the tip, but to future actions of third parties ordinarily not easily predicted. The letter writer's accurate information as to the travel plans of each of the Gates was of a character likely obtained only from the Gates themselves, or from someone familiar with their not entirely ordinary travel plans. If the informant had access to accurate information of this type a magistrate could properly conclude that it was not unlikely that he also had access to reliable information of the Gates' alleged illegal activities.[14] Of

13. The Illinois Supreme Court thought that the verification of details contained in the anonymous letter in this case amounted only to "the corroboration of innocent activity," and that this was insufficient to support a finding of probable cause. We are inclined to agree, however, with the observation of Justice Moran in his dissenting opinion that "In this case, just as in *Draper,* seemingly innocent activity became suspicious in the light of the initial tip." And it bears noting that *all* of the corroborating detail established in *Draper, supra,* was of entirely innocent activity—a fact later pointed out by the Court in both *Jones v. United States, and* Ker v. California.

This is perfectly reasonable. As discussed previously, probable cause requires only a probability or substantial chance of criminal activity, not an actual showing of such activity. By hypothesis, therefore, innocent behavior frequently will provide the basis for a showing of probable cause; to require otherwise would be to *sub silentio* impose a drastically more rigorous definition of probable cause than the

security of our citizens demands. We think the Illinois court attempted a too rigid classification of the types of conduct that may be relied upon in seeking to demonstrate probable cause. In making a determination of probable cause the relevant inquiry is not whether particular conduct is "innocent" or "guilty," but the degree of suspicion that attaches to particular types of non-criminal acts.

14. The dissent seizes on one inaccuracy in the anonymous informant's letter—its statement that Sue Gates would fly from Florida to Illinois, when in fact she drove—and argues that the probative value of the entire tip was undermined by this allegedly "material mistake." We have never required that informants used by the police be infallible, and can see no reason to impose such a requirement in this case. Probable cause, particularly when police have obtained a warrant, simply does not require the perfection the dissent finds necessary.

Likewise, there is no force to the dissent's argument that the Gates' action in leaving course, the Gates' travel plans might have been learned from a talkative neighbor or travel agent; under the "two-pronged test" developed from *Spinelli,* the character of the details in the anonymous letter might well not permit a sufficiently clear inference regarding the letter writer's "basis of knowledge." But, as discussed previously, probable cause does not demand the certainty we associate with formal trials. It is enough that there was a fair probability that the writer of the anonymous letter had obtained his entire story either from the Gates or someone they trusted. And corroboration of major portions of the letter's predictions provides just this probability. It is apparent, therefore, that the judge issuing the warrant had a "substantial basis for * * * conclud[ing]" that probable cause to search the Gates' home and car existed. The judgment of the Supreme Court of Illinois therefore must be

Reversed.

Justice WHITE, concurring in the judgment.[a]

* * * Although I agree that the warrant should be upheld, I reach this conclusion in accordance with the *Aguilar-Spinelli* framework.

For present purposes, the *Aguilar-Spinelli* rules can be summed up as follows. First, an affidavit based on an informer's tip, standing alone, cannot provide probable cause for issuance of a warrant unless the tip includes information that apprises the magistrate of the informant's basis for concluding that the contraband is where he claims it is (the "basis of knowledge" prong), *and* the affiant informs the magistrate of his basis for believing that the informant is credible (the "veracity" prong).[20] Second, if a tip fails under either or both of the two prongs,

their home unguarded undercut the informant's claim that drugs were hidden there. Indeed, the line-by-line scrutiny that the dissent applies to the anonymous letter is akin to that we find inappropriate in reviewing magistrate's decisions. The dissent apparently attributes to the magistrate who issued the warrant in this case the rather implausible notion that persons dealing in drugs always stay at home, apparently out of fear that to leave might risk intrusion by criminals. If accurate, one could not help sympathizing with the self-imposed isolation of people so situated. In reality, however, it is scarcely likely that the magistrate ever thought that the anonymous tip "kept one spouse" at home, much less that he relied on the theory advanced by the dissent. The letter simply says that Sue would fly from Florida to Illinois, without indicating whether the Gates' made the bitter choice of leaving the drugs in their house, or those in their car, unguarded. The magistrate's determination that there might be drugs or evidence of criminal activity in the Gates' home was well-supported by the less speculative theory, noted in text, that if the informant could predict with considerable accuracy the somewhat unusual travel plans of the Gates, he probably also had a reliable basis for his statements that the Gates' kept a large quantity of drugs in their home and frequently were visited by other drug traffickers there.

a. In an omitted portion of his opinion, Justice White argued for adoption of a "good-faith" exception to the exclusionary rule.

20. The "veracity" prong is satisfied by a recitation in the affidavit that the informant previously supplied accurate information to the police, see *McCray v. Illinois,* [p. 204], or by proof that the informant gave his information against his penal interest, see *United States v. Harris,* 403 U.S. 573, 91 S.Ct. 2075, 29 L.Ed.2d 723 (1971) (plurality opinion). [Editor's Note: In *Harris,* the informant said that he had purchased illicit whiskey from defendant for two years, most recently within the past two weeks, and had often seen defendant get the whiskey for him and others from a certain building. The plurality opinion concluded that because "people do not lightly admit a crime and place critical evidence in the hands of the police in the form of their own admissions," such admissions "carry their own indicia of credibility—sufficient at least to support finding of probable cause to search" when, as here, the basis of knowledge is also indicated (as almost inevitably will be the case when there is such an admission). The four dissenters objected that "the effect of adopting such a rule would be to encourage the Government to prefer as informants participants in criminal enterprises rather than ordinary citizens, a goal the Government specifically eschews in its brief in this case upon the explicit premise that such persons are often less reliable than those who obey the law."] The "basis of knowledge" prong is satisfied by a statement from the informant that he personally observed the criminal activity, or, if he came by the information indirectly, by a satisfactory explanation of probable cause may yet be established by independent police investigatory work that corroborates the tip to such an extent that it supports "both the inference that the informer was generally trustworthy and that he made his charge on the basis of information obtained in a reliable way." In instances where the officers rely on corroboration, the ultimate question is whether the corroborated tip "is as trustworthy as a tip which would pass *Aguilar's* tests without independent corroboration."

In the present case, it is undisputed that the anonymous tip, by itself, did not furnish probable cause. The question is whether those portions of the affidavit describing the results of the police investigation of the respondents, when considered in light of the tip, "would permit the suspicions engendered by the informant's report to ripen into a judgment that a crime was probably being committed." * * *

In my view, the lower court's characterization of the Gates' activity here as totally "innocent" is dubious. In fact, the behavior was quite suspicious. I agree with the Court that Lance Gates' flight to Palm Beach, an area known to be a source of narcotics, the brief overnight stay in a motel, and apparent immediate return North, suggest a pattern that trained law-enforcement officers have recognized as indicative of illicit drug-dealing activity.

Even, however, had the corroboration related only to completely innocuous activities, this fact alone would not preclude the issuance of a valid warrant. The critical issue is not whether the activities observed by the police are innocent or suspicious. Instead, the proper focus should be on whether the actions of the suspects, whatever their nature, give rise to an inference that the informant is credible and that he obtained his information in a reliable manner.

Thus, in *Draper v. United States* an informant stated on Sept. 7 that Draper would be carrying narcotics when he arrived by train in Denver on the morning of Sept. 8 or Sept. 9. The informant also provided the police with a detailed physical description of the clothes Draper would be wearing when he alighted from the train. The police observed Draper leaving a train on the morning of Sept. 9, and he was wearing the precise clothing described by the informant. The Court held that the police had probable cause to arrest Draper at this point, even though the police had seen nothing more than the totally innocent act of a man getting off a train carrying a briefcase. As we later explained in *Spinelli,* the important point was that the corroboration showed both that the informant was credible, *i.e.* that he "had not been fabricating his report out of whole cloth," and that he had an adequate basis of knowledge for his allegations, "since the report was of the sort which in common experience may be recognized as having been obtained in a reliable way." The fact that the informer was able to predict, two days in advance, the exact clothing Draper would be wearing dispelled the possibility that his tip was just based on rumor or "an off-hand remark heard at a neighborhood bar." Probably Draper had planned in advance to wear these specific clothes so that an accomplice could identify him. A clear inference could therefore be drawn that the informant was either involved in the criminal scheme himself or that he otherwise had access to reliable, inside information.[22]

why his sources were reliable, or, in the absence of a statement detailing the manner in which the information was gathered, by a description of the accused's criminal activity in sufficient detail that the magistrate may infer that the informant is relying on something more substantial than casual rumor or an individual's general reputation. *Spinelli v. United States.*

22. Thus, as interpreted in *Spinelli,* the Court in *Draper* held that there was probable cause because "the kind of information related by the informant [was] not generally sent

As in *Draper,* the police investigation in the present case satisfactorily demonstrated that the informant's tip was as trustworthy as one that would alone satisfy the *Aguilar* tests. The tip predicted that Sue Gates would drive to Florida, that Lance Gates would fly there a few days after May 3, and that Lance would then drive the car back. After the police corroborated these facts, the magistrate could reasonably have inferred, as he apparently did, that the informant, who had specific knowledge of these unusual travel plans, did not make up his story and that he obtained his information in a reliable way. It is theoretically possible, as respondents insist, that the tip could have been supplied by a "vindictive travel agent" and that the Gates' activities, although unusual, might not have been unlawful. But *Aguilar* and *Spinelli,* like our other cases, do not require that certain guilt be established before a warrant may properly be issued. "[O]nly the probability, and not a prima facie showing, of criminal activity is the standard of probable cause." I therefore conclude that the judgment of the Illinois Supreme Court invalidating the warrant must be reversed.

The Court agrees that the warrant was valid, but, in the process of reaching this conclusion, it overrules the *Aguilar-Spinelli* tests and replaces them with a "totality of the circumstances" standard. As shown above, it is not at all necessary to overrule *Aguilar-Spinelli* in order to reverse the judgment below. Therefore, because I am inclined to believe that, when applied properly, the *Aguilar-Spinelli* rules play an appropriate role in probable cause determinations, and because the Court's holding may foretell an evisceration of the probable cause standard, I do not join the Court's holding.

The Court reasons that the "veracity" and "basis of knowledge" tests are not independent, and that a deficiency as to one can be compensated for by a strong showing as to the other. Thus, a finding of probable cause may be based on a tip from an informant "known for the unusual reliability of his predictions" or from "an unquestionably honest citizen," even if the report fails thoroughly to set forth the basis upon which the information was obtained. If this is so, then it must follow *a fortiori* that "the affidavit of an officer, known by the magistrate to be honest and experienced, stating that [contraband] is located in a certain building" must be acceptable. It would be "quixotic" if a similar statement from an honest informant, but not one from an honest officer, could furnish probable cause. But we have repeatedly held that the unsupported assertion or belief of an officer does not satisfy the probable cause requirement. Thus, this portion of today's holding can be read as implicitly rejecting the teachings of these prior holdings.

---

ahead of a person's arrival in a city except to those who are intimately connected with making careful arrangements for meeting him." *Spinelli* (White, J., concurring). As I said in *Spinelli,* the conclusion that *Draper* itself was based on this fact is far from inescapable. Prior to *Spinelli, Draper* was susceptible to the interpretation that it stood for the proposition that "the existence of the tenth and critical fact is made sufficiently probable to justify the issuance of a warrant by verifying nine other facts coming from the same source." *Spinelli* (White, J., concurring). But it now seems clear that the Court in *Spinelli* rejected this reading of *Draper.*

Justice Brennan erroneously interprets my *Spinelli* concurrence as espousing the view that "corroboration of certain details in a tip may be sufficient to satisfy the veracity, but not the basis of knowledge, prong of *Aguilar.*" I did not say that corroboration could *never* satisfy the basis of knowledge prong. My concern was, and still is, that the prong might be deemed satisfied on the basis of corroboration of information that does not in any way suggest that the informant had an adequate basis of knowledge for his report. If, however, as in *Draper,* the police corroborate information from which it can be inferred that the informant's tip was grounded on inside information, this corroboration is sufficient to satisfy the basis of knowledge prong. *Spinelli* (White, J., concurring). The rules would indeed be strange if, as Justice Brennan suggests, the basis of knowledge prong could be satisfied by detail in the tip alone, but not by independent police work.

The Court may not intend so drastic a result. Indeed, the Court expressly reaffirms the validity of cases such as *Nathanson* that have held that, no matter how reliable the affiant-officer may be, a warrant should not be issued unless the affidavit discloses supporting facts and circumstances. The Court limits these cases to situations involving affidavits containing only "bare conclusions" and holds that, if an affidavit contains anything more, it should be left to the issuing magistrate to decide, based solely on "practical[ity]" and "common-sense," whether there is a fair probability that contraband will be found in a particular place.

Thus, as I read the majority opinion, it appears that the question whether the probable cause standard is to be diluted is left to the common-sense judgments of issuing magistrates. I am reluctant to approve any standard that does not expressly require, as a prerequisite to issuance of a warrant, some showing of facts from which an inference may be drawn that the informant is credible and that his information was obtained in a reliable way. The Court is correctly concerned with the fact that some lower courts have been applying *Aguilar-Spinelli* in an unduly rigid manner. I believe, however, that with clarification of the rule of corroborating information, the lower courts are fully able to properly interpret *Aguilar-Spinelli* and avoid such unduly-rigid applications. I may be wrong; it ultimately may prove to be the case that the only profitable instruction we can provide to magistrates is to rely on common sense. But the question whether a particular anonymous tip provides the basis for issuance of a warrant will often be a difficult one, and I would at least attempt to provide more precise guidance by clarifying *Aguilar-Spinelli* and the relationship of those cases with *Draper* before totally abdicating our responsibility in this area. Hence, I do not join the Court's opinion rejecting the *Aguilar-Spinelli* rules.

Justice BRENNAN, with whom Justice MARSHALL joins, dissenting.

Although I join Justice Stevens' dissenting opinion and agree with him that the warrant is invalid even under the Court's newly announced "totality of the circumstances" test, I write separately to dissent from the Court's unjustified and ill-advised rejection of the two-prong test for evaluating the validity of a warrant based on hearsay announced in *Aguilar v. Texas,* and refined in *Spinelli v. United States.*

* * * In *Spinelli,* the Court reviewed a search warrant based on an affidavit that was "more ample" than the one in *Aguilar.* The affidavit in *Spinelli* contained not only a tip from an informant, but also a report of an independent police investigation that allegedly corroborated the informant's tip. Under these circumstances, the Court stated that it was "required to delineate the manner in which *Aguilar's* two-pronged test should be applied * * *."

The Court held that the *Aguilar* test should be applied to the tip, and approved two additional ways of satisfying that test. First, the Court suggested that if the tip contained sufficient detail describing the accused's criminal activity it might satisfy *Aguilar's* basis of knowledge prong. Such detail might assure the magistrate that he is "relying on something more substantial than a casual rumor circulating in the underworld or an accusation based merely on an individual's general reputation." Although the tip in the case before it did not meet this standard, "[t]he detail provided by the informant in *Draper v. United States* provide[d] a suitable benchmark" because "[a] magistrate, when confronted with such detail, could reasonably infer that the informant had gained his information in a reliable way."

Second, the Court stated that police corroboration of the details of a tip could provide a basis for satisfying *Aguilar.* The Court's opinion is not a model of clarity on this issue since it appears to suggest that corroboration can satisfy both the basis of knowledge and veracity prongs of *Aguilar*. Justice White's concurring opinion, however, points the way to a proper reading of the Court's opinion. After reviewing the Court's decision in *Draper v. United States*, Justice White concluded that "[t]he thrust of *Draper* is not that the verified facts have independent significance with respect to proof of [another unverified fact]." In his view, "[t]he argument instead relates to the reliability of the source: because an informant is right about some things, he is more probably right about other facts, usually the critical, unverified facts." Justice White then pointed out that prior cases had rejected "the notion that the past reliability of an officer is sufficient reason for believing his current assertions." Justice White went on to state:

"Nor would it suffice, I suppose, if a reliable informant states there is gambling equipment in Apartment 607 and then proceeds to describe in detail Apartment 201, a description which is verified before applying for the warrant. He was right about 201, but that hardly makes him more believable about the equipment in 607. But what if he states that there are narcotics locked in a safe in Apartment 300, which is described in detail, and the apartment manager verifies everything but the contents of the safe? I doubt that the report about the narcotics is made appreciably more believable by the verification. The informant could still have gotten his information concerning the safe from others about whom nothing is known or could have inferred the presence of narcotics from circumstances which a magistrate would find unacceptable."

I find this reasoning persuasive. Properly understood, therefore, *Spinelli* stands for the proposition that corroboration of certain details in a tip may be sufficient to satisfy the veracity, but not the basis of knowledge, prong of *Aguilar*. As noted, *Spinelli* also suggests that in some limited circumstances considerable detail in an informant's tip may be adequate to satisfy the basis of knowledge prong of *Aguilar*. * * *

In rejecting the *Aguilar-Spinelli* standards, the Court * * * relies on * * * the "practical, nontechnical" nature of probable cause.

[O]ne can concede that probable cause is a "practical, nontechnical" concept without betraying the values that *Aguilar* and *Spinelli* reflect. As noted, *Aguilar* and *Spinelli* require the police to provide magistrates with certain crucial information. They also provide structure for magistrates' probable cause inquiries. In so doing, *Aguilar* and *Spinelli* preserve the role of magistrates as independent arbiters of probable cause, insure greater accuracy in probable cause determinations, and advance the substantive value of precluding findings of probable cause, and attendant intrusions, based on anything less than information from an honest or credible person who has acquired his information in a reliable way. Neither the standards nor their effects are inconsistent with a "practical, nontechnical" conception of probable cause. Once a magistrate has determined that he has information before him that he can reasonably say has been obtained in a reliable way by a credible person, he has ample room to use his common sense and to apply a practical, nontechnical conception of probable cause. * * *

The Court also insists that the *Aguilar-Spinelli* standards must be abandoned because they are inconsistent with the fact that non-lawyers frequently serve as magistrates. To the contrary, the standards help to structure probable cause inquiries and, properly interpreted, may actually help a non-lawyer magistrate in making a probable cause determination. * * *

The Court's complete failure to provide any persuasive reason for rejecting *Aguilar* and *Spinelli* doubtlessly reflects impatience with what it perceives to be "overly technical" rules governing searches and seizures under the Fourth Amendment. Words such as "practical," "nontechnical," and "commonsense," as used in the Court's opinion, are but code words for an overly permissive attitude towards police practices in derogation of the rights secured by the Fourth Amendment. Everyone shares the Court's concern over the horrors of drug trafficking, but under our Constitution only measures consistent with the Fourth Amendment may be employed by government to cure this evil. * * *

Justice STEVENS, with whom Justice BRENNAN joins, dissenting.

* * * The informant had indicated that "Sue drives their car to Florida *where she leaves it to be loaded up with drugs* * * *. *Sue flies back after she drops the car off in Florida.*" (emphasis added). Yet Detective Mader's affidavit reported that she "left the West Palm Beach area driving the Mercury northbound."

The discrepancy between the informant's predictions and the facts known to Detective Mader is significant for three reasons. First, it cast doubt on the informant's hypothesis that the Gates already had "over $100,000 worth of drugs in their basement." The informant had predicted an itinerary that always kept one spouse in Bloomingdale, suggesting that the Gates did not want to leave their home unguarded because something valuable was hidden within. That inference obviously could not be drawn when it was known that the pair was actually together over a thousand miles from home.

Second, the discrepancy made the Gates' conduct seem substantially less unusual than the informant had predicted it would be. It would have been odd if, as predicted, Sue had driven down to Florida on Wednesday, left the car, and flown right back to Illinois. But the mere facts that Sue was in West Palm Beach with the car,[1] that she was joined by her husband at the Holiday Inn on Friday,[2] and that the couple drove north together the next morning[3] are neither unusual nor probative of criminal activity.

Third, the fact that the anonymous letter contained a material mistake undermines the reasonableness of relying on it as a basis for making a forcible entry into a private home.

Of course, the activities in this case did not stop when the magistrate issued the warrant. The Gates drove all night to Bloomingdale, the officers searched the car and found 400 pounds of marijuana, and then they searched the house. However, none of these subsequent events may be considered in evaluating the warrant, and the search of the house was legal only if the warrant was valid. I cannot accept the Court's casual conclusion that, *before the Gates arrived in Bloomingdale,* there was probable cause to justify a valid entry and search of a

---

1. The anonymous note suggested that she was going down on Wednesday, but for all the officers knew she had been in Florida for a month.

2. Lance does not appear to have behaved suspiciously in flying down to Florida. He made a reservation in his own name and gave an accurate home phone number to the airlines. And Detective Mader's affidavit does not report that he did any of the other things drug couriers are notorious for doing, such as paying for the ticket in cash, dressing casually, looking pale and nervous, improperly filling out baggage tags, carrying American Tourister luggage, not carrying any luggage, or changing airlines en route.

3. Detective Mader's affidavit hinted darkly that the couple had set out upon "that interstate highway commonly used by travelers to the Chicago area." But the same highway is also commonly used by travelers to Disney World, Sea World, and Ringling Brothers and Barnum and Bailey Circus World. It is also the road to Cocoa Beach, Cape Canaveral, and Washington, D.C. I would venture that each year dozens of perfectly innocent people fly to Florida, meet a waiting spouse, and drive off together in the family car.

private home. No one knows who the informant in this case was, or what motivated him or her to write the note. Given that the note's predictions were faulty in one significant respect, and were corroborated by nothing except ordinary innocent activity, I must surmise that the Court's evaluation of the warrant's validity has been colored by subsequent events. * * *[a]

Notes and Questions

1. In MASSACHUSETTS v. UPTON, 466 U.S. 727, 104 S.Ct. 2085, 80 L.Ed.2d 721 (1984), police Lt. Beland assisted in the execution of a search warrant for a motel room reserved by one Richard Kelleher, which produced several items of identification belonging to two persons whose homes had recently been burglarized. Other items taken in the burglaries, such as jewelry, silver and gold, were not found. A few hours later Beland received a call from an unidentified female who told him that there was "a motor home full of stolen stuff," including jewelry, silver and gold, at George Upton's premises. After verifying that a motor home was parked there, Beland prepared an application for a search warrant, to which he attached the police reports on the two prior burglaries, along with lists of the stolen property, and his affidavit with the above information and the following:

"She further stated that George Upton was going to move the motor home any time now because of the fact that Ricky Kelleher's motel room was raided and that George Upton had purchased these stolen items from Ricky Kelleher. This unidentified female stated that she had seen the stolen items but refused to identify herself because 'he'll kill me,' referring to George Upton. I then told this unidentified female that I knew who she was, giving her the name of Lynn Alberico, who I had met on May 16, 1980, at George Upton's repair shop off Summer St., in Yarmouthport. She was identified to me by George Upton as being his girlfriend, Lynn Alberico. The unidentified female admitted that she was the girl that I had named, stating that she was surprised that I knew who she was. She then told me that she'd broken up with George Upton and wanted to burn him. She also told me that she wouldn't give me her address or phone number but that she would contact me in the future, if need be."

A magistrate issued the warrant, and a subsequent search of the motor home produced the described items. The Supreme Court, per curiam upheld the warrant:

"Examined in light of Gates, Lt. Beland's affidavit provides a substantial basis for the issuance of the warrant. No single piece of evidence in it is conclusive. But the pieces fit neatly together and, so viewed, support the magistrate's determination that there was 'a fair probability that contraband or evidence of crime' would be found in Upton's motor home. The informant claimed

---

a. For criticism of *Gates*, see Yale Kamisar, *Gates, "Probable Cause," "Good Faith," and Beyond*, 69 Iowa L.Rev. 557 (1984); Wayne R. LaFave, *Fourth Amendment Vagaries (of Improbable Cause, Imperceptible Plain View, Notorious Privacy, and Balancing Askew)*, 74 J.Crim.L. & C. 1171, 1186–99 (1983); Arnold H. Loewy, *Protecting Citizens from Cops and Crooks: An Assessment of the Supreme Court's Interpretation of the Fourth Amendment During the 1982 Term*, 62 N.C.L.Rev. 329, 336–45 (1984) (criticizing the Court's handling of "probable cause," but not its abandonment of

the "two-pronged test"); Silas J. Wasserstrom, *The Incredible Shrinking Fourth Amendment*, 21 Am.Crim.L.Rev. 257, 274–75, 329–40 (1984) (same). Cf. Charles A. Moylan, *Illinois v. Gates: What It Did and Did Not Do*, 20 Crim.L.Bull. 93 (1984) (criticizing the Court's "rhetoric," but maintaining that, on its facts, *Gates* is an exceedingly narrow holding). For a strong defense of *Gates*, see Joseph D. Grano, *Probable Cause and Common Sense: A Reply to the Critics of Illinois v. Gates*, 17 U.Mich.J.L.Ref. 465 (1984).

to have seen the stolen goods and gave a description of them which tallied with the items taken in recent burglaries. She knew of the raid on the motel room—which produced evidence connected to those burglaries—and that the room had been reserved by Kelleher. She explained the connection between Kelleher's motel room and the stolen goods in Upton's motor home. And she provided a motive both for her attempt at anonymity—fear of Upton's retaliation—and for furnishing the information—her recent breakup with Upton and her desire 'to burn him.' "[b]

2. It is apparent from the language of the Fourth Amendment that a valid arrest warrant or search warrant may only be issued upon facts establishing probable cause. However, as we will see later, police are often permitted to make arrests and searches without first obtaining a warrant, to which the Fourth Amendment's protection against "unreasonable searches and seizures" applies. But, because a "principal incentive" for the procurement of warrants would be destroyed if police needed less evidence when acting without a warrant, the requirements in such instances "surely cannot be less stringent" than when a warrant is obtained. *Wong Sun v. United States*, 371 U.S. 471, 83 S.Ct. 407, 9 L.Ed.2d 441 (1963). Thus probable cause is also required for warrantless arrests and searches.[c]

3. It is generally assumed that the same quantum of evidence is required whether one is concerned with probable cause to arrest or probable cause to search. However, probable cause for search requires a somewhat different kind of conclusion than probable cause for arrest. For arrest, there must be a substantial probability that a crime has been committed and that the person to be arrested committed it; for search, there must be a substantial probability that certain items are the fruits, instrumentalities or evidence of crime and that these items are presently to be found at a certain place.

Because the latter type of probable cause has to do with the *present* location of certain objects, it may be found to be lacking because the time of the facts relied upon is unknown or highly uncertain. Does this mean, as held in *Schmidt v. State*, 659 S.W.2d 420 (Tex.Crim.App.1983), that there was no probable cause to search defendant's car for drugs when the affidavit said defendant, "presently under medical attention," had been found in that vehicle in need of medical attention and had said then that he "had been sniffing cocaine," in that the only reference to time is ambiguous because it is not clear whether defendant had been under medical attention "for a few hours or a few months'"? When the time of the facts is given probable cause will sometimes be lacking because that information has become "stale."[d] See, e.g., *United States v. Steeves*, 525 F.2d 33 (8th Cir.1975) (warrant to search for clothing, ski mask, hand gun, money and money bag, all

b. Brennan and Marshall, JJ., dissented from the summary disposition of the case and would have denied the petition for certiorari. After remand, *Commonwealth v. Upton*, 476 N.E.2d 548 (Mass.1985), held that *Aguilar* and *Spinelli* "provide a more appropriate structure for probable cause inquiries" under the *state* constitution, and concluded that the affidavit failed to establish probable cause.

c. However, as discussed in §§ 7, 9 of this chapter, certain kinds of searches and seizures, because they involve a lesser degree of intrusion or interference, are permitted upon less than the traditional amount of probable cause.

d. In contrast to the "stale" information problem, the question is sometimes raised whether the information is premature, in the sense that it only shows that certain goods are to be at a certain place at some future time. Most courts agree with *People v. Glen*, 282 N.E.2d 614 (N.Y.1972), noted in 19 Wayne L.Rev. 1339 (1973) (search warrant issued on information that package containing narcotics would arrive at designated premises on future date; held: "as long as the evidence creates substantial probability that the seizable property will be on the premises when searched, the warrant should be sustained").

sought as evidence of bank robbery which occupant of premises participated in three months earlier; held, there was no probable cause the money or bag would still be there, but there was probable cause the other items would be there, as "a highly incriminating or consumable item of personal property is less likely to remain in one place as long as an item of property which is not consumable or which is innocuous in itself or not particularly incriminating"). Finally, even if no such problems are present, it must be remembered that to have probable cause to search there must be a sufficient connection of the items sought with a particular place. Thus, while a valid search warrant can sometimes issue even when the perpetrator of the crime is unknown, it does not necessarily follow that probable cause to arrest a person will likewise constitute probable cause to search that person's residence for evidence of that crime. See, e.g., *United States v. Lalor*, 996 F.2d 1578 (4th Cir.1993) (where informants gave information re defendant's drug sales at certain street corner, probable cause to search defendant's residence elsewhere lacking where affidavit does not "explain the geographic relationship between the area where the drug sales occurred" and defendant's residence).

4. Does "probable cause" always (or sometimes) mean more probable than not? Consider *State v. Thomas*, 421 S.E.2d 227 (W.Va.1992), where police, investigating a sexual assault-murder apparently committed by one person acting alone, obtained separate search warrants to search the homes and cars of Mosier and Thomas, each of whom was known to have had contact with the victim on the night of her death and to fit the FBI psychological profile of a possible perpetrator of such crimes. As the court recognized, such facts starkly present this issue: "If the same facts can be used to implicate more than one person in a crime that could have been committed by one of them, can probable cause be found to exist?" Relying on the *Gates* assertion that no "numerically precise degree of certainty" is required to show probable cause, the *Thomas* court answered in the affirmative and thus upheld the search warrant which resulted in discovery of a minute portion of the victim's type of blood in defendant's car.

5. When the police act without a warrant, they initially make the probable cause decision themselves, although it is subject to after-the-fact review by a judicial officer upon a motion to suppress evidence found because of the arrest or search. When the police act with a warrant, the probable cause decision is made by a magistrate in the first instance, but his decision may likewise be challenged in an adversary setting upon a motion to suppress (except insofar as the question is avoided entirely by reliance on *United States v. Leon*, p. 129. In a warrant case, the issue upon the motion to suppress is usually cast in terms of whether the facts set out in the complaint or affidavit upon which the warrant was issued establish probable cause.[e] However, the dissenters in *Aguilar* suggested that a defective affidavit might be cured by what the judge was told at the time the warrant was sought, and they would also resuscitate the affidavit on the basis of the officer's subsequent testimony on the motion to suppress.

As to the first possibility, consider *United States v. Clyburn*, 24 F.3d 613 (4th Cir.1994) (the "Fourth Amendment does not require that the basis for probable cause be established in a written affidavit," and thus "magistrates may consider sworn, unrecorded oral testimony in making probable cause determinations during warrant proceedings," even though "presentation of written affidavits or recorded testimony provides a preferable way of securing a search warrant";

---

e. But consider *United States v. Marin–Buitrago*, 734 F.2d 889 (2d Cir.1984), holding that police are required "to report [to the magistrate who issued the warrant] any mate-rial changes in the facts contained in a warrant affidavit that occur before the warrant is executed."

Fed.R.Crim.P. 41(c)(1) requirement that all information showing probable cause be in affidavit not applicable here, as warrant at issue obtained by local police from local magistrate). As to the second possibility, consider *Whiteley v. Warden,* 401 U.S. 560, 91 S.Ct. 1031, 28 L.Ed.2d 306 (1971): "Under the cases of this Court, an otherwise insufficient affidavit cannot be rehabilitated by testimony concerning information possessed by the affiant when he sought the warrant but not disclosed to the issuing magistrate. * * * A contrary rule would, of course, render the warrant requirements of the Fourth Amendment meaningless."

6.   Does it follow that the defendant may not challenge an affidavit which is sufficient on its face? No, the Court answered in FRANKS v. DELAWARE, 438 U.S. 154, 98 S.Ct. 2674, 57 L.Ed.2d 667 (1978). Reasoning that (i) "a flat ban on impeachment of veracity could denude the probable cause requirement of all real meaning," (ii) "the hearing before the magistrate not always will suffice to discourage lawless or reckless misconduct," (iii) "the alternative sanctions of a perjury prosecution, administrative discipline, contempt, or a civil suit are not likely to fill the gap," (iv) "allowing an evidentiary hearing, after a suitable preliminary proffer of material falsity, will not diminish the importance and solemnity of the warrant-issuing process," (v) "the claim that a post-search hearing will confuse the issue of the defendant's guilt with the issue of the State's possible misbehavior is footless," and (vi) allowing impeachment does not really extend the exclusionary rule "to a 'new' area," the Court, per BLACKMUN, J., held "that, where the defendant makes a substantial preliminary showing that a false statement knowingly and intentionally, or with reckless disregard for the truth, was included by the affiant in the warrant affidavit, and if the allegedly false statement is necessary to the finding of probable cause, the Fourth Amendment requires that a hearing be held at the defendant's request. In the event that at that hearing the allegation of perjury or reckless disregard is established by the defendant by a preponderance of the evidence, and, with the affidavit's false material set to one side, the affidavit's remaining content is insufficient to establish probable cause, the search warrant must be voided and the fruits of the search excluded to the same extent as if probable cause was lacking on the face of the affidavit."[f]

Shouldn't the same result obtain if the false statement was negligently made, as reasoned in *Theodor v. Superior Court,* 501 P.2d 234 (Cal.1972), given "the overriding principle of reasonableness which governs the application of the Fourth Amendment"? Shouldn't the same result follow even as to innocently made falsehoods, where "[a]n honestly-erring individual * * * has substituted his erroneous judgment for that of the magistrate," as argued in Comment, 19 U.C.L.A.L.Rev. 96, 140 (1971)? If there was a deliberate false statement, then why shouldn't this *always* invalidate the warrant because, as stated in *United States v. Carmichael,* 489 F.2d 983 (7th Cir.1973), "[t]he fullest deterrent sanctions of the exclusionary rule should be applied to such serious and deliberate government wrongdoing"?

Should *Franks* apply where defendant's objection is that the police left out of the affidavit some additional information which would have put into question the probable cause shown by the information included? If so, what constitutes a material omission for this purpose, and what is the applicable mental state regarding the affiant's failure to include that information?

---

f.   Rehnquist, J., joined by the Chief Justice, dissenting, argued: "If the function of the warrant requirement is to obtain the determination of a neutral magistrate as to whether sufficient grounds have been urged to support the issuance of a warrant, that function is fulfilled at the time the magistrate concludes that the requirement has been met."

NOTES ON THE INFORMER'S PRIVILEGE

1. In McCRAY v. ILLINOIS, 386 U.S. 300, 87 S.Ct. 1056, 18 L.Ed.2d 62 (1967), petitioner was arrested and found to have heroin on his person. At the suppression hearing, the arresting officers testified that an informant who had supplied reliable information in about 20 previous cases told them that he had observed McCray selling narcotics at a certain corner and then accompanied them to that corner and pointed him out. Both officers were asked for the name and address of the informant, but objections to these questions were sustained. Petitioner's motion was denied, and he was subsequently convicted. The Court, per STEWART, J., affirmed:

"When the issue is not guilt or innocence, but, as here, the question of probable cause for an arrest or search, the Illinois Supreme Court has held that police officers need not invariably be required to disclose an informant's identity if the trial judge is convinced, by evidence submitted in open court and subject to cross-examination, that the officers did rely in good faith upon credible information supplied by a reliable informant. This Illinois evidentiary rule is consistent with the law of many other States. * * *

"The reasoning of the Supreme Court of New Jersey in judicially adopting the same basic evidentiary rule was instructively expressed by Chief Justice Weintraub in *State v. Burnett*, 42 N.J. 377, 201 A.2d 39 [1964]:

" 'If a defendant may insist upon disclosure of the informant in order to test the truth of the officer's statement that there is an informant or as to what the informant related or as to the informant's reliability, we can be sure that every defendant will demand disclosure. He has nothing to lose and the prize may be the suppression of damaging evidence if the State cannot afford to reveal its source, as is so often the case. And since there is no way to test the good faith of a defendant who presses the demand, we must assume the routine demand would have to be routinely granted. The result would be that the State could use the informant's information only as a lead and could search only if it could gather adequate evidence of probable cause apart from the informant's data. Perhaps that approach would sharpen investigatorial techniques, but we doubt that there would be enough talent and time to cope with crime upon that basis. Rather we accept the premise that the informer is a vital part of society's defensive arsenal. The basic rule protecting his identity rests upon that belief. * * *

" 'We must remember also that we are not dealing with the trial of the criminal charge itself. There the need for a truthful verdict outweighs society's need for the informer privilege. Here, however, the accused seeks to avoid the truth. The very purpose of a motion to suppress is to escape the inculpatory thrust of evidence in hand, not because its probative force is diluted in the least by the mode of seizure, but rather as a sanction to compel enforcement officers to respect the constitutional security of all of us under the Fourth Amendment. * * * If the motion to suppress is denied, defendant will still be judged upon the untarnished truth. * * *

" 'The Fourth Amendment is served if a judicial mind passes upon the existence of probable cause. Where the issue is submitted upon an application for a warrant, the magistrate is trusted to evaluate the credibility of the affiant in an *ex parte* proceeding. As we have said, the magistrate is concerned, not with whether the informant lied, but with whether the affiant is truthful in his recitation of what he was told. If the magistrate doubts the credibility of the affiant, he may require that the informant be identified or even produced. It seems to us that the same approach is equally sufficient where the search was without a warrant, that is to say, that it should rest entirely with the judge who hears the motion to suppress to decide whether he needs such disclosure as to the informant in order to decide whether the officer is a believable witness.' * * *

"[W]e are now asked to hold that the Constitution somehow compels Illinois to abolish the informer's privilege from its law of evidence, and to require disclosure of the informer's identity in every such preliminary hearing where it appears that the officers made the arrest or search in reliance upon facts supplied by an informer they had reason to trust. The argument is based upon the Due Process Clause of the Fourteenth Amendment, and upon the Sixth Amendment right of confrontation, applicable to the States through the Fourteenth Amendment. * * *

"Nothing in the Due Process Clause of the Fourteenth Amendment requires a state court judge in every such hearing to assume the arresting officers are committing perjury. * * *

"The petitioner does not explain precisely how he thinks his Sixth Amendment right to confrontation and cross-examination was violated by Illinois' recognition of the informer's privilege in this case. If the claim is that the State violated the Sixth Amendment by not producing the informer to testify against the petitioner, then we need no more than repeat the Court's answer to that claim a few weeks ago: 'Petitioner also presents the contention here that he was unconstitutionally deprived of the right to confront a witness against him, because the State did not produce the informant to testify against him. This contention we consider absolutely devoid of merit.'

"On the other hand, the claim may be that the petitioner was deprived of his Sixth Amendment right to cross-examine the arresting officers themselves, because their refusal to reveal the informer's identity was upheld. But it would follow from this argument that no witness on cross-examination could ever constitutionally assert a testimonial privilege, including the privilege against compulsory self-incrimination guaranteed by the Constitution itself. We have never given the Sixth Amendment such a construction, and we decline to do so now."

DOUGLAS, J., joined by The Chief Justice, and Justices Brennan and Fortas, dissented:

"There is no way to determine the reliability of Old Reliable, the informer, unless he is produced, at the trial and cross-examined. Unless he is produced, the Fourth Amendment is entrusted to the tender mercies of the police. What we do today is to encourage arrests and searches without warrants. The whole momentum of criminal law administration should be in precisely the opposite direction, if the Fourth Amendment is to remain a vital force. Except in rare and emergency cases, it requires magistrates to make the findings of 'probable cause.' We should be mindful of its command that a judicial mind should be interposed between the police and the citizen. We should also be mindful that 'disclosure, rather than suppression, of relevant materials ordinarily promotes the proper administration of criminal justice.' "

2. How valid is the following criticism of *McCray* by Irving Younger, a former federal prosecutor, in *The Perjury Routine,* The Nation, May 8, 1967, pp. 596–97:

"[The *McCray* majority] said that 'nothing in the Due Process Clause of the Fourteenth Amendment requires a state court judge in every such hearing to assume the arresting officers are committing perjury.' Why not? Every lawyer who practices in the criminal courts knows that police perjury is commonplace.

"The reason is not hard to find. Policemen see themselves as fighting a two-front war—against criminals in the street and against 'liberal' rules of law in court. All's fair in this war, including the use of perjury to subvert 'liberal' rules of law that might free those who 'ought' to be jailed. * * *

"Far from adopting a presumption of perjury, the *McCray* case almost guarantees wholesale police perjury. When his conduct is challenged as constituting an unreasonable search and seizure, all the policeman need say is that an unnamed 'reliable informant' told him that the defendant was committing a crime. Henceforth, every policeman will have a genie-like informer to legalize his master's arrests."

3. Appellate decisions reversing a trial judge's denial of disclosure are extremely rare, and typically involve a situation in which the court could have simply said that probable cause had not been shown. But a growing number of cases are to be found along the lines of *People v. Darden,* 313 N.E.2d 49 (N.Y.1974), concluding it is "fair and wise, in a case such as this, where there is insufficient evidence to establish probable cause apart from the testimony of the arresting officer as to communications received from an informer, when the issue of identity of the informer is raised at the suppression hearing, for the suppression judge then to conduct an in camera inquiry. The prosecution should be required to make the informer available for interrogation before the Judge. The prosecutor may be present but not the defendant or his counsel. Opportunity should be afforded counsel for defendant to submit in writing any questions which he may desire the Judge to put to the informer. The Judge should take testimony, with recognition of the special need for protection of the interests of the absent defendant, and make a summary report as to the existence of the informer and with respect to the communications made by the informer to the police to which the police testify. That report should be made available to the defendant and to the People and the transcript of testimony should be sealed to be available to the appellate courts if the occasion arises." Contra: *State v. Richardson,* 529 A.2d 1236 (Conn.1987): "Requiring an informant to attend an in camera hearing involves a substantial risk that his identity will be discovered."

NOTES ON OTHER SOURCES OF PROBABLE CAUSE

The probable cause decisions of the United States Supreme Court, almost exclusively concerned with when information from an informant, with or without some corroborating facts, is sufficient for arrest or search, are not fairly representative of the full range of probable cause issues confronted by the police. Consider these situations:

1. *Information from an alleged victim of, or witness to, a crime.* A major distinction between the victim-witness cases and the informant cases is that prior reliability need not be shown as to the former. As explained in *State v. Paszek,* 184 N.W.2d 836 (Wis.1971): "Information supplied to officers by the traditional police informer is not given in the spirit of a concerned citizen, but often is given in exchange for some concession, payment, or simply out of revenge against the subject. The nature of these persons and the information which they supply convey a certain impression of unreliability, and it is proper to demand that some evidence of their credibility and reliability be shown. * * *

"However, an ordinary citizen who reports a crime which has been committed in his presence, or that a crime is being or will be committed, stands on much different ground than a police informer. He is a witness to criminal activity who acts with an intent to aid the police in law enforcement because of his concern for society or for his own safety. He does not expect any gain or concession in exchange for his information. An informer of this type usually would not have more than one opportunity to supply information to the police, thereby precluding proof of his reliability by pointing to previous accurate information which he has supplied."

In the victim-witness cases, the critical question usually is whether the general description given by the victim or witness is sufficient to justify the arrest of any one person. For example, in *Brown v. United States,* 365 F.2d 976 (D.C.Cir.1966), the police received a radio report at 4:30 a.m. of a recent armed robbery, and were told to be on the lookout for a heavily built black male driving a maroon 1954 Ford. Shortly thereafter, 20 blocks from the robbery scene, the police saw what they thought to be such a car (actually, it was a 1952 Ford), and radioed for details about the robber. They were told that the robber was about five feet five inches, and that he was wearing a brown jacket and cream-colored straw hat. The suspect was about five feet eleven inches, was wearing blue, and had only a felt hat, but he was nonetheless arrested. Held: "These discrepancies, which can be the result of the victim's excitement or poor visibility or of the suspect's changing clothes, did not destroy the ascertainment made on the basis of the accurate portion of the identification, which was by itself enough to constitute probable cause."

2. *Direct observations by police.* Most troublesome, because the situations are so varied, are those cases in which the probable cause determination must be made solely upon suspicious conduct observed by police. For example, in *Brooks v. United States,* 159 A.2d 876 (D.C.Mun.App.1960), an officer observed two men, both known to have prior convictions for larceny, carrying a console-type record player in the commercial area at 6:30 p.m. The officer noted that the player was new and still bore store tags. Upon questioning, one of the suspects said the machine belonged to his mother and that he was taking it in to be repaired. When the officer pointed out the tags, the suspect changed his story and said that the machine had been given to him by an unknown person, whom he was unable to describe. The officer then placed the two men under arrest. The court, noting that "the probabilities must be measured by the standards of the reasonable, cautious and prudent peace officer as he sees them, and not those of the casual passerby," held that the officer had acted on probable cause.

What if the officer had not known of the suspects' past records? What if the suspects had refused to answer any questions? Or, what if the suspect had not changed his first story? If the officer had been aware of the fact that larcenies were common in that area, would this be relevant?[a] What if the suspects had

---

a. Consider *United States v. Davis,* 458 F.2d 819 (D.C.Cir.1972): "Although no presumption of guilt arises from the activities of inhabitants of an area in which the police know that narcotics offenses frequently occur, the syndrome of criminality in those areas cannot realistically go unnoticed by the judiciary. It too is a valid consideration when coupled with other reliable indicia or suspicious circumstances. We make this statement warily, for it is all too clear that few live in these areas by choice."

Compare Jerome H. Skolnick, *Justice Without Trial* 217–18 (1966): "If an honest citizen resides in a neighborhood heavily populated by criminals, just as the chances are high that he might be one, so too are the chances high that he might be mistaken for one. The probabilities, from the point of view of the individual, are always the same—either he is or is not culpable. Thus, behavior which seems 'reason-taken flight upon being stopped? Cf. Note 7, p. 324. What if they had engaged in "furtive gestures" upon seeing the police? To what extent, if at all, should account be taken of the expertise of the police in ascertaining what is probably criminal conduct?[b]

3. *Information and orders from official channels.* In *Whiteley v. Warden,* 401 U.S. 560, 91 S.Ct. 1031, 28 L.Ed.2d 306 (1971), Laramie, Wyoming police arrested two men fitting a description given in a police bulletin emanating from the office of the Carbon County Sheriff and transmitted over the state police radio network, indicating that the two described men were wanted for breaking and entering and that a warrant had been issued for their arrest. Although the warrant had not issued on probable cause, the state claimed that the arrests made by the Laramie officers were nonetheless legal because "they reasonably assumed that whoever authorized the bulletin had probable cause to direct Whiteley's and Daley's arrest." The Court, per Justice Harlan, disagreed: "We do not of course question that the Laramie police were entitled to act on the strength of the radio bulletin. Certainly police officers called upon to aid other officers in executing arrest warrants are entitled to assume that the officers requesting aid offered the magistrate the information requisite to support an independent judicial assessment of probable cause. Where, however, the contrary turns out to be true, an otherwise illegal arrest cannot be insulated from challenge by the decision of the instigating officer to rely on fellow officers to make the arrest."[c] What is the status of *Whiteley* after *Evans,* p. 150, where the Court distinguished *Whiteley,* relied upon by the defendant, because it mistakenly "treated identification of a Fourth Amendment violation as synonymous with application of the exclusionary rule to evidence secured incident to that violation"?

SECTION 4. SEARCH WARRANTS

A. Issuance of the Warrant

1. *The "neutral and detached magistrate" requirement.* In *Coolidge v. New Hampshire,* 403 U.S. 443, 91 S.Ct. 2022, 29 L.Ed.2d 564 (1971), the State Attorney General (authorized by state law to issue search warrants as a justice of the peace) issued a search warrant for the defendant's car in the course of a murder investigation of which he had taken personal charge and for which he later served as chief prosecutor at trial. The Court, per Stewart, J., held that this procedure "violated a fundamental premise of both the Fourth and Fourteenth Amendments" because "the state official who was the chief investigator and prosecutor in this case * * * was not the neutral and detached magistrate required by the Constitution," and summarily rejected "the proposition that the existence of probable cause renders noncompliance with the warrant procedure an irrelevance."

able' to the police because of the character of the neighborhood is seen by the honest citizen in it as irresponsible and unreasonable. About *him,* more errors will necessarily be made under a 'reasonableness' standard."

b. Compare *United States v. 1964 Ford Thunderbird,* 445 F.2d 1064 (3d Cir.1971) ("The standard is not what a police officer trained in a particular field would conclude, but rather it is what a reasonable prudent man would conclude"); with *United States v. Hoyos,* 892 F.2d 1387 (9th Cir.1989) (the "experience

and expertise of the officers involved in the investigation and arrest may be considered in determining probable cause").

c. Compare *United States v. Webster,* 750 F.2d 307 (5th Cir.1984) (arrest illegal notwithstanding probable cause at the source of the request, as defendant was arrested in response to a request which merely asked that anyone discovered in the area of the crime be picked up).

Compare *Shadwick v. City of Tampa,* 407 U.S. 345, 92 S.Ct. 2119, 32 L.Ed.2d 783 (1972), where a unanimous Court, per Powell, J., upheld a city charter provision authorizing municipal court clerks to issue *arrest* warrants for municipal ordinance violations. Rejecting the notion "that all warrant authority must reside exclusively in a lawyer or judge" (and noting that "even within the federal system warrants were until recently widely issued by nonlawyers"), the Court concluded that "an issuing magistrate must meet two tests. He must be neutral and detached, and he must be capable of determining whether probable cause exists for the requested arrest or search." The clerk possesses the requisite detachment, as he "is removed from prosecutor or police and works within the judicial branch subject to the supervision of the municipal court judge."[a] As to capacity: "We presume from the nature of the clerk's position that he would be able to deduce from the facts on an affidavit before him whether there was probable cause to believe a citizen guilty of impaired driving, breach of peace, drunkenness, trespass or the multiple other common offenses covered by a municipal code. There has been no showing that this is too difficult a task for a clerk to accomplish. Our legal system has long entrusted nonlawyers to evaluate more complex and significant factual data than that in the case at hand. Grand juries daily determine probable cause prior to rendering indictments, and trial juries assess whether guilt is proved beyond a reasonable doubt." On the basis of *Shadwick,* could court clerks be authorized to issue arrest warrants in all cases? To issue search warrants? If so, can *Shadwick* be reconciled with *Leon,* p. 129?

In *Connally v. Georgia,* 429 U.S. 245, 97 S.Ct. 546, 50 L.Ed.2d 444 (1977), a unanimous Court held that the search warrant had not been issued by a "neutral and detached magistrate" where the issuing justice of the peace was unsalaried and, so far as search warrants were concerned, was paid a fee of $5 if he issued a warrant but nothing if he denied the application.

In *Rooker v. Commonwealth,* 508 S.W.2d 570 (Ky.App.1974), the court, in ruling that evidence obtained in execution of a search warrant must be suppressed, held: "Where a judge issues a search warrant based upon an affidavit which he does not read, he makes no determination of probable cause but merely serves as a rubber stamp for the police. Such action is improper even though the affidavit actually shows probable cause for the issuance of the warrant."

United States v. Davis, 346 F.Supp. 435 (S.D.Ill.1972), involved these facts: A Treasury agent, accompanied by an assistant U.S. attorney, went to Magistrate Ghiglieri and presented an affidavit for a search warrant. The agent did not swear to the affidavit, but the magistrate dated and signed the affidavit and indicated that it was denied. The following day the agent, again accompanied by the assistant, went to Magistrate Giffin and presented the same affidavit. Giffin, after being apprised of the proceedings before Ghiglieri, issued a search warrant. The court found this procedure to be "highly improper" and concluded: "Magistrate Ghiglieri's decision was final and binding, and his denial of the application * * * equitably estopped Magistrate Giffin from issuing a search warrant on the exact same showing." Is this a desirable result, in that it limits magistrate-shopping? If the first magistrate was in error, what recourse should be open to the affiant-officer?

---

a. Is the magistrate sufficiently detached from the police if it is his practice to assist the police in the preparation of search warrant affidavits? See *United States v. Steed,* 465 F.2d 1310 (9th Cir.1972); *Albitez v. Beto,* 465 F.2d 954 (5th Cir.1972). If he assists the police in execution of the warrant? See *Lo-Ji Sales, Inc. v. New York,* 442 U.S. 319, 99 S.Ct. 2319, 60 L.Ed.2d 920 (1979).

2. *Particular description of the place to be searched.* As for the Fourth Amendment requirement of particularity in the description of the place to be searched, it "is enough if the description is such that the officer with a search warrant can, with reasonable effort ascertain and identify the place intended." *Steele v. United States,* 267 U.S. 498, 45 S.Ct. 414, 69 L.Ed. 757 (1925). The common practice is to identify premises in an urban area by street address, which is sufficient. Less particularity is required for rural premises; for example, description of a farm by the name of the owner and general directions for reaching the farm is adequate.

Most of the problems which arise concerning the particularity of description occur not because the warrant description is facially vague, but rather because upon execution it proves to be not as certain as theretofore assumed. One possibility is that the description will turn out not to be sufficiently precise, as where the warrant refers to apartment 3 in a certain building but the officers find apartments with that number on each floor. In this kind of case, courts are receptive to a showing that the executing officers had other information (e.g., the occupant's name), via the affidavit or otherwise, which made it apparent which place was intended.

Another type of case is that in which the executing officers find that some but not all of the descriptive facts fit the same place. Illustrative is *State v. Blackburn,* 511 P.2d 381 (Or.1973), where the apartment in a particular building was said to be apartment number 2 with "the letters ECURB on the door," but the officer found one apartment with the numeral 2 on the door and another with no numeral but the letters ECURB on the door. In upholding the search of the latter apartment, the court held that "there could be no real doubt as to which of the premises was intended" because "[n]o one could have made a mistake or been confused about a word like ECURB, but anyone could easily have made a mistake about a numeral."

In the absence of a probable cause showing as to all the separate living units in a multiple-occupancy structure, the warrant for such a building must describe the particular unit to be searched. But, if the building in question from its outward appearance would be taken to be a single-occupancy structure and neither the affiant nor other investigating officers nor the executing officers knew or had reason to know otherwise until execution of the warrant was under way, then the warrant is not defective for failure to specify a unit within the building.

A similar situation, was involved in MARYLAND v. GARRISON, 480 U.S. 79, 107 S.Ct. 1013, 94 L.Ed.2d 72 (1987), where police obtained a search warrant to search the person of one McWebb and "the premises known as 2036 Park Avenue third floor apartment," but discovered only after uncovering contraband during execution that they were in respondent's separate apartment. The Court, per STEVENS, J., concluded: (i) that the search warrant authorized search of the entire third floor but yet "was valid when it issued," for such validity "must be assessed on the basis of the information that the officers disclosed, or had a duty to discover and to disclose, to the issuing magistrate"; (ii) that the execution of the search warrant was valid because "the officers' failure to realize the overbreadth of the warrant was objectively understandable and reasonable." BLACKMUN, J., for the three dissenters, objected: (i) that the search warrant did not authorize search of the entire third floor, but only the apartment on that floor belonging to McWebb; and (ii) that the police knew the building was a multiple-occupancy structure and should have known before obtaining the search warrant and did know before executing it that there were seven apartments in the 3–story building, and thus unreasonably assumed the third floor was but one apartment.

3. *Particular description of the things to be seized.* The Fourth Amendment requirement of particularity in the description of the things to be seized is intended to prevent general searches, to prevent the seizure of objects on the mistaken assumption that they fall within the magistrate's authorization, and to prevent "the issuance of warrants on loose, vague or doubtful bases of fact." *Go-Bart Importing Co. v. United States,* 282 U.S. 344, 51 S.Ct. 153, 75 L.Ed. 374 (1931). As noted in LaFave, § 4.6:

"Consistent with these three purposes are certain general principles which may be distilled from the decided cases in this area. They are: (1) A greater degree of ambiguity will be tolerated when the police have done the best that could be expected under the circumstances, by acquiring all the descriptive facts which reasonable investigation of this type of crime could be expected to uncover and by ensuring that all of those facts were included in the warrant.[18] (2) A more general type of description will be sufficient when the nature of the objects to be seized are such that they could not be expected to have more specific characteristics.[19] (3) A less precise description is required of property which is, because of its particular character, contraband. (4) Failure to provide all of the available descriptive facts is not a basis for questioning the adequacy of the description when the omitted facts could not have been expected to be of assistance to the executing officer.[21] (5) An error in the statement of certain descriptive facts is not a basis for questioning the adequacy of the description if the executing officer was nonetheless able to determine, from the other facts provided, that the object seized was that intended by the description.[22] (6) Greater care in description is ordinarily called for when the type of property sought is generally in lawful use in substantial quantities.[23] (7) A more particular description than otherwise might be necessary is required when other objects of the same general classification are likely to be found at the particular place to be searched.[24] (8) The greatest care in description is required when the consequences of a seizure of innocent articles by mistake is most substantial, as when the objects to be seized are books or films or indicia of membership in an association, or where the place to be searched is an attorney's office. (9) The mere fact that some items were admittedly improperly seized in execution of the warrant 'does not mean that the warrant was not sufficiently particular.' "

4. *Neutrality, particularity, and "good faith."* Consider the impact of *United States v. Leon,* p. 129, and *Massachusetts v. Sheppard,* p. 142, in this context.

B. EXECUTION OF THE WARRANT

18. * * * Compare * * *United States v. Blakeney,* 942 F.2d 1001 (6th Cir.1991) ("jewelry" insufficient where inventory available of what taken in jewelry store robbery) * * *.

19. * * * *State v. Salsman,* 290 A.2d 618 (N.H.1972) (description of 42 sheets of plywood sufficient, "considering the nature of these items"). * * *

21. * * * *United States v. Scharfman,* 448 F.2d 1352 (2d Cir.1971) (any effort to describe more particularly which furs in fur stores were stolen "would have required a legion of fur experts" to execute the warrant).

22. *United States v. Rytman,* 475 F.2d 192 (5th Cir.1973) (compressor of described brand and with serial number approximating that stated in the warrant could be seized); * * *

23. * * * *People v. Prall,* 145 N.E. 610 (Ill.1924) (thus description of "certain automobile tires and tubes" insufficient); * * *

24. * * * *United States v. Cook,* 657 F.2d 730 (5th Cir.1981) ("cassettes onto which * * * copyrighted films * * * have been electronically transferred" insufficient as to place with many other cassettes). * * *

1. *Time of execution.* Statutes and court rules commonly provide that a search warrant must be executed within a certain time, such as 10 days. Execution within that time is proper, "provided that the probable cause recited in the affidavit continues until the time of execution, giving consideration to the intervening knowledge of the officers and the passage of time." *United States v. Nepstead,* 424 F.2d 269 (9th Cir.1970) (execution of warrant, for seizure of equipment used to manufacture LSD, 6 days after issuance timely, as premises under daily surveillance and no activity noted until after first 5 days).[b] Compare *State v. Neely,* 862 P.2d 1109 (Mont.1993) (where probable cause for search warrant not stale when it issued, warrant may be lawfully executed any time within 10–day statutory period); and consider the somewhat reverse situation in *State v. Miller,* 429 N.W.2d 26 (S.D.1988) (where violation of statutory 10–day rule but probable cause had not dissipated, suppression not necessary, as "the letter, not the spirit, of the law was broken").

Also, in many jurisdictions a search warrant may be served only in the daytime unless it expressly states to the contrary, and a warrant so stating often can be obtained only by meeting special requirements—e.g., obtaining the concurrence of two magistrates, showing that the property is definitely in the place to be searched, or showing some need for prompt action. In GOODING v. UNITED STATES, 416 U.S. 430, 94 S.Ct. 1780, 40 L.Ed.2d 250 (1974), holding that the federal statute relating to searches for controlled substances required no special showing for a nighttime search other than that the contraband is likely to be on the property at that time, Justice MARSHALL, joined by Douglas and Brennan, JJ., noted in dissent that while the "constitutional question is not presented in this case and need not be resolved here," the principle that nighttime searches "involve a greater intrusion than ordinary searches and therefore require a greater justification * * * may well be a constitutional imperative. It is by now established Fourth Amendment doctrine that increasingly severe standards of probable cause are necessary to justify increasingly intrusive searches. In *Camara v. Municipal Court* [p. 339], after holding that search warrants were required to authorize administrative inspections, we held that the quantum of probable cause required for issuance of an inspection warrant must be determined in part by the reasonableness of the proposed search. As Justice White stated, 'there can be no ready test for determining reasonableness other than by balancing the need to search against the invasion which the search entails.' The Court in *Camara* thus approved the issuance of area inspection warrants in part because such searches 'involve a relatively limited invasion of the urban citizen's privacy.' I do not regard this principle as a one-way street, to be used only to water down the requirement of probable cause when necessary to authorize governmental intrusions. In some situations—and the search of a private home during nighttime would seem to be a paradigm example—this principle requires a showing of additional justification for a search over and above the ordinary showing of probable cause."

In *United States v. Gervato,* 474 F.2d 40 (3d Cir.1973), the court emphasized the various protections provided by Fed.R.Crim.P. 41 in rejecting the district court's holding "that a search warrant executed in the absence of the occupant constitutes an unreasonable search because there exists the possibility of a general search and 'pilferage by officers of the law.' "

b. See also *United States v. Marin–Buitrago,* fn. e at p. 202.

2. *Gaining entry.* In *Wilson v. Arkansas*, 514 U.S. 927, 115 S.Ct. 1914, 131 L.Ed.2d 976 (1995), a unanimous Court, per Thomas, J., proceeded "to resolve the conflict among the lower courts" by holding that the common law doctrine which "recognized a law enforcement officer's authority to break open the doors of a dwelling, but generally indicated that he first ought to announce his presence and authority," "forms a part of the reasonableness inquiry under the Fourth Amendment." The Court cautioned that the "Fourth Amendment's flexible requirement of reasonableness should not be read to mandate a rigid rule of announcement that ignores countervailing law enforcement interests," for "the common-law principle of announcement was never stated as an inflexible rule."

In RICHARDS v. WISCONSIN, 520 U.S. 385, 117 S.Ct. 1416, 137 L.Ed.2d 615 (1997), a unanimous Court, per STEVENS, J., rejected the state supreme court's holding that police officers are *never* required to knock and announce their presence when executing a search warrant in a felony drug investigation:

"The Wisconsin court explained its blanket exception as necessitated by the special circumstances of today's drug culture, and the State asserted at oral argument that the blanket exception was reasonable in 'felony drug cases because of the convergence in a violent and dangerous form of commerce of weapons and the destruction of drugs.' But creating exceptions to the knock-and-announce rule based on the 'culture' surrounding a general category of criminal behavior presents at least two serious concerns.

"First, the exception contains considerable overgeneralization. For example, while drug investigation frequently does pose special risks to officer safety and the preservation of evidence, not every drug investigation will pose these risks to a substantial degree. For example, a search could be conducted at a time when the only individuals present in a residence have no connection with the drug activity and thus will be unlikely to threaten officers or destroy evidence. Or the police could know that the drugs being searched for were of a type or in a location that made them impossible to destroy quickly. In those situations, the asserted governmental interests in preserving evidence and maintaining safety may not outweigh the individual privacy interests intruded upon by a no-knock entry. Wisconsin's blanket rule impermissibly insulates these cases from judicial review.

"A second difficulty with permitting a criminal-category exception to the knock-and-announce requirement is that the reasons for creating an exception in one category can, relatively easily, be applied to others. Armed bank robbers, for example, are, by definition, likely to have weapons, and the fruits of their crime may be destroyed without too much difficulty. If a per se exception were allowed for each category of criminal investigation that included a considerable—albeit hypothetical—risk of danger to officers or destruction of evidence, the knock-and-announce element of the Fourth Amendment's reasonableness requirement would be meaningless.

"Thus, the fact that felony drug investigations may frequently present circumstances warranting a no-knock entry cannot remove from the neutral scrutiny of a reviewing court the reasonableness of the police decision not to knock and announce in a particular case. Instead, in each case, it is the duty of a court confronted with the question to determine whether the facts and circumstances of the particular entry justified dispensing with the knock-and-announce requirement.

"In order to justify a 'no-knock' entry, the police must have a reasonable suspicion that knocking and announcing their presence, under the particular circumstances, would be dangerous or futile, or that it would inhibit the effective investigation of the crime by, for example, allowing the destruction of evidence. This standard—as opposed to a probable cause requirement—strikes the appropriate balance between the legitimate law enforcement concerns at issue in the execution of search warrants and the individual privacy interests affected by no-knock entries. * * * This showing is not high, but the police should be required to make it whenever the reasonableness of a no-knock entry is challenged."

The Court concluded with two additional points: (1) The trial judge had correctly concluded that the police were excused from the knock-and-announce requirement because of the facts of the particular case. The officer who knocked at the door of defendant's hotel room claimed to be a maintenance man, defendant opened the door slightly and upon seeing a uniformed officer slammed the door, at which the police kicked the door in and entered. As the Court explained, once "the officers reasonably believed that Richards knew who they were * * * it was reasonable for them to force entry immediately given the disposable nature of the drugs." (2) The refusal of the magistrate issuing the search warrant to issue a no-knock warrant[c] did not alter this conclusion, as "a magistrate's decision not to authorize a no-knock entry should not be interpreted to remove the officers' authority to exercise independent judgment concerning the wisdom of a no-knock entry at the time the warrant is being executed."

In light of the test set out in *Richards* and the illustrations therein of what would *not* suffice, which of the following bits of information would justify an unannounced entry to execute a search warrant for drugs: (a) that the small amount of narcotics was always kept near a toilet; (b) that there was but a small amount of drugs; (c) that there was an unknown quantity of drugs; (d) that the person who planned to sell the drugs was present; (e) that the person who used the drugs was present; (f) that a person whose relationship to the drugs was unknown was present.

In UNITED STATES v. RAMIREZ, 523 U.S. 65, 118 S.Ct. 992, 140 L.Ed.2d 191 (1998), the Court, per REHNQUIST, C.J., unanimously held that whether the *Richards* reasonable suspicion test has been met "depends in no way on whether police must destroy property in order to enter." The Court then concluded that no Fourth Amendment violation had occurred in the instant case, where police executing a search warrant authorizing entry to seize a wanted person broke a garage window in order to deter the occupants of the premises (who thereafter exited and surrendered) from entering the garage to obtain weapons thought to be stored there: "A reliable confidential informant had notified the police that Alan Shelby might be inside respondent's home, and an officer had confirmed this possibility. Shelby was a prison escapee with a violent past who reportedly had access to a large supply of weapons. He had vowed that he would 'not do federal time.' The police certainly had a 'reasonable suspicion' that knocking and announcing their presence might be dangerous to themselves or to others."

3. *Detention and search of persons on the premises.* On the basis of information from an informant that he had frequently and recently observed tinfoil

c. Wisconsin is among those few jurisdictions specifically authorizing magistrates to issue such search warrants, allowing entry without prior announcement, upon a sufficient showing to the magistrate of a need to do so. A "reverse twist" on the *Richards* view regarding a magistrate's *refusal* to issue such a warrant is the position, stated in *Parsley v. Superior Court*, 513 P.2d 611 (Cal.1973), that a magistrate's *issuance* of such a warrant is of no effect because "unannounced entry is excused only on the basis of exigent circumstances existing at the time an officer approached a site to make an arrest or execute a warrant," and thus "can be judged only in light of circumstances of which the officer is aware at the latter moment."

packets of heroin behind the bar and on the person of the bartender of a certain tavern and that the bartender told him he would that day have heroin for sale, a warrant authorizing search of the tavern and bartender for heroin was issued. The warrant was executed during the late afternoon by 7–8 officers, who proceeded to pat down each of the 9–13 customers then present. A cigarette package was located and retrieved from customer Ybarra's pocket, and tinfoil packets of heroin were found therein. State courts held the heroin admissible because found in a search authorized by a statute[d] deemed constitutional as applied in the instant case. In YBARRA v. ILLINOIS, 444 U.S. 85, 100 S.Ct. 338, 62 L.Ed.2d 238 (1979), the Court, in a 6–3 decision, reversed. STEWART, J., for the majority, stated:

"There is no reason to suppose that, when the search warrant was issued on March 1, 1976, the authorities had probable cause to believe that any person found on the premises of the Aurora Tap Tavern, aside from [bartender] 'Greg,' would be violating the law. The Complaint for Search Warrant did not allege that the bar was frequented by persons illegally purchasing drugs. It did not state that the informant had ever seen a patron of the tavern purchase drugs from 'Greg' or from any other person. Nowhere, in fact, did the complaint even mention the patrons of the Aurora Tap Tavern.

"Not only was probable cause to search Ybarra absent at the time the warrant was issued; it was still absent when the police executed the warrant. Upon entering the tavern, the police did not recognize Ybarra and had no reason to believe that he had committed, was committing or was about to commit any offense under state or federal law. Ybarra made no gestures indicative of criminal conduct, made no movements that might suggest an attempt to conceal contraband, and said nothing of a suspicious nature to the police officers. * * *

"It is true that the police possessed a warrant based on probable cause to search the tavern in which Ybarra happened to be at the time the warrant was executed. But, a person's mere propinquity to others independently suspected of criminal activity does not, without more, give rise to probable cause to search that person. * * *[5] "

As for the state's claim "that the first patdown search of Ybarra constituted a reasonable frisk for weapons under the doctrine of *Terry v. Ohio*," p. 304, the Court responded that the frisk was "not supported by a reasonable belief that he was armed and presently dangerous, a belief which this Court has invariably held must form the predicate to a patdown of a person for weapons. * * * Upon seeing Ybarra, [the police] neither recognized him as a person with a criminal history nor had any particular reason to believe that he might be inclined to assault them. Moreover, as police agent Johnson later testified, Ybarra, whose hands were empty, gave no indication of possessing a weapon, made no gestures or other actions indicative of an intent to commit an assault, and acted generally in a manner that was not threatening."

Emphasizing "the ease with which the evidence of narcotics possession may be concealed or moved around from person to person," the State next contended that the *Terry* standard "should be made applicable to aid the evidence-gathering

---

d. This statute, Ill.Comp.Stat. ch. 725, § 5/108–9, reads: "In the execution of the warrant the person executing the same may reasonably detain to search any person in the place at the time: (a) To protect himself from attack, or (b) To prevent the disposal or concealment of any instruments, articles or things particularly described in the warrant."

5. [W]e need not consider situations where the warrant itself authorizes the search of unnamed persons in a place and is supported by probable cause to believe that persons who will be in the place at the time of the search will be in possession of illegal drugs.

function of the search warrant." The Court answered: "The 'long prevailing' constitutional standard of probable cause embodies " 'the best compromise that has been found for accommodating the [ ] often opposing interests" in "safe-guard[ing] citizens from rash and unreasonable interferences with privacy" and in "seek[ing] to give fair leeway for enforcing the law in the community's protection." ' "

REHNQUIST, J., for the dissenters, reasoned that the *Terry* individualized suspicion standard, "important in the case of an on-the-street stop, where the officer must articulate some reason for singling the person out of the general population", was of "less significance in the present situation" for two reasons: (i) "in place of the requirement of 'individualized suspicion' as a guard against arbitrary exercise of authority, we have here the determination of a neutral and detached magistrate that a search was necessary"; and (ii) "the task performed by the officers executing a search warrant is inherently more perilous than is a momentary encounter on the street."

4. *Detention of persons on the premises.* MICHIGAN v. SUMMERS, 452 U.S. 692, 101 S.Ct. 2587, 69 L.Ed.2d 340 (1981), involved these facts: "As Detroit police officers were about to execute a warrant to search a house for narcotics, they encountered respondent descending the front steps. They requested his assistance in gaining entry and detained him while they searched the premises. After finding narcotics in the basement and ascertaining that respondent owned the house, the police arrested him, searched his person, and found in his coat pocket an envelope containing 8.5 grams of heroin." The Court, per STEVENS, J., upheld the seizure on the basis of the principle derived from *Terry* and related cases, namely, that "some seizures * * * constitute such limited intrusions on the personal security of those detained and are justified by such substantial law enforcement interests that they may be made on less than probable cause, so long as police have an articulable basis for suspecting criminal activity":

"Of prime importance in assessing the intrusion is the fact that the police had obtained a warrant to search respondent's house for contraband. A neutral and detached magistrate had found probable cause to believe that the law was being violated in that house and had authorized a substantial invasion of the privacy of the persons who resided there. The detention of one of the residents while the premises were searched, although admittedly a significant restraint on his liberty, was surely less intrusive than the search itself. Indeed, we may safely assume that most citizens—unless they intend flight to avoid arrest—would elect to remain in order to observe the search of their possessions. Furthermore, the type of detention imposed here is not likely to be exploited by the officer or unduly prolonged in order to gain more information, because the information the officers seek normally will be obtained through the search and not through the detention. Moreover, because the detention in this case was in respondent's own residence, it could add only minimally to the public stigma associated with the search itself and would involve neither the inconvenience nor the indignity associated with a compelled visit to the police station. * * *

"In assessing the justification for the detention of an occupant of premises being searched for contraband pursuant to a valid warrant, both the law enforcement interest and the nature of the "articulable facts" supporting the detention are relevant. Most obvious is the legitimate law enforcement interest in preventing flight in the event that incriminating evidence is found. Less obvious, but sometimes of greater importance, is the interest in minimizing the risk of harm to the officers. Although no special danger to the police is suggested by the evidence in this record, the execution of a warrant to search for narcotics is the kind of transaction that may give rise to sudden violence or frantic efforts to conceal or destroy evidence. The risk of harm to both the police and the occupants is minimized if the officers routinely exercise unquestioned command of the situation. Finally, the orderly completion of the search may be facilitated if the occupants of the premises are present. Their self-interest may induce them to open locked doors or locked containers to avoid the use of force that is not only damaging to property but may also delay the completion of the task at hand.

"It is also appropriate to consider the nature of the articulable and individualized suspicion on which the police base the detention of the occupant of a home subject to a search warrant. We have already noted that the detention represents only an incremental intrusion on personal liberty when the search of a home has been authorized by a valid warrant. The existence of a search warrant, however, also provides an objective justification for the detention. A judicial officer has determined that police have probable cause to believe that someone in the home is committing a crime. Thus a neutral magistrate rather than an officer in the field has made the critical determination that the police should be given a special authorization to thrust themselves into the privacy of a home. The connection of an occupant to that home gives the police officer an easily identifiable and certain basis for determining that suspicion of criminal activity justifies a detention of that occupant."

STEWART, J., joined by Brennan and Marshall, JJ., dissenting, objected that *Terry* and related cases required "some governmental interest independent of the ordinary interest in investigating crime and apprehending suspects," which was not present here, and also that the majority's "view that the detention here is of the limited, unintrusive sort" required under *Terry* was in error, as "a detention 'while a proper search is being conducted' can mean a detention of several hours."

5. *Intensity and duration of the search.* Although a search under a search warrant may extend to all parts of the premises described in the warrant, it does not follow that the executing officers may look everywhere within the described premises; they may only look where the items described in the warrant might be concealed. For example, if a search warrant indicated that the items sought were stolen television sets, the officer would not be authorized to rummage through desk drawers and other places too small to hold these items. Once the items named in the search warrant have been found, the search must cease.

6. *Seizure of items not named in the search warrant.* In HORTON v. CALIFORNIA, 496 U.S. 128, 110 S.Ct. 2301, 110 L.Ed.2d 112 (1990), a police officer's affidavit established probable cause to search defendant's home for the proceeds of a robbery (including three specified rings) and for the weapons used in that robbery, but the magistrate issued a warrant only for the proceeds. They were not found in execution of the warrant, but the guns were; they were seized. The defendant claimed this seizure did not come within Justice Stewart's plurality decision in *Coolidge v. New Hampshire*, 403 U.S. 443, 91 S.Ct. 2022, 29 L.Ed.2d 564 (1971), that items found in "plain view" may be seized "where it is immediately apparent to the police that they have evidence before them," because he also required "that the discovery of evidence in plain view must be inadvertent." The Court in *Horton*, 7–2, disagreed. STEVENS, J., explained:

"Justice Stewart concluded that the inadvertence requirement was necessary to avoid a violation of the express constitutional requirement that a valid warrant must particularly describe the things to be seized. He explained:

'The rationale of the exception to the warrant requirement, as just stated, is that a plain-view seizure will not turn an initially valid (and therefore limited) search into a "general" one, while the inconvenience of procuring a warrant to cover an inadvertent discovery is great. But where the discovery is anticipated, where the police know in advance the location of the evidence and intend to seize it, the situation is altogether different. The requirement of a warrant to seize imposes no inconvenience whatever, or at least none which is constitutionally cognizable in a legal system that regards warrantless searches as "*per se* unreasonable" in the absence of "exigent circumstances."

'If the initial intrusion is bottomed upon a warrant that fails to mention a particular object, though the police know its location and intend to seize it, then there is a violation of the express constitutional requirement of "Warrants . . . particularly describing . . . [the] things to be seized." '

"We find two flaws in this reasoning. First, evenhanded law enforcement is best achieved by the application of objective standards of conduct, rather than standards that depend upon the subjective state of mind of the officer. The fact that an officer is interested in an item of evidence and fully expects to find it in the course of a search should not invalidate its seizure if the search is confined in area and duration by the terms of a warrant or a valid exception to the warrant requirement. If the officer has knowledge approaching certainty that the item will be found, we see no reason why he or she would deliberately omit a particular description of the item to be seized from the application for a search warrant. Specification of the additional item could only permit the officer to expand the scope of the search. On the other hand, if he or she has a valid warrant to search for one item and merely a suspicion concerning the second, whether or not it amounts to probable cause, we fail to see why that suspicion should immunize the second item from seizure if it is found during a lawful search for the first. The hypothetical case put by Justice White in his dissenting opinion in *Coolidge* is instructive:

'Let us suppose officers secure a warrant to search a house for a rifle. While staying well within the range of a rifle search, they discover two photographs of the murder victim, both in plain sight in the bedroom. Assume also that the discovery of the one photograph was inadvertent but finding the other was anticipated. The Court would permit the seizure of only one of the photographs. But in terms of the "minor" peril to Fourth Amendment values there is surely no difference between these two photographs: the interference with possession is the same in each case and the officers' appraisal of the photograph they expected to see is no less reliable than their judgment about the other. And in both situations the actual inconvenience and danger to evidence remain identical if the officers must depart and secure a warrant.'

"Second, the suggestion that the inadvertence requirement is necessary to prevent the police from conducting general searches, or from converting specific warrants into general warrants, is not persuasive because that interest is already served by the requirements that no warrant issue unless it 'particularly describ[es] the place to be searched and the persons or things to be seized,' and that a warrantless search be circumscribed by the exigencies which justify its initiation. Scrupulous adherence to these requirements serves the interests in limiting the area and duration of the search that the inadvertence requirement inadequately protects. Once those commands have been satisfied and the officer has a lawful right of access, however, no additional Fourth Amendment interest is furthered by requiring that the discovery of evidence be inadvertent. If the scope of the search exceeds that permitted by the terms of a validly issued warrant or the character of the relevant exception from the warrant requirement, the subsequent seizure is unconstitutional without more."

BRENNAN, J., joined by Marshall, J. dissenting, asserted: "When an officer with probable cause to seize an item fails to mention that item in his application for a search warrant—for whatever reason—and then seizes the item anyway, his conduct is *per se* unreasonable. * * *

* * * It is true that the inadvertent discovery requirement furthers no privacy interests. The requirement in no way reduces the scope of a search or the number of places into which officers may look. But it does protect possessory interests. Cf. *Illinois v. Andreas,* [p. 289] ('The plain-view doctrine is grounded on the proposition that once police are lawfully in a position to observe an item first-hand, its owner's privacy interest in that item is lost; *the owner may retain the incidents of title and possession* but not privacy') (emphasis added). The inadvertent discovery requirement is essential if we are to take seriously the Fourth Amendment's protection of possessory interests as well as privacy interests. The Court today eliminates a rule designed to further possessory interests on the ground that it fails to further privacy interests. I cannot countenance such constitutional legerdemain."

In determining whether the discovered article is incriminating in nature, how carefully may the police examine it? See *Stanley v. Georgia,* 394 U.S. 557, 89 S.Ct. 1243, 22 L.Ed.2d 542 (1969) (obscene films suppressed where police found reels of film while searching for gambling paraphernalia and then viewed the film on a projector and screen found in another room); cf. *Arizona v. Hicks,* p. 260; and compare *State v. Ruscoe,* 563 A.2d 267 (Conn.1989) (where in executing warrant for silver "candlesticks, napkin holders and a silver mug" police moved a TV, 2 VCR's and a tape deck and noticed they without serial numbers, this a lawful discovery under *Hicks,* as "the police moved items in the course of searching for items listed in the warrant").

C. THE "PREFERENCE" FOR WARRANTS

1. The Supreme Court has long expressed a strong preference for searches made pursuant to a search warrant, e.g., *United States v. Ventresca,* 380 U.S. 102, 85 S.Ct. 741, 13 L.Ed.2d 684 (1965), and on occasion has even asserted "that the police must, whenever practicable, obtain advance judicial approval of searches and seizures."*Terry v. Ohio,* p. 304. But this is far from being an accurate portrayal of current law or practice; the fact of the matter is that a great majority of police seizures and searches are made and upheld notwithstanding the absence of a warrant.

This is so because, as is elaborated upon in the following sections in this Chapter, the Supreme Court has recognized a considerable variety of circumstances in which the police may lawfully make a search or a seizure without the prior approval of a magistrate. A warrant is excused in situations other than those in which there existed genuine exigent circumstances making it unfeasible for the police to utilize the often time-consuming warrant process. Sometimes this is explained by the Court on the ground that the police activity being permitted without a warrant intrudes only upon lesser Fourth Amendment values. Illustrative is *California v. Carney,* p. 275, allowing warrantless search of vehicles because of the "diminished expectation of privacy" in them. Sometimes warrant excusal is rationalized on the ground that the permitted police activity is merely "routine," as with the inventory allowed in *Colorado v. Bertine*, p. 296. On other occasions the Supreme Court has recognized an exception to the warrant requirement because of a purported need for "bright lines" in the rules governing police conduct. Illustrative is *United States v. Watson*, p. 221, holding a warrant is never needed to arrest in a public place because a contrary holding would "encumber criminal prosecutions with endless litigation with respect to the existence of exigent circumstances, whether it was practicable to get a warrant, whether the suspect was about to flee, and the like." The tension between these and other considerations has not always produced predictable or consistent results in the Court's decisions concerning what is permissible warrantless police action.

2. The preference for the warrant process is commonly explained on the ground that it, more so than the post-search suppression process, *prevents* illegal searches. Compare William S. Stuntz, *Warrants and Fourth Amendment Remedies,* 77 Va.L.Rev. 881, 893 (1991): "Unfortunately, given our existing system, warrants may not have the desired preventive effect. Police officers are not the only ones who can get the relevant legal standards wrong; other actors in the system make mistakes as well. And while requiring warrants does reduce the odds of police mistake in applying the relevant legal standards, it also creates additional opportunities for error by magistrates. This is no small problem. Magistrates (1) may do a bad job of applying the probable cause standard because of deficiencies in the warrant process (review is ex parte and cursory), and (2) nevertheless receive a great deal of deference by judges after the fact. Requiring warrants therefore may lead to many *more* bad searches than would a simple system of police decisionmaking followed by after-the-fact review.

"And even if warrants do prevent bad searches, so do after-the-fact sanctions. An ounce of prevention may indeed be worth a pound of cure, but the pound of cure—after-the-fact sanctions—is itself a preventive device, since the threat of ex post penalties affects behavior ex ante. This is a simple point, but an important one. Police officers, like other regulated actors, respond to legal signals and alter their behavior in order to avoid after-the-fact sanctions. In most other contexts, that is thought to be the cheapest means of achieving a given level of deterrence * * *. Thus, to defend warrants, one must point to some reason why after-the-fact deterrence will work unusually poorly in the search and seizure context—some argument that explains why search and seizure law should be treated *differently* than most other regulatory regimes."

Stuntz, id. at 884, suggests some other reasons—that "the exclusionary rule generates an additional pair of problems for fourth amendment law, problems that warrants might plausibly help solve. Exclusion * * * may bias judges' after-the-fact probable cause determinations by requiring that they be made in cases where the officer actually found incriminating evidence. Similarly, the lack of a credible opponent (the defendant has, after all, been found with incriminating evidence) invites the police to subvert the governing legal standard by testifying falsely at suppression hearings. Warrants can reduce both problems by forcing the necessary judicial decision to be made, and the police officer's account of the facts to be given, before the evidence is found."

3. Craig M. Bradley, *Two Models of the Fourth Amendment*, 83 Mich.L.Rev. 1468, 1471–72 (1985), after noting that extant Fourth Amendment doctrine on when a warrant is required is "mired in exceptions and modifications (with resultant confusion)," asserts that there "are two, and only two, ways of looking at the fourth amendment which will provide the police with reasonably coherent direction as to how they must proceed and the courts with a consistent basis for

decision": (1) The "no lines" model, i.e., that a "search or seizure must be reasonable, considering all relevant factors on a case-by-case basis," considering such factors as "whether probable cause existed, whether a warrant was obtained, whether exigent circumstances existed, and the nature of the intrusion, the quantum of evidence possessed by the police, and the seriousness of the offense under investigation." This model, "by presenting an unabashedly *unclear* rule that provides no guidelines, will never have to be modified to suit an unusual fact situation," and thus will "work considerably better than the present system where the Court purports to set forth clear rules but does not actually do so." (2) The "bright line" model, i.e., that "a warrant is always required for every search and seizure when it is practicable to obtain one," but "the warrant need not be in writing but rather may be phoned or radioed into a magistrate * * * who will authorize or forbid the search orally." Under this model, "the police would know what is expected of them and would be able to conform their conduct to the requirement of the law, much as they have accommodated their behavior to the *Miranda* requirements

SECTION 5. WARRANTLESS ARRESTS AND SEARCHES OF THE PERSON

UNITED STATES v. WATSON
423 U.S. 411, 96 S.Ct. 820, 46 L.Ed.2d 598 (1976).

Justice WHITE delivered the opinion of the Court.

[Reliable informant Khoury told a federal postal inspector that Watson had supplied him with a stolen credit card and had agreed to furnish additional cards at their next meeting, scheduled for a few days later. At that meeting, which occurred in a restaurant, Khoury signaled the inspector that Watson had the cards, at which point the inspector arrested Watson without a warrant, as he was authorized to do under 18 U.S.C. § 3061 and applicable postal regulations. The court of appeals held the arrest unconstitutional because the inspector had failed to secure an arrest warrant although he concededly had time to do so, and this was a significant factor in the court's additional holding that Watson's consent to a search of his car was not voluntary.]

* * * Section 3061 represents a judgment by Congress that it is not unreasonable under the Fourth Amendment for postal inspectors to arrest without a warrant provided they have probable cause to do so. This was not an isolated or quixotic judgment of the legislative branch. Other federal law enforcement officers have been expressly authorized by statute for many years to make felony arrests on probable cause but without a warrant. * * *

Because there is a "strong presumption of constitutionality due to an Act of Congress, especially when it turns on what is 'reasonable,' * * * [o]bviously the Court should be reluctant to decide that a search thus authorized by Congress was unreasonable and that the Act was therefore unconstitutional." Moreover, there is nothing in the Court's prior cases indicating that under the Fourth Amendment a warrant is required to make a valid arrest for a felony. Indeed, the relevant prior decisions are uniformly to the contrary. * * *[a]

---

a. The Court noted by way of footnote that because the arrest here was in a public place, it did not have to resolve the "still unsettled question" of whether a warrant is needed to enter private premises to make an arrest. This issue is considered at p. 266.

The cases construing the Fourth Amendment thus reflect the ancient common-law rule that a peace officer was permitted to arrest without a warrant for a misdemeanor or felony committed in his presence as well as for a felony not committed in his presence if there was reasonable grounds for making the arrest. This has also been the prevailing rule under state constitutions and statutes. * * *

Because the common-law rule authorizing arrests without warrant generally prevailed in the States, it is important for present purposes to note that in 1792 Congress invested United States Marshals and their deputies with "the same powers in executing the laws of the United States, as sheriffs and their deputies in their several states have by law, in executing the laws of their respective states." The Second Congress thus saw no inconsistency between the Fourth Amendment and giving United States Marshals the same power as local peace officers to arrest for a felony without a warrant.[8] * * *

The balance struck by the common law in generally authorizing felony arrests on probable cause, but without a warrant, has survived substantially intact. It appears in almost all of the States in the form of express statutory authorization. * * *

This is the rule Congress has long directed its principal law enforcement officers to follow. Congress has plainly decided against conditioning warrantless arrest power on proof of exigent circumstances. Law enforcement officers may find it wise to seek arrest warrants where practicable to do so, and their judgments about probable cause may be more readily accepted where backed by a warrant issued by a magistrate. But we decline to transform this judicial preference into a constitutional rule when the judgment of the Nation and Congress has for so long been to authorize warrantless public arrests on probable cause rather than to encumber criminal prosecutions with endless litigation with respect to the existence of exigent circumstances, whether it was practicable to get a warrant, whether the suspect was about to flee, and the like. * * *

Reversed.

Justice STEVENS took no part in the consideration or decision of this case.

Justice POWELL, concurring. * * *

On its face, our decision today creates a certain anomaly. There is no more basic constitutional rule in the Fourth Amendment area than that which makes a warrantless search unreasonable except in a few "jealously and carefully drawn" exceptional circumstances. * * * In short, the course of judicial development of the Fourth Amendment with respect to searches has remained true to the principles so well expressed by Justice Jackson:

> "Any assumption that evidence sufficient to support a magistrate's disinterested determination to issue a search warrant will justify the officers in making a search without a warrant would reduce the Amendment to a nullity and leave the people's homes secure only in the discretion of police officers. * * * When the right of privacy must reasonably yield to the right of search is, as a rule, to be decided by a judicial officer, not by a policeman or Government enforcement agent." *Johnson v. United States,* 333 U.S. 10, 14, 68 S.Ct. 367, 369, 92 L.Ed. 436 (1948).

8. Of equal import is the rule recognized by this Court that even in the absence of a federal statute granting or restricting the authority of federal law enforcement officers, "the law of the state where an arrest without warrant takes place determines its validity." *United States v. Di Re,* 332 U.S. 581, 68 S.Ct. 222, 92 L.Ed. 210 (1948). * * *

Since the Fourth Amendment speaks equally to both searches and seizures, and since an arrest, the taking hold of one's person, is quintessentially a seizure, it would seem that the constitutional provision should impose the same limitations upon arrests that it does upon searches. Indeed, as an abstract matter an argument can be made that the restrictions upon arrest perhaps should be greater. A search may cause only annoyance and temporary inconvenience to the law-abiding citizen, assuming more serious dimension only when it turns up evidence of criminality. An arrest, however, is a serious personal intrusion regardless of whether the person seized is guilty or innocent. Although an arrestee cannot be held for a significant period without some neutral determination that there are grounds to do so, no decision that he should go free can come quickly enough to erase the invasion of his privacy that already will have occurred. Logic therefore would seem to dictate that arrests be subject to the warrant requirement at least to the same extent as searches.

But logic sometimes must defer to history and experience. The Court's opinion emphasizes the historical sanction accorded warrantless felony arrests. * * *

Moreover, a constitutional rule permitting felony arrests only with a warrant or in exigent circumstances could severely hamper effective law enforcement. Good police practice often requires postponing an arrest, even after probable cause has been established, in order to place the suspect under surveillance or otherwise develop further evidence necessary to prove guilt to a jury. Under the holding of the Court of Appeals such additional investigative work could imperil the entire prosecution. Should the officers fail to obtain a warrant initially, and later be required by unforeseen circumstances to arrest immediately with no chance to procure a last-minute warrant, they would risk a court decision that the subsequent exigency did not excuse their failure to get a warrant in the interim since they first developed probable cause. If the officers attempted to meet such a contingency by procuring a warrant as soon as they had probable cause and then merely held it during their subsequent investigation, they would risk a court decision that the warrant had grown stale by the time it was used.[5] Law enforcement personnel caught in this squeeze could ensure validity of their arrests only by obtaining a warrant and arresting as soon as probable cause existed, thereby foreclosing the possibility of gathering vital additional evidence from the suspect's continued actions. * * *

Justice STEWART, concurring in the result. * * *

Justice MARSHALL, with whom Justice BRENNAN joins, dissenting. * * *

The signal of the reliable informant that Watson was in possession of stolen credit cards gave the postal inspectors probable cause to make the arrest. * * * When law enforcement officers have probable cause to believe that an offense is taking place in their presence and that the suspect is at that moment in possession of the evidence, exigent circumstances exist. Delay could cause the escape of the suspect or the destruction of the evidence. Accordingly, Watson's warrantless arrest was valid under the recognized exigent circumstances exception

---

5. The probable cause to support issuance of an arrest warrant normally would not grow stale as easily as that which supports a warrant to search a particular place for particular objects. This is true because once there is probable cause to believe that someone is a felon the passage of time often will bring new supporting evidence. But in some cases the original grounds supporting the warrant could be disproved by subsequent investigation that at the same time turns up wholly new evidence supporting probable cause on a different theory. In those cases the warrant could be stale because based upon discredited information.

to the warrant requirement, and the Court has no occasion to consider whether a warrant would otherwise be necessary. * * *

[T]he substance of the ancient common-law rule provides no support for the far-reaching modern rule that the Court fashions on its model. * * *

* * * Only the most serious crimes were felonies at common law, and many crimes now classified as felonies under federal or state law were treated as misdemeanors. * * * To make an arrest for any of these crimes at common law, the police officer was required to obtain a warrant, unless the crime was committed in his presence. Since many of these same crimes are commonly classified as felonies today however, under the Court's holding a warrant is no longer needed to make such arrests, a result in contravention of the common law.

[T]he only clear lesson of history is contrary to the one the Court draws: the common law considered the arrest warrant far more important than today's decision leaves it. * * *

[W]e must now consider (1) whether the privacy of our citizens will be better protected by ordinarily requiring a warrant to be issued before they may be arrested; and (2) whether a warrant requirement would unduly burden legitimate governmental interests.

The first question is easily answered. Of course the privacy of our citizens will be better protected by a warrant requirement. We have recognized that "the Fourth Amendment protects people, not places." Indeed, the privacy guaranteed by the Fourth Amendment is quintessentially personal. Thus a warrant is required in search situations not because of some high regard for property, but because of our regard for the individual, and *his* interest in his possessions and person. * * *

The Government's assertion that a warrant requirement would impose an intolerable burden stems, in large part, from the specious supposition that procurement of an arrest warrant would be necessary as soon as probable cause ripens. There is no requirement that a search warrant be obtained the moment police have probable cause to search. The rule is only that present probable cause be shown and a warrant obtained before a search is undertaken. The same rule should obtain for arrest warrants, where it may even make more sense. Certainly, there is less need for prompt procurement of a warrant in the arrest situation. Unlike probable cause to search, probable cause to arrest, once formed will continue to exist for the indefinite future, at least if no intervening exculpatory facts come to light.

This sensible approach obviates most of the difficulties that have been suggested with an arrest warrant rule. Police would not have to cut their investigation short the moment they obtain probable cause to arrest, nor would undercover agents be forced suddenly to terminate their work and forfeit their covers. Moreover, if in the course of the continued police investigation exigent circumstances develop that demand an immediate arrest, the arrest may be made without fear of unconstitutionality, so long as the exigency was unanticipated and not used to avoid the arrest warrant requirement. Likewise, if in the course of the continued investigation police uncover evidence tying the suspect to another crime, they may immediately arrest him for that crime if exigency demands it, and still be in full conformity with the warrant rule. This is why the arrest in this case was not improper.[15] Other than where police attempt to evade the warrant

15. Although the postal inspectors here anticipated the occurrence of the second crime, they could not have obtained a warrant for Watson's arrest for that crime until probable

requirement, the rule would invalidate an arrest only in the obvious situation: where police, with probable cause but without exigent circumstances, set out to arrest a suspect. Such an arrest must be void, even if exigency develops in the course of the arrest that would ordinarily validate it; otherwise the warrant requirement would be reduced to a toothless prescription. * * *

It is suggested, however, that even if application of this rule does not require police to secure a warrant as soon as they obtain probable cause, the confused officer would nonetheless be prone to do so. If so, police "would risk a court decision that the warrant had grown stale by the time it was used." (Powell, J., concurring). This fear is groundless. First, as suggested above, the requirement that police procure a warrant before an arrest is made is rather simple of application. Thus, there is no need for the police to find themselves in this "squeeze." Second, the "squeeze" is nonexistent. Just as it is virtually impossible for probable cause for an arrest to grow stale between the time of formation and the time a warrant is procured, it is virtually impossible for probable cause to become stale between procurement and arrest. Delay by law enforcement officers in executing an arrest warrant does not ordinarily affect the legality of the arrest. * * *

Notes and Questions

1. Consider LaFave, § 5.1: "A study conducted for the President's Commission on Law Enforcement and Administration of Justice indicated that, while nearly fifty percent of all arrests are made within two hours of the crime as a result of a 'hot' search of the crime scene or a 'warm' search of the general vicinity of the crime, very few additional arrests occur immediately thereafter. Rather, there is a delay while further investigation is conducted; about 45 percent of all arrests occur more than a day after the crime, and nearly 35 percent of all arrests are made after the passage of over a week. In these latter instances, * * * the risk is negligible that the defendant will suddenly flee between the time the police solve the case and the time which would be required to obtain and serve an arrest warrant. Indeed, in such cases the need to arrest before an arrest warrant can be obtained is likely to be considerably less apparent than the need to search before a search warrant can be acquired and executed; the defendant is unlikely suddenly to decide to flee or go into hiding at that point, but he well might have reached the stage where he is about to dispose of the fruits of his crime or destroy or abandon items of physical evidence which might link him with the crime."

2. As for the *Watson* dissenters' conclusion that "the privacy of our citizens will be better protected by ordinarily requiring a warrant to be issued before they may be arrested," consider Barrett, *Criminal Justice: The Problem of Mass Production,* in The American Assembly, Columbia University, The Courts, the Public, and the Law Explosion 85, 117–18 (H.W. Jones ed. 1965): "How can a magistrate be more than a 'rubber stamp' in signing warrants unless he devotes at least some minutes in each case to reading the affidavits submitted to him in support of the request for a warrant, and inquiring into the background of the conclusions stated therein? And where is the judicial time going to be found to make such inquiries in the generality of cases? The Los Angeles Municipal Court with annual filings of about 130,000 (excluding parking and traffic) *finds itself so pressed that in large areas of its caseload it averages but a minute per case in receiving pleas and imposing sentence.* How could it cope with the added burden

cause formed, just moments before the arrest. A warrant based on anticipated facts is prema-ture and void. *United States v. Roberts,* 333 F.Supp. 786 (E.D.Tenn.1971).

that would be involved in the issuance of warrants to govern the approximately 200,000 arrests made per year in Los Angeles for offenses other than traffic"?

3. Is the "preference" for arrest warrants nonetheless justified on the ground that, at least the police must make a record before the event of the basis for their actions? Consider Skolnick, *Justice Without Trial* 214–15 (1966): "[T]he policeman perceives * * * the need to be able to reconstruct a set of complex happenings in such a way that, subsequent to the arrest, probable cause can be found according to appellate court standards. In this way, as one district attorney expressed it, 'the policeman fabricates probable cause.' By saying this, he did not mean to assert that the policeman is a liar, but rather that he finds it necessary to construct an *ex post facto* description of the preceding events so that these conform to legal arrest requirements, whether in fact the events actually did so or not at the time of the arrest. Thus, the policeman respects the necessity for 'complying' with the arrest laws. His 'compliance,' however, may take the form of *post hoc* manipulation of the facts rather than before-the-fact behavior."

4. Given the concern regarding "*post hoc* manipulation of the facts," should the arrest of a person booked for one offense be upheld on the ground that the police actually had sufficient evidence of a quite different offense? No, argued Chief Justice Warren, dissenting from the dismissal of the writ of certiorari in *Wainwright v. New Orleans,* 392 U.S. 598, 88 S.Ct. 2243, 20 L.Ed.2d 1322 (1968): "I see no more justification for permitting the State to disregard its own booking record than for permitting any other administrative body to disregard its own records. Quite the contrary. In the 'low-visibility' sphere of police investigatory practices, there are obvious and compelling reasons why official records should prevail over the second guessing of lawyers and judges. Nor would holding the police to official records frustrate any legitimate interest of society. If the police in this case really believed that petitioner was the murder suspect, and if they had probable cause to so believe, all they had to do was to arrest and book him for murder." Compare *Hatcher v. State,* 410 N.E.2d 1187 (Ind.1980) ("public policy in detecting and prosecuting criminal offenders outweighs the value of having arresting officers choose and enunciate the correct legal theory for the arrest").[b]

5. The common law "in presence" requirement for a warrantless misdemeanor arrest has sometimes caused the courts difficulties. Consider *People v. Burdo,* 223 N.W.2d 358 (Mich.App.1974) (officer could not arrest for misdemeanor of driving under influence of liquor when he came on scene of auto accident and found defendant there, even though defendant obviously was intoxicated and admitted he had been driving); *People v. Dixon,* 222 N.W.2d 749 (Mich.1974) (after stopping noisy vehicle, officer could arrest driver for misdemeanor of driving without a license after being advised via police radio that defendant's license had been suspended).

6. In *Street v. Surdyka,* 492 F.2d 368 (4th Cir.1974), it was held that the Fourth Amendment should not "be interpreted to prohibit warrantless arrests for misdemeanors committed outside an officer's presence." Is this so after *Watson?* Consider that some states now use the felony-arrest rule for *all* offenses, while some have redefined the misdemeanor arrest power in terms of need, as in Neb.Rev.Stat. § 29–404.02, which permits an officer to arrest a person without a warrant if he "has reasonable cause to believe that such person has committed

b. A somewhat different problem arises when the booking entry indicates that the defendant was arrested "on suspicion of" or "for investigation of" a certain offense. A few courts have taken the position that such an entry makes the arrest illegal, although in practice such entries are often made solely as a means of identifying those cases which require the attention of the detective division.

* * * [a] misdemeanor, and the officer has reasonable cause to believe that such person either (a) will not be apprehended unless immediately arrested; (b) may cause injury to himself or others or damage to property unless immediately arrested; (c) may destroy or conceal evidence of the commission of such misdemeanor; or (d) has committed a misdemeanor in the presence of the officer."

7. Rejecting the contention that if the *Watson* probable cause "requirement is satisfied the Fourth Amendment has nothing to say about *how* that seizure is made," the Court in TENNESSEE v. GARNER, 471 U.S. 1, 105 S.Ct. 1694, 85 L.Ed.2d 1 (1985), held that the use of deadly force to arrest a fleeing felon is sometimes unreasonable under the Fourth Amendment. WHITE, J., stated for the majority:

"The use of deadly force to prevent the escape of all felony suspects, whatever the circumstances, is constitutionally unreasonable. It is not better that all felony suspects die than that they escape. Where the suspect poses no immediate threat to the officer and no threat to others, the harm resulting from failing to apprehend him does not justify the use of deadly force to do so. It is no doubt unfortunate when a suspect who is in sight escapes, but the fact that the police arrive a little late or are a little slower afoot does not always justify killing the suspect. A police officer may not seize an unarmed, nondangerous suspect by shooting him dead. The Tennessee statute is unconstitutional insofar as it authorizes the use of deadly force against such fleeing suspects.

"It is not, however, unconstitutional on its face. Where the officer has probable cause to believe that the suspect poses a threat of serious physical harm, either to the officer or to others, it is not constitutionally unreasonable to prevent escape by using deadly force. Thus, if the suspect threatens the officer with a weapon or there is probable cause to believe that he has committed a crime involving the infliction or threatened infliction of serious physical harm, deadly force may be used if necessary to prevent escape, and if, where feasible, some warning has been given. As applied in such circumstances, the Tennessee statute would pass constitutional muster."

O'CONNOR, J., joined by the Chief Justice and Rehnquist, J., dissenting, objected:

"A proper balancing of the interests involved suggests that use of deadly force as a last resort to apprehend a criminal suspect fleeing from the scene of a nighttime burglary is not unreasonable within the meaning of the Fourth Amendment. Admittedly, the events giving rise to this case are in retrospect deeply regrettable. No one can view the death of an unarmed and apparently nonviolent 15–year old without sorrow, much less disapproval. Nonetheless, the reasonableness of Officer Hymon's conduct for purposes of the Fourth Amendment cannot be evaluated by what later appears to have been a preferable course of police action. The officer pursued a suspect in the darkened backyard of a house that from all indications had just been burglarized. The police officer was not certain whether the suspect was alone or unarmed; nor did he know what had transpired inside the house. He ordered the suspect to halt, and when the suspect refused to obey and attempted to flee into the night, the officer fired his weapon to prevent escape. The reasonableness of this action for purposes of the Fourth Amendment is not determined by the unfortunate nature of this particular case; instead, the question is whether it is constitutionally impermissible for police officers, as a last resort, to shoot a burglary suspect fleeing the scene of the crime."[c]

c. See H. Richard Uviller, *Seizure by Gunshot: The Riddle of the Fleeing Felon,* 14 N.Y.U.Rev.L. & Soc.Chg. 705 (1986).

The Fourth Amendment reasonableness standard, the Court later declared in *Graham v. Connor,* 490 U.S. 386, 109 S.Ct. 1865, 104 L.Ed.2d 443 (1989), (1) applies to "*all* claims that law enforcement officers have used excessive force—deadly or not—in the course of an arrest, investigatory stop, or other 'seizure' of a free citizen"; (2) "requires careful attention to the facts and circumstances of each particular case, including the severity of the crime at issue, whether the suspect poses an immediate threat to the safety of the officers or others, and whether he is actively resisting arrest or attempting to evade arrest by flight"; (3) "must embody allowance for the fact that police officers are often forced to make split-second judgments—in circumstances that are tense, uncertain, and rapidly evolving—about the amount of force that is necessary in a particular situation"; and (4) asks "whether the officers' actions are 'objectively reasonable' in light of the facts and circumstances confronting them, without regard to their underlying intent or motivation."

If the police conduct causing death or bodily harm was not a search or seizure, then the Fourteenth Amendment due process shocks-the-conscience test, rather than the Fourth Amendment reasonableness test, applies. See *County of Sacramento v. Lewis,* p. 43.

What is the meaning of the term "deadly force" in *Garner*? In *Vera Cruz v. City of Escondido,* 139 F.3d 659 (9th Cir.1997), an officer acting solely to terminate a person's flight released his "K–9 companion," who bit the fleeing party on the arm and held him until the officer took away the arrestee's knife, resulting in wounds requiring surgery and eight days of hospitalization. In a § 1983 action, plaintiff argued for the Model Penal Code definition, "force that the actor uses with the purpose of causing or that he knows to create a substantial risk of causing death or serious bodily injury," but the court ruled that "deadly force is that force which is reasonably likely to cause death." Which is correct?

8. In GERSTEIN v. PUGH, 420 U.S. 103, 95 S.Ct. 854, 43 L.Ed.2d 54 (1975), the Court, per POWELL, J., held:

"[A] policeman's on-the-scene assessment of probable cause provides legal justification for arresting a person suspected of crime, and for a brief period of detention to take the administrative steps incident to arrest. Once the suspect is in custody, however, the reasons that justify dispensing with the magistrate's neutral judgment evaporate. There no longer is any danger that the suspect will escape or commit further crimes while the police submit their evidence to a magistrate. And, while the State's reasons for taking summary action subside, the suspect's need for a neutral determination of probable cause increases significantly. The consequences of prolonged detention may be more serious than the interference occasioned by arrest. Pretrial confinement may imperil the suspect's job, interrupt his source of income, and impair his family relationships. Even pretrial release may be accompanied by burdensome conditions that effect a significant restraint on liberty. When the stakes are this high, the detached judgment of a neutral magistrate is essential if the Fourth Amendment is to furnish meaningful protection from unfounded interference with liberty. Accordingly, we hold that the Fourth Amendment requires a judicial determination of probable cause as a prerequisite to extended restraint on liberty following arrest.[d]

d. In a subsequent footnote, the Court indicated that a grand jury determination to indict would provide such a "judicial determination." In distinguishing the prosecutor's determination that probable cause exists, the Court not-

ed: "By contrast, the Court has held that an indictment, 'fair upon its face,' and returned by a 'properly constituted grand jury' conclusively determines the existence of probable

"This result has historical support in the common law that has guided interpretation of the Fourth Amendment. At common law it was customary, if not obligatory, for an arrested person to be brought before a justice of the peace shortly after arrest. The justice of the peace would 'examine' the prisoner and the witnesses to determine whether there was reason to believe the prisoner had committed a crime. If there was, the suspect would be committed to jail or bailed pending trial. If not, he would be discharged from custody. The initial determination of probable cause also could be reviewed by higher courts on a writ of habeas corpus. This practice furnished the model for criminal procedure in America immediately following the adoption of the Fourth Amendment, and there are indications that the Framers of the Bill of Rights regarded it as a model for a 'reasonable' seizure."

The Court then concluded the Court of Appeals had erred in holding "that the determination of probable cause must be accompanied by the full panoply of adversary safeguards—counsel, confrontation, cross-examination, and compulsory process for witnesses." The Court of Appeals had required that the state provide, in effect, a "full preliminary hearing * * * modeled after the procedure used in many States to determine whether the evidence justifies going to trial under an information or presenting the case to a grand jury." The Fourth Amendment, the Court noted, did not require such an adversary proceeding:

"The sole issue is whether there is probable cause for detaining the arrested person pending further proceedings. This issue can be determined reliably without an adversary hearing. That standard—probable cause to believe the suspect has committed a crime—traditionally has been decided by a magistrate in a nonadversary proceeding on hearsay and written testimony, and the Court has approved these informal modes of proof. * * * The use of an informal procedure is justified not only by the lesser consequences of a probable cause determination but also by the nature of the determination itself. It does not require the fine resolution of conflicting evidence that a reasonable-doubt or even a preponderance standard demands, and credibility determinations are seldom crucial in deciding whether the evidence supports a reasonable belief in guilt. This is not to say that confrontation and cross-examination might not enhance the reliability of probable cause determinations in some cases. In most cases, however, their value would be too slight to justify holding, as a matter of constitutional principle, that these formalities and safeguards designed for trial must also be employed in making the Fourth Amendment determination of probable cause."[e]

cause and requires issuance of an arrest warrant without further inquiry. The willingness to let a grand jury judgment substitute for that of a neutral and detached magistrate is attributable to the grand jury's relationship to the courts and its historical role of protecting individuals from unjust prosecution."

e. Stewart, J., joined by Douglas, Brennan and Marshall, JJ., refused to join this portion of the Court's opinion. Justice Stewart noted: "I see no need in this case for the Court to say that the Constitution extends less procedural protection to an imprisoned human being than is required to test the propriety of garnishing a commercial bank account, *North Georgia Finishing, Inc. v. Di–Chem, Inc.,* 419 U.S. 601, 95 S.Ct. 719, 42 L.Ed.2d 751 [(1975)], the custody of a refrigerator, *Mitchell v. W. T. Grant Co.,* 416 U.S. 600, 94 S.Ct. 1895, 40 L.Ed.2d 406

[(1974)], the temporary suspension of a public school student, *Goss v. Lopez,* 419 U.S. 565, 95 S.Ct. 729, 42 L.Ed.2d 725 [(1975)], or the suspension of a driver's license, *Bell v. Burson,* 402 U.S. 535, 91 S.Ct. 1586, 29 L.Ed.2d 90 [(1971)]. Although it may be true that the Fourth Amendment's 'balance between individual and public interests always has been thought to define the "process that is due" for seizures of person or property in criminal cases,' this case does not involve an initial arrest, but rather the continuing incarceration of a presumptively innocent person. Accordingly, I cannot join the Court's effort to foreclose any claim that the traditional requirements of constitutional due process are applicable in the context of pretrial detention."

" * * * There is no single preferred pretrial procedure, and the nature of the probable cause determination usually will be shaped to accord with a State's pretrial procedure viewed as a whole. * * * It may be found desirable, for example, to make the probable cause determination at the suspect's first appearance before a judicial officer,[24] the determination may be incorporated into the procedure for setting bail or fixing other conditions of pretrial release. * * * Whatever procedure a State may adopt, it must provide a fair and reliable determination of probable cause as a condition for any significant pretrial restraint on liberty,[26] and this determination must be made by a judicial officer either before or promptly after arrest.[27]"

9. Is it clear from *Gerstein* which defendants are entitled to a prompt judicial review of probable cause? Consider *In re Walters,* 543 P.2d 607 (Cal.1975): "As the posting of bail may impose an unwarranted burden on an accused if probable cause to detain is lacking, the accused is entitled to have that determination made prior to electing to post or not to post bail."

10. In COUNTY OF RIVERSIDE v. McLAUGHLIN, 500 U.S. 44, 111 S.Ct. 1661, 114 L.Ed.2d 49 (1991), the Court confronted the question of "what is 'prompt' under *Gerstein* "and concluded, 5–4, per O'CONNOR, J., that "it is important to provide some degree of certainty so that States and counties may establish procedures with confidence that they fall within constitutional bounds. Taking into account the competing interests articulated in *Gerstein,* we believe that a jurisdiction that provides judicial determinations of probable cause within 48 hours of arrest will, as a general matter, comply with the promptness requirement of *Gerstein.* For this reason, such jurisdictions will be immune from systemic challenges.

"This is not to say that the probable cause determination in a particular case passes constitutional muster simply because it is provided within 48 hours. Such a hearing may nonetheless violate *Gerstein* if the arrested individual can prove that his or her probable cause determination was delayed unreasonably. Examples of unreasonable delay are delays for the purpose of gathering additional evidence to justify the arrest, a delay motivated by ill will against the arrested individual, or delay for delay's sake. In evaluating whether the delay in a particular case is

---

24. Several States already authorize a determination of probable cause at this stage or immediately thereafter. This Court has interpreted the Federal Rules of Criminal Procedure to require a determination of probable cause at the first appearance.

26. Because the probable cause determination is not a constitutional prerequisite to the charging decision, it is required only for those suspects who suffer restraints on liberty other than the condition that they appear for trial. There are many kinds of pretrial release and many degrees of conditional liberty. We cannot define specifically those that would require a prior probable cause determination, but the key factor is significant restraint on liberty.

27. In his concurring opinion, Mr. Justice Stewart objects to the Court's choice of the Fourth Amendment as the rationale for decision and suggests that the Court offers less procedural protection to a person in jail than it requires in certain civil cases. Here we deal with the complex procedures of a criminal case

and a threshold right guaranteed by the Fourth Amendment. The historical basis of the probable cause requirement is quite different from the relatively recent application of variable procedural due process in debtor-creditor disputes and termination of government-created benefits. The Fourth Amendment was tailored explicitly for the criminal justice system, and its balance between individual and public interests always has been thought to define the "process that is due" for seizures of person or property in criminal cases, including the detention of suspects pending trial. Moreover, the Fourth Amendment probable cause determination is in fact only the *first* stage of an elaborate system, unique in jurisprudence, designed to safeguard the rights of those accused of criminal conduct. The relatively simple civil procedures (e.g., prior interview with school principal before suspension) presented in the cases cited in the concurring opinion are inapposite and irrelevant in the wholly different context of the criminal justice system. * * *

unreasonable, however, courts must allow a substantial degree of flexibility. Courts cannot ignore the often unavoidable delays in transporting arrested persons from one facility to another, handling late-night bookings where no magistrate is readily available, obtaining the presence of an arresting officer who may be busy processing other suspects or securing the premises of an arrest, and other practical realities.

"Where an arrested individual does not receive a probable cause determination within 48 hours, the calculus changes. In such a case, the arrested individual does not bear the burden of proving an unreasonable delay. Rather, the burden shifts to the government to demonstrate the existence of a bona fide emergency or other extraordinary circumstance. The fact that in a particular case it may take longer than 48 hours to consolidate pretrial proceedings does not qualify as an extraordinary circumstance. Nor, for that matter, do intervening weekends. A jurisdiction that chooses to offer combined proceedings must do so as soon as is reasonably feasible, but in no event later than 48 hours after arrest."

SCALIA, J., dissenting, reasoned that "the only element bearing upon the reasonableness of delay was * * * the arresting officer's ability, once the prisoner had been secured, to reach a magistrate who could issue the needed warrant for further detention,"and that consequently the time at which the presumption should shift ought to be only 24 hours.

11. Assuming a *Gerstein* violation, what bearing should it have if the individual is later prosecuted? In *Powell v. Nevada*, 511 U.S. 79, 114 S.Ct. 1280, 128 L.Ed.2d 1 (1994), holding *McLaughlin* retroactive to that case, the Court, per Ginsburg, J., noted: "It does not necessarily follow, however, that Powell must 'be set free' or gain other relief, for several questions remain open for decision on remand," including "the appropriate remedy for a delay in determining probable cause (an issue not resolved by *McLaughlin*)." In *Powell,* an untimely probable cause determination was made four days after defendant's arrest, shortly after he gave the police an incriminating statement. In declaring that "whether a suppression remedy applies in that setting remains an unresolved question," Justice Ginsburg took note of two arguably analogous rules pointing in opposite directions: (i) that an after-the-fact judicial determination of probable cause does not make admissible evidence obtained in a search in violation of the Fourth Amendment's search warrant requirement; and (ii) that under *Harris,* p. 791, suppression of a statement subsequently obtained elsewhere is not required because of defendant's warrantless arrest inside premises in violation of the Fourth Amendment.

12. The governor of Michigan issued an arrest warrant for Doran pursuant to a request for extradition from the governor of Arizona. Attached to the Arizona requisition were an arrest warrant for theft, two supporting affidavits, and the original complaint on which the charge was based. Relying upon *Gerstein* and language of the Uniform Criminal Extradition Act that the "indictment, information, or affidavit made before the magistrate must substantially charge the person demanded with having committed a crime," the state supreme court held that Doran could not be extradited because the "complaint and arrest warrant are both phrased in conclusory language" and "the two supporting affidavits fail to set out facts which could justify a Fourth Amendment finding of probable cause." But in *Michigan v. Doran,* 439 U.S. 282, 99 S.Ct. 530, 58 L.Ed.2d 521 (1978), the Court, per Burger, C.J., held "that once the governor of the asylum state has acted on a requisition for extradition based on the demanding state's judicial determination that probable cause existed, no further judicial inquiry may be had on that issue

in the asylum state." Emphasizing that the Extradition Clause[f] "was intended to enable each state to bring offenders to trial as swiftly as possible in the state where the alleged offense was committed," the Court concluded that to "allow plenary review in the asylum state of issues that can be fully litigated in the charging state would defeat the plain purposes of the summary and mandatory procedure authorized by" the Clause.

Three concurring Justices, after noting the absence of any discussion in the majority opinion of the significance of the Fourth Amendment, reasoned that the "extradition process involves an 'extended restraint of liberty following arrest' even more severe than that accompanying detention within a single State. [T]herefore, the Amendment's language and the holding in *Gerstein* mean that, even in the extradition context, where the demanding State's 'charge' rests upon something less than an indictment, there must be a determination of probable cause by a detached and neutral magistrate, and that the asylum State need not grant extradition unless that determination has been made. The demanding State, of course, has the burden of so demonstrating." They then concluded that this burden had been met in the instant case because the Arizona arrest warrant declared that a probable cause finding had been made.

UNITED STATES v. ROBINSON
414 U.S. 218, 94 S.Ct. 467, 38 L.Ed.2d 427 (1973).

Justice REHNQUIST delivered the opinion of the Court.

Respondent Robinson was convicted in United States District Court for the District of Columbia of the possession and facilitation of concealment of heroin. * * * [T]he Court of Appeals *en banc* reversed the judgment of conviction, holding that the heroin introduced in evidence against respondent had been obtained as a result of a search which violated the Fourth Amendment to the United States Constitution.

On April 23, 1968, at approximately 11 o'clock p.m., Officer Richard Jenks, a 15–year veteran of the District of Columbia Metropolitan Police Department, observed the respondent driving a 1965 Cadillac near the intersection of 8th and C Streets, Southeast, in the District of Columbia. Jenks, as a result of previous investigation following a check of respondent's operator's permit four days earlier, determined there was reason to believe that respondent was operating a motor vehicle after the revocation of his operator's permit. This is an offense defined by statute in the District of Columbia which carries a mandatory minimum jail term, a mandatory minimum fine, or both.

Jenks signaled respondent to stop the automobile, which respondent did, and all three of the occupants emerged from the car. At that point Jenks informed respondent that he was under arrest for "operating after revocation and obtaining a permit by misrepresentation." It was assumed by the majority of the Court of Appeals, and is conceded by the respondent here, that Jenks had probable cause to arrest respondent, and that he effected a full custody arrest.

In accordance with procedures prescribed in Police Department instructions,[2] Jenks then began to search respondent. He explained at a subsequent hearing

---

f. U.S. Const., Art. IV, § 2: "A Person charged in any State with Treason, Felony, or other Crime, who shall flee from Justice, and be found in another State, shall on Demand of the executive Authority of the State from which he fled, be delivered up, to be removed to the State having Jurisdiction of the Crime."

2. The government introduced testimony at the evidentiary hearing upon the original remand by the Court of Appeals as to certain that he was "face to face" with the respondent, and "placed [his] hands on [the respondent], my right hand to his left breast like this (demonstrating) and proceeded to pat him down thus (with the right hand)." During this patdown, Jenks felt an object in the left breast pocket of the heavy coat respondent was wearing, but testified that he "couldn't tell what it was" and also that he "couldn't actually tell the size of it." Jenks then reached into the pocket and pulled out the object, which turned out to be a "crumpled up cigarette package." Jenks testified that at this point he still did not know what was in the package:

> "As I felt the package I could feel objects in the package but I couldn't tell what they were. * * * I knew they weren't cigarettes."

The officer then opened the cigarette pack and found 14 gelatin capsules of white powder which he thought to be, and which later analysis proved to be, heroin. Jenks then continued his search of respondent to completion, feeling around his waist and trouser legs, and examining the remaining pockets. The heroin seized from the respondent was admitted into evidence at the trial which resulted in his conviction in the District Court. * * *

It is well settled that a search incident to a lawful arrest is a traditional exception to the warrant requirement of the Fourth Amendment. This general exception has historically been formulated into two distinct propositions. The first is that a search may be made of the *person* of the arrestee by virtue of the lawful arrest. The second is that a search may be made of the area within the control of the arrestee.

Examination of this Court's decisions in the area show that these two propositions have been treated quite differently. The validity of the search of a person incident to a lawful arrest has been regarded as settled from its first enunciation, and has remained virtually unchallenged until the present case. The validity of the second proposition, while likewise conceded in principle, has been subject to differing interpretations as to the extent of the area which may be searched. * * *

Throughout the series of cases in which the Court has addressed the second proposition relating to a search incident to a lawful arrest—the permissible area beyond the person of the arrestee which such a search may cover—no doubt has been expressed as to the unqualified authority of the arresting authority to search the person of the arrestee. * * *

Thus the broadly stated rule, and the reasons for it, have been repeatedly affirmed in the decisions of this Court since *Weeks v. United States* nearly 60 years ago. Since the statements in the cases speak not simply in terms of an exception to the warrant requirement, but in terms of an affirmative authority to search, they clearly imply that such searches also meet the Fourth Amendment's requirement of reasonableness. * * *

standard operating procedures of the Metropolitan Police Department. Sergeant Dennis C. Donaldson, a Training Division Instructor, testified that when a police officer makes "a full custody arrest" which he defined as where an officer "would arrest a subject and subsequently transport him to a police facility for booking," the officer is trained to make a full "field type search" * * *. Sergeant Donaldson testified that officers are instructed to examine the "contents of all of the pockets" of the arrestee in the course of the field search. * * * Those regulations also provide that in the case of some traffic offenses, including the crime of operating a motor vehicle after revocation of an operator's permit, the officer shall make a summary arrest of the violator and take the violator, in custody, to the stationhouse for booking. D.C.Metropolitan Police Department General Order No. 3, series 1959 (April 24, 1959). Such operating procedures are not, of course, determinative of the constitutional issues presented by this case.

Virtually all of the statements of this Court affirming the existence of an unqualified authority to search incident to a lawful arrest are dicta. We would not therefore be foreclosed by principles of *stare decisis* from further examination into history and practice in order to see whether the sort of qualifications imposed by the Court of Appeals in this case were in fact intended by the Framers of the Fourth Amendment or recognized in cases decided prior to *Weeks*. Unfortunately such authorities as exist are sparse. * * *

While these earlier authorities are sketchy, they tend to support the broad statement of the authority to search incident to arrest found in the successive decisions of this Court, rather than the restrictive one which was applied by the Court of Appeals in this case. * * *

The Court of Appeals in effect determined that the *only* reason supporting the authority for a *full* search incident to lawful arrest was the possibility of discovery of evidence or fruits. Concluding that there could be no evidence or fruits in the case of an offense such as that with which respondent was charged, it held that any protective search would have to be limited by the conditions laid down in *Terry* [*v. Ohio*, p. 304] for a search upon less than probable cause to arrest. Quite apart from the fact that *Terry* clearly recognized the distinction between the two types of searches, and that a different rule governed one than governed the other, we find additional reason to disagree with the Court of Appeals.

The justification or reason for the authority to search incident to a lawful arrest rests quite as much on the need to disarm the suspect in order to take him into custody as it does on the need to preserve evidence on his person for later use at trial. The standards traditionally governing a search incident to lawful arrest are not, therefore, commuted to the stricter *Terry* standards by the absence of probable fruits or further evidence of the particular crime for which the arrest is made.

Nor are we inclined, on the basis of what seems to us to be a rather speculative judgment, to qualify the breadth of the general authority to search incident to a lawful custodial arrest on an assumption that persons arrested for the offense of driving while their license has been revoked are less likely to be possessed of dangerous weapons than are those arrested for other crimes.[5] It is scarcely open to doubt that the danger to an officer is far greater in the case of the extended exposure which follows the taking of a suspect into custody and transporting him to the police station than in the case of the relatively fleeting contact resulting from the typical *Terry*-type stop. This is an adequate basis for treating all custodial arrests alike for purposes of search justification.

But quite apart from these distinctions, our more fundamental disagreement with the Court of Appeals arises from its suggestion that there must be litigated in each case the issue of whether or not there was present one of the reasons supporting the authority for a search of the person incident to a lawful arrest. We do not think the long line of authorities of this Court dating back to *Weeks*, nor

---

5. Such an assumption appears at least questionable in light of the available statistical data concerning assaults on police officers who are in the course of making arrests. The danger to the police officer flows from the fact of the arrest, and its attendant proximity, stress and uncertainty, and not from the grounds for arrest. One study concludes that approximately 30% of the shootings of police officers occur when the officer approaches a person seated in a car. Bristow, *Police Officer Shootings—A Tactical Evaluation*, 54 J.Crim.L.C. & P.S. 93 (1963). The Government in its brief notes that the Uniform Crime Reports, prepared by the Federal Bureau of Investigation, indicate that a significant percentage of police officers murders occur when the officers are making traffic stops. Brief for the United States, at 23. Those reports indicate that during January–March, 1973, 35 police officers were murdered; 11 of those officers were killed while engaged in traffic stops. Ibid.

what we can glean from the history of practice in this country and in England, requires such a case by case adjudication. A police officer's determination as to how and where to search the person of a suspect whom he has arrested is necessarily a quick *ad hoc* judgment which the Fourth Amendment does not require to be broken down in each instance into an analysis of each step in the search. The authority to search the person incident to a lawful custodial arrest, while based upon the need to disarm and to discover evidence, does not depend on what a court may later decide was the probability in a particular arrest situation that weapons or evidence would in fact be found upon the person of the suspect. A custodial arrest of a suspect based on probable cause is a reasonable intrusion under the Fourth Amendment; that intrusion being lawful, a search incident to the arrest requires no additional justification. It is the fact of the lawful arrest which establishes the authority to search, and we hold that in the case of a lawful custodial arrest a full search of the person is not only an exception to the warrant requirement of the Fourth Amendment, but is also a "reasonable" search under that Amendment.

The search of respondent's person conducted by Officer Jenks in this case and the seizure from him of the heroin, were permissible under established Fourth Amendment law. * * * Since it is the fact of custodial arrest which gives rise to the authority to search, it is of no moment that Jenks did not indicate any subjective fear of the respondent or that he did not himself suspect that respondent was armed.[7] Having in the course of a lawful search come upon the crumpled package of cigarettes, he was entitled to inspect it; and when his inspection revealed the heroin capsules, he was entitled to seize them as "fruits, instrumentalities, or contraband" probative of criminal conduct. The judgment of the Court of Appeals holding otherwise is reversed.

Reversed.

Justice MARSHALL, with whom Justice DOUGLAS and Justice BRENNAN join, dissenting. * * *

The majority's attempt to avoid case-by-case adjudication of Fourth Amendment issues is not only misguided as a matter of principle, but is also doomed to fail as a matter of practical application. As the majority itself is well aware, the powers granted the police in this case are strong ones, subject to potential abuse. Although, in this particular case, Officer Jenks was required by Police Department regulation to make an in-custody arrest rather than to issue a citation, in most jurisdictions and for most traffic offenses the determination of whether to issue a citation or effect a full arrest is discretionary with the officer. There is always the possibility that a police officer, lacking probable cause to obtain a search warrant, will use a traffic arrest as a pretext to conduct a search. I suggest this possibility not to impugn the integrity of our police, but merely to point out that case-by-case adjudication will always be necessary to determine whether a full arrest was effected for purely legitimate reasons or, rather, as a pretext for searching the arrestee.

The majority states that "A police officer's determination as to how and where to search the person of a suspect whom he has arrested is necessarily a quick *ad hoc* judgment which the Fourth Amendment does not require to be

---

7. The United States concedes that "in searching respondent, [Officer Jenks] was not motivated by a feeling of imminent danger and was not specifically looking for weapons." Brief for the United States. Officer Jenks testified, "I just searched him [Robinson]. I didn't think about what I was looking for. I just searched him." Officer Jenks also testified that upon removing the cigarette package from the respondent's custody, he was still unsure what was in the package, but that he knew it was not cigarettes.

broken down in each instance into an analysis of each step in the search." No precedent is cited for this broad assertion—not surprisingly, since there is none. Indeed, we only recently rejected such "a rigid all-or-nothing model of justification and regulation under the Amendment, [for] it obscures the utility of limitations upon the scope, as well as the initiation, of police action as a means of constitutional regulation. This Court has held in the past that a search which is reasonable at its inception may violate the Fourth Amendment by virtue of its intolerable intensity and scope." *Terry v. Ohio.* As we there concluded, "in determining whether the seizure and search were 'unreasonable' our inquiry is a dual one—whether the officer's action was justified at its inception, and whether it was reasonably related in scope to the circumstances which justified the interference in the first place."

As I view the matter, the search in this case divides into three distinct phases: the patdown of respondent's coat pocket; the removal of the unknown object from the pocket; and the opening of the crumpled up cigarette package.

No question is raised here concerning the lawfulness of the patdown of respondent's coat pocket. The Court of Appeals unanimously affirmed the right of a police officer to conduct a limited frisk for weapons when making an in-custody arrest, regardless of the nature of the crime for which the arrest was made. As it said,

> "it would seem clearly unreasonable to expect a police officer to place a suspect in his squad car for transportation to the station house without first taking reasonable measures to insure that the suspect is unarmed. We therefore conclude that whenever a police officer, acting within the bounds of his authority, makes an in-custody arrest, he may also conduct a limited *frisk* of the suspect's outer clothing in order to remove any weapons the suspect may have in his possession."

With respect to the removal of the unknown object from the coat pocket, * * * Officer Jenks had no reason to believe and did not in fact believe that the object in respondent's coat pocket was a weapon. He admitted later that the object did not feel like a gun. * * *

Since the removal of the object from the pocket cannot be justified as part of a limited *Terry* weapons frisk, the question arises whether it is reasonable for a police officer, when effecting an in-custody arrest of a traffic offender, to make a fuller search of the person than is permitted pursuant to *Terry.* * * *

The Government does not now contend that the search of respondent's pocket can be justified by any need to find and seize evidence in order to prevent its concealment or destruction, for as the Court of Appeals found, there are no evidence or fruits of the offense with which respondent was charged. The only rationale for a search in this case, then, is the removal of weapons which the arrestee might use to harm the officer and attempt an escape. This rationale, of course, is identical to the rationale of the search permitted in *Terry.* * * *

Since the underlying rationale of a *Terry* search and the search of a traffic violator are identical, the Court of Appeals held that the scope of the searches must be the same. * * *

The problem with this approach, however, is that it ignores several significant differences between the context in which a search incident to arrest for a traffic violation is made, and the situation presented in *Terry.* Some of these differences would appear to suggest permitting a more thorough search in this case than was permitted in *Terry;* other differences suggest a narrower, more limited right to search than was there recognized.

The most obvious difference between the two contexts relates to whether the officer has cause to believe that the individual he is dealing with possesses weapons which might be used against him. *Terry* did not permit an officer to conduct a weapons frisk of anyone he lawfully stopped on the street, but rather, only where "he has reason to believe that he is dealing with an armed and dangerous individual. * * * "While the policeman who arrests a suspected rapist or robber may well have reason to believe he is dealing with an armed and dangerous person, certainly this does not hold true with equal force with respect to persons arrested for motor vehicle violations of the sort involved in this case.

Nor was there any particular reason in this case to believe that respondent was dangerous. He had not attempted to evade arrest, but had quickly complied with the police both in bringing his car to a stop after being signalled to do so and in producing the documents Officer Jenks requested. In fact, Jenks admitted that he searched respondent face-to-face rather than in spread-eagle fashion because he had no reason to believe respondent would be violent.

While this difference between the situation presented in *Terry* and the context presented in this case would tend to suggest a lesser authority to search here than was permitted in *Terry,* other distinctions between the two contexts suggest just the opposite. As the Court of Appeals noted, a crucial feature distinguishing the in-custody arrest from the *Terry* context "is not the greater likelihood that a person taken into custody is armed, but rather the increased likelihood of danger to the officer *if* in fact the person is armed." A *Terry* stop involves a momentary encounter between officer and suspect, while an in-custody arrest places the two in close proximity for a much longer period of time. If the individual happens to have a weapon on his person, he will certainly have much more opportunity to use it against the officer in the in-custody situation. The prolonged proximity also makes it more likely that the individual will be able to extricate any small hidden weapon which might go undetected in a weapons frisk, such as a safety pin or razor blade. In addition, a suspect taken into custody may feel more threatened by the serious restraint on his liberty than a person who is simply stopped by an officer for questioning, and may therefore be more likely to resort to force.

Thus, in some senses there is less need for a weapons search in the in-custody traffic arrest situation than in a *Terry* context, while in other ways, there is a greater need. Balancing these competing considerations in order to determine what is a reasonable warrantless search in the traffic arrest context is a difficult process, one for which there may be no easy analytical guideposts. We are dealing in factors not easily quantified and, therefore, not easily weighed one against the other. And the competing interests we are protecting—the individual's interest in remaining free from unnecessarily intrusive invasions of privacy and society's interest that police officers not take unnecessary risks in the performance of their duties—are each deserving of our most serious attention and do not themselves tip the balance in any particular direction. * * *

The majority relies on statistics indicating that a significant percentage of police officer murders occur when the officers are making traffic stops. But these statistics only confirm what we recognized in *Terry*—that "American criminals have a long tradition of armed violence, and every year in this country many law enforcement officers are killed in the line of duty, and thousands more are wounded." As the very next sentence in *Terry* recognized, however, "Virtually all of these deaths and a substantial portion of the injuries are inflicted with guns and knives." The statistics relied on by the Government in this case support this observation. Virtually all of the killings are caused by guns and knives, the very type of weapons which will not go undetected in a properly conducted weapons frisk.[5] * * *

The majority opinion fails to recognize that the search conducted by Officer Jenks did not merely involve a search of respondent's person. It also included a separate search of effects found on his person. And even were we to assume, *arguendo,* that it was reasonable for Jenks to remove the object he felt in respondent's pocket, clearly there was no justification consistent with the Fourth Amendment which would authorize his opening the package and looking inside.

To begin with, after Jenks had the cigarette package in his hands, there is no indication that he had reason to believe or did in fact believe that the package contained a weapon. More importantly, even if the crumpled up cigarette package had in fact contained some sort of small weapon, it would have been impossible for respondent to have used it once the package was in the officer's hands. Opening the package therefore did not further the protective purpose of the search. * * *

It is suggested, however, that since the custodial arrest itself represents a significant intrusion into the privacy of the person, any additional intrusion by way of opening or examining effects found on the person is not worthy of constitutional protection. But such an approach was expressly rejected by the Court in *Chimel.* There it was suggested that since the police had lawfully entered petitioner's house to effect an arrest, the additional invasion of privacy stemming from an accompanying search of the entire house was inconsequential. The Court answered: "[W]e see no reason why, simply because some interference with an individual's privacy and freedom of movement has lawfully taken place, further intrusions should automatically be allowed despite the absence of a warrant that the Fourth Amendment would otherwise require." * * *

The Government argues that it is difficult to see what constitutionally protected "expectation of privacy" a prisoner has in the interior of a cigarette pack. One wonders if the result in this case would have been the same were respondent a businessman who was lawfully taken into custody for driving without a license and whose wallet was taken from him by the police. Would it be reasonable for the police officer, because of the possibility that a razor blade was hidden somewhere in the wallet, to open it, remove all the contents, and examine each item carefully? Or suppose a lawyer lawfully arrested for a traffic offense is found to have a sealed envelope on his person. Would it be permissible for the arresting officer to tear open the envelope in order to make sure that it did not contain a clandestine weapon—perhaps a pin or a razor blade? Would it not be more consonant with the purpose of the Fourth Amendment and the legitimate needs of the police to require the officer, if he has any question whatsoever about what the wallet or letter contains, to hold onto it until the arrestee is brought to the precinct station?

I, for one, cannot characterize any of these intrusions into the privacy of an individual's papers and effects as being negligible incidents to the more serious intrusion into the individual's privacy stemming from the arrest itself. Nor can any principled distinction be drawn between the hypothetical searches I have

5. The Uniform Crime Reports prepared by the Federal Bureau of Investigation which are relied on by the majority, see ante, at n. 5, indicate that 112 police officers were killed nationwide in 1972. Of these, 108 were killed by firearms. Two of the remaining four were killed with knives, and the last two cases involved a bomb and an automobile.

posed and the search of the cigarette package in this case. The only reasoned distinction is between warrantless searches which serve legitimate protective and evidentiary functions and those that do not.

NOTES AND QUESTIONS ON UNLAWFUL, PRETEXT, AND ARBITRARY ARRESTS

1. In the companion case of GUSTAFSON v. FLORIDA, 414 U.S. 260, 94 S.Ct. 488, 38 L.Ed.2d 456 (1973), petitioner was arrested for failure to have an operator's license after the car he was driving was observed weaving across the center line several times, and was then searched, resulting in the discovery of a cigarette box within which the arresting officer found marijuana cigarettes. Petitioner contended his case was different from *Robinson* in that (a) he had experienced no previous encounters with the officer; (b) the offense for which he was arrested was "benign or trivial in nature," carrying with it no mandatory minimum sentence; and (c) there were no police regulations which required the officer to take petitioner into custody or which required full scale body searches upon arrest in the field. The Court, per REHNQUIST, J., did "not find these differences determinative of the constitutional issue," and thus upheld the search on the basis of *Robinson*.

MARSHALL, Douglas, and Brennan, JJ., dissented for the reasons stated in *Robinson*. STEWART, J., concurring, noted "that a persuasive claim might have been made in this case that the custodial arrest of the petitioner for a minor traffic offense violated his rights under the Fourth and Fourteenth Amendments," but since petitioner had "fully conceded the constitutional validity of his custodial arrest," the search of his person should be accepted as incidental to that arrest. POWELL, J., concurring in both cases, emphasized that for him the "essential premise" of both decisions was "that an individual lawfully subjected to a custodial arrest retains no significant Fourth Amendment interest in the privacy of his person."

2. In what sense could a "persuasive claim" have been made in *Gustafson* that the arrest violated the Fourth Amendment? Was it because the arrest there was what the *Robinson* dissenters called a "pretext" arrest? Or did Stewart, J., mean that the *Gustafson* arrest, unlike the *Robinson* arrest, was subject to attack on Fourth Amendment grounds because no statute[a] or police regulations guided the officer as to when a "custodial arrest" was to be employed instead of a citation? Compare the "standard criteria" requirement in *Colorado v. Bertine*, p. 296. Or, did Stewart mean the *Gustafson* arrest was subject to attack because it was unnecessary in the sense that the "lesser intrusion" of a citation would have sufficed? Did *Zurcher v. Stanford Daily*, p. 297, later foreclose such a contention?

a. Note, in this regard, the variation in state law governing traffic "arrests." Some states require that persons halted for violations of misdemeanor traffic laws be released upon issuance of a citation unless they fall within certain exceptions. The exceptions usually are divided into two categories: (1) persons who must be arrested and taken before a magistrate—usually those violating several specified laws (e.g., driving with a suspended license, or driving under the influence of alcohol); and (2) person who may be released on citation or taken before a magistrate at the option of the police officer—e.g., those who have violated several other specified laws (e.g., reckless driving or failure to submit to vehicle inspection), who fail to have a license in their possession, or who fail to furnish satisfactory evidence of identification. Other states require that persons in certain categories be taken into custody, but grant the officer discretion as to whether to take other misdemeanor violators into custody or to release them upon issuance of a citation. Special requirements are often imposed for release of nonresident drivers.

3. In *United States v. Mota,* 982 F.2d 1384 (9th Cir.1993), state officers found counterfeit money in the search of two brothers incident to their custodial arrest for the municipal ordinance violation of operating a food cart without a license. Because a state statute required that such violators merely be given a citation, the court ruled the Fourth Amendment required suppression of their money. Is this because the *arrest* (not claimed to be pretextual) violated the Fourth Amendment? The *Mota* court seemed to think so, stating: "Given the state's expression of disinterest in allowing warrantless arrests for mere infractions, we conclude that a custodial arrest for such infractions is unreasonable, and thus unlawful under the Fourth Amendment." Note that there is considerable authority to the contrary,[a] and that the Supreme Court has to date *never* taken the position that an arrest made on probable cause violates the Fourth Amendment merely because a taking of custody is deemed unnecessary (as a matter of state law or otherwise). Should the court in *Mota* instead have said that it was the search and not the arrest which violated the Fourth Amendment because *Robinson* upholds a search on incident-to-arrest grounds only when the arrest is a "lawful custodial arrest," which must mean lawful as a matter of state law? And what is the current status of *Mota* in light of *Whren*, infra?

4. Nearly a quarter of a century passed before the Supreme Court finally addressed the pretext and police regulation issues in a traffic seizure context in WHREN v. UNITED STATES, 517 U.S. 806, 116 S.Ct. 1769, 135 L.Ed.2d 89 (1996). Justice SCALIA delivered the opinion of a unanimous Court:

"On the evening of June 10, 1993, plainclothes vice-squad officers of the District of Columbia Metropolitan Police Department were patrolling a 'high drug area' of the city in an unmarked car. Their suspicions were aroused when they passed a dark Pathfinder truck with temporary license plates and youthful occupants waiting at a stop sign, the driver looking down into the lap of the passenger at his right. The truck remained stopped at the intersection for what seemed an unusually long time—more than 20 seconds. When the police car executed a U-turn in order to head back toward the truck, the Pathfinder turned suddenly to its right, without signalling, and sped off at an 'unreasonable' speed. The policemen followed, and in a short while overtook the Pathfinder when it stopped behind other traffic at a red light. They pulled up alongside, and Officer Ephraim Soto stepped out and approached the driver's door, identifying himself as a police officer and directing the driver, petitioner Brown, to put the vehicle in park. When Soto drew up to the driver's window, he immediately observed two large plastic bags of what appeared to be crack cocaine in petitioner Whren's hands. Petitioners were arrested, and quantities of several types of illegal drugs were retrieved from the vehicle.

"Petitioners were charged in a four-count indictment with violating various federal drug laws. At a pretrial suppression hearing, they challenged the legality of the stop and the resulting seizure of the drugs. They argued that the stop had not been justified by probable cause to believe, or even reasonable suspicion, that petitioners were engaged in illegal drug-dealing activity; and that Officer Soto's asserted ground for approaching the vehicle—to give the driver a warning concerning traffic violations—was pretextual. The District Court denied the suppression motion * * *.

a. See, e.g., *Barry v. Fowler,* 902 F.2d 770 (9th Cir.1990), holding that in a § 1983 action claiming an unconstitutional arrest, the plaintiff cannot prevail if the arrest was made on probable cause but was in violation of state law.

"Petitioners were convicted of the counts at issue here. The Court of Appeals affirmed the convictions, holding with respect to the suppression issue that, 'regardless of whether a police officer subjectively believes that the occupants of an automobile may be engaging in some other illegal behavior, a traffic stop is permissible as long as a reasonable officer in the same circumstances could have stopped the car for the suspected traffic violation.'

"The Fourth Amendment guarantees '[t]he right of the people to be secure in their persons, houses, papers, and effects, against unreasonable searches and seizures.' Temporary detention of individuals during the stop of an automobile by the police, even if only for a brief period and for a limited purpose, constitutes a 'seizure' of 'persons' " within the meaning of this provision. An automobile stop is thus subject to the constitutional imperative that it not be 'unreasonable' under the circumstances. As a general matter, the decision to stop an automobile is reasonable where the police have probable cause to believe that a traffic violation has occurred.

"Petitioners accept that Officer Soto had probable cause to believe that various provisions of the District of Columbia traffic code [regarding inattentive driving, speeding, and turning without signalling] had been violated. They argue, however, that 'in the unique context of civil traffic regulations' probable cause is not enough. Since, they contend, the use of automobiles is so heavily and minutely regulated that total compliance with traffic and safety rules is nearly impossible, a police officer will almost invariably be able to catch any given motorist in a technical violation. This creates the temptation to use traffic stops as a means of investigating other law violations, as to which no probable cause or even articulable suspicion exists. Petitioners, who are both black, further contend that police officers might decide which motorists to stop based on decidedly impermissible factors, such as the race of the car's occupants. To avoid this danger, they say, the Fourth Amendment test for traffic stops should be, not the normal one (applied by the Court of Appeals) of whether probable cause existed to justify the stop; but rather, whether a police officer, acting reasonably, would have made the stop for the reason given.

"Petitioners contend that the standard they propose is consistent with our past cases' disapproval of police attempts to use valid bases of action against citizens as pretexts for pursuing other investigatory agendas. We are reminded that in *Florida v. Wells,* [p. 302], we stated that 'an inventory search must not be used as a ruse for a general rummaging in order to discover incriminating evidence'; that in *Colorado v. Bertine,* [p. 296], in approving an inventory search, we apparently thought it significant that there had been 'no showing that the police, who were following standard procedures, acted in bad faith or for the sole purpose of investigation'; and that in *New York v. Burger,* [p. 340], we observed, in upholding the constitutionality of a warrantless administrative inspection, that the search did not appear to be 'a "pretext" for obtaining evidence of . . . violation of . . . penal laws.' But only an undiscerning reader would regard these cases as endorsing the principle that ulterior motives can invalidate police conduct that is justifiable on the basis of probable cause to believe that a violation of law has occurred. In each case we were addressing the validity of a search conducted in the absence of probable cause. Our quoted statements simply explain that the exemption from the need for probable cause (and warrant), which is accorded to searches made for the purpose of inventory or administrative regulation, is not accorded to searches that are not made for those purposes.

" * * * Not only have we never held, outside the context of inventory search or administrative inspection (discussed above), that an officer's motive invalidates objectively justifiable behavior under the Fourth Amendment; but we have repeatedly held and asserted the contrary. In *United States v. Villamonte–Marquez,* 462 U.S. 579, 584, n. 3, 103 S.Ct. 2573, 2577, n. 3, 77 L.Ed.2d 22 (1983), we held that an otherwise valid warrantless boarding of a vessel by customs officials was not rendered invalid 'because the customs officers were accompanied by a Louisiana state policeman, and were following an informant's tip that a vessel in the ship channel was thought to be carrying marihuana.' We flatly dismissed the idea that an ulterior motive might serve to strip the agents of their legal justification. In *United States v. Robinson,* [p.232], we held that a traffic-violation arrest (of the sort here) would not be rendered invalid by the fact that it was 'a mere pretext for a narcotics search,' and that a lawful postarrest search of the person would not be rendered invalid by the fact that it was not motivated by the officer-safety concern that justifies such searches. And in *Scott v. United States,* [p. 378], in rejecting the contention that wiretap evidence was subject to exclusion because the agents conducting the tap had failed to make any effort to comply with the statutory requirement that unauthorized acquisitions be minimized, we said that '[s]ubjective intent alone . . . does not make otherwise lawful conduct illegal or unconstitutional.' We described *Robinson* as having established that 'the fact that the officer does not have the state of mind which is hypothecated by the reasons which provide the legal justification for the officer's action does not invalidate the action taken as long as the circumstances, viewed objectively, justify that action.'

"We think these cases foreclose any argument that the constitutional reasonableness of traffic stops depends on the actual motivations of the individual officers involved. We of course agree with petitioners that the Constitution prohibits selective enforcement of the law based on considerations such as race. But the constitutional basis for objecting to intentionally discriminatory application of laws is the Equal Protection Clause, not the Fourth Amendment. Subjective intentions play no role in ordinary, probable-cause Fourth Amendment analysis.

"Recognizing that we have been unwilling to entertain Fourth Amendment challenges based on the actual motivations of individual officers, petitioners disavow any intention to make the individual officer's subjective good faith the touchstone of 'reasonableness.' They insist that the standard they have put forward—whether the officer's conduct deviated materially from usual police practices, so that a reasonable officer in the same circumstances would not have made the stop for the reasons given—is an 'objective' one.

"But although framed in empirical terms, this approach is plainly and indisputably driven by subjective considerations. Its whole purpose is to prevent the police from doing under the guise of enforcing the traffic code what they would like to do for different reasons. Petitioners' proposed standard may not use the word 'pretext,' but it is designed to combat nothing other than the perceived 'danger' of the pretextual stop, albeit only indirectly and over the run of cases. Instead of asking whether the individual officer had the proper state of mind, the petitioners would have us ask, in effect, whether (based on general police practices) it is plausible to believe that the officer had the proper state of mind.

"Why one would frame a test designed to combat pretext in such fashion that the court cannot take into account actual and admitted pretext is a curiosity that can only be explained by the fact that our cases have foreclosed the more sensible option. If those cases were based only upon the evidentiary difficulty of establishing subjective intent, petitioners' attempt to root out subjective vices through objective means might make sense. But they were not based only upon that, or indeed even principally upon that. Their principal basis—which applies equally to attempts to reach subjective intent through ostensibly objective means—is simply that the Fourth Amendment's concern with 'reasonableness' allows certain actions to be taken in certain circumstances, whatever the subjective intent. See, e.g., *Robinson,* supra ('Since it is the fact of custodial arrest which gives rise to the authority to search, it is of no moment that [the officer] did not indicate any subjective fear of the [arrestee] or that he did not himself suspect that [the arrestee] was armed'). But even if our concern had been only an evidentiary one, petitioners' proposal would by no means assuage it. Indeed, it seems to us somewhat easier to figure out the intent of an individual officer than to plumb the collective consciousness of law enforcement in order to determine whether a 'reasonable officer' would have been moved to act upon the traffic violation. While police manuals and standard procedures may sometimes provide objective assistance, ordinarily one would be reduced to speculating about the hypothetical reaction of a hypothetical constable—an exercise that might be called virtual subjectivity.

"Moreover, police enforcement practices, even if they could be practicably assessed by a judge, vary from place to place and from time to time. We cannot accept that the search and seizure protections of the Fourth Amendment are so variable, and can be made to turn upon such trivialities. The difficulty is illustrated by petitioners' arguments in this case. Their claim that a reasonable officer would not have made this stop is based largely on District of Columbia police regulations which permit plainclothes officers in unmarked vehicles to enforce traffic laws 'only in the case of a violation that is so grave as to pose an immediate threat to the safety of others.' This basis of invalidation would not apply in jurisdictions that had a different practice. And it would not have applied even in the District of Columbia, if Officer Soto had been wearing a uniform or patrolling in a marked police cruiser.

"Petitioners argue that our cases support insistence upon police adherence to standard practices as an objective means of rooting out pretext. They cite no holding to that effect, and dicta in only two cases. In *Abel v. United States,* 362 U.S. 217, 80 S.Ct. 683, 4 L.Ed.2d 668 (1960), the petitioner had been arrested by the Immigration and Naturalization Service (INS), on the basis of an administrative warrant that, he claimed, had been issued on pretextual grounds in order to enable the Federal Bureau of Investigation (FBI) to search his room after his arrest. We regarded this as an allegation of 'serious misconduct,' but rejected Abel's claims on the ground that '[a] finding of bad faith is . . . not open to us on th[e] record' in light of the findings below, including the finding that ' "the proceedings taken by the [INS] differed in no respect from what would have been done in the case of an individual concerning whom [there was no pending FBI investigation]." ' But it is a long leap from the proposition that following regular procedures is some evidence of lack of pretext to the proposition that failure to follow regular procedures proves (or is an operational substitute for) pretext. *Abel,* moreover, did not involve the assertion that pretext could invalidate a search or seizure for which there was probable cause—and even what it said about pretext in other contexts is plainly inconsistent with the views we later stated in [the cases summarized above]. In the other case claimed to contain supportive dicta, *United States v. Robinson,* in approving a search incident to an arrest for driving without a license, we noted that the arrest was 'not a departure from established police department practice.' That was followed, however, by the statement that '[w]e leave for another day questions which would arise on facts different from these.' This is not even a dictum that purports to provide an answer, but merely one that leaves the question open.

"In what would appear to be an elaboration on the 'reasonable officer' test, petitioners argue that the balancing inherent in any Fourth Amendment inquiry requires us to weigh the governmental and individual interests implicated in a traffic stop such as we have here. That balancing, petitioners claim, does not support investigation of minor traffic infractions by plainclothes police in un-marked vehicles; such investigation only minimally advances the government's interest in traffic safety, and may indeed retard it by producing motorist confusion and alarm—a view said to be supported by the Metropolitan Police Department's own regulations generally prohibiting this practice. And as for the Fourth Amend-ment interests of the individuals concerned, petitioners point out that our cases acknowledge that even ordinary traffic stops entail 'a possibly unsettling show of authority'; that they at best 'interfere with freedom of movement, are inconven-ient, and consume time' and at worst 'may create substantial anxiety.' That anxiety is likely to be even more pronounced when the stop is conducted by plainclothes officers in unmarked cars.

"It is of course true that in principle every Fourth Amendment case, since it turns upon a 'reasonableness' determination, involves a balancing of all relevant factors. With rare exceptions not applicable here, however, the result of that balancing is not in doubt where the search or seizure is based upon probable cause. That is why petitioners must rely upon cases like *Prouse* to provide examples of actual 'balancing' analysis. There, the police action in question was a random traffic stop for the purpose of checking a motorist's license and vehicle registration, a practice that—like the practices at issue in the inventory search and administrative inspection cases upon which petitioners rely in making their 'pretext' claim—involves police intrusion without the probable cause that is its traditional justification. Our opinion in *Prouse* expressly distinguished the case from a stop based on precisely what is at issue here: 'probable cause to believe that a driver is violating any one of the multitude of applicable traffic and equipment regulations.' It noted approvingly that '[t]he foremost method of enforcing traffic and vehicle safety regulations ... is acting upon observed violations,' which afford the ' "quantum of individualized suspicion" ' necessary to ensure that police discretion is sufficiently constrained. What is true of *Prouse* is also true of other cases that engaged in detailed 'balancing' to decide the constitutionality of automobile stops: the detailed 'balancing' analysis was neces-sary because they involved seizures without probable cause.

"Where probable cause has existed, the only cases in which we have found it necessary actually to perform the 'balancing' analysis involved searches or sei-zures conducted in an extraordinary manner, unusually harmful to an individual's privacy or even physical interests—such as, for example, seizure by means of deadly force, see *Tennessee v. Garner,* [p. 227], unannounced entry into a home, see *Wilson v. Arkansas,* [p. 213], entry into a home without a warrant, see *Welsh v. Wisconsin,* [p. 271], or physical penetration of the body, see *Winston v. Lee,* [p. 250]. The making of a traffic stop out-of-uniform does not remotely qualify as such an extreme practice, and so is governed by the usual rule that probable cause to believe the law has been broken 'outbalances' private interest in avoiding police contact.

"Petitioners urge as an extraordinary factor in this case that the 'multitude of applicable traffic and equipment regulations' is so large and so difficult to obey perfectly that virtually everyone is guilty of violation, permitting the police to single out almost whomever they wish for a stop. But we are aware of no principle that would allow us to decide at what point a code of law becomes so expansive and so commonly violated that infraction itself can no longer be the ordinary measure of the lawfulness of enforcement. And even if we could identify such exorbitant codes, we do not know by what standard (or what right) we would decide, as petitioners would have us do, which particular provisions are sufficiently important to merit enforcement.

"For the run-of-the-mine case, which this surely is, we think there is no realistic alternative to the traditional common-law rule that probable cause justifies a search and seizure. * * *

"Here the District Court found that the officers had probable cause to believe that petitioners had violated the traffic code. That rendered the stop reasonable under the Fourth Amendment, the evidence thereby discovered admissible, and the upholding of the convictions by the Court of Appeals for the District of Columbia Circuit correct."

5. As the Supreme Court was advised in the briefs of the petitioners and amici, the tactic at issue in *Whren* is one which has been commonly employed by police in recent years in their "war against drugs." Both in urban areas and on the interstates, police are on the watch for "suspicious" travellers, and once one is spotted it is only a matter of time before some technical or trivial offense produces the necessary excuse for pulling him over. Perhaps because the offenses are so often insignificant, the driver is typically told at the outset that he will merely be given a warning. But then things often turn ugly. The driver and passengers are usually closely questioned about their identities, the reason for their travels, their intended destination, and the like. The subject of drugs comes up, and often the driver is induced to "consent" to a full search of the vehicle and all effects therein for drugs. If such consent is not forthcoming, another police vehicle with a drug-sniffing dog may appear on the scene. See, e.g., *United States v. Mesa,* 62 F.3d 159 (6th Cir.1995); *United States v.* Roberson, 6 F.3d 1088 (5th Cir.1993) (noting the trooper's "remarkable record" of turning traffic stops into drug arrests on 250 prior occasions), *State v. Dominguez-Martinez,* 895 P.2d 306 (Or.1995).

6. Two illustrations from the many reported cases of this genre reveal how little it takes to supply grounds for a traffic stop acceptable to the courts. In one, a Texas state trooper passing a van noticed it had four black occupants, so the officer crested a hill, pulled onto the shoulder and doused his lights. When the van approached, the driver cautiously changed lanes to distance the van from the vehicle on the shoulder, but failed to signal—hardly surprising considering that the van was the only moving vehicle on that stretch of road. Yet the stop for an illegal lane change was upheld. *United States v. Roberson,* supra. In the other case, the stop occurred after a Utah deputy patrolling Interstate 70 saw an automobile driven by a black man straddle the center line for about one second before proceeding to the other lane of traffic. The stop was upheld on the grounds that the officer had sufficient suspicion the operator was driving while impaired. *United States v. Lee,* 73 F.3d 1034 (10th Cir.1996).

7. "As part of the settlement of a civil rights lawsuit, the Maryland State Police tracked the race of drivers stopped since January 1995.

"Statistics released last November showed that 73 percent of drivers who were stopped and searched on Interstate 95 between Baltimore and Delaware were African–American. A corresponding American Civil Liberties Union study concluded that only 14 percent of drivers on the highway were black.

"And in central Florida, black drivers on the Florida Turnpike were 6.5 times more likely to be searched than white drivers, according to an analysis by the *Orlando Sentinel*, which studied more than 3,800 traffic stops between January 1996 and April 1997." Michael Higgins, *Looking the Part*, 48 A.B.A.J. 48, 49 (Nov.1997). See also David A. Harris, *"Driving While Black" and All Other Traffic Offenses: The Supreme Court and Pretextual Traffic Stops*, 87 J.Crim.L. & Criminology 544 (1997).

8. The dissent by Chief Judge Seymour in *United States v. Botero–Ospina*, 71 F.3d 783 (10th Cir.1995), a pre-*Whren* decision which squares with the *Whren* holding, provides an interesting contrast to the later Scalia opinion in *Whren*. That dissent states in part:

"In addition to producing the intrusion any individual experiences when subjected to a traffic stop, the majority's standard frees a police officer to target members of minority communities for the selective enforcement of otherwise unenforced statutes. The Supreme Court recognized in *Terry [v. Ohio*, p. 394] that the harassment of minority groups by certain elements of the police population does occur, and that 'the degree of community resentment aroused by particular practices is clearly relevant to an assessment of the quality of the intrusion upon reasonable expectations of personal security caused by those practices.' By refusing to examine either the arbitrariness with which a particular statute is enforced or the motivation underlying its enforcement in a particular case, the majority standard does nothing to curb the ugly reality that minority groups are sometimes targeted for selective enforcement. As a result, the majority standard adds the onus of discrimination and resentment to the already significant burden imposed by traffic stops generally. * * *

"The Supreme Court held in *Terry* that to justify a particular intrusion, a 'police officer must be able to point to specific and articulable facts which, taken together with the rational inferences from those facts, reasonably warrant that intrusion.' It is difficult to justify a stop as reasonable, even if supported by an observed violation, if the undisputed facts indicate that the violation does not ordinarily result in a stop. Moreover, the Court in *Terry* described in detail the appropriate reasonableness inquiry in language that is utterly irreconcilable with the majority standard. The Court stated that in assessing the reasonableness of a particular stop 'it is imperative that the facts be judged against an objective standard: would the facts available to the officer at the moment of the seizure or the search "warrant a man of reasonable caution in the belief" that the action taken was appropriate?' It would hardly seem necessary to point out that the Court's mandate to determine what a reasonable officer would do in the circumstances cannot be fulfilled by merely ascertaining in a vacuum what a particular officer could do under state law.

"Given the 'multitude of applicable traffic and equipment regulations' in any jurisdiction, upholding a stop on the basis of a regulation seldom enforced opens the door to the arbitrary exercise of police discretion condemned in *Terry* and its progeny. 'Anything less [than the reasonable officer standard] would invite intrusions upon constitutionally guaranteed rights based on nothing more substantial than inarticulate hunches, a result this Court has consistently refused to sanction.' *Terry*."

9. Is Chief Judge Seymour's concern about harassment of minorities met by Justice Scalia's observation that selective enforcement based on race is barred by the Equal Protection Clause? How could the petitioners in *Whren* have proved such an equal protection violation? Does/should the "rigorous standard for discov-

ery" against the government upon a defendant's claim of race-based selective prosecution, see *United States v. Armstrong*, CH. 13, § 3, also apply in this setting? And even if the *Whren* petitioners *did* prove that the traffic stop was itself a violation of the Equal Protection Clause, would that bar prosecution on the *drug* charges? Would it require suppression of the drugs? Cf. *United v. Jennings,* 985 F.2d 562 (6th Cir.1993) (dictum by majority that if defendant had proved he had been selected for a consensual encounter solely because of his race, then the evidence obtained in a consent search during that encounter ought to be excluded, as "evidence seized in violation of the Equal Protection Clause should be suppressed"; concurring opinion notes that the case cited in support by the majority, *Elkins v. United States,* p. 127, "provides absolutely no support for the majority's position").

10. Does Justice Scalia ever respond directly to the *Whren* petitioners' argument that probable cause is not enough "in the unique context of civil traffic regulations" because it is possible for a police officer to catch any given motorist in a technical violation? Is the proper response, as Scalia says at one point, that the matter of police purpose is relevant only in situations represented by *Wells, Bertine* and *Burger,* where the search is allowed without probable cause? Is the risk of pretext greater in those situations, where the police must show they complied with "standard procedures" or "reasonable legislative or administrative standards," than as to traffic stops?

NOTES AND QUESTIONS ON OTHER
SEARCHES OF THE PERSON

1. Full searches of an arrested person are more typically made when that person has been delivered to the place of his forthcoming detention. These searches are typically upheld on two bases: (1) as a delayed *Robinson* search incident to arrest; and (2) as an inventory incident to booking to safeguard the property of the accused and to ensure that weapons and contraband are not introduced into the jail. However, some jurisdictions have rejected the *Robinson* rule and have also limited the extent of permissible inventory. See, e.g., *State v. Kaluna,* 520 P.2d 51 (Hawaii 1974) (police matron subjected female arrested for armed robbery to strip search, resulting in discovery of packet of drugs in her bra; held, not a valid search incident to arrest because no reason to believe weapons or evidence of the crime there, and not valid inventory because the packet could have been inventoried without opening it). Also, in some jurisdictions a search at the station is deemed unlawful if the defendant was not afforded a sufficient opportunity to gain his release. See, e.g., *Zehrung v. State,* 569 P.2d 189 (Alaska 1977), on rehearing, 573 P.2d 858 (1978) ("when one is arrested and brought to a jail for a minor offense for which bail has already been set in a bail schedule, he should be allowed a reasonable opportunity to attempt to raise bail before being subjected to remand and booking procedures and the incidental inventory search"; but on rehearing court admits state may be correct in saying this impractical in smaller communities with no separate holding cells in unsecured area, and that there the search may be proper unless defendant presently has the bail money).

2. ILLINOIS v. LAFAYETTE, 462 U.S. 640, 103 S.Ct. 2605, 77 L.Ed.2d 65 (1983), concerned the admissibility of amphetamines found in respondent's shoulder bag during an at-the-station inventory of his effects following his arrest for disturbing the peace. The Court, per BURGER, C.J., concluded:

"The governmental interests underlying a stationhouse search of the arrestee's person and possessions may in some circumstances be even greater than those supporting a search immediately following arrest. Consequently, the scope of a stationhouse search will often vary from that made at the time of arrest. Police conduct that would be impractical or unreasonable—or embarrassingly intrusive—on the street can more readily—and privately—be performed at the station. For example, the interests supporting a search incident to arrest would hardly justify disrobing an arrestee on the street, but the practical necessities of routine jail administration may even justify taking a prisoner's clothes before confining him, although that step would be rare. This was made clear in *United States v. Edwards, * * *.*[2]

"At the stationhouse, it is entirely proper for police to remove and list or inventory property found on the person or in the possession of an arrested person who is to be jailed. A range of governmental interests support an inventory process. It is not unheard of for persons employed in police activities to steal property taken from arrested persons; similarly, arrested persons have been known to make false claims regarding what was taken from their possession at the stationhouse. A standardized procedure for making a list or inventory as soon as reasonable after reaching the stationhouse not only deters false claims but also inhibits theft or careless handling of articles taken from the arrested person. Arrested persons have also been known to injure themselves—or others—with belts, knives, drugs or other items on their person while being detained. Dangerous instrumentalities—such as razor blades, bombs, or weapons—can be concealed in innocent-looking articles taken from the arrestee's possession. The bare recital of these mundane realities justifies reasonable measures by police to limit these risks—either while the items are in the police possession or at the time they are returned to the arrestee upon his release. Examining all the items removed from the arrestee's person or possession and listing or inventorying them is an entirely reasonable administrative procedure. It is immaterial whether the police actually fear any particular package or container; the need to protect against such risks arises independent of a particular officer's subjective concerns. Finally, inspection of an arrestee's personal property may assist the police in ascertaining or verifying his identity. In short, every consideration of orderly police administration benefiting both police and the public points toward the appropriateness of the examination of respondent's shoulder bag prior to his incarceration.

"Our prior cases amply support this conclusion. In *South Dakota v. Opperman,* [p. 296], we upheld a search of the contents of the glove compartment of an abandoned automobile lawfully impounded by the police. We held that the search was reasonable because it served legitimate governmental interests that outweighed the individual's privacy interests in the contents of his car. Those measures protected the owner's property while it was in the custody of the police and protected police against possible false claims of theft. We found no need to consider the existence of less intrusive means of protecting the police and the property in their custody—such as locking the car and impounding it in safe storage under guard. Similarly, standardized inventory procedures are appropriate to serve legitimate governmental interests at stake here.

"The Illinois court held that the search of respondent's shoulder bag was unreasonable because 'preservation of the defendant's property and protection of police from claims of lost or stolen property, "could have been achieved in a less intrusive manner." For example, * * * the defendant's shoulder bag could easily have been secured by sealing it within a plastic bag or box and placing it in a

---

2. We were not addressing in *Edwards,* and do not discuss here, the circumstances in   which a strip search of an arrestee may or may not be appropriate.

secured locker.' Perhaps so, but the real question is not what 'could have been achieved,' but whether the Fourth Amendment *requires* such steps; it is not our function to write a manual on administering routine, neutral procedures of the stationhouse. Our role is to assure against violations of the Constitution.

" * * * We are hardly in a position to second-guess police departments as to what practical administrative method will best deter theft by and false claims against its employees and preserve the security of the stationhouse. It is evident that a stationhouse search of every item carried on or by a person who has lawfully been taken into custody by the police will amply serve the important and legitimate governmental interests involved.

"Even if less intrusive means existed of protecting some particular types of property, it would be unreasonable to expect police officers in the everyday course of business to make fine and subtle distinctions in deciding which containers or items may be searched and which must be sealed as a unit.[b] * * * "[3]

3. UNITED STATES v. EDWARDS, 415 U.S. 800, 94 S.Ct. 1234, 39 L.Ed.2d 771 (1974), concerned the admissibility of paint chips obtained from defendant's clothing, taken from him without a warrant while he was in jail about 10 hours after his arrest for attempted breaking and entering. The clothing was seized because investigation subsequent to the arrest showed that paint had been chipped from a window when entry was attempted with a pry bar. The Court, per WHITE, J., concluded "that once the defendant is lawfully arrested and is in custody, the effects in his possession at the place of detention that were subject to search at the time and place of his arrest may lawfully be searched and seized without a warrant even though a substantial period of time has elapsed between the arrest and subsequent administrative processing on the one hand and the taking of the property for use as evidence on the other. This is true where the clothing or effects are immediately seized upon arrival at the jail, held under the defendant's name in the 'property room' of the jail and at a later time searched and taken for use at the subsequent criminal trial. The result is the same where the property is not physically taken from the defendant until sometime after his incarceration."[c] The Court added it was not holding "that the warrant clause of the Fourth Amendment is never applicable to postarrest seizures of the effects of an arrestee," and by footnote to that caveat stated it was expressing no view "concerning those circumstances surrounding custodial searches incident to incarceration which might 'violate the dictates of reason either because of their number or their manner of perpetration.' "

STEWART, J., joined by Douglas, Brennan, and Marshall, JJ., dissented, arguing that they could "see no justification for dispensing with the warrant requirement here. The police had ample time to seek a warrant, and no exigent circumstances were present to excuse their failure to do so," as the government

---

b. Marshall and Brennan, JJ., concurring, asserted: "A very different case would be presented if the State had relied solely on the fact of arrest to justify the search of respondent's shoulder bag."

3. The record is unclear as to whether respondent was to have been incarcerated after being booked for disturbing the peace. That is an appropriate inquiry on remand.

c. Of course, if the search incident to arrest is made at the station, it will be unlawful if the grounds for the arrest have dissipated prior to the time of the search. See *United States v.*

Coughlin, 338 F.Supp. 1328 (E.D.Mich.1972) (defendant arrested upon leaving house at which mailman had just delivered package containing narcotics; at the station, police put his hands under fluorescent light and determined that defendant had handled the narcotics which the police had previously dusted with fluorescent powder; held, search illegal because promptly after arrest police learned that defendant was not the addressee of the package, so that there was not probable cause for further detention).

"has not even suggested that [the defendant] was aware of the presence of the paint chips on his clothing."

4. After *Robinson, Lafayette* and *Edwards,* is a person in custody following a lawful arrest "fair game" for a search for evidence of crimes other than the crime for which the arrest was made? Compare *People v. Trudeau,* 187 N.W.2d 890 (Mich.1971) (defendant was under arrest for breaking and entering, in recent attempted burglary with similar modus operandi watchman was killed and heel print was left at scene, police subsequently took defendant's shoe and matched it with heel print; held, seizure illegal because police "had no probable cause to believe that the seized shoes were evidence linked to the crime").

5. In SCHMERBER v. CALIFORNIA, [the facts and other aspects of which are discussed at p. 42], the Court per BRENNAN, J., observed:

"Although the facts which established probable cause to arrest in this case also suggested the required relevance and likely success of a test of petitioner's blood for alcohol, the question remains whether the arresting officer was permitted to draw these inferences himself, or was required instead to procure a warrant before proceeding with the test. Search warrants are ordinarily required for searches of dwellings, and, absent an emergency, no less could be required where intrusions into the human body are concerned. * * *

"The officer in the present case, however, might reasonably have believed that he was confronted with an emergency, in which the delay necessary to obtain a warrant, under the circumstances, threatened 'the destruction of evidence' * * *. We are told that the percentage of alcohol in the blood begins to diminish shortly after drinking stops, as the body functions to eliminate it from the system. Particularly in a case such as this, where time had to be taken to bring the accused to a hospital and to investigate the scene of the accident, there was no time to seek out a magistrate and secure a warrant. Given these special facts, we conclude that the attempt to secure evidence of blood-alcohol content in this case was an appropriate incident to petitioner's arrest."[d]

6. Applying the *Schmerber* balancing test, the Court in WINSTON v. LEE, 470 U.S. 753, 105 S.Ct. 1611, 84 L.Ed.2d 662 (1985), held that the proposed court-ordered surgery on defendant, for the purpose of removing a bullet expected to show that defendant was the robber hit by the victim's gunfire, would constitute an unreasonable search. "The reasonableness of surgical intrusions beneath the skin," the Court stated per BRENNAN, J., "depends on a case-by-case approach, in which the individual's interests in privacy and security are weighed against society's interests in conducting the procedure." Taking into account medical evidence that the operation would require a general anesthetic, might last over two hours, and could require probing of muscle tissue which might cause injury to the muscle as well as to nerves, blood vessels and other tissue, the Court concluded the "operation sought will intrude substantially on respondent's protected interests." Such an intrusion would not be reasonable, the Court then decided, given the state's failure "to demonstrate a compelling need for it." No such need was deemed to be present, as the state had considerable other evidence

---

d. Is it essential that this be characterized as a search incident to arrest? What if the defendant had not been arrested and the blood sample was taken while he was in the emergency room of the hospital for treatment of injuries he received in an accident in which he was involved, because it reasonably appeared to the police investigating the accident that he was intoxicated? Is this issue resolved by *Cupp v. Murphy,* discussed in Note 10 infra?

connecting defendant with the robbery, including a prompt identification of him by the victim and his location near the robbery shortly after it occurred.[e]

7. In light of *Schmerber* and *Winston,* what about other scientific tests and intrusions into the body after arrest? Consider *United States ex rel. Guy v. McCauley,* 385 F.Supp. 193 (E.D.Wis.1974), concerning a stationhouse search of the vagina of an incarcerated female which resulted in the discovery of a packet of narcotics. The court held the search violated due process because not conducted "by skilled medical technicians." But what if it had been so conducted? In *Guy,* the defendant also objected that the search was not made upon probable cause, but the court, while noting that the search was apparently prompted by "vague information several years old that [she] was known to carry heroin in her vagina," asserted that this objection "missed the mark" in light of *Robinson* and *Edwards.* Is that so? What then of other warrantless searches of the body of an arrestee which have been upheld, including "the placing of the arrestee's hands under an ultraviolet lamp; examining the arrestee's arms to determine the age of burn marks; swabbing the arrestee's hands with a chemical substance; taking scrapings from under the arrestee's fingernails; taking a small sample of hair from the arrestee's head; obtaining a urine sample from the arrestee; giving the arrestee a breathalyzer examination; swabbing the arrestee's penis; taking dental impressions from the arrestee; or taking pubic hair combings from him." LaFave at § 5.3(c).

8. In KNOWLES v. IOWA, ___ U.S. ___, 119 S.Ct. 484, 142 L.Ed.2d 492 (1998), a policeman stopped Knowles for speeding and then, pursuant to a statute authorizing (but not requiring) him to issue a citation in lieu of arrest for most bailable offenses, issued Knowles a citation. The officer then made a full search of Knowles car and found a bag of marijuana. That search was upheld by the state courts on the ground that because an Iowa statute declared that issuance of a citation in lieu of arrest "does not affect the officer's authority to conduct an otherwise lawful search," it sufficed here that the officer had probable cause to make a custodial arrest. A unanimous Supreme Court, per REHNQUIST, C.J., reversed. Looking at the two historical rationales for search incident to arrest discussed in *Robinson,* the Court reasoned. (i) The "threat to officer safety from issuing a traffic citation * * * is a good deal less than in the case of a custodial arrest," where (as it was put in *Robinson*) there is "the extended exposure which follows the taking of a suspect into custody and transporting him to the police station," and thus the "concern for officer safety" incident to a traffic stop is sufficiently met by the officer's authority to order the driver and passengers out of the car,[f] to "perform a 'patdown' of a driver and any passengers upon reasonable

---

e. See Ronald J. Bacigal, *Dodging a Bullet, But Opening Old Wounds in Fourth Amendment Jurisprudence,* 16 Seton Hall L.Rev. 597 (1986).

f. In *Pennsylvania v. Mimms,* 434 U.S. 106, 98 S.Ct. 330, 54 L.Ed.2d 331 (1977), officers stopped a vehicle with an expired license plate for the purpose of issuing a traffic summons and then ordered the driver out of the car, which resulted in the observation of a large bulge under his pocket, and this prompted a frisk and discovery of a gun. Rejecting the state court's holding that the driver could be directed to get out of the car only upon a reasonable suspicion he "posed a threat to police safety," the Court reasoned that "this additional intrusion can only be described as de minimis" and was justified because it "reduces the likelihood that the officer will be the victim of an assault." In *Maryland v. Wilson,* 519 U.S. 408, 117 S.Ct. 882, 137 L.Ed.2d 41 (1997), the Court held "that an officer making a traffic stop may order passengers to get out of the car pending completion of the stop." The Court agreed that "there is not the same basis for ordering the passengers out of the car as there is for ordering the driver out," but yet deemed "the additional intrusion on the passenger" to be "minimal" and justified in light of the fact that "danger to an officer from a traffic stop is likely to be greater when there are passengers in addition to the driver in the stopped car."

suspicion that they may be armed and dangerous,"[g] and to conduct a patdown "of the passenger compartment of a vehicle upon reasonable suspicion that an occupant is dangerous and may gain immediate control of a weapon."[h] (ii) The "need to discover and preserve evidence" does not exist here, as "no further evidence of excessive speed was going to be found either on the person of the offender or in the passenger compartment of the car," and any concern with destruction of evidence as to identity can be met by arresting the driver whenever the officer is not satisfied with his identification.

Considering that Knowles "did not argue * * * that the statute could never be lawfully applied" and that the Court only passed upon "the search at issue," are there circumstances in which a search made under this statute would be lawful? Consider *State v. Greenslit*, 559 A.2d 672 (Vt.1989) (upholding search of person incident to issuance of notice to appear for present use of marijuana). What if Iowa reformulated its statute to conform to language used in some other states, i.e., that if an officer makes an arrest, the lawfulness of a search incident thereto is not affected by a subsequent decision at the scene to issue a citation and release the arrestee? Or, even absent such reformulation, may Iowa police, given their broad statutory authority to elect either citation or arrest as they wish, merely delay that decision until after a search, and then justify productive searches under the principle of the *Rawlings* case, note i infra?

9. As for search of the person without any arrest at all, consider CUPP v. MURPHY, 412 U.S. 291, 93 S.Ct. 2000, 36 L.Ed.2d 900 (1973). The Court, per STEWART, J., held that where Murphy voluntarily appeared at the station for questioning concerning the strangulation of his wife, at which time the police noticed what appeared to be blood on his finger, and the police had probable cause to arrest him but did not formally place him under arrest,[i] the warrantless taking of scrapings from his fingernails "was constitutionally permissible." Noting that Murphy was aware of the police suspicion and tried to wipe his fingers clean, the Court concluded that "the rationale of *Chimel* * * * justified the police in subjecting him to the very limited search necessary to preserve the highly evanescent evidence they found under his fingernails." But, because a person not under formal arrest "might well be less hostile to the police and less likely to take conspicuous, immediate steps to destroy incriminating evidence on his person," the Court emphasized it was *not* holding "that a full *Chimel* search would have been justified in this case without a formal arrest and without a warrant." MARSHALL, J., concurring, noted that the police could not have preserved the evidence by "close surveillance" and that detaining Murphy while a warrant was sought "would have been as much a seizure as detaining him while his fingernails were scraped." DOUGLAS, J., dissenting, argued: "There was time to get a warrant; Murphy could have been detained while one was sought; and that detention would have preserved the perishable evidence the police sought."

---

g. As authorized by *Terry v. Ohio*, p. 304.

h. As authorized by *Michigan v. Long*, p. 334.

i. Murphy was not arrested until over a month later, and thus the case is unlike those in which the arrest followed the search by a matter of minutes. The prevailing view is that a search "incident" to arrest may actually come before the formal making of an arrest if the police had grounds to arrest at the time the search was made. As stated in *Rawlings v. Kentucky* (other aspects of which are discussed at p. 777): "Where the formal arrest followed quickly on the heels of the challenged search of petitioner's person, we do not believe itparticularly important that the search preceded the arrest rather than vice versa."

SECTION 6. WARRANTLESS SEARCHES OF PREMISES, VEHICLES, AND CONTAINERS

CHIMEL v. CALIFORNIA
395 U.S. 752, 89 S.Ct. 2034, 23 L.Ed.2d 685 (1969).

Justice STEWART delivered the opinion of the Court. * * *

The relevant facts are essentially undisputed. Late in the afternoon of September 13, 1965, three police officers arrived at the Santa Ana, California, home of the petitioner with a warrant authorizing his arrest for the burglary of a coin shop. The officers knocked on the door, identified themselves to the petitioner's wife, and asked if they might come inside. She ushered them into the house, where they waited 10 or 15 minutes until the petitioner returned home from work. When the petitioner entered the house, one of the officers handed him the arrest warrant and asked for permission to "look around." The petitioner objected, but was advised that "on the basis of the lawful arrest," the officers would nonetheless conduct a search. No search warrant had been issued.

Accompanied by the petitioner's wife, the officers then looked through the entire three-bedroom house, including the attic, the garage, and a small workshop. In some rooms the search was relatively cursory. In the master bedroom and sewing room, however the officers directed the petitioner's wife to open drawers and "to physically move contents of the drawers from side to side so that [they] might view any items that would have come from [the] burglary." After completing the search, they seized numerous items—primarily coins, but also several medals, tokens, and a few other objects. The entire search took between 45 minutes and an hour.

At the petitioner's subsequent state trial on two charges of burglary, the items taken from his house were admitted into evidence against him, over his objection that they had been unconstitutionally seized. He was convicted, and the judgments * * * affirmed * * *.

Without deciding the question, we proceed on the hypothesis that the California courts were correct in holding that the arrest of the petitioner was valid under the Constitution. This brings us directly to the question whether the warrantless search of the petitioner's entire house can be constitutionally justified as incident to that arrest. The decisions of this Court bearing upon that question have been far from consistent, as even the most cursory review makes evident.[a]

***

a. In an omitted portion of the opinion, the Court described how dictum on search incident to arrest broadened from search of the "person," *Weeks v. United States*, 232 U.S. 383, 34 S.Ct. 341, 58 L.Ed. 652 (1914), to search for what is "upon his person or in his control," *Carroll v. United States*, 267 U.S. 132, 45 S.Ct. 280, 69 L.Ed. 543 (1925), to search of "persons lawfully arrested" and "the place where the arrest is made," *Agnello v. United States*, 269 U.S. 20, 46 S.Ct. 4, 70 L.Ed. 145 (1925). Then, in *Marron v. United States*, 275 U.S. 192, 48 S.Ct. 74, 72 L.Ed. 231 (1927), concerning seizure of evidence at a place where illegal liquor sales were occurring, the Court held that because the police had made an arrest on the premises they "had a right without a warrant contemporaneously to search the place in order to find and seize the things used to carry on the criminal enterprise." But in *Go-Bart Importing Co. v. United States*, 282 U.S. 344, 51 S.Ct. 153, 75 L.Ed. 374 (1931), *Marron* was limited to where the items seized "were visible and accessible and in the offender's immediate custody" and there "was no threat of force or general search or rummaging of the place." This limitation was reiterated in *United States v. Lefkowitz*, 285 U.S. 452, 52 S.Ct. 420, 76 L.Ed. 877 (1932), which, like *Go-Bart*, held unlawful a search of a desk despite the fact the search had accompanied a lawful arrest, but was abandoned in *Harris v. United States*, 331 U.S. 145, 67 S.Ct. 1098, 91 L.Ed. 1399 (1947), upholding the search of a four-room apartment as "incident to arrest." But *Harris* was not followed in *Trupiano v. United States*, 334 U.S.

In 1950 * * * came *United States v. Rabinowitz,* 339 U.S. 56, 70 S.Ct. 430, 94 L.Ed. 653 (1950), the decision upon which California primarily relies in the case now before us. In *Rabinowitz,* federal authorities had been informed that the defendant was dealing in stamps bearing forged overprints. On the basis of that information they secured a warrant for his arrest, which they executed at his one-room business office. At the time of the arrest, the officers "searched the desk, safe, and file cabinets in the office for about an hour and a half," and seized 573 stamps with forged overprints. The stamps were admitted into evidence at the defendant's trial, and this Court affirmed his conviction, rejecting the contention that the warrantless search had been unlawful. The Court held that the search in its entirety fell within the principle giving law enforcement authorities "[t]he right 'to search the place where the arrest is made in order to find and seize things connected with the crime * * *.'" * * * The test, said the Court, "is not whether it is reasonable to procure a search warrant, but whether the search was reasonable."

Rabinowitz has come to stand for the proposition, inter alia, that a warrantless search "incident to a lawful arrest" may generally extend to the area that is considered to be in the "possession" or under the "control" of the person arrested. And it was on the basis of that proposition that the California courts upheld the search of the petitioner's entire house in this case. That doctrine, however, at least in the broad sense in which it was applied by the California courts in this case, can withstand neither historical nor rational analysis.

Even limited to its own facts, the *Rabinowitz* decision was, as we have seen, hardly founded on an unimpeachable line of authority. * * *

Nor is the rationale by which the State seeks here to sustain the search of the petitioner's house supported by a reasoned view of the background and purpose of the Fourth Amendment. Justice Frankfurter wisely pointed out in his *Rabinowitz* dissent that the Amendment's proscription of "unreasonable searches and seizures" must be read in light of "the history that gave rise to the words"—a history of "abuses so deeply felt by the Colonies as to be one of the potent causes of the Revolution * * *." The Amendment was in large part a reaction to the general warrants and warrantless searches that had so alienated the colonists and had helped speed the movement for independence. In the scheme of the Amendment, therefore, the requirement that "no Warrants shall issue, but upon probable cause," plays a crucial part. * * * Even in the *Agnello* case the Court relied upon the rule that "[b]elief, however well founded, that an article sought is concealed in a dwelling house furnishes no justification for a search of that place without a warrant. And such searches are held unlawful notwithstanding facts unquestionably showing probable cause." Clearly, the general requirement that a search warrant be obtained is not lightly to be dispensed with, and "the burden is on those seeking [an] exemption [from the requirement] to show the need for it * * *."

* * * When an arrest is made, it is reasonable for the arresting officer to search the person arrested in order to remove any weapons that the latter might seek to use in order to resist arrest or effect his escape. Otherwise, the officer's safety might well be endangered, and the arrest itself frustrated. In addition, it is entirely reasonable for the arresting officer to search for and seize any evidence on the arrestee's person in order to prevent its concealment or destruction. And the area into which an arrestee might reach in order to grab a weapon or evidentiary

699, 68 S.Ct. 1229, 92 L.Ed. 1663 (1948), declaring that "law enforcement agents must secure and use search warrants wherever reasonably practicable."

items must, of course, be governed by a like rule. A gun on a table or in a drawer in front of one who is arrested can be as dangerous to the arresting officer as one concealed in the clothing of the person arrested. There is ample justification, therefore, for a search of the arrestee's person and the area "within his immediate control"—construing that phrase to mean the area from within which he might gain possession of a weapon or destructible evidence.

There is no comparable justification, however, for routinely searching rooms other than that in which an arrest occurs—or, for that matter, for searching through all the desk drawers or other closed or concealed areas in that room itself. Such searches, in the absence of well-recognized exceptions, may be made only under the authority of a search warrant. The "adherence to judicial processes" mandated by the Fourth Amendment requires no less. * * *

It is argued in the present case that it is "reasonable" to search a man's house when he is arrested in it. But that argument is founded on little more than a subjective view regarding the acceptability of certain sorts of police conduct, and not on considerations relevant to Fourth Amendment interests. Under such an unconfined analysis, Fourth Amendment protection in this area would approach the evaporation point. It is not easy to explain why, for instance, it is less subjectively "reasonable" to search a man's house when he is arrested on his front lawn—or just down the street—than it is when he happens to be in the house at the time of arrest. * * *

It would be possible, of course, to draw a line between *Rabinowitz* and *Harris* on the one hand, and this case on the other. For *Rabinowitz* involved a single room, and *Harris* a four-room apartment, while in the case before us an entire house was searched. But such a distinction would be highly artificial. The rationale that allowed the searches and seizures in *Rabinowitz* and *Harris* would allow the searches and seizures in this case. No consideration relevant to the Fourth Amendment suggests any point of rational limitation, once the search is allowed to go beyond the area from which the person arrested might obtain weapons or evidentiary items. The only reasoned distinction is one between a search of the person arrested and the area within his reach on the one hand, and more extensive searches on the other.[12]

The petitioner correctly points out that one result of decisions such as *Rabinowitz* and *Harris* is to give law enforcement officials the opportunity to engage in searches not justified by probable cause, by the simple expedient of arranging to arrest suspects at home rather than elsewhere. We do not suggest that the petitioner is necessarily correct in his assertion that such a strategy was

---

12. It is argued in dissent that so long as there is probable cause to search the place where an arrest occurs, a search of that place would be permitted even though no search warrant has been obtained. This position seems to be based principally on two premises: first, that once an arrest has been made, the additional invasion of privacy stemming from the accompanying search is "relatively minor"; and second, that the victim of the search may "shortly thereafter" obtain a judicial determination of whether the search was justified by probable cause. With respect to the second premise, one may initially question whether all of the States in fact provide the speedy suppression procedures the dissent assumes. More fundamentally, however, we cannot accept the view that Fourth Amendment interests are vindicated so long as "the rights of the criminal" are "protect[ed] * * * against introduction of evidence seized without probable cause." The Amendment is designed to prevent, not simply to redress, unlawful police action. In any event, we cannot join in characterizing the invasion of privacy that results from a top-to-bottom search of a man's house as "minor." And we can see no reason why, simply because some interference with an individual's privacy and freedom of movement has lawfully taken place, further intrusions should automatically be allowed despite the absence of a warrant that the Fourth Amendment would otherwise require.

utilized here, but the fact remains that had he been arrested earlier in the day, at his place of employment rather than at home, no search of his house could have been made without a search warrant. In any event, even apart from the possibility of such police tactics, the general point so forcefully made by Judge Learned Hand in *United States v. Kirschenblatt,* 16 F.2d 202 [2d Cir.1926], remains:

> "After arresting a man in his house, to rummage at will among his papers in search of whatever will convict him, appears to us to be indistinguishable from what might be done under a general warrant; indeed, the warrant would give more protection, for presumably it must be issued by a magistrate. True, by hypothesis the power would not exist, if the supposed offender were not found on the premises; but it is small consolation to know that one's papers are safe only so long as one is not at home."

Rabinowitz and *Harris* have been the subject of critical commentary for many years, and have been relied upon less and less in our own decisions. It is time, for the reasons we have stated, to hold that on their own facts, and insofar as the principles they stand for are inconsistent with those that we have endorsed today, they are no longer to be followed.

Application of sound Fourth Amendment principles to the facts of this case produces a clear result. The search here went far beyond the petitioner's person and the area from within which he might have obtained either a weapon or something that could have been used as evidence against him. There was no constitutional justification, in the absence of a search warrant, for extending the search beyond that area. The scope of the search was, therefore, "unreasonable" under the Fourth and Fourteenth Amendments, and the petitioner's conviction cannot stand.

Reversed.

Justice HARLAN, concurring. * * *

The only thing that has given me pause in voting to overrule *Harris* and *Rabinowitz* is that as a result of *Mapp v. Ohio,* every change in Fourth Amendment law must now be obeyed by state officials facing widely different problems of local law enforcement. We simply do not know the extent to which cities and towns across the Nation are prepared to administer the greatly expanded warrant system which will be required by today's decision; nor can we say with assurance that in each and every local situation, the warrant requirement plays an essential role in the protection of those fundamental liberties protected against state infringement by the Fourteenth Amendment. * * *

Justice WHITE, with whom Justice BLACK joins, dissenting.

* * * The Court has always held, and does not today deny, that when there is probable cause to search and it is "impracticable" for one reason or another to get a search warrant, then a warrantless search may be reasonable. This is the case whether an arrest was made at the time of the search or not. * * *

This case provides a good illustration of my point that it is unreasonable to require police to leave the scene of an arrest in order to obtain a search warrant when they already have probable cause to search and there is a clear danger that the items for which they may reasonably search will be removed before they return with a warrant. Petitioner was arrested in his home after an arrest whose validity will be explored below, but which I will now assume was valid. There was doubtless probable cause not only to arrest petitioner, but to search his house. He had obliquely admitted both to a neighbor, and to the owner of the burglarized store, that he had committed the burglary. In light of this, and the fact that the neighbor had seen other admittedly stolen property in petitioner's house, there was surely probable cause on which a warrant could have issued to search the house for the stolen coins. Moreover, had the police simply arrested petitioner, taken him off to the station house, and later returned with a warrant,[5] it seems very likely that petitioner's wife, who in view of petitioner's generally garrulous nature must have known of the robbery, would have removed the coins. For the police to search the house while the evidence they had probable cause to search out and seize was still there cannot be considered unreasonable.

This line of analysis, supported by the precedents of this Court, hinges on two assumptions. One is that the arrest of petitioner without a valid warrant[7] was constitutional as the majority assumes;[b] the other is that the police were not required to obtain a search warrant in advance, even though they knew that the effect of the arrest might well be to alert petitioner's wife that the coins had better be removed soon.

* * * It must very often be the case that by the time probable cause to arrest a man is accumulated, the man is aware of police interest in him or for other good reasons is on the verge of flight. Moreover, it will likely be very difficult to determine the probability of his flight. Given this situation, it may be best in all cases simply to allow the arrest if there is probable cause, especially since that issue can be determined very shortly after the arrest. * * *

If circumstances so often require the warrantless arrest that the law generally permits it, the typical situation will find the arresting officers lawfully on the premises without arrest or search warrant. * * * [W]here as here the existence of probable cause is independently established and would justify a warrant for a broader search for evidence, I would follow past cases and permit such a search to be carried out without a warrant, since the fact of arrest supplies an exigent circumstance justifying police action before the evidence can be removed, and also alerts the suspect to the fact of the search so that he can immediately seek judicial determination of probable cause in an adversary proceeding, and appropriate redress. * * *

NOTES ON SEARCH OF PREMISES INCIDENT TO AND AFTER ARREST THEREIN

1. Is the *Chimel* dissent strengthened or weakened by the Court's later decision in *Watson?*

2. Some of the cases which have applied the *Chimel* "immediate control" test seem to assume that defendants maintain control over a considerable area even after they have been arrested. See, e.g., *People v. Perry*, 266 N.E.2d 330 (Ill.1971) (4 officers broke into a 10 by 12 foot motel room, saw defendant place

---

5. There were three officers at the scene of the arrest, one from the city where the coin burglary had occurred, and two from the city where the arrest was made. Assuming that one policeman from each city would be needed to bring the petitioner in and obtain a search warrant, one policeman could have been left to guard the house. However, if he not only could have remained in the house against petitioner's wife's will, but followed her about to assure that no evidence was being tampered with, the invasion of her privacy would be almost as great as that accompanying an actual search. Moreover, had the wife summoned an accomplice, one officer could not have watched them both.

7. An arrest warrant was in fact issued, but it was issued on an inadequate supporting affidavit and was therefore invalid, so that the case must be considered as though no warrant had issued.

b. But see the later decision in *Payton v. New York*, p. 266.

something in a dresser drawer, handcuffed him, and took him out into the corridor; their immediately subsequent search of the partially open dresser drawer and a purse on the bed was within *Chimel* rule, "since it was within the area from which defendant could have obtained a weapon or something that could have been used as evidence against him"). Are such cases best explained on the ground that *Chimel* should be construed so as to give the police a "bright line" rule (cf. *New York v. Belton*, p. 290), one which, as concluded in *People v. Hufnagel*, 745 P.2d 242 (Colo.1987), makes it irrelevant whether "the arrestee was physically able to reach the exact place searched at the exact second it was searched"?

3. *Chimel* also requires attention to the question of when, if ever, officers may look into other areas of the defendant's home *after* the defendant has been placed under arrest there. Consider:

(a) *When it is necessary for the arrestee to put on street clothes.* See, e.g., *Giacalone v. Lucas,* 445 F.2d 1238 (6th Cir.1971) (defendant arrested at front door went into bedroom to change into street clothes; held, police could look into dresser drawer defendant was about to open, and gun found therein admissible; dissent argues defendant initially told police he was ready to go immediately, thereby expressing "his desire to limit the officers' intrusion into the privacy of his home," and that he went to get dressed upon order of the police).

(b) *When the officers are acting for their own protection.* The question of when a "protective sweep" is permissible reached the Court in MARYLAND v. BUIE, 494 U.S. 325, 110 S.Ct. 1093, 108 L.Ed.2d 276 (1990), where the state court had required full probable cause of a dangerous situation. By analogy to *Terry v. Ohio,* p. 304, and *Michigan v. Long,* p. 334, the Court opted for a less demanding reasonable suspicion test. The state had argued for a "bright-line rule" to the effect that "police should be permitted to conduct a protective sweep whenever they make an in-home arrest for a violent crime"; the Court responded that *Terry* requires individualized suspicion, but then adopted a two-part sweep rule which included another kind of bright line. Specifically, the Court (7–2), per WHITE, J., concluded:

"We agree with the State, as did the court below, that a warrant was not required. We also hold that as an incident to the arrest the officers could, as a precautionary matter and without probable cause or reasonable suspicion, look in closets and other spaces immediately adjoining the place of arrest from which an attack could be immediately launched. Beyond that, however, we hold that there must be articulable facts which, taken together with the rational inferences from those facts, would warrant a reasonable prudent officer in believing that the area to be swept harbors an individual posing a danger to those on the arrest scene. * * *

"We should emphasize that such a protective sweep, aimed at protecting the arresting officers, if justified by the circumstances, is nevertheless not a full search of the premises, but may extend only to a cursory inspection of those spaces where a person may be found. The sweep lasts no longer than is necessary to dispel the reasonable suspicion of danger and in any event no longer than it takes to complete the arrest and depart the premises."

The Court remanded for application of this test. The facts, as stated in the Supreme Court opinions, are these: Two men (one wearing a red running suit) committed an armed robbery of a restaurant on Feb. 3; warrants for them (Buie and Allen) were issued that day, and Buie's home was immediately placed under surveillance. On Feb. 5, after a police department secretary called the residence and verified that Buie was there, 6 or 7 officers proceeded to the house and fanned out through the first and second floors. Officer Rozar said he would "freeze" the basement so that no one could come up; he drew his weapon and twice shouted into the basement for anyone there to come out, and Buie then emerged from the basement. He was arrested, searched and handcuffed by Rozar. Once Buie was outside the house, Officer Frolich entered the basement, noticed a red running suit in plain view and seized it. Rozar testified he was not worried about any possible danger when he arrested Buie; Frolich said he entered the basement "in case there was someone else" down there, though he "had no idea who lived there." What should the result be on remand?

(c) *When the officers are seeking other offenders.* See, e.g., *People v. Block,* 491 P.2d 9 (Cal.1971) (officers knocked on door to check out tip concerning narcotics suspect, when door was opened they detected smell of burning marijuana, five persons in living room and two in dining room with odor of marijuana on their breath were arrested, after which one of the officers went upstairs and looked into bedrooms, where he found marijuana; held, in view of "undetermined number of participants" and fact upstairs light was on, officers had "reasonable cause to believe" other participants might be present; dissent objects there was not probable cause here and distinguishes *Guevara v. Superior Court,* 86 Cal.Rptr. 657 (App.1970), where informant had told police confederates were probably present). If a "potential accomplice" is located, should the police then be allowed to search areas within *his* immediate control?

4. In some circumstances, the Court concluded in WASHINGTON v. CHRISMAN, 455 U.S. 1, 102 S.Ct. 812, 70 L.Ed.2d 778 (1982), a warrantless *entry* of premises will be permissible incident to and following an arrest elsewhere. There, a campus policeman arrested an apparently underage student as he left a campus dormitory carrying a half-gallon bottle of gin, accompanied the student back to his room so that he could obtain his identification, and there observed marijuana seeds and a marijuana pipe. The state court had held that the entry was unlawful, but the Supreme Court, per BURGER, C.J., disagreed:

"Every arrest must be presumed to present a risk of danger to the arresting officer. Cf. *United States v. Robinson,* [p. 232], n. 5. There is no way for an officer to predict reliably how a particular subject will react to arrest or the degree of the potential danger. Moreover, the possibility that an arrested person will attempt to escape if not properly supervised is obvious. Although the Supreme Court of Washington found little likelihood that Overdahl could escape from his dormitory room, an arresting officer's custodial authority over an arrested person does not depend upon a reviewing court's after-the-fact assessment of the particular arrest situation. Cf. *New York v. Belton* [p. 290].

"We hold, therefore, that it is not 'unreasonable' under the Fourth Amendment for a police officer, as a matter of routine, to monitor the movements of an arrested person, as his judgment dictates, following the arrest."[c]

NOTES ON WARRANTLESS SEIZURES WHILE IN PREMISES TO ARREST

1. If an officer is lawfully present within premises to make an arrest, he may observe certain items not within the "immediate control" of the arrestee which will nonetheless be subject to warrantless seizure under the so-called "plain view"

---

c. White, Brennan and Marshall, JJ., dissenting, could "perceive no justification for what is in effect a per se rule that an officer in Daugherty's circumstances could always enter the room and stay at the arrestee's elbow."

doctrine. But, as cautioned in *Coolidge v. New Hampshire,* 403 U.S. 443, 91 S.Ct. 2022, 29 L.Ed.2d 564 (1971), such "extension of the original justification is legitimate only where it is immediately apparent[a] to the police that they have evidence before them; the 'plain view' doctrine may not be used to extend a general exploratory search from one object to another until something incriminating at last emerges."

2. In ARIZONA v. HICKS, 480 U.S. 321, 107 S.Ct. 1149, 94 L.Ed.2d 347 (1987), police lawfully entered premises from which a weapon was fired, and within one officer "noticed two sets of expensive stereo components, which seemed out of place in the squalid and otherwise ill-appointed four-room apartment. Suspecting that they were stolen, he read and recorded their serial numbers— moving some of the components, including a Bang and Olufsen turntable, in order to do so—which he then reported by phone to his headquarters. On being advised that the turntable had been taken in an armed robbery, he seized it immediately. It was later determined that some of the other serial numbers matched those on other stereo equipment taken in the same armed robbery, and a warrant was obtained and executed to seize that equipment as well." SCALIA, J., for a 6–3 majority, concluded the moving of the equipment was an unreasonable search, while the dissenters relied on the fact that "the overwhelming majority of both state and federal courts have held that probable cause is not required for a minimal inspection of an item in plain view." The majority responded:

"Justice O'Connor's dissent suggests that we uphold the action here on the ground that it was a cursory inspection rather than a full-blown search, and could therefore be justified by reasonable suspicion instead of probable cause. As already noted, a truly cursory inspection—one that involves merely looking at what is already exposed to view, without disturbing it—is not a 'search' for Fourth Amendment purposes, and therefore does not even require reasonable suspicion. We are unwilling to send police and judges into a new thicket of Fourth Amendment law, to seek a creature of uncertain description that is neither a plain-view inspection nor yet a full-blown search. Nothing in the prior opinions of this Court supports such a distinction * * *.

"Justice Powell's dissent reasonably asks what it is we would have had Officer Nelson do in these circumstances. The answer depends, of course, upon whether he had probable cause to conduct a search, a question that was not preserved in this case. If he had, then he should have done precisely what he did. If not, then he should have followed up his suspicions, if possible, by means other than a search—just as he would have had to do if, while walking along the street, he had noticed the same suspicious stereo equipment sitting inside a house a few feet away from him, beneath an open window. It may well be that, in such circumstances, no effective means short of a search exist. But there is nothing new in the realization that the Constitution sometimes insulates the criminality of a few in order to protect the privacy of us all. Our disagreement with the dissenters pertains to where the proper balance should be struck; we choose to adhere to the textual and traditional standard of probable cause."

NOTES ON WARRANTLESS SEARCH OF PREMISES UNDER EXIGENT CIRCUMSTANCES

a. In *Texas v. Brown,* p. 288, the plurality opinion asserted that this phrase "was very likely an unhappy choice of words, since it can be taken to imply that an unduly high degree of certainty as to the incriminating character of evidence is necessary for an application of the 'plain view' doctrine," and then concluded it was intended to be merely a "statement of the rule * * * requiring probable cause for seizure in the ordinary case."

1. In VALE v. LOUISIANA, 399 U.S. 30, 90 S.Ct. 1969, 26 L.Ed.2d 409 (1970), officers possessing two warrants for Vale's arrest and having information that he was residing at a specified address set up a surveillance of the house in an unmarked car. After about 15 minutes they observed a car drive up and sound the horn twice. A man they recognized as Vale then came out of the house and walked up to the car, had a brief conversation with the driver, looked up and down the street and then returned to the house. A few minutes later he reappeared on the porch, looked cautiously up and down the street, and then proceeded to the car and leaned through the window. Convinced that a narcotics sale had just occurred, the officers approached. Vale retreated toward the house while the driver of the car began driving off. The police blocked the car and saw the driver, one Saucier, place something in his mouth. Vale was then arrested on his front steps and the police advised him they were going to search the house. An officer made a cursory inspection of the house to ascertain if anyone else was present, after which Vale's mother and brother entered the house and were told of the arrest and impending search. A quantity of narcotics were found in a rear bedroom. The Court, per STEWART, J., concluded (without deciding whether *Chimel* should be accorded retroactive effect[a]) that "no precedent of this Court can sustain the constitutional validity of the search in the case before us":

"A search may be incident to an arrest 'only if it is substantially contemporaneous with the arrest and is confined to the *immediate* vicinity of the arrest.' If a search of a house is to be upheld as incident to an arrest, that arrest must take place *inside* the house, not somewhere outside—whether two blocks away, twenty feet away, or on the sidewalk near the front steps. 'Belief, however well founded, that an article sought is concealed in a dwelling house furnishes no justification for a search of that place without a warrant.' That basic rule 'has never been questioned in this Court.'

"The Louisiana Supreme Court thought the search independently supportable because it involved narcotics, which are easily removed, hidden, or destroyed. It would be unreasonable, the Louisiana court concluded, 'to require the officers under the facts of the case to first secure a search warrant before searching the premises, as time is of the essence inasmuch as the officers never know whether there is anyone on the premises to be searched who could very easily destroy the evidence.' Such a rationale could not apply to the present case, since by their own account the arresting officers satisfied themselves that no one else was in the house when they first entered the premises. But entirely apart from that point, our past decisions make clear that only in 'a few specifically established and well-delineated' situations, may a warrantless search of a dwelling withstand constitutional scrutiny, even though the authorities have probable cause to conduct it. The burden rests on the State to show the existence of such an exceptional situation. And the record before us discloses none. * * *

"The officers were able to procure two warrants for the appellant's arrest. They also had information that he was residing at the address where they found him. There is thus no reason, so far as anything before us appears, to suppose that it was impracticable for them to obtain a search warrant as well. We decline to hold that an arrest on the street can provide its own 'exigent circumstance' so as to justify a warrantless search of the arrestee's house."

Justice BLACK, joined by The Chief Justice, dissented:

---

a. *Chimel* was later held not to be retroactive in *Williams v. United States*, 401 U.S. 646,   91 S.Ct. 1148, 28 L.Ed.2d 388 (1971).

"[When Vale and Saucier were arrested,] the police had probable cause to believe that Vale was engaged in a narcotics transfer, and that a supply of narcotics would be found in the house, to which Vale had returned after his first conversation, from which he had emerged furtively bearing what the police could readily deduce was a supply of narcotics, and toward which he hurried after seeing the police. But the police did not know then who else might be in the house. Vale's arrest took place near the house, and anyone observing from inside would surely have been alerted to destroy the stocks of contraband which the police believed Vale had left there. The police had already seen Saucier, the narcotics addict, apparently swallow what Vale had given him. Believing that some evidence had already been destroyed and that other evidence might well be, the police were faced with the choice of risking the immediate destruction of evidence or entering the house and conducting a search. I cannot say that their decision to search was unreasonable. Delay in order to obtain a warrant would have given an accomplice just the time he needed.

"That the arresting officers did, in fact, believe that others might be in the house is attested to by their actions upon entering the door left open by Vale. The police at once checked the small house to determine if anyone else was present. Just as they discovered the house was empty, however, Vale's mother and brother arrived. Now what had been a suspicion became a certainty: Vale's relatives were in possession and knew of his arrest. To have abandoned the search at this point, and left the house with Vale, would not have been the action of reasonable police officers. * * *

"Moreover, the circumstances here were sufficiently exceptional to justify a search, even if the search was not strictly 'incidental' to an arrest. The Court recognizes that searches to prevent the destruction or removal of evidence have long been held reasonable by this Court. Whether the 'exceptional circumstances' justifying such a search exist or not is a question which may be, as it is here, quite distinct from whether or not the search was incident to a valid arrest. It is thus unnecessary to determine whether the search was valid as incident to the arrest * * *.

"[T]he Court seems to argue that the search was unreasonable because the police officers had time to obtain a warrant. I agree that the opportunity to obtain a warrant is one of the factors to be weighed in determining reasonableness. But the record conclusively shows that there was no such opportunity here. As I noted above, once the officers had observed Vale's conduct in front of the house they had probable cause to believe that a felony had been committed and that immediate action was necessary. At no time after the events in front of Mrs. Vale's house would it have been prudent for the officers to leave the house in order to secure a warrant.

"The Court asserts, however, that because the police obtained two warrants for Vale's arrest there is 'no reason * * * to suppose that it was impracticable for them to obtain a search warrant as well.' The difficulty is that the two arrest warrants on which the Court seems to rely so heavily were not issued because of any present misconduct of Vale's; they were issued because the bond had been increased for an earlier narcotics charge then pending against Vale. When the police came to arrest Vale, they knew only that his bond had been increased. There is nothing in the record to indicate that, absent the increased bond, there would have been probable cause for an arrest, much less a search. Probable cause for the search arose for the first time when the police observed the activity of Vale and Saucier in and around the house."

2. What *should* the officers have done in *Vale?* Consider *United States v. Grummel,* 542 F.2d 789 (9th Cir.1976) (defendant picked up package known to contain heroin at post office; 10 minutes after taking the package into his home he was arrested there; because his mother was home, agent gave her the option of leaving the premises or remaining inside with him while another agent left to get a search warrant; held, it was proper on these facts to "secure the premises to the extent necessary to prevent destruction of the evidence until a warrant could be obtained"). Consider, in assessing the reasonableness of this alternative, the possibility of obtaining a warrant very promptly via telephone, as authorized in some jurisdictions (see, e.g., Fed.R.Crim.P. 41(c)(2)).

In SEGURA v. UNITED STATES, 468 U.S. 796, 104 S.Ct. 3380, 82 L.Ed.2d 599 (1984), the police, upon confirming that they had in fact observed a drug sale by Colon and Segura, went to their apartment building. Segura was arrested in the lobby, and when Colon answered a knock on the door she was also arrested. Police made a warrantless entry of the apartment and remained there until a search warrant was issued, which occurred some 19 hours later because of "administrative delay." The Court held "that where officers, having probable cause, enter premises, and with probable cause, arrest the occupants who have legitimate possessory interests in its contents and take them into custody and, for no more than the period here involved, secure the premises from within to preserve the status quo while others, in good faith, are in the process of obtaining a warrant, they do not violate the Fourth Amendment's proscription against unreasonable seizures." The Court also held that the evidence first discovered in execution of the warrant was not a fruit of the illegal entry. (See p. 793.) The first holding was explicated in a portion of an opinion by BURGER, C.J., in which only O'Connor, J., joined. Without deciding whether the petitioners were correct in characterizing the police action as a seizure of the entire contents of the apartment, they concluded any such seizure was not unreasonable. Noting that in other contexts the Court had approved warrantless seizures in circumstances where a warrantless search could not have been held (see the *Chadwick* and *Sanders* cases, discussed in *California v. Acevedo,* p. 281), they could see "no reason * * * why the same principle should not apply when a dwelling is involved." These two Justices continued:

"In this case, the agents entered and secured the apartment from within. Arguably, the wiser course would have been to depart immediately and secure the premises from the outside by a 'stakeout' once the security check revealed that no one other than those taken into custody were in the apartment. But the method actually employed does not require a different result under the Fourth Amendment, insofar as the *seizure* is concerned. As the Court of Appeals held, absent exigent circumstances, the entry may have constituted an illegal *search*, or interference with petitioners' privacy interests, requiring suppression of all evidence observed during the entry. Securing of the premises from within, however, was no more an interference with the petitioners' possessory interests in the contents of the apartment than a perimeter 'stakeout.' In other words, the initial entry—legal or not—does not affect the reasonableness of the seizure. Under either method—entry and securing from within or a perimeter stakeout—agents control the apartment pending arrival of the warrant; both an internal securing and a perimeter stakeout interfere to the same extent with the possessory interests of the owners. * * *

"Of course, a seizure reasonable at its inception because based upon probable cause may become unreasonable as a result of its duration or for other reasons. Here, because of the delay in securing the warrant, the occupation of the apartment continued throughout the night and into the next day. Such delay in securing a warrant in a large metropolitan center unfortunately is not uncommon; this is not, in itself, evidence of bad faith. And there is no suggestion that the officers, in bad faith, purposely delayed obtaining the warrant. The asserted explanation is that the officers focused first on the task of processing those whom they had arrested before turning to the task of securing the warrant. It is not unreasonable for officers to believe that the former should take priority, given, as was the case here, that the proprietors of the apartment were in the custody of the officers throughout the period in question.

"There is no evidence that the agents in any way exploited their presence in the apartment; they simply awaited issuance of the warrant. Moreover, more than half of the 19–hour delay was between 10 p.m. and 10 a.m. the following day, when it is reasonable to assume that judicial officers are not as readily available for consideration of warrant requests. Finally, and most important, we observed in *United States v. Place,* [p. 331], that '[t]he intrusion on possessory interests occasioned by a seizure * * * can vary both in its nature and extent. The seizure may be made after the owner has relinquished control of the property to a third party or * * * from the immediate custody and control of the owner.' Here, of course, Segura and Colon, whose possessory interests were interfered with by the occupation, were under arrest and in the custody of the police throughout the entire period the agents occupied the apartment. The actual interference with their possessory interests in the apartment and its contents was, thus, virtually nonexistent. We are not prepared to say under these limited circumstances that the seizure was unreasonable under the Fourth Amendment."

The four dissenters, per STEVENS, J., argued that the occupation was an unreasonable search, infringing upon a reasonable expectation of privacy, and an unreasonable seizure, involving exercise of "complete dominion and control over the apartment and its contents"; that the Fourth Amendment protects possessory interests in a residence even when the occupants are in custody; and that "what is even more strange about the Chief Justice's conclusion is that it permits the authorities to benefit from the fact that they had unlawfully arrested" an occupant of the apartment.[b]

3. Although in *Vale* the Court noted in passing that "the goods ultimately seized were not in the process of destruction," many lower courts have not taken that language too seriously in light of the Court's assumption that not even a threat of destruction was present.[c] In *United States v. Rubin,* 474 F.2d 262 (3d Cir.1973), the court upheld a warrantless search[d] pursuant to this test:

---

b. For criticism of *Segura,* see Joshua Dressler, *A Lesson in Incaution, Overwork, and Fatigue: The Judicial Miscraftsmanship of Segura v. United States,* 26 Wm. & Mary L.Rev. 375 (1985).

c. See Barbara Salken, *Balancing Exigency and Privacy in Warrantless Searches to Prevent Destruction of Evidence,* 39 Hastings L.J. 283 (1988).

d. The facts in *Rubin* were as follows: Customs agents received reliable information that a bronze statute containing a large shipment of illicit drugs would be shipped to a hospital in a certain area. Agents were posted at the airport and waterfront, and finally a crate answering the general description given by the informant arrived at the airport from abroad. It was inspected and found to contain narcotics. Agents observed one Agnes pick up the crate and take it to a certain address, where it was unloaded at about 5 p.m. After one agent was dispatched to secure a search warrant, Agnes left the premises in his car but without the crate. He was tailed for a short distance, but when his evasive actions led agents to believe he was aware of the tail, they arrested him. When he was placed under arrest about six blocks from the house in question, he yelled to spectators to call his brother. At this point the agents, fearing disposal of the narcotics if they waited for the search warrant, entered the house and searched for and seized the narcotics.

"When Government agents, however, have probable cause to believe contraband is present and, in addition, based on the surrounding circumstances or the information at hand, they reasonably conclude that the evidence will be destroyed or removed before they can secure a search warrant, a warrantless search is justified. The emergency circumstances will vary from case to case, and the inherent necessities of the situation at the time must be scrutinized. Circumstances which have seemed relevant to courts include (1) the degree of urgency involved and the amount of time necessary to obtain a warrant * * *; (2) reasonable belief that the contraband is about to be removed * * *; (3) the possibility of danger to police officers guarding the site of the contraband while a search warrant is sought * * *; (4) information indicating the possessors of the contraband are aware that the police are on their trail * * *; and (5) the ready destructibility of the contraband and the knowledge 'that efforts to dispose of narcotics and to escape are characteristic behavior of persons engaged in the narcotics traffic.' "

4. Assuming no such exigent circumstances, is it permissible for police to engage in a subterfuge which causes an occupant to remove the evidence to another place where warrantless search is permissible? See *State v. Hendrix*, 782 S.W.2d 833 (Tenn.1989) (proper for police to telephone residence with anonymous false "tip" that police were on their way there with search warrant, causing defendant to leave with drugs in car, which was then stopped and searched). What if the telephoning police had falsely reported a gas leak and likely explosion?

5. Although several courts had held that when the police are summoned to the scene of a homicide they may remain on those premises without a warrant (and, perhaps, return after a brief absence) to conduct a general investigation into the cause of the death, in *Mincey v. Arizona*, 437 U.S. 385, 98 S.Ct. 2408, 57 L.Ed.2d 290 (1978), the Court, confronted with a rather broad variation of the so-called homicide scene exception to the warrant requirement (the criminal nature and perpetrator of the homicide were known from the outset, no occupant of the premises had summoned the police, and the searches upheld by the lower court continued for four days), "decline[d] to hold that the seriousness of the offense under investigation itself creates exigent circumstances of the kind that under the Fourth Amendment justify a warrantless search." *Mincey* was later applied in *Thompson v. Louisiana*, 469 U.S. 17, 105 S.Ct. 409, 83 L.Ed.2d 246 (1984), to invalidate a two-hour general search of premises to which police were summoned because of defendant's attempt to get medical assistance after shooting her husband. The Court noted the authorities, "while they were in petitioner's house to offer her assistance," could have seized evidence in plain view and could also have made a limited search for a suspect or for other victims.

6. When evidence of crime is fortuitously discovered by the police without a warrant while they are performing other functions, courts find it necessary to assess the reasonableness of the police conduct under the Fourth Amendment. Compare *Geimer v. State*, 591 N.E.2d 1016 (Ind.1992) (evidence admissible, as entry was on "a reasonable belief that a person within the premises is in need of aid" where one of missing person's sons said "it was unlike his father to leave town for a period of time without notifying anyone" and other son, who lived with father, "told various persons differing stories regarding the victim's sudden absence"); with *State v. Geisler*, 610 A.2d 1225 (Conn.1992) (evidence suppressed, as where car at accident scene suffered minor damage, key left in ignition, car door left open, and no response when officer rang bell and knocked at home of car owner, such "facts could not reasonably lead to the conclusion that the driver might have suffered the type of injury that would require emergency aid").

PAYTON v. NEW YORK

445 U.S. 573, 100 S.Ct. 1371, 63 L.Ed.2d 639 (1980).

Justice STEVENS delivered the opinion of the Court. * * *

On January 14, 1970, after two days of intensive investigation, New York detectives had assembled evidence sufficient to establish probable cause to believe that Theodore Payton had murdered the manager of a gas station two days earlier. At about 7:30 a.m. on January 15, six officers went to Payton's apartment in the Bronx, intending to arrest him. They had not obtained a warrant. Although light and music emanated from the apartment, there was no response to their knock on the metal door. They summoned emergency assistance and, about 30 minutes later, used crowbars to break open the door and enter the apartment. No one was there. In plain view, however, was a 30–caliber shell casing that was seized and later admitted into evidence at Payton's murder trial. * * *

On March 14, 1974, Obie Riddick was arrested for the commission of two armed robberies that had occurred in 1971. He had been identified by the victims in June of 1973 and in January 1974 the police had learned his address. They did not obtain a warrant for his arrest. At about noon on March 14, a detective, accompanied by three other officers, knocked on the door of the Queens house where Riddick was living. When his young son opened the door, they could see Riddick sitting in bed covered by a sheet. They entered the house and placed him under arrest. Before permitting him to dress, they opened a chest of drawers two feet from the bed in search of weapons and found narcotics and related paraphernalia. Riddick was subsequently indicted on narcotics charges. * * *

The New York Court of Appeals, in a single opinion, affirmed the convictions of both Payton and Riddick. * * *[a]

It is a "basic principle of Fourth Amendment law" that searches and seizures inside a home without a warrant are presumptively unreasonable. Yet it is also well-settled that objects such as weapons or contraband found in a public place may be seized by the police without a warrant. The seizure of property in plain view involves no invasion of privacy and is presumptively reasonable, assuming that there is probable cause to associate the property with criminal activity. * * *

As the late Judge Leventhal recognized, this distinction has equal force when the seizure of a person is involved. Writing on the constitutional issue now before us for the United States Court of Appeals for the District of Columbia Circuit sitting en banc, *Dorman v. United States,* 435 F.2d 385 (D.C.Cir.1970), Judge Leventhal first noted the settled rule that warrantless arrests in public places are valid. He immediately recognized, however, that

"[a] greater burden is placed [ ] on officials who enter a home or dwelling without consent. Freedom from intrusion into the home or dwelling is the archetype of the privacy protection secured by the Fourth Amendment."

His analysis of this question then focused on the long-settled premise that, absent exigent circumstances, a warrantless entry to search for weapons or contraband is unconstitutional even when a felony has been committed and there

---

a. At this point, the Court "put to one side other related problems that are *not* presented today": whether there were exigent circumstances justifying a warrantless entry; whether police can "enter a third party's home to arrest a suspect"; whether "the police lacked probable cause to believe that the suspect was at home when they entered"; and whether the entry was consented to.

is probable cause to believe that incriminating evidence will be found within. He reasoned that the constitutional protection afforded to the individual's interest in the privacy of his own home is equally applicable to a warrantless entry for the purpose of arresting a resident of the house; for it is inherent in such an entry that a search for the suspect may be required before he can be apprehended. Judge Leventhal concluded that an entry to arrest and an entry to search for and to seize property implicate the same interest in preserving the privacy and the sanctity of the home, and justify the same level of constitutional protection. * * * We find this reasoning to be persuasive and in accord with this Court's Fourth Amendment decisions.

The majority of the New York Court of Appeals, however, suggested that there is a substantial difference in the relative intrusiveness of an entry to search for property and an entry to search for a person. It is true that the area that may legally be searched is broader when executing a search warrant than when executing an arrest warrant in the home. See *Chimel v. California,* [p. 253]. This difference may be more theoretical than real, however, because the police may need to check the entire premises for safety reasons, and sometimes they ignore the restrictions on searches incident to arrest.

But the critical point is that any differences in the intrusiveness of entries to search and entries to arrest are merely ones of degree rather than kind. The two intrusions share this fundamental characteristic: the breach of the entrance to an individual's home. * * * In terms that apply equally to seizures of property and to seizures of persons, the Fourth Amendment has drawn a firm line at the entrance to the house. Absent exigent circumstances, that threshold may not reasonably be crossed without a warrant. * * *[b]

The parties have argued at some length about the practical consequences of a warrant requirement as a precondition to a felony arrest in the home. In the absence of any evidence that effective law enforcement has suffered in those States that already have such a requirement, we are inclined to view such arguments with skepticism. More fundamentally, however, such arguments of policy must give way to a constitutional command that we consider to be unequivocal.

Finally, we note the State's suggestion that only a search warrant based on probable cause to believe the suspect is at home at a given time can adequately protect the privacy interests at stake, and since such a warrant requirement is manifestly impractical, there need be no warrant of any kind. We find this

b. At this point, Stevens, J., observed that New York argued that "the reasons supporting the *Watson* [p. 221] holding require a similar result here. In *Watson* the Court relied on (a) the well-settled common-law rule that a warrantless arrest in a public place is valid if the arresting officer had probable cause to believe the suspect is a felon; (b) the clear consensus among the States adhering to that well-settled common-law rule; and (c) the expression of the judgment of Congress that such an arrest is 'reasonable.' We consider each of these reasons as it applies to a warrantless entry into a home for the purpose of making a routine felony arrest."

In an extended analysis, the *Payton* majority concluded (a) that "the relevant common law does not provide the same guidance that was present in *Watson,*" as there is "no direct authority supporting forcible entries into a home to make a routine arrest and the weight of the scholarly opinion is somewhat to the contrary"; (b) that presently 24 states permit such warrantless entries, 15 prohibit them, and 11 have taken no position, with "a significant decline during the last decade in the number of States permitting warrantless entries for arrest"; and (c) that "no congressional determination that warrantless entries into the home are 'reasonable' has been called to our attention." While the majority then concluded from this that "neither history nor this Nation's experience" lent support to the New York position, the *Payton* dissenters read essentially the same data as supporting their position.

ingenious argument unpersuasive. It is true that an arrest warrant requirement may afford less protection than a search warrant requirement, but it will suffice to interpose the magistrate's determination of probable cause between the zealous officer and the citizen. If there is sufficient evidence of a citizen's participation in a felony to persuade a judicial officer that his arrest is justified, it is constitutionally reasonable to require him to open his doors to the officers of the law. Thus, for Fourth Amendment purposes, an arrest warrant founded on probable cause implicitly carries with it the limited authority to enter a dwelling in which the suspect lives when there is reason to believe the suspect is within.

Because no arrest warrant was obtained in either of these cases, the judgments must be reversed * * *.

Justice BLACKMUN, concurring. * * *

Justice WHITE, with whom THE CHIEF JUSTICE and Justice REHNQUIST join, dissenting. * * *

Today's decision ignores the carefully crafted restrictions on the common-law power of arrest entry and thereby overestimates the dangers inherent in that practice. At common law, absent exigent circumstances, entries to arrest could be made only for felony. Even in cases of felony, the officers were required to announce their presence, demand admission, and be refused entry before they were entitled to break doors. Further, it seems generally accepted that entries could be made only during daylight hours. And, in my view, the officer entering to arrest must have reasonable grounds to believe, not only that the arrestee has committed a crime, but also that the person suspected is present in the house at the time of the entry.[13]

These four restrictions on home arrests—felony, knock and announce, daytime, and stringent probable cause—constitute powerful and complementary protections for the privacy interests associated with the home. The felony requirement guards against abusive or arbitrary enforcement and ensures that invasions of the home occur only in case of the most serious crimes. The knock and announce and daytime requirement protect individuals against the fear, humiliation and embarrassment of being aroused from the beds in states of partial or complete undress. And these requirements allow the arrestee to surrender at his front door, thereby maintaining his dignity and preventing the officers from entering other rooms of the dwelling. The stringent probable cause requirement would help ensure against the possibility that the police would enter when the suspect was not home, and, in searching for him, frighten members of the family or ransack parts of the house, seizing items in plain view. In short, these requirements, taken together, permit an individual suspected of a serious crime to surrender at the front door of his dwelling and thereby avoid most of the humiliation and indignity that the Court seems to believe necessarily accompany a house arrest entry. Such a front door arrest, in my view, is no more intrusive on personal privacy than the public warrantless arrests which we found to pass constitutional muster in *Watson*.[14]

---

13. I do not necessarily disagree with the Court's discussion of the quantum of probable cause necessary to make a valid home arrest. The Court indicates that only an arrest warrant, and not a search warrant, is required. To obtain the warrant, therefore, the officers need only show probable cause that a crime has been committed and that the suspect committed it. However, under today's decision, the officers apparently need an extra increment of

probable cause when executing the arrest warrant, namely grounds to believe that the suspect is within the dwelling.

14. If the suspect flees or hides, of course, the intrusiveness of the entry will be somewhat greater; but the policeman's hands should not be tied merely because of the possibility that the suspect will fail to cooperate with legitimate actions by law enforcement personnel.

All of these limitations on warrantless arrest entries are satisfied on the facts of the present cases. The arrests here were for serious felonies—murder and armed robbery—and both occurred during daylight hours. The authorizing statutes required that the police announce their business and demand entry; neither Payton nor Riddick makes any contention that these statutory requirements were not fulfilled. And it is not argued that the police had no probable cause to believe that both Payton and Riddick were in their dwellings at the time of the entries. Today's decision, therefore, sweeps away any possibility that warrantless home entries might be permitted in some limited situations other than those in which exigent circumstances are present. The Court substitutes, in one sweeping decision, a rigid constitutional rule in place of the common-law approach, evolved over hundreds of years, which achieved a flexible accommodation between the demands of personal privacy and the legitimate needs of law enforcement.

A rule permitting warrantless arrest entries would not pose a danger that officers would use their entry power as a pretext to justify an otherwise invalid warrantless search. A search pursuant to a warrantless arrest entry will rarely, if ever, be as complete as one under authority of a search warrant. If the suspect surrenders at the door, the officers may not enter other rooms. Of course, the suspect may flee or hide, or may not be at home, but the officers cannot anticipate the first two of these possibilities and the last is unlikely given the requirement of probable cause to believe that the suspect is at home. Even when officers are justified in searching other rooms, they may seize only items within the arrestee's position [sic] or immediate control or items in plain view discovered during the course of a search reasonably directed at discovering a hiding suspect. Hence a warrantless home entry is likely to uncover far less evidence than a search conducted under authority of a search warrant. Furthermore, an arrest entry will inevitably tip off the suspects and likely result in destruction or removal of evidence not uncovered during the arrest. I therefore cannot believe that the police would take the risk of losing valuable evidence through a pretextual arrest entry rather than applying to a magistrate for a search warrant.

While exaggerating the invasion of personal privacy involved in home arrests, the Court fails to account for the danger that its rule will "severely hamper effective law enforcement." The policeman on his beat must now make subtle discriminations that perplex even judges in their chambers. As Justice Powell noted, concurring in *United States v. Watson*, police will sometimes delay making an arrest, even after probable cause is established, in order to be sure that they have enough evidence to convict. Then, if they suddenly have to arrest, they run the risk that the subsequent exigency will not excuse their prior failure to obtain a warrant. This problem cannot effectively be cured by obtaining a warrant as soon as probable cause is established because of the chance that the warrant will go stale before the arrest is made.

Further, police officers will often face the difficult task of deciding whether the circumstances are sufficiently exigent to justify their entry to arrest without a warrant. This is a decision that must be made quickly in the most trying of circumstances. If the officers mistakenly decide that the circumstances are exigent, the arrest will be invalid and any evidence seized incident to the arrest or in plain view will be excluded at trial. On the other hand, if the officers mistakenly determine that exigent circumstances are lacking, they may refrain from making the arrest, thus creating the possibility that a dangerous criminal will escape into the community. The police could reduce the likelihood of escape by staking out all possible exits until the circumstances become clearly exigent or a warrant is obtained. But the costs of such a stakeout seem excessive in an era of rising crime and scarce police resources.

The uncertainty inherent in the exigent circumstances determination burdens the judicial system as well. In the case of searches, exigent circumstances are sufficiently unusual that this Court has determined that the benefits of a warrant outweigh the burdens imposed, including the burdens on the judicial system. In contrast, arrests recurringly involve exigent circumstances, and this Court has heretofore held that a warrant can be dispensed with without undue sacrifice in Fourth Amendment values. The situation should be no different with respect to arrests in the home. Under today's decision, whenever the police have made a warrantless home arrest there will be the possibility of "endless litigation with respect to the existence of exigent circumstances, whether it was practicable to get a warrant, whether the suspect was about to flee, and the like."

* * * It would be far preferable to adopt a clear and simple rule: after knocking and announcing their presence, police may enter the home to make a daytime arrest without a warrant when there is probable cause to believe that the person to be arrested committed a felony and is present in the house. * * *[c]

Notes and Questions

1. The Supreme Court has approved of warrantless entries to arrest under some circumstances. In *Warden v. Hayden,* 387 U.S. 294, 87 S.Ct. 1642, 18 L.Ed.2d 782 (1967), where police were reliably informed that an armed robbery had taken place and that the perpetrator had entered a certain house five minutes earlier, the Court concluded they "acted reasonably when they entered the house and began to search for a man of the description they had been given and for weapons which he had used in the robbery or might use against them.[d] The Fourth Amendment does not require police officers to delay in the course of an investigation if to do so would gravely endanger their lives or the lives of others." And in *United States v. Santana,* 427 U.S. 38, 96 S.Ct. 2406, 49 L.Ed.2d 300 (1976), it was held that *United States v. Watson,* p. 221, permitted the police to attempt a warrantless arrest of the defendant when she was found "standing directly in the doorway—one step forward would have put her outside, one step backward would have put her in the vestibule of her residence." The Court reasoned that she "was in a public place," as she "was not merely visible to the public but was exposed to public view, speech, hearing and touch as if she had been standing completely outside her house." Thus, under the *Hayden* "hot pursuit" rule the police could pursue her without a warrant when she sought refuge within upon their approach.

What then if the person to be arrested answers a knock on the door by the police but does not step onto or over the threshold? What if he does because of a police request or subterfuge which conceals their purpose in being there? Or, what if the police use such tactics to gain entry into the premises?

2. In *Dorman,* relied upon in *Payton,* the court found that exceptional circumstances were present by assessing these considerations:

"First, that a grave offense is involved, particularly one that is a crime of violence. * * *

c. See Joseph D. Harbaugh & Nancy L. Faust, *"Knock on Any Door"—Home Arrests After Payton and Steagald,* 86 Dick.L.Rev. 191 (1982).

d. Thus, the Court held admissible clothing found in a washing machine, where an officer looked for weapons "prior to or immediately contemporaneous with Hayden's arrest."

"Second, * * * that the suspect is reasonably believed to be armed. * * *

"Third, that there exists not merely the minimum of probable cause, that is requisite even when a warrant has been issued, but beyond that a clear showing of probable cause, including 'reasonably trustworthy information,' to believe that the suspect committed the crime involved.

"Fourth, strong reason to believe that the suspect is in the premises being entered.

"Fifth, a likelihood that the suspect will escape if not swiftly apprehended.

"Sixth, the circumstance that the entry, though not consented, is made peaceably. * * *

"Another factor to be taken into account, though it works in more than one direction, relates to time of entry—whether it is made at night. On the one hand, as we shall later develop, the late hour may underscore the delay (and perhaps impracticability of) obtaining a warrant and hence serve to justify proceeding without one. On the other hand, the fact that an entry is made at night raises a particular concern over its reasonableness * * * and may elevate the degree of probable cause required, both as implicating the suspect, and as showing that he is in the place entered."

Judge Wright, disagreed: "The police, while waiting for a judicial officer to authorize entry into the home, could simply stake out the apartment."

3. The Supreme Court focused upon the first *Dorman* factor in WELSH v. WISCONSIN, 466 U.S. 740, 104 S.Ct. 2091, 80 L.Ed.2d 732 (1984), where Welsh was arrested within his own home minutes after a witness had seen him nearby driving erratically and then departing on foot in an apparently inebriated condition after driving off the road into a field. The Court, per BRENNAN, J., held "that an important factor to be considered when determining whether any exigency exists is the gravity of the underlying offense for which the arrest is being made. Moreover, although no exigency is created simply because there is probable cause to believe that a serious crime has been committed, see *Payton,* application of the exigent-circumstances exception in the context of a home entry should rarely be sanctioned when there is probable cause to believe that only a minor offense, such as the kind at issue in this case, has been committed.

"Application of this principle to the facts of the present case is relatively straightforward. The petitioner was arrested in the privacy of his own bedroom for a noncriminal, traffic offense. The State attempts to justify the arrest by relying on the hot-pursuit doctrine, on the threat to public safety, and on the need to preserve evidence of the petitioner's blood-alcohol level. On the facts of this case, however, the claim of hot pursuit is unconvincing because there was no immediate or continuous pursuit of the petitioner from the scene of a crime. Moreover, because the petitioner had already arrived home, and had abandoned his car at the scene of the accident, there was little remaining threat to the public safety. Hence, the only potential emergency claimed by the State was the need to ascertain the petitioner's blood-alcohol level.

"Even assuming, however, that the underlying facts would support a finding of this exigent circumstance, mere similarity to other cases involving the imminent destruction of evidence is not sufficient. The State of Wisconsin has chosen to classify the first offense for driving while intoxicated as a noncriminal, civil forfeiture offense for which no imprisonment is possible. This is the best indication of the state's interest in precipitating an arrest, and is one that can be easily identified both by the courts and by officers faced with a decision to arrest. Given this expression of the state's interest, a warrantless home arrest cannot be upheld simply because evidence of the petitioner's blood-alcohol level might have dissipated while the police obtained a warrant. To allow a warrantless home entry on these facts would be to approve unreasonable police behavior that the principles of the Fourth Amendment will not sanction.''

WHITE, J., joined by Rehnquist, J., dissenting, agreed that the gravity of the offense is "a factor to be considered," but asserted that "if, under all the circumstances of a particular case, an officer has probable cause to believe that the delay involved in procuring an arrest warrant will gravely endanger the officer or other persons or will result in the suspect's escape, I perceive no reason to disregard those exigencies on the ground that the offense for which the suspect is sought is a 'minor' one." By like reasoning, they concluded that "nothing in our previous decisions suggests that the fact that a State has defined an offense as a misdemeanor for a variety of social, cultural, and political reasons necessarily requires the conclusion that warrantless in-home arrests designed to prevent the imminent destruction or removal of evidence of that offense are always impermissible. * * * A test under which the existence of exigent circumstances turns on the perceived gravity of the crime would significantly hamper law enforcement and burden courts with pointless litigation concerning the nature and gradation of various crimes.''

Would the result in *Welsh* have been different if the police were in immediate hot pursuit? See *State v. Bolte,* 560 A.2d 644 (N.J.1989) (rejecting state's argument answer is yes because "citizens should not be encouraged to elude arrest by retreating into their homes'').

4. MINNESOTA v. OLSON, 495 U.S. 91, 110 S.Ct. 1684, 109 L.Ed.2d 85 (1990) (also discussed at p. 780), another warrantless entry to arrest case, involved these facts: "Shortly before 6 a.m. on Saturday, July 18, 1987, a lone gunman robbed an Amoco gasoline station in Minneapolis, Minnesota, and fatally shot the station manager. A police officer heard the police dispatcher report and suspected Joseph Ecker. The officer and his partner drove immediately to Ecker's home, arriving at about the same time that an Oldsmobile arrived. The Oldsmobile took evasive action, spun out of control, and came to a stop. Two men fled the car on foot. Ecker, who was later identified as the gunman, was captured shortly thereafter inside his home. The second man escaped.

"Inside the abandoned Oldsmobile, police found a sack of money and the murder weapon. They also found a title certificate with the name Rob Olson crossed out as a secured party, a letter addressed to a Roger R. Olson of 3151 Johnson Street, and a videotape rental receipt made out to Rob Olson and dated two days earlier. The police verified that a Robert Olson lived at 3151 Johnson Street.

"The next morning, Sunday, July 19, a woman identifying herself as Dianna Murphy called the police and said that a man by the name of Rob drove the car in which the gas-station killer left the scene and that Rob was planning to leave town by bus. About noon, the same woman called again, gave her address and phone number, and said that a man named Rob had told a Maria and two other women, Louanne and Julie, that he was the driver in the Amoco robbery. The caller stated that Louanne was Julie's mother and that the two women lived at 2406 Fillmore Northeast. The detective-in-charge who took the second phone call sent police officers to 2406 Fillmore to check out Louanne and Julie. When police arrived they determined that the dwelling was a duplex and that Louanne Bergstrom and her daughter Julie lived in the upper unit but were not home. Police spoke to

Louanne's mother, Helen Niederhoffer, who lived in the lower unit. She confirmed that a Rob Olson had been staying upstairs but was not then in the unit. She promised to call the police when Olson returned. At 2 p.m., a pickup order, or 'probable cause arrest bulletin,' was issued for Olson's arrest. The police were instructed to stay away from the duplex.

"At approximately 2:45 p.m., Niederhoffer called police and said Olson had returned. The detective-in-charge instructed police officers to go to the house and surround it. He then telephoned Julie from headquarters and told her Rob should come out of the house. The detective heard a male voice say 'tell them I left.' Julie stated that Rob had left, whereupon at 3 p.m. the detective ordered the police to enter the house. Without seeking permission and with weapons drawn, the police entered the upper unit and found respondent hiding in a closet."

The Court, per WHITE, J., determined that "the Minnesota Supreme Court was correct in holding that there were no exigent circumstances that justified the warrantless entry into the house to make the arrest.

"The Minnesota Supreme Court applied essentially the correct standard in determining whether exigent circumstances existed. The court observed that 'a warrantless intrusion may be justified by hot pursuit of a fleeing felon, or imminent destruction of evidence, or the need to prevent a suspect's escape, or the risk of danger to the police or to other persons inside or outside the dwelling.' The court also apparently thought that in the absence of hot pursuit there must be at least probable cause to believe that one or more of the other factors justifying the entry were present and that in assessing the risk of danger, the gravity of the crime and likelihood that the suspect is armed should be considered. Applying this standard, the state court determined that exigent circumstances did not exist.

"We are not inclined to disagree with this fact-specific application of the proper legal standard. The court pointed out that although a grave crime was involved, respondent 'was known not to be the murderer but thought to be the driver of the getaway car,' and that the police had already recovered the murder weapon. 'The police knew that Louanne and Julie were with the suspect in the upstairs duplex with no suggestion of danger to them. Three or four Minneapolis police squads surrounded the house. The time was 3 p.m., Sunday.... It was evident the suspect was going nowhere. If he came out of the house he would have been promptly apprehended.' We do not disturb the state court's judgment that these facts do not add up to exigent circumstances."

5. In STEAGALD v. UNITED STATES, 451 U.S. 204, 101 S.Ct. 1642, 68 L.Ed.2d 38 (1981), police entered Steagald's home in an effort to find one Lyons, for whom they had an arrest warrant; they did not find Lyons but did find drugs in plain view, resulting in Steagald's prosecution and conviction. In reversing the conviction, the Court, per MARSHALL, J., reasoned that "whether the arrest warrant issued in this case adequately safeguarded the interests protected by the Fourth Amendment depends upon what the warrant authorized the agents to do. To be sure, the warrant embodied a judicial finding that there was probable cause to believe that Ricky Lyons had committed a felony, and the warrant therefore authorized the officers to seize Lyons. However, the agents sought to do more than use the warrant to arrest Lyons in a public place or in his home; instead, they relied on the warrant as legal authority to enter the home of a third person based on their belief that Ricky Lyons might be a guest there. Regardless of how reasonable this belief might have been, it was never subjected to the detached scrutiny of a judicial officer. Thus, while the warrant in this case may have protected Lyons from an unreasonable seizure, it did absolutely nothing to protect

petitioner's privacy interest in being free from an unreasonable invasion and search of his home. Instead, petitioner's only protection from an illegal entry and search was the agent's personal determination of probable cause. In the absence of exigent circumstances, we have consistently held that such judicially untested determinations are not reliable enough to justify an entry into a person's home to arrest him without a warrant, or a search of a home for objects in the absence of a search warrant. We see no reason to depart from this settled course when the search of a home is for a person rather than an object.

"A contrary conclusion—that the police, acting alone and in the absence of exigent circumstances, may decide when there is sufficient justification for searching the home of a third party for the subject of an arrest warrant—would create a significant potential for abuse. Armed solely with an arrest warrant for a single person, the police could search all the homes of that individual's friends and acquaintances. See, e.g., *Lankford v. Gelston,* 364 F.2d 197 (C.A.4 1966) (enjoining police practice under which 300 homes searched pursuant to arrest warrants for two fugitives). Moreover, an arrest warrant may serve as the pretext for entering a home in which the police have a suspicion, but not probable cause to believe, that illegal activity is taking place."

Though the majority went on to conclude that this result was not contrary to common law precedent and "will not significantly impede effective law enforcement efforts," in that "the situations in which a search warrant will be necessary are few" and in those situations "the inconvenience incurred by the police is simply not that significant," REHNQUIST and White, JJ., dissenting, argued that "the common law as it existed at the time of the framing of the Fourth Amendment" did not support such a result, and concluded:

"The genuinely unfortunate aspect of today's ruling is not that fewer fugitives will be brought to book, or fewer criminals apprehended, though both of these consequences will undoubtedly occur; the greater misfortune is the increased uncertainty imposed on police officers in the field, committing magistrates, and trial judges, who must confront variations and permutations of this factual situation on a day-to-day basis. They will, in their various capacities, have to weigh the time during which a suspect for whom there is an outstanding arrest warrant has been in the building, whether the dwelling is the suspect's home, how long he has lived there, whether he is likely to leave immediately, and a number of related and equally imponderable questions. Certainty and repose, as Justice Holmes said, may not be the destiny of man, but one might have hoped for a higher degree of certainty in this one narrow but important area of the law than is offered by today's decision."

6. An unannounced entry of premises to make an arrest therein is subject to the Fourth Amendment limitations like those regarding unannounced entry to execute a search warrant, as set out in *Richards v. Wisconsin,* p. 213. See, e.g., *United States v. Fields*, 113 F.3d 313 (2d Cir.1997). State statutes declaring an officer may not enter to arrest unless he has been denied admittance after giving "notice of his office and purpose" have usually been interpreted as codifying the common law exception for "exigent circumstances" when there is a reasonable belief compliance "would increase his peril, frustrate an arrest, or permit the destruction of evidence." *People v. Rosales*, 437 P.2d 489 (Cal.1968).

CALIFORNIA v. CARNEY
471 U.S. 386, 105 S.Ct. 2066, 85 L.Ed.2d 406 (1985).

Chief Justice BURGER delivered the opinion of the Court. * * *

On May 31, 1979, Drug Enforcement Agency Agent Robert Williams watched respondent, Charles Carney, approach a youth in downtown San Diego. The youth accompanied Carney to a Dodge Mini Motor Home parked in a nearby lot. Carney and the youth closed the window shades in the motor home, including one across the front window. Agent Williams had previously received uncorroborated information that the same motor home was used by another person who was exchanging marihuana for sex. Williams, with assistance from other agents, kept the motor home under surveillance for the entire one and one-quarter hours that Carney and the youth remained inside. When the youth left the motor home, the agents followed and stopped him. The youth told the agents that he had received marijuana in return for allowing Carney sexual contacts.

At the officers' request, the youth returned to the motor home and knocked on its door; Carney stepped out. The agents identified themselves as law enforcement officers. Without a warrant or consent, one agent entered the motor home and observed marihuana, plastic bags, and a scale of the kind used in weighing drugs on a table. Agent Williams took Carney into custody and took possession of the motor home. A subsequent search of the motor home at the police station revealed additional marihuana in the cupboards and refrigerator.

Respondent was charged with possession of marihuana for sale. At a preliminary hearing, he moved to suppress the evidence discovered in the motor home. The Magistrate denied the motion, [but later the state supreme court reversed the conviction, holding the search was unreasonable because no warrant was obtained.]

* * * There are, of course, exceptions to the general rule that a warrant must be secured before a search is undertaken; one is the so-called "automobile exception" at issue in this case. This exception to the warrant requirement was first set forth by the Court 60 years ago in *Carroll v. United States,* 267 U.S. 132, 45 S.Ct. 280, 69 L.Ed. 543 (1925). There, the Court recognized that the privacy interests in an automobile are constitutionally protected; however, it held that the ready mobility of the automobile justifies a lesser degree of protection of those interests. The Court rested this exception on a long-recognized distinction between stationary structures and vehicles:

> "[T]he guaranty of freedom from unreasonable searches and seizures by the Fourth Amendment has been construed, practically since the beginning of Government, as recognizing a necessary difference between a search of a store, dwelling house or other structure in respect of which a proper official warrant readily may be obtained, and a search of a ship, motor boat, wagon or automobile, for contraband goods, where it is not practicable to secure a warrant because the vehicle can be *quickly moved* out of the locality or jurisdiction in which the warrant must be sought."

The capacity to be "quickly moved" was clearly the basis of the holding in *Carroll,* and our cases have consistently recognized ready mobility as one of the principal bases of the automobile exception. * * *

However, although ready mobility alone was perhaps the original justification for the vehicle exception, our later cases have made clear that ready mobility is not the only basis for the exception. The reasons for the vehicle exception, we have said, are twofold. "Besides the element of mobility, less rigorous warrant requirements govern because the expectation of privacy with respect to one's automobile is significantly less than that relating to one's home or office."

Even in cases where an automobile was not immediately mobile, the lesser expectation of privacy resulting from its use as a readily mobile vehicle justified application of the vehicular exception. In some cases, the configuration of the vehicle contributed to the lower expectations of privacy; for example, we held in *Cardwell v. Lewis,* 417 U.S. [583], 94 S.Ct. [2464, 41 L.Ed.2d 325 (1974)], that, because the passenger compartment of a standard automobile is relatively open to plain view, there are lesser expectations of privacy. But even when enclosed "repository" areas have been involved, we have concluded that the lesser expectations of privacy warrant application of the exception. We have applied the exception in the context of a locked car trunk, *Cady v. Dombrowski,* 413 U.S. 433, 93 S.Ct. 2523, 37 L.Ed.2d 706 (1973), a sealed package in a car trunk, *United States v. Ross,* [p. 281], a closed compartment under the dashboard, *Chambers v. Maroney,* [p. 279], the interior of a vehicle's upholstery, *Carroll, supra,* or sealed packages inside a covered pickup truck, *United States v. Johns,* [p. 283].

These reduced expectations of privacy derive not from the fact that the area to be searched is in plain view, but from the pervasive regulation of vehicles capable of traveling on the public highways. As we explained in *South Dakota v. Opperman,* an inventory search case:

"Automobiles, unlike homes, are subjected to pervasive and continuing governmental regulation and controls, including periodic inspection and licensing requirements. As an everyday occurrence, police stop and examine vehicles when license plates or inspection stickers have expired, or if other violations, such as exhaust fumes or excessive noise, are noted, or if headlights or other safety equipment are not in proper working order."

The public is fully aware that it is accorded less privacy in its automobiles because of this compelling governmental need for regulation. Historically, "individuals always [have] been on notice that movable vessels may be stopped and searched on facts giving rise to probable cause that the vehicle contains contraband, without the protection afforded by a magistrate's prior evaluation of those facts." In short, the pervasive schemes of regulation, which necessarily lead to reduced expectations of privacy, and the exigencies attendant to ready mobility justify searches without prior recourse to the authority of a magistrate so long as the overriding standard of probable cause is met.

When a vehicle is being used on the highways, or if it is readily capable of such use and is found stationary in a place not regularly used for residential purposes—temporary or otherwise—the two justifications for the vehicle exception come into play. First, the vehicle is obviously readily mobile by the turn of a switch key, if not actually moving. Second, there is a reduced expectation of privacy stemming from its use as a licensed motor vehicle subject to a range of police regulation inapplicable to a fixed dwelling. At least in these circumstances, the overriding societal interests in effective law enforcement justify an immediate search before the vehicle and its occupants become unavailable.

While it is true that respondent's vehicle possessed some, if not many of the attributes of a home, it is equally clear that the vehicle falls clearly within the scope of the exception laid down in *Carroll* and applied in succeeding cases. Like the automobile in *Carroll,* respondent's motor home was readily mobile. Absent the prompt search and seizure, it could readily have been moved beyond the reach of the police. Furthermore, the vehicle was licensed to "operate on public streets; [was] serviced in public places; * * * and [was] subject to extensive regulation and inspection." And the vehicle was so situated that an objective observer would conclude that it was being used not as a residence, but as a vehicle.

Respondent urges us to distinguish his vehicle from other vehicles within the exception because it was *capable of functioning as a home.* In our increasingly mobile society, many vehicles used for transportation can be and are being used not only for transportation but for shelter, i.e., as a "home" or "residence." To distinguish between respondent's motor home and an ordinary sedan for purposes of the vehicle exception would require that we apply the exception depending upon the size of the vehicle and the quality of its appointments. Moreover, to fail to apply the exception to vehicles such as a motor home ignores the fact that a motor home lends itself easily to use as an instrument of illicit drug traffic and other illegal activity. In *United States v. Ross,* we declined to distinguish between "worthy" and "unworthy" containers, noting that "the central purpose of the Fourth Amendment forecloses such a distinction." We decline today to distinguish between "worthy" and "unworthy" vehicles which are either on the public roads and highways, or situated such that it is reasonable to conclude that the vehicle is not being used as a residence.

Our application of the vehicle exception has never turned on the other uses to which a vehicle might be put. The exception has historically turned on the ready mobility of the vehicle, and on the presence of the vehicle in a setting that objectively indicates that the vehicle is being used for transportation.[3] These two requirements for application of the exception ensure that law enforcement officials are not unnecessarily hamstrung in their efforts to detect and prosecute criminal activity, and that the legitimate privacy interests of the public are protected. Applying the vehicle exception in these circumstances allows the essential purposes served by the exception to be fulfilled, while assuring that the exception will acknowledge legitimate privacy interests. * * *

This search was not unreasonable; it was plainly one that the magistrate could authorize if presented with these facts. * * *

The judgment of the California Supreme Court is reversed * * *.

Justice STEVENS, with whom Justice BRENNAN and Justice MARSHALL join, dissenting. * * *

As we explained in *Ross,* the automobile exception * * * has been developed to ameliorate the practical problems associated with the search of vehicles that have been stopped on the streets or public highways because there was probable cause to believe they were transporting contraband. Until today, however, the Court has never decided whether the practical justifications that apply to a vehicle that is stopped in transit on a public way apply with the same force to a vehicle parked in a lot near a court house where it could easily be detained while a warrant is issued.[15]

---

3. We need not pass on the application of the vehicle exception to a motor home that is situated in a way or place that objectively indicates that it is being used as a residence. Among the factors that might be relevant in determining whether a warrant would be required in such a circumstance is its location, whether the vehicle is readily mobile or instead, for instance, elevated on blocks, whether the vehicle is licensed, whether it is connected to utilities, and whether it has convenient access to a public road.

15. In *Coolidge v. New Hampshire,* 403 U.S. 443, 91 S.Ct. 2022, 29 L.Ed.2d 564 (1971), a plurality refused to apply the automobile exception to an automobile that was seized while parked in the driveway of the suspect's house, towed to a secure police compound, and later searched:

"The word 'automobile' is not a talisman in whose presence the Fourth Amendment fades away and disappears. And surely there is nothing in this case to invoke the meaning and purpose of the rule of *Carroll v. United States*—no alerted criminal bent on flight, no fleeting opportunity on an open highway after a hazardous chase, no contraband or stolen goods or weapons, no confederates waiting to move the evidence, not even the inconvenience of a special police detail to guard the immobi-

In this case, the motor home was parked in an off-the-street lot only a few blocks from the courthouse in downtown San Diego where dozens of magistrates were available to entertain a warrant application.[16] The officers clearly had the element of surprise with them, and with curtains covering the windshield, the motor home offered no indication of any imminent departure. The officers plainly had probable cause to arrest the petitioner and search the motor home, and on this record, it is inexplicable why they eschewed the safe harbor of a warrant.

In the absence of any evidence of exigency in the circumstances of this case, the Court relies on the inherent mobility of the motor home to create a conclusive presumption of exigency. This Court, however, has squarely held that mobility of the place to be searched is not a sufficient justification for abandoning the warrant requirement. In *United States v. Chadwick*, 433 U.S. 1, 97 S.Ct. 2476, 53 L.Ed.2d 538 (1977), the Court held that a warrantless search of a footlocker violated the Fourth Amendment even though there was ample probable cause to believe it contained contraband. The Government had argued that the rationale of the automobile exception applied to movable containers in general, and that the warrant requirement should be limited to searches of homes and other "core" areas of privacy. We categorically rejected the Government's argument observing that there are greater privacy interests associated with containers than with automobiles, and that there are less practical problems associated with the temporary detention of a container than with the detention of an automobile.

* * * It is perfectly obvious that the citizen has a much greater expectation of privacy concerning the interior of a mobile home than of a piece of luggage such as a footlocker. If "inherent mobility" does not justify warrantless searches of containers, it cannot rationally provide a sufficient justification for the search of a person's dwelling place.

Unlike a brick bungalow or a frame Victorian, a motor home seldom serves as a permanent lifetime abode. The motor home in this case, however, was designed to accommodate a breadth of ordinary everyday living. Photographs in the record indicate that its height, length and beam provided substantial living space inside: stuffed chairs surround a table; cupboards provide room for storage of personal effects; bunk-beds provide sleeping space; and a refrigerator provides ample space for food and beverages. Moreover, curtains and large opaque walls inhibit viewing the activities inside from the exterior of the vehicle. The interior configuration of the motor home establishes that the vehicle's size, shape, and mode of construction should have indicated to the officers that it was a vehicle containing mobile living quarters.

The State contends that officers in the field will have an impossible task determining whether or not other vehicles contain mobile living quarters. It is not necessary for the Court to resolve every unanswered question in this area in a single case, but common English usage suggests that we already distinguish

lized automobile. In short, by no possible stretch of the legal imagination can this be made into a case where 'it is not practicable to secure a warrant,' and the 'automobile exception' despite its label, is simply irrelevant." (opinion of Stewart, J., joined by Douglas, Brennan and Marshall, JJ.).

In *Cardwell v. Lewis,* 417 U.S. 583, 94 S.Ct. 2464, 41 L.Ed.2d 325 (1974), a different plurality approved the seizure of an automobile from a public parking lot, and a later examination of its exterior. (opinion of Blackmun, J.). Here, of course, we are concerned with the reasonableness of the search, not the seizure. Even if the diminished expectations of privacy associated with an automobile justify the warrantless search of a parked automobile notwithstanding the diminished exigency, the heightened expectations of privacy in the interior of motor home require a different result.

16. In addition, a telephonic warrant was only 20 cents and the nearest phone booth away.

between a "motor home" which is "equipped as a self-contained traveling home," a "camper" which is only equipped for "casual travel and camping," and an automobile which is "designed for passenger transportation." Surely the exteriors of these vehicles contain clues about their different functions which could alert officers in the field to the necessity of a warrant.[21] * * *

In my opinion, searches of places that regularly accommodate a wide range of private human activity are fundamentally different from searches of automobiles which primarily serve a public transportation function. Although it may not be a castle, a motor home is usually the functional equivalent of a hotel room, a vacation and retirement home, or a hunting and fishing cabin. These places may be as spartan as a humble cottage when compared to the most majestic mansion, but the highest and most legitimate expectations of privacy associated with these temporary abodes should command the respect of this Court. In my opinion, a warrantless search of living quarters in a motor home is "presumptively unreasonable absent exigent circumstances."

I respectfully dissent.

Notes and Questions

1. As the Court's earlier cases make clear, the "ready mobility" language in *Carney* does *not* refer to the actual likelihood that the vehicle would be moved if a search warrant were sought. In *Chambers v. Maroney*, 399 U.S. 42, 90 S.Ct. 1975, 26 L.Ed.2d 419 (1970), police stopped a station wagon on probable cause the occupants had just committed a robbery; the occupants were arrested and the car was driven to the police station, where a thorough search revealed a revolver under the dashboard and other evidence. Although Harlan, J., dissenting, reasoned that there was no need for a warrantless search because the car could simply be held in police custody until a warrant was obtained, the majority, per White, J., responded with this syllogism: (i) "the blue station wagon could have been searched on the spot when it was stopped since there was probable cause to search and it was a fleeting target for a search"; (ii) it "was not unreasonable * * * to take the car to the station house," as the arrests were made "in a dark parking lot in the middle of the night"; (iii) once the car was at the station, "there is little to choose in terms of practical consequences between an immediate search without a warrant and the car's immobilization until a warrant is obtained." But in *Texas v. White*, 423 U.S. 67, 96 S.Ct. 304, 46 L.Ed.2d 209 (1975), *Chambers* was deemed applicable to an at-the-station vehicle search though, as the two dissenters noted, "the arrest took place at 1:30 in the afternoon, and there is no indication that an immediate search would have been either impractical or unsafe for the arresting officers."

Consider also *Colorado v. Bannister*, 449 U.S. 1, 101 S.Ct. 42, 66 L.Ed.2d 1 (1980) (unanimous Court concludes that where probable cause to search developed after the car was stopped for a traffic violation, "it would be especially unreasonable to require a detour to a magistrate before the unanticipated evidence could be lawfully seized"); *Michigan v. Thomas*, 458 U.S. 259, 102 S.Ct. 3079, 73 L.Ed.2d 750 (1982) (Court stresses that "the justification to conduct such a warrantless search does not vanish once the car has been immobilized; nor does it depend

---

21. In refusing to extend the California Supreme Court's decision in *Carney* beyond its context, the California Courts of Appeals have had no difficulty in distinguishing the motor home involved there from a Ford van and a cab-high camper shell on the back of a pick-up truck. There is no reason to believe that trained officers could not make similar distinctions between different vehicles, especially when state vehicle laws already require them to do so.

upon a reviewing court's assessment of the likelihood in each particular case that the car would have been driven away, or that its contents would have been tampered with, during the period required for the police to obtain a warrant"); *Florida v. Meyers,* 466 U.S. 380, 104 S.Ct. 1852, 80 L.Ed.2d 381 (1984) (Court holds on authority of *Thomas* that lower court erred in concluding warrantless search of car improper where, as here, the car had been impounded eight hours earlier and was presently stored in a secure area).

2.　In *Chambers* the Court stated that what is required, even if no warrant need first be obtained, is "probable cause to search a particular auto for particular articles." Consider the following cases, both holding that the facts stated justified a warrantless search of the car under *Chambers: United States v. Jones,* 452 F.2d 884 (8th Cir.1971) (defendant was stopped after he made illegal turn and ran red light while driving car without plates, as officer approached he saw defendant tear paper into small pieces and push them between seat and back cushions, defendant was arrested and placed in squad car after he displayed driver's license of another person, officer then retrieved the pieces of paper, which turned out to be stolen welfare check); *People v. Hering,* 327 N.E.2d 583 (Ill.App.1975) (trooper stopped car because one headlight out, as he was writing ticket defendant drove off and, when overtaken, could not explain why he did so, trooper then searched the car).

Compare *United States v. Coleman,* 322 F.Supp. 550 (E.D.Pa.1971) (officer checking out two suspicious persons obtained consent to look in trunk of car owned by one of them and found a gun, after which the two were arrested; later a detective came to scene of arrests and searched the car and seized a revolver, two ski masks and two shopping bags; held, evidence suppressed: "Knowing all this, we have no idea what [the detective] reasonably expected to find inside the car other than its interior").

3.　The probable cause to search must also be assessed in order to ascertain whether an otherwise lawful warrantless search of a vehicle was properly limited in scope and intensity, as is illustrated by *Maldonado v. State,* 528 S.W.2d 234 (Tex.Crim.1975) (truck searched on probable cause it was stolen, officers pulled up flooring and found false compartment containing 650 packages of marijuana; held, that part of search illegal because it "could not reasonably be expected that evidence of theft might be uncovered by these means"); *Wimberly v. Superior Court,* 547 P.2d 417 (Cal.1976) (after vehicle stopped for traffic violation, officer saw pipe and 12 marijuana seeds on floor and smelled odor of marijuana, passenger compartment was searched and bag with very small amount of marijuana was found in jacket pocket, trunk of car then searched and several pounds of marijuana found there; held, latter search illegal, as police had probable cause occupants of car were occasional users rather than dealers, and thus "it was not reasonable to infer that petitioners had additional contraband hidden in the trunk"). Compare *United States v. Loucks,* 806 F.2d 208 (10th Cir.1986) (such user-dealer distinction is "illogical and unreasonable").

4.　Assuming grounds to make a warrantless search of a car, but the absence of grounds to arrest some occupant of the car, may that occupant also be searched if the items sought are of such a nature that they could be concealed on his person? No, the Supreme Court held in *United States v. Di Re* [p. 222]. However, *Model Pre–Arraignment Code* § SS 260.3 provides otherwise (except as to passengers in a common carrier) if the officer has not found the items sought in the vehicle and has "reason to suspect that one or more of the occupants of the vehicle may have the things subject to seizure so concealed." The Reporters argue that "it seems absurd to say that the occupants can take the narcotics out of the glove compartment and stuff them in their pockets, and drive happily away after the vehicle has been fruitlessly searched." Can that position be squared with *Ybarra v. Illinois,* p. 215?

CALIFORNIA v. ACEVEDO
500 U.S. 565, 111 S.Ct. 1982, 114 L.Ed.2d 619 (1991).

Justice BLACKMUN delivered the opinion of the Court.

[One Daza picked up a package the police knew contained marijuana from a Federal Express office and took it to his apartment. About two hours later, Acevedo entered that apartment and shortly thereafter left carrying a brown paper bag the size of one of the wrapped marijuana packages. He placed the bag in the trunk of his car and drove off; the police then stopped him, opened the trunk and bag, and found marijuana. The California Court of Appeal held the marijuana should have been suppressed, the state supreme court denied review, and the Supreme Court then granted certiorari.]

In *United States v. Ross,* 456 U.S. 798, 102 S.Ct. 2157, 72 L.Ed.2d 572, decided in 1982, we held that a warrantless search of an automobile under the *Carroll* doctrine could include a search of a container or package found inside the car when such a search was supported by probable cause. The warrantless search of Ross' car occurred after an informant told the police that he had seen Ross complete a drug transaction using drugs stored in the trunk of his car. The police stopped the car, searched it, and discovered in the trunk a brown paper bag containing drugs. We decided that the search of Ross' car was not unreasonable under the Fourth Amendment: "The scope of a warrantless search based on probable cause is no narrower—and no broader—than the scope of a search authorized by a warrant supported by probable cause." Thus, "[i]f probable cause justifies the search of a lawfully stopped vehicle, it justifies the search of every part of the vehicle and its contents that may conceal the object of the search." In *Ross,* therefore, we clarified the scope of the *Carroll* doctrine as properly including a "probing search" of compartments and containers within the automobile so long as the search is supported by probable cause.

In addition to this clarification, *Ross* distinguished the *Carroll* doctrine from the separate rule that governed the search of closed containers. The Court had announced this separate rule, unique to luggage and other closed packages, bags, and containers, in *United States v. Chadwick,* 433 U.S. 1, 97 S.Ct. 2476, 53 L.Ed.2d 538 (1977). In *Chadwick,* federal narcotics agents had probable cause to believe that a 200–pound double-locked footlocker contained marijuana. The agents tracked the locker as the defendants removed it from a train and carried it through the station to a waiting car. As soon as the defendants lifted the locker into the trunk of the car, the agents arrested them, seized the locker, and searched it. In this Court, the United States did not contend that the locker's brief contact with the automobile's trunk sufficed to make the *Carroll* doctrine applicable. Rather, the United States urged that the search of movable luggage could be considered analogous to the search of an automobile.

The Court rejected this argument because, it reasoned, a person expects more privacy in his luggage and personal effects than he does in his automobile. Moreover, it concluded that as "may often not be the case when automobiles are seized," secure storage facilities are usually available when the police seize luggage.

In *Arkansas v. Sanders,* 442 U.S. 753, 99 S.Ct. 2586, 61 L.Ed.2d 235 (1979), the Court extended *Chadwick*'s rule to apply to a suitcase actually being transported in the trunk of a car. In *Sanders,* the police had probable cause to believe a suitcase contained marijuana. They watched as the defendant placed the suitcase in the trunk of a taxi and was driven away. The police pursued the taxi for several blocks, stopped it, found the suitcase in the trunk, and searched it. Although the Court had applied the *Carroll* doctrine to searches of integral parts of the automobile itself, (indeed, in *Carroll,* contraband whiskey was in the upholstery of the seats), it did not extend the doctrine to the warrantless search of personal luggage "merely because it was located in an automobile lawfully stopped by the police." Again, the *Sanders* majority stressed the heightened privacy expectation in personal luggage and concluded that the presence of luggage in an automobile did not diminish the owner's expectation of privacy in his personal items.

In *Ross,* the Court endeavored to distinguish between *Carroll,* which governed the *Ross* automobile search, and *Chadwick,* which governed the *Sanders* automobile search. It held that the *Carroll* doctrine covered searches of automobiles when the police had probable cause to search an entire vehicle but that the *Chadwick* doctrine governed searches of luggage when the officers had probable cause to search only a container within the vehicle. Thus, in a *Ross* situation, the police could conduct a reasonable search under the Fourth Amendment without obtaining a warrant, whereas in a *Sanders* situation, the police had to obtain a warrant before they searched.

The dissent is correct, of course, that *Ross* involved the scope of an automobile search. *Ross* held that closed containers encountered by the police during a warrantless search of a car pursuant to the automobile exception could also be searched. Thus, this Court in *Ross* took the critical step of saying that closed containers in cars could be searched without a warrant because of their presence within the automobile. Despite the protection that *Sanders* purported to extend to closed containers, the privacy interest in those closed containers yielded to the broad scope of an automobile search. * * *

This Court in *Ross* rejected *Chadwick*'s distinction between containers and cars. It concluded that the expectation of privacy in one's vehicle is equal to one's expectation of privacy in the container, and noted that "the privacy interests in a car's trunk or glove compartment may be no less than those in a movable container." It also recognized that it was arguable that the same exigent circumstances that permit a warrantless search of an automobile would justify the warrantless search of a movable container. In deference to the rule of *Chadwick* and *Sanders,* however, the Court put that question to one side. It concluded that the time and expense of the warrant process would be misdirected if the police could search every cubic inch of an automobile until they discovered a paper sack, at which point the Fourth Amendment required them to take the sack to a magistrate for permission to look inside. We now must decide the question deferred in *Ross:* whether the Fourth Amendment requires the police to obtain a warrant to open the sack in a movable vehicle simply because they lack probable cause to search the entire car. We conclude that it does not.

Dissenters in *Ross* asked why the suitcase in *Sanders* was "more private, less difficult for police to seize and store, or in any other relevant respect more properly subject to the warrant requirement, than a container that police discover in a probable-cause search of an entire automobile?" We now agree that a container found after a general search of the automobile and a container found in a car after a limited search for the container are equally easy for the police to store and for the suspect to hide or destroy. In fact, we see no principled distinction in terms of either the privacy expectation or the exigent circumstances between the paper bag found by the police in *Ross* and the paper bag found by the police here. Furthermore, by attempting to distinguish between a container for which the police are specifically searching and a container which they come across in a car, we have provided only minimal protection for privacy and have impeded effective law enforcement.

The line between probable cause to search a vehicle and probable cause to search a package in that vehicle is not always clear, and separate rules that govern the two objects to be searched may enable the police to broaden their power to make warrantless searches and disserve privacy interests. * * * At the moment when officers stop an automobile, it may be less than clear whether they suspect with a high degree of certainty that the vehicle contains drugs in a bag or simply contains drugs. If the police know that they may open a bag only if they are actually searching the entire car, they may search more extensively than they otherwise would in order to establish the general probable cause required by *Ross*.

Such a situation is not far fetched. In *United States v. Johns,* 469 U.S. 478, 105 S.Ct. 881, 83 L.Ed.2d 890 (1985), customs agents saw two trucks drive to a private airstrip and approach two small planes. The agents drew near the trucks, smelled marijuana, and then saw in the backs of the trucks packages wrapped in a manner that marijuana smugglers customarily employed. The agents took the trucks to headquarters and searched the packages without a warrant. Relying on *Chadwick,* the defendants argued that the search was unlawful. The defendants contended that *Ross* was inapplicable because the agents lacked probable cause to search anything but the packages themselves and supported this contention by noting that a search of the entire vehicle never occurred. We rejected that argument and found *Chadwick* and *Sanders* inapposite because the agents had probable cause to search the entire body of each truck, although they had chosen not to do so.[a] We cannot see the benefit of a rule that requires law enforcement officers to conduct a more intrusive search in order to justify a less intrusive one.

To the extent that the *Chadwick–Sanders* rule protects privacy, its protection is minimal. Law enforcement officers may seize a container and hold it until they obtain a search warrant. "Since the police, by hypothesis, have probable cause to seize the property, we can assume that a warrant will be routinely forthcoming in the overwhelming majority of cases." And the police often will be able to search containers without a warrant, despite the *Chadwick–Sanders* rule, as a search incident to a lawful arrest [under] *Belton*. * * *

Finally, the search of a paper bag intrudes far less on individual privacy than does the incursion sanctioned long ago in *Carroll*. In that case, prohibition agents slashed the upholstery of the automobile. This Court nonetheless found their

a. However, "the central issue" in *Johns* was whether the warrantless search was permissible in light of the fact that the packages were not opened until three days after they had been removed from the trucks. The majority answered in the affirmative:

"We do not suggest that police officers may indefinitely retain possession of a vehicle and its contents before they complete a vehicle search. Nor do we foreclose the possibility that the owner of a vehicle or its contents might attempt to prove that delay in the completion of a vehicle search was unreasonable because it adversely affected a privacy or possessory interest. We note that in this case there was probable cause to believe that the trucks contained contraband and there is no plausible argument that the object of the search could not have been concealed in the packages. Respondents do not challenge the legitimacy of the seizure of the trucks or the packages, and they never sought return of the property. Thus, respondents have not even alleged, much less proved, that the delay in the search of packages adversely affected legitimate interests protected by the Fourth Amendment."

search to be reasonable under the Fourth Amendment. If destroying the interior of an automobile is not unreasonable, we cannot conclude that looking inside a closed container is. In light of the minimal protection to privacy afforded by the *Chadwick–Sanders* rule, and our serious doubt whether that rule substantially serves privacy interests, we now hold that the Fourth Amendment does not compel separate treatment for an automobile search that extends only to a container within the vehicle.

The *Chadwick–Sanders* rule not only has failed to protect privacy but it has also confused courts and police officers and impeded effective law enforcement. * * *

The discrepancy between the two rules has led to confusion for law enforcement officers. For example, when an officer, who has developed probable cause to believe that a vehicle contains drugs, begins to search the vehicle and immediately discovers a closed container, which rule applies? The defendant will argue that the fact that the officer first chose to search the container indicates that his probable cause extended only to the container and that *Chadwick* and *Sanders* therefore require a warrant. On the other hand, the fact that the officer first chose to search in the most obvious location should not restrict the propriety of the search. The *Chadwick* rule, as applied in *Sanders,* has developed into an anomaly such that the more likely the police are to discover drugs in a container, the less authority they have to search it. * * *

The interpretation of the *Carroll* doctrine set forth in *Ross* now applies to all searches of containers found in an automobile. In other words, the police may search without a warrant if their search is supported by probable cause. * * * In the case before us, the police had probable cause to believe that the paper bag in the automobile's trunk contained marijuana. That probable cause now allows a warrantless search of the paper bag. The facts in the record reveal that the police did not have probable cause to believe that contraband was hidden in any other part of the automobile and a search of the entire vehicle would have been without probable cause and unreasonable under the Fourth Amendment. * * *

Justice SCALIA, concurring in the judgment.

I agree with the dissent that it is anomalous for a briefcase to be protected by the "general requirement" of a prior warrant when it is being carried along the street, but for that same briefcase to become unprotected as soon as it is carried into an automobile. On the other hand, I agree with the Court that it would be anomalous for a locked compartment in an automobile to be unprotected by the "general requirement" of a prior warrant, but for an unlocked briefcase within the automobile to be protected. I join in the judgment of the Court because I think its holding is more faithful to the text and tradition of the Fourth Amendment, and if these anomalies in our jurisprudence are ever to be eliminated that is the direction in which we should travel. * * *

Although the Fourth Amendment does not explicitly impose the requirement of a warrant, it is of course textually possible to consider that implicit within the requirement of reasonableness. For some years after the (still continuing) explosion in Fourth Amendment litigation that followed our announcement of the exclusionary rule in *Weeks v. United States,* [p. 122], our jurisprudence lurched back and forth between imposing a categorical warrant requirement and looking to reasonableness alone. * * *

The victory was illusory. Even before today's decision, the "warrant requirement" had become so riddled with exceptions that it was basically unrecognizable.

In 1985, one commentator cataloged nearly 20 such exceptions, including "searches incident to arrest ... automobile searches ... border searches ... administrative searches of regulated businesses ... exigent circumstances ... search[es] incident to nonarrest when there is probable cause to arrest ... boat boarding for document checks ... welfare searches ... inventory searches ... airport searches ... school search[es].... " Bradley, *Two Models of the Fourth Amendment*, 83 Mich.L.Rev. 1468, 1473–1474 (1985) (footnotes omitted). Since then, we have added at least two more. *California v. Carney* [p. 275] (searches of mobile homes); *O'Connor v. Ortega* [p. 163] (searches of offices of government employees). Our intricate body of law regarding "reasonable expectation of privacy" has been developed largely as a means of creating these exceptions, enabling a search to be denominated not a Fourth Amendment "search" and therefore not subject to the general warrant requirement.

Unlike the dissent, therefore, I do not regard today's holding as some momentous departure, but rather as merely the continuation of an inconsistent jurisprudence that has been with us for years. There can be no clarity in this area unless we make up our minds, and unless the principles we express comport with the actions we take.

In my view, the path out of this confusion should be sought by returning to the first principle that the "reasonableness" requirement of the Fourth Amendment affords the protection that the common law afforded. I have no difficulty with the proposition that that includes the requirement of a warrant, where the common law required a warrant; and it may even be that changes in the surrounding legal rules (for example, elimination of the common-law rule that reasonable, good-faith belief was no defense to absolute liability for trespass), may make a warrant indispensable to reasonableness where it once was not. But the supposed "general rule" that a warrant is always required does not appear to have any basis in the common law, and confuses rather than facilitates any attempt to develop rules of reasonableness in light of changed legal circumstances, as the anomaly eliminated and the anomaly created by today's holding both demonstrate.

And there are more anomalies still. Under our precedents (as at common law), a person may be arrested outside the home on the basis of probable cause, without an arrest warrant. *United States v. Watson* [p. 221]. Upon arrest, the person, as well as the area within his grasp, may be searched for evidence related to the crime. *Chimel v. California* [p. 253]. Under these principles, if a known drug dealer is carrying a briefcase reasonably believed to contain marijuana (the unauthorized possession of which is a crime), the police may arrest him and search his person on the basis of probable cause alone. And, under our precedents, upon arrival at the station house, the police may inventory his possessions, including the briefcase, even if there is no reason to suspect that they contain contraband. *Illinois v. Lafayette* [p. 247]. According to our current law, however, the police may not, on the basis of the same probable cause, take the less intrusive step of stopping the individual on the street and demanding to see the contents of his briefcase. That makes no sense *a priori,* and in the absence of any common-law tradition supporting such a distinction, I see no reason to continue it.

I would reverse the judgment in the present case, not because a closed container carried inside a car becomes subject to the "automobile" exception to the general warrant requirement, but because the search of a closed container, outside a privately owned building, with probable cause to believe that the container contains contraband, and when it in fact does contain contraband, is not one of those searches whose Fourth Amendment reasonableness depends upon a warrant. For that reason I concur in the judgment of the Court.

Justice WHITE, dissenting.

Agreeing as I do with most of Justice Stevens' opinion and with the result he reaches, I dissent and would affirm the judgment below.

Justice STEVENS, with whom Justice MARSHALL joins, dissenting.

At the end of its opinion, the Court pays lip service to the proposition that should provide the basis for a correct analysis of the legal question presented by this case: It is " 'a cardinal principle that "searches conducted outside the judicial process, without prior approval by judge or magistrate, are *per se* unreasonable under the Fourth Amendment—subject only to a few specifically established and well-delineated exceptions." ' * * * "

[The warrant] requirement * * * reflects the sound policy judgment that, absent exceptional circumstances, the decision to invade the privacy of an individual's personal effects should be made by a neutral magistrate rather than an agent of the Executive. * * *

In *Chadwick,* the Department of Justice had mounted a frontal attack on the warrant requirement. The Government's principal contention was that "the Fourth Amendment Warrant Clause protects only interests traditionally identified with the home." We categorically rejected that contention, relying on the history and text of the amendment, the policy underlying the warrant requirement, and a line of cases spanning over a century of our jurisprudence. We also rejected the Government's alternative argument that the rationale of our automobile search cases demonstrated the reasonableness of permitting warrantless searches of luggage.

We concluded that neither of the justifications for the automobile exception could support a similar exception for luggage. We first held that the privacy interest in luggage is "substantially greater than in an automobile." Unlike automobiles and their contents, we reasoned, "[l]uggage contents are not open to public view, except as a condition to a border entry or common carrier travel; nor is luggage subject to regular inspections and official scrutiny on a continuing basis." Indeed, luggage is specifically intended to safeguard the privacy of personal effects, unlike an automobile, "whose primary function is transportation."

We then held that the mobility of luggage did not justify creating an additional exception to the Warrant Clause. Unlike an automobile, luggage can easily be seized and detained pending judicial approval of a search. Once the police have luggage "under their exclusive control, there [i]s not the slightest danger that the [luggage] or its contents could [be] removed before a valid search warrant could be obtained.... With the [luggage] safely immobilized, it [i]s unreasonable to undertake the additional and greater intrusion of a search without a warrant" (footnote omitted). * * *

[W]e recognized in *Ross* that *Chadwick* and *Sanders* had not created a special rule for container searches, but rather had merely applied the cardinal principle that warrantless searches are per se unreasonable unless justified by an exception to the general rule. *Ross* dealt with the scope of the automobile exception; *Chadwick* and *Sanders* were cases in which the exception simply did not apply.

In its opinion today, the Court recognizes that the police did not have probable cause to search respondent's vehicle and that a search of anything but the paper bag that respondent had carried from Daza's apartment and placed in the trunk of his car would have been unconstitutional. Moreover, as I read the opinion, the Court assumes that the police could not have made a warrantless inspection of the bag before it was placed in the car. Finally, the Court also does not question the fact that, under our prior cases, it would have been lawful for the police to seize the container and detain it (and respondent) until they obtained a search warrant. Thus, all of the relevant facts that governed our decisions in *Chadwick* and *Sanders* are present here whereas the relevant fact that justified the vehicle search in *Ross* is not present.

The Court does not attempt to identify any exigent circumstances that would justify its refusal to apply the general rule against warrantless searches. Instead, it advances these three arguments: First, the rules identified in the foregoing cases are confusing and anomalous. Second, the rules do not protect any significant interest in privacy. And, third, the rules impede effective law enforcement. None of these arguments withstands scrutiny. * * *

The Court summarizes the alleged "anomaly" created by the coexistence of *Ross, Chadwick,* and *Sanders* with the statement that "the more likely the police are to discover drugs in a container, the less authority they have to search it." This juxtaposition is only anomalous, however, if one accepts the flawed premise that the degree to which the police are likely to discover contraband is correlated with their authority to search *without a warrant.* Yet, even proof beyond a reasonable doubt will not justify a warrantless search that is not supported by one of the exceptions to the warrant requirement. And, even when the police have a warrant or an exception applies, once the police possess probable cause, the extent to which they are more or less certain of the contents of a container has no bearing on their authority to search it.

To the extent there was any "anomaly" in our prior jurisprudence, the Court has "cured" it at the expense of creating a more serious paradox. For, surely it is anomalous to prohibit a search of a briefcase while the owner is carrying it exposed on a public street yet to permit a search once the owner has placed the briefcase in the locked trunk of his car. One's privacy interest in one's luggage can certainly not be diminished by one's removing it from a public thoroughfare and placing it—out of sight—in a privately owned vehicle. Nor is the danger that evidence will escape increased if the luggage is in a car rather than on the street. In either location, if the police have probable cause, they are authorized to seize the luggage and to detain it until they obtain judicial approval for a search. Any line demarking an exception to the warrant requirement will appear blurred at the edges, but the Court has certainly erred if it believes that, by erasing one line and drawing another, it has drawn a clearer boundary.

The Court's statement that *Chadwick* and *Sanders* provide only "minimal protection to privacy" is also unpersuasive. Every citizen clearly has an interest in the privacy of the contents of his or her luggage, briefcase, handbag or any other container that conceals private papers and effects from public scrutiny. That privacy interest has been recognized repeatedly in cases spanning more than a century.

Under the Court's holding today, the privacy interest that protects the contents of a suitcase or a briefcase from a warrantless search when it is in public view simply vanishes when its owner climbs into a taxicab. Unquestionably the rejection of the *Sanders* line of cases by today's decision will result in a significant loss of individual privacy.

To support its argument that today's holding works only a minimal intrusion on privacy, the Court suggests that "[i]f the police know that they may open a bag only if they are actually searching the entire car, they may search more extensively than they otherwise would in order to establish the general probable cause required by *Ross*." As I have already noted, this fear is unexplained and inexplicable. Neither evidence uncovered in the course of a search nor the scope of the search conducted can be used to provide *post hoc* justification for a search unsupported by probable cause at its inception.

The Court also justifies its claim that its holding inflicts only minor damage by suggesting that, under *New York v. Belton,* the police could have arrested respondent and searched his bag if respondent had placed the bag in the passenger compartment of the automobile instead of the trunk. In *Belton,* however, the justification for stopping the car and arresting the driver had nothing to do with the subsequent search, which was based on the potential danger to the arresting officer. The holding in *Belton* was supportable under a straightforward application of the automobile exception. I would not extend *Belton's* holding to this case, in which the container—which was protected from a warrantless search before it was placed in the car—provided the only justification for the arrest. Even accepting *Belton's* application to a case like this one, however, the Court's logic extends its holding to a container placed in the *trunk* of a vehicle, rather than in the passenger compartment. And the Court makes this extension without any justification whatsoever other than convenience to law enforcement. * * *

Despite repeated claims that *Chadwick* and *Sanders* have "impeded effective law enforcement," the Court cites no authority for its contentions. * * *

Even if the warrant requirement does inconvenience the police to some extent, that fact does not distinguish this constitutional requirement from any other procedural protection secured by the Bill of Rights. It is merely a part of the price that our society must pay in order to preserve its freedom. * * *

Notes and Questions

1.   Reassess the law and facts of *Chadwick* in light of *Acevedo*. Absent true exigent circumstances, is a search warrant still required for a container having no connection with a vehicle? If so, is there actually a sufficient container-vehicle connection in *Chadwick* to make the *Acevedo* no-warrant rule applicable?

2.   If there *is* a general rule that absent exigent circumstances search warrants are needed for the search of containers not sufficiently connected with vehicles, are there exceptions? Consider:

(a) Fn. 13 in *Sanders:* "Not all containers and packages found by police during the course of a search will deserve the full protection of the Fourth Amendment. Thus, some containers (for example a kit of burglar tools or a gun case) by their very nature cannot support any reasonable expectation of privacy because their contents can be inferred from their outward appearance. Similarly, in some cases the contents of a package will be open to 'plain view,' thereby obviating the need for a warrant."

(b) In *Texas v. Brown,* 460 U.S. 730, 103 S.Ct. 1535, 75 L.Ed.2d 502 (1983), involving a warrantless search of a knotted opaque party balloon found with several plastic vials, a quantity of loose white powder, and a bag of balloons, Stevens, J., for three members of the Court, after characterizing the plurality's explanation for why no search warrant was needed to search the balloon as "incomplete," speculated that the balloon "could be one of those rare single-purpose containers which 'by their very nature cannot support any reasonable expectation of privacy because their contents can be inferred from their outward appearance.' Whereas a suitcase or a paper bag may contain an almost infinite variety of items, a balloon of this kind might be used only to transport drugs. Viewing it where he did could have given the officer a degree of certainty that is equivalent to the plain view of the heroin itself. If that be true, I would conclude that the plain view doctrine supports the search as well as the seizure even though the contents of the balloon were not actually visible to the officer.

"This reasoning leads me to the conclusion that the Fourth Amendment would not require exclusion of the balloon's contents in this case if, but only if, there was probable cause to search the entire vehicle or there was virtual certainty that the balloon contained a controlled substance.[5]"

(c) After customs agents found marijuana inside a table shipped into the country, it was repackaged and delivered to defendant by police posing as delivery men. Surveilling police saw defendant pull the container into his apartment, and when he reemerged with it 30 to 45 minutes later he was arrested and the package searched without a warrant. The state court, relying upon *Sanders* and *Chadwick,* held the marijuana inadmissible, but the Supreme Court, in ILLINOIS v. ANDREAS, 463 U.S. 765, 103 S.Ct. 3319, 77 L.Ed.2d 1003 (1983), disagreed. The Court, per BURGER, C.J., first addressed the threshold question of "whether an individual has a legitimate expectation of privacy in the contents of a previously lawfully searched container. It is obvious that the privacy interest in the contents of a container diminishes with respect to a container that law enforcement authorities have already lawfully opened and found to contain illicit drugs. No protected privacy interest remains in contraband in a container once government officers lawfully have opened that container and identified its contents as illegal. The simple act of resealing the container to enable the police to make a controlled delivery does not operate to revive or restore the lawfully invaded privacy rights.

"This conclusion is supported by the reasoning underlying the 'plain view' doctrine. The plain view doctrine authorizes seizure of illegal or evidentiary items visible to a police officer whose access to the object has some prior Fourth Amendment justification and who has probable cause to suspect that the item is connected with criminal activity. The plain view doctrine is grounded on the proposition that once police are lawfully in a position to observe an item firsthand, its owner's privacy interest in that item is lost; the owner may retain the incidents of title and possession but not privacy. That rationale applies here; once a container has been found to a certainty to contain illicit drugs, the contraband becomes like objects physically within the plain view of the police, and the claim to privacy is lost. Consequently the subsequent opening is not a 'search' within the intendment of the Fourth Amendment."

The Court then noted that "perfect" controlled deliveries are often impossible, so that there may result "a gap in surveillance" during which "it is possible that the container will be put to other uses—for example, the contraband may be removed or other items may be placed inside." On the resulting question of "at what point after an interruption of control or surveillance, courts should recognize the individual's expectation of privacy in the container as a legitimate right protected by the Fourth Amendment," the Court adopted the "workable," "reasonable" and "objective" standard of "whether there is a substantial likelihood

---

5. Sometimes there can be greater certainty about the identity of a substance within a container than about the identity of a substance that is actually visible. One might actually see a white powder without realizing that it is heroin, but be virtually certain a balloon contains such a substance in a particular context. It seems to me that in evaluating whether a person's privacy interests are infringed, "virtual certainty" is a more meaningful indicator than visibility.

that the contents of the container have been changed during the gap in surveillance. We hold that absent a substantial likelihood that the contents have been changed, there is no legitimate expectation of privacy in the contents of a container previously opened under lawful authority." The Court then concluded there was no substantial likelihood in the instant case. "The unusual size of the container, its specialized purpose, and the relatively short break in surveillance, combine to make it substantially unlikely that the respondent removed the table or placed new items inside the container while it was in his apartment."

BRENNAN and Marshall, JJ., dissenting, objected that while after the customs search "any reasonable expectation respondent may have had that the existence of the contraband would remain secret was lost, and could not be regained," he still had a Fourth Amendment right "to be 'let alone' " which "is, at the very least, the right not to have one's repose and possessions disturbed" without a warrant. Moreover, "if a person has no reasonable expectation of privacy in a package whose contents are already legally known to the authorities, a reasonable expectation of privacy should reattach if the person has unobserved access to the package and any opportunity to change its contents." STEVENS, J., dissenting separately, would remand for reconsideration under his "virtual certainty" test in *Texas v. Brown.*

NEW YORK v. BELTON
453 U.S. 454, 101 S.Ct. 2860, 69 L.Ed.2d 768 (1981).

Justice STEWART delivered the opinion of the Court. * * *

On April 9, 1978, Trooper Douglas Nicot, a New York State policeman driving an unmarked car on the New York Thruway, was passed by another automobile travelling at an excessive rate of speed. Nicot gave chase, overtook the speeding vehicle, and ordered its driver to pull it over to the side of the road and stop. There were four men in the car, one of whom was Roger Belton, the respondent in this case. The policeman asked to see the driver's license and automobile registration, and discovered that none of the men owned the vehicle or was related to its owner. Meanwhile, the policeman had smelled burnt marihuana and had seen on the floor of the car an envelope marked "Supergold" that he associated with marihuana. He therefore directed the men to get out of the car, and placed them under arrest for the unlawful possession of marihuana. He patted down each of the men and "split them up into four separate areas of the Thruway at this time so they would not be in physical touching area of each other." He then picked up the envelope marked "Supergold" and found that it contained marihuana. After giving the arrestees the warnings required by *Miranda v. Arizona,* the state policeman searched each one of them. He then searched the passenger compartment of the car. On the back seat he found a black leather jacket belonging to Belton. He unzipped one of the pockets of the jacket and discovered cocaine. Placing the jacket in his automobile, he drove the four arrestees to a nearby police station.

Belton was subsequently indicted for criminal possession of a controlled substance. In the trial court he moved that the cocaine the trooper had seized from the jacket pocket be suppressed. The court denied the motion. Belton then pleaded guilty to a lesser included offense, but preserved his claim that the cocaine had been seized in violation of the Fourth and Fourteenth Amendments. The Appellate Division of the New York Supreme Court upheld the constitutionality of the search and seizure, reasoning that "[o]nce defendant was validly arrested for possession of marihuana, the officer was justified in searching the immediate area for other contraband."

The New York Court of Appeals reversed, holding that "[a] warrantless search of the zippered pockets of an unaccessible jacket may not be upheld as a search incident to a lawful arrest where there is no longer any danger that the arrestee or a confederate might gain access to the article." * * *

It is a first principle of Fourth Amendment jurisprudence that the police may not conduct a search unless they first convince a neutral magistrate that there is probable cause to do so. This Court has recognized, however, that "the exigencies of the situation" may sometimes make exemption from the warrant requirement "imperative." Specifically, the Court held in *Chimel v. California* [p. 253], that a lawful custodial arrest creates a situation which justifies the contemporaneous search without a warrant of the person arrested and of the immediately surrounding area. Such searches have long been considered valid because of the need "to remove any weapons that [the arrestee] might seek to use in order to resist arrest or effect his escape" and the need to prevent the concealment or destruction of evidence.

The Court's opinion in *Chimel* emphasized the principle that, "The scope of [a] search must be 'strictly tied to and justified by' the circumstances which rendered its initiation permissible." Thus while the Court in *Chimel* found "ample justification" for a search of "the area from within which [an arrestee] might gain possession of a weapon or destructible evidence," the Court found "no comparable justification * * * for routinely searching any room other than that in which an arrest occurs—or, for that matter, for searching through all the desk drawers or other closed or concealed areas in that room itself."

Although the principle that limits a search incident to a lawful custodial arrest may be stated clearly enough, courts have discovered the principle difficult to apply in specific cases. Yet, as one commentator has pointed out, the protection of the Fourth and Fourteenth Amendments "can only be realized if the police are acting under a set of rules which, in most instances, makes it possible to reach a correct determination beforehand as to whether an invasion of privacy is justified in the interest of law enforcement." LaFave, *"Case-by-Case Adjudication" versus "Standardized Procedures": The Robinson Dilemma*, 1974 Sup.Ct.Rev. 127, 142. This is because

> "Fourth Amendment doctrine, given force and effect by the exclusionary rule, is primarily intended to regulate the police in their day-to-day activities and thus ought to be expressed in terms that are readily applicable by the police in the context of the law enforcement activities in which they are necessarily engaged. A highly sophisticated set of rules, qualified by all sorts of ifs, ands, and buts and requiring the drawing of subtle nuances and hairline distinctions, may be the sort of heady stuff upon which the facile minds of lawyers and judges eagerly feed, but they may be 'literally impossible of application by the officer in the field.' "Id., at 141.

In short, "A single, familiar standard is essential to guide police officers, who have only limited time and expertise to reflect on and balance the social and individual interests involved in the specific circumstances they confront." *Dunaway v. New York* [p. 337].

So it was that, in *United States v. Robinson* [p. 232], the Court hewed to a straightforward rule, easily applied, and predictably enforced: "[I]n the case of a lawful custodial arrest a full search of the person is not only an exception to the warrant requirement, but it is also a 'reasonable' search under that amendment." In so holding, the Court rejected the suggestion "that there must be litigated in each case the issue of whether or not there was present one of the reasons supporting the authority for a search of the person incident to a lawful arrest."

But no straightforward rule has emerged from the litigated cases respecting the question involved here—the question of the proper scope of a search of the interior of an automobile incident to a lawful custodial arrest of its occupants. The difficulty courts have had is reflected in the conflicting views of the New York judges who dealt with the problem in the present case, and is confirmed by a look at even a small sample drawn from the narrow class of cases in which courts have decided whether, in the course of a search incident to the lawful custodial arrest of the occupants of an automobile, police may search inside the automobile after the arrestees are no longer in it. * * *

When a person cannot know how a court will apply a settled principle to a recurring factual situation, that person cannot know the scope of his constitutional protection, nor can a policeman know the scope of his authority. While the *Chimel* case established that a search incident to an arrest may not stray beyond the area within the immediate control of the arrestee, courts have found no workable definition of "the area within the immediate control of the arrestee" when that area arguably includes the interior of an automobile and the arrestee is its recent occupant. Our reading of the cases suggests the generalization that articles inside the relatively narrow compass of the passenger compartment of an automobile are in fact generally, even if not inevitably, within "the area into which an arrestee might reach in order to grab a weapon or evidentiary item." In order to establish the workable rule this category of cases requires, we read *Chimel* 's definition of the limits of the area that may be searched in light of that generalization. Accordingly, we hold that when a policeman has made a lawful custodial arrest of the occupant of an automobile, he may, as a contemporaneous incident of that arrest, search the passenger compartment of that automobile.[3]

It follows from this conclusion that the police may also examine the contents of any containers found within the passenger compartment, for if the passenger compartment is within reach of the arrestee, so also will containers in it be within his reach.[4] Such a container may, of course, be searched whether it is open or closed, since the justification for the search is not that the arrestee has no privacy interest in the container, but that the lawful custodial arrest justifies the infringement of any privacy interest the arrestee may have. Thus, while the Court in *Chimel* held that the police could not search all the drawers in an arrestee's house simply because the police had arrested him at home, the Court noted that drawers within an arrestee's reach could be searched because of the danger their contents might pose to the police.

It is true, of course, that these containers will sometimes be such that they could hold neither a weapon nor evidence of the criminal conduct for which the suspect was arrested. However, in *United States v. Robinson,* the Court rejected

---

3. Our holding today does no more than determine the meaning of *Chimel*'s principles in this particular and problematic content. It in no way alters the fundamental principles established in the *Chimel* case regarding the basic scope of searches incident to lawful custodial arrests.

4. "Container" here denotes any object capable of holding another object. It thus in-

cludes closed or open glove compartments, consoles, or other receptacles located anywhere within the passenger compartment, as well as luggage, boxes, bags, clothing, and the like. Our holding encompasses only the interior of the passenger compartment of an automobile and does not encompass the trunk.

the argument that such a container—there a "crumpled up cigarette package"—
located during a search of Robinson incident to his arrest could not be searched:
"The authority to search the person incident to a lawful custodial arrest, while
based upon the need to disarm and to discover evidence, does not depend on what
a court may later decide was the probability in a particular arrest situation that
weapons or evidence would in fact be found upon the person of the suspect. A
custodial arrest of a suspect based on probable cause is a reasonable intrusion
under the Fourth Amendment; that intrusion being lawful, a search incident to
the arrest requires no additional justification." * * *

It is not questioned that the respondent was the subject of a lawful custodial
arrest on a charge of possessing marihuana. The search of the respondent's jacket
followed immediately upon that arrest. The jacket was located inside the passenger compartment of the car in which the respondent had been a passenger just
before he was arrested. The jacket was thus within the area which we have
concluded was "within the arrestee's immediate control" within the meaning of
the *Chimel* case.[6] The search of the jacket, therefore, was a search incident to a
lawful custodial arrest, and it did not violate the Fourth and Fourteenth Amendments. Accordingly, the judgment is reversed.

Justice REHNQUIST, concurring.

Because it is apparent that a majority of the Court is unwilling to overrule
Mapp v. Ohio, and because the Court does not find it necessary to consider the
"automobile exception" in its disposition of this case, I join the opinion of the
Court.

Justice STEVENS, concurring in the judgment.

For the reasons stated in my dissenting opinion in *Robbins v. California,* I
agree [that] this judgment should be reversed. [That opinion follows.—ed.]

The Court's careful and repeated use of the term "lawful custodial arrest"
seems to imply that a significant distinction between custodial arrests and
ordinary arrests exists. I am familiar with the distinction between a "stop," see,
e.g., *Terry v. Ohio,* [p. 304], and an "arrest," but I am not familiar with any
difference between custodial arrests and any other kind of arrest.[a] It is, of course,
true that persons apprehended for traffic violations are frequently not required to
accompany the arresting officer to the police station before they are permitted to
leave on their own recognizance or by using their driver's licenses as a form of
bond. It is also possible that state law or local regulations may in some cases
forbid police officers from taking persons into custody for violation of minor traffic
laws. As a matter of constitutional law, however, any person lawfully arrested for
the pettiest misdemeanor may be temporarily placed in custody.[11] Indeed, as the

---

6. Because of this disposition of the case,
there is no need here to consider whether the
search and seizure were permissible under the
so-called "automobile exception."

a. Consider in this regard the search-of-
vehicle-incident-to-citation case of *Knowles v.
Iowa,* p. 251.

11. Justice Stewart apparently believes
that the Fourth and Fourteenth Amendments
might provide some impediment to police taking a defendant into custody for violation of a
"minor traffic offense." See *Gustafson v. Florida* (Stewart, J. concurring). Although I agree
that a police officer's authority to restrain an

individual's liberty should be limited in the
context of stops for routine traffic violations,
the Court has not directly considered the question whether "there are constitutional limits
upon the use of 'custodial arrests' as the
means for invoking the criminal process when
relatively minor offenses are involved." See 2
W. LaFave, *Search and Seizure* § 5.2, p. 290
(1978); see also id. § 5.1, p. 256–260, § 5.2, p.
281–291. To the extent that the Court has
considered the scope of an officer's authority in
making routine traffic stops, the Court has not
imposed constitutional restrictions on that authority. Thus the Court may be assuming that

Court has repeatedly held, every arrest is a seizure of the person within the meaning of the Fourth Amendment. The rule of constitutional law the Court fashions today therefore potentially applies to every arrest of every occupant of an automobile.[12]

After the vehicle in which respondent was riding was stopped, the officer smelled marihuana and thereby acquired probable cause to believe that the vehicle contained contraband. A thorough search of the car was therefore reasonable. But if there were no reason to believe that anything more than a traffic violation had occurred, I should think it palpably unreasonable to require the driver of a car to open his briefcase or his luggage for inspection by the officer. The driver so compelled, however, could make no constitutional objection to a decision by the officer to take the driver into custody and thereby obtain justification for a search of the entire interior of the vehicle. Indeed, under the Court's new rule, the arresting officer may find reason to follow that procedure whenever he sees an interesting looking briefcase or package in a vehicle that has been stopped for a traffic violation. That decision by a police officer will therefore provide the constitutional predicate for broader vehicle searches than any neutral magistrate could authorize by issuing a warrant. * * *

Justice BRENNAN, with whom Justice MARSHALL joins, dissenting.

* * *

By approving the constitutionality of the warrantless search in this case, the Court carves out a dangerous precedent that is not justified by the concerns underlying *Chimel*. Disregarding the principle "that the scope of a warrantless search must be commensurate with the rationale that excepts the search from the warrant requirement," the Court for the first time grants police officers authority to conduct a warrantless "area" search under circumstances where there is no chance that the arrestee "might gain possession of a weapon or destructible evidence." Under the approach taken today, the result would presumably be the same even if Officer Nicot had handcuffed Belton and his companions in the patrol car before placing them under arrest, and even if his search had extended to locked luggage or other inaccessible containers located in the back seat of the car. * * *

The Court seeks to justify its departure from the principles underlying *Chimel* by proclaiming the need for a new bright line rule to guide the officer in the field. As we pointed out in *Mincey v. Arizona,* [p. 265], however, "the mere fact that law enforcement may be made more efficient can never by itself justify disregard of the Fourth Amendment." Moreover, the Court's attempt to forge a "bright line" rule fails on its own terms. * * * The Court's new approach leaves open too many questions and, more important, it provides the police and the courts with too few tools with which to find the answers.

its new rule will be limited by a constitutional restriction that does not exist.

12. After today, the driver of a vehicle stopped for a minor traffic violation must look to state law for protection from unreasonable searches. Such protection may come from two sources. Statutory law may provide some protection. Legislatures in some states permit officers to take traffic violators into custody only for certain violations. In some states, however, the police officer has the discretion to make a "custodial arrest" for violation of any motor vehicle law. Additionally, the failure to produce a satisfactory bond will often justify "detention and custodial arrest." Given the incomplete protection afforded by statutory law, drivers in many States will have to persuade state supreme courts to interpret their state constitution's equivalent to the Fourth Amendment to prohibit the unreasonable searches permitted by the Court here.

Thus, although the Court concludes that a warrantless search of a car may take place even though the suspect was arrested outside the car, it does not indicate how long after the suspect's arrest that search may validly be conducted. Would a warrantless search incident to arrest be valid if conducted five minutes after the suspect left his car? Thirty minutes? Three hours? Does it matter whether the suspect is standing in close proximity to the car when the search is conducted? Does it matter whether the police formed probable cause to arrest before or after the suspect left his car? And *why* is the rule announced today necessarily limited to searches of cars? What if a suspect is seen walking out of a house where the police, peering in from outside, had formed probable cause to believe a crime was being committed? Could the police then arrest that suspect and enter the house to conduct a search incident to arrest? Even assuming today's rule is limited to searches of the "interior" of cars—an assumption not demanded by logic—what is meant by "interior"? Does it include locked glove compartments, the interior of door panels, or the area under the floorboards? Are special rules necessary for station wagons and hatchbacks, where the luggage compartment may be reached through the interior, or taxicabs, where a glass panel might separate the driver's compartment from the rest of the car? Are the only containers that may be searched those that are large enough to be "capable of holding another object"? Or does the new rule apply to any container, even if it "could hold neither a weapon nor evidence of the criminal conduct for which the suspect was arrested"?

The Court does not give the police any "bright line" answers to these questions. More important, because the Court's new rule abandons the justifications underlying *Chimel, it offers no guidance to the police officer seeking to work out these answers for himself.* * * *

The standard announced in *Chimel* is not nearly as difficult to apply as the Court suggests. To the contrary, I continue to believe that *Chimel* provides a sound, workable rule for determining the constitutionality of a warrantless search incident to arrest. Under *Chimel,* searches incident to arrest may be conducted without a warrant only if limited to the person of the arrestee, or to the area within the arrestee's "immediate control." While it may be difficult in some cases to measure the exact scope of the arrestee's immediate control, relevant factors would surely include the relative number of police officers and arrestees, the manner of restraint placed on the arrestee, and the ability of the arrestee to gain access to a particular area or container.[5] Certainly there will be some close cases, but when in doubt the police can always turn to the rationale underlying *Chimel*—the need to prevent the arrestee from reaching weapons or contraband—before exercising their judgment. A rule based on that rationale should provide more guidance than the rule announced by the Court today. Moreover, unlike the Court's rule, it would be faithful to the Fourth Amendment.

Justice WHITE, with whom Justice MARSHALL joins, dissenting.

---

5. The Court sets up a straw man when it claims that under the "exclusive control" approach taken by the Court of Appeals, "no search or seizure incident to a lawful custodial arrest would ever be valid; by seizing an article even on the arrestee's person, an officer may be said to have reduced that article to his 'exclusive control.'"

If a police officer could obtain exclusive control of an article by simply holding it in his hand, I would certainly agree with the Court.

But as we recognized in *United States v. Chadwick,* exclusive control means more than that. It means sufficient control such that there is no significant risk that the arrestee or his confederates "might gain possession of a weapon or destructible evidence." *Chimel v. California.* The issue of exclusive control presents a question of fact to be decided under the circumstances of each case, just as the New York Court of Appeals has decided it here.

* * * The Court now holds that as incident to the arrest of the driver or any other person in an automobile, the interior of the car and any container found therein, whether locked or not, may not only be seized but also searched even absent probable cause to believe that contraband or evidence of crime will be found. As to luggage, briefcases or other containers, this seems to me an extreme extension of *Chimel* and one to which I cannot subscribe. * * *[a]

COLORADO v. BERTINE
479 U.S. 367, 107 S.Ct. 738, 93 L.Ed.2d 739 (1987).

Chief Justice REHNQUIST delivered the opinion of the Court.

On February 10, 1984, a police officer in Boulder, Colorado arrested respondent Steven Lee Bertine for driving while under the influence of alcohol. After Bertine was taken into custody and before the arrival of a tow truck to take Bertine's van to an impoundment lot,[1] a backup officer inventoried the contents of the van. The officer opened a closed backpack in which he found controlled substances, cocaine paraphernalia, and a large amount of cash. Bertine was subsequently charged with driving while under the influence of alcohol, unlawful possession of cocaine with intent to dispense, sell, and distribute, and unlawful possession of methaqualone. We are asked to decide whether the Fourth Amendment prohibits the State from proving these charges with the evidence discovered during the inventory of Bertine's van. We hold that it does not. * * *

After Bertine was charged with the offenses described above, he moved to suppress the evidence found during the inventory search on the ground, *inter alia,* that the search of the closed backpack and containers [therein] exceeded the permissible scope of such a search under the Fourth Amendment. The Colorado trial court * * * determined that the inventory search did not violate Bertine's rights under the Fourth Amendment of the United States Constitution. The court, nevertheless, granted Bertine's motion to suppress, holding that the inventory search violated the Colorado Constitution.

On the State's interlocutory appeal, the Supreme Court of Colorado affirmed. In contrast to the District Court, however, the Colorado Supreme Court premised its ruling on the United States Constitution. The court recognized that in *South Dakota v. Opperman,* 428 U.S. 364, 96 S.Ct. 3092, 49 L.Ed.2d 1000 (1976), we had held inventory searches of automobiles to be consistent with the Fourth Amendment, and that in *Illinois v. Lafayette,* [p. 247], we had held that the inventory search of personal effects of an arrestee at a police station was also permissible under that Amendment. The Supreme Court of Colorado felt, however, that our decisions in *Arkansas v. Sanders,* [p. 282], and *United States v. Chadwick,* [p. 281], holding searches of closed trunks and suitcases to violate the Fourth Amendment, meant that *Opperman* and *Lafayette* did not govern this case.

a. For close analyses of *Belton,* see Joseph D. Grano, *Rethinking the Fourth Amendment Warrant Requirement,* 19 Am.Crim.L.Rev. 603 (1982); Lewis R. Katz, *Automobile Searches and Diminished Expectations in the Warrant Clause,* 19 Am.Crim.L.Rev. 557 (1982); David S. Rudstein, *The Search of an Automobile Incident to an Arrest: An Analysis of New York v. Belton,* 67 Marq.L.Rev. 205 (1984).

1. Section 7–7–2(a)(4) of the Boulder Revised Code authorizes police officers to im-

pound vehicles when drivers are taken into custody. Section 7–7–2(a)(4) provides:

"A peace officer is authorized to remove or cause to be removed a vehicle from any street, parking lot, or driveway when:

. . .

(4) The driver of a vehicle is taken into custody by the police department." Boulder Rev.Code § 7–7–2(a)(4) (1981).

[I]nventory searches are now a well-defined exception to the warrant requirement of the Fourth Amendment. The policies behind the warrant requirement are not implicated in an inventory search, nor is the related concept of probable cause:

> "The standard of probable cause is peculiarly related to criminal investigations, not routine, noncriminal procedures.... The probable-cause approach is unhelpful when analysis centers upon the reasonableness of routine administrative caretaking functions, particularly when no claim is made that the protective procedures are a subterfuge for criminal investigations."

For these reasons, the Colorado Supreme Court's reliance on *Arkansas v. Sanders* and *United States v. Chadwick* was incorrect. Both of these cases concerned searches solely for the purpose of investigating criminal conduct, with the validity of the searches therefore dependent on the application of the probable cause and warrant requirements of the Fourth Amendment.

By contrast, an inventory search may be "reasonable" under the Fourth Amendment even though it is not conducted pursuant to warrant based upon probable cause. In *Opperman,* this Court assessed the reasonableness of an inventory search of the glove compartment in an abandoned automobile impounded by the police. We found that inventory procedures serve to protect an owner's property while it is in the custody of the police, to insure against claims of lost, stolen, or vandalized property, and to guard the police from danger. In light of these strong governmental interests and the diminished expectation of privacy in an automobile, we upheld the search. In reaching this decision, we observed that our cases accorded deference to police caretaking procedures designed to secure and protect vehicles and their contents within police custody.

In our more recent decision, *Lafayette,* a police officer conducted an inventory search of the contents of a shoulder bag in the possession of an individual being taken into custody. In deciding whether this search was reasonable, we recognized that the search served legitimate governmental interests similar to those identified in *Opperman.* We determined that those interests outweighed the individual's Fourth Amendment interests and upheld the search.

In the present case, as in *Opperman* and *Lafayette,* there was no showing that the police, who were following standardized procedures, acted in bad faith or for the sole purpose of investigation. In addition, the governmental interests justifying the inventory searches in *Opperman* and *Lafayette* are nearly the same as those which obtain here. In each case, the police were potentially responsible for the property taken into their custody. By securing the property, the police protected the property from unauthorized interference. Knowledge of the precise nature of the property helped guard against claims of theft, vandalism, or negligence. Such knowledge also helped to avert any danger to police or others that may have been posed by the property.[5]

The Supreme Court of Colorado opined that *Lafayette* was not controlling here because there was no danger of introducing contraband or weapons into a jail facility. Our opinion in *Lafayette,* however, did not suggest that the station-house setting of the inventory search was critical to our holding in that case. Both in the

---

5. In arguing that the latter two interests are not implicated here, the dissent overlooks the testimony of the back-up officer who conducted the inventory of Bertine's van. According to the officer, the vehicle inventory procedures of the Boulder Police Department are designed for the "[p]rotection of the police department" in the event that an individual later claims that "there was something of value taken from within the vehicle." The officer added that inventories are also conducted in order to check "[f]or any dangerous items such as explosives [or] weapons." The officer testified that he had found such items in vehicles.

present case and in *Lafayette*, the common governmental interests described above were served by the inventory searches.

The Supreme Court of Colorado also expressed the view that the search in this case was unreasonable because Bertine's van was towed to a secure, lighted facility and because Bertine himself could have been offered the opportunity to make other arrangements for the safekeeping of his property. But the security of the storage facility does not completely eliminate the need for inventorying; the police may still wish to protect themselves or the owners of the lot against false claims of theft or dangerous instrumentalities. And while giving Bertine an opportunity to make alternate arrangements would undoubtedly have been possible, we said in *Lafayette:*

> "[t]he real question is not what 'could have been achieved,' but whether the Fourth Amendment *requires* such steps ... The reasonableness of any particular governmental activity does not necessarily or invariably turn on the existence of alternative 'less intrusive' means."

We conclude that here, as in *Lafayette*, reasonable police regulations relating to inventory procedures administered in good faith satisfy the Fourth Amendment, even though courts might as a matter of hindsight be able to devise equally reasonable rules requiring a different procedure.[6]

The Supreme Court of Colorado also thought it necessary to require that police, before inventorying a container, weigh the strength of the individual's privacy interest in the container against the possibility that the container might serve as a repository for dangerous or valuable items. We think that such a requirement is contrary to our decisions in *Opperman* and *Lafayette:*

> "Even if less intrusive means existed of protecting some particular types of property, it would be unreasonable to expect police officers in the everyday course of business to make fine and subtle distinctions in deciding which containers or items may be searched and which must be sealed as a unit."
> *Lafayette*, supra.

Bertine finally argues that the inventory search of his van was unconstitutional because departmental regulations gave the police officers discretion to choose between impounding his van and parking and locking it in a public parking place. The Supreme Court of Colorado did not rely on this argument in reaching its conclusion, and we reject it. Nothing in *Opperman* or *Lafayette* prohibits the exercise of police discretion so long as that discretion is exercised according to standard criteria and on the basis of something other than suspicion of evidence of criminal activity. Here, the discretion afforded the Boulder police was exercised in light of standardized criteria, related to the feasibility and appropriateness of parking and locking a vehicle rather than impounding it.[7] There was no showing

---

6. We emphasize that, in this case, the trial court found that the police department's procedures mandated the opening of closed containers and the listing of their contents. Our decisions have always adhered to the requirement that inventories be conducted according to standardized criteria.

By quoting a portion of the Colorado Supreme Court's decision out of context, the dissent suggests that the inventory here was not authorized by the standard procedures of the Boulder Police Department. Yet that court specifically stated that the procedure followed here was "officially authorized." In addition, the court did not disturb the trial court's finding that the police procedures for impounding vehicles required a detailed inventory of Bertine's van.

7. In arguing that the Boulder Police Department procedures set forth no standardized criteria guiding an officer's decision to impound a vehicle, the dissent selectively quotes from the police directive concerning the care and security of vehicles taken into police custody. The dissent fails to mention that the directive establishes several conditions that must that the police chose to impound Bertine's van in order to investigate suspected criminal activity. * * *

Reversed.

Justice BLACKMUN, with whom Justice POWELL and Justice O'CONNOR join, concurring. * * * I join the Court's opinion, but write separately to underscore [that] it is permissible for police officers to open closed containers in an inventory search only if they are following standard police procedures that mandate the opening of such containers in every impounded vehicle. * * *

Justice MARSHALL, with whom Justice BRENNAN joins, dissenting. * * *

As the Court acknowledges, inventory searches are reasonable only if conducted according to standardized procedures. In both *Opperman* and *Lafayette,* the Court relied on the absence of police discretion in determining that the inventory searches in question were reasonable. * * *

The Court today attempts to evade these clear prohibitions on unfettered police discretion by declaring that "the discretion afforded the Boulder police was exercised in light of standardized criteria, related to the feasibility and appropriateness of parking and locking a vehicle rather than impounding it." This vital assertion is flatly contradicted by the record in this case. The officer who conducted the inventory, Officer Reichenbach, testified at the suppression hearing that the decision not to "park and lock" respondent's vehicle was his "own individual discretionary decision." Indeed, application of these supposedly standardized "criteria" upon which the Court so heavily relies would have yielded a different result in this case. Since there was ample public parking adjacent to the intersection where respondent was stopped, consideration of "feasibility" would certainly have militated in favor of the "park and lock" option, not against it. I do not comprehend how consideration of "appropriateness" serves to channel a field officer's discretion; nonetheless, the "park and lock" option would seem particularly appropriate in this case, where respondent was stopped for a traffic offense and was not likely to be in custody for a significant length of time.

Indeed, the record indicates that *no* standardized criteria limit a Boulder police officer's discretion. According to a departmental directive,[1] after placing a driver under arrest, an officer has three options for disposing of the vehicle. First, he can allow a third party to take custody. Second, the officer or the driver (depending on the nature of the arrest) may take the car to the nearest public parking facility, lock it, and take the keys.[3] Finally, the officer can do what was

be met before an officer may pursue the park and lock alternative. For example, police may not park and lock the vehicle where there is reasonable risk of damage or vandalism to the vehicle or where the approval of the arrestee cannot be obtained. Not only do such conditions circumscribe the discretion of individual officers, but they also protect the vehicle and its contents and minimize claims of property loss.

1. Subsections 7–7–2(a)(1) and 7–7–2(a)(4) of the Boulder Revised Code authorize police to impound a vehicle if the driver is taken into custody or if the vehicle obstructs traffic. A departmental directive authorizes inventory searches of impounded vehicles. See General Procedure issued from the office of the Chief of Police, Boulder Police Department, concerning Motor Vehicle Impounds, effective September 7, 1977.

3. If the vehicle and its contents are not evidence of a crime and the owner consents, § III of the General Procedure provides, in relevant part:

"A. Upon placing the operator of a motor vehicle in custody, Officers *may* take the following steps in securing the arrestee's vehicle and property ...:

. . .

"4. The Officer shall drive the vehicle off the roadway and legally park the vehicle in the nearest PUBLIC parking area. The date, time, and location where the vehicle is parked shall be indicated on the IMPOUND FORM.

done in this case: impound the vehicle, and search and inventory its contents, including closed containers.[4]

Under the first option, the police have no occasion to search the automobile. Under the "park and lock" option, "[c]losed containers that give no indication of containing either valuables or a weapon *may not be opened and the contents searched* (i.e., inventoried)." Only if the police choose the third option are they entitled to search closed containers in the vehicle. Where the vehicle is not itself evidence of a crime, as in this case, the police apparently have totally unbridled discretion as to which procedure to use. Consistent with this conclusion, Officer Reichenbach testified that such decisions were left to the discretion of the officer on the scene.

Once a Boulder police officer has made this initial completely discretionary decision to impound a vehicle, he is given little guidance as to which areas to search and what sort of items to inventory. The arresting officer, Officer Toporek, testified at the suppression hearing as to what items would be inventoried: "That would I think be very individualistic as far as what an officer may or may not go into. I think whatever arouses his suspicious [*sic*] as far as what may be contained in any type of article in the car." In application, these so-called procedures left the breadth of the "inventory" to the whim of the individual officer. Clearly, "[t]he practical effect of this system is to leave the [owner] subject to the discretion of the official in the field."

Inventory searches are not subject to the warrant requirement because they are conducted by the government as part of "community caretaking" function, "totally divorced from the detection, investigation, or acquisition of evidence relating to the violation of a criminal statute." Standardized procedures are necessary to ensure that this narrow exception is not improperly used to justify, after the fact, a warrantless investigative foray. Accordingly, to invalidate a search that is conducted without established procedures, it is not necessary to establish that the police actually acted in bad faith, or that the inventory was in fact a "pretext." By allowing the police unfettered discretion, Boulder's discretionary scheme is unreasonable because of the " 'grave danger' of abuse of discretion."

In *South Dakota v. Opperman,* and *Illinois v. Lafayette,* both of which involved inventories conducted pursuant to standardized procedures, we balanced the individual's expectation of privacy against the government's interests to determine whether the search was reasonable. Even if the search in this case did

"5. The Officer shall remove the ignition keys, and lock all doors of the vehicle.

"6. During the booking process, the arrestee shall be given a continuation form for his signature which indicates the location of his vehicle. One copy of the continuation form is to be retained in the case file." (emphasis added).

4. Section II(A) of the General Procedure establishes the following impoundment procedures:

"1. If the vehicle or its contents have been used in the commission of a crime or are themselves the fruit of a crime, the Officer shall conduct a detailed vehicle inspection and inventory and record it upon the VEHICLE IMPOUND FORM.

"2. Personal items of value should be removed from the vehicle and subsequently placed into Property for safekeeping.

"3. The Officer shall request a Tow Truck, and upon its arrival have the Tow Truck operatory sign the IMPOUND FORM, keeping one copy in his possession, before the Officer releases the vehicle for impoundment in the City of Boulder impoundment facility."

Subsection (B) of the directive provides that this procedure is also to be followed when a vehicle involved in a traffic accident is to be held for evidentiary purposes.

constitute a legitimate inventory, it would nonetheless be unreasonable under this analysis.

The Court greatly overstates the justifications for the inventory exception to the Fourth Amendment. Chief Justice Burger, writing for a plurality in *Opperman,* relied on three governmental interests to justify the inventory search of an unlocked glove compartment in an automobile impounded for overtime parking: (i) "the protection of the owner's property while it remains in police custody"; (ii) "the protection of the police against claims or disputes over lost or stolen property"; and (iii) "the protection of the police from potential danger." The majority finds that "nearly the same" interests obtain in this case. As Justice Powell's concurring opinion in *Opperman* reveals, however, only the first of these interests is actually served by an automobile inventory search.

The protection-against-claims interest did not justify the inventory search either in *Opperman* or in this case. As the majority apparently concedes, the use of secure impoundment facilities effectively eliminates this concern.[6] As to false claims, "inventories are [not] a completely effective means of discouraging false claims, since there remains the possibility of accompanying such claims with an assertion that an item was stolen prior to the inventory or was intentionally omitted from the police records."

Officer Reichenbach's inventory in this case would not have protected the police against claims lodged by respondent, false or otherwise. Indeed, the trial court's characterization of the inventory as "slip-shod" is the height of under-statement. For example, Officer Reichenbach failed to list $150 in cash found in respondent's wallet or the contents of a sealed envelope marked "rent," $210, in the relevant section of the property form. His reports make no reference to other items of value, including respondent's credit cards, and a converter, a hydraulic jack, and a set of tire chains, worth a total of $125. The $700 in cash found in respondent's backpack, along with the contraband, appeared only on a property form completed later by someone other than Officer Reichenbach. The interior of the vehicle was left in disarray, and the officer "inadvertently" retained respondent's keys—including his house keys—for two days following his arrest.

The third interest—protecting the police from potential danger—failed to receive the endorsement of a majority of the Court in *Opperman.* After noting that "there is little danger associated with impounding unsearched vehicles," Justice Powell recognized that "there does not appear to be any effective way of identifying in advance those circumstances or classes of automobile impoundments which represent a greater risk." As with the charge of overtime parking in *Opperman,* there is nothing in the nature of the offense for which respondent was arrested that suggests he was likely to be carrying weapons, explosives, or other dangerous items.

Thus, only the government's interest in protecting the owner's property actually justifies an inventory search of an impounded vehicle. While I continue to believe that preservation of property does not outweigh the privacy and security interests protected by the Fourth Amendment, I fail to see how preservation can even be asserted as a justification for the search in this case. In *Opperman,* the owner of the impounded car was not available to safeguard his possessions, and it could plausibly be argued that, in his absence, the police were entitled to act for his presumed benefit. When the police conducted the inventory in *Opperman,* they

---

6. The impoundment lot in *South Dakota v. Opperman* was "the old county highway yard. It ha[d] a wooden fence partially around part of it, and kind of a dilapidated wire fence, a makeshift fence."

could not predict how long the car would be left in their possession. In this case, however, the owner was "present to make other arrangements for the safekeeping of his belongings," yet the police made no attempt to ascertain whether in fact he wanted them to "safeguard" his property. Furthermore, since respondent was charged with a traffic offense, he was unlikely to remain in custody for more than a few hours. He might well have been willing to leave his valuables unattended in the locked van for such a short period of time.

Thus, the government's interests in this case are weaker than in *Opperman,* but the search here is much more intrusive. *Opperman* did not involve a search of closed containers or other items that " 'touch upon intimate areas of an individual's personal affairs' "; nor can the Court's opinion be read to authorize the inspection of "containers which might themselves be sealed, removed and secured without further intrusion." To expand the *Opperman* rationale to include containers in which the owner clearly has a reasonable expectation of privacy, the Court relies on *Illinois v. Lafayette.* Such reliance is fundamentally misplaced, however; the inventory in *Lafayette* was justified by considerations which are totally absent in this context.

In *Lafayette,* we upheld a station house inventory search of an arrestee's shoulder bag. Notwithstanding the Court's assertions to the contrary, the inventory in that case *was* justified primarily by compelling governmental interests unique to the station house, preincarceration context. There is a powerful interest in preventing the introduction of contraband or weapons into a jail.

Notes and Questions

1. A narrower view is taken in some jurisdictions. For example, the South Dakota Supreme Court held on remand in *Opperman* that the inventory search violated the search and seizure guarantee of the South Dakota Constitution, the language of which "is almost identical to that found in the Fourth Amendment." *State v. Opperman,* 247 N.W.2d 673 (S.D.1976). Under the state constitutional provision, warrantless inventory searches of automobiles "must be restricted to safeguarding those articles which are within plain view of the officer's vision."

2. Consider the dissent of Ely, J., in *United States v. Mitchell,* 458 F.2d 960 (9th Cir.1972), suggesting that an "effective compromise" would be "to permit extensive inventory searches of seized vehicles, so as fully to protect the police, but to forbid, over the objection of one having standing, the use of any item seized in the search as evidence against the objector."

3. Evidence found in an otherwise lawful inventory must be suppressed if the prior impoundment of the vehicle was not justified. See, e.g., *Dyke v. Taylor Implement Mfg. Co.,* 391 U.S. 216, 88 S.Ct. 1472, 20 L.Ed.2d 538 (1968) (search of car outside courthouse while driver, arrested for reckless driving, inside to post bond was improper, as "there is no indication that the police had purported to impound or to hold the car [or] that they were authorized by any state law to do so"); *State v. Simpson,* 622 P.2d 1199 (Wash.1980) (where defendant arrested at home, impoundment of his truck lawfully parked in front of house illegal).

4. In *Florida v. Wells,* 495 U.S. 1, 110 S.Ct. 1632, 109 L.Ed.2d 1 (1990), all members of the Court agreed that the inventory of a locked suitcase found in an impounded vehicle was unlawful under *Bertine* because "the Florida Highway Patrol had no policy whatever with respect to the opening of closed containers encountered during an inventory search." The Chief Justice, for five members of the Court, went on to say that the state court erred in saying *Bertine* requires a policy either mandating or barring inventory of all containers:

"But in forbidding uncanalized discretion to police officers conducting inventory searches, there is no reason to insist that they be conducted in a totally mechanical 'all or nothing' fashion. * * * A police officer may be allowed sufficient latitude to determine whether a particular container should or should not be opened in light of the nature of the search and characteristics of the container itself. Thus, while policies of opening all containers or of opening no containers are unquestionably permissible, it would be equally permissible, for example, to allow the opening of closed containers whose contents officers determine they are unable to ascertain from examining the containers' exteriors. The allowance of the exercise of judgment based on concerns related to the purposes of an inventory search does not violate the Fourth Amendment."

Brennan and Marshall, JJ., concurring, declined to join the majority opinion because, in "pure dictum given the disposition of the case," it "goes on to suggest that a State may adopt an inventory policy that vests individual police officers with *some* discretion to decide whether to open such containers." Blackmun, J., concurring, agreed that the Fourth Amendment did not impose an "all or nothing" requirement, so that a state "probably could adopt a policy which requires the opening of all containers that are not locked, or a policy which requires the opening of all containers over or under a certain size, even though these policies do not call for the opening of all or no containers," but objected it was "an entirely different matter, however, to say, as this majority does, that an individual policeman may be afforded discretion in conducting an inventory search." Stevens, J., concurring separately, agreed with the Blackmun opinion.

5. If the inventory cannot be upheld when the department has no policy (as in *Wells*) or when the only standard practice identified is that of the individual officer (as in *United States v. Kordosky,* 909 F.2d 219 (7th Cir.1990)), then what if (unlike *Bertine*) the purported department policy followed was not in writing but was merely testified to by the inventorying officer? Most courts, e.g., *United States v. Ford,* 986 F.2d 57 (4th Cir.1993), have held that is sufficient, but this result has been questioned: "A primary concern, of course, is the possibility of undetected arbitrariness, a risk which takes on much greater proportions when the supposed 'standardized procedures' are established only by the self-serving and perhaps inaccurate oral statements of a police officer, and are not memorialized in the department's previous written instructions to its officers. Another * * * is that what is represented as department policy may constitute nothing more than a custom, hardly deserving the deference which an actual policy receives." Wayne R. LaFave, *Controlling Discretion by Administrative Regulations: The Use, Misuse, and Nonuse of Police Rules and Policies in Fourth Amendment Adjudication,* 89 Mich.L.Rev. 442, 456–57 (1990).

6. Consider *Ex parte Boyd,* 542 So.2d 1276 (Ala.1989): "We are unaware of any case, federal or state, that presents the issue of whether a search can be valid as an inventory notwithstanding a four-day lapse of time between the impoundment and the inventory. We are of the opinion that the Fourth Amendment requires that, without a demonstrable justification based upon exigent circumstances other than the mere nature of automobiles, the inventory be conducted either contemporaneously with the impoundment or as soon thereafter as would be safe, practical, *and* satisfactory in light of the objectives for which this exception to the Fourth Amendment warrant requirement was created. In other words, to be valid, there must be a sufficient temporal proximity between the impoundment and the inventory. * * * The justifications for the intrusion— protecting the owner's property, protecting the police from false claims or disputes, and protecting the police from danger—are simply not served, however,

when the inventory is inexcusably postponed; in that circumstance, the inventory becomes unreasonable.''

SECTION 7. STOP AND FRISK

TERRY v. OHIO

392 U.S. 1, 88 S.Ct. 1868, 20 L.Ed.2d 889 (1968).

Chief Justice WARREN delivered the opinion of the court.

[Officer McFadden, a Cleveland plainclothes detective, became suspicious of two men standing on a street corner in the downtown area at about 2:30 in the afternoon. One of the suspects walked up the street, peered into a store, walked on, started back, looked into the same store, and then joined and conferred with his companion. The other suspect repeated this ritual, and between them the two men went through this performance about a dozen times. They also talked with a third man, and then followed him up the street about ten minutes after his departure. The officer, thinking that the suspects were "casing" a stickup and might be armed, followed and confronted the three men as they were again conversing. He identified himself and asked the suspects for their names. The men only mumbled something, and the officer spun Terry around and patted his breast pocket. He felt a pistol, which he removed. A frisk of Terry's companion also uncovered a pistol; a frisk of the third man did not disclose that he was armed, and he was not searched further. Terry was charged with carrying a concealed weapon, and he moved to suppress the weapon as evidence. The motion was denied by the trial judge, who upheld the officer's actions on a stop-and-frisk theory. The Ohio court of appeals affirmed, and the state supreme court dismissed Terry's appeal.]

* * * The question is whether in all the circumstances of this on-the-street encounter, [Terry's] right to personal security was violated by an unreasonable search and seizure.

We would be less than candid if we did not acknowledge that this question thrusts to the fore difficult and troublesome issues regarding a sensitive area of police activity—issues which have never before been squarely presented to this Court. * * *

On the one hand, it is frequently argued that in dealing with the rapidly unfolding and often dangerous situations on city streets the police are in need of an escalating set of flexible responses, graduated in relation to the amount of information they possess. For this purpose it is urged that distinctions should be made between a "stop" and an "arrest" (or a "seizure" of a person), and between a "frisk" and a "search." Thus, it is argued, the police should be allowed to "stop" a person and detain him briefly for questioning upon suspicion that he may be connected with criminal activity. Upon suspicion that the person may be armed, the police should have the power to "frisk" him for weapons. If the "stop" and the "frisk" give rise to probable cause to believe that the suspect has committed a crime, then the police should be empowered to make a formal "arrest," and a full incident "search" of the person. This scheme is justified in part upon the notion that a "stop" and a "frisk" amount to a mere "minor inconvenience and petty indignity," which can properly be imposed upon the citizen in the interest of effective law enforcement on the basis of a police officer's suspicion.

On the other side the argument is made that the authority of the police must be strictly circumscribed by the law of arrest and search as it has developed to date in the traditional jurisprudence of the Fourth Amendment. It is contended with some force that there is not—and cannot be—a variety of police activity which does not depend solely upon the voluntary cooperation of the citizen and yet which stops short of an arrest based upon probable cause to make such an arrest. The heart of the Fourth Amendment, the argument runs, is a severe requirement of specific justification for any intrusion upon protected personal security, coupled with a highly developed system of judicial controls to enforce upon the agents of the State the commands of the Constitution. * * *

* * * The State has characterized the issue here as "the right of a police officer * * * to make an on-the-street stop, interrogate and pat down for weapons (known in the street vernacular as 'stop and frisk')." But this is only partly accurate. For the issue is not the abstract propriety of the police conduct, but the admissibility against petitioner of the evidence uncovered by the search and seizure. * * * [I]n our system evidentiary rulings provide the context in which the judicial process of inclusion and exclusion approves some conduct as comporting with constitutional guarantees and disapproves other actions by state agents. A ruling admitting evidence in a criminal trial, we recognize, has the necessary effect of legitimizing the conduct which produced the evidence, while an application of the exclusionary rule withholds the constitutional imprimatur.

The exclusionary rule has its limitations, however, as a tool of judicial control. It cannot properly be invoked to exclude the products of legitimate police investigative techniques on the ground that much conduct which is closely similar involves unwarranted intrusions upon constitutional protections. Moreover, in some contexts the rule is ineffective as a deterrent. Street encounters between citizens and police officers are incredibly rich in diversity. They range from wholly friendly exchanges of pleasantries or mutually useful information to hostile confrontations of armed men involving arrests, or injuries, or loss of life. Moreover, hostile confrontations are not all of a piece. Some of them begin in a friendly enough manner, only to take a different turn upon the injection of some unexpected element into the conversation. Encounters are initiated by the police for a wide variety of purposes, some of which are wholly unrelated to a desire to prosecute for crime. Doubtless some police "field interrogation" conduct violates the Fourth Amendment. But a stern refusal by this Court to condone such activity does not necessarily render it responsive to the exclusionary rule. Regardless of how effective the rule may be where obtaining convictions is an important objective of the police, it is powerless to deter invasions of constitutionally guaranteed rights where the police either have no interest in prosecuting or are willing to forego successful prosecution in the interest of serving some other goal.

Proper adjudication of cases in which the exclusionary rule is invoked demands a constant awareness of these limitations. The wholesale harassment by certain elements of the police community, of which minority groups, particularly Negroes, frequently complain, will not be stopped by the exclusion of any evidence from any criminal trial. Yet a rigid and unthinking application of the exclusionary rule, in futile protest against practices which it can never be used effectively to control, may exact a high toll in human injury and frustration of efforts to prevent crime. No judicial opinion can comprehend the protean variety of the street encounter, and we can only judge the facts of the case before us. * * *

[W]e turn our attention to the quite narrow question posed by the facts before us: whether it is always unreasonable for a policeman to seize a person and subject him to a limited search for weapons unless there is probable cause for an arrest.

* * * It is quite plain that the Fourth Amendment governs "seizures" of the person which do not eventuate in a trip to the station house and prosecution for crime—"arrests" in traditional terminology. It must be recognized that whenever a police officer accosts an individual and restrains his freedom to walk away, he has "seized" that person. And it is nothing less than sheer torture of the English language to suggest that a careful exploration of the outer surfaces of a person's clothing all over his or her body in an attempt to find weapons is not a "search." Moreover, it is simply fantastic to urge that such a procedure performed in public by a policeman while the citizen stands helpless, perhaps facing a wall with his hands raised, is a "petty indignity."[13] It is a serious intrusion upon the sanctity of the person, which may inflict great indignity and arouse strong resentment, and it is not to be undertaken lightly.

* * * We therefore reject the notions that the Fourth Amendment does not come into play at all as a limitation upon police conduct if the officers stop short of something called a "technical arrest" or a "full-blown search."

In this case there can be no question, then, that Officer McFadden "seized" petitioner and subjected him to a "search" when he took hold of him and patted down the outer surfaces of his clothing. We must decide whether at that point it was reasonable for Officer McFadden to have interfered with petitioner's personal security as he did.[16] And in determining whether the seizure and search were "unreasonable" our inquiry is a dual one—whether the officer's action was justified at its inception, and whether it was reasonably related in scope to the circumstances which justified the interference in the first place.

If this case involved police conduct subject to the Warrant Clause of the Fourth Amendment, we would have to ascertain whether "probable cause" existed to justify the search and seizure which took place. However, that is not the case. We do not retreat from our holdings that the police must, whenever practicable, obtain advance judicial approval of searches and seizures through the warrant procedure, * * * or that in most instances failure to comply with the warrant requirement can only be excused by exigent circumstances. * * * But we deal here with an entire rubric of police conduct—necessarily swift action predicated upon the on-the-spot observations of the officer on the beat—which historically has not been, and as a practical matter could not be, subjected to the warrant procedure. Instead, the conduct involved in this case must be tested by the Fourth Amendment's general proscription against unreasonable searches and seizures.

Nonetheless, the notions which underlie both the warrant procedure and the requirement of probable cause remain fully relevant in this context. In order to

---

13. Consider the following apt description: "[T]he officer must feel with sensitive fingers every portion of the prisoner's body. A thorough search must be made of the prisoner's arms and armpits, waistline and back, the groin and area about the testicles, and entire surface of the legs down to the feet." Priar & Martin, *Searching and Disarming Criminals,* 45 J.Crim.L.C. & P.S. 481 (1954).

16. We thus decide nothing today concerning the constitutional propriety of an investigative "seizure" upon less than probable cause for purposes of "detention" and/or interroga-

tion. Obviously, not all personal intercourse between policemen and citizens involves "seizures" of persons. Only when the officer, by means of physical force or show of authority, has in some way restrained the liberty of a citizen may we conclude that a "seizure" has occurred. We cannot tell with any certainty upon this record whether any such "seizure" took place here prior to Officer McFadden's initiation of physical contact for purposes of searching Terry for weapons, and we thus may assume that up to that point no intrusion upon constitutionally protected rights had occurred.

assess the reasonableness of Officer McFadden's conduct as a general proposition, it is necessary "first to focus upon the governmental interest which allegedly justifies official intrusion upon the constitutionally protected interests of the private citizen," for there is "no ready test for determining reasonableness other than by balancing the need to search [or seize] against the invasion which the search [or seizure] entails." *Camara v. Municipal Court* [p. 339]. And in justifying the particular intrusion the police officer must be able to point to specific and articulable facts which, taken together with rational inferences from those facts, reasonably warrant that intrusion. The scheme of the Fourth Amendment becomes meaningful only when it is assured that at some point the conduct of those charged with enforcing the laws can be subjected to the more detached, neutral scrutiny of a judge who must evaluate the reasonableness of a particular search or seizure in light of the particular circumstances. And in making that assessment it is imperative that the facts be judged against an objective standard: would the facts available to the officer at the moment of the seizure or the search "warrant a man of reasonable caution in the belief" that the action taken was appropriate? * * * Anything less would invite intrusions upon constitutionally guaranteed rights based on nothing more substantial than inarticulate hunches, a result this Court has consistently refused to sanction. * * *

Applying these principles to this case, we consider first the nature and extent of the governmental interests involved. One general interest is of course that of effective crime prevention and detection; it is this interest which underlies the recognition that a police officer may in appropriate circumstances and in an appropriate manner approach a person for purposes of investigating possibly criminal behavior even though there is no probable cause to make an arrest. It was this legitimate investigative function Officer McFadden was discharging when he decided to approach petitioner and his companions. He had observed Terry, Chilton, and Katz go through a series of acts, each of them perhaps innocent in itself, but which taken together warranted further investigation. There is nothing unusual in two men standing together on a street corner, perhaps waiting for someone. Nor is there anything suspicious about people in such circumstances strolling up and down the street, singly or in pairs. Store windows, moreover, are made to be looked in. But the story is quite different where, as here, two men hover about a street corner for an extended period of time, at the end of which it becomes apparent that they are not waiting for anyone or anything; where these men pace alternately along an identical route, pausing to stare in the same store window roughly 24 times; where each completion of this route is followed immediately by a conference between the two men on the corner; where they are joined in one of these conferences by a third man who leaves swiftly; and where the two men finally follow the third and rejoin him a couple of blocks away. It would have been poor police work indeed for an officer of 30 years' experience in the detection of thievery from stores in this same neighborhood to have failed to investigate this behavior further.

The crux of this case, however, is not the propriety of Officer McFadden's taking steps to investigate petitioner's suspicious behavior, but rather, whether there was justification for McFadden's invasion of Terry's personal security by searching him for weapons in the course of that investigation. We are now concerned with more than the governmental interest in investigating crime; in addition, there is the more immediate interest of the police officer in taking steps to assure himself that the person with whom he is dealing is not armed with a weapon that could unexpectedly and fatally be used against him. Certainly it would be unreasonable to require that police officers take unnecessary risks in the performance of their duties. American criminals have a long tradition of armed violence, and every year in this country many law enforcement officers are killed in the line of duty, and thousands more are wounded. Virtually all of these deaths and a substantial portion of the injuries are inflicted with guns and knives.

In view of these facts, we cannot blind ourselves to the need for law enforcement officers to protect themselves and other prospective victims of violence in situations where they may lack probable cause for an arrest. When an officer is justified in believing that the individual whose suspicious behavior he is investigating at close range is armed and presently dangerous to the officer or to others, it would appear to be clearly unreasonable to deny the officer the power to take necessary measures to determine whether the person is in fact carrying a weapon and to neutralize the threat of physical harm. * * *

Petitioner * * * does not say that an officer is always unjustified in searching a suspect to discover weapons. Rather, he says it is unreasonable for the policeman to take that step until such time as the situation evolves to a point where there is probable cause to make an arrest. * * *

There are two weaknesses in this line of reasoning however. First, it fails to take account of traditional limitations upon the scope of searches, and thus recognizes no distinction in purpose, character, and extent between a search incident to an arrest and a limited search for weapons. The former, although justified in part by the acknowledged necessity to protect the arresting officer from assault with a concealed weapon, is also justified on other grounds, and can therefore involve a relatively extensive exploration of the person. A search for weapons in the absence of probable cause to arrest, however, must, like any other search, be strictly circumscribed by the exigencies which justify its initiation. Thus it must be limited to that which is necessary for the discovery of weapons which might be used to harm the officer or others nearby, and may realistically be characterized as something less than a "full" search, even though it remains a serious intrusion.

A second, and related, objection to petitioner's argument is that it assumes that the law of arrest has already worked out the balance between the particular interests involved here—the neutralization of danger to the policeman in the investigative circumstance and the sanctity of the individual. But this is not so. An arrest is a wholly different kind of intrusion upon individual freedom from a limited search for weapons, and the interests each is designed to serve are likewise quite different. An arrest is the initial stage of a criminal prosecution. It is intended to vindicate society's interest in having its laws obeyed, and it is inevitably accompanied by future interference with the individual's freedom of movement, whether or not trial or conviction ultimately follows. The protective search for weapons, on the other hand, constitutes a brief, though far from inconsiderable intrusion upon the sanctity of the person. It does not follow that because an officer may lawfully arrest a person only when he is apprised of facts sufficient to warrant a belief that the person has committed or is committing a crime, the officer is equally unjustified, absent that kind of evidence, in making any intrusions short of an arrest. Moreover, a perfectly reasonable apprehension of danger may arise long before the officer is possessed of adequate information to justify taking a person into custody for the purpose of prosecuting him for a crime. * * *

Our evaluation of the proper balance that has to be struck in this type of case leads us to conclude that there must be a narrowly drawn authority to permit a reasonable search for weapons for the protection of the police officer, where he has reason to believe that he is dealing with an armed and dangerous individual, regardless of whether he has probable cause to arrest the individual for a crime. The officer need not be absolutely certain that the individual is armed; the issue is whether a reasonably prudent man in the circumstances would be warranted in the belief that his safety or that of others was in danger. * * * And in determining whether the officer acted reasonably in such circumstances, due weight must be given, not to his inchoate and unparticularized suspicion or "hunch", but to the specific reasonable inferences which he is entitled to draw from the facts in light of his experience.

We must now examine the conduct of Officer McFadden in this case to determine whether his search and seizure of petitioner were reasonable, both at their inception and as conducted. He had observed Terry, together with Chilton and another man, acting in a manner he took to be preface to a "stick-up." We think on the facts and circumstances Officer McFadden detailed before the trial judge a reasonably prudent man would have been warranted in believing petitioner was armed and thus presented a threat to the officer's safety while he was investigating his suspicious behavior. The actions of Terry and Chilton were consistent with McFadden's hypothesis that these men were contemplating a daylight robbery—which, it is reasonable to assume, would be likely to involve the use of weapons—and nothing in their conduct from the time he first noticed them until the time he confronted them and identified himself as a police officer gave him sufficient reason to negate that hypothesis. Although the trio had departed the original scene, there was nothing to indicate abandonment of an intent to commit a robbery at some point. Thus, when Officer McFadden approached the three men gathered before the display window at Zucker's store he had observed enough to make it quite reasonable to fear that they were armed; and nothing in their response to his hailing them, identifying himself as a police officer, and asking their names served to dispel that reasonable belief. We cannot say his decision at that point to seize Terry and pat his clothing for weapons was the product of a volatile or inventive imagination, or was undertaken simply as an act of harassment; the record evidences the tempered act of a policeman who in the course of an investigation had to make a quick decision as to how to protect himself and others from possible danger, and took limited steps to do so.

The manner in which the seizure and search were conducted is, of course, as vital a part of the inquiry as whether they were warranted at all. The Fourth Amendment proceeds as much by limitations upon the scope of governmental action as by imposing preconditions upon its initiation. The entire deterrent purpose of the rule excluding evidence seized in violation of the Fourth Amendment rests on the assumption that "limitations upon the fruit to be gathered tend to limit the quest itself." * * * Thus, evidence may not be introduced if it was discovered by means of a seizure and search which were not reasonably related in scope to the justification for their initiation.

[A protective search for weapons,] unlike a search without a warrant incident to a lawful arrest, is not justified by any need to prevent the disappearance or destruction of evidence of crime. The sole justification of the search in the present situation is the protection of the police officer and others nearby, and it must therefore be confined in scope to an intrusion reasonably designed to discover guns, knives, clubs, or other hidden instruments for the assault of the police officer.

The scope of the search in this case presents no serious problem in light of these standards. Officer McFadden patted down the outer clothing of petitioner and his two companions. He did not place his hands in their pockets or under the outer surface of their garments until he had felt weapons, and then he merely reached for and removed the guns. He never did invade Katz's person beyond the outer surfaces of his clothes, since he discovered nothing in his pat down which might have been a weapon. Officer McFadden confined his search strictly to what was minimally necessary to learn whether the men were armed and to disarm them once he discovered the weapons. He did not conduct a general exploratory search for whatever evidence of criminal activity he might find.

We conclude that the revolver seized from Terry was properly admitted in evidence against him. At the time he seized petitioner and searched him for weapons, Officer McFadden had reasonable grounds to believe that petitioner was armed and dangerous, and it was necessary for the protection of himself and others to take swift measures to discover the true facts and neutralize the threat of harm if it materialized. The policeman carefully restricted his search to what was appropriate to the discovery of the particular items which he sought. Each case of this sort will, of course, have to be decided on its own facts. We merely hold today that where a police officer observes unusual conduct which leads him reasonably to conclude in light of his experience that criminal activity may be afoot and that the persons with whom he is dealing may be armed and presently dangerous; where in the course of investigating this behavior he identifies himself as a policeman and makes reasonable inquiries; and where nothing in the initial stages of the encounter serves to dispel his reasonable fear for his own or others' safety, he is entitled for the protection of himself and others in the area to conduct a carefully limited search of the outer clothing of such persons in an attempt to discover weapons which might be used to assault him. Such a search is a reasonable search under the Fourth Amendment, and any weapons seized may properly be introduced in evidence against the person from whom they were taken.

Affirmed.

Justice HARLAN, concurring.

* * * The holding has * * * two logical corollaries that I do not think the Court has fully expressed.

In the first place, if the frisk is justified in order to protect the officer during an encounter with a citizen, the officer must first have constitutional grounds to insist on an encounter, to make a *forcible* stop. Any person, including a policeman, is at liberty to avoid a person he considers dangerous. If and when a policeman has a right instead to disarm such a person for his own protection, he must first have a right not to avoid him but to be in his presence. That right must be more than the liberty (again, possessed by every citizen) to address questions to other persons, for ordinarily the person addressed has an equal right to ignore his interrogator and walk away; he certainly need not submit to a frisk for the questioner's protection. I would make it perfectly clear that the right to frisk in this case depends upon the reasonableness of a forcible stop to investigate a suspected crime.

Where such a stop is reasonable, however, the right to frisk must be immediate and automatic if the reason for the stop is, as here, an articulable suspicion of a crime of violence. Just as a full search incident to a lawful arrest requires no additional justification, a limited frisk incident to a lawful stop must often be rapid and routine. There is no reason why an officer, rightfully but forcibly confronting a person suspected of a serious crime, should have to ask one question and take the risk that the answer might be a bullet. * * *

Justice WHITE, concurring.

* * * I think an additional word is in order concerning the matter of interrogation during an investigative stop. There is nothing in the Constitution which prevents a policeman from addressing questions to anyone on the streets. Absent special circumstances, the person approached may not be detained or frisked but may refuse to cooperate and go on his way. However, given the proper circumstances, such as those in this case, it seems to me the person may be briefly detained against his will while pertinent questions are directed to him. Of course, the person stopped is not obliged to answer, answers may not be compelled, and refusal to answer furnishes no basis for an arrest, although it may alert the officer to the need for continued observation. * * *

Justice DOUGLAS, dissenting.

* * * Had a warrant been sought, a magistrate would, therefore, have been unauthorized to issue one, for he can act only if there is a showing of "probable cause." We hold today that the police have greater authority to make a "seizure" and conduct a "search" than a judge has to authorize such action. We have said precisely the opposite over and over again. * * *

The infringement on personal liberty of any "seizure" of a person can only be "reasonable" under the Fourth Amendment if we require the police to possess "probable cause" before they seize him. Only that line draws a meaningful distinction between an officer's mere inkling and the presence of facts within the officer's personal knowledge which would convince a reasonable man that the person seized has committed, is committing, or is about to commit a particular crime. * * *

THE SIGNIFICANCE OF THE STOP–AND–FRISK CASES

A. The Utility of the Balancing Test

1. What qualifies a particular police practice for assessment under the *Terry* balancing test?[a] In *Michigan v. Summers,* p. 216, Stewart, J., joined by Brennan and Marshall, JJ., dissenting, objected to the majority's use of the balancing test in holding that a warrant to search premises for contraband authorizes police to detain the occupants while the warrant is executed. They reasoned "that before a court can uphold a detention on less than probable cause on the ground that it is 'reasonable' in the light of the competing interests, the government must demonstrate an important purpose beyond the normal goals of criminal investigation,[b] or must demonstrate an extraordinary obstacle to such investigation," which they believed had not been done in the instant case.

2. Should the balancing test also be used to keep the evidentiary requirements for a given police practice "flexible," so that, for example, less evidence would be required when the crime being investigated is a serious one? Consider Justice Jackson, dissenting in *Brinegar v. United States,* 338 U.S. 160, 69 S.Ct. 1302, 93 L.Ed. 1879 (1949): "If we assume, for example, that a child is kidnapped and the officers throw a roadblock about the neighborhood and search every outgoing car, it would be a drastic and undiscriminating use of the search. The officers might be unable to show probable cause for searching any particular car. However, I should candidly strive hard to sustain such an action, executed fairly

a. See Scott E. Sundby, *A Return to Fourth Amendment Basics: Undoing the Mischief of Camara and Terry,* 72 Minn.L.Rev. 383 (1988).

b. See § 8 of this Chapter.

and in good faith, because it might be reasonable to subject travelers to that indignity if it was the only way to save a threatened life and detect a vicious crime. But I should not strain to sustain such a roadblock and universal search to salvage a few bottles of bourbon and catch a bootlegger."[c]

B. POLICE ACTION SHORT OF A SEIZURE

1. FLORIDA v. BOSTICK, 501 U.S. 429, 111 S.Ct. 2382, 115 L.Ed.2d 389 (1991), involved these facts, as stated by the state supreme court: "Two officers, complete with badges, insignia and one of them holding a recognizable zipper pouch, containing a pistol, boarded a bus bound from Miami to Atlanta during a stopover in Fort Lauderdale. Eyeing the passengers, the officers admittedly without articulable suspicion, picked out the defendant passenger and asked to inspect his ticket and identification. The ticket, from Miami to Atlanta, matched the defendant's identification and both were immediately returned to him as unremarkable. However, the two police officers persisted and explained their presence as narcotics agents on the lookout for illegal drugs. In pursuit of that aim, they then requested the defendant's consent to search his luggage. Needless to say, there is a conflict in the evidence about whether the defendant consented to the search of the second bag in which the contraband was found and as to whether he was informed of his right to refuse consent. However, any conflict must be resolved in favor of the state, it being a question of fact decided by the trial judge." That court ruled that "an impermissible seizure result[s] when police mount a drug search on buses during scheduled stops and question boarded passengers without articulable reasons for doing so, thereby obtaining consent to search the passengers' luggage." The Supreme Court reversed; O'CONNOR, J., for the majority, stated:

"Our cases make it clear that a seizure does not occur simply because a police officer approaches an individual and asks a few questions. So long as a reasonable person would feel free 'to disregard the police and go about his business,' the encounter is consensual and no reasonable suspicion is required. The encounter will not trigger Fourth Amendment scrutiny unless it loses its consensual nature. * * *

"There is no doubt that if this same encounter had taken place before Bostick boarded the bus or in the lobby of the bus terminal, it would not rise to the level of a seizure. The Court has dealt with similar encounters in airports and has found them to be 'the sort of consensual encounter[s] that implicat[e] no Fourth Amendment interest.' We have stated that even when officers have no basis for suspecting a particular individual, they may generally ask questions of that individual, ask to examine the individual's identification, and request consent to search his or her luggage—as long as the police do not convey a message that compliance with their requests is required.

c. Compare *Dunaway v. New York,* p. 338.

On the use of roadblocks, consider *Model Pre-Arraignment Code* § 110.2, providing in part:

"(2) *Stopping of Vehicles at Roadblock.* A law enforcement officer may if

"(a) he has reasonable cause to believe that a felony has been committed; and

"(b) stopping all or most vehicles moving in a particular direction or directions is reason-

ably necessary to permit a search for the perpetrator or victim of such felony in view of the seriousness and special circumstances of such felony,

order the drivers of such vehicles to stop, and may search such vehicles to the extent necessary to accomplish such purpose. Such action shall be accomplished as promptly as possible under the circumstances."

"Bostick insists that this case is different because it took place in the cramped confines of a bus. A police encounter is much more intimidating in this setting, he argues, because police tower over a seated passenger and there is little room to move around. Bostick claims to find support in cases indicating that a seizure occurs when a reasonable person would believe that he or she is not 'free to leave.' Bostick maintains that a reasonable bus passenger would not have felt free to leave under the circumstances of this case because there is nowhere to go on a bus. Also, the bus was about to depart. Had Bostick disembarked, he would have risked being stranded and losing whatever baggage he had locked away in the luggage compartment.

"The Florida Supreme Court found this argument persuasive, so much so that it adopted a *per se* rule prohibiting the police from randomly boarding buses as a means of drug interdiction. The state court erred, however, in focusing on whether Bostick was 'free to leave', rather than on the principle that those words were intended to capture. When police attempt to question a person who is walking down the street or through an airport lobby, it makes sense to inquire whether a reasonable person would feel free to continue walking. But when the person is seated on a bus and has no desire to leave, the degree to which a reasonable person would feel that he or she could leave is not an accurate measure of the coercive effect of the encounter.

"Here, for example, the mere fact that Bostick did not feel free to leave the bus does not mean that the police seized him. Bostick was a passenger on a bus that was scheduled to depart. He would not have felt free to leave the bus even if the police had not been present. Bostick's movements were 'confined' in a sense, but this was the natural result of his decision to take the bus; it says nothing about whether or not the police conduct at issue was coercive.

"In this respect, the Court's decision in *INS v. Delgado,* [466 U.S. 210, 104 S.Ct. 1758, 80 L.Ed.2d 247 (1984)] is dispositive. At issue there was the INS' practice of visiting factories at random and questioning employees to determine whether any were illegal aliens. Several INS agents would stand near the building's exits, while other agents walked through the factory questioning workers. The Court acknowledged that the workers may not have been free to leave their worksite, but explained that this was not the result of police activity: 'Ordinarily, when people are at work their freedom to move about has been meaningfully restricted, not by the actions of law enforcement officials, but by the workers' voluntary obligations to their employers.' We concluded that there was no seizure because, even though the workers were not free to leave the building without being questioned, the agents' conduct should have given employees 'no reason to believe that they would be detained if they gave truthful answers to the questions put to them or if they simply refused to answer.'

"The present case is analytically indistinguishable from *Delgado.* Like the workers in that case, Bostick's freedom of movement was restricted by a factor independent of police conduct—*i.e.,* by his being a passenger on a bus. Accordingly, the 'free to leave' analysis on which Bostick relies is inapplicable. In such a situation, the appropriate inquiry is whether a reasonable person would feel free to decline the officers' requests or otherwise terminate the encounter. This formulation follows logically from prior cases and breaks no new ground. We have said before that the crucial test is whether, taking into account all of the circumstances surrounding the encounter, the police conduct would 'have communicated to a reasonable person that he was not at liberty to ignore the police presence and go about his business.' Where the encounter takes place is one factor, but it is not the only one. And, as the Solicitor General correctly observes, an individual may decline an officer's request without fearing prosecution. We have consistently held that a refusal to cooperate, without more, does not furnish the minimal level of objective justification needed for a detention or seizure.

"The facts of this case, as described by the Florida Supreme Court, leave some doubt whether a seizure occurred. Two officers walked up to Bostick on the bus, asked him a few questions, and asked if they could search his bags. As we have explained, no seizure occurs when police ask questions of an individual, ask to examine the individual's identification, and request consent to search his or her luggage—so long as the officers do not convey a message that compliance with their requests is required. Here, the facts recited by the Florida Supreme Court indicate that the officers did not point guns at Bostick or otherwise threaten him and that they specifically advised Bostick that he could refuse consent.

"Nevertheless, we refrain from deciding whether or not a seizure occurred in this case. The trial court made no express findings of fact, and the Florida Supreme Court rested its decision on a single fact—that the encounter took place on a bus—rather than on the totality of the circumstances. We remand so that the Florida courts may evaluate the seizure question under the correct legal standard. We do reject, however, Bostick's argument that he must have been seized because no reasonable person would freely consent to a search of luggage that he or she knows contains drugs. This argument cannot prevail because the 'reasonable person' test presupposes an *innocent* person. * * *

"The dissent also attempts to characterize our decision as applying a lesser degree of constitutional protection to those individuals who travel by bus, rather than by other forms of transportation. This, too, is an erroneous characterization. Our Fourth Amendment inquiry in this case—whether a reasonable person would have felt free to decline the officers' requests or otherwise terminate the encounter—applies equally to police encounters that take place on trains, planes, and city streets. It is the dissent that would single out this particular mode of travel for differential treatment by adopting a *per se* rule that random bus searches are unconstitutional."

MARSHALL, J., for the three dissenters, interpreted the state court holding as not a "*per se* rule" but rather as a decision based on all the facts, but then added that in any event the Supreme Court could determine the "question of law" of whether *all* the facts set forth in the state court opinion add up to a Fourth Amendment seizure. Accepting the majority's "free to decline" test, Marshall continued:

"Unlike the majority, I have no doubt that the answer to this question is no. Apart from trying to accommodate the officers, respondent had only two options. First, he could have remained seated while obstinately refusing to respond to the officers' questioning. But in light of the intimidating show of authority that the officers made upon boarding the bus, respondent reasonably could have believed that such behavior would only arouse the officers' suspicions and intensify their interrogation. Indeed, officers who carry out bus sweeps like the one at issue here frequently admit that this is the effect of a passenger's refusal to cooperate. The majority's observation that a mere refusal to answer questions, 'without more,' does not give rise to a reasonable basis for seizing a passenger, is utterly beside the point, because a passenger unadvised of his rights and otherwise unversed in constitutional law *has no reason to know* that the police cannot hold his refusal to cooperate against him.

"Second, respondent could have tried to escape the officers' presence by leaving the bus altogether. But because doing so would have required respondent to squeeze past the gun-wielding inquisitor who was blocking the aisle of the bus, this hardly seems like a course that respondent reasonably would have viewed as available to him. The majority lamely protests that nothing in the stipulated facts shows that the questioning officer '*point[ed]* [his] gu[n] at [respondent] or otherwise *threatened* him' with the weapon. Our decisions recognize the obvious point, however, that the choice of the police to 'display' their weapons during an encounter exerts significant coercive pressure on the confronted citizen. We have never suggested that the police must go so far as to put a citizen in immediate apprehension of *being shot* before a court can take account of the intimidating effect of being questioned by an officer with weapon in hand.

"Even if respondent had perceived that the officers would *let* him leave the bus, moreover, he could not reasonably have been expected to resort to this means of evading their intrusive questioning. For so far as respondent knew, the bus' departure from the terminal was imminent. Unlike a person approached by the police on the street or at a bus or airport terminal after reaching his destination, a passenger approached by the police at an intermediate point in a long bus journey cannot simply leave the scene and repair to a safe haven to avoid unwanted probing by law-enforcement officials. The vulnerability that an intrastate or interstate traveler experiences when confronted by the police outside of his 'own familiar territory' surely aggravates the coercive quality of such an encounter.

"The case on which the majority primarily relies, *INS v. Delgado*, is distinguishable in every relevant respect. In *Delgado*, this Court held that workers approached by law-enforcement officials inside of a factory were not 'seized' for purposes of the Fourth Amendment. The Court was careful to point out, however, that the presence of the agents did not furnish the workers with a reasonable basis for believing that they were not free to leave the factory, as at least some of them did. Unlike passengers confronted by law-enforcement officials on a bus stopped temporarily at an intermediate point in its journey, workers approached by law-enforcement officials at their workplace need not abandon personal belongings and venture into unfamiliar environs in order to avoid unwanted questioning. Moreover, the workers who did not leave the building in *Delgado* remained free to move about the entire factory, a considerably less confining environment than a bus. Finally, contrary to the officer who confronted respondent, the law-enforcement officials in *Delgado* did not conduct their interviews with guns in hand.

"Rather than requiring the police to justify the coercive tactics employed here, the majority blames respondent for his own sensation of constraint. The majority concedes that respondent 'did not feel free to leave the bus' as a means of breaking off the interrogation by the Broward County officers. But this experience of confinement, the majority explains, 'was the natural result of *his* decision to take the bus.' Thus, in the majority's view, because respondent's 'freedom of movement was restricted by a factor independent of police conduct—*i.e.,* by his being a passenger on a bus,' respondent was not seized for purposes of the Fourth Amendment.

"This reasoning borders on sophism and trivializes the values that underlie the Fourth Amendment. Obviously, a person's 'voluntary decision' to place himself in a room with only one exit does not authorize the police to force an encounter upon him by placing themselves in front of the exit. It is no more acceptable for the police to force an encounter on a person by exploiting his 'voluntary decision' to expose himself to perfectly legitimate personal or social constraints. By consciously deciding to single out persons who have undertaken interstate or intrastate travel, officers who conduct suspicionless, dragnet-style sweeps put passengers to the choice of cooperating or of exiting their buses and possibly being stranded in unfamiliar locations. It is exactly because this 'choice' is no 'choice' at all that police engage this technique."

2. In CALIFORNIA v. HODARI D., 499 U.S. 621, 111 S.Ct. 1547, 113 L.Ed.2d 690 (1991), Hodari fled upon seeing an approaching police car, only to be pursued on foot by Officer Pertoso, after which Hodari tossed away what appeared to be a small rock but which when retrieved by the police proved to be crack cocaine. The state court suppressed the cocaine as the fruit of a seizure made without reasonable suspicion, but the Supreme Court, per SCALIA, J., reversed:

"To say [as the common law authorities do] that an arrest is effected by the slightest application of physical force, despite the arrestee's escape, is not to say that for Fourth Amendment purposes there is a *continuing* arrest during the period of fugitivity. If, for example, Pertoso had laid his hands upon Hodari to arrest him, but Hodari had broken away and had *then* cast away the cocaine, it would hardly be realistic to say that that disclosure had been made during the course of an arrest. Cf. *Thompson v. Whitman,* 18 Wall. 457, 471 (1874) ('A seizure is a single act, and not a continuous fact'). The present case, however, is even one step further removed. It does not involve the application of any physical force; Hodari was untouched by Officer Pertoso at the time he discarded the cocaine. His defense relies instead upon the proposition that a seizure occurs 'when the officer, by means of physical force *or show of authority,* has in some way restrained the liberty of a citizen.' *Terry v. Ohio,* [p. 304]. Hodari contends (and we accept as true for purposes of this decision) that Pertoso's pursuit qualified as a 'show of authority' calling upon Hodari to halt. The narrow question before us is whether, with respect to a show of authority as with respect to application of physical force, a seizure occurs even though the subject does not yield. We hold that it does not.

"The language of the Fourth Amendment, of course, cannot sustain respondent's contention. The word 'seizure' readily bears the meaning of a laying on of hands or application of physical force to restrain movement, even when it is ultimately unsuccessful. ('She seized the purse-snatcher, but he broke out of her grasp.') It does not remotely apply, however, to the prospect of a policeman yelling 'Stop, in the name of the law!' at a fleeing form that continues to flee. That is no seizure. Nor can the result respondent wishes to achieve be produced—indirectly, as it were—by suggesting that Pertoso's uncomplied-with show of authority was a common-law arrest, and then appealing to the principle that all common-law arrests are seizures. An arrest requires *either* physical force (as described above) *or,* where that is absent, *submission* to the assertion of authority. * * *

"We do not think it desirable, even as a policy matter, to stretch the Fourth Amendment beyond its words and beyond the meaning of arrest, as respondent urges. Street pursuits always place the public at some risk, and compliance with police orders to stop should therefore be encouraged. Only a few of those orders, we must presume, will be without adequate basis, and since the addressee has no ready means of identifying the deficient ones it almost invariably is the responsible course to comply. Unlawful orders will not be deterred, moreover, by sanctioning through the exclusionary rule those of them that are *not* obeyed. Since policemen do not command 'Stop!' expecting to be ignored, or give chase hoping to be outrun, it fully suffices to apply the deterrent to their genuine, successful seizures.

STEVENS, J., for the two dissenters, objected: "The deterrent purposes of the exclusionary rule focus on the conduct of law enforcement officers, and on discouraging improper behavior on their part, and not on the reaction of the citizen to the show of force. In the present case, if Officer Pertoso had succeeded in tackling respondent before he dropped the rock of cocaine, the rock unquestionably would have been excluded as the fruit of the officer's unlawful seizure. Instead, under the Court's logic-chopping analysis, the exclusionary rule has no application because an attempt to make an unconstitutional seizure is beyond the coverage of the Fourth Amendment, no matter how outrageous or unreasonable the officer's conduct may be.

"It is too early to know the consequences of the Court's holding. If carried to its logical conclusion, it will encourage unlawful displays of force that will frighten countless innocent citizens into surrendering whatever privacy rights they may still have. It is not too soon, however, to note the irony in the fact that the Court's own justification for its result is its analysis of the rules of the common law of arrest that antedated our decisions in *Katz* [p. 155] and *Terry*. Yet, even in those days the common law provided the citizen with protection against an attempt to make an unlawful arrest. The central message of *Katz* and *Terry* was that the protection the Fourth Amendment provides to the average citizen is not rigidly confined by ancient common-law precept. The message that today's literal-minded majority conveys is that the common law, rather than our understanding of the Fourth Amendment as it has developed over the last quarter of a century, defines, and limits, the scope of a seizure. The Court today defines a seizure as commencing, not with egregious police conduct, but rather, with submission by the citizen. Thus, it both delays the point at which 'the Fourth Amendment becomes relevant' to an encounter and limits the range of encounters that will come under the heading of 'seizure.' Today's qualification of the Fourth Amendment means that innocent citizens may remain 'secure in their persons ... against unreasonable searches and seizures' only at the discretion of the police."[d]

3. After citing *Hodari D.* to support the conclusion "that a police pursuit in attempting to seize a person does not amount to a 'seizure' within the meaning of the Fourth Amendment," the Court in *County of Sacramento v. Lewis*, p. 43, also concluded "that no Fourth Amendment seizure would take place where a 'pursuing police car sought to stop the suspect only by the show of authority represented by flashing lights and continuing pursuit,' but accidentally stopped the suspect by crashing into him." This is because for a Fourth Amendment seizure there must be "a governmental termination of freedom of movement *through means intentionally applied*."

4. What result would the Court have reached if, before Hodari threw away the cocaine, Officer Pertoso had (a) fired his pistol at Hodari, barely missing him; (b) fired his pistol at Hodari, causing a wound which slowed down but did not stop him; (c) cornered Hodari in a dead-end alley; or (d) grabbed the collar of Hodari's jacket, only to have him slip out of the garment? Compare *United States v. Lender*, 985 F.2d 151 (4th Cir.1993) (officer called defendant to stop, defendant responded "you don't want me" and continued walking, officer again called defendant to stop and defendant did stop, at which loaded pistol fell to the ground, which officer prevented defendant from picking up; no prior seizure of defendant, as court refuses "to characterize as capitulation conduct that is fully consistent with preparation to whirl and shoot the officers"); with *United States v. Wood*, 981

---

d. For criticism of *Bostick* and *Hodari D.*, see Wayne R. LaFave, *Pinguitudinous Police, Pachydermatous Prey: Whence Fourth Amendment "Seizures"?*, 1991 U.Ill.L.Rev. 729.

F.2d 536 (D.C.Cir.1992) (when officer ordered defendant to stop, defendant "froze in his tracks and immediately dropped the [theretofore unobserved] weapon between his feet," there was a prior seizure; court "cannot imagine a more submissive response"). Compare *Tom v. Voida,* 963 F.2d 952 (7th Cir.1992) (where flight and pursuit and, when suspect fell on ice, officer kneeled on him but suspect violently resisted and broke away, seizure occurred when officer "overtook him on the ice and physically touched him"); with *United States v. Holloway,* 962 F.2d 451 (5th Cir.1992) (where after defendant's car boxed in by police cars defendant accelerated into police car behind him, no prior seizure, as no "touching" of defendant and no submission given that he then "decided to flee").

5.   What result under *Bostick* and *Hodari D.* if, when an intercity bus has stopped for an equipment change, necessitating that all passengers leave the bus with their luggage, the police board the bus and announce that they have a narcotics canine outside the bus and that the dog will "alert" to anyone carrying narcotics? Does it depend upon whether "the tenor and tone of [the] announcement was informative rather than confrontational"? On whether the passengers are told to exit "in a normal fashion with your carry-on," or instead to disembark "with all their carry-on luggage in their right hand so that the luggage would pass by the dog"? Compare *United States v. Jones,* 914 F.Supp. 421 (D.Colo.1996); with *United States v. Brumfield,* 910 F.Supp. 1528 (D.Colo.1996).

6.   In *United States v. Wilson,* 953 F.2d 116 (4th Cir.1991), involving an airport encounter between a DEA agent and a drug courier suspect, Wilson granted the agent's request to speak with him and submitted to questioning, produced identification upon request, and allowed the agent and an associate to search his bag and his person. But when the agent asked to search the two coats Wilson was carrying, Wilson angrily refused and walked away. The agent stayed with him, repeatedly requesting that Wilson consent to search of the coats and repeatedly asking Wilson to explain why he would not allow the search. Wilson continued walking through the terminal and then outside on the sidewalk, objecting the entire time to the harassment, but he finally consented to the search, which uncovered a bag of cocaine. If Wilson claims his consent to the search was the fruit of an illegal seizure, what result under *Bostick* and *Hodari D.?*

7.   In *Bostick* and *Hodari D.* the defendants were black. Is that relevant? Consider Tracey Maclin, *"Black and Blue Encounters"—Some Preliminary Thoughts About Fourth Amendment Seizures: Should Race Matter?,* 26 Val. U.L.Rev. 243, 250 (1991): "I submit that the dynamics surrounding an encounter between a police officer and a black male are quite different from those that surround an encounter between an officer and the so-called average, reasonable person. My tentative proposal is that the Court should disregard the notion that there is an average, hypothetical, reasonable person out there by which to judge the constitutionality of police encounters. When assessing the coercive nature of an encounter, the Court should consider the race of the person confronted by the police, and how that person's race might have influenced his attitude toward the encounter."

Cf. *In re J.M.,* 619 A.2d 497 (D.C.App.1992) (majority, applying *Bostick* objective standard, concludes 14–year–old bus passenger had not been seized during his on-bus interrogation which culminated in the youth's supposed consent to a search of his bag and pat-down of his person; two concurring judges argue it "consistent with the teaching of the Supreme Court opinions that specific, objectively observable characteristics of the person who is the object of police conduct be considered by a court in determining whether a seizure has occurred," so that issue here is "whether a reasonable person who is a child would have thought that he or she was free to leave under the circumstances"; another judge "would factor into the totality of the circumstances the relevant characteristics of age and race," and suggests "that no reasonable innocent black male (with any knowledge of American history) would feel free to ignore or walk away from a drug interdicting team").

C. GROUNDS FOR TEMPORARY SEIZURE FOR INVESTIGATION

1. Under *Terry,* what grounds are needed for a stop, and how do they differ from those needed for a full-fledged arrest? Shortly after *Terry,* one commentator suggested that for arrest it must be "more probable than not that the person is the offender," while for a *Terry* stop "it should be sufficient that there is a substantial possibility that a crime has been or is about to be committed and that the suspect is the person who committed or is planning the offense."[e] Compare the Court's later elaboration in UNITED STATES v. CORTEZ, 449 U.S. 411, 101 S.Ct. 690, 66 L.Ed.2d 621 (1981):

"Courts have used a variety of terms to capture the elusive concept of what cause is sufficient to authorize police to stop a person. Terms like 'articulable reasons' and 'founded suspicion' are not self-defining; they fall short of providing clear guidance dispositive of the myriad factual situations that arise. But the essence of all that has been written is that the totality of the circumstances—the whole picture—must be taken into account. Based upon that whole picture the detaining officers must have a particularized and objective basis for suspecting the particular person stopped of criminal activity.

"The idea that an assessment of the whole picture must yield a particularized suspicion contains two elements, each of which must be present before a stop is permissible. First, the assessment must be based upon all the circumstances. The analysis proceeds with various objective observations, information from police reports, if such are available, and consideration of the modes or patterns of operation of certain kinds of lawbreakers. From these data, a trained officer draws inferences and makes deductions—inferences and deductions that might well elude an untrained person.

"The process does not deal with hard certainties, but with probabilities. Long before the law of probabilities was articulated as such, practical people formulated certain common sense conclusions about human behavior; jurors as factfinders are permitted to do the same—and so are law enforcement officers. Finally, the evidence thus collected must be seen and weighed not in terms of library analysis by scholars, but as understood by those versed in the field of law enforcement.

"The second element contained in the idea that an assessment of the whole picture must yield a particularized suspicion is the concept that the process just described must raise a suspicion that the particular individual being stopped is engaged in wrongdoing."

e. Wayne R. LaFave, *"Street Encounters" and the Constitution: Terry, Sibron, Peters and Beyond,* 67 Mich.L.Rev. 40, 73–75 (1968). An excellent illustration is provided by *Luckett v. State,* 284 N.E.2d 738 (Ind.1972), where an officer stopped for investigation a green car bearing a license plate prefix 82J upon information that such a car had been used by persons fleeing from a burglary earlier in the evening. The court concluded that the officer had "probable cause to stop the automobile" even though it was "readily apparent" that he "did not have probable cause to stop every green automobile with an 82J license prefix and formally arrest its occupants."

2. In SIBRON v. UNITED STATES, 392 U.S. 40, 88 S.Ct. 1889, 20 L.Ed.2d 917 (1968), a companion case to *Terry,* the facts as stated by the Court were as follows: "At the hearing on the motion to suppress, Officer Martin testified that while he was patrolling his beat in uniform on March 9, 1965, he observed Sibron 'continually from the hours of 4:00 P.M. to 12:00, midnight * * * in the vicinity of 742 Broadway.' He stated that during this period of time he saw Sibron in conversation with six or eight persons whom he (Patrolman Martin) knew from past experience to be narcotics addicts. The officer testified that he did not overhear any of these conversations, and that he did not see anything pass between Sibron and any of the others. Late in the evening Sibron entered a restaurant. Patrolman Martin saw Sibron speak with three more known addicts inside the restaurant. Once again, nothing was overheard and nothing was seen to pass between Sibron and the addicts. Sibron sat down and ordered pie and coffee, and as he was eating, Patrolman Martin approached him and told him to come outside. Once outside, the officer said to Sibron, 'You know what I am after.' According to the officer, Sibron 'mumbled something and reached into his pocket.' Simultaneously, Patrolman Martin thrust his hand into the same pocket, discovering several glassine envelopes, which, it turned out, contained heroin."

Though the Court, per WARREN, C.J., focused primarily upon the lack of grounds for and the improper manner of the frisk (see Notes 1 and 3, pp. 333–34), it was intimated that there were not even grounds for a stop because "Patrolman Martin was completely ignorant regarding the content of these conversations, and that he saw nothing pass between Sibron and the addicts. So far as he knew, they might indeed 'have been talking about the World Series.' The inference that persons who talk to narcotics addicts are engaged in the criminal traffic in narcotics is simply not the sort of reasonable inference required to support an intrusion by the police upon an individual's personal security."

Do you believe that Officer Martin was less certain of what Sibron was up to than Officer McFadden was as to what Terry and his companions were up to? Are there other considerations at play here? HARLAN, J., concurring in *Sibron,* observed that "in *Terry,* the police officer judged that his suspect was about to commit a violent crime and that he had to assert himself in order to prevent it. Here there was no reason for Officer Martin to think that an incipient crime, or flight, or the destruction of evidence would occur if he stayed his hand; indeed, there was no more reason for him to intrude upon Sibron at the moment when he did than there had been four hours earlier, and no reason to think the situation would have changed four hours hence. While no hard-and-fast rule can be drawn, I would suggest that one important factor, missing here, that should be taken into account in determining whether there are reasonable grounds for a forcible intrusion is whether there is any need for immediate action."

3. ALABAMA v. WHITE, 496 U.S. 325, 110 S.Ct. 2412, 110 L.Ed.2d 301 (1990), involved these facts: "On April 22, 1987, at approximately 3 p.m., Corporal B.H. Davis of the Montgomery Police Department received a telephone call from an anonymous person, stating that Vanessa White would be leaving 235–C Lynwood Terrace Apartments at a particular time in a brown Plymouth station wagon with the right taillight lens broken, that she would be going to Dobey's Motel, and that she would be in possession of about an ounce of cocaine inside a brown attaché case. Corporal Davis and his partner, Corporal P.A. Reynolds, proceeded to the Lynwood Terrace Apartments. The officers saw a brown Plymouth station wagon with a broken right taillight in the parking lot in front of the 235 building. The officers observed respondent leave the 235 building, carrying nothing in her hands, and enter the station wagon. They followed the vehicle as it

drove the most direct route to Dobey's Motel. When the vehicle reached the Mobile Highway, on which Dobey's Motel is located, Corporal Reynolds requested a patrol unit to stop the vehicle. The vehicle was stopped at approximately 4:18 p.m., just short of Dobey's Motel. Corporal Davis asked respondent to step to the rear of her car, where he informed her that she had been stopped because she was suspected of carrying cocaine in the vehicle. He asked if they could look for cocaine and respondent said they could look. The officers found a locked brown attaché case in the car and, upon request, respondent provided the combination to the lock." In upholding the stop, the Court, per WHITE, J., reasoned:

"The opinion in [*Illinois v.*] *Gates* [p. 186] recognized that an anonymous tip alone seldom demonstrates the informant's basis of knowledge or veracity inasmuch as ordinary citizens generally do not provide extensive recitations of the basis of their everyday observations and given that the veracity of persons supplying anonymous tips is 'by hypothesis largely unknown, and unknowable.' This is not to say that an anonymous caller could never provide the reasonable suspicion necessary for a *Terry* stop.[f] But the tip in *Gates* was not an exception to the general rule, and the anonymous tip in this case is like the one in *Gates:* '[i]t provides virtually nothing from which one might conclude that [the caller] is either honest or his information reliable; likewise, the [tip] gives absolutely no indication of the basis for the [caller's] predictions regarding [Vanessa White's] criminal activities.' * * *

"As there was in *Gates,* however, in this case there is more than the tip itself. The tip was not as detailed, and the corroboration was not as complete, as in *Gates,* but the required degree of suspicion was likewise not as high. * * *

"Reasonable suspicion is a less demanding standard than probable cause not only in the sense that reasonable suspicion can be established with information that is different in quantity or content than that required to establish probable cause, but also in the sense that reasonable suspicion can arise from information that is less reliable than that required to show probable cause. * * * Reasonable suspicion, like probable cause, is dependent upon both the content of information possessed by police and its degree of reliability. Both factors—quantity and quality—are considered in the 'totality of the circumstances—the whole picture' that must be taken into account when evaluating whether there is reasonable suspicion. Thus, if a tip has a relatively low degree of reliability, more information will be required to establish the requisite quantum of suspicion than would be required if the tip were more reliable. The *Gates* Court applied its totality of the circumstances approach in this manner, taking into account the facts known to the officers from personal observation, and giving the anonymous tip the weight it deserved in light of its indicia of reliability as established through independent police work. The same approach applies in the reasonable suspicion context, the only difference being the level of suspicion that must be established. Contrary to the court below, we conclude that when the officers stopped respondent, the anonymous tip had been sufficiently corroborated to furnish reasonable suspicion that respondent was engaged in criminal activity and that the investigative stop therefore did not violate the Fourth Amendment.

f. In *United States v. Clipper,* 973 F.2d 944 (D.C.Cir.1992), defendant interpreted *White* "as requiring anonymous tips to include, and the police to corroborate, predictive information," but the court responded that while this might be so in a drug case, the "careful balancing of interests" contemplated by *Terry* would permit taking into account the "hazards that the illegal use of firearms presents to officer and citizen alike," so that a gun suspect could be stopped even absent a corroborated prediction of future (as compared with ongoing) events.

"It is true that not every detail mentioned by the tipster was verified, such as the name of the woman leaving the building or the precise apartment from which she left; but the officers did corroborate that a woman left the 235 building and got into the particular vehicle that was described by the caller. With respect to the time of departure predicted by the informant, Corporal Davis testified that the caller gave a particular time when the woman would be leaving, but he did not state what that time was. He did testify that, after the call, he and his partner proceeded to the Lynwood Terrace Apartments to put the 235 building under surveillance. Given the fact that the officers proceeded to the indicated address immediately after the call and that respondent emerged not too long thereafter, it appears from the record before us that respondent's departure from the building was within the time frame predicted by the caller. As for the caller's prediction of respondent's destination, it is true that the officers stopped her just short of Dobey's Motel and did not know whether she would have pulled in or continued on past it. But given that the four-mile route driven by respondent was the most direct route possible to Dobey's Motel, but nevertheless involved several turns, we think respondent's destination was significantly corroborated.

"The Court's opinion in *Gates* gave credit to the proposition that because an informant is shown to be right about some things, he is probably right about other facts that he has alleged, including the claim that the object of the tip is engaged in criminal activity. Thus, it is not unreasonable to conclude in this case that the independent corroboration by the police of significant aspects of the informer's predictions imparted some degree of reliability to the other allegations made by the caller.

"We think it also important that, as in *Gates,* 'the anonymous [tip] contained a range of details relating not just to easily obtained facts and conditions existing at the time of the tip, but to future actions of third parties ordinarily not easily predicted.' The fact that the officers found a car precisely matching the caller's description in front of the 235 building is an example of the former. Anyone could have 'predicted' that fact because it was a condition presumably existing at the time of the call. What was important was the caller's ability to predict respondent's *future behavior,* because it demonstrated inside information—a special familiarity with respondent's affairs. The general public would have had no way of knowing that respondent would shortly leave the building, get in the described car, and drive the most direct route to Dobey's Motel. Because only a small number of people are generally privy to an individual's itinerary, it is reasonable for police to believe that a person with access to such information is likely to also have access to reliable information about that individual's illegal activities. When significant aspects of the caller's predictions were verified, there was reason to believe not only that the caller was honest but also that he was well informed, at least well enough to justify the stop."

STEVENS, J., for the three dissenters, objected: "Anybody with enough knowledge about a given person to make her the target of a prank, or to harbor a grudge against her, will certainly be able to formulate a tip about her like the one predicting Vanessa White's excursion. In addition, under the Court's holding, every citizen is subject to being seized and questioned by any officer who is prepared to testify that the warrantless stop was based on an anonymous tip predicting whatever conduct the officer just observed. Fortunately, the vast majority of those in our law enforcement community would not adopt such a practice. But the Fourth Amendment was intended to protect the citizen from the overzealous and unscrupulous officer as well as from those who are conscientious and truthful. This decision makes a mockery of that protection."

4. In UNITED STATES v. SOKOLOW, 490 U.S. 1, 109 S.Ct. 1581, 104 L.Ed.2d 1 (1989), the defendant was stopped at the Honolulu airport by agents who knew "that (1) he paid $2,100 for two airplane tickets from a roll of $20 bills; (2) he traveled under a name that did not match the name under which his telephone number was listed; (3) his original destination was Miami, a source city for illicit drugs; (4) he stayed in Miami for only 48 hours, even though a round-trip flight from Honolulu to Miami takes 20 hours; (5) he appeared nervous during his trip; and (6) he checked none of his luggage." The Court, per REHNQUIST, C.J., held this amounted to reasonable suspicion (said to be a level of suspicion "considerably less than proof of wrongdoing by a preponderance of the evidence") defendant was a drug courier:

"We do not agree with respondent that our analysis is somehow changed by the agents' belief that his behavior was consistent with one of the DEA's 'drug courier profiles.' A court sitting to determine the existence of reasonable suspicion must require the agent to articulate the factors leading to that conclusion, but the fact that these factors may be set forth in a 'profile' does not somehow detract from their evidentiary significance as seen by a trained agent."

MARSHALL, J., joined by Brennan, J., dissenting, objected: "It is highly significant that the DEA agents stopped Sokolow because he matched one of the DEA's 'profiles' of a paradigmatic drug courier. In my view, a law enforcement officer's mechanistic application of a formula of personal and behavioral traits in deciding whom to detain can only dull the officer's ability and determination to make sensitive and fact-specific inferences 'in light of his experience,' *Terry*, particularly in ambiguous or borderline cases. Reflexive reliance on a profile of drug courier characteristics runs a far greater risk than does ordinary, case-by-case police work, of subjecting innocent individuals to unwarranted police harassment and detention. This risk is enhanced by the profile's 'chameleon-like way of adapting to any particular set of observations.' "

5. Should either the seriousness of the suspected crime or the time of its apparent commission have any bearing on whether a *Terry* stop is permissible? In UNITED STATES v. HENSLEY, 469 U.S. 221, 105 S.Ct. 675, 83 L.Ed.2d 604 (1985), the Court, per O'CONNOR, J., held by analogy to *Whiteley v. Warden*, p. 208, "that, if a flyer or bulletin has been issued on the basis of articulable facts supporting a reasonable suspicion that the wanted person has committed an offense, then reliance on that flyer or bulletin justifies a stop to check identification, to pose questions to the person, or to detain the person briefly while attempting to obtain further information." But the Court first rejected the lower court's position that *Terry* is limited to ongoing criminal activity:

" * * * The precise limits on investigatory stops to investigate past criminal activity are more difficult to define. The proper way to identify the limits is to apply the same test already used to identify the proper bounds of intrusions that further investigations of imminent or ongoing crimes. That test, which is grounded in the standard of reasonableness embodied in the Fourth Amendment, balances the nature and quality of the intrusion on personal security against the importance of the governmental interests alleged to justify the intrusion. When this balancing test is applied to stops to investigate past crimes, we think that probable cause to arrest need not always be required.

"The factors in the balance may be somewhat different when a stop to investigate past criminal activity is involved rather than a stop to investigate ongoing criminal conduct. This is because the governmental interest and the nature of the intrusions involved in the two situations may differ. As we noted in

Terry, one general interest present in the context of ongoing or imminent criminal activity is 'that of effective crime prevention and detection.' A stop to investigate an already completed crime does not necessarily promote the interest of crime prevention as directly as a stop to investigate suspected ongoing criminal activity. Similarly, the exigent circumstances which require a police officer to step in before a crime is committed or completed are not necessarily as pressing long afterwards. Public safety may be less threatened by a suspect in a past crime who now appears to be going about his lawful business than it is by a suspect who is currently in the process of violating the law. Finally, officers making a stop to investigate past crimes may have a wider range of opportunity to choose the time and circumstances of the stop.

"Despite these differences, where police have been unable to locate a person suspected of involvement in a past crime, the ability to briefly stop that person, ask questions, or check identification in the absence of probable cause promotes the strong government interest in solving crimes and bringing offenders to justice. Restraining police action until after probable cause is obtained would not only hinder the investigation, but might also enable the suspect to flee in the interim and to remain at large. Particularly in the context of felonies or crimes involving a threat to public safety, it is in the public interest that the crime be solved and the suspect detained as promptly as possible. The law enforcement interests at stake in these circumstances outweigh the individual's interest to be free of a stop and detention that is no more extensive than permissible in the investigation of imminent or ongoing crimes.

"We need not and do not decide today whether *Terry* stops to investigate all past crimes, however serious, are permitted. It is enough to say that, if police have a reasonable suspicion, grounded in specific and articulable facts, that a person they encounter was involved in or is wanted in connection with a completed felony, then a *Terry* stop may be made to investigate that suspicion."[g]

6.   Are there grounds for the stops made on the following facts, essentially those in *United States v. Feliciano,* 45 F.3d 1070 (7th Cir.1995)? An officer on patrol near a train station at midnight saw *F* and *M* walking in an area of a parking lot where there were no cars and which led to the river embankment. *M* then approached *K,* who was standing near the tracks with a suitcase, spoke with him for a while, and then left, rejoined *F,* and departed the scene in a direction opposite of that *K* then headed. The officer approached *K,* who told the officer that *M* had tried to lure him to the embankment to help an injured friend, but that *K* had refused. *K* explained that he had also seen *F* earlier and thus knew he was not injured; *K* surmised that the two had been planning to mug him. The officer asked his backup officer to stop *F* and *M.* The backup officer, who recognized *F* as a gang member recently released from prison, where *F* had served time for robbery, then stopped *F* and *M* as they walked toward their homes through the apparently deserted downtown area.

7.   In *Hodari D.,* p. 316, did Officer Pertoso have grounds to seize Hodari *before* the cocaine was discarded? In a footnote, Justice Scalia, though noting this issue had not been decided by the Court, commented: "That it would be unreason-

---

g.   But, what if the stop is made other than at a crime scene because the individual is thought to have information about the criminal activity of others? A stop for such a purpose was involved in *United States v. Ward,* 488 F.2d 162 (9th Cir.1973), where FBI agents used their siren to stop a person driving a car, after which he displayed a false draft card. The court held that the seizure was improper because there was no emergency requiring the interview of that person at that particular time, and went on to note that *Terry* "cannot be stretched so far as to allow detentive stops for generalized criminal inquiries."

able to stop, for brief inquiry, young men who scatter in panic upon the mere sighting of the police is not self-evident, and arguably contradicts proverbial common sense. See Proverbs 28:1 ('The wicked flee when no man pursueth')."

Compare Tracey Maclin, supra, at 276: "Of course, this viewpoint never considers that Hodari, a black youth, may have had alternative reasons for wanting to avoid the cops. Many persons who have never committed a crime have ambivalent or negative attitudes about the police. Perhaps a youth like Hodari flees at the sight of police because he does not wish to drop his pants, as many black youth in Boston have been forced to do, just because the cops suspect he belongs to a gang or is selling drugs. Or maybe Hodari has had an older sibling or friend roughed up by the police, and does not wish to undergo a similar experience with the approaching officers."

Compare also David A. Harris, *Factors for Reasonable Suspicion: When Black and Poor Means Stopped and Frisked,* 69 Ind.L.J. 659, 674, 687 (1994), noting there are many lower court cases holding that "presence in a high crime location" plus "evasion" are together "enough to sustain a *Terry* stop," and proposing that instead "the law should require that something more than a location of high crime or drug activity and evasion of the police be present, something clearly indicative of criminality. For example, gestures known to be characteristic of drug activity, such as using particular hand signals to indicate the availability of contraband, in addition to location and evasion, could be enough."

8. *Terry* relied upon the *Camara* case, p. 339, allowing safety inspections of buildings without such individualized suspicion when pursuant to an established scheme or plan. And in *Brown v. Texas,* 443 U.S. 47, 99 S.Ct. 2637, 61 L.Ed.2d 357 (1979), a unanimous Court declared that the Fourth Amendment requires that a brief detention for investigation "be based on specific, objective facts indicating that society's legitimate interests require the seizure of the particular individual, or that the seizure must be carried out pursuant to a plan embodying explicit, neutral limitations on the conduct of individual officers." Does this mean that such a plan is a sufficient substitute for individualized suspicion? How might such a plan be drafted?

D.   PERMISSIBLE EXTENT OF TEMPORARY SEIZURE

1. Assuming that the police only have grounds to make a temporary seizure on the street for purposes of investigation, what limits must be observed by them to prevent the seizure from becoming illegal? What if the officer approaches with a drawn gun and orders the suspect to raise his hands? What if the officer asserts that the suspect is under arrest? And what of the length of detention? Compare *United States v. Jennings,* 468 F.2d 111 (9th Cir.1972) (25 minutes too long where suspect cooperated fully and no greater suspicion developed); with *United States v. Richards,* 500 F.2d 1025 (9th Cir.1974) (1 hour not too long where suspects gave implausible responses to questions, thereby adding to initial suspicion, and police diligently pursued the most plausible means of clarifying the situation). What if the suspect was transported to a nearby crime scene for possible identification as the perpetrator, held impermissible in *People v. Harris,* 540 P.2d 632 (Cal.1975), whenever the witnesses could be transported to the detention scene?[h] As for detention at the police station, see pp. 336–39.

---

h. Compare *People v. Bloyd,* 331 N.W.2d 447 (Mich.1982), concluding that because transportation of a suspect even a short dis- tance is more intrusive than a mere stop, it "should be dependent upon knowledge that a crime has been committed" and impermissible

2. In FLORIDA v. ROYER, 460 U.S. 491, 103 S.Ct. 1319, 75 L.Ed.2d 229 (1983), the detectives asked Royer to accompany them to a small room about 40 feet away. His luggage was retrieved from the airline and brought to that room, and Royer was then asked to consent to a search of the suitcases, which he did. About 15 minutes had elapsed since the initial encounter. The *Royer* plurality[i] first commented:

"The predicate permitting seizures on suspicion short of probable cause is that law enforcement interests warrant a limited intrusion on the personal security of the suspect. The scope of the intrusion permitted will vary to some extent with the particular facts and circumstances of each case. This much, however, is clear: an investigative detention must be temporary and last no longer than is necessary to effectuate the purpose of the stop. Similarly, the investigative methods employed should be the least intrusive means reasonably available to verify or dispel the officer's suspicion in a short period of time. It is the State's burden to demonstrate that the seizure it seeks to justify on the basis of a reasonable suspicion was sufficiently limited in scope and duration to satisfy the conditions of an investigative seizure."

The plurality then concluded "that at the time Royer produced the key to his suitcase, the detention to which he was then subjected was a more serious intrusion on his personal liberty than is allowable on mere suspicion of criminal activity." They stressed: (i) that the situation "had escalated into an investigatory procedure in a police interrogation room," so that "[a]s a practical matter, Royer was under arrest"; and (ii) that "the officers' conduct was more intrusive than necessary to effectuate an investigative detention otherwise authorized by the *Terry* line of cases," as while "there are undoubtedly reasons of safety and security that would justify moving a suspect from one location to another during an investigatory detention, such as from an airport concourse to a more private area," there was "no indication in this case that such reasons prompted the officers to transfer the site of the encounter from the concourse to the interrogation room. It appears, rather, that the primary interest of the officers was not in having an extended conversation with Royer but in the contents of his luggage, a matter which the officers did not pursue orally with Royer until after the encounter was relocated to the police room. The record does not reflect any facts which would support a finding that the legitimate law enforcement purposes which justified the detention in the first instance were furthered by removing Royer to the police room prior to the officer's attempt to gain his consent to a search of his luggage. As we have noted, had Royer consented to a search on the spot, the search could have been conducted with Royer present in the area where the bags were retrieved by Officer Johnson and any evidence recovered would have been admissible against him. If the search proved negative, Royer would have been free to go much earlier and with less likelihood of missing his flight, which in itself can be a very serious matter in a variety of circumstances.

"Third, the State has not touched on the question whether it would have been feasible to investigate the contents of Royer's bags in a more expeditious way. The courts are not strangers to the use of trained dogs to detect the presence of controlled substances in luggage. There is no indication here that this means was not feasible and available. If it had been used, Royer and his luggage could have been momentarily detained while this investigative procedure was carried

when the defendant's conduct was suspicious but "there has not been any report of a crime" recently in the vicinity.

i. White, J., joined by Marshall, Powell and Stevens, JJ.

out. Indeed, it may be that no detention at all would have been necessary. A negative result would have freed Royer in short order; a positive result would have resulted in his justifiable arrest on probable cause."[j]

BRENNAN, J., concurring, addressed this point in a footnote reading as follows: "I interpret the plurality's requirement that the investigative methods employed pursuant to a *Terry* stop be 'the least intrusive means reasonably available to verify or dispel the officer's suspicion in a short period of time,' to mean that the availability of a less intrusive means may make an otherwise reasonable stop unreasonable. I do not interpret it to mean that the absence of a less intrusive means can make an otherwise unreasonable stop reasonable."

BLACKMUN, J., dissenting because he believed that Royer consented to go to the room, added that he could not "accept the 'least intrusive' alternative analysis the plurality would impose on the law of the Fourth Amendment." REHNQUIST, J., joined by the Chief Justice and O'Connor, J., dissenting, also found no support in prior cases for the plurality's "least intrusive means" principle and concluded that the plurality's analysis "adds up to little more than saying that if my aunt were a man, she would be my uncle. The officers might have taken different steps than they did to investigate Royer, but the same may be said of virtually every investigative encounter that has more than one step to it. The question we must decide is what was *unreasonable* about the steps which *these officers* took with respect to *this* suspect in the Miami Airport on this particular day."

3. What limits, if any, does *Royer* place upon *Terry* stops? Does the case justify the conclusion (i) that such a stop may not extend as long as 15 minutes? (ii) that the person detained may never be moved to another location? (iii) that the person detained may not be moved from a public area to a private one? (iv) that the police must opt for the most expeditious means of investigation? Consider UNITED STATES v. SHARPE, 470 U.S. 675, 105 S.Ct. 1568, 84 L.Ed.2d 605 (1985). There, a federal drug agent, patrolling in an unmarked car in a highway area under surveillance for drug trafficking, saw an apparently overloaded camper truck traveling in tandem with a Pontiac. He radioed for assistance, and when a highway patrolman responded they attempted to stop the two vehicles. The Pontiac pulled over, but the truck continued on, pursued by the patrolman. Once the drug agent obtained identification from the driver of the Pontiac, he sought without success to reach the patrolman by radio. He then radioed for more assistance, and when local police appeared he left them with the Pontiac and drove ahead to where the patrolman had stopped the truck. After smelling the odor of marijuana coming from the vehicle, he opened it and saw bales of marijuana and then arrested the driver of the truck, one Savage. The Court of Appeals held that the 20–minute detention of Savage "failed to meet the [Fourth Amendment's] requirement of brevity," but the Supreme Court, per BURGER, C.J., disagreed:

" * * * Obviously, if an investigative stop continues indefinitely, at some point it can no longer be justified as an investigative stop. But our cases impose no rigid time limitation on *Terry* stops. * * * Much as a 'bright line' rule would be desirable, in evaluating whether an investigative detention is unreasonable, common sense and ordinary human experience must govern over rigid criteria.[k]

---

j. The plurality then concluded "that probable cause to arrest Royer did not exist at the time he consented to the search of his luggage," so that the consent was the fruit of an illegal arrest. The dissenters, believing the detention in the room was permissible under *Terry,* found it unnecessary to address the probable cause issue.

k. Compare *Model Code of Pre–Arraignment Procedure* § 110.2(1), recommending a maximum of 20 minutes for a *Terry* stop.

"In assessing whether a detention is too long in duration to be justified as an investigative stop, we consider it appropriate to examine whether the police diligently pursued a means of investigation that was likely to confirm or dispel their suspicions quickly, during which time it was necessary to detain the defendant. A court making this assessment should take care to consider whether the police are acting in a swiftly developing situation, and in such cases the court should not indulge in unrealistic second-guessing. A creative judge engaged in *post hoc* evaluation of police conduct can almost always imagine some alternative means by which the objectives of the police might have been accomplished. But '[t]he fact that the protection of the public might, in the abstract, have been accomplished by "less intrusive" means does not, in itself, render the search unreasonable.' The question is not simply whether some other alternative was available, but whether the police acted unreasonably in failing to recognize or to pursue it."

Stressing that the "delay in this case was attributable almost entirely to the evasive actions of Savage," that most of the 20 minutes was consumed by the agent trying to reach the patrolman and to obtain additional assistance, and that when the agent reached Savage "he proceeded expeditiously," the majority in *Sharpe* concluded the delay was not unreasonable. MARSHALL, J., though concurring because the "prolonged encounter" was attributable to "the evasive actions" of Savage, argued that "fidelity to the rationales that justify *Terry* stops require that the intrusiveness of the stop be measured independently of law enforcement needs. A stop must first be found not unduly intrusive, particularly in its length, before it is proper to consider whether law enforcement aims warrant limited investigation." BRENNAN, J., dissenting, objected that record did not clearly show that Savage had tried to elude the police, and that the government had not met its burden under *Royer* to "show at a minimum that the 'least intrusive means reasonably available' were used in carrying out the stop."

4. Will the most common investigative technique, interrogation, ordinarily be the most expeditious? Does that depend upon the significance which can be attached to noncooperation? Cf. KOLENDER v. LAWSON, 461 U.S. 352, 103 S.Ct. 1855, 75 L.Ed.2d 903 (1983), where the Court overturned on void for vagueness grounds a statute which, as construed, made it a criminal offense for a person lawfully stopped under *Terry* to fail to provide "credible and reliable" identification and to account for his presence, as the statute "contains no standard for determining what a suspect has to do in order to satisfy the requirement to provide a 'credible and reliable' identification." The majority thus found it unnecessary to address other issues, but BRENNAN, J., concurring, asserted that "under the Fourth Amendment, police officers with reasonable suspicion that an individual has committed or is about to commit a crime may detain that individual, using some force if necessary, for the purpose of asking investigative questions. They may ask their questions in a way calculated to obtain an answer. But they may not *compel* an answer, and they must allow the person to leave after a reasonably brief period of time unless the information they have acquired during the encounter has given them probable cause sufficient to justify an arrest.[4]"

---

4. * * * In some circumstances it is even conceivable that the mere fact that a suspect refuses to answer questions once detained, viewed in the context of the facts that gave rise to reasonable suspicion in the first place, would be enough to provide probable cause. A court confronted with such a claim, however, would have to evaluate it carefully to make certain that the person arrested was not being penalized for the exercise of his right to refuse to answer.

5. Reconsider the pretext traffic stop tactic discussed in Notes 5–10, pp. 245–47. To what extent does the *Terry* requirement that the seizure be "reasonably related in scope to the circumstances which justified the interference in the first place" provide meaningful limits upon the opportunity for the police to conduct a narcotics investigation during a traffic stop? For example, on the following facts, taken from *United States v. Ramos,* 20 F.3d 348 (8th Cir.1994), on reh. 42 F.3d 1160 (8th Cir.1994), at what point, if at all, did the officer cross the line?

At 7 a.m. the trooper stopped a pickup on Interstate 80 when he saw the passenger was not wearing a seat belt. The trooper asked the passenger for identification, and the passenger produced his driver's license. The trooper then asked for the driver for his license as well, which was also produced. (The trooper later testified he needed only the passenger's identification to prepare a citation.) The trooper then asked the driver to accompany him to the patrol car, where the trooper radioed for a computer check on the two men and the truck. While awaiting a response, the trooper questioned the driver about various matters, including his precise destination, the purpose of his trip, and his employment. When a negative response was received from the computer inquiry, the trooper returned the driver's license and then asked him to stay in the patrol car while he gave the warning ticket to the passenger. The trooper gave the warning ticket, which bore the time 7:40 a.m., to the passenger and then asked him about his destination and whether there were any drugs in the truck. The trooper then went back to his patrol car and questioned the driver again about where he was from and his destination, and asked if there were drugs in the truck. The trooper then asked the driver to consent to a search of the truck, and the driver signed a consent form which also bore the time 7:40 a.m. The trooper then called for a second officer, who arrived at the scene 10 minutes later, and then the searched commenced.

6. The cases analyzing such traffic stops usually take the view that if the officer who made the stop has checked out the driver's license and vehicle registration and has written up the traffic citation or warning, then any *extension* of the stop thereafter for the purpose of questioning about drugs or seeking consent to search for drugs is illegal. See, e.g., *United States v. Fernandez,* 18 F.3d 874 (10th Cir.1994); *People v. Banks,* 650 N.E.2d 833 (N.Y.1995). Dictum in some cases, e.g., *United States v. Cummins,* 920 F.2d 498 (8th Cir.1990), suggests that *all* of the officer's investigative activity must be limited to the offense for which the stop was made unless reasonable suspicion develops as to other criminality, e.g., drug possession. However, courts often deem questioning on unrelated matters absent such suspicion as unobjectionable *provided* it is accomplished within the permissible time span of the traffic stop. See, e.g., *United States v. Crain,* 33 F.3d 480 (5th Cir.1994).

It is thus sometimes necessary to determine whether a traffic stop was extended or instead terminated at a certain point. Even if it is apparent to the defendant that the officer has completed writing up the ticket or warning, that does not terminate the stop if the officer continues to hold the defendant's license, vehicle registration, or other credentials. *United States v. Fernandez,* supra. But if, on the other hand, the officer *has* returned those credentials, does this mean that the seizure has terminated even if the officer then uses the Lt. Colombo gambit ("Oh, one more thing, . . .") in order to question the defendant about drugs? See *United States v. Werking,* 915 F.2d 1404 (10th Cir.1990) (return of his papers manifested to the driver that he "was free to leave the scene," so that when he instead remained and responded to the questions he "chose to engage in a consensual encounter").

7. OHIO v. ROBINETTE, 519 U.S. 33, 117 S.Ct. 417, 136 L.Ed.2d 347 (1996), involved these facts: a sheriff's deputy on "drug interdiction patrol" stopped defendant for speeding. The deputy examined defendant's license, ran a computer check indicting no previous violations, issued a verbal warning and returned defendant's license, and then immediately asked defendant if he had drugs in the car; when defendant answered in the negative, the deputy asked to search the car and defendant consented, resulting in a search which uncovered a small amount of marijuana and a single pill which was a controlled substance. The state supreme court concluded the evidence must be suppressed, reasoning that the "right to be secure in one's person and property requires that citizens stopped for traffic offenses be clearly informed by the detaining officer when they are free to go after a valid detention, before an officer attempts to engage in a consensual interrogation." The Supreme Court, per REHNQUIST, C.J., focused on the issue stated in the certiorari petition, whether such a warning is a prerequisite to a voluntary consent, and answered in the negative. The state court's per se rule was deemed inconsistent with the approach to Fourth Amendment issues by the Supreme Court, which has "consistently eschewed bright-line rules, instead emphasizing the fact-specific nature of the reasonableness inquiry." Moreover, the Court reasoned in *Robinette*, requiring such warnings would be just as impractical as the right-to-refuse-consent warnings held unnecessary by the Court in *Schneckloth v. Bustamonte* [p. 343].

Only Justice STEVENS, dissenting, fully considered an alternative characterization of the state court's holding, namely, that (i) the officer's failure to tell defendant he was free to leave meant that a reasonable person would continue to believe he was not free to leave, so that the seizure had not yet ended at the time the consent was obtained; (ii) the seizure by that time was illegal, as it had exceeded its lawful purpose, the giving of a warning about the traffic offense; and (iii) consequently the evidence obtained via the voluntary consent was a suppressible fruit of that poisonous tree. He concluded that the evidence in the case (including the fact that this deputy had used this tactic to make 786 consent searches in one year) supported that conclusion, so that the suppression of evidence by the state court was justified.

The *Robinette* majority was not totally silent regarding this theory. The defendant argued the Court could not reach the voluntariness issue because the state court decision set out a valid alternative ground in the following language: "When the motivation behind a police officer's continued detention of a person stopped for a traffic violation is not related to the purpose of the original, constitutional stop, and when that continued detention is not based on articulable facts giving rise to a suspicion of some separate illegal activity justifying an extension of the detention, the continued detention constitutes an illegal seizure." Relying on the *Whren* case, p. 240, the Chief Justice declared that the state court was in error because "the subjective intentions of the officer did not make the continued detention of respondent illegal under the Fourth Amendment." Is this a proper application of *Whren*? Does it mean that in applying the *Terry* scope limitation, the fact the officer decided only to give a warning is irrelevant? Or, is Justice Stevens correct in concluding that the irrelevant subjective motivation was drug interdiction, but that the subjective purpose of warning bears on the justification for the continued detention, so that by the time the consent was obtained "the lawful traffic stop had come to an end" because the defendant "had been given his warning"?

E.   Temporary Seizure of Effects

1. In *United States v. Van Leeuwen*, 397 U.S. 249, 90 S.Ct. 1029, 25 L.Ed.2d 282 (1970) a postal clerk in Mt. Vernon, Washington, advised a policeman that he was suspicious of two packages of coins just mailed. The policeman immediately noted that the return address was fictitious and that the individual who mailed the packages had Canadian license plates, and later investigation disclosed that the addressees (one in California, the other in Tennessee) were under investigation for trafficking in illegal coins. Upon this basis a search warrant for both packages was obtained, but not until the packages had been held for slightly more than a day. A unanimous Court, although acknowledging that "detention of mail could at some point become an unreasonable seizure of 'papers' or 'effects' within the meaning of the Fourth Amendment," cited *Terry* in upholding this "detention, without a warrant, while an investigation was made." The Court emphasized that the investigation was conducted promptly and that most of the delay was attributable to the fact that because of the time differential the Tennessee authorities could not be reached until the following day.

2. In UNITED STATES v. PLACE, 462 U.S. 696, 103 S.Ct. 2637, 77 L.Ed.2d 110 (1983), federal agents stopped respondent, a suspected drug courier, at LaGuardia Airport, seized his luggage for the purported purpose of taking it to a judge while a warrant was sought, and then allowed respondent to go his way. They took the bags to Kennedy Airport, where a trained narcotics dog reacted positively to one of them and ambiguously to the other, but because it was late Friday afternoon held the bags until Monday morning, when a warrant was obtained for the first bag and cocaine was found in execution of the warrant. The Court, per O'CONNOR, J., first recognized "the reasonableness under the Fourth Amendment of warrantless seizures of personal luggage from the custody of the owner on the basis of less than probable cause for the purpose of pursuing a limited course of investigation, short of opening the luggage, that would quickly confirm or dispel the authorities' suspicion." Applying the *Terry* balancing of interests approach, the Court concluded that "the governmental interest in seizing the luggage briefly to pursue further investigation is substantial," and that because "seizures of property can vary in intrusiveness, some brief detentions of personal effects may be so minimally intrusive of Fourth Amendment interests that strong countervailing governmental interests will justify a seizure based only on specific articulable facts that the property contains contraband or evidence of a crime.

"* * * Particularly in the case of detention of luggage within the traveler's immediate possession, the police conduct intrudes on both the suspect's possessory interest in his luggage as well as his liberty interest in proceeding with his itinerary. The person whose luggage is detained is technically still free to continue his travels or carry out other personal activities pending release of the luggage. Moreover, he is not subjected to the coercive atmosphere of a custodial confinement or to the public indignity of being personally detained. Nevertheless, such a seizure can effectively restrain the person since he is subjected to the possible disruption of his travel plans in order to remain with his luggage or to arrange for its return.[8] Therefore, when the police seize luggage from the suspect's custody,

---

8. "At least when the authorities do not make it absolutely clear how they plan to reunite the suspect and his possessions at some future time and place, seizure of the object is tantamount to seizure of the person. This is because that person must either remain on the we think the limitations applicable to investigative detentions of the person should define the permissible scope of an investigative detention of the person's luggage on less than probable cause. Under this standard, it is clear that the police conduct here exceeded the permissible limits of a *Terry*-type investigative stop.

"The length of the detention of respondent's luggage alone precludes the conclusion that the seizure was reasonable in the absence of probable cause. Although we have recognized the reasonableness of seizures longer than the momentary ones involved in *Terry,* the brevity of the invasion of the individual's Fourth Amendment interests is an important factor in determining whether the seizure is so minimally intrusive as to be justifiable on reasonable suspicion. Moreover, in assessing the effect of the length of the detention, we take into account whether the police diligently pursue their investigation. We note that here the New York agents knew the time of Place's scheduled arrival at LaGuardia, had ample time to arrange for their additional investigation at that location, and thereby could have minimized the intrusion on respondent's Fourth Amendment interests. Thus, although we decline to adopt any outside time limitation for a permissible *Terry* stop, we have never approved a seizure of the person for the prolonged 90–minute period involved here and cannot do so on the facts presented by this case.

"Although the 90–minute detention of respondent's luggage is sufficient to render the seizure unreasonable, the violation was exacerbated by the failure of the agents to accurately inform respondent of the place to which they were transporting his luggage, of the length of time he might be dispossessed, and of what arrangements would be made for return of the luggage if the investigation dispelled the suspicion."

BRENNAN, J., joined by Marshall, J., concurring in the result, objected that the majority's approval of brief detention of luggage was "unnecessary to the Court's judgment" and "finds no support in *Terry* or its progeny and significantly dilutes the Fourth Amendment's protections against government interference with personal property." They contended that when the officers "did not develop probable cause to arrest respondent during their encounter with him," "they had to let him go" and could not then subject him "to an independent dispossession of his personal effects based simply on reasonable suspicion." They argued that the *Terry* "balancing inquiries should not be conducted except in the most limited circumstances," while BLACKMUN, J., concurring separately, similarly expressed concern "with what appears to me to be an emerging tendency on the part of the Court to convert the *Terry* decision into a general statement that the Fourth Amendment requires only that any seizure be reasonable."

F.   PROTECTIVE SEARCH

1.   After *Terry,* what is the test for determining whether an officer may conduct a "frisk"? Consider *Sibron,* p. 320, where the Court stated: "In the case of the self-protective search for weapons, [the officer] must be able to point to particular facts from which he reasonably inferred that the individual was armed and dangerous. Patrolman Martin's testimony reveals no such facts. The suspect's mere act of talking with a number of known narcotics addicts over an eight-hour period no more gives rise to reasonable fear of life or limb on the part of the police

scene or else seemingly surrender his effects   *Search and Seizure* § 9.6, p. 61 (1982 Supp.).
permanently to the police." 3 W. LaFave,

officer than it justifies an arrest for committing a crime. Nor did Patrolman Martin urge that when Sibron put his hand in his pocket, he feared that he was going for a weapon and acted in self-defense. His opening statement to Sibron— 'You know what I am after'—made it abundantly clear that he sought narcotics, and his testimony at the hearing left no doubt that he thought there were narcotics in Sibron's pocket."

Compare *Adams v. Williams,* 407 U.S. 143, 92 S.Ct. 1921, 32 L.Ed.2d 612 (1972), where the majority concluded the officer "had ample reason to fear for his own safety"[k] upon being told by an informant that defendant, seated in a nearby car, was carrying narcotics and had a gun at his waist. Marshall, J., joined by Douglas, J., dissenting, objected: "The fact remains that Connecticut specifically authorizes persons to carry guns so long as they have a permit. Thus, there was no reason for the officer to infer from anything that the informant said that the respondent was dangerous."

2. Consider David A. Harris, *Frisking Every Suspect: The Withering of Terry,* 28 U.C. Davis L.Rev. 1, 5, 43–44 (1994): "Perhaps as a result of the high-visibility use of frisks as a contemporary crime control device, or because of general public antipathy to crime, lower courts have stretched the law governing frisks to the point that the Supreme Court might find it unrecognizable. Lower courts have consistently expanded the *types of offenses* always considered violent regardless of the individual circumstances. At the same time, lower courts have also found that certain *types of persons and situations* always pose a danger of armed violence to police [e.g., those present in a high-crime or drug-involved location who engage in allegedly evasive behavior toward the police]. When confronted with these offenses, persons, or situations, police may *automatically* frisk, whether or not any individualized circumstances point to danger. * * *

" * * * African–Americans and Hispanic–Americans pay a higher personal price for [these] contemporary stop and frisk practices than whites do."

3. As for the requisite search procedure, the Court in *Sibron* stated: "The search for weapons approved in *Terry* consisted solely of a limited patting of the outer clothing of the suspect for concealed objects which might be used as instruments of assault. Only when he discovered such objects did the officer in *Terry* place his hands in the pockets of the men he searched. In this case, with no attempt at an initial limited exploration for arms, Patrolman Martin thrust his hand into Sibron's pocket and took from him envelopes of heroin. His testimony shows that he was looking for narcotics, and he found them. The search was not reasonably limited in scope to the accomplishment of the only goal which might conceivably have justified its inception—the protection of the officer by disarming a potentially dangerous man."

Compare *Adams v. Williams,* where the officer immediately reached into the car and removed a theretofore concealed gun from defendant's waistband. The Court stated: "When Williams rolled down his window, rather than complying with the policeman's request to step out of the car so that his movements could more easily be seen, the revolver allegedly at Williams' waist became an even

---

k. The Court footnoted that statement with the following:

"Figures reported by the Federal Bureau of Investigation indicate that 125 policemen were murdered in 1971, with all but five of them having been killed by gunshot wounds. Federal Bureau of Investigation *Law En-*

forcement Bulletin, February 1972, p. 33. According to one study, approximately 30% of police shootings occurred when a police officer approached a suspect seated in an automobile. Bristow, *Police Officer Shootings—A Tactical Evaluation,* 54 J.Crim.L.C. & P.S. 93 (1963)."

greater threat. Under these circumstances the policeman's action in reaching to the spot where the gun was thought to be hidden constituted a limited intrusion designed to insure his safety, and we conclude that it was reasonable."

4. Assuming that there are grounds for a protective search, how extensive a "patting down" of the suspect is permissible? Consider the description quoted in note 13 of *Terry*. Is the right to make a protective search limited to the person of the suspect? What if the suspect is carrying an attache case, a shopping bag, a purse, or similar object?

In *Minnesota v. Dickerson*, 508 U.S. 366, 113 S.Ct. 2130, 124 L.Ed.2d 334 (1993), the frisking officer felt a small lump in the suspect's front pocket and then, upon further tactile examination, concluded the lump was a lump of crack cocaine in a plastic or cellophane bag, which the officer removed from the suspect's pocket. Noting the state court's findings that the officer "determined that the lump was contraband only after 'squeezing, sliding and otherwise manipulating the outside of the defendant's pocket' "*after* the officer knew it contained no weapon, the Supreme Court held the state court "was correct in holding that the police officer in this case overstepped the bounds of the 'strictly circumscribed' search for weapons allowed under *Terry*."

5. In MICHIGAN v. LONG, 463 U.S. 1032, 103 S.Ct. 3469, 77 L.Ed.2d 1201 (1983), two deputies saw a car swerve into a ditch and stopped to investigate. Long, the only occupant of the car, met the deputies at the rear of the car, supplied his driver's license upon demand, and started back toward the open door when asked for his vehicle registration. The officers saw a large hunting knife on the floorboard, so Long was frisked and one officer then entered the vehicle and found an open pouch of marijuana under an armrest. The Supreme Court, per O'CONNOR, J., held:

"Our past cases indicate then that protection of police and others can justify protective searches when police have a reasonable belief that the suspect poses a danger, that roadside encounters between police and suspects are especially hazardous, and that danger may arise from the possible presence of weapons in the area surrounding a suspect. These principles compel our conclusion that the search of the passenger compartment of an automobile, limited to those areas in which a weapon may be placed or hidden, is permissible if the police officer possesses a reasonable belief based on 'specific and articulable facts which, taken together with the rational inferences from those facts, reasonably warrant' the officers in believing that the suspect is dangerous and the suspect may gain immediate control of weapons. * * *

"The circumstances of this case clearly justified Deputies Howell and Lewis in their reasonable belief that Long posed a danger if he were permitted to reenter his vehicle. The hour was late and the area rural. Long was driving his automobile at excessive speed, and his car swerved into a ditch. The officers had to repeat their questions to Long, who appeared to be 'under the influence' of some intoxicant. Long was not frisked until the officers observed that there was a large knife in the interior of the car into which Long was about to reenter. The subsequent search of the car was restricted to those areas to which Long would generally have immediate control, and that could contain a weapon. The trial court determined that the leather pouch containing marijuana could have contained a weapon. It is clear that the intrusion was 'strictly circumscribed by the exigencies which justifi[ed] its initiation.' * * *

"The Michigan Supreme Court appeared to believe that it was not reasonable for the officers to fear that Long could injure them, because he was effectively under their control during the investigative stop and could not get access to any weapons that might have been located in the automobile. This reasoning is mistaken in several respects. During any investigative detention, the suspect is 'in the control' of the officers in the sense that he 'may be briefly detained against his will * * *.' Just as a *Terry* suspect on the street may, despite being under the brief control of a police officer, reach into his clothing and retrieve a weapon, so might a *Terry* suspect in Long's position break away from police control and retrieve a weapon from his automobile. In addition, if the suspect is not placed under arrest, he will be permitted to reenter his automobile, and he will then have access to any weapons inside. Or, as here, the suspect may be permitted to reenter the vehicle before the *Terry* investigation is over, and again, may have access to weapons. In any event, we stress that a *Terry* investigation, such as the one that occurred here, involves a police investigation 'at close range,' when the officer remains particularly vulnerable in part *because* a full custodial arrest has not been effected, and the officer must make a 'quick decision as to how to protect himself and others from possible danger * * *.' In such circumstances, we have not required that officers adopt alternate means to ensure their safety in order to avoid the intrusion involved in a *Terry* encounter."

BRENNAN and Marshall, JJ., dissenting, objected: "Putting aside the fact that the search at issue here involved a far more serious intrusion than that 'involved in a *Terry* encounter,' and as such might suggest the need for resort to 'alternate means,' the Court's reasoning is perverse. The Court's argument in essence is that the *absence* of probable cause to arrest compels the conclusion that a broad search, traditionally associated in scope with a search incident to arrest, must be permitted based on reasonable suspicion. But *United States v. Robinson, supra,* stated: 'It is scarcely open to doubt that the danger to an officer is far greater in the case of the extended exposure which follows the taking of a suspect into custody and transporting him to the police station than in the case of the relatively fleeting contact resulting from the typical *Terry*-type stop.' In light of *Robinson*'s observation, today's holding leaves in grave doubt the question of whether the Court's assessment of the relative dangers posed by given confrontations is based on any principled standard."

6. Can a limited search for any other reason ever be undertaken incident to a lawful stop? In *State v. Flynn,* 285 N.W.2d 710 (Wis.1979), one of two suspects lawfully stopped for investigation of a just-completed burglary admitted he had identification in his wallet but refused to identify himself, so the officer removed the wallet and examined it to the extent necessary to find the suspect's name and then arrested the suspect when a radio check revealed he was wanted for an earlier crime. Reasoning that "unless the officer is entitled to at least ascertain the identity of the suspect, the right to stop him can serve no useful purpose at all," that the search was a very limited one, and "that defendant could himself have substantially avoided the intrusion simply by producing the identification himself as his companion did," the court held the officer's actions reasonable under the *Terry* balancing test. Compare *People v. Williams,* 234 N.W.2d 541 (Mich.App.1975) (even though officer had good reason to believe lawfully stopped suspect was lying when he said he had no identification, looking in his wallet at driver's license violated the Fourth Amendment). Cf. *Arizona v. Hicks,* p. 260; and *Ybarra v. Illinois,* p. 215.

What then of on-the-scene fingerprinting? In *Hayes v. Florida,* 470 U.S. 811, 105 S.Ct. 1643, 84 L.Ed.2d 705 (1985), the majority in dictum opined this would be permissible "if there is reasonable suspicion that the suspect has committed a criminal act, if there is a reasonable basis for believing that fingerprinting will establish or negate the suspect's connection with that crime, and if the procedure is carried out with dispatch." Brennan and Marshall, JJ., concurring, responded "that on-site fingerprinting (apparently undertaken in full view of any passerby) would involve a singular intrusion on the suspect's privacy, an intrusion that would not be justifiable (as was the patdown in *Terry*) as necessary for the officer's protection."

G.   OTHER BRIEF DETENTION FOR INVESTIGATION

1.   In DAVIS v. MISSISSIPPI, 394 U.S. 721, 89 S.Ct. 1394, 22 L.Ed.2d 676 (1969), petitioner and 24 other black youths were detained for questioning and fingerprinting in connection with a rape for which the only leads were a general description given by the victim and a set of fingerprints around the window through which the assailant entered. Petitioner's prints were found to match those at the scene of the crime, and this evidence was admitted at his trial. The Court, per BRENNAN, J., held that the prints should have been excluded as the fruits of a seizure of petitioner in violation of the Fourth Amendment, but intimated that a detention for such a purpose might sometimes be permissible on evidence insufficient for arrest:

"Detentions for the sole purpose of obtaining fingerprints are no less subject to the constraints of the Fourth Amendment. It is arguable, however, that because of the unique nature of the fingerprinting process, such detentions might, under narrowly defined circumstances, be found to comply with the Fourth Amendment even though there is no probable cause in the traditional sense. Detention for fingerprinting may constitute a much less serious intrusion upon personal security than other types of police searches and detentions. Fingerprinting involves none of the probing into an individual's private life and thoughts which marks an interrogation or search. Nor can fingerprint detention be employed repeatedly to harass any individual, since the police need only one set of each person's prints. Furthermore, fingerprinting is an inherently more reliable and effective crime-solving tool than eyewitness identifications or confessions and is not subject to such abuses as the improper line-up[l] and the 'third degree.' Finally, because there is no danger of destruction of fingerprints, the limited detention need not come unexpectedly or at an inconvenient time. For this same reason, the general requirement that the authorization of a judicial officer be obtained in advance of detention would seem not to admit of any exception in the fingerprinting context.

"We have no occasion in this case, however, to determine whether the requirements of the Fourth Amendment could be met by narrowly circumscribed procedures for obtaining, during the course of a criminal investigation, the fingerprints of individuals for whom there is no probable cause to arrest. For it is clear that no attempt was made here to employ procedures which might comply with the requirements of the Fourth Amendment: the detention at police headquarters of petitioner and the other young Negroes was not authorized by a judicial officer; petitioner was unnecessarily required to undergo two fingerprinting sessions; and petitioner was not merely fingerprinted during the December 3 detention but also subjected to interrogation."[m]

l.   In *Wise v. Murphy*, 275 A.2d 205 (D.C.App.1971), the court noted the negative reference in *Davis* was only to an "improper line-up" and thus concluded that upon a proper showing, lacking in the instant case, a court could order a person to appear in a lineup even if grounds for arrest were lacking, at least for investigation of "serious felonies involving grave personal injuries."

m.   *Davis* was reaffirmed in *Hayes v. Florida*, p. 335, where the Court again suggested "the Fourth Amendment might permit the ju-

2. *United States v. Dionisio,* p. 695, holds that the Fourth Amendment was not violated by subpoenaing witnesses to appear before a grand jury to give voice exemplars. No preliminary showing of "probable cause" or "reasonableness" is required in such a case, as: (a) "a subpoena to appear before a grand jury is not a 'seizure' in the Fourth Amendment sense," and thus "*Davis* is plainly inapposite"; and (b) the requirement that the witness give exemplars does not infringe upon Fourth Amendment rights, as "the physical characteristics of a person's voice, its tone and manner, as opposed to the content of a specific conversation, are constantly exposed to the public," so that "no person can have a reasonable expectation that others will not know the sound of his voice." *United States v. Mara,* p. 698, reached the same result as to the subpoenaing of a witness to give handwriting exemplars.

3. A few jurisdictions have adopted statutes or rules of court which authorize brief detention at the station (usually pursuant to court order), on less than the grounds needed to arrest, for the purpose of conducting certain identification procedures. Such provisions have been upheld by the courts, and some other cases have upheld similar procedures even absent such a provision. For example, in *In re Fingerprinting of M.B.,* 309 A.2d 3 (N.J.Super.1973), the court affirmed an order requiring all 22 male members of the eighth grade class of a particular school to submit to fingerprinting. A ring of that elementary school's graduating class was found near the body of a homicide victim, and later the victim's car was located. Fingerprints other than those of the victim were found both inside and outside the vehicle. Upon request of the prosecutor, the court ordered all male members of that graduating class to submit to fingerprinting; the order permitted the pupils to be accompanied by a parent, guardian or attorney, directed that the prints be used only in the investigation of the homicide, and specified further that upon completion of the investigation the prints should be destroyed. The appellate court, in affirming commented:

"[T]here [is] a substantial basis to suspect that a member of the school class in question may have had some implication in or material knowledge of the homicide such that fingerprinting of all the male members of the class was reasonable, having in mind the protective provision of the order for destruction of the prints after completion of the investigation. Under all the circumstances extant and the terms of the order below we find the existence of such 'narrowly circumscribed procedures' as render the order reasonable within the view of the Fourth Amendment adumbrated in *Davis.*"

4. In DUNAWAY v. NEW YORK, 442 U.S. 200, 99 S.Ct. 2248, 60 L.Ed.2d 824 (1979), the police, lacking grounds to arrest petitioner but suspecting he was implicated in an attempted robbery and homicide, had him "picked up" for questioning. He was placed in an interrogation room at police headquarters, where he was questioned by officers after being given the *Miranda* warnings. Petitioner waived counsel and within an hour gave incriminating statements. His conviction following a trial at which those statements were admitted was affirmed by the state court on the ground that officers "may detain an individual upon reasonable suspicion for questioning for a reasonable and brief period of time under carefully controlled conditions which are ample to protect the individual's Fifth and Sixth Amendment Rights." The Supreme Court, per BRENNAN, J., reversed:

diciary to authorize the seizure of a person on less than probable cause and his removal to the police station for the purpose of fingerprinting."

"In contrast to the brief and narrowly circumscribed intrusions involved in [*Terry* and its progeny], the detention of petitioner was in important respects indistinguishable from a traditional arrest. Petitioner was not questioned briefly where he was found. Instead, he was taken from a neighbor's home to a police car, transported to a police station, and placed in an interrogation room. He was never informed that he was 'free to go'; indeed, he would have been physically restrained if he had refused to accompany the officers or had tried to escape their custody. The application of the Fourth Amendment's requirement of probable cause does not depend on whether an intrusion of this magnitude is termed an 'arrest' under state law. The mere facts that petitioner was not told he was under arrest, was not 'booked,' and would not have had an arrest record if the interrogation had proved fruitless, * * * obviously do not make petitioner's seizure even roughly analogous to the narrowly defined intrusions involved in *Terry* and its progeny. Indeed, any 'exception' that could cover a seizure as intrusive as that in this case would threaten to swallow the general rule that Fourth Amendment seizures are 'reasonable' only if based on probable cause. * * *

"In effect, respondents urge us to adopt a multifactor balancing test of 'reasonable police conduct under the circumstances' to cover all seizures that do not amount to technical arrests. But the protections intended by the Framers could all too easily disappear in the consideration and balancing of the multifarious circumstances presented by different cases, especially when that balancing may be done in the first instance by police officers engaged in the 'often competitive enterprise of ferreting out crime.' A single, familiar standard is essential to guide police officers, who have only limited time and expertise to reflect on and balance the social and individual interests involved in the specific circumstances they confront. Indeed, our recognition of these dangers, and our consequent reluctance to depart from the proven protections afforded by the general rule, is reflected in the narrow limitations emphasized in the cases employing the balancing test. For all but those narrowly defined intrusions, the requisite 'balancing' has been performed in centuries of precedent and is embodied in the principle that seizures are 'reasonable' only if supported by probable cause."

Justice Brennan then concluded "that the treatment of petitioner, whether or not it is technically characterized as an arrest, must be supported by probable cause" because "detention for custodial interrogation—regardless of its label—intrudes so severely on interests protected by the Fourth Amendment as necessarily to trigger the traditional safeguards against illegal arrest."

WHITE, J., concurring, cautioned that the majority opinion should not be read to mean that *Terry* "is an almost unique exception to a hard-and-fast standard of probable cause," and added that it was "enough, for me, that the police conduct here is similar enough to an arrest that the normal level of probable cause is necessary before the interests of privacy and personal security must give way." REHNQUIST, J., joined by the Chief Justice in dissent, indicated he "would have little difficulty joining" the opinion of the Court but for his conclusion that no Fourth Amendment seizure had occurred: "After learning that the person who answered the door was petitioner, the officer asked him if he would accompany the officers to police headquarters for questioning, and petitioner responded that he would. Petitioner was not told that he was under arrest or in custody and was not warned not to resist or flee. No weapons were displayed and petitioner was not handcuffed. Each officer testified that petitioner was not touched or held during the trip downtown; his freedom of action was not in any way restrained by the police. In short, the police behavior in this case was entirely free of 'physical force or show of authority.' "

SECTION 8. ADMINISTRATIVE INSPECTIONS AND REGULATORY SEARCHES: MORE ON BALANCING THE NEED AGAINST THE INVASION OF PRIVACY

The Supreme Court has upheld a rather broad range of searches and seizures even when conducted without the traditional quantum of probable cause. These decisions manifest further application of the *Camara* balancing test, also used by the Court in *Terry,* p. 304, to assay the discrete police practice of stop-and-frisk. But *Camara* itself was an administrative inspection type of case, and thus it is not surprising that this balancing process has since been utilized most often regarding various other administrative inspections and regulatory searches, where the Court typically has emphasized certain "special needs" beyond those present in the more typical law enforcement context.

Collectively, the cases briefly summarized below reflect two kinds of departures from the traditional probable cause requirement. One, as in *Terry,* is to require individualized suspicion (typically referred to as reasonable suspicion) less compelling than is need for the usual arrest or search. (In contrast to the rule in a regular law enforcement context, see *Ybarra,* p. 215, and *Hicks,* p. 260, such reasonable suspicion sometimes suffices even to search for incriminating evidence.) Another kind of departure is to require no individualized suspicion whatsoever, but instead to require that the seizure or search be conducted pursuant to some neutral criteria which guard against arbitrary selection of those subjected to such procedures (similar to the impoundment-inventory process approved in *Bertine,* p. 296).

1. *Safety inspections.* In *Camara v. Municipal Court,* 387 U.S. 523, 87 S.Ct. 1727, 18 L.Ed.2d 930 (1967), dealing with fire, health, and housing code inspection programs directed at dwellings, the Court concluded that if an occupant did not consent to an inspection the authorities would ordinarily have to get a warrant,[a] but "that 'probable cause' to issue a warrant to inspect must exist if reasonable legislative or administrative standards for conducting an area inspection are satisfied with respect to a particular dwelling. Such standards, which will vary with the municipal program being enforced, may be based upon the passage of time, the nature of the building (e.g., a multi-family apartment house), or the condition of the entire area, but they will not necessarily depend upon specific knowledge of the condition of the particular dwelling." Among the "persuasive factors" identified by the Court "to support the reasonableness of area code-enforcement inspections" were (i) doubt "that any other canvassing technique would achieve acceptable results," and (ii) that the contemplated inspections "involve a relatively limited invasion of the urban citizen's privacy" as compared to execution of the more traditional search warrant.[b]

a. Three dissenters objected: "This boxcar warrant will be identical as to every dwelling in the area, save the street number itself. I daresay they will be printed up in pads of a thousand or more—with space for the street number to be inserted—and issued by magistrates in broadcast fashion as a matter of course."

b. Another type of safety inspection is that conducted after a fire. In *Michigan v. Clifford,* 464 U.S. 287, 104 S.Ct. 641, 78 L.Ed.2d 477 (1984), four Justices concluded that a burning building creates exigent circumstances justifying authorities to enter to fight the blaze and to remain a reasonable time to investigate the cause of the fire, but that later entries without consent require a warrant—an administrative

A *Camara*-type warrant "showing that a specific business has been chosen * * * on the basis of a general administrative plan * * * derived from neutral sources" also suffices for inspection of business premises. *Marshall v. Barlow's, Inc.,* 436 U.S. 307, 98 S.Ct. 1816, 56 L.Ed.2d 305 (1978). But the Court has often upheld warrantless business inspections by emphasizing the "closely regulated" nature of the business and that the inspection permitted by statute or regulations is "carefully limited in time, place, and scope," as in *New York v. Burger,* 482 U.S. 691, 107 S.Ct. 2636, 96 L.Ed.2d 601 (1987). In *Burger,* the Court upheld such warrantless inspections of junkyards even though the administrative scheme concerned a social problem (stolen property) also addressed in the penal law, police officers were allowed to make the inspections, and the inspections would often uncover evidence of crime.

2. *Border searches.* In *United States v. Ramsey,* 431 U.S. 606, 97 S.Ct. 1972, 52 L.Ed.2d 617 (1977), upholding a customs inspection of mail entering the United States (which, by regulation, could not extend to reading of correspondence), the Court stressed (i) that the search was constitutional under the longstanding rule generally applicable to border searches, namely, that such searches are "considered to be 'reasonable' by the single fact that the person or item in question had entered into our country from outside"; and (ii) that the lower court was wrong in concluding a warrant would be needed as to mail, for "the 'border search' exception is not based on the doctrine of 'exigent circumstances' at all."

As for nonroutine border inspections, lower courts have generally held that "a real suspicion" is needed for a strip search, and the "clear indication" of *Schmerber,* p. 42, for a body cavity search. See, e.g., *Henderson v. United States,* 390 F.2d 805 (9th Cir.1967). In *United States v. Montoya de Hernandez,* 473 U.S. 531, 105 S.Ct. 3304, 87 L.Ed.2d 381 (1985), the Court held that when customs agents "reasonably suspect that the traveler is smuggling contraband in her alimentary canal" she may be detained so long as is "necessary to either verify or dispel the suspicion" (i.e., if the suspect declines to submit to an x-ray, until a bowel movement occurs).

3. *Vehicle checkpoints.* In a series of cases dealing with the stopping of vehicles away from the border to see if they were occupied by illegal aliens, the Court held that while roving patrols could stop and search vehicles for illegal aliens only on probable cause, *Almeida–Sanchez v. United States,* 413 U.S. 266, 93 S.Ct. 2535, 37 L.Ed.2d 596 (1973), only *Terry*-type reasonable suspicion was needed for such patrols to engage in the more "modest" interference with Fourth Amendment interests which attends the stopping of motorists and inquiring briefly as to their residential status. Even at a permanent checkpoint away from the border, search of a vehicle for aliens is not permissible absent probable cause, *United States v. Ortiz,* 422 U.S. 891, 95 S.Ct. 2585, 45 L.Ed.2d 623 (1975), but the brief questioning of vehicle occupants at such checkpoints is permissible without

warrant "to determine the cause and origin of a recent fire" on the showing "that a fire of undetermined origin has occurred on the premises, that the scope of the proposed search is reasonable and will not intrude unnecessarily on the fire victim's privacy, and that the search will be executed at a reasonable and convenient time"; or a conventional search warrant on probable cause if the "primary objective of the search is to gather evidence of criminal activity." A fifth Justice, concurring, opined that a "traditional criminal search warrant" should be required for any later entry without advance notice to the owner. The four dissenters agreed that a conventional warrant was required to search the balance of the home, but declared that a warrantless inspection of the fire scene was permissible because "the utility of requiring a magistrate to evaluate the grounds for a search following a fire is so limited that the incidental protection of an individual's privacy interests simply does not justify imposing a warrant requirement."

any individualized suspicion whatsoever. *United States v. Martinez–Fuerte,* 428 U.S. 543, 96 S.Ct. 3074, 49 L.Ed.2d 1116 (1976). As to the latter practice, the Court emphasized (i) that "the potential interference with legitimate traffic is minimal"; and (ii) that such checkpoint operations "involve less discretionary enforcement activity," as "the officer may stop only those cars passing the checkpoint," which "is not chosen by officers in the field, but by officials responsible for making overall decisions as to the most effective allocation of limited enforcement resources."[c] The Court in *Martinez–Fuerte* also concluded that if more than the briefest inquiry was needed in a particular instance the vehicle could be referred to a secondary inspection area "on the basis of criteria that would not sustain a roving-patrol stop."

Consistent with those cases, the Court held in *Delaware v. Prouse,* 440 U.S. 648, 99 S.Ct. 1391, 59 L.Ed.2d 660 (1979), that absent reasonable suspicion the police may not stop individual vehicles for the purpose of checking the driver's license and the registration of the automobile. But the Court stressed it was not precluding states "from developing methods for spot checks that involve less intrusion or that do not involve the unconstrained exercise of discretion," and gave as "one possible alternative" the "questioning of all oncoming traffic at roadblock-type stops."

Then came *Michigan Dep't of State Police v. Sitz,* 496 U.S. 444, 110 S.Ct. 2481, 110 L.Ed.2d 412 (1990), upholding the sobriety checkpoint program there at issue. Important ingredients in that conclusion were: (i) the intrusion upon motorists is "slight"; (ii) the program sufficiently limited officers' discretion, as "checkpoints are selected pursuant to the guidelines, and uniformed police officers stop every approaching vehicle"; (iii) the program addressed the very serious "drunken driving problem"; and (iv) there was support in the record for the law enforcement judgment that such checkpoints were among the "reasonable alternatives" available for dealing with that problem. The Court emphasized it was addressing "only the initial stop of each motorist passing through a checkpoint and the associated preliminary questioning and observation by checkpoint officers," and cautioned that "detention of particular motorists for more extensive field sobriety testing may require satisfaction of an individualized suspicion standard."

4. *Search of students.* Utilizing the *Camara* balancing test, the Court in *New Jersey v. T.L.O.,* 469 U.S. 325, 105 S.Ct. 733, 83 L.Ed.2d 720 (1985), struck "the balance between the school child's legitimate expectations of privacy and the school's equally legitimate needs to maintain an environment in which learning can take place" by holding: (i) "that school officials need not obtain a warrant before searching a student who is under their authority"; (ii) that ordinarily "a search of a student by a teacher or other school official will be 'justified at its inception' when there are reasonable grounds for suspecting that the search will turn up evidence that the student has violated or is violating either the law or the rules of the school"; and (iii) that such a search "will be permissible in its scope when the measures adopted are reasonably related to the objectives of the search and not excessively intrusive in light of the age and sex of the student and the nature of the infraction."

c. The Court also rejected the argument "that routine stops at a checkpoint are permissible only if a warrant has given judicial authorization to the particular checkpoint location." As for defendant's reliance on *Camara* in this connection, the Court answered that there but not here a warrant was necessary to provide assurance to the individual involved that the government agent was acting under proper authorization.

5. *Supervision of parolees and probationers.* In *Griffin v. Wisconsin,* 483 U.S. 868, 107 S.Ct. 3164, 97 L.Ed.2d 709 (1987), the Court concluded that a "State's operation of a probation system * * * likewise presents 'special needs' beyond normal law enforcement that may justify departures from the usual warrant and probable cause requirements." No warrant was required for search of the probationer's home, for it would not only "make it more difficult for probation officials to respond quickly to evidence of misconduct," but also would interfere with the probation officer's judgment as to "how close a supervision the probationer requires." Moreover, full probable cause was not required either, as such a requirement would also "reduce the deterrent effect of the supervisory arrangement" and would be "both unrealistic and destructive of the * * * continuing probation relationship."

6. *Drug testing.* While lower courts have approved government-mandated drug testing of government or private employees upon individualized reasonable suspicion, two programs not requiring such suspicion have been upheld by the Supreme Court. In *National Treasury Employees Union v. Von Raab,* 489 U.S. 656, 109 S.Ct. 1384, 103 L.Ed.2d 685 (1989), the Court held "that the suspicionless testing of employees who apply for promotion to positions directly involving the interdiction of illegal drugs, or to positions which require the incumbent to carry a firearm, is reasonable." The Court reasoned that because the testing program at issue "is not designed to serve the ordinary needs of law enforcement," a balancing process was proper, in which the "Government's compelling interests in preventing the promotion of drug users to positions where they might endanger the integrity of our Nation's borders or the life of the citizenry" outweighed the "diminished expectation of privacy" of "those who seek promotion to these positions."[d]

By similar balancing, the Court in *Skinner v. Railway Labor Executives' Ass'n,* 489 U.S. 602, 109 S.Ct. 1402, 103 L.Ed.2d 639 (1989), upheld blood and urine testing of railroad employees following major train accidents or incidents and the breath and urine testing of railroad employees who violate certain safety rules. In allowing such testing even "in the absence of * * * reasonable suspicion that any particular employee may be impaired," the Court emphasized (i) the special danger presented by the performance of "certain sensitive tasks while under the influence"; (ii) the "diminished expectation of privacy that attaches to information pertaining to the fitness of covered employees"; and (iii) "the limited discretion" railroad employers had regarding who and when to test.

In *Vernonia School District 47J v. Acton,* 515 U.S. 646, 115 S.Ct. 2386, 132 L.Ed.2d 564 (1995), the Court upheld the district's policy under which each week 10% of the students then participating in school athletics were randomly selected for urinalysis. In reaching this conclusion, the Court emphasized (i) that "students within the school environment have a lesser expectation of privacy than members of the population generally," especially as to medical examinations and procedures; (ii) that "legitimate privacy expectations are even less with regard to student athletes," who by going out for a team "voluntarily subject themselves to a degree of regulation even higher than that imposed on students generally"; (iii) that the "privacy-invasive aspect of urinalysis" was kept at a minimum; (iv) that the district court's findings that a large segment of the student body was "in a state of rebellion * * * fueled by alcohol and drug abuse" manifested "an

---

d. Two Justices who joined the Court's decision in *Skinner* because of "the demonstrated frequency of drug and alcohol use by the targeted class of employees, and the demonstrated connection between such use and grave harm," dissented in *Von Raab* because the government was unable to cite "even a single instance" of such use or connection to harm.

immediate crisis of greater proportions than existed" in *Skinner* or *Von Raab*; and (v) "that a drug problem largely fueled by the 'role model' effect of athletes' drug use, and of particular danger to athletes, is effectively addressed by making sure that athletes do not use drugs." But the Court in *Acton* then "caution[ed] against the assumption that suspicionless drug testing will readily pass constitutional muster in other contexts."[e]

SECTION 9. CONSENT SEARCHES

Consent searches are frequently relied upon by the police because they involve no time-consuming paper work and offer an opportunity to search even when probable cause is lacking. Thus, the constitutional protection against unreasonable search and seizure widens or narrows, depending on the difficulty or ease with which the prosecution can establish that the defendant (or some other authorized person) has "consented" to what would otherwise be an unconstitutional invasion of his privacy.

A. THE NATURE OF "CONSENT"

SCHNECKLOTH v. BUSTAMONTE
412 U.S. 218, 93 S.Ct. 2041, 36 L.Ed.2d 854 (1973).

Justice STEWART delivered the opinion of the Court. * * *

[A police officer stopped a car containing six men when he observed that one headlight and the license plate light were burned out. After the driver could not produce a license, the officer asked a passenger who claimed he was the vehicle owner's brother if he could search the car, and the passenger replied, "Sure, go ahead." The driver "helped in the search of the car, by opening the trunk and glove compartment." Stolen checks were found under a seat, leading to charges against passenger Bustamonte, whose motion to suppress was denied. His conviction was affirmed on appeal; the federal district court denied his petition for a writ of habeas corpus, but the 9th Circuit court of appeals set aside the district court's order.]

The precise question in this case, then, is what must the state prove to demonstrate that a consent was "voluntarily" given. * * *

The most extensive judicial exposition of the meaning of "voluntariness" has been developed in those cases in which the Court has had to determine the "voluntariness" of a defendant's confession for purposes of the Fourteenth Amendment. * * * It is to that body of case law to which we turn for initial guidance on the meaning of "voluntariness" in the present context. * * *

The significant fact about all of these decisions is that none of them turned on the presence or absence of a single controlling criterion; each reflected a careful

---

e. Compare *Chandler v. Miller*, 520 U.S. 305, 117 S.Ct. 1295, 137 L.Ed.2d 513 (1997), invalidating a Georgia statute requiring each candidate for public office to submit to drug testing, where the Court stated: "Georgia asserts no evidence of a drug problem among the State's elected officials, those officials typically do not perform high-risk, safety-sensitive tasks, and the required certification immediately aids no interdiction effort. The need revealed, in short, is symbolic, not 'special,' as that term draws meaning from our case law." As for the state's reliance on *Von Raab*, the Court noted that there the affected employees and their work product were not amenable to "day-to-day scrutiny," and then concluded: "Candidates for public office, in contrast, are subject to relentless scrutiny—by their peers, the public, and the press. Their day-to-day conduct attracts attention notable beyond the norm in ordinary work environments."

scrutiny of all the surrounding circumstances. In none of them did the Court rule that the Due Process Clause required the prosecution to prove as part of its initial burden that the defendant knew he had a right to refuse to answer the questions that were put. While the state of the accused's mind, and the failure of the police to advise the accused of his rights, were certainly factors to be evaluated in assessing the "voluntariness" of an accused's responses, they were not in and of themselves determinative.

Similar considerations lead us to agree with the courts of California that the question whether a consent to a search was in fact "voluntary" or was the product of duress or coercion, express or implied, is a question of fact to be determined from the totality of all the circumstances. While knowledge of the right to refuse consent is one factor to be taken into account, the government need not establish such knowledge as the *sine qua non* of an effective consent. As with police questioning, two competing concerns must be accommodated in determining the meaning of a "voluntary" consent—the legitimate need for such searches and the equally important requirement of assuring the absence of coercion.

In situations where the police have some evidence of illicit activity, but lack probable cause to arrest or search, a search authorized by a valid consent may be the only means of obtaining important and reliable evidence. In the present case for example, while the police had reason to stop the car for traffic violations, the State does not contend that there was probable cause to search the vehicle or that the search was incident to a valid arrest of any of the occupants. Yet, the search yielded tangible evidence that served as a basis for a prosecution, and provided some assurance that others, wholly innocent of the crime, were not mistakenly brought to trial. And in those cases where there is probable cause to arrest or search, but where the police lack a warrant, a consent search may still be valuable. If the search is conducted and proves fruitless, that in itself may convince the police that an arrest with its possible stigma and embarrassment is unnecessary, or that a far more extensive search pursuant to a warrant is not justified. In short a search pursuant to consent may result in considerably less inconvenience for the subject of the search, and, properly conducted, is a constitutionally permissible and wholly legitimate aspect of effective police activity.

But the Fourth and Fourteenth Amendments require that a consent not be coerced, by explicit or implicit means, by implied threat or covert force. For, no matter how subtly the coercion were applied, the resulting "consent" would be no more than a pretext for the unjustified police intrusion against which the Fourth Amendment is directed. * * *

The problem of reconciling the recognized legitimacy of consent searches with the requirement that they be free from any aspect of official coercion cannot be resolved by an infallible touchstone. To approve such searches without the most careful scrutiny would sanction the possibility of official coercion; to place artificial restrictions upon such searches would jeopardize their basic validity. Just as was true with confessions, the requirement of a "voluntary" consent reflects a fair accommodation of the constitutional requirements involved. In examining all the surrounding circumstances to determine if in fact the consent to search was coerced, account must be taken of subtly coercive police questions, as well as the possibly vulnerable subjective state of the person who consents. Those searches that are the product of police coercion can thus be filtered out without undermining the continuing validity of consent searches. In sum, there is no reason for us to depart in the area of consent searches, from the traditional definition of "voluntariness."

The approach of the Court of Appeals for the Ninth Circuit finds no support in any of our decisions that have attempted to define the meaning of "voluntariness." Its ruling, that the State must affirmatively prove that the subject of the search knew that he had a right to refuse consent, would, in practice, create serious doubt whether consent searches could continue to be conducted. There might be rare cases where it could be proved from the record that a person in fact affirmatively knew of his right to refuse—such as a case where he announced to the police that if he didn't sign the consent form, "you [police] are going to get a search warrant;" or a case where by prior experience and training a person had clearly and convincingly demonstrated such knowledge. But more commonly where there was no evidence of any coercion, explicit or implicit, the prosecution would nevertheless be unable to demonstrate that the subject of the search in fact had known of his right to refuse consent.

The very object of the inquiry—the nature of a person's subjective understanding—underlines the difficulty of the prosecution's burden under the rule applied by the Court of Appeals in this case. Any defendant who was the subject of a search authorized solely by his consent could effectively frustrate the introduction into evidence of the fruits of that search by simply failing to testify that he in fact knew he could refuse to consent. And the near impossibility of meeting this prosecutorial burden suggests why this Court has never accepted any such litmus-paper test of voluntariness. * * *

One alternative that would go far towards proving that the subject of a search did know he had a right to refuse consent would be to advise him of that right before eliciting his consent. That, however, is a suggestion that has been almost universally repudiated by both federal and state courts, and, we think, rightly so. For it would be thoroughly impractical to impose on the normal consent search the detailed requirements of an effective warning.[a] Consent searches are part of the standard investigatory techniques of law enforcement agencies. They normally occur on the highway, or in a person's home or office, and under informal and unstructured conditions. The circumstances that prompt the initial request to search may develop quickly or be a logical extension of investigative police questioning. The police may seek to investigate further suspicious circumstances or to follow up leads developed in questioning persons at the scene of a crime. These situations are a far cry from the structured atmosphere of a trial where, assisted by counsel if he chooses, a defendant is informed of his trial rights. And, while surely a closer question, these situations are still immeasurably far removed from "custodial interrogation" where, in *Miranda v. Arizona* [p. 475], we found that the Constitution required certain now familiar warnings as a prerequisite to police interrogation. * * *

It is said, however, that a "consent" is a "waiver" of a person's rights under the Fourth and Fourteenth Amendments. The argument is that by allowing the police to conduct a search, a person "waives" whatever right he had to prevent the police from searching. It is argued that under the doctrine of *Johnson v. Zerbst,* 304 U.S. 458, 58 S.Ct. 1019, 82 L.Ed. 1461 (1938), to establish such a "waiver" the state must demonstrate "an intentional relinquishment or abandonment of a known right or privilege." * * *

---

a. Relying upon this language, the Court later held in *Ohio v. Robinette*, 519 U.S. 33, 117 S.Ct. 417, 136 L.Ed.2d 347 (1996), that if a person has been lawfully seized, for example, because of commission of a traffic violation, and following the point at which the detainee would be free to go he consents to a search, that consent is not involuntary because the officer failed to specifically advise the detainee that he was free to go, as a requirement of such warnings would be equally "unrealistic."

Almost without exception the requirement of a knowing and intelligent waiver has been applied only to those rights which the Constitution guarantees to a criminal defendant in order to preserve a fair trial. Hence, and hardly surprisingly in view of the facts of *Johnson* itself, the standard of a knowing and intelligent waiver has most often been applied to test the validity of a waiver of counsel, either at trial, or upon a guilty plea. And the Court has also applied the *Johnson* criteria to assess the effectiveness of a waiver of other trial rights such as the right to confrontation, to a jury trial, and to a speedy trial, and the right to be free from twice being placed in jeopardy. Guilty pleas have been carefully scrutinized to determine whether the accused knew and understood all the rights to which he would be entitled at trial, and that he had intentionally chosen to forgo them. And the Court has evaluated the knowing and intelligent nature of the waiver of trial rights in trial-type situations, such as the waiver of the privilege against compulsory self-incrimination before an administrative agency or a congressional committee, or the waiver of counsel in a juvenile proceeding.

The guarantees afforded a criminal defendant at trial also protect him at certain stages before the actual trial, and any alleged waiver must meet the strict standard of an intentional relinquishment of a "known" right. But the "trial" guarantees that have been applied to the "pretrial" stage of the criminal process are similarly designed to protect the fairness of the trial itself. * * *[b]

The standards of *Johnson* were, therefore, found to be a necessary prerequisite to a finding of a valid waiver.[29] * * *

A strict standard of waiver has been applied to those rights guaranteed to a criminal defendant to insure that he will be accorded the greatest possible opportunity to utilize every facet of the constitutional model of a fair criminal trial. Any trial conducted in derogation of that model leaves open the possibility that the trial reached an unfair result precisely because all the protections specified in the Constitution were not provided. A prime example is the right to counsel. For without that right, a wholly innocent accused faces the real and substantial danger that simply because of his lack of legal expertise he may be convicted. * * *

The protections of the Fourth Amendment are of a wholly different order, and have nothing whatever to do with promoting the fair ascertainment of truth at a criminal trial. Rather, as Justice Frankfurter's opinion for the Court put it in *Wolf v. Colorado* [p. 122], the Fourth Amendment protects the "security of one's privacy against arbitrary intrusion by the police...." * * *

Nor can it even be said that a search, as opposed to an eventual trial, is somehow "unfair" if a person consents to a search. While the Fourth and Fourteenth Amendments limit the circumstances under which the police can

b. At this point, the Court noted that "the standard of a knowing and intelligent waiver" applies to waiver of counsel at a lineup under *United States v. Wade,* p. 641, and *Gilbert v. California,* p. 641, because counsel is provided to protect the right of cross-examination at trial; and that the same standard applies to waiver of counsel at custodial interrogation under *Miranda v. Arizona,* p. 475, because counsel is provided to ensure that the safeguards concerning the giving of testimony at trial do not "become empty formalities."

29. As we have already noted, *Miranda* itself involved interrogation of a suspect de-

tained in custody and did not concern the investigatory procedures of the police in general on-the-scene questioning. By the same token, the present case does not require a determination of the proper standard to be applied in assessing the validity of a search authorized solely by an alleged consent that is obtained from a person after he has been placed in custody. We do note, however, that other courts have been particularly sensitive to the heightened possibilities for coercion when the "consent" to a search was given by a person in custody.

conduct a search, there is nothing constitutionally suspect in a person voluntarily allowing a search. The actual conduct of the search may be precisely the same as if the police had obtained a warrant. And, unlike those constitutional guarantees that protect a defendant at trial, it cannot be said every reasonable presumption ought to be indulged against voluntary relinquishment. We have only recently stated: "[I]t is no part of the policy underlying the Fourth and Fourteenth Amendments to discourage citizens from aiding to the utmost of their ability in the apprehension of criminals." *Coolidge v. New Hampshire*, [p. 217]. Rather the community has a real interest in encouraging consent, for the resulting search may yield necessary evidence for the solution and prosecution of crime, evidence that may insure that a wholly innocent person is not wrongly charged with a criminal offense.

Those cases that have dealt with the application of the *Johnson v. Zerbst* rule make clear that it would be next to impossible to apply to a consent search the standard of "an intentional relinquishment or abandonment of a known right or privilege." To be true to *Johnson* and its progeny, there must be examination into the knowing and understanding nature of the waiver, an examination that was designed for a trial judge in the structured atmosphere of a courtroom. * * * It would be unrealistic to expect that in the informal, unstructured context of a consent search, a policeman, upon pain of tainting the evidence obtained, could make the detailed type of examination demanded by *Johnson*. And, if for this reason a diluted form of "waiver" were found acceptable, that would itself be ample recognition of the fact that there is no universal standard that must be applied in every situation where a person forgoes a constitutional right.[33]

Similarly, a "waiver" approach to consent searches would be thoroughly inconsistent with our decisions that have approved "third party consents." In *Coolidge v. New Hampshire*, where a wife surrendered to the police guns and clothing belonging to her husband, we found nothing constitutionally impermissible in the admission of that evidence at trial since the wife had not been coerced. *Frazier v. Cupp*, [p. 359], held that evidence seized from the defendant's duffel bag in a search authorized by his cousin's consent was admissible at trial. We found that the defendant had assumed the risk that his cousin with whom he shared the bag would allow the police to search it. And in *Hill v. California*, 401 U.S. 797, 91 S.Ct. 1106, 28 L.Ed.2d 484 (1971), we held that the police had validly seized evidence from the petitioner's apartment incident to the arrest of a third party, since the police had probable cause to arrest the petitioner and reasonably though mistakenly believed the man they had arrested was he. Yet it is inconceivable that the Constitution could countenance the waiver of a defendant's right to counsel by a third party, or that a waiver could be found because a trial judge reasonably though mistakenly believed a defendant had waived his right to plead not guilty. * * *

Much of what has already been said disposes of the argument that the Court's decision in the *Miranda* case requires the conclusion that knowledge of a right to refuse is an indispensable element of a valid consent. The considerations that

---

33. It seems clear that even a limited view of the demands of "an intentional relinquishment or abandonment of a known right or privilege" standard would inevitably lead to a requirement of detailed warnings before any consent search—a requirement all but universally rejected to date. As the Court stated in *Miranda* with respect to the privilege against compulsory self-incrimination: "[W]e will not pause to inquire in individual cases whether the defendant was aware of his rights without a warning being given. Assessments of the knowledge the defendant possessed, based on information as to his age, education, intelligence, or prior contact with authorities, can never be more than speculation; a warning is a clearcut fact."

informed the Court's holding in *Miranda* are simply inapplicable in the present case. In *Miranda* the Court found that the techniques of police questioning and the nature of custodial surroundings produce an inherently coercive situation. The Court concluded that "[u]nless adequate protective devices are employed to dispel the compulsion inherent in custodial surroundings, no statement obtained from the defendant can truly be the product of his free choice." And at another point the Court noted that "without proper safeguards the process of in-custody interrogation of persons suspected or accused of crime contains inherently compelling pressures which work to undermine the individual's will to resist and to compel him to speak where he would not otherwise do so freely."

In this case there is no evidence of any inherently coercive tactics—either from the nature of the police questioning or the environment in which it took place. Indeed, since consent searches will normally occur on a person's own familiar territory, the spectre of incommunicado police interrogation in some remote station house is simply inapposite. There is no reason to believe, under circumstances such as are present here, that the response to a policeman's question is presumptively coerced; and there is, therefore, no reason to reject the traditional test for determining the voluntariness of a person's response. *Miranda*, of course, did not reach investigative questioning of a person not in custody, which is most directly analogous to the situation of a consent search, and it assuredly did not indicate that such questioning ought to be deemed inherently coercive.

It is also argued that the failure to require the Government to establish knowledge as a prerequisite to a valid consent, will relegate the Fourth Amendment to the special province of "the sophisticated, the knowledgeable, and the privileged." We cannot agree. The traditional definition of voluntariness we accept today has always taken into account evidence of minimal schooling, low intelligence, and the lack of any effective warnings to a person of his rights; and the voluntariness of any statement taken under those conditions has been carefully scrutinized to determine whether it was in fact voluntarily given.

Our decision today is a narrow one. We hold only that when the subject of a search is not in custody and the State attempts to justify a search on the basis of his consent, the Fourth and Fourteenth Amendments require that it demonstrate that the consent was in fact voluntarily given, and not the result of duress or coercion, express or implied. Voluntariness is a question of fact to be determined from all the circumstances, and while the subject's knowledge of a right to refuse is a factor to be taken into account, the prosecution is not required to demonstrate such knowledge as a prerequisite to establishing a voluntary consent.[c]

Justice MARSHALL, dissenting. * * *

The Fifth Amendment, in terms, provides that no person "shall be compelled in any criminal case to be a witness against himself." Nor is the interest protected by the Due Process Clause of the Fourteenth Amendment any different. The inquiry in a case where a confession is challenged as having been elicited in an

---

c. Powell, J., joined by the Chief Justice and Rehnquist, J., concurred on the ground "that federal collateral review of a state prisoner's Fourth Amendment claims—claims which rarely bear on innocence—should be confined solely to the question of whether the petitioner was provided a fair opportunity to raise and have adjudicated the question in state courts." Blackmun, J., concurred to ex- press substantial agreement with the Powell opinion. Douglas, J., dissenting, would have remanded for a determination of whether Alcala knew he had the right to refuse. Brennan, J., dissenting, declared: "It wholly escapes me how our citizens can meaningfully be said to have waived something as precious as a constitutional guarantee without ever being aware of its existence."

unconstitutional manner is, therefore, whether the behavior of the police amounted to compulsion of the defendant. * * *

In contrast, this case deals not with "coercion," but with "consent," a subtly different concept to which different standards have been applied in the past. Freedom from coercion is a substantive right, guaranteed by the Fifth and Fourteenth Amendments. Consent, however, is a mechanism by which substantive requirements, otherwise applicable, are avoided. * * * Thus, consent searches are permitted not because such an exception to the requirements of probable cause and warrant is essential to proper law enforcement, but because we permit our citizens to choose whether or not they wish to exercise their constitutional rights. Our prior decisions simply do not support the view that a meaningful choice has been made solely because no coercion was brought to bear on the subject. * * *

If consent to search means that a person has chosen to forego his right to exclude the police from the place they seek to search, it follows that his consent cannot be considered a meaningful choice unless he knew that he could in fact exclude the police. * * * I would therefore hold, at a minimum, that the prosecution may not rely on a purported consent to search if the subject of the search did not know that he could refuse to give consent. Where the police claim authority to search yet in fact lack such authority, the subject does not know that he may permissibly refuse them entry, and it is this lack of knowledge that invalidates the consent. * * *

The burden on the prosecutor would disappear, of course, if the police, at the time they requested consent to search, also told the subject that he had a right to refuse consent and thus his decision to refuse would be respected. The Court's assertions to the contrary notwithstanding, there is nothing impractical about this method of satisfying the prosecution's burden of proof. * * *

The Court contends that if an officer paused to inform the subject of his rights, the informality of the exchange would be destroyed. I doubt that a simple statement by an officer of an individual's right to refuse consent would do much to alter the informality of the exchange, except to alert the subject to a fact that he surely is entitled to know. It is not without significance that for many years the agents of the Federal Bureau of Investigation have routinely informed subjects of their right to refuse consent, when they request consent to search. The reported cases in which the police have informed subject of their right to refuse consent show, also, that the information can be given without disrupting the casual flow of events. What evidence there is, then, rather strongly suggests that nothing disastrous would happen if the police, before requesting consent, informed the subject that he had a right to refuse consent and that his refusal would be respected.[12]

I must conclude, with some reluctance, that when the Court speaks of practicality, what it really is talking of is the continued ability of the police to capitalize on the ignorance of citizens so as to accomplish by subterfuge what they could not achieve by relying only on the knowing relinquishment of constitutional rights. * * *

12. The Court's suggestion that it would be "unrealistic" to require the officers to make "the detailed type of examination" involved when a court considers whether a defendant has waived a trial right, deserves little comment. The question before us relates to the inquiry to be made in court when the prosecution seeks to establish that consent was given. I therefore do not address the Court's strained argument that one may waive constitutional rights without making a knowing and intentional choice so long as the rights do not relate to the fairness of a criminal trial. I would suggest, however, that that argument is fundamentally inconsistent with the law of unconstitutional conditions.

NOTES ON THE RELEVANT FACTORS IN DETERMINING
THE VALIDITY OF A CONSENT

1. *What is the issue?* Some courts, as did the court of appeals in *Bustamonte,* 448 F.2d 699 (9th Cir.1971), characterize a consent to search as "a waiver of a constitutional right" and thus focus upon the state of mind of the person allegedly giving the consent. Some other courts look instead to the state of mind of the officer seeking the consent; the question is said to be whether "the officers, as reasonable men, could conclude that defendant's consent was given," e.g., *People v. Henderson,* 210 N.E.2d 483 (Ill.1965). Does *Bustamonte* clearly indicate a choice of either of these theories? Cf. *Florida v. Jimeno,* p. 352, and *Illinois v. Rodriguez,* p. 353. An illustration of how the choice of one of these theories over the other might affect the outcome is provided by *United States v. Elrod,* 441 F.2d 353 (5th Cir.1971), holding: "No matter how genuine the belief of the officers is that the consenter is apparently of sound mind and deliberately acting, the search depending upon his consent fails if it is judicially determined that he lacked mental capacity. It is not that the actions of the officers were imprudent or unfounded. It is that the key to validity—consent—is lacking for want of mental capacity, no matter how much concealed."

2. *Claim or show of authority.* In *Bumper v. North Carolina,* 391 U.S. 543, 88 S.Ct. 1788, 20 L.Ed.2d 797 (1968), defendant's grandmother allowed the police to search her house after one of them announced, "I have a search warrant to search your house." At the hearing on the motion to suppress the rifle found therein, the prosecutor did not rely upon a warrant to justify the search. The Supreme Court was advised that the officers did have a warrant, but none was ever returned and nothing was known about the conditions under which it was issued. The Court held, 7–2, per Stewart, J., that a search cannot be justified on the basis of consent "when that 'consent' has been given only after the official conducting the search has asserted that he possesses a warrant," as when "a law enforcement officer claims authority to search a home under a warrant, he announces in effect that the occupant has no right to resist the search. The situation is instinct with coercion—albeit colorably lawful coercion. Where there is coercion there cannot be consent."

What if the grandmother had responded to the police, "You don't need a search warrant, go ahead"? What if the officer in *Bumper* had merely threatened to obtain a search warrant? Consider *United States v. Boukater,* 409 F.2d 537 (5th Cir.1969) (coercive unless the officer actually had grounds to obtain a warrant or he merely said he would seek a search warrant). The "claim of lawful authority" referred to in *Bumper* need not involve mention of a search warrant; a flat assertion by the police that they have come to search will suffice. *Amos v. United States,* 255 U.S. 313, 41 S.Ct. 266, 65 L.Ed. 654 (1921).

3. *Prior illegal police action.* Under the "fruit of the poisonous tree" doctrine of *Wong Sun,* p. 786, a consent may be held ineffective because obtained in exploitation of a prior illegal arrest.

4. *Mental or emotional state of the person.* Compare *United States v. Elrod,* Note 1 supra; and *Commonwealth v. Angivoni,* 417 N.E.2d 422 (Mass.1981) (voluntary consent of defendant in hospital emergency room with dislocated hip not established, as "defendant's understanding and ability to reason reflectively may have been impaired by intoxication or as a result of his injuries or an emotional trauma attendant to his just having been in an accident"); with the

Supreme Court's more recent application of the voluntariness test in *Colorado v. Connelly,* p. 614.

5. *Denial of guilt.* Doesn't the ready discovery of incriminating evidence pursuant to the "consent" of a person who has denied his guilt manifest that the consent must have been involuntary? Yes, concluded the court in *Higgins v. United States,* 209 F.2d 819 (D.C.Cir.1954): "No sane man who denies his guilt would actually be willing that policemen search his room for contraband which is certain to be discovered." But in *Florida v. Bostick,* p. 31, in response to the defendant's contention that "no reasonable person would freely consent to a search of luggage that he or she knows contains drugs," the Court responded that such an "argument cannot prevail because the 'reasonable person' test presupposes an *innocent* person."

6. *Custody; Warning of Fourth Amendment rights.* In *United States v. Watson,* p. 221, the majority concluded that the failure to give the defendant Fourth Amendment warnings "is not to be given controlling significance" where, as there, the defendant "had been arrested and was in custody, but his consent was given while on a public street, not in the confines of the police station." Marshall and Brennan, JJ., dissenting, objected that the case should be remanded for reconsideration of the consent issue by the court of appeals in light of the fact that the "lack of custody was of decisional importance in *Schneckloth,* which repeatedly distinguished the case before it from one involving a suspect in custody."

In *Gentile v. United States,* 419 U.S. 979, 95 S.Ct. 241, 42 L.Ed.2d 191 (1974), where consent was obtained from the defendant during stationhouse custodial interrogation after the giving of the *Miranda* warnings but without Fourth Amendment warnings, Douglas and Marshall, JJ., dissenting from the denial of certiorari, noted: "When a suspect is in custody the situation is in control of the police. The pace of events will not somehow deny them an opportunity to give a warning, as the [*Schneckloth*] Court apparently feared would happen in noncustodial settings. Moreover, the custodial setting will permit easy documentation of both the giving of a warning and the arrestee's response."

7. *Warning of Fifth Amendment rights.* It has sometimes been held that a valid consent to search, given by a person in custody, must be preceded by *Miranda* warnings because "the request to search is a request that defendant be a witness against himself which he is privileged to refuse under the Fifth Amendment." *State v. Williams,* 432 P.2d 679 (Or.1967). But the prevailing view, as stated in *United States v. LaGrone,* 43 F.3d 332 (7th Cir.1994), is that "because requesting consent to search is not likely to elicit an incriminating statement, such questioning is not interrogation, and thus *Miranda* warnings are not required."

8. *Right to counsel.* In *Tidwell v. Superior Court,* 95 Cal.Rptr. 213 (App. 1971), the police asked petitioner, who was in jail, if they could search his car, which had been impounded. Petitioner allegedly replied, "Go ahead and search." The court held that petitioner's consent was ineffective since at the time he had been arraigned on a burglary charge and counsel had been appointed, yet the police had asked him to consent to the search without notifying his lawyer. Rejecting the argument that *Massiah* [p. 460] should apply only to "statements elicited and not to consents given," the court observed: "This distinction is very thin considering the incriminating effect a consent to search may have. The reasoning of [the cases protecting] defendants' right to effective aid of counsel applies equally to a consent given at the instigation of the police."

9. *"Consent" by deception.* In contrast to the type of deception allegedly used in *Bumper,* Note 2 supra, the police sometimes obtain evidence of criminal activity by acting in an undercover capacity and obtaining a "consent" which the defendant would not have given had he known the officer's true identity; see *Lewis v. United States,* p. 386, upholding this practice upon the facts presented. A third situation is that in which the officer's true identity is known but he misleads the suspect as to his intentions. Compare *Graves v. Beto,* 424 F.2d 524 (5th Cir.1970) (rape defendant's consent to blood test which resulted in matching his blood with that at crime scene not freely and intelligently given where his acquiescence was obtained by intimating that test was to be taken simply to determine whether he had a sufficient quantity of alcohol in his blood stream to be detained on a charge of public drunkenness); with *United States v. Andrews,* 746 F.2d 247 (5th Cir.1984) (federal agents asked to see shotgun on ruse they were trying to connect it with robberies, actual purpose was to establish defendant's crime of illegal possession of firearm by convicted felon; consent voluntary, *Graves* distinguished because "there is no evidence indicating that Andrews was assured his production of the guns would only be used to investigate the robberies").

10. *Scope of consent.* The standard for measuring the scope of a suspect's consent, the Court concluded in *Florida v. Jimeno,* 500 U.S. 248, 111 S.Ct. 1801, 114 L.Ed.2d 297 (1991), is neither the suspect's intent nor the officer's perception thereof but rather "that of 'objective' reasonableness—what would the typical reasonable person have understood by the exchange between the officer and the suspect?" Given the officer's statement in *Jimeno* that he would be looking for narcotics, "it was objectively reasonable for the police to conclude that the general consent to search respondent's car included consent to search containers within that car which might bear drugs." But, the nature of the container is also relevant. "It is very unreasonable to think that a suspect, by consenting to the search of his trunk, has agreed to the breaking open of a locked briefcase within the trunk, but it is otherwise with respect to a closed paper bag."

Does the *Jimeno* principle, that "the scope of the search is generally defined by its expressed object," suffice as to consent searches of the person? Consider *United States v. Rodney,* 956 F.2d 295 (D.C.Cir.1992) (sweeping motion over crotch area during consent search for drugs lawful, as it no more intrusive than a *Terry* frisk; court distinguishes *United States v. Blake,* 888 F.2d 795 (11th Cir.1989), suppressing drugs found on person, as that case involved "a direct 'frontal touching' of the defendant's private parts").

Does a consent, voluntary when given, justify a second search of the same place at a later time after a fruitless first search? Compare *People v. Nawrocki,* 148 N.W.2d 211 (Mich.App.1967) (defendant's consent to search his car construed as "permission to search the car at any time," thus justifying second search hours later after the car was impounded and the defendant was in jail); with *State v. Brochu,* 237 A.2d 418 (Me.1967) (contra where passage of time was greater, second search involved re-entry of defendant's home, and defendant's status had changed from suspect to accused in interim).

B. Third Party Consent[c]

ILLINOIS v. RODRIGUEZ
497 U.S. 177, 110 S.Ct. 2793, 111 L.Ed.2d 148 (1990).

Justice SCALIA delivered the opinion of the Court. * * *

On July 26, 1985, police were summoned to the residence of Dorothy Jackson on South Wolcott in Chicago. They were met by Ms. Jackson's daughter, Gail

c. See Mary I. Coombs, *Shared Privacy and the Fourth Amendment, or the Right of Relationships,* 75 Calif.L.Rev. 1593 (1987).

Fischer, who showed signs of a severe beating. She told the officers that she had been assaulted by respondent Edward Rodriguez earlier that day in an apartment on South California. Fischer stated that Rodriguez was then asleep in the apartment, and she consented to travel there with the police in order to unlock the door with her key so that the officers could enter and arrest him. During this conversation, Fischer several times referred to the apartment on South California as "our" apartment, and said that she had clothes and furniture there. It is unclear whether she indicated that she currently lived at the apartment, or only that she used to live there.

The police officers drove to the apartment on South California, accompanied by Fischer. They did not obtain an arrest warrant for Rodriguez, nor did they seek a search warrant for the apartment. At the apartment, Fischer unlocked the door with her key and gave the officers permission to enter. They moved through the door into the living room, where they observed in plain view drug paraphernalia and containers filled with white powder that they believed (correctly, as later analysis showed) to be cocaine. They proceeded to the bedroom, where they found Rodriguez asleep and discovered additional containers of white powder in two open attaché cases. The officers arrested Rodriguez and seized the drugs and related paraphernalia.

Rodriguez was charged with possession of a controlled substance with intent to deliver. He moved to suppress all evidence seized at the time of his arrest, claiming that Fischer had vacated the apartment several weeks earlier and had no authority to consent to the entry. The Cook County Circuit Court granted the motion, holding that at the time she consented to the entry Fischer did not have common authority over the apartment. The Court concluded that Fischer was not a "usual resident" but rather an "infrequent visitor" at the apartment on South California, based upon its findings that Fischer's name was not on the lease, that she did not contribute to the rent, that she was not allowed to invite others to the apartment on her own, that she did not have access to the apartment when respondent was away, and that she had moved some of her possessions from the apartment. The Circuit Court also rejected the State's contention that, even if Fischer did not possess common authority over the premises, there was no Fourth Amendment violation if the police *reasonably believed* at the time of their entry that Fischer possessed the authority to consent. * * *

The Fourth Amendment generally prohibits the warrantless entry of a person's home, whether to make an arrest or to search for specific objects. The prohibition does not apply, however, to situations in which voluntary consent has been obtained, either from the individual whose property is searched, or from a third party who possesses common authority over the premises, see *United States v. Matlock,* [415 U.S. 164, 94 S.Ct. 988, 39 L.Ed.2d 242 (1974)]. The State of Illinois contends that that exception applies in the present case.

As we stated in *Matlock,* "[c]ommon authority" rests "on mutual use of the property by persons generally having joint access or control for most purposes."[a]

---

a. Where there is such "common authority," the Court went on to say in *Matlock,* "it is reasonable to recognize that any of the co-inhabitants has the right to permit the inspection in his own right and that the others have assumed the risk that one of their number

The burden of establishing that common authority rests upon the State. On the basis of this record, it is clear that burden was not sustained. The evidence showed that although Fischer, with her two small children, had lived with Rodriguez beginning in December 1984, she had moved out on July 1, 1985, almost a month before the search at issue here, and had gone to live with her mother. She took her and her children's clothing with her, though leaving behind some furniture and household effects. During the period after July 1 she sometimes spent the night at Rodriguez's apartment, but never invited her friends there, and never went there herself when he was not home. Her name was not on the lease nor did she contribute to the rent. She had a key to the apartment, which she said at trial she had taken without Rodriguez's knowledge (though she testified at the preliminary hearing that Rodriguez had given her the key). On these facts the State has not established that, with respect to the South California apartment, Fischer had "joint access or control for most purposes." To the contrary, the Appellate Court's determination of no common authority over the apartment was obviously correct.

[R]espondent asserts that permitting a reasonable belief of common authority to validate an entry would cause a defendant's Fourth Amendment rights to be "vicariously waived." We disagree.

We have been unyielding in our insistence that a defendant's waiver of his trial rights cannot be given effect unless it is "knowing" and "intelligent." We would assuredly not permit, therefore, evidence seized in violation of the Fourth Amendment to be introduced on the basis of a trial court's mere "reasonable belief"—derived from statements by unauthorized persons—that the defendant has waived his objection. But one must make a distinction between, on the one hand, trial rights that *derive* from the violation of constitutional guarantees and, on the other hand, the nature of those constitutional guarantees themselves. * * *

What Rodriguez is assured by the trial right of the exclusionary rule, where it applies, is that no evidence seized in violation of the Fourth Amendment will be introduced at his trial unless he consents. What he is assured by the Fourth Amendment itself, however, is not that no government search of his house will occur unless he consents; but that no such search will occur that is "unreasonable." There are various elements, of course, that can make a search of a person's house "reasonable"—one of which is the consent of the person or his cotenant. The essence of respondent's argument is that we should impose upon this element a requirement that we have not imposed upon other elements that regularly compel government officers to exercise judgment regarding the facts: namely, the requirement that their judgment be not only responsible but correct.[b]

[I]n order to satisfy the "reasonableness" requirement of the Fourth Amendment, what is generally demanded of the many factual determinations that must regularly be made by agents of the government—whether the magistrate issuing a warrant, the police officer executing a warrant, or the police officer conducting a search or seizure under one of the exceptions to the warrant requirement—is not that they always be correct, but that they always be reasonable. As we put it in *Brinegar v. United States,* [p. 311]:

might permit the common area to be searched."

b. In an omitted portion of the opinion, illustrations were given: (i) the probable cause requirement for a warrant, as to which the magistrate may act on "seemingly reliable but factually inaccurate information"; (ii) the war-

rant requirement, as to which the officer may be reasonably mistaken as to the warrant's scope, *Maryland v. Garrison,* p. 210; and (iii) the search incident to arrest doctrine, where the officer may be reasonably mistaken as to the person to be arrested, *Hill v. California,* p. 347.

"Because many situations which confront officers in the course of executing their duties are more or less ambiguous, room must be allowed for some mistakes on their part. But the mistakes must be those of reasonable men, acting on facts leading sensibly to their conclusions of probability."

We see no reason to depart from this general rule with respect to facts bearing upon the authority to consent to a search. Whether the basis for such authority exists is the sort of recurring factual question to which law enforcement officials must be expected to apply their judgment; and all the Fourth Amendment requires is that they answer it reasonably. The Constitution is no more violated when officers enter without a warrant because they reasonably (though erroneously) believe that the person who has consented to their entry is a resident of the premises, than it is violated when they enter without a warrant because they reasonably (though erroneously) believe they are in pursuit of a violent felon who is about to escape.

Stoner v. California, [p. ___] is in our view not to the contrary. There, in holding that police had improperly entered the defendant's hotel room based on the consent of a hotel clerk, we stated that "the rights protected by the Fourth Amendment are not to be eroded ... by unrealistic doctrines of 'apparent authority.'" It is ambiguous, of course, whether the word "unrealistic" is descriptive or limiting—that is, whether we were condemning as unrealistic all reliance upon apparent authority, or whether we were condemning only such reliance upon apparent authority as is unrealistic. Similarly ambiguous is the opinion's earlier statement that "there [is no] substance to the claim that the search was reasonable because the police, relying upon the night clerk's expressions of consent, had a reasonable basis for the belief that the clerk had authority to consent to the search." Was there no substance to it because it failed as a matter of law, or because the facts could not possibly support it? At one point the opinion does seem to speak clearly:

> "It is important to bear in mind that it was the petitioner's constitutional right which was at stake here, and not the night clerk's nor the hotel's. It was a right, therefore, which only the petitioner could waive by word or deed, either directly or through an agent."

But as we have discussed, what is at issue when a claim of apparent consent is raised is not whether the right to be free of searches has been *waived,* but whether the right to be free of *unreasonable* searches has been *violated.* Even if one does not think the *Stoner* opinion had this subtlety in mind, the supposed clarity of its foregoing statement is immediately compromised, as follows:

> "It is true that the night clerk clearly and unambiguously consented to the search. But there is nothing in the record to indicate that *the police had any basis whatsoever to believe that* the night clerk had been authorized by the petitioner to permit the police to search the petitioner's room."

The italicized language should have been deleted, of course, if the statement two sentences earlier meant that an appearance of authority could never validate a search. In the last analysis, one must admit that the rationale of *Stoner* was ambiguous—and perhaps deliberately so. It is at least a reasonable reading of the case, and perhaps a preferable one, that the police could not rely upon the obtained consent because they knew it came from a hotel clerk, knew that the room was rented and exclusively occupied by the defendant, and could not reasonably have believed that the former had general access to or control over the latter. * * *

As *Stoner* demonstrates, what we hold today does not suggest that law enforcement officers may always accept a person's invitation to enter premises. Even when the invitation is accompanied by an explicit assertion that the person lives there, the surrounding circumstances could conceivably be such that a reasonable person would doubt its truth and not act upon it without further inquiry. As with other factual determinations bearing upon search and seizure, determination of consent to enter must "be judged against an objective standard: would the facts available to the officer at the moment . . . 'warrant a man of reasonable caution in the belief' " that the consenting party had authority over the premises? If not, then warrantless entry without further inquiry is unlawful unless authority actually exists. But if so, the search is valid.

In the present case, the Appellate Court found it unnecessary to determine whether the officers reasonably believed that Fischer had the authority to consent, because it ruled as a matter of law that a reasonable belief could not validate the entry. Since we find that ruling to be in error, we remand for consideration of that question. * * *

Justice MARSHALL, with whom Justice BRENNAN and Justice STEVENS join, dissenting. * * *

Unlike searches conducted pursuant to the recognized exceptions to the warrant requirement, third-party consent searches are not based on an exigency and therefore serve no compelling social goal. Police officers, when faced with the choice of relying on consent by a third party or securing a warrant, should secure a warrant, and must therefore accept the risk of error should they instead choose to rely on consent. * * *

Acknowledging that the third party in this case lacked authority to consent, the majority seeks to rely on cases suggesting that reasonable but mistaken factual judgments by police will not invalidate otherwise reasonable searches. The majority reads these cases as establishing a "general rule" that "what is generally demanded of the many factual determinations that must regularly be made by agents of the government—whether the magistrate issuing a warrant, the police officer executing a warrant, or the police officer conducting a search or seizure under one of the exceptions to the warrant requirement—is not that they always be correct, but that they always be reasonable."

The majority's assertion, however, is premised on the erroneous assumption that third-party consent searches are generally reasonable. The cases the majority cites thus provide no support for its holding. In *Brinegar v. United States,* for example, the Court confirmed the unremarkable proposition that police need only probable cause, not absolute certainty, to justify the arrest of a suspect on a highway. As *Brinegar* makes clear, the possibility of factual error is built into the probable cause standard, and such a standard, by its very definition, will in some cases result in the arrest of a suspect who has not actually committed a crime. Because probable cause defines the reasonableness of searches and seizures outside of the home, a search is reasonable under the Fourth Amendment whenever that standard is met, notwithstanding the possibility of "mistakes" on the part of police. In contrast, our cases have already struck the balance against warrantless home intrusions in the absence of an exigency. Because reasonable factual errors by law enforcement officers will not validate unreasonable searches, the reasonableness of the officer's mistaken belief that the third party had authority to consent is irrelevant. * * * *c

c. As for the other illustrations given by the majority, the dissenters explained that

"*Hill* should be understood no less than *Brinegar* as simply a gloss on the meaning of 'proba-

NOTES ON WHO MAY CONSENT

1. *Husband-wife.* In *United States v. Duran,* 957 F.2d 499 (7th Cir.1992), holding defendant's wife could consent to search of a separate building on their farm which he used as a gym, the court concluded the requisite access was established by the wife's testimony that she could have entered that building at any time, though the wife had not theretofore done so and had none of her personal effects there. This is not to say, the court cautioned, that there is "a per se rule that common spousal authority extends to every square inch of property upon which a couple's residence is built"; such an approach "presumes that spouses, in forging a marital bond, remove any and all boundaries between them," which "does not reflect reality, either in practice or in the eyes of the law." The *Duran* court thus opted for this position: "In the context of a more intimate marital relationship [as compared to other co-occupants], the burden upon the government should be lighter. We hold that a spouse presumptively has authority to consent to a search of all areas of the homestead; the nonconsenting spouse may rebut this presumption only by showing that the consenting spouse was denied access to the particular area searched." Query, what is the effect of the rebuttal in light of *Rodriguez?*

2. *Parent-child.* If a child is living at the home of his parents, the courts are in agreement that the head of the household may give consent to a search of the child's living quarters. A contrary result is sometimes reached if the "child" living with his parents has reached adulthood. A child may not give consent to a full search of the parent's house. However, where it is not unusual or unauthorized for the child to admit visitors into the home, the mere entry of police on the premises with the consent of the child is not improper.

3. *Landlord-tenant; co-tenants.* A landlord may not consent to a search of his tenant's premises (as compared to areas of common usage), and this is so even though the landlord may have some right of entry for purposes of inspecting or cleaning the premises. *Chapman v. United States,* 365 U.S. 610, 81 S.Ct. 776, 5 L.Ed.2d 828 (1961). Hotel employees may not consent to the search of a particular room during the period in which it has been rented by a guest. *Stoner v. California,* 376 U.S. 483, 84 S.Ct. 889, 11 L.Ed.2d 856 (1964). But "where two or more persons occupy a dwelling place jointly, the general rule is that a joint tenant can consent to police entry and search of the entire house or apartment, even though they occupy separate bedrooms." *State v. Thibodeau,* 317 A.2d 172 (Me.1974).

4. *Employer-employee.* As to consent by defendant's employer, compare *Gillard v. Schmidt,* 579 F.2d 825 (3d Cir.1978) (consent invalid as to search of defendant's desk; protection of the Fourth Amendment "does not turn on the nature of the property interest in the searched premises, but on the reasonableness of the person's privacy expectation," and defendant had a high expectation concerning his desk because he worked "in an office secured by a locked door and a desk containing psychological profiles and other confidential student records"); with *Commonwealth v. Glover,* 405 A.2d 945 (Pa.Super.1979) (factory owner could consent to search of items on top of work bench, as it not an area assigned to defendant or used exclusively by him).

ble cause,' " while *Garrison* "was premised on the [fact that] searches based on warrants are generally reasonable," and "like *Brinegar,* thus tells us nothing about the reasonableness under the Fourth Amendment of a warrantless arrest."

Whether an employee can give a valid consent to a search of his employer's premises depends upon the scope of his authority. Generally, the courts have been of the view that the average employee, such as a clerk, janitor, driver, or other person temporarily in charge, may not give consent. However, if the employee is a manager or other person of considerable authority who is left in complete charge for a substantial period of time, then the prevailing view is that such a person can waive his employer's rights.

5. *Bailor-bailee.* If a person leaves his car at a garage for repairs, does he assume the risk that the repairman might permit police to look inside the car to determine whether it is stolen, as held in *State v. Baker,* 310 S.E.2d 101 (N.C.App.1983)? If so, is a different result called for if the repairman turns the vehicle over to the police so that they can inspect it more closely at another location, as in *State v. Farrell,* 443 A.2d 438 (R.I.1982)?

NOTES ON LIMITS ON THIRD-PARTY CONSENT

Even if the consent was given by a third party who, at least in some circumstances, could give effective consent, it may still be questioned whether other circumstances of the particular case made that person's consent ineffective vis-a-vis the defendant. Consider:

1. *Antagonism.* What if, for example, a wife calls the police into the house and points out incriminating evidence because she is angry at her husband? Compare *State v. Gonzalez–Valle,* 385 So.2d 681 (Fla.App.1980) (where "the motive of the defendant's wife in consenting to the search was clearly one of spite," she "had no right to waive her husband's protection against unreasonable searches and seizures"); with *Commonwealth v. Martin,* 264 N.E.2d 366 (Mass. 1970) ("while they are both living in the premises the equal authority does not lapse and revive with the lapse and revival of amicable relations between the spouses").

2. *Defendant's instructions.* If the defendant had previously instructed the third party not to allow a search, should those instructions be controlling? In *People v. Fry,* 76 Cal.Rptr. 718 (App.1969), the court held: "When the officers solicited consent of the wife to enter for the purpose of seizing property they knew her husband had instructed her not to consent and, under these circumstances, were not entitled to rely upon her consent as justification for their conduct" in searching the family home. *Fry* was distinguished in *People v. Reynolds,* 127 Cal.Rptr. 561 (App.1976), because in the later case the police were unaware of the husband's instructions to his wife. Is the *Matlock* test relevant on this issue?

3. *Defendant's refusal or failure to consent.* In *Matter of Welfare of D.A.G.,* 484 N.W.2d 787 (Minn.1992), the court concluded: "The 'waiver' and 'assumption of risk' rationales, however, are not compelling in a case such as this, where the person against whom the search is directed is present and the consenting joint occupant is not. First, an absent third-party's consent should not be used to 'waive' another individual's constitutional rights when that individual is present at the search to give or withhold consent in his or her own right. Similarly, the risk that one co-inhabitant might permit the common area of a jointly occupied premises to be searched in the absence of another is qualitatively different from the risk that a warrantless search will be conducted over the objection of a present joint occupant: A present, objecting joint occupant cannot be said to have assumed the risk that an absent third party will vicariously waive his or her constitutional rights. We agree that 'the risk assumed by joint occupancy is merely an inability

to control access to the premises during one's absence.' * * * We do not, however, decide what the result would be where both consenting and non-consenting joint occupants are present when the police request permission to search a premises."

4. *Exclusive control by defendant of effects or areas within shared premises or objects.* In *State v. Evans,* 372 P.2d 365 (Hawaii 1962), the court held the wife could not consent to a search of personal items found in a cuff link case located in her husband's dresser drawer. Is this holding consistent with the *Matlock* test? Consider also the relevance of *Frazier v. Cupp,* 394 U.S. 731, 89 S.Ct. 1420, 22 L.Ed.2d 684 (1969), where the Court concluded that one of petitioner's contentions, namely, that the police illegally searched and seized clothing from his duffel bag, could "be dismissed rather quickly":

"This duffel bag was being used jointly by petitioner and his cousin Rawls and it had been left in Rawls' home. The police, while arresting Rawls, asked him if they could have his clothing. They were directed to the duffel bag and both Rawls and his mother consented to its search. During this search, the officers came upon petitioner's clothing and it was seized as well. Since Rawls was a joint user of the bag, he clearly had authority to consent to its search. The officers therefore found evidence against petitioner while in the course of an otherwise lawful search. * * * Petitioner argues that Rawls only had actual permission to use one compartment of the bag and that he had no authority to consent to a search of the other compartments. We will not, however, engage in such metaphysical subleties in judging the efficacy of Rawls' consent. Petitioner, in allowing Rawls to use the bag and in leaving it in his house, must be taken to have assumed the risk that Rawls would allow someone else to look inside."

Chapter 6

WIRETAPPING, ELECTRONIC EAVES- DROPPING, THE USE OF SECRET AGENTS TO OBTAIN INCRIMINA- TING STATEMENTS, AND THE FOURTH AMENDMENT[a]

SECTION 1. HISTORICAL BACKGROUND

A. CONSTITUTIONAL PERMISSION

OLMSTEAD v. UNITED STATES, 277 U.S. 438, 48 S.Ct. 564, 72 L.Ed. 944 (1928), held (5–4), per Chief Justice TAFT, that wiretapping did not amount to a search and seizure for reasons that have since been rejected by the Court. The Fourth Amendment itself, observed Taft, "shows that the search is to be of material things—the person, the house, his papers or his effects. The description of the warrant necessary to make the proceeding lawful, is that it must specify the place to be searched and the person or *things* to be seized." Moreover, not only did the police fail to violate the amendment by tapping, as such, but neither did they do so at any point along the way, in the course of gaining access to the wiretap evidence: "The evidence was secured by the use of the sense of hearing and that only. There was no entry of the houses or offices of the defendants."

Although the evidence which led to the conviction for conspiracy to violate the National Prohibition Act was obtained by federal prohibition agents in violation of a statute of the state of Washington, which made it a misdemeanor to "intercept" telegraphic or telephonic messages, the Chief Justice pointed out that "this statute does not declare that evidence obtained by such interception shall be inadmissible, and by the common law [it] would not be." Moreover, "clearly a [state statute] cannot affect the rules of evidence applicable in courts of the United States."[b]

---

a. This chapter does not attempt to cover in detail Title III of the Crime Control Act of 1968, as amended by the Electronic Communication Privacy Act of 1986, and the extensive litigation these statutes have generated. For more comprehensive treatment, see James Carr, *The Law of Electronic Surveillance* (1977); Clifford S. Fishman, *Wiretapping and Eavesdropping* (1978); Michael Goldsmith, *The Supreme Court and Title III: Rewriting the Law of Electronic Surveillance*, 74 J.Crim.L. & C. 1 (1983). For a fairly brief but very helpful examination of various aspects of Title III, and of electronic surveillance generally, see Chap-ter 14 of Charles H. Whitebread & Christopher Slobogin, *Criminal Procedure* (3d ed. 1993).

b. "Taft did not challenge the fourth amendment exclusionary rule; he *confined* it. Rejecting the argument that 'unethically,' as well as unconstitutionally, secured evidence should be barred, he concluded that 'the exclusion of evidence should be confined to cases where *rights under the Constitution* would be violated by *admitting* it' [emphasis added.] Kamisar, *Does (Did) (Should) the Exclusionary Rule Rest on a "Principled Basis" Rather than an "Empirical Proposition"?*, 16 Creighton L.Rev. 565, 603 (1983).

In an exhaustive dissenting opinion, Justice BRANDEIS observed:

"The progress of science in furnishing the government with means of espionage is not likely to stop with wire tapping. Ways may some day be developed by which the government, without removing papers from secret drawers, can reproduce them in court, and by which it will be enabled to expose to a jury the most intimate occurrences of the home. Advances in the psychic and related sciences may bring means of exploring unexpressed beliefs, thoughts and emotions. * * * Can it be that the Constitution affords no protection against such invasions of individual security?

"[In] *Ex parte Jackson*, 96 U.S. 727, 24 L.Ed. 877 [1877], it was held that a sealed letter intrusted to the mail is protected by the amendments. The mail is a public service furnished by the government. The telephone is a public service furnished by its authority. There is, in essence, no difference between the sealed letter and the private telephone message.

"[The] evil incident to invasion of the privacy of the telephone is far greater than that involved in tampering with the mails. Whenever a telephone line is tapped, the privacy of the persons at both ends of the line is invaded, and all conversations between them upon any subject, and although proper, confidential, and privileged, may be overheard. Moreover, the tapping of one man's telephone line involves the tapping of the telephone of every other person whom he may call, or who may call him. As a means of espionage, writs of assistance and general warrants are but puny instruments of tyranny and oppression when compared with wire tapping.

"Time and again this court, in giving effect to the principle underlying the Fourth Amendment, has refused to place an unduly literal construction upon it. * * * No court which looked at the words of the amendment rather than at its underlying purpose would hold, as this court did in *Ex parte Jackson*, that its protection extended to letters in the mails.

"[The] makers of our Constitution * * * conferred, as against the government, the right to be let alone—the most comprehensive of rights and the right most valued by civilized men. To protect that right, every unjustifiable intrusion by the government upon the privacy of the individual, whatever the means employed, must be deemed a violation of the Fourth Amendment. And the use, as evidence in a criminal proceeding, of facts ascertained by such intrusion must be deemed a violation of the Fifth. * * *

"Independently of the constitutional question, I am of opinion that the judgment should be reversed. By the laws of Washington, wire tapping is a crime. To prove its case, the government was obliged to lay bare the crimes committed by its officers on its behalf. A federal court should not permit such a prosecution to continue. * * *

"Decency, security, and liberty alike demand that government officials shall be subjected to the same rules of conduct that are commands to the citizen. In a government of laws, existence of the government will be imperiled if it fails to observe the law scrupulously. Our government is the potent, the omnipresent teacher. For good or for ill, it teaches the whole people by its example. Crime is contagious. If the government becomes a lawbreaker, it breeds contempt for law; it invites every man to become a law unto himself; it invites anarchy. To declare that in the administration of the criminal law the end justifies the means—to declare that the government may commit crimes in order to secure the conviction of a private criminal—would bring terrible retribution. Against that pernicious doctrine this court should resolutely set its face."

In a brief separate dissent, Justice HOLMES commented:

"While I do not deny it I am not prepared to say that the penumbra of the Fourth and Fifth Amendments covers the defendants, although I fully agree that courts are apt to err by sticking too closely to the words of a law where these words import a policy that goes beyond them. [But] I think, as Justice Brandeis says, that apart from the Constitution the government ought not to use evidence obtained and only obtainable by a criminal act. * * * It is desirable that criminals should be detected, and to that end that all available evidence should be used. It also is desirable that the government should not itself foster and pay for other crimes, when they are the means by which the evidence is to be obtained. * * * We have to choose, and for my part I think it is a less evil that some criminals should escape than that the government should play an ignoble part.

"For those who agree with me no distinction can be taken between the government as prosecutor and the government as judge. If the existing code does not permit district attorneys to have a hand in such dirty business it does not permit the judge to allow such iniquities to succeed. [And] if all that I have said so far be accepted it makes no difference that in this case wire tapping is made a crime by the law of the state, not by the law of the United States. * * * I am aware of the often-repeated statement that in a criminal proceeding the court will not take notice of the manner in which papers offered in evidence have been obtained. But that somewhat rudimentary mode of disposing of the question has been overthrown by *Weeks*. [T]he reason for excluding evidence obtained by violating the Constitution seems to me logically to lead to excluding evidence obtained by a crime of the officers of the law."

Notes and Questions

1. *Different views of constitutional interpretation.* For a close study of the opinions of Chief Justice Taft and Justice Brandeis in the *Olmstead* case and an insightful discussion of the two Justices' different views of constitutional interpretation, see James Boyd White, *Judicial Criticism,* 20 Ga.L.Rev. 835, 847–70 (1986).

2. *Shedding light on the original bases of the exclusionary rule.* Although often quoted by proponents of the fourth amendment exclusionary rule, the most famous passages in the Holmes–Brandeis dissents are arguments for extending the exclusionary rule to situations where the federal government has not violated the Constitution, or even federal law, but only a state anti-wiretapping law. "Nevertheless," observes Kamisar, fn. b, p. 360, "these famous dissents shed light on the original bases and purposes of the exclusionary rule. [They] underscore that the exclusionary rule is [or at least was thought to be] based on principle— one might also say that it has an important symbolic quality—not on estimates of how substantially the exclusion of evidence affects police behavior."

B.   STATUTORY PROHIBITION: § 605 OF THE 1934 FEDERAL COMMUNICATIONS ACT[a]

Chief Justice Taft noted in his *Olmstead* opinion that "Congress may of course protect the secrecy of telephone messages by making them when intercept-

a. Section 605 of the 1934 Act was "amend- ed" by Title III of the Crime Control Act of 1968, permitting court-approved wiretapping ed, inadmissible in evidence in federal criminal trials, by direct legislation, and thus depart from the common law of evidence." Such a development occurred with the passage of the Federal Communications Act of 1934. Section 605 of the Act read in part: "[N]o person not being authorized by the sender shall intercept any communication and divulge or publish the existence, contents, substance, purport, effect, or meaning of such intercepted communication to any person * * *." This wording was held to cover wiretapping by state or federal officers as well as by private persons, *Nardone v. United States,* 302 U.S. 379, 58 S.Ct. 275, 82 L.Ed. 314 (1937), 308 U.S. 338, 60 S.Ct. 266, 84 L.Ed. 307 (1939); *Benanti v. United States,* 355 U.S. 96, 78 S.Ct. 155, 2 L.Ed.2d 126 (1957); and to apply to intrastate as well as interstate communications, *Weiss v. United States,* 308 U.S. 321, 60 S.Ct. 269, 84 L.Ed. 298 (1939).

The Department of Justice and the FBI took the position that Section 605 did not prohibit wiretapping *alone,* only tapping *followed by* "divulgence," and, further, that it was not a "divulgence" when one member of the government communicated to another, but only when he communicated outside the government, e.g., sought to introduce the wiretap information into evidence. See e.g., William P. Rogers, *The Case for Wire Tapping,* 63 Yale L.J. 792, 793 (1954). For sharp criticism of this view see, e.g., Edward Bennett Williams, *The Wiretapping–Eavesdropping Problem; A Defense Counsel's View,* 44 Minn.L.Rev. 855, 860 (1960).

C.   WIRETAPPING, § 605 AND FEDERAL–STATE RELATIONS

Since it involved the use of state-gathered wiretap evidence in a state prosecution, *Schwartz v. Texas,* 344 U.S. 199, 73 S.Ct. 232, 97 L.Ed. 231 (1952), posed the wiretapping counterpart of *Wolf v. Colorado.* Although the Court recognized that "the problem under '605 is somewhat different [than *Wolf*] because the introduction of the intercepted communication would itself be a violation of the statute," i.e., a prohibited "divulgence," it nevertheless relied on *Wolf* to hold the evidence admissible. Only Douglas, J., dissented.

More weight was given to the Federal Communication Act's "built-in" exclusionary rule in *Benanti v. United States, supra,* which barred state-gathered wiretap evidence proffered in a *federal* prosecution, even though at the time the great weight of authority (later overruled in *Elkins,* p. 148) allowed federal prosecutors to use evidence obtained by illegal state searches so long as there was no "collusion" between the two "sovereignties."

Two days before the electronic surveillance provisions of the Crime Control Act of 1968 were signed into law, *Schwartz* was overruled by *Lee v. Florida,* 392 U.S. 378, 88 S.Ct. 2096, 20 L.Ed.2d 1166 (1968): "*Schwartz* cannot survive the demise of *Wolf.* [*Mapp*] imposed a judicially devised exclusionary rule. [In] the present case the federal law itself explicitly protects intercepted communications from divulgence, in a court or any other place."

D.   NON-TELEPHONIC ELECTRONIC EAVESDROPPING

1. *Brandeis' fears become a reality.* Several studies in the 1950s and 60s, e.g., Samuel Dash, Robert Knowlton & Richard Schwartz, *The Eavesdroppers* 339–79 (1959); Allan F. Westin, *Privacy and Freedom* 69–89 (1967); indicated that modern

and electronic eavesdropping by federal and state law enforcement officials in the investigation of many listed offenses.

developments in electronic eavesdropping had made the prophetic fears voiced by Justice Brandeis in his *Olmstead* dissent a reality. According to these studies: Tiny microphones can be secreted behind a picture or built into a coat button. Highly directive microphones known as "parabolic microphones" are capable of eavesdropping on a conversation taking place in an office on the *opposite side of a busy street* or on a park bench or outdoor restaurant terrace hundreds of feet away. Laser beams can pick sound waves off closed windows. A small, continuously operating transmitter can be placed beneath the fender of an automobile and its signal picked up by a receiver in another car or in a fixed plant. A special gun developed for American military authorities can shoot a small dart containing a wireless radio microphone into a tree, window pane, awning or any other object near the subject of investigation.

However, while electronic eavesdropping appeared to be "the ultimate invasion of privacy," Williams, supra, at 866, for decades the law furnished much less protection against this danger than it did against wiretapping. The Federal Communications Act applied only when telephone, telegraph, or radiotelegraph conversations were overheard and until the 1960's the constitutional protection against unreasonable search and seizure applied only when electronic snooping was accomplished by a physical invasion or "trespass". No such "trespass" occurred in *Olmstead* (the taps from house lines were made in the streets near the house) or in *Goldman v. United States,* 316 U.S. 129, 62 S.Ct. 993, 86 L.Ed. 1322 (1942) (where federal officers placed a detectaphone *against the wall* of a private office) or in *On Lee v. United States* (1952) (Sec. 3, infra) (where incriminating statements were picked up via a "wired for sound" former acquaintance of petitioner).

That the Constitution does furnish *some* protection against the electronic seizure of conversations as well as the seizure of "papers and effects" was made plain by *Silverman v. United States,* 365 U.S. 505, 81 S.Ct. 679, 5 L.Ed.2d 734 (1961). There, a unanimous Court, per Stewart, J., held that listening to incriminating conversations within a house by inserting an electronic device (a so-called "spike mike") into a party wall and making contact with a heating duct serving the house occupied by petitioners, "thus converting their entire heating system into a conductor of sound," amounted to an illegal search and seizure.

Justice Douglas concurred, maintaining: "The depth of the penetration of the electronic device—even the degree of its remoteness from the inside of the house—is not measure of the injury. * * * Our concern should not be with the trivialities of the local law of trespass, as the opinion of the Court indicates. But neither should the command of the Fourth Amendment be limited by nice distinctions turning on the kind of electronic equipment employed. Rather our sole concern should be with whether the privacy of the home was invaded."

Silverman not only established that conversations could be "seized" within the meaning of the Fourth Amendment, but suggested that a Fourth Amendment "search" for them might occur without any trespass. This seemed even more certain when three years later, in *Clinton v. Virginia,* 377 U.S. 158, 84 S.Ct. 1186, 12 L.Ed.2d 213 (1964) (per curiam), the Court summarily rejected the state court's holding that *Silverman* did not apply where the spike mike "was not driven into the wall but was 'stuck in' it." Any lingering doubts were dispelled by *Katz v. United States* (p. 155).

SECTION 2. *BERGER AND KATZ*; THE WISDOM AND CONSTITUTIONALITY OF TITLE III OF THE CRIME CONTROL ACT

A.　The Implications of *Berger* and *Katz*

BERGER v. NEW YORK, 388 U.S. 41, 87 S.Ct. 1873, 18 L.Ed.2d 1040 (1967),[a] left the dissenting Justices (and many others) wondering whether *any* wiretapping or electronic eavesdropping statute could pass constitutional muster. The Court, per CLARK, J., struck down a New York electronic surveillance statute,[b] calling it a "blanket grant of permission to eavesdrop * * * without adequate supervision or protective procedures."

The statute, observed Justice Clark, (1) permitted a court order to issue merely on reasonable grounds to believe that evidence of crime may be obtained, without specifying what crime has been or is being committed and without describing what conversations are to be overheard—thus failing to "particularly [describe] the place to be searched, and the person or things to be seized," as required by the Fourth Amendment[c]—(2) permitted installation and operation of surveillance equipment for 60 days—"the equivalent of a series of intrusions, searches and seizures pursuant to a single showing of probable cause"—(3) permitted renewal of the order on the basis of the original grounds on which the initial order was issued—"this we believe insufficient without a showing of present probable cause for continuance of the eavesdrop"—(4) placed no termination on the eavesdrop once the conversation sought is seized—"this is left entirely to the discretion of the officer"—and (5) did not provide for a return on the warrant—"thereby leaving full discretion in the officer as to the use of seized conversations of innocent as well as guilty parties."

The Court contrasted the New York statute's "broadside authorization" of electronic surveillance with the "precise and discriminate" procedures followed in *Osborn v. United States*, 385 U.S. 323, 87 S.Ct. 429, 17 L.Ed.2d 394 (1966), where,

a. The case grew out of a state investigation of alleged bribery of state liquor authority officials. Pursuant to the challenged New York statute, a court order was obtained permitting the installation of a recording device in a lawyer's office for up to 60 days. On the basis of information gathered from this eavesdrop, a second order was obtained, authorizing the installation of a recording device in another person's office. As a result of evidence obtained from the second eavesdrop, petitioner was indicted for, and convicted of, conspiracy to bribe the chairman of the state liquor authority.

b. The statute, N.Y.Code Crim.P. § 813–a, provided in part: "An ex parte order for eavesdropping * * * may be issued by any justice of the supreme court [a trial court in New York] or judge of a county court [upon] oath or affirmation of a district attorney [or police officer above the rank of sergeant] that there is reasonable ground to believe that evidence of crime may be thus obtained, and particularly describing the person or persons whose communications, conversations or discussions are to be overheard or recorded and the purpose

thereof * * *. Any such order shall be effective for the time specified therein but not for a period of more than two months unless extended or renewed by [the judge who issued the original order] upon satisfying himself that such extension or renewal is in the public interest. Any such order, together with the papers upon which the application was based, shall be delivered to and retained by the applicant as authority for the eavesdropping authorized therein. A true copy of such order [or denial of any application for such an order] shall at all times be retained [by the judge issuing the order or denying the application]."

c. The statute did require the naming of "the person or persons whose communications, conversations or discussions are to be overheard or recorded," but, said the Court, "this does no more than identify the person whose constitutionally protected area is to be invaded rather than 'particularly describing' the communications, conversations, or discussions to be seized. As with general warrants, this leaves too much to the discretion of the officer executing the order."

on the basis of a detailed affidavit alleging that an attorney was attempting to bribe a juror, two federal judges authorized a tape recorder to be concealed on the person of the attorney's "employee" (actually a secret government agent) for a specific meeting with the attorney.[d] Because *Osborn* involved such a rare fact situation, one atypical of police electronic surveillance, the Court's reference to this case raised further doubts about the constitutionality of most electronic surveillance.[e]

DOUGLAS, J., concurred in the result, maintaining that electronic surveillance is "a search for 'mere evidence,' "which is a violation of the Fourth and Fifth Amendments regardless of "the nicety and precision with which a warrant may be drawn."[f] "If a statute were to authorize placing a policeman in every home or office where it was shown that there was probable cause to believe that evidence would be obtained," he observed, "there is little doubt that it would be struck down as a bald invasion of privacy, far worse than the general warrants prohibited by the Fourth Amendment. I can see no difference between such a statute and one authorizing electronic surveillance, which, in effect, places an invisible policeman in the home. If anything, the latter is more offensive because the homeowner is completely unaware of the invasion of privacy."[g]

STEWART, J., concurred in the result. He fully agreed with the dissenters that the challenged New York law was constitutional, but he concluded that "the affidavits on which the judicial order issued in this case did not constitute a showing of probable cause adequate to justify the authorizing order." The standard of reasonableness embodied in the Fourth Amendment, "he observed," demands that the showing of justification match the degree of intrusion."The affidavits" "might be enough to satisfy the standards of the Fourth Amendment for a conventional search or arrest," but not "an intrusion of the scope and duration that was permitted in this case."

Responding to the contentions that court-ordered electronic surveillance fails to specify with adequate particularity the conversations to be seized and allows a general and indiscriminate search and seizure, Justice HARLAN observed: "Just as some exercise of dominion, beyond mere perception, is necessary for the seizure of tangibles, so some use of the conversation beyond the initial listening process is required for the seizure of the spoken word."

Similarly, dissenting Justice WHITE maintained that an electronic surveillance that is continued over a span of time is no more a "general search" barred by the Fourth Amendment than the typical execution of a search warrant over a

d. Is there a "certain irony" in the *Berger* Court's approval of *Osborn?* If the *Osborn* order was properly issued without any statutory authorization, why didn't the *Berger* Court consider the particularity of the order issued in this case without regard to the constitutionality of the New York statute? See Kent Greenawalt, *The Consent Problem in Wiretapping and Eavesdropping*, 68 Colum.L.Rev. 189, 201–02 (1968).

e. See Samuel Dash, *Katz—Variations on a Theme by Berger*, 17 Cath.L.Rev. 296, 311–13 (1968).

f. Since *Berger* was briefed and argued prior to *Warden v. Hayden* (p. 174), petitioner argued at some length that the New York statute authorized "general searches" for "mere evidence." But the Court, per Clark, J., rejected the contention in a brisk footnote (fn.

2), stating that it had been "disposed of in *Hayden* adversely to petitioner's assertion here." For the view that it had not, that *Hayden* had been careful to leave open the possibility of some "testimonial limit" on the permissible objects of seizure, see Telford Taylor, *Two Studies in Constitutional Interpretation* 68–71, 101–03 (1969).

g. How can this argument be met? Could a police officer lawfully hide in the closet of a suspect's home for 30 days? Ten? Twenty-four hours? Does it matter whether the officer looks through the keyhole as well as listens? As you limit the area of the search, may the time be increased? May a tap be distinguished from a bug on the ground that the former is a "search" of a much narrower "area"?

described area: "Petitioner suggests that the search is inherently overbroad because the eavesdropper will overhear conversations which do not relate to criminal activity. But the same is true of almost all searches of private property which the Fourth Amendment permits. In searching for seizable matters, the police must necessarily see or hear, and comprehend, items which do not relate to the purpose of the search. That this occurs, however, does not render the search invalid, so long as it is authorized by a suitable search warrant and so long as the police, in executing that warrant, limit themselves to searching for items which may constitutionally be seized."

A short time after *Berger,* the Court, per STEWART, J., made plain in KATZ v. UNITED STATES (p. 155) that the "trespass" doctrine enunciated in *Olmstead* and *Goldman* was no longer viable and that the "penetration" of the governmental intrusion "can have no constitutional significance." But the *Katz* Court thought it "clear that [the surveillance involved in this case] was so narrowly circumscribed that a duly authorized magistrate, properly notified of the need for such investigation, specifically informed of the basis on which it was to proceed, and clearly apprised of the precise intrusion it would entail, could constitutionally have authorized, with appropriate safeguards, the very limited search and seizure that the Government asserts in fact took place."[a]

The Court likened the "discriminate circumstances" of the electronic surveillance in *Katz* to those in *Osborn* where, the *Berger* Court had said, the court order "afforded similar protections to those [of] conventional warrants authorizing the seizure of tangible evidence." "Here, too," observed the *Katz* Court, "a similar judicial order could have accommodated 'the legitimate needs of law enforcement' by authorizing the carefully limited use of electronic surveillance."

Although he dissented in *Katz,* Justice BLACK was encouraged: "[T]oday's opinion differs sharply from *Berger,* [which] set up what appeared to be insuperable obstacles to the valid passage [of] wiretapping laws. [The] Court's opinion [in] this case [removes] the doubts about state power in this field and abates to a large extent the confusion and near paralyzing effect of the *Berger* holding."

The basis for Justice Black's view that the *Katz* opinion "differs sharply from *Berger*" is unclear. *Both opinions* referred to *Osborn* with approval. And the surveillance in *Katz* itself, as well as in *Osborn,* was very narrowly circumscribed. But the Congress seemed to read *Katz* the same way Justice Black did. Within seven months of *Katz,* in Title III of the Omnibus Crime Control and Safe Streets Act of 1968 (commonly referred to as Title III), discussed immediately below, Congress adopted legislation granting law enforcement officials extensive powers to conduct wiretapping and electronic surveillance.

a. FBI agents had attached an electronic listening and recording device to the outside of the public phone booth from which petitioner had placed his calls. The agents "did not begin their electronic surveillance until investigation had established a strong possibility that he was using the telephone in question to transmit gambling information [in] violation of federal law. Moreover, the surveillance was limited, both in scope and in duration, to the specific purpose of establishing the contents of the petitioner's unlawful telephone communications. The agents confined their surveillance to the brief periods during which he used the telephone booth, and they took great care to overhear only the conversations of the petitioner himself."

B. Title III: An Overview

The text of Title III is set forth in Supp. App. B. For useful summaries of Title III, on which the following brief discussion relies heavily, see LaFave & Israel, § 4.2; Michael Goldsmith, *The Supreme Court and Title III: Rewriting the Law of Electronic Surveillance,* 74 J.Crim.L. & C. 1, 39?56 (1983) (hereinafter referred to as Goldsmith); Charles H. Whitebread & Christopher Slobogin, *Criminal Procedure* 302–330 (3d ed. 1993) (hereinafter referred to as Whitebread & Slobogin).

Title III was designed to regulate all *"nonconsensual"* electronic surveillance (i.e., electronic surveillance when *none* of the parties overheard have consented to the interception),[a] except "national security" eavesdropping.[b] The states are free to adopt laws of their own authorizing court-ordered electronic surveillance, but compliance with federal statutory standards is essential. See § 2516(2).

Title III is concerned only with orders "authorizing or approving the *interception* of a wire or oral communication," '2518(1) (emphasis added), and the statute defines "intercept" to mean "the *aural* acquisition of the contents of any wire or oral *communication* through the use of any electronic, mechanical, or other device." § 2410(4) (emphasis added). Thus, until recently,[c] because "pen registers

---

a. Section 2511(2)(c) provides that "it shall not be unlawful under this chapter for a person acting under color of law to intercept a wire or oral communication where such person is a party to the communication or *one of the parties* to the communication has given prior consent to such interception." (Emphasis added.) Consensual electronic surveillance is not restricted by the Fourth Amendment. See *Lopez v. United States* (1963) (p. 384); *United States v. White* (1971) (p. 391).

The National Wiretap Commission, *Majority Report* (1976) found that consensual electronic surveillance "is especially vital for the investigation of certain criminal activities, particularly official corruption, extortion, and loansharking," and that "it also serves to protect police officers, informants, and complainants, or whoever is the consenting participant to the conversation." The Majority Report deemed court authorization for such surveillance "unnecessary for the protection of privacy because it is not a 'search' within the meaning of the Fourth Amendment" and because "it serves not to intercept conversations, but merely to corroborate them, improving the accuracy of evidence for use in court."

b. Section 2511(3) states that nothing in Title III "shall limit the constitutional power of the President to take such measures as he deems necessary to protect the Nation against actual or potential attack or other hostile acts of a foreign power, to obtain foreign intelligence information deemed essential to the security of the United States, or to protect national security information against foreign intelligence activities. Nor shall anything contained in this chapter be deemed to

limit the constitutional power of the President to take such measures as he deems necessary to protect the United States against the overthrow of the Government by force or other unlawful means, or against any other clear and present danger to the structure or existence of the Government." *United States v. United States District Court,* 407 U.S. 297, 92 S.Ct. 2125, 32 L.Ed.2d 752 (1972) (often called *Keith* after then District Judge Damon Keith), held that the President lacked power to conduct warrantless surveillance in "domestic security" cases, but left open the question whether there could be warrantless surveillance of foreign powers or their agents. In response, Congress enacted the Foreign Intelligence Surveillance Act (FISA) of 1978. The Act, inter alia, provides that under certain circumstances the President, through the Attorney General, may authorize electronic surveillance for periods up to one year to acquire foreign intelligence information. The FISA was upheld in *United States v. Belfield,* 692 F.2d 141 (D.C.Cir.1982). See generally Senate Select Committee on Intelligence, *The Foreign Surveillance Act of 1978: The First Five Years,* S.Doc. No. 660, 98th Cong., 2d Sess. 3 (1984); William Webster, *Sophisticated Surveillance—Intolerable Intrusion or Prudent Protection?,* 63 Wash.U.L.Q. 351 (1985); Note, 71 Mich.L.Rev. 1116 (1980).

c. Under the 1986 Electronic Communications Privacy Act, 18 U.S.C. § 3121, pen register surveillance must be court-approved, but is not subject to all the safeguards governing court-ordered electronic surveillance. Moreover, apparently no exclusionary rule applies.

do not accomplish the 'aural acquisition' of anything,"[d] these devices (which do not record phone conversations, but only the numbers dialed from a given phone and the times the number was dialed) were not governed by Title III. Nor does Title III cover video surveillance i.e., surreptitious *television* surveillance, although some courts have applied Title III's provisions by analogy.[e]

Criminal penalties and civil remedies are available against one who willfully intercepts, uses or discloses information in violation of the statute. See §§ 2511(a), 2520. Aside from specific provisions requiring exclusion of the evidence, Title III also has a general exclusion provision, § 2515, that "transcends its constitutional counterpart by being applicable to all governmental judicial, quasi-judicial, and administrative proceedings." Goldsmith 40.[f] This exclusion provision also applies to private, as well as government, interceptions.

Suppression of the evidence, however, is not the consequence of *every* failure to follow the provisions of Title III. Suppression is required only when the particular statutory provision violated "was intended to play a central role in the statutory scheme." Compare *United States v. Giordano*, 416 U.S. 505, 94 S.Ct. 1820, 40 L.Ed.2d 341 (1974) with *United States v. Chavez*, 416 U.S. 562, 94 S.Ct. 1849, 40 L.Ed.2d 380 (1974).

Federal applications may be authorized only by the Attorney General or a specially designated Assistant Attorney General, see § 2516(1), a requirement designed to ensure that discretion is exercised by a senior and politically accountable executive official before a court is asked to pass on an application. (When authorized by state law, the "principal prosecuting attorney of any state or political subdivision thereof" may apply to a state judge for an electronic surveillance order. The state provisions are thus less centralized, but this was deemed necessitated by realities of state law enforcement systems.) Only federal district and appellate judges and their state counterparts may issue surveillance orders. See § 2510(9).

Except for "emergencies"—§ 2518(7) permits warrantless electronic surveillance when "an emergency situation exists" involving "conspiratorial activities threatening the national security interest" or "conspiratorial activities characteristic of organized crime" or (pursuant to a 1984 amendment) "immediate danger of death or serious physical injury to any person"[g]—no electronic surveillance is permitted without a properly authorized application. See § 2518(1).

---

d. *United States v. New York Telephone Co.*, 434 U.S. 159, 98 S.Ct. 364, 54 L.Ed.2d 376 (1977). The Court subsequently held, *Smith v. Maryland* (1979) (p. 161), that the use of a pen register did not constitute a "search" within the meaning of the Fourth Amendment, observing, inter alia: Although petitioner's conduct "may have been calculated to keep the *contents* of his conversation private, his conduct was not and could not have been calculated to preserve the privacy of the number he dialed."

e. See pp. 371-74.

f. *Calandra* (1974) (p. 146), it will be recalled, refused to allow a grand jury witness to invoke the Fourth Amendment exclusionary rule. In *Gelbard v. United States*, 408 U.S. 41, 92 S.Ct. 2357, 33 L.Ed.2d 179 (1972), however, a 5–4 majority, per Brennan, J., held that grand jury witnesses may refuse to testify where their testimony is sought on the basis of illegal electronic surveillance.

g. There must be "grounds upon which an order could be entered under this chapter to authorize such interception"; the situation must require an interception before a court order "can with due diligence be obtained"; and, within 48 hours after the interception has begun to occur, an application must be filed seeking retroactive approval for such interception.

See generally Clifford Fishman, *Interception of Communications in Exigent Circumstances*, 22 Ga.L.Rev. 1, 35–48 (1987). The "emergency surveillance" provision "has been invoked only rarely, and there has been virtually no judicial discussion or interpretation of it." Id. at 35.

Each application must be in writing and under oath; disclose the identity of the officer making the application and the officer authorizing it (see *United States v. Chavez,* supra); and include a "full and complete" statement of the circumstances justifying the belief that an order should be issued, including (i) details as to the particular offense, (ii) a particular description of the communication facility, (iii) a particular description of "the type of communication" sought to be intercepted, and (iv) "the identity of the person, if known, committing the offense, and whose conversation is to be intercepted."[h] "In other words," comments Goldsmith at 42, "there must be probable cause to believe that a particular person involved in a designated crime will have discussion pertinent to that crime using a particular phone (or at a particular place) during a specified time period."

Moreover, to discourage routine use of tapping or electronic eavesdropping, the application must include "full and complete" statements as to "whether or not other investigative procedures have been tried or failed or why they reasonably appear to be unlikely to succeed if tried or to be too dangerous"[i] and of the facts concerning all previous applications "involving any of the same persons, facilities or places specified in the application, and the action taken by the judge on each such application." See § 2518(1)(c), (e).

The judge may enter an order as requested or as modified upon determining, on the basis of the facts submitted, that "normal investigative procedures" are not a viable alternative and that there is probable cause for believing three things: an individual has committed or is about to commit a particular offense enumerated in the statute; "particular communications concerning that offense will be obtained through such interception"; and the facilities or place where the communications are to be intercepted are being, or about to be, used in connection with the offense or "are leased to, listed in the name of, or commonly used by such person." See § 2518(3).

The court order must designate the personnel authorized to conduct the surveillance, identify both the person (if known) and the facilities or place targeted for interception, specify the period of surveillance, and furnish a "particular description of the type of communication sought to be intercepted, and a statement of the particular offense to which it relates."[j] See § 2518(4). In addition, each order must provide, § 2518(5), that the authorization to intercept "shall be executed as soon as practicable, shall be conducted in such a way as to *minimize the interception of communications not otherwise subject to interception*" (emphasis added),[k] and "must terminate upon attainment of the authorized objective, or in any event in thirty days."

---

h. On the obligation of the government to discover and name the person to be heard, see *United States v. Kahn,* 415 U.S. 143, 94 S.Ct. 977, 39 L.Ed.2d 225 (1974). For the consequences of noncompliance with this provision, see *United States v. Donovan,* 429 U.S. 413, 97 S.Ct. 658, 50 L.Ed.2d 652 (1977).

i. In practice, maintains James Carr, *The Law of Electronic Surveillance* 179 (1977), this requirement has been watered down to "one of investigatory utility, rather than necessity."

j. What was intended by "type of communication" is unclear. It now "appears to be generally accepted that [this requirement] can be fulfilled by indicating the offense under inves-

tigation, without further details about the anticipated conversations," Carr, fn. i supra, at 173.

k. But see *Scott v. United States* (1978) (p. 378), rejecting the contention that the failure of the surveilling officers to make any effort to comply with a minimization requirement was alone a basis for suppression. The Court took the position that "subjective intent alone does not make otherwise lawful conduct illegal," meaning that the officers' presumed failure to make even a good-faith effort to comply with the requirement was not itself a reason for excluding the evidence obtained.

Title III does meet at least some of the objections voiced by the *Berger* Court when it invalidated the state law involved in that case. The federal statute requires that surveillance cease once "the objective of the authorization" is achieved, § 2815(5), and it permits electronic surveillance extensions only upon a new showing of probable cause and only by resort to the procedures required in obtaining the initial order. (See id.) But Title III does allow continued electronic surveillance for up to 30 days on the basis of a single showing of probable cause, id., and it permits an unlimited number of 30 day extensions, albeit on renewed showings of probable cause. See id.

"Allowing such lengthy surveillance, possibly for years," argues a leading critic of police electronic eavesdropping, Herman Schwartz, *The Legitimation of Electronic Eavesdropping*: *The Politics of "Law and Order,"* 67 Mich.L.Rev. 455, 461 (1969), "conflicts sharply with *Berger's* clear disapproval of the two-month authorization permitted by the New York statute. Moreover, sections 2518(1)(d) and 4(e) of the Act do not limit the eavesdropping to specific points in time, unlike the [situation] in *Katz* and the cases approvingly cited in *Berger,* but rather allow uninterrupted eavesdropping over a 'period of time.' Under such a provision, officers may install a tap or a bug which will be in *continuous* operation throughout the days or months for which the interception is authorized. This would seem to pose a rather clear conflict with the Supreme Court's holding in *Berger,* which disapproved the uninterrupted interception as allowing 'indiscriminate' seizure and approved the *Osborn* interception because 'the order authorized one limited intrusion rather [than] a continuous surveillance'."[1]

Section 2518(8)(d) provides that "within a reasonable period but not later than ninety days" after the filing of an application has been denied or the authorized surveillance terminated, the issuing or denying judge shall serve on "the persons *named* in the order or the application, and *such other parties* to intercepted communication as the judge *may determine in his discretion that is in the interest of justice"* (emphasis added) an "inventory" including (1) the fact of the entry of the order or the application; (2) the date of the entry and the period of interception, or the denial of the application; and (3) the fact that during the period communications were or were not intercepted. However, upon "an ex parte showing of good cause," the serving of the inventory may be postponed.[m]

That only "named" individuals are guaranteed statutory notice, comments Goldsmith at 55, "is not constitutionally objectionable. * * * Congress realized that at times notice of interception might be a source of considerable distress. For example, eavesdropping targets could be embarrassed if their innocent conversations resulted in disclosure of the surveillance to uninvolved parties. The possibility also existed that notice mailed to one's home or business could cause domestic or professional discomfiture respectively. Accordingly, Congress decided to give notice to those most obviously affected by the investigation; others would receive it upon a proper exercise of judicial discretion."

C. SILENT VIDEO SURVEILLANCE

Because "a man televised while silently making a bomb is not engaged in any form of communication, let alone 'wire or oral communication,'" and "a visual

---

l. But see *United States v. Cafero,* p. 374.

m. "The 'reasonable time' requirement has been broadly construed. As for the 'good cause' for postponement, it has been held to include such reasons as protecting the integrity of an ongoing investigation or ensuring that persons would not flee to avoid arrest." LaFave & Israel at 399.

observation is in no possible sense an 'aural acquisition,' " *United States v. Torres,* infra, Title III does not cover video surveillance (and various attempts to legislate such surveillance have failed). Yet "[n]othing more dramatically conjures up the image of an 'Orwellian society' than a surreptitiously planted government 'eye' in one's living room." Whitebread & Slobogin 326.

Consider UNITED STATES v. TORRES, 751 F.2d 875 (7th Cir.1984), which arose as follows: The FBI obtained judicial authorization to install cameras in "safehouses" being used by members of FALN, a Puerto Rico separatist group suspected of making explosives for terrorist purposes. (The government had not invoked the Foreign Intelligence Surveillance Act.) The videotapes had no sound-tracks, but at the same time that the FBI was televising the interior of the house (in some respects more like a business than a home) it was recording the sounds on different equipment. (The admissibility of the sound tapes was not an issue in this appeal.) As Judge Posner, author of the Seventh Circuit majority opinion in the case, explained, "the FBI wanted to see as well as hear because it had reason to believe that the [suspects], concerned that they might be bugged, would play the radio loudly when they were speaking to each other and also would speak in code and that the actual assembly of the bombs would be carried out in silence." The district court held that Title III did not authorize such surveillance and in the absence of any statutory basis for the authorizing order, the videotaping had violated the Fourth Amendment.

The Seventh Circuit reversed. A majority of the court, per POSNER, J., agreed that there was no statutory authorization for the court order to install the cameras, but held that the district court nevertheless had the authority—under both Fed.R.Crim.P. 41(b) and its inherent judicial power to issue warrants—to issue a warrant authorizing the television surveillance. Although the court concluded that Title III neither authorized nor prohibited silent video surveillance, it made clear that, "because television surveillance is potentially so menacing to personal privacy," a warrant that failed to satisfy (as the government *did* satisfy in this case) the provisions of Title III would violate the Fourth Amendment.

"The usual way in which judges interpreting the Fourth Amendment take account of the fact that searches vary in the degree to which they invade personal privacy," observed Judge Posner, "is by requiring a higher degree of probable cause (to believe that the search will yield incriminating evidence), and by being more insistent that a warrant be obtained if at all feasible, the more intrusive the search is. But maybe in dealing with so intrusive a technique as television surveillance, other methods of control as well, such as banning the technique outright from use in the home in connection with minor crimes, will be required in order to strike a proper balance between public safety and personal privacy. That question is not before us, but we mention it to make clear that in declining to hold televison surveillance unconstitutional *per se* we do not suggest that the Constitution must be interpreted to allow it to be used as generally as less intrusive techniques can be. * * * [A] search could be unreasonable, though conducted pursuant to an otherwise valid warrant, by intruding on personal privacy to an extent disproportionate to the likely benefits from obtaining fuller compliance with the law. '[T]here can be no ready test for determining reasonable-ness other than by balancing the need to search against the invasion which the search entails.' *Camara v. Municipal Court* [p. 339]."

Professor Whitebread and Slobogin (supra, at 327–28) consider the willing-ness of the Seventh Circuit and other courts to apply Title III guidelines to video surveillance "unfortunate" because even Title III's restrictions "are not stringent enough for monitoring investigative use of cameras":

"If video surveillance is to be permitted, several rules should be followed at a *minimum*. First, because the intrusion they seek is so significant, the police should have to show more than ordinary probable cause, * * *. Second, particularity requirements should be heightened as well; only those rooms in which essential elements of the crime are to take place should be observed. In *Torres*, the FBI planted bugs and cameras in every room of the 'safehouses.' If evidence of bombmaking was all that was being sought, this arrangement was not necessary. Third, because minimization is particularly difficult to enforce where cameras are involved, a stringent prohibition against bad faith viewing of activities which are innocent or which do not involve the suspects [is] appropriate. Given the invasion of privacy involved, perhaps even negligent failures to minimize should result in exclusion. One appropriate minimization method [is] prohibition of video surveillance until audio surveillance indicates criminal activity is taking place.

"Fourth, a warrant should not be issued unless no other method, including eavesdropping, can accomplish the investigative objective. In *Torres*, for instance, there may have been probable cause sufficient to obtain a search warrant authorizing entry of the safehouses while the bombs were being made. This alternative may not have produced as much evidence as video surveillance but may still have been preferable to it. In *People v. Teicher*,[31] on the other hand, there probably was no alternative to installing a camera focused on the dental chair of a dentist suspected of sexually abusing his patients. [Furthermore,] stated the court, 'the use of a police decoy without the protection of visual surveillance would not have produced the needed evidence in this case, since the decoy, of necessity, would have been heavily sedated and might not have been able to relate what transpired.' * * *

"If evidence of criminal activity sufficient to make a case is not obtained within a very short time—perhaps even within a single day—police should have to justify further surveillance. Finally, at least one court has rightly held that, in contrast to the rule for other types of surveillance, warrantless video surveillance should be prohibited even when one of those surveilled consents to it.[32] The assumption that a person assumes the risk that government will seize everything another person hears, which is questionable enough, should not be extended to permit government observation of everything another person sees. Moreover, of course, what a video camera 'observes' may be quite different from what a government agent might see."

See also *United States v. Koyomejian*, 970 F.2d 536 (9th Cir.1992) (en banc). The court, per Trott, J., agreed that the federal electronic surveillance statute neither authorizes nor prohibits domestic silent video surveillance. (It noted, however, that the Foreign Intelligence Surveillance Act (FISA) does regulate such surveillance for foreign intelligence purposes.) Turning to the federal electronic surveillance statute "for guidance in implementing the fourth amendment," the court adopted four requirements of the statute "in addition to the ordinary requirement of a finding of probable cause":

(1) the judge issuing the warrant must find that "normal investigative procedures have been tried and have failed or reasonably appear to be unlikely to

31. 422 N.E.2d 506 (N.Y.1981).   **32.** *People v. Henderson*, 270 Cal.Rptr. 248 (1990).

succeed if tried" (a "least intrusive means" requirement); (2) the warrant must contain "a particular description" of the type of activity to videotape and "a statement of the particular offense to which it relates"; (3) the warrant must not allow the period of surveillance to be "longer than is necessary to achieve the objective of the authorization"; and (4) the warrant must require that the surveillance "be conducted in such a way as to minimize the [videotaping of activity] not otherwise subject to [surveillance]."

Concurring Judge Kozinski voiced "serious doubt whether the Constitution requires all of the rules the majority plucks from" the federal electronic surveillance statute. Judge Kozinski maintained that the first requirement, the "least intrusive means" requirement, "clearly has no constitutional moorings."

D. THE FACIAL VALIDITY OF TITLE III

Surprisingly, the Supreme Court has never explicitly considered the facial validity of Title III. But there is no hint in the Court's many decisions interpreting various provisions of Title III that the statute is facially invalid. And the lower federal courts have consistently upheld the statute against constitutional challenge.

Lower court decisions reconciling continuing electronic surveillance up to 30 days, permitted by Title III, with the Fourth Amendment, "rely upon the analysis of Justices Harlan and White, [both of whom] dissented in *Berger*. [See p. 366]. Their contention was that an electronic surveillance which is continued over a span of time is no more a general search than the typical execution of a search warrant over a described area." LaFave & Israel 369. Illustrative of the lower federal courts' rejection of constitutional challenges to Title III is UNITED STATES v. CAFERO, 473 F.2d 489 (3d Cir.1973), (ALDISERT, J.):

As for the contention that the statute is unconstitutional because it permits as much as 30 days of surveillance: "[W]e interpret § 2518(5) as requiring automatic termination upon attainment of the objective of the authorization irrespective of whether a statement to this effect has been included by the authorizing judge. [The] thirty-day period is merely a statutory limitation on the life of any authorization, which terminates every authorization at the end of thirty days regardless of whether the objective of the authorization has been achieved."

As for the argument that Title III is fatally defective because it fails to require prompt notice to those people whose conversations have been intercepted after authorized surveillance has been completed: "We find it difficult to accept the proposition that a search may be deemed reasonable, and therefore constitutional, during the various stages of application for authorization, execution, supervision of the interception, and termination, only to be invalidated *ab initio* because of the operation of some condition subsequent, to wit, a failure to give notice of the items seized. In the context of traditional search warrants, a failure to comply with certain procedural requirements of Fed.R.Crim.P. 41 [e.g., a failure to deliver promptly a copy of the warrant to the party whose premises were searched] has been held not to amount to deprivation of Fourth Amendment rights necessitating suppression."

As for the complaint that the inventory procedure set forth in § 2518(8)(d) lacks the degree of promptness required by the Constitution: "[The] constitutional standard for searches and seizures relating to both tangible objects and communications is the reasonableness of the governmental action. [A] statute which requires an inventory to be filed within 'a reasonable time' cannot, without more, be said to offend this test. If, in a given case there is undue delay, that contention may be pressed in an appropriate averment alleging non-compliance with the statute."

"[The] same analysis should apply to inspection of the contents of the interception, [which § 2518(8)(d)] leaves to the discretion of the issuing court 'as the judge determines to be in the interest of justice.' The parameters of 'the interests of justice' within the statutory schema and the Federal Constitution remain to be fashioned on a case-by-case basis. [The] Congressional decision to entrust this inspection to the judicial process is not offensive to the Fourth Amendment."

It will be recalled that, concurring in the result in *Berger,* Justice Stewart concluded that although the evidence might have been adequate "for a conventional search or arrest," it was "constitutionally insufficient to constitute probable cause to justify an intrusion of the scope and duration that was permitted in this case." (See p. 366.) This argument, however, has not prevailed. Illustrative is *United States v. Falcone,* 505 F.2d 478 (3d Cir.1974): "Probable cause is not a matter of degree. Although *Berger* and *Katz* call for extra vigilance in the supervision of electronic eavesdropping, neither case separates probable cause into degrees. Moreover, no special probable cause requirement can be found in the statutory scheme."[a]

E.   The Need For, and Utility of, Title III

As pointed out in Goldsmith at 35–37: "[A year before Title III was enacted into law, the President's Crime Commission's task force on organized crime had] noted that traditional evidence gathering techniques are relatively ineffectual in organized crime cases. [The] Commission provided several examples of successful New York organized crime prosecutions that purportedly could not have been made without electronic surveillance. Indeed, the Commission observed that only in New York, where electronic surveillance had been used for more than two decades, 'have law enforcement officials achieved some level of success in bringing prosecutions against organized crime.' It was these findings, together with a concern for controlling abuses, which prompted a majority of the Commission members to recommend the adoption of legislation authorizing electronic surveillance under a system of strict controls.

"[T]he drafters of Title III relied heavily upon the Commission's analysis in determining that such legislation was necessary for modern law enforcement. The legislative history noted that crime was a 'national catastrophe' and that organized crime, in particular, had a pervasive influence upon American society which previous law enforcement efforts had been unable to control. * * * Congress suggested that police misconduct had been responsible for few unlawful invasions of privacy, and implicitly concluded that providing the police with a carefully controlled, lawful means for conducting electronic surveillance would remove the incentive for abuse.

"[It] has been suggested that Title III was the product of a hysterical Congress responding to conservative political pressure during a national climate of

a. But consider Posner, J., in *United States*   372.
v. Torres, p. 372; Whitebread & Slobogin, p.

fear. No doubt the debate over electronic surveillance was at times emotional, and it is probably true that the assassination of Martin Luther King and Robert F. Kennedy contributed somewhat to Title III's expedited approval. Overall, however, the measure appears to have been a bipartisan effort designed to accommodate the demands of modern society's need for privacy and law enforcement."[a]

The wisdom, as well as the constitutionality, of various provisions of Title III are forcefully challenged in Herman Schwartz, *The Legitimation of Electronic Eavesdropping: The Politics of "Law and Order,"* 67 Mich.L.Rev. 455 (1969). Professor Schwartz observes, inter alia, at 481–82:

"[S]ection 2516 allows federal officials to tap and bug not only for such common activities of organized crime as extortion, corruption, interstate gambling, loan sharking, labor racketeering, and the like, but also for any offense involving marijuana, riots, obstruction of a criminal investigation, counterfeiting, and theft from interstate shipments.

"State officers are treated even more generously, despite the fact that the states have a far smaller role than the federal government in fighting organized crime. Indeed, one of the greatest problems in fighting organized crime is [that] few state or local law enforcement agencies show any interest in the enterprise. Yet states are given authority to use electronic surveillance for [a practically unlimited number of offenses, referring to § 2516(2)].[b] [Yet] even with respect to certain serious offenses, the case for eavesdropping authority is feeble, for the technique is of little use in solving murder cases and of almost no use in investigating robbery, rape, or any other crimes of violence that usually involved sudden, nonrepetitive encounters. [Thus] Title III grants authority to use eavesdropping almost as freely as any other standard investigative tool. In this respect, it is not very different from the New York statute which allows eavesdropping for any crime, and under which some eighty per cent of police wiretapping was for the investigation of minor gambling and vice offenses."

Professor Schwartz also maintains that Title III "will turn out to be either a provision of relatively little value in the struggle against organized crime or a verbal smoke screen for continuing illegality" (id. at 468–69, 471–72):

"According to its proponents, the special advantage of electronic surveillance is that it is a valuable tool for gathering strategic intelligence about organized crime and that it thus enables law enforcement officials to obtain 'a look at the overall picture' for 'prevention' purposes. The techniques of fighting organized crime differ from those used in ordinary criminal investigation. The former involves accumulating a great deal of superficially irrelevant information which is then collated. Furthermore, in investigating organized crime the police do not

---

a. But see Herman Schwartz, *Taps, Bugs, and Fooling the People* 13 (1977): "[Title III was enacted at a time when] Americans were frightened as rarely before in a time of official peace. They feared street crime, black rebellions, radicals, young people, organized crime. Overhanging everything was Vietnam.

"Congress had a pretty good idea of how bad the bill was. As Richard Harris reported, 'all those who voted against it, many of those who voted for it, and most of those who didn't vote at all [believed] the bill was a piece of demagoguery, devised out of malevolence and enacted in hysteria.' Nevertheless, records Harris,

'in the House, only 17 members voted against it, and in the Senate only four.' "

Professor Schwartz's reference to Harris is to a detailed, critical account of the political and legislative history of Title III, Harris, *Annals of Legislation—The Turning Point,* New Yorker, Dec. 14, 1968, pp. 68, 152–63.

b. Section 2516(2) of Title III invites the states to pass legislation modeled on the federal act, but many states have not done so and thus their law enforcement officials lack statutory authority to apply for an electronic surveillance order.

work from a known crime to an unknown or suspected criminal, but 'backwards' from a 'known criminal' to a hoped-for discovery of an as-yet-unknown crime.

"[The] fact is that searches for strategic intelligence, without a specific crime as the objective, cannot be squared with *Berger, Katz,* and *Osborn.* Judging by the language used by the Court, the facts at issue in those cases, and the kinds of permissible electronic surveillance cited in the various opinions, it would seem that gathering tactical intelligence is the only kind of surveillance that is justifiable under present theories of the fourth amendment. And in this respect, [Title III] is verbally consistent with the cases in limiting eavesdropping to such tactical intelligence purposes.

"[This] is surely an odd result, for if the war against organized crime—the justification for Title III—really requires strategic intelligence, how will that war be advanced by legislation which seems to permit the acquisition of only tactical intelligence? And if the Act does not grant law enforcement officers the power to obtain allegedly crucial strategic information, will we not again experience the same kind of widespread flouting of clear legal limitations that has recently come to light? In sum, even the very loose Title III is too restrictive to accomplish the purposes advanced by its proponents, and this raises serious questions about the reasons for their support of the legislation, and about how meaningful they expect its ostensible limitations to be."[c]

But see National Wiretap Commission, *Majority Report* (1976),[d] "vigorously reaffirm[ing] the findings and statements of policy made by Congress in 1968 that organized criminals make extensive use of wire and oral communications in their criminal activities" and that "the interception of such communications to obtain evidence of the commission of crimes or to prevent their commission is an indispensable aid to law enforcement and the administration of justice."

"We have, for example," reports the Commission, "seen much of the major organized criminal activity in an entire state—New Jersey—weeded out through the astute use of electronic surveillance in coordination with other investigative techniques. Notable in the use of Title III by the New Jersey Attorney General's office is the technique of 'working up the ladder' of an organized crime group through successive wiretaps, each based on probable cause, each leading to higher echelons of criminality, each being promptly shut down when it achieved its object. [In] Washington, D.C., we have seen how the Capital City's major narcotics dealer, who had survived all conventional efforts to gather evidence for his apprehension, was finally convicted by the use of wiretap evidence.

"[On the other hand], the inability of Illinois investigators to use court-authorized electronic surveillance [because they lacked such authority][e] foreclosed the possibility of identifying and indicting the top leaders of [a large theft and fencing ring].[f] There is no doubt that the use of court-authorized electronic

---

c. Professor Goldsmith maintains, however, Goldsmith at 52 n. 322, that Professor Schwartz's contention that Title III's limitation on surveillance for purely strategic intelligence is inconsistent with its drafters' goal of providing a means to combat organized crime on a long term basis "overlooks [that] strategic intelligence is often legitimately overheard during the course of actual surveillance."

d. Title III was enacted as a compromise of various conflicting views of the form any legislation regulating electronic surveillance should take. The National Commission for the Review of Federal and State Laws Relating to Wiretapping and Electronic Surveillance (National Wiretap Commission) was created, as part of the compromise, to, among other duties, conduct a comprehensive study and review of the operation of Title III in the first six years after its enactment. The majority and minority reports issued in 1976 were the result of two years of work by the Commission.

e. See fn. b supra.

f. But see Schwartz, fn. a supra, at 33, urging an end to state authority for electronic surveillance because "the results are meager, surveillance has accomplished a great deal for law enforcement that could not have been done without it."

The Majority Report called for *more* extensive use of electronic surveillance, "particularly in the investigation of narcotics importation and distribution and theft and fencing." It also found that "federal officials responsible for administering wiretap application review procedures have shown a commendable concern for adhering to the requirements of Title III." Indeed, "it appears that these review procedures for authorizing an electronic-surveillance application have in some instances been *too* time-consuming" (emphasis added).[g]

SECTION 3. SOME APPLICATIONS OF TITLE III

After considerable discussion, Professor Michael Goldsmith concludes that Title III is constitutional on its face, Goldsmith at 55, but he quickly adds: "The real question today * * * is not Title III's facial validity, but the manner in which it has been applied. Congress intended that the statute be strictly enforced under careful judicial supervision. Indeed, given the many questions raised about its facial validity, the law's ultimate constitutionality was said by some to depend upon such enforcement. Yet, ironically, the Supreme Court, which originally took the initiative in advising Congress as to the drafting of electronic surveillance legislation, has since failed to enforce Title III in a consistently scrupulous manner." Consider the following:

A.   "MINIMIZ[ING] THE INTERCEPTION OF COMMUNICATIONS NOT OTHERWISE SUBJECT TO INTERCEPTION"; WHAT WEIGHT, IF ANY, SHOULD BE GIVEN TO THE OFFICER'S UNDERLYING INTENT OR MOTIVATION?

One of the limiting provisions of Title III is found in § 2518(5), requiring every order to contain a provision that the authorization to intercept "be conducted in such a way as to minimize the interception of communications not otherwise subject to interception." In SCOTT v. UNITED STATES, 436 U.S. 128, 98 S.Ct. 1717, 56 L.Ed.2d 168 (1978), pursuant to a court wiretap order requiring "minimization," government agents intercepted for a one-month period virtually all conversations over a particular telephone suspected of being used in furtherance of a conspiracy to import and distribute narcotics. Only forty percent of the conversations were shown to be narcotics related and the Special Agent who conducted the wiretap testified that "he and the agents working under him knew

---

the abuses are great, judicial scrutiny is poor and not likely to improve, and few states are really eager for the authority."

g. A minority of the Commission differed sharply on the conclusions to be drawn from the evidence. The Minority Report observed, for example, that "in seven years Title III has been responsible, directly or indirectly, for only nine federal convictions and three pending indictments against leading Organized Crime figures. The actual impact of these cases on an organization with over 5,000 known members nationwide must be regarded as minimal at best."

The Minority Report also noted that "electronic surveillance has been used since 1968 against a very great number of low-level gamblers with very little success in reaching up

into the hierarchy of any major gambling or related Organized Crime operation. Despite seven years of court-ordered electronic surveillance, illegal gambling continues to flourish in every major city in the country and in many rural areas as well. [E]ven if convicted, the gambler virtually never receives a prison sentence * * *. Finally, the Commission found no evidence to support the theory, advanced by some, that gambling wiretaps lead the authorities to more serious crimes."

See also Schwartz, fn. a supra, at 33, urging that "[e]lectronic surveillance in gambling and drug cases should be stopped, if only for fiscal reasons. This alone would eliminate more than 80% of the taps and bugs."

of the minimization requirement but made no attempt to comply therewith." Rejecting petitioners' argument that the failure to make good-faith efforts to comply with the minimization requirement is itself a violation of § 2518(5), a 7–2 majority per REHNQUIST, J., agreed with the Court of Appeals that an evaluation of compliance with the minimization requirement, like evaluation of all alleged violations of the Fourth Amendment, should "be based on the reasonableness of the actual interceptions and not on whether the agents subjectively intended to minimize their interceptions." Observed the Court:

"The Government [contends] that petitioners' argument fails to properly distinguish between what is necessary to establish a statutory or constitutional violation and what is necessary to support a suppression remedy once a violation has been established. In view of the deterrent purposes of the exclusionary rule, consideration of official motives may play some part in determining whether application of the exclusionary rule is appropriate *after* a statutory or constitutional violation has been established. But the existence *vel non* of such a violation turns on an objective assessment of the officer's actions in light of the facts and circumstances confronting him at the time. Subjective intent alone, the Government contends, does not make otherwise lawful conduct illegal or unconstitutional.

"[The Government's position] embodies the proper approach for evaluating compliance with the minimization requirement. [A]lmost without exception in evaluating alleged violations of the Fourth Amendment the Court has first undertaken an objective assessment of an officer's actions in light of the facts and circumstances then known to him. The language of the Amendment itself proscribes only 'unreasonable' searches and seizures.

"[In] the very section in which it directs minimization, Congress, by its use of the word 'conducted,' made it clear that the focus was to be on the agents' actions, not their motives. Any lingering doubt is dispelled by the legislative history [which declares that] § 2515 was not 'intended generally to press the scope of the suppression role beyond present search and seizure law.' "[13]

Analyzing the reasonableness of the agents' conduct, the Court observed: "[B]lind reliance on the percentage of nonpertinent calls intercepted is not a sure guide to the correct answer. Such percentages may provide assistance, but there are surely cases, such as the one at bar, where the percentage of nonpertinent calls is relatively high and yet their interception was still reasonable. The reasons for this may be many. Many of the nonpertinent calls may have been very short. Others may have been one-time only calls. Still others may have been ambiguous in nature or involve guarded or coded language. In all these circumstances agents can hardly be expected to know that their calls are not pertinent prior to their termination.

"[W]hen the investigation is focusing on what is thought to be a widespread conspiracy more extensive surveillance may be justified in an attempt to deter-

---

13. This is not to say, of course, that the question of motive plays absolutely no part in the suppression inquiry. On occasion, the motive with which the officer conducts an illegal search may have some relevance in determining the propriety of applying the exclusionary rule. [This] focus on intent, however, becomes relevant only after it has been determined that the Constitution was in fact violated. We also have little doubt that as a practical matter the judge's assessment of the motives of the officers may occasionally influence his judgment regarding the credibility of the officers' claims with respect to what information was or was not available to them at the time of the incident in question. But the assessment and use of motive in this limited manner is irrelevant to our analysis of the questions at issue in this case.

mine the precise scope of the enterprise. [The] type of use to which the telephone is normally put may also have some bearing on the extent of minimization required. For example, if the agents are permitted to tap a public telephone because one individual is thought to be placing bets over the phone, substantial doubts as to minimization may arise if the agents listen to every call which goes out over that phone regardless of who places the call. On the other hand, if the phone is located [as in the case at bar] in the residence of a person who is thought to be the head of a major drug ring, a contrary conclusion may be indicated.

"[We] find nothing to persuade us that the Court of Appeals was wrong in its rejection of [the minimization] claims. Forty percent of the calls were clearly narcotics related * * *. Many of the remaining calls were very short, such as wrong number calls [and] calls to persons who were not available to come to the phone. [In] a case such as this, involving a wide-ranging conspiracy with a large number of participants, even a seasoned listener would have been hard pressed to determine with any precision the relevancy of many of the calls before they were completed. A large number were ambiguous in nature, making characterization virtually impossible until the completion of these calls. * * *

"We are thus left with the seven calls between [petitioner] Jenkins and her mother. [After pointing out that most of the calls were intercepted at the beginning of the surveillance and that several indicated that the mother may have known of the conspiracy, the Court concluded that] [a]lthough none of these conversations turned out to be material to the investigation at hand, we cannot say that the Court of Appeals was incorrect in concluding that the agents did not act unreasonably at the time they made these interceptions."

Dissenting Justice BRENNAN, joined by Marshall, J., maintained that the Court's reasoning "is thrice flawed":

"First, and perhaps most significant, it totally disregards the explicit congressional command that the wiretap be *conducted* so as to minimize interception of communications not subject to interception. Second, it blinks reality by accepting as a substitute for the good-faith exercise of judgment as to which calls should not be intercepted by the agent most familiar with the investigation, the *post hoc* conjectures of the Government as to how the agent would have acted had he exercised his judgment. [In] the nature of things it is impossible to know how many fewer interceptions would have occurred had a good-faith judgment been exercised, and it is therefore totally unacceptable to permit the failure to exercise the congressionally imposed duty to be excused by the difficulty in predicting what might have occurred had the duty been exercised. Finally, the Court's holding permits government agents deliberately to flout the duty imposed upon them by Congress. In a linguistic *tour de force* the Court converts the mandatory language that the interception shall be conducted to a precatory suggestion."

Notes and Questions

1. Consider the criticism of *Scott* in John Burkoff, *The Court that Devoured the Fourth Amendment: The Triumph of an Inconsistent Exclusionary Doctrine*, 58 Or.L.Rev. 151, 187–88 (1979): "In the fourth amendment exclusionary context, since there is only one effective remedy for violation of fourth amendment rights, the distinction between right and remedy is semantic, not substantive. * * *

"Ironically, the *Scott* Court's use of one test for determining the existence of a fourth amendment violation and a second test for application of an exclusionary remedy appears to have as its casuistic end the exclusion of deterrence from the first test although deterrence is the key element of the second test. After all, law enforcement deterrence is the issue that raises the question of the ill-motivated subjective intent of law enforcement agents; for unintended unlawful acts cannot be deterred, whereas if any unlawful acts can be deterred, consciously undertaken ones can be. Given, however, the objection to distinguishing right from remedy in this context, the real issue is not whether deterrence should be part of the test for one, but not the other; rather, the issue is whether deterrence should be a part of both elements of fourth amendment analysis or neither."

2. But see LaFave & Israel, § 3.1(d), taking the view that *Scott* properly rejected the contention that "lack of good faith efforts" required suppression even if no minimization would have been feasible in this case. As a general matter, they maintain, deciding the Fourth Amendment claim, as the *Scott* Court did, by "an objective assessment of an officer's action in the light of the facts and circumstances then known to him," without regard to the officer's underlying intent or motivation, is a sound approach. See also LaFave § 1.4.

3. But consider Goldsmith at 108–09: "[Whatever the rule should be with respect to conventional searches], [g]iven the greater intrusion occasioned by electronic surveillance, [the] fourth amendment's reasonableness clause would seem to require such searches to be undertaken in good faith. Moreover, from a statutory perspective [*Scott*] directly contravened basis Title III principles. Section 2518(5) requires that execution of the order be '*conducted* in such a way as to minimize the interception of [nonpertinent] communications' [emphasis supplied by Goldsmith]. Given the broad deterrent purpose underlying Title III, there is no reason to read the term 'conducted' as excluding subjective intent. [P]rovision for criminal prohibitions in section 2511(1), outlawing willful misconduct, demonstrates that intent was an integral aspect of the overall statutory scheme—indeed by 'willfully' intercepting or 'endeavor[ing]' to intercept in a manner unauthorized by Title III, the agents [in *Scott*] appear to have committed statutory felonies."

Adds Goldsmith (at 109): "Certainly, conformance to a court order should be evaluated in subjective terms. For example, assume that, for the sake of efficiency, surveillance agents decide to put their equipment on 'automatic record,' thereby allowing them to devote their energies to other aspects of the investigation. Even if all the resulting interceptions could be justified subsequently under prevailing minimization standards, would any judge be satisfied that the authorization had been conducted in compliance with his order?"

4. *Should the minimization provision be amended?* Consider Clifford Fishman, *The "Minimization" Requirement in Electronic Surveillance: Title III, the Fourth Amendment and the Dread Scott Decision*, 28 Am.U.L.Rev. 315, 354–55 (1979):

"[A] purely objective analysis of reasonableness may be adequate to decide whether an officer was justified in making an isolated arrest, stop, frisk, search or seizure. Such an analysis, however, is wholly inadequate when several weeks of continuous, surreptitious interceptions of otherwise private conversations are at issue. Particularly in complex investigations, where the government, with superficial plausibility can retroactively defend total interception, it is unlikely that any minimization will be achieved unless a good-faith effort is made to do so. [The] minimization provision should be amended to read: 'Every order and extension thereof shall contain a provision that the [interception] shall be conducted in a *good faith and reasonable manner in order to* minimize the interception of communications not otherwise subject to interception under this chapter."

B.   ELECTRONIC SURVEILLANCE WHICH INVOLVES COVERT ENTRY INTO PRIVATE
PREMISES TO INSTALL EQUIPMENT; HAS THE COURT'S STATUTORY
PERSPECTIVE UNDERGONE A FUNDAMENTAL CHANGE?

DALIA v. UNITED STATES, 441 U.S. 238, 99 S.Ct. 1682, 60 L.Ed.2d 177
(1979), arose as follows: Finding reasonable cause to believe that petitioner was
conspiring to steal goods being shipped in interstate commerce and that his
business office was being used by petitioner and others in connection with the
alleged conspiracy, a federal district court authorized the interception of all oral
communications concerning the conspiracy at petitioner's office. Although the
court order did not explicitly authorize entry into petitioner's office, FBI agents
secretly entered the office one midnight by prying open a window and spent three
hours in the building installing a listening device in the ceiling. All electronic
surveillance of petitioner ended some six weeks later, at which time the agents
secretly re-entered petitioner's office and removed the bug. Partly on the basis of
conversations intercepted pursuant to this order, petitioner was convicted of
receiving stolen goods and related charges. The Court, per POWELL, J., upheld
the electronic surveillance:

First, "[t]he Fourth Amendment does not prohibit *per se* a covert entry
performed for the purpose of installing otherwise legal electronic bugging equipment." *Second,* the Court rejected the contention that, even if it could have
constitutionally done so, Congress had not given the courts statutory authority to
approve covert entries for electronic surveillance purposes: "In the face of [the
legislative history of Title III], one simply cannot assume that Congress, aware
that most bugging requires covert entry, nonetheless wished to except surveillance
requiring such entries from the broad authorization of Title III, and that it
resolved to do so by remaining silent on the subject. On the contrary, the language
and history of Title III convey quite a different explanation for Congress' failure
to distinguish between surveillance that requires covert entry and that which does
not. Those considering the surveillance legislation understood that, by authorizing
electronic interception of oral communications in addition to wire communications, they were necessarily authorizing surreptitious entries."

Third, the Court rejected the contention that, because the authorizing court
did not explicitly set forth its approval of covert entries, the entry violated
petitioner's Fourth Amendment privacy rights: The Warrant Clause of the Fourth
Amendment requires only that warrants be issued by "neutral, disinterested
magistrates"; that they be based on probable cause to believe that " 'the evidence
sought will aid in a particular apprehension or conviction' for a particular
offense"; and that they "particularly describe" the things to be seized as well as
the place to be searched. Nothing in [the] Fourth Amendment or the Court's
decisions "suggests that, in addition to [these three requirements], search warrants also must include a specification of the precise manner in which they are to
be executed."

Dissenting Justice STEVENS, joined by Brennan and Marshall, JJ., thought
the majority's conclusion that Title III implicitly authorizes breaking and entering
"especially anomalous because the statutory scheme in all other respects is
exhaustive and explicit * * * Only one relevant conclusion can be drawn from a
review of the entire legislative history of Title III. The legislators never even
considered the possibility that they were passing a statute that would authorize
federal agents to break into private premises without any finding of necessity by a
neutral and detached magistrate. Congressional silence should not be construed to

authorize the Executive to violate state criminal laws or to encroach upon constitutionally protected privacy interests. * * * Without a legislative mandate that is both explicit and specific, I would presume that this flagrant invasion of the citizen's privacy is prohibited."

In a separate opinion, concurring in part and dissenting in part, Justice BRENNAN, joined by Stewart, J., maintained that "even reading Title III to authorize covert entries, the Justice Department's present practice of securing specific authorization for covert entries is not only preferable, but also constitutionally required": "Breaking and entering into private premises for the purpose of planting a bug cannot be characterized as a mere mode of warrant execution to be left to the discretion of the executing officer. The practice entails an invasion of privacy of constitutional significance distinct from that which attends nontrespassory surveillance; indeed, it is tantamount to an independent search and seizure. [Since] premises may be bugged through means less drastic than home invasion, requiring police to secure prior approval for covert entries may well prevent unnecessary and improper intrusions."

Notes and Questions

1. Consider, Comment, 70 J.Crim.L. & C. 510, 526–27 (1979): "[The *Dalia* majority's approach] is inconsistent with the overall emphasis of Title III—an emphasis upon minimizing the intrusiveness of an intercept order. [By] construing the statutory language—or the absence thereof so as to require that breaking and entering be employed only when alternative means have been tried and have failed or else reasonably appear too unlikely to succeed if tried, the Supreme Court would merely have been extending the express requirement of sections 2518(1)(c) and 2518(3)(c). Moreover, such a position would have substantially minimized the potential for abuse, the threat to personal security, and the invasion of personal privacy [posed by covert entries]. Only when efforts to minimize the intrusion have proven unacceptable would breaking and entering to plant listening devices be authorized."

2. "In all likelihood," observes Goldsmith at 116–18, "the [*Dalia*] majority's pragmatic analysis more closely reflected congressional intent; [it] is inconceivable that, after years of debate, Congress would have failed to realize that most bugs necessitate covert entries. * * * Nevertheless, as enacted the statute contained a potential defect which had to be remedied. Ultimately, in *Dalia*, judicial process was used to rectify this legislative interstice. Hence, the true significance of *Dalia* lay not in the Court's holding that Title III conferred authority to effect covert entries, but in the manner in which this decision was made. * * * *Dalia* abandoned the mode of analysis adopted in *District Court* [p. 368, fn. b] to remedy what Congress might otherwise have made explicit. In the process, the Court's statutory perspective seems to have undergone a fundamental change; although Title III had been designed to constitute a blanket prohibition against electronic surveillance, subject to narrowly tailored statutory exceptions, Justice Powell's analysis now suggested that the law conferred a general grant of authority subject to narrowly tailored prohibitions. Thus, analytically and perhaps philosophically, *Dalia* symbolized the extent to which the Supreme Court had changed direction since 1968 when Title III was enacted."

C. "ROVING SURVEILLANCE"

Prior to recent amendment by the Electronic Communications Privacy Act of 1986, Title III required that all eavesdropping warrants specify the facility or place of the anticipated communication. As amended in 1986, however, Title III orders need not designate the surveillance site—

(a) if in the case of an application with respect to the interception of an *oral* communication "the application contains a full and complete statement as to why such specification is *not practical*" and the judge finds such specification "*not practical*", § 2518(11)(a) (emphasis added); and

(b) if "in the case of an application with respect to a *wire* or *electronic* communication, [the] applicable makes a showing of *a purpose,* on the part of [the targeted] person, *to thwart interception* by changing facilities and the judge finds that *such purpose* has been adequately shown," § 2518(11)(b) (emphasis added).

Michael Goldsmith, *Eavesdropping Reform: The Legality of Roving Surveillance,* 1987 U.Ill.L.Rev. 401, 413 (hereinafter Goldsmith), notes that "[t]he legislative history's only attempt to illustrate [the meaning of the 'not practical'] concept involves 'a suspect who moves from room to room in a hotel to avoid a bug and who sets up a meeting with another suspect for a beach or field. [This] observation is undoubtedly accurate, but fails to provide guidance in other situations."

Why did the 1986 amendment impose more stringent requirements on roving wiretapping interceptions (a showing of "a purpose [to] thwart interception") than on roving oral interceptions? According to Clifford Fishman, *Interception of Communications in Exigent Circumstances,* 22 Ga.L.Rev. 1, 55–56 (1987) (hereinafter Fishman), it was "because of concerns expressed by lobbyists for the nation's telephone companies, [who] wanted statutory protection for their clients, who might suddenly be told to 'wire up' large numbers of pay telephones on short notice." Goldsmith 414 regards the "purpose [to] thwart interception" requirement unduly restrictive and voices concern that "courts may interpret the 'thwart' restriction for wiretaps as evincing congressional intent to construe the term 'not practical' [the term governing roving oral interceptions] narrowly as well."

Can the roving surveillance provision be reconciled with the command of the Fourth Amendment that "no warrants shall issue" which fail to "particularly describe the place to be searched [and] things to be seized"? See Goldsmith at 416–28. On this issue, do *Steagald v. United States* (p. 273) and *United States v. Karo* (p. 171) point in opposite directions? See Fishman at 66–69.

SECTION 4. THE USE OF SECRET AGENTS (WITH AND WITHOUT ELECTRONIC DEVICES) TO OBTAIN INCRIMINATING STATEMENTS

In LOPEZ v. UNITED STATES, 373 U.S. 427, 83 S.Ct. 1381, 10 L.Ed.2d 462 (1963), petitioner made an unsolicited bribe offer to Davis, an IRS agent, who, following his superiors' instructions to "pretend to play along with the scheme," met petitioner in the latter's office and recorded his subsequent bribe offers by means of a concealed wire recorder. Relying heavily on *On Lee v. United States*[a]

---

a. In *On Lee,* 343 U.S. 747, 72 S.Ct. 967, 96 L.Ed. 1270 (1952), Chin Poy, an old acquaintance and former employee of defendant, entered the latter's laundry and engaged him in conversation, in the course of which defendant made incriminating statements. Unknown to defendant, Chin Poy was a "wired for sound" secret government agent, and the microphone concealed on his person transmitted all sounds to a narcotics agent stationed outside. Chin Poy was not called to testify about defendant's incriminating statements—probably because and *Rathbun v. United States*,[b] the Court, per HARLAN, J., rejected the argument that considering the agent's falsification of his mission, he gained access to Lopez's office by misrepresentation and consequently illegally "seized" Lopez's words:

"[T]his case involves no 'eavesdropping' whatever in any proper sense of that term. The Government did not use an electronic device to listen in on conversations it could not otherwise have heard. Instead, the device was used only to obtain the most reliable evidence possible of a conversation in which the Government's own agent was a participant and which that agent was fully entitled to disclose. And the device was not planted by means of an unlawful physical invasion of petitioner's premises under circumstances which would violate the Fourth Amendment. It was carried in and out by an agent who was there with petitioner's assent, and it neither saw nor heard more than the agent himself. * * *

"Stripped to its essentials, petitioner's argument amounts to saying that he has a constitutional right to rely on possible flaws in the agent's memory, or to challenge the agent's credibility without being beset by corroborating evidence that is not susceptible of impeachment. For no other argument can justify excluding an accurate version of a conversation that the agent could testify to from memory. We think the risk that petitioner took in offering a bribe to Davis fairly included the risk that the offer would be accurately reproduced in court, whether by faultless memory or mechanical recording."

Chief Justice WARREN concurred separately, agreeing with the *Lopez* dissenters that *On Lee* was wrongly decided, but finding *On Lee* and the instant case "quite dissimilar constitutionally":

"The only purpose the recording served [in the instant case] was to protect the credibility of [Agent] Davis against that of a man who wished to corrupt a public servant in the performance of his public trust. I find nothing unfair in this procedure. [The] use and purpose of the transmitter in *On Lee* was substantially different from the use of the recorder here. Its advantage was not to corroborate the testimony of Chin Poy, but rather, to obviate the need to put him on the stand. [Had] Chin Poy been available for cross-examination, [the defense could have explored] the possibility of entrapments, police pressure brought to bear to persuade Chin Poy to turn informer, and Chin Poy's own recollection of the contents of the conversation. His testimony might not only have seriously discred-

"the very defects of character and blemishes of record which [led defendant to confide in him] would make a jury distrust his testimony"— but the narcotics agent was allowed to relate the conversations he overheard. A 5–4 majority, per Jackson, J., rejected the claim that Chin Poy had committed a trespass because consent to enter defendant's laundry was obtained by fraud. And the Court dismissed as "verging on the frivolous" the further contention that the agent stationed outside the laundry was "a trespasser" because, by virtue of the microphone concealed on Chin Poy, he overheard what went on inside. "It would be a dubious service to the genuine liberties protected by the Fourth Amendment," observed the Court, "to make them bedfellows with spurious liberties improvised by farfetched analogies which would liken eavesdropping on a conversation, with the connivance of one of the parties, to an unreasonable search and seizure."

b. In *Rathbun*, 355 U.S. 107, 78 S.Ct. 161, 2 L.Ed.2d 134 (1957), the Court held, per Warren, C.J., that the overhearing of a conversation on a regularly used telephone extension with the consent of one party to the conversation was not a violation of § 605 of the Federal Communications Act: "Each party to a telephone conversation takes the risk that the other party may have an extension telephone and may allow another to overhear the conversation. When such takes place there has been no violation of any privacy of which the parties may complain. Consequently, one element of Section 605, *interception*, has not occurred."

ited the prosecution, but might also have raised questions of constitutional proportions."

Justice BRENNAN, joined by Douglas and Goldberg, JJ., dissented, finding *On Lee* indistinguishable from the instant case and maintaining that the evidence should have been excluded in both cases:

"[Not] all communications are privileged. On Lee assumed the risk that his acquaintance would divulge their conversation; Lopez assumed the same risk *vis-à-vis* Davis. The risk inheres in all communications which are not in the sight of the law privileged. [But] the risk which both *On Lee* and today's decision impose is of a different order. It is the risk that third parties, whether mechanical auditors like the Minifon or human transcribers of mechanical transmissions as in *On Lee*—third parties who cannot be shut out of a conversation as conventional eavesdroppers can be, merely by a lowering of voices, or withdrawing to a private place—may give independent evidence of any conversation. There is only one way to guard against such a risk, and that is to keep one's mouth shut on all occasions.

"[There] is a qualitative difference between electronic surveillance [and] conventional police stratagems such as eavesdropping and disguise. The latter do not so seriously intrude upon the right of privacy. The risk of being overheard by an eavesdropper or betrayed by an informer or deceived as to the identity of one with whom one deals is probably inherent in the conditions of human society. It is the kind of risk we necessarily assume whenever we speak. But as soon as electronic surveillance comes into play, the risk changes crucially. There is no security from that kind of eavesdropping, no way of mitigating the risk, and so not even a residuum of true privacy."

Notes and Questions

1. If conversations are within the protection of the Fourth Amendment, why should it matter whether the conversation was "seized" by an electronic device? Was the police practice involved in *On Lee* any dirtier business than it would have been had the defendant's old acquaintance simply elicited the incriminating admissions and then testified? Why does the fact that On Lee would have been better able to attack the acquaintance's credibility than he was to challenge that of the narcotics bureau agent make the original deceit more moral? See Kent Greenawalt, *The Consent Problem in Wiretapping and Eavesdropping,* 68 Colum.L.Rev. 189, 193 (1968); Edmund W. Kitch, *Katz v. United States: The Limits of the Fourth Amendment,* 1968 Supreme Court Rev. 133, 141–42.

2. Is the issue not whether secret agents and informers can be monitored, but whether a warrant is necessary for such monitoring? To what extent is Justice Brennan's position based on the premise that "the warrant procedure can be adapted to electronic surveillance of specific persons at specific places for a limited period of time," but—inasmuch as informers and secret agents "must be developed or placed over a long period of time and the objectives of their 'search' will almost always be broad and impossible to delineate with any precision in advance"?the Fourth Amendment warrant requirement would "prevent altogether the use of informers and secret agents"? See Kitch, supra, at 142.

———

In LEWIS v. UNITED STATES, 385 U.S. 206, 87 S.Ct. 424, 17 L.Ed.2d 312 (1966), decided the same day as *Hoffa,* infra, a federal narcotics agent, by misrepresenting his identity as "Jimmy the Pollack [sic]" and expressing a willingness to purchase narcotics, was invited into petitioner's home where an unlawful narcotics transaction took place. At petitioner's trial, the agent testified as to what occurred in petitioner's home and the narcotics were introduced. Petitioner relied on *Gouled v. United States*, 255 U.S. 298, 41 S.Ct. 261, 65 L.Ed. 647 (1921) (other aspects of which are discussed at p. 174), which excluded incriminating documents obtained when, acting under federal officers' orders, a business acquaintance of defendant obtained entry into defendant's office by pretending that he intended only to pay a social visit, but in defendant's absence searched the office. The *Gouled* Court held that "whether entrance to the home or office of a [suspect] be obtained by a [government agent] by stealth or through social acquaintance, or in the guise of a business call, and whether the owner be present or not when he enters, any search and seizure subsequently and secretly made in his absence falls within the scope of the prohibition of the Fourth Amendment * * *"

Distinguishing *Gouled,* the Court, per WARREN, C.J., stressed that "in the instant case [the] petitioner invited the undercover agent to his home for the specific purpose of executing a felonious sale of narcotics. [During] neither of his visits to petitioner's home did the agent see, hear, or take anything that was not contemplated and in fact intended by petitioner as a necessary part of his illegal business. Were we to hold the deceptions of the agent in this case constitutionally prohibited, we would come near to a rule that the use of undercover agents in any manner is virtually unconstitutional per se.[a] [W]hen, as here, the home is converted into a commercial center to which outsiders are invited for purposes of transacting unlawful business, that business is entitled to no greater sanctity than if it were carried on in a store, a garage, a car or on the street. [This case has been well summarized by the Government as follows:] '[T]he only statements repeated were those that were willingly made to the agent and the only things taken were the packets of marihuana voluntarily transferred to him. The pretense resulted in no breach of privacy; it merely encouraged the suspect to say things which he was willing and anxious to say to anyone who would be interested in purchasing marihuana.' "[b]

Why didn't the *Lewis* Court dismiss petitioner's argument out of hand with a citation to *Lopez?* Why instead, in a case in which no electronic device was used,

---

a. Consider Daniel Rotenberg, *The Police Detection Practice of Encouragement: Lewis v. United States and Beyond,* 4 Houston L.Rev. 609, 614 (1967): "To say that public encouragement [the author defines 'encouragement' as the activity of police or their agents acting in the capacity of 'victims' and communicating this feigned willingness to be a victim to the suspect] is proper, but private encouragement is not, is to tell narcotics sellers to 'move indoors.' [Where] the *modus operandi* of the criminal includes both public and private places, the encouraging officer, if he is to complete the encouragement detection, has no choice except to enter the defendant's private quarters. Observations of the practices of prostitutes show that some of them operate out of hotel rooms or private residences using the telephone to make appointments. If a policeman is to detect the prostitute's commission of a solicitation he must, playing the role of a client, enter her private room or residence and encourage her. It follows that, if the narcotics

seller were, in effect, told to 'move indoors,' he would. Copying the homosexual [in a jurisdiction where only public solicitation by a homosexual is criminal] and prostitute, he would use the telephone to set up sales, or would roam the streets locating buyers and then retreat into privacy before making the outlawed sale. The [*Lewis*] Court obviously appreciated the inseparable relationship of public and private encouragement."

As Professor Rotenberg has observed, id. at 612, "the practice [of police encouragement], although not the label," was before the Court in *Lewis,* but what significance, if any, the case has for police encouragement and the defense of entrapment is unclear for, as the Court noted, "petitioner does not argue that he was entrapped, as he could not on the facts of this case." See generally Ch. 7, infra.

b. Only Justice Douglas dissented. See p. 389.

did the Court assume that the use of a secret agent raised a serious Fourth Amendment problem. See Kitch, supra, at 141–43.

———

James Hoffa was convicted for endeavoring to bribe members of a jury, during the so-called Test Fleet trial, which ended in a hung jury. A substantial element in the government's proof was the testimony of one Partin, a local union official. After being released from jail where he had been held pending state and federal charges, Partin had made frequent visits to the Hoffa hotel suite, on which occasions he was continually in the company of Hoffa and his associates. Proceeding upon the premise that Partin was a "governmental informer" from the time he first arrived on the scene in the Test Fleet and that the government had compensated him for his services as such, the Court nevertheless affirmed the conviction, HOFFA v. UNITED STATES, 385 U.S. 293, 87 S.Ct. 408, 17 L.Ed.2d 374 (1966),[a] in an opinion by Justice STEWART:

"The argument is that Partin's failure to disclose his role as a government informer vitiated the consent that the petitioner gave to Partin's repeated entries into [Hoffa's hotel] suite, and that by listening to the petitioner's statements Partin conducted an illegal 'search' for verbal evidence. [Where] the argument falls is in its misapprehension of the fundamental nature and scope of Fourth Amendment protection. What the Fourth Amendment protects is the security a man relies upon when he places himself or his property within a constitutionally protected area, be it his home or his office, his hotel room or his automobile.[b]

"[In] the present case, however, it is evident that no interest legitimately protected by the Fourth Amendment is involved. [Partin] was in the suite by invitation, and every conversation which he heard was either directed to him or knowingly carried on in his presence. The petitioner, in a word, was not relying on the security of the hotel room; he was relying upon his misplaced confidence that Partin would not reveal his wrongdoing. * * * Neither this Court nor any member of it has ever expressed the view that the Fourth Amendment protects a wrongdoer's misplaced belief that a person to whom he voluntarily confides his wrongdoing will not reveal it. Indeed, the Court unanimously rejected that very contention less than four years ago in *Lopez*. [The] Court was divided [on the admissibility of the surreptitious recording]. But there was no dissent from the view that testimony about the conversation by Davis himself was clearly admissible. [In] the words of the dissenting opinion in *Lopez*, 'the risk of being overheard by an eavesdropper or betrayed by an informer or deceived to the identity of one with whom one deals is probably inherent in the conditions of human society. It is the kind of risk we necessarily assume whenever we speak.' "[c]

Chief Justice WARREN dissented, deeming it unnecessary to reach any constitutional questions "for the affront to the quality and fairness of federal law which this case presents is sufficient to require an exercise of our supervisory powers":

a. *Hoffa* was decided the same day as *Lewis* and *Osborn* (p. 365), where, on the basis of a tape recorded meeting between defendant and his "employee" (a secret government agent), one of Hoffa's lawyers was convicted of attempting to bribe a juror.

b. But compare the same Justice's analysis for the Court a year later in *Katz*, p. 155.

c. Note well that at the time the meetings at which Partin was present occurred Hoffa had not been indicted for bribing a juror nor had judicial proceedings otherwise commenced against him with respect to this crime. If they had, Hoffa would have had the benefit of the *Massiah* doctrine. See generally Ch. 8, § 5.

"Here, Edward Partin, a jailbird languishing in a Louisiana jail under indictments for such state and federal crimes as embezzlement, kidnapping, and manslaughter (and soon to be charged with perjury and assault), contacted federal authorities and told them he was willing to become, and would be useful as, an informer against Hoffa who was then about to be tried in the Test Fleet case. A motive for his doing this is immediately apparent—namely, his strong desire to work his way out of jail and out of his various legal entanglements with the State and Federal Governments. And it is interesting to note that, if this was his motive, he has been uniquely successful in satisfying it. In the four years since he first volunteered to be an informer against Hoffa he has not been prosecuted on any of the serious federal charges for which he was at that time jailed, and the state charges have apparently vanished into thin air. This type of informer and the uses to which he was put in this case evidence a serious potential for undermining the integrity of the truth-finding process in the federal courts. Given the incentives and background of Partin, no conviction should be allowed to stand when based heavily on his testimony. And that is exactly the quicksand upon which these convictions rest.

"[In] performing its duty to prosecute crime the Government must take the witnesses as it finds them. [But here] the Government reaches into the jailhouse to employ a man who was himself facing indictments far more serious (and later including one for perjury) than the one confronting the man against whom he offered to inform. It employed him not for the purpose of testifying to something that had already happened, but rather for the purpose of infiltration to see if crimes would in the future be committed. * * * Certainly if a criminal defendant insinuated his informer into the prosecution's camp in this manner he would be guilty of obstructing justice. * * * "

Justice Clark, joined by Justice Douglas, would have dismissed the writs of certiorari as improvidently granted for the reason that the district court's finding that the government did *not* "place" Partin in the defendant's midst could not be regarded "clearly erroneous." However, in the companion case of *Osborn*, fn. a, p. 388, Justice DOUGLAS, the lone dissenter in that case, made it plain that if he had been satisfied in *Hoffa* that the government had "placed" Partin in Hoffa's councils he would have voted to reverse the conviction: "[A] person may take the risk that a friend will turn on him and report to the police. But that is far different from the Government's 'planting' a friend in a person's entourage so that he can secure incriminating evidence. In the one case the Government has merely been the willing recipient of information supplied by a fickle friend. In the other, the Government has actively encouraged and participated in a breach of privacy by sending in an undercover agent. [T]he Government unlawfully enters a man's home when its agent crawls through a window, breaks down a door, enters surreptitiously, or, as alleged here, gets in by trickery and fraud."[d]

Notes and Questions

1. Had Hoffa opened his hotel suite for the conduct of any business? Did any specificity of purpose or duration limit Partin's presence there? Why "while so carefully limiting its holding in *Lewis*," did the Court "at the same time approve the extensive intrusion in *Hoffa* without even acknowledging the substantial differences in the breadth of the searches involved in the two cases"? See *The Supreme Court, 1966 Term*, 81 Harv.L.Rev. 69, 192–93 (1967).

---

d. Justices Fortas and White took no part in the case.

2. Was Hoffa, as the majority put it, "relying upon his misplaced confidence that Partin would not reveal his wrongdoing" or also on the assumption that the government would not attempt to spy on him in the privacy of his hotel room? Was Partin a friend who later "revealed wrongdoing" or was he working for the government at the very time Hoffa spoke? Must people take the risk that their "friends" or associates are "government agents," i.e., have been "planted" by the government or have already promised to report whatever they see or hear to the government? See Kitch, supra, at 151–52; Note, 76 Yale L.J. 994, 1009–13 (1967).

If so, then why does one using the phone not "assume the risk" that the police will be tapping the wire? And why does one using the mails not assume that the police will be reading his letters? Are these other risks small only because the Court has made them so? Should the inquiry be not whether a person has "assumed the risk," but what risks of governmental intrusion citizens of a free society *should have to assume?* Is the view that one "assumes the risk" that the friend in whom he confides is a "government agent" anything more than a conclusion that the probability of accomplishing some social good by such a tactic outweighs the invasion of privacy and therefore the risk is tolerable in a free society? Consider Harlan, J., dissenting in *United States v. White,* p. 391.

3. Consider Note, 76 Yale L.J. 994, 1010 (1967):

"Though rejected by the Court in Lopez, Brennan's dichotomy between bugging and secret agents became in *Hoffa* the basis of the Court's decision that secret agents do not threaten privacy enough to merit Fourth Amendment limitation. But it is difficult to accept, at least without explanation, [this reasoning]. Consider, for example, the likely reactions of the citizenry if asked to rank the offensiveness of three practices:

"(1) the police will be allowed to search your home, without force during daylight hours;

"(2) the police will be allowed to offer your friends very strong inducements to report to them any illegal activities on your part;

"(3) the police will be allowed to employ agents, who may be strangers, business associates or friends, to invite or encourage you to take part in a criminal venture.

"The clear state of the constitutional law after *Hoffa* and its companion cases is that (1) represents an invasion of privacy abhorrent to the American way of life, but (2) and (3) are quite proper. The average citizen would hardly agree."

Does an undercover agent's participation in a pretrial meeting between defendant and his lawyer constitute a *per se* violation of defendant's right to the effective assistance of counsel with respect to the pending criminal action? If not, under what circumstances does such governmental activity fatally taint the trial? Consider WEATHERFORD v. BURSEY, 429 U.S. 545, 97 S.Ct. 837, 51 L.Ed.2d 30 (1977): Bursey and Weatherford (a state undercover agent) vandalized a selective service office. Weatherford reported the incident to the police, but in order to maintain his undercover status and his usefulness on other current matters in that capacity, he was arrested and charged along with Bursey. Both were released on bond and retained separate attorneys. Then, at the request of Bursey's attorney, who sought Weatherford's presence in order to discuss his client's defense, Weatherford attended two pretrial meetings with Bursey and his attorney. Weatherford had no discussions either with his superiors or the prosecution concerning anything said at the attorney-client meetings. Although Weatherford had not expected to be a witness at the trial, and had so told Bursey, on the day of the trial (because Weatherford had been seen in the company of police officers shortly before and his effectiveness as an undercover agent thus impaired), the prosecution decided to call him as a witness.[a] Weatherford's testimony related only to events prior to the meetings with Bursey and his lawyer and did not refer to anything said at these meetings. Nor was there any evidence that any of Weatherford's testimony was the product of anything said at these meetings. Bursey was convicted. After he had served his sentence, he brought an action against Weatherford under 42 U.S.C. § 1983, alleging that the latter's participation in the pretrial meetings had deprived him of the effective assistance of counsel as well as his right to a fair trial. The Court, per WHITE, J., held that Bursey's constitutional rights were not violated and that the right to counsel establishes no *per se* rule forbidding an undercover agent to meet with a defendant's counsel:

"[As] long as the information possessed by Weatherford remained uncommunicated, he posed no substantial threat to Bursey's Sixth Amendment rights. Nor do we believe [that] prosecutors will be so prone to lie or the difficulties of proof so great that we must always assume not only that an informant communicates what he learns from an encounter with the defendant and his counsel but also that what he communicates has the potential for detriment or benefit to the prosecutor's case.

"[That a *per se* rule] would operate prophylactically and effectively is very likely true; but it would require the informant to refuse to participate in attorney-client meetings, even though invited, and thus for all practical purposes to unmask himself. Our cases, however, have recognized the unfortunate necessity of undercover work and the value it often is to effective law enforcement.

"[There] being no tainted evidence in this case, no communication of defense strategy to the prosecution, and no purposeful intrusion by Weatherford, there was no violation of the [right to counsel]."

Justice MARSHALL, joined by Brennan, J., dissented, unable to "join in providing even the narrowest of openings to the practice of spying upon attorney-client communications":

"[E]ven if I could agree that unintended and undisclosed interceptions by government witness-employers [violate no constitutional rights], I still could not join in upholding the practice. For [the] precious constitutional rights at stake here, like other constitutional rights, need 'breathing space to survive' and a prophylactic prohibition on all intrusions of this sort is therefore essential. A rule that offers defendants relief only when they can prove 'intent' or 'disclosure' is, I fear, little better than no rule at all. Establishing [an intent or desire to spy] will seldom be possible * * *. Proving that an informer reported to the prosecution on defense strategy will be equally difficult * * *."

UNITED STATES v. WHITE
401 U.S. 745, 91 S.Ct. 1122, 28 L.Ed.2d 453 (1971).

Justice WHITE announced the judgment of the Court and an opinion in which The Chief Justice, Justice STEWART, and Justice BLACKMUN join.

a. Bursey's contention that the government was constitutionally forbidden to conceal Weatherford's identity from him during his trial preparation and to permit Weatherford to "deny" that he would testify against him is treated in Ch. 22, § 5.

[On numerous occasions a government informer, carrying a concealed radio transmitter, engaged defendant in conversations which were electronically overheard by federal narcotics agents. The conversations in a restaurant, defendant's home and in the informer's car were overheard by the use of radio equipment. A number of conversations in the informer's home were not only electronically overheard by an agent stationed outside the house but by another agent who, with the informer's consent, concealed himself in the latter's kitchen closet.[a] At no time did the agents obtain a warrant or court order. The informer was not produced at the trial, but the testimony of the "eavesdropping" agents was admitted and led to defendant's conviction of narcotics violations. The U.S. Court of Appeals for the Seventh Circuit read *Katz* as overruling *On Lee* and interpreted the Fourth Amendment as prohibiting testimony about the electronically overheard statements.]

[The *Hoffa* case], left undisturbed by *Katz*, held that however strongly a defendant may trust an apparent colleague, his expectations in this respect are not protected by the Fourth Amendment when it turns out that the colleague is a government agent regularly communicating with the authorities. * * *

Conceding that *Hoffa, Lewis,* and *Lopez* remained unaffected by *Katz*, the Court of Appeals nevertheless read both *Katz* and the Fourth Amendment to require a different result if the agent not only records his conversations with the defendant but instantaneously transmits them electronically to other agents equipped with radio receivers.

[To] reach this result it was necessary for the Court of Appeals to hold that *On Lee* was no longer good law. In that case, [the] Court first rejected claims of a Fourth Amendment violation because the informer had not trespassed when he entered the defendant's premises and conversed with him. To this extent the Court's rationale cannot survive *Katz*. But the Court announced a second and independent ground for its decision; for it went on to say that overruling *Olmstead* and *Goldman* [which the Court subsequently did in *Katz*] would be of no aid to On Lee since he "was talking confidentially and indiscreetly with one he trusted, and he was overheard. * * * " We see no indication in *Katz* that the Court meant to disturb that understanding of the Fourth Amendment or to disturb the result reached in the *On Lee* case, nor are we now inclined to overturn this view of the Fourth Amendment.

Concededly a police agent who conceals his police connections may write down for official use his conversations with a defendant and testify concerning them, without a warrant authorizing his encounters with the defendant and without otherwise violating the latter's Fourth Amendment rights. *Hoffa*. For constitutional purposes, no different result is required if the agent instead of immediately reporting and transcribing his conversations with defendant, either (1) simultaneously records them with electronic equipment which he is carrying on his person, *Lopez;* (2) or carries radio equipment which simultaneously transmits the conversations either to recording equipment located elsewhere or to other agents monitoring the transmitting frequency. *On Lee*. If the conduct and revelations of an agent operating without electronic equipment do not invade the defendant's constitutionally justifiable expectations of privacy, neither does a simultaneous recording of the same conversations made by the agent or by others from transmissions received from the agent to whom the defendant is talking and whose trustworthiness the defendant necessarily risks.

---

a. No testimony by this agent was offered at trial. See Note 4 following this case.

Our problem is not what the privacy expectations of particular defendants in particular situations may be or the extent to which they may in fact have relied on the discretion of their companions. Very probably, individual defendants neither know nor suspect that their colleagues have gone or will go to the police or are carrying recorders or transmitters. Otherwise, conversation would cease and our problem with these encounters would be nonexistent or far different from those now before us. Our problem, in terms of the principles announced in *Katz,* is what expectations of privacy are constitutionally "justifiable"—what expectations the Fourth Amendment will protect in the absence of a warrant. So far, the law permits the frustration of actual expectations of privacy by permitting authorities to use the testimony of those associates who for one reason or another have determined to turn to the police, as well as by authorizing the use of informants in the manner exemplified by *Hoffa* and *Lewis.* If the law gives no protection to the wrongdoer whose trusted accomplice is or becomes a police agent, neither should it protect him when that same agent has recorded or transmitted the conversations which are later offered in evidence to prove the State's case.

Inescapably, one contemplating illegal activities must realize and risk that his companions may be reporting to the police. If he sufficiently doubts their trustworthiness, the association will very probably end or never materialize. But if he has no doubts, or allays them, or risks what doubt he has, the risk is his. In terms of what his course will be, what he will or will not do or say, we are unpersuaded that he would distinguish between probable informers on the one hand and probable informers with transmitters on the other.

[It is] untenable to consider the activities and reports of the police agent himself, though acting without a warrant, to be a "reasonable" investigative effort and lawful under the Fourth Amendment but to view the same agent with a recorder or transmitter as conducting an "unreasonable" and unconstitutional search and seizure. * * * No different result should obtain where, as in *On Lee* and the instant case, the informer disappears and is unavailable at trial; for the issue of whether specified events on a certain day violate the Fourth Amendment should not be determined by what later happens to the informer. [R]eversed.[b]

Justice DOUGLAS, dissenting. * * *

On Lee and *Lopez* are of a vintage opposed to *Berger* and *Katz.* However they may be explained, they are products of the old common-law notions of trespass. *Katz,* on the other hand, emphasized that with few exceptions "searches conducted outside the judicial process, without prior approval by judge or magistrate, are *per se* unreasonable under the Fourth Amendment. * * * "

Monitoring, if prevalent, certainly kills free discourse and spontaneous utterances. Free discourse—a First Amendment value—may be frivolous or serious, humble or defiant, reactionary or revolutionary, profane or in good taste; but it is not free if there is surveillance. Free discourse liberates the spirit, though it may produce only froth. The individual must keep some facts concerning his thoughts within a small zone of people. At the same time he must be free to pour out his

---

b. The plurality opinion also upheld the admissibility of the evidence of defendant's incriminating statements on another ground: the events in question took place long prior to *Katz* and *Desist,* p. 46, had held that *Katz* applied only to those electronic surveillances which occurred subsequent to the date of that decision. Justice Brennan, whose concurring opinion is summarized infra, concurred in the result, agreeing that *Desist* required affirmance, but differing on the issue of the continued viability of *On Lee.* Justice Black concurred in the result for the reasons set forth in his *Katz* dissent, but adhered to his view that *Katz* should be applied retroactively. Dissenting Justices Douglas, Harlan and Marshall would apply *Katz* retroactively and viewed it as overruling *On Lee.*

woes or inspirations or dreams to others. He remains the sole judge as to what must be said and what must remain unspoken. This is the essence of the idea of privacy implicit in the First and Fifth Amendments as well as in the Fourth. * * *

Justice HARLAN, dissenting.

[The] plurality opinion seeks to erase the crucial distinction between the facts before us and [the holdings in *Lopez, Lewis* and *Hoffa*] by the following reasoning: if A can relay verbally what is revealed to him by B (as in *Lewis* and *Hoffa*), or record and later divulge it (as in *Lopez*), what difference does it make if A conspires with another to betray B by contemporaneously transmitting to the other all that is said? The contention is, in essence, an argument that the distinction between third-party monitoring and *other* undercover techniques is one of form and not substance. The force of the contention depends on the evaluation of two separable but intertwined assumptions: first, that there is no greater invasion of privacy in the third-party situation, and, second, that uncontrolled consensual surveillance in an electronic age is a tolerable technique of law enforcement, given the values and goals of our political system.

The first of these assumptions takes as a point of departure the so-called "risk analysis" approach of *Lewis,* and *Lopez,* and to a lesser extent *On Lee,* or the expectations approach of *Katz.* While these formulations represent an advance over the unsophisticated trespass analysis of the common law, they too have their limitations and can, ultimately, lead to the substitution of words for analysis. The analysis must, in my view, transcend the search for subjective expectations or legal attribution of assumptions of risk. Our expectations, and the risks we assume, are in large part reflections of laws that translate into rules the customs and values of the past and present.

Since it is the task of the law to form and project, as well as mirror and reflect, we should not, as judges, merely recite the expectations and risks without examining the desirability of saddling them upon society. The critical question, therefore, is whether under our system of government, as reflected in the Constitution, we should impose on our citizens the risks of the electronic listener or observer without at least the protection of a warrant requirement.

[The] impact of the practice of third-party bugging, must, I think, be considered such as to undermine that confidence and sense of security in dealing with one another that is characteristic of individual relationships between citizens in a free society. It goes beyond the impact on privacy occasioned by the ordinary type of "informer" investigation upheld in *Lewis* and *Hoffa.* The argument of the plurality opinion, to the effect that it is irrelevant whether secrets are revealed by the mere tattletale or the transistor, ignores the differences occasioned by third-party monitoring and recording which insures full and accurate disclosure of all that is said, free of the possibility of error and oversight that inheres in human reporting.

[I]t is too easy to forget—and, hence, too often forgotten—that the issue here is whether to interpose a search warrant procedure between law enforcement agencies engaging in electronic eavesdropping and the public generally. By casting its "risk analysis" solely in terms of the expectations and risks that "wrongdoers" or "one contemplating illegal activities" ought to bear, the plurality opinion, I think, misses the mark entirely. *On Lee* does not simply mandate that criminals must daily run the risk of unknown eavesdroppers prying into their private affairs; it subjects each and every law-abiding member of society to that risk. * * * Abolition of *On Lee* would not end electronic eavesdropping. It would prevent public officials from engaging in that practice unless they first had probable cause to suspect an individual of involvement in illegal activities and had tested their version of the facts before a detached judicial officer. The interest *On Lee* fails to protect is the expectation of the ordinary citizen, who has never engaged in illegal conduct in his life, that he may carry on his private discourse freely, openly, and spontaneously without measuring his every word against the connotations it might carry when instantaneously heard by others unknown to him and unfamiliar with his situation or analyzed in a cold, formal record played days, months, or years after the conversation. Interposition of a warrant requirement is designed not to shield "wrongdoers," but to secure a measure of privacy and a sense of personal security throughout our society. * * *

Justice MARSHALL, dissenting.

I am convinced that the correct view of the Fourth Amendment in the area of electronic surveillance is one that brings the safeguards of the warrant requirement to bear on the investigatory activity involved in this case. In this regard I agree with the dissents of Justice Douglas and Justice Harlan. In short, I believe that *On Lee* cannot be considered viable in light of the constitutional principles articulated in *Katz* and other cases. * * *

[Justice BRENNAN concurred in the result, agreeing that *Katz* should not be applied retroactively but emphasizing that on the issue of the viability of *On Lee,* neither the dissenters' views nor Justice White's "commands the support of a majority of the Court."[c] He would "go further" than the dissenters; their reasoning "compels the conclusion" that *Lopez,* as well as *On Lee,* is "no longer sound law. [C]urrent Fourth Amendment jurisprudence interposes a warrant requirement not only in cases of third-party electronic monitoring (the situation in *On Lee* and in this case) but also in cases of electronic recording by a government agent of a face-to-face conversation with a criminal suspect, which was the situation in *Lopez.*" As he viewed it, *Katz* had adopted the "doctrinal basis" of his *Lopez* dissent and that meant that both *On Lee* and *Lopez,* which presented "rationally indistinguishable" situations,[d] should now be regarded as overruled.[e]]

Notes and Questions

1. After *White,* what, if anything, is left of anyone's "justifiable reliance" on the privacy of his conversation (*Katz*)? Did *Katz* mean that a citizen must adjust his expectations of privacy to new laws and electronic techniques or that these new laws and techniques should conform to present expectations? Did *Katz* mean, or should it be read as meaning, that the individual only "assumes the risk" that he objectively perceives and no more? That *reasonable* reliance on the privacy of one's conversation suffices to invoke the protection of the Fourth Amendment? See Note, 52 B.U.L.Rev. 831, 838–44 (1972).

c. Aren't there "five votes" in *White* sustaining *On Lee?* Recall that the "fifth Justice," Black, concurred in the *White* result for the reasons advanced in his *Katz* dissent, where he viewed Fourth Amendment protection of privacy as extending only to "unreasonable searches and seizures of 'persons, houses, papers and effects.'"Recall, too, Justice Black's *Berger* dissent, where he could not read the Fourth Amendment as applying to "the spoken word" as well as "tangible things."

Justice Black did dissent in *On Lee*—solely on the ground that the Court should reject the evidence in the exercise of its supervisory authority over federal criminal justice. Why didn't he make that argument in *White?*

d. Did they?

e. As to whether the government has a constitutional obligation to retain tapes of conversations for the defendant's possible use, see Ch. 25, § 3.

Didn't defendant White take reasonable steps to protect against governmental intrusion by choosing the locations he did for his private conversations? Didn't federal agents employ an informer and conceal a radio transmitter on his person for the very reason that they anticipated defendant White would make reasonable efforts to avoid being overheard? Does the *White* plurality opinion mean the privacy of one's conversation is unprotected if one can anticipate *any* risk that his words might be disclosed to third parties? If so, how does the Fourth Amendment protect the privacy of one's conversations unless one *completely stops* communicating to others? See Note, 85 Harv.L.Rev. 250, 254 (1971). See also Hufstedler, J., dissenting in *Holmes v. Burr,* 486 F.2d 55, 61, 71–76 (9th Cir.1973).

2. Did the *White* plurality opinion refuse to recognize normal expectations of privacy because to do so would restrict a "normal" police stratagem? Is the "reasonableness" of privacy expectations to be measured by how the average person views a given situation or by whether affording Fourth Amendment protection would "unreasonably" impede the police? See 52 B.U.L.Rev. at 838; Note, Harv.L.Rev. 63, 192–93 (1968).

3. The *White* plurality opinion observes that "the law gives no protection to the wrongdoer whose trusted accomplice [*unequipped* with an electronic device] *is* or *becomes* a police agent." (Emphasis added.) Should the law distinguish between (1) a "trusted accomplice" who, absent prior arrangements with the police, *subsequently* supplies them with evidence; and (2) a "trusted accomplice" who was a "police agent" all along, who was "planted" by the government to secure incriminating evidence? Reconsider Chief Justice Warren's dissenting opinion in *Hoffa,* p. 388; and Justice Douglas' dissenting opinion in *Osborn* and *Lewis,* p. 389.

Might the *White* dissenters have read *Katz* more broadly than they did? Might they have argued, alternatively, that if, as the *White* plurality opinion maintains, "the difference between the electronically equipped [governmental 'plant'] and the unequipped [governmental 'plant'] is [not] substantial enough to require discrete constitutional recognition," then *Katz* should be read as overruling *Hoffa* as well as *On Lee?* May it be said of the *Hoffa* case—using the language in *Katz*—that the government's use of defendant's trusted friend to obtain evidence against him "violated the privacy upon which [defendant] justifiably relied" and thus constituted a "search" or "seizure"?

4. Both the Seventh Circuit and Supreme Court opinions in *White* dealt only with the use of *electronically* overheard conversations because only such evidence was offered at trial. If the *White* dissenters had prevailed, would their reasoning also have led to the exclusion of the testimony of the narcotics agent (not equipped with an electronic device) who had overheard defendant's conversations from his hiding place in the informer's kitchen closet? Why (not)?

5. *Renewed doubts about the validity of White.* In *Marshall v. Barlow's* (p. 340), the government maintained that the pervasiveness of state and national safety regulations refuted the view that an employer can have a "realistic privacy interest" in employee work areas. Rejecting this argument, the Court, per White, J., observed: "Employees are not prohibited from reporting OSHA violations. What they observe in their daily functions is undoubtedly beyond the employer's reasonable expectation of privacy. The Government inspector, however, is not an employee. Without a warrant he stands in no better position than a member of the public. [That] an employee is free to report, and the Government is free to use, any evidence of noncompliance with OSHA that the employee observes furnishes

no justification for federal agents to enter a place of business from which the public is restricted and to conduct their own warrantless search."

Does *Barlow's* raise serious questions and renewed doubts about the validity of *White* and other cases dealing with participant monitoring? By talking to a confidant, did the defendant in *White* consent to government information-gathering any more than the defendant in *Barlow's* did, by permitting employees to observe his premises? See Joseph D. Grano, *Perplexing Questions About Three Basic Fourth Amendment Issues*, 69 J.Crim.L. & C. 425, 435–38 (1978).

Chapter 7

POLICE "ENCOURAGEMENT"
AND THE DEFENSE OF
ENTRAPMENT

"The mode adopted [to] bring to light the malfeasance of the defendant, had no necessary connection with his violation of law. He exercised his own volition * * *. Even if inducements to commit crime could be assumed to exist in this case, the allegation of the defendant would be but the repetition of the plea as ancient as the world, and first interposed in Paradise: 'The serpent beguiled me and I did eat.' That defense was overruled by the great Lawgiver, and whatever estimate we may form, or whatever judgment pass upon the character or conduct of the tempter, this plea has never since availed to shield crime or give indemnity to the culprit, and it is safe to say that under any code of civilized, not to say christian ethics, it never will."

—Bacon, J., in *Board of Commissioners v. Backus,* 29 How.Pr. 33, 42 (N.Y.Sup.Ct.1864).

"[T]wo deeply seated and widely shared intuitive judgments [explain the creation and survival of the entrapment defense]. The first is that a person is somewhat less culpable if tempted into crime by certain kinds of inducements. The second is that it is extremely dangerous to allow government the power to stress test the morality of ordinary citizens by dangling substantial inducements before them. [But] where do [these] intuitions come from?"

—Seidman, *The Supreme Court, Entrapment, and Our Criminal Justice Dilemma,* 1981 Sup.Ct.Rev. 111, 146.

" 'Encouragement' is descriptive of an intentional technique of police agencies used in the detection of a certain class of crimes. [It] denotes activity of the police or their agent: (1) acting in the capacity of a victim, (2) intending by his actions to suggest his willingness to be a victim, (3) actually communicating this feigned willingness to the suspect, and (4) thereby having some influence upon his commission of the crime. It is not necessarily a single act; it usually consists of a series of acts by the officer which are part of the normal interplay between victim and suspect in the specific crime. It is utilized as a device in dealing with certain crimes having the common element of vice—prostitution, homosexuality, liquor sales, narcotics, and gambling. The reason that the same technique is adapted to all these crimes is suggested by the 'vice' label applicable to all of them, that these offenses are committed privately with a willing victim who will not complain, making normal detection virtually impossible. 'Encouragement,' to state it more succinctly, is a process of persuasion. * * *

"[It] is by no means a wholesome police practice. It is founded upon deception. Not only must the participating officer deliberately deceive, but he must often say and do things that are vulgar, profane and indecent. However, to condemn the characteristics is to condemn the practice, because deception, vulgarity, profanity, and indecency are often essential to the simulation of reality which encouragement attempts to achieve. When to these characteristics is added the unfortunate fact that on occasion encouragement induces persons to commit crime who ordinarily would not, it is understandable that the practice is roundly criticized. But if there is no way to protect society effectively from certain criminal harms except through detection by encouragement, then it is as idle to criticize the practice continually as it would be to criticize surgery for its efforts to eliminate disease because the surgical method, of necessity, cuts and hurts the body. The fact should not be overlooked that the fault lies more with the social harm and the human hurt and their causes than with the methods of eradication."

—Rotenberg, *The Police Detection Practice of Encouragement,* 49 Va.L.Rev. 871, 874 (1963).

———

"Manifestly, [the function of law enforcement] does not include the manufacturing of crime. Criminal activity is such that stealth and strategy are necessary weapons in the arsenal of the police officer. However, 'A different question is presented when the criminal design originates with the officials of the government, and they implant in the mind of an innocent person the disposition to commit the alleged offense and induce its commission in order that they may prosecute.' Then stealth and strategy become as objectionable police methods as the coerced confession and the unlawful search. * * * To determine whether entrapment has been established a line must be drawn between the trap for the unwary innocent and the trap for the unwary criminal."

—Warren, C.J., for the Court in *Sherman v. United States,* 356 U.S. 369, 372 (1958).

———

"That [the defendant] was induced, provoked or tempted to [commit the crime] by government agents does not make him any more innocent or any less predisposed than he would be if he had been induced, provoked or tempted by a private person—which, of course, would not entitle him to cry 'entrapment.' Since the only difference between these situations is the identity of the tempter, it follows that the significant focus must be on the conduct of the government agents, and not on the predisposition of the defendant.

"The purpose of the entrapment defense * * * must be to prohibit unlawful governmental activity in instigating crime. [If] so, then whether the particular defendant was 'predisposed' or 'otherwise innocent' is irrelevant; and the important question becomes whether the Government's conduct in inducing the crime was beyond judicial toleration."

—Stewart, J., dissenting in *United States v. Russell,* 411 U.S. 423, 442 (1973).

———

"If the police entice someone to commit a crime who would not have done so without their blandishments, and then arrest him and he is prosecuted, convicted, and punished, law enforcement resources are squandered in the following sense: resources that could and should have been used in an effort to reduce the nation's unacceptably high crime rate are used instead in the entirely sterile activity of first inciting and then punishing a crime. However, if the police are just inducing someone to commit sooner a crime he would have committed eventually, but to do so in controlled circumstances where the costs to the criminal justice system of apprehension and conviction are minimized, the police are economizing on resources. It is particularly difficult to catch arsonists, so if all the police were doing here was making it easier to catch an arsonist—not inducing someone to become an arsonist—they were using law enforcement resources properly and there is no occasion for judicial intervention. * * *

"Thus in my view 'entrapment' is merely the name we give to a particularly unproductive use of law enforcement resources, which our system properly condemns. If this is right, the implementing concept of 'predisposition to crime' calls less for psychological conjecture than for a common-sense assessment of whether it is likely that the defendant would have committed the crime anyway—without the blandishments the police used on him—but at a time and place where it would have been more difficult for them to apprehend him and the state to convict him, or whether the police used threats or promises so powerful that a law-abiding individual was induced to commit a crime. If the latter is the case, the police tactics do not merely affect the timing and location of a crime; they cause crime."

—Posner, J., concurring in *United States v. Kaminski,* 703 F.2d 1004, 1010 (7th Cir.1983).

———

"If the investigators were too creative or squandered their limited resources, this is a political problem. Congress can hold oversight hearings or pass a law; we shouldn't apply a chancellor's foot veto. Dissipating law enforcement resources injures persons who become victims of crime when the deterrent force of the law declines. Reversing convictions of the guilty cannot apply balm to these wounds. Those who protest that social interests would have been served by prosecuting someone else (or some additional, similarly situated persons) routinely lose. We deem it enough to support punishment that this person committed this offense, leaving to other institutions the redirection of investigative or prosecutorial resources. So it should be here."

—Easterbrook, J., concurring in *United States v. Miller,* 891 F.2d 1265, 1271–72 (7th Cir.1989).

———

"The central evil of entrapment is discriminatory law enforcement, whether the police zero in on a 'politician' or a 'drug dealer.' The act of selecting a subject for temptation is always, even at a minor level, a political act."

—Chevigny, *A Rejoinder,* The Nation, Feb. 23, 1980, p. 205.

"Our national integrity has been on a downhill slide for seven years; we really don't need the FBI to grease the skids with Operation ABSCAM.[a] Where no crime has been contemplated, the FBI has, through entrapment, induced to crime men who were previously involved in no wrongdoing. Aren't there enough naturally encouraging crimes to keep the FBI busy? Must they spend astronomical sums creating crime?"

—Letter to the Editor, Newsweek, Mar. 1, 1980, p. 5.

"House Speaker Thomas P. (Tip) O'Neill may have thundered that '[Operation ABSCAM] was a setup, a goddam setup,' but a crook is a crook is a crook. Whether set up or not, honest people do not take bribes."

—Letter to the Editor, Newsweek Mar. 1, 1980, p. 5.

SECTION 1. THE TESTS FOR ENTRAPMENT[a]

UNITED STATES v. RUSSELL

411 U.S. 423, 93 S.Ct. 1637, 36 L.Ed.2d 366 (1973).

Justice REHNQUIST delivered the opinion of the Court.

[After] a jury trial in the District Court, in which his sole defense was entrapment, respondent was convicted [of] having unlawfully manufactured and processed methamphetamine ("speed") and of having unlawfully sold and delivered that drug. [On] appeal, the United States Court of Appeals for the Ninth Circuit [reversed] the conviction solely for the reason that an undercover agent

a. "Abscam" is an acronym combining the first two letters of Abdul Enterprises, a fictitious Middle Eastern corporation, and "scam," a slang term for swindle or confidence game. Abscam began as a standard "sting" operation, i.e., an FBI undercover scheme to recover stolen securities and paintings. In 1978, the operation shifted to political corruption in the New Jersey area. A year later, it had turned its attention to the "Asylum Scenario"; unsuspecting "middlemen" (private persons unaware that they were part of a government undercover operation) passed the word to various Congressmen, or to their aides and acquaintances, that wealthy Arabs were willing to bribe members of Congress in order to ensure that they would introduce private immigration bills on the Arabs' behalf if and when necessary. In early 1980, shortly before shutting down, the operation shifted to political corruption in Philadelphia.

As a result of Abscam, a U.S. Senator, six U.S. Representatives and a number of other public officials and lawyers were convicted of various corrupt acts. Although many of the defendants (and many critics of the operation both in and out of Congress) charged that the FBI's methods constituted entrapment and/or violated the due process rights of the individuals caught in the operation, not a single Abscam defendant prevailed in the courts. See, e.g., *United States v. Kelly* (D.C.Cir.1983), p. 417, which discusses one phase of the Abscam operation at considerable length.

a. "Entrapment" is sometimes confused with, but should be distinguished from, "estoppel," which occurs when defendants rely on the assurances of government authorities that their contemplated conduct is lawful only to be prosecuted for such conduct. See *Cox v. Louisiana*, 379 U.S. 559, 85 S.Ct. 476, 13 L.Ed.2d 487 (1965) (to sustain appellant's conviction "for demonstrating where [public officials] told him he could 'would be to sanction an indefensible sort of entrapment by the State * * *'"); *Raley v. Ohio*, 360 U.S. 423, 79 S.Ct. 1257, 3 L.Ed.2d 1344 (1959); *People v. Donovan*, 279 N.Y.S.2d 404 (Ct.Spec.Sess. 1967), 81 Harv. L.Rev. 895 (1968).

supplied an essential chemical for manufacturing the methamphetamine which formed the basis of respondent's conviction. * * *

There is little dispute concerning the essential facts in this case. On December 7, 1969, Joe Shapiro, an undercover agent for the Federal Bureau of Narcotics and Dangerous Drugs, went to respondent's home [where] he met with respondent and his two codefendants, John and Patrick Connolly. Shapiro's assignment was to locate a laboratory where it was believed that methamphetamine was being manufactured illicitly. He told the respondent and the Connollys that he represented an organization [that] was interested in controlling the manufacture and distribution of methamphetamine. He then made an offer to supply the defendants with the chemical phenyl–2–propanone, an essential ingredient in the manufacture of methamphetamine, in return for one-half of the drug produced. This offer was made on the condition that Agent Shapiro be shown a sample of the drug which they were making and the laboratory where it was being produced.

During the conversation, Patrick Connolly revealed that he had been making the drug since May 1969 and since then had produced three pounds of it. John Connolly gave the agent a bag containing a quality of methamphetamine that he represented as being from "the last batch that we made." Shortly thereafter, Shapiro and Patrick Connolly left respondent's house to view the laboratory which was located in the Connolly house on Whidbey Island. At the house, Shapiro observed an empty bottle bearing the chemical label phenyl–2–propanone.

By prearrangement, Shapiro returned to the Connolly house on December 9, 1969, to supply 100 grams of propanone and observe the manufacturing process. When he arrived he observed Patrick Connolly and the respondent cutting up pieces of aluminum foil and placing them in a large flask. There was testimony that some of the foil pieces accidentally fell on the floor and were picked up by the respondent and Shapiro and put into the flask. Thereafter, Patrick Connolly added all of the necessary chemicals, including the propanone brought by Shapiro, to make two batches of methamphetamine. The manufacturing process having been completed the following morning, Shapiro was given one-half of the drug and respondent kept the remainder. Shapiro offered to buy, and the respondent agreed to sell, part of the remainder for $60.

About a month later, Shapiro returned to the Connolly house and met with Patrick Connolly to ask if he was still interested in their "business arrangement." Connolly replied that he was interested but that he had recently obtained two additional bottles of phenyl–2–propanone and would not be finished with them for a couple of days. He provided some additional methamphetamine to Shapiro at that time. Three days later Shapiro returned to the Connolly house with a search warrant and, among other items, seized an empty 500–gram bottle of propanone and a 100–gram bottle, not the one he had provided, that was partially filled with the chemical.

There was testimony at the trial of respondent and Patrick Connolly that phenyl–2–propanone was generally difficult to obtain. At the request of the Bureau of Narcotics and Dangerous Drugs, some chemical supply firms had voluntarily ceased selling the chemical.

At the close of the evidence, and after receiving the District Judge's standard entrapment instruction,[4] the jury found the respondent guilty on all counts

---

4. The District Judge stated the governing law on entrapment as follows: "Where a person already has the willingness and the readiness to break the law, the mere fact that the government agent provides what appears to be a favorable opportunity is not entrapment."

charged. On appeal, the respondent conceded that the jury could have found him predisposed to commit the offenses, but argued that on the facts presented there was entrapment as a matter of law. The Court of Appeals agreed, although it did not find the District Court had misconstrued or misapplied the traditional standards governing the entrapment defense. Rather, the court in effect expanded the traditional notion of entrapment, which focuses on the predisposition of the defendant, to mandate dismissal of a criminal prosecution whenever the court determines that there has been "an intolerable degree of governmental participation in the criminal enterprise." In this case the court decided that the conduct of the agent in supplying a scarce ingredient essential for the manufacture of a controlled substance established that defense.

This new defense was held to rest on either of two alternative theories. One theory is based on two lower court decisions which have found entrapment, regardless of predisposition, whenever the government supplies contraband to the defendants. The second theory, a non-entrapment rationale, is based on a recent Ninth Circuit decision that reversed a conviction because a government investigator was so enmeshed in the criminal activity that the prosecution of the defendants was held to be repugnant to the American criminal justice system. The court below held that these two rationales constitute the same defense, and that only the label distinguishes them. In any event, it held that "[b]oth theories are premised on fundamental concepts of due process and evince the reluctance of the judiciary to countenance 'overzealous law enforcement.'"

This Court first recognized and applied the entrapment defense in *Sorrells v. United States,* 287 U.S. 435, 53 S.Ct. 210, 77 L.Ed. 413 (1932), [where] a federal prohibition agent visited the defendant while posing as a tourist and engaged him in conversation about their common war experiences. After gaining the defendant's confidence, the agent asked for some liquor, was twice refused, but upon asking a third time the defendant finally capitulated, and was subsequently prosecuted for violating the National Prohibition Act.

Chief Justice Hughes, speaking for the Court, held that as a matter of statutory construction the defense of entrapment should have been available to the defendant. Under the theory propounded by the Chief Justice, the entrapment defense prohibits law enforcement officers from instigating a criminal act by persons "otherwise innocent in order to lure them to its commission and to punish them." Thus, the thrust of the entrapment defense was held to focus on the intent or predisposition of the defendant to commit the crime. "[I]f the defendant seeks acquittal by reason of entrapment he cannot complain of an appropriate and searching inquiry into his own conduct and predisposition as bearing upon that issue."

Justice Roberts concurred but was of the view "that courts must be closed to the trial of a crime instigated by the government's own agents." The difference in the view of the majority and the concurring opinions is that in the former the inquiry focuses on the predisposition of the defendant, whereas in the latter the inquiry focuses on whether the government "instigated the crime."

In *Sherman v. United States,* 356 U.S. 369, 78 S.Ct. 819, 2 L.Ed.2d 848 (1958) the Court again considered the theory underlying the entrapment defense and expressly reaffirmed the view expressed by the *Sorrells* majority. In *Sherman* the

He then instructed the jury to acquit respondent if it had a "reasonable doubt whether the defendant had the previous intent or purpose to commit the offense * * * and did so only because he was induced or persuaded by some officer or agent of the government." No exception was taken by respondent to this instruction.

defendant was convicted of selling narcotics to a Government informer. As in *Sorrells,* it appears that the Government agent gained the confidence of the defendant and, despite initial reluctance, the defendant finally acceded to the repeated importunings of the agent to commit the criminal act. On the basis of *Sorrells,* this Court [overturned the] conviction.

In affirming the theory underlying *Sorrells,* [the Court, per Chief Justice Warren] held that "[t]o determine whether entrapment has been established, a line must be drawn between the trap for the unwary innocent and the trap for the unwary criminal." Justice Frankfurter [maintained in a concurring opinion that] Justice Roberts had the better view in *Sorrells* and [thus] would have framed the question to be asked in an entrapment defense in terms of "whether the police conduct revealed in the particular case falls below standards [for] the proper use of governmental power."

In the instant case, respondent asks us to reconsider the theory of the entrapment defense [as] set forth [in] *Sorrells* and *Sherman.* His principal contention is that the defense should rest on constitutional grounds. He argues that the level of Shapiro's involvement in the manufacture of the methamphetamine was so high that a criminal prosecution for the drug's manufacture violates the fundamental principles of due process. [He] contends that the same factors that led this Court to apply the exclusionary rule to illegal searches and seizures [and] confessions should be considered here. But he would have the Court go further in deterring undesirable official conduct by requiring that any prosecution be barred absolutely because of the police involvement in criminal activity. The analogy is imperfect in any event, for the principal reason behind the adoption of the exclusionary rule was the Government's "failure to observe its own laws." [Here, however, the government's conduct] violated no independent constitutional right of the respondent. Nor did Shapiro violate any federal statute or rule or commit any crime in infiltrating the respondent's drug enterprise.

Respondent would overcome this basic weakness in his analogy to the exclusionary rule cases by having the Court adopt a rigid constitutional rule that would preclude any prosecution when it is shown that the criminal conduct would not have been possible had not an undercover agent "supplied an indispensable means to the commission of the crime that could not have been obtained otherwise, through legal or illegal channels." Even if we were to surmount the difficulties attending the notion that due process of law can be embodied in fixed rules, and those attending respondent's particular formulation, the rule he proposes would not appear to be of significant benefit to him. For, on the record presented, it appears that he cannot fit within the terms of the very rule he proposes.

[The] defendants admitted making the drug both before and after those batches made with the propanone supplied by Shapiro. [Thus, the record amply demonstrates] that the propanone used in the illicit manufacture of methamphetamine not only *could* have been obtained without the intervention of Shapiro but was in fact obtained by these defendants.

While we may some day be presented with a situation in which the conduct of law enforcement agents is so outrageous that due process principles would absolutely bar the government from invoking judicial processes to obtain a conviction, the instant case is distinctly not of that breed. Shapiro's contribution of propanone to the criminal enterprise already in process was scarcely objectionable. The chemical is by itself a harmless substance and its possession is legal. While the Government may have been seeking to make it more difficult for drug rings, such as that of which respondent was a member, to obtain the chemical, the evidence described above shows that it nonetheless was obtainable. The law enforcement conduct here stops far short of violating that "fundamental fairness, shocking to the universal sense of justice," mandated by the Due Process Clause of the Fifth Amendment.

The illicit manufacture of drugs is not a sporadic, isolated criminal incident, but a continuing, though illegal, business enterprise. In order to obtain convictions for illegally manufacturing drugs, the gathering of evidence of past unlawful conduct frequently proves to be an all but impossible task. Thus in drug-related offenses law enforcement personnel have turned to one of the only practicable means of detection: the infiltration of drug rings and a limited participation in their unlawful present practices. Such infiltration is a recognized and permissible means of investigation; if that be so, then the supply of some item of value that the drug ring requires must, as a general rule, also be permissible. For an agent will not be taken into the confidence of the illegal entrepreneurs unless he has something of value to offer them. Law enforcement tactics such as this can hardly be said to violate "fundamental fairness" or "shocking to the universal sense of justice."

[This] Court's opinions in *Sorrells* and *Sherman* held that the principal element in the defense of entrapment was the defendant's predisposition to commit the crime. Respondent conceded [that] "he may have harbored a predisposition to commit the charged offenses." Yet he argues that the jury's refusal to find entrapment under the charge submitted to it by the trial court should be overturned and the views of Justices Roberts and Frankfurter, in *Sorrells* and *Sherman,* respectively, which make the essential element of the defense turn on the type and degree of governmental conduct, be adopted as the law. We decline to overrule these cases. [Since] the defense is not of a constitutional dimension, Congress may address itself to the question and adopt any substantive definition of the defense that it may find desirable.

Critics of the rule laid down in *Sorrells* and *Sherman* have suggested that its basis in the implied intent of Congress is largely fictitious, and have pointed to what they conceive to be the anomalous difference between the treatment of a defendant who is solicited by a private individual and one who is entrapped by a government agent. Questions have been likewise raised as to whether "predisposition" can be factually established with the requisite degree of certainty. [Such arguments] have been twice previously made to this Court, and twice rejected by it, first in *Sorrells* and then in *Sherman.*

We believe that at least equally cogent criticism has been made of the concurring views in these cases. Commenting in *Sherman* on Mr. Justice Roberts' position in *Sorrells* that "although the defendant could claim that the Government had induced him to commit the crime, the Government could not reply by showing that the defendant's criminal conduct was due to his own readiness and not to the persuasion of government agents," Mr. Chief Justice Warren quoted the observation of Judge Learned Hand in an earlier stage of that proceeding:

> " 'Indeed, it would seem probable that, if there were no reply [to the claim of inducement], it would be impossible ever to secure convictions of any offences which consist of transactions that are carried on in secret.' "

Nor does it seem particularly desirable for the law to grant complete immunity from prosecution to one who himself planned to commit a crime, and then committed it, simply because government undercover agents subjected him to inducements which might have seduced a hypothetical individual who was not so predisposed.

[Several lower federal court decisions] have undoubtedly gone beyond this Court's opinions in *Sorrells* and *Sherman* in order to bar prosecutions because of what they thought to be, for want of a better term, "overzealous law enforcement." But the defense of entrapment enunciated in those opinions was not intended to give the federal judiciary a "chancellor's foot" veto over law enforcement practices of which it did not approve. The execution of the federal laws under our Constitution is confided primarily to the Executive Branch of the Government, subject to applicable constitutional and statutory limitations and to judicially fashioned rules to enforce those limitations. We think that the decision of the Court of Appeals in this case quite unnecessarily introduces an unmanageably subjective standard which is contrary to the holdings of this Court in *Sorrells* and *Sherman*.

[In light of *Sorrells* and *Sherman*, respondent's concession] that the jury finding as to predisposition was supported by the evidence [is], therefore, fatal to his claim of entrapment. He was an active participant in an illegal drug manufacturing enterprise which began before the Government agent appeared on the scene, and continued after the Government agent had left the scene. He was, in the words of *Sherman*, not an "unwary innocent" but an "unwary criminal."
* * *

Reversed.

Justice STEWART, with whom Justice BRENNAN and Justice MARSHALL join, dissenting.

[In] *Sorrells* and *Sherman* the Court took what might be called a "subjective" approach to the defense of entrapment. [This] approach focuses on the conduct and propensities of the particular defendant in each individual case: if he is "otherwise innocent," he may avail himself of the defense; but if he had the "predisposition" to commit the crime, or if the "criminal design" originated with him, then—regardless of the nature and extent of the Government's participation—there has been no entrapment. And, in the absence of a conclusive showing one way or the other, the question of the defendant's "predisposition" to the crime is a question of fact for the jury. The Court today adheres to this approach.

The concurring opinion of Justice Roberts, joined by Justices Brandeis and Stone, in the *Sorrells* case, and that of Justice Frankfurter, joined by Justices Douglas, Harlan, and Brennan, in the *Sherman* case, took a different view of the entrapment defense. In their concept, the defense is [grounded] on the belief that "the methods employed on behalf of the Government to bring about conviction cannot be countenanced." Thus, the focus of this approach is not on the propensities and predisposition of a specific defendant, but on "whether the police conduct revealed in the particular case falls below standards, to which common feelings respond, for the proper use of governmental power." Phrased another way, the question is whether—regardless of the predisposition to crime of the particular defendant involved—the governmental agents have acted in such a way as is likely to instigate or create a criminal offense. Under this approach, the determination of the lawfulness of the Government's conduct must be made—as it is on all questions involving the legality of law enforcement methods—by the trial judge, not the jury.

In my view, this objective approach to entrapment [is] the only one truly consistent with the underlying rationale of the defense.[1] * * * I find it impossible

1. Both the Proposed New Federal Criminal Code (1971), Final Report of the National Commission on Reform of Federal Criminal to believe that the purpose of the defense is to effectuate some unexpressed congressional intent to exclude from its criminal statutes persons who committed a prohibited act, but would not have done so except for the Government's inducements.

[Furthermore,] to say that such a defendant is "otherwise innocent" or not "predisposed" to commit the crime is misleading, at best. The very fact that he has committed an act that Congress has determined to be illegal demonstrates conclusively that he is not innocent of the offense. He may not have originated the precise plan or the precise details, but he was "predisposed" in the sense that he has proved to be quite capable of committing the crime. That he was induced, provoked, or tempted to do so by government agents does not make him any more innocent or any less predisposed than he would be if he had been induced, provoked, or tempted by a private person—which, of course, would not entitle him to cry "entrapment." Since the only difference between these situations is the identity of the tempter, it follows that the significant focus must be on the conduct of the government agents, and not on the predisposition of the defendant.

[Moreover,] a test that makes the entrapment defense depend on whether the defendant had the requisite predisposition permits the introduction into evidence of all kinds of hearsay, suspicion, and rumor—all of which would be inadmissible in any other context—in order to prove the defendant's predisposition. It allows the prosecution, in offering such proof, to rely on the defendant's bad reputation or past criminal activities, including even rumored activities of which the prosecution may have insufficient evidence to obtain an indictment, and to present the agent's suspicions as to why they chose to tempt this defendant. This sort of evidence is not only unreliable, as the hearsay rule recognizes; but it is also highly prejudicial, especially if the matter is submitted to the jury, for, despite instructions to the contrary, the jury may well consider such evidence as probative not simply of the defendant's predisposition, but of his guilt of the offense with which he stands charged.

More fundamentally, focusing on the defendant's innocence or predisposition has the direct effect of making what is permissible or impermissible police conduct depend upon the past record and propensities of the particular defendant involved. Stated another way, this subjective test means that the Government is permitted to entrap a person with a criminal record or bad reputation, and then to prosecute him for the manufactured crime, confident that his record or reputation itself will be enough to show that he was predisposed to commit the offense anyway. [In] my view, a person's alleged "predisposition" to crime should not expose him to government participation in the criminal transaction that would be otherwise unlawful.

* * * [G]overnment agents may engage in conduct that is likely, when objectively considered, to afford a person ready and willing to commit the crime an opportunity to do so. But when the agents' involvement in criminal activities goes beyond the mere offering of such an opportunity, and when their conduct is of a kind that could induce or instigate the commission of a crime by one not ready and willing to commit it, then—regardless of the character or propensities of the particular person induced—I think entrapment has occurred. For in that situation, the Government has engaged in the impermissible manufacturing of crime, and the federal courts should bar the prosecution in order to preserve the institutional integrity of the system of federal criminal justice.

Laws § 702, and the American Law Institute's Model Penal Code § 2.13 (Proposed Official Draft, 1962), adopt this objective approach.

[What] the agent did here was to meet with a group of suspected producers of methamphetamine, including the respondent; to request the drug; to offer to supply the chemical phenyl–2–propanone in exchange for one-half of the methamphetamine to be manufactured therewith; and, when that offer was accepted, to provide the needed chemical ingredient, and to purchase some of the drug from the respondent. [Although] the Court of Appeals found that the phenyl–2–propanone could not have been obtained without the agent's intervention—that "there could not have been the manufacture, delivery, or sale of the illicit drug had it not been for the Government's supply of one of the essential ingredients"— the Court today rejects this finding as contradicted by the facts revealed at trial. The record, as the Court states, discloses that one of the respondent's accomplices, though not the respondent himself, had obtained phenyl–2–propanone from independent sources both before and after receiving the agent's supply, and had used it in the production of methamphetamine. This demonstrates, it is said, that the chemical was obtainable other than through the government agent; and hence the agent's furnishing it for the production of the methamphetamine involved in this prosecution did no more than afford an opportunity for its production to one ready and willing to produce it. Thus, the argument seems to be, there was no entrapment here, any more than there would have been if the agent had furnished common table salt, had that been necessary to the drug's production.

It cannot be doubted that if phenyl–2–propanone had been wholly unobtainable from other sources, the agent's undercover offer to supply it to the respondent in return for part of the illicit methamphetamine produced therewith—an offer initiated and carried out by the agent for the purpose of prosecuting the respondent for producing methamphetamine—would be precisely the type of governmental conduct that constitutes entrapment under any definition. For the agent's conduct in that situation would make possible the commission of an otherwise totally impossible crime, and, I should suppose, would thus be a textbook example of instigating the commission of a criminal offense in order to prosecute someone for committing it.[a]

But assuming in this case that the phenyl–2–propanone was obtainable through independent sources, the fact remains that that used for the particular batch of methamphetamine involved in all three counts of the indictment with which the respondent was charged [was] supplied by the Government. [The] chemical ingredient was available only to licensed persons, and the Government itself had requested suppliers not to sell that ingredient even to people with a license. Yet the Government agent readily offered, and supplied, that ingredient to an unlicensed person and asked him to make a certain illegal drug with it. The Government then prosecuted that person for making the drug produced *with the very ingredient* which its agent had so helpfully supplied. This strikes me as the very pattern of conduct that should be held to constitute entrapment as a matter of law. * * *[b]

COMMENTARY ON THE "SUBJECTIVE" AND "OBJECTIVE" TESTS

a. But see *Hampton v. United States*, p. 413.

b. In a separate dissent, Justice Douglas, joined by Brennan, J., maintained that "[f]ederal agents play a debased role when they become the instigators of the crime, or partners in its commission, or the creative brain behind the illegal scheme. That is what the federal agent did here when he furnished the accused with one of the chemical ingredients needed to manufacture the unlawful drug."

1. *Support for the "hypothetical person" or "objective" test.* As pointed out in LaFave & Israel, § 5.2(b), "the objective test is favored by most commentators, and is reflected in the formulation of the entrapment defense appearing in the *Model Penal Code* '2.13. Its first authoritative acceptance came by judicial decision in *Grossman v. State,* 457 P.2d 226 (Alaska 1969), and now a dozen other states have adopted it either by statute or case law. See Piccaretta & Keenan, *Entrapment Targets and Tactics: Jacobson v. United States,* 29 Crim.L.Bull. 241, 252 (1993).

See, e.g., People v. Barraza, 591 P.2d 947 (Cal.1979), per Mosk, J., holding that the proper test of entrapment in California is: "was the [police conduct] likely to induce a normally law-abiding person to commit the offense?" Observed the court:

"[W]e presume that [a normally law-abiding] person would resist the temptation to commit a crime presented by the simple opportunity to act unlawfully. [But] it is impermissible for the police or their agents to pressure the suspect by overbearing conduct such as badgering, cajoling, importuning, or other affirmative acts likely to induce a normally law-abiding person to commit the crime."

"[G]uidance will generally be found in the application of one or both of two principles. First, if the [police conduct] would generate in a normally law-abiding person a motive for the crime other than ordinary criminal intent, entrapment will be established. An example of such conduct would be an appeal by the police that would induce such a person to commit the act because of friendship or sympathy, instead of a desire for personal gain or other typical criminal purpose. Second, affirmative police conduct that would make commission of the crime unusually attractive to a normally law-abiding person will likewise constitute entrapment. Such conduct would include, for example, a guarantee that the act is not illegal or the offense will go undetected, an offer of exorbitant consideration, or any similar enticement."[a]

2. *Doubts about the efficacy of the "objective" test.* Roger Park, *The Entrapment Controversy,* 60 Minn.L.Rev. 163, 270–71 (1976), voices doubts that the "hypothetical person" test could control the conduct of police and informers: "Standardized procedures cannot govern the sundry and unpredictable events that occur during encounters between target and tempter. Moreover, even if such procedures could be formulated and somehow taught to the army of addicts and criminals used by police to set up controlled offenses, it is doubtful that they would be followed—particularly since the rules would inevitably become known to targets as well as police agents.

" * * * Because many targets are professional criminals, judges will be reluctant to rule that entrapment has occurred simply because an agent found it necessary to appeal to friendship, make multiple requests, or offer a substantial profit. Yet approval of such conduct would lead to unfair results in cases where the target was law-abiding but ductile. For example, conviction of someone who has been solicited by a friend may be fair enough in the general run of cases, but unfair if the target was a nondisposed person who would not have committed the type of crime charged but for a request from that particular friend.

"The danger of acquitting wolves and convicting lambs would be ameliorated if courts following the hypothetical-person test allow predisposition evidence to be

---

a. Under this test, emphasized the court, "the character of the suspect, his predisposition to commit the offense, and his subjective intent are irrelevant." On this point, see Note 3 infra.

introduced for its bearing on the propriety of the agent's inducement. The degree of persistence permitted would then depend upon whether the agent had sound reasons to believe that his target was already engaged in criminal enterprise. However, this approach would create even greater uncertainty about the boundaries of permissible inducement and further limit the defense's utility as a guide to police conduct.

"[The federal defense] attempts to distinguish between persons who are blameworthy and persons who are not. In the absence of extraordinary circumstances, that should be the goal of our law of crimes."

3. *Should the "subjective" test be retained, but stripped of its indiscriminate attitude toward "predisposition" evidence?* The "subjective" test, protested Stewart, J., dissenting in *United States v. Russell,* permits the use of otherwise inadmissible "hearsay, suspicion and rumor" to prove defendant's predisposition.[b] The defendant, in effect, is "put on trial for his past offenses and character." *Grossman v. State,* 457 P.2d 226, 229 (Alaska 1969) (adopting the objective test).

But, maintains Park, supra, at 272, "the indiscriminate attitude toward predisposition evidence"—"the greatest fault" of the subjective test—"is by no means a necessary feature of the subjective test. If the accused was already engaged in a course of criminal conduct, the prosecution should be able to develop an arsenal of reliable predisposition evidence. If it cannot, the danger of wrongful acquittal is outweighed by the danger of convicting a person whose only real vice is a bad reputation. Reputation and other hearsay evidence should not become admissible merely because the accused has raised the defense of entrapment. If construed to exclude such testimony, the subjective defense should present more reliable evidence to the fact-finder than the hypothetical-person defense. The latter focuses upon the nature of the inducement offered; consequently, trials are likely to be reduced to a swearing match between unreliable witnesses about words said in private."

4. *Is the distinction between the objective and subjective approaches overstated?* Consider Louis Michael Seidman, *The Supreme Court, Entrapment, and Our Criminal Justice Dilemma,* 1981 Sup.Ct.Rev. 111, 118–20:

"The [subjective test] is premised on the notion that it is possible to isolate the class of 'unwary criminals' who are 'ready and willing' to engage in crime apart from the inducements offered by the government. But whether a person is 'ready and willing' to break the law depends on what the person expects to get in return—that is, on the level of inducement. Like the rest of us, criminals do not generally work for free. Their willingness to take the risks of crime varies with the incentive which is provided. To be sure, the less cynical among us may believe that there is still a class of people who 'have no price.' [But] even if one concedes that such people can be found somewhere, they are, by definition, not among the ranks of entrapped defendants, since such defendants must have succumbed to some inducement in order to be entrapped.

"Consequently, so long as one equates 'predisposition' with a readiness to commit crime, no definition of 'predisposition' can be complete without an articulation of the level of inducement to which a 'predisposed' defendant would respond. Furthermore, the 'predisposed' cannot be distinguished from the 'nondisposed' without focusing on the propriety of the government's conduct—the very

b. Not only prior convictions, but prior arrests, acts of prior misconduct, "reputation testimony" and "suspicious conduct" have been admitted on this issue. See LaFave & Israel, § 5.2(c).

factor that the subjective approach professes to ignore. This is true because a defendant who responds favorably to a 'proper' inducement has thereby conclusively demonstrated that he is disposed to crime when such an inducement is offered.[c] It would seem, then, that so long as government agents restrict themselves to 'proper' inducements, they run no risk of violating the entrapment rules. The entrapment test is 'subjective' only in the sense that even if the government offers an 'excessive' inducement, the defendant may nonetheless be convicted under such a test if he would have responded favorably to a proper one."

5. *Was the distinction between the subjective and objective tests smudged in the DeLorean case?* Because John DeLorean was prosecuted for drug violations in federal court, the judge instructed the jury to consider the entrapment claim in accordance with the subjective test. However, points out Maura Whelan, *Lead Us Not Into (Unwarranted) Temptation: A Proposal to Replace the Entrapment Defense with a Reasonable Suspicion Requirement,* 133 U.Pa.L.Rev. 1193, 1199–1200 (1985), "it seems from the jurors' remarks" after the acquittal that "they followed the objective approach instead. Those jurors who discussed the entrapment issue with reporters emphasized the impropriety of the operation, not DeLorean's character. One juror expressed the view that the FBI went after DeLorean only because he was an influential person. There were several indications that the agents viewed DeLorean as a highly desirable arrest. [It] was undoubtedly the spirit of the hunt that led [one agent] to report to FBI headquarters that DeLorean was 'involved in large scale narcotics transactions, in addition to the laundering [of] large amounts of illegally received income,' although he knew it wasn't true. His explanation for this message? 'I thought it sounded pretty good.' "[d]

OTHER ISSUES RAISED BY THE ENTRAPMENT DEFENSE[a]

1. *Contingent fee arrangements.* In *Williamson v. United States,* 311 F.2d 441 (5th Cir.1962), the informer had been promised $200 and $100, respectively,

---

c. In the Abscam cases, observes Bennett Gershman, *Abscam, the Judiciary, and the Ethics of Entrapment,* 91 Yale L.J. 1565, 1581 (1982), "the jury was allowed to infer predisposition simply from the defendant's affirmative response to the government's inducements. For instance, that [two defendants] readily accepted cash payments was found to constitute sufficient evidence that they had a *preexisting* intention to take a bribe. In other words, the defendant is said to be predisposed because he committed the act, and then is held responsible for the act because he was predisposed. The pernicious circularity of this approach is obvious."

d. According to newspaper accounts of the DeLorean trial, summarized in Whelan, supra, at 1197–99, by 1980 DeLorean desperately needed ten million dollars to save his automobile company. About this time, he was invited to participate in a major cocaine transaction by FBI informant James Hoffman, a former neighbor of DeLorean and an admitted perjurer and occasional drug dealer. The FBI had no reason to believe that DeLorean was involved in drugs in any way until Hoffman came forward with his allegation that DeLorean wanted

to make money quickly in a big narcotics deal and hoped that Hoffman could arrange something.

According to the original scenario, DeLorean would invest two million dollars toward the purchase of the cocaine and make as much as sixty million dollars. When DeLorean reported that he would have to withdraw from the operation because of his inability to raise the money, either Hoffman or an FBI agent proposed an alternative: simply put up two million dollars of collateral, which included various property. DeLorean also signed over the entire voting stock of his company to the federal agents who were posing as drug dealers. An FBI agent recommended that DeLorean "launder" any profits from the operation through one of his companies.

The jury's acquittal of DeLorean was based both on disapproval of the FBI's methods and the conclusion that the government had failed to prove that DeLorean had committed a crime.

a. Because three issues—(1) when a private person should be considered a "government agent" for purposes of the entrapment defense;

for producing legally admissible evidence that two specified persons were engaged in illicit liquor dealings. Using its supervisory powers over the administration of federal criminal justice,[b] the court held that absent a special justification for its use in a particular case, a conviction is invalid if it rests on evidence of informants hired on such a basis. *Williamson* "could have been construed to limit the widespread practice of offering leniency to arrested persons who agree to incriminate others by making purchases of contraband," but the case "has had virtually no impact. Courts faced with a defense based on it have almost invariably found a way to distinguish it." Park, supra, at 175.

Williamson was, in effect, disapproved in *United States v. Grimes,* 438 F.2d 391 (6th Cir.1971), reasoning that a contingent fee informer is "no more likely to [lie and manufacture crimes] than witnesses acting for other, more common reasons," such as a codefendant hoping for leniency or an informant who feels that his future employment may depend upon success on this occasion. But are not contingent fee informers likely to be more desperate then informers generally? Are they not likely to have a stronger incentive for overreaching and falsification? See LaFave & Israel, § 5.4(a).

2. *"Inconsistent" defenses.* The traditional view had been that the defense of entrapment is not available to one who denies commission of the criminal act with which he is charged, for the reason that the denial is inconsistent with the assertion of such a defense. But *Mathews v. United States,* 485 U.S. 58, 108 S.Ct. 883, 99 L.Ed.2d 54 (1988) holds that "even if the defendant denies one or more elements of the crime, he is entitled to an entrapment instruction whenever there is sufficient evidence from which a reasonable jury could find entrapment."

3. *Triable by court or jury.* Recall that *Sorrells* rejected, and *Sherman* declined to reconsider, the argument that the issue of entrapment should be tried separately to the court without a jury. Although most commentators favor a judicial determination of the issue, the defense has traditionally been regarded as a matter for the jury, except in those unusual cases where entrapment is established as a matter of law. It has been argued, in support of this position, that a jury has special, or at least traditional, competence to judge matters of credibility and motivation and to assess the subjective response to the stimulus of police encouragement. Moreover, if the matter is placed in the hands of the jury, there is an opportunity for "jury nullification" if the police conduct evokes "moral revulsion." See generally LaFave & Israel § 5.3(b).

On the other hand, it has been said that where the subjective test prevails "the most urgent considerations" support judicial determination of the issue—to avoid the great impact on the jury of prior convictions, prior arrests and "reputation testimony"—but that in those jurisdictions that follow the objective approach "the case for separate trial to the court is more evenly balanced." See Comment to *Model Penal Code* § 2.10(2) (Tent. Draft No. 9, 1959). It has been argued, however, that here, too, the case for having the matter decided by the court is a strong one: It is the function of the court to preserve its own purity; to the extent that the objective approach is based on a deterrence-of-police rationale, this is the function of the court, just as it is when the court rules on suppression motions;

(2) whether a government agent should be allowed to solicit an offense absent "probable cause" or at least "reasonable suspicion" that his target is engaged in criminal activity; and (3) whether judicial authorization should be required for an undercover operation—received prominent attention as a result of the Abscam cases, treatment of these issues is postponed until the Notes and Questions following *United States v. Kelly,* p. 422.

b. See generally pp. 51–55.

and, as Frankfurter, J., maintained in *Sherman*, only the court can provide government agents with the necessary guidance. See LaFave & Israel, supra.

4. *Burden of proof.* In those jurisdictions following the subjective approach, it is generally agreed that the defendant must establish the fact of inducement by a government agent. Once the defendant satisfies this threshold requirement (and it is unclear whether he need only produce "some evidence" of inducement or sustain a burden of persuasion by a preponderance of the evidence), the burden is then on the government to negate the defense by establishing the defendant's "predisposition" beyond a reasonable doubt. See LaFave & Israel, § 5.3(d).

In states where the objective test prevails, entrapment is viewed as an "affirmative defense" rather than something that negates the existence of an element of the crime charged, and the entire burden of production and persuasion is on the defendant. The defendant must establish the defense by a preponderance of the evidence. The *Model Penal Code* § 2.13(2) also takes this position. For criticism of this approach, see Park, 1 supra, at 265–67, suggesting that the real basis for placing the burden of persuasion on the defendant is that entrapment is a disfavored defense.

SECTION 2. MORE ON THE DUE PROCESS DEFENSE TO GOVERNMENT "OVERINVOLVEMENT" IN A CRIMINAL ENTERPRISE[a]

HAMPTON v. UNITED STATES, 425 U.S. 484, 96 S.Ct. 1646, 48 L.Ed.2d 113 (1976), grew out of the following facts: Petitioner was convicted of distributing heroin in violation of federal law. The district court refused to give petitioner's requested instruction that if it were found, as he claimed, that the narcotics he sold to government agents (posing as narcotics buyers) had been supplied to him by a government informant[b] he must be acquitted as a matter of law regardless of his predisposition to commit the offense charged. On appeal, petitioner conceded that he was "predisposed." A majority of the Court rejected petitioner's contention, but there was no opinion of the Court. Justice REHNQUIST, who announced the judgment of the Court in an opinion in which Burger, C.J., and White, J., joined, observed:

"In *Russell* [we] ruled out the possibility that the defense of entrapment could ever be based upon governmental misconduct in a case, such as this one, where the predisposition of the defendant to commit the crime was established.

a. Although the claim that the government has unduly "dominated" or become impermissibly "overinvolved" in the criminal activity has often been viewed as a species of the objective test entrapment, it seems preferable to view it as the basis for a separate test for entrapment or as a due process defense independent of general entrapment theory.

b. According to petitioner's version of the events, the informant not only supplied the narcotics but was the first to propose the criminal enterprise. Petitioner alleged that when he stated that he was short of cash, the informant responded by proposing they sell drugs that he could get from a pharmacist friend. Evidently, petitioner did not deem this particular aspect of his version of the facts significant. Evident-

ly, too, a majority of the Court considered it irrelevant so long as petitioner was "predisposed" to commit the offense and the governmental activity had not "implant[ed] in the mind of an *innocent* person the disposition to commit the alleged offense." (Emphasis added.) No member of the majority disputed dissenting Justice Brennan's characterization of the case as one where "the two sales for which petitioner was convicted were allegedly instigated by Government agents." See also Judge Adams's dissent in *United States v. Twigg* (p. 415, fn. a infra) (describing *Hampton* as a case where the government "suggested the operation"). But see the majority opinion in *Twigg* and Note, 67 Geo.L.J. 1455, 1464 & fn. 73, 1466 (1979).

[In] view of [*Sorrells, Sherman* and *Russell*], petitioner correctly recognizes that his case does not qualify as one involving 'entrapment' at all, [but] relies on the language in *Russell* that 'we may some day be presented with a situation in which the conduct of law enforcement agents is so outrageous that due process principle would absolutely bar the government from invoking judicial processes to obtain a conviction.'

"[In] urging that this [is such a case], petitioner misapprehends the meaning of the quoted language in *Russell*. Admittedly petitioner's case is different from Russell's but the difference is one of degree, not of kind. In *Russell* the ingredient supplied by the government agent was a legal drug which the defendants demonstrably could have obtained from other sources besides the Government. Here the drug which the government informant allegedly supplied [was] both illegal and constituted the *corpus delicti* for the sale of which the petitioner was convicted. The Government obviously played a more significant role in enabling petitioner to sell contraband in this case than it did in *Russell*.

"But in each case the government agents were acting in concert with the defendant, and in each case either the jury found or the defendant conceded that he was predisposed to commit the crime for which he was convicted. The remedy of the criminal defendant with respect to the acts of government agents, which, far from being resisted, are encouraged by him, lies solely in the defense of entrapment. But, as noted, petitioner's conceded predisposition rendered this defense unavailable to him.

"To sustain petitioner's contention here would run directly contrary to our statement in *Russell* that the defense of entrapment is not intended 'to give the federal judiciary a "chancellor's foot" veto over law enforcement practices of which it did not approve. * * * ' " [The limitations of the Due Process Clause of the Fifth Amendment come into play only when the Government activity in question violates some protected right of the defendant. [If] the police engage in illegal activity in concert with a defendant beyond the scope of their duties the remedy lies, not in freeing the equally culpable defendant, but in prosecuting the police under the applicable provisions of state or federal law. But the police conduct here no more deprived defendant of any right secured to him by the United States Constitution than did the police conduct in *Russell* deprive Russell of any rights."

Concurring Justice POWELL, joined by Blackmun, J., agreed that "this case is controlled completely by *Russell*," but was "unwilling to join the plurality in concluding that, no matter what the circumstances, neither due process principles nor our supervisory power could support a bar to conviction in any case where the Government is able to prove disposition": "[Disposition of the claims in *Russell* and earlier cases] did not require the Court to consider whether overinvolvement of government agents in contraband offenses could ever reach such proportions as to bar conviction of a predisposed defendant as a matter of due process. Nor have we had occasion yet to confront Government overinvolvement in areas outside the realm of contraband offenses. In these circumstances, I am unwilling to conclude that an analysis other than one limited to predisposition would never be appropriate under due process principles."[c]

c. At this point Justice Powell quotes from Judge Friendly's view in *United States v. Archer*, 486 F.2d 670, 676 (2d Cir.1973), that "it would be unthinkable, for example, to permit government agents to instigate robberies and beatings merely to gather evidence to convict other members of a gang of hoodlums."

Justice BRENNAN, joined by Stewart and Marshall, JJ., dissented, urging that conviction be "barred as a matter of law where the subject of the criminal charge is the sale of contraband provided to the defendant by a Government agent."[d] The dissenters reiterated their support for the "objective" approach to entrapment, under which, they maintained, petitioner's claims "would plainly be held to constitute entrapment as a matter of law," but considered reversal compelled even "for those who follow the 'subjective' approach." Where the Government's agent "deliberately sets up the accused by supplying him with contraband and then bringing him to another agent as a potential purchaser," protested the dissent, "the Government's role has passed the point of toleration. The Government is doing nothing less than buying contraband from itself through an intermediary and jailing the intermediary."[e]

Notes and Questions

1. "The depth of our confusion concerning the proper limits on government power in this area," observes Louis Michael Seidman, *The Supreme Court, Entrapment, and Our Criminal Justice Dilemma,* 1981 Sup.Ct.Rev. 111, 116 n. 20, "is illustrated by comparing the intuitions of Justice Powell with those of the authors of the Model Penal Code. Justice Powell hints that his objective, due process test would be violated if the government induced beatings or armed robberies. [See fn. c to his concurring opinion in *Hampton.*] Yet the Model Penal Code [' 2.13(3)] makes an entrapment defense unavailable in precisely those cases where the defendant causes or threatens bodily injury."

2. Leslie Abramson & Lisa Lindeman, *Entrapment and Due Process in the Federal Courts,* 8 Am.J.Crim.Law 139, 180–82 (1980), concludes, inter alia: "Many courts treat the constitutional due process defense as an illegitimate offspring of entrapment, and recognize the issue reluctantly when it is presented in the pleadings. It is then granted only cursory review. The better approach, therefore, is to plead the defense independently of the general entrapment defense, with police misconduct as the exclusive basis. In that case, the due process defense cannot later be dismissed by a finding of predisposition, because a defendant can prove police misconduct and overreaching without having to disprove his own predisposition. The trial court can then decide the due process question as a matter of law." [The] due process defense requires a stricter scrutiny of government conduct than the traditional entrapment defense. Possibly, as in *United States v. Twigg,*[a] lower courts will soon accept the need for a constitutional due

d. The dissent deemed it sufficient "for present purposes" to adopt this rule "under our supervisory power and leave to another day whether it ought to be made applicable to the States under the Due Process Clause." For a general discussion of the federal court's supervisory power over criminal justice, see pp. 51–55.

e. Stevens, J., took no part in the consideration or decision of the case.

a. 588 F.2d 373 (3d Cir.1978). In *Twigg,* apparently the only post-*Hampton* federal court of appeals decision to invalidate a conviction on the basis of the due process defense, the informant contacted an old acquaintance, defendant Neville, and proposed that they set up a "speed" laboratory. Neville assumed responsibility for raising the capital and arrang-

ing for distribution of the product. The informant assumed responsibility for acquiring the necessary equipment, raw materials, and a production site. The DEA assisted the informant in carrying out his part of the operation by providing two and one-half gallons of the essential and hard to obtain ingredient, propanone; some glassware; and a rented farmhouse for the laboratory site. Defendant Twigg joined the operation, at the invitation of Neville. The laboratory operated for one week, producing about six pounds of speed. The informant alone had the expertise to manufacture the drug and thus was completely in charge of the laboratory.

Neville and Twigg were convicted of conspiracy to manufacture speed. On appeal, a 2–1 majority, per Rosenn, J., reversed. Distinguishing *Russell* as a case in which the defendant process defense independent of the general entrapment theory. To protect the constitutional rights of an individual does not necessarily require application of a 'chancellor's foot.' "

3. *Is the due process defense in entrapment cases so unruly and so subjective that it should no longer be considered?* As a strong proponent of the due process defense in entrapment cases, Paul Marcus, recognizes, *The Due Process Defense in Entrapment Cases: The Journey Back,* 27 Am.Crim.L.Rev. 457, 458 (1990): "It will take a great deal to persuade courts that entrapment-like schemes violate due process. Some courts have announced that they have *never* overturned convictions on this basis."

See, e.g., *United States v. Simpson,* 813 F.2d 1462 (9th Cir.1987), holding that (1) the FBI's "manipulation" of a prostitute (Helen Miller), who was a heroin user and a fugitive from drug charges, into becoming an informant; (2) the fact that Ms. Miller continued to use heroin and engage in acts of prostitution during the investigation of defendant; (3) Ms. Miller's "use of sex" to deceive defendant into believing she was "an intimate friend" so that she could "lure him into selling heroin to undercover FBI agents"; and (4) the FBI's continued use of Ms. Miller as an informant even after learning of her sexual involvement with defendant was "not so shocking as to violate the due process clause." Although Simpson "may have suffered severe emotional trauma and felt stripped of his dignity upon learning that [Ms. Miller's] apparent affection for him was contrived," his treatment by her "falls short of the brutality and coercion underlying previous successful outrageous conduct challenges."

See also *United States v. Miller* 891 F.2d 1265 (7th Cir.1989), where the undercover agent had a contingent fee arrangement with the government, had been a cocaine addict both before and during her employment and had earlier been sexually intimate with the defendant. But these factors "neither separately or combined" amounted to " 'truly outrageous' government conduct." Concurring

was an active participant before the government agent arrived on the scene, and *Hampton* as concerned with the sale of an illegal drug—"a much more fleeting and elusive crime to detect than the operation of an illicit drug laboratory"—the *Twigg* majority concluded that the government involvement was so "overreaching," "egregious" and "outrageous" as to bar prosecution as a matter of due process. The court emphasized (a) that the "illicit plan did not originate with the criminal defendants"; (b) that the informant's expertise was "an indispensable requisite to this criminal enterprise"; and (c) that Neville was "lawfully and peacefully minding his own affairs" until approached by the defendant.

As dissenting Judge Adams read the relevant Supreme Court cases, due process analysis "was not intended simply to reestablish the objective approach to entrapment under a new name." He dissented because he did not believe that "this situation presents the intolerable set of circumstances necessary to warrant resort to the due process clause." He thought the facts less persuasive for reversal than were those in *Hampton* because none of the chemicals, equipment or skill provided by

the government "was itself contraband." The government, through its agent, did suggest the operation, "but that is the situation in many undercover operations, and was the case in *Hampton.*"

Twigg suggests that the oft-proposed but rarely applied "reasonable suspicion" requirement (see p. 422) "may on occasion emerge as an aspect of the due process limits upon encouragement activity. The point seems to be that overinvolvement by the government to the extent reflected in *Twigg* is permissible, if at all, only against a person who is 'reasonably suspected of criminal conduct or design.' "LaFave & Israel, § 5.4(c). See also Note, 67 Geo. L.J. 1455, 1461, 1467 (1979).

Another important principle recognized in *Twigg* is that "the practicalities of combatting" a certain type of criminal activity must be considered in determining whether "more extreme methods of investigation" are constitutionally permissible. But *Twigg* may have misapplied this principle. Consider Note, 67 Geo.L.J. at 1463: "[A] drug laboratory, which by nature is sophisticated and covert, arguably is *more* difficult to detect than the sale of drugs."

Judge Easterbrook would have gone farther. He argued that there should not even be a due process defense in entrapment cases:

" 'Outrageousness' "as a defense * * * creates serious problems of consistency. [How] much is 'too much'? The nature of the question exposes it as (a) unanswerable, and (b) political. What, if anything, could separate stirring up of crime in unpalatable ways here [from] Operation Greylord [or] the 'creative' endeavors in Abscam? From any of the 'sting' operations? [Any] line we draw would be unprincipled and therefore not judicial in nature. More likely there would be no line; judges would vote their lower intestines. Such a meandering, personal approach is the antithesis of justice under law, and we ought not indulge it. Inability to describe in general terms just what makes tactics too outrageous to tolerate suggests that there is no definition?—and 'I know it when I see it' is not a rule of any kind, let alone a command of the Due Process Clause.

"The kinds of prosecution that trouble me most are not those like Operation Greylord or offers of sex in exchange for cocaine, but those that impose costs on the innocent. Take for example a sting in which the FBI sets up a fence and buys stolen goods. The money the government pumps into the business must lead people to steal things to sell to the FBI—with misery for the victims of the burglary and potential violence in the process. Stings have been upheld consistently, however * * *. Methods such as those used to ensnare [the defendant in this case] do not trouble me. Other judges are offended by immorality (such as sponsoring an informant's use of sexual favors as currency) or by acts that endanger informants (such as supplying them with drugs for personal use) but not by a traditional sting. This shows the subjective basis of the concern—all the more reason not to have such a doctrine in our law."[b]

But consider Marcus, supra, at 465: "[The due process defense in entrapment cases] is important because it creates outer limits on appropriate law enforcement techniques and because it clearly demonstrates to the legal and law enforcement communities, and to society at large, that courts are indeed willing to draw some lines that cannot be crossed even in pursuit of criminals. [As for Judge Easterbrook's argument that the inability of reasonable people to agree on the application of the defense indicates that it is not a rule of any kind,] it is not factually accurate. There will be fact situations where reasonable people could agree that the law enforcement behavior was utterly outrageous. Certainly, Judge Friendly's hypothetical problem of government agents beating some members of a gang in order to get to other members of a gang is just such a case."

UNITED STATES v. KELLY

707 F.2d 1460 (D.C.Cir.1983).

[The phase of the Abscam operation that resulted in the indictment of Kelly and other Congressmen was conceived by convicted confidence man Weinberg and approved by the FBI. It was to spread the word that wealthy Arabs were willing to bribe members of Congress to ensure that they would introduce private immigration legislation on the Arabs' behalf if and when necessary.

[Among those to whom the word was passed was codefendant Ciuzio, an acquaintance of Congressman Kelly. At a November, 1979 meeting, Ciuzio told Kelly that he had some Arab clients with immigration difficulties and asked Kelly

---

b. Some courts have followed Judge Easterbrook's lead in rejecting or greatly restricting the "outrageous governmental conduct" de-fense. See *United States v. Gaviria*, 116 F.3d 1498 (D.C.Cir.1997); *United States v. Tucker*, 28 F.3d 1420 (6th Cir.1994).

if he could help them. Kelly indicated that he would be glad to do so, particularly since Ciuzio indicated the Arabs might invest in his district. Ciuzio told Kelly that he—Ciuzio—would receive a large fee if Kelly helped the Arabs. Kelly replied that the fee would cause no difficulties. Ciuzio then told codefendant Weisz, who was a business associate of Rosenberg (who was helping Weinberg locate politicians willing to assist the latter's "Arab-employers"), that Kelly would be happy to help the Arabs. The word was passed via the Abscam "middlemen" to Weinberg that a "candidate" was available who would assist with the Arabs' immigration problems and that he wanted $250,000. Weinberg suggested that the Congressman be paid $25,000 down, with the balance paid when legislation was required.

[At a December 19 meeting among Ciuzio, Weinberg and FBI agent Amoroso (Weinberg's immediate supervisor), Ciuzio was told what assistance would be expected of the Congressman. Ciuzio indicated that the Congressman was Kelly and intimated that he and Kelly had had previous dealings of a similar nature. Ciuzio suggested that he had told Kelly of the offer and claimed that Kelly had left the arrangements to him. But Ciuzio opposed direct payment to Kelly and suggested that the money instead be escrowed through Weisz.

[A January 8, 1980 meeting was arranged between Kelly and the "Arabs' representatives" at the FBI's townhouse in Washington, D.C. Soon after his arrival, Ciuzio, in a private meeting with Weinberg and Amoroso, sought to dissuade them from attempting to bribe Kelly directly. It was ultimately agreed that Kelly would acknowledge that the money was in exchange for his agreement to assist the Arabs, but that Ciuzio would actually take the money from the meeting.

[Finally, later that evening, Congressman Kelly met with Amoroso alone. When Amoroso proposed a payoff, Kelly told him that he was interested in the investment in his district, that he didn't "know anything about" Amoroso's arrangement with Ciuzio and others—"I'm not involved with it"—but that Amoroso's arrangement with Ciuzio and others was "fine."

[After Amoroso received a phone call from an Assistant United States Attorney who was monitoring the meeting and who told Amoroso that Kelly was "being cute," Amoroso sought to clarify Kelly's position. Kelly maintained that he wanted the money given to Ciuzio. Amoroso indicated that all of the money was supposed to go to Kelly, that Ciuzio would be compensated separately, and that giving the money directly to Kelly would avoid witnesses, thus protecting Kelly. The Congressman then agreed that that was "the best way of doing it." Amoroso then gave Kelly $25,000 in packets of $100 bills and Kelly stuffed the money in the pockets of his suit.]

PER CURIAM: Judge MacKinnon files an opinion in Parts I, II, III(A), and IV of which Chief Judge Robinson concurs.[a] Judge Ginsburg files an opinion in which Chief Judge Robinson concurs. Thus Parts I, II, III(A) and IV of Judge MacKinnon's opinion together with Judge Ginsburg's opinion constitute the opinion of the court. * * *

MacKinnon, Circuit Judge. [On] January 8, 1980, Congressman Richard Kelly accepted $25,000 from an agent of the FBI who was posing as a representative of two wealthy Arabs as part of the FBI's elaborate Abscam investigation. In return, Kelly agreed to use his position in Congress to assist the Arabs to become

---

a. Part I, a detailed discussion of the facts, and Part II, a discussion of the district court   opinion dismissing the indictment, are omitted.

permanent residents of the United States. Unbeknownst to Kelly, the FBI recorded the entire illegal transaction on video tape.

On the basis of this and other evidence, Kelly and [Ciuzio and Weisz] were charged with [bribery and other federal offenses]. A jury found each defendant guilty on all counts. However, the district court granted Kelly's motion to dismiss the indictment, entering a judgment of acquittal in his favor, because it concluded that the FBI's actions in furtherance of Abscam were so outrageous that prosecution of Kelly was barred by principles of due process. * * *

III. ANALYSIS

A. *The Due Process Defense*

"[Our task] is to assess whether the FBI's conduct in Abscam reached a "demonstrable level of outrageousness" [Powell, J., concurring in *Hampton*], while keeping in mind the difficulties inherent in detecting corrupt public officials. Measured against this standard, the FBI's conduct did not violate due process.

B. *Abscam*

[S]tripped of [its] trappings of wealth, Abscam was no more than an "opportunity for the commission of crime by those willing to do so." *United States v. Myers*, 692 F.2d 823, 837 (2d Cir.1982). Amoroso and Weinberg let it be known that they would pay substantial sums of money to congressmen willing to promise to assist the wealthy Arabs with their immigration difficulties. Thereafter, the FBI operatives simply waited for the grapevine to work and to see who appeared to take bribes. No congressmen were targeted for investigation; rather, Abscam pursued all who were brought to the operation by the grapevine.[50] In essence, then, Abscam was *not* significantly different from an undercover drug or fencing operation offering to buy from all who appear at its door.[51] Instead of buying stolen goods or contraband drugs, Abscam bought corrupt official influence in Congress. Such government involvement in crime does not violate principles of due process.

We need not determine the exact limits on government involvement in crime imposed by the due process clause for it is clear that the FBI's involvement in

---

50. However, not all officials brought to Abscam were offered bribes. The Abscam operatives recognized that they had no control over the representations made by intermediaries such as Ciuzio, Rosenberg, and Weisz. Accordingly, the FBI *always* discussed the asylum scenario with the officials prior to the offer of a bribe. That was certainly the case with Kelly; Amoroso carefully discussed the details of the asylum scenario with Kelly *before* any bribe money was paid. See discussion infra. In one instance, where this discussion revealed that the official was unaware of the corrupt nature of the proposal, the FBI terminated the meeting.

51. The district court concluded that Abscam was unlike ordinary, "passive" undercover operations because it used "recruiting agents" to spread the word that bribes were available. I disagree. I seriously doubt that the government would establish an undercover drug or fencing operation without spreading the word, through informants and criminal

elements (labeled "recruiting agents" by the district court), that its services were available. The Abscam investigators did no more.

My colleagues term Abscam an extraordinary operation. It was extraordinary only in the positions of some of the individuals involved and in the intangible nature of the "commodity" purchased. Otherwise, it is strikingly similar to ordinary undercover operations. * * *

My colleagues also criticize the failure of the FBI to closely supervise the Abscam operation. To the extent that this criticism extends to the non-FBI middlemen, such as Ciuzio, Rosenberg and Weisz, involved in Abscam, their activities could hardly be "supervised" because they did not know Abscam was an undercover investigation. The FBI took considerable precautions to compensate for its inability to control the representations of the middlemen. See note 50 supra. * * *

Abscam was less than that government involvement found unobjectionable by the Supreme Court.[52]

[In *Russell* and *Hampton*] the government not only provided an *opportunity* to commit a crime, but also provided the *means* to commit that crime. Nevertheless, in each case the Supreme Court concluded that the government's conduct did not violate due process. Where, as in Abscam, the government simply provides the opportunity to commit a crime, prosecution of a defendant does not violate principles of due process. This conclusion is in accord with decisions of the Second and Third Circuits upholding Abscam convictions challenged on due process grounds. *United States v. Williams,* 705 F.2d 603 (2d Cir.1983); *Myers,* supra; *United States v. Alexandro,* 675 F.2d 34 (2d Cir.); *United States v. Jannotti,* 673 F.2d 578 (3d Cir.) (en banc).[53]

C. Specific Claims

1. Reasonable Suspicion[b]

Nor do any of the specifically challenged FBI actions in furtherance of Abscam reach that "demonstrable level of outrageousness" which would bar Kelly's prosecution. The district court stressed that Abscam's asylum scenario was not triggered by any suspicion of corruption in government. [But] prior to the January 8 meeting with Kelly, the Abscam operatives had evidence from which they could conclude that Kelly was, in fact, corrupt. [Thus,] the FBI had [the requisite reasonable suspicion] to justify pursuing the asylum scenario and Kelly, if such suspicion was necessary.[58] * * *

2. Utilization of Weinberg

[The] argument that the FBI violated due process by utilizing the services of an admitted confidence man, Melvin Weinberg, in Abscam should likewise be rejected. Successful creation of an "elaborate hoax" such as Abscam may well *require* employment of "experts" such as Weinberg to give the operation an aura of "credibility" and "contacts" with criminal elements. The employment of a convicted confidence man in Abscam is analogous to the entirely proper employment of a convicted seller of drugs to purchase drugs from a suspected distributor. * * *

4. Multiple Bribe Offers

Finally, Kelly contends that the FBI operatives violated due process when they persisted in offering a bribe after what he characterizes as his initial rejection. *Kelly asserts that he rejected the bribe at his meeting with Ciuzio on December 23, that Ciuzio informed Amoroso and Weinberg of that fact at the townhouse on January 8, and that he rejected the bribe several times in his meeting with Amoroso.* Kelly argues, and the district court agreed, that under these

---

52. For this reason, we need not decide the validity of the due process test formulated by the district court—whether the temptation offered is "one which the individual is likely to encounter in the ordinary course." It is suggested, however, that criminal conduct being as highly varied as it is that such test is unduly speculative.

53. The Third Circuit's decision in *Jannotti* is particularly significant because it held that *Twigg,* the only post-*Hampton* case to uphold a due process challenge to prosecution because of

excessive government involvement, did not control its consideration of Abscam. Thus Kelly's reliance on *Twigg* is misplaced.

b. See Notes 1–3 following this case.

58. Although we need not decide the question, both the Second and Third Circuits have rejected the argument that the government must have reasonable suspicion of wrongdoing before proceeding with an undercover operation such as Abscam.

circumstances Amoroso's several bribe offers to Kelly were outrageous and violated due process. I cannot agree.

The evidence in this case clearly demonstrates that at no time did Kelly reject Abscam's corrupt immigration proposal. On both December 23 and January 8, Kelly agreed to assure the wealthy Arabs that he would help them with their immigration problems as a favor to Ciuzio, despite the fact that Kelly knew that in return the Arabs would pay substantial sums to Ciuzio [and others]. It is also clear that Kelly understood that part of the arrangement was that the Arabs would make substantial investments in his district. Such agreements, which would benefit Kelly indirectly, constitute violations of the bribery statute. Furthermore, the discussions between Ciuzio, Kelly, and the Abscam operatives at the town-house of January 8 focused on the *manner* in which the bribe would be paid, not on whether it would be paid. Ciuzio told Weinberg not to bribe Kelly directly, but agreed that he would take the money for Kelly. After agreeing that Amoroso was going to give him some money at the meeting, Kelly asked Amoroso to pay the bribe to Ciuzio?to "deal with [Ciuzio] about it." In my view, Congressman Kelly "did not reject a bribe, he [initially] rejected its payment under circumstances he feared would be incriminating." *Myers.*

I likewise reject Kelly's characterization of his conversation with Amoroso on January 8 as a *series* of bribe offers. Although the terms of the corrupt Abscam proposal were mentioned several times during that conversation, Amoroso's discussion reflects the evasive and circumspect negotiation to be expected of a person seeking to corrupt a public official. In my view, Amoroso's conversation with Kelly on January 8 can be fairly characterized only as a *single offer* of a corrupt proposal to Kelly. For these reasons I reject Kelly's contention that he initially rejected a bribe, that the Abscam agents persisted in offering him a bribe, and that they thus violated due process.

IV. CONCLUSION

[The] Supreme Court has made it clear that "a successful due process defense must be predicated on *intolerable government conduct* which goes beyond that necessary to sustain an entrapment defense." *Jannotti* (emphasis added). Considering the genuine need to detect corrupt public officials, as well as the difficulties inherent in doing so, we conclude that the FBI's conduct in furtherance of its Abscam operation, insofar as it involved Kelly, simply did not reach intolerable levels. * * *

RUTH BADER GINSBURG, Circuit Judge: ["Abscam"] was an extraordinary operation. The investigation was steered in large part by a convicted swindler; it relied upon con men to identify and attract targets, to whom legitimate as well as illegitimate inducements were offered; it proceeded without close supervision by responsible officials.[1]

---

1. * * * We do not share Judge Mac-Kinnon's view that, apart from "trappings of wealth," Abscam "was *not* significantly different from" run-of-the-mill "passive" undercover operations. As the District Court's opinion sets out in painstaking detail, the Abscam actors did a good deal more than simply "spread the word." Nor can we agree with Judge Mac-Kinnon that the FBI "had ample suspicion of corruption to justify pursuing * * * Kelly." That suspicion, as Judge MacKinnon recites, was based on Ciuzio's report to Amoroso and

Weinberg that "Kelly was, in fact, corrupt." But as the District Court observed:

"Ciuzio went to great lengths to make it appear that he had virtual control over the Congressman, indicating at the time that Kelly was dishonest and was already taking money and had various other weaknesses. He indicated that he had known and cultivated Kelly for about 2 1/2 years. None of this was true. No attempt was made to verify it; and there is no indication that Weinberg and Amoroso believed it."

[The] District Court stated and attempted to apply an objective test to determine when government investigation exceeds tolerable limits: Was the crime-inducing conduct in which the government engaged, the temptation presented to the target, modeled on reality? This test, the District Court indicated, should apply when the government had no knowledge of prior wrongdoing by the target and no reason to believe the target was about to commit a crime; it would serve as a check against government creation (rather than apprehension) of criminals by offers or importuning that would never occur in the real world.

The real-world test, as applied by the District Court, is speculative. The District Judge assumed that a person who offers a bribe would retreat upon encountering an initial rejection and would not "have the audacity" to press on "for fear of being reported." But the first overture renders the party offering the bribe vulnerable to prosecution. "In for a calf," such a person might press on if he perceives any chance of ultimate success.[9] Nonetheless, were the slate clean, we might be attracted to an approach similar to the District Court's, and would perhaps ask whether, in real-world circumstances, the person snared would ever encounter bait as alluring as the offer the government tendered.

However, our slate contains references that lower courts are not positioned to erase. We may not alter the contours of the entrapment defense under a due process cloak,[11] and we lack authority, where no *specific* constitutional right of the defendant has been violated, to dismiss indictments as an exercise of supervisory power over the conduct of federal law enforcement agents. *See United States v. Payner* [p. 52]. Precedent dictates that we refrain from applying the general due process constraint to bar a conviction except in the rare instance of "[p]olice overinvolvement in crime" that reaches "a demonstrable level of outrageousness." *Hampton* (Powell, J., concurring) * * *; *Russell*. The requisite level of outrageousness, the Supreme Court has indicated, is not established [unless there is] "coercion, violence or brutality to the person."[c]

The importuning of Congressman Kelly and the offers made to him, extraordinary and in excess of real-world opportunities as they appear to have been, did not involve the infliction of pain or physical or psychological coercion. We are therefore constrained to reverse, although we share the District Court's grave concern that the Abscam drama, both in its general tenor, and in "the [particular] manner in which Kelly was handled," unfolded as "an unwholesome spectacle."

Notes and Questions

1. *The "reasonable suspicion" requirement.* A number of commentators have maintained that the government should not be permitted to solicit an offense absent "probable cause" or at least "reasonable suspicion" that the target is engaged in criminal activity, but current lower federal court authority "overwhelmingly holds that no 'reasonable cause' requirement exits." Note, 67 Geo.L.J. 1455, 1467 (1979). Moreover, "*Russell* seems to have sapped [this theory] of any remaining vitality by indicating that the entrapment defense is intended to protect nondisposed defendants rather than to control police conduct." Roger Park, *The Entrapment Controversy,* 60 Minn.L.Rev. 163, 197 (1976).[a]

9. As the government points out, parties to real-world transactions could readily adjust to a one-refusal rule: the bribe taker would always resist the first overture.

11. See *Twigg* (Adams, J., dissenting).

c. See Note 3, p. 416.

a. It should be noted, however, that in *United States v. Luttrell,* 889 F.2d 806 (9th Cir.1989), a panel opinion by Judge Dorothy Nelson of the Ninth Circuit took the position that government agents violate due process when, lacking "reasoned grounds" for believing their targets are involved in crime, they

Operation Abscam, however, has prompted renewed interest in this issue, for there a convicted swindler and other "middlemen," themselves under investigation, decided which politicians would be offered bribes. Congressman Don Edwards, a former FBI agent, voiced concern about "free-floating surveyors, middlemen, who work with the FBI and are the ones who finger people," and his colleague, Representative John Seiberling, balked at "the idea of giving some people of dubious ethical standards free rein to entice anyone they can entice to commit a crime." See N.Y. Times, Feb. 17, 1980, pp. 1, 20. Indeed, Professor Paul Chevigny maintains that "Abscam shows [that the] central evil of entrapment is discriminatory law enforcement, whether the police zero in on a 'politician' or a 'drug dealer.'" *A Rejoinder*, The Nation, Feb. 23, 1980, p. 205 [b]. Consider, too, Bennett Gershman, *Abscam, the Judiciary, and the Ethics of Entrapment*, 91 Yale L.J. 1565, 1584–85 (1982), who emphasizes that, although Operation Abscam intruded on people's privacy and autonomy to a much greater degree than the typical search and seizure, the operation was not restricted by procedural safeguards such as the requirement of a warrant: "Government agents secretly monitored the Abscam defendants for many months, recorded their intimate conversations and surreptitiously videotaped meetings they attended. No judge authorized such procedures; indeed it is unlikely that any judge would have authorized this type of surveillance absent prior suspicion."

Professor Gershman proposes a federal entrapment statute that, inter alia, requires government agents to offer inducements "only to individuals currently engaged in, or reasonably suspected of engaging in, criminal activity." Id. at 1588. Such a requirement would allow courts "to dispense with the predisposition inquiry and to use instead the concept of 'reasonable suspicion' to test whether an individual is 'nondisposed.'" Id.

2. *Are official corruption investigations different?* Katherine Goldwasser, *After Abscam: An Examination of Congressional Proposals to Limit Targeting Discretion in Federal Undercover Investigations*, 36 Emory L.J. 75, 124–25 (1987); balks at imposing a probable cause or reasonable suspicion requirement for undercover targeting: "[D]eterrence is not the only societal benefit to be derived from targeting [public officials] without a factual basis. Such targeting—integrity testing—usually provides no other societal benefit because the integrity of most potential undercover targets is not particularly important to society. But integrity testing of public officials is different. Public officials routinely are confronted with tests of their corruptibility because of the official power they wield. Those who 'fail' cause considerable harm to society. In short, [the] testing of public officials does serve significant societal ends. [Such testing] without a factual basis would provide a strong deterrent against corruption, but would pose little risk to the personal privacy of public officials and would generate no generalized atmosphere of suspicion and mistrust throughout society."

3. *When is a private person a "government agent" for entrapment purposes? The use of "unwitting agents."* Defending Operation Abscam, then Assistant Attorney General Phillip Heymann emphasized: "No one associated with the United States ever picked any politician for the investigation. The middlemen did all that." N.Y. Times, Mar. 5, 1980 p. 18. But this raises another problem. Many

approach them and provide them with a specific opportunity to engage in criminal conduct. But the Ninth Circuit, sitting en banc, vacated the portion of the panel opinion discussing a "reasoned grounds" or "reasonable suspicion" requirement, noting that a number of other circuits had explicitly rejected such a requirement. See 923 F.2d 764 (9th Cir.1991).

b. But compare the views of Chevigny's colleague, Professor Stephen Gillers, *In Defense of Abscam: Entrapment, Where is Thy Sting?*, The Nation, Feb. 23, 1980, p. 203.

of the people involved in Abscam were "unsuspecting middlemen," i.e., private persons who were unaware that they were working with, or for, government agents. But because entrapment is ultimately concerned with government conduct, it offers no defense to those who succumb to the inducements of private individuals acting alone. For entrapment purposes, should "unsuspecting middlemen," such as those utilized in Abscam, be regarded as agents of the government, albeit "unwitting agents"?

When government agents have persuaded a "middleman" to induce *a particular target selected by the agents* to commit a crime, the courts generally extend the entrapment defense to the ultimate targets. See, e.g., *People v. McIntire*, 591 P.2d 527 (Cal.1979), where a narcotics agent, posing as a high school student, importuned a classmate, the brother of the defendant, to obtain marijuana from his sister. Rejecting the prosecution's argument that entrapment cannot be effected through an "unwitting agent" (in this case, the defendant's brother), the court, per Mosk, J., observed: "The purposes of the entrapment defense can be fulfilled only if it is understood that one can act as a [government agent] without realizing the identity of his principal; the unwitting agent, though he may not appreciate the true nature of his role, is nonetheless being manipulated as the officer's tool in a plan to foster a crime and entrap its perpetrator."

However, when investigations are not aimed at a specific target, even though there is "substantial certainty that the person solicited by the police for the commission of a crime will seek the participation of another," such as when the agent requests the middleman to seek unidentified public officials who will accept bribes, the federal courts have "sharply disagreed" on how to apply the law of entrapment. See Note, 95 Harv.L.Rev. 1122, 1126–27 (1982). "Whenever it is reasonable to expect that the investigation will result in a secondary target's committing an offense," maintains the Harvard Note, "whether the secondary target was selected by [a government agent] or [the unsuspecting middleman], the additional offense must be considered 'the creature of [the agent's] purpose' unless the government can prove that the defendant was predisposed to commit a similar crime." Id. at 1128.

Moreover, "even when the government has no reason to expect that [the initial target] of an investigation will induce a nonessential [third party] to join in criminal activity, the third party should still be able to plead entrapment if it is found that the initial target was himself entrapped. If the original target was entrapped, the government has by definition created the actions that the initial target took in pursuing the illegal activity." Id. at 1129.

SECTION 3. CONTINUING CONTROVERSY OVER THE ENTRAPMENT DEFENSE

JACOBSON v. UNITED STATES
503 U.S. 540, 112 S.Ct. 1535, 118 L.Ed.2d 174 (1992).

Justice WHITE delivered the opinion of the Court.

On September 24, 1987, [petitioner] was indicted for violating a provision of the Child Protection Act of 1984, which criminalizes the knowing receipt through the mails of a "visual depiction [that] involves the use of a minor engaging in sexually explicit conduct...." Petitioner defended on the ground that the Government entrapped him into committing the crime through a series of communications from undercover agents that spanned the 26 months preceding his arrest.

[He was found guilty after a jury trial. The Eighth Circuit, sitting en banc, affirmed, concluding that "Jacobson was not entrapped as a matter of law."]

Because the Government overstepped the line between setting a trap for the "unwary innocent" and the "unwary criminal," and as a matter of law failed to establish that petitioner was independently predisposed to commit the crime for which he was arrested, we reverse * * *.

[In] February 1984, petitioner, a 56–year-old veteran-turned-farmer who supported his elderly father in Nebraska, ordered two magazines and a brochure from a California adult bookstore. The magazines, entitled *Bare Boys I* and *Bare Boys II*, contained photographs of nude preteen and teenage boys. The contents of the magazines startled petitioner, who testified that he had expected to receive photographs of "young men 18 years or older." [The] young men depicted in the magazines were not engaged in sexual activity, and petitioner's receipt of the magazines was legal under both federal and Nebraska law. Within three months, the law with respect to child pornography changed; Congress passed the Act illegalizing the receipt through the mails of sexually explicit depictions of children. In the very month that the new provision became law, postal inspectors found petitioner's name on the mailing list of the California bookstore that had mailed him *Bare Boys I* and *II*. There followed over the next 2½ years, repeated efforts by two Government agencies, through five fictitious organizations and a bogus pen pal, to explore petitioner's willingness to break the new law by ordering sexually explicit photographs of children through the mail.

The Government began its efforts in January 1985 when a postal inspector sent petitioner a letter supposedly from the American Hedonist Society, which in fact was a fictitious organization. The letter included a membership application and stated the Society's doctrine: that members had the "right to read what we desire, the right to discuss similar interests with those who share our philosophy, and finally that we have the right to seek pleasure without restrictions being placed on us by outdated puritan morality." Petitioner enrolled in the organization and returned a sexual attitude questionnaire that asked him to rank on a scale of one to four his enjoyment of various sexual materials, with one being "really enjoy," two being "enjoy," three being "somewhat enjoy," and four being "do not enjoy." Petitioner ranked the entry "[p]re-teen sex" as a two, but indicated that he was opposed to pedophilia.

For a time, the Government left petitioner alone. But then a new "prohibited mail specialist" in the Postal Service found petitioner's name in a file and in May 1986 petitioner received a solicitation from a second fictitious consumer research company, "Midlands Data Research," seeking a response from those who "believe in the joys of sex and the complete awareness of those lusty and youthful lads and lasses of the neophite *[sic]* age." The letter never explained whether "neophite" referred to minors or young adults. Petitioner responded: "Please feel free to send me more information, I am interested in teenage sexuality. Please keep my name confidential."

Petitioner then heard from yet another Government creation, "Heartland Institute for a New Tomorrow" (HINT), which proclaimed that it was "an organization founded to protect and promote sexual freedom and freedom of choice. We believe that arbitrarily imposed legislative sanctions restricting your sexual freedom should be rescinded through the legislative process." The letter also enclosed a second survey. Petitioner indicated that his interest in "[p]reteen sex-homosexual" material was above average, but not high. In response to another question, petitioner wrote: "Not only sexual expression but freedom of the press is under attack. We must be ever vigilant to counter attack right wing fundamentalists who are determined to curtail our freedoms."

"HINT" replied, portraying itself as a lobbying organization seeking to repeal "all statutes which regulate sexual activities, except those laws which deal with violent behavior, such as rape. HINT is also lobbying to eliminate any legal definition of 'the age of consent'." These lobbying efforts were to be funded by sales from a catalog to be published in the future "offering the sale of various items which we believe you will find to be both interesting and stimulating." HINT also provided computer matching of group members with similar survey responses; and, although petitioner was supplied with a list of potential "pen pals," he did not initiate any correspondence.

Nevertheless, the Government's "prohibited mail specialist" began writing to petitioner, using the pseudonym "Carl Long." The letters employed a tactic known as "mirroring," which the inspector described as "reflect[ing] whatever the interests are of the person we are writing to." Petitioner responded at first, indicating that his interest was primarily in "male-male items." Inspector "Long" wrote back:

"My interests too are primarily male-male items. Are you satisfied with the type of VCR tapes available? Personally, I like the amateur stuff better if its [sic] well produced as it can get more kinky and also seems more real. I think the actors enjoy it more."

Petitioner responded:

"As far as my likes are concerned, I like good looking young guys (in their late teens and early 20's) doing their thing together."

Petitioner's letters to "Long" made no reference to child pornography. After writing two letters, petitioner discontinued the correspondence.

By March 1987, 34 months had passed since the Government obtained petitioner's name from the mailing list of the California bookstore, and 26 months had passed since the Postal Service had commenced its mailings to petitioner. Although petitioner had responded to surveys and letters, the Government had no evidence that petitioner had ever intentionally possessed or been exposed to child pornography. The Postal Service had not checked petitioner's mail to determine whether he was receiving questionable mailings from persons—other than the Government—involved in the child pornography industry.

At this point, a second Government agency, the Customs Service, included petitioner in its own child pornography sting, "Operation Borderline," after receiving his name on lists submitted by the Postal Service. Using the name of a fictitious Canadian company called "Produit Outaouais," the Customs Service mailed petitioner a brochure advertising photographs of young boys engaging in sex. Petitioner placed an order that was never filled.

The Postal Service also continued its efforts in the Jacobson case, writing to petitioner as the "Far Eastern Trading Company Ltd." The letter began:

"As many of you know, much hysterical nonsense has appeared in the American media concerning 'pornography' and what must be done to stop it from coming across your borders. This brief letter does not allow us to give much comments; however, why is your government spending millions of dollars to exercise international censorship while tons of drugs, which makes yours the world's most crime ridden country are passed through easily."

The letter went on to say:

"[W]e have devised a method of getting these to you without prying eyes of U.S. Customs seizing your mail. . . . After consultations with American solicitors, we have been advised that once we have posted our material through your system, it cannot be opened for any inspection without authorization of a judge."

The letter invited petitioner to send for more information. [He] responded. A catalogue was sent and petitioner ordered *Boys Who Love Boys,* a pornographic magazine depicting young boys engaged in various sexual activities. Petitioner was arrested after a controlled delivery of a photocopy of the magazine.

When petitioner was asked at trial why he placed such an order, he explained that the Government had succeeded in piquing his curiosity:

"Well, the statement was made of all the trouble and the hysteria over pornography and I wanted to see what the material was. * * * I didn't know for sure what kind of sexual action they were referring to in the Canadian letter. . . ."

In petitioner's home, the Government found the *Bare Boys* magazines and materials that the Government had sent to him in the course of its protracted investigation, but no other materials that would indicate that petitioner collected or was actively interested in child pornography. * * *

The trial court instructed the jury on [the] entrapment defense,[1] petitioner was convicted, and [the] Eighth Circuit affirmed * * *.

[In] their zeal to enforce the law [the Government] may not originate a criminal design, implant in an innocent person's mind the disposition to commit a criminal act, and then induce commission of the crime so that the Government may prosecute. Where the Government has induced an individual to break the law and the defense of entrapment is at issue, as it was in this case, the prosecution must prove beyond reasonable doubt that the defendant was disposed to commit the criminal act prior to first being approached by Government agents.[2]

---

1. The jury was instructed:

"As mentioned, one of the issues in this case is whether the defendant was entrapped. If the defendant was entrapped he must be found not guilty. The government has the burden of proving beyond a reasonable doubt that the defendant was not entrapped.

"If the defendant before contact with law-enforcement officers or their agents did not have any intent or disposition to commit the crime charged and was induced or persuaded by law-enforcement officers o[r] their agents to commit that crime, then he was entrapped. On the other hand, if the defendant before contact with law-enforcement officers or their agents did have an intent or disposition to commit the crime charged, then he was not entrapped even though law-enforcement officers or their agents provided a favorable opportunity to commit the crime or made committing the crime easier or even participated in acts essential to the crime."

2. Inducement is not at issue in this case. The Government does not dispute that it induced petitioner to commit the crime. The sole issue is whether the Government carried its burden of proving that petitioner was predis-

posed to violate the law *before* the Government intervened. The dissent is mistaken in claiming that this is an innovation in entrapment law and in suggesting that the Government's conduct prior to the moment of solicitation is irrelevant. * * * Indeed, the proposition that the accused must be predisposed prior to contact with law enforcement officers is so firmly established that the Government conceded the point at oral argument, submitting that the evidence it developed during the course of its investigation was probative because it indicated petitioner's state of mind *prior* to the commencement of the Government's investigation.

This long-established standard in no way encroaches upon Government investigatory activities. Indeed, the Government's internal guidelines for undercover operations provide that an inducement to commit a crime should not be offered unless:

"(a) there is a reasonable indication, based on information developed through informants or other means, that the subject is engaging, has engaged, or is likely to engage in illegal activity of a similar type; *or*

"(b) The opportunity for illegal activity has been structured so that there is reason for

Thus, an agent deployed to stop the traffic in illegal drugs may offer the opportunity to buy or sell drugs, and, if the offer is accepted, make an arrest on the spot or later. In such a typical case, or in a more elaborate "sting" operation involving government-sponsored fencing where the defendant is simply provided with the opportunity to commit a crime, the entrapment defense is of little use because the ready commission of the criminal act amply demonstrates the defendant's predisposition. Had the agents in this case simply offered petitioner the opportunity to order child pornography through the mails, and petitioner—who must be presumed to know the law—had promptly availed himself of this criminal opportunity, it is unlikely that his entrapment defense would have warranted a jury instruction.

But that is not what happened here. By the time petitioner finally placed his order, he had already been the target of 26 months of repeated mailings and communications from Government agents and fictitious organizations. Therefore, although he had become predisposed to break the law by May 1987, it is our view that the Government did not prove that this predisposition was independent and not the product of the attention that the Government had directed at petitioner since January 1985.

The prosecution's evidence of predisposition falls into two categories: evidence developed prior to the Postal Service's mail campaign, and that developed during the course of the investigation. The sole piece of preinvestigation evidence is petitioner's 1984 order and receipt of the Bare Boys magazines. But this is scant if any proof of petitioner's predisposition to commit an illegal act, the criminal character of which a defendant is presumed to know. It may indicate a predisposition to view sexually-oriented photographs that are responsive to his sexual tastes; but evidence that merely indicates a generic inclination to act within a broad range, not all of which is criminal, is of little probative value in establishing predisposition.

Furthermore, petitioner was acting within the law at the time he received these magazines. * * * Evidence of predisposition to do what once was lawful is not, by itself, sufficient to show predisposition to do what is now illegal, for there is a common understanding that most people obey the law even when they disapprove of it. [Hence,] the fact that petitioner legally ordered and received the *Bare Boys* magazines does little to further the Government's burden of proving that petitioner was predisposed to commit a criminal act. This is particularly true given petitioner's unchallenged testimony was that he did not know until they arrived that the magazines would depict minors.

The prosecution's evidence gathered during the investigation also fails to carry the Government's burden. Petitioner's responses to the many communications prior to the ultimate criminal act were at most indicative of certain personal inclinations, including a predisposition to view photographs of preteen sex and a willingness to promote a given agenda by supporting lobbying organizations. Even so, petitioner's responses hardly support an inference that he would commit the crime of receiving child pornography through the mails.[3]

believing that persons drawn to the opportunity, or brought to it, are predisposed to engage in the contemplated illegal activity." *Attorney General's Guidelines on FBI Undercover Operations* (Dec. 31, 1980).

3. We do not hold, as the dissent suggests, that the Government was required to prove that petitioner knowingly violated the law. We simply conclude that proof that petitioner engaged in legal conduct and possessed certain generalized personal inclinations is not sufficient evidence to prove beyond a reasonable doubt that he would have been predisposed to commit the crime charged independent of the Government's coaxing.

[On] the other hand, the strong arguable inference is that, by waving the banner of individual rights and disparaging the legitimacy and constitutionality of efforts to restrict the availability of sexually explicit materials, the Government not only excited petitioner's interest in sexually explicit materials banned by law but also exerted substantial pressure on petitioner to obtain and read such material as part of a fight against censorship and the infringement of individual rights. * * *

Petitioner's ready response to these solicitations cannot be enough to establish beyond reasonable doubt that he was predisposed, prior to the Government acts intended to create predisposition, to commit the crime of receiving child pornography through the mails. The evidence that petitioner was ready and willing to commit the offense came only after the Government had devoted 2½ years to convincing him that he had or should have the right to engage in the very behavior proscribed by law. Rational jurors could not say beyond a reasonable doubt that petitioner possessed the requisite predisposition prior to the Government's investigation and that it existed independent of the Government's many and varied approaches to petitioner. As was explained in *Sherman,* where entrapment was found as a matter of law, "the Government [may not] pla[y] on the weaknesses of an innocent party and beguil[e] him into committing crimes which he otherwise would not have attempted."

Law enforcement officials go too far when they "implant in the mind of an innocent person the *disposition* to commit the alleged offense and induce its commission in order that they may prosecute." *Sorrells* (emphasis added). [When] the Government's quest for convictions leads to the apprehension of an otherwise law-abiding citizen who, if left to his own devices, likely would have never run afoul of the law, the courts should intervene. * * *

Justice O'CONNOR, with whom The Chief Justice and Justice KENNEDY join, and with whom Justice SCALIA joins except as to Part II, dissenting.

Keith Jacobson was offered only two opportunities to buy child pornography through the mail. Both times, he ordered. Both times, he asked for opportunities to buy more. He needed no Government agent to coax, threaten, or persuade him; no one played on his sympathies, friendship, or suggested that his committing the crime would further a greater good. In fact, no Government agent even contacted him face-to-face. The Government contends that from the enthusiasm with which Mr. Jacobson responded to the chance to commit a crime, a reasonable jury could permissibly infer beyond a reasonable doubt that he was predisposed to commit the crime. I agree.

[The] first time the Government sent Mr. Jacobson a catalog of illegal materials, he ordered a set of photographs advertised as picturing "young boys in sex action fun." He enclosed the following note with his order: "I received your brochure and decided to place an order. If I like your product, I will order more later." For reasons undisclosed in the record, Mr. Jacobson's order was never delivered.

The second time the Government sent a catalog of illegal materials, Mr. Jacobson ordered a magazine called "Boys Who Love Boys," described as: "11 year old and 14 year old boys get it on in every way possible. Oral, anal sex and heavy masturbation. If you love boys, you will be delighted with this." Along with his order, Mr. Jacobson sent the following note: "Will order other items later. I want to be discreet in order to protect you and me."

Government agents admittedly did not offer Mr. Jacobson the chance to buy child pornography right away. Instead, they first sent questionnaires in order to make sure that he was generally interested in the subject matter. Indeed, a "cold call" in such a business would not only risk rebuff and suspicion, but might also shock and offend the uninitiated, or expose minors to suggestive materials. Mr. Jacobson's responses to the questionnaires gave the investigators reason to think he would be interested in photographs depicting preteen sex.

The Court, however, concludes that a reasonable jury could not have found Mr. Jacobson to be predisposed beyond a reasonable doubt on the basis of his responses to the Government's catalogs, even though it admits that, by that time, he was predisposed to commit the crime. The Government, the Court holds, failed to provide evidence that Mr. Jacobson's obvious predisposition at the time of the crime "was independent and not the product of the attention that the Government had directed at petitioner." In so holding, I believe the Court fails to acknowledge the reasonableness of the jury's inference from the evidence, redefines "predisposition," and introduces a new requirement that Government sting operations have a reasonable suspicion of illegal activity before contacting a suspect.

This Court has held previously that a defendant's predisposition is to be assessed as of the time the Government agent first suggested the crime, not when the Government agent first became involved. * * * [Even] in *Sherman,* [where entrapment was found] as a matter of law, the Government agent had repeatedly and unsuccessfully coaxed the defendant to buy drugs, ultimately succeeding only by playing on the defendant's sympathy. The Court found lack of predisposition based on the Government's numerous unsuccessful attempts to induce the crime, not on the basis of preliminary contacts with the defendant.

Today, the Court holds that Government conduct may be considered to create a predisposition to commit a crime, even before any Government action to induce the commission of the crime. In my view, this holding changes entrapment doctrine. Generally, the inquiry is whether a suspect is predisposed before the Government induces the commission of the crime, not before the Government makes initial contact with him. There is no dispute here that the Government's questionnaires and letters were not sufficient to establish inducement; they did not even suggest that Mr. Jacobson should engage in any illegal activity. If all the Government had done was to send these materials, Mr. Jacobson's entrapment defense would fail. Yet the Court holds that the Government must prove not only that a suspect was predisposed to commit the crime before the opportunity to commit it arose, but also before the Government came on the scene.

The rule that preliminary Government contact can create a predisposition has the potential to be misread by lower courts as well as criminal investigators as requiring that the Government must have sufficient evidence of a defendant's predisposition *before it ever seeks to contact him.* Surely the Court cannot intend to impose such a requirement, for it would mean that the Government must have a reasonable suspicion of criminal activity before it begins an investigation, a condition that we have never before imposed. The Court denies that its new rule will affect run-of-the-mill sting operations and one hopes that it means what it says. Nonetheless, after this case, every defendant will claim that something the Government agent did before soliciting the crime "created" a predisposition that was not there before. For example, a bribe taker will claim that the description of the amount of money available was so enticing that it implanted a disposition to accept the bribe later offered. A drug buyer will claim that the description of the drug's purity and effects was so tempting that it created the urge to try it for the first time. In short, the Court's opinion could be read to prohibit the Government from advertising the seductions of criminal activity as part of its sting operation, for fear of creating a predisposition in its suspects. That limitation would be especially likely to hamper sting operations such as this one, which mimic the advertising done by genuine purveyors of pornography. No doubt the Court would protest that its opinion does not stand for so broad a proposition, but the apparent lack of a principled basis for distinguishing these scenarios exposes a flaw in the more limited rule the Court today adopts.

The Court's rule is all the more troubling because it does not distinguish between Government conduct that merely highlights the temptation of the crime itself, and Government conduct that threatens, coerces, or leads a suspect to commit a crime in order to fulfill some other obligation. For example, in *Sorrells,* the Government agent repeatedly asked for illegal liquor, coaxing the defendant to accede on the ground that "one former war buddy would get liquor for another." In *Sherman,* the Government agent played on the defendant's sympathies, pretending to be going through drug withdrawal and begging the defendant to relieve his distress by helping him buy drugs.

The Government conduct in this case is not comparable. While the Court states that the Government "exerted substantial pressure on petitioner to obtain and read such material as part of a fight against censorship and the infringement of individual rights," one looks at the record in vain for evidence of such "substantial pressure." The most one finds is letters advocating legislative action to liberalize obscenity laws, letters which could easily be ignored or thrown away. * * * Nowhere did the Government suggest that the proceeds of the sale of the illegal materials would be used to support legislative reforms. * * * Mr. Jacobson's curiosity to see what " 'all the trouble and the hysteria' " was about is certainly susceptible of more than one interpretation. And it is the jury that is charged with the obligation of interpreting it. In sum, the Court fails to construe the evidence in the light most favorable to the Government, and fails to draw all reasonable inferences in the Government's favor. It was surely reasonable for the jury to infer that Mr. Jacobson was predisposed beyond a reasonable doubt, even if other inferences from the evidence were also possible.

The second puzzling thing about the Court's opinion is its redefinition of predisposition. The Court acknowledges that "[p]etitioner's responses to the many communications prior to the ultimate criminal act [were] indicative of certain personal inclinations, including a predisposition to view photographs of preteen sex...." If true, this should have settled the matter; Mr. Jacobson was predisposed to engage in the illegal conduct. Yet, the Court concludes, "petitioner's responses hardly support an inference that he would commit the crime of receiving child pornography through the mails."

The Court seems to add something new to the burden of proving predisposition. Not only must the Government show that a defendant was predisposed to engage in the illegal conduct, here, receiving photographs of minors engaged in sex, but also that the defendant was predisposed to break the law knowingly in order to do so. The statute violated here, however, does not require proof of specific intent to break the law; it requires only knowing receipt of visual depictions produced by using minors engaged in sexually explicit conduct. Under the Court's analysis, however, the Government must prove *more* to show predisposition than it need prove in order to convict.

[The] crux of the Court's concern in this case is that the Government went too far and "abused" the "processes of detection and enforcement" by luring an innocent person to violate the law. Consequently, the Court holds that the Government failed to prove beyond a reasonable doubt that Mr. Jacobson was predisposed to commit the crime. It was, however, the jury's task, as the conscience of the community, to decide whether or not Mr. Jacobson was a willing participant in the criminal activity here or an innocent dupe. [There] is no dispute that the jury in this case was fully and accurately instructed on the law of entrapment, and nonetheless found Mr. Jacobson guilty. Because I believe there was sufficient evidence to uphold the jury's verdict, I respectfully dissent.

Notes and Questions

1. *Unproductive use of law enforcement resources.* Consider Note, 61 U.Cin.L.Rev. 1067, 1090–91 (1993): "To allow law enforcement officials to go on 'fishing expeditions' based on only the most generalized suspicion is to allow a tremendous waste of resources and to risk the targeting of unpopular groups, such as gay men. Judge Posner has indicated that entrapment is, at its most basic, a label given to the unproductive use of law enforcement resources. [*United States v. Kaminski,* 703 F.2d 1004, 1010 (7th Cir.1983) (concurring opinion.)][a] [The] *Jacobson* case exemplifies this inefficient use of law enforcement resources, in that an individual with no apparent history of dealing in child pornography became the focus of an investigation lasting two and one-half years, culminating in his arrest and conviction for receiving a single magazine that was supplied by the government. The government's stated purpose in investigations of this sort is to eliminate child pornography, yet the only child pornography present in this case was that manufactured and distributed by the government."

Should second-guessing the government's use of its law enforcement resources be the business of the courts? See Adams, J., dissenting in *United States v. Twigg,* 588 F.2d 373 (3d Cir.1978). If government investigators squander their limited resources, should this be regarded as a political problem to be addressed by oversight hearings? See Easterbrook, J., concurring in *United States v. Miller,* 891 F.2d 1265, 1271–72 (7th Cir.1989).[b]

2. *"Reasonable suspicion" that the target was predisposed to commit the crime.* Is *Jacobson* likely, as Justice O'Connor suggests, to be interpreted by lower courts and criminal investigators "as requiring that the Government must have sufficient evidence of a defendant's predisposition *before it ever seeks to contact him*"? The majority observes that when Jacobson was arrested the government found no evidence—aside from the *Bare Boys* magazines and the material the government had sent him—indicating that he "collected or was actively interested in child pornography." Suppose government agents *had* found other material establishing that Jacobson collected child pornography *even though they were unaware* that such evidence existed before they arrested him? Wouldn't the prosecution have been able to defeat Jacobson's entrapment claim by establishing that his predisposition was independent and not the product of the government's many and varied approaches to him?

Note, too, the majority points out that if, absent any prior dealings between the government and Jacobson, federal agents had simply offered him the opportunity to order child pornography through the mails and he had promptly agreed, Jacobson's entrapment defense would have failed. For in such a case "the ready

---

a. For an extract from Judge Posner's opinion see p. 400.

b. For an extract from Judge Easterbrook's opinion see p. 400.

commission of the criminal act amply demonstrates the defendant's predisposition." But wouldn't this be so *regardless* of whether government agents had any indication of Jacobson's predisposition before they offered him the opportunity to obtain child pornography?

3. *What must the government prove before it "comes on the scene"?* Does *Jacobson* hold, as the dissenters maintain, that "the Government must prove not only that a suspect was predisposed to commit the crime before the opportunity to [do so] arose, but also before the Government came on the scene"?

If an undercover agent gradually became a close friend of a target but never brought up the subject of drugs in the first ten months of their acquaintanceship (during which time the agent simply socialized with, and gained the confidence of, the target), would it matter whether there was any evidence that the target was predisposed to commit a drug offense when the government agent initiated contact with the target or first "came on the scene"? Is *Jacobson* a different case because when a fictitious organization first sent Jacobson a mailing, the government had not *merely* initiated contact with him or arrived on the scene but (as far as a majority of the Court was concerned) had begun "working on" Jacobson?

4. *Did the Jacobson Court blend the "subjective" and "objective" entrapment tests?* As noted by Michael L. Piccarreta & Jefferson Keenan, *Entrapment Targets and Tactics: Jacobson v. United States*, 29 Crim.L.Bull. 241, 249 (1993), *Jacobson* "is the first Supreme Court opinion concerning entrapment in which none of the Justices even adverted to the 'objective' theory of entrapment." However, although the *Jacobson* majority purported to be applying the "subjective" test of entrapment, it also seemed quite offended by the tactics used by the government to induce Jacobson to order pornographic material. As the majority described it, some of the literature sent to Jacobson by the fictitious organizations created by the government disparaged the legitimacy of efforts to restrict the availability of sexually explicit material and came close to *challenging* Jacobson to assert his right to obtain and read such material. Does this feature of the case fit more easily within the framework of the "objective" test? Might it even constitute reprehensible or offensive conduct under that test?

But consider Note, 68 Wash.L.Rev. 185, 198–99 (1993): "Although the fictitious organizations did decry the criminalization of some forms of pornography, that very message signaled the illegality of the material. That Jacobson was aware that he was committing an unlawful act was not disputed. As the [Court's] opinion states, 'there is a common understanding that most people obey the law even when they disapprove of it.' If we analogize this fact pattern to a bribery sting, it is fantastic to suggest that a defendant could support an entrapment claim by avowing that the undercover agent avouched, 'Bribery is illegal—but it really shouldn't be.' "

5. *In "reverse sting" cases, should the objective and subjective approaches be combined?* Unlike the traditional "sting" (where undercover agents pose as buyers of illicit goods or services), in "reverse sting" cases, such as *Jacobson*, government agents act as sellers. According to Damon D. Camp, *Out of the Quagmire after Jacobson v. United States: Toward a More Balanced Entrapment Standard,* 83 J.Crim.L. & C. 1055, 1056 (1993), the subjective entrapment test works reasonably well in traditional sting cases. In such cases proclivity to engage in criminal conduct is difficult to deny because the defendant actually provides contraband to a government agent. In reverse stings, however, "the notion of predisposition becomes a significant issue, and the role of enforcement officers in securing cooperation becomes critical." In such cases, maintains Professor Camp, the key

question should be whether predisposition to commit the crime or the government's conduct was a more important influence on the defendant's participation in crime.

HOW ARE THE FEDERAL COURTS INTERPRETING *JACOBSON*?

In UNITED STATES v. GENDRON, 18 F.3d 955 (1st Cir.1994), in the course of holding that defendant was not entrapped into receiving child pornography, Chief Judge (now Supreme Court Justice) BREYER observed:

"As the Supreme Court has recently stated: 'When the Government's quest for conviction leads to the apprehension of an *otherwise law-abiding citizen* who, *if left to his own devices*, likely would never have been afoul of the law, the courts should intervene.' *Jacobson v. United States* (emphasis added). Since the Court has repeatedly expressed concern about *both* government 'abuse' of its enforcement powers (or the like) *and* the 'otherwise law-abiding citizen' (or the like), it is not surprising that the defense has two parts, one that focuses upon government 'inducement' and the other upon the defendant's 'predisposition.'

"[The Supreme Court] saw in the entrapment defense not so much a sanction used to control police conduct, but rather a protection of the ordinary law-abiding citizen against government overreaching. Consequently, it saw no need to permit a defendant to take advantage of that defense unless he himself was such a citizen. The upshot is that we must find out just who that 'innocent person' is. Who is the *'otherwise* law-abiding citizen' who would not 'otherwise' have committed the crime?

"[The] right way to ask the question, it seems to us, is to abstract from—to assume away—the present circumstances *insofar as they reveal government overreaching*. That is to say, we should ask how the defendant likely would have reacted to an *ordinary* opportunity to commit the crime. *See Jacobson*, n. 2. By using the word 'ordinary,' we mean an opportunity that lacked those special features of the government's conduct that made of it an 'inducement,' or an 'overreaching.' Was the defendant 'predisposed' to respond affirmatively to a *proper*, not to an *improper*, lure? * * *

"We turn now to *Jacobson* * * *. In three respects [government agents] did more than provide an ordinary opportunity to buy child pornography: First, the solicitations reflected a psychologically 'graduated' set of responses to Jacobson's own noncriminal responses, beginning with innocent lures and progressing to frank offers. [Second,] the government's soliciting letters sometimes depicted their senders as 'free speech' lobbying organizations and fighters for the 'right to read what we desire'; they asked Jacobson to 'fight against censorship and the infringement of individual rights.' Third, the government's effort to provide an 'opportunity' to buy child pornography stretched out over two and a half years. Taken together, one might find in these three sets of circumstances—the graduated response, the long time period, the appeal to a proper (free speech) motive—a substantial risk of inducing an ordinary law-abiding person to commit the crime. Indeed, the government conceded in *Jacobson*, that its methods amounted, for entrapment purposes, to an improper 'inducement.' Id. at n. 2.

"*Jacobson's* importance, however, concerns the 'predisposition' part of the entrapment defense. The Court held that the evidence, as a matter of law, required acquittal because a reasonable jury would have had to doubt Jacobson's predisposition. [The government] failed to show 'predisposition' (beyond a reasonable doubt). That means (as we understand it) that the government's evidence did not show how Jacobson would have acted had he been faced with an ordinary 'opportunity' to commit the crime rather than a special 'inducement.'

"[The evidence in this case,] taken together, reveals a defendant who met an initial opportunity to buy child pornography with enthusiasm, who responded to each further government initiative with a purchase order, and who, unlike Jacobson, showed no particular interest in an anti-censorship campaign. [This evidence] permits a jury to find (beyond a reasonable doubt) that Gendron would have responded affirmatively to the most ordinary of opportunities, and hence, was 'predisposed' to commit the crime. We therefore find the jury's entrapment decision lawful."

Compare UNITED STATES v. HOLLINGSWORTH, 27 F.3d 1196 (7th Cir. 1994) (en banc). In the course of holding that the defendants, Pickard (an orthodontist) and Hollingsworth (a farmer), had been entrapped as a matter of law into engaging in a money laundering scheme, a 6–5 majority, per POSNER, C.J., observed:

"[Had] the Court in *Jacobson* believed that the legal concept of predisposition is exhausted in the demonstrated willingness of the defendant to commit the crime without threats or promises by the government, then Jacobson was predisposed, in which event the Court's reversal of his conviction would be difficult to explain. The government did not offer Jacobson any inducements to buy pornographic magazines or threaten him with harm if he failed to buy them. It was not as if the government had had to badger Jacobson for 26 months in order to overcome his resistance to committing a crime. He *never* resisted.

"* * * [W]e are naturally reluctant to suppose that [*Jacobson*] is limited to the precise facts before the Court, or to ignore the Court's definition of entrapment, which concludes the analysis portion of the opinion and is not found in previous opinions, as 'the apprehension of an otherwise law-abiding citizen who, if left to his own devices, likely would have never run afoul of the law.' That was Jacobson. However impure his thoughts, he was law abiding. A farmer in Nebraska, his access to child pornography was limited. As far as the government was aware, over the period of more than two years in which it was playing cat and mouse with him, he did not receive any other solicitations to buy pornography. So, had he been 'left to his own devices,' in all likelihood he would 'have never run afoul of the law.' If the same can be said of [the defendants in this case,] Pickard and Hollingsworth, they too are entitled to be acquitted. * * *

"Recently the First Circuit, struggling as are we to understand the scope of *Jacobson*, suggested that all it stands for is that the government may not, in trying to induce the target of a sting to commit a crime, confront him with circumstances that are different from the ordinary or typical circumstances of a private inducement. *Gendron*. The [First Circuit] thought that the government's attempt to persuade Jacobson that he had a First Amendment right to consume child pornography had departed from typicality. We are not so sure. Just as the gun industry likes to wrap itself in the mantle of the Second Amendment, so the pornography industry likes to wrap itself in the mantle of the First Amendment. But however that may be, the government made no effort in *this* case to show that a real customer for money laundering would have responded to an advertisement to sell a Grenadan bank * * *.

"We put the following hypothetical case to the government's lawyer at the reargument. Suppose the government went to someone and asked him whether he would like to make money as a counterfeiter, and the reply was, 'Sure, but I don't know anything about counterfeiting.' Suppose the government then bought him a printer, paper, and ink, showed him how to make the counterfeit money, hired a staff for him, and got everything set up so that all he had to do was press a button to print the money; and then offered him $10,000 for some quantity of counterfeit bills. The government's lawyer acknowledged that the counterfeiter would have a strong case that he had been entrapped, even though he was perfectly willing to commit the crime once the government planted the suggestion and showed him how and the government neither threatened him nor offered him an overwhelming inducement.[a]

"We do not suggest that *Jacobson* adds a new element to the entrapment defense—'readiness' or 'ability' or 'dangerousness' on top of inducement and, most important, predisposition. Predisposition is not a purely mental state, the state of being willing to swallow the government's bait. It has positional as well as dispositional force. [The] defendant must be so situated by reason of previous training or experience or occupation or acquaintances that it is likely that if the government had not induced him to commit the crime some criminal would have done so; only then does a sting or other arranged crime take a dangerous person out of circulation. A public official is in a position to take bribes; a drug addict to deal drugs; a gun dealer to engage in illegal gun sales. For these and other traditional targets of stings all that must be shown to establish the predisposition and thus defeat the defense of entrapment is willingness to violate the law without extraordinary inducements; ability can be presumed. It is different when the defendant is not in a position without the government's help to become involved in illegal activity. * * *

"There is no evidence that before 'Hinch' began his campaign to inveigle them into a money-laundering scheme either Pickard or Hollingsworth had contemplated engaging in such behavior. [When] the opportunity to become *crooked* international financiers beckoned, they were willing enough, though less willing than Jacobson had been to violate the federal law against purchasing child pornography through the mails—Jacobson never evinced reluctance, even though he had received no financial inducements. Pickard and Hollingsworth had no prayer of becoming money launderers without the government's aid.

"[The] point is not that Pickard and Hollingsworth were *incapable* of engaging in the act of money laundering. Obviously they were capable of the act. [But] to get into the international money-laundering business you need underworld contacts, financial acumen or assets, access to foreign banks or bankers, or other assets. Pickard and Hollingsworth had none. [They] were objectively harmless.

"We do not wish to be understood as holding that lack of *present* means to commit a crime is alone enough to establish entrapment if the government supplies the means. [Suppose] that before Hinch chanced on the scene (for *Jacobson* makes clear [that] a predisposition *created* by the government cannot be used to defeat a defense of entrapment), Pickard had decided to smuggle arms to Cuba but didn't know where to buy a suitable boat. On a hunch, a government agent sidles up to Pickard and gives him the address of a boat dealer; and Pickard is arrested after taking possession of the boat and setting sail, and is charged with attempted smuggling. That would be a case in which the defendant had the idea for the crime all worked out and lacked merely the present means to commit it, and if the government had not supplied them someone else very well might have. It would be a case in which the government had merely furnished the opportunity to commit the crime to someone already predisposed to commit it. * * *

a. Did the government's lawyer concede too much?

"Our two would-be international financiers were at the end of their tether, making it highly unlikely that if Hinch had not providentially appeared someone else would have guided them into money laundering. No real criminal would do business with such tyros. Or so it appears * * *."[b]

Consider, too, UNITED STATES v. KNOX, 112 F.3d. 802 (5th Cir. 1997), which arose as follows: Defendant Brace was the pastor of a church that was heavily in debt. In an effort to raise $10 million to pay the church's creditors, Brace hired a financial advisor, who in turn contacted other people. At the same time, undercover federal agents were conducting a sting operation designed to catch money launderers. Brace's financial advisor and the advisor's contacts told the undercover agents that they knew of a minister who would be interested in laundering drug money. Finally, the undercover agents met with Brace himself and told him that he was being asked to launder money that came from the sale of cocaine. Brace replied that he had no trouble with that. The jury rejected the entrapment defense and convicted Brace of laundering drug proceeds. "Because the government failed to prove that the preacher was likely to engage in money laundering absent the government's conduct," the Fifth Circuit, per DeMOSS, J., held that Brace was entrapped "as a matter of law":

"The en banc Seventh Circuit recently wrestled with the meaning of *Jacobson* [in the *Hollingsworth* case]. Writing for the majority, Chief Judge Posner stated that in examining predisposition, we must ask ourselves what the defendant would have done had the government not been involved. To properly answer the question, we must look to more than the defendant's mental state; we must also consider the defendant's skills, background and contacts. * * *

"We recognize that the Seventh Circuit's reading of *Jacobson* has not been universally embraced. The Ninth Circuit has rejected the Seventh Circuit's positional predisposition requirement and the First Circuit has adopted a different test. In *Gendron*, then Chief Judge (now Justice) Breyer held that *Jacobson* stands for the proposition that in trying to induce the target of a sting to commit a crime, the government may not confront him with circumstances that are different from the ordinary circumstances a real criminal would use in inducing one to engage in wrongdoing. [Thus,] the Government must show that a defendant would have committed the crime when 'faced with an ordinary "opportunity" to commit the crime rather than a special "inducement." ' "

"Nonetheless, we are persuaded that the Seventh Circuit's Hollingsworth decision is correct. See Paul Marcus, *Presenting Back From the [Almost] Dead, the Entrapment Defense*, 47 Fla.L.Rev. 205, 233–34 (1995) (arguing *Hollingsworth* is proper approach to entrapment law). The Supreme Court instructs that in determining predisposition we are to ask what the defendant would have done absent government involvement. To give effect to that command, we must look not only to the defendant's mental state (his 'disposition'), but also to whether the defendant was able and likely, based on experience, training, and contacts, to actually commit the crime (his 'position').[c]

"[We] are called upon to determine whether the government proved beyond a reasonable doubt that Brace was predisposed to launder money. Following *Holl-*

---

b. In three separate dissents, Judges Coffey, Easterbrook and Ripple voiced strong disagreement with the majority's interpretation of *Jacobson*.

c. The court noted that "in this case the result would not differ under the First Circuit's *Gendron* test. The government failed to prove that real drug dealers would provide the same, or even similar, terms to a launderer as the undercover agents offered Brace. Thus, the government failed to offer any evidence that Brace would accept an 'ordinary opportunity' to launder money."

ingsworth, we look to Brace's position, as well as his mental disposition. [The] government failed to prove that Brace, absent government involvement, was in a position to launder money. Therefore, the evidence is insufficient to prove that Brace was predisposed to launder money.

"[When] we ask the question of what Brace would have done if he had never met the undercover agents, we cannot answer 'launder money for real drug dealers.' In all likelihood, Brace never would have laundered money * * *."

Chapter 8

POLICE INTERROGATION
AND CONFESSIONS

SECTION 1. SOME DIFFERENT PERSPECTIVES

FRED E. INBAU: POLICE INTERROGATION—
A PRACTICAL NECESSITY
52 J.Crim.L.C. & P.S. 16 (1961), reprinted in Police Power
and Individual Freedom 147 (Sowle ed. 1962).

One completely false assumption accounts for most of the legal restrictions on police interrogations. It is this, and the fallacy is certainly perpetuated to a very considerable extent by mystery writers, the movies, and TV: whenever a crime is committed, if the police will only look carefully at the crime scene they will almost always find some clue that will lead them to the offender and at the same time establish his guilt; and once the offender is located, he will readily confess or disclose his guilt by trying to shoot his way out of the trap. But this is pure fiction; in actuality the situation is quite different. As a matter of fact, the art of criminal investigation has not developed to a point where the search for and the examination of physical evidence will always, or even in most cases, reveal a clue to the identity of the perpetrator or provide the necessary proof of his guilt. In criminal investigations, even of the most efficient type, there are many, many instances where physical clues are entirely absent, and the only approach to a possible solution of the crime is the interrogation of the criminal suspect himself, as well as others who may possess significant information. Moreover, in most instances these interrogations, particularly of the suspect himself, must be conducted under conditions of privacy and for a reasonable period of time; and they frequently require the use of psychological tactics and techniques that could well be classified as "unethical," if we are to evaluate them in terms of ordinary, everyday social behavior.

To protect myself from being misunderstood, I want to make it unmistakably clear that I am not an advocate of the so-called "third degree," for I am unalterably opposed to the use of any interrogation tactic or technique that is apt to make an innocent person confess. I am opposed, therefore, to the use of force, threats, or promises of leniency—all of which might well induce *an innocent person* to confess; but I do approve of such psychological tactics and techniques as trickery and deceit that are not only helpful but frequently necessary in order to secure incriminating information from the guilty, or investigate leads from otherwise uncooperative witnesses or informants.

My position, then, is this, and it may be presented in the form of three separate points, each accompanied by case illustrations:

1. *Many criminal cases, even when investigated by the best qualified police departments, are capable of solution only by means of an admission or confession from the guilty individual or upon the basis of information obtained from the questioning of other criminal suspects.*

As to the validity of this statement, I suggest that consideration be given to the situation presented by cases such as these. A man is hit on the head while walking home late at night. He did not see his assailant, nor did anyone else. A careful and thorough search of the crime scene reveals no physical clues. Then take the case of a woman who is grabbed on the street at night and dragged into an alley and raped. Here, too, the assailant was unaccommodating enough to avoid leaving his hat or other means of identification at the crime scene; and there are no other physical clues. All the police have to work on is the description of the assailant given by the victim herself. She described him as about six feet tall, white, and wearing a dark suit. Or consider this case, an actual recent one in Illinois. Three women are vacationing in a wooded resort area. Their bodies were found dead alongside a foot trail, the result of physical violence, and no physical clues are present.

In cases of this kind—and they all typify the difficult investigation problem that the police frequently encounter—how else can they be solved, if at all, except by means of the interrogation of suspects or of others who may possess significant information?

There are times, too, when a police interrogation may result not only in the apprehension and conviction of the guilty, but also in the release of the innocent from well-warranted suspicion. Here is one such actual case within my own professional experience.

The dead body of a woman was found in her home. Her skull had been crushed, apparently with some blunt instrument. A careful police investigation of the premises did not reveal any clues to the identity of the killer. No fingerprints or other significant evidence were located; not even the lethal instrument itself could be found. None of the neighbors could give any helpful information. Although there was some evidence of a slight struggle in the room where the body lay, there were no indications of a forcible entry into the home. The deceased's young daughter was the only other resident of the home and she had been away in school at the time of the crime. The daughter could not give the police any idea of what, if any, money or property had disappeared from the home.

For several reasons the police considered the victim's husband a likely suspect. He was being sued for divorce; he knew his wife had planned on leaving the state and taking their daughter with her; and the neighbors reported that the couple had been having heated arguments, and that the husband was of a violent temper. He also lived conveniently near—in a garage adjoining the home. The police interrogated him and although his alibi was not conclusive his general behavior and the manner in which he answered the interrogator's questions satisfied the police of his innocence. Further investigation then revealed that the deceased's brother-in-law had been financially indebted to the deceased; that he was a frequent gambler; that at a number of social gatherings which he had attended money disappeared from some of the women's purses; that at his place of employment there had been a series of purse thefts; and that on the day of the killing he was absent from work. The police apprehended and questioned him. As the result of a few hours of competent interrogation—unattended by any abusive methods, but yet conducted during a period of delay in presenting the suspect before a committing magistrate as required by state statute—the suspect confessed to the murder. * * *

Without an opportunity for interrogation the police could not have solved this case. The perpetrator of the offense would have remained at liberty, perhaps to repeat his criminal conduct.

2. *Criminal offenders, except, of course, those caught in the commission of their crimes, ordinarily will not admit their guilt unless questioned under conditions of privacy, and for a period of perhaps several hours.*

* * * Self-condemnation and self-destruction not being normal behavior characteristics, human beings ordinarily do not utter unsolicited, spontaneous confessions. They must first be questioned regarding the offense. In some instances, a little bit of information inadvertently given to a competent interrogator by the suspect may suffice to start a line of investigation which might ultimately establish guilt. Upon other occasions, a full confession, with a revelation of details regarding a body, the loot, or the instruments used in the crime, may be required to prove the case. But whatever the possible consequences may be, it is impractical to expect any but a very few confessions to result from a guilty conscience unprovoked by an interrogation. It is also impractical to expect admissions or confessions to be obtained under circumstances other than privacy. Here again recourse to our everyday experience will support the basic validity of this requirement. For instance, in asking a personal friend to divulge a secret, or embarrassing information, we carefully avoid making the request in the presence of other persons, and seek a time and place when the matter can be discussed in private. The very same psychological factors are involved in a criminal interrogation, and even to a greater extent. For related psychological considerations, if an interrogation is to be had at all, it must be one based upon an unhurried interview, the necessary length of which will in many instances extend to several hours, depending upon various factors such as the nature of the case situation and the personality of the suspect. * * *

If the right to counsel arises only at the time of trial, or even when the judicial process begins, as at a preliminary hearing or at the time of indictment, the police have at least some opportunity for an interrogation. On the other hand, if the right is considered to exist immediately upon arrest, the interrogation opportunity, for all practical purposes, is gone—because of the prevailing concept that the role of defense counsel is to advise his client, "keep your mouth shut; don't say anything to anybody." * * *

In my judgment the right to counsel at the time of trial, or even at the very start of the judicial process, should be accorded *and provided* to all indigent defendants, insofar as practicable, regardless of whether the case involves a capital or non-capital offense, or even if it amounts only to a misdemeanor. What I do object to is an extension of the right to arrestees, indigent or non-indigent, prior to the start of the judicial process. It is not constitutionally required, and practical considerations will not tolerate such an extension, and particularly so if the extension is supplemented by a rule of court that would nullify, as a violation of due process, a confession obtained during a period of police detention before the start of the judicial process. Moreover, sometime in the near future we will have to come to grips with this interrogation problem and consider the passage of legislation, by all the states as well as the federal government, which will specifically provide for a reasonable period of police detention for the interrogation of suspects who are not otherwise unwilling to talk. * * *

Regarding the routine advice of counsel to an arrestee to remain silent and refuse to answer questions put to him by the police, it is my suggestion that the legal profession give serious consideration to the adoption of an alternative practice, which would require counsel to say to his client, the arrestee: "Although you do not have to say anything, my advice to you is that you discuss this matter with the police and that you tell them the truth; I'll stand by to protect you from any harm or abuse." With the advent of such a change in the ethical concept of the role of counsel, we might then be able to say that all arrestees should be entitled to counsel from the time of their arrest. As matters now stand, however, public protection and safety require that we adhere to the present viewpoint that there is no right to counsel during the investigative, non-judicial stage of the case.

3. *In dealing with criminal offenders, and consequently also with criminal suspects who may actually be innocent, the interrogator must of necessity employ less refined methods than are considered appropriate for the transaction of ordinary, everyday affairs by and between law-abiding citizens.*

To illustrate this point, permit me to revert to the previously discussed case of the woman who was murdered by her brother-in-law. His confession was obtained largely as a result of the interrogator adopting a friendly attitude in questioning the suspect, when concededly no such genuine feeling existed; by pretending to sympathize with the suspect because of his difficult financial situation; by suggesting that perhaps the victim had done or said something which aroused his anger and which would have aroused the anger of anyone else similarly situated to such an extent as to provoke a violent reaction; and by resorting to other similar expressions, or even overtures of friendliness and sympathy such as a pat on the suspect's shoulder or knee. In all of this, of course, the interrogation was "unethical" according to the standards usually set for professional, business and social conduct. But the pertinent issue in this case was no ordinary, lawful, professional, business or social matter. It involved the taking of a human life by one who abided by no code of fair play toward his fellow human beings. The killer would not have been moved one bit toward a confession by subjecting him to a reading or lecture regarding the morality of his conduct. It would have been futile merely to give him a pencil and paper and trust that his conscience would impel him to confess. Something more was required—something which was in its essence an "unethical" practice on the part of the interrogator. But, under the circumstances involved in this case, how else would the murderer's guilt have been established? Moreover, let us bear this thought in mind. From the criminal's point of view, *any* interrogation of him is objectionable. To *him* it may be a "dirty trick" to be talked into a confession, for surely it was not done for his benefit. Consequently, any interrogation of him might be labeled as deceitful or unethical.

Of necessity, criminal interrogators must deal with criminal offenders on a somewhat lower moral plane than that upon which ethical, law-abiding citizens are expected to conduct their everyday affairs. That plane, in the interest of innocent suspects need only be subject to the following restriction: Although both "fair" and "unfair" interrogation practices are permissible, nothing shall be done or said to the subject that will be apt to make an innocent person confess.

If all this be so, why then the withholding of this essential interrogation opportunity from the police? And we do, insofar as the stated law is concerned. It comes in the form of statutes or rules that require the prompt delivery of an arrested person before a magistrate for a preliminary hearing or arraignment. Moreover, the United States Supreme Court has decreed that in federal cases no confession is to be received in evidence, regardless of its voluntariness or trustworthiness, if it was obtained during a period of unnecessary delay in delivering the arrestee to a federal commissioner or judge for arraignment. In the federal jurisdiction of Washington, D.C., which must cope with a variety of criminal offenses and problems similar to any other city of comparable size, this federal court rule has had a very crippling effect on police investigations.[6]

One incongruity of the prompt arraignment rule is this. It is lawful for the police to arrest upon *reasonable belief* that the arrestee has committed the offense, following which they must take him before a magistrate, without unnecessary delay, and charge him with the crime; but for legal proof of the charge, his guilt at the time of trial must be established *beyond reasonable doubt*. Moreover, when the accused gets into the hands of a magistrate for the preliminary hearing, the opportunity for an effective interrogation is ended, many times because of the advice he receives from his attorney to keep his mouth shut.

If we view this whole problem realistically, we must come to the conclusion that an interrogation opportunity is necessary and that legislative provision ought to be made for a privately conducted police interrogation, covering a reasonable period of time, of suspects who are not unwilling to be interviewed, and that the only tactics or techniques that are to be forbidden are those which are apt to make an innocent person confess. * * *

The only real, practically attainable protection we can set up for ourselves against police interrogation abuses (just as with respect to arrest and detention abuses) is to see to it that our police are selected and promoted on a merit basis, that they are properly trained, adequately compensated, and that they are permitted to remain substantially free from politically inspired interference. In the hands of men of this competence there will be a minimum degree of abusive practices. And once again I suggest that the real interest that should be exhibited by the legislatures and the courts is with reference to the protection of the innocent from the hazards of tactics and techniques that are apt to produce confessions of guilt or other false information. Individual civil liberties can survive in such an atmosphere, alongside the protective security of the public.[a]

YALE KAMISAR— EQUAL JUSTICE IN THE GATEHOUSES AND MANSIONS OF AMERICAN CRIMINAL PROCEDURE

In Kamisar, Inbau & Arnold, Criminal Justice in Our Time 19–36 (Howard ed. 1965).

The Show in the "Gatehouse" vs. the Show in the "Mansion" * * *

The courtroom is a splendid place where defense attorneys bellow and strut and prosecuting attorneys are hemmed in at many turns. But what happens before an accused reaches the safety and enjoys the comfort of this veritable mansion? Ah, there's the rub. Typically he must first pass through a much less pretentious edifice, a police station with bare back rooms and locked doors.

---

6. In addition, some concern should be exhibited over the risk involved in freeing obviously guilty offenders as a result of the courts' efforts to discipline the police. For instance, following the Supreme Court's reversal of his rape conviction, and his release from custody, the defendant in *Mallory* [p. 458] committed two other offenses against female victims. For the latest one he was found guilty and sentenced to the penitentiary by a Pennsylvania Court. * * *

a. See also Inbau, Reid & Buckley, Criminal Interrogation and Confessions xiii (3d ed. 1986) (introduction); Grano, *Selling the Idea to Tell the Truth: The Professional Interrogator and Modern Confessions Law,* 84 Mich.L.Rev. 662 (1986) (essay review of Inbau, Reid & Buckley, supra) (new edition of Inbau book is "a manual for successful interrogation that a free, civilized, and just society can and should endorse without apology").

In this "gatehouse" of American criminal procedure—through which most defendants journey and beyond which many never get—the enemy of the state is a depersonalized "subject" to be "sized up" and subjected to "interrogation tactics and techniques most appropriate for the occasion";[55] he is "game" to be stalked and cornered.[56] Here, ideals are checked at the door, "realities" faced, and the prestige of law enforcement vindicated. Once he leaves the "gatehouse" and enters the "mansion"—if he ever gets there—the enemy of the state is repersonalized, even dignified, the public invited, and a stirring ceremony in honor of individual freedom from law enforcement celebrated.

I suspect it is not so much that society knows and approves of the show in the gatehouse, but that society does not know or care. "[S]ociety, by its insouciance, has divested itself of a moral responsibility and unloaded it on to the police. Society doesn't want to know about criminals, but it does want them put away, and it is incurious how this can be done provided it is done. Thus society, in giving the policeman power and wishing to ignore what his techniques must be, has made over to him part of its own conscience."[57]

True, the man in the street would have considerable difficulty explaining why the Constitution requires so much in the courtroom and means so little in the police station, but that is not his affair. "The task of keeping the two shows going at the same time without losing the patronage or the support of the Constitution for either," as Thurman Arnold once observed, is "left to the legal scholar."[58] Perhaps this is only fitting and proper, for as Thomas Reed Powell used to say, if you can think about something that is related to something else without thinking about the thing to which it is related, then you have the legal mind.

That the legal mind passes by or shuts out the *de facto* inquisitorial system which has characterized our criminal procedure for so long is bad enough. What is worse is that such an attitude leads many—perhaps requires many—to recoil with horror and dismay at any proposal which recognizes the grim facts of the criminal process and seeks to do something about them.

[At this point, the author discusses suggestions in the late 1920's that (rather than a police officer) a magistrate, or a prosecutor in the presence of a magistrate, do the interrogation, and a proposal in the early 1940's that in federal cases a commissioner do the interrogation at preliminary hearings, but only after advising the suspect of his right to counsel and his right to remain silent. Both proposals were "beaten down to the accompaniment of cries" that they were "opposed to our traditions of fair play," "contrary to the basic traditions of Anglo–American procedure" and violative of the constitutional guarantee against self-incrimination.]

Evidently, so long as neither the proceedings nor the presiding officer is "judicial," basic traditions are honored and self-incrimination problems avoided.
* * *

55. Inbau & Reid, *Criminal Interrogation and Confessions* 20 (1962).

56. "[T]he interrogator's task is somewhat akin to that of a hunter stalking his game. Each must patiently maneuver himself into a position from which the desired objective may be attained; and in the same manner that the hunter may lose his game by a noisy dash through the bush, can the interrogator fail by not exercising the proper degree of patience."

Inbau & Reid, *Lie Detection and Criminal Interrogation* 185 (3d ed. 1953). The authors have dropped this graphic language from their later work.

57. MacInnes, *The Criminal Society,* in The Police and the Public 101 (Rolph ed. 1962).

58. Arnold, *The Symbols of Government* 156 (Harbinger ed. 1962).

Four score years ago, Sir James Fitzjames Stephen noted with pride that the fact that "the prisoner is absolutely protected against all judicial questioning before or at the trial * * * contributes greatly to the dignity and apparent humanity of a criminal trial. It effectually avoids the appearance of harshness, not to say cruelty, which often shocks an English spectator in a French court of justice." Whatever the case then, one would have to underscore the "apparent" and "the appearance" in that statement today. Stephen also told us that "the fact that the prisoner cannot be questioned stimulates the search for independent evidence." Whatever the case then, one cannot but wonder today how often the only thing "stimulated" by the inability of judicial officers to question a prisoner is questioning by police officers. One cannot but wonder how often the availability of the privilege (or, perhaps more aptly, the inability of the State to undermine the privilege), once the accused reaches the safety and comfort of the mansion, only furnishes the State with an *additional incentive* for proving the charge against him out of his own mouth before he leaves the gatehouse.

IS THE PRIVILEGE CHECKED AT THE "GATEHOUSE" DOOR?

[O]ne who would apply the privilege to the police station may select from the vast conglomerate of determinants which form its history the fact that the maxim "no man shall be compelled to accuse himself" first meant (and until the seventeenth century probably only meant) that no man shall be compelled to make the *first charge* against himself, to submit to a "fishing" interrogation about his crimes, to furnish his own indictment from his own lips. Until the 1600's all parties concerned seemed to have operated on the premise that *after* pleading to the indictment, the accused could be compelled to incriminate himself. * * * When we apply the privilege to "arrests for investigation" or "routine pickups," do we disguise a revolutionary idea in the garb of the past or do we restore the privilege to its primordial state?

Nor should it be forgotten that for many centuries there were simply no "police interrogators" to whom the privilege could be applied. Although what Dean Wigmore calls "the first part" of the history of the privilege, the opposition to the ex officio oath of the ecclesiastical courts, began in the 1200's "criminal investigation by the police, with its concomitant of police interrogation, is a product of the late nineteenth century";[82] in eighteenth-century America as in eighteenth-century England "there were no police [in the modern sense] and, though some states seem to have had prosecutors, private prosecution was the rule rather than the exception."[83] In fact as well as in theory, observes Professor Edmond M. Morgan, "there can be little question that the modern American police have taken over the functions performed originally by the English committing magistrates [and at least by some colonial magistrates]; they are in a real sense administrative officers and their questioning of the person under arrest is an investigative proceeding in which testimony is taken." If modern police are permitted to interrogate under the coercive influence of arrest and secret detention, then, insists Professor Albert R. Beisel, "they are doing the very same acts which historically the judiciary was doing in the seventeenth century but which the privilege against self-incrimination abolished."

I do not contend that "the implications of a tangled and obscure history" dictate that the privilege apply to the police station, only that they permit it. I do

---

82. Note, *An Historical Argument for the Right to Counsel During Police Interrogation,* 73 Yale L.J. 1000, 1034 (1964).

83. Id. at 1041. See also Barrett, *Police Practices and the Law—From Arrest to Release or Charge,* 50 Calif.L.Rev. 11, 16–19 (1962). * * *

not claim that this long and involved history displaces judgment, only that it liberates it. I do not say that the distinct origins of the confession and self-incrimination rules are irrelevant, only that it is more important (if we share Dean Charles T. McCormick's views) that "the kinship of the two rules is too apparent for denial" and that "such policy as modern writers are able to discover as a basis for the self-incrimination privilege * * * pales to a flicker beside the flaming demands of justice and humanity for protection against extorted confessions."

Those who applaud the show in the mansion without hissing the show in the gatehouse may also:

Find refuge in the notion that compulsion to testify means *legal* compulsion. Since he is threatened neither with perjury for testifying falsely nor contempt for refusing to testify at all, it cannot be said, runs the argument, that the man in the back room of the police station is being "compelled" to be a "witness against himself" within the meaning of the privilege. Since the police have no legal right to make him answer, "there is no legal obligation to which a privilege in the technical sense can apply."[91]

Can we accept this analysis without forgetting as lawyers and judges what we know as men? Without permitting logic to triumph over life? So long as "what on their face are merely words of request take on color from the officer's badge, gun and demeanor";[94] so long as his interrogators neither advise him of his rights nor permit him to consult with a lawyer who will; can there be any doubt that many a "subject" will *assume* that the police have a legal right to an answer? That many an incriminating statement will be extracted under "color" of law? So long as the interrogator is instructed to "get the idea across [that he] has 'all the time in the world' "; so long as "the power [legal or otherwise] to extract answers begets a forgetfulness of the just limitations of the power" and "the simple and peaceful process of questioning breeds a readiness to resort to bullying and to physical force"; can there be any doubt that many a subject will assume that there is an *illegal* sanction for contumacy?

If these inferences are unfair, if very few "subjects" are misled to believe that there is either a legal obligation to talk or unlimited time and illegal means available to make them do so—if, in short, they know they can "shut up"—why are the police so bent on preventing counsel from telling them what they already know? Why, at least, don't the officers themselves tell their "subjects" plainly and emphatically that they need not and cannot be made to answer? That they will be permitted to consult with counsel, or be brought before a magistrate in short order? And why is the "subject" questioned in *secret?* Why does the modest proposal that a suspect be interrogated by or before an impartial functionary immediately after arrest "meet with scant favor in police circles, even from the most high-minded and highly respected elements in those circles"?[99]

Finally, those who have learned to live with the widespread practices in the gatehouse may take the "waiver" tack. They may:

Concede that the privilege against self-incrimination exists in the police station, but maintain that when (instead of exercising his right to remain silent or

---

91. See Mayers, *Shall We Amend the Fifth Amendment?* 82–83, 223–33 (1959); 8 Wigmore, *Evidence* 329 n. 27 (McNaughton rev. 1961). But both authors are quick to marshal the contrary arguments.

94. Foote, *The Fourth Amendment: Obstacle or Necessity in the Law of Arrest?* in Police Power and Individual Freedom 29, 30 (Sowle ed. 1962).

99. Mayers 90.

to make only self-serving remarks) a suspect "volunteers" damaging statements he has *waived* his rights. This is not much of a concession for "if the privilege is easily waived, there is really no privilege at all."[100] However, if "when the state is putting questions, the answers to which will disclose criminal activities by the witness, there is likely to be an especially high insistence checked by an especially high reluctance," then there is likely to be an especially low incidence of valid waiving of the privilege.

So long as "the classic definition of waiver enumerated in *Johnson v. Zerbst*—'an intelligent relinquishment or abandonment of a known right or privilege' furnishes the controlling standard,"[102] so long as the courts "indulge every reasonable presumption against [such] waiver," it is difficult to see how the contention that an unadvised suspect waives the privilege simply by talking even presents a substantial question. "The Fourteenth Amendment," announced the Supreme Court only a year ago, "secures against state invasion the same privilege that the Fifth Amendment guarantees against federal infringement—the right of a person to remain silent unless he chooses to speak in the unfettered exercise of his own will."[104] Can it seriously be said of the routine police interrogation that the suspect so speaks? Again, only a year ago, the Court pointed out that "no system of criminal justice can, or should, survive if it comes to depend for its continued effectiveness on the citizens' abdication through unawareness of their constitutional rights."[105] On what else does the existing system depend?

[The] trouble with both the "waiver" and "no legal compulsion" rationalizations of the existing *de facto* inquisitorial system is this: when we expect the police dutifully to notify a suspect of the very means he may utilize to frustrate them—when we rely on them to advise a suspect unbegrudgingly and unequivocally of the very rights he is being counted on *not* to assert—we demand too much of even our best officers. As Dean Edward L. Barrett has asked: "[I]s it the duty of the police to persuade the suspect to talk or persuade him not to talk? They cannot be expected to do both."[110]

Suspects there are who feel in a "pleading guilty" mood, for some of the many reasons most defendants do plead guilty. Suspects there are who would intentionally relinquish their rights for some hoped-for favor from the state. I do not deny this. I do deny that such suspects do not need a lawyer.

Surely the man who, in effect, is pleading guilty in the gatehouse needs a lawyer no less than one who arrives at the same decision only after surviving the perilous journey through that structure.[a]

JOSEPH D. GRANO—CONFESSIONS, TRUTH, AND THE LAW

129–36 (1993).

100. Note, 5 Stan.L.Rev. 459, 477 (1953).

102. *Fay v. Noia* [Ch. 28, § 2].

104. *Malloy v. Hogan* [p. 468].

105. *Escobedo v. Illinois* [p. 462].

110. Brief Amicus Curiae, p. 9, *People v. Dorado*, 398 P.2d 361 (1965) (on rehearing).

a. Compare Stephen A. Saltzburg, *Miranda v. Arizona Revisited: Constitutional Law or Judicial Fiat*, 26 Washburn L.J. 1, 14 (1986) (drafters of self-incrimination clause could not have intended to prohibit any magistrate or judge from compelling a person to answer questions, but to permit other officials to do so in secret sessions and without any judicial protection against the nature and manner of questioning) with Joseph D. Grano, *Selling the Idea to Tell the Truth: The Professional Interrogator and Modern Confessions Law*, 84 Mich.L.Rev. 662, 683–84, 686 (1986) (in an historical sense, no "compulsion" within meaning of self-incrimination clause is present in the stationhouse; moreover, "mere questioning by itself" is hardly equivalent to compulsion).

[Professor Laurence Benner] correctly noted that English judges in the nineteenth century came to regard it as their duty to advise suspects at the pretrial examination that they need not respond to questions, a requirement ultimately codified in 1848.[90] Because these developments occurred after the Fifth Amendment's adoption, however, they do not shed much light on the principle that the framers thought they were constitutionalizing. Moreover, judicial questioning of the accused at the preliminary examination persisted in some American states, such as New York, until the middle of the nineteenth century. At least one commentator has speculated that the privilege came to be viewed as a bar to judicial questioning at the pretrial examination only after the examination court ceased to perform an investigatory function and assumed more of an ordinary judicial role. This thesis finds support in the observation of a British Home Office working group that the nineteenth-century development of organized police forces made possible the separation of the investigative and judicial functions that had previously been combined in the pretrial examination court.

[It] should not be surprising [that] the mid-nineteenth-century statutory restrictions on judicial questioning of the accused created in some quarters "a sense of resistance to police interrogation"; in Professor Mark Berger's words, "[h]aving given up the role of interrogator, the justices of the peace were uncertain whether police could be allowed to perform that function."[99] As already seen, however, the development of organized police forces and the concomitant ban on judicial questioning, at least at the pretrial examination, did not take hold either in Britain or in this country until well after the Fifth Amendment was adopted. In any event, uncertainty about the propriety of police interrogation and a ban on police interrogation are two different matters, and the former never evolved into the latter. On the contrary, as Professor George Dix has documented, nineteenth-century voluntariness law in England tolerated confessions induced by trickery and made exceptions to the rule excluding confessions induced by promises, while American courts displayed even "less enthusiasm" for the common-law rules.[100]

[Thus, the *Miranda* Court] erred, at least from a historical perspective, in perceiving an "intimate connection"[a] between the privilege, which prohibited compulsory oaths and mandatory judicial questioning of the accused, and the issues pertaining to the admissibility of extrajudicial confessions. [Although] the common law had developed a voluntariness requirement for confessions prior to the adoption of the Fifth Amendment, neither the voluntariness rule nor its underlying trustworthiness rationale referred to the protection against compulsory self-incrimination. Concededly, some voices did question how police interrogation could be deemed consistent with the mid-nineteenth-century ban on mandatory judicial questioning of the accused at the pretrial examination, but in neither Great Britain nor the United States did the voluntariness rule or the privilege

90. Benner, *Requiem for Miranda: The Rehnquist Court's Voluntariness Doctrine in Historical Perspective,* 67 Wash. U.L.Q. 59, 81–82.

99. Berger, *Legislating Confession Law in Great Britain: A Statutory Approach to Police Interrogations,* 24 U.Mich.J.L.Ref. 1, 10 n. 34 (1990).

100. Dix, *Mistake, Ignorance, Expectation of Benefit, and the Modern Law of Confessions,* 1975 Wash.U.L.Q. 275, 282–84.

a. After quoting extensively from several police interrogation manuals which recommended and spelled out various methods of obtaining incriminating statements from a suspect taken into custody, the *Miranda* Court commented (384 U.S. at 458, 86 S.Ct. at 1619): "From the foregoing, we can readily perceive an intimate connection between the privilege against self-incrimination and police custodial questioning."

evolve to the point of prohibiting police interrogation. Indeed, not even [the *Miranda* case] went that far. * * *

Some may contend that the privilege, if applied to the police station, should make police-initiated interrogation unlawful. This would make the privilege in the police station coextensive with the privilege at trial, where both the prosecutor and judge are forbidden from questioning an accused who does not "waive" Fifth Amendment rights by taking the stand in his own defense. If this is the privilege to be applied, however, the "kinship" between it and the common-law voluntariness rule, far from being "too apparent for denial," is difficult to fathom, for the common-law voluntariness rule, as the previous section indicated, never condemned police interrogation as such.

Still, some may find it incongruous to bar interrogation at trial but to permit police questioning before trial. [Some 30 years ago] Bernard Weisberg complained in an influential article that we "would be hard put to explain to visitors from a legal Mars how ... secret questioning in a police station fits into a system of criminal law which recognizes the privilege against self-incrimination," and he specifically contrasted the scope of an accused's protections at trial with the absence of corresponding protections in the police station.[106] Building on this theme, Professor Kamisar similarly contrasted in colorful, metaphoric prose the "show in the gatehouse," where "ideals are checked at the door and 'realities' faced," and the "show in the mansion," where "the defendant is 'even dignified, the public invited, and a stirring ceremony in honor of individual freedom from law enforcement celebrated.' "

[The] answer to the charge of incongruity is rooted both in history and in the "realities" that Professor Kamisar disparagingly referred to. Despite the questions that were raised, nineteenth-century courts in both Great Britain and this country refused to prohibit police interrogation or to render it ineffective by onerous restrictions. Although debate has never abated, courts in both countries, particularly in recent years, have continued to recognize the importance of police interrogation. Indeed, [the] transformation of the judicial role that occurred in the nineteenth century was probably made possible by the development of police forces that assumed the investigative function previously performed by the pretrial examination court.

[The] division of the investigative and adjudicative functions makes sense from a separation of powers perspective. Moreover, reflecting their own perceptions of fairness, American criminal justice systems in particular have deemed it important to separate the prosecutorial and the judicial roles. Whatever a system's structure or underlying ideology, however, the investigative authority must be lodged somewhere for the system to be viable. Because successful investigation often depends on the questioning of reluctant witnesses and suspects, and on other intrusive strategies as well, the investigative stage, as a practical matter, cannot be subject to the same restraints that govern the adjudicative stage. The operative rules will be different because the institutions that dominate the successive stages of the process have dissimilar functions and responsibilities. Simply put, an investigation is not, and cannot be, a trial. * * *

One might still object [that] an argument invoking history and practical considerations does not provide a principled response to the gatehouse-mansion dichotomy. After all, the fact remains that the accused is not subject to interroga-

---

106. Weisberg, *Police Interrogation of Arrested Persons: A Skeptical View*, 52 J.Crim.L. & P.S. 21 (1961).

tion at trial unless he elects to testify, and on principle the institution of police interrogation seems inconsistent with this limitation. The answer to this is that the alleged inconsistency is not nearly as obvious as it seems. Rather than referring to a single rule, the "privilege ... embraces several distinct rules of law, each having an independent development." Nonetheless, in most situations, the "privilege is merely an *option of refusal,* not a prohibition of inquiry."

Thus, * * * a grand jury may subpoena even a target of its investigation, and the targeted individual has the burden of invoking the privilege on a question-by-question basis. Similarly, even under *Miranda,* targets of police interrogation who are not in custody are not entitled to warnings and have the burden of affirmatively invoking the privilege when questioned.

If] the privilege cannot plausibly be viewed as a ban on police-initiated questioning, what can it mean in the context of police interrogation, and what establishes its "kinship" to the voluntariness rule for confessions? [O]ne might concede that the privilege would prohibit any attempt formally to require suspects, in custody or not, to answer questions. Such a prohibition would be vacuous, however, if governmental officials could force suspects to answer questions by the use of physical or psychological coercion. Not surprisingly, therefore, although the privilege did not play a significant role in the abolition of torture to secure statements in English procedure, various individuals on both sides of the Atlantic came to regard torture as inconsistent with the privilege. Viewed in this light, an obvious kinship exists between the privilege and the voluntariness requirement; indeed, had a voluntariness requirement not independently developed, one might early have been inferred as a logical imperative of the privilege. All this leads, however, to the unremarkable conclusion that the Fifth Amendment, if properly applied to police interrogation at all, prohibits coerced or involuntary confessions. That is, in the context of police interrogation, to "compel" a suspect to become a witness against himself can only mean to "coerce" a suspect to become a witness against himself.

This conclusion, however, is bothersome for *Miranda's* supporters. For example, Professors Irene and Yale Rosenberg have asserted that "it seems unlikely that the long struggle culminating in the incorporation of the Fifth Amendment prohibition against compelled testimony could have been simply an heroic effort to provide an official synonym for involuntariness."[128] Likewise, regarding it as almost self-evident that the privilege was "more than the 'voluntary' test masquerading under a different label," Professor Kamisar has declared that it takes "real dexterity" to purport to apply the Fifth Amendment to the police station and "yet conclude that [this] does not change things very much." But, to repeat, unless the Fifth Amendment is read as a prohibition on all police questioning, custodial and noncustodial, it can be read in the context of police interrogation only as providing protection against involuntariness or coercion. Indeed, the *Miranda* Court read the Fifth Amendment this way, for it found the Fifth Amendment applicable to the "informal compulsion" exerted by the police, concluded that "custodial" interrogation was "inherently compelling," and distinguished on-the-scene questioning, which it exempted from its holding, on the ground that "the compelling atmosphere inherent in the process of in-custody interrogation is not necessarily present."

128. Rosenberg & Rosenberg, *A Modest Proposal for the Abolition of Custodial Confes-* sions, 68 N.C.L.Rev. 69, 108–9 (1989).

The possibility remains, of course, that *coercion* for Fifth Amendment purposes should be a less demanding concept than *coercion* for due process purposes and that, accordingly, *involuntariness* should have different meanings under the two amendments. The Court in *Miranda* took such an approach, for none of its previous due process voluntariness cases had sought to protect the suspect merely from the inherent pressures of custodial questioning. Indeed, the Court candidly admitted, even if it understated the point, that it "might not find the defendants' statements to have been involuntary in traditional terms." The question that *Miranda* did not answer, however, is why the concepts of coercion and involuntariness should have different meanings in the Fifth Amendment and due process contexts.

SECTION 2. HISTORICAL BACKGROUND[a]

A.   THE INTERESTS PROTECTED BY THE DUE PROCESS "VOLUNTARINESS"
TEST FOR ADMITTING CONFESSIONS

The first rules governing the admissibility of confessions were laid down in the eighteenth and nineteenth centuries, a time when illegal police methods were relevant only insofar as they affected the trustworthiness of the evidence. Whatever the meaning of the elusive terms "involuntary" and "coerced" confessions since 1940, for centuries the rule that a confession was admissible so long as it was "voluntary" was more or less an alternative statement of the rule that a confession was admissible so long as it was free of influence which made it untrustworthy or "probably untrue." See generally Charles T. McCormick, *Evidence* 226 (1954); 3 John Henry Wigmore, *Evidence* § 822 (3d ed. 1940).

Indeed, Dean Wigmore condemned the use of the "voluntary" terminology for the reason that "there is nothing in the mere circumstance of compulsion to speak in general * * * which create any risk of untruth." 3 Wigmore, § 843. But the courts' continued reference to the term "voluntariness" in enunciating the requisites for the admissibility of a confession under the due process clause was defended by Dean McCormick, who suggested that it might be prompted "not only by a liking for its convenient brevity, but also by a recognition that there is an interest here to be protected closely akin to the interest of a witness or of an accused person which is protected by the privilege against compulsory self-incrimination." McCormick, *The Scope of Privilege in the Law of Evidence*, 16 Texas L.Rev. 447, 453 (1938).

At least in its advanced stage (the early 1960s), the "due process" or "involuntariness" test appeared to have *three* underlying values or goals. It barred the use of confessions (a) which were of doubtful reliability because of the police methods used to obtain them;[b] (b) which were produced by offensive methods even

---

a. For a much more detailed treatment of the subject matter of this Note, see Mark Berger, *Taking the Fifth* 99–124 (1980); Joseph D. Grano, *Confessions, Truth, and the Law* 59–172 (1993); Otis Stephens, *The Supreme Court and Confessions of Guilt* 17–119 (1973); 3 Wigmore, *Evidence* §§ 817–26 (Chadbourn rev. 1970); Anthony G. Amsterdam, *The Supreme Court and the Rights of Suspects in Criminal Cases*, 45 N.Y.U. L.Rev. 785, 803–10 (1970); Laurence A. Benner, *Requiem for Miranda: The Rehnquist's Court's Voluntariness Doctrine in Historical Perspective*, 67 Wash. U.L.Q.

59 (1989); Gerald M. Caplan, *Questioning Miranda*, 38 Vand.L.Rev. 1417, 1427–43 (1985); Catherine Hancock, *Due Process before Miranda*, 70 Tul.L.Rev. 2195 (1996); Yale Kamisar, *What is an "Involuntary" Confession?*, 17 Rutgers L.Rev. 728 (1963); Welsh S. White, *What is an Involuntary Confession Now?*, 50 Rutgers L.Rev. 2001 (1998).

b. But see *Colorado v. Connelly* (1986) (p. 614), viewing the unreliability of a confession as "a matter to be governed by the evidentiary though the reliability of the confession was not in question; and (c) which were involuntary *in fact* (e.g., obtained from a drugged person) even though the confession was entirely trustworthy and not the product of any conscious police wrongdoing.[c]

At the outset, however, the primary (and perhaps the exclusive) basis for excluding confessions under the due process "voluntariness" test was the "untrustworthiness" rationale, the view that the confession rule was designed merely to protect the integrity of the fact-finding process. This rationale sufficed to explain the exclusion of the confession in *Brown v. Mississippi*, 297 U.S. 278, 56 S.Ct. 461, 80 L.Ed. 682 (1936), the first fourteenth amendment due process confession case (where the deputy who had presided over the beating of the defendants conceded that one prisoner had been whipped but "not too much for a Negro; not as much as I would have done if it were left to me"), and the cases which immediately followed for they, too, were pervaded by threats of, or outright, physical violence. "But when cases involving the more subtle 'psychological' pressures began to appear—usually instances of prolonged interrogation [it] was no longer possible easily to assume that the confessions exacted were unreliable as evidence of guilt. [In *Ashcraft v. Tennessee*, 322 U.S. 143, 64 S.Ct. 921, 88 L.Ed. 1192 (1944)] a conviction was reversed where a confession had been obtained after some thirty-six hours of continuous interrogation of the defendant by the police. In effect, the Court ruled that the extended questioning raised a conclusive presumption of 'coercion.' Considering the facts as revealed in the record of the *Ashcraft* case, it is fair to suggest that the result reached by the Court reflected less a concern with the reliability of the confession as evidence of guilt in the particular case than disapproval of police methods which a majority of the Court conceived as generally dangerous and subject to serious abuse." Francis Allen, *The Supreme Court, Federalism, and State Systems of Criminal Justice,* 8 DePaul L.Rev. 213, 235 (1959). See also Monrad Paulsen, *The Fourteenth Amendment and the Third Degree,* 6 Stan.L.Rev. 411, 418–19 (1954).

As Professor Catherine Hancock has recently observed, *Due Process Before Miranda*, 70 Tul. 2195, 2226 (1996), "*Ashcraft* was a milestone because it prefigured *Miranda*'s recognition of the coercion inherent in all custodial interrogations. [In] a prophetic dictum, [dissenting Justice Jackson] declared that 'even one hour' of interrogation would be inherently coercive, and so there could be no stopping point to the *Ashcraft* doctrine. However, more than twenty years elapsed before this prophecy came to pass in the form of *Miranda*'s presumption that even a few moments of custodial interrogation are inherently coercive."

In *Watts v. Indiana*, 338 U.S. 49, 69 S.Ct. 1347, 93 L.Ed. 1801 (1949) and the companion cases of *Harris v. South Carolina*, 338 U.S. 68, 69 S.Ct. 1354, 93 L.Ed. 1815 (1949) and *Turner v. Pennsylvania*, 338 U.S. 62, 69 S.Ct. 1352, 93 L.Ed. 1810 (1949), the Court reversed three convictions resting on coerced confessions without disputing the accuracy of Justice Jackson's observation (concurring in *Watts* and dissenting in the other cases) that "checked with external evidence they [the

laws of the forum and not by the Due Process Clause."

c. As for the third underlying value, see *Townsend v. Sain,* 372 U.S. 293, 83 S.Ct. 745, 9 L.Ed.2d 770 (1963), excluding a confession obtained from one given a drug with the properties of a truth serum, even though the police were unaware of the drug's effect and had engaged in no conscious wrongdoing (although they may have been negligent), and even though the confession was apparently reliable. "Any questioning by police officers which *in fact* produces a confession which is not the product of free intellect," observed the Court, "renders the confession inadmissible."

However, in *Colorado v. Connelly* (1986) (p. 614), the Court looked back at *Townsend* as a case that "presented [an] instance of police wrongdoing."

confessions in each case] are inherently believable and were not shaken as to truth by anything that occurred at the trial."

The majority, per Frankfurter, J., commented: "In holding that the Due Process Clause *bars police procedure* which violates the basic notions of our accusatorial mode of prosecuting crime and vitiates a conviction based on the fruits of such procedure, we apply the Due Process Clause to its historic function of *assuring appropriate procedure* before liberty is curtailed or life is taken." (Emphasis added.) And three years later, in the famous "stomach-pumping" case of *Rochin v. California,* p. 40, the Court, again speaking through Justice Frankfurter, viewed the coerced confession cases as "only instances of the general requirement that States in their prosecutions respect certain decencies of civilized conduct," pointing out: "Use of involuntary verbal confessions in State criminal trials is constitutionally obnoxious not only because of their unreliability. They are inadmissible under the Due Process Clause even though statements contained in them may be independently established as true. Coerced confessions offend the community's sense of fair play and decency."

That the Court was applying a "police methods"—as well as a "trustworthiness"—test was made clear by *Spano v. New York,* 360 U.S. 315, 79 S.Ct. 1202, 3 L.Ed.2d 1265 (1959); *Blackburn v. Alabama,* 361 U.S. 199, 80 S.Ct. 274, 4 L.Ed.2d 242 (1960) and *Rogers v. Richmond,* 365 U.S. 534, 81 S.Ct. 735, 5 L.Ed.2d 760 (1961). Thus, the Court, per Warren, C.J., pointed out in *Spano* that the ban against "involuntary" confessions turns not only on their reliability but on the notion that "the police must obey the law while enforcing the law." And the Court, again speaking through the Chief Justice, acknowledged in *Blackburn* that "a *complex of values* underlies the strictures against use by the state of confessions which, by way of *convenient shorthand,* this Court terms involuntary." (Emphasis added.)

Perhaps the most emphatic statement of the point that the untrustworthiness of a confession was not (or no longer) the principal reason for excluding it appears in one of Justice Frankfurter's last opinions on the subject. Writing for the Court in *Rogers,* he observed: "Our decisions under [the Fourteenth Amendment] have made clear that convictions following the admission into evidence of [involuntary confessions] cannot stand * * * not so much because such confessions are unlikely to be true but because the methods used to extract them offend an underlying principle in the enforcement of our criminal law: that ours is an accusatorial and not an inquisitorial system. * * * Indeed, in many of the cases [reversing] state convictions involving the use of confessions obtained by impermissible methods, independent corroborating evidence left little doubt of the truth of what the defendant had confessed."[d]

Although, theoretically, the "police methods" and "trustworthiness" standards for admitting confessions are to be applied independently of each other, in practice they often overlap. Even though it might be conclusively demonstrated that "offensive" police interrogation methods did not produce an "untrustworthy" confession *in the particular case* before the Court, the continued use of such methods is likely to create a substantial risk that other suspects subjected to

d. In admitting the confession, the *Rogers* trial court had found that the interrogation tactics "had no tendency to produce a confession that was not in accord with the truth." The Supreme Court did not consider the finding *unwarranted,* but *irrelevant.* The admissibility of the confession had been decided "by reference to a legal standard which took into account the circumstance of probable truth or falsity"—"and this is not a permissible standard under the Due Process Clause." See Stephen J. Schulhofer, *Confessions and the Court,* 79 Mich.L.Rev. 865, 867 (1981).

similar tactics would falsely confess. See Kamisar, *What is an "Involuntary" Confession?*, 17 Rutgers L.Rev. 728, 754–55 (1963), reprinted in Kamisar, Police Interrogation and Confessions 1, 20–22 (1980) (hereinafter referred to as Kamisar Essays).

What *are* the objectionable police methods which render a resulting confession "involuntary"? In the advanced stages of the test, at least, the use or threatened use of physical violence or the kind of protracted relay interrogation that occurred in *Ashcraft,* supra, rendered any resulting confession inadmissible *per se.* In the main, however, it is difficult to isolate any particular interrogation tactic and say that, standing alone, it is so "coercive" or so "offensive" that it requires the exclusion of any resulting confession. For the significant fact about the great bulk of the "involuntary confessions" cases is that "none of them turned on the presence or absence of a single controlling criterion; each reflected a careful scrutiny of all the surrounding circumstances" *Schneckloth v. Bustamonte* (p. 343) at 226, 93 S.Ct. at 2047. And the totality of the surrounding circumstances included "both the characteristics of the accused [many of whom were uneducated, of low mentality or emotionally unstable] and the details of the interrogation." Ibid.

Nevertheless, the pre-*Escobedo,* pre-*Miranda* cases reveal numerous police practices which, if not impermissible *per se,* certainly militate heavily against the "voluntariness" of any resulting confession: stripping off defendant's clothes and keeping him naked for several hours, *Malinski v. New York,* 324 U.S. 401, 65 S.Ct. 781, 89 L.Ed. 1029 (1945); informing defendant that state financial aid for her infant children would be cut off, and her children taken from her, if she failed to "cooperate" with police, *Lynumn v. Illinois,* 372 U.S. 528, 83 S.Ct. 917, 9 L.Ed.2d 922 (1963); after defendant persisted in his denial of guilt, pretending to "bring in" defendant's wife (who suffered from arthritis) for questioning, *Rogers v. Richmond,* supra; repeatedly rejecting defendant's requests to phone his wife and repeatedly informing him that he would not be able to call her or anyone else unless and until he gave the police a statement, *Haynes v. Washington,* 373 U.S. 503, 83 S.Ct. 1336, 10 L.Ed.2d 513 (1963); removing defendant from jail to a distant place in order to thwart the efforts of his friends or relatives to secure his release, or at least to contact him, *Ward v. Texas,* 316 U.S. 547, 62 S.Ct. 1139, 86 L.Ed. 1663 (1942); utilization of a state-employed psychiatrist, with considerable knowledge of hypnosis, who posed as a "general practitioner" who would provide defendant with the medical relief he needed and succeeded in obtaining a confession from defendant by skillful and suggestive questioning, *Leyra v. Denno,* 347 U.S. 556, 74 S.Ct. 716, 98 L.Ed. 948 (1954); utilization of defendant's "childhood friend," then a fledgling police officer, who, pursuant to his superiors' instructions, pretended that defendant's phone call had gotten his "friend" "in a lot of trouble," so much so that his "friend's" job was in jeopardy, and loss of his job would prove disastrous to his "friend's" wife and children, *Spano,* supra.

Consider Albert Alschuler, *Constraint and Confessions,* 74 Denv.U.L.Rev. 957 (1997): "The Court should define the term coerced confession to mean a confession caused by offensive governmental conduct, period. * * * Shifting their attention almost entirely from the minds of suspects to the conduct of government officers, courts should abandon the search for 'overborne wills' and attempts to assess the quality of individual choices."

B. The Shortcomings of the "Voluntariness" Test

Although the Supreme Court customarily used the terms "voluntariness" and "involuntariness" in explaining and applying the due process test for the admissibility of confessions, the "voluntariness" concept seems to be at once too wide and too narrow. In one sense, in the sense of wanting to confess, or doing so in a completely spontaneous manner, "in the sense of a confession to a priest merely to rid one's soul of a sense of guilt" (Jackson, J., dissenting in *Ashcraft v. Tennessee*), few criminal confessions reviewed by the courts, if any, had been "voluntary." On the other hand, in the sense that the situation always presents a "choice" between two alternatives, either one disagreeable, to be sure, *all* confessions are "voluntary." See 3 Wigmore, § 824.

Moreover, as the rationales for the Court's coerced confession cases evolved, it became increasingly doubtful that terms such as "voluntariness," "coercion," and "breaking the will" were very helpful in resolving the issue. For such terms do not focus directly on either the risk of untrue confessions or the offensiveness of police interrogation methods employed in eliciting the confession. See Paulsen, supra, at 429–30.

As the Court, per O'Connor, J., observed in *Miller v. Fenton*, 474 U.S. 104, 106 S.Ct. 445, 88 L.Ed.2d 405 (1985) (holding that the "voluntariness" of a confession is not a "factual issue" but "a legal question meriting independent consideration in a federal habeas corpus proceeding"): "[T]he admissibility of a confession turns as much on whether the techniques for extracting the statements, as applied to *this* suspect, are compatible with a system that presumes innocence and assures that a conviction will not be secured by inquisitorial means as on whether the defendant's will was in fact overborne. [The] hybrid quality of the voluntariness inquiry, subsuming, as it does, a 'complex of values,' *Blackburn*, itself militates against treating the question as one of simple historical fact." As the *Miller* Court also noted, "[t]he voluntariness rubric has been variously condemned as 'useless,' 'perplexing,' and 'legal "double-talk."' "

Nor was "the elusive, measureless standard of psychological coercion heretofore developed in this Court by accretion on almost an ad hoc, case-by-case basis," as Justice Clark described it, dissenting in *Reck v. Pate*, 367 U.S. 433, 81 S.Ct. 1541, 6 L.Ed.2d 948 (1961); a test which seemed to permit constitutionally permissible police interrogation to vary widely according to how dull or alert or soft or tough the particular suspect, see e.g., Maguire, *Evidence of Guilt* 134 fn. 5 (1959); likely to guide or to shape police conduct very much, if at all.

Moreover, as pointed out in Schulhofer, fn. d supra, at 869–70, because of its ambiguity and "its subtle mixture of factual and legal elements," the "voluntariness" test "virtually invited [trial judges] to give weight to their subjective preferences" and "discouraged review even by the most conscientious appellate judges." See also Kamisar Essays at 12–25, 69–76; LaFave & Israel, § 6.2(d); Herman, *The Supreme Court, the Attorney General, and the Good Old Days of Police Interrogation*, 48 Ohio St.L.J. 733, 745–55 (1987); Stone, *The Miranda Doctrine in the Burger Court*, 1977 Sup.Ct.Rev. 99, 102–03; W. White, *Defending Miranda: A Reply to Professor Caplan*, 39 Vand.L.Rev. 1, 7–9, 11–16 (1986).[a]

---

a. But consider Gerald Caplan, *Questioning Miranda*, 38 Vand.L.Rev. 1417, 1433–34 (1985): "[The voluntariness test] allowed the Court to move carefully, to feel its way, and to make its judgments without fear of prematurely constitutionalizing interrogation practices. [The] Court's failure to state the basis for a particular decision or its blurring of a holding in the veiled attire of the 'totality of the circumstances' can be seen as shrewd and responsible pragmatism. Pragmatism may have been preferable to principles at a time when there was little general agreement on the principles to be applied. [If] the development of the voluntariness test had not come to a near end with the advent of *Miranda*, perhaps the test would have continued to achieve definition and improved serviceability."

As police interrogators made greater use of "psychological" techniques over the years, the always difficult problems of proof confronting the alleged victims of improper interrogation practices became increasingly arduous. Disputes over whether physical violence occurred are not always easy to resolve, but evidence of "mental" or "psychological" coercion is especially elusive. Frequently, the defendant was inarticulate, which aggravated the difficulties of recreating the tenor and atmosphere of the police questioning or the *manner* in which the appropriate advice about the suspect's rights might have been given or, if properly given, subsequently undermined.

Moreover, the local courts almost always resolved the almost inevitable "swearing contest" over what happened behind the closed doors in favor of the police, perhaps for the reasons suggested by Walter Schaefer, *Federalism and State Criminal Procedure,* 70 Harv.L.Rev. 1, 7 (1956): "In the field of criminal procedure [a] strong local interest competes only against an ideal. Local interest is concerned with the particular case and with the guilt or innocence of the particular individual. * * * While it is hard indeed for any judge to set apart the question of the guilt or innocence of a particular defendant and focus solely upon the procedural aspect of the case, it becomes easier [in] a reviewing court where the impact of the evidence is diluted. The more remote the court, the easier it is to consider the case in terms of a hypothetical defendant accused of crime, instead of a particular man whose guilt has been established."[b]

Under the old case-by-case approach, however, the defendant could not often avail himself of the "remoteness" of the U.S. Supreme Court. In the thirty years since *Brown v. Mississippi,* the Court had taken an average of about one state confession case per year and *two-thirds of these* had been "death penalty" cases.

---

b. This may help to explain the strikingly different reactions of the state courts and the U.S. Supreme Court to the situation in *Mincey v. Arizona,* 437 U.S. 385, 98 S.Ct. 2408, 57 L.Ed.2d 290 (1978) (other aspects of which are discussed at p. 265). Just a few hours before the interrogation occurred, Mincey had been seriously wounded during a narcotics raid which resulted in the death of a police officer. According to the attending physician, Mincey had arrived at the hospital "depressed almost to the point of coma." At the time Detective Hust questioned him, Mincey's condition was still sufficiently serious that he was in the intensive care unit. Lying on his back on a hospital bed, encumbered by tubes, needles and breathing apparatus, Mincey (according to the Supreme Court) clearly and repeatedly expressed his wish not to be interrogated, but Hust continued to question him. Unable to speak because of the tube in his mouth, Mincey responded to Hust's questions by writing answers on pieces of paper provided by the hospital, at one point writing: "This is all I can say without a lawyer." (In a written report dated about a week later, Hust transcribed Mincey's answers and added the questions he believed he had asked.)

Under these circumstances, the trial court found "with unmistakable clarity" that Mincey's statements were "voluntary" and thus, despite being obtained in violation of *Miranda,* admissible for impeachment purposes. (On this point, see Ch. 11, § 4 infra). The state supreme court unanimously affirmed. On the basis of its independent evaluation of the record, the Court, per Stewart, J., reversed. It noted, inter alia, that "the reliability of Hust's report [reconstructing the interrogation] is uncertain." It concluded that "the undisputed evidence makes clear that Mincey wanted *not* to answer Detective Hust" but that—"weakened by pain and shock, isolated from family, friends and legal counsel, and barely conscious"—Mincey's "will was simply overborne."

Rehnquist, J., dissented from the holding that Mincey's statements were involuntary and—as was true of so many of the older "involuntariness" cases—disputed the Court's reading of the record: "[The Court] ignores entirely some evidence of voluntariness and distinguishes away yet other testimony. * * * Despite the contrary impression given by the Court, [the state supreme court's] opinion casts no doubt on the testimony or report of Detective Hust. The Court is thus left solely with its own conclusions as to the reliability of various witnesses based on a re-examination of the record on appeal. * * * I believe that the trial court was entitled to conclude that, notwithstanding Mincey's medical condition, his statements in the intensive care unit were admissible. [T]hat the same court might have been equally entitled to reach the opposite conclusion does not justify this Court's adopting the opposite conclusion."

Indeed, the Court's workload was so great that it even denied a hearing in most "death penalty" cases. See Kamisar Essays 75. Almost no garden-variety criminal defendant who cried "coerced confession" but lost the "swearing contest" below was likely to survive the winnowing process above. Not surprisingly, Justice Black remarked in the course of the oral arguments in *Miranda:* "[I]f you are going to determine [the admissibility of the confession] each time on the circumstances, [if] this Court will take them one by one [it] is more than we are capable of doing."

Although the 1964 *Massiah* and *Escobedo* cases and the 1966 *Miranda* case (all discussed infra) were to catch heavy criticism, "[g]iven the Court's inability to articulate a clear and predictable definition of 'voluntariness,' the apparent persistence of state courts in utilizing the ambiguity of the concept to validate confessions of doubtful constitutionality, and the resultant burden on its own workload, it seemed inevitable that the Court would seek 'some automatic device by which the potential evils of incommunicado interrogation [could] be controlled.' "Stone, *The Miranda Doctrine in the Burger Court,* 1977 Sup.Ct.Rev. 102–03 (quoting from Schaefer, *The Suspect and Society* 10 (1967)).[c]

C. THE McNABB-MALLORY RULE: SUPERVISORY AUTHORITY OVER FEDERAL CRIMINAL JUSTICE VS. FOURTEENTH AMENDMENT DUE PROCESS

As Justice FRANKFURTER pointed out for the majority in the famous case of McNABB v. UNITED STATES, 318 U.S. 332, 63 S.Ct. 608, 87 L.Ed. 819 (1943), while the power of the Court to upset *state* convictions is limited to the enforcement of fourteenth amendment due process, the standards of *federal* criminal justice "are not satisfied merely by observance of those minimal historic safeguards." Rather, the Court can, and has, formulated rules of evidence in the exercise of its "supervisory authority" over the administration of federal criminal justice which go well beyond due process requirements.[a] A good example was the significance given to the fact that incriminating statements were obtained during illegal detention, i.e., while the suspect was held in violation of federal statutory requirements that he be promptly taken before a committing magistrate to

c. *The continued vitality of the pre-Miranda voluntariness test.* Since the landmark *Miranda* case, the police must give a suspect the now familiar warnings and obtain a waiver of his rights before subjecting him to "custodial interrogation." However, the "old" due process-voluntariness test is still important in a number of situations, e.g., when the police question a suspect not in "custody"; when the police question a suspect who waives his rights and agrees to talk, but denies any involvement in the crime. See generally this Ch., § 4. Moreover, the distinction between an "involuntary" confession and one obtained only in violation of *Miranda* is important in a number of procedural contexts, e.g., use of the confession for impeachment purposes. See generally Ch. 11, § 4.

Thus, "[c]areful attention to the voluntariness issue remains an imperative, though sometimes overlooked, obligation of court and counsel," Schulhofer, supra, at 878. To illustrate his point, Professor Schulhofer refers to *United States v. Mesa,* discussed at pp. 517, 526, ___. The *Mesa* court's rejection of a *Miranda* challenge, observes Schulhofer, id. at

878 n. 58, was "based on particularities of *Miranda's* rationale and would by no means preclude a voluntariness claim. Yet the defense never argued, and so the [Third Circuit] never considered, whether the statements made by this psychologically distraught suspect, on the verge of suicide, [who had barricaded himself in a motel room and threatened that he would not surrender peacefully], in the course of a three-and-one-half-hour conversation [with an FBI crisis negotiator] under highly charged circumstances, were admissible under the due process test."

a. For a long, hard look at the federal courts' exercise of "supervisory powers" over the administration of federal criminal justice generally and a look back at *McNabb,* regarded by many as the first supervisory power decision, see Sara Sun Beale, *Reconsidering Supervisory Power in Criminal Cases: Constitutional and Statutory Limits on the Authority of the Federal Courts,* 84 Colum.L.Rev. 1433 (1984). Extracts from Professor Beale's article appear at p. 51.

ascertain whether good cause exists to hold him for trial. Although, during this period, an otherwise voluntary confession was not rendered inadmissible in a *state* prosecution solely because it was elicited during prolonged and hence illegal precommitment detention (this was only *one* of many factors in determining whether a confession was voluntary), the 1943 *McNabb* case, although hardly free from ambiguity, seemed to hold that such a confession had to be excluded from *federal* prosecutions.

The *McNabb* rule was heavily criticized by law enforcement spokesmen and many members of Congress and begrudgingly interpreted by most lower federal courts. See generally James E. Hogan & Joseph M. Snee, *The McNabb–Mallory Rule: Its Rise, Rationale and Rescue,* 47 Geo.L.J. 1 (1958). However, it was emphatically reaffirmed in MALLORY v. UNITED STATES, 354 U.S. 449, 77 S.Ct. 1356, 1 L.Ed.2d 1479 (1957), where, speaking for a unanimous Court, Justice FRANKFURTER observed:

"We cannot sanction this extended delay [some seven hours], resulting in confession, without subordinating [Fed.R.Crim.P. 5(a), requiring that an arrestee be taken 'without unnecessary delay' to the nearest available committing officer] to the discretion of arresting officers in finding exceptional circumstances for its disregard. [There is no escape] from the constraint laid upon the police by that Rule in that two other suspects were involved for the same crime. Presumably, whomever the police arrest they must arrest on 'probable cause.' It is not the function of the police to arrest, as it were, at large and to use an interrogating process at police headquarters in order to determine whom they should charge before a committing magistrate on 'probable cause.' "

Only a handful of states adopted the *McNabb-Mallory* rule or its equivalent on their own initiative.[b] But many hoped (and many others feared) that some day the Court would apply the rule to the states as a matter of fourteenth amendment due process. The Court never did. Instead, in the years since the 1957 *Mallory* decision, the last of the *McNabb* line of cases, the Court closed in on the state confession problem by making increasing resort to the right to counsel and the privilege against self-incrimination. By such means the state confession rules were eventually to *go beyond* the *McNabb-Mallory* doctrine in a number of respects.[c]

b. It was not until 1960 that the states' unanimity in refusing to follow the Supreme Court's lead in the *McNabb-Mallory* line of cases was broken. See *People v. Hamilton,* 102 N.W.2d 738, 741–43 (Mich.1960); Rothblatt & Rothblatt, *Police Interrogation: The Right to Counsel and to Prompt Arraignment,* 27 Brooklyn L.Rev. 24, 40–44 (1960). On the eve of *Miranda,* two more states adopted an equivalent of the rule, Delaware, see *Webster v. State,* 213 A.2d 298, 301 (Del.1965); and Connecticut, by legislation, see *State v. Vollhardt,* 244 A.2d 601, 607 (Conn.1968) (subsequent case construing statute). In recent years at least three more state courts—Maryland, Montana, and Pennsylvania—adopted some equivalent of the rule. See *Johnson v. State,* 384 A.2d 709, 714–18 (Md.1978); *State v. Benbo,* 570 P.2d 894, 899–900 (Mont.1977); *Commonwealth v. Davenport,* 370 A.2d 301, 306 (Pa.1977); *Commonwealth v. Futch,* 290 A.2d 417, 418–19 (Pa. 1972).

The life of Maryland's version of the *McNabb-Mallory* rule, adopted in the 1978

Johnson case, "was short and unhappy." Donald E. Wilkes, *The New Federalism in Criminal Procedure in 1984: Death of the Phoenix?,* in Developments in State Constitutional Law 166, 170 (B. McGraw ed. 1985). The *Johnson* rule was usually interpreted begrudgingly and—in a "legislative blow to the new federalism"—repealed by statute in 1981. See id. at 169–171.

For a close examination and strong criticism of the "state court revival" *McNabb-Mallory* rule, see Note, 72 J.Crim.L. & C. 204 (1981). The Note maintains, id. at 241, that "current constitutional law addresses many of the original concerns underlying delay statutes, obviating the need for reliance on a doctrine of implied statutory exclusion."

c. Title II of the Omnibus Crime Control and Safe Streets Act of 1968 purports to repeal (among other judicial doctrines) the *McNabb-Mallory* rule. Because the possible constitutional vulnerability of this 1968 provision turns in part on an appraisal of *Miranda,* treatment of this point is postponed until p. 499.

D.   The Right to Counsel and the Analogy
to the Accusatorial, Adversary Trial

CROOKER v. CALIFORNIA, 357 U.S. 433, 78 S.Ct. 1287, 2 L.Ed.2d 1448 (1958), involved a petitioner who attended one year of law school, during which time he studied criminal law, and who indicated in his dealings with the police that he was fully aware of his right to remain silent. On the basis of a challenged confession, he was convicted of murder of his paramour and sentenced to death. He contended that by persisting in interrogating him after denying his specific request to contact his lawyer the police violated his due process right to legal representation and advice and that therefore use of any confession obtained from him under these circumstances should be barred even though "freely" and "voluntarily" made under traditional standards. Such a rule retorted the Court, per CLARK, J., "would have [a] devastating effect on enforcement of criminal law, for it would effectively preclude police questioning—*fair as well as unfair*—until the accused was afforded opportunity to call his attorney. Due process, a concept 'less rigid and more fluid than those envisaged in other specific and particular provisions of the Bill of Rights,' *Betts v. Brady*, demands no such rule."

In his dissenting opinion, Justice DOUGLAS, with whom Warren, C.J., and Black and Brennan, JJ., joined, insisted: "The right to have counsel at the pretrial stage is often necessary to give meaning and protection to the right to be heard at the trial itself. It may also be necessary as a restraint on the coercive power of the police. [The] demands of our civilization expressed in the Due Process Clause require that the accused who wants a counsel should have one at any time after the moment of arrest."

In the companion case of CICENIA v. LA GAY, 357 U.S. 504, 78 S.Ct. 1297, 2 L.Ed.2d 1523 (1958), not only did petitioner unsuccessfully ask to see his lawyer while he was being questioned by the police, but his lawyer, who arrived at the police station while petitioner was being interrogated, repeatedly (and unsuccessfully) asked to see his client. Moreover, petitioner was not well educated as was Crooker. Nevertheless, the Court affirmed the murder conviction (which led to a life sentence), disposing of petitioner's contention that he had a constitutional right to confer with counsel on the authority of *Crooker*. With the exception of Justice Brennan, who took no part in the case, the Court split along the same lines it had in *Crooker*.

The following year, however, by virtue of SPANO v. NEW YORK, it appeared that the Court had reached the view that once a person was *formally charged* by indictment or information his constitutional right to counsel had "begun"—at least his right to the assistance of counsel he himself had retained. Four concurring Justices took this position in *Spano:* Justices Black, Douglas and Brennan, all of whom had dissented in *Crooker;* and newly appointed Justice Stewart, who had replaced Justice Burton.

In separate concurring opinions both Justice Douglas (joined by Black and Brennan, JJ.) and Justice Stewart (joined by Douglas and Brennan, JJ.) stressed that *Spano* was not a case where the police were questioning a suspect in the course of investigating an unsolved crime but one where the subject of interrogation was already under indictment for murder when he surrendered to the authorities. Both concurring opinions also measured the proceedings in the "interrogation" room against the standard of a public trial and formal judicial proceedings. Thus Justice STEWART observed: "Under our system of justice an indictment is supposed to be followed by an arraignment and a trial. * * * What followed the petitioner's surrender in this case was not arraignment in a court of law, but an all-night inquisition in a prosecutor's office, a police station, and an automobile. * * * Our Constitution guarantees the assistance of counsel to a man on trial for his life in an orderly courtroom, presided over by a judge, open to the public, and protected by all the procedural safeguards of the law. Surely a Constitution which promises that much can vouchsafe no less to the same man under midnight inquisition in the squad room of a police station."

As we have already seen, a majority of the *Spano* Court did not go off on "right to counsel" grounds, finding the confession inadmissible on straight "coerced confession" grounds, but the Chief Justice, who wrote the majority opinion, had taken the position, a year earlier in *Crooker,* that the right to counsel should "begin" even earlier than at the point of indictment. Thus, counting heads, it appeared that by 1959 the view of the concurring Justices in *Spano* commanded a majority of the Court.

E. *MASSIAH AND ESCOBEDO:* THE COURT CLOSES IN ON THE "CONFESSION PROBLEM"

"There is a case in the Supreme Court now from Illinois, *People v. Escobedo,* that involves this very issue [of when the right to counsel begins] and I am scared that the Court is going to hold that this right exists from the time of arrest—if a person asks for counsel and he is not given counsel, anything you get from him after that has to be excluded."

—Fred E. Inbau, *A Forum on the Interrogation of the Accused,* 49 Corn.L.Q. 382, 401 (January 31, 1964).

Five years after *Spano,* in MASSIAH v. UNITED STATES, 377 U.S. 201, 84 S.Ct. 1199, 12 L.Ed.2d 246 (1964), a 6–3 majority (consisting of the four concurring Justices in *Spano,* Chief Justice Warren, and newly appointed Justice Goldberg) adopted the view advanced in the *Spano* concurring opinions. *Massiah* arose as follows: After he had been indicted for federal narcotics violations, Massiah retained a lawyer, pled not guilty, and was released on bail. A codefendant, Colson, invited him to discuss the pending case in Colson's car, parked on a city street. Unknown to Massiah, Colson had decided to cooperate with federal agents in their continuing investigation of the case. A radio transmitter was installed under the front seat of Colson's car, enabling a nearby agent (Murphy), who was equipped with a recording device, to overhear the Massiah–Colson conversation. As expected, Massiah made several damaging admissions.

It is hardly surprising that the *Massiah* dissenters considered the facts of the case a "peculiarly inappropriate" setting for a major breakthrough on the "police interrogation"-"confession" front. Even if the *Spano* concurring opinions had come to represent the majority view, argued then Solicitor General Archibald Cox, Massiah's statements should still be admissible because at the time he made them he was neither in "custody"—not even in the loosest sense—nor undergoing "police interrogation." He was under no "official pressure" to answer questions or even to engage in conversation; his conversation "was not affected by even that degree of constraint which may result from a suspect's knowledge that he is talking to a law enforcement officer."[a] Moreover, Colson, a layman unskilled in

---

a. Extensive extracts from the Government's brief and oral argument in *Massiah* appear in Kamisar Essays 171–73.

the art of interrogation, did not and probably could not utilize any of the standard techniques to induce Massiah to incriminate himself.[b]

Nevertheless, as the *Massiah* majority, per STEWART, J., saw it, the decisive feature of the case was that after he had been indicted—"and therefore at a time when he was clearly entitled to a lawyer's help" and at a time when he was awaiting trial "in an orderly courtroom, presided over by a judge, open to the public, and protected by all the procedural safeguards of the law"—Massiah had been subjected to a "completely extrajudicial" police-orchestrated proceeding designed to obtain incriminating statements from him. Besides, if in one respect— the lack of an inherently or potentially "coercive atmosphere"—Massiah had been less seriously imposed upon than the average "confession" defendant, he was more seriously imposed upon in another respect—he did not, and could not be expected to, keep his guard up because he was not even aware that he was dealing with a government agent[c]: "We hold that the petitioner was denied the basic protections of [the right to counsel] when there was used against him at his trial evidence of his own incriminating words, which federal agents had deliberately elicited from him after he had been indicted and in the absence of his counsel. It is true that in the *Spano* case the defendant was interrogated in a police station, while here the damaging testimony was elicited from [him] without his knowledge while he was free on bail. But, as Judge Hays pointed out in his dissent in the [Second Circuit], 'if such a rule is to have any efficacy it must apply to indirect and surreptitious interrogations as well as those conducted in the jailhouse. In this case, Massiah was more seriously imposed upon * * * because he did not even know that he was under interrogation by a government agent.' * * *

"We do not question that in this case, as in many cases, it was entirely proper to continue an investigation of the suspected criminal activities of the defendant and his alleged confederates, even though the defendant had already been indicted. All that we hold is that the defendant's own incriminating statements, obtained by federal agents under the circumstances here disclosed, could not constitutionally be used by the prosecution as evidence against *him* at his trial."

Dissenting Justice WHITE, joined by Clark and Harlan, JJ., protested: "[H]ere there was no substitution of brutality for brains, no inherent danger of police coercion justifying the prophylactic effect of another exclusionary rule. Massiah was not being interrogated in a police station, was not surrounded by numerous officers or questioned in relays, and was not forbidden access to others. Law enforcement may have the elements of a contest about it, but it is not a game."

The dissenters were "unable to see how this case presents an unconstitutional interference with Massiah's right to counsel. Massiah was not prevented from consulting with counsel as often as he wished. No meetings with counsel were

---

b. The Massiah–Colson conversation was not only broadcast to a nearby federal agent, but secretly tape-recorded by Colson. In the district court, however, Massiah successfully objected to the admission of these tapes on the ground that they implicated other defendants and contained privileged matters. The Government maintained that the recording confirmed the testimony of Agent Murphy that Colson did not coerce Massiah into making any incriminating statements or even induce him by appeals to talk in the guise of friendship and filed the recording with the clerk of the Court. Colson

did not testify himself. Massiah did not testify either or otherwise contradict Murphy's testimony about the meeting. See Kamisar Essays at 278 fn. 202.

c. Massiah's unawareness that he was, in effect, talking to the police, and thus his inability to protect himself, "was a nice point (or counterpoint), but it was hardly the decisive one." Kamisar Essays 174. Any doubts that the *Massiah* doctrine also applies when the suspect realizes he is in the presence of the police were removed in *Brewer v. Williams* (1977), p. 619.

disturbed or spied upon. Preparation for trial was in no way obstructed. It is only a sterile syllogism—an unsound one besides—to say that because Massiah had a right to counsel's aid before and during the trial, his out-of-court conversations and admissions must be excluded if obtained without counsel's consent or presence."

"This case," maintained the dissenters, "cannot be analogized to [Canon 9 of the ABA's Canons of Professional Ethics] forbidding an attorney to talk to the opposing party litigant outside the presence of his counsel.[d] Aside from the fact that [the canons] are not of constitutional dimensions, [Canon 9] deals with the conduct of lawyers and not with the conduct of investigators.[e] Lawyers are forbidden to interview the opposing party because of the supposed imbalance of legal skill and acumen between the lawyer and the party litigant; the reason for the rule does not apply to nonlawyers and certainly not to Colson, Massiah's codefendant."

Were the *Massiah* dissenters right when they observed that "the reason given for the result here—the admissions were obtained in the absence of counsel—would seem equally pertinent to statements obtained at any time after the right to counsel attaches, whether there has been an indictment or not"? Does a suspect who has not yet been indicted need "a lawyer's help" every bit as much as one who has been formally charged? By drawing the line at the initiation of formal judicial proceedings, had Justice Stewart (author of *Massiah,* but a dissenter in *Escobedo,* infra) "painted himself into a corner [from] which he could extricate himself only by a highly formalistic reading of the Sixth Amendment"? See Lawrence Herman, *The Supreme Court and Restrictions on Police Interrogation,* 25 Ohio St.L.J. 449, 491 (1964).

As made plain a short five weeks later in the same Term, ESCOBEDO v. ILLINOIS, 378 U.S. 478, 84 S.Ct. 1758, 12 L.Ed.2d 977 (1964), a majority of the Court was not about to give the Sixth Amendment a formalistic reading. Escobedo's interrogation had occurred before "judicial" or "adversary" proceedings had commenced against him, but, as dissenting Justice Stewart characterized the *Escobedo* majority's reasoning, "[t]he Court disregards this basic difference between the present case and Massiah's, with the bland assertion that 'that fact should make no difference.' "

Escobedo arose as follows: On the night of January 19, petitioner's brother-in-law was fatally shot. A few hours later petitioner was taken into custody for questioning, but he made no statement and was released the following afternoon pursuant to a writ of habeas corpus obtained by his retained counsel. On January 30, one Di Gerlando, who was then in police custody and who was later indicted for the murder along with petitioner, stated that petitioner had fired the shots which killed his brother-in-law. That evening petitioner was again arrested and taken to police headquarters. En route to the police station he was told that Di Gerlando had named him as the one who fired the fatal shots and that he might as well admit it, but petitioner replied (probably because his attorney had obtained

---

d. Does (should) this ethical rule apply to criminal proceedings? See Note 5, p. 632.

e. But consider Breitel, C.J., in *People v. Hobson,* 348 N.E.2d 894, 898 (N.Y.1976): "[I]t would not be rational, logical, moral or realistic to make any distinction between a lawyer acting for the State who [by seeking a waiver of the right to counsel from a suspect in the absence of, and without notification to, his lawyer] violates [the Code of Professional Responsibility] directly and one who indirectly uses the admissions improperly obtained by a police officer, who is the badged and uniformed representative of the State." See also *United States v. Springer,* 460 F.2d 1344, 1354–55 (7th Cir.1972) (Judge (now Justice) Stevens, dissenting).

his release from police custody only 11 days earlier or because he had consulted with his attorney in the meantime): "I am sorry but I would like to have advice from my lawyer." Shortly after petitioner reached police headquarters, his retained lawyer arrived and spent the next several hours trying unsuccessfully to speak to his client. He talked to every officer he could find, but was repeatedly told that he could not see his client and that he would have to get a writ of habeas corpus. In the meantime, petitioner repeatedly but unsuccessfully asked to speak to his lawyer. Instead, the police arranged a confrontation between petitioner and Di Gerlando. Petitioner denied that he had fired the fatal shots, claiming that Di Gerlando had done so, but thereby implicated himself in the murder plot. Petitioner's subsequent statement, to an assistant prosecutor who asked carefully framed questions, was admitted into evidence and he was convicted of murder. The Supreme Court of Illinois affirmed.

When certiorari was granted, the lawyers involved realized, as did close students of the problem, that *Escobedo* might be a momentous case. Bernard Weisberg, author of an important article on police interrogation, *Police Interrogation of Arrested Persons: A Skeptical View*, 52 J.Crim.L. & P.S. 21 (1961), argued the case for the ACLU, as *amicus curiae*. Because he thought it "playing Hamlet without the ghost to discuss police questioning without knowing what such questioning is really like," in his article Weisberg had made very extensive use of the interrogation manuals. He did the same in his *Escobedo* brief, maintaining that these books "are invaluable because they vividly describe the kind of interrogation practices which are accepted as lawful and proper under the best current standards of professional police work." What these manuals reveal, argued Weisberg, "is that 'fair and reasonable' and 'effective interrogation' is basically unfair and inherently coercive."[f]

Former Northwestern University law professor James Thompson (who later became Governor of Illinois) argued the *Escobedo* case for the state. He warned the U.S. Supreme Court: "[A decision that the right to counsel begins at the moment of arrest] means the end of confessions as a tool of law enforcement. [For] once this petitioner's claim with Illinois is settled, the inevitable progression of the law must follow:

"*First*, if the right to counsel attaches at the moment of arrest [as the dissent in *Crooker* maintained], then it can hardly be denied that this right must be available to the poor as well as to the rich. * * *

"*Second*, if indigent criminal defendants are entitled to counsel from the moment of arrest, then already established law makes it clear that such a right does not depend upon a request. [N]ot only must the state furnish counsel to the indigent defendant at this stage of the criminal proceeding, it must make sure that he does not waive the right through ignorance of its existence. * * *"[g]

f. Weisberg's article on confessions, apparently the first to make extensive use of the interrogation manuals, and his *Escobedo* brief set the fashion for civil libertarians. The ACLU brief in *Miranda*, primarily the work of Professors Anthony Amsterdam and Paul Mishkin, reprinted a full chapter from one interrogation manual. In turn, Chief Justice Warren's opinion for the Court in *Miranda*, infra, devoted six full pages to extracts from various police manuals and texts "document[ing] procedures employed with success in the past, [and] recommend[ing] various other effective tactics."

Many of the examples selected by the *Miranda* Court in 1966 were the same ones Weisberg used in his 1961 article and his 1964 *Escobedo* brief.

g. Thompson's discussion of "the inevitable progression of the law" was, of course, the statement of an advocate; Illinois deemed it advantageous to underscore the extent to which the rule espoused by its adversaries would "cripple" law enforcement. But Escobedo's lawyers were advocates, too, and they could not, or at least did not try to, minimize the impact of the rule they sought. Neither the

Added Thompson: "Criminal defendants, rich as well as poor, enjoy more protection from unjust conviction today than at any time in our history. 'The terrible engine' of the criminal law has been repeatedly braked by this Court, by state courts and legislatures and by fair and honest administration of the law by prosecutors and police. We need to guard against its derailment. * * * "

A 5–4 majority of the Court, per GOLDBERG, J., struck down Escobedo's confession, but, until *Miranda* moved *Escobedo* off center stage two years later, the scope and meaning of the decision was a matter of strong and widespread disagreement. In large part this was due to the accordion-like quality of the *Escobedo* opinion. At some places the opinion launched so broad an attack on the use of confessions in general and rejected the arguments for an "effective interrogation opportunity" so forcefully that it threatened (or promised) to eliminate virtually all police interrogation. At other places, however, the language of the opinion was so narrow and confining that it arguably limited the case to its special facts:

"The interrogation here was conducted before petitioner was formally indicted. But in the context of this case, that fact should make no difference. When petitioner requested, and was denied, an opportunity to consult with his lawyer, the investigation had ceased to be a general investigation of 'an unsolved crime.' Petitioner had become the accused, and the purpose of the interrogation was to 'get him' to confess his guilt despite his constitutional right not to do so. At the time of his arrest and throughout the course of the interrogation, the police told petitioner that they had convincing evidence that he had fired the fatal shots. Without informing him of his absolute right to remain silent in the face of this accusation, the police urged him to make a statement. * * *

"Petitioner, a layman, was undoubtedly unaware that under Illinois law an admission of 'mere' complicity in the murder plot was legally as damaging as an admission of firing of the fatal shots. The 'guiding hand of counsel' was essential to advise petitioner of his rights in this delicate situation. This was the 'stage when legal aid and advice' were most critical to petitioner. *Massiah.* * * *

"[It] is argued that if the right to counsel is afforded prior to indictment, the number of confessions obtained by the police will diminish significantly, because most confessions are obtained during the period between arrest and indictment, and 'any lawyer worth his salt will tell the suspect in no uncertain terms to make no statement to police under any circumstances.' This argument, of course, cuts two ways. The fact that many confessions are obtained during this period points up its critical nature as a 'stage when legal aid and advice' are surely needed. *Massiah.* The right to counsel would indeed be hollow if it began at a period when few confessions were obtained. * * *

"We have learned the lesson of history, ancient and modern, that a system of criminal law enforcement which comes to depend on the 'confession' will, in the long run, be less reliable and more subject to abuses than a system which depends on extrinsic evidence independently secured through skillful investigation. * * *

"We have also learned the companion lesson of history that no system of criminal justice can, or should, survive if it comes to depend for its continued effectiveness on the citizens' abdication through unawareness of their constitu-

ACLU brief nor the brief filed by Escobedo's own lawyers ever cited *Gideon, Douglas, Griffin,* or *Carnley.*

Moreover, shortly after *Escobedo* was decided, Thompson continued to view the case essentially the same way, now not as an advocate, but as assistant director of the Northwestern University Law School's Criminal Law Program. See fn. i infra.

tional rights. No system worth preserving should have to *fear* that if an accused is permitted to consult with a lawyer, he will become aware of, and exercise, these rights. If the exercise of constitutional rights will thwart the effectiveness of a system of law enforcement, then there is something very wrong with that system.[h]

"We hold, therefore, that where, as here, the investigation is no longer a general inquiry into an unsolved crime but has begun to focus on a particular suspect, the suspect has been taken into police custody, the police carry out a process of interrogations that lends itself to eliciting incriminating statements, the suspect has requested and been denied an opportunity to consult with his lawyer, and the police have not effectively warned him of his absolute constitutional right to remain silent, the accused has been denied 'the Assistance of Counsel' in violation of the Sixth Amendment to the Constitution as 'made obligatory upon the States by the Fourteenth Amendment,' *Gideon*, and that no statement elicited by the police during the interrogation may be used against him at a criminal trial. * * *

"Nothing we have said today affects the power of the police to investigate 'an unsolved crime' by gathering information from witnesses and by other 'proper investigative efforts.' We hold only that when the process shifts from investigatory to accusatory—when its focus is on the accused and its purpose is to elicit a confession—our adversary system begins to operate, and, under the circumstances here, the accused must be permitted to consult with his lawyer."[i]

Dissenting Justice STEWART protested:

"*Massiah* is not in point here. * * * Putting to one side the fact that the case now before us is not a federal case, the vital fact remains that this case does not involve the deliberate interrogation of a defendant after the initiation of judicial proceedings against him. The Court disregards this basic difference between the present case and Massiah's, with the bland assertion that 'that fact should make no difference.'

"It is 'that fact,' I submit, which makes all the difference. Under our system of criminal justice the institution of formal, meaningful judicial proceedings, by way of indictment, information, or arraignment, marks the point at which a criminal investigation has ended and adversary litigative proceedings have com-

---

h. But consider Gerald Caplan, *Questioning Miranda*, 38 Vand.L.Rev. 1417, 1440 (1985): "This statement is misleading because the right that the Court was defending, far from being of long standing, was newly discovered, indeed created, in this very opinion. What may have been 'very wrong' was not the extant 'system,' but the right the Court just announced."

i. As to whether *Escobedo* extended the constitutional role of counsel to the preindictment stage "when the process shifts from investigatory to accusatory—when its focus is on the accused and its purpose is to elicit a confession"—or when the process so shifts *and* one or some combination or all of the limiting facts in *Escobedo* are also present, see the summary of the wide disagreement over the probable meaning of the case in Kamisar Essays at 161 fn. 26.

Although many lower courts construed *Escobedo* quite narrowly, James Thompson, who had the distinction of making the losing argument in the case, read it quite broadly. He told a group of prosecuting attorneys attending a criminal law program that "in all cases where the police desire to obtain a confession from a suspect under circumstances like those in *Escobedo* [and] the suspect does not have retained counsel and does not request counsel, the police should, before interrogation, (a) inform him of his right not to say anything; and (b) inform him that anything he does say might be used against him." He also observed: [I]n dealing with [a suspect who, unlike Danny Escobedo,] has not expressly indicated that he is aware of his right to counsel, absolute compliance with the *Escobedo* rule may well require a warning of the right to counsel along with the warning of the privilege against self-incrimination." See the extensive extracts from Thompson's analysis of *Escobedo* in Kamisar Essays, at 66–68.

menced. It is at this point that the constitutional guarantees attach which pertain to a criminal trial."

In a separate dissent, Justice WHITE, joined by Stewart and Clark, JJ., observed:

"[*Massiah*] held that as of the date of the indictment the prosecution is disentitled to secure admissions from the accused. The Court now moves that date back to the time when the prosecution begins to 'focus' on the accused. Although the opinion purports to be limited to the facts of this case, it would be naive to think that the new constitutional right announced will depend upon whether the accused has retained his own counsel, or has asked to consult with counsel in the course of interrogation. At the very least the Court holds that once the accused becomes a suspect and, presumably, is arrested, any admission made to the police thereafter is inadmissible in evidence unless the accused has waived his right to counsel. * * *

"It is incongruous to assume that the provision for counsel in the Sixth Amendment was meant to amend or supersede the self-incrimination provision of the Fifth Amendment, which is now applicable to the States. That amendment addresses itself to the very issue of incriminating admissions of an accused and resolves it by proscribing only compelled statements.

"[The] Court chooses [to] rely on the virtues and morality of a system of criminal law enforcement which does not depend on the 'confession.' No such judgment is to be found in the Constitution. The only 'inquisitions' the Constitution forbids are those which compel incrimination. Escobedo's statements were not compelled and the Court does not hold that they were. * * *

"[The] Court may be concerned with a narrower matter: the unknowing defendant who responds to police questioning because he mistakenly believes that he must and that his admissions will not be used against him. But this worry hardly calls for the broadside the Court has now fired. [If] an accused is told he must answer and did not know better, it would be very doubtful that the resulting admissions could be used against him. When the accused has not been informed of his rights at all the Court characteristically and properly looks very closely at the surrounding circumstances. I would continue to do so. But, in this case Danny Escobedo knew full well that he need not answer and knew full well that his lawyer had advised him not to answer."[j]

ON THE MEANING OF *ESCOBEDO*

1. *What right comes into play?* Once the investigation has ceased to be "a general inquiry of an unsolved crime but has begun to focus on a particular suspect," what right comes into play? The right of the suspect to consult with his lawyer before resuming the interrogation or the right to enjoy his attorney's *continued presence* and *constant advice* from that point on, as a protection in the face of any further police interrogation? Cf. *Massiah*.

2. *The role of counsel.* Consider Gerald Caplan, *Questioning Miranda*, 38 Vand.L.Rev. 1417, 1440–41 (1985): "Danny Escobedo's lawyer had advised him not to say anything to the police. If the homicide detectives had granted Escobedo's request to see his attorney again, there would have been nothing additional

---

j. In a brief separate dissent, Justice Harlan agreed with Justice White that "the rule announced today is most ill-conceived and that it seriously and unjustifiably fetters perfectly legitimate methods of criminal law enforcement."

for his attorney to communicate. Escobedo had already been given all the assistance his counsel could provide without actually being present to assist his client on a question-by-question basis. Was Escobedo's attorney seeking the right to be present during the interrogation? Probably not. His intent in seeking entry to the homicide bureau was most likely to bring the interrogation to a close. Given that a defense attorney's usual objective is to stop the interrogation, it is hard to understand why the Court was so certain that 'no system worth preserving should have to fear that if an accused person is permitted to consult with a lawyer, he will become aware of, and exercise [his] rights,' unless the Court simply believed that there was no social utility in police interrogation. The *Escobedo* opinion contains no hint of anxiety that harm may accrue from a right to counsel: that there may be fewer confessions, and more crime."

3. *The "right to remain silent."* As we have seen, *Escobedo* refers to a suspect's "absolute constitutional right to remain silent." Where does this right come from? Does the privilege against self-incrimination confer (or was it intended to confer) a right to remain silent or a right to refuse to respond to incriminating questions or only the right to be free of compulsion? See Albert W. Alschuler, *A Peculiar Privilege in Historical Perspective: The Right to Remain Silent*, 94 Mich.L.Rev. 2625, 2630–32 (1996); Joseph D. Grano, *Confessions, Truth, and the Law* 141–43 (1993).

Does the Court simply mean that since the police lack legislative authorization to compel answers, a suspect is not required to provide any? Does the Court mean more—that the Constitution would prevent a legislature from investing police with the power to compel non-incriminating answers? Or does the Court mean that since a layperson cannot be expected to know what statements may be incriminating, if *in the absence of counsel*, she chooses not to incriminate herself, the only practical way she can assure that she will not do so is to remain completely silent?

F. A LATE ARRIVAL ON THE SCENE: THE PRIVILEGE AGAINST SELF-INCRIMINATION

"[Despite] a great deal of emotional writing which elevates the privilege against self-incrimination to 'one of the great landmarks in man's struggle to make himself civilized,' [the] most abundant proof [that it does not prohibit pretrial interrogation] is to be found in the United States. There the privilege is in the Federal Constitution and in [forty-eight state constitutions]. But in none of the forty-nine jurisdictions does it apply to what happens in the police station. The police interrogate freely, sometimes for seven to eight hours on end. The statements thus extracted are given in evidence. [O]nly statements made voluntarily may be given in evidence, but that seems to be interpreted rather liberally, judged by our standards."

—Judge V.G. Hiemstra of the Supreme Court of South Africa, *Abolition of the Right Not to be Questioned*, 80 South African L.J. 187, 194–95 (1963).

As long ago as 1931, Ernest Hopkins, a member of the Wickersham Commission staff, forcefully argued that the "third degree"-indeed, all secret police interrogation as typically practiced-was fundamentally in violation of the privilege against self-incrimination. Ernest Hopkins, *Our Lawless Police* 193–95 (1931). As we have seen, however, the concurring justice in *Spano* and the majorities in *Massiah* and *Escobedo* relied primarily on the right to counsel, not the privilege against self-incrimination-the other essential mainstay of the accusatorial, adversary system. But the "prime suspect"-"focal point"-"accusatory state" test(s) of *Escobedo* threatened the admissibility of even "volunteered" statements. There was reason to think that the Court might be in the process of shaping "a novel right not to confess except knowingly and with the tactical assistance of counsel," Arnold Enker & Sheldon Elsen, *Counsel for the Suspect: Massiah v. United States and Escobedo v. Illinois,* 49 Minn.L.Rev. 47, 60–61, 69, 83 (1964). Thus *critics* of *Escobedo* turned to the privilege against self-incrimination as a less restrictive alternative. Dissenting in *Escobedo,* Justice White, joined by Clark and Stewart, JJ., observed:

"It is incongruous to assume that the provision for counsel in the Sixth Amendment was meant to amend or supersede the self-incrimination provision of the Fifth Amendment which is now applicable to the States. [*Malloy v. Hogan,* infra.] That amendment addresses itself to the very issue of incriminating admissions and resolves it by proscribing only compelled statements. [That amendment provides no support] for the idea that an accused has an absolute constitutional right not to answer even in the absence of compulsion, [no support for the view that he has] the constitutional right not to incriminate himself by making voluntary disclosures."

Even as Justice White spoke, there was reason to think that, at long last, the privilege against self-incrimination was knocking on the door of the interrogation room. Only a few months before *Escobedo* had been decided, the Court, in MALLOY v. HOGAN, 378 U.S. 1, 84 S.Ct. 1489, 12 L.Ed.2d 653 (1964) (per Brennan, J.), had performed "what might have seemed to some a shotgun wedding of the privilege [against self-incrimination] to the confession rule," Lawrence Herman, *The Supreme Court and Restrictions on Police Interrogation,* 25 Ohio St.L.J. 449, 465 (1965), by declaring that "today the admissibility of a confession in a state criminal prosecution is tested by the same standard applied in federal prosecutions since 1897, when in *Bram v. United States,* 168 U.S. 532, 18 S.Ct. 183, 42 L.Ed. 568, the Court held that '[i]n criminal trials, in the courts of the United States, wherever a question arises whether a confession is incompetent because not voluntary, the issue is controlled by [the self-incrimination] portion of the Fifth Amendment.' "[a]

Whether or not this approach to police interrogation and confessions makes good sense it constitutes very questionable history—at least since *Brown v. Mississippi* (1936). The old *Bram* case might well have furnished a steppingstone to the standard advanced in *Malloy,* but until *Escobedo,* at any rate, it only seemed to amount to an early excursion from the prevailing multifactor or "totality of circumstances" approach. In none of the dozens of federal *or* state confession cases decided by the Court in the 1930's, 1940's and 1950's had the privilege against self-incrimination, certainly not as it applied to judicial proceedings, been the basis for judgment (although it had occasionally been mentioned in an opinion). If the privilege against self-incrimination had been the way to resolve the confession problem, then all the state courts and lower federal courts that had admitted confessions would have been reversed *per curiam.* For it was plain that law enforcement officers could, and without hesitation did, resort to methods they would never consider utilizing at the trial, that they had much greater power over

---

a. Until the 1960's *Bram* had become a largely forgotten case, but in recent years it has been the subject of close analysis and spirited debate. Compare Lawrence A. Benner, *Requiem for Miranda: The Rehnquist Court's Voluntariness Doctrine in Historical Perspective,* 67 Wash.U.L.Q. 59, 107–11 (1989) and Stephen A. Saltzburg, *Miranda v. Arizona Revisited: Constitutional Law or Judicial Fiat,* 26 Washburn L.J. 1, 4–14 (1986) with Joseph D. Grano, *Confessions, Truth, and the Law* 123–31 (1993).

a suspect or defendant away from the restraining influence of a public trial in an open courtroom.

Although certain factors, such as the length of pre-arraignment detention, had been taking on increasing significance, as Justice Frankfurter described the situation in *Culombe v. Connecticut* (1961), neither the privilege against self-incrimination nor any other "single litmus-paper test for constitutionally impermissible interrogation [had] been evolved: neither extensive cross-questioning-deprecated by the English judges; nor undue delay in arraignment-proscribed by *McNabb;* nor failure to caution a prisoner-enjoined by the [English] Judges' Rules; nor refusal to permit communication with friends and legal counsel at stages in the proceedings when the prisoner is still only a suspect-prohibited by several state statutes." That was why, as Justice Goldberg put it for a majority in *Haynes v. Washington,* 373 U.S. 503, 83 S.Ct. 1336, 10 L.Ed.2d 513 (1963) (only a year before he wrote the opinion of the Court in *Escobedo*), "the line between proper and permissible police conduct and techniques and methods offensive to due process is, at best, a difficult one to draw, particularly in cases such as this where it is necessary to make fine judgments as to the effect of psychologically coercive pressures and inducements on the mind and will of an accused."

Why had the privilege against self-incrimination been excluded from the stationhouse all these years? The legal reasoning was that compulsion to testify meant *legal* compulsion. Since he is threatened neither with perjury for testifying falsely nor contempt for refusing to testify at all, it cannot be said, ran the argument, that the subject of police interrogation is being "compelled" to be "a witness against himself" within the meaning of the privilege-even though he may assume or be led to believe that there *are* legal (or extralegal) sanctions for contumacy. Since the police have no *legal right* to make a suspect answer, there is no legal obligation to answer to which a privilege in the technical sense can apply. For an appraisal of this argument, see Lewis Mayers, *Shall We Amend the Fifth Amendment?,* 82–83, 223–33 (1959); Walter Schaefer, *The Suspect and Society* 16–18 (1967); 8 John Henry Wigmore, *Evidence* 329 fn. 27 (McNaughton rev. 1961).

It has been suggested that the reasoning above "had a great deal more to commend it than merely the inherent force of its 'logic' or the self-restraint and tenderness of the exempted class of interrogators," Kamisar Essays 59–60; and that among the forces at work were *"necessity"*—the conviction that police interrogation without advising the suspect of his rights was "indispensable" in law enforcement—and the *invisibility* of the process, which made it easy for society to be complacent about what was really going on and to readily accept police-prosecution "sanitized" versions of what was going on. Id. at 60–63.

How the *Malloy* opinion looked back, however, was not as important as how it looked forward. Whatever one thought of the manner in which *Malloy* had recorded the recent past, one could not treat lightly the way it anticipated the near future.

SECTION 3. THE *MIRANDA* "REVOLUTION"

ORAL ARGUMENTS IN *MIRANDA* AND COMPANION CASES[a]

* * *

MR. DUANE R. NEDRUD, on behalf of the National District Attorneys Association, *Amicus Curiae.* * * *

---

a. These extracts from the oral arguments are not taken from an "official transcript"—no such transcript is available–but from a tran-script the Institute of Criminal Law and Procedure of the Georgetown University Law Center and several private parties, including the edi-

THE CHIEF JUSTICE: May I ask you this, please, Mr. Nedrud: if you agree on the facts that *Escobedo* should not be overruled, what would you say as to the man who did not have a lawyer, but who said he wanted a lawyer before he talked?

MR. NEDRUD: If he asked for a lawyer, and he does not waive his right to counsel, I think that he should have a lawyer. [I] would go so far as to say that I think the state should appoint a lawyer if he asks for a lawyer. I do not think, however, that we should in effect encourage him to have a lawyer.

THE CHIEF JUSTICE: Why do you say we should not encourage him to have a lawyer? Are lawyers a menace? * * *

MR. NEDRUD: I think [a lawyer] is not a menace at the trial level. He is not a menace, per se, but he is, in doing his duty, going to prevent a confession from being obtained. * * *

JUSTICE DOUGLAS: * * * [A lawyer] needs time to prepare for the trial, so the appointment must be at some point anterior to the trial. Our question here is how far anterior. * * *

MR. NEDRUD: The question comes down I think, Mr. Justice Douglas, to whether or not we are going to allow the trial court to determine guilt or innocence?or the defense counsel. If the defense counsel comes in at the arrest stage, he will, as he should, prevent the defendant from confessing to his crime, and you will have fewer convictions. If this is what is wanted, this is what will occur.

JUSTICE BLACK: I guess there is no doubt, is there, as to the effect of the provision which provides for protection against compelling him to give testimony. Is it not fewer convictions?

MR. NEDRUD: [I believe] there is a point of diminishing returns and at some stage the police must be in a position to protect us.

JUSTICE BLACK: * * * Can you think of any time when [a person] needs a lawyer more than [at] the point of detention?

MR. NEDRUD: Mr. Justice Black, again, the question is are we interested in convicting the defendant, or are we interested in protecting or acquitting him? This is the only point that I can, in effect, make, if you say that this defendant needs counsel at this time.

For example, if I may use this illustration, I worked when I was a professor of law, which I was prior to taking this position, I worked on the defense project for the American Bar Association. In the questionnaire there was a statement, "When is the ideal time for counsel to be appointed for the defendant?"

Actually, the question is, "When is the ideal time for whom, the people or the defendant?" If it is for the defendant, then it is the earliest possible opportunity; if it is for the people, it should not be until a critical stage. * * *

JUSTICE BLACK: I have found out over many years a very critical stage is when a person is taken to the police headquarters. * * *

tors of this book, arranged to have made. Substantial extracts from the oral arguments also appear in Richard J. Medalie, *From Escobedo* *to Miranda: The Anatomy of a Supreme Court Decision* (1966) (Inst. Of Crim.L&P., Geo.U.).

A person is taken to police headquarters and placed under arrest or detention. He can't leave, if he wants to, unless they let him. Would you call that voluntary for him, then, for [the police] to have him there in that situation and probe him about probable conviction of crime? Would you think of that as voluntary?

MR. NEDRUD: As being voluntarily in the police station, no. * * *

MR. VICTOR M. EARLE, III on behalf of the petitioner in VIGNERA v. NEW YORK. * * *

JUSTICE FORTAS: [Are you saying] that when the point of time comes where it appears that the police have enough information to satisfy themselves that the fellow really did the act, then the right to arrange for counsel or to give the warning attaches?

MR. EARLE: I think that is correct, although we don't have to look into the mind of police necessarily to be able to determine that. * * * If in doubt, push it out on the other side of the warning. That is why I don't see that it should pose so much of a problem. I think the FBI Agents give warnings on this proceeding.

JUSTICE STEWART: What should this warning contain? What should this warning be?

MR. EARLE: The Chief of Police in the District of Columbia last August promulgated a warning which, I understand, is now being given by all police officials in the District. It goes something like this: You have been placed under arrest. You are not required to say anything to us any time or to answer any questions. Anything you say may be used as evidence in court. You may call a lawyer or a relative or a friend. Your lawyer may be present here, and you may talk with him. If you cannot obtain a lawyer, one will be appointed for you when your case first goes to court.

I might have a little quibble with that third point, because it suggests a little bit that you might not be able to get a lawyer now.

JUSTICE FORTAS: Much more than a little bit of quibble on the basis of what you have argued so far—that he has an absolute right for a lawyer to be appointed for him at that point, unless he waives it.

MR. EARLE: Yes, sir, unless he waives it. The question might come up of how do the police, or what do the police do when the fellow says, "Thanks. I would like a lawyer now that you mention it, but I don't happen to have any money." They have a choice. They can give him ten cents and the number of a legal aid society.

They have another alternative—just stop interrogating. That alternative was never mentioned. * * *

JUSTICE WHITE: They give him the warning, and he nods his head, yes. (laughter)

JUSTICE WHITE: What happens?

MR. EARLE: It takes a conscious relinquishing of his known rights, those rights I have been telling you about, Justice White.

JUSTICE WHITE: I thought that is what you would say. What happens then if the fellow just nods his head and just looks at him?

MR. EARLE: If we can believe he nodded his head, it is possible that he waives it. I would be very reluctant to come to that conclusion on [that] hypothesis.

JUSTICE WHITE: What else besides giving a warning and right to counsel?

MR. EARLE: I think if he writes down in his own handwriting, "I have been warned, I understand that I have a right to a lawyer now, to talk to him this minute, if I want to, or the right to say nothing if I want to. I understand that. I would like to go ahead and cooperate with the police. Signed: Michael Vignera." That would be enough.

JUSTICE WHITE: That is just barely the first stage.

MR. EARLE: That is what the police have to say.

JUSTICE WHITE: Sure, but if they want to rely on a waiver at any time, is this the only ground that you would accept for a lawyer not being present, a written waiver? Isn't that right?

MR. EARLE: I think that is right. It should be definitely recorded.

JUSTICE WHITE: It should be a written waiver?

MR. EARLE: Absolutely. It shouldn't be something he is conned into giving.

* * *

JUSTICE WHITE: What if he doesn't waive? He says, "I do want counsel," and the state says, "Fine. Here is a dime, and there is the legal aid number," and the fellow calls him. He talks to the lawyer, and he comes back and sits down, and you ask him some questions, and he answers them.

MR. EARLE: Without his lawyer being present, for example?

JUSTICE WHITE: Yes.

MR. EARLE: I take it that would be a decision made by his lawyer, and the lawyer can waive rights for his client.

JUSTICE WHITE: Is that a waiver in your book? What is it, a waiver of the right to consult counsel or a waiver of the right to have counsel present?

MR. EARLE: I think it is a waiver to have a counsel in all the ways it is meant. The lawyer can make the determination of whether he should be present or not. Lawyers have waived many rights, like not filing the 30th day and the notice of appeal and the like * * *

JUSTICE WHITE: My question is really going to what you think the scope of the right is. You think the scope of the right is to have counsel present and that you must waive not only the right to consult counsel, but the right to have counsel present?

MR. EARLE: I think that is right, Mr. Justice White. I want to elaborate on it, if I might. In a deposition in a civil case, for example, customarily, the plaintiff and the defendant can have counsel present. I can certainly conceive that one lawyer will not be present. The client, through him, would, therefore, waive that right. It would seem that the only way we could distinguish this case from *Escobedo* is the fact that Vignera did not make a request. What we have been talking about is doing that.

Obviously, it wasn't the request of the individual that made the right attach. The significance of the request, I think, in *Escobedo* was that it was a subjective piece of evidence to show that a stage had been reached. * * *

JUSTICE STEWART: How can there be a waiver, if these are Constitutional rights and are important? How can anybody waive them without the consent of counsel or without the advice of counsel? Doesn't he need a lawyer before he can waive them, if you are right?

MR. EARLE: You are entitled to waive in other situations. It is true in court when they want to plead guilty, for example, the judge will decline assignment of counsel, and the judge will, typically, interrogate him to some length to realize the significance of his act, and that is a lot more advisable a situation than—and more conducive to our being receptive to the idea of a waiver than the police station. I agree that is the worst place for waiver. The party alleging waiver has control of the party alleged to have waived.

JUSTICE STEWART: It seems to follow that he needs a lawyer before he can waive his right to a lawyer.

MR. EARLE: I wouldn't be unhappy to have lawyers in the police station.

JUSTICE STEWART: It follows naturally.

MR. EARLE: It doesn't follow naturally, because a majority of the court in *Escobedo* said these rights can be waived. I think we do have to recognize some of the realities of law enforcement. They do have to investigate. They do have the public duty of—if crimes are being committed by the minute, they do have to operate out of the police station. * * *

JUSTICE HARLAN: Is there a claim that the confession was coerced?

MR. EARLE: In no sense. I don't think it was coerced at all. Mr. Justice White asked yesterday a question about compelling someone to give up his Fifth Amendment privilege. I think there is a substantial difference between that and coercing a confession. I mean, it wasn't until 1964 that the Fifth Amendment privilege applied to the states, and so * * * all through until the § 60's, really, state convictions were overturned only by looking to the generality of the totality of the circumstances under the due process clause.

Now, we have specific Constitutional guarantees that are applied in branch to the states, of both the Fifth and Sixth Amendment rights. It is true that the word "compel" is used in the Fifth Amendment with respect to the privilege, but it is quite different to say that the privilege is cut down and impaired by detention and to say a man's will has been so overborne a confession is forced from him. * * *

I hate to sound cynical, but if we go back to the totality of circumstances, that means this Court will sit all by itself as it has so many years to overturn the few confessions it can take, necessarily, by the bulk of the work. The lower courts won't do their job. We need some specific guidelines as *Escobedo* to help them along the way. * * *

MR. WILLIAM I. SIEGEL, on behalf of the respondent in VIGNERA v. NEW YORK. * * *

JUSTICE FORTAS: Mr. Siegel, [the problem presented by these cases] really affects the basic relationship of the individual and the state. It really goes beyond the administration of justice, and that has been the history of mankind. * * *

MR. SIEGEL: [T]here is an immediate objective, also, and the immediate objective is to protect society; because, if society isn't protected, it, in one degree or another, lapses into anarchy because of crime and then the opportunity to reach this beautiful ideal is gone. It is the function of the police—.

JUSTICE FORTAS: (Interrupting) * * * The problem is to reconcile a good many objectives that are not totally consonant.

I am a little troubled, I must say, when I sit here and hear so much reference to this problem as if it were merely a pragmatic problem of convicting people who did a crime, because there are many more dimensions, I suggest, to the problem than just that simple statement.

MR. SIEGEL: * * * The problem that is before this Court, it seems to me, is just how to keep the balance between the ultimate necessity of the civilized, peaceful society and the constitutional rights of a specific defendant.

JUSTICE BLACK: Don't you think that the Bill of Rights has something to do with making that balance?

MR. SIEGEL: Yes, sir.

JUSTICE BLACK: There is not any doubt, is there, that no person should be convicted on evidence he has been compelled to give? Why do we have to get into a discussion of society or the beauties of the ideal civilization when that is the issue before us?

MR. SIEGEL: Because the Bill of Rights only says that [one] shall not be compelled, but the word "compelled" is not self-defining. We, for many, many years, were told [by] a great majority of Your Honors' predecessors, that compelled meant that which couldn't make a man talk by the exercise of process.

JUSTICE BLACK: By what?

MR. SIEGEL: By the exercise of process. You couldn't subpoena him into a court and, under pain of punishment, make him talk. * * *

SOLICITOR GENERAL THURGOOD MARSHALL, on behalf of the government in WESTOVER v. UNITED STATES. * * *

JUSTICE BLACK: [As] I understand you to say, of course, any person that has a lawyer or has the money to get a lawyer could get one immediately. This man has no lawyer and has no money to get one. The only reason he doesn't have a lawyer is for that reason. Does that raise any principles as to what an indigent is entitled to? He is certainly not getting treated like a man who has the money to get a lawyer.

MR. MARSHALL: He is not being denied anything. The state is not affirmatively denying anything. The state is just not furnishing him anything. * * *

JUSTICE BLACK: I understood you to say if he had the money he would have the right to have the lawyer but the man that has no money has no chance to. That is the situation that we had in *Griffin*.

MR. MARSHALL: *Griffin* was a different point. You can't equalize the whole thing. I don't believe that we can. * * *

———

"I was introduced for my accomplishments primarily as being of counsel in *Miranda*, and consistently I must disabuse everyone of the accomplishment * * *. When certiorari was granted and we were asked by the ACLU to prepare and file the brief, we had a meeting in our law office in which we agreed that the briefs should be written with the entire focus on the Sixth Amendment [right to counsel] because that is where the Court was headed after *Escobedo*, and, as you are all aware, in the very first paragraph [of the *Miranda* opinion] Chief Justice Warren said, 'It is the Fifth Amendment to the Constitution that is at issue today.' That was Miranda's effective use of counsel."

—John J. Flynn, *Panel Discussion on the Exclusionary Rule*, 61 F.R.D. 259, 278 (1972).

MIRANDA v. ARIZONA (NO. 759)*
384 U.S. 436, 86 S.Ct. 1602, 16 L.Ed.2d 694 (1966).

Chief Justice WARREN delivered the opinion of the Court.

The cases before us raise questions which go to the roots of American criminal jurisprudence: the restraints society must observe [in] prosecuting individuals for crime. More specifically, we deal with the admissibility of statements obtained from an individual who is subjected to custodial police interrogation and the necessity for procedures which assure that the individual is accorded his privilege under the Fifth Amendment to the Constitution not to be compelled to incriminate himself. * * *

We start here, as we did in *Escobedo* with the premise that our holding is not an innovation in our jurisprudence, but is an application of principles long recognized and applied in other settings. We have undertaken a thorough re-examination of the *Escobedo* decision and the principles it announced, and we reaffirm it. That case was but an explication of basic rights that are enshrined in our Constitution—that "No person * * * shall be compelled in any criminal case to be a witness against himself," and that "the accused [shall] have the Assistance of Counsel"—rights which were put in jeopardy in that case through official overbearing. * * *

Our holding will be spelled out with some specificity in the pages which follow but briefly stated it is this: the prosecution may not use statements, whether exculpatory or inculpatory, stemming from custodial interrogation of the defendant unless it demonstrates the use of procedural safeguards effective to secure the privilege against self-incrimination. By custodial interrogation, we mean questioning initiated by law enforcement officers after a person has been taken into custody or otherwise deprived of his freedom of action in any significant way.[4] As for the procedural safeguards to be employed, unless other fully effective means are devised to inform accused persons of their right of silence and to assure a continuous opportunity to exercise it, the following measures are required. Prior to any questioning, the person must be warned that he has a right to remain silent, that any statement he does make may be used as evidence against him, and that he has a right to the presence of an attorney, either retained or appointed. The defendant may waive effectuation of these rights, provided the waiver is made voluntarily, knowingly and intelligently. If, however, he indicates in any manner and at any stage of the process that he wishes to consult with an attorney before speaking there can be no questioning. Likewise, if the individual is alone and indicates in any manner that he does not wish to be interrogated, the police may not question him. The mere fact that he may have answered some questions or volunteered some statements on his own does not deprive him of the right to refrain from answering any further inquiries until he has consulted with an attorney and thereafter consents to be questioned.

The constitutional issue we decide in each of these cases is the admissibility of statements obtained from a defendant questioned while in custody and deprived of

---

* Together with No. 760, *Vignera v. New York* [and] No. 761, *Westover v. United States* [and] No. 584, *California v. Stewart* * * *.

4. This is what we meant in *Escobedo* when we spoke of an investigation which had focused on an accused.

his freedom of action in any significant way. In each, the defendant was questioned by police officers, detectives, or a prosecuting attorney in a room in which he was cut off from the outside world. In none of these cases was the defendant given a full and effective warning of his rights at the outset of the interrogation process. In all the cases, the questioning elicited oral admissions, and in three of them, signed statements as well which were admitted at their trials. They all thus share salient features—incommunicado interrogation of individuals in a police-dominated atmosphere, resulting in self-incriminating statements without full warnings of constitutional rights. * * *

Again we stress that the modern practice of in-custody interrogation is psychologically rather than physically oriented. * * * Interrogation still takes place in privacy. Privacy results in secrecy and this in turn results in a gap in our knowledge as to what in fact goes on in the interrogation rooms. A valuable source of information about present police practices, however, may be found in various police manuals and texts which document procedures employed with success in the past, and which recommend various other effective tactics. These texts are used by law enforcement agencies themselves as guides.[9] It should be noted that these texts professedly present the most enlightened and effective means presently used to obtain statements through custodial interrogation. By considering these texts and other data, it is possible to describe procedures observed and noted around the country. * * *

To highlight the isolation and unfamiliar surroundings, the manuals instruct the police to display an air of confidence in the suspect's guilt and from outward appearance to maintain only an interest in confirming certain details. The guilt of the subject is to be posited as a fact. The interrogator should direct his comments toward the reasons why the subject committed the act, rather than court failure by asking the subject whether he did it. Like other men, perhaps the subject has had a bad family life, had an unhappy childhood, had too much to drink, had an unrequited desire for women. The officers are instructed to minimize the moral seriousness of the offense, to cast blame on the victim or on society. These tactics are designed to put the subject in a psychological state where his story is but an elaboration of what the police purport to know already—that he is guilty. Explanations to the contrary are dismissed and discouraged.

The texts thus stress that the major qualities an interrogator should possess are patience and perseverance. * * *

[When other techniques] prove unavailing, the texts recommend they be alternated with a show of some hostility. One ploy often used has been termed the "friendly-unfriendly" or the "Mutt and Jeff" act:

> "[In] this technique, two agents are employed. Mutt, the relentless investigator, who knows the subject is guilty and is not going to waste any time. He's sent a dozen men away for this crime and he's going to send the

---

9. The methods described in Inbau and Reid, *Criminal Interrogation and Confessions* (1962), are a revision and enlargement of material presented in three prior editions of a predecessor text, *Lie Detection and Criminal Interrogation* (3d ed. 1953). The authors and their associates are officers of the Chicago Police Scientific Crime–Detection Laboratory and have had extensive experience in writing, lecturing and speaking to law enforcement authorities over a 20–year period. They say that the techniques portrayed in their manuals reflect their experiences and are the most effective psychological stratagems to employ during interrogations. Similarly, the techniques described in O'Hara, *Fundamentals of Criminal Investigation* (1959), were gleaned from long service as observer, lecturer in police science, and work as a federal criminal investigator. All these texts have had rather extensive use among law enforcement agencies and among students of police science, with total sales and circulation of over 44,000.

subject away for the full term. Jeff, on the other hand, is obviously a kindhearted man. He has a family himself. He has a brother who was involved in a little scrape like this. He disapproves of Mutt and his tactics and will arrange to get him off the case if the subject will cooperate. He can't hold Mutt off for very long. The subject would be wise to make a quick decision. The technique is applied by having both investigators present while Mutt acts out his role. Jeff may stand by quietly and demur at some of Mutt's tactics. When Jeff makes his plea for cooperation, Mutt is not present in the room."

The interrogators sometimes are instructed to induce a confession out of trickery. The technique here is quite effective in crimes which require identification or which run in series. In the identification situation, the interrogator may take a break in his questioning to place the subject among a group of men in a line-up. "The witness or complainant (previously coached, if necessary) studies the line-up and confidently points out the subject as the guilty party." Then the questioning resumes "as though there were now no doubt about the guilt of the subject." A variation on this technique is called the "reverse line-up":

"The accused is placed in a line-up, but this time he is identified by several fictitious witnesses or victims who associated him with different offenses. It is expected that the subject will become desperate and confess to the offense under investigation in order to escape from the false accusations."

The manuals also contain instructions for police on how to handle the individual who refuses to discuss the matter entirely, or who asks for an attorney or relatives. The examiner is to concede him the right to remain silent. "This usually has a very undermining effect. First of all, he is disappointed in his expectation of an unfavorable reaction on the part of the interrogator. Secondly, a concession of this right to remain silent impresses the subject with the apparent fairness of his interrogator." After this psychological conditioning, however, the officer is told to point out the incriminating significance of the suspect's refusal to talk:

"Joe, you have a right to remain silent. That's your privilege and I'm the last person in the world who'll try to take it away from you. If that's the way you want to leave this, O.K. But let me ask you this. Suppose you were in my shoes and I were in yours and you called me in to ask me about this and I told you, 'I don't want to answer any of your questions.' You'd think I had something to hide, and you'd probably be right in thinking that. That's exactly what I'll have to think about you, and so will everybody else. So let's sit here and talk this whole thing over."

Few will persist in their initial refusal to talk, it is said, if this monologue is employed correctly.

In the event that the subject wishes to speak to a relative or an attorney, the following advice is tendered:

"[T]he interrogator should respond by suggesting that the subject first tell the truth to the interrogator himself rather than get anyone else involved in the matter. If the request is for an attorney, the interrogator may suggest that the subject save himself or his family the expense of any such professional service, particularly if he is innocent of the offense under investigation. The interrogator may also add, 'Joe, I'm only looking for the truth, and if you're telling the truth, that's it. You can handle this by yourself.' "

From these representative samples of interrogation techniques, the setting prescribed by the manuals and observed in practice becomes clear. In essence, it is this: To be alone with the subject is essential to prevent distraction and to deprive him of any outside support. The aura of confidence in his guilt undermines his will to resist. He merely confirms the preconceived story the police seek to have him describe. Patience and persistence, at times relentless questioning, are employed. To obtain a confession, the interrogator must "patiently maneuver himself or his quarry into a position from which the desired object may be obtained." When normal procedures fail to produce the needed result, the police may resort to deceptive stratagems such as giving false legal advice. It is important to keep the subject off balance, for example, by trading on his insecurity about himself or his surroundings. The police then persuade, trick, or cajole him out of exercising his constitutional rights.

Even without employing brutality, the "third degree" or the specific stratagems described above, the very fact of custodial interrogation exacts a heavy toll on individual liberty and trades on the weakness of individuals.

In the cases before us today, given this background, we concern ourselves primarily with this interrogation atmosphere and the evils it can bring. In *Miranda v. Arizona,* the police arrested the defendant and took him to a special interrogation room where they secured a confession. In *Vignera v. New York,* the defendant made oral admissions to the police after interrogation in the afternoon, and then signed an inculpatory statement upon being questioned by an assistant district attorney later the same evening. In *Westover v. United States,* the defendant was handed over to the Federal Bureau of Investigation by local authorities after they had detained and interrogated him for a lengthy period, both at night and the following morning. After some two hours of questioning, the federal officers had obtained signed statements from the defendant. Lastly, in *California v. Stewart,* the local police held the defendant five days in the station and interrogated him on nine separate occasions before they secured his inculpatory statement.

In these cases, we might not find the defendants' statements to have been involuntary in traditional terms. Our concern for adequate safeguards to protect precious Fifth Amendment rights is, of course, not lessened in the slightest. In each of the cases, the defendant was thrust into an unfamiliar atmosphere and run through menacing police interrogation procedures. The potentiality for compulsion is forcefully apparent, for example, in *Miranda,* where the indigent Mexican defendant was a seriously disturbed individual with pronounced sexual fantasies, and in *Stewart,* in which the defendant was an indigent Los Angeles Negro who had dropped out of school in the sixth grade. To be sure, the records do not evince overt physical coercion or patented psychological ploys. The fact remains that in none of these cases did the officers undertake to afford appropriate safeguards at the outset of the interrogation to insure that the statements were truly the product of free choice.

It is obvious that such an interrogation environment is created for no purpose other than to subjugate the individual to the will of his examiner. This atmosphere carries its own badge of intimidation. To be sure, this is not physical intimidation, but it is equally destructive of human dignity. The current practice of incommunicado interrogation is at odds with one of our Nation's most cherished principles—that the individual may not be compelled to incriminate himself. Unless adequate protective devices are employed to dispel the compulsion inherent in custodial surroundings, no statement obtained from the defendant can truly be the product of his free choice.

From the foregoing, we can readily perceive an intimate connection between the privilege against self-incrimination and police custodial questioning. It is fitting to turn to history and precedent underlying the Self–Incrimination Clause to determine its applicability in this situation.

We sometimes forget how long it has taken to establish the privilege against self-incrimination, the sources from which it came and the fervor with which it was defended. Its roots go back into ancient times.[27] * * *

[W]e may view the historical development of the privilege as one which groped for the proper scope of governmental power over the citizen. As a "noble principle often transcends its origins," the privilege has come rightfully to be recognized in part as an individual's substantive right, a "right to a private enclave where he may lead a private life. That right is the hallmark of our democracy." We have recently noted that the privilege against self-incrimination—the essential mainstay of our adversary system—is founded on a complex of values. *Murphy v. Waterfront Comm'n* [p. 716]. All these policies point to one overriding thought: the constitutional foundation underlying the privilege is the respect a government—state or federal—must accord to the dignity and integrity of its citizens. To maintain a "fair state-individual balance," to require the government "to shoulder the entire load," 8 Wigmore, *Evidence* (McNaughton rev., 1961), to respect the inviolability of the human personality, our accusatory system of criminal justice demands that the government seeking to punish an individual produce the evidence against him by its own independent labors, rather than by the cruel, simple expedient of compelling it from his own mouth. In sum, the privilege is fulfilled only when the person is guaranteed the right "to remain silent unless he chooses to speak in the unfettered exercise of his own will." *Malloy v. Hogan* [p. 468].

* * * We are satisfied that all the principles embodied in the privilege apply to informal compulsion exerted by law-enforcement officers during in-custody questioning. An individual swept from familiar surroundings into police custody, surrounded by antagonistic forces, and subjected to the techniques of persuasion described above cannot be otherwise than under compulsion to speak. As a practical matter, the compulsion to speak in the isolated setting of the police station may well be greater than in courts or other official investigations, where there are often impartial observers to guard against intimidation or trickery.

This question in fact could have been taken as settled in federal courts almost seventy years ago [by] *Bram v. United States* (1897) [discussed at pp. 468 & 468n.a, ___]. Because of the adoption by Congress of Rule 5(a) of the Federal Rules of Criminal Procedure, and this Court's effectuation of that Rule in *McNabb* and *Mallory*, we have had little occasion in the past quarter century to reach the constitutional issues in dealing with federal interrogations. These supervisory rules, requiring production of an arrested person before a commissioner "without unnecessary delay" and excluding evidence obtained in default of that statutory obligation, were nonetheless responsive to the same considerations of Fifth Amendment policy that unavoidably face us now as to the States. In [the *McNabb* and *Mallory* cases] we recognized both the dangers of interrogation and the

---

27. Thirteenth century commentators found an analogue to the privilege grounded in the Bible. * * * [See generally Irene Rosenberg & Yale Rosenberg, *In the Beginning: The Tal-* *mudic Rule Against Self–Incrimination*, 63 N.Y.U.L.Rev. 955 (1988) and the authorities discussed therein].

appropriateness of prophylaxis stemming from the very fact of interrogation itself.[32]

Our decision in *Malloy v. Hogan* necessitates an examination of the scope of the privilege in state cases as well. In *Malloy,* we squarely held the privilege applicable to the States, and held that the substantive standards underlying the privilege applied with full force to state court proceedings. The implications [of *Malloy*] were elaborated in our decision in *Escobedo,* decided one week after *Malloy* applied the privilege to the States.

[In *Escobedo*], as in the cases today, we sought a protective device to dispel the compelling atmosphere of the interrogation. In *Escobedo,* however, the police did not relieve the defendant of the anxieties which they had created in the interrogation rooms. Rather, they denied his request for the assistance of counsel.[35] This heightened his dilemma, and made his later statements the product of this compulsion. [The] denial of the defendant's request for his attorney thus undermined his ability to exercise the privilege—to remain silent if he chose or to speak without any intimidation, blatant or subtle. The presence of counsel, in all the cases before us today, would be the adequate protective device necessary to make the process of police interrogation conform to the dictates of the privilege. His presence would insure that statements made in the government-established atmosphere are not the product of compulsion.

* * * Without the protections flowing from adequate warnings and the rights of counsel, "all the careful safeguards erected around the giving of testimony, whether by an accused or any other witness, would become empty formalities in a procedure where the most compelling possible evidence of guilt, a confession, would have already been obtained at the unsupervised pleasure of the police." *Mapp v. Ohio* (Harlan, J., dissenting).

Today, then, there can be no doubt that the Fifth Amendment privilege is available outside of criminal court proceedings and serves to protect persons in all settings in which their freedom of action is curtailed from being compelled to incriminate themselves. We have concluded that without proper safeguards the process of in-custody interrogation of persons suspected or accused of crime contains inherently compelling pressures which work to undermine the individual's will to resist and to compel him to speak where he would not otherwise do so freely. In order to combat these pressures and to permit a full opportunity to exercise the privilege against self-incrimination, the accused must be adequately and effectively apprised of his rights and the exercise of those rights must be fully honored.

It is impossible for us to foresee the potential alternatives for protecting the privilege which might be devised by Congress or the States in the exercise of their creative rule-making capacities. Therefore we cannot say that the Constitution necessarily requires adherence to any particular solution for the inherent compulsions of the interrogation process as it is presently conducted. Our decision in no way creates a constitutional straitjacket which will handicap sound efforts at reform, nor is it intended to have this effect. We encourage Congress and the

---

32. Our decision today does not indicate in any manner, of course, that these rules can be disregarded. When federal officials arrest an individual, they must as always comply with the dictates of the congressional legislation and cases thereunder. * * *

35. The police also prevented the attorney from consulting with his client. Independent of any other constitutional proscription, this action constitutes a violation of the Sixth Amendment right to the assistance of counsel and excludes any statement obtained in its wake. See *People v. Donovan,* 13 N.Y.2d 148, 243 N.Y.S.2d 841, 193 N.E.2d 628 (N.Y.1963) (Fuld, J.).

States to continue their laudable search for increasingly effective ways of protecting the rights of the individual while promoting efficient enforcement of our criminal laws. However, unless we are shown other procedures which are at least as effective in apprising accused persons of their right of silence and in assuring a continuous opportunity to exercise it, the following safeguards must be observed.

At the outset, if a person in custody is to be subjected to interrogation, he must first be informed in clear and unequivocal terms that he has the right to remain silent. For those unaware of the privilege, the warning is needed simply to make them aware of it?the threshold requirement for an intelligent decision as to its exercise. More important, such a warning is an absolute prerequisite in overcoming the inherent pressures of the interrogation atmosphere. It is not just the subnormal or woefully ignorant who succumb to an interrogator's imprecations, whether implied or expressly stated, that the interrogation will continue until a confession is obtained or that silence in the face of accusation is itself damning and will bode ill when presented to a jury.[37] Further, the warning will show the individual that his interrogators are prepared to recognize his privilege should he choose to exercise it.

The Fifth Amendment privilege is so fundamental to our system of constitutional rule and the expedient of giving an adequate warning as to the availability of the privilege so simple, we will not pause to inquire in individual cases whether the defendant was aware of his rights without a warning being given. Assessments of the knowledge the defendant possessed, based on information as to his age, education, intelligence, or prior contact with authorities, can never be more than speculation;[38] a warning is a clearcut fact. More important, whatever the background of the person interrogated, a warning at the time of the interrogation is indispensable to overcome its pressures and to insure that the individual knows he is free to exercise the privilege at that point in time.

The warning of the right to remain silent must be accompanied by the explanation that anything said can and will be used against the individual in court. This warning is needed in order to make him aware not only of the privilege, but also of the consequences of forgoing it. It is only through an awareness of these consequences that there can be any assurance of real understanding and intelligent exercise of the privilege. Moreover, this warning may serve to make the individual more acutely aware that he is faced with a phase of the adversary system—that he is not in the presence of persons acting solely in his interest.

The circumstances surrounding in-custody interrogation can operate very quickly to overbear the will of one merely made aware of his privilege by his interrogators. Therefore, the right to have counsel present at the interrogation is indispensable to the protection of the Fifth Amendment privilege under the system we delineate today. Our aim is to assure that the individual's right to choose between silence and speech remains unfettered throughout the interrogation process. A once-stated warning, delivered by those who will conduct the interrogation, cannot itself suffice to that end among those who most require knowledge of their rights. A mere warning given by the interrogators is not alone sufficient to accomplish that end. Prosecutors themselves claim that the admon-

---

37. [In] accord with this decision, it is impermissible to penalize an individual for exercising his Fifth Amendment privilege when he is under police custodial interrogation. The prosecution may not, therefore, use at trial the fact that he stood mute or claimed his privilege in the face of accusation.

38. Cf. *Betts v. Brady,* and the recurrent inquiry into special circumstances it necessitated. * * *

ishment of the right to remain silent without more "will benefit only the recidivist and the professional." Brief for the National District Attorneys Association as *amicus curiae*. Even preliminary advice given to the accused by his own attorney can be swiftly overcome by the secret interrogation process. Thus, the need for counsel to protect the Fifth Amendment privilege comprehends not merely a right to consult with counsel prior to questioning but also to have counsel present during any questioning if the defendant so desires.

The presence of counsel at the interrogation may serve several significant subsidiary functions as well. If the accused decides to talk to his interrogators, the assistance of counsel can mitigate the dangers of untrustworthiness. With a lawyer present the likelihood that the police will practice coercion is reduced, and if coercion is nevertheless exercised the lawyer can testify to it in court. The presence of a lawyer can also help to guarantee that the accused gives a fully accurate statement to the police and that the statement is rightly reported by the prosecution at trial.

An individual need not make a preinterrogation request for a lawyer. While such request affirmatively secures his right to have one, his failure to ask for a lawyer does not constitute a waiver. No effective waiver of the right to counsel during interrogation can be recognized unless specifically made after the warnings we here delineate have been given. The accused who does not know his rights and therefore does not make a request may be the person who most needs counsel. * * *

Accordingly we hold that an individual held for interrogation must be clearly informed that he has the right to consult with a lawyer and to have the lawyer with him during interrogation under the system for protecting the privilege we delineate today. As with the warnings of the right to remain silent and that anything stated can be used in evidence against him, this warning is an absolute prerequisite to interrogation. No amount of circumstantial evidence that the person may have been aware of this right will suffice to stand in its stead. Only through such a warning is there ascertainable assurance that the accused was aware of this right.

If an individual indicates that he wishes the assistance of counsel before any interrogation occurs, the authorities cannot rationally ignore or deny his request on the basis that the individual does not have or cannot afford a retained attorney. The financial ability of the individual has no relationship to the scope of the rights involved here. The privilege against self-incrimination secured by the Constitution applies to all individuals. The need for counsel in order to protect the privilege exists for the indigent as well as the affluent. In fact, were we to limit these constitutional rights to those who can retain an attorney, our decisions today would be of little significance. The cases before us as well as the vast majority of confession cases with which we have dealt in the past involve those unable to retain counsel. While authorities are not required to relieve the accused of his poverty, they have the obligation not to take advantage of indigence in the administration of justice.[41] Denial of counsel to the indigent at the time of interrogation while allowing an attorney to those who can afford one would be no more supportable by reason or logic than the similar situation at trial and on appeal struck down in *Gideon* and *Douglas v. California*.

41. See Kamisar, *Equal Justice in the Gatehouses and Mansions of American Criminal Procedure,* in Criminal Justice in Our Time (1965), 64–81; * * * Report of the Attorney General's Committee on *Poverty and the Administration of Federal Criminal Justice* (1963), p. 9 * * *.

In order fully to apprise a person interrogated of the extent of his rights under this system then, it is necessary to warn him not only that he has the right to consult with an attorney, but also that if he is indigent a lawyer will be appointed to represent him. Without this additional warning, the admonition of the right to consult with counsel would often be understood as meaning only that he can consult with a lawyer if he has one or has the funds to obtain one. The warning of a right to counsel would be hollow if not couched in terms that would convey to the indigent—the person most often subjected to interrogation—the knowledge that he too has a right to have counsel present. As with the warnings of the right to remain silent and of the general right to counsel, only by effective and express explanation to the indigent of this right can there be assurance that he was truly in a position to exercise it.[43]

Once warnings have been given, the subsequent procedure is clear. If the individual indicates in any manner, at any time prior to or during questioning, that he wishes to remain silent, the interrogation must cease.[44] At this point he has shown that he intends to exercise his Fifth Amendment privilege; any statement taken after the person invokes his privilege cannot be other than the product of compulsion, subtle or otherwise. Without the right to cut off questioning, the setting of in-custody interrogation operates on the individual to overcome free choice in producing a statement after the privilege has been once invoked. If the individual states that he wants an attorney, the interrogation must cease until an attorney is present. At that time, the individual must have an opportunity to confer with the attorney and to have him present during any subsequent questioning. If the individual cannot obtain an attorney and he indicates that he wants one before speaking to police, they must respect his decision to remain silent.

This does not mean, as some have suggested, that each police station must have a "station house lawyer" present at all times to advise prisoners. It does mean, however, that if police propose to interrogate a person they must make known to him that he is entitled to a lawyer and that if he cannot afford one, a lawyer will be provided for him prior to any interrogation. If authorities conclude that they will not provide counsel during a reasonable period of time in which investigation in the field is carried out, they may do so without violating the person's Fifth Amendment privilege so long as they do not question him during that time.

If the interrogation continues without the presence of an attorney and a statement is taken, a heavy burden rests on the Government to demonstrate that the defendant knowingly and intelligently waived his privilege against self-incrimination and his right to retained or appointed counsel. This Court has always set high standards of proof for the waiver of constitutional rights, *Johnson v. Zerbst,* and we reassert these standards as applied to in-custody interrogation. Since the State is responsible for establishing the isolated circumstances under which the interrogation takes place and has the only means of making available

43. While a warning that the indigent may have counsel appointed need not be given to the person who is known to have an attorney or is known to have ample funds to secure one, the expedient of giving a warning is too simple and the rights involved too important to engage in *ex post facto* inquiries into financial ability when there is any doubt at all on that score.

44. If an individual indicates his desire to remain silent, but has an attorney present, there may be some circumstances in which further questioning would be permissible. In the absence of evidence of overbearing, statements then made in the presence of counsel might be free of the compelling influence of the interrogation process and might fairly be construed as a waiver of the privilege for purposes of these statements.

corroborated evidence of warnings given during incommunicado interrogation, the burden is rightly on its shoulders.

An express statement that the individual is willing to make a statement and does not want an attorney followed closely by a statement could constitute a waiver. But a valid waiver will not be presumed simply from the silence of the accused after warnings are given or simply from the fact that a confession was in fact eventually obtained [referring to *Carnley v. Cochran,* 369 U.S. 506, 82 S.Ct. 884, 8 L.Ed.2d 70 (1962)].

* * * Moreover, where in-custody interrogation is involved, there is no room for the contention that the privilege is waived if the individual answers some questions or gives some information on his own prior to invoking his right to remain silent when interrogated.[45]

Whatever the testimony of the authorities as to waiver of rights by an accused, the fact of lengthy interrogation or incommunicado incarceration before a statement is made is strong evidence that the accused did not validly waive his rights. In these circumstances the fact that the individual eventually made a statement is consistent with the conclusion that the compelling influence of the interrogation finally forced him to do so. It is inconsistent with any notion of a voluntary relinquishment of the privilege. Moreover, any evidence that the accused was threatened, tricked, or cajoled into a waiver will, of course, show that the defendant did not voluntarily waive his privilege. The requirement of warnings and waiver of rights is a fundamental with respect to the Fifth Amendment privilege and not simply a preliminary ritual to existing methods of interrogation.

The warnings required and the waiver necessary in accordance with our opinion today are, in the absence of a fully effective equivalent, prerequisites to the admissibility of any statement made by a defendant. No distinction can be drawn between statements which are direct confessions and statements which amount to "admissions" of part or all of an offense. The privilege against self-incrimination protects the individual from being compelled to incriminate himself in any manner; it does not distinguish degrees of incrimination. Similarly, for precisely the same reason, no distinction may be drawn between inculpatory statements and statements alleged to be merely "exculpatory." If a statement made were in fact truly exculpatory it would, of course, never be used by the prosecution. In fact, statements merely intended to be exculpatory by the defendant are often used to impeach his testimony at trial or to demonstrate untruths in the statement given under interrogation and thus to prove guilt by implication. These statements are incriminating in any meaningful sense of the word and may not be used without the full warnings and effective waiver required for any other statement. In *Escobedo* itself, the defendant fully intended his accusation of another as the slayer to be exculpatory as to himself.

The principles announced today deal with the protection which must be given to the privilege against self-incrimination when the individual is first subjected to police interrogation while in custody at the station or otherwise deprived of his freedom of action in any significant way. It is at this point that our adversary system of criminal proceedings commences, distinguishing itself at the outset from

---

45. Although this Court held in *Rogers v. United States,* 340 U.S. 367, 71 S.Ct. 438, 95 L.Ed. 344 (1951), over strong dissent, that a witness before a grand jury may not in certain circumstances decide to answer some questions and then refuse to answer others that decision has no application to the interrogation situation we deal with today. No legislative or judicial fact-finding authority is involved here, nor is there a possibility that the individual might make self-serving statements of which he could make use at trial while refusing to answer incriminating statements.

the inquisitorial system recognized in some countries. Under the system of warnings we delineate today or under any other system which may be devised and found effective, the safeguards to be erected about the privilege must come into play at this point.

Our decision is not intended to hamper the traditional function of police officers in investigating crime. When an individual is in custody on probable cause, the police may, of course, seek out evidence in the field to be used at trial against him. Such investigation may include inquiry of persons not under restraint. General on-the-scene questioning as to facts surrounding a crime or other general questioning of citizens in the fact-finding process is not affected by our holding. It is an act of responsible citizenship for individuals to give whatever information they may have to aid in law enforcement. In such situations the compelling atmosphere inherent in the process of in-custody interrogation is not necessarily present.[46]

In dealing with statements obtained through interrogation, we do not purport to find all confessions inadmissible. Confessions remain a proper element in law enforcement. Any statement given freely and voluntarily without any compelling influences is, of course, admissible in evidence. The fundamental import of the privilege while an individual is in custody is not whether he is allowed to talk to the police without the benefit of warnings and counsel, but whether he can be interrogated. There is no requirement that police stop a person who enters a police station and states that he wishes to confess to a crime, or a person who calls the police to offer a confession or any other statement he desires to make. Volunteered statements of any kind are not barred by the Fifth Amendment and their admissibility is not affected by our holding today.

To summarize, we hold that when an individual is taken into custody or otherwise deprived of his freedom by the authorities in any significant way and is subjected to questioning, the privilege against self-incrimination is jeopardized. Procedural safeguards must be employed to protect the privilege, and unless other fully effective means are adopted to notify the person of his right of silence and to assure that the exercise of the right will be scrupulously honored, the following measures are required. He must be warned prior to any questioning that he has the right to remain silent, that anything he says can be used against him in a court of law, that he has the right to the presence of an attorney, and that if he cannot afford an attorney one will be appointed for him prior to any questioning if he so desires. Opportunity to exercise these rights must be afforded to him throughout the interrogation. After such warnings have been given, and such opportunity afforded him, the individual may knowingly and intelligently waive these rights and agree to answer questions or make a statement. But unless and until such warnings and waiver are demonstrated by the prosecution at trial, no evidence obtained as a result of interrogation can be used against him. * * *

If the individual desires to exercise his privilege, he has the right to do so. This is not for the authorities to decide. An attorney may advise his client not to talk to police until he has had an opportunity to investigate the case, or he may wish to be present with his client during any police questioning. In doing so an

---

46. The distinction and its significance has been aptly described in the opinion of a Scottish court:

"In former times such questioning, if undertaken, would be conducted by police officers visiting the house or place of business of the suspect and there questioning him, probably in the presence of a relation or friend. However convenient the modern practice may be, it must normally create a situation very unfavorable to the suspect." *Chalmers v. H.M. Advocate,* [1954] Sess.Cas. 66, 78 (J.C.).

attorney is merely exercising the good professional judgment he has been taught. This is not cause for considering the attorney a menace to law enforcement. He is merely carrying out what he is sworn to do under his oath—to protect to the extent of his ability the rights of his client. In fulfilling this responsibility the attorney plays a vital role in the administration of criminal justice under our Constitution.

In announcing these principles, we are not unmindful of the burdens which law enforcement officials must bear, often under trying circumstances. * * * This Court, while protecting individual rights, has always given ample latitude to law enforcement agencies in the legitimate exercise of their duties. The limits we have placed on the interrogation process should not constitute an undue interference with a proper system of law enforcement. [Although] confessions may play an important role in some convictions, the cases before us present graphic examples of the overstatement of the "need" for confessions. In each case authorities conducted interrogations ranging up to five days in duration despite the presence, through standard investigating practices, of considerable evidence against each defendant.[51] Further examples are chronicled in our prior cases.

It is also urged that an unfettered right to detention for interrogation should be allowed because it will often redound to the benefit of the person questioned. When police inquiry determines that there is no reason to believe that the person has committed any crime, it is said, he will be released without need for further formal procedures. The person who has committed no offense, however, will be better able to clear himself after warnings, with counsel present than without. It can be assumed that in such circumstances a lawyer would advise his client to talk freely to police in order to clear himself.

Custodial interrogation, by contrast, does not necessarily afford the innocent an opportunity to clear themselves. A serious consequence of the present practice of the interrogation alleged to be beneficial for the innocent is that many arrests "for investigation" subject large numbers of innocent persons to detention and interrogation. In one of the cases before us, *California v. Stewart,* police held four persons, who were in the defendant's house at the time of the arrest, in jail for five days until defendant confessed. At that time they were finally released. Police stated that there was "no evidence to connect them with any crime." Available statistics on the extent of this practice where it is condoned indicate that these four are far from alone in being subjected to arrest, prolonged detention, and interrogation without the requisite probable cause.

[The] experience in some other countries * * * suggests that the danger to law enforcement in curbs on interrogation is overplayed. The English procedure since 1912 under the Judges' Rules is significant. As recently strengthened, the Rules require that a cautionary warning be given an accused by a police officer as soon as he has evidence that affords reasonable grounds for suspicion; they also require that any statement made be given by the accused without questioning by police.[57] The right of the individual to consult with an attorney during this period is expressly recognized. * * *

---

51. Miranda, Vignera, and Westover were identified by eyewitnesses. Marked bills from the bank robbed were found in Westover's car. Articles stolen from the victim as well as from several other robbery victims were found in Stewart's home at the outset of the investigation.

57. [1964] Crim.L.Rev. 166–170. These Rules provide in part:

"II. As soon as a police officer has evidence which would afford reasonable grounds for suspecting that a person has committed an offence, he shall caution that person or cause him to be cautioned before putting to him any

Because of the nature of the problem and because of its recurrent significance in numerous cases, we have to this point discussed the relationship of the Fifth Amendment privilege to police interrogation without specific concentration on the facts of the cases before us. We turn now to these facts to consider the application to these cases of the constitutional principles discussed above. In each instance, we have concluded that statements were obtained from the defendant under circumstances that did not meet constitutional standards for protection of the privilege.

No. 759. *Miranda v. Arizona.*

On March 13, 1963, petitioner, Ernesto Miranda, was arrested at his home and taken in custody to a Phoenix police station. He was there identified by the complaining witness. The police then took him to "Interrogation Room No. 2" of

questions, or further questions, relating to that offence.

"The caution shall be in the following terms:

" 'You are not obliged to say anything unless you wish to do so but what you say may be put into writing and given in evidence.'

"When after being cautioned a person is being questioned, or elects to make a statement, a record shall be kept of the time and place at which any such questioning or statement began and ended and of the persons present.

* * *

"(b) It is only in exceptional cases that questions relating to the offence should be put to the accused person after he has been charged or informed that he may be prosecuted.

* * *

"IV. All written statements made after caution shall be taken in the following manner:

"(a) If a person says that he wants to make a statement he shall be told that it is intended to make a written record of what he says.

"He shall always be asked whether he wishes to write down himself what he wants to say; if he says that he cannot write or that he would like someone to write it for him, a police officer may offer to write the statement for him. * * *

"(b) Any person writing his own statement shall be allowed to do so without any prompting as distinct from indicating to him what matters are material.

* * *

"(d) Whenever a police officer writes the statement, he shall take down the exact words spoken by the person making the statement, without putting any questions other than such as may be needed to make the statement coherent, intelligible and relevant to the material matters: he shall not prompt him." * * *

Ed. Note–*England curtails the right to silence.* In the fall of 1994, the British Parliament adopted various restrictions on the right to silence, effective March 1, 1995. These restrictions were similar to those Parliament had imposed on Northern Ireland in 1988. The new law permits judges and jurors to draw adverse inferences when, during interrogation, suspects do not tell the police any fact subsequently relied upon in their defense at trial, if under the circumstances, the suspects would have "been "reasonably expected" to mention that fact to the police. (This section corresponds to a provision of the Northern Ireland Order, which, according to the government, was designed to end terrorists' use of the "ambush defense," whereby terrorists would remain silent during interrogation and thus prevent the prosecution from preparing a rebuttal to subsequent defense claims.)

[The new law also permits judges and jurors to draw adverse inferences when suspects fail to respond to police questions about any suspicious objects, substances, or marks which are found on their persons or clothing or when suspects do not explain to the police why they were present at a place at or about the time of the crime for which they were arrested. Finally, if the defendant fails to testify at trial, the new law permits the jury to draw such adverse inferences "as appear proper"–including the "common sense" inference that there is no explanation for the evidence produced against the defendant and that the defendant is guilty. See generally, Mark Berger, *Of Policy, Politics, and Parliament: The Legislative Rewriting of the British Right to Silence*, 22 Am.J.Crim.L. 391 (1995); Gregory W. O'Reilly, *England Limits the Right to Silence and Moves Toward an Inquisitional System of Justice*, 85 J.Crim.L. & C. 402 (1994).

[For the view that silence during police interrogation does not cause police to drop charges or prosecutors to dismiss cases or courts to acquit defendants; that using adverse inferences will not induce suspects to talk to the police or to reveal their defenses; that there is no indication that in the past a defendant's right to silence has been frequently invoked at trial; and that adverse inferences about a defendant's failure to testify at trial will not foster testimony by defendants, see O'Reilly, supra, at 431–42.]

the detective bureau. There he was questioned by two police officers. The officers admitted at trial that Miranda was not advised that he had a right to have an attorney present. Two hours later, the officers emerged from the interrogation room with a written confession signed by Miranda. At the top of the statement was a typed paragraph stating that the confession was made voluntarily, without threats or promises of immunity and "with full knowledge of my legal rights, understanding any statement I make may be used against me."[67]

[Miranda] was found guilty of kidnapping and rape. [On] appeal, the Supreme Court of Arizona held that Miranda's constitutional rights were not violated in obtaining the confession and affirmed the conviction. In reaching its decision, the court emphasized heavily the fact that Miranda did not specifically request counsel.

We reverse. From the testimony of the officers and by the admission of respondent, it is clear that Miranda was not in any way apprised of his right to consult with an attorney and to have one present during the interrogation, nor was his right not to be compelled to incriminate himself effectively protected in any other manner. Without these warnings the statements were inadmissible. The mere fact that he signed a statement which contained a typed-in clause stating that he had "full knowledge" of his legal rights does not approach the knowing and intelligent waiver required to relinquish constitutional rights. * * *

No. 760. *Vignera v. New York.*

Petitioner, Michael Vignera, was picked up by New York police on October 14, 1960, in connection with the robbery three days earlier of a Brooklyn dress shop. They took him to the 17th Detective Squad headquarters in Manhattan. Sometime thereafter he was taken to the 66th Detective Squad. There a detective questioned Vignera with respect to the robbery. Vignera orally admitted the robbery to the detective. [T]he defense was precluded from making any showing that warnings had not been given. While at the 66th Detective Squad, Vignera was identified by the store owner and a saleslady as the man who robbed the dress shop. At about 3:00 p.m. he was formally arrested. The police then transported him to still another station, the 70th Precinct in Brooklyn, "for detention". At 11:00 p.m. Vignera was questioned by an assistant district attorney in the presence of a hearing reporter who transcribed the questions and Vignera's answers. This verbatim account of these proceedings contains no statement of any warnings given by the assistant district attorney. * * *

Vignera was [convicted of first degree robbery]. We reverse. The foregoing indicates that Vignera was not warned of any of his rights before the questioning by the detective and by the assistant district attorney. No other steps were taken to protect these rights. Thus he was not effectively apprised of his Fifth Amendment privilege or of his right to have counsel present and his statements are inadmissible.

No. 761. *Westover v. United States.*

At approximately 9:45 p.m. on March 20, 1963, petitioner, Carl Calvin Westover, was arrested by local police in Kansas City as a suspect in two Kansas City robberies. A report was also received from the FBI that he was wanted on a felony charge in California. * * * Kansas City police interrogated Westover on the night of his arrest. He denied any knowledge of criminal activities. The next day local officers interrogated him again throughout the morning. Shortly before noon

---

67. One of the officers testified that he read this paragraph to Miranda. Apparently, however, he did not do so until after Miranda had confessed orally.

they informed the FBI that they were through interrogating Westover and that the FBI could proceed to interrogate him. There is nothing in the record to indicate that Westover was ever given any warning as to his rights by local police. At noon, three special agents of the FBI continued the interrogation in a private interview room of the Kansas City Police Department, this time with respect to the robbery of a savings and loan association and a bank in Sacramento, California. After two or two and one-half hours, Westover signed separate confessions to each of these two robberies which had been prepared by one of the agents during the interrogation. At trial one of the agents testified, and a paragraph on each of the statements states, that the agents advised Westover that he did not have to make a statement, that any statement he made could be used against him, and that he had the right to see an attorney.

[We reverse Westover's federal conviction of the California robberies.] On the facts of this case we cannot find that Westover knowingly and intelligently waived his right to remain silent and his right to consult with counsel prior to the time he made the statement. At the time the FBI agents began questioning Westover, he had been in custody for over 14 hours and had been interrogated at length during that period. The FBI interrogation began immediately upon the conclusion of the interrogation by Kansas City police and was conducted in local police headquarters. Although the two law enforcement authorities are legally distinct and the crimes for which they interrogated Westover were different, the impact on him was that of a continuous period of questioning. There is no evidence of any warning given prior to the FBI interrogation nor is there any evidence of an articulated waiver of rights after the FBI commenced their interrogation. The record simply shows that the defendant did in fact confess a short time after being turned over to the FBI following interrogation by local police. Despite the fact that the FBI agents gave warnings at the outset of their interview, from Westover's point of view the warnings came at the end of the interrogation process. In these circumstances an intelligent waiver of constitutional rights cannot be assumed.

We do not suggest that law enforcement authorities are precluded from questioning any individual who has been held for a period of time by other authorities and interrogated by them without appropriate warnings. A different case would be presented if an accused were taken into custody by the second authority, removed both in time and place from his original surroundings, and then adequately advised of his rights and given an opportunity to exercise them. But here the FBI interrogation was conducted immediately following the state interrogation in the same police station—in the same compelling surroundings. Thus, in obtaining a confession from Westover the federal authorities were the beneficiaries of the pressure applied by the local in-custody interrogation. In these circumstances the giving of warnings alone was not sufficient to protect the privilege.

No. 584. *California v. Stewart.*

In the course of investigating a series of purse-snatch robberies in which one of the victims had died of injuries inflicted by her assailant, respondent, Roy Allen Stewart, was pointed out to Los Angeles police as the endorser of dividend checks taken in one of the robberies. At about 7:15 p.m., January 31, 1963, police officers went to Stewart's house and arrested him. One of the officers asked Stewart if they could search the house, to which he replied, "Go ahead." The search turned up various items taken from the five robbery victims. At the time of Stewart's arrest, police also arrested Stewart's wife and three other persons who were visiting him. These four were jailed along with Stewart and were interrogated.

490 POLICE INTERROGATION Pt. 2

Stewart was taken to the University Station of the Los Angeles Police Department where he was placed in a cell. During the next five days, police interrogated Stewart on nine different occasions. Except during the first interrogation session, when he was confronted with an accusing witness, Stewart was isolated with his interrogators.

During the ninth interrogation session, Stewart admitted that he had robbed the deceased and stated that he had not meant to hurt her. Police then brought Stewart before a magistrate for the first time. Since there was no evidence to connect them with any crime, the police then released the other four persons arrested with him.

Nothing in the record specifically indicates whether Stewart was or was not advised of his right to remain silent or his right to counsel. In a number of instances, however, the interrogating officers were asked to recount everything that was said during the interrogations. None indicated that Stewart was ever advised of his rights.

[The] jury found Stewart guilty of robbery and first degree murder and fixed the penalty as death. On appeal, the Supreme Court of California reversed. It held that under this Court's decision in *Escobedo*, Stewart should have been advised of his right to remain silent and of his right to counsel and that it would not presume in the face of a silent record that the police advised Stewart of his rights.

We affirm. In dealing with custodial interrogation, we will not presume that a defendant has been effectively apprised of his rights and that his privilege against self-incrimination has been adequately safeguarded on a record that does not show that any warnings have been given or that any effective alternative has been employed. Nor can a knowing and intelligent waiver of these rights be assumed on a silent record. Furthermore, Stewart's steadfast denial of the alleged offenses through eight of the nine interrogations over a period of five days is subject to no other construction than that he was compelled by persistent interrogation to forgo his Fifth Amendment privilege.

Therefore, in accordance with the foregoing, [*Miranda*,[a] *Vignera*, and *Westover* are reversed and *Stewart* is affirmed].[b]

Justice CLARK, dissenting in [*Miranda*, *Vignera*, and *Westover*, and concurring in the result in *Stewart*.]

[I cannot] agree with the Court's characterization of the present practices of police and investigatory agencies as to custodial interrogation. The materials referred to as "police manuals" are not shown by the record here to be the official manuals of any police department, much less in universal use in crime detection. Moreover, the examples of police brutality mentioned by the Court are rare exceptions to the thousands of cases that appear every year in the law reports.
* * *

[The Court's] strict constitutional specific inserted at the nerve center of crime detection may well kill the patient. Since there is at this time a paucity of information and an almost total lack of empirical knowledge on the practical

a. On retrial, *Miranda* was again convicted of kidnapping and rape. The conviction was affirmed in *State v. Miranda*, 450 P.2d 364 (Ariz.1969). For a rich narrative of *Miranda* from arrest to reconviction, see L. Baker, *Miranda: Crime, Law & Politics* (1983).

b. A week later, the Court ruled that *Escobedo* and *Miranda* applied only to trials begun after the decisions were announced.

operation of requirements truly comparable to those announced by the majority, I would be more restrained lest we go too far too fast. * * *

Rather than employing the arbitrary Fifth Amendment rule which the Court lays down I would follow the more pliable dictates of Due Process Clauses of the Fifth and Fourteenth Amendments which we are accustomed to administering and which we know from our cases are effective instruments in protecting persons in police custody. In this way we would not be acting in the dark nor in one full sweep changing the traditional rules of custodial interrogation which this Court has for so long recognized as a justifiable and proper tool in balancing individual rights against the rights of society. It will be soon enough to go further when we are able to appraise with somewhat better accuracy the effect of such a holding. * * *

Justice HARLAN, whom Justice STEWART and Justice WHITE join, dissenting. * * *

While the fine points of [the Court's new constitutional code of rules for confessions] are far less clear than the Court admits, the tenor is quite apparent. The new rules are not designed to guard against police brutality or other unmistakably banned forms of coercion. Those who use third-degree tactics and deny them in court are equally able and destined to lie as skillfully about warnings and waivers. Rather, the thrust of the new rules is to negate all pressures, to reinforce the nervous or ignorant suspect, and ultimately to discourage any confession at all. The aim in short is toward "voluntariness" in a utopian sense, or to view it from a different angle, voluntariness with a vengeance.

To incorporate this notion into the Constitution requires a strained reading of history and precedent and a disregard of the very pragmatic concerns that alone may on occasion justify such strains. I believe that reasoned examination will show that the Due Process Clauses provide an adequate tool for coping with confessions and that, even if the Fifth Amendment privilege against self-incrimination be invoked, its precedents taken as a whole do not sustain the present rules. Viewed as a choice based on pure policy, these new rules prove to be a highly debatable if not one-sided appraisal of the competing interests, imposed over wide-spread objection, at the very time when judicial restraint is most called for by the circumstances. * * *

[The] Court's asserted reliance on the Fifth Amendment [is] an approach which I frankly regard as a *trompe l'oeil*. The Court's opinion in my view reveals no adequate basis for extending the Fifth Amendment's privilege against self-incrimination to the police station. Far more important, it fails to show that the Court's new rules are well supported, let alone compelled, by Fifth Amendment precedents. Instead, the new rules actually derive from quotation and analogy drawn from precedents under the Sixth Amendment, which should properly have no bearing on police interrogation. * * *

Having decided that the Fifth Amendment privilege does apply in the police station, the Court reveals that the privilege imposes more exacting restrictions than does the Fourteenth Amendment's voluntariness test. It then emerges from a discussion of *Escobedo* that the Fifth Amendment requires for an admissible confession that it be given by one distinctly aware of his right not to speak and shielded from "the compelling atmosphere" of interrogation. From these key premises, the Court finally develops the safeguards of warning, counsel, and so forth. I do not believe these premises are sustained by precedents under the Fifth Amendment.[9]

The more important premise is that pressure on the suspect must be eliminated though it be only the subtle influence of the atmosphere and surroundings. The Fifth Amendment, however, has never been thought to forbid *all* pressure to incriminate one's self in the situations covered by it. * * *

A closing word must be said about the Assistance of Counsel Clause of the Sixth Amendment, which is never expressly relied on by the Court but whose judicial precedents turn out to be linchpins of the confession rules announced today.

[The] only attempt in this Court to carry the right to counsel into the station house occurred in *Escobedo,* the Court repeating several times that that stage was no less "critical" than trial itself. * * * This is hardly persuasive when we consider that a grand jury inquiry, the filing of a certiorari petition, and certainly the purchase of narcotics by an undercover agent from a prospective defendant may all be equally "critical" yet provision of counsel and advice on that score have never been thought compelled by the Constitution in such cases. The sound reason why this right is so freely extended for a criminal trial is the severe injustice risked by confronting an untrained defendant with a range of technical points of law, evidence, and tactics familiar to the prosecutor but not to himself. This danger shrinks markedly in the police station where indeed the lawyer in fulfilling his professional responsibilities of necessity may become an obstacle to truthfinding. See infra, n. 12.

[The] Court's new rules aim to offset [the] minor pressures and disadvantages intrinsic to any kind of police interrogation. The rules do not serve due process interests in preventing blatant coercion since, as I noted earlier, they do nothing to contain the policeman who is prepared to lie from the start. The rules work for reliability in confessions almost only in the Pickwickian sense that they can prevent some from being given at all.[12] * * *

What the Court largely ignores is that its rules impair, if they will not eventually serve wholly to frustrate, an instrument of law enforcement that has long and quite reasonably been thought worth the price paid for it. There can be little doubt that the Court's new code would markedly decrease the number of confessions. To warn the suspect that he may remain silent and remind him that his confession may be used in court are minor obstructions. To require also an express waiver by the suspect and an end to questioning whenever he demurs must heavily handicap questioning. And to suggest or provide counsel for the suspect simply invites the end of the interrogation. See supra, n. 12. * * *

While passing over the costs and risks of its experiment, the Court portrays the evils of normal police questioning in terms which I think are exaggerated. Albeit stringently confined by the due process standards interrogation is no doubt often inconvenient and unpleasant for the suspect. However, it is no less so for a man to be arrested and jailed, to have his house searched, or to stand trial in

---

9. I lay aside *Escobedo* itself; it contains no reasoning or even general conclusions addressed to the Fifth Amendment and indeed its citation in this regard seems surprising in view of *Escobedo's* primary reliance on the Sixth Amendment.

12. The Court's vision of a lawyer "mitigat[ing] the dangers of untrustworthiness" by witnessing coercion and assisting accuracy in the confession is largely a fancy; for if counsel arrives, there is rarely going to be a police station confession. *Watts v. Indiana* (separate opinion of Jackson, J.): "[A]ny lawyer worth his salt will tell the suspect in no uncertain terms to make no statement to police under any circumstances."

court, yet all this may properly happen to the most innocent given probable cause, a warrant, or an indictment. Society has always paid a stiff price for law and order, and peaceful interrogation is not one of the dark moments of the law.

This brief statement of the competing considerations seems to me ample proof that the Court's preference is highly debatable at best and therefore not to be read into the Constitution. However, it may make the analysis more graphic to consider the actual facts of one of the four cases reversed by the Court. *Miranda* serves best, being neither the hardest nor easiest of the four under the Court's standards.[15]

On March 3, 1963, an 18–year-old girl was kidnapped and forcibly raped near Phoenix, Arizona. Ten days later, on the morning of March 13, petitioner Miranda was arrested and taken to the police station. At this time Miranda was 23 years old, indigent, and educated to the extent of completing half the ninth grade. He had "an emotional illness" of the schizophrenic type, according to the doctor who eventually examined him; the doctor's report also stated that Miranda was "alert and oriented as to time, place, and person", intelligent within normal limits, competent to stand trial, and sane within the legal definition. At the police station, the victim picked Miranda out of a lineup, and two officers then took him into a separate room to interrogate him, starting about 11:30 a.m. Though at first denying his guilt, within a short time Miranda gave a detailed oral confession and then wrote out in his own hand and signed a brief statement admitting and describing the crime. All this was accomplished in two hours or less without any force, threats or promises and—I will assume this though the record is uncertain * * *—without any effective warnings at all.

Miranda's oral and written confessions are now held inadmissible under the Court's new rules. One is entitled to feel astonished that the Constitution can be read to produce this result. These confessions were obtained during brief, daytime questioning conducted by two officers and unmarked by any of the traditional indicia of coercion. They assured a conviction for a brutal and unsettling crime, for which the police had and quite possibly could obtain little evidence other than the victim's identifications, evidence which is frequently unreliable. There was, in sum, a legitimate purpose, no perceptible unfairness, and certainly little risk of injustice in the interrogation. Yet the resulting confessions, and the responsible course of police practice they represent, are to be sacrificed to the Court's own finespun conception of fairness which I seriously doubt is shared by many thinking citizens in this country.

[It is] instructive to compare the attitude in this case of those responsible for law enforcement with the official views that existed when the Court undertook three major revisions of prosecutorial practice prior to this case, *Johnson v. Zerbst*, *Mapp*, and *Gideon*. In *Johnson*, which established that appointed counsel must be offered the indigent in federal criminal trials, the Federal Government all but conceded the basic issue, which had in fact been recently fixed as Department of Justice policy. In *Mapp*, which imposed the exclusionary rule on the States for Fourth Amendment violations, more than half of the States had themselves already adopted some such rule. In *Gideon*, which extended *Johnson v. Zerbst* to the States, an *amicus* brief was filed by 22 States and Commonwealths urging that course; only two States beside the respondent came forward to protest. By

---

15. In *Westover*, a seasoned criminal was practically given the Court's full complement of warnings and did not heed them. The *Stewart* case, on the other hand, involves long detention and successive questioning. In *Vignera*, the facts are complicated and the record somewhat incomplete.

contrast, in this case new restrictions on police questioning have been opposed by the United States and in an *amicus* brief signed by 27 States and Commonwealths, not including the three other States who are parties. No State in the country has urged this Court to impose the newly announced rules, nor has any State chosen to go nearly so far on its own.

[The] law of the foreign countries described by the [majority] reflects a more moderate conception of the rights of the accused as against those of society when other data is considered. Concededly, the English experience is most relevant. In that country, a caution as to silence but not counsel has long been mandated by the "Judges' Rules," which also place other somewhat imprecise limits on police cross-examination of suspects. However, in the court's discretion confessions can be and apparently quite frequently are admitted in evidence despite disregard of the Judges' Rules, so long as they are found voluntary under the common-law test. Moreover, the check that exists on the use of pretrial statements is counterbalanced by the evident admissibility of fruits of an illegal confession and by the judge's often-used authority to comment adversely on the defendant's failure to testify. * * *

[S]ome reference must be made to [the] ironic untimeliness [of these confession rules]. There is now in progress in this country a massive re-examination of criminal law enforcement procedures on a scale never before witnessed. Participants in this undertaking include a Special Committee of the American Bar Association, under the chairmanship of Chief Judge Lumbard of the Court of Appeals for the Second Circuit; a distinguished study group of the American Law Institute, headed by Professor Vorenberg of the Harvard Law School; and the President's Commission on Law Enforcement and Administration of Justice, under the leadership of the Attorney General of the United States. Studies are also being conducted by [other groups] equipped to do practical research.

[It] is no secret that concern has been expressed lest long-range and lasting reforms be frustrated by this Court's too rapid departure from existing constitutional standards. Despite the Court's disclaimer, the practical effect of the decision made today must inevitably be to handicap seriously sound efforts at reform, not least by removing options necessary to a just compromise of competing interests. [T]he legislative reforms when they came would have the vast advantage of empirical data and comprehensive study, they would allow experimentation and use of solutions not open to the courts, and they would restore the initiative in criminal law reform to those forums where it truly belongs. * * *

Justice WHITE, with whom Justice HARLAN and Justice STEWART join, dissenting.

The proposition that the privilege against self-incrimination forbids in-custody interrogation without the warnings specified in the majority opinion and without a clear waiver of counsel has no significant support in the history of the privilege or in the language of the Fifth Amendment. As for the English authorities and the common-law history, the privilege, firmly established in the second half of the seventeenth century, was never applied except to prohibit compelled judicial interrogations. The rule excluding coerced confessions matured about 100 years later, "[b]ut there is nothing in the reports to suggest that the theory has its roots in the privilege against self-incrimination. And so far as the cases reveal, the privilege, as such, seems to have been given effect only in judicial proceedings, including the preliminary examinations by authorized magistrates." Morgan, *The Privilege Against Self–Incrimination*, 34 Minn.L.Rev. 1, 18 (1949).

[That] the Court's holding today is neither compelled nor even strongly suggested by the language of the Fifth Amendment, is at odds with American and English legal history, and involves a departure from a long line of precedent does not prove either that the Court has exceeded its powers or that the Court is wrong or unwise in its present reinterpretation of the Fifth Amendment. It does, however, underscore the obvious—that the Court has not discovered or found the law in making today's decision, nor has it derived it from some irrefutable sources; what it has done is to make new law and new public policy in much the same way that it has in the course of interpreting other great clauses of the Constitution. This is what the Court historically has done. Indeed, it is what it must do and will continue to do until and unless there is some fundamental change in the constitutional distribution of governmental powers.

But if the Court is here and now to announce new and fundamental policy to govern certain aspects of our affairs, it is wholly legitimate to examine the mode of this or any other constitutional decision in this Court and to inquire into the advisability of its end product in terms of the long-range interest of the country. At the very least the Court's text and reasoning should withstand analysis and be a fair exposition of the constitutional provision which its opinion interprets. Decisions like these cannot rest alone on syllogism, metaphysics or some ill-defined notions of natural justice, although each will perhaps play its part.

[The Court] extrapolates a picture of what it conceives to be the norm from police investigatorial manuals, published in 1959 and 1962 or earlier, without any attempt to allow for adjustments in police practices that may have occurred in the wake of more recent decisions of state appellate tribunals or this Court. But even if the relentless application of the described procedures could lead to involuntary confessions, it most assuredly does not follow that each and every case will disclose this kind of interrogation or this kind of consequence.[2] Insofar as it appears from the Court's opinion, it has not examined a single transcript of any police interrogation, let alone the interrogation that took place in any one of these cases which it decides today. Judged by any of the standards for empirical investigation utilized in the social sciences the factual basis for the Court's premises is patently inadequate.

Although in the Court's view in-custody interrogation is inherently coercive, it says that the spontaneous product of the coercion of arrest and detention is still to be deemed voluntary. An accused, arrested on probable cause, may blurt out a confession which will be admissible despite the fact that he is alone and in custody, without any showing that he had any notion of his right to remain silent or of the consequences of his admission. Yet, under the Court's rule, if the police ask him a single question such as "Do you have anything to say?" or "Did you kill your wife?" his response, if there is one, has somehow been compelled, even if the accused has been clearly warned of his right to remain silent. Common sense informs us to the contrary. While one may say that the response was "involuntary" in the sense the question provoked or was the occasion for the response and thus the defendant was induced to speak out when he might have remained silent

---

2. In fact, the type of sustained interrogation described by the Court appears to be the exception rather than the rule. A survey of 399 cases in one city found that in almost half of the cases the interrogation lasted less than 30 minutes. Barrett, *Police Practices and the Law—From Arrest to Release or Charge*, 50 Calif.L.Rev. 11, 41–45 (1962). Questioning tends to be confused and sporadic and is usual-ly concentrated on confrontations with witnesses or new items of evidence, as these are obtained by officers conducting the investigation. See generally LaFave, *Arrest: The Decision to Take a Suspect into Custody* 386 (1965); ALI, *Model Pre-Arraignment Procedure Code*, Commentary § 5.01, at 170, n. 4 (Tent.Draft No. 1, 1966).

if not arrested and not questioned, it is patently unsound to say the response is compelled.

[If] the rule announced today were truly based on a conclusion that all confessions resulting from custodial interrogation are coerced, then it would simply have no rational foundation. * * * Even if one were to postulate that the Court's concern is not that all confessions induced by police interrogation are coerced but rather that some such confessions are coerced and present judicial procedures are believed to be inadequate to identify the confessions that are coerced and those that are not, it would still not be essential to impose the rule that the Court has now fashioned. Transcripts or observers could be required, specific time limits, tailored to fit the cause, could be imposed, or other devices could be utilized to reduce the chances that otherwise indiscernible coercion will produce an inadmissible confession.

On the other hand, even if one assumed that there was an adequate factual basis for the conclusion that all confessions obtained during in-custody interrogation are the product of compulsion, the rule propounded by the Court would still be irrational, for, apparently, it is only if the accused is also warned of his right to counsel and waives both that right and the right against self-incrimination that the inherent compulsiveness of interrogation disappears. But if the defendant may not answer without a warning a question such as "Where were you last night?" without having his answer be a compelled one, how can the court ever accept his negative answer to the question of whether he wants to consult his retained counsel or counsel whom the court will appoint? And why if counsel is present and the accused nevertheless confesses, or counsel tells the accused to tell the truth, and that is what the accused does, is the situation any less coercive insofar as the accused is concerned? The court apparently realizes its dilemma of foreclosing questioning without the necessary warnings but at the same time permitting the accused, sitting in the same chair in front of the same policemen, to waive his right to consult an attorney. It expects, however, that not too many will waive the right; and if it is claimed that he has, the State faces a severe, if not impossible burden of proof.

All of this makes very little sense in terms of the compulsion which the Fifth Amendment proscribes. That amendment deals with compelling the accused himself. It is his free will that is involved. Confessions and incriminating admissions, as such, are not forbidden evidence; only those which are compelled are banned. I doubt that the Court observes these distinctions today. By considering any answers to any interrogation to be compelled regardless of the content and course of examination and by escalating the requirements to prove waiver, the Court not only prevents the use of compelled confessions but for all practical purposes forbids interrogation except in the presence of counsel. That is, instead of confining itself to protection of the right against compelled self-incrimination the Court has created a limited Fifth Amendment right to counsel—or, as the Court expresses it, a "right to counsel to protect the Fifth Amendment privilege * * *." The focus then is not on the will of the accused but on the will of counsel and how much influence he can have on the accused. Obviously there is no warrant in the Fifth Amendment for thus installing counsel as the arbiter of the privilege.

In sum, for all the Court's expounding on the menacing atmosphere of police interrogation procedures it has failed to supply any foundation for the conclusions it draws or the measures it adopts.

Criticism of the Court's opinion, however, cannot stop at a demonstration that the factual and textual bases for the rule it propounds are, at best, less than compelling. Equally relevant is an assessment of the rule's consequences measured against community values. The Court's duty to assess the consequences of its action is not satisfied by the utterance of the truth that a value of our system of criminal justice is "to respect the inviolability of the human personality" and to require government to produce the evidence against the accused by its own independent labors. More than the human dignity of the accused is involved; the human personality of others in the society must also be preserved. Thus the values reflected by the privilege are not the sole desideratum; society's interest in the general security is of equal weight.

The obvious underpinning of the Court's decision is a deep-seated distrust of all confessions. As the Court declares that the accused may not be interrogated without counsel present, absent a waiver of the right to counsel, and as the Court all but admonishes the lawyer to advise the accused to remain silent, the result adds up to a judicial judgment that evidence from the accused should not be used against him in any way, whether compelled or not. This is the not so subtle overtone of the opinion?that it is inherently wrong for the police to gather evidence from the accused himself. And this is precisely the nub of this dissent. I see nothing wrong or immoral, and certainly nothing unconstitutional, with the police asking a suspect whom they have reasonable cause to arrest whether or not he killed his wife or with confronting him with the evidence on which the arrest was based, at least where he has been plainly advised that he may remain completely silent. * * * Particularly when corroborated, as where the police have confirmed the accused's disclosure of the hiding place of implements or fruits of the crime, such confessions have the highest reliability and significantly contribute to the certitude with which we may believe the accused is guilty.

[The] rule announced today [is] a deliberate calculus to prevent interrogations, to reduce the incidence of confessions and pleas of guilty and to increase the number of trials. [Under] the present law, the prosecution fails to prove its case in about 30% of the criminal cases actually tried in the federal courts. But it is something else again to remove from the ordinary criminal case all those confessions which heretofore have been held to be free and voluntary acts of the accused and to thus establish a new constitutional barrier to the ascertainment of truth by the judicial process. There is, in my view, every reason to believe that a good many criminal defendants, who otherwise would have been convicted on what this Court has previously thought to be the most satisfactory kind of evidence, will now, under this new version of the Fifth Amendment, either not be tried at all or acquitted if the State's evidence, minus the confession, is put to the test of litigation.

I have no desire whatsoever to share the responsibility for any such impact on the present criminal process. * * *

There is another aspect to the effect of the Court's rule on the person whom the police have arrested on probable cause. The fact is that he may not be guilty at all and may be able to extricate himself quickly and simply if he were told the circumstances of his arrest and were asked to explain. This effort, and his release, must now await the hiring of a lawyer or his appointment by the court, consultation with counsel and then a session with the police or the prosecutor. Similarly, where probable cause exists to arrest several suspects as where the body of the victim is discovered in a house having several residents, it will often be true that a suspect may be cleared only through the results of interrogation of other suspects. Here too the release of the innocent may be delayed by the Court's rule.

Much of the trouble with the Court's new rule is that it will operate indiscriminately in all criminal cases, regardless of the severity of the crime or the circumstances involved. It applies to every defendant whether the professional criminal or one committing a crime of momentary passion who is not part and parcel of organized crime. It will slow down the investigation and the apprehension of confederates in those cases where time is of the essence, such as kidnapping, [those] involving the national security, [and] some organized crime situations. In the latter context the lawyer who arrives may also be the lawyer for the defendants' colleagues and can be relied upon to insure that no breach of the organization's security takes place even though the accused may feel that the best thing he can do is to cooperate.

At the same time, the Court's *per se* approach may not be justified on the ground that it provides a "bright line" permitting the authorities to judge in advance whether interrogation may safely be pursued without jeopardizing the admissibility of any information obtained as a consequence. Nor can it be claimed that judicial time and effort, assuming that is a relevant consideration, will be conserved because of the ease of application of the new rule. Today's decision leaves open such questions as whether the accused was in custody, whether his statements were spontaneous or the product of interrogation, whether the accused has effectively waived his rights, and whether nontestimonial evidence introduced at trial is the fruit of statements made during a prohibited interrogation, all of which are certain to prove productive of uncertainty during investigation and litigation during prosecution. For all these reasons, if further restrictions on police interrogation are desirable at this time, a more flexible approach makes much more sense than the Court's constitutional strait-jacket which forecloses more discriminating treatment by legislative or rule-making pronouncements. * * *[a]

TITLE II OF THE OMNIBUS CRIME CONTROL AND SAFE STREETS ACT OF 1968—ADMISSIBILITY OF CONFESSIONS—MAY CONGRESS REPEAL *MIRANDA?*[b]

Title II of the Crime Control Act of 1968, which purports to "repeal" *Miranda* and the *McNabb-Mallory* rule in federal prosecutions, amends Chapter 223, title 18, United States Code, by adding the following new sections:

"§ 3501. Admissibility of confessions

"(a) In any criminal prosecution brought by the United States or by the District of Columbia, a confession, as defined in subsection (e) hereof, shall be admissible in evidence if it is voluntarily given. Before such confession is received

---

a. At this point, the instructor (or student) may wish to consider the different views on the desirability, efficacy and legitimacy of *Miranda* that appear at pp. 500 and 505 to 509. Because some of these materials refer to various post-*Miranda* developments discussed in the succeeding pages, it seemed preferable to the editors to postpone consideration of the materials until the end of the *Miranda* section. But a case can be made for taking up these materials (at least some of them) immediately after *Miranda*.

b. For a detailed account of congressional reaction to *Miranda* and related decisions, see Breckenridge, *Congress Against the Court* (1970). For other accounts of congressional, and Presidential Candidate Nixon's, hostility to *Miranda*, see Graham, *The Self-Inflicted Wound* 305–32 (1970); Kamisar, *How to Use, Abuse—and Fight Back with—Crime Statistics,* 25 Okla.L.Rev. 239 (1972).

in evidence, the trial judge shall, out of the presence of the jury, determine any issue as to voluntariness. If the trial judge determines that the confession was voluntarily made it shall be admitted in evidence and the trial judge shall permit the jury to hear relevant evidence on the issue of voluntariness and shall instruct the jury to give such weight to the confession as the jury feels it deserves under all the circumstances.

"(b) The trial judge in determining the issue of voluntariness shall take into consideration all the circumstances surrounding the giving of the confession, including (1) the time elapsing between arrest and arraignment of the defendant making the confession, if it was made after arrest and before arraignment, (2) whether such defendant knew the nature of the offense with which he was charged or of which he was suspected at the time of making the confession, (3) whether or not such defendant was advised or knew that he was not required to make any statement and that any such statement could be used against him, (4) whether or not such defendant had been advised prior to questioning of his right to the assistance of counsel; and (5) whether or not such defendant was without the assistance of counsel when questioned and when giving such confession.

"The presence or absence of any of the above-mentioned factors to be taken into consideration by the judge need not be conclusive on the issue of voluntariness of the confession.

"(c) In any criminal prosecution by the United States or by the District of Columbia, a confession made or given by a person who is a defendant therein, while such person was under arrest or other detention in the custody of any law-enforcement officer or law-enforcement agency, shall not be inadmissible solely because of delay in bringing such person before a commissioner or other officer empowered to commit persons charged with offenses against the laws of the United States or of the District of Columbia if such confession is found by the trial judge to have been made voluntarily and if the weight to be given the confession is left to the jury and if such confession was made or given by such person within six hours immediately following his arrest or other detention: *Provided,* That the time limitation contained in this subsection shall not apply in any case in which the delay in bringing such person before such commissioner or other officer beyond such six-hour period is found by the trial judge to be reasonable considering the means of transportation and the distance to be traveled to the nearest available such commissioner or other officer.

"(d) Nothing contained in this section shall bar the admission in evidence of any confession made or given voluntarily by any person to any other person without interrogation by anyone, or at any time at which the person who made or gave such confession was not under arrest or other detention.

"(e) As used in this section, the term 'confession' means any confession of guilt of any criminal offense or any self-incriminating statement made or given orally or in writing."

Does § 3501 (c) codify a limited form of the McNabb–Mallory rule or does it repudiate the rule in its entirety? Consider *United States v. Alvarez–Sanchez,* 511 U.S. 350, 114 S.Ct. 1599, 128 L.Ed.2d 319 (1994). Respondent was arrested on state drug charges on Friday and spent the weekend in the custody of Los Angeles police. When the police found counterfeit currency on respondent, they notified U.S. Secret Service agents, who questioned respondent Monday (when he was still in the custody of the Los Angeles police). After waiving his *Miranda* rights, respondent made incriminating statements. Shortly thereafter, the Secret Service agents arrested respondent and took him to their field office for booking. Respondent was then convicted of counterfeiting charges after a jury trial at which his incriminating statements were admitted.

The U.S. Court of Appeals for the Ninth Circuit reversed, reasoning that, by negative implication, § 3501 (c) must in some circumstances allow suppression of a confession made *more than* six hours after arrest solely on the basis of pre-presentment delay and regardless of the voluntariness of the confession. The government argued, on the other hand, that § 3501 repudiated the *McNabb-Mallory* rule in its entirety and that the admissibility of a confession obtained beyond the six-hour is controlled by § 3501 (a), which provides that a confession is admissible so long as "it is voluntarily given." The Supreme Court, per Thomas, J., reversed the Ninth Circuit without resolving (and seeing no need to resolve) the dispute, because "the terms of § 3501 (c) were never triggered in this case":

"[T]here can be no 'delay' in bringing a person before a federal magistrate until, at a minimum, there is some obligation to bring the person before such a judicial officer in the first place. Plainly, a duty to present a person to a federal magistrate does not arise until the person has been arrested for a *federal* offense. [Until then] no 'delay' under § 3501 (c) can occur."[a]

On signing the Crime Control Act into law on June 19, 1968, President Johnson commented that "the provisions of Title II, vague and ambiguous as they are, can, I am advised by the Attorney General, be interpreted in harmony with the Constitution." (N.Y. Times, June 20, 1968, p. 23, col. 1.) Insofar as the Act attempts to repeal *Massiah, Escobedo* and *Miranda,* how?

So far, § 3501 (a) has not provoked the collision between Congress and the Court that might have been expected because, as Justice Scalia noted, concurring in *Davis v. United States* (1994) (discussed at p.561), "with limited exceptions the provision has been studiously avoided by every Administration, not only in this Court, but in the lower courts, since its enactment." The Justice Department's repeated refusal to invoke § 3501, "combined with the Court's traditional (albeit merely prudential) refusal to consider arguments not raised," complained Justice Scalia, "has caused the federal judiciary to confront a host of 'Miranda' issues that might be entirely irrelevant under federal law." Scalia recognized that the executive branch "has the power (whether or not it has the right) to avoid application of § 3501 by simply declining to introduce into evidence confessions admissible under its terms." But he added:

"[O]nce a prosecution has been commenced and a confession introduced, the Executive assuredly has neither the power nor the right to determine what objections to admissibility of the confession are valid in law. Section 3501 is a provision of law directed *to the courts*, reflecting the people's assessment of the proper balance to be struck between concern for persons interrogated in custody and the needs of effective law enforcement. We shirk our duty if we systematically

a. The Court declined to discuss the effect of § 3501 (c), if any, in the event that local authorities, acting in collusion with federal officers, were to arrest and detain a suspect in order to allow the federal officers to interrogate him in violation of his right to a prompt federal presentment. Because there was "no evidence" of such collusion in the instant case.

disregard that statutory command simply because the Justice Department systematically declines to remind us of it."

(Justice Scalia's comments did not go unnoticed. Five years later, a panel of the Fourth Circuit upheld the constitutionality of § 3501 and ruled that it had overturned *Miranda*. See *United States v. Dickerson*, p. 507.)

Are the *Miranda* warnings "constitutional rules" or congressionally reversible "constitutionally inspired common law"? Compare Monaghan, *The Supreme Court, 1974 Term—Foreword: Constitutional Common Law*, 89 Harv.L.Rev. 1, 18–23, 30–34, 42 n. 217 (1975) with Schrock, Welsh & Collins, *Interrogational Rights: Reflections on Miranda v. Arizona*, 52 So.Cal.L.Rev. 1 (1978). See also Robert A. Burt, *Miranda and Title II: A Morganatic Marriage*, 1967 Sup.Ct.Rev. 81; Archibald Cox, *The Role of Congress in Constitutional Determinations*, 40 U.Cinn.L.Rev. 199 (1971).

Has the case for upholding § 3501 grown a good deal stronger with the passage of years because, starting in 1974 (see cases discussed at pp. 502–05), the Court has repeatedly called the *Miranda* rules "not themselves rights protected by the Constitution" but only "procedural safeguards" or "prophylactic rules"? Does this way of thinking about *Miranda* render it especially susceptible to congressional "repeal"? Make *Miranda* an "illegitimate" decision? See the extracts from the writings of Professors Grano, Schulhofer and Strauss at pp. 505–06.

LETTER FROM JUSTICE BRENNAN TO CHIEF JUSTICE WARREN, COMMENTING ON AN EARLY DRAFT OF THE *MIRANDA* OPINION

This portion of Justice Brennan's long letter, perhaps better described
as a lengthy memorandum, is reprinted in Charles Weisselberg,
Saving Miranda, 84 Cornell L.Rev. 109, 123–24 (1998).

You may recall that at the initial conference to select the cases for argument, I offered the following: that the extension of the privilege against the states by *Malloy v. Hogan* [p. 468] inevitably required that we consider whether police interrogation should be hedged about with procedural safeguards effective to secure the privilege ... This is not the first time the Court has had to consider the imposition of a requirement that the states provide procedural safeguards effective to secure a specific of the Bill of Rights extended against the states. A familiar recent example is in the obscenity area,[a] [where] we held that the states were constitutionally required to provide procedures effective to safeguard nonobscene expression from suppression. In the Fourth Amendment area, our imposition of the exclusionary rule in *Mapp v. Ohio* is of the same order.

Before *Malloy*, when the problem was only that of federal interrogation, we fashioned the safeguards ourselves, through the criminal rules and the exercise of our supervisory power. We went pretty far ... Here, however, our powers are more limited. We cannot prescribe rigid rules for the same reason that we did not do so in *Freedman v. Maryland*: we are justified in policing interrogation practices only to the extent required to prevent denial of the right against compelled self-incrimination as we defined that right in *Malloy*. I therefore do not think, as your draft seems to suggest, that there is only a single constitutionally required solution to the problems of testimonial compulsion inherent in custodial interroga-

a. At this point Justice Brennan referred to *Marcus v. Search Warrant of Property*, 367 U.S. 717 (1961); *Quantity of Copies of Books v.* *Kansas*, 378 U.S. 205 (1964); and *Freedman v. Maryland*, 380 U.S. 51 (1965).

tions. I agree that, largely for the reasons you have stated, all four cases must be reversed for lack of any safeguards against denial of the right. I also agree that warnings and the help of counsel are appropriate. But should we not leave Congress and the States latitude to devise other means (if they can) which might also create an interrogation climate which has the similar effect of preventing the fettering of a person's own will? . . .

I agree fully that the opinion must demonstrate . . . the dangers necessarily inherent in custodial questioning . . . We may thus establish that safeguards against those effects are constitutionally required to give substance to the [Fifth Amendment] right.

―――――――

Chief Justice Warren reworked his draft opinion of *Miranda* to accommodate Justice Brennan's suggestions. Years later, the language Warren had added caught the attention of newly appointed Justice Rehnquist. When, writing for the Court in *Michigan v. Tucker* (a case discussed under the next heading), Justice Rehnquist characterized *Miranda*'s rules as not constitutionally required, he relied upon language in *Miranda* that Chief Justice Warren had used at Justice Brennan's request. See Charles D. Weisselberg, *Saving Miranda* 109, 128–29 (1998).

THE IMPLICATIONS OF THE *TUCKER–QUARLES–ELSTAD* WAY OF THINKING ABOUT *MIRANDA*

MICHIGAN v. TUCKER, 417 U.S. 433, 94 S.Ct. 2357, 41 L.Ed.2d 182 (1974), dealt with the admissibility of the testimony of a witness whose identity had been learned by questioning defendant without giving him the full *Miranda* warnings.[a] The questioning occurred before *Miranda* was decided, but defendant's trial took place afterwards. Thus, *Miranda* was applicable to the case[b] and, accordingly, defendant's own statements to the police were excluded; but the witness' testimony was not. In the course of holding that under the circumstances the witness' testimony was admissible,[c] the Court, per REHNQUIST, J., viewed the *Miranda* warnings as "not themselves rights protected by the Constitution" but only "prophylactic standards" designed to "safeguard" or to "provide practical reinforcement" for the privilege against self-incrimination:[d]

"[T]he Court in *Miranda,* for the first time, expressly declared that the Self–Incrimination Clause was applicable to state interrogations at a police station, and

a. Defendant had been told that he had a right to the presence of counsel, but had not been informed that if he could not afford a lawyer but desired one, a lawyer would be appointed for him prior to any questioning.

b. The Court held, a week after *Miranda,* that *Miranda* affects only those cases in which *the trial* began after the date of that decision. Should the Court have held that *Miranda* only applies to *police interrogations* conducted after the date of that decision? See generally Ch. 2, § 3.

c. The Court noted, inter alia, that since the police action "was pursued in complete good faith," the deterrent purpose of the exclusionary rule "loses much of its force"; and deemed it "significant [that] the officers' fail-

ure to advise [defendant] of his right to appointed counsel occurred prior [to] *Miranda.*"

d. As noted in Laurence Herman, *The Supreme Court, the Attorney General and the Good Old Days of Police Interrogation,* 48 Ohio St.L.J. 733, 738–39 fn. 44 (1987), in June, 1969, the Department of Justice sent to the U.S. Attorneys a memorandum drafted in the Office of Legal Counsel—an office then headed by future Supreme Court Justice Rehnquist— which viewed the *Miranda* warnings as "not themselves constitutional absolutes" and characterized *Miranda* as "a protective measure"; "a means, suggested by the Court, by which the accused's Fifth Amendment privilege may be safeguarded."

that a defendant's statements might be excluded at trial despite their voluntary character under traditional principles.

"To supplement this new doctrine, and to help police officers conduct interrogations without facing a continued risk that valuable evidence would be lost, the [*Miranda* Court] established a set of specific guidelines, now commonly known as the *Miranda* rules.

"[The *Miranda* Court] recognized that these procedural safeguards were not themselves rights protected by the Constitution but were instead measures to insure that the right against compulsory self-incrimination was protected. As [it] remarked: '[W]e cannot say that the Constitution necessarily requires adherence to any particular solution for the inherent compulsions of the interrogation process as it is presently conducted.' The suggested safeguards were not intended to 'create a constitutional straitjacket,' *Miranda,* but rather to provide practical reinforcement for the right against compulsory self-incrimination.[e]

"A comparison of the facts in this case with the historical circumstances underlying the privilege against compulsory self-incrimination strongly indicates that the police conduct here did not deprive [Tucker] of his privilege against self-incrimination as such, but rather failed to make available to him the full measure of procedural safeguards associated with that right since *Miranda*. Certainly no one could contend that the interrogation faced by [Tucker] bore any resemblance to the historical practices at which the right against compulsory self-incrimination was aimed. [H]is statements could hardly be termed involuntary as that term has been defined in the decisions of this Court. * * *

"Our determination that the interrogation in this case involved no compulsion sufficient to breach the right against compulsory self-incrimination does not mean there was not a disregard, albeit an inadvertent disregard, of the procedural rules later established in *Miranda*. The question for decision is how sweeping the judicially imposed consequences of this disregard shall be."[f]

A decade later, first in New York v. Quarles (1984) (p. 532), and then in Oregon v. Elstad (1985) (p. 803), the Court reiterated *Tucker's* way of looking at, and thinking about, *Miranda*. *Quarles* recognized a "public safety" exception to the *Miranda* warnings and thus held both the suspect's statement, "the gun is over there," and the gun found as a result admissible. *Elstad* ruled that the fact

---

e. But as Justice Douglas observed in his *Tucker* dissent, the Court, per Rehnquist, J., overlooked other language in the *Miranda* opinion. For example, in the same paragraph from *Miranda* quoted by Justice Rehnquist in *Tucker,* the *Miranda* Court added: "However, unless we are shown other procedures which are at least as effective in apprising accused persons of their right of silence and in assuring a continuous opportunity to exercise it, the following safeguards [the *Miranda* warnings] must be observed." Moreover, later in the opinion, the *Miranda* Court reiterated: "The warnings required and the waiver necessary in accordance with our opinion today are, in the absence of a fully effective equivalent, prerequisites to the admissibility of any statements made by a defendant. * * * Procedural safeguards must be employed to protect the privilege, and unless other fully effective means are adopted to notify the person of his right of silence and to assure that the exercise of the

right will be scrupulously honored, the following measures [the *Miranda* warnings] are required."

f. Consider, also *Brown v. Illinois* (p. 787) where the Court, per Blackmun, J., observed: "This Court has described the *Miranda* warnings as a 'prophylactic rule' and as a 'procedural safeguard' employed to protect Fifth Amendment rights against 'the compulsion inherent in custodial surroundings.' The function of the warnings relates to the Fifth Amendment's guarantee against coerced self-incrimination, and the exclusion of a statement made in the absence of the warnings, it is said, serves to deter the taking of an incriminating statement without first informing the individual of his Fifth Amendment rights." Note, too, that dissenting in *Brewer v. Williams* (p. 619), Justice Blackmun, joined by White and Rehnquist, JJ., described *Miranda* as "this Court's procedural (as distinguished from constitutional) ruling."

that the police had earlier obtained a statement from defendant in violation of his *Miranda* rights (when they questioned him in his home) did not bar the admissibility of a subsequent confession (at the station house) when, this time, the police complied with *Miranda*. In both cases the Court underscored the distinction between statements that are *actually* "coerced" or "compelled" and those obtained *merely* in violation of *Miranda's* "procedural safeguards" or "prophylactic rules."

In QUARLES, the Court, per REHNQUIST, J., relied heavily on Justice Rehnquist's opinion for the Court in *Tucker:*

"The prophylactic *Miranda* warnings * * * are 'not themselves rights protected by the Constitution but [are] instead measures to insure that the right against compulsory self-incrimination [is] protected' *Tucker*. Requiring *Miranda* warnings before custodial interrogation provides 'practical reinforcement' for the Fifth Amendment right. *Tucker*.

"In this case we have before us no claim that [Quarles'] statements were actually compelled by police conduct which overcame his will to resist. Thus the only issue before us is whether [the officer] was justified in failing to make available to [Quarles] the procedural safeguards associated with the privilege against compulsory self-incrimination since *Miranda*. * * *

"We conclude that the need for answers to questions in a situation posing a threat to the public safety outweighs the need for the prophylactic rule protecting the Fifth Amendment's privilege against self-incrimination."

In ELSTAD, defendant relied on the "fruit of the poisonous tree" doctrine, a rule first developed in the search and seizure area that bars the use of evidence derived from and "tainted" by a prior constitutional violation. (See Ch. 11, § 3.) Defendant contended that the second confession, although immediately preceded by *Miranda* warnings and a valid waiver of rights, should be excluded as the "fruit" of the earlier *Miranda* violation. The Court disagreed: The "fruit of the poisonous tree" doctrine assumes the existence of an underlying constitutional violation. However, unlike a Fourth Amendment violation or an "actually coerced" confession (i.e., one inadmissible under the "due-process"-"voluntariness" test), a failure to give the *Miranda* warnings, when called for, is not in itself a violation of the fifth amendment. Observed the Court per O'CONNOR, J.:

"If errors are made by law enforcement officers in administering the prophylactic *Miranda* procedures, they should not breed the same irremediable consequences as police infringement of the Fifth Amendment itself. [There] is a vast difference between the direct consequences flowing from coercion of a confession by physical violence or other deliberate means calculated to break the suspect's will and the uncertain consequences of disclosure of a 'guilty secret' freely given in response to an unwarned but noncoercive question, as in this case. [A]bsent deliberately coercive or improper tactics in obtaining the initial statement, the mere fact that a suspect has made an unwarned admission does not warrant a presumption of compulsion. A subsequent administration of *Miranda* warnings to a suspect who has given a voluntary but unwarned statement ordinarily should suffice to remove the conditions that precluded admission of the earlier statement."

Dissenting Justice BRENNAN, joined by Marshall, J., protested:

"[Assertions in recent cases that the *Miranda* safeguards are not themselves rights guaranteed by the Fifth Amendment] are erroneous. *Miranda* 's requirement of warnings and an effective waiver was not merely an exercise of supervisory authority over interrogation practices. * * * *Miranda* clearly emphasized that warnings and an informed waiver are essential to the Fifth Amendment privilege itself.

"[The] Court today refuses to apply the derivative-evidence rule even to the extent necessary to deter objectively unreasonable failures by the authorities to honor a suspect's *Miranda* rights. * * * How can the Court possibly expect the authorities to obey *Miranda* when they have every incentive now to interrogate suspects without warnings or an effective waiver, knowing that the fruits of such interrogations 'ordinarily' will be admitted * * * ?"

In a separate dissent, STEVENS, J., maintained:

"[T]he Court's attempt to fashion a distinction between actual coercion 'by physical violence or other deliberate means calculated to break the suspect's will' and irrebuttably presumed coercion cannot succeed. The presumption is only legitimate if it is assumed that there is always a coercive aspect to custodial interrogation that is not preceded by adequate advice of the constitutional right to remain silent.

"[The] Court appears ambivalent on the question whether there was any constitutional violation [in this case]. This ambivalence is either disingenuous or completely lawless. This Court's power to require state courts to exclude probative self-incriminatory statements rests entirely on the premise that the use of such evidence violates the Federal Constitution. The same constitutional analysis applies whether the custodial interrogation is actually coercive or irrebuttably presumed to be coercive. If the Court does not accept that premise, it must regard the holding in the *Miranda* case itself, as well as all the Federal jurisprudence that has evolved from that decision, as nothing more than an illegitimate exercise of raw judicial power."

———

By equating "compulsion" within the meaning of the self-incrimination clause with "coercion" or "involuntariness" under the pre-*Miranda* due process "totality of the circumstances" test for admitting confessions, did the post-Warren Court overlook that in pre-*Miranda* days the terms "coercion" and "involuntariness" were not used in their ordinary sense, but as terms of art? Does it overlook, too, that *much greater* pressures were necessary to render a confession "coerced" or "involuntary" under the old test for admitting confessions than are needed (or were deemed needed at the time of *Miranda*) to render a confession "compelled" within the meaning of the privilege? Was that not a principal reason for abandoning the old test in favor of *Miranda*? If, as the Court now seems to say, a violation of the self-incrimination clause *itself* occurs only when a confession is "involuntary" under traditional standards, is this "an outright rejection of the core premise of *Miranda*"? See Geoffrey R. Stone, *The Miranda Doctrine in the Burger Court,* 1977 Sup.Ct.Rev. 99, 118.

PROPHYLACTIC RULES, SUPERVISORY POWERS AND THE CONSTITUTIONALITY OF § 3501

According to Joseph D. Grano, *Confessions, Truth and the Law* 173–98 (1993), *Miranda* is an "illegitimate" decision. Pointing to the *Tucker*, *Quarles* and *Elstad* cases, Professor Grano argues that what the Court *now* characterizes what it did in *Miranda* was to promulgate a "prophylactic rule" that does not conform to the *Marbury v. Madison* model of judicial review:

"To permit federal courts to impose prophylactic rules on the states [is] to say in essence that federal courts have supervisory power over state courts. [The Fifth Amendment] does not proscribe self-incrimination that is not compelled, nor does it proscribe custody, interrogation, or custodial interrogation as such. By supposedly adopting a conclusive presumption of compulsion (Y) from the mere fact of unwarned custodial interrogation (X), *Miranda* eliminated compulsion (Y) from the legal standard. [To] explain, applaud, or defend *Miranda* in terms of a conclusive presumption rationale [is] to assert for the Supreme Court the power of constitutional amendment."

But Stephen Schulhofer, *Reconsidering Miranda,* 54 U.Chi.L.Rev. 435, 453 (1987), considers *Miranda*'s conclusive presumption of compulsion "a responsible reaction to the problems of the voluntariness test, to the rarity of cases in which compelling pressures are truly absent, and to the adjudicatory costs of case-by-case decisions in this area. Indeed, in any ranking of the issues that properly demand some form of prophylactic rule, the problem of determining compulsion in the context of custodial interrogation wins the prize hands down."

Supporting Schulhofer, Professor David A. Strauss, *The Ubiquity of Prophylactic Rules,* 55 U.Chi.L.Rev. 190, 194–95, 208–09 (1988), argues that prophylactic rules are "a central and necessary feature of constitutional law":

"If it is legitimate for a court to create a rebuttable presumption or burden of proof rule, why is it illegitimate for a court to decide that the sum of error costs and administrative costs will be minimized by making certain evidence legally immaterial? Moreover, there is a sense in which a rebuttable presumption makes certain evidence immaterial as well—in the case of a rebuttable version of *Miranda,* any evidence that tends to show that a confession was voluntary, but that is not quite enough to overcome the presumption. * * *

"Judges do not have a general authority to implement their visions of the best world, unless, of course, those visions are validated by the Constitution. But judges do, necessarily, consider institutional concerns when they apply the Constitution in specific cases. This means that the critics of *Miranda* must meet it on its own terms; they must show that the constitutional and institutional values at stake do not justify the conclusive presumption that *Miranda* established. They cannot say that it is illegitimate just because it established a conclusive presumption."

The failure of the Justice Department to invoke § 3501, which purports to "repeal" *Miranda* in the federal courts (see Justice Scalia's concurring opinion in *Davis v. United States,* p. 561) did not discourage two conservative legal groups, the Washington Legal Foundation (WLF) and the Safe Streets Coalition. Led by the indefatigable Paul Cassell, a Utah Law School professor who has become the nation's leading critic of *Miranda,*[a] these groups repeatedly urged the federal courts to inject § 3501 into their cases. They maintained that confessions obtained in violation of *Miranda* should be admitted unless they failed to satisfy the more lenient standard for admissibility set forth in § 3501. They also criticized the federal government for failing to assert the applicability of § 3501.

For example, in UNITED STATES v. LEONG, 116 F.3d 1474 (4th Cir. 1997), the WLF moved to proceed as *amicus* in the U.S. Court of Appeals for the Fourth

---

a. See, e.g., Paul G. Cassell, *Miranda's Social Costs: An Empirical Reassessment,* 90 Nw. U.L.Rev. 387 (1996); Paul G. Cassell, *Miranda's "Negligible" Effect on Law Enforcement: Some Skeptical Observations,* 20 Harv. J.L.Pub.Pol'y 327 (1997); Paul G. Cassell & Richard Fowles, *Handcuffing the Cops? A Thirty-Year Perspective on Miranda's Harmful Effects on Law Enforcement,* 50 Stan.L.Rev. 1055 (1998).

Circuit, recalling that in 1986, after a comprehensive analysis of the issue, the Justice Department's Office of Legal Policy had concluded, in a lengthy report to the Attorney General (see 22 Mich.J.L. Ref. 437, 549 (1989)): "[Because of the enactment of § 3501] *Miranda* should no longer be regarded as controlling [in federal cases]. Since the Supreme Court now holds that *Miranda's* rules are merely prophyllactic, and that the fifth amendment is not violated by the admission of a defendant's voluntary statements despite non-compliance with *Miranda*, a decision by the Court invalidating [§ 3501] would require some extraordinary legal theorizing of an unpredictable legal nature."

The Burger and Rehnquist Court's description of the *Miranda* rules as "prophylactic," emphasized Justice, "does not require the conclusion that the rules are therefore extra-constitutional. The appellation may simply reflect the notion that *Miranda*, in the interest of avoiding constitutional violations,structured a regime that 'overprotects the value at stake,' and thus excludes some statements that are not 'compelled' within the meaning of the Self-Incrimination Clause. [That] a 'prophylactic' rule is not necessarily a non-constitutional rule is confirmed by the Supreme Court's description of *Edwards v. Arizona* (1981)[p. 548]. [The] Court has both characterized the *Edwards* rule as 'a second layer of prophylaxis' to protect a suspect's right to counsel under *Miranda* and also unmistakably described [it] as a constitutional decision."

Moreover, argued Justice, even if cases such as *Tucker, Quarles* and *Elstad* "are viewed as having eroded *Miranda's* basic constitutional premise," it would be inappropriate for any lower court "to apply § 3501 to admit a defendant's statement in a case in which *Miranda* would require its suppression or for the Department of Justice to urge the lower courts to do so": "[A lower court] may not disregard controlling Supreme Court precedent. *Miranda* has never expressly been overruled, and it is the Supreme Court's sole province to pass on the continuing validity of its decisions."

In response, the WLF warned the Fourth Circuit: "If the [Justice] Department's position is left unreviewed, [the] Department will have succeeded in frustrating the constitutional scheme of separated powers—by obtaining for itself not simply a role in executing the laws but effectively in writing them as well. It has long been established that the executive branch's charge to execute the law does not carry with it a power *not* to execute."

Since the federal government had not pressed § 3501 before the district court or the court of appeals as a basis for a determination that defendant's confession was inadmissible, the Fourth Circuit declined to rehear the appeal. But the court voiced strong disagreement with the Justice Department's view that *Miranda* "remains binding on lower federal courts notwithstanding § 3501 unless or until it is modified by the Supreme Court."

A year and a half later, in UNITED STATES v. DICKERSON, 166 F.3d 667 (4th Cir. 1999), a panel of the Fourth Circuit gave the WLF and the Safe Streets Coalition a stunning victory. Although the dissenting judge protested that the ruling was made "without the benefit of any briefing in opposition" and "against the express wishes of the Department of Justice," a 2–1 majority per KAREN WILLIAMS, J., held that the pre-*Miranda* due process-voluntariness test set forth in § 3501, rather than the *Miranda* case, governs the admissibility of confessions in the federal courts. Therefore, the district court had erred when it had suppressed a voluntary confession simply because it was obtained in violation of *Miranda*. In upholding the constitutionality of § 3501, the *Dickerson* majority relied heavily on the fact that the Burger and Rehnquist Courts had "consistently referred to the *Miranda* warnings as 'prophylactic' and 'not themselves rights protected by the Constitution' ":

"[The] Department of Justice, elevating politics over law, prohibited the U.S. Attorney's Office from arguing that Dickerson's confession is admissible under the mandate of § 3501. Fortunately, we are a court of law and not politics. Thus, the Department of Justice cannot prevent us from deciding this case under the governing law simply by refusing to argue it. * * *

"Determining whether Congress possesses the authority to enact § 3501 is relatively straightforward. Congress has the power to overrule judicially created rules of evidence and procedure that are not required by the Constitution. Thus, whether Congress has the authority to enact § 3501 turns on whether the rule set forth by the Supreme Court in Miranda is required by the Constitution. Clearly, it is not. At no point did the Supreme Court in *Miranda* refer to the warnings as constitutional rights. Indeed, the Court acknowledged that the Constitution did not require the warnings, disclaimed any intent to create a 'constitutional straightjacket,' referred to the warnings as 'procedural safeguards,' and invited Congress and the States 'to develop their own safeguards for [protecting] the privilege.' Since deciding *Miranda*, the Supreme Court has consistently referred to the *Miranda* warnings as 'prophylactic,' *Quarles* and 'not themselves rights protected by the Constitution,' *Tucker*. We have little difficulty concluding, therefore, that § 3501, enacted at the invitation of the Supreme Court and pursuant to Congress's unquestioned power to establish the rules of procedure and evidence in the federal courts, is constitutional. As a consequence, we hold that the admissibility of confessions in federal court is governed by § 3501, rather than the judicially created rule of *Miranda*.

"Although Congress enacted § 3501 with the express purpose of restoring voluntariness as the test for admitting confessions in federal court, it is important to note that Congress did not completely abandon the central holding of *Miranda*, i.e., the four warnings are important safeguards in protecting the Fifth Amendment privilege against self-incrimination. Indeed, § 3501 specifically lists the *Miranda* warnings as factors that a district court should consider when determining whether a confession was voluntarily given. Congress simply provided that the failure to administer the warnings to a suspect would no longer create an irrebuttable presumption that a subsequent confession was involuntarily given. * * *

"[L]est there be any confusion on the matter, nothing in today's opinion provides those in law enforcement with an incentive to stop giving the now familiar *Miranda* warnings. As noted above, those warnings are among the factors a district court should consider when determining whether a confession was voluntarily given. Indeed, federal courts rarely find confessions obtained in technical compliance with *Miranda* to be involuntary under the Fifth Amendment. [Thus,] providing the four *Miranda* warnings is still the best way to guarantee a finding of voluntariness."

Dissenting Judge MICHAEL observed:

"* * * I cannot agree with the majority's accusation that the Department of Justice 'elevat[ed] politics over law' when it prevented the United States Attorney from invoking § 3501 in an effort to save Dickerson's confession. A move to admit more confessions could be touted as aggressive prosecution, so I would think it might be better politics to invoke § 3501. In any event, I see no evidence that the Department of Justice is putting politics over law when it comes to § 3501. The

Department's view—that § 3501 cannot be used to admit confessions that *Miranda* would exclude—is a view that I accept as genuine.

"* * * We perform our role as neutral arbiter best when we let the parties raise the issues, and both sides brief and argue them fully. That did not happen here. By invoking § 3501, the majority injects into this case the overriding constitutional question of whether § 3501 can supersede *Miranda*. It then decides the question against the defendant, when the only briefing we have on the issue is about two pages from *amici* that the majority agrees with. * * * I don't know whether [or not *Miranda* is a constitutional rule], but before I had to decide, I would want thoughtful lawyers on *both* sides to answer one question for me. If *Miranda* is not a constitutional rule, why does the Supreme Court continue to apply it in prosecutions arising in state courts? [This] question illustrates that the § 3501 issue is so sweeping that we should not be delving into it on our own."

THREE DECADES WITH *MIRANDA:* AN OVERVIEW

Because *Miranda* was the centerpiece of the Warren Court's "revolution in American criminal procedure" and the prime target of those who thought the courts were "soft" on criminals, almost everyone expected the so-called Burger Court to treat *Miranda* unkindly. And it did—at first. But it must also be said that the new Court has interpreted *Miranda* fairly generously in some important respects.

The first blows the Burger Court dealt *Miranda* were the impeachment cases, *Harris v. New York* (1971) (Ch. 11, § 4) and *Oregon v. Hass* (1975) (Ch. 11, § 4). *Harris* held that statements preceded by defective warnings, and thus inadmissible to establish the prosecution's case-in-chief, could nevertheless be used to impeach the defendant's credibility if he chose to take the stand in his own defense. The Court noted, but seemed unperturbed by the fact, that some language in the *Miranda* opinion could be read as barring the use of statements obtained in violation of *Miranda* for *any* purpose.

The Court went a step beyond *Harris* in the *Hass* case. In this case, after being advised of his rights, the defendant *asserted* them. Nevertheless, the police refused to honor the defendant's request for a lawyer and continued to question him. The Court ruled that here, too, the resulting incriminating statements could be used for impeachment purposes. Since many suspects make incriminating statements even after the receipt of complete *Miranda* warnings, *Harris* might have been explained—and contained—on the ground that permitting impeachment use of statements acquired without complete warnings would not greatly encourage the police to violate *Miranda*. But now that *Hass* is on the books, when a suspect asserts his rights, it seems the police have virtually nothing to lose and everything to gain by continuing to question him.[a]

Although language in *Miranda* could be read as establishing a *per se* rule against any further questioning of one who has asserted his "right to silence" (as opposed to his *right to counsel,* discussed below), *Michigan v. Mosley* (1975) (p. 547) held that under certain circumstances (and what they are is unclear), if they

a. More recently, the Court held that a defendant's prior silence could be used to impeach him when he testified in his own defense, *Jenkins v. Anderson* (1980) (Ch. 11, § 4), and that even a defendant's *post*arrest silence (so long as he was not given the *Miranda* warnings) could be used for impeachment purposes, *Fletcher v. Weir* (1982) (Ch. 11, § 4). Both *Jenkins* and *Weir* distinguished *Doyle v. Ohio* (1976) (Ch. 11, § 4), which deemed it a violation of due process to use a defendant's silence for impeachment purposes when the defendant remained silent *after* being given *Miranda* warnings.

cease questioning on the spot, the police may "try again," and succeed at a later interrogation session. At the very least, it seems, the police must promptly terminate the original interrogation, resume questioning after the passage of a significant period of time, and give the suspect a fresh set of warnings at the outset of the second session. Whether *Mosley* requires more is a matter of dispute.

The Court has read "custody" or "*custodial* interrogation" rather narrowly. *Oregon v. Mathiason* (1977) (p. 518) and *California v. Beheler* (1983) (p. 518) illustrate that even *police station* questioning designed to produce incriminating statements is not necessarily "custodial interrogation." The result in *Mathiason* is more easily defensible because the suspect went down to the station house on his own after an officer had requested that he meet him there at a convenient time and he had agreed to do so. In *Beheler,* however, the suspect went to the station house in the company of the police. (He was said to have "voluntarily agreed" to accompany the police.)

In *Brown v. Illinois* (1975) (Ch. 11, § 3), the Court declined an invitation to do serious damage to the Fourth Amendment by making the *Miranda* warnings, in effect, a "cure-all." The Court rejected the contention that the giving of the warnings should purge the taint of any preceding illegal arrest—a view that would have permitted the admissibility at trial of any resulting incriminating statements to be considered without regard to the illegal arrest and thus would have encouraged such arrests.[b]

In the early 1980's *Miranda* seemed to enjoy a "second honeymoon." Considering the alternatives (e.g., a mechanical approach to "interrogation," one limited to situations where the police directly address a suspect), the Court gave the key term "interrogation" a fairly generous reading in *Rhode Island v. Innis* (1980) (p. 519). Although the *Innis* case itself involved police "speech," the Court's definition of "interrogation" embraces interrogation techniques that do not. The following year, in *Edwards v. Arizona* (1981) (p. 548), the Court reinvigorated *Miranda* in an important respect. In effect, it added a "bright line" test to the "bright line" *Miranda* rules. Sharply distinguishing *Mosley,* the *Edwards* Court held that when a suspect asserts his right to counsel (as opposed to his right to remain silent), the police *cannot* "try again." Under these circumstances, a suspect cannot be questioned anew "*until* counsel has been made available to him, *unless* [he] himself *initiates* further communication, exchanges or conversations with the police" (emphasis added).[c]

But then, as discussed earlier, Justice Rehnquist's way of thinking about *Miranda,* which had first surfaced in *Michigan v. Tucker* (1974), reappeared—first in *New York v. Quarles* (1984) and then, more prominently, in Justice O'Connor's opinion for the Court in *Oregon v. Elstad* (1985). This left defenders of *Miranda* somewhat in disarray.

APPLYING AND EXPLAINING *MIRANDA*

1. **"*Exploiting a criminal's ignorance or stupidity*"; "*intelligent*" waivers vs. "*wise*" ones.** Consider State v. McKnight, 243 A.2d 240 (N.J.1968), per WEINTRAUB, C.J.:

b. *Brown* was reaffirmed and fortified in *Dunaway v. New York* (1979) and *Taylor v. Alabama* (1982), both discussed in Ch. 11, § 3.

c. In recent years the Court has read *Edwards* expansively. See *Arizona v. Roberson* (1988) (p. 548) and *Minnick v. Mississippi* (1990) (p. 549). But see *Oregon v. Bradshaw* (1983) (p. 557).

"The Constitution is not at all offended when a guilty man stubs his toe. On the contrary, it is decent to hope that he will. [T]he Fifth Amendment does not say that a man shall not be permitted to incriminate himself, or that he shall not be persuaded to do so. It says no more than that a man shall not be 'compelled' to give evidence against himself. [It] is consonant with good morals, and the Constitution, to exploit a criminal's ignorance or stupidity in the detectional process. This must be so if Government is to succeed in its primary mission to live free from criminal attack.

" * * * Nowhere does *Miranda* suggest that the waiver of counsel at the detectional stage would not be 'knowing' or 'intelligent' if the suspect did not understand the law relating to the crime, the possible defenses, and the hazards of talking without the aid of counsel, or if the suspect was not able to protect his interests without such aid, [or] if it was not 'wise' of the prisoner to forego counsel or the right to silence. * * * However relevant to 'waiver' of the right to counsel at trial or in connection with a plea of guilty, those factors are foreign to the investigational scene where the detection of crime is the legitimate aim.

"Hence if a defendant has been given the *Miranda* warnings, if the coercion of custodial interrogation was thus dissipated, his 'waiver' was no less 'voluntary' and 'knowing' and 'intelligent' because he misconceived the inculpatory thrust of the facts he admitted, or because he thought that what he said could not be used because it was only oral or because he had his fingers crossed, or because he could well have used a lawyer. A man need not have the understanding of a lawyer to waive one. Such matters, irrelevant when the defendant volunteers his confession to a friend or to a policeman passing on his beat, are equally irrelevant when the confession is made in custody after the coercion of custodial interrogation has been dispelled by the *Miranda* warnings. With such warnings, the essential fact remains that defendant understood he had the right to remain silent and thereby to avoid the risk of self-incrimination. That is what the Fifth Amendment privilege is about."

See also *Collins v. Brierly,* 492 F.2d 735 (3d Cir.1974) (en banc): "*Miranda* speaks of 'intelligent' waiver [in the sense] that the individual must know of his available options before deciding what he thinks best suits his particular situation. In this context intelligence is not equated with wisdom." Consider, too, James J. Tomkovicz, *Standards for Invocation and Waiver of Counsel in Confession Contexts,* 71 Iowa L.Rev. 975, 1049 (1986): "The policies of the fifth amendment privilege do not demand rationality, intelligence, or knowledge, but only a voluntary choice not to remain silent." Is this (ought this be) so?

2. *Adequacy of warnings.* Consider DUCKWORTH v. EAGAN, 492 U.S. 195, 109 S.Ct. 2875, 106 L.Ed.2d 166 (1989), which arose as follows: Respondent Eagan, suspected of murdering a woman, denied any involvement in the crime. He agreed to go to police headquarters for further questioning. At the stationhouse an officer read him a waiver form which provided, inter alia:

"You have a right to talk to a lawyer for advice before we ask you any questions, and to have him with you during questioning. You have the right to the advice and presence of a lawyer even if you cannot afford to hire one. *We have no way of giving you a lawyer, but one will be appointed for you, if you wish, if and when you go to court.* If you wish to answer questions now without a lawyer present, you have the right to stop answering questions at any time. You also have the right to stop answering at any time until you've talked to a lawyer." (Emphasis added.)

Eagan signed the waiver form, but again denied any involvement in the crime. He was then placed in the "lock up" at police headquarters. Some 29 hours later, the police met with Eagan again. Before questioning him, an officer read from a differently worded waiver form. Eagan signed it and then confessed to stabbing the woman. A 5–4 majority, per REHNQUIST, C.J., concluded that the initial warnings given to Eagan at police headquarters "touched all of the bases required by *Miranda*":

"*Miranda* has not been limited to station-house questioning, and the officer in the field may not always have access to printed *Miranda* warnings, or he may inadvertently depart from routine practice, particularly if a suspect requests an elaboration of the warnings. The prophylactic *Miranda* warnings are 'not themselves rights protected by the Constitution but [are] instead measures to insure that the right against compulsory self-incrimination [is] protected.' *Michigan v. Tucker*. Reviewing courts therefore need not examine *Miranda* warnings as if construing a will or defining the terms of an easement. The inquiry is simply whether the warnings reasonably 'conve[y] to [a suspect] his rights as required by *Miranda*.' *California v. Prysock*, 453 U.S. 355, 101 S.Ct. 2806, 69 L.Ed.2d 696 (1981) (per curium) [where, in the course of upholding the challenged warnings, the Supreme Court observed: "This Court has never indicated that the 'rigidity' of *Miranda* extends to the precise formulation of the warnings given a criminal defendant."]

"[On federal habeas corpus, the U.S. Court of Appeals for the Seventh Circuit thought that the] 'if and when you go to court' language suggested that 'only those accused who can afford an attorney have the right to have one present before answering any questions,' and 'implie[d] that if the accused does not 'go to court,' i.e., the government does not file charges, the accused is not entitled to [counsel] at all.'

"In our view, the Court of Appeals misapprehended the effect of the inclusion of 'if and when you go to court' language * * *. First, this instruction accurately described the procedure for the appointment of counsel in Indiana, [where] counsel is appointed at the defendant's initial appearance in court and formal charges must be filed at or before that hearing. We think it must be relatively commonplace for a suspect, after receiving *Miranda* warnings, to ask *when* he will obtain counsel. The 'if and when you go to court' advice simply anticipates that question. Second, *Miranda* does not require that attorneys be producible on call, but only that the suspect be informed, as here, that he has the right to an attorney before and during questioning, and that an attorney would be appointed for him if he could not afford one. The Court in *Miranda* emphasized that it was not suggesting that 'each police station must have a "station house lawyer" present at all times to advise prisoners.' If the police cannot provide appointed counsel, *Miranda* requires only that the police not question a suspect unless he waives his right to counsel. Here, respondent did just that. * * *."

Dissenting Justice MARSHALL, joined by Brennan, Blackmun and Stevens, JJ., maintained:

"Under *Miranda,* a police warning must '*clearly infor[m]*' a suspect taken into custody 'that if he cannot afford an attorney one will be appointed for him *prior to any questioning* if he so desires.' (Emphasis added.) A warning qualified by an 'if and when you go to court' caveat does nothing of the kind; instead, it leads the suspect to believe that a lawyer will not be provided until some indeterminate time in the future *after questioning*. I refuse to acquiesce in the continuing debasement of this historic precedent * * *.

"Even if the typical suspect could draw the inference [from the initial warning that] the majority does—that questioning will not commence until a lawyer is provided at a later court appearance—a warning qualified by an 'if and when' caveat still fails to give a suspect any indication of *when* he will be taken to court. Upon hearing the warnings given in this case, a suspect would likely conclude that no lawyer would be provided until trial. In common parlance, 'going to court' is synonymous with 'going to trial.' Furthermore, the negative implication of the caveat is that, if the suspect is never taken to court, he 'is not entitled to an attorney at all.' An unwitting suspect harboring uncertainty on this score is precisely the sort of person who may feel compelled to talk 'voluntarily' to the police, without the presence of counsel, in an effort to extricate himself from his predicament * * *."

Notes and Questions

(a) *Access to a Miranda card.* An officer "in the field," notes the Court, "may not always have access to printed *Miranda* warnings" or may "inadvertently depart from routine practice, particularly if a suspect requests an elaboration of the warnings." What bearing should this have on a case like *Duckworth v. Eagan,* where the suspect was questioned at police headquarters and never asked for an elaboration of the warnings? Moreover, would it be burdensome or unreasonable to require police officers always to carry a standard *Miranda* card?

(b) *Anticipating a suspect's questions.* Should it be the business of the police to "anticipate" a suspect's questions? Does this confuse the role of the police officer with that of the defense lawyer?

"Anticipating" a question by Eagan, the police informed him that if he could not afford a lawyer "we have no way of giving you a lawyer" before or during questioning. What impact could that information have other than to make it *less likely* that Eagan would assert his right to appointed counsel?

Should the police have "anticipated" *another* question: "If you cannot give me a lawyer now, what happens if I ask for one now?" Under *Edwards v. Arizona* (1981) (p. 548), would the truthful answer to that question have been: "Then, we would be very restricted as to how we could proceed. We would have to cease questioning on the spot. And we could not resume questioning at a later time. We could not talk to you any more about this case unless and until you yourself initiated further communication with us." What would the impact of that information be other than to make it *more likely* that Eagan would assert his right to appointed counsel?

Are the police likely to "anticipate" any questions the answers to which further the suspect's interests, not theirs? Are the police (should the police be) free to "anticipate" those questions they would like to answer and free *not* to "anticipate" those questions they would rather not answer? Does *Duckworth* give them that freedom? See Kamisar, *Duckworth v. Eagan: A Little–Noticed Miranda Case that May Cause Much Mischief,* 25 Crim.L.Bull. 550 (1989).

(c) *Complying with Miranda.* According to *Miranda,* "if police propose to interrogate a person they must make known to him that he is entitled to a lawyer and that if he cannot afford one, a lawyer will be provided for him prior to any interrogation." Was Eagan told, in effect, that if he could not afford a lawyer, one would *not* be—and *could not* be—provided for him prior to (or during) any questioning?

3. *Need for police admonitions in addition to the four Miranda warnings.*

(a) *The consequences of silence.* If, as *Miranda* points out, many suspects will assume that "silence in the face of accusation is itself damning and will bode ill when presented to a jury" (text at fn. 37), should the suspect be explicitly advised not only that any statement he makes may be used against him but that his silence may *not* be used against him? Isn't a suspect likely to ask himself most urgently: "How do I get out of this mess and avoid looking guilty?" Absent assurance on this point, are many suspects likely to stand by their *Miranda* rights? An interrogator can truthfully tell a suspect that once the police advise him of his right to remain silent the prosecution may not comment at trial on his reliance on that right, but can he truthfully tell him that his silence will not be used against him *in any way?* For example, won't the suspect's silence affect the decision to prosecute? See Sheldon Elsen & Arthur Rosett, *Protections for the Suspect under Miranda v. Arizona,* 67 Colum.L.Rev. 645, 654–55 (1967).

(b) *The right to be made aware of the subject matter of the questioning.*

In COLORADO v. SPRING, 479 U.S. 564, 107 S.Ct. 851, 93 L.Ed.2d 954 (1987), a 7–2 majority, per POWELL, J., held that "a suspect's awareness of all the possible subjects of questioning in advance of interrogation is not relevant to determining whether the suspect voluntarily, knowingly, and intelligently waived his Fifth Amendment privilege." The case arose as follows:

An informant told agents of the Bureau of Alcohol, Tobacco and Firearms (ATF) that Spring (a) was engaged in the interstate shipment of stolen firearms and (b) had been involved in a Colorado killing. The ATF agents set up an undercover operation to purchase firearms from Spring. On March 30, ATF agents arrested Spring in Missouri during the undercover purchase. Spring was advised of his *Miranda* rights and signed a written waiver form.

The agents first questioned Spring about the firearms transactions that led to his arrest. They then asked him if he had ever shot anyone. Spring admitted that he had "shot [a] guy once." On May 26, Colorado officers visited Spring in jail and advised him of his *Miranda* rights. He again signed a written waiver form. The officers then informed Spring that they wanted to question him about the Colorado homicide. Spring confessed to the crime and was convicted of murder.

Spring contended that his waiver of *Miranda* rights before the March 30 statement was invalid because the ATF agents had not informed him that he would be questioned about the Colorado murder and that the May 26 confession was the illegal "fruit" of the March 30 admission. The Colorado Supreme Court agreed, but the U.S. Supreme Court reversed:

"[There] is no doubt that Spring's [March 30 waiver] was knowingly and intelligently made: that is, that Spring understood that he had the right to remain silent and that anything he said could be used as evidence against him. The Constitution does not require that a criminal suspect know and understand every possible consequence of a waiver of the Fifth Amendment privilege." Nor, held that Court, does the failure to inform a suspect of the potential subjects of interrogation constitute the police trickery and deception condemned in *Miranda:*

"This Court has never held that mere silence by law enforcement officials as to the subject matter of an interrogation is 'trickery' sufficient to invalidate a suspect's waiver of *Miranda* rights, and we expressly decline so to hold today. Once *Miranda* warnings are given, it is difficult to see how official silence could cause a suspect to misunderstand the nature of his constitutional right? 'his right to refuse to answer any question which might incriminate him.' '[W]e have never read the Constitution to require that the police supply a suspect with a flow of information to help him calibrate his self-interest in deciding whether to speak or stand by his rights.' *Moran v. Burbine* [p. 571]. Here, the additional information could affect only the wisdom of a *Miranda* waiver, not its essentially voluntary and knowing nature. Accordingly, the failure [to] inform Spring of the subject matter of the interrogation could not affect [his] decision to waive his Fifth Amendment privilege in a constitutionally significant manner."

MARSHALL, joined by Brennan, J., dissented:

"The interrogation tactics utilized in this case demonstrate the relevance of the information Spring did not receive. The [ATF] agents evidently hoped to obtain from Spring a valid confession to the federal firearms charge for which he was arrested and then parlay this admission into an additional confession of first degree murder. Spring could not have expected questions about the latter, separate offense when he agreed to waive his rights, as it occurred in a different state and was a violation of state law outside the normal investigative focus of federal [ATF] agents.

"[The] coercive aspects of the psychological ploy intended in this case, when combined with an element of surprise which may far too easily rise to a level of deception, cannot be justified in light of *Miranda*'s strict requirements that the suspect's waiver and confession be voluntary, knowing, and intelligent. If a suspect has signed a waiver form with the intention of making a statement regarding a specifically alleged crime, the Court today would hold this waiver valid with respect to questioning about any other crime, regardless of its relation to the charges the suspect believes he will be asked to address. Yet once this waiver is given and the intended statement made, the protections afforded by *Miranda* against the 'inherently compelling pressures' of the custodial interrogation have effectively dissipated. Additional questioning about entirely separate and more serious suspicions of criminal activity can take unfair advantage of the suspect's psychological state, as the unexpected questions cause the compulsive pressures suddenly to reappear. Given this technique of interrogation, a suspect's understanding of the topics planned for questioning is, therefore, at the very least 'relevant' to assessing whether his decision to talk to the officers was voluntarily, knowingly, and intelligently made."

Notes and Questions

(i) Should the *Spring* Court have given weight to the fact that the ATF agents had deprived defendant of information regarding the *more serious charge?* Since the agents had arrested Spring in the act of selling illegal firearms, is it likely that Spring decided to talk to the agents because he felt he had nothing more to lose? See Note, 30 Ariz.L.Rev. 551, 564 (1988).

(ii) Would the Court have reached the same result if Spring had asked the ATF agents what crimes they planned to question him about and the agents (a) had remained silent or (b) had replied that the firearms transactions were the only crimes under investigation? If so, why? If not, is it sound "to fashion a confession law doctrine which turns on the fortuity of a suspect asking the right questions"? See id. at 560–61.

4. *"Custody" vs. "focus."* After defining "custodial interrogation" in the text, the *Miranda* Court, as one commentator put it, Kenneth W. Graham, *What Is "Custodial Interrogation"?,* 14 U.C.L.A.Rev. 59, 114 (1966), dropped an "obfuscating footnote [4]": "This is what we meant in *Escobedo* when we spoke of an investigation which has focused on an accused." This footnote led some to think that "custody" and "focus" were alternative grounds for requiring the warnings, but these are different events and they have very different consequences.[a] The likely explanation for footnote 4 was the *Miranda* Court's understandable effort to maintain some continuity with a recent precedent. Despite that footnote, however, *Miranda* actually marked a fresh start in describing the circumstances under which constitutional protections first come into play.

The "focus" test, as it had generally been understood at the time of *Escobedo* was expressly rejected in BECKWITH v. UNITED STATES, 425 U.S. 341, 96 S.Ct. 1612, 48 L.Ed.2d 1 (1976). Agents of the Intelligence Division of the IRS did not arrest petitioner, but met with him in a private home where he occasionally stayed. Petitioner argued that the "interview," which produced incriminating statements, should have been preceded by full *Miranda* warnings (instead of the modified *Miranda* warning which petitioner received) because the taxpayer is clearly the "focus" of a criminal investigation when a case is assigned to the Intelligence Division and such a confrontation "places the taxpayer under 'psychological restraints' which are the functional, and therefore, the legal equivalent of custody." The Court per BURGER, C.J., was "not impressed with this argument in the abstract nor as applied to the particular facts of [petitioner's] interrogation":

"An interview with government agents in a situation such as [this one] simply does not present the elements which the *Miranda* Court found so inherently coercive as to require its holding. Although the 'focus' of an investigation may indeed have been on [petitioner] at the time of the interview in the sense that it was his tax liability which was under scrutiny, he hardly found himself in the custodial situation described by the *Miranda* Court as the basis for its holding. *Miranda* specifically defined 'focus,' for its purposes, as 'questioning initiated by law enforcement officers *after* a person has been taken into custody or otherwise deprived of his freedom of action in any significant way.' "[b]

In *Stansbury v. California*, 511 U.S. 318, 114 S.Ct. 1526, 128 L.Ed.2d 293 (1994) (per curium), the Court held, "not for the first time, that an officer's subjective and undisclosed view concerning whether the person being interrogated is a suspect is irrelevant to the assessment whether the person is in custody." Unless they are communicated to the person being questioned, emphasized the Court, "an officer's evolving but unarticulated suspicions do not affect the objective circumstances of an interrogation or interview, and thus cannot affect the *Miranda* custody inquiry."

5. *What constitutes "custody" or "custodial interrogation"?* According to Israel, *Criminal Procedure, the Burger Court and the Legacy of the Warren Court,* 75 Mich.L.Rev. 1320, 1383–84 (1977), "difficulties [with *Miranda*] have arisen primarily in situations involving questioning 'on the street.' [P]olice can easily identify what constitutes 'custodial interrogation' where that concept is

a. *Hoffa v. United States,* p. 388, emphasized, albeit not in a *Miranda* context, that "there is no constitutional right to be arrested" and that the police "are under no constitutional duty to call a halt to a criminal investigation the moment they have the minimum evidence to establish probable cause."

b. See also Chief Justice Burger's plurality opinion in *United States v. Mandujano,* p. 718, rejecting the argument that a "putative" or "virtual" defendant called before the grand jury is entitled to full *Miranda* warnings and stressing that the *Miranda* warnings "were

aimed at the evils seen by the Court as endemic to police interrogation of a person in custody. [*Miranda*] recognized that many official investigations, such as grand jury questioning, take place in a setting wholly different from custodial police interrogation. [To] extend [*Miranda*] concepts to questioning before a grand jury inquiring into criminal activity under the guidance of a judge is an extravagant expansion [of that case]." But see Justice Brennan's concurring opinion in *Mandujano.*

limited to questioning at the police station or a similar setting." In the main, the concept has been so limited.

Most courts have concluded that absent special circumstances (such as arresting a suspect at gunpoint or forcibly subduing him),[a] police questioning "on the street," in a public place or in a person's home or office is not "custodial." Cf. *Schneckloth v. Bustamonte* (p. 532) (warning requirement need not be imposed on "normal consent searches" because they occur on highways, homes or offices and "under informal and unstructured conditions" "immeasurably far removed from 'custodial interrogations.' ")[b]

---

a. See *Orozco v. Texas,* 394 U.S. 324, 89 S.Ct. 1095, 22 L.Ed.2d 311 (1969) (applying *Miranda* to a situation where defendant was questioned in his bedroom by four police officers at 4:00 a.m., circumstances that produced a "potentiality for compulsion" equivalent to police station interrogation); *New York v. Quarles* (1984) (p. 343) (defendant in "custody" when questioned in a supermarket minutes after arrested at gunpoint, surrounded by four officers, "frisked" and handcuffed, but "public safety" exception to *Miranda* applied).

The "custodial interrogation" issue arose in a unique setting in *United States v. Mesa,* 638 F.2d 582 (3d Cir.1980). After shooting and wounding both his wife and daughter, Mesa barricaded himself in a motel room. FBI agents cleared the area and repeatedly called to him, through a bullhorn, to surrender. Mesa did not respond. Believing that Mesa was armed (he was) and not knowing whether he had hostages (he did not), the FBI brought in a "hostage negotiator." Mesa agreed to take a mobile phone into his room. Before Mesa finally surrendered peacefully, the negotiator and Mesa conversed over the mobile phone for three and a half hours. The conversation consisted mainly of long narrative monologues by Mesa, but in the course of his exchange of remarks with the negotiator Mesa did make some incriminating statements about the shootings. At no time was he given the *Miranda* warnings. A 2–1 majority of the Third Circuit held that Mesa's statements were admissible, but because one judge decided the case solely on the ground that the exchange between Mesa and the negotiator did not constitute "interrogation" (see p. 526), there was no majority opinion on the "custody" issue.

Maintaining that *Miranda's* description of the custodial setting "demonstrates that, at a minimum, the police must have immediate control over the suspect," Chief Judge Seitz concluded that Mesa had not been subjected to *custodial* interrogation: "Mesa successfully had barricaded himself [in] such a way that he prevented [the police] from exercising immediate control over his actions. They could not compel [him] even to listen to any questions they might want to ask, much less subject him to the interviewing techniques or 'tricks' that concerned the *Miranda* Court. They had no power to handcuff him or [otherwise] confine him in such a manner that he had no choice

but to listen. * * * Furthermore, implicit in [*Miranda*] is the notion that the police are in a position to give a suspect his warnings. [But here] no one would suggest that [the negotiator] should have given Mesa [the warnings]. [*Miranda*] should not be expanded to encompass the present situation where the giving of warnings could have disastrous effects on the suspect and perhaps on others in the vicinity."

Dissenting Judge Weiner appraised the situation quite differently: "Mesa was isolated in his room and in communication only with law enforcement officers. [In] a very real sense, therefore, he was under the direct and immediate control of the authorities and was effectively being restrained by them in his freedom of movement. [He] could have left the room in only one of three possible ways: dead, injured and under arrest, or uninjured and under arrest. It is thus of little import that he was not actually placed under arrest. [Although] a person barricaded in a motel room with a gun retains some ability to 'call the shots,' the overall 'balance of power' was with the authorities surrounding the motel, who were clearly in command of the situation. [The] mere ability to terminate [police questioning] does not abrogate one's rights under the Fifth Amendment and the *Miranda* rule; rather it is the need to assure that those who in fact possess Fifth Amendment rights are actually informed of their rights and ability to exercise them that gives rise to the required [warnings]."

Did the judges who addressed the "custody" issue in *Mesa* make the "logical error" of assuming that exclusion of the incriminating statements would somehow *require* the police to give *Miranda* warnings in such situations? Is the best resolution of "standoff situations" for the police "simply [to] decide, as they probably did here, that it [is] better to withhold the *Miranda* warnings and do without the evidence obtained during the conversation"? See Gibbons, J., dissenting from the denial of a petition for rehearing en banc in *Mesa*. See also Note, 91 Yale L.J. 344 (1981).

b. Consider *Minnesota v. Murphy,* 465 U.S. 420, 104 S.Ct. 1136, 79 L.Ed.2d 409 (1984). Murphy, a probationer, arranged to meet with his probation officer in her office as she had requested. He then admitted, in response to her questioning, that he had com-

Indeed, *Oregon v. Mathiason,* 429 U.S. 492, 97 S.Ct. 711, 50 L.Ed.2d 714 (1977) (per curiam), makes it plain that *Miranda* may not apply even when police questioning *does* take place in the station house. Mathiason, a suspect in a burglary, agreed over the phone to meet with a police officer at a convenient time and place (the state patrol office, only two blocks from the suspect's apartment). Mathiason went to the patrol office on his own. When he arrived the officer told him he was not under arrest. The officer then said he wanted to talk to the suspect about a burglary. When Mathiason confessed a few moments later he was not, held the Court, being subjected to "custodial interrogation."

There was some reason to think that *Mathiason* might be limited to situations where suspects go to the station house *unaccompanied* by police officers. But *California v. Beheler,* 463 U.S. 1121, 103 S.Ct. 3517, 77 L.Ed.2d 1275 (1983) (per curiam), made it plain that *Mathiason* could not be read that narrowly. Some hours after the murder weapon (which defendant claimed others had hidden) was found in his backyard, Beheler, as the Court described it, "voluntarily agreed to accompany police to the station house, although the police specifically told [him] that he was not under arrest." At the station house, Beheler agreed to talk about the murder, but the police did not advise him of his *Miranda* rights. The incriminating statements made at the police station, ruled the Court, were not the product of "custodial interrogation."

Illustrative of the current approach to what constitutes "custody" or "custodial interrogation" is BERKEMER v. McCARTY, 468 U.S. 420, 104 S.Ct. 3138, 82 L.Ed.2d 317 (1984), where the Court, per MARSHALL, J., one of *Miranda*'s strongest defenders, held that "the roadside questioning of a motorist detained pursuant to a routine traffic stop" does not amount to "custodial interrogation":

"Two features of an ordinary traffic stop mitigate the danger that a person questioned will be induced 'to speak where he would not otherwise do so freely,' *Miranda.* First, detention of a motorist pursuant to a traffic stop is presumptively temporary and brief. The vast majority of roadside detentions last only a few minutes. A motorist's expectations, when he sees a policeman's light flashing behind him, are that he will be obliged to spend a short period of time answering questions and waiting while the officer checks his license and registration, that he may then be given a citation, but that in the end he most likely will be allowed to

mitted a rape and a murder a number of years earlier. Although the terms of his probation required Murphy to report to his probation officer periodically and to respond truthfully to all her questions, and although the officer had substantial reason to believe that Murphy's answers to her questions were likely to be incriminating, a 6–3 majority, per White, J., concluded that Murphy could not claim the "in custody" exception to the general rule that the privilege against self-incrimination is not self-executing:

"Custodial arrest is said to convey to the suspect a message that he has no choice but to submit to the officers' will and to confess. It is unlikely that a probation interview, arranged by appointment at a mutually convenient time, would give rise to a similar impression. Moreover, custodial arrest thrusts an individual [into] 'an interrogation environment * * * created for no purpose other than to subjugate the

individual to the will of his examiner.' Many of the psychological ploys discussed in *Miranda* capitalize on the suspect's unfamiliarity with the officers and the environment. Murphy's regular meetings with his probation officer should have served to familiarize him with her and her office and to insulate him from psychological intimidation that might overbear his desire to claim the privilege. Finally, the coercion inherent in custodial interrogation derives in large measure from an interrogator's insinuations that the interrogation will continue until a confession is obtained. [Since] Murphy was not physically restrained and could have left the office, any compulsion he might have felt from the possibility that terminating the meeting would have led to revocation of probation was not comparable to the pressure on a suspect who is painfully aware that he literally cannot escape a persistent custodial interrogator."

continue on his way. In this respect, questioning incident to an ordinary traffic stop is quite different from stationhouse interrogation * * *.

"Second, circumstances associated with the typical traffic stop are not such that the motorist feels completely at the mercy of the police. * * * Perhaps most importantly, the typical traffic stop is public, at least to some degree. [This] exposure to public view both reduces the ability of an unscrupulous policeman to use illegitimate means to elicit self-incriminating statements and diminishes the motorist's fear that, if he does not cooperate, he will be subjected to abuse. [In] short, the atmosphere surrounding an ordinary traffic stop is substantially less 'police dominated' than that surrounding the kinds of interrogation at issue in *Miranda* itself and in the subsequent cases in which we have applied *Miranda*.

"In both of these respects, the usual traffic stop is more analogous to a so-called '*Terry* stop' than to a formal arrest. [Typically, an officer who makes a *Terry* stop] may ask the detainee a moderate number of questions to determine his identity and to try to obtain information confirming or dispelling the officer's suspicions. But the detainee is not obliged to respond. And, unless the detainee's answers provide the officer with probable cause to arrest him, he must then be released. The comparatively nonthreatening character of detentions of this sort explains the absence of any suggestion in our opinions that *Terry* stops are subject to the dictates of *Miranda*. * * *

"Turning to the case before us, we find nothing in the record that indicates that respondent should have been given *Miranda* warnings at any point prior to the time Trooper Williams placed him under arrest. [Although] Trooper Williams apparently decided as soon as respondent stepped out of his car that respondent would be taken into custody and charged with a traffic offense, Williams never communicated his intention to respondent. A policeman's unarticulated plan has no bearing on the question whether a suspect was 'in custody' at a particular time; the only relevant inquiry is how a reasonable man in the suspect's position would have understood his situation."[a]

When an officer stops a motorist, must all of the officer's activity be limited to the offense for which the stop was made? Unless reasonable suspicion develops as to other criminality, is it improper for the police to question a motorist about matters unrelated to the offense for which he was stopped? See Note 7, p. 330.

6. *What constitutes interrogation within the meaning of Miranda?*

RHODE ISLAND v. INNIS

446 U.S. 291, 100 S.Ct. 1682, 64 L.Ed.2d 297 (1980).

Justice STEWART delivered the opinion of the Court.

[*Miranda*] held that, once a defendant in custody asks to speak with a lawyer, all interrogation must cease until a lawyer is present. The issue in this case is whether the respondent was "interrogated" in violation [of *Miranda*].[a]

a. The Court rejected the argument that *Miranda* does not apply to misdemeanor traffic offenses and held that one subjected to custodial interrogation is entitled to the *Miranda* warnings "regardless of the nature or severity of the offense of which he is suspected or for which he was arrested." Thus, since it was clear that McCarty was "in custody" when he was formally placed under arrest and ordered into the police car, and he had not been informed of his rights at that point, his subsequent admission should not have been used against him.

a. Why is *this* the issue? Since respondent asserted his right to counsel, why isn't the issue whether the police "scrupulously honored" the exercise of that right? Cf. *Michigan v. Mosley* (p. 547). Or why isn't the issue (a)

[At approximately 4:30 a.m., a patrolman arrested respondent, suspected of robbing a taxicab driver and murdering him with a shotgun blast to the back of the head. Respondent was unarmed. He was advised of his rights. Within minutes a sergeant (who advised respondent of his rights) and then a captain arrived at the scene of the arrest. The captain also gave respondent the *Miranda* warnings, whereupon respondent asked to speak with a lawyer. The captain then directed that respondent be placed in a police vehicle with a wire screen mesh between the front and rear seats and be driven to the police station. Three officers were assigned to accompany the arrestee. Although the record is somewhat unclear, it appears that Patrolman Williams was in the back seat with respondent and that Patrolmen Gleckman and McKenna were in front.]

While enroute to the central station, Patrolman Gleckman initiated a conversation with Patrolman McKenna concerning the missing shotgun.[1] As Patrolman Gleckman later testified:

> "A.   At this point, I was talking back and forth with Patrolman McKenna stating that I frequent this area while on patrol and [that because a school for handicapped children is located nearby,] there's a lot of handicapped children running around in this area, and God forbid one of them might find a weapon with shells and they might hurt themselves."

Patrolman McKenna apparently shared his fellow officer's concern:

> "A.   I more or less concurred with him [Gleckman] that it was a safety factor and that we should, you know, continue to search for the weapon and try to find it."

[Respondent then interrupted the conversation, stating that he would show the officers where the gun was located. The police vehicle then returned to the scene of the arrest where a search for the shotgun was in progress. There, the captain again advised respondent of his rights. He replied that he understood his rights, but "wanted to get the gun out of the way because of the kids in the area in the school." He then led the police to a nearby field, where he pointed out the shotgun under some rocks.

[Respondent was convicted of murder. The trial judge admitted the shotgun and testimony related to its discovery. On appeal, the Rhode Island Supreme Court concluded that the police had "interrogated" respondent without a valid waiver of his right to counsel; the conversation in the police vehicle had constituted "subtle coercion" that was the equivalent of *Miranda* "interrogation."

[Since the parties agree that respondent was fully informed of his *Miranda* rights, that he asserted his right to counsel, and that he was "in custody" while being driven to the police station, the issue is whether he was "interrogated" in violation of *Miranda*.] In resolving this issue, we first define the term "interrogation" under *Miranda* before turning to a consideration of the facts of this case.

[Various references throughout the *Miranda* opinion] to "questioning" might suggest that the *Miranda* rules were to apply only to those police interrogation practices that involve express questioning of a defendant while in custody.

---

whether the police impermissibly "prompted" respondent to change his mind after he invoked his right to counsel or (b) whether respondent "*himself initiate[d]* further communication, exchanges or conversations with the police," *Edwards v. Arizona* (p. 548) (emphasis

added), after initially invoking his right to counsel?

1.   Although there was conflicting testimony about the exact seating arrangements, it is clear that everyone in the vehicle heard the conversation.

We do not, however, construe the *Miranda* opinion so narrowly. The concern of the Court in *Miranda* was that the "interrogation environment" created by the interplay of interrogation and custody would "subjugate the individual to the will of his examiner" and thereby undermine the privilege against compulsory self-incrimination. The police practices that evoked this concern included several that did not involve express questioning [such as] the so-called "reverse lineup" in which a defendant would be identified by coached witnesses as the perpetrator of a fictitious crime, [to induce] him to confess to the actual crime of which he was suspected in order to escape the false prosecution. [It] is clear that these techniques of persuasion, no less than express questioning, were thought, in a custodial setting, to amount to interrogation.[3]

This is not to say, however, that all statements obtained by the police after a person has been taken into custody are to be considered the product of interrogation. [The *Miranda* warnings] are required not where a suspect is simply taken into custody, but rather where a suspect in custody is subjected to interrogation. "Interrogation," as conceptualized [in *Miranda*], must reflect a measure of compulsion above and beyond that inherent in custody itself.[4]

We conclude that the *Miranda* safeguards come into play whenever a person in custody is subjected to either express questioning or its functional equivalent. That is to say, the term "interrogation" under *Miranda* refers not only to express questioning, but also to any words or actions on the part of the police (other than those normally attendant to arrest and custody)[a] that the police should know are reasonably likely to elicit an incriminating response from the suspect. The latter portion of this definition focuses primarily upon the perceptions of the suspect, rather than the intent of the police. This focus reflects the fact that the *Miranda* safeguards were designed to vest a suspect in custody with an added measure of protection against coercive police practices, without regard to objective proof of

---

3.　To limit the ambit of *Miranda* to express questioning would "place a premium on the ingenuity of the police to devise methods of indirect interrogation, rather than to implement the plain mandate of *Miranda*." *Commonwealth v. Hamilton,* 445 Pa. 292, 297, 285 A.2d 172, 175 [(1971)].

4.　There is language in the opinion of the Rhode Island Supreme Court in this case suggesting that the definition of "interrogation" under *Miranda* is informed by this Court's decision in *Brewer v. Williams,* [p. 619, reaffirming and expansively interpreting the *Massiah* doctrine]. This suggestion is erroneous. Our decision in *Brewer* rested solely on the Sixth and Fourteenth Amendment right to counsel. That right, as we held in *Massiah,* prohibits law enforcement officers from "deliberately elicit[ing]" incriminating information from a defendant in the absence of counsel after a formal charge against the defendant has been filed. Custody in such a case is not controlling; indeed, the petitioner in *Massiah* was not in custody. By contrast, the right to counsel at issue in the present case is based not on the Sixth and Fourteenth Amendments, but rather on the Fifth and Fourteenth Amendments as interpreted in the *Miranda* opinion. The definitions of "interrogation" under the Fifth and Sixth Amendments, if indeed the term "interrogation" is even apt in the

Sixth Amendment context, are not necessarily interchangeable, since the policies underlying the two constitutional protections are quite distinct. See Kamisar, *Brewer v. Williams, Massiah and Miranda: What is "Interrogation"? When Does it Matter?,* 67 Geo.L.J. 1, 41–55 (1978).

a.　In *South Dakota v. Neville,* 459 U.S. 553, 103 S.Ct. 916, 74 L.Ed.2d 748 (1983), the Court noted (fn. 15) that "in the context of an arrest for driving while intoxicated, a police inquiry of whether the suspect will take a blood-alcohol test is not an interrogation within the meaning of *Miranda*." Recalling that *Innis* had excluded "police words or actions 'normally attendant to arrest and custody' "from the definition of "interrogation," the *Neville* Court added: "The police inquiry here is highly regulated by state law, and is presented in virtually the same words to all suspects. It is similar to a police request to submit to fingerprinting or photography. Respondent's choice of refusal thus enjoys no prophylactic *Miranda* protection outside the basic Fifth Amendment protection. See generally Peter Arenella, *Schmerber and the Privilege Against Self–Incrimination: A Reappraisal,* 20 Am. Crim.L.Rev. 31, 56?58 (1982)."

the underlying intent of the police. A practice that the police should know is reasonably likely to evoke an incriminating response from a suspect thus amounts to interrogation.[7] But, since the police surely cannot be held accountable for the unforeseeable results of their words or actions, the definition of interrogation can extend only to words or actions on the part of police officers that they *should have known* were reasonably likely to elicit an incriminating response.[8]

Turning to the facts of the present case, we conclude that the respondent was not "interrogated" within the meaning of *Miranda*. It is undisputed that the first prong of the definition of "interrogation" was not satisfied, for the [Gleckman–McKenna conversation] included no express questioning of the respondent. Rather, that conversation was, at least in form, nothing more than a dialogue between the two officers to which no response from the respondent was invited.

Moreover, it cannot be fairly concluded that the respondent was subjected to the "functional equivalent" of questioning. It cannot be said, in short, that [the officers] should have known that their conversation was reasonably likely to elicit an incriminating response from the respondent. There is nothing in the record to suggest that the officers were aware that the respondent was peculiarly susceptible to an appeal to his conscience concerning the safety of handicapped children [or that] the police knew that the respondent was unusually disoriented or upset at the time of his arrest.[9]

The case thus boils down to whether, in the context of a brief conversation, the officers should have known that the respondent would suddenly be moved to make a self-incriminating response. Given the fact that the entire conversation appears to have consisted of no more than a few off-hand remarks, we cannot say that the officers should have known that it was reasonably likely that Innis would so respond. This is not a case where the police carried on a lengthy harangue in the presence of the suspect. Nor does the record support the respondent's contention that, under the circumstances, the officers' comments were particularly "evocative."

[The] Rhode Island Supreme Court erred, in short, in equating "subtle compulsion" with interrogation. That the officers' comments struck a responsive cord is readily apparent. Thus, it may be said, as the Rhode Island Supreme Court did say, that the respondent was subjected to "subtle compulsion." But that is not the end of the inquiry. It must also be established that a suspect's incriminating response was the product of words or actions on the part of the police that they should have known were reasonably likely to elicit an incriminating response.[10] This was not established in the present case. * * *

7. This is not to say that the intent of the police is irrelevant, for it may well have a bearing on whether the police should have known that their words or actions were reasonably likely to evoke an incriminating response. In particular, where a police practice is designed to elicit an incriminating response from the accused, it is unlikely that the practice will not also be one which the police should have known was reasonably likely to have that effect.

8. Any knowledge the police may have had concerning the unusual susceptibility of a defendant to a particular form of persuasion might be an important factor in determining whether the police should have known that their words or actions were reasonably likely to elicit an incriminating response from the suspect.

9. The record in no way suggests that the officers' remarks were *designed* to elicit a response. It is significant that the trial judge, after hearing the officers' testimony, concluded that it was "entirely understandable that [the officers] would voice their concern [for the safety of the handicapped children] to each other."

10. By way of example, if the police had done no more than to drive past the site of the concealed weapon while taking the most direct route to the police station, and if the respondent, upon noticing for the first time the proximity of the school for handicapped children,

Chief Justice BURGER, concurring in the judgment.

Since the result is not inconsistent with *Miranda,* I concur in the judgment.

The meaning of *Miranda* has become reasonably clear and law enforcement practices have adjusted to its strictures; I would neither overrule *Miranda,* disparage it, nor extend it at this late date. I fear, however, that [the Court's opinion] may introduce new elements of uncertainty; under the Court's test, a police officer, in the brief time available, apparently must evaluate the suggestibility and susceptibility of an accused. * * *

Justice MARSHALL, with whom Justice BRENNAN joins, dissenting.

I am substantially in agreement with the Court's definition of "interrogation" within the meaning of *Miranda.* In my view, the *Miranda* safeguards apply whenever police conduct is intended or likely to produce a response from a suspect in custody. As I read the Court's opinion, its definition of "interrogation" for *Miranda* purposes is equivalent, for practical purposes, to my formulation, since it contemplates that "where a police practice is designed to elicit an incriminating response from the accused, it is unlikely that the practice will not also be one which the police should have known was reasonably likely to have that effect" [fn. 7]. Thus, the Court requires an objective inquiry into the likely effect of police conduct on a typical individual, taking into account any special susceptibility of the suspect to certain kinds of pressure of which the police know or have reason to know.

I am utterly at a loss, however, to understand how this objective standard as applied to the facts before us can rationally lead to the conclusion that there was no interrogation. * * *

One can scarcely imagine a stronger appeal to the conscience of a suspect—*any* suspect—than the assertion that if the weapon is not found an innocent person will be hurt or killed. And not just any innocent person, but an innocent child—a little girl—a helpless, handicapped little girl on her way to school. The notion that such an appeal could not be expected to have any effect unless the suspect were known to have some special interest in handicapped children verges on the ludicrous. As a matter of fact, the appeal to a suspect to confess for the sake of others, to "display some evidence of decency and honor," is a classic interrogation technique.

Gleckman's remarks would obviously have constituted interrogation if they had been explicitly directed to petitioner, and the result should not be different because they were nominally addressed to McKenna. [The officers] knew petitioner would hear and attend to their conversation, and they are chargeable with knowledge of and responsibility for the pressures to speak which they created.

I firmly believe that this case is simply an aberration, and that in future cases the Court will apply the standard adopted today in accordance with its plain meaning.

Justice STEVENS, dissenting.

[In] my view any statement that would normally be understood by the average listener as calling for a response is the functional equivalent of a direct question, whether or not it is punctuated by a question mark. The Court, however, takes a much narrower view. It holds that police conduct is not the

had blurted out that he would show the officers where the gun was located, it could not seriously be argued that this "subtle compulsion" would have constituted "interrogation" within the meaning of the *Miranda* opinion.

"functional equivalent" of direct questioning unless the police should have known that what they were saying or doing was likely to elicit an incriminating response from the suspect. This holding represents a plain departure from the principles set forth in *Miranda*.

[From] the suspect's point of view, the effectiveness of the warnings depends on whether it appears that the police are scrupulously honoring his rights. Apparent attempts to elicit information from a suspect after he has invoked his right to cut off questioning necessarily demean that right and tend to reinstate the imbalance between police and suspect that the *Miranda* warnings are designed to correct. Thus, if the rationale for requiring those warnings in the first place is to be respected, any police conduct or statements that would appear to a reasonable person in the suspect's position to call for a response must be considered "interrogation."

In short, in order to give full protection to a suspect's right to be free from any interrogation at all, the definition of "interrogation" must include any police statement or conduct that has the same purpose or effect as a direct question. Statements that appear to call for a response from the suspect, as well as those that are designed to do so, should be considered interrogation. By prohibiting only those relatively few statements or actions that a police officer should know are likely to elicit an incriminating response, the Court today accords a suspect considerably less protection. Indeed, since I suppose most suspects are unlikely to incriminate themselves even when questioned directly, this new definition will almost certainly exclude every statement that is not punctuated with a question mark from the concept of "interrogation."

The difference between the approach required by a faithful adherence to *Miranda* and the stinted test applied by the Court today can be illustrated by comparing three different ways in which Officer Gleckman could have communicated his fears about the possible dangers posed by the shotgun to handicapped children. He could have:

(1) directly asked Innis:

Will you please tell me where the shotgun is so we can protect handicapped schoolchildren from danger?

(2) announced to the other officers in the wagon:

If the man sitting in the back seat with me should decide to tell us where the gun is, we can protect handicapped children from danger.

or (3) stated to the other officers:

It would be too bad if a little handicapped girl would pick up the gun that this man left in the area and maybe kill herself.

In my opinion, all three of these statements should be considered interrogation because all three appear to be designed to elicit a response from anyone who in fact knew where the gun was located.[12] Under the Court's test, on the other hand, the form of the statements would be critical. The third statement would not be interrogation because in the Court's view there was no reason for Officer Gleckman to believe that Innis was susceptible to this type of an implied appeal; therefore, the statement would not be reasonably likely to elicit an incriminating response. Assuming that this is true, then it seems to me that the first two

---

12. See Welsh White, *Rhode Island v. Innis: The Significance of a Suspect's Assertion of His Right to Counsel*, 17 Amer.Crim.L.Rev. 53, 68 (1979), where the author proposes the same test and applies it to the facts of this case * * *.

statements, which would be just as unlikely to elicit such a response, should also not be considered interrogation. But, because the first statement is clearly an express question, it *would* be considered interrogation under the Court's test. The second statement, although just as clearly a deliberate appeal to Innis to reveal the location of the gun, would presumably not be interrogation because (a) it was not in form a direct question and (b) it does not fit within the "reasonably likely to elicit an incriminating response" category that applies to indirect interrogation.

As this example illustrates, the Court's test creates an incentive for police to ignore a suspect's invocation of his rights in order to make continued attempts to extract information from him. If a suspect does not appear to be susceptible to a particular type of psychological pressure, the police are apparently free to exert that pressure on him despite his request for counsel, so long as they are careful not to punctuate their statements with question marks. And if, contrary to all reasonable expectations, the suspect makes an incriminating statement, that statement can be used against him at trial. The Court thus turns *Miranda*'s unequivocal rule against any interrogation at all into a trap in which unwary suspects may be caught by police deception.

* * * I think the Court is clearly wrong in holding, as a matter of law, that Officer Gleckman should not have realized that his statement was likely to elicit an incriminating response. [Moreover,] there is evidence in the record to support the view that Officer Gleckman's statement was intended to elicit a response from Innis. Officer Gleckman, who was not regularly assigned to the caged wagon, was directed by a police captain to ride with respondent to the police station. [The] record does not explain why, notwithstanding the fact that respondent was handcuffed, unarmed, and had offered no resistance when arrested by an officer acting alone, the captain ordered Officer Gleckman to ride with respondent. It is not inconceivable that two professionally trained police officers concluded that a few well-chosen remarks might induce respondent to disclose the whereabouts of the shotgun. This conclusion becomes even more plausible in light of the emotionally charged words chosen by Officer Gleckman ("God forbid" that a "little girl" should find the gun and hurt herself).[19] * * *

Notes and Questions

(a) If Officer Gleckman's remarks had been explicitly directed to Innis, would they have constituted "interrogation" regardless of whether they were reasonably likely—or at all likely—to elicit an incriminating response? If so, why should words or actions that are the "functional equivalent" of express questioning have to satisfy a "reasonable likelihood" or "apparent probability" of success standard? Why isn't it sufficient that the police speech or conduct—unlike "administrative questioning" (routine questions asked of all arrestees "booked" or otherwise processed) and unlike casual conversation in no way related to the case—would normally be understood as *calling for* a response about the merits of the case or be *likely to be viewed* as *having the same force and effect* as a question about the merits of the case? See Welsh White, *Interrogation without Questions*, 78 Mich. L.Rev. 1209, 1227–36 (1980); Jesse H. Choper, Yale Kamisar & Laurence H. Tribe, *The Supreme Court: Trends and Developments, 1979–80* at 88–89, 92–95 (1981) (remarks of Professor Kamisar).

---

19. In his article [fn. 12,] Professor White also points out that the officers were probably aware that the chances of a handicapped child finding the weapon at a time when police were not present were relatively slim. Thus, he concluded that it was unlikely that the true purpose of the conversation was to voice a genuine concern over the children's welfare. [See also Note (d), following this case].

(b) If Gleckman *had admitted* that his remarks to McKenna were *designed* to get Innis to make incriminating statements, would (should) they have constituted "interrogation" regardless of Gleckman's apparent likelihood of success? Why (not)? Reconsider fns. 7 & 9 to the majority opinion. But see fn. 6 to *New York v. Quarles,* p. 532. Did it (should it) matter whether the "Christian burial speech" delivered in *Brewer v. Williams,* p. 619, was reasonably likely to elicit an incriminating response from Williams? Why (not)?

(c) To what extent does the *Innis* result turn on the fact that "the officers involved were ordinary patrolmen as opposed to detectives specifically trained in the art of interrogation"? That their "only assignment" was to transport the suspect? That "indeed, they had specific instructions not to question him during the trip"? See White, at 1235 fn. 161. To what extent does the result turn on the fact that there was a *plausible basis* for believing that Gleckman's remarks were made for a purpose *other than* that of eliciting an incriminating response? See id. at 1234–35.

(e) In *United States v. Mesa,* discussed at p. 517, fn. a, involving a lengthy conversation between a barricaded suspect and a "hostage negotiator," Judge Adams concurred in the result on the ground that "Mesa's statements were made in the course of a colloquy that is not an 'interrogation,' as that term was recently defined in *Innis*"; the conversation was "nonadversarial and noninquisitive in nature"; the negotiator "acted not as a questioner, but primarily as a listener"; and the comments interjected by the negotiator "were not designed to elicit an incriminating response, [but] calculated to convey sympathy and understanding, to indicate that [the negotiator] was still listening, and to keep Mesa from dwelling on thoughts of suicide."

But dissenting Judge Weiner maintained that the negotiator's comments were "frequently investigatory" and "appear[ed] calculated to both bring about a peaceful end to the standoff [and] to elicit incriminating statements about the shootings. [I]t seems inconceivable that [the negotiator] could not have known that the entire conversation itself, as well as the specific questions related to the shootings, would be reasonably likely to elicit an incriminating response."

(f) In ARIZONA v. MAURO, 481 U.S. 520, 107 S.Ct. 1931, 95 L.Ed.2d 458 (1987), a 5–4 majority, per POWELL, J., held that it was not "custodial interrogation" within the meaning of *Miranda* for the police to accede to the request of defendant's wife, also a suspect in the murder of their son, to speak with defendant (being held in a room at the station house) in the presence of a police officer (Detective Manson), who placed a tape recorder in plain sight on a desk. (Defendant had been given the *Miranda* warnings and had asserted his right to counsel.) Observed the Court:

"There is no evidence that the officers sent Mrs. Mauro in to see her husband for the purpose of eliciting incriminating statements. [T]he officers tried to discourage her from talking to her husband, but finally 'yielded to her insistent demands.' Nor was Detective Manson's presence improper. [There were] a number of legitimate reasons—not related to securing incriminating statements—for having a police officer present. Finally, the weakness of Mauro's claim that he was interrogated is underscored by examining the situation from his perspective. * * * We doubt that a suspect, told by officers that his wife will be allowed to speak to him, would feel that he was being coerced to incriminate himself in any way.

"[The state supreme court] was correct to note that there was a 'possibility' that Mauro would incriminate himself while talking to his wife [and] that the officers were aware of that possibility. [But] the actions in this case were far less questionable than the 'subtle compulsion' [held] *not* to be interrogation in *Innis*. Officers do not interrogate a suspect simply by hoping that he will incriminate himself. * * *

"[In] deciding whether particular police conduct is interrogation, we must remember the purpose behind [*Miranda*]: preventing government officials from using the coercive nature of confinement to extract confessions that would not be given in an unrestrained environment. The government actions in this case do not implicate the purpose in any way."

Dissenting Justice STEVENS, joined by Brennan, Marshall and Blackmun, JJ., maintained:

"[The] facts compel the conclusion that the police took advantage of Mrs. Mauro's request to visit her husband, setting up a confrontation between them at a time when he manifestly desired to remain silent. Because they allowed [Mauro's] conversation with his wife to commence at a time when they knew it was reasonably likely to produce an incriminating statement, the police interrogated him.

"[The] intent of the detectives is clear from their own testimony. They both knew that if the conversation took place, incriminating statements were likely to be made. With that in mind, they decided to take in a tape recorder, sit near [Mauro] and his wife and allow the conversation to commence. * * *

"It is undisputed that a police decision to place two suspects in the same room and then to listen to or record their conversation may constitute a form of interrogation even if no questions are asked by any police officers.[a] That is exactly what happened here. [The Mauros] were both suspects in the murder of their son. Each of them had been interrogated separately before the officers decided to allow them to converse, an act that surely did not require a tape recorder or the presence of a police officer within hearing range. Under the circumstances, the police knew or should have known that [this encounter] was reasonably likely to produce an incriminating statement. * * *

"[Under] the circumstances, the mere fact that [Mrs. Mauro] made the initial request leading to the conversation does not alter [the fact that the police violated *Miranda*]. [They] exercised exclusive control over whether and when the suspects spoke with each other; the police knew that whatever Mauro wished to convey to his wife at that moment, he would have to say under the conditions unilaterally imposed by the officers. In brief, the police exploited the custodial situation and the understandable desire of Mrs. Mauro to speak with [her husband] to conduct an interrogation."

Notes and Questions

(i) *Likelihood of incrimination.* According to the *Mauro* majority, the meeting between Mauro and his wife did not "present a sufficient likelihood of incrimination" to satisfy the *Innis* standard [fn. 6]. What if it did? What if, as the dissenters maintained, the police did know or should have known that the meeting between Mauro and his wife was likely to produce an incriminating statement. Should this be decisive in a case like *Mauro*?

a. Does Justice Stevens mean that this situation may constitute a form of interrogation within the meaning of *Miranda* even if the suspects are *unaware* that the police are listening to, or recording, their conversation? If so, why? Where is the "compulsion"? See the discussion following this case and the discussion in Note 8.

Should the *Innis* language defining police interrogation or its functional equivalent be taken literally? Did the *Innis* Court assume a basic factual setting—police conduct equivalent to direct police questioning in terms of its compulsion or pressure? Did the *Innis* Court have in mind conduct *by the police* and in *the presence of the suspect,* such as confronting the suspect with a report indicating that he "flunked" a lie detector exam or confronting him with the confession of an accomplice or bringing an effusive and accusing accomplice into the same room with the police and the suspect?[b]

(ii) *"Police blue" compulsion.* If a spouse or parent or friend meets with someone in custody, does that add significantly to the *official* compulsion, the *"police blue"* compulsion? If not, why should this conduct be considered the equivalent of "custodial *police* interrogation"?

(iii) *The purpose of the police.* The *Mauro* majority emphasizes the lack of any evidence that the police sent Mrs. Mauro to see her husband "for the purpose of eliciting incriminating statements." What if the detectives had asked Mrs. Mauro to try to get her husband to confess and she had agreed to do so? Would she have become an "agent" of the police? Why does this matter for *Miranda* purposes? If defendant *were unaware* of his wife's or the detectives' purpose, how would that purpose render defendant's environment more "compelling" or make him more likely to feel that he was being "coerced" to incriminate himself? How would the undisclosed purpose of the police alter the situation *from the defendant's perspective?*

(iv) *The suspect's awareness that the police are present.* Is the key factor in a case like *Mauro* not the intent of the police but the suspect's awareness that the police are present, or listening, when he meets with a spouse or friend? If Detective Manson had not been physically present, but the police had *secretly recorded* defendant's meeting with his wife, would *Mauro* have been a much easier case? Why (not)? See next Note.

7. The "jail plant" situation; "surreptitious interrogation." Suppose a secret government agent, posing as a fellow-prisoner, is placed in the same cell or cellblock with an incarcerated suspect and induces him to discuss the crime for which he has been arrested. Does this constitute "custodial interrogation"? No, answered the Court in ILLINOIS v. PERKINS, 496 U.S. 292, 110 S.Ct. 2394, 110 L.Ed.2d 243 (1990); "*Miranda* warnings are not required when the suspect is unaware that he is speaking to a law enforcement officer and gives a voluntary statement."

The case arose as follows: Respondent Perkins, who was suspected of committing the Stephenson murder, was incarcerated on charges unrelated to the murder. The police placed Charlton (who had been a fellow inmate of Perkins in another prison) and Parisi (an undercover officer) in the same cellblock with Perkins. The secret government agents were instructed to engage Perkins in casual conversation and to report anything he said about the Stephenson murder. The cellblock consisted of 12 separate cells that opened onto a common room. When Charlton met Perkins in the prison he introduced Parisi by his alias. Parisi

b. Although the *Innis* case involved police "speech," the Court's definition of "interrogation" embraces police tactics that do not. Thus, the Court seems to have repudiated the position taken by a number of courts prior to *Innis* that *confronting* a suspect with physical or documentary evidence (e.g., a ballistics report or a bank surveillance photograph) or *arrang-* ing a meeting in the presence of the police between an arrestee and an accomplice who has already confessed is not "interrogation" because it does not involve verbal conduct on the part of the police. For criticism of these pre-*Innis* cases, see Kamisar Essays at 156–58 n. 21.

suggested that the three of them escape. There was further conversation. Parisi asked Perkins if he had ever "done" anybody. Perkins replied that he had and proceeded to describe his involvement in the Stephenson murder in detail.

In an opinion joined by six other Justices, KENNEDY, J., explained why Perkins' statements were not barred by *Miranda:*

"The essential ingredients of a 'police-dominated atmosphere' and compulsion are not present when an incarcerated person speaks freely to someone that he believes to be a fellow inmate. Coercion is determined from the perspective of the suspect. [When] a suspect considers himself in the company of cellmates and not officers, the coercive atmosphere is lacking.

"[It] is the premise of *Miranda* that the danger of coercion results from the interaction of custody and official interrogation. We reject the argument that *Miranda* warnings are required whenever a suspect is in custody in a technical sense and converses with someone who happens to be a government agent. [When] the suspect has no reason to think that the listeners have official power over him, it should not be assumed that his words are motivated by the reaction he expects from his listeners. '[W]hen the agent carries neither badge nor gun and wears not "police blue," but the same prison gray' as the suspect, there is no '*interplay* between police interrogation and police custody.' Kamisar, *Brewer v. Williams, Massiah and Miranda: What is 'Interrogation?' When Does it Matter?,* 67 Geo.L.J. 1, 67, 63 (1978). [The] only difference between this case and *Hoffa* is that the suspect here was incarcerated, but detention, whether or not for the crime in question, does not warrant a presumption that the use of an undercover agent to speak with an incarcerated suspect makes any confession thus obtained involuntary. * * *

"[This] Court's Sixth Amendment decisions in [the *Massiah* line of cases] also do not avail respondent. [No] charges had been filed [against him] on the subject of the interrogation, and our Sixth Amendment precedents are not applicable."[a]

Only MARSHALL, J., dissented, maintaining that "[t]he conditions that require the police to apprise a defendant of his constitutional rights—custodial interrogation conducted by an agent of the police—were present in this case. Because [respondent] received no *Miranda* warnings before he was subjected to custodial interrogation, his confession was not admissible." Continued Justice Marshall:

"Because Perkins was interrogated by police while he was in custody, *Miranda* required that the officer inform him of his rights. In rejecting that conclusion, the Court finds that 'conversations' between undercover agents and suspects are devoid of the coercion inherent in stationhouse interrogations conducted by law enforcement officials who openly represent the State. *Miranda* was not, however, concerned solely with police *coercion.* It dealt with *any* police tactics that may operate to compel a suspect in custody to make incriminating statements without full awareness of his constitutional rights. [Thus,] when a law enforcement agent structures a custodial interrogation so that a suspect feels compelled

a. Brennan, J., concurred in the judgment of the Court, "agree[ing] that when a suspect does not know that his questioner is a police agent, such questioning does not amount to 'interrogation' in an 'inherently coercive' environment so as to require application of *Miranda*"—"the only issue raised at this stage of the litigation." But he went on to say that "the deception and manipulation practiced on re-spondent raise a substantial claim that the confession was obtained in violation of the Due Process Clause." For "the deliberate use of deception and manipulation by the police appears to be incompatible 'with a system that presumes innocence and assures that a conviction will not be secured by inquisitional means' and raises serious concerns that respondent's will was overborne."

to reveal incriminating information, he must inform the suspect of his constitutional rights and give him an opportunity to decide whether or not to talk. * * *

"[The] psychological pressures inherent in confinement increase the suspect's anxiety, making him likely to seek relief by talking with others. [The] inmate is thus more susceptible to efforts by undercover agents to elicit information from him. Similarly, where the suspect is incarcerated, the constant threat of physical danger peculiar to the prison environment may make him demonstrate his toughness to other inmates by recounting or inventing past violent acts. [In] this case, the police deceptively took advantage of Perkins' psychological vulnerability by including him in a sham escape plot, a situation in which he would feel compelled to demonstrate his willingness to shoot a prison guard by revealing his past involvement in a murder.

"[Thus,] the pressures unique to custody allow the police to use deceptive interrogation tactics to compel a suspect to make an incriminating statement. The compulsion is not eliminated by the suspect's ignorance of his interrogator's true identity. The Court therefore need not inquire past the bare facts of custody and interrogation to determine whether *Miranda* warnings are required. * * *

Notes and Questions

(a) Is *Perkins* a case where, as dissenting Justice Marshall maintains, "a law enforcement agent structures a custodial interrogation so that a suspect feels compelled to reveal incriminating information" or is it a case where a law enforcement agent structures a situation so that a suspect feels free to reveal incriminating information?

(b) Consider Fred Cohen, *Miranda and Police Deception in Interrogation,* 26 Crim.L.Bull. 534, 543–44 (1990): "Can it be that the *Miranda* rule was intended to be responsive only to force while leaving in place and indeed encouraging the refinement of other methods for achieving an *uninformed* confession? The word *uninformed* is emphasized because I believe strongly that *Miranda* was intended to achieve some form of rough informational equivalency between the state and the accused during the interrogative phase of the investigatory stage in a criminal proceeding. [If] *Miranda* was fashioned solely to ameliorate the inherent coercion associated with a police-dominated environment, then *Perkins* was correctly decided. If *Miranda* was concerned also with informational equivalency and with giving suspects an opportunity to obtain counsel and, in effect, barter information, instead of making an uninformed gift, then *Perkins* was wrongly decided."

8. More on "custodial interrogation" and the "booking question exception" to Miranda. Consider PENNSYLVANIA v. MUNIZ, 496 U.S. 582, 110 S.Ct. 2638, 110 L.Ed.2d 528 (1990). The case arose as follows:

Respondent Muniz was arrested for driving while intoxicated. Without advising him of his *Miranda* rights, Officer Hosterman asked Muniz to perform three standard field sobriety tests. Muniz performed poorly and then admitted that he had been drinking. Muniz was taken to a Booking Center. Following its routine practice for receiving persons suspected of driving under the influence, the Booking Center videotaped the ensuing proceedings. Muniz was told that his action and voice were being recorded, but again he was not advised of his *Miranda* rights. Officer Hosterman first asked Muniz his name, address, height, weight, eye color, date of birth, and current age (the "first seven questions" or the seven "booking" questions). Both the delivery and content of his answers were incriminating. Next the officer asked Muniz what the Court called "the sixth birthday question": "Do you know what the date was of your sixth birthday?" Muniz responded, "No, I don't."

The officer then requested Muniz to perform the same sobriety tests that he had been asked to do earlier during the initial roadside stop. While performing the tests, Muniz made several audible and incriminating statements. Finally, Muniz was asked to submit to a breathalyzer test. He refused. At this point, for the first time, Muniz was advised of his *Miranda* rights. Both the video and audio portions of the videotape were admitted into evidence, along with the arresting officer's testimony that Muniz failed the roadside sobriety tests and made incriminating statements at the time. Muniz was convicted of driving while intoxicated.

The Court excluded only Muniz's response to the "sixth birthday question" (by a 5–4 vote). BRENNAN, J., wrote the opinion of the Court, except as to the grounds for admitting Muniz's answers to the first seven questions or "booking" questions.

Some of the issues raised by the case were relatively easy. Muniz's answers to direct questions were not barred by *Miranda* "merely because the slurred nature of his speech was incriminating." Under *Schmerber v. California* (discussed at pp. 42, 641) and its progeny, "any slurring of speech and other evidence of lack of muscular coordination revealed by Muniz's responses * * * constitute nontestimonial components of those responses." Muniz's incriminating utterances during the physical sobriety tests were also admissible because "not prompted by an interrogation within the meaning of *Miranda*." Officer Hosterman's conversation with Muniz concerning the tests "consisted primarily of carefully scripted instructions as to how the tests were to be performed," instructions "not likely to be perceived as calling for any verbal response" and thus "not 'words or actions' constituting custodial interrogation."[a]

More difficult issues were whether Muniz's response to the sixth birthday question should be allowed into evidence and whether Muniz's answers to the first seven questions asked him at the Booking Center (the seven "booking" questions) were admissible—and if not, *why* not.

In contrast to a number of other questions Muniz was asked, the sixth birthday question, observed the Court, per Brennan, J., "required a testimonial response. When Officer Hosterman asked Muniz if he knew the date of his sixth birthday and Muniz, for whatever reason, could not remember or calculate that date, he was [placed in a predicament the self-incrimination clause was designed to prevent]. By hypothesis, the inherently coercive environment created by the custodial interrogation precluded the option of remaining silent. Muniz was left with the choice of incriminating himself by admitting that he did not then know the date of his sixth birthday, or answering untruthfully by reporting a date that he did not then believe to be accurate (an incorrect guess would be incriminating as well as truthful). [The] incriminating inference of impaired mental facilities stemmed, not just from the fact that Muniz slurred his response, but also from a testimonial aspect of that response."

a. "Similarly," added the Court, "*Miranda* does not require suppression of the statements Muniz made when asked to submit to a breathalyzer examination." The officer who requested Muniz to take the breathalyzer test "carefully limited her role to providing Muniz with relevant information about [the] test and the implied consent law. She questioned Muniz only as to whether he understood her instructions and wished to submit to the test. These limited and focused inquiries were necessarily 'attendant to' the legitimate police procedure [and] not likely to be perceived as calling for any incriminating response."

The Court noted that "Muniz does not and cannot challenge the introduction into evidence of his refusal to submit to the breathalyzer test." See *South Dakota v. Neville* (p. 521).

REHNQUIST, C.J., joined by White, Blackmun and Stevens, JJ., disagreed:

"The sixth birthday question here was an effort on the part of the police to check how well Muniz was able to do a simple mathematical exercise. Indeed, had the question related only to the date of his birthday, it presumably would have come under the 'booking exception' to *Miranda* to which the Court refers elsewhere in its opinion. [See discussion below.] [If] the police may require Muniz to use his body in order to demonstrate the level of his physical coordination, there is no reason why they should not be able to require him to speak or write in order to determine his mental coordination. That was all that was sought here. Since it was permissible for the police to extract and examine a sample of Schmerber's blood to determine how much that part of his system had been affected by alcohol, I see no reason why they may not examine the functioning of Muniz's mental processes for the same purpose."

Eight members of the Court agreed that the answers to the "booking" questions were admissible, but they differed as to the reason. Four Justices (Rehnquist, C.J., joined by White, Blackmun and Stevens, JJ.) did not consider the questions "testimonial." Thus, they did not address the issue whether, even if the questions were "testimonial," they came under a "booking exception" to *Miranda*. The other four Justices (Brennan, J., joined by O'Connor, Scalia and Kennedy, JJ.,) believed the first seven questions were "testimonial" and did amount to "custodial interrogation" within the meaning of *Miranda*. Nonetheless, they concluded that Muniz's answers were admissible because of a "routine booking question" exception to *Miranda*—one that permits questions "to secure the 'biographical data necessary to complete booking or pretrial services.' "The state court had found that the first seven questions were "requested for record-keeping purposes only"; thus, "the questions appear reasonably related to the police's administrative concerns."

Only MARSHALL, J., would have kept out the answers to the first seven questions. He rejected both the Brennan group's and the Rehnquist group's rationales for admitting Muniz's answers to these questions:

"[The questions] sought 'testimonial' responses for the same reason the sixth birthday question did: because the content of the answers would indicate Muniz's state of mind. The booking questions, like the sixth birthday question, required Muniz to (1) answer correctly, indicating lucidity, (2) answer incorrectly, implying that his mental facilities were impaired, or (3) state that he did not know the answer, also indicating impairment. Muniz's initial incorrect response to the question about his age and his inability to give his address without looking at his license, like his inability to answer the sixth birthday question, in fact gave rise to the incriminating inference that his mental facilities were impaired."

As for the Brennan group's rationale for admitting Muniz's answers—the questions fell within a "routine booking question" exception to *Miranda*—even if such an exception was appropriate in some instances, responded Marshall, J., the exception "should not extend to booking questions [asked in circumstances, such as the instant case, which] the police should know are reasonably likely to elicit incriminating responses." More generally, Justice Marshall balked at creating "yet another exception" to *Miranda* because "[s]uch exceptions undermine *Miranda's* fundamental principle that the doctrine should be clear so that it can be easily applied by both police and courts."

9. *Questioning prompted by concern for "public safety."*

NEW YORK v. QUARLES

467 U.S. 649, 104 S.Ct. 2626, 81 L.Ed.2d 550 (1984).

Justice REHNQUIST delivered the opinion of the Court.

[At approximately 12:30 a.m., police apprehended respondent in the rear of a supermarket. He matched the description of the man who had just raped a woman. The woman had told the police that the rapist had just entered the supermarket and that he was carrying a gun. Apparently upon seeing Officer Kraft enter the store, respondent turned and ran toward the rear. Officer Kraft pursued him with a drawn gun and, upon regaining sight of him, ordered him to stop and put his hands over his head. Although several other officers had arrived at the scene by then, Kraft was the first to reach respondent. He frisked him and discovered he was wearing an empty shoulder holster. After handcuffing him, the officer asked where the gun was. Respondent nodded in the direction of some empty cartons and responded, "the gun is over there." At that time, emphasized the New York Court of Appeals, respondent was surrounded by four officers whose guns had been returned to their holsters because, as one testified, the situation was under control.

[The gun was not visible, but Officer Kraft reached into one of the cartons and retrieved a loaded revolver. Respondent was then formally placed under arrest and advised of his *Miranda* rights. Respondent waived his rights. In response to questions, he then stated that he owned the revolver and had purchased it in Miami.

[In the subsequent prosecution of respondent for criminal possession of a weapon (the record does not reveal why the state failed to pursue the rape charge), the New York courts suppressed the statement "the gun is over there" as well as the gun itself because they had been obtained in violation of respondent's *Miranda* rights. Respondent's statements about his ownership of the gun and the place of purchase were also excluded as having been fatally tainted by the seizure of the gun and the prewarning response as to its location.]

* * * We conclude that under the circumstances involved in this case, overriding considerations of public safety justify the officer's failure to provide *Miranda* warnings before he asked questions devoted to locating the abandoned weapon.

[In] this case we have before us no claim that respondent's statements were actually compelled by police conduct which overcame his will to resist. Thus the only issue before us is whether Officer Kraft was justified in failing to make available to respondent the procedural safeguards associated with the privilege against compulsory self-incrimination since *Miranda*.[5]

The New York Court of Appeals was undoubtedly correct in deciding that the facts of this case come within the ambit of the *Miranda* decision as we have subsequently interpreted it. [The] New York Court of Appeals' majority declined to express an opinion as to whether there might be an exception to the *Miranda*

---

5. The dissent curiously takes us to task for "endors[ing] the introduction of coerced self-incriminating statements in criminal prosecutions." [Of] course our decision today does nothing of the kind. [R]espondent is certainly free on remand to argue that his statement was coerced under traditional due process stan- dards. Today we merely reject the only argu- ment that respondent has raised to support the exclusion of his statement, that the statement must be *presumed* compelled because of Officer Kraft's failure to read him his *Miranda* warn- ings.

rule if the police had been acting to protect the public, because the lower courts in New York had made no factual determination that the police had acted with that motive.

We hold that on these facts there is a "public safety" exception to the requirement that *Miranda* warnings be given before a suspect's answers may be admitted into evidence, and that the availability of that exception does not depend upon the motivation of the individual officers involved. In a kaleidoscopic situation such as the one confronting these officers, where spontaneity rather than adherence to a police manual is necessarily the order of the day, the application of the exception which we recognize today should not be made to depend on *post hoc* findings at a suppression hearing concerning the subjective motivation of the arresting officer.[6] Undoubtedly most police officers, if placed in Officer Kraft's position, would act out of a host of different, instinctive, and largely unverifiable motives—their own safety, the safety of others, and perhaps as well the desire to obtain incriminating evidence from the suspect.

Whatever the motivation of individual officers in such a situation, we do not believe that the doctrinal underpinnings of *Miranda* require that it be applied in all its rigor to a situation in which police officers ask questions reasonably prompted by a concern for the public safety.

[The] police in this case, in the very act of apprehending a suspect, were confronted with the immediate necessity of ascertaining the whereabouts of a gun which they had every reason to believe the suspect had just removed from his empty holster and discarded in the supermarket. So long as the gun was concealed somewhere in the supermarket, with its actual whereabouts unknown, it obviously posed more than one danger to the public safety: an accomplice might make use of it, a customer or employee might later come upon it.

In such a situation, if the police are required to recite the familiar *Miranda* warnings before asking the whereabouts of the gun, suspects in Quarles' position might well be deterred from responding. Procedural safeguards which deter a suspect from responding were deemed acceptable in *Miranda* in order to protect the Fifth Amendment privilege; when the primary social cost of those added protections is the possibility of fewer convictions, the *Miranda* majority was willing to bear that cost. Here, had *Miranda* warnings deterred Quarles from responding to Officer Kraft's question about the whereabouts of the gun, the cost would have been something more than merely the failure to obtain evidence useful in convicting Quarles. Officer Kraft needed an answer to his question not simply to make his case against Quarles but to insure that further danger to the public did not result from the concealment of the gun in a public area.

We conclude that the need for answers to questions in a situation posing a threat to the public safety outweighs the need for the prophylactic rule protecting the Fifth Amendment's privilege against self-incrimination. We decline to place officers such as Officer Kraft in the untenable position of having to consider, often in a matter of seconds, whether it best serves society for them to ask the necessary questions without the *Miranda* warnings and render whatever probative evidence they uncover inadmissible, or for them to give the warnings in order

---

6. Similar approaches have been rejected in other contexts. See *Innis* (officer's subjective intent to incriminate not determinative of whether "interrogation" occurred); *Mendenhall* (opinion of Stewart, J.) (officer's subjective intent to detain not determinative of whether a "seizure" occurred within the meaning of the Fourth Amendment); *Robinson* (officer's subjective fear not determinative of necessity for "search incident to arrest" exception to the Fourth Amendment warrant requirement).

to preserve the admissibility of evidence they might uncover but possibly damage or destroy their ability to obtain that evidence and neutralize the volatile situation confronting them.[7]

[This exception] will not be difficult for police officers to apply because in each case it will be circumscribed by the exigency which justifies it. We think police officers can and will distinguish almost instinctively between questions necessary to secure their own safety or the safety of the public and questions designed solely to elicit testimonial evidence from a suspect.

The facts of this case clearly demonstrate that distinction and an officer's ability to recognize it. Officer Kraft asked only the question necessary to locate the missing gun before advising respondent of his rights. It was only after securing the loaded revolver and giving the warnings that he continued with investigatory questions about the ownership and place of purchase of the gun. The exception which we recognize today, far from complicating the thought processes and the on-the-scene judgments of police officers, will simply free them to follow their legitimate instincts when confronting situations presenting a danger to the public safety.[8]

We hold that the [court below] erred in excluding the statement, "the gun is over there," and the gun because of the officer's failure to read respondent his *Miranda* rights before attempting to locate the weapon. Accordingly [it] also erred in excluding the subsequent statements as illegal fruits of a *Miranda* violation.[9]

* * *

Justice O'CONNOR, concurring in part in the judgment and dissenting in part. * * *

[Justice O'Connor would suppress the respondent's initial statement, "the gun is over there"—but not the gun itself because "nothing in *Miranda* or the privilege itself requires exclusion of nontestimonial evidence derived from informal custodial interrogation." Justice O'Connor's views on why *Miranda* requires that respondent's initial statement be suppressed are set forth below. Her views

---

7. The dissent argues that a public safety exception to *Miranda* is unnecessary because in every case an officer can simply ask the necessary questions to protect himself or the public, and then the prosecution can decline to introduce any incriminating responses at a subsequent trial. But absent actual coercion by the officer, there is no constitutional imperative requiring the exclusion of the evidence that results from police inquiry of this kind; and we do not believe that the doctrinal underpinnings of *Miranda* require us to exclude the evidence, thus penalizing officers for asking the very questions which are the most crucial to their efforts to protect themselves and the public.

8. Although it involves police questions in part relating to the whereabouts of a gun, *Orozco v. Texas* [p. 516, fn. a] is in no sense inconsistent with our disposition of this case. [In *Orozco,*] the questions about the gun were clearly investigatory; they did not in any way relate to an objectively reasonable need to protect the police or the public from any immediate danger associated with the weapon. In short there was no exigency requiring immedi-

ate action by the officers beyond the normal need expeditiously to solve a serious crime.

Innis also involved the whereabouts of a missing weapon, but our holding in that case depended entirely on our conclusion that no police interrogation took place so as to require consideration of the applicability of the *Miranda* prophylactic.

9. Because we hold that there is no violation of *Miranda* in this case, we have no occasion to [decide whether] the gun is admissible either because it is nontestimonial or because the police would inevitably have discovered it absent their questioning.

[A year earlier, in *Nix v. Williams (Williams II)*, p. 797, the Court had held that the "fruit of the poisonous tree" doctrine did not bar the use of evidence derived from a constitutional violation if such evidence would "ultimately" or "inevitably" have been discovered even if the police had acted lawfully. The "fruits" doctrine, formulated initially in applying the Fourth Amendment exclusionary rule, prohibits the use of evidence derived from, and thus "tainted" by, a constitutional violation.]

on the admissibility of the gun itself and her thoughts about the statements elicited after the *Miranda* warnings were given are set forth at p. 802. See also Justice O'Connor's discussion of the application (or nonapplication) of the "fruit of the poisonous tree" doctrine in her opinion for the Court in *Oregon v. Elstad,* p. 803.]

In my view, a "public safety" exception unnecessarily blurs the edges of the clear line heretofore established and makes *Miranda's* requirements more difficult to understand. In some cases, police will benefit because a reviewing court will find that an exigency excused their failure to administer the required warnings. But in other cases, police will suffer because, though they thought an exigency excused their noncompliance, a reviewing court will view the "objective" circumstances differently and require exclusion of admissions thereby obtained. The end result will be a finespun new doctrine on public safety exigencies incident to custodial interrogation, complete with the hair-splitting distinctions that currently plague our Fourth Amendment jurisprudence.

[The] justification the Court provides for upsetting the equilibrium that has finally been achieved—that police cannot and should not balance considerations of public safety against the individual's interest in avoiding compulsory testimonial self-incrimination—really misses the critical question to be decided. *Miranda* has never been read to prohibit the police from asking questions to secure the public safety. Rather, the critical question *Miranda* addresses is who shall bear the cost of securing the public safety when such questions are asked and answered: the defendant or the State. *Miranda,* for better or worse, found the resolution of that question implicit in the prohibition against compulsory self-incrimination and placed the burden on the State. When police ask custodial questions without administering the required warnings, *Miranda* quite clearly requires that the answers received be presumed compelled and that they be excluded from evidence at trial. * * *

Justice MARSHALL, with whom Justice BRENNAN and Justice STEVENS join, dissenting * * *.

The majority's entire analysis rests on the factual assumption that the public was at risk during Quarles' interrogation. This assumption is completely in conflict with the facts as found by New York's highest court. * * * Contrary to the majority's speculations, Quarles was not believed to have, nor did he in fact have, an accomplice to come to his rescue. When the questioning began, the arresting officers were sufficiently confident of their safety to put away their guns.

[The] New York court's conclusion that neither Quarles nor his missing gun posed a threat to the public's safety is amply supported by the evidence presented at the suppression hearing. [Although] the supermarket was open to the public, Quarles' arrest took place during the middle of the night when the store was apparently deserted except for the clerks at the checkout counter. The police could easily have cordoned off the store and searched for the missing gun. Had they done so, they would have found the gun forthwith. [As] the State acknowledged before the New York Court of Appeals: "After Officer Kraft had handcuffed and frisked the defendant in the supermarket, *he knew with a high degree of certainty that the defendant's gun was within the immediate vicinity of the encounter.* He undoubtedly would have searched for it in the carton a few feet away without the defendant having looked in that direction and saying that it was there." (Emphasis added.)

[This] case is illustrative of the chaos the "public-safety" exception will unleash. The circumstances of Quarles' arrest have never been in dispute. [T]he

New York Court of Appeals concluded that there was "no evidence in the record before us that there were exigent circumstances posing a risk to the public safety." Upon reviewing the same facts and hearing the same arguments, a majority of this Court has come to precisely the opposite conclusion * * *.[4]

Though unfortunate, the difficulty of administering the "public-safety" exception is not the most profound flaw in the majority's decision. The majority has lost sight of the fact that *Miranda* and our earlier custodial-interrogation cases all implemented a constitutional privilege against self-incrimination. The rules established in these cases were designed to protect criminal defendants against prosecutions based on coerced self-incriminating statements. The majority today turns its back on these constitutional considerations, and invites the government to prosecute through the use of what necessarily are coerced statements.

The majority's error stems from a serious misunderstanding of *Miranda* and of the Fifth Amendment upon which that decision was based. The majority implies that *Miranda* consisted of no more than a judicial balancing act in which the benefits of "enlarged protection for the Fifth Amendment privilege" were weighed against "the cost to society in terms of fewer convictions of guilty suspects." Supposedly because the scales tipped in favor of the privilege against self-incrimination, the *Miranda* Court erected a prophylactic barrier around statements made during custodial interrogations. The majority now proposes to return to the scales of social utility to calculate whether *Miranda*'s prophylactic rule remains cost-effective when threats to public's safety are added to the balance.

[The] majority misreads *Miranda*. Though the *Miranda* dissent prophesized dire consequences, the *Miranda* Court refused to allow such concerns to weaken the protections of the Constitution * * *.

Whether society would be better off if the police warned suspects of their rights before beginning an interrogation or whether the advantages of giving such warnings would outweigh their costs did not inform the *Miranda* decision. On the contrary, the *Miranda* Court was concerned with the proscriptions of the Fifth Amendment, and, in particular, whether the Self–Incrimination Clause permits the government to prosecute individuals based on statements made in the course of custodial interrogations.

[In] fashioning its "public-safety" exception to *Miranda,* the majority makes no attempt to deal with the constitutional presumption established by that case. [The] majority's only contention is that police officers could more easily protect the public if *Miranda* did not apply to custodial interrogations concerning the public's safety.[7] But *Miranda* was not a decision about public safety; it was a

---

4. One of the peculiarities of the majority's decision is its suggestion that police officers can "distinguish almost instinctively" questions tied to public safety and questions designed to elicit testimonial evidence. Obviously, these distinctions are extraordinarily difficult to draw. In many cases—like this one—custodial questioning may serve both purposes. It is therefore wishful thinking for the majority to suggest that the intuitions of police officers will render its decision self-executing.

7. The majority elsewhere attempts to disguise its decision as an effort to cut back on the overbreadth of *Miranda*'s prophylactic standard. The disguise is transparent. Although *Miranda* was overbroad in that its ap-

plication excludes some statements made during custodial interrogations that are not in fact coercive, the majority is not dealing with a class of cases affected by *Miranda*'s overbreadth. The majority is exempting from *Miranda*'s prophylactic rule incriminating statements that were elicited to safeguard the public's safety. As is discussed below, the majority supports the "public safety" exception because "public-safety" interrogations can be coercive. In this respect, the Court's decision differs greatly from *Michigan v. Tucker*, in which the Court sanctioned the admission of the fruits of a *Miranda* violation, but only because the violation was technical and the interrogation itself noncoercive.

decision about coerced confessions. Without establishing that interrogations concerning the public's safety are less likely to be coercive than other interrogations, the majority cannot endorse the "public-safety" exception and remain faithful to the logic of *Miranda*.

[That] the application of the "public-safety" exception in this case entailed coercion is no happenstance. The majority's *ratio decidendi* is that interrogating suspects about matters of public safety *will* be coercive. In its cost-benefit analysis, the Court's strongest argument in favor of a public-safety exception to *Miranda* is that the police would be better able to protect the public's safety if they were not always required to give suspects their *Miranda* warnings. The crux of this argument is that, by deliberately withholding *Miranda* warnings, the police can get information out of suspects who would refuse to respond to police questioning were they advised of their constitutional rights. The "public-safety" exception is efficacious precisely because it permits police officers to coerce criminal defendants into making involuntary statements.

[The] irony of the majority's decision is that the public's safety can be perfectly well protected without abridging the Fifth Amendment. If a bomb is about to explode or the public is otherwise imminently imperiled, the police are free to interrogate suspects without advising them of their constitutional rights. [If] trickery is necessary to protect the public, then the police may trick a suspect into confessing. While the Fourteenth Amendment sets limits on such behavior, nothing in the Fifth Amendment or our decision in *Miranda* proscribes this sort of emergency questioning. All the Fifth Amendment forbids is the introduction of coerced statements at trial. * * *[b]

Notes and Questions

(a) If a case like *Innis* or *Mesa* (the "hostage negotiator" case) arose today, would the courts quickly dispose of it under the "public safety" exception to *Miranda* without ever reaching the question whether the suspect had been subjected to "custodial interrogation" in violation of *Miranda?*

(b) *Quarles* and *Miranda*. The *Quarles* case, observes Charles Weisselberg, *Saving Miranda*, 84 Cornell L.Rev. 109, 129 (1998), "struck at the Court's original version of *Miranda* in several respects": It "reinforced the notion that the warning requirement was divorced from the Fifth Amendment"; the majority's cost-benefit analysis "represents a wholly different view of the value of the Fifth Amendment than was expressed in *Miranda*"; and "[t]hird, by creating a vague and ill-defined exception to the warning requirement, the Court reduced the efficacy of *Miranda*'s bright-line rules." However, adds Professor Weisselberg, *Quarles* "did not—as it turns out—open the door to other large exceptions to the *Miranda* rule. In the fourteen years since *Quarles* was decided, the Supreme Court has not approved any other instances of custodial interrogations in which warnings need not be given."

(c) Is the *Quarles* Court's attempt to distinguish *Orozco* (see fn. 8) convincing? In *Orozco,* the police entered a sleeping defendant's room and questioned him about a gun used in a murder several hours earlier. They had ample cause to believe that defendant was the murderer and, as it turned out, the murder weapon *was* hidden in his room. There was no need to protect *the public* from immediate danger, but why wasn't there a need to protect *the police?* Does the Court's treatment of *Orozco* mean that, at least where there is no threat to members of

---

b. For the portion of Justice Marshall's dissenting opinion dealing with the admissibility of the gun discovered as a result of Quarles' statement, see p. 803.

the public, *Quarles* only permits the police to ask about the location of a gun when they come upon the scene in "hot pursuit?"

(d) *The "rescue doctrine."* Somewhat similar to the "public safety" exception is the "rescue doctrine." Should statements obtained in violation of *Miranda* be admissible if police interrogation of a suspected kidnapper is motivated primarily by a desire to save the victim's life? Yes, answer *People v. Dean,* 114 Cal.Rptr. 555 (Cal.App.1974) and *People v. Krom,* 461 N.E.2d 276 (N.Y.1984). See generally William T. Pizzi, *The Privilege Against Self–Incrimination in a Rescue Situation,* 76 J.Crim.L. & C. (1985). It is unsound, maintains Professor Pizzi, id. at 595–603, to approach the scope of the privilege against self-incrimination "solely from the defendant's point of view while totally ignoring the threat to the lives of others and the purpose and function of the police conduct"; the privilege and its attendant rules should not control "where the police are functioning in a situation which is primarily noninvestigative and where life is at stake."

Are there (should there be) any limits on what a police officer may do to a suspected kidnapper in order to get him to reveal the location of a kidnap victim? Cf. *Leon v. State,* 410 So.2d 201 (Fla.App.1982), holding, over a forceful dissent, that the use of police threats and physical violence at the scene of arrest in order to ascertain the kidnap victim's whereabouts "did not constitutionally infect the later confessions." Consider Pizzi, supra, at 606: "[T]here are [due process] limits on the conduct of the police in their treatment of suspects even in an emergency situation where life is at stake," but "[i]n determining those limits [the] traditional scope of police conduct permitted in a purely investigative context is only a starting point."

10. *Meeting the "heavy burden" of demonstrating waiver: should tape recordings of the warnings and police questioning be required?* Five years *before* the *Miranda* case, one close student of the problem, Bernard Weisberg, *Police Interrogation of Arrested Persons: A Skeptical View,* 52 J. Crim.L. & P.S. 21, 48 (1961), attacked the secrecy surrounding police interrogation: "No other case comes to mind in which an administrative official is permitted the broad discretionary power assumed by the police interrogator, together with the power to prevent objective recordation of the facts. The absence of a record makes disputes inevitable about the conduct of the police and, sometimes, about what the prisoner has actually said. It is secrecy, not privacy, which accounts for the absence of a reliable record of interrogation proceedings in a police station. If the need for some pre-judicial questioning is assumed, privacy may be defended on grounds of necessity; secrecy cannot be defended on this or any other ground."

Recall, too, that before turning to the police manuals for valuable information about current police practices, the *Miranda* Court noted that the secrecy surrounding police questioning "results in a gap in our knowledge as to what in fact goes on in the interrogation rooms." (See p. 476.) However, as pointed out by Richard A. Leo, *Inside the Interrogation Room,* 86 J. Crim.L. & Criminology 266 (1996), three decades after *Miranda*, we know "scant more" about actual police interrogation practices than we did at the time that famous case was decided.

At one point, the *Miranda* opinion (see p. 483) came to the very edge of requiring law enforcement officers to tape, where feasible, the warning, waiver and subsequent questioning and statements made in response: "If the interrogation continues without the presence of an attorney and a statement is taken, a heavy burden rests on the Government to demonstrate that the defendant knowingly and intelligently waived his [rights]. Since the State is responsible for establishing the isolated circumstances under which the interrogation takes place and *has the only means of making available corroborated evidence* of warnings given during incommunicado interrogation, the burden is rightly on its shoulders." (Emphasis added.) However, the *Miranda* Court fell short of imposing a tape recording requirement on police interrogators—perhaps because it was well aware that such a requirement would add much fuel to the criticism that it was exercising undue control over police practices—that it was "legislating."

Despite the references to "heavy burden" and "corroborated evidence" in the *Miranda* opinion and the strong support for video, or at least audio, taping in the literature, all but two state courts have held that—even when taping the proceedings in the interrogation room is feasible—the uncorroborated testimony of an officer that he gave complete *Miranda* warnings and obtained a waiver is sufficient. The two exceptions are *Stephan v. State*, 711 P.2d 1156 (Alaska 1985) and *State v. Scales*, 518 N.W.2d 587 (Minn.1994).

PAUL G. CASSELL, *Miranda's Social Costs: An Empirical Assessment*, 90 Nw. U.L.Rev. 387, 486–97 (1996), has forcefully argued that a recording requirement should be viewed as an *alternative* to *Miranda*:

"Videotaping interrogations would certainly be as effective as *Miranda* in preventing police coercion and probably more so. The *Miranda* regime appears to have had little effect on the police misconduct that does exist. In contrast, videotaping, when used, has often reduced claims of police coercion and probably real coercion as well. To be sure, police conceivably could alter tapes or deploy force off-camera. But if you were facing a police officer with a rubber hose, would you prefer a world in which he was required to mumble the *Miranda* warnings and have you waive your rights, all as reported by him in later testimony? Or a world in which the interrogation is videorecorded and the burden is on law enforcement to explain if it is not; where date and time are recorded on the videotape; where your physical appearance and demeanor during the interrogation are permanently recorded?

"[While] recording maintains, and in many ways exceeds, *Miranda's* supposed benefits of deterring coercion and preventing false confessions, it has the advantage over *Miranda* of not significantly impeding law enforcement. In 1992 the National Institute of Justice (NIJ) published a nationwide survey of representative samples of police agencies about videotaping interrogations. The survey found that about one-sixth of all police and sheriff's departments in the United States videotaped at least some confessions. The survey found that 59.8% of the agencies believed that they obtained more incriminating information from suspects, 26.9% the same amount, while 13.2% thought they obtained less. Also, 8.6% thought suspects were more willing to talk to police, 63.1% thought there was no difference, while 28.3% reported suspects less willing to talk. Videotaping also had many other benefits, such as improving police interrogation practices, rendering confessions more convincing, facilitating their introduction into evidence, assisting prosecutors in negotiating more acceptable plea bargains and obtaining guilty pleas, and helping in securing convictions.[a]

a. "Recent and substantial experience with a mandatory recording requirement in Britian," added Cassell, "suggests that such a requirement would not significantly harm police efforts to obtain confessions." In 1988, a Code of Practice went into effect that generally required the police to tape record interviews with suspects. A review of this requirement five years later by the Royal Commission on Criminal Justice reported that tape recording in the stationhouse had "proved to be a strikingly successful innovation providing better safeguards for the suspect and the police officer alike." According to one survey, some 90 percent of police officers approval of the practice, with two-thirds reporting "very favorable" news about it.

A[In] light of the benefits of videotaping and the costly features of *Miranda*, what might a replacement for *Miranda* look like? Suspects could continue to be advised of their rights as follows:

(1) You do not have to say anything.

(2) Anything you do say may be used as evidence.

(3) You have the right to be represented by a lawyer when we bring you before a judge.

(4) If you cannot afford a lawyer, the judge will appoint one for you without charge.

(5) We are required to bring you before a judge without unnecessary delay.

"While adding a new, fifth warning that is not required by *Miranda*, the modified warnings would dispense with the *Miranda* offer of counsel, identified as a particularly harmful aspect of *Miranda* and, in any event, a right that has proven to be purely theoretical since police always terminate questioning rather than finding a lawyer. Also, the alternative would dispense with the requirement that police obtain an affirmative waiver of rights from suspects, another particularly harmful feature of *Miranda*. However, police could continue to ask suspects whether they understood the rights communicated to them, since nothing in the empirical literature identifies this aspect of *Miranda* as being particularly harmful. Also eliminated would be the requirement that police immediately terminate an interview whenever the suspect requests an end to the interview or an opportunity to meet with counsel. These features have been identified as harming the confession rate.[634]

"[Since] police are still required to give modified warnings and since they will be videotaped while conducting interrogations, police will not gain the mistaken impression that any judicial supervision of the interrogation process has ended.[b]

Professor Cassell's article evoked a response from STEPHEN J. SCHULHOF-ER, *Miranda's Practical Effect: Substantial Benefits and Vanishingly Small Social Costs*, 90 Nw. U.L.Rev. 556–60 (1996). Professor Schulhofer agreed that videotaping is an extremely valuable tool—for both the police interrogator and the

---

Consider, too, William A. Geller, *Videotaping Interrogations and Confessions* (1990), in Miranda: Law, Justice and Policing 303 (Richard A. Leo & George C. Thomas eds. 1998). In 1990, reports Geller, approximately one-third of all police and sheriffs departments in town or cities of 50,000 or more were doing some videotaping of police interrogation. According to Geller, the great majority of the agencies who have used videotaping had positive things to say about it.

If procedures relating to tape recordings are established, should the police inform the suspect that what he says is being recorded? Would such a requirement inhibit too many from talking? On the other hand, would such a requirement bring home to suspects the seriousness of their situations? See Kamisar Essays at 133 n. 22.

634. Continued persistence to convince a suspect to change his mind will, at some point, render a confession involuntary and thus inad-missable under Fifth Amendment principles. * * *

b. See also Richard A. Leo, *The Impact of Miranda Revisited*, 86 J. Crim. L. & Criminology 621, 680–82 (1996). Although he believes *Miranda* should neither be overruled nor strengthened doctrinally, Professor Leo maintains that substantive due process requires the electronic recording of custodial interrogations in all felony cases and that such a requirement constitutes the most adequate solution to the problems *Miranda* failed to resolve, "problems that continue to bedevil the constitutional law of criminal procedure." According to Leo, these are "the problems of adjudicating the 'swearing contest' between officer and suspect in court; the problem of false allegations of police improprieties; the problem of police perjury; the problem of false confessions; and most notably, the problem of determining the voluntariness of a confession."

suspect—but rejected the notion that videotaping could be *a* substitute for *Miranda*. He maintained that Cassell's proposed replacement for *Miranda* would expose suspects to violations of their constitutional rights:

"No doubt a videotaped record would often prevent police abuse and manipulation of the 'swearing contest.' But without clear substantive requirements against which to test the police behavior that the videotape will reveal, the objective record will lack any specific legal implications.

"The heart of the Cassell proposals is his recommendation to strip arrested suspects of their right to consult counsel during pre-arraignment interrogation, to eliminate the requirement that interrogation be preceded by an explicit waiver of rights, and to eliminate *Miranda*'s requirement that interrogation cease if a suspect makes a clear request to break off questioning or to consult with counsel. The requirements he would eliminate are not only central to the *Miranda* safeguards but have now become entrenched in the interrogation procedures of many countries around the world.[242]

"[Under Cassell's proposal,] [s]uspects would have no right to consult with counsel prior to formal arraignment. They would be told they have a right to remain silent, but the protective effect of that warning would be immediately negated by police actions. Instead of "scrupulously honoring" a suspect's decision to remain silent, as *Miranda* requires, police would be authorized to ignore the suspect's decision and press forward with the interrogation. Will suspects treated this way really have (or think they have) the right to remain silent? All they will have (mixed messages notwithstanding) is the legally sanctioned obligation to submit to an unwanted custodial interrogation.

"The distinction Cassell needs to draw here, to render his proposal plausible, is the distinction between compelling the suspect *to answer,* which the Constitution clearly forbids, and compelling him to *submit to questions,* which Cassell thinks should be permissible. Involuntary *statements* would be ruled out, but not involuntary *interrogation.* In the context of custodial police interrogation, there is only a slender conceptual difference here, not a practical difference that can possibly matter. If the suspect in police custody chooses to make no statement and asks for questioning to cease, if the interrogators who hold him in their power ignore that request and continue asking him to say something, are they merely compelling him *to listen?* Or are they not, in every practical sense, compelling (or trying to compel) him *to answer?* * * *

"[The Cassell proposal would bring about a] return to the vague due process test [one that] would compel hundreds of thousands of unwilling suspects (roughly half a million suspects per year) to submit to involuntary questioning, and it would leave police (and courts) without any predictable framework for judging how long such an involuntary interrogation could last and what kinds of tactics could be used. Worse yet, since the murky boundaries for dealing with recalcitrant suspects would sometimes be overstepped, serious instances of physical and

242. See Craig M. Bradley, *The Emerging International Consensus as to Criminal Procedure Rules,* 14 Mich.J.Int'l L. 171, 185 (1993) ("England's interrogation rules are *more stringent* than *Miranda.*") (emphasis added); id. at 197–98 (noting that in Canada, a suspect must be informed upon arrest of his right to counsel, and that police "must refrain from attempting to elicit evidence from the detainee until he has a reasonable opportunity to retain and instruct counsel") (quoting Martin's Annual Criminal Code CH–21 (1991); id. at 214–15 (Germany requires warning of rights to silence and right "*at all times, even before his examination,* to consult with defense counsel of his choice") (emphasis added) (quoting German Code of Criminal Procedure § 136); id. at 217–18 (noting that Italian interrogation rules prohibit use of statements made in the absence of counsel).

psychological abuse would inevitably occur even among the best-intentioned officers.

"All to what end? Is it the hope that law enforcement practices would eventually settle into the new regime, that truly egregious abuses would not occur too often, that society will tolerate subjecting arrested suspects to pressures the Fifth Amendment clearly forbids in every other context, and that a microscopically small increase in the net conviction rate would eventually be realized as a result? With or without a video camera to record the process, persistent custodial questioning of unwilling suspects is pragmatically undesirable and constitutionally indefensible."[a]

11. Implied waiver. Although a waiver is not established merely by showing that a defendant was given complete *Miranda* warnings and thereafter made an incriminating statement, *Tague v. Louisiana,* 444 U.S. 469, 100 S.Ct. 652, 62 L.Ed.2d 622 (1980), this does not mean that a waiver of *Miranda* rights will never be recognized unless "specifically made" after the warnings are given. As the Court, per STEWART, J., observed in NORTH CAROLINA v. BUTLER, 441 U.S. 369, 99 S.Ct. 1755, 60 L.Ed.2d 286 (1979):

"The question is not one of form, but rather whether the defendant knowingly and voluntarily waived [his *Miranda* rights]. [Although] mere silence is not enough [that] does not mean that the defendant's silence, coupled with an understanding of his rights and a course of conduct indicating waiver, may never support a conclusion that a defendant has waived his rights. The courts must presume that a defendant did not waive his rights; the prosecution's burden is great; but in at least some cases waiver can be clearly inferred from the actions and words of the person interrogated."[a]

Dissenting Justice BRENNAN, joined by Marshall and Stevens, JJ., protested: "[The Court] shrouds in half-light the question of waiver, allowing courts to construct inferences from ambiguous word and gestures. But the very premise of *Miranda* requires that ambiguity be interpreted against the interrogator. [Under the conditions inherent in custodial interrogation], only the most explicit waiver of rights can be considered knowingly and freely given. [S]ince the Court agrees that *Miranda* requires the police to obtain some kind of waiver—whether express

---

a. In *All Benefits, No Costs: The Grand Illusion of Miranda's Defenders,* 90 Nw. U.L.Rev. 1084, 1121B22 (1996), a rejoinder to Professor Schulhofer's response, Professor Cassell comments, inter alia:

" * * * Schulhofer appears to agree [that] videotaping would be more effective than *Miranda* in preventing police brutality and identifying fine points of coercion, but he offers no specific explanation for his conclusion that this benefit is outweighed by what he sees as the costs of modifying *Miranda.* Nor does he offer any response to my argument that videotaping would eliminate the problem of false confessions that convict the innocent. * * *

"Instead of engaging on these issues, Professor Schulhofer moves swiftly and predictably to the one part of my proposal that is designed to reduce *Miranda*'s social costs: the abolition of the prophylactic rules that require an affirmative waiver of rights and give suspects an unqualified right to avoid questioning. Here Professor Schulhofer's approach to the *Miranda*

compromise is revealed to be intransigent. In essence, his stance is: 'What's mine is mine, and what's yours is negotiable.'"

a. After reading the FBI's "Advice of Rights" form, defendant was asked whether he understood his rights. He replied that he did, but refused to sign the waiver at the bottom of the form. He was then told that he need neither speak nor sign the form, but that the agents would like him to talk to them. He replied, "I will talk to you but I am not signing any form." He then made incriminating statements. Because defendant had said nothing when advised of his right to counsel, and because the state supreme court read *Miranda* as requiring a specific waiver of each right, it concluded that defendant had not waived his right to counsel. The U.S. Supreme Court disagreed: "By creating an inflexible rule that no implicit waiver [of *Miranda* rights] can ever suffice, the [state court] has gone beyond the requirements of federal organic law."

or implied—the requirement of an express waiver would impose no burden on the police not imposed by the Court's interpretation. It would merely make that burden explicit. Had [the agent] simply elicited a clear answer to the question, 'Do you waive your right to a lawyer?' this journey through three courts would not have been necessary."

Notes and Questions

(a) *The "intelligent and knowing" test in practice.* Consider Mark Berger, *Compromise and Continuity: Miranda Waivers, Confession Admissibility, and the Retention of Interrogation Protections,* 49 U.Pitt.L.Rev. 1007, 1063 (1988): "Current indications are that [the requirement that *Miranda* waivers meet an intelligent and knowing test] extends no further than a general awareness by the suspect that he has the right to remain silent and have the assistance of counsel, and that anything he says can be used against him. Of course, these are the elements contained in the *Miranda* warning itself, and there is no sign that the Supreme Court is likely to require anything more to meet the knowing test. In practice, it appears that as long as the warnings are given and the suspect exhibits no overt signs of a lack of capacity to understand them, his waiver will be upheld."

(b) *Should the Johnson v. Zerbst standard apply to Miranda waivers?* Under *Johnson v. Zerbst* (1938) (quoted at p. 64), the prosecution must demonstrate "an intentional relinquishment or abandonment of a known right" in order to establish a waiver of counsel *at trial*. The *Miranda* Court (p. 483) cited *Zerbst* for the proposition that "this Court has always set high standards of proof for the waiver of constitutional rights." As noted in Berger, supra, at 1031, however, the *Miranda* Court "did not specifically adopt the *Zerbst* criteria." But in the same paragraph citing *Zerbst* the Court stated that "a heavy burden rests on the Government to demonstrate that the defendant knowingly and intelligently waived" his *Miranda* rights. Was *this* an adoption of the *Zerbst* "intentional relinquishment" standard? If so, did the *Miranda* Court too hurriedly lump together *Miranda* rights and the right to counsel at trial? Should the *Zerbst* criteria and "waiver" terminology be expelled from *Miranda* law? Yes, maintains James Tomkovicz, *Standards for Invocation and Waiver of Counsel in Confession Contexts,* 71 Iowa L.Rev. 975, 1050–53 (1986):

"Elimination of the *Zerbst* formula [is] preferable not only because *Zerbst* does not accurately capture fifth amendment decisions in the abstract, but also because actual applications in fifth amendment cases prove that the formula does not describe the waivers that have been acceptable. Furthermore, those interpretations threaten to dilute the demands of the 'voluntary and knowing' standard and thereby to undermine its ability to shelter other constitutional rights for which it is appropriate. A weakened *Zerbst* waiver standard for *Miranda*'s fifth amendment counsel, for example, is easily borrowed for sixth amendment counsel waiver determinations. The vigor of that guarantee, however, depends on more stringent protection against surrender than the *Butler* dilution of *Zerbst* affords."

12. *"Qualified" waiver.* As *North Carolina v. Butler* itself illustrates (see fn. a supra), a suspect may refuse to sign a waiver but nonetheless indicate that he is willing to talk.[a] Or he may object to any notetaking by an officer but agree to talk about the case or indicate that he will talk only if a tape recorder is turned off. Are oral waivers effective in the face of such objections? A number of courts

---

a. The *Butler* Court did not hold that this constituted a valid waiver, but only rejected the state court's view that nothing short of an express waiver would satisfy *Miranda*.

have held that they are. See, e.g., *United States v. Frazier*, 476 F.2d 891 (D.C.Cir.1973) (en banc) (*Frazier II*). But see LaFave & Israel, § 6.9(f) (in these situations defendant probably acted as he did "because of a mistaken impression that an oral confession which was not contemporaneously recorded could not be used against him"; therefore, police should be required to "clear up misunderstandings of this nature which are apparent to any reasonable observer").[b]

The Court addressed this general problem in CONNECTICUT v. BARRETT, 479 U.S. 523, 107 S.Ct. 828, 93 L.Ed.2d 920 (1987). While in custody, respondent, a suspect in a sexual assault case, was thrice advised of his *Miranda* rights. On each occasion, after signing an acknowledgment that he had been informed of his rights, respondent indicated that he would not make a written statement, but that he was willing to talk about the incident that led to his arrest. On the second and third such occasions, respondent added that he would not make a written statement outside the presence of counsel, and then orally admitted his involvement in the crime. An officer reduced to writing his recollection of respondent's last such statement, and the confession was admitted into evidence at respondent's trial. The Court, per REHNQUIST, C.J., rejected the contention that respondent's expressed desire for counsel before making a written statement served as an invocation of the right for all purposes:

"[W]e know of no constitutional objective that would be served by suppression in this case. It is undisputed that Barrett desired the presence of counsel before making a written statement. [His] limited requests for counsel, however, were accompanied by affirmative announcements of his willingness to speak with the authorities. The fact that officials took [this opportunity] to obtain an oral confession is quite consistent with the Fifth Amendment. *Miranda* gives the defendant a right to choose between speech and silence, and Barrett chose to speak.

" * * * Barrett made clear his intentions and they were honored. [To] conclude that [he] invoked his right to counsel for all purposes requires not a broad interpretation of an ambiguous statement, but disregard of the ordinary meaning of respondent's statement. [The] fact that some might find Barrett's decision illogical is irrelevant, for we have never 'embraced the theory that a defendant's ignorance of the full consequences of his decisions vitiates their voluntariness.' "

BRENNAN, J., concurred in the judgment. Although "Barrett's contemporaneous waiver of his right to silence and limited invocation of his right to counsel (for the purpose of making a written statement) suggested that he did not understand that anything he *said* could be used against him," he testified that "he understood his *Miranda* rights, i.e., he knew that he need not talk to the police without a lawyer and that anything he said could be used against him. Under these circumstances, the waiver of the right to silence and the limited invocation of the right to counsel were valid."

Had the prosecution been without Barrett's trial testimony, Brennan would have dissented: "As a general matter, I believe that this odd juxtaposition (a willingness to talk and an unwillingness to have anything preserved) militates against finding a knowing or intelligent waiver of the right to silence. [But] the

b. One study indicates that 45 percent of post-*Miranda* defendants mistakenly believed that oral statements could not be used against them. See Lawrence S. Leiken, *Police Interrogation in Colorado: The Implementation of Miranda*, 47 Denver L.J. 1, 15–16, 33 (1970). If so many people do not realize the significance of an oral statement, should the warning take this form: "You have a right to remain silent and anything you say, *orally or* in writing, may (will) be used against you"? *Unif.R.Crim.P.* 212(b) and 243 so provide.

State has carried its 'heavy burden' of demonstrating waiver. It has shown that Barrett received the *Miranda* warnings, that he had the capacity to understand them and *in fact* understood them, and that he expressly waived his right to silence. [In] my view, each of these findings was essential to the conclusion that a voluntary, knowing, and intelligent waiver of the *Miranda* rights occurred."[a]

13. *What constitutes an invocation of Miranda rights?* In FARE v. MICHAEL C., 442 U.S. 707, 99 S.Ct. 2560, 61 L.Ed.2d 197 (1979), after being fully advised of his *Miranda* rights, a juvenile, who had been taken into custody on suspicion of murder, asked, "Can I have my probation officer here?" The police officer replied that he was "not going to call [the probation officer] right now," then continued: "If you want to talk to us without an attorney present, you can. If you don't want to, you don't have to." The juvenile then agreed to talk to the police without an attorney being present and made incriminating statements. The Court, per BLACKMUN, J., held the statements admissible, deeming the request to see a probation officer not a *per se* invocation of *Miranda* rights—not the equivalent of asking for a lawyer. The admissibility of the statements on the basis of waiver turned on "the totality of the circumstance surrounding the interrogation" (e.g., evaluation of the juvenile's age, experience, background and intelligence).

"The *per se* aspect of *Miranda*," emphasized the Court, was "based on the unique role the lawyer plays in the adversarial system of criminal justice in this country. [A] probation officer is not in the same posture with regard to either the accused or the system of justice as a whole. * * * Moreover, [he] is the employee of the State which seeks to prosecute the alleged offender. He is a peace officer, and as such is allied, to a greater or lesser extent, with his fellow peace officers. [It is the] pivotal role of legal counsel [in the administration of criminal justice] that justifies the *per se* rule established in *Miranda* and that distinguishes the request for counsel from the request for a probation officer, a clergyman, or a close friend."

Justice MARSHALL, joined by Brennan and Stevens, JJ., dissented. Noting that the California Supreme Court had "determined that probation officers have a statutory duty to represent minors' interests and, indeed, are 'trusted guardian figure[s]' to whom a juvenile would likely turn for assistance," the dissenters maintained that "*Miranda* requires that interrogation cease whenever a juvenile requests an adult who is obligated to represent his interests." Such request "constitutes both an attempt to obtain advice and a general invocation of the right to silence. For, as the California Supreme Court recognized, 'it is fatuous to assume that a minor in custody will be in a position to call an attorney for assistance,' or that he will trust the police to obtain an attorney for him. A juvenile in these circumstances will likely turn to his parents, or another adult responsible for his welfare, as the only means of securing legal counsel. Moreover, a request for such adult assistance is surely inconsistent with a present desire to speak freely."[a]

Does *Fare v. Michael C.* stand for the broad proposition that a request by any suspect (with the possible exception of a young, inexperienced juvenile; Michael C. was an "experienced" 16½ year old) to see anyone *other than an attorney,* whether

---

a. Stevens, J., joined by Marshall, J., dissented, deeming respondent's request for the assistance of counsel indistinguishable from the request in *Edwards.*

a. Justice Powell wrote a separate dissent, "not satisfied that this particular 16–year-old boy, in this particular situation was subjected to a fair interrogation free from inherently coercive circumstances."

it be a parent, spouse or best friend, does not *per se* constitute an assertion or invocation of *Miranda* rights? If so, is this because neither parent, spouse or best friend has the "unique ability to protect the Fifth Amendment rights" of a suspect undergoing custodial interrogation? How much weight, if any, should be given to the fact that the mother, father or husband requested by the suspect plays a "unique role" in the life of the particular suspect?

14. *The scope of "second-level" Miranda safeguards—the procedures that must be followed when suspects do assert their rights—and the distinction between invoking the right to remain silent and the right to counsel.* In most *Miranda* cases, the issue is the need for the *Miranda* warnings or the adequacy of the warnings given or the suspect's alleged waiver in response to the warnings. But different issues arise when the suspect *asserts* his rights— thereby triggering what have been called "second level" *Miranda* safeguards. Although this development may have surprised the *Miranda* Court, it turns out that the procedures that must be followed when a suspect invokes his rights depends on whether he asserted the right to remain silent or the right to counsel.

The Court first addressed this issue in MICHIGAN v. MOSLEY, 423 U.S. 96, 96 S.Ct. 321, 46 L.Ed.2d 313 (1975). Mosley was arrested in connection with certain robberies. After being given *Miranda* warnings by a robbery detective, Mosley declined to talk about the robberies (but he did not request a lawyer). The detective promptly ceased questioning and made no effort to persuade Mosley to reconsider his position. Mosley was then taken to a cell block in the building. After a two-hour interval, a homicide detective brought Mosley from the cell block to the homicide bureau for questioning about "an unrelated holdup murder." Mosley was again advised of his rights. This time he waived them and made an incriminating statement. A 7–2 majority, per STEWART, J., held the statement admissible.

After studying the *Miranda* opinion, the Court concluded that "the admissibility of statements obtained after the person in custody has decided to remain silent depends [on] whether his 'right to cut off questioning' was 'scrupulously honored.' " After examining the facts, the Court concluded that Mosley's right had been honored. The questioning by the homicide detective, emphasized the Court, had "focused exclusively on [a] crime different in nature and in time and place by occurrence from the robberies for which Mosley had been arrested and interrogated by [the robbery detective]" and the subsequent questioning by another detective about an unrelated homicide was "quite consistent with a reasonable interpretation of Mosley's earlier refusal to answer any questions about the robberies." Therefore, "this is not a case [where] the police failed to honor a decision [to] cut off questioning, either by refusing to discontinue the interrogation upon request or by persisting in repeated efforts to wear down [the suspect's] resistance and make him change his mind. [The] police here immediately ceased the interrogation, resumed questioning only after the passage of a significant period of time and the provision of a fresh set of warnings, and restricted the second interrogation to a crime that had not been a subject of the earlier interrogation."

Concurring Justice WHITE foreshadowed his opinion for the Court six years later in *Edwards v. Arizona,* below, by observing: "[The *Miranda* Court showed in its opinion] that when it wanted to create a *per se* rule against further interrogation after assertion of a right, it knew how to do so. The Court there said 'if the individual states that he wants an attorney, the interrogation must cease *until an attorney is present.'* [Emphasis added by White, J.]"

Three factors seem to be *minimal requirements* for the resumption of questioning once a suspect asserts his right to remain silent: (1) immediately ceasing the interrogation; (2) suspending questioning entirely for a significant period; (3) giving a fresh set of *Miranda* warnings at the outset of the second interrogation. May these three circumstances also be *the only* critical factors? May *Mosley* mean that these three circumstances suffice without more to eliminate the coercion inherent in the continuing custody and the renewed questioning? How significant is it that a different officer resumed the questioning? That the second interrogation occurred at another location? That the second interrogation was limited to a separate and "unrelated" crime? Compare Geoffrey Stone, *The Miranda Doctrine in the Burger Court*, 1977 Sup.Ct.Rev. 99, 134 (last factor "seems critical") with Kamisar, *The Warren Court (Was It Really So Defense–Minded?), the Burger Court (Is It Really So Prosecution–Oriented?) and Police Investigatory Practices*, in The Burger Court: The Counter–Revolution That Wasn't 62, 83 & n. 133 (V. Blasi ed. 1983) (not at all clear that *Mosley* was meant to be or will be so limited).

Distinguishing the *Mosley* case, EDWARDS v. ARIZONA, 451 U.S. 477, 101 S.Ct. 1880, 68 L.Ed.2d 378 (1981), held that once a suspect has invoked his right to counsel he may not be "subject[ed] to further interrogation [until] counsel has been made available to him unless [he] himself initiates further communication, exchanges or conversations with the police."

Edwards was arrested for burglary, robbery and murder and taken to the police station. He waived his rights and agreed to talk about these crimes. But some time later he asserted his right to counsel. At this point, questioning ceased and Edwards was taken to jail. The next morning, two detectives, colleagues of the officer who had questioned Edwards the previous day, came to the jail, met with Edwards and again informed him of his rights.[a] This time Edwards agreed to talk about the same crimes. He then made incriminating statements which led to his conviction for these crimes. The state supreme court held that although Edwards had asserted his right to counsel the day before, he waived this right the following day when he agreed to talk after again being given his *Miranda* warnings. The Court, per WHITE, J., disagreed:

"[H]owever sound the conclusion of the state courts as to the voluntariness of Edwards' admission may be, [neither court] undertook to focus on whether Edwards understood his right to counsel and intelligently and knowingly relinquished it. It is thus apparent that the decision below misunderstood the requirement for finding a valid waiver of the right to counsel, once invoked.

"[A]dditional safeguards [for waiver] are necessary when the accused asks for counsel; and we now hold that when an [in-custody suspect does assert this right a valid waiver of it] cannot be established by showing only that he responded to further police-initiated custodial interrogation even if he has been advised of his rights. [An] accused, such as Edwards, having expressed his desire to deal with the police only through counsel, is not subject to further interrogation by the authori-

---

a. When a guard informed Edwards that two detectives wanted to talk to him, Edwards replied that he did not want to talk to anyone. But the guard told him "he had" to talk to the detectives and then took him to meet with them. The opinion of the Court, however, seems to be written without regard to these particular facts.

ties until counsel has been made available to him, unless the accused himself initiates further communication, exchanges or conversations with the police."[b]

15. ***Clarification (and extension?) of the Edwards rule.*** In ARIZONA v. ROBERSON, 486 U.S. 675, 108 S.Ct. 2093, 100 L.Ed.2d 704 (1988), a 6–2 majority, per STEVENS, J., held that once a suspect effectively asserts his *Miranda-Edwards* right to counsel, the police cannot even initiate interrogation about crimes *other than* the one for which the suspect has invoked his right to counsel:

"[The] presumption raised by a suspect's request for counsel—that he considers himself unable to deal with the pressure of custodial interrogation without legal assistance—does not disappear simply because the police have approached the suspect, still in custody, still without counsel, about a separate investigation. [We] also disagree with [the] contention that fresh sets of *Miranda* warnings will 'reassure' a suspect who has been denied the counsel he has clearly requested that his rights have remained untrammeled. Especially in a case such as this, in which a period of three days elapsed between the unsatisfied request for counsel and the interrogation about a second offense, there is a serious risk that the mere repetition of the *Miranda* warnings would not overcome the presumption of coercion that is created by prolonged police custody."[a]

Newly appointed Justice KENNEDY, joined by Chief Justice Rehnquist, dissented, emphasizing that "*Edwards* is our rule, not a constitutional command; and it is our obligation to justify its expansion." According to Justice Kennedy the majority's approach was not "consistent with the practical realities of suspects' rights and police investigations":

"It is a frequent occurrence that [a custodial suspect] is wanted for questioning with respect to crimes unrelated to the one for which he has been apprehended. The rule announced today will bar law enforcement officials, even those from [some] other jurisdiction, from questioning a suspect about an unrelated matter if he is in custody and has requested counsel to assist in answering questions put to him about the crime for which he was arrested.

"[Having] observed that his earlier invocation of rights was effective in terminating questioning and having been advised that further questioning may not relate to that crime, [the suspect] would understand that he may invoke his rights again with respect to the new investigation, and so terminate questioning regarding that investigation as well. Indeed, the new warnings and explanations will reinforce his comprehension of a suspect's rights." [b]

When, two years later, the Court read the *Edwards* rule still more expansively in *Minnick,* set forth below, many Court watchers were surprised to learn that Justice Kennedy, the forceful dissenter in *Roberson,* had written the opinion of the Court.

b. Chief Justice Burger and Justices Powell and Rehnquist concurred in the result.

a. The Court "attach[ed] no significance to the fact that the officer who conducted the second interrogation did not know that respondent had made a request for counsel. In addition to the fact that *Edwards* focuses on the state of mind of the suspect and not of the police, custodial interrogation must be conducted pursuant to established procedures, and those procedures in turn must enable an officer who proposes to initiate an interrogation to determine whether the suspect has previously requested counsel."

b. O'Connor, J., took no part in the consideration or decision of the case.

MINNICK v. MISSISSIPPI
498 U.S. 146, 111 S.Ct. 486, 112 L.Ed.2d 489 (1990).

Justice KENNEDY delivered the opinion of the Court.

* * * The issue in the case before us is whether *Edwards'* protection ceases once the suspect has consulted with an attorney.

[Petitioner Minnick and fellow prisoner Dykes escaped from a Mississippi jail and broke into a trailer in search of weapons. In the course of the burglary, they killed two people. Minnick and Dykes fled to Mexico, where they fought, and Minnick then proceeded alone to California where, some four months after the murders, he was arrested by local police and placed in a San Diego jail. The day following his arrest, Saturday, two FBI agents came to the jail to interview him. After being advised of his rights and acknowledging that he understood them, Minnick refused to sign a rights waiver form, but agreed to answer some questions. He maintained that Dykes had killed one victim and forced him to shoot the other, but otherwise he hesitated to discuss what happened at the trailer.]

[At this point] the [FBI] agents reminded him he did not have to answer questions without a lawyer present. According to the [FBI] report, "Minnick stated that he would make a more complete statement then with his lawyer present." The FBI interview ended.

After the FBI interview, an appointed attorney met with petitioner. [He] spoke with the lawyer on two or three occasions, though it is not clear from the record whether all of these conferences were in person.

On Monday [Denham, a Mississippi deputy sheriff,] came to the San Diego jail to question Minnick. Minnick testified that his jailers * * * told him he would "have to talk" to Denham and that he "could not refuse." Denham advised petitioner of his rights, and petitioner again declined to sign a rights waiver form. [However, Minnick agreed to answer some questions and made a number of incriminating statements].

Minnick was tried for murder in Mississippi. He moved to suppress all statements given to the FBI or other police officers, including Denham. The trial court denied the motion with respect to petitioner's statements to Denham, but suppressed his other statements. Petitioner was convicted on two counts of capital murder and sentenced to death. [The state supreme court affirmed.]

[The *Edwards* rule] is "designed to prevent police from badgering a defendant into waiving his previously asserted *Miranda* rights." [The rule] ensures that any statement made in subsequent interrogation is not the result of coercive pressures. *Edwards* conserves judicial resources which would otherwise be expended in making difficult determinations of voluntariness, and implements the protections of *Miranda* in practical and straightforward terms.

The merit of the *Edwards* decision lies in the clarity of its command and the certainty of its application. [The] rule provides " 'clear and unequivocal' guidelines to the law enforcement profession."

[A] fair reading of *Edwards* and subsequent cases demonstrates that we have interpreted the rule to bar police-initiated interrogation unless the accused has counsel with him at the time of questioning. Whatever the ambiguities of our earlier cases on this point, we now hold that when counsel is requested, interrogation must cease, and officials may not reinitiate interrogation without counsel present, whether or not the accused has consulted with his attorney.

We consider our ruling to be an appropriate and necessary application of the *Edwards* rule. A single consultation with an attorney does not remove the suspect from persistent attempts by officials to persuade him to waive his rights, or from the coercive pressures that accompany custody and that may increase as custody is prolonged. The case before us well illustrates the pressures, and abuses, that may be concomitants of custody. Petitioner testified that though he resisted, he was required to submit to both the FBI and the Denham interviews. In the latter instance, the compulsion to submit to interrogation followed petitioner's unequivocal request during the FBI interview that questioning cease until counsel was present. The case illustrates also that consultation is not always effective in instructing the suspect of his rights. One plausible interpretation of the record is that petitioner thought he could keep his admissions out of evidence by refusing to sign a formal waiver of rights. If the authorities had complied with Minnick's request to have counsel present during interrogation, the attorney could have corrected Minnick's misunderstanding, or indeed counseled him that he need not make a statement at all. We decline to remove protection from police-initiated questioning based on isolated consultations with counsel who is absent when the interrogation resumes.

The exception to *Edwards* here proposed is inconsistent with *Edwards'* purpose to protect the suspect's right to have counsel present at custodial interrogation. It is inconsistent as well with *Miranda*, where we specifically rejected respondent's theory that the opportunity to consult with one's attorney would substantially counteract the compulsion created by custodial interrogation. We noted in *Miranda* that "[e]ven preliminary advice given to the accused by his own attorney can be swiftly overcome by the secret interrogation process. Thus the need for counsel to protect the Fifth Amendment privilege comprehends not merely a right to consult with counsel prior to questioning, but also to have counsel present during any questioning if the defendant so desires."

The exception proposed, furthermore, would undermine the advantages flowing from *Edwards'* "clear and unequivocal" character. Respondent concedes that even after consultation with counsel, a second request for counsel should reinstate the *Edwards* protection. We are invited by this formulation to adopt a regime in which *Edwards'* protection could pass in and out of existence multiple times prior to arraignment, at which point the same protection might reattach by virtue of our Sixth Amendment jurisprudence, see *Michigan v. Jackson* [p. 565]. Vagaries of this sort spread confusion through the justice system and lead to a consequent loss of respect for the underlying constitutional principle.

In addition, adopting the rule proposed would leave far from certain the sort of consultation required to displace *Edwards*. Consultation is not a precise concept, for it may encompass variations from a telephone call to say that the attorney is in route, to a hurried interchange between the attorney and client in a detention facility corridor, to a lengthy in-person conference in which the attorney gives full and adequate advice respecting all matters that might be covered in further interrogations.

[Added] to these difficulties in definition and application of the proposed rule is our concern over its consequence that the suspect whose counsel is prompt would lose the protection of *Edwards*, while the one whose counsel is dilatory would not. There is more than irony to this result. There is a strong possibility that it would distort the proper conception of the attorney's duty to the client and set us on a course at odds with what ought to be effective representation. * * *

Justice SCALIA, with whom The Chief Justice joins, dissenting.

The Court today establishes an irrebuttable presumption that a criminal suspect, after invoking his *Miranda* right to counsel, can *never* validly waive that right during any police-initiated encounter, even after the suspect has been provided multiple *Miranda* warnings and has actually consulted his attorney. This holding builds on foundations already established in *Edwards,* but "the rule of *Edwards* is our rule, not a constitutional command; and it is our obligation to justify its expansion." *Arizona v. Roberson* (Kennedy, J., dissenting). Because I see no justification for applying the *Edwards* irrebuttable presumption when a criminal suspect has actually consulted with his attorney, I respectfully dissent.

[According to the Court, that] Minnick's original request to see an attorney had been honored, that Minnick had consulted with his attorney on several occasions, and that the attorney had specifically warned Minnick not to speak to the authorities, are irrelevant. That Minnick was familiar with the criminal justice system in general or *Miranda* warnings in particular (he had previously been convicted of robbery in Mississippi and assault with a deadly weapon in California) is also beside the point. The confession must be suppressed, not because it was "compelled," nor even because it was obtained from an individual who could realistically be assumed to be unaware of his rights, but simply because this Court sees fit to prescribe as a "systemic assuranc[e]" that a person in custody who has once asked for counsel cannot thereafter be approached by the police unless counsel is present. Of course the Constitution's proscription of compelled testimony does not remotely authorize this incursion upon state practices; and even our recent precedents are not a valid excuse. * * *

Notwithstanding our acknowledgment that *Miranda* rights are "not themselves rights protected by the Constitution [but] measures to insure that the right against compulsory self-incrimination [is] protected," *Michigan v. Tucker,* we have adhered to the principle that nothing less than the *Johnson v. Zerbst* standard for the waiver of constitutional rights [see pp. 483–84] applies to the waiver of *Miranda* rights. Until *Edwards,* however, we refrained from imposing on the States a *higher* standard for the waiver of *Miranda* rights. For example, in *Michigan v. Mosley,* we rejected a proposed irrebuttable presumption that a criminal suspect, after invoking the *Miranda* right to remain silent, could not validly waive the right during any subsequent questioning by the police. * * *

Edwards, however, broke with this approach * * *. The case stands as a solitary exception to our waiver jurisprudence. [In] the narrow context in which it applies, it provides 100% assurance against confessions that are "the result of coercive pressures"; it " 'prevent[s] police from badgering a defendant' "; it "conserves judicial resources which would otherwise be expended in making difficult determinations of voluntariness"; and it provides " ' "clear and unequivocal" guidelines to the law enforcement profession.' " But so would a rule that simply excludes all confessions by all persons in police custody. The value of any prophylactic rule (assuming the authority to adopt a prophylactic rule) must be assessed not only on the basis of what is gained, but also on the basis of what is lost. In all other contexts we have thought the above-described consequences of abandoning *Zerbst* outweighed by " 'the need for police questioning as a tool for effective enforcement of criminal laws,' " *Moran v. Burbine* [p. 571].

[In] this case, of course, we have not been called upon to reconsider *Edwards,* but simply to determine whether its irrebuttable presumption should continue after a suspect has actually consulted with his attorney. Whatever justifications might support *Edwards* are even less convincing in this context.

Most of the Court's discussion of *Edwards*—which stresses repeatedly, in various formulations, the case's emphasis upon "the 'right to have counsel *present* during custodial interrogation' "(emphasis added by the Court)—is beside the point. The existence and the importance of the *Miranda*-created right "to have counsel *present*" are unquestioned here. What *is* questioned is why a State should not be given the opportunity to prove (under *Zerbst*) that the right was *voluntarily waived* by a suspect who, after having been read his *Miranda* rights twice and having consulted with counsel at least twice, chose to speak to a police officer (and to admit his involvement in two murders) without counsel present.

[The *Edwards* rule] should not, in my view, extend beyond the circumstances present in *Edwards* itself—where the suspect in custody asked to consult an attorney, and was interrogated before that attorney had ever been provided. In those circumstances, the *Edwards* rule rests upon an assumption similar to that of *Miranda* itself: that when a suspect in police custody is first questioned he is likely to be ignorant of his rights and to feel isolated in a hostile environment. This likelihood is thought to justify special protection against unknowing or coerced waiver of rights. After a suspect has seen his request for an attorney honored, however, and has actually spoken with that attorney, the probabilities change. The suspect then knows that he has an advocate on his side, and that the police will permit him to consult that advocate. He almost certainly also has a heightened awareness (above what the *Miranda* warning itself will provide) of his right to remain silent—since at the earliest opportunity "any lawyer worth his salt will tell the suspect in no uncertain terms to make no statement to the police under any circumstances." * * *

One should not underestimate the extent to which the Court's expansion of *Edwards* constricts law enforcement. Today's ruling, that the invocation of a right to counsel permanently prevents a police-initiated waiver, makes it largely impossible for the police to urge a prisoner who has initially declined to confess to change his mind—or indeed, even to ask whether he has changed his mind. Many persons in custody will invoke the *Miranda* right to counsel during the first interrogation, so that the permanent prohibition will attach at once. Those who do not do so will almost certainly request or obtain counsel at arraignment. We have held that a general request for counsel, after the Sixth Amendment right has attached, also triggers the *Edwards* prohibition of police-solicited confessions, see *Michigan v. Jackson* [p. 565], and I presume that the perpetuality of prohibition announced in today's opinion applies in that context as well. "Perpetuality" is not too strong a term, since, although the Court rejects one logical moment at which the *Edwards* presumption might end, it suggests no alternative. In this case Minnick was reapproached by the police three days after he requested counsel, but the result would presumably be the same if it had been three months, or three years, or even three decades.[b] This perpetual irrebuttable presumption will apply, I might add, not merely to interrogations involving the original crime but to those involving other subjects as well. See *Roberson*.

* * * Clear and simple rules are desirable, but only in pursuance of authority that we possess. We are authorized by the Fifth Amendment to exclude confessions that are "compelled," which we have interpreted to include confessions that the police obtain from a suspect in custody without a knowing and voluntary waiver of his right to remain silent. Undoubtedly some bright-line rules can be

---

b. See *United States v. Green*, Note (c), following this case.

adopted to implement that principle, marking out the situations in which knowledge or voluntariness cannot possibly be established—for example, a rule excluding confessions obtained after five hours of continuous interrogation. But a rule excluding all confessions that follow upon even the slightest police inquiry cannot conceivably be justified on this basis. It does not rest upon a reasonable prediction that all such confessions, or even most such confessions, will be unaccompanied by a knowing and voluntary waiver.

It can be argued that the same is true of the category of confessions excluded by the *Edwards* rule itself. I think that is so, but, as I have discussed above, the presumption of involuntariness is at least more plausible for that category. There is, in any event, a clear and rational line between that category and the present one, and I see nothing to be said for expanding upon a past mistake. Drawing a distinction between police-initiated inquiry before consultation with counsel and police-initiated inquiry after consultation with counsel is assuredly more reasonable than other distinctions *Edwards* has already led us into—such as the distinction between police-initiated inquiry after assertion of the *Miranda* right to remain silent, and police-initiated inquiry after assertion of the *Miranda* right to counsel, see Kamisar, The *Edwards* and *Bradshaw* Cases: The Court Giveth and the Court Taketh Away, in 5 The Supreme Court: Trends and Developments 157 (J. Choper, Y. Kamisar, & L. Tribe eds. 1984) ("[E]ither *Mosley* was wrongly decided or *Edwards* was"); or the distinction between what is needed to prove waiver of the *Miranda* right to have counsel present and what is needed to prove waiver of rights found in the Constitution.

[As] for the "irony" that "the suspect whose counsel is prompt would lose the protection of *Edwards,* while the one whose counsel is dilatory would not": There seems to me no irony in applying a special protection only when it is needed. The *Edwards* rule is premised on an (already tenuous) assumption about the suspect's psychological state, and when the event of consultation renders that assumption invalid the rule should no longer apply. One searching for ironies in the state of our law should consider, first, the irony created by *Edwards* itself: The suspect in custody who says categorically "I do not wish to discuss this matter" can be asked to change his mind; but if he should say, more tentatively, "I do not think I should discuss this matter without my attorney present" he can no longer be approached. To that there is added, by today's decision, the irony that it will be far harder for the state to establish a knowing and voluntary waiver of Fifth Amendment rights by a prisoner who has already consulted with counsel than by a newly arrested suspect. * * *

Today's extension of the *Edwards* prohibition is the latest stage of prophylaxis built upon prophylaxis, producing a veritable fairyland castle of imagined constitutional restriction upon law enforcement. This newest tower, according to the Court, is needed to avoid "inconsisten[cy] with [the] purpose" of *Edwards'* prophylactic rule, which was needed to protect *Miranda*'s prophylactic right to have counsel present, which was needed to protect the right against *compelled self-incrimination* found (at last!) in the Constitution.

[Both *Edwards* and today's decision] are explicable, in my view, only as an effort to protect suspects against what is regarded as their own folly. The sharp-witted criminal would know better than to confess; why should the dull-witted suffer for his lack of mental endowment? Providing him an attorney at every stage where he might be induced or persuaded (though not coerced) to incriminate himself will even the odds. Apart from the fact that this protective enterprise is beyond our authority under the Fifth Amendment or any other provision of the

Constitution, it is unwise. [That] some clever criminals may employ those protections to their advantage is poor reason to allow criminals who have not done so to escape justice.

Thus, even if I were to concede that an honest confession is a foolish mistake, I would welcome rather than reject it; a rule that foolish mistakes do not count would leave most offenders not only unconvicted but undetected. More fundamentally, however, it is wrong, and subtly corrosive of our criminal justice system, to regard an honest confession as a "mistake." [Not] only for society, but for the wrongdoer himself, "admissio[n] of guilt [if] not coerced, [is] inherently desirable," because it advances the goals of both "justice *and* rehabilitation." *Michigan v. Tucker* (emphasis added). A confession is rightly regarded by the sentencing guidelines as warranting a reduction of sentence, because it "demonstrates a recognition and affirmative acceptance of personal responsibility [for] criminal conduct," U.S. Sentencing Commission, Guidelines Manual '3E1.1 (1988), which is the beginning of reform. [We should] rejoice at an honest confession, rather than pity the "poor fool" who has made it; and we should regret the attempted retraction of that good act, rather than seek to facilitate and encourage it. To design our laws on premises contrary to these is to abandon belief in either personal responsibility or the moral claim of just government to obedience. Cf. Caplan, Questioning *Miranda*, 38 Vand.L.Rev. 1417, 1471–1473 (1985). * * *

Notes and Questions

(a) *Do the opinions in Minnick reflect the attitudes of the majority opinion and the Harlan and White dissenting opinions in Miranda?* Consider Note, 82 J.Crim.L. & C. 878, 893–94 (1992): "The [*Minnick*] majority recognized that police have a duty to try to make suspects talk. [The majority,] therefore, views the realities of interrogation beyond the stationhouse door with due skepticism. [In] contrast, Justice Scalia based his dissent [on] an underlying belief that police conduct during custodial [interrogation] is not as harsh and abusive as the Court contended. [He] also apparently believed that feelings of guilt motivate confessions more than custodial interrogation by the police. The opinions in *Minnick* thus reflect the attitudes of the majority and [dissenting opinions] in *Miranda* in the way the Justices differ on the realities of custodial interrogation."

(b) *The need to prevent the police from "badgering" a suspect who has previously asserted his rights.* The *Minnick* majority reiterates that the *Edwards* rule is "designed to prevent police from badgering a defendant into waiving his previously asserted" *right to counsel* and to "ensure that any statement made in subsequent interrogation is not the result of coercive pressures." But why isn't there a comparable need for a rule designed to prevent the police from badgering or pressuring a suspect into waiving his previously asserted *right to remain silent?*

16. When does the "question-proof status" of a person who has asserted his right to counsel come to an end? Does a sentenced prisoner who has settled into the routine of his new life in the prison population need the extra protection of *Edwards*? Consider UNITED STATES v. GREEN, 592 A.2d 985 (D.C.App.1991), *cert. granted*, 504 U.S. 908 *vacated and cert. dismissed*, 507 U.S. 545 (1993). When arrested on a drug charge on July 18, 1989, defendant refused to answer any questions without having a lawyer present. The next day an attorney was appointed to represent him. Defendant remained incarcerated. On September 27, he pled guilty to a lesser included offense. He was then moved to a juvenile facility while a presentence report was being prepared (On Feb. 26, 1990, he was sentenced on the drug charge.) On January 4, 1990, the police obtained an arrest warrant charging defendant with an unrelated murder that had occurred six months before he had been arrested on the drug charge. The next day, January 5th, defendant was taken to the homicide division. After being advised of his rights he agreed to talk to a detective about the murder and admitted his involvement in that crime. He was then indicted for first degree murder.

Defendant contended that his confession to the murder had been obtained in violation of *Edwards* in view of his original refusal at the time of his arrest on the drug charge to answer questions without counsel being present—an event that occurred more than five months before he had been advised of his rights in connection with the murder and had agreed to talk about his involvement in that crime. The trial judge initially denied the motion to suppress. Three days after the court's initial ruling, however, the Supreme Court handed down *Minnick*. The trial judge then reversed his earlier ruling and suppressed the confession.

A 2–1 majority of the District of Columbia Court of Appeals, per FARRELL, J., affirmed. True, defendant had confessed to the murder more than three months after he had pled guilty in the drug case, the case in which he had requested, and obtained, counsel. But his plea in the drug case was "consistent with his election to communicate with the police only through counsel." Thus his guilty plea in the drug case "cannot be the pivotal break in events that *Edwards* demands before a waiver can be regarded as an initial election by the accused to deal with the authorities on his own." True, too, between the time the defendant asserted his right to counsel in the drug case and the time he agreed to talk about the unrelated murder, more than five months had elapsed. But assigning decisive weight to the passage of time between an invocation of the right to counsel and a subsequent confession would blur a rule that the Supreme Court had insisted should be kept "clear and unequivocal":

"If five months in custody without evidence of 'badgering' is held sufficient to dispel *Edwards'* presumption that any new waiver of rights is involuntary, then why not three months or three weeks? At what point in time—and in conjunction with what other circumstances—does it make doctrinal sense to treat the defendant's invocation of his right to counsel as countermanded without any initiating activity on his part. * * * Ultimately, given its emphasis on the need for a bright-line rule in this area, we think only the Supreme Court can explain whether the *Edwards* rule is time-tethered and whether a five-month interval, during which no efforts at custodial interrogation took place, is too long a period to justify a continuing irrebuttable presumption that any police-initiated waiver was invalid."

When defendant died in March of 1993, the Supreme Court vacated the order granting certiorari—but not before oral arguments had been heard in the case. See 52 Crim.L.Rep. 3096. The government maintained that "a dramatic change of circumstances that changes the position of the suspect * * * makes it unreasonable to continue application of *Edwards'* irrebuttable presumption of coercion." Thus, when the suspect pleads guilty to the charge which prompted him to assert his right to counsel or a substantial period of time has elapsed between his initial invocation of rights and the second interrogation or there has been "a break in the custody of the suspect," the police may approach the suspect, in counsel's absence, to ask questions about unrelated offenses. Do you agree?

Consider LAURIE MAGID, *Questioning the Question–Proof Inmate: Defining Miranda Custody for Incarcerated Suspects*, 58 Ohio State L.J. 883, 889, 892–93 (1997):

"The situation presented in *Green*, that of the long question-proof suspect [*i.e.*, an inmate unapproachable for any police questioning, even if fresh *Miranda* warnings are given] is likely to become even more common, given current trends in law enforcement. New York and other large cities have enacted specific policies requiring officers to arrest people for minor, quality of life crimes partly in the hope that the arrestee will turn out to be a suspect in some much more serious, unsolved crime. The efficacy of this much applauded policy will be greatly diminished if arrestees invoke the right to counsel when approached about the initial minor crime, fail to make bail, and are then deemed question-proof before the police even have a chance to learn what serious crime the arrestee is suspected of committing. * * *

"Miranda and its progeny do not support, much less compel, the finding that an inmate who once invoked the right to counsel and remains continuously incarcerated also remains forever question-proof. The balance sought in *Miranda* between individual rights and the needs of law enforcement is not met by conferring a question-proof status on some inmates that can last as long as their natural life. Examination of the Court's existing *Miranda* jurisprudence reveals that lower courts have taken an unnecessarily narrow view of the authority of law enforcement officials to approach and question incarcerated suspects who earlier invoked the right to counsel.

"Moreover, the cases that have equated continuous incarceration with continuous custody in order to bar the questioning of those inmates who happened to have invoked the right to counsel are squarely in conflict with a large and growing body of law decided in another context. This other body of cases concludes clearly and persuasively that inmates are not in custody for *Miranda* purposes during every moment of their incarceration. These numerous cases have arisen in the situation where an inmate who had never invoked his right to counsel, and thus could be properly approached for questioning, was questioned in prison without having been given the *Miranda* warnings. Many courts have admitted the resulting, unwarned statements by concluding that at the moment of questioning, the inmate was not in custody for *Miranda* purposes and, thus, was not entitled to the *Miranda* warnings. Courts have reached this conclusion [by] applying an 'additional restraint' test to determine custody [*i.e.*, by focusing on whether the inmate was subjected to some restraint in addition to those normally imposed on a prison inmate, such as being handcuffed or taken from his cell to an isolation wing].

"The traditional 'free to leave' test, used to determine custody in settings such as the police station house, is not particularly useful in a prison setting where none of the inmates are free to leave the facility. The cases relying on the additional restraint test to define custody stand for the important principle that a person can be incarcerated yet not be in custody for *Miranda* purposes. Thus, these cases provide ample support for the premise of this Article—that a continuously incarcerated inmate can experience a break in custody that will end the question-proof status he obtained upon his earlier invocation of the right to counsel. That break in custody will leave the inmate approachable for questioning about new crimes under investigation.

"In fact, a sentenced inmate experiences not just some brief 'break in custody' but is generally not in *Miranda* custody for most of the term of incarceration. An inmate who has been sentenced and has settled into the routine of prison life is not in *Miranda* custody, and will return to custody for *Miranda* purposes only when he is subjected to some additional restraint beyond those of his normal life as an inmate. Imposition of an additional restraint will return him to a custodial state and entitle him to be given the *Miranda* warnings before any interrogation. However, the question-proof status that bars officials from approaching a suspect for questioning will have ended, because the inmate will have experienced a long period of non-custodial incarceration before any additional restraint was imposed on him."

17. What constitutes "initiating" further communication with the police? The *Edwards* rule was deemed inapplicable in OREGON v. BRADSHAW, 462 U.S. 1039, 103 S.Ct. 2830, 77 L.Ed.2d 405 (1983). Bradshaw, suspected of causing the death of Reynolds, a minor, by drunken driving, was arrested for furnishing liquor to Reynolds. Bradshaw agreed to talk to an officer about the fatal crash, but when the officer suggested that Bradshaw had been behind the wheel of the truck when Reynolds died, Bradshaw denied his involvement and expressed a desire to talk to a lawyer. The officers immediately terminated the conversation.

A few minutes later, either while still at the police station or enroute to the jail, Bradshaw asked the officer: "Well, what is going to happen to me now?" In response, the officer said that Bradshaw didn't have to talk to him and, because he had requested a lawyer, he didn't want Bradshaw to talk to him unless he decided to do so as a matter of his "own free will." Bradshaw said he understood. General conversation followed, in the course of which there was a discussion about where Bradshaw was being taken and the crime(s) for which he would be charged. The officer reiterated his own theory of how Bradshaw had caused Reynolds' death and then suggested that Bradshaw take a lie detector test to "clean the matter up." Bradshaw agreed.[a]

a. Should Bradshaw have been advised of his rights and a valid waiver obtained at this point (not the next day, just before Bradshaw took the lie-detector test)? Does the critical moment occur when a suspect *agrees* to take a lie detector test (or agrees to submit to further interrogation) regardless of whether the test is given (or further interrogation takes place) then or later? Compare *Bradshaw* with *Wyrick v. Fields,* 459 U.S. 42, 103 S.Ct. 394, 74 L.Ed.2d 214 (1982) (per curiam), which arose as follows: After discussing the matter with his private counsel and with a military attorney, Fields, a soldier charged with rape, requested a polygraph examination. Prior to undergoing the examination, Fields signed a waiver-of-rights form. He was also told: "If you are now going to discuss the offense under investigation, which is rape, with or without a lawyer present, you have a right to stop answering questions at any time or speak to a lawyer before answering further, even if you sign a waiver certificate. Do you want a lawyer at this time?" Fields answered: "No."

At the conclusion of the polygraph examination, which took less than two hours, a CID agent told Fields that there had been some deceit and asked him if he could explain why his answers were bothering him. Fields then made some incriminating statements. On federal habeas corpus, the Eighth Circuit found that the State had failed to satisfy its burden of proving that Fields knowingly and intelligently waived his right to have counsel present at the *post*-test interrogation. The Supreme Court disagreed:

"The only plausible explanation for the [Eighth Circuit's] holding is that, encouraged by what it regarded as a *per se* rule established in *Edwards,* it fashioned another rule of its own: that, notwithstanding a voluntary, knowing, and intelligent waiver of the right to have counsel present at a polygraph examination, and notwithstanding clear evidence that the suspect understood that right and was aware of his power to stop questioning at any time or to speak to an attorney at any time, the police again must advise the suspect of his rights before questioning him at the same interrogation about the results of the polygraph. [This approach] certainly finds no support in *Edwards,* which emphasizes that the totality of the circumstances, including the fact that the suspect initiated the questioning, is controlling. Nor is the rule logical; the questions put to Fields after the examination would not have caused him to forget the rights of which he had been advised and which he had understood moments before. The rule is simply an unjustifiable restriction on reasonable police questioning."

Dissenting Justice Marshall underscored the distinction between "an agreement to submit to a polygraph examination" and "the initiation of an ordinary conversation with the authorities": "[A] polygraph examination is a discrete test. It has a readily identifiable beginning and end. An individual who submits to such an examination does not necessarily have any reason whatsoever to expect that he will be subjected to a post-examination interrogation." In any event, Justice Marshall did "not believe

The next day, just before he took the lie detector test, Bradshaw was given another set of *Miranda* warnings and he signed a written waiver of his rights. At the conclusion of the test, the polygraph examiner told Bradshaw that he had not been truthful in response to certain questions. Bradshaw then admitted that he had been driving the vehicle in which Reynolds was killed and that he had consumed a considerable amount of alcohol before passing out at the wheel.

The Supreme Court held that under the circumstances Bradshaw could not avail himself of the *Edwards* rule, but there was no opinion of the Court. Justice REHNQUIST, joined by Burger, C.J., and White and O'Connor, JJ., observed:

"There are some inquiries, such as a request for a drink of water or a request to use a telephone that are so routine that they cannot be fairly said to represent a desire on the part of an accused to open up a more generalized discussion relating directly or indirectly to the investigation. Such inquiries or statements, by either an accused or a police officer, relating to routine incidents of the custodial relationship, will not generally 'initiate' a conversation in the sense in which that word was used in *Edwards*.

"Although ambiguous, the respondent's question in this case as to what was going to happen to him evinced a willingness and a desire for a generalized discussion about the investigation; it was not merely a necessary inquiry arising out of the incidents of the custodial relationship. It could reasonably have been interpreted by the officer as relating generally to the investigation. That the police officer so understood it is apparent from the fact that he immediately reminded the accused that 'you do not have to talk to me,' and only after the accused told him that he 'understood' did they have a generalized conversation. On these facts we believe that there was not a violation of the *Edwards* rule.

"[The next inquiry, therefore] was 'whether a valid waiver of [Bradshaw's rights] had occurred, that is, whether the purported waiver was knowing and intelligent and found to be so under the totality of the circumstances, including the necessary fact that the accused, not the police, reopened the dialogue with the authorities.' *Edwards*.

"[The] state trial court [found that a valid waiver of defendant's rights did occur and] we have no reason to dispute these conclusions * * *."

Concurring Justice POWELL, whose vote was decisive, agreed that Bradshaw had knowingly and intelligently waived his right to counsel, but saw no need for a two-step analysis—whether the suspect "initiated" a conversation with the police, and if so, whether under the "totality of circumstances" a valid waiver of rights followed. According to Powell, J.: "Fragmenting the standard into a novel two-step analysis—if followed literally—often would frustrate justice as well as common sense. Courts should engage in more substantive inquiries than 'who said what first.' [The *Edwards* rule] cannot in my view fairly be reduced to this."

MARSHALL, J., joined by Brennan, Blackmun and Stevens, JJ., dissented, "agree[ing] with the plurality that, in order to constitute 'interrogation' under *Edwards*, an accused's inquiry must demonstrate a desire to discuss the subject matter of the criminal investigation," but expressing "baffle[ment] [at] the plurality's application of that standard to the facts of this case":

"The plurality asserts that respondent's question, 'What is going to happen to me now?', evinced both 'a willingness and a desire for a generalized discussion about the investigation.' If respondent's question had been posed by Jean-Paul

that this substantial constitutional question   should be disposed of summarily."

Sartre before a class of philosophy students, it might well have evinced a desire for a 'generalized' discussion. But under the circumstances of this case, it is plain that respondent's only 'desire' was to find out where the police were going to take him. As the Oregon Court of Appeals stated, respondent's query came only minutes after his invocation of the right to counsel and was simply 'a normal reaction to being taken from the police station and placed in a police car, obviously for transport to some destination.'

"[To] hold that respondent's question in this case opened a dialogue with the authorities flies in the face of the basic purpose of the *Miranda* safeguards. When someone in custody asks, 'What is going to happen to me now?', he is surely responding to his custodial surroundings. The very essence of custody is the loss of control over one's freedom of movement. [To] allow the authorities to recommence an interrogation based on such a question is to permit them to capitalize on the custodial setting. Yet *Miranda's* procedural protections were adopted precisely in order 'to dispel the compulsion inherent in custodial surroundings.' "

Notes and Questions

(i) *Is the Edwards–Bradshaw test for "initiating" further communication with the police a satisfactory one?* Consider James Tomkovicz, *Standards for Invocation and Waiver of Counsel in Confession Contexts*, 74 Iowa L.Rev. 975, 1033–34 (1986), maintaining that the *Edwards-Bradshaw* test, "which at most demands evidence of a generalized desire or willingness to discuss the investigation" is too broad and too spongy because "it allows officers to recommence interrogation in many situations in which suspects may not have changed their minds [about desiring counsel]." According to Professor Tomkovicz, a definition of suspect initiation of further communication with the police "must describe conduct by the individual that revokes the earlier claim [of counsel] and conveys the message that the added support of counsel is not desired."

(ii) *The suspect's counterpart to "administrative questioning."* Should a "natural response" to arrest or transportation to a jail or police station be viewed as the suspect's counterpart to "administrative questioning"? Consider the remarks of Professor Kamisar in Choper, Kamisar & Tribe, *The Supreme Court: Trends and Developments 1982–83* (1984) at 165–66:

"When the [*Innis* Court defined 'police interrogation'] it *excluded* police words or actions 'normally attendant to arrest and custody' and properly so. Such statements, often called 'administrative questioning,' e.g., the routine questions asked of all persons 'booked' or otherwise processed, do not enhance the pressures and anxiety generated by arrest and detention. Thus, any incriminating statements in response to administrative questioning is, and should be, viewed as a 'volunteered' statement.

"The suspect's counterpart to 'administrative questioning' [is] an expression of fear, anxiety or confusion *normally attendant* to arrest, removal from the scene of arrest, or transportation to the stationhouse or jail. These expressions, such as, Where am I being taken? When can I call my lawyer? and, yes, What's going to happen to me? should not count as "initiation of dialogue" for *Edwards* purposes.

"Of course, if the officer *answers* one of the arrestee's questions about what's going to happen to him by *telling him* where he is being taken [or] when he will be able to meet with an attorney that should not count either. But when the officer's response to the suspect's expression of concern or confusion clearly goes beyond the scope of the suspect's question—when the officer exploits the situation, as he did in [*Bradshaw*]—that *should* count as 'police interrogation.' [Under] such circumstances, the suspect did not 'invite' or 'initiate' conversation about the merits of the case—the officer 'initiated' a *new* conversation."

18. How direct, assertive and unambiguous must a suspect be in order to invoke the right to counsel? A year before the decision in *Davis v. United States*, set forth immediately below, Professor Janet Ainsworth pointed out that sociolinguistic research indicates that certain discrete segments of the population (women and a majority of minority racial and ethnic groups) are far more likely than other groups to avoid strong, assertive means of expression and to use indirect and hedged speech patterns that give the impression of uncertainty or equivocality. See Janet E. Ainsworth, *In a Different Register: The Pragmatics of Powerlessness in Police Interrogation*, 103 Yale L.J. 259 (1993). However, observed Ainsworth, in determining whether a suspect had effectively invoked his or her right to counsel, a majority of the lower courts assumed that "direct and assertive speech—a mode of expression more characteristic of men than women—is or should be, the norm." This assumption not only manifests a "kind of gender bias"; it "does not serve the interests of the many speech communities whose discourse patterns deviate from the implicit norms in standard, 'male register' English."

Moreover, since the custodial police interrogation setting involves an imbalance of power between the suspect and his or her interrogator(s), such a setting increases the likelihood that a suspect will adopt an indirect or hedged—and thus ambiguous—means of expression. Even within speech communities whose members do not ordinarily use indirect modes of expression, one who is situationally powerless, that is, aware of the dominant power of the person he or she is addressing (and it is hard to think of a better example than a custodial suspect confronting one or more police interrogators), may also adopt a hedging or otherwise deferential speech register. According to Professor Ainsworth, only a *per se* invocation standard, a rule requiring all police questioning to cease upon any request for or reference to counsel, however equivocal or ambiguous, would provide "both assertive and deferential suspects with equivalent protection" and furnish "the powerless [the] same constitutional protections as the powerful."

However, in DAVIS v. UNITED STATES, 512 U.S. 452, 114 S.Ct. 2350, 129 L.Ed.2d 362 (1994), Justice O'CONNOR, speaking for five members of the Court rejected the view that (a) the courts should not place a premium on suspects making direct, assertive unqualified invocations of the right to counsel and (b) all arguable references to counsel should be treated as valid invocations of the right. The *Davis* case arose as follows:

Davis, a member of the U.S. Navy, was suspected of murdering another sailor. When interviewed by agents of the Naval Investigative Service (NIS) at the NIS office, he initially waived his *Miranda* rights. About an hour and a half into the interview, he said: "Maybe I should talk to a lawyer." At this point, according to the uncontradicted testimony of one of the agents, "we made it very clear [that] we weren't going to pursue the matter unless we have it clarified is he asking for a lawyer or is he just making a comment about a lawyer" and Davis replied, "No, I'm not asking for a lawyer" and then said, "No, I don't want a lawyer."

After a short break, the agents then reminded Davis of his *Miranda* rights and the interview continued for another hour—until Davis said, "I think I want a lawyer before I say anything." At this point, questioning ceased. A military judge admitted Davis's statements and he was convicted of murder. The U.S. Court of Appeals affirmed the conviction—as did the U.S. Supreme Court:

"The applicability of the ' "rigid" prophylactic rule' of *Edwards* requires courts to 'determine whether the accused *actually invoked* his right to counsel.' *Smith v. Illinois*, 469 U.S. 91, 105 S.Ct. 490, 83 L.Ed.2d 488 (1984) (emphasis added). To avoid difficulties of proof and to provide guidance to officers conducting interrogations, this is an objective inquiry. Invocation of the *Miranda* right to counsel 'requires, at a minimum, some statement that can reasonably be construed to be an expression of a desire for the assistance of an attorney.' But if a suspect makes a reference to an attorney that is ambiguous or equivocal in that a reasonable officer in light of the circumstances would have understood only that the suspect *might* be invoking the right to counsel, our precedents do not require the cessation of questioning. * * *

"Rather, the suspect must unambiguously request counsel. As we have observed, 'a statement either is such an assertion of the right to counsel or it is not.' *Smith v. Illinois*. Although a suspect need not 'speak with the discrimination of an Oxford don' (Souter, J., concurring in judgment), he must articulate his desire to have counsel present sufficiently clearly that a reasonable police officer in the circumstances would understand the statement to be a request for an attorney. If the statement fails to meet the requisite level of clarity, *Edwards* does not require that the officers stop questioning the suspect. * * *

"We decline petitioner's invitation to extend *Edwards* and require law enforcement officers to cease questioning immediately upon the making of an ambiguous or equivocal reference to an attorney. [When] the officers conducting the questioning reasonably do not know whether or not the suspect wants a lawyer, a rule requiring the immediate cessation of questioning 'would transform the *Miranda* safeguards into wholly irrational obstacles to legitimate police investigative activity,' because it would needlessly prevent the police from questioning a suspect in the absence of counsel even if the suspect did not wish to have a lawyer present. Nothing in *Edwards* requires the provision of counsel to a suspect who consents to answer questions without the assistance of a lawyer. * * *

"We recognize that requiring a clear assertion of the right to counsel might disadvantage some suspects who—because of fear, intimidation, lack of linguistic skills, or a variety of other reasons—will not clearly articulate their right to counsel although they actually want to have a lawyer present. But the primary protection afforded suspects subject to custodial interrogation is the *Miranda* warnings themselves. [A] suspect who knowingly and voluntarily waives his right to counsel after having that right explained to him has indicated his willingness to deal with the police unassisted. Although *Edwards* provides an additional protection—if a suspect subsequently requests an attorney, questioning must cease—it is one that must be affirmatively invoked by the suspect.

"In considering how a suspect must invoke the right to counsel, we must consider the other side of the *Miranda* equation: the need for effective law enforcement. Although the courts ensure compliance with the *Miranda* requirements through the exclusionary rule, it is police officers who must actually decide whether or not they can question a suspect. The *Edwards* rule—questioning must cease if the suspect asks for a lawyer—provides a bright line that can be applied by officers in the real world of investigation and interrogation without unduly hampering the gathering of information. But if we were to require questioning to cease if a suspect makes a statement that *might* be a request for an attorney, this clarity and ease of application would be lost. Police officers would be forced to make difficult judgment calls about whether the suspect in fact wants a lawyer even though he hasn't said so, with the threat of suppression if they guess wrong. We therefore hold that, after a knowing and voluntary waiver of the *Miranda* rights, law enforcement officers may continue questioning until and unless the suspect clearly requests an attorney.

"[To] recapitulate: We held in *Miranda* that a suspect is entitled to the assistance of counsel during custodial interrogation even though the Constitution does not provide for such assistance. We held in *Edwards* that if the suspect invokes the right to counsel at any time, the police must immediately cease questioning him until an attorney is present. But we are unwilling to create a third layer of prophylaxis to prevent police questioning when the suspect *might* want a lawyer. Unless the suspect actually requests an attorney, questioning may continue."[a]

Justice SOUTER, joined by Blackmun, Stevens and Ginsburg, JJ., wrote a separate opinion. Although he concurred in the judgment affirming Davis's conviction, "resting partly on evidence of statements given after agents ascertained that he did not wish to deal with them through counsel," Justice Souter could not join the majority's "further conclusion that if the investigators here had been so inclined, they were at liberty to disregard Davis's reference to a lawyer entirely, in accordance with a general rule that interrogators have no legal obligation to discover what a custodial subject meant by an ambiguous statement that could reasonably be understood to express a desire to consult a lawyer":

"[While] the question we address today is an open one, its answer requires coherence with nearly three decades of case law addressing the relationship between police and criminal suspects in custodial interrogation. Throughout that period, two precepts have commanded broad assent: that the *Miranda* safeguards exist 'to assure that *the individual's right to choose* between speech and silence remains unfettered throughout the interrogation process,' and that the justification for *Miranda* rules, intended to operate in the real world, 'must be consistent [with] practical realities.' *Arizona v. Roberson* (Kennedy, J., dissenting). A rule barring government agents from further interrogation until they determine whether a suspect's ambiguous statement was meant as a request for counsel fulfills both ambitions. It assures that a suspect's choice whether or not to deal with police through counsel will be 'scrupulously honored' and it faces both the real-world reasons why misunderstandings arise between suspect and interrogator and the real-world limitations on the capacity of police and trial courts to apply fine distinctions and intricate rules.

"Tested against the same two principles, the approach the Court adopts does not fare so well. First, as the majority expressly acknowledges, criminal suspects who may (in *Miranda*'s words) be 'thrust into an unfamiliar atmosphere and run through menacing police interrogation procedures,' would seem an odd group to single out for the Court's demand of heightened linguistic care. A substantial percentage of them lack anything like a confident command of the English language, many are 'woefully ignorant,' and many more will be sufficiently intimidated by the interrogation process or overwhelmed by the uncertainty of

---

a. The Court noted that "the Government has not sought to rely in this case on § 3501 [and] we therefore decline the invitation of some *amici* to consider it. Although we will consider arguments raised only in an *amicus* brief, we are reluctant to do so when the issue is one of first impression involving the interpretation of a federal statute on which the Department of Justice expressly declines to take a position." Justice Scalia wrote a concurring opinion, quoted at p. 500, discussing the applicability of § 3501 to *Miranda* issues and concluding that the Court's continuing refusal to consider § 3501 was inconsistent with "the Third Branch's obligation to decide according to the law."

their predicament that the ability to speak assertively will abandon them.[4] Indeed, the awareness of just these realities has, in the past, dissuaded the Court from placing any burden of clarity upon individuals in custody, but has led it instead to require that requests for counsel be 'give[n] a broad, rather than a narrow, interpretation' and that courts 'indulge every reasonable presumption,' *Johnson v. Zerbst,* that a suspect has not waived his right to counsel under *Miranda.*

"[Nor] may the standard governing waivers as expressed in these statements be deflected away by drawing a distinction between initial waivers of *Miranda* rights and subsequent decisions to reinvoke them, on the theory that so long as the burden to demonstrate waiver rests on the government, it is only fair to make the suspect shoulder a burden of showing a clear subsequent assertion. *Miranda* itself discredited the legitimacy of any such distinction. The opinion described the object of the warning as being to assure 'a continuous opportunity to exercise [the right of silence].' '[C]ontinuous opportunity' suggests an unvarying one, governed by a common standard of effectiveness.

"[The] Court defends as tolerable the certainty that some poorly expressed requests for counsel will be disregarded on the ground that *Miranda* warnings suffice to alleviate the inherent coercion of the custodial interrogation. But, 'a once-stated warning, delivered by those who will conduct the interrogation cannot itself suffice' to 'assure that [the] right to choose between silence and speech remains unfettered throughout the interrogation process.' *Miranda.*

"[It] is easy, amidst the discussion of layers of protection, to lose sight of a real risk in the majority's approach, going close to the core of what the Court has held that the Fifth Amendment provides. [When] a suspect understands his (expressed) wishes to have been ignored (and by hypothesis, he has said something that an objective listener could 'reasonably,' although not necessarily, take to be a request), in contravention of the 'rights' just read to him by his interrogator, he may well see further objection as futile and confession (true or not) as the only way to end his interrogation.

"Nor is it enough to say [as the majority does] that a 'statement either is [an] assertion of the right to counsel or it is not' [quoting *Smith v. Illinois*]. In *Smith,* we neither denied the possibility that a reference to counsel could be ambiguous nor suggested that particular statements should be considered in isolation.

"[The] other justifications offered for the 'requisite level of clarity' rule are that, whatever its costs, it will further society's strong interest in 'effective law enforcement,' and maintain the 'ease of application' that has long been a concern of our *Miranda* jurisprudence. With respect to the first point, the margin of difference between the clarification approach advocated here and the one the Court adopts is defined by the class of cases in which a suspect, if asked, would make it plain that he meant to request counsel (at which point questioning would cease). While these lost confessions do extract a real price from society, it is one that *Miranda* itself determined should be borne.

"[As] for practical application, while every approach, including the majority's, will involve some 'difficult judgment calls,'[7] the rule argued for here would relieve

---

4. Social science confirms what common sense would suggest, that individuals who feel intimidated or powerless are more likely to speak in equivocal or nonstandard terms when no ambiguity or equivocation is meant. Suspects in police interrogation are strong candidates for these effects. Even while resort by the police to the 'third degree' has abated since *Miranda,* the basic forms of psychological pressure applied by police appear to have changed less. * * *

7. In the abstract, nothing may seem more clear than a "clear statement" rule, but in police stations and trial courts the question, the officer of any responsibility for guessing 'whether the suspect in fact wants a lawyer even though he hasn't said so.' To the contrary, it would assure that the 'judgment call' will be made by the party most competent to resolve the ambiguity, who our case law has always assumed should make it: the individual suspect. * * *

"Our cases are best respected by a rule that when a suspect under custodial interrogation makes an ambiguous statement that might reasonably be understood as expressing a wish that a lawyer be summoned (and questioning cease), interrogators' questions should be confined to verifying whether the individual meant to ask for a lawyer. While there is reason to expect that trial courts will apply today's ruling sensibly (without requiring criminal suspects to speak with the discrimination of an Oxford don) and that interrogators will continue to follow what the Court rightly calls 'good police practice' (compelled up to now by a substantial body of state and Circuit law), I believe that the case law under *Miranda* does not allow them to do otherwise."

Ascertaining the suspect's choice vs. influencing that choice. Sometimes a police officer will respond to a suspect's ambiguous reference to a lawyer *not* by asking questions designed to clarify the suspect's wishes, but by making statements designed to *convey the message* that the suspect has no need for a lawyer or that obtaining a lawyer will not be in the suspect's best interest. See, e.g., *Mueller v. Commonwealth*, 422 S.E.2d 380 (Va.1992). Mueller waived his *Miranda* rights and agreed to talk to a detective. Two hours into the interrogation, Mueller asked the detective: "Do you think I need an attorney here?" The detective responded by shaking his head slightly, holding his arms out and his palms up in a shrug-like manner, and replying: "You're just talking to us." Several moments later, Mueller confessed to the crime (rape-murder) for which he was later sentenced to death.

The Supreme Court of Virginia held that (a) Mueller's question did not constitute the unambiguous request for counsel needed to invoke the *Edwards* rule and (b) the detective's response did not violate Mueller's *Miranda* rights. But in the brief it filed in the *Davis* case, the United States specifically disapproved of the *Mueller* ruling because the detective's response to Mueller's question conveyed the message that he did not really need a lawyer. Once a suspect has made an ambiguous reference to counsel, observed the United States, the officer's questions "must be objectively neutral and limited to ascertaining, not influencing, the choice that the suspect is entitled to make freely under *Miranda* and *Edwards*." See also *Collazo v. Estelle*, 940 F.2d 411 (9th Cir.1991) (en banc), where a 7–4 majority per Trott, J., emphasized that the police cannot attempt to discourage a suspect from speaking to a lawyer, cannot lead him to think that he can "reap some legal benefit" by excluding a defense lawyer from the process or suggest that somehow he will be "penalized" if he invokes his right to a lawyer.

"how clear is clear?" is not so readily answered. When a suspect says, "uh, yeah, I'd like to do that" after being told he has a right to a lawyer, has he "clearly asserted" his right? Compare *Smith v. Illinois (per curiam)* (statement was " 'neither indecisive nor ambiguous' ") with [Justice Rehnquist's dissent in that case]. * * * (questioning clarity). * * *

As a practical matter, of course, the primary arbiters of "clarity" will be the interrogators themselves, who tend as well to be courts' preferred source in determining the precise words a suspect used. And when an inculpatory statement has been obtained as a result of an unrecorded, incommunicado interrogation, these officers rarely lose "swearing matches" against criminal defendants at suppression hearings.

19.   *Application of Edwards rule to Sixth Amendment right to counsel.* In *Michigan v. Jackson,* 475 U.S. 625, 106 S.Ct. 1404, 89 L.Ed.2d 631 (1986), defendants had waived their rights and agreed to talk to the police without counsel before their "arraignments" (in the setting of the *Jackson* case, this proceeding is often called the "first appearance"). When brought before the magistrate, however, defendants requested that counsel be appointed for them because they were indigent. After the "arraignment" and before defendants had an opportunity to consult with counsel, the police again advised them of their rights, obtained written waivers, questioned them and obtained confessions. The Court, per Stevens, J., agreed with the state supreme court that "the *Edwards* rule 'applies by analogy to those situations where an accused requests counsel before the arraigning magistrate * * *.' [The] reasons for prohibiting the interrogation of an uncounseled prisoner who has asked for the help of a lawyer are even stronger after he has been formally charged with an offense than before." Thus, because the police initiated the questioning, the post-arraignment waivers of Sixth Amendment rights were invalid.

The Court rejected the argument that defendants' requests for appointed counsel may have encompassed only representation at trial and in other formal legal proceedings, not during further questioning by the police: "[The State] has the burden of establishing a valid waiver. Doubts must be resolved in favor of protecting the constitutional claim. This settled approach to questions of waiver requires us to give a broad, rather than a narrow, interpretation to a defendant's request for counsel—we presume that the defendant requests the lawyer's services at every critical stage of the prosecution."[a]

However, as demonstrated by *McNeil v. Wisconsin,* immediately below, because (unlike the *Miranda-Edwards–Roberson* rule) the Sixth Amendment right to counsel is "offense-specific," one who invokes her Sixth Amendment right at a formal legal proceeding has less protection than one who asserts her *Miranda-Edwards* right at a custodial interrogation.

In MCNEIL v. WISCONSIN, 501 U.S. 171, 111 S.Ct. 2204, 115 L.Ed.2d 158 (1991), a 6–3 majority held that a suspect's assertion of his Sixth Amendment right to counsel, by his appearance with counsel at a bail hearing concerning an offense with which he had been charged, does not serve as an invocation of the Fifth Amendment-based *Miranda-Edwards–Roberson* right to have counsel present during custodial interrogation. Thus, although assertion of the Sixth Amendment right protects a suspect from police-initiated questioning without counsel about the crime for which he has been charged, it does not prevent the police from initiating counselless interrogation about unrelated and uncharged crimes. The Sixth Amendment right is "offense specific" and the *Michigan v. Jackson* ban on counselless interrogation—unlike the *Edwards-Roberson* rule—is similarly limited.

The case arose as follows: After his arrest, pursuant to a warrant charging him with an armed robbery in West Allis (the West Allis crime), McNeil was represented by a public defender at a bail hearing. The commissioner set bail and scheduled a preliminary examination. Later that evening, a deputy sheriff, who

---

a. Dissenting Justice Rehnquist, joined by Powell and O'Connor, JJ., maintained that "the prophylactic rule set forth in *Edwards* makes no sense at all except when linked to the Fifth Amendment's prohibition against compelled self-incrimination." Chief Justice Burger concurred in the judgment, observing that although "stare decisis calls for my following the rule of *Edwards* in the context," "plainly the subject calls for reexamination." For forceful criticism of *Jackson,* see H. Richard Uviller, *Evidence from the Mind of the Criminal Suspect,* 87 Colum.L.Rev. 1137, 1190 (1987).

had been investigating a murder, attempted murder and burglary in Caledonia (the Caledonia crimes), visited McNeil in jail. McNeil waived his *Miranda* rights, but said he had not been involved in the Caledonia crimes. On two subsequent occasions (two days and four days later) the deputy sheriff returned with Caledonia detectives. On each occasion McNeil waived his rights and made incriminating statements. He was then formally charged with the Caledonia crimes. After his pretrial motion to suppress the incriminating statements was denied, McNeil was convicted, *inter alia*, of murder and attempted murder. The Court, per SCALIA, J., rejected his contention that his appearance at the bail hearing for the West Allis crime constituted an invocation of the *Miranda-Edwards–Roberson* right to counsel:

"The Sixth Amendment [right to counsel] is offense-specific. It cannot be invoked once for all future prosecutions, for it does not attach until a prosecution is commenced * * *. And just as the right is offense-specific, so also its *Michigan v. Jackson* effect of invalidating subsequent waivers in police-initiated interviews is offense-specific. * * * Because petitioner provided the statements at issue here before his Sixth Amendment right to counsel with respect to the *Caledonia* offenses had been (or even could have been) invoked, the right poses no bar to the admission of the statements in this case.

" * * * Petitioner seeks to prevail by combining the [*Miranda-Edwards* right to counsel and the Sixth Amendment right]. He contends that, although he expressly waived his *Miranda* right to counsel on every occasion he was interrogated, those waivers were the invalid product of impermissible approaches, because his prior invocation of the offense-specific right with regard to the West Allis burglary was also an invocation of the non-offense-specific *Miranda-Edwards* right. We think that is false as a matter of fact and inadvisable (even if permissible) as a contrary-to-fact presumption of policy.

"As to the former: The purpose of the Sixth Amendment counsel guarantee—and hence the purpose of invoking it—is to 'protec[t] the unaided layman at critical confrontations' with his 'expert adversary,' the government, *after* 'the adverse positions of government and defendant have solidified' with respect to a particular alleged crime. The purpose of the *Miranda-Edwards* guarantee, on the other hand—and hence the purpose of invoking it—is to protect a quite different interest: the suspect's 'desire to deal with the police only through counsel,' *Edwards*. [To] invoke the Sixth Amendment interest is, as a matter of *fact, not* to invoke the *Miranda-Edwards* interest. One might be quite willing to speak to the police without counsel present concerning many matters, but not the matter under prosecution. It can be said, perhaps, that it is *likely* that one who has asked for counsel's assistance in defending against a prosecution would want counsel present for all custodial interrogation, even interrogation unrelated to the charge. [But] even if [that] were true, the *likelihood* that a suspect would wish counsel to be present is not the test for applicability of *Edwards*. [That rule] requires, at a minimum, some statement that can reasonably be construed to be expression of a desire for the assistance of an attorney *in dealing with custodial interrogation by the police*. Requesting the assistance of an attorney at a bail hearing does not bear that construction. * * *

"There remains to be considered the possibility that, even though the assertion of the Sixth Amendment right to counsel does not *in fact* imply an assertion of the *Miranda* 'Fifth Amendment' right, we should declare it to be such as a matter of sound policy. Assuming we have such an expansive power under the Constitution, it would not wisely be exercised. Petitioner's proposed rule has only insignificant advantages. If a suspect does not wish to communicate with the police except through an attorney, he can simply tell them that when they give him the *Miranda* warnings. There is not the remotest chance that he will feel 'badgered' by their asking to talk to him without counsel present, since the subject will not be the charge on which he has already requested counsel's assistance (for in that event *Jackson* would preclude initiation of the interview) and he will not have rejected uncounseled interrogation on *any* subject before (for in that event *Edwards* would preclude initiation of the interview). The proposed rule would, however, seriously impede effective law enforcement. The Sixth Amendment right to counsel attaches at the first formal proceeding against an accused, and in most States, at least with respect to serious offenses, free counsel is made available at that time and ordinarily requested. Thus, if we were to adopt petitioner's rule, most persons in pretrial custody for serious offenses would be *unapproachable* by police officers suspecting them of involvement in other crimes, *even though they have never expressed any unwillingness to be questioned*. Since the ready ability to obtain uncoerced confessions is not an evil but an unmitigated good, society would be the loser. * * *[2]

"We like [guidelines for judicial review] to be 'clear and unequivocal,' but only when they guide sensibly, and in a direction we are authorized to go. Petitioner's proposal would in our view do much more harm than good, and is not contained within, or even in furtherance of, the Sixth Amendment's right to counsel or the Fifth Amendment's right against compelled self-incrimination. * * *"[3]

Dissenting Justice STEVENS, joined by Marshall and Blackmun, JJ., protested:

"The Court's opinion demeans the importance of the right to counsel. As a practical matter, the opinion probably will have only a slight impact on current

---

2. The dissent condemns these sentiments as "revealing a preference for an inquisitorial system of justice." We cannot imagine what this means. What makes a system adversarial rather than inquisitorial is not the presence of counsel, much less the presence of counsel where the defendant has not requested it; but rather, the presence of a judge who does not (as an inquisitor does) conduct the factual and legal investigation himself, but instead decides on the basis of facts and arguments pro and con adduced by the parties. In the inquisitorial criminal process of the civil law, the defendant ordinarily has counsel; and in the adversarial criminal process of the common law, he sometimes does not. Our system of justice is, and has always been, an inquisitorial one at the investigatory stage (even the grand jury is an inquisitorial body), and no other disposition is conceivable. Even if detectives were to bring impartial magistrates around with them to all interrogations, there would be no decision for the impartial magistrate to umpire. If all the dissent means by a "preference for an inquisitorial system" is a preference not to require the presence of counsel during an investigatory interview where the interviewee has not requested it—that is a strange way to put it, but we are guilty.

3. The dissent predicts that the result in this case will routinely be circumvented when,

"[i]n future preliminary hearings, competent counsel ... make sure that they, or their clients, make a statement on the record" invoking the *Miranda* right to counsel. We have in fact never held that a person can invoke his *Miranda* rights anticipatorily, in a context other than "custodial interrogation"—which a preliminary hearing will not always, or even usually, involve, cf. *Pennsylvania v. Muniz* (plurality opinion); *Rhode Island v. Innis*. If the *Miranda* right to counsel can be invoked at a preliminary hearing, it could be argued, there is no logical reason why it could not be invoked by a letter prior to arrest, or indeed even prior to identification as a suspect. Most rights must be asserted when the government seeks to take the action they protect against. The fact that we have allowed the *Miranda* right to counsel, once asserted, to be effective with respect to future custodial interrogation does not necessarily mean that we will allow it to be asserted initially outside the context of custodial interrogation, with similar future effect. Assuming, however, that an assertion at arraignment would be effective, and would be routinely made, the mere fact that adherence to the principle of our decisions will not have substantial consequences is no reason to abandon that principle. It would remain intolerable that a person in custody who had expressed *no* objection to being questioned would be unapproachable.

custodial interrogation procedures. As a theoretical matter, the Court's innovative development of an 'offense-specific' limitation on the scope of the attorney-client relationship can only generate confusion in the law and undermine the protections that undergird our adversarial system of justice. As a symbolic matter, today's decision is ominous because it reflects a preference for an inquisitorial system that regards the defense lawyer as an impediment rather than a servant to the cause of justice.

"The predicate for the Court's entire analysis is the failure of the defendant at the preliminary hearing to make a 'statement that can reasonably be construed to be expression of a desire for the assistance of an attorney *in dealing with custodial interrogation by the police.*' If petitioner in this case had made such a statement indicating that he was invoking his Fifth Amendment right to counsel as well as his Sixth Amendment right to counsel, the entire offense-specific house of cards that the Court has erected today would collapse, pursuant to our holding in *Roberson,* that a defendant who invokes the right to counsel for interrogation on one offense may not be reapproached regarding any offense unless counsel is present.

"In future preliminary hearings, competent counsel can be expected to make sure that they, or their clients, make a statement on the record that will obviate the consequences of today's holding. That is why I think this decision will have little, if any, practical effect on police practices.

"[In] the final analysis, the Court's decision is explained by its fear that making counsel available to persons held in custody would 'seriously impede effective law enforcement.' [The Court's] fears are exaggerated because, as I have explained, today's holding will probably affect very few cases in the future. The fears are misguided because a contrary rule would not make all pretrial detainees 'unapproachable'; it would merely serve to ensure that a suspect's statements during custodial interrogation are truly voluntary.

"A contrary rule would also comport with respect to tradition. Undergirding our entire line of cases requiring the police to follow fair procedures when they interrogate presumptively innocent citizens suspected of criminal wrongdoing is the longstanding recognition that an adversarial system of justice can function effectively only when the adversaries communicate with one another through counsel and when laypersons are protected from overreaching by more experienced and skilled professionals. Whenever the Court ignores the importance of fair procedure in this context and describes the societal interest in obtaining 'uncoerced confessions' from pretrial detainees as an 'unmitigated good,' the Court is revealing a preference for an inquisitorial system of justice. * * *

"The Court's refusal to acknowledge any 'danger of "subtle compulsion" '[2] in a case of this kind evidences an inability to recognize the difference between an inquisitorial and an adversarial system of justice."

---

2. In his opinion dissenting for himself and two other members of the Wisconsin Supreme Court, Chief Justice Heffernan wrote:

"It is apparent that there is danger of 'subtle compulsion' when a defendant requests the assistance of an attorney at an initial appearance and is nevertheless subjected to further interrogation while custody continues. Whether a request for an attorney is made to a police officer or to a judge, whether in the jail or during an initial appearance, the dangers of the inherent pressure of custodial interrogation when not having an attorney present are the same. Just as the *Edwards* protection is not dependent upon the subject matter of the interrogation, neither is this protection dependent upon whether the request for assistance of counsel is made to a police officer while in custody or to a magistrate at an initial appearance before the defendant is interrogated."

Notes and Questions

(a) *Footnote 3.* At the outset of his opinion for the Court, Justice Scalia states that the question presented is whether "an accused's invocation of his Sixth Amendment right to counsel during a judicial proceeding constitutes an invocation of his *Miranda* right to counsel." But footnote 3 to Scalia's opinion suggests that (1) an accused *cannot* invoke her *Miranda-Edwards* right to counsel at a judicial proceeding *even if* she (or her lawyer) makes an unambiguous statement on the record invoking such a right and suggests further that (2) a person taken into police custody *cannot* "anticipatorily" assert her *Miranda-Edwards* right to counsel "in a context other than 'custodial *interrogation.*'"(Emphasis added.) Is this so? Should it be?

(b) *"Anticipatorily" invoking the Miranda–Edwards right to counsel.* Consider the following *alternative* hypothetical situations:

(1) A murder suspect is arrested in his apartment and told he is being taken to police headquarters where he will be questioned by the lieutenant in charge of the case. He tells the arresting officers: "Before I leave my apartment and go with you, I want to make one thing perfectly clear. When I get to the police station, I'm not talking to the lieutenant or anybody else unless my lawyer is present."

(2) Same facts as above except that the suspect says nothing until he arrives at the police station and is ushered into the office of the lieutenant in charge of the case. At this point, the suspect tells the lieutenant: "Before you ask me anything, I want you to know that I am well aware that I have a right to a lawyer and I want one at my side before I answer any questions."

(3) Same facts as above except that when the suspect enters the lieutenant's office, the lieutenant tells him: "I'm in charge of this case. I want you to know that I am going to treat you fairly and squarely. As soon as you take off your coat and sit down in that chair next to my desk I am going to advise you fully of your rights." The suspect, who has said nothing to any officer up to this point, remains standing and replies: "Don't bother to read me my rights. I know my rights and I want a lawyer right now. I'm not going to answer a single question without a lawyer being present."

Assume further that in each of these alternative hypothetical situations the lieutenant proceeds to give the suspect the *Miranda* warnings and in each instance the suspect *agrees* to talk to the police about his involvement in the murder when he is advised of his rights. In which instance, if any, has the suspect effectively invoked his *Miranda-Edwards* right to counsel?

(c) *The position taken by the lower courts.* Relying heavily on footnote 3 to Justice Scalia's opinion in *McNeil,* most courts that have addressed the issue have balked at the notion that *Miranda-Edwards* protections can be triggered anticipatorily. However, they have left open the possibility that a suspect might be able to invoke the *Miranda-Edwards* right to counsel if custodial interrogation is about to begin or is "imminent." See *Alston v. Redman,* 34 F.3d 1237 (3d Cir.1994); *United States v. LaGrone,* 43 F.3d 332 (7th Cir.1994); *United States v. Wright,* 962 F.2d 953 (9th Cir.1992); *Sapp v. State,* 690 So.2d 581 (Fla.1997).[a]

---

a. But cf. *United States v. Goodson,* 18 M.J. 243 (Ct.Mil.App.1984), vac'd and remanded for further consideration in light of *Smith v. Illinois* (p. 561). Goodson was one of nine soldiers arrested for drug violations and taken to a military police station for interrogation by Mil-

itary Police Investigator Allinder. While waiting his turn to be interrogated (Allinder didn't get around to him until nine hours later), Goodson asked a sergeant whether he could contact a lawyer. But when his turn came to be questioned and he was advised of his rights by

20. *If a suspect has not requested a lawyer but, unbeknownst to him, somebody else has retained one for him, does the failure to inform the suspect that a lawyer is trying to see him vitiate the waiver of his Miranda rights? If the police mislead the attorney about whether her client will be questioned or otherwise deceive an inquiring attorney, should the confession be excluded?*

MORAN v. BURBINE
475 U.S. 412, 106 S.Ct. 1135, 89 L.Ed.2d 410 (1986).

Justice O'CONNOR delivered the opinion of the Court.

After being informed of his rights pursuant to *Miranda* and after executing a series of written waivers, respondent confessed to the murder of a young woman. At no point during the course of the interrogation, which occurred prior to arraignment, did he request an attorney. While he was in police custody, his sister attempted to retain a lawyer to represent him. The attorney telephoned the police station and received assurances that respondent would not be questioned further until the next day. In fact, the interrogation session that yielded the inculpatory statements began later that evening. The question presented is whether either the conduct of the police or respondent's ignorance of the attorney's efforts to reach him taints the validity of the waivers and therefore requires exclusion of the confessions.

On the morning of March 3, 1977, Mary Jo Hickey was found unconscious in a factory parking lot in Providence, Rhode Island. Suffering from injuries to her skull apparently inflicted by a metal pipe found at the scene, she was rushed to a nearby hospital. Three weeks later she died from her wounds.

Several months after her death, the Cranston, Rhode Island police arrested respondent and two others in connection with a local burglary. Shortly before the arrest, Detective Ferranti of the Cranston police force had learned from a confidential informant that the man responsible for Ms. Hickey's death lived at a certain address and went by the name of "Butch." Upon discovering that respondent lived at that address and was known by that name, Detective Ferranti informed respondent of his *Miranda* rights. When respondent refused to execute a written waiver, Detective Ferranti spoke separately with the two other suspects arrested on the breaking and entering charge and obtained statements further implicating respondent in Ms. Hickey's murder. At approximately 6:00 p.m., Detective Ferranti telephoned the police in Providence to convey the information he had uncovered. An hour later, three officers from that department arrived at

Allinder, Goodson signed a waiver-of-rights form. He then made an incriminating statement. Goodson never indicated to Allinder that he wanted, or had previously requested, counsel. And Allinder did not recall anyone telling him that Goodson had requested counsel.

In upholding the admissibility of Goodson's statement, a 2–1 majority, per Cook, J., distinguished *Edwards* on the ground that "Goodson made all of his requests for counsel *before* he was advised of his rights and while the case was still in the investigatory state. [T]he right to appointed counsel does not arise until in-custody interrogation has begun. The corollary is that a waiver of the *Miranda* rights cannot

occur unless there has been a full advisement of rights."

Dissenting Chief Judge Everett maintained that "even if a waiver of *Miranda* rights cannot proceed without full advisement of those rights," it does not follow "that a request for counsel which precedes this advice can be ignored, as was done here." Moreover, the Court's approach "is an invitation to hairsplitting." By vacating the judgment and remanding the case for further consideration in light of *Smith v. Illinois,* did the Supreme Court indicate support for dissenting Chief Judge Everett's views?

the Cranston headquarters for the purpose of questioning respondent about the murder.

That same evening, at about 7:45 p.m., respondent's sister telephoned the Public Defender's Office to obtain legal assistance for her brother. Her sole concern was the breaking and entering charge, as she was unaware that respondent was then under suspicion for murder. [She tried to contact the attorney who was to represent her brother on the breaking and entering charge, but when unable to do so, wound up talking to another Assistant Public Defender (Ms. Munson) about her brother's situation. At 8:15 p.m. Ms. Munson phoned the Cranston police station, asked that her call be transferred to the detective division, and stated that she would act as Burbine's counsel in the event the police intended to put him in a lineup or question him. An unidentified person told her that neither act would occur and that the police were "through" with Burbine "for the night." Ms. Munson was told neither that the Providence police were at the stationhouse nor that Burbine was a suspect in Mary's murder.]

At all relevant times, respondent was unaware of his sister's efforts to retain counsel and of the fact and contents of Ms. Munson's telephone conversation.

Less than an hour later, the police brought respondent to an interrogation room and conducted the first of a series of interviews concerning the murder. Prior to each session, respondent was informed of his *Miranda* rights, and on three separate occasions he signed a written form acknowledging that he understood his right to the presence of an attorney and explicitly indicating that he "[did] not want an attorney called or appointed for [him]" before he gave a statement. Uncontradicted evidence at the suppression hearing indicated that at least twice during the course of the evening, respondent was left in a room where he had access to a telephone, which he apparently declined to use. Eventually, respondent signed three written statements fully admitting to the murder.

Prior to trial, respondent moved to suppress the statements. The court denied the motion, finding that respondent had received the *Miranda* warnings and had "knowingly, intelligently, and voluntarily waived his privilege against self-incrimination [and] his right to counsel." [Even if Ms. Munson had phoned the police, held the court], the constitutional right to request the presence of an attorney belongs solely to the defendant and may not be asserted by his lawyer. Because the evidence was clear that respondent never asked for the services of an attorney, the telephone call had no relevance to the validity of the waiver or the admissibility of the statements.

The jury found respondent guilty of murder in the first degree, and [the Supreme Court of Rhode Island affirmed]. [The state supreme court] noted that because two different police departments were operating in the Cranston station house on the evening in question, the record supported the trial court's finding that there was no "conspiracy or collusion" to prevent Ms. Munson from seeing respondent. In any case, the court held, the right to the presence of counsel belongs solely to the accused and may not be asserted by "benign third parties, whether or not they happen to be attorneys." [On federal habeas corpus, the First Circuit, per Coffin, J.,] held that the police's conduct had fatally tainted respondent's "otherwise valid" waiver of his Fifth Amendment privilege against self incrimination and right to counsel. The court reasoned that by failing to inform respondent that an attorney had called and that she had been assured that no questioning would take place until the next day, the police had deprived respondent of information crucial to his ability to waive his rights knowingly and intelligently. * * *

We granted certiorari to decide whether a pre-arraignment confession preceded by an otherwise valid waiver must be suppressed either because the police misinformed an inquiring attorney about their plans concerning the suspect or because they failed to inform the suspect of the attorney's efforts to reach him.

We now reverse. * * *

Respondent does not dispute that the Providence police followed [the *Miranda* procedures] with precision [and] that he at no point requested the presence of a lawyer. He contends instead that the confessions must be suppressed because the police's failure to inform him of the attorney's telephone call deprived him of information essential to his ability to knowingly waive his Fifth Amendment rights. In the alternative, he suggests that to fully protect the Fifth Amendment values served by *Miranda,* we should extend that decision to condemn the conduct of the Providence police. We address each contention in turn.

Echoing the standard first articulated in *Johnson v. Zerbst, Miranda* holds that "[t]he defendant may waive effectuation" of the rights conveyed in the warnings "provided the waiver is made voluntarily, knowingly and intelligently." The inquiry has two distinct dimensions. First the relinquishment of the right must have been voluntary in the sense that it was the product of a free and deliberate choice rather than intimidation, coercion or deception. Second, the waiver must have been made with a full awareness both of the nature of the right being abandoned and the consequences of the decision to abandon it.

[Under] this standard, we have no doubt that respondent validly waived his right to remain silent and to the presence of counsel. [Nonetheless, on federal habeas corpus, the First Circuit] believed that the "[d]eliberate or reckless" conduct of the police, in particular their failure to inform respondent of the telephone call, fatally undermined the validity of the otherwise proper waiver. We find this conclusion untenable as a matter of both logic and precedent.

Events occurring outside of the presence of the suspect and entirely unknown to him surely can have no bearing on the capacity to comprehend and knowingly relinquish a constitutional right. Under the analysis of the Court of Appeals, the same defendant, armed with the same information and confronted with precisely the same police conduct, would have knowingly waived his *Miranda* rights had a lawyer not telephoned the police station to inquire about his status. Nothing in any of our waiver decisions or in our understanding of the essential components of a valid waiver requires so incongruous a result. No doubt the additional information would have been useful to respondent; perhaps even it might have affected his decision to confess. But we have never read the Constitution to require that the police supply a suspect with a flow of information to help him calibrate his self interest in deciding whether to speak or stand by his rights. Once it is determined that a suspect's decision not to rely on his rights was uncoerced, that he at all times knew he could stand mute and request a lawyer, and that he was aware of the state's intention to use his statements to secure a conviction, the analysis is complete and the waiver is valid as a matter of law.[1] The Court of Appeals' conclusion to the contrary was in error.

---

1. The dissent incorrectly reads our analysis of the components of a valid waiver to be inconsistent [with] *Edwards.* [But the] dissent never comes to grips with the crucial distinguishing feature of this case—that Burbine at no point requested the presence of counsel, as was his right under *Miranda* to do. [We reject] the dissent's entirely undefended suggestion that the Fifth Amendment "right to counsel" requires anything more than that the police inform the suspect of his right to representation and honor his request that the interrogation cease until his attorney is present.

Nor do we believe that the level of the police's culpability in failing to inform respondent of the telephone call has any bearing on the validity of the waiver. [W]hether intentional or inadvertent, the state of mind of the police is irrelevant to the question of the intelligence and voluntariness of respondent's election to abandon his rights. Although highly inappropriate, even deliberate deception of an attorney could not possibly affect a suspect's decision to waive his *Miranda* rights unless he were at least aware of the incident. Compare *Escobedo* (excluding confession where police incorrectly told the *suspect* that his lawyer " 'didn't want to see' him"). Nor was the failure to inform respondent of the telephone call the kind of "trick[ery]" that can vitiate the validity of a waiver. *Miranda.* Granting that the "deliberate or reckless" withholding of information is objectionable as a matter of ethics, such conduct is only relevant to the constitutional validity of a waiver if it deprives a defendant of knowledge essential to his ability to understand the nature of his rights and the consequences of abandoning them. Because respondent's voluntary decision to speak was made with full awareness and comprehension of all the information *Miranda* requires the police to convey, the waivers were valid.

* * * Regardless of any issue of waiver, [contends respondent], the Fifth Amendment requires the reversal of a conviction if the police are less than forthright in their dealings with an attorney or if they fail to tell a suspect of a lawyer's unilateral efforts to contact him. Because the proposed modification ignores the underlying purposes of the *Miranda* rules and because we think that the decision as written strikes the proper balance between society's legitimate law enforcement interests and the protection of the defendant's Fifth Amendment rights, we decline the invitation to further extend *Miranda*'s reach.

At the outset, while we share respondent's distaste for the deliberate misleading of an officer of the court, reading *Miranda* to forbid police deception of an *attorney* "would cut [the decision] completely loose from its own explicitly stated rationale."

[The] purpose of the *Miranda* warnings * * * is to dissipate the compulsion inherent in custodial interrogation and, in so doing, guard against abridgement of the suspect's Fifth Amendment rights. Clearly, a rule that focuses on how the police treat an attorney—conduct that has no relevance at all to the degree of compulsion experienced by the defendant during interrogation—would ignore both *Miranda*'s mission and its only source of legitimacy.

Nor are we prepared to adopt a rule requiring that the police inform a suspect of an attorney's efforts to reach him. While such a rule might add marginally to *Miranda*'s goal of dispelling the compulsion inherent in custodial interrogation, overriding practical considerations counsel against its adoption. As we have stressed on numerous occasions, "[o]ne of the principal advantages" of *Miranda* is the ease and clarity of its application. We have little doubt that the approach urged by respondent and endorsed by the Court of Appeals would have the inevitable consequence of muddying *Miranda*'s otherwise relatively clear waters. The legal questions it would spawn are legion: To what extent should the police be held accountable for knowing that the accused has counsel? Is it enough that someone in the station house knows, or must the interrogating officer himself know of counsel's efforts to contact the suspect? Do counsel's efforts to talk to the suspect concerning one criminal investigation trigger the obligation to inform the defendant before interrogation may proceed on a wholly separate matter? We are unwilling to modify *Miranda* in a manner that would so clearly undermine the decision's central "virtue of informing police and prosecutors with specificity

[what] they may do in conducting [a] custodial interrogation, and of informing courts under what circumstances statements obtained during such interrogation are not admissible." *Fare v. Michael C.*

Moreover, problems of clarity to one side, reading *Miranda* to require the police in each instance to inform a suspect of an attorney's efforts to reach him would work a substantial and, we think, inappropriate shift in the subtle balance struck in that decision. Custodial interrogations implicate two competing concerns. On the one hand, "the need for police questioning as a tool for effective enforcement of criminal laws" cannot be doubted. Admissions of guilt [are] essential to society's compelling interest in finding, convicting and punishing those who violate the law. On the other hand, the Court has recognized that the interrogation process is "inherently coercive" and that, as a consequence, there exists a substantial risk that the police will inadvertently traverse the fine line between legitimate efforts to elicit admissions and constitutionally impermissible compulsion. *Miranda* attempted to reconcile these opposing concerns by giving the *defendant* the power to exert some control over the course of the interrogation. Declining to adopt the more extreme position that the actual presence of a lawyer was necessary to dispel the coercion inherent in custodial interrogation, the Court found that the suspect's Fifth Amendment rights could be adequately protected by less intrusive means. Police questioning, often an essential part of the investigatory process, could continue in its traditional form, the Court held, but only if the suspect clearly understood that, at any time, he could bring the proceeding to a halt or, short of that, call in an attorney to give advice and monitor the conduct of his interrogators.

The position urged by respondent would upset this carefully drawn approach in a manner that is both unnecessary for the protection of the Fifth Amendment privilege and injurious to legitimate law enforcement. Because, as *Miranda* holds, full comprehension of the rights to remain silent and request an attorney are sufficient to dispel whatever coercion is inherent in the interrogation process, a rule requiring the police to inform the suspect of an attorney's efforts to contact him would contribute to the protection of the Fifth Amendment privilege only incidentally, if at all. This minimal benefit, however, would come at a substantial cost to society's legitimate and substantial interest in securing admissions of guilt. Indeed, the very premise of the Court of Appeals was not that awareness of Ms. Munson's phone call would have dissipated the coercion of the interrogation room, but that it might have convinced respondent not to speak at all. Because neither the letter nor purposes of *Miranda* require this additional handicap on otherwise permissible investigatory efforts, we are unwilling to expand the *Miranda* rules to require the police to keep the suspect abreast of the status of his legal representation. * * *

Respondent also contends that the Sixth Amendment requires exclusion of his three confessions. [The] difficulty for respondent is that the interrogation sessions that yielded the inculpatory statements took place *before* the initiation of "adversary judicial proceedings." He contends, however, that this circumstance is not fatal to his Sixth Amendment claim. [The] right to noninterference with an attorney's dealings with a criminal suspect, he asserts, arises the moment that the relationship is formed, or, at the very least, once the defendant is placed in custodial interrogation.

We are not persuaded. At the outset, subsequent decisions foreclose any reliance on *Escobedo* and *Miranda* for the proposition that the Sixth Amendment right, in any of its manifestations, applies prior to the initiation of adversary judicial proceedings. Although *Escobedo* was originally decided as a Sixth Amendment case, "the Court in retrospect perceived that the 'prime purpose' of *Escobedo* was not to vindicate the constitutional right to counsel as such, but, like *Miranda,* 'to guarantee full effectuation of the privilege against self-incrimination....'" *Kirby v. Illinois* [p. 655]. Clearly then, *Escobedo* provides no support for respondent's argument. Nor, of course, does *Miranda,* the holding of which rested exclusively on the Fifth Amendment.

[Precedent aside,]we find respondent's understanding of the Sixth Amendment both practically and theoretically unsound. As a practical matter, it makes little sense to say that the Sixth Amendment right to counsel attaches at different times depending on the fortuity of whether the suspect or his family happens to have retained counsel prior to interrogation. More importantly, the suggestion that the existence of an attorney-client relationship itself triggers the protections of the Sixth Amendment misconceives the underlying purposes of the right to counsel. The Sixth Amendment's intended function is not to wrap a protective cloak around the attorney-client relationship for its own sake any more than it is to protect a suspect from the consequences of his own candor. [By] its very terms, [the Sixth Amendment] becomes applicable only when the government's role shifts from investigation to accusation. * * *

Finally, respondent contends that the [police treatment of Assistant Public Defender Munson] was so offensive as to deprive him of the fundamental fairness guaranteed by [due process]. We do not question that on facts more egregious than those presented here police deception might rise to a level of a due process violation. Accordingly, Justice Stevens' apocalyptic suggestion that we have approved any and all forms of police misconduct is demonstrably incorrect.[4] We hold only that, on these facts, the challenged conduct falls short of the kind of misbehavior that so shocks the sensibilities of civilized society as to warrant a federal intrusion into the criminal processes of the States. * * *

Justice STEVENS, with whom Justice BRENNAN and Justice MARSHALL join, dissenting.

---

4. Among its other failings, the dissent declines to follow *Oregon v. Elstad* [p. 803], a decision that categorically forecloses Justice Stevens' major premise—that *Miranda* requires the police to inform a suspect of any and all information that would be useful to a decision whether to remain silent or speak with the police. The dissent also launches a novel "agency" theory of the Fifth Amendment under which any perceived deception of a lawyer is automatically treated as deception of his or her client. This argument entirely disregards the elemental and established proposition that the privilege against compulsory self-incrimination is, by hypothesis, a personal one that can only be invoked by the individual whose testimony is being compelled.

Most importantly, the dissent's misreading of *Miranda* itself is breathtaking in its scope. For example, it reads *Miranda* as creating an undifferentiated right to the presence of an attorney that is triggered automatically by the initiation of the interrogation itself. [The] dissent condemns us for embracing "incommuni-cado questioning [as] a societal goal of the highest order that justifies police deception of the shabbiest kind." We, of course, do nothing of the kind. As any reading of *Miranda* reveals, the decision, rather than proceeding from the premise that the rights and needs of the defendant are paramount to all others, embodies a carefully crafted balance designed to fully protect *both* the defendant's and society's interests. The dissent may not share our view that the Fifth Amendment rights of the defendant are amply protected by application of *Miranda as written*. But the dissent is "simply wrong" in suggesting that exclusion of Burbine's three confessions follows perfunctorily from *Miranda's* mandate. Y. Kamisar, *Police Interrogation and Confessions* 217–218, n. 94 (1980).

Quite understandably, the dissent is outraged by the very idea of police deception of a lawyer. Significantly less understandable is its willingness to misconstrue this Court's constitutional holdings in order to implement its subjective notions of sound policy.

[The] Court's holding focuses on the period after a suspect has been taken into custody and before he has been charged with an offense. The core of the Court's holding is that police interference with an attorney's access to her client during that period is not unconstitutional. The Court reasons that a State has a compelling interest, not simply in custodial interrogation, but in lawyer-free, incommunicado custodial interrogation. Such incommunicado interrogation is so important that a lawyer may be given false information that prevents her presence and representation; it is so important that police may refuse to inform a suspect of his attorney's communications and immediate availability.[8] [Until] today, incommunicado questioning has been viewed with the strictest scrutiny by this Court; today, incommunicado questioning is embraced as a societal goal of the highest order that justifies police deception of the shabbiest kind. * * * Police interference with communications between an attorney and his client is a recurrent problem. [The] near-consensus of state courts and the [ABA Standards of Criminal Justice] about this recurrent problem lends powerful support to the conclusion that police may not interfere with communications between an attorney and the client whom they are questioning. Indeed, at least two opinions from this Court seemed to express precisely that view.[20] The Court today flatly rejects that widely held view and [adopts] the most restrictive interpretation of the federal constitutional restraints on police deception, misinformation, and interference in attorney-client communications. * * *

Well-settled principles of law lead inexorably to the conclusion that the failure to inform Burbine of the call from his attorney makes the subsequent waiver of his constitutional rights invalid. Analysis should begin with an acknowledgment that the burden of proving the validity of a waiver of constitutional rights is always on the *government*. When such a waiver occurs in a custodial setting, that burden is an especially heavy one because custodial interrogation is inherently coercive, because disinterested witnesses are seldom available to describe what actually happened, and because history has taught us that the danger of overreaching during incommunicado interrogation is so real. * * *

Miranda established that a waiver is not valid in the absence of certain warnings. *Edwards* similarly established that a waiver is not valid if police initiate questioning after the defendant has invoked his right to counsel. In these circumstances, the waiver is invalid as a matter of law even if the evidence overwhelmingly establishes, as a matter of fact, that "a suspect's decision not to rely on his rights was uncoerced, that he at all times knew that he could stand mute and request a lawyer, and that he was aware of the state's intention to use his statement to secure a conviction." In light of our decision in *Edwards*, the Court is simply wrong in stating that "the analysis is complete and the waiver is

---

8. This kind of police-maintained incommunicado questioning becomes, in the Court's rendition, "an essential part of the investigatory process." Police interference in communications between a lawyer and her client are justified because "[a]dmissions of guilt [are] essential to society's compelling interest in finding, convicting, and punishing those who violate the law." It is this overriding interest in obtaining self-incriminatory statements in the lawyer-free privacy of the police interrogation room that motivates the Court's willingness to swallow its admitted "distaste for the deliberate misleading of an officer of the court."

20. See *Miranda* at n. 35 (in *Escobedo*, "[t]he police also prevented the attorney from consulting with his client. Independent of any other constitutional proscription, this action constitutes a violation of the Sixth Amendment right to the assistance of counsel and excludes any statement obtained in its wake"); *Escobedo* ("[I]t 'would be highly incongruous if our system of justice permitted the district attorney, the lawyer representing the State, to extract a confession from the accused while his own lawyer, seeking to speak with him, was kept from him by the police' ").

valid as a matter of law" when these facts have been established. Like the failure to give warnings and like police initiation of interrogation after a request for counsel, police deception of a suspect through omission of information regarding attorney communications greatly exacerbates the inherent problems of incommunicado interrogation and requires a clear principle to safeguard the presumption against the waiver of constitutional rights. As in those situations, the police deception should render a subsequent waiver invalid.

Indeed, as *Miranda* itself makes clear, proof that the required warnings have been given is a necessary, but by no means sufficient, condition for establishing a valid waiver. As the Court plainly stated in *Miranda,* "any evidence that the accused was threatened, tricked, or cajoled into a waiver will, of course, show that the defendant did not voluntarily waive his privilege. The requirement of warnings and waiver of rights is a fundamental with respect to the Fifth Amendment privilege and not simply a preliminary ritual to existing methods of interrogation."

[*Miranda*] clearly condemns threats or trickery that cause a suspect to make an unwise waiver of his rights even though he fully understands those rights. In my opinion there can be no constitutional distinction—as the Court appears to draw—between a deceptive misstatement and the concealment by the police of the critical fact that an attorney retained by the accused or his family has offered assistance, either by telephone or in person.

Thus, the Court's truncated analysis, which relies in part on a distinction between deception accomplished by means of an omission of a critically important fact and deception by means of a misleading statement, is simply untenable. If, as the Court asserts, "the analysis is at an end" as soon as the suspect is provided with enough information to have the *capacity* to understand and exercise his rights, I see no reason why the police should not be permitted to make the same kind of misstatements to the suspect that they are apparently allowed to make to his lawyer. *Miranda,* however, clearly establishes that both kinds of deception vitiate the suspect's waiver of his right to counsel. * * *[42]

[In] short, settled principles about construing waivers of constitutional rights and about the need for strict presumptions in custodial interrogations, as well as a plain reading of the *Miranda* opinion itself, overwhelmingly support the conclusion reached by almost every state court that has considered the matter—a suspect's waiver of his right to counsel is invalid if police refuse to inform the suspect of his counsel's communications.

The Court makes the alternative argument that requiring police to inform a suspect of his attorney's communications to and about him is not required because it would upset the careful "balance" of *Miranda.* Despite its earlier notion that the attorney's call is an "outside event" that has "no bearing" on a knowing and intelligent waiver, the majority does acknowledge that information of attorney Munson's call "would have been useful to respondent" and "might have affected his decision to confess." Thus, a rule requiring the police to inform a suspect of an attorney's call would have two predictable effects. It would serve *"Miranda '*s goal of dispelling the compulsion inherent in custodial interrogation" and it would

---

42. * * * The majority mischaracterizes this dissent by stating that its "major premise" is that *"Miranda* requires the police to inform a suspect of any and all information that would be useful to a decision whether to remain silent or speak with police." The majority's response ignores the fact that the police action here is not simply a failure to provide "useful" information; rather, it is affirmative police interference in a communication between an attorney and a suspect. Moreover, the "information" intercepted by the police bears directly on the right to counsel that police are asking the suspect to waive. * * *

disserve the goal of custodial interrogation because it would result in fewer confessions. By a process of balancing these two concerns, the Court finds the benefit to the individual outweighed by the "substantial cost to society's legitimate and substantial interest in securing admissions of guilt."

The Court's balancing approach is profoundly misguided. The cost of suppressing evidence of guilt will always make the value of a procedural safeguard appear "minimal," "marginal," or "incremental." Indeed, the value of any trial at all seems like a "procedural technicality" when balanced against the interest in administering prompt justice to a murderer or a rapist caught redhanded. The individual interest in procedural safeguards that minimize the risk of error is easily discounted when the fact of guilt appears certain beyond doubt.

What is the cost of requiring the police to inform a suspect of his attorney's call? It would decrease the likelihood that custodial interrogation will enable the police to obtain a confession. This is certainly a real cost, but it is the same cost that this Court has repeatedly found necessary to preserve the character of our free society and our rejection of an inquisitorial system. * * *

[At] the time attorney Munson made her call to the Cranston Police Station, she was acting as Burbine's attorney. Under ordinary principles of agency law the deliberate deception of Munson was tantamount to deliberate deception of her client.

[The] majority brushes aside the police deception involved in the misinformation of attorney Munson. It is irrelevant to the Fifth Amendment analysis, concludes the majority, because that right is personal; it is irrelevant to the Sixth Amendment analysis, continues the majority, because the Sixth Amendment does not apply until formal adversary proceedings have begun.

In my view, as a matter of law, the police deception of Munson was tantamount to deception of Burbine himself. It constituted a violation of Burbine's right to have an attorney present during the questioning that began shortly thereafter. The existence of that right is undisputed. Whether the source of that right is the Sixth Amendment, the Fifth Amendment, or a combination of the two is of no special importance, for I do not understand the Court to deny the existence of the right.

[The] possible reach of the Court's opinion is stunning. For the majority seems to suggest that police may deny counsel all access to a client who is being held. At least since *Escobedo*, it has been widely accepted that police may not simply deny attorneys access to their clients who are in custody. This view has survived the recasting of *Escobedo* from a Sixth Amendment to a Fifth Amendment case that the majority finds so critically important. That this prevailing view is shared *by the police* can be seen in the state court opinions detailing various forms of police deception of attorneys. For, if there were no obligation to give attorneys access, there would be no need to take elaborate steps to avoid access, such as shuttling the suspect to a different location, or taking the lawyer to different locations; police could simply refuse to allow the attorneys to see the suspects. But the law enforcement profession has apparently believed, quite rightly in my view, that denying lawyers access to their clients is impermissible. The Court today seems to assume that this view was error?that, from the federal constitutional perspective, the lawyer's access is, as a question from the Court put it in oral argument, merely "a matter of prosecutorial grace." Certainly, nothing in the Court's Fifth and Sixth Amendments analysis acknowledges that there is *any* federal constitutional bar to an absolute denial of lawyer access to a suspect who is in police custody.

[In] my judgment, police interference in the attorney-client relationship is the type of governmental misconduct on a matter of central importance to the administration of justice that the Due Process Clause prohibits. Just as the police cannot impliedly promise a suspect that his silence will not be used against him and then proceed to break that promise, so too police cannot tell a suspect's attorney that they will not question the suspect and then proceed to question him. Just as the government cannot conceal from a suspect material and exculpatory evidence, so too the government cannot conceal from a suspect the material fact of his attorney's communication.

[This] case turns on a proper appraisal of the role of the lawyer in our society. If a lawyer is seen as a nettlesome obstacle to the pursuit of wrongdoers—as in an inquisitorial society—then the Court's decision today makes a good deal of sense. If a lawyer is seen as an aid to the understanding and protection of constitutional rights?as in an accusatorial society?then today's decision makes no sense at all.
* * *

Notes and Questions

(a) *"Incommunicado questioning."* Consider Note, 100 Harv.L.Rev. 125, 126 (1986): *"Burbine* betrays the spirit of *Miranda* by placing a judicial seal of approval on official deception, thereby encouraging incommunicado interrogation and suggesting that police may deny counsel all access to a detained client." Do you agree? May the police tell a suspect no attorney has called, when in fact one has? If a suspect has not requested a lawyer, but someone else has retained a lawyer for him, how long may the police deny that lawyer access to the suspect? What exactly is meant by "incommunicado" or "incommunicado questioning" (terms used frequently by dissenting Justice Stevens)? These terms may mean either (1) preventing a prisoner from communicating with or meeting with counsel; or (2) not informing the outside world of the prisoner's whereabouts; or (3) denying a prisoner's friends, relatives or lawyers access to him. In which sense, if any, was Burbine held "incommunicado"?

(b) *The Miranda warnings and the need for a lawyer's advice.* Consider the Harvard Note, supra, at 133: "[T]o the extent that the population at large is unaware of its fifth and sixth amendment rights, the role of the lawyer—possibly the only one capable of safeguarding these rights—must be protected." Is *a suspect advised of his rights* (as opposed to "the population at large") unaware of his rights? If a lawyer is "the only one capable of safeguarding these rights," did the *Miranda* Court commit grievous error by not requiring that a suspect first consult with a lawyer or actually have a lawyer present in order for his waiver of rights to be effective?

(c) *The Burbine dissent's reliance on fn. 35 to Miranda.* In fn. 20 to his dissenting opinion, Justice Stevens maintains that the majority opinion cannot be reconciled with fn. 35 to *Miranda,* which, discussing *Escobedo,* states that "prevent[ing] [an] attorney from consulting with his client" violates the Sixth Amendment "independent of any other constitutional proscription." Should this statement be read in light of *Escobedo*'s particular facts? Consider Kamisar, Essays 217 n. 94 (1980):

"It is hard to believe that in the course of writing a 60–page opinion *based on the premise* that police-issued warnings can adequately protect a suspect's rights the [*Miranda*] Court would say in the next breath that such warnings are insufficient when, but only when, a suspect's lawyer is not allowed to consult with him—that even though a suspect has been emphatically and unequivocally advised of his rights and insists on talking, what he says is inadmissible [when] a lawyer *whose services he has not requested* has, *unbeknown to him,* entered the picture.

"Although the police did not advise Escobedo of any of his rights, 'he repeatedly asked to speak to his lawyer.' * * * Indeed, [the *Escobedo*] opinion begins: 'The critical issue in this case is whether [the] refusal by the police to honor petitioner's request to consult with his lawyer during the course of an interrogation constitutes a denial of "the Assistance of Counsel." ' [If the refusal of the police to let Escobedo's lawyer meet with him] has any relevance, it is only because Escobedo became *aware of the fact* that the police were preventing his lawyer from talking to him, and this realization may well have underscored the police domination of the situation and the gravity of his plight."

(d) *Does the Burbine case dramatize "the Court's changed vision of Miranda"?* According to William Stuntz, *Self-Incrimination and Excuse,* 88 Colum.L.Rev. 1227, 1268 n. 141 (1988) the *Burbine* case "offers a striking example of the Court's changed vision of *Miranda.* Justice Steven's dissent in that case argues forcefully that *Miranda* is designed to prevent police from obtaining confessions by taking advantage of suspects' ignorance or bad judgment, and thereby to ensure that waivers of the right to remain silent result only from rational, self-interested choices by suspects. [This] reasoning is quite consistent with the reasoning of [the *Miranda* majority opinion]. On the other hand, Justice O'Connor's majority opinion in *Burbine* argues that station house confessions are essential to the proper enforcement of the criminal law [and] that the Constitution in no way protects suspects against unwise decisions to confess. [This] line of argument tracks not Warren's *Miranda* majority, but rather Justice White's *Miranda* dissent. *Burbine* thus exemplifies a (perhaps *the*) central truth about modern *Miranda* doctrine: while the holding of *Miranda* remains intact, it has been shaped to serve very different ends than those its original authors had in mind." See also Joshua Dressler, *Understanding Criminal Procedure,* 418–19 (2d ed. 1997) (*Burbine* case demonstrates the considerable distance the Court has traveled since the days of *Escobedo* and *Miranda*).

(e) *Should Burbine dishearten or encourage Miranda's defenders?* Consider Kamisar, *The "Police Practice" Phases of the Criminal Process and the Three Phases of the Burger Court,* in The Burger Years (Herman Schwartz ed. 1987) at 143, 150: "[The *Burbine* Court's view of *Miranda* as not 'proceeding from the premise that the rights and needs of the defendant are paramount to all others, [but as a case that] embodies a carefully crafted balance designed to fully protect *both* the defendant's and society's interests'] [see fn. 4 to the Court's opinion] is the way *Miranda*'s defenders—not its critics—have talked about the case for the past twenty years. [The *Burbine* Court's view of *Miranda* as a serious effort to strike a proper 'balance,' between, or to 'reconcile,' competing interests may turn out to be more important than its specific ruling." See also Kamisar, *Remembering the "Old World" of Criminal Procedure: A Reply to Professor Grano,* 23 U.Mich.J.L.Ref. 537, 575–84 (1990).

(f) *What result if, before being taken away by the police, a suspect asks a relative to contact a lawyer?* Would the result in *Burbine* have been different if, before being taken to the police station (a) the defendant had asked his sister to contact the Public Defender's Office and get somebody in the office to represent him; (b) his sister had done so; (c) the assistant public defender who had agreed to represent defendant had told the police she wanted to meet with her client immediately; but (d) the police had failed to inform defendant of this development? Why (not)? Cf. *People v. Griggs,* 604 N.E.2d 257 (Ill. 1992).

(g) *Reaction of the state courts.* Can a person fully comprehend the nature of his right to counsel and the consequences of a decision to waive this right without being informed that a lawyer, who could explain the consequences of a waiver, has been retained to represent him and is immediately able to consult with him? Relying on independent state grounds, a number of state courts have answered in the negative, thereby rejecting the U.S. Supreme Court's reasoning in *Burbine*. See *State v. Stoddard*, 537 A.2d 446 (Conn.1988); *Haliburton v. State*, 514 So.2d 1088 (Fla.1987); *People v. McCauley*, 645 N.E.2d 923 (Ill. 1994); *People v. Bender*, 551 N.W.2d 71 (1996); *People v. McCauley*, 645 N.E.2d 923 (Ill.1994).

21. ***Use of a pretrial psychiatric examination at a capital sentencing proceeding.*** ESTELLE v. SMITH, 451 U.S. 454, 101 S.Ct. 1866, 68 L.Ed.2d 359 (1981), arose as follows: Respondent was indicted for murder. The state announced its intention to seek the death penalty. Thereafter, although defense counsel had not put into issue his client's competency to stand trial or his sanity at the time of the offense, a judge informally ordered the prosecution to arrange a psychiatric examination of respondent by Dr. Grigson to determine respondent's capacity to stand trial. But Dr. Grigson did not merely report to the court on the issue of competence to stand trial; after respondent was convicted of murder the doctor also testified—on the basis of his pretrial examination of respondent—as to respondent's "future dangerousness," one of the critical issues to be resolved by a jury at the capital sentencing proceeding.[a] The jury answered the "future dangerousness" question and other requisite questions in the affirmative and, thus, under Texas law, the death penalty for respondent was mandatory.

Dr. Grigson did not obtain permission from respondent's attorneys to examine him. Nor was respondent advised before the pretrial psychiatric examination that he had a right to remain silent or that any statement he made could be used against him at a sentencing proceeding. The state argued, however, that the privilege against self-incrimination was inapplicable because (a) Dr. Grigson's testimony was used only to determine punishment after conviction, not to establish guilt; and (b) respondent's communications to Dr. Grigson were "nontestimonial" in nature. Rejecting these contentions, the Court held, per BURGER, C.J., that both respondent's Fifth and Sixth Amendment rights were violated by the use of Dr. Grigson's testimony at the penalty phase of the case:

"In this case, the ultimate penalty of death was a potential consequence of what respondent told the examining psychiatrist. Just as the Fifth Amendment prevents a criminal defendant from being made 'the deluded instrument of his own conviction,' it protects him as well from being made the 'deluded instrument' of his own execution."

As for the argument that respondent's communications to the examining psychiatrist were "nontestimonial" in nature, "Dr. Grigson's prognosis as to future dangerousness rested on statements respondent made and remarks he omitted, in reciting the details of the crime. [Thus,] the State used as evidence against respondent the substance of his disclosures during the pretrial psychiatric examination."[b]

a. In Texas, if the defendant is found guilty of a capital offense, a separate proceeding is held to determine the punishment. If, at the penalty phase, the jury affirmatively answers three questions on which the state has the burden of proof beyond a reasonable doubt, the judge must impose the death sentence. One of the three critical questions is "whether there is a probability that the defendant would commit criminal acts of violence that would constitute a continuing threat to society."

b. Because respondent had been indicted and assigned counsel before Dr. Grigson examined him and the examination had taken place without notice to respondent's counsel, Stew-

22. *Use of psychiatric examinations in proceedings to commit indi-viduals found to be "sexually dangerous persons."* ALLEN v. ILLINOIS, 478 U.S. 364, 106 S.Ct. 2988, 92 L.Ed.2d 296 (1986), arose as follows: The state sought to commit Allen under the Illinois Sexually Dangerous Persons Act to declare Allen "sexually dangerous" under the Act. Pursuant to the Act, the trial court ordered Allen to submit to two psychiatric examinations. The trial court ruled that Allen's statements to the psychiatrists were not themselves admissible, but allowed each psychiatrist to give his opinion based on his interview work with Allen. Partly on the basis of the psychiatrists' testimony, the trial court found Allen to be a sexually dangerous person under the Act. Although (a) the state cannot file a sexually-dangerous-person petition unless it has already brought criminal charges against the person in question and (b) proceedings under the Act are accompanied by safeguards usually found in criminal trials (e.g., the right to counsel, the right to demand a jury trial, the requirement that the prosecution prove its case beyond a reasonable doubt), a 5–4 majority, per REHNQUIST, J., concluded that the proceedings were not "criminal" within the meaning of the Fifth Amendment privilege against compelled self-incrimination:

"[P]etitioner places great reliance on the fact that proceedings under the Act are accompanied by procedural safeguards usually found in criminal trials. [But the] State has indicated quite clearly its intent that these commitment proceed-ings be civil in nature; [providing] some of the safeguards applicable in criminal trials cannot itself turn these proceedings into criminal prosecutions requiring the full panoply of rights applicable there."

Dissenting Justice STEVENS, joined by Brennan, Marshall and Blackmun, JJ., protested: "In many respects, [this] proceeding is virtually identical to Illinois' proceeding for prosecution of sex-related crimes. When the criminal law casts so long a shadow on a putatively civil proceeding, I think it clear that the procedure must be deemed a 'criminal case' within the meaning of the Fifth Amendment. [The] sexually-dangerous-person proceeding [may] not escape a characterization as 'criminal' simply because a goal is 'treatment.' If this were not the case, moreover, nothing would prevent a State from creating an entire corpus of 'dangerous person' statutes to shadow its criminal code."

23. *Comparing and contrasting Miranda with (a) the prohibition against the use of involuntary or compelled statements and (b) the Fourth Amendment exclusionary rule.*

WITHROW v. WILLIAMS
507 U.S. 680, 113 S.Ct. 1745, 123 L.Ed.2d 407 (1993).

Justice SOUTER delivered the opinion of the Court.

In *Stone v. Powell* [p. 130], we held that when a State has given a full and fair chance to litigate a Fourth Amendment claim, federal habeas review is not available to a state prisoner alleging that his conviction rests on evidence obtained through an unconstitutional search or seizure. Today we hold [that *Stone*] does

art, J., joined by Powell, J., concurred in the judgment on *Massiah* grounds without reach-ing the *Miranda* issue. Although he dissented, in effect, on the *Miranda* issue, Rehnquist, J., also concurred in the result of *Massiah* grounds. Thus, the Court's judgment that re-spondent's Sixth Amendment right to counsel had been violated was unanimous.

See also *Powell v. Texas,* 492 U.S. 680, 109 S.Ct. 3146, 106 L.Ed.2d 551 (1989) (that defen-dant raised insanity defense "no basis for con-cluding" he waived Sixth Amendment right to counsel set out in *Estelle*).

not extend to a state prisoner's claim that his conviction rests on statements obtained in violation [of] *Miranda*.

[Although respondent Williams, a murder suspect, was not advised of his *Miranda* rights until the police had taken him into custody and questioned him for some 40 minutes, during which time he made incriminating statements, a Michigan court declined to suppress any of these statements. He was then convicted on two counts of murder. After these convictions were affirmed, Williams turned to the federal courts. A federal district court found that his *Miranda* rights had been violated. The court also concluded, although neither party had addressed the issue, that Williams' statements, after receiving the *Miranda* warnings, were involuntary and thus likewise subject to suppression.[a] The U.S. Court of Appeals for the Sixth Circuit affirmed], summarily rejecting the argument that [*Stone*] should apply to bar habeas review of Williams' *Miranda* claim. We granted certiorari to review the significant issue thus presented.[2]

We have made it clear that *Stone*'s limitations on federal habeas relief was not jurisdictional in nature, but rested on prudential concerns counseling against the application of the Fourth Amendment exclusionary rule on collateral review. * * * We simply concluded in *Stone* that the costs of applying the exclusionary rule on collateral review outweighed any potential advantage to be gained by applying it there. * * *

Over the years, we have repeatedly declined to extend the rule in *Stone* beyond its original bounds. In *Jackson v. Virginia* [Ch. 28, § 2], for example, we denied a request to apply *Stone* to bar habeas consideration of a Fourteenth Amendment due process claim of insufficient evidence to support a state conviction. We stressed that the issue was "central to the basic question of guilt or innocence," unlike a claim that a state court had received evidence in violation of the Fourth Amendment exclusionary rule, and we found that to review such a claim on habeas imposed no great burdens on the federal courts.

After a like analysis, in *Rose v. Mitchell* [Ch. 28, § 2], we decided against extending *Stone* to foreclose habeas review of an equal protection claim of racial discrimination in selecting a state grand-jury foreman. A charge that state adjudication had violated the direct command of the Fourteenth Amendment implicated the integrity of the judicial process, we reasoned, and failed to raise the "federalism concerns" that had driven the Court in *Stone*.

[In] a third instance, in *Kimmelman v. Morrison* [Ch. 28, § 2], we again declined to extend *Stone*, in that case to bar habeas review of certain claims of ineffective assistance of counsel under the Sixth Amendment. We explained that unlike the Fourth Amendment, which confers no "trial right," the Sixth confers a "fundamental right" on criminal defendants, one that "assures the fairness, and thus the legitimacy, of our adversary process." [In] this case, the argument for extending *Stone* again falls short.

[Petitioner] argues that *Miranda*'s safeguards are not constitutional in character, but merely "prophylactic," and that in consequence habeas review should not extend to a claim that a state conviction rests on statements obtained in the

a. The Court later noted, in a portion of the opinion that has been deleted, that the district court acted incorrectly in reaching this issue without giving the state an opportunity to address it.

2. Justice Scalia argues in effect that the rule in *Stone* should extend to all claims on federal habeas review. With respect, that reasoning goes beyond the question on which we granted certiorari [and] we see no good reason to address it in this case.

absence of those safeguards. We accept petitioner's premise for purposes of this case, but not her conclusion.

The *Miranda* Court did of course caution that the Constitution requires no "particular solution for the inherent compulsions of the interrogation process," and left it open to a State to meet its burden by adopting "other procedures [at] least as effective in apprising accused persons" of their rights. The Court indeed acknowledged that, in barring introduction of a statement obtained without the required warnings, *Miranda* might exclude a confession that we would not condemn as "involuntary in traditional terms," and for this reason we have sometimes called the *Miranda* safeguards "prophylactic" in nature. * * * Calling the *Miranda* safeguards "prophylactic," however, is a far cry from putting *Miranda* on all fours with *Mapp,* or from rendering *Miranda* subject to *Stone.*

As we explained in *Stone,* the *Mapp* rule "is not a personal constitutional right," but serves to deter future constitutional violations; although it mitigates the juridical consequences of invading the defendant's privacy, the exclusion of evidence at trial can do nothing to remedy the completed and wholly extrajudicial Fourth Amendment violation. Nor can the *Mapp* rule be thought to enhance the soundness of the criminal process by improving the reliability of evidence introduced at trial.

Miranda differs from *Mapp* in both respects. "Prophylactic" though it may be, in protecting a defendant's Fifth Amendment privilege against self-incrimination *Miranda* safeguards "a fundamental *trial* right." [The privilege] reflects "many of our fundamental values and most noble aspirations" [quoting *Murphy v. Waterfront Comm'n,* pp. 479, 716].

Nor does the Fifth Amendment "trial right" protected by *Miranda* serve some value necessarily divorced from the correct ascertainment of guilt. [By] bracing against "the possibility of unreliable statements in every instance of in-custody interrogation," *Miranda* serves to guard against "the use of unreliable statements at trial."

Finally, and most importantly, eliminating review of *Miranda* claims would not significantly benefit the federal courts in their exercise of habeas jurisdiction, or advance the cause of federalism in any substantial way. [For it] would not prevent a state prisoner from simply converting his barred *Miranda* claim into a due process claim that his conviction rested on an involuntary confession. Indeed, although counsel could provide us with no empirical basis for projecting the consequence of adopting petitioner's position, it seems reasonable to suppose that virtually all *Miranda* claims would simply be recast in this way.[5]

If that is so, the federal courts would certainly not have heard the last of *Miranda* on collateral review. Under the due process approach, [courts] look to the totality of circumstances to determine whether a confession was voluntary. Those potential circumstances include [the] failure of police to advise the defendant of his rights to remain silent and to have counsel present during custodial interrogation. * * * We could lock the front door against *Miranda,* but not the back.

We thus fail to see how abdicating *Miranda*'s bright-line (or, at least, brighter-line) rules in favor of an exhaustive totality-of-circumstances approach on habeas would do much of anything to lighten the burdens placed on busy federal courts. * * * We likewise fail to see how purporting to eliminate *Miranda* issues from federal habeas would go very far to relieve such tensions as *Miranda* may

---

5. Justice O'Connor is confident that many such claims would be unjustified, but that is beside the point. Justifiability is not much of a gatekeeper on habeas.

now raise between the two judicial systems. Relegation of habeas petitioners to straight involuntariness claims would not likely reduce the amount of litigation, and each such claim would in any event present a legal question requiring an "independent federal determination" on habeas.

One might argue that tension results between the two judicial systems whenever a federal habeas court overturns a state conviction on finding that the state court let in a voluntary confession obtained by the police without the *Miranda* safeguards. And one would have to concede that this has occurred in the past, and doubtless will occur again. It is not reasonable, however, to expect such occurrences to be frequent enough to amount to a substantial cost of reviewing *Miranda* claims on habeas or to raise federal-state tensions to an appreciable degree. We must remember in this regard that *Miranda* came down some 27 years ago. In that time, law enforcement has grown in constitutional as well as technological sophistication, and there is little reason to believe that the police today are unable, or even generally unwilling, to satisfy *Miranda*'s requirements.[6] And if, finally, one should question the need for federal collateral review of requirements that merit such respect, the answer simply is that the respect is sustained in no small part by the existence of such review. * * *

Justice O'CONNOR, with whom The Chief Justice joins, concurring in part and dissenting in part.

Today the Court permits the federal courts to overturn on habeas the conviction of a double-murderer, not on the basis of an inexorable constitutional or statutory command, but because it believes the result desirable from the standpoint of equity and judicial administration. Because the principles that inform our habeas jurisprudence—finality, federalism, and fairness—counsel decisively against the result the Court reaches, I respectfully dissent from this holding. * * *

Today we face the question whether alleged violations of the prophylactic rule of *Miranda* should be cognizable on habeas. Continuing the tradition of caution in this area, the Court answers that question in the negative. This time I must disagree. In my view, the "prudential concerns" that inform our habeas jurisprudence counsel the exclusion of *Miranda* claims just as strongly as they did the exclusionary rule claims at issue in *Stone* itself.

* * * Like the suppression of the fruits of an illegal search or seizure, the exclusion of statements obtained in violation of *Miranda* is not constitutionally required. This Court repeatedly has held that *Miranda*'s warning requirement is not a dictate of the Fifth Amendment itself, but a prophylactic rule. * * * Because *Miranda* "sweeps more broadly than the Fifth Amendment itself," it excludes some confessions even though the Constitution would not. * * * *Miranda*'s overbreadth, of course, is not without justification. [But,] like the exclusionary rule for illegally seized evidence, *Miranda*'s prophylactic rule does so at a substantial cost. Unlike involuntary or compelled statements?which are of dubious reliability and are therefore inadmissible for any purpose?confessions obtained in violation of *Miranda* are not necessarily untrustworthy. In fact, because *voluntary* statements are "trustworthy" even when obtained without proper warnings, their suppression actually *impairs* the pursuit of truth by concealing probative information from the trier of fact.

6. It should indeed come as no surprise that one of the submissions arguing against the extension of *Stone* in this case comes to us from law enforcement organizations. See Brief for the Police Foundation et al. as *Amici Curiae.*

[When] the case is on direct review, that damage to the truth-seeking function is deemed an acceptable sacrifice for the deterrence and respect for constitutional values that the *Miranda* rule brings. But once a case is on collateral review, the balance between the costs and benefits shifts; the interests of federalism, finality, and fairness compel *Miranda*'s exclusion from habeas. The benefit of enforcing *Miranda* through habeas is marginal at best. * * *

Despite its meager benefits, the relitigation of *Miranda* claims on habeas imposes substantial costs. Just like the application of the exclusionary rule, application of *Miranda*'s prophylactic rule on habeas consumes scarce judicial resources on an issue unrelated to guilt or innocence. No less than the exclusionary rule, it undercuts finality. It creates tension between the state and federal courts. And it upsets the division of responsibilities that underlies our federal system. But most troubling of all, *Miranda*'s application on habeas sometimes precludes the just application of law altogether. The order excluding the statement will often be issued "years after trial, when a new trial may be a practical impossibility." *Duckworth* (O'Connor, J., concurring). Whether the Court admits it or not, the grim result of applying *Miranda* on habeas will be, time and time again, "the release of an admittedly guilty individual who may pose a continuing threat to society."

[The] Court identifies a number of differences that, in its view, distinguishes this case from *Stone v. Powell*. I am sympathetic to the Court's concerns but find them misplaced nonetheless.

The first difference the Court identifies concerns the nature of the right protected. *Miranda*, the Court correctly points out, fosters Fifth Amendment rather than Fourth Amendment values. [The] Court's spirited defense of the Fifth Amendment is, of course, entirely beside the point. The question is not whether *true* Fifth Amendment claims—the extraction and use of *compelled* testimony— should be cognizable on habeas. It is whether violations of *Miranda*'s prophylactic rule, which excludes from trial voluntary confessions obtained without the benefit of *Miranda*'s now-familiar warnings, should be. * * * Excluding violations of *Miranda*'s prophylactic suppression requirement from habeas would not leave true Fifth Amendment violations unredressed. * * *

Excluding *Miranda* claims from habeas, then, denies collateral relief only in those cases in which the prisoner's statement was neither compelled nor involuntary but merely obtained without the benefit of *Miranda*'s prophylactic warnings. The availability of a suppression remedy in such cases cannot be labeled a "fundamental trial right," for there is no constitutional right to the suppression of *voluntary* statements. [If] the principles of federalism, finality, and fairness ever counsel in favor of withholding relief on habeas, surely they do so where there is no constitutional harm to remedy.

Similarly unpersuasive is the Court's related argument, that the Fifth Amendment trial right is not "necessarily divorced" from the interest of reliability. Whatever the Fifth Amendment's relationship to reliability, *Miranda*'s prophylactic rule is not merely "divorced" from the quest for truth but at war with it as well. The absence of *Miranda* warnings does not by some mysterious alchemy convert a voluntary and trustworthy statement into an involuntary and unreliable one. To suggest otherwise is both unrealistic and contrary to precedent.

[The] consideration the Court identifies as being "most importan[t]" of all, is an entirely pragmatic one. Specifically, the Court "project[s] that excluding *Miranda* questions from habeas will not significantly promote efficiency or federalism because some *Miranda* issues are relevant to a statement's voluntariness. It is true that barring *Miranda* claims from habeas poses no barrier to the adjudication of voluntariness questions. But that does not make it "reasonable to suppose that virtually all *Miranda* claims [will] simply be recast" and litigated as voluntariness claims. [A] *Miranda* claim [requires] no evidence of police overreaching whatsoever; it is enough that law enforcement officers commit a technical error. Even the forgetful failure to issue warnings to the most wary, knowledgeable, and seasoned of criminals will do. [If, as the Court maintains,] the police have truly grown in "constitutional * * * sophistication," then certainly it is reasonable to suppose that most technical errors in the administration of *Miranda*'s warnings are just that.

In any event, I see no need to resort to supposition. The published decisions of the lower federal courts show that what the Court assumes to be true demonstrably is not. In case after case, the courts are asked on habeas to decide purely technical *Miranda* questions that contain not even a hint of police overreaching. [Whether] the suspect was in "custody," whether or not there was "interrogation," whether warnings were given or were adequate, whether the defendant's equivocal statement constituted an invocation of rights, whether waiver was knowing and intelligent—this is the stuff that *Miranda* claims are made of.

[Even] assuming that many *Miranda* claims could "simply be recast" as voluntariness claims, it does not follow that barring *Miranda*'s prophylactic rule from habeas would unduly complicate their resolution. * * * *Miranda* creates as many close questions as it resolves. The task of determining whether a defendant is in "custody" has proved to be "a slippery one." And the supposedly "bright" lines that separate interrogation from spontaneous declaration, the exercise of a right from waiver, and the adequate warning from the inadequate, likewise have turned out to be rather dim and ill-defined. [Yet] *Miranda* requires those lines to be drawn with precision in each case.

The totality-of-the-circumstances approach, on the other hand, permits each fact to be taken into account without resort to formal and dispositive labels. [Thus,] it is true that the existence of warnings is still a consideration under the totality-of-the-circumstances approach, but it is unnecessary to determine conclusively whether "custody" existed and triggered the warning requirement, or whether the warnings given were sufficient. It is enough that the habeas court look to the warnings or their absence, along with all other factors, and consider them in deciding what is, after all, the ultimate question: whether the confession was compelled and involuntary or the product of a free and unimpaired will.

[The] Court's final rationale is that, because the federal courts rarely issue writs for *Miranda* violations, eliminating *Miranda* claims from *habeas* will not decrease state-federal tensions to an appreciable degree. [The] relative infrequency of relief, however, does not diminish the intrusion on state sovereignty; it diminishes only our justification for intruding in the first place. After all, even if relief is denied at the end of the day, the State still must divert its scarce prosecutorial resources to defend an otherwise final conviction. If relief is truly rare, efficiency counsels in favor of dispensing with the search for the prophylactic rule violation in a haystack; instead, the federal courts should concentrate on the search for true Fifth Amendment violations by adjudicating the questions of voluntariness and compulsion directly. I therefore find it of little moment that the Police Foundation, et al., support respondent. (Opinion of the Court at n. 6). Those who bear the primary burden of defending state convictions in federal courts—including 36 States and the National District Attorneys Association—resoundingly support the opposite side.

[As] the Court emphasizes today, *Miranda*'s prophylactic rule is now 26 years old; the police and the state courts have indeed grown accustomed to it. But it is precisely because the rule is well accepted that there is little further benefit to enforcing it on habeas. We can depend on law enforcement officials to administer warnings in the first instance and the state courts to provide a remedy when law enforcement officers err. * * *

Justice SCALIA, with whom Justice THOMAS joins, concurring in part and dissenting in part.

The issue in this case—whether the extraordinary remedy of federal habeas corpus should routinely be available for claimed violations of *Miranda* rights—involves not *jurisdiction* to issue the writ, but the *equity* of doing so. In my view, both the Court and Justice O'Connor disregard the most powerful equitable consideration: that Williams has already had full and fair opportunity to litigate this claim. He had the opportunity to raise it in the Michigan trial court; he did so and lost. He had the opportunity to seek review of the trial court's judgment in the Michigan Court of Appeals; he did so and lost. Finally, he had the opportunity to seek discretionary review of that Court of Appeals judgment in both the Michigan Supreme Court and this Court; he did so and review was denied. The question at this stage is whether, given all that, a federal habeas court should now reopen the issue and adjudicate the *Miranda* claim anew. The answer seems to me obvious: it should not. That would be the course followed by a federal habeas court reviewing a *federal* conviction; it mocks our federal system to accord state convictions less respect. * * *

As the Court today acknowledges, the rule of *Stone* is simply one application of equitable discretion. It does not deny a federal habeas court jurisdiction over Fourth Amendment claims, but merely holds that the court ought not to entertain them when the petitioner has already had an opportunity to litigate them fully and fairly. It is therefore not correct to say that applying *Stone* to the present case involves "eliminating review of *Miranda* claims" from federal habeas, (opinion of the Court) or that the Court is being "asked to exclude a substantive category of issues from relitigation on habeas," (opinion of O'Connor, J.). And it is therefore unnecessary to discuss at length the value of *Miranda* rights, as though it has been proposed that since they are particularly worthless they deserve specially disfavored treatment. The proposed rule would treat *Miranda* claims no differently from *all other claims*, taking account of all equitable factors, including the opportunity for full and fair litigation, in determining whether to provide habeas review. Wherein *Miranda* and Fourth Amendment claims differ from some other claims, is that the most significant countervailing equitable factor (possibility that the assigned error produced the conviction of an innocent person) will ordinarily not exist.

At common law, the opportunity for full and fair litigation of an issue at trial and (if available) direct appeal was not only a factor weighing against reaching the merits of an issue on habeas; it was a *conclusive* factor, unless the issue was a legal issue going to the jurisdiction of the trial court. See *Ex parte Watkins,* [28 U.S. (3 Pet.) 193 (1830)]. Beginning in the late 19th century, however, that rule was gradually relaxed, by the device of holding that various illegalities deprived the trial court of jurisdiction. Finally, the jurisdictional line was openly abandoned in *Waley v. Johnston,* 316 U.S. 101, 104–105, 62 S.Ct. 964, 965–966, 86 L.Ed. 1302 (1942).

But to say that prior opportunity for full and fair litigation no longer *automatically* precludes from consideration even nonjurisdictional issues is not to say that such prior opportunity is no longer a relevant equitable factor. Reason would suggest that it must be, and *Stone* establishes that it is. Thus, the question before us is not whether a holding unique to Fourth Amendment claims (and resting upon nothing more principled than our estimation that Fourth Amendment exclusion claims are not very important) should be expanded to some other arbitrary category beyond that; but rather, whether the general principle that is the only valid justification for *Stone* should for some reason *not* be applied to *Miranda* claims. I think the answer to that question is clear: Prior opportunity to litigate an issue should be an important equitable consideration in *any* habeas case, and should ordinarily preclude the court from reaching the merits of a claim, unless it goes to the fairness of the trial process or to the accuracy of the ultimate result.

Our case law since *Stone* is entirely consistent with this view. As the Court notes, we have held that the rule in *Stone* does not apply in three cases. *Kimmelman v. Morrison* involved alleged denial of the Sixth Amendment right to counsel, which unquestionably goes to the fairness of the trial process. *Rose v. Mitchell* involved alleged discrimination by the trial court in violation of the Fourteenth Amendment. [And] *Jackson v. Virginia* involved a claim that "no rational trier of fact could have found proof of guilt beyond a reasonable doubt," which is obviously a direct challenge to the accuracy of the ultimate result.

The rule described above—or indeed a rule even somewhat more limiting of habeas review than that—is followed in federal postconviction review of *federal* convictions under 28 U.S.C. § 2255. In *Kaufman v. United States* [Ch. 29, § 2], which held that res judicata does not bar § 2255 habeas review of constitutional issues, we stated that a district court had "discretion" to refuse to reach the merits of a constitutional claim that had already been raised and resolved against the prisoner at trial and on direct review. Since *Kaufman,* federal courts have uniformly held that, absent countervailing considerations, district courts may refuse to reach the merits of a constitutional claim previously raised and rejected on direct appeal. [Thus,] a prior opportunity for full and fair litigation is normally dispositive of a federal prisoner's habeas claim. If the claim was raised and rejected on direct review, the habeas court will not readjudicate it absent countervailing equitable considerations; if the claim was not raised, it is procedurally defaulted and the habeas court will not adjudicate it absent countervailing equitable considerations (*e.g.,* actual innocence or cause and prejudice, see *United States v. Frady* [Ch. 29, § 3]).

Because lower federal courts have not generally recognized their discretion to deny habeas relief in state cases where opportunity for full and fair litigation was accorded, the peculiar state of current federal habeas practice is this: State courts routinely see their criminal convictions vacated by federal district judges, but federal courts see their criminal convictions afforded a substantial measure of finality and respect. * * * Only one theory can possibly justify this disparity—the theory advanced in *Fay v. Noia* [Ch. 29, § 2] that a federal forum must be afforded for every federal claim of a state criminal defendant. In my view, that theory is profoundly wrong for several reasons.

First, it has its origin in a misreading of our early precedents. * * * Worse than [that], however, the federal right/federal forum theory misperceives the basic structure of our national system. That structure establishes this Court as the supreme judicial interpreter of the Federal Constitution and laws, but gives other federal courts no higher or more respected a role than state courts in applying that "Law of the Land"—which it says all state courts are bound by, and all state judges must be sworn to uphold. U.S. Const., Art. VI.

[A] federal court entertaining collateral attack against a state criminal conviction should accord the same measure of respect and finality as it would to a federal criminal conviction. [The] distinction that has arisen in lower-court practice is unsupported in law, utterly impractical and demeaning to the States in its consequences, and must be eliminated. * * *

Notes and Questions

(a) *Does Withrow affirm that the Miranda rule contains a constitutional command?* "If the Court had viewed *Miranda* as truly non-constitutional," comments Charles D. Weisselberg, *Saving Miranda*, 84 Cornell L.Rev. 109, 130–31 (1998), "then it had little reason to refuse *Withrow's* invitation to take mere *Miranda* violations out of federal habeas corpus. The Court in *Withrow* thus kept the universe of *Miranda* claims within the Constitution."

(b) *Do Fifth Amendment violations occur only at trial? Withrow* talks about "the Fifth Amendment 'trial right' " and about *"Miranda* safeguard[ing] 'a fundamental *trial* right.' " However, Weisselberg, supra at 180, observes that "a number of cases have found Fifth Amendment violations in circumstances in which witnesses suffered penalties for asserting the privilege against self-incrimination, even though they faced no criminal charges and had no criminal trial." [He refers to such cases as *Lefkowitz v. Cunningham*, 431 U.S. 801, 97 S.Ct. 2132, 53 L.Ed.2d 1 (1977), holding that a grand jury witness cannot be divested of political office as a penalty for exercising his Fifth Amendment privilege; and *Gardner v. Broderick*, 392 U.S. 273, 88 S.Ct. 1913, 20 L.Ed.2d 1082 (1968), holding that a police officer cannot lose his job for asserting the privilege before a grand jury.] These cases are impossible to square with the notion that Fifth Amendment violations occur only at trial."

According to Professor Weisselberg, if police question a suspect at the police station in violation of *Miranda* "the best view" may be that "the violation occurs at the station house, but continues or recurs at trial. The values that underlie the Fifth Amendment include preserving autonomy, maintaining our adversarial system, curtailing inhumane treatment and police misconduct, avoiding false confessions, and complying with our sense of fair play. Custodial interrogation can undermine most of these values in the station house at the time that the questioning occurs."

24. Other Miranda problems discussed elsewhere in the book. Is *Miranda's* prohibition against police trickery and deception confined to their use in obtaining a waiver of rights or does it also bar such tactics *after* a person has validly waived his rights? See the next section.

If a defendant takes the stand in his own defense, may the prosecution impeach him by using statements obtained from him in violation of *Miranda*? See Ch. 11, § 4, infra. May a defendant's *prior silence,* even his *post* arrest silence, be used to impeach his credibility when he chooses to testify at his trial? See id.

Suppose, after a suspect is illegally arrested, he is advised of his rights, waives them, and confesses? Do the *Miranda* warnings "cure" the illegality of the arrest? See Ch. 11, § 3, infra.

Suppose, a couple of hours after the police obtain an incriminating statement from a suspect in violation of *Miranda,* they give him the complete warnings and the suspect waives his rights and confesses? Is the "second confession" admissible or is it "the fruit" of the first inadmissible statement? See Ch. 11, § 3, infra. Suppose, as the result of a statement obtained in violation of *Miranda,* the police find the murder weapon or locate an important witness. Is the testimony of the witness or the murder weapon admissible? Or is it the "fruit of the poisonous tree"? See id.

THE IMPACT OF *MIRANDA* IN PRACTICE

In 1988, a special committee of the ABA's Criminal Justice Section—Special Committee on Criminal Justice in a Free Society, *Criminal Justice in Crisis* 28 (1988)—reported that "a very strong majority of those surveyed—prosecutors, judges, and police officers—agree that compliance with *Miranda* does not present serious problems for law enforcement." This report, taken together with many earlier empirical studies indicating that *Miranda* posed no significant barrier to effective law enforcement, appeared to be, as the ABA Special Committee put it, "a strong repudiation of the claim that law enforcement would be greatly improved if *Miranda* were repealed or overruled."[a]

However, in *Miranda's Social Costs: An Empirical Reassessment*, 90 Nw. U.L.Rev. 387 (1996), Professor Paul G. Cassell attacked the general consensus, contending that despite the "conventional academic wisdom" to the contrary, "*Miranda* has significantly harmed law enforcement efforts in this country." According to Cassell, who reexamined many of the before-and-after studies conducted shortly after the *Miranda* decision, "the existing empirical data supports the tentative estimate that *Miranda* has led to lost cases against almost four percent [3.8%] of all criminal suspects in this country who are questioned"—an apparently small percentage figure that when "multiplied across the run of criminal cases constitutes a large number of criminals."[b]

Responding to Professor Cassell's article, Stephen J. Schulhofer, *Miranda's Practical Effect: Substantial Benefits and Vanishingly Small Social Costs*, 90 N.W.U.L.Rev. 500 (1996), maintains that if one reexamines the old studies with all necessary qualifications in mind, "the properly adjusted attrition rate is not 3.8%, but *at most* only .78%." Moreover, emphasizes Professor Schulhofer, "even if we can assume that the studies [Cassell relies on] give a reliable picture of *Miranda's* costs thirty years ago, there is strong reason to believe that such costs were transitory and that confession rates have since rebounded from any temporary decline."

In his rejoinder, *All Benefits, No Costs: The Grand Illusion of Miranda's Defenders*, 90 Nw.U.L.Rev. 1084 (1996), Professor Cassell maintains that both clearance rate data and confession rate data demonstrate that "over the long haul, law enforcement never recovered from the blow inflicted by *Miranda*." Cassell

a. See also Donald Dripps, *Foreword: Against Police Interrogation—and the Privilege Against Self–Incrimination*, 78 J. Crim.L. & C. 699, 722 (1988); Lawrence Herman, *The Supreme Court, the Attorney General, and the Good Old Days of Police Interrogation*, 48 Ohio St. L.J. 733, 737 (1987); Stephen J. Schulhofer, *Reconsidering Miranda*, 54 U.Chi.L.Rev. 435, 456 (1987); Welsh White, *Defending Miranda: A Reply to Professor Caplan*, 39 Vand.L.Rev.

17–20 (especially White's summary of various empirical studies at p. 19).

b. Professor Cassell's article and Professor Schulhofer's response, as well as other articles on *Miranda's* impact in the police station by Richard A. Leo, George C. Thomas III, and Cassell and Bret S. Hayman are reprinted in large part in Richard A. Leo & George C. Thomas III, *The Miranda Debate* (1998).

relies, inter alia, on a 1994 study of police interrogation in Salt Lake City that he co-authored, Cassell & Bret Hayman, *Police Interrogation in the 1990s: An Empirical Study of the Effects of Miranda*, 43 UCLA L.Rev. 839 (1996), a study which found that suspects gave incriminating statements in only about a third of all cases presented for prosecution, a confession rate well below the average rate before *Miranda*.[c]

However, according to Schulhofer, supra at 509, the Salt Lake County study's low confession rate "results from a good deal of unjustified juggling of the numbers": it includes cases in which suspects were never questioned at all, non-custodial interrogations (although the best reading of the pre-*Miranda* studies is that they involved only custodial interrogation) and it *excludes* cases in which the suspect gave "denials with explanation" although a substantial number of such "denials" probably should have been classified as incriminating statements.

As already indicated, Professor Thomas, fn. c supra, criticizes the Cassell–Hayman Salt Lake County study on grounds similar to Schulhoffer's. Thomas concludes that if the adjustments to the Cassell–Hayman study he would make were accepted, "the Salt Lake County data looks remarkably like the pre-*Miranda* studies" and support the hypothesis that *Miranda* has had no effect on confession rates. Adds Professor Thomas:

"Cassell and Hayman conclude that 12.1% of felony suspects 'who were questioned invoked their rights before police were successful in interrogation.' Two observations can be made about this figure. First, if the *Miranda*-dissenters and the police in 1966 had been told that the effect of *Miranda* would be limited to 12.1% of felony suspects, they would have cheered in relief. Thus, while significant, 12.1% is hardly crippling to the law enforcement enterprise.

"But another observation must be made: There is no way to credit *Miranda* with all of that 12.1%. Some suspects refused to cooperate with police prior to *Miranda*. The 12.1% who invoke their rights includes that category of suspects, now given an easier way to refuse to cooperate. On this point, though, Cassell and Hayman can find support among *Miranda*'s defenders. If *Miranda* is to have any of the effects envisioned by its supporters (reduce pressure in the interrogation room, level the playing field, increase equality among suspects), it simply must cause more invocations. Otherwise, *Miranda* is (as some cynics have charged) merely about symbolism and appearances.[d] Thus, *Miranda* supporters should cheer an increase in invocations. Though the paucity of the pre-*Miranda* data makes hazardous any guess as to the magnitude of the difference, the Cassell–

---

c. Professor Cassell recognizes that a 1994 study of interrogation by detectives in three California cities found an incriminating rate of about 64%. See Richard A. Leo, *Inside the Interrogation Room*, 86 J.Crim.L. & Criminology 266, 280 (1996); Richard A. Leo, Police Interrogation in America: A Study of Violence, Civility, and Social Change (1994) (unpublished Ph.D. dissertation, University of California (Berkeley)). But Cassell argues that Leo's sample "needs to be adjusted to reflect suspects who are never questioned, suspects questioned in less productive noncustodial settings, and suspects questioned not only by detectives but also by less effective patrol officers. Such adjustments produce a confession rate of somewhere below 38.7%, quite close to what we found." Cassell rejoinder at 1091–92.

However, George C. Thomas III, *Plain Talk About the Miranda Empirical Debate: A "Steady–State" Theory of Confessions*, 43 UCLA L.Rev. 933 (1996) maintains that Professor Leo's methodology "is consistent with the pre-*Miranda* studies, and that the attempt by Cassell to whittle down Leo's confession rate on methodological grounds "must be rejected." Id. at 954. According to Professor Thomas, it is not the Leo confession rate, that needs to be adjusted downward, but the Cassell–Hayman rate that should be adjusted upward. See id. at 946–55.

d. See, e.g., Louis Michael Seidman, *Brown and Miranda*, 80 Calif.L.Rev. 673, 743–47 (1992).

Hayman data, together with Leo's data, suggest that the effect may be rather substantial.[93]

"The available data thus seems to demonstrate that more suspects invoke their right to remain silent, and the rate of confessions is roughly the same. This divergence supports my steady-state theory: *Miranda* encourages some suspects not to talk and encourages others to talk too much. It is possible that, in the pre-*Miranda* era, fewer suspects refused to talk but more suspects gave terse answers. Perhaps more suspects refuse to talk today, but those who do talk have a *Miranda*-created incentive to tell a fuller story. The *Miranda* warnings might make suspects believe they can avoid being prosecuted only in they tell a story close enough to the truth that the police will be fooled in letting them go. In the NIJ study, for example, more robbery suspects admitted being at the scene of the crime than gave an outright confession."[e]

In 1997, the Cassell–Schulhofer debate continued in the pages of another law journal. As evidence of Miranda's harmful effects, Professor Cassell noted that in 1965 the clearance rate for violent crime had been stable for several years and stood at nearly 60 percent—only to plunge more than twelve percentage points in the next three years. See Paul G. Cassell, *Miranda's "Negligible" Effect on Law Enforcement: Some Skeptical Observations*, 20 Harv.J.L.Pub.Pol'y 327, 333–35 (1997). Professor Schulhofer responded that clearance capacity (the number of officers and dollars available to investigate each reported crime) collapsed in the late 1960s as crime rose sharply and that the dramatic reduction in clearance *capacity* provides "the most likely explanation" for the significant decline in the clearance *rates* that occurred at the same time. Schulhofer points out that after *Miranda* the *number* of crimes cleared continued to rise. See Stephen J. Schulhofer, *Bashing Miranda is Unjustified—and Harmful*, 20 Harv.J.L.Pub.Pol'y 347, 357–62 (1997).

At this point, another law professor joined the debate, Peter Arenella, *Miranda Stories*, 20 Harv.J.L.Pub.Pol'y 375 (1997), observing: "Neither the 'conservative' nor the 'liberal' tale provides a fully plausible account of *Miranda*'s impact on our criminal justice system because both stories commit the same fundamental error: exaggerating either *Miranda*'s costs (Cassell) or benefits (Schulhofer). Moreover, each story generates an obvious question that neither author answers persuasively. If Cassell's account is accurate, why have the police and a conservative Supreme Court shown no interest in eliminating the *Miranda* regime? Conversely, if Schulhofer is right (and I believe he is) that the *Miranda* regime has not impaired law enforcement's ability to secure incriminating admissions, how exactly does *Miranda*'s negligible impact demonstrate its success in eliminating the 'inherent coerciveness' of police interrogation?"

In 1998, the controversy, revivified by Professor Cassell, over *Miranda*'s costs and benefits, spilled into the *Stanford Law Review* and a new critic of Cassell's work, Professor John J. Donohue III, entered the fray. After conducting a multiple regression analysis of crime clearance rates from 1950 to 1995, Cassell and Richard Fowles, *Handcuffing the Cops? A Thirty–Year Perspective on Miranda's Harmful Effects on Law Enforcement*, 50 Stan.L.Rev. 1055 (1998), contend that

---

93. Leo's study finds an even greater rate of invocation: 21.7%. [See Richard A. Leo, *Inside the Interrogation Room*, 86 J.Crim.L. & Criminology 266, 275–76, 286 (1996).]

e. See also George C. Thomas III, *Is Miranda A Real–World Failure? A Plea for More (and Better) Empirical Evidence*, 43 UCLA L.Rev. 821, 823–24 (1996): "I believe the *Miranda* warnings have simultaneous, and roughly off-setting effects. The warnings discourage suspects from making outright acknowledgments of guilt, but they encourage suspects to talk to police and thus often incriminate themselves indirectly."

Miranda has had a statistically significant adverse and long-term effect on clearance rates for total violent and total property crimes generally and for certain individual crimes, such as robbery and burglary. In response, *Did Miranda Diminish Police Effectiveness?*, 50 Stan.L.Rev. 1147 (1998), Professor Donohue maintains that the Cassell–Fowles regression study itself does not identify *Miranda* as the event that led to a significant decline in clearance rates for certain crimes and, in any case, their study shows no significant relationship between *Miranda* and the clearance rate for murder—the most accurately reported crime. Donohue suggests that *Miranda*'s only real impact upon clearance rates may be that it prevents the police from obtaining information from custodial suspects about crimes other than the one(s) for which the suspects have been arrested.

Finally, consider Charles D. Weisselberg, *Saving Miranda*, 84 Cornell L.Rev. 109, 172–77 (1998). Although he calls Cassell's writings "the most detailed and determined empirical effort to measure *Miranda*'s costs," Weisselberg notes that no methodology can assess *Miranda*'s "benefits." Indeed, he continues, "in arguing that *Miranda* costs too much to maintain, [Cassell] largely avoids any analysis of *Miranda*'s virtues." "The *Miranda* debate," concludes Weisselberg, "can have no empirical resolution. That *Miranda* has an impact may mean nothing more than it works as the Court intended."[f]

HOW TO GET PEOPLE TO CONFESS IN THE POST–*MIRANDA* WORLD: HAVE MODERN POLICE INTERROGATORS "ADAPTED" TO *MIRANDA* OR ARE THEY VIOLATING IT?

In 1988, after persuading the Baltimore police department to grant him unlimited access to the city's homicide unit for a full year, David Simon, a *Baltimore Sun* reporter who had spent four years on the police beat, took a leave of absence from the *Sun* and followed one shift of detectives as they traveled from interrogations to autopsies and from crime scenes to hospital emergency rooms. Simon's 1991 book, *Homicide: A Year on the Killing Streets*, was the result. In an author's note, Simon tells us that *Homicide* is a "work of journalism" and that the events he has written about "occurred in the manner described."

How, despite the seemingly formidable obstacle of *Miranda*, do the Baltimore police manage to get so many suspects to incriminate themselves? According to Simon (see pp. 194–207 of his book), the following, or something close to it, occurs:

(1) The detective produces an "Explanation of Rights" sheet, reads the warnings one at a time and when the suspect responds that he understands them, gets the suspect to initial each warning.

(2) Next, the detective gets the suspect to sign his name just below a sentence that reads: "I have read the explanation of my rights and fully understand it."

(3) At this point—and before the suspect is asked whether he wants to waive his rights and talk about the case—the detective assures the suspect that he will honor his rights if he invokes them, but in the next breath warns him that asserting his rights would make matters worse for him. For it would prevent his

---

f. Elsewhere in his article, (p. 174), Professor Weisselberg observes: "Even if one accepts Cassell's conclusion that *Miranda* has led to a decrease in statements to the police, *Miranda* still might accomplish its purpose efficiently. If *Miranda* significantly reduces the incidence of coerced or false confessions and leads police to respect Fifth Amendment values, it functions exactly as the Court intended, even if it reduces the number of cases that face prosecution."

friend, the detective, from writing up the case as manslaughter or perhaps even self-defense, rather than first degree murder. The detective emphasizes that he is affording the suspect the opportunity to tell his side of the story (Did the man you stabbed come at you? Was it self-defense?), "but once you up and call for that lawyer, son, we can't do a damn thing for you ... [T]he next authority figure to scan your case will be a tie-wearing, three-piece bloodsucker—a no-nonsense prosecutor from the Violent Crimes Unit [and] God help you then, son ... Now's the time to speak up ... because once I walk out of this room any chance you have of telling your side of the story is gone."

(4) In a typical case, the detective also tells the suspect (falsely) that the evidence against him is overwhelming, and the only reason he is interested in hearing the suspect's version of what happened is "to make sure that there ain't nothing you can say for yourself before I write it all up" (as murder in the first degree).

(5) The suspect cautiously indicates a willingness to talk about the case or at least to consider talking about it. The suspect also indicates that he likes the suggestion that the slain man had "come at him." The detective smiles inwardly. He has given the suspect "the Out" and the suspect has taken it.

(6) The suspect is now eager to tell his story, but the detective cuts him off. Before proceeding any further, there is some "paperwork" to be completed—to do this the right way the suspect must first sign a form stating that he is willing to answer police questions without having a lawyer present and that his decision to do so has been "free and voluntary" on his part.

(7) The suspect signs the form and the detective encourages him to resume telling his story. At the same time, the detective tells himself: "End of the road, pal. It's over. It's history."

Recent articles indicate that the Baltimore detectives' tactics described by Simon are utilized by detectives in many other police departments as well. See Richard A. Leo, *Miranda's Revenge: Police Interrogation as a Confidence Game*, 30 Law & Society Rev. 259 (1996) (based on 500 hours of participant observation in three police departments); Richard A. Leo & Welsh S. White, *Adapting to Miranda: Modern Interrogators' Strategies for Dealing with the Obstacles Posed by Miranda* (1999) (forthcoming); Peter Carlson, *You Have the Right to Remain Silent* ..., Washington Post Magazine, Sept. 13, 1998, pp. 6–11, 19–24 (based largely on interviews with police interrogators from Washington, D.C., and surrounding Maryland and Virginia suburbs).[a]

It is unclear whether Baltimore detectives (or police interrogators from other cities who use similar tactics) think their methods can be reconciled with *Miranda* or whether they realize they are "at war" with *Miranda*. There is reason to believe that Mr. Simon (and many members of the Baltimore homicide unit) think that the aforementioned interrogation techniques are permitted by *Miranda*. At

---

a. Thus, Professors White and Leo observe that "[o]ne of the most powerful [*Miranda*] de-emphasizing strategies involves focusing the suspect's attention on the importance of telling his story to the interrogator. The interrogators communicate to the suspect that they want to hear his 'side of the story' but they will not be able to do so until the suspect waives his *Miranda* rights." Still another common way to de-emphasize *Miranda*, report Leo and White, "is to create the appearance of a non-adver- sarial relationship between the interrogator and a suspect. An interrogator employing this strategy portrays himself as the suspect's friend, confidant or guardian, whose goal is not to obtain incriminating statements but rather to help the suspect improve his situation." This strategy, continue Leo and White, "not only de-emphasizes the *Miranda* warnings but also suggest to the suspect that waiving his *Miranda* warnings will be to his advantage."

one point, for example, Simon observes that, forced to deal with *Miranda*, a detective "follows the requirements of the law to the letter—or close enough so as not to jeopardize his case. Just as carefully, he ignores the law's spirit and intent. He becomes a salesman, a huckster as thieving and silver-tongued as any man who ever moved used cars or aluminum siding * * *." But consider the following:

YALE KAMISAR—KILLING *MIRANDA* IN BALTIMORE: REFLECTIONS ON DAVID SIMON'S *HOMICIDE*

JURIST: Books-on-Law, Feb. 1999, vol.2, no.2
(http://jurist.law.pitt.edu/lawbooks/) (archived).

"[I]f the admissibility of a statement obtained as a result of the methods described [by Mr. Simon] were challenged by a defense lawyer, a Baltimore prosecutor would be in a strong position. For she would be armed with a signed waiver of rights form (and a signed explanation of rights form as well). But she would be in a strong position only if—as would hardly be surprising—the detective(s) involved in the case lied about, or conveniently failed to remember, how the suspect was induced to sign the waiver of rights form. If all the facts were known—if, for example, the entire transaction had been tape recorded—no court could or would admit the statement unless it was prepared to overrule *Miranda* itself.

Despite Mr. Simon's comments to the contrary, the Baltimore police do not follow the requirements of *Miranda* closely enough to avoid jeopardizing their cases, nor do they merely ignore *Miranda*'s spirit. Indeed, it would be more accurate to say they flout the substance of that famous case.

One of the principal purposes of the warning is, to quote from the *Miranda* opinion, "to make the individual more acutely aware that he is faced with a phase of the adversary system—that he is not in the presence of persons acting solely in his interest." But the Baltimore detectives seriously undermine this purpose by leading the suspect to believe that it is in his best interest to waive his rights and to talk to "your friends in the city homicide unit" about the case, and by pretending to be not only the suspect's friend but his protector (or at least a buffer) against the detectives' heartless superiors and the zealous prosecutor waiting outside the door, a prosecutor who has no compunctions about charging the suspect with first degree murder without bothering to hear his "side of the story."

Early in its *Miranda* opinion, the Warren Court vents its judicial ire at the interrogation manuals which instruct the police to "persuade, trick, or cajole" suspects out of exercising their constitutional rights. Twenty pages later, the Court returns to this point: "[A]ny evidence that the accused was threatened, tricked, or cajoled into a waiver will, of course, show that the defendant did not voluntarily waive his privilege. The requirement of warnings and waiver of rights is a fundamental [and] not simply a preliminary ritual to existing methods of interrogation."

Unfortunately, the very police conduct that *Miranda* tried to forbid seems to be occurring in Baltimore police stations. The police *are* threatening the suspect: they are telling him that unless he talks to them about the homicide, they will write it up as first degree murder and turn him over to a "bloodsucking" assistant state's attorney. They *are* tricking the suspect: they are leading him to believe that it is in his best interest to tell them his side of the story; indeed, they are pretending that this is the suspect's only chance to get the homicide charge reduced (or perhaps even dismissed).

To quote Mr. Simon, in a typical interrogation session a detective warns the suspect: "[O]nce I walk out of this room, any chance you have of telling your side of the story is gone and I gotta write it up the way it looks [and] it looks right now [like] first-degree murder." And all along the way, the detectives are cajoling suspects into waiving their rights.

To quote the *Miranda* opinion again, transforming its requirements of warnings and waiver of rights into "simply a preliminary ritual to existing methods of interrogation" is also a pretty good description of what is taking place in Baltimore police stations. Indeed, to put it somewhat differently, although the police are not supposed to subject a custodial suspect to interrogation *unless and until* they obtain a waiver of his rights, what they are really doing in Baltimore (and who knows how many other places) is subjecting individuals to "interrogation" *before* they waive their rights.

At one point, Mr. Simon notes that "[t]he fraud that claims it is somehow in a suspect's interest to talk with police will forever be the catalyst in any criminal interrogation." Exactly right. This is why the methods used by the Baltimore police to get a suspect to waive his rights—methods that simultaneously manipulate him into talking about the case and, eventually, incriminating himself—should be classified as "interrogation." Whatever deception, seduction and trickery a police interrogator may be able to utilize *after* the suspect effectively waives his rights and agrees to talk (and, more than 30 years after *Miranda*, what the interrogator may do at this stage is still far from clear), the police cannot resort to any of these techniques *before* the suspect waives his rights, and they cannot use any of these techniques to *get him* to waive his rights.

Once the police have taken a suspect into custody, there is no such thing (at least there is no lawful basis for any such thing) as a "pre-interview' or 'pre-waiver" interrogation. The waiver of rights transaction is supposed to take place as soon as the curtain goes up, not postponed until the second or third act.

Mr. Simon's graphic description of how the Baltimore Homicide Unit (and who knows how many other police departments?) goes about getting custodial suspects to make incriminating statements underscores the need to record on video or audio tape the entire proceedings in the police station—the reading of rights, the waiver transactions and any subsequent interrogation. Perhaps because it feared that requiring electronic recording of police questioning, whenever feasible, would have added fuel to the criticism that it was "legislating," the *Miranda* Court permitted the police to obtain waivers of a person's constitutional rights without the presence of any disinterested observer and without any objective recording of the proceedings.

Since *Miranda*, the great majority of state courts has held that the testimony of an officer that she complied with *Miranda* is sufficient and need not be corroborated. Nevertheless, there is nothing new or startling about tape-recording police questioning. Virtually all of the nation's leading criminal procedure commentators—critics and defenders of *Miranda* alike—favor the idea. Why, then, is tape-recording not [the uniform practice] in American police stations today? * * *

The only startling thing about this issue is that, after all these years, American law enforcement officials are still able to prevent objective recordation of all the facts of police "interviews" or "conversations" with a suspect and, of course, how the warnings are delivered and how the waiver of rights is obtained.

But if you were a member of the Baltimore homicide unit (or a member of other police departments employing the same interrogation methods), would you favor tape-recording (and making available for public inspection) what really happens in the interrogation room?

———

David Simon describes how Baltimore interrogators manage to get custodial suspects to sign waivers of their *Miranda* rights, but what happens if a suspect *invokes* his right to remain silent or her right to counsel? There is reason to think that some detectives in some police departments continue to question the suspects in order (a) to obtain incriminating statements which will enable the prosecution to impeach the suspect if he subsequently takes the stand in his own defense or (b) to obtain evidence *derived from* statements made in violation of *Miranda*, derivative evidence such as the existence of an eyewitness or the location of the murder weapon. Discussion of these police tactics is postponed until Chapter 11, which contains materials on the "fruit of the poisonous tree" and the use of illegally obtained evidence for impeachment purposes. See pp. 825-27.

———

SHOULD POLICE INTERROGATION BE REPLACED BY A SYSTEM OF JUDICIALLY SUPERVISED QUESTIONING?

Even before the Supreme Court decided *Brown v. Mississippi* (1936), the first Fourteenth Amendment "coerced" confession case, several commentators proposed eliminating or greatly restricting police interrogation in favor of judicial or judicially supervised questioning. Paul Kauper, *Judicial Examination of the Accused—A Remedy for the Third Degree*, 30 Mich.L.Rev. 1224 (1932), seems to have been the first commentator to spell out the desirability of, and historical support for, such a procedure, as well as the first to marshal, and to evaluate with any degree of thoroughness, the policy and constitutional arguments against such a procedure. See Kamisar, *Kauper's "Judicial Examination of the Accused" Forty Years Later—Some Comments on a Remarkable Article*, 73 Mich.L.Rev. 15 (1974).

In the wake of *Miranda*, two eminent judges in effect returned to the Kauper proposal and built upon it. See Walter Schaefer, *The Suspect and Society* 76–81 (1967); Henry Friendly, *The Fifth Amendment Tomorrow: The Case for Constitutional Change*, 37 U.Cin.L.Rev. 671, 713–16 (1968). Under what has been called the "Kauper–Schaefer–Friendly" model, discussed at length in Kamisar, supra, a suspect questioned either by or before a judicial officer would have the assistance of counsel and be informed that she need not answer any questions. But she would also be told that if subsequently prosecuted her refusal to answer questions at the earlier proceeding would be disclosed at trial.

Judges Friendly and Schaefer both assumed that their proposal could not be effectuated without a constitutional amendment, as have more recent commentators. See Donald A. Dripps, *Foreword: Against Police Interrogation—and the Privilege Against Self–Incrimination*, 78 J.Crim.L. & C. 699, 730 (1988); Phillip E. Johnson, *A Statutory Replacement for the Miranda Doctrine*, 24 Am.Crim.L.Rev. 303, 309 (1987); Stephen A. Saltzburg, *Miranda v. Arizona Revisited: Constitutional Law or Judicial Fiat*, 26 Washburn L.J.1, 25 (1986). But former federal judge Marvin Frankel, *From Private Rights to Public Justice*, 51 N.Y.U.L.Rev.

516, 531 (1976), has expressed the hope that the proposal could be adopted without constitutional amendment:

"Only one recent decision seems to stand squarely in the way [*Griffin v. California* (1965), set forth in Ch. 25, § 4, which forbids comment on a defendant's failure to testify at trial]. But that ruling should not be deemed so central and inevitable as to preclude restudy in an altered context. If custodial admissions in the absence of either counsel or a presiding judicial officer were totally excluded, protecting the luckless or entrapped multitudes who currently 'waive' as well as those who do not waive, we may be certain that the amount of truly 'compelled' self-incrimination in our society would be sharply diminished. The suggested *quid pro quo*—allowing comment upon [a defendant's silence at a preliminary judicial examination to be made at her trial] would 'compel' testimony only in a strained, ahistorical, unrealistic sense of compulsion. It is permissible to hope that constitutional statesmanship will sustain this rearrangement as more thoroughly consistent with the fifth amendment privilege, and less conducive to genuinely unacceptable coercion, than in the existing situation."

See also Albert W. Alschuler, *A Peculiar Privilege in Historical Perspective: The Right to Remain Silent*, 94 Mich.L.Rev. 2625, 2670–72 (1996): "A suspect's answers to orderly questioning in a safeguarded courtroom environment should not be regarded as the product of compulsion. * * * Interrogation before a judicial officer would be likely to promote accurate fact-finding both when accurate fact-finding would help the suspect and when it would hurt her. * * * The procedure also would be consistent with the original understanding of the Fifth Amendment privilege, for the Framers saw no tension between the privilege and their own interrogation practices—practices that differed from the proposal only in that they lacked some of its safeguards. [When] neither text, history, nor sensible policy condemns a practice, a court should find it constitutional; and if the practice seems inconsistent with the right to remain silent, courts should read the Constitution again."

Recently Professor Akhil Reed Amar and Ms. Renée B. Lettow, *Fifth Amendment First Principles: The Self–Incrimination Clause*, 93 Mich.L.Rev. 857, 908–909 (1995), revisited and revised the "Kauper–Schaefer–Friendly" proposal. Amar and Lettow maintain that the best way to "rein in unsupervised police officers who might be tempted to abuse suspects" is "to shift interrogation from police stations to magistrates' hearing rooms. [I]n light of this civilized alternative [to the present system], courts might well choose to police the police even more strictly than today, enforcing a prophylactic rule that no police-station confession by a defendant is ever allowed in, unless volunteered by a suspect in the presence of an on-duty defense lawyer or ombudsman in the police station, or unless the defendant consents to its introduction at trial." See also Akhil Reed Amar, *The Constitution and Criminal Procedure* 76–77 (1997).

Under the Amar–Lettow proposal, the suspect at a judicially supervised pretrial hearing who failed to answer truthfully, could be held in contempt. If he did answer, he would only be entitled to "testimonial immunity," *i.e.*, his compelled *words* could not be introduced in a criminal trial, but the evidence derived from these words—such as the whereabouts of damaging physical evidence or the existence and location of potential witnesses for the prosecution—would be admissible. See 93 Mich.L.Rev. at 858–59, 898–99. By empowering the government, at a pretrial hearing presided over by a judicial officer to compel a suspect, under penalty of contempt, to provide links in the chain of evidence to convict him, the Amar–Lettow proposal differs significantly from the Kauper–Schaefer–

Friendly plan. Under the latter plan, *the only sanction* for a suspect's silence at the pretrial judicially supervised proceeding would be to permit the trier of fact to consider that silence for whatever bearing it has on guilt or innocence. Amar and Lettow, 93 Mich.L.Rev. at 909, maintain that if their judicially supervised interrogation proposal went into effect, and was accompanied by a prohibition against all police station confessions, "this strict regime would create powerful incentives to conduct interrogation before magistrates rather than in police stations." Would it? Consider Kamisar, *On the "Fruits" of Miranda Violations, Coerced Confessions, and Compelled Testimony*, 93 Mich.L.Rev. 929, 932–33 (1995): "Amar and Lettow can't have it both ways. If, as they maintain, '[o]nly the defendant's compelled *testimony* should be protected by the [Fifth] Amendment'—a view upon which their proposal depends—then only the coerced or otherwise improperly obtained stationhouse confessions or incriminating statements, *not their 'fruits,'* would be protected by the Fifth Amendment. But how can we expect to discourage the police from proceeding in an irregular manner in the stationhouse when they know that any evidence their improper questioning brings to light will be admissible?"

SECTION 4. THE "DUE PROCESS"–"VOLUNTARINESS" TEST REVISITED

Although one might say (and many commentators have) that *Miranda* displaced the due process-totality of circumstances-voluntariness test, in a number of important situations "the primary criterion of [confession] admissibility under *current* law is [still] the 'old' due process voluntariness test." Stephen J. Schulhofer, *Confessions and the Court*, 79 Mich.L.Rev. 865, 877 (1981). For one thing, empirical studies indicate that most suspects waive their rights and submit to police questioning. "Because the admissibility of statements given after a valid waiver of *Miranda* rights must be determined on the basis of the voluntariness test, that test remains vitally important." Welsh S. White, *What is an Involuntary Confession Now?*, 50 Rutgers L.Rev. 2001, 2004 (1998). Moreover, as Schulhofer, supra, points out, the voluntariness test is important when suspects *not* in custody are questioned by the police; when suspects in a custody-like situation are questioned (or threatened) by private citizens (e.g. *Commonwealth v. Mahnke*, 335 N.E.2d 660 (Mass.1975)); or when the prosecution seeks to use a confession to impeach a defendant's testimony at trial or to use the "fruits" of the confession (e.g., the murder weapon), but not the confession itself. As discussed in Ch. 11, §§ 2,3, although statements obtained in violation of *Miranda* may be used for impeachment purposes, "coerced" or "involuntary" statements may not. Moreover, although the distinctions have not yet been fully developed, the Court has left little doubt that it is much more likely to permit the use of evidence *derived from* a *Miranda* violation than the "fruits" of an "involuntary" confession.

A. *MILLER v. FENTON*: WHAT KINDS OF TRICKERY OR DECEPTION, IF ANY, MAY THE POLICE EMPLOY *AFTER* A SUSPECT HAS WAIVED HIS RIGHTS?

Is *Miranda*'s prohibition against police deception and trickery limited to their use *in obtaining a waiver* of *Miranda* rights or does it also bar such police techniques *after* a person has validly waived his rights? Suppose a suspect waives his rights and expresses a willingness to talk, but denies any involvement in the case. May the police then display apparent sympathy? Turn the suspect over to a

friendly, gentle interrogator and then to a hostile, short-tempered one (the "Mutt
and Jeff" routine)? Although such techniques seemed to have vented Chief Justice
Warren's judicial ire in *Miranda*, that landmark case "did not condemn any
specific techniques as such or hold that evidence obtained by use of them would be
inadmissible. Reliance was placed on warning and counsel to protect the suspect."
Sheldon Elsen & Arthur Rosett, *Protections for the Suspect under Miranda v.
Arizona,* 67 Colum.L.Rev. 645, 667 (1967). More than two decades after *Miranda,*
the issue has yet to be clearly resolved.[a]

A year after *Miranda,* Professor Fred Inbau and Mr. John Reid published a
new edition of their leading interrogation manual and maintained that "all but a
very few of the interrogation techniques presented in our earlier [pre-*Escobedo,*
pre-*Miranda*] publication are still valid if used after the recently prescribed
warnings have been given to the suspect under interrogation, and after he has
waived his self-incriminating privilege and his right to counsel." See *Criminal
Interrogation and Confessions,* (2d ed. 1967). See also Inbau, Reid & Buckley,
Criminal Interrogation and Confessions 216 (3d ed. 1986), maintaining that,
although the Court did not explicitly address the issue in *Frazier v. Cupp,* fn. a
supra, that case "implicitly recognized" the essentiality of interrogation practices
involving trickery or deceit, and approved of them. [Moreover,] there are many
appellate court cases holding that a confession is admissible even when it was
obtained by trickery and deceit, [provided that the trickery does not] 'shock the
conscience' [or is not] apt to induce a false confession."[b]

Welsh S. White, *Police Trickery in Inducing Confessions,* 127 U.Pa.L.Rev.
581–90, 599–600, 628–29 (1979), takes a very different view of police use of
trickery in the post-*Miranda* era, maintaining that, because they are likely to
render a resulting confession involuntary *or* because they distort the meaning or
vitiate the effect of the *Miranda* warnings *or* because they "undermine [a]
suspect's independent right to an attorney," "several widely employed interrogation tactics * * * should be absolutely prohibited." Among the techniques Professor White considers "impermissible *per se*" are deception that distorts the
seriousness of the matter under investigation (e.g., falsely informing a murder
suspect that the victim is still alive), the "assumption of non-adversary roles" by
interrogating officers (e.g., assuming the role of a father figure or religious

a. Cf. *Frazier v. Cupp,* 394 U.S. 731, 89
S.Ct. 1420, 22 L.Ed.2d 684 (1969) (admitting a
confession in a pre-*Miranda* case although the
police had falsely told the defendant that another had confessed and had also "sympathet-
ically" suggested that the victim's homosexual
advances may have started the fight). See also
Oregon v. Mathiason (p. 518) (interrogator's
false statement to defendant that his fingerprints were found at scene may have bearing
on other issues in case, but "has nothing to do
with whether [defendant] was in custody for
[*Miranda*] purposes").

b. Although agreeing that a goodly number
of lower courts have interpreted *Frazier* as
"definitively ruling that police trickery is a
mere factor to be included in a court's assessment of a confession's involuntariness under a
totality of the circumstances analysis," Note,
40 Stan.L.Rev. 1593, 1607–08 (1988), maintains that "several factors make *Frazier* a particularly bad case for a definitive ruling on
police trickery":

"First, the opinion does not recognize as
trickery the detective's feigned sympathy in his
suggestion that a homosexual advance was a
reason for the fight. Also, *Frazier* was tried
and decided before the *Miranda* decision, and
so the Court's indictment of police misconduct
in *Miranda* did not apply. * * * Third, apart
from the one recognized and one unrecognized
instances of police trickery, the interrogators' behavior was exemplary. The police gave
coercive conduct a wide berth, questioning Frazier for only forty-five minutes immediately
after he was brought to the police station. In
addition, the interrogation was tape-recorded
and the tape played for the trial judge, who
subsequently concluded that the confession
was voluntary. Last and most important, the
police lie that [another person] had confessed,
the only trickery recognized by the Court, does
not seem to have induced Frazier's confession."

counselor), repeated assurances that the suspect is known to be guilty, and the "Mutt and Jeff" routine. See also Note, 40 Stan.L.Rev. 1593, 1612–15 (1988).

But police deception and trickery did not prevent the admissibility of the resulting confession in *Miller v. Fenton,* below. *Miller* is a dramatic illustration that the problems raised by the old "totality of the circumstances"—"due process"—"voluntariness" test have not disappeared in the post-*Miranda* era.

When he accompanied the police to a state police barracks, Miller, the prime suspect in the brutal murder of Ms. Margolin, was advised of his rights and signed "a *Miranda* card," waiving his rights.[a] Thus, the issue in MILLER v. FENTON, 796 F.2d 598 (3d Cir.1986), was the "voluntariness" of the defendant's murder confession.[b] A 2–1 majority, per BECKER, J. (joined by Seitz, J.), framed the issue in terms of whether the tactics of Detective Boyce during the 53–minute interrogation "were sufficiently manipulative to overbear the will of a person with [defendant's] characteristics" and viewed the limits of permissible interrogation as turning on "a weighing of the circumstances of pressure [applied by the police] against the power of resistance of the person confessing." After listening to Detective Boyce's questions and defendant Miller's responses (the police had taped the interrogation), the majority concluded that "under the totality of circumstances of this case" Miller's confession was "voluntarily given":

"It is clear that Boyce made no threats and engaged in no physical coercion of Miller. To the contrary, throughout the interview, Detective Boyce assumed a friendly, understanding manner and spoke in a soft tone of voice. He repeatedly assured Miller that he was sympathetic to him and wanted to help him unburden his mind. [The detective's] statements of sympathy at times approached the maudlin. [E.g., 'This hurts me more than it hurts you because I love people * * * I'm on your side, Frank * * * I'm your brother, you and I are brothers, Frank [and] I want to help my brother.']

"Boyce also gave Miller certain factual information, some of which was untrue. At the beginning of the interrogation, for example, Boyce informed Miller that the victim was still alive; this was false. During the interview, Boyce told Miller that Ms. Margolin had just died, although in fact she had been found dead several hours earlier.

"Detective Boyce's major theme throughout the interrogation was that whoever had committed such a heinous crime had mental problems and was desperately in need of psychological treatment. [The] Detective stated several times that Miller was not a criminal who should be punished, but a sick individual who should receive help. * * *

"Boyce also appealed to Miller's conscience and described the importance of Miller's purging himself of the memories that must be haunting him. [E.g., 'First thing we have to do is let it all come out. Don't fight it because it's worse * * * It's hurting me because I feel it. I feel it wanting to come out, but it's hurting me,

---

a. Several hours earlier, Miller had been questioned by the police for about 45 minutes at his place of employment, but had denied any involvement in the murder.

b. The case has a long procedural history. After a New Jersey trial court admitted his confession, Miller was convicted of murder. A three-judge panel of an intermediate state appellate court reversed, holding Miller's confession "involuntary." But a 4–3 majority of the New Jersey Supreme Court reinstated the con-

viction, deeming the confession "voluntary." On federal habeas corpus, the Third Circuit, deferring to the state court's finding of "voluntariness," upheld the admissibility of the confession. The U.S. Supreme Court reversed (see p. 455), holding that on federal habeas corpus the "voluntariness" of a confession is a matter for independent federal court determination, and remanding the case for a fuller analysis under the correct standard.

Frank. * * * I know how you feel inside, Frank, it's eating you up, am I right? * * * You've got to come forward. You've got to do it for yourself, for your family, for your father, this is what's important, the truth, Frank.']

"When Miller at last confessed [almost an hour after the interrogation session began], he collapsed in a state of shock. He slid off his chair and onto the floor with a blank stare on his face. The police officers sent for a first aid squad that took him to the hospital. * * *

"[Psychological] ploys may play a part in the suspect's decision to confess, but as long as that decision is a product of the suspect's own balancing of competing considerations, the confession is voluntary. The question we must answer [is] whether [the detective's] statements were so manipulative or coercive that they deprived Miller of his ability to make an unconstrained autonomous decision to confess. To that inquiry we now turn. * * *

"Miller is a mature adult, thirty-two years of age [and] has some high school education. Such a person is more resistant to interrogation than a person who is very young, uneducated or weak-minded. [Moreover,] Miller [had] served a jail sentence. Thus, he was aware of the consequences of confessing. [He had also] received *Miranda* warnings. Detective Boyce's interrogation of Miller lasted less than an hour. [I]t is thus distinguishable from the lengthy interrogations during incommunicado detention that have been held to result in involuntary confessions. * * *

"Boyce's supportive, encouraging manner was an interrogation tactic aimed at winning Miller's trust and making him feel comfortable about confessing. Excessive friendliness on the part of an interrogator can be deceptive. In some instances, in combination with other tactics, it might create an atmosphere in which a suspect forgets that his questioner is in an adversarial role, and thereby prompt admissions that the suspect would ordinarily make only to a friend, not to the police. [But] the 'good guy' approach is recognized as a permissible interrogation tactic. * * *

"[While an officer's] lie [about] an important aspect of the case may affect the voluntariness of the confession, the effect of the lie must be analyzed in the context of all the circumstances of the interrogation. See, e.g., *Frazier v. Cupp* * * *. We do not believe that the lie about the time of Ms. Margolin's death, by itself, constituted sufficient trickery to overcome Miller's will. [The] drama of the announcement of the victims death [during the interrogation] might have prompted particularly acute feelings in Miller, which could have helped to induce his confession. However, the record suggests that this emotional reaction did not occur, for it appears that Miller was not affected at all by the news of the death. Indeed, he remained quite impassive. * * *

"Detective Boyce's statements that Miller was not a criminal, but rather a mentally ill individual not responsible for his actions, and Boyce's promises to help Miller raise a more serious question about the voluntariness of Miller's confession. By telling Miller that he was not responsible for anything he might have done, Boyce may have been understood to be making an implied promise to Miller that [he] would not be prosecuted, or that if he were prosecuted Boyce would aid him in presenting the insanity defense. Similarly, the promises of psychiatric help might have suggested to Miller that he would be treated, rather than prosecuted. If these promises, implicit and explicit, tricked Miller into confessing, his confession may have been involuntary. To determine whether Boyce's promises affected the voluntariness of Miller's confession, we must consider how manipulative these tactics in fact were.

"In *Bram v. United States,* (1897) [p. 468] [the Court] endorsed the view that to be voluntary a confession must not have been 'extracted by any sort of threats or violence, *nor obtained by any direct or implied promises, however slight.*' [Emphasis added.] Although the *Bram* test has been reaffirmed [it] has not been interpreted as a *per se* proscription against promises made during interrogation.[c] Nor does the Supreme Court even use a but-for test when promises have been made during an interrogation.

"[At] no time did Detective Boyce state that Miller would not be prosecuted or that he could successfully avail himself of the insanity defense. [While] innuendo might rise to the level of trickery, it is not so likely to break down resistance as is a promise that is spelled out. Indeed, Boyce's statements that Miller was 'not a criminal' need not be understood as assurances of leniency at all. Since [Boyce's] strategy was to present himself as a friend to whom Miller could unburden himself, he of course attempted throughout the interview to persuade Miller to trust him and confide in him. The statement at issue can be viewed as a means of convincing Miller that Boyce was sympathetic, no matter what the state's reaction might be. 'You are not responsible' and 'You are not a criminal' thus would mean 'In my eyes, you are not responsible or a criminal and therefore you should relieve your conscience by talking to me, who understands you.'

"While such a statement might have made Miller feel more comfortable about speaking to Boyce, it would not render his confession the product of a mistaken belief that the state would grant him leniency. Detective Boyce never stated that anyone but he thought that Miller was 'not a criminal' nor did he state that he had any authority to affect the charges brought against Miller. Miller's confession may have been made in the hope of leniency, but that does not mean that it was made in response to a promise of leniency.

"[While] Boyce's promises of psychiatric help and statements that Miller was 'not a criminal,' in combination with his friendly manner, may have been a form of psychological trickery, we do not believe that these elements of the interrogation affected the voluntariness of the confession. Miller's personal characteristics support a conclusion that the confession was voluntary, for Miller does not seem to be the type of person whose will would be easily overborne by Boyce's remarks. Miller's age, intelligence and experience rendered him resistant to the level of persuasiveness that Boyce employed.

"Moreover, throughout the interview, Miller made remarks that indicate that he knew that this was an ordinary police interrogation rather than an encounter with a compassionate friend, and that he was aware that a confession would result in criminal prosecution and possibly in conviction and sentence. Throughout the session, he appears to have retained a suspicious, guarded attitude. * * *

"[In light of some statements by Miller indicating that his] prior experience with the law had made him wary of policemen [it] is difficult for us to believe that [he] was tricked into confessing. Rather, it seems that Miller made an uncoerced decision to unburden his inner tensions and to acknowledge his guilt. Indeed, from

---

c. But cf. LaFave & Israel, § 6.2(c): "[L]ower courts have rather consistently held that a confession is involuntary if made in response to a promise that the result will be nonprosecution, the dropping of some charges, or a certain reduction in the punishment defendant may receive. But the cases go both ways on the question of what the result should be when a confession has been obtained in response to a police assertion that cooperation would facilitate prompt release on bail or would mean that the defendant would fare better in subsequent proceedings. Especially as to the latter situation, '[m]uch of the difficulty arises from failure to reconcile the voluntariness requirement with the plea bargaining process and especially the role of the police in that practice.'"

the tape of the interrogation, it clearly appears that the precipitating cause of Miller's confession was a desire to make a clean breast of it, rather than a reliance on any promise of leniency or psychiatric help. * * *

"We have little doubt that Detective Boyce's encouraging words, perhaps in contribution with the sad announcement that the victim had just died, helped Miller to reach his decision to unburden himself. However, the test for voluntariness is not a but-for test, but a question of whether the confession was a product of free choice. * * * Many criminals experience an urge during interrogation to own up to their crimes. * * * Boyce's manner and his statements may have stirred this urge in Miller, but, in our view, they did not produce psychological pressure strong enough to overbear the will of a mature, experienced man, who was suffering from no mental or physical illness and was interrogated for less than an hour at a police station close to his home.

"Detective Boyce's method of interrogation might have overborne the will of another detainee, for example, a young, inexperienced person of lower intelligence than Miller, or a person suffering from a painful physical ailment. It might have overcome the will of Miller himself if the interrogation had been longer or if Miller had been refused food, sleep, or contact with a person he wished to see. Moreover, if Miller had made remarks that indicated that he truly believed that the state would treat him leniently because he was 'not responsible' for what he had done or that he believed that he would receive psychiatric help rather than punishment, we might not find the confession voluntary. We hold simply that, under the totality of the circumstances of this case, the confession was voluntarily given."

Dissenting Judge GIBBONS protested:

"[B]y endorsing a thoroughly bad piece of police work, the majority sends a signal to the police community * * * likely to have the harmful consequence of encouraging coercion of defendants in place of acceptable methods of investigation. [T]he police did not need to conduct an interrogation directed at investigating the murder; [they had acquired so much information pointing to Miller that the case] was already solved so far as they were concerned. [They] conducted an interrogation directed at obtaining a confession from the sole suspect, and that investigation was designed to assure Miller's prosecution for felony murder rather than a lesser offense.

"For me, although obviously not for the majority, the most significant circumstance in this case supporting the conclusion that Miller's admission was obtained in a manner inconsistent with the Constitution is the complete absence of any legitimate investigative purpose for the interrogation. The circumstances of this case provide a classic illustration of the once common practice of obtaining guilty pleas in the back rooms of police stations rather than in open court. Moreover, the evidence of the method of interrogation must be examined in light of Officer Boyce's sole purpose—the obtaining of admissions of guilt, not the solution of a crime which Boyce believed to be solved already. * * *

"The majority stresses that Boyce 'repeatedly assured Miller that he was sympathetic to him and wanted to help him unburden his mind.' Admittedly, Boyce did feign sympathy for Miller, but clearly unburdening Miller's mind was not Boyce's purpose. The repeated assurances, the friendly, understanding manner, and the soft tone of voice to which the majority makes reference were all directed to a single purpose—making an unwilling defendant admit his guilt. Referring to the detective's statement of sympathy as 'maudlin' is deceptive. Every word, every nuance of expression, every change in tone of voice, was calculated toward one end, and one end only—obtaining an admission of guilt.

From the tone of the majority opinion one might believe that its author actually credits these deceptive expressions of sympathy. But as the majority well knows the state police are not in the business of acting as religious or psychiatric counselors. Boyce was not sympathetic. He was no more interested in helping Miller 'unburden his inner tensions' than he was in any other aspect of Miller's health. Instead Boyce was determined and ultimately successful in obtaining from an unwilling defendant the one thing that was his purpose—a confession. * * *

"The majority, acknowledging that the police had previously lied to Miller that Ms. Margolin had survived and that Boyce repeated the lie about the time of her death, attempts to put the deliberate trickery in a positive light, observing,

'We do not believe that the lie about the time of Ms. Margolin's death, by itself, constituted sufficient trickery to overcome Miller's will. Because Boyce never suggested that the time of Ms. Margolin's death might be relevant in linking Miller to the crime, the only possible effect of Boyce's initial statement that she was alive, followed by his report that she had just died, would be an emotional response in Miller.'

"There are several glaring deficiencies in this attempted justification. First, it ignores the plain fact that, by initially suggesting to Miller that Ms. Margolin survived, the police intended to leave him with the impression that she would eventually identify him. When that ploy proved to be unsuccessful in breaking down his will, Boyce shifted to a different tactic, by announcing, falsely, that she had just died. Boyce hoped, as the majority concedes, to evoke an emotional response in Miller. Admitting that this was an attempt at psychological coercion, the majority explains it away with the preposterous statement, 'However, the record suggests that this emotional reaction did not occur, for it appears that Miller was not affected at all by the news of the death.' What the record actually discloses is that the interrogation continued as follows:

BOYCE: Are you, do you feel what I feel right now?

MILLER: I feel pretty bad.

BOYCE: Do you want to talk to me about it?

MILLER: There's nothing I can tell . . .

BOYCE: About how you feel?

MILLER: . . . there's nothing I can talk, I mean I feel sorry for this girl, I mean, uh, this is something that, you know

. . .

BOYCE: That what?

MILLER: Well, it's a shame, uh . . .

* * *

BOYCE: Frank, you're very, very nervous. Now, I, I don't, you know, you, you're, you understand what I'm saying?

MILLER: Yeah, I know what you're saying.

BOYCE: Now, there's a reason for that, isn't there?

MILLER: Yes.

BOYCE: Do you want to tell me about it?

MILLER: Being involved in something like this is . . .

BOYCE: Is what, does it, does it, does it visibly shake you physically?

MILLER: Yes, it does, * * *.

"At this point, twenty-seven minutes into the second interrogation, it was briefly interrupted while the recording cassette was turned over. Boyce had by then spent seven minutes attempting to capitalize on the emotional response he attempted to elicit by his staged phone call about Ms. Margolin's recent death. I leave it to the reader to judge whether this colloquy establishes that, in the words of the majority opinion, Miller 'remained quite impassive.' Having listened to the tape recording on several occasions, I represent that Miller sounds, at this point of the interrogation, increasingly tense and emotional. So emotional, indeed, that the interrogator, Boyce, stated, 'Frank, you're very, very nervous.'

"The colloquy above, occurring immediately following Boyce's lie about the time of death, is not mentioned by the majority in connection with the police lies because the majority, bent on a result, has chosen to judge the police conduct not in light of the totality of the circumstances, but by subdividing each instance of police misconduct and discussing it in isolation. Thus, it chooses to treat the colloquy that immediately followed Boyce's lies under the heading of Boyce's promises. These are dismissed with the observation, 'While such a statement might have made Miller feel more comfortable about speaking to Boyce, it would not render his confession the product of a mistaken belief that the state would grant him leniency.' The total unfairness of that cavalier dismissal of the *intended* effect upon Miller's will may best be judged in light of the colloquy that continued as soon as the tape recorder was turned on:

BOYCE: Now listen to me Frank. This hurts me more than it hurts you, because I love people.

MILLER: It can't hurt you anymore than it hurts me. * * *

BOYCE: Okay, listen Frank. *If I promise to, you know, do all I can with the psychiatrist and everything, and we get the proper help for you, and get the proper help for you, will you talk to me about it?*

MILLER: I can't talk to you about something I'm not ...

BOYCE: Alright, listen Frank, alright, honest. I know, I know what's going on inside you, Frank. I want to help you, you know, between us right now. I know what going on inside you, Frank, you've got to come forward and tell me that you want to help yourself. You've got to talk to me about it. This is the only way we'll be able to work it out. I mean, you know, listen, I want to help you, because you are in my mind, *you are not responsible. You are not responsible, Frank. Frank, what's the matter?*

MILLER: I feel bad.

BOYCE: Frank, listen to me, honest to God, I'm I'm telling you, Frank (inaudible). I know, it's going to bother you, Frank, it's going to bother you. It's there, it's not going to go away, it's there. It's right in front of you, Frank. Am I right or wrong?

MILLER: Yeah.

BOYCE: You can see it Frank, you can feel it, you can feel it, *but you are not responsible.* This is what I'm trying to tell you, but you've got to come forward and tell me. Don't, don't, don't let it eat you up, don't, don't fight it. You've got to rectify it, Frank. We've got to get together on this thing, or I, I mean really, *you need help, you need proper help and you know it, my God, you know, in God's name you, you, you know it. You are not a criminal, you are not a criminal.*

MILLER: Alright. Yes, I was over there and I talked to her about the cow and left. I left in my car and I stopped up on the road where, you know, where the cow had been and she followed me in her car . . .

"Thus, approximately thirty minutes into the second interrogation, Miller made his first incriminating statement. By far the largest part of that thirty minutes is comprised of lies and promises by Boyce. The majority's suggestion that these lies and promises had no effect upon Miller's will is utter speculation. The lies and promises were directed to the sole purpose of obtaining a confession. There is nothing in the record from which it can be inferred that Miller's abandonment of his self-interested denials of involvement in the homicide was the product of any other influence. The majority opinion describes Boyce's conduct as if he were a confessor, offering solace under the seal of the confessional, or a psychiatrist offering relief from anxiety under the shelter of a physician-patient privilege, rather than what he was—a wily interrogator determined to break down Miller's resistance by lies and false promises. The majority's treatment of the police tactics leading to Miller's collapse is about as fair as those tactics. Confession may be good for the soul, but it was Miller's freedom, not his soul, that was at stake, and it was his freedom, not his soul, that interested Boyce. * * *

"The reason why the state had to preserve and make use of the tape-recorded interrogation appears in Boyce's testimony at the suppression hearing:

Q. I gather that [a] statement was never taken, is that right?

A. It was not.

Q. Why was that, Officer?

A. Momentarily after terminating this particular interview Mr. Miller went into as I can best define it a state of shock.

Q. What do you mean by that, sir?

A. He was sitting on a chair? . . . Mr. Miller had been sitting on a chair, had slid off the chair on the floor maintaining a blank stare on his face, staring straight ahead and we were unable to get any type of verbal response from him. * * *

"Incredibly, the only reference in the majority's opinion to Miller's collapse is the cryptic sentence [that] 'One hour into the interrogation, Miller confessed to the murder of Deborah Margolin, then passed out.' The majority does not even recognize Miller's collapse into a catatonic state and his transportation to a hospital as relevant circumstances in its totality of the circumstances analysis! This most telling of all indications as to the effect on Miller of Boyce's tactics is simply ignored. Instead the majority opinion perversely reasons that Boyce's manner and statements may have stirred in Miller the urge to confess, 'but, in our view, they did not produce psychological pressure strong enough to overbear the will of a mature, experienced man, who was suffering from no mental or physical illness. . . .' The reasoning is perverse because it ignores the fact that at the end of the interrogation Miller collapsed and was taken to a hospital. How can it be honestly represented that he was suffering from no mental or physical illness? And, unless the majority identifies some other reason for Miller's abrupt abandonment of his self-interested denials of guilt than the psychological coercion exercised by Boyce, what other cause is left? * * *

"It has long been established that confessions obtained by virtue of even implied promises of leniency are deemed to be inadmissible. See *Bram v. United States* (1897). The majority attempts to undercut the authority of the *Bram* rule by suggesting that it is no longer interpreted as a *per se* proscription against promises made during interrogations. [But the] Supreme Court has never retreated from the *Bram* holding. Indeed, other federal circuit courts of appeals have consistently cited the *Bram* test as the standard by which voluntariness will be evaluated. [Thus,] when promises, however slight, are made in the interrogation room rather than in the presence of counsel, those promises render the resulting confession inadmissible.

"Boyce's second interrogation cannot be read in pieces. Its effect was cumulative, as it was intended to be. From the moment he began it, Boyce put relentless psychological pressure on Miller. Boyce repeatedly assured Miller that he only wanted to help Miller, that Miller was not a criminal, that Miller was not responsible for his actions, and that Miller would not be punished. In addition to these express promises, Boyce confused Miller by lying to him about the time of Ms. Margolin's death and the strength of the evidence against Miller.

"The majority emphasizes that the key issue is whether, in the totality of the circumstances, Miller's will was overborne. While I agree with the majority's general focus, I disagree with the majority's method of analysis. In ascertaining the effects of Boyce's interrogation tactics on Miller, the majority attempts to place itself in Miller's position and thereby evaluate the impact of Boyce's promises and lies. Unfortunately, we cannot know what effects those promises and lies had on Miller's will. Instead what we can know is that when, as in this case, the record reveals a series of repeated promises of psychological help and assurances that the suspect will not be punished, *Bram* requires as a matter of law that we hold the resulting confession to be coerced. Any other rule leads to the kind of subjective speculation that the majority engages in. Thus applying the *Bram* rule within the totality of the circumstances of Miller's interrogation, the confession used to commit Miller must be declared inadmissible as a violation of Miller's fifth amendment right to remain silent."

Notes and Questions

1. *Should "police trickery" in obtaining confessions be barred? What is "trickery" in the confession context?* Consider Note, 40 Stan.L.Rev. 1593, 1594–95 (1988): "The courts have not clearly defined the term 'trickery' and 'trickery' has been used interchangeably with 'misrepresentation,' 'artifice,' 'deception,' 'fraud,' and 'subterfuge.' This note argues that the term trickery, when used in the confessions context, should be defined as police elicitation of a confession by deliberate distortion of material fact, by failure to disclose to the defendant a material fact, or by playing on a defendant's emotions or scruples. Police trickery should be viewed as a type of fraud, the use of which as an interrogation tool is inconsistent with our adversarial system of criminal justice because it allows the prosecution an unfair, indeed an unconstitutional, advantage at trial."

2. *The relationship between Miller and Detective Boyce.* At one point the *Miller* majority observes that Boyce's statements to Miller that he is "not a criminal" who should be punished, and "not responsible" for anything he might have done "need not be understood as assurances of leniency" but could be viewed as the expression of sympathy by "a friend"—"a means of convincing Miller that Boyce [personally] was sympathetic, no matter what the state's reaction might be." At another point, however, the majority opinion observes that Miller's

responses indicated "he knew that this was an ordinary police interrogation, rather than an encounter with a compassionate friend." Which is it?

To avoid the prohibition against obtaining confessions by promises of leniency, one might say, as the majority does at one point, that Boyce's "interrogation strategy was to present himself as a friend to whom Miller would unburden," and that, as the majority suggests at several places, the detective's strategy succeeded. If so, however, doesn't this raise another problem? If Boyce led Miller to believe he was a sympathetic friend didn't Boyce cause Miller to forget that his questioner was in an adversarial role and thus negate the effect of the *Miranda* warnings?

3. *Drawing a line between expressions of sympathy and implied promises of leniency.* Compare the Stanford Note with Phillip Johnson, *A Statutory Replacement for the Miranda Doctrine,* 24 Am.Crim.L.Rev. 303, 305 (1987), proposing that the police be forbidden to make "any statement which is intended to imply or may reasonably be understood as implying that the suspect will not be prosecuted or punished," but approving police expressions of sympathy and compassion, whether real or feigned; police appeals to the suspect's conscience, religious or otherwise; and police appeals to the suspect's sympathy for the victim or other affected persons.

Observes Professor Johnson, id. at 310–11: "Offers of leniency can be made later in the plea bargaining process, where the accused is represented by counsel and can properly evaluate what is being offered. Promises of leniency from the police during interrogation are too likely to be deceptive, and too likely to give even an innocent suspect the impression that confession is the only way to escape conviction or mitigate the punishment. [However, police expressions of sympathy and compassion should be permitted because] a pose of sympathy is not overbearing or coercive, nor is it likely by itself to encourage an innocent person to provide a confession. A difficulty in this area is that the difference between expressions of compassionate understanding on the one hand, and implied promises of leniency on the other, is at the margin sometimes a matter of emphasis and nuance." Did Detective Boyce cross the line in the *Miller* case? See id. at 311.

4. *How should the law respond to empirical data indicating that the interrogation tactics of threatening harsh punishment if the suspect does not confess and/or significant leniency if he does are likely to induce false confessions?* According to studies of the interrogation process and of sixty known and probable false confession cases by Professors Richard J. Ofshe and Richard A. Leo, see *The Consequences of False Confessions,* 88 J.Crim.L. & C. 429 (1998) and *The Social Psychology of Police Interrogation,* 16 Studies in Law, Politics & Society 189 (1997), threatening a suspect with harsh punishment if he does not confess and/or promising him leniency if he does are "coercive" police interrogation tactics likely to induce false confessions. What follows from this? See Welsh S. White, *What Is a Voluntary Confession Now?,* 50 Rutgers L.Rev. 2001, 2052–53 (1998). After discussing *Leyra v. Denno* (1954) (p. 454) and *Lynumn v. Illinois* (1963) (p. 454), two pre-*Miranda* "voluntariness" cases "which suggest that interrogation tactics that threaten the suspect with harsh punishments if she does not confess or offer express or implied promises of significant sentencing advantages if she does may exert such unfair pressure on the suspect as to render the resulting confession involuntary," Profess White comments: "[T]he Court could establish the rule that interrogation tactics that threaten harsh consequences if the suspect does not confess or suggest that she will receive significant leniency in terms of disposition [citing *Miller v. Fenton*] or sentence if she does will generally be sufficient to render a resulting confession involuntary."

5. *Distinguishing among different kinds of trickery.* The Ofshe–Leo studies, supra Note 4, indicate that in certain situations the tactic of misrepresenting evidence of the suspect's guilt is likely to produce an untrustworthy confession and that "false evidence ploys based on scientific procedures" are more likely to produce a false confession than similar ploys based on eyewitness reports. Professor White, supra Note 4, at 2055, believes that the Leo–Ofshe data "provide a clear basis for distinguishing among different kinds of trickery. Based on [this data], a court applying the Due Process test could properly hold that certain types of misrepresentation should be strongly condemned and perhaps sufficient in themselves to render a resulting confession involuntary. Specifically, misrepresentations designed to convince the suspect that his guilt has been established by either forensic evidence or his failure to pass a lie detector test should be prohibited, or at least viewed as likely to render a resulting confession involuntary."

6. *More on false verbal assertions by the police vs. the fabrication of scientific evidence.* Interestingly, long before the Leo–Ofshe empirical studies had been published, one lower court drew a line between police deception generally (which does not render a confession involuntary per se) and the "manufacturing" of false documents or scientific evidence by the police (which "has no place in our criminal justice system"). *State v. Layward,* 552 So.2d 971 (Fla.App.1989). The case arose as follows: The police suspected defendant of sexually assaulting and killing his five-year-old niece. They intentionally fabricated laboratory reports indicating that a scientific test established that the semen stains on the victim's underwear came from defendant and showed the reports to him. He confessed soon after. In upholding the trial court's suppression of the confession, the District Court of Appeal of Florida observed:

"We think [that] both the suspect's and the public's expectations concerning the built-in adversariness of police interrogations do not encompass the notion that the police will knowingly fabricate tangible documentation or physical evidence against an individual. [The] manufacturing of false documents by police officials offends our traditional notions of due process. [Moreover,] manufactured documents have the potential of indefinite life and the facial appearance of authenticity." Thus, they "might be disclosed to the media as a result of the public records law" or find their way into the courtroom.

Is there, as the Florida court believed, an "intrinsic" or "qualitative" difference between police lying, e.g., the false assertion that the suspect's fingerprints were found at the scene of the crime, and manufactured evidence? If, as the Florida court maintained, sanctioning police fabrication of documents "would greatly lessen the respect the public has for the criminal justice system and for those sworn to uphold and enforce the law," doesn't this concern apply to false verbal assertions by police interrogators as well? See Jerome H. Skolnick and Richard A. Leo, *The Ethics of Deceptive Interrogation,* Crim.Justice Ethics, Winter/Spring 1992, pp. 3, 7–9.

7. *Offering to protect a prisoner from physical harm at the hands of other inmates.* Consider ARIZONA v. FULMINANTE, 499 U.S. 279, 111 S.Ct. 1246, 113 L.Ed.2d 302 (1991) (other aspects of which are discussed in Ch. 27). The case arose as follows: After defendant Fulminante's 11–year-old stepdaughter, Jeneane, was murdered, he was convicted of an unrelated federal crime and incarcerated in a federal prison. There he was befriended by another inmate, Sarivola, who was a paid informant for the FBI masquerading as an organized crime figure. Upon hearing a rumor that defendant had killed his stepdaughter, Sarivola brought up

the subject several times, but defendant repeatedly denied any involvement in the murder. Then Sarivola told defendant that he knew he was "starting to get some tough treatment" from other inmates because of the rumor that he had killed his stepdaughter but that he, Sarivola, would protect defendant from his fellow inmates if he told him the truth about the murder. Defendant then confessed to Sarivola that he had sexually molested and killed Jeneane. The confession was admitted at defendant's trial and he was convicted of murder and sentenced to death. On appeal, the state supreme court held that the confession was coerced. Although it considered the question "a close one," a 5–4 majority of the Supreme Court, per WHITE, J., agreed with the state supreme court:

"In applying the totality of the circumstances test to determine that the confession to Sarivola was coerced, the Arizona Supreme Court focused on a number of relevant facts. First, the court noted that 'because [Fulminante] was an alleged child murderer, he was in physical harm at the hands of other inmates.' In addition, Sarivola was aware that Fulminante was receiving 'rough treatment from the guys.' Using his knowledge of these threats, Sarivola offered to protect Fulminante in exchange for a confession to Jeneane's murder and 'in response to Sarivola's offer of protection [Fulminante] confessed.' Agreeing with Fulminante that 'Sarivola's promise was "extremely coercive," ' the Arizona Court declared: '[T]he confession was obtained as a direct result of extreme coercion and was tendered in the belief that the defendant's life was in jeopardy if he did not confess. * * * '

"We normally give great deference to the factual findings of the state court. Nevertheless, 'the ultimate issue of "voluntariness" is a legal question requiring independent federal determination.' Although the question is a close one, we agree [that] Fulminante's confession was coerced. The Arizona Supreme Court found a credible threat of physical violence unless Fulminante confessed. [A] finding of coercion need not depend upon actual violence by a government agent; a credible threat is sufficient. [As] in *Payne v. Arkansas,* 356 U.S. 560, 78 S.Ct. 844, 2 L.Ed.2d 975 (1958)], where the Court found that a confession was coerced because the interrogating police officer had promised that if the accused confessed, the officer would protect the accused from an angry mob outside the jailhouse door, so too here, the Arizona Supreme Court found that it was fear of physical violence, absent protection from his friend (and Government agent) Sarivola, which motivated Fulminante to confess. Accepting the Arizona court's finding, permissible on this record, that there was a credible threat of physical violence, we agree that Fulminante's will was overborne in such a way as to render his confession the product of coercion."

Dissenting on this issue, REHNQUIST, C.J., joined by O'Connor, Kennedy and Souter, JJ., was "at a loss to see how the Supreme Court of Arizona reached the conclusion that it did":

"Fulminante offered no evidence that he believed his life was in danger or that he in fact confessed to Sarivola in order to obtain the proffered protection. Indeed, he had stipulated that '[a]t no time did the defendant indicate he was in fear of other inmates nor did he ever seek Mr. Sarivola's "protection." ' Sarivola's testimony that he told Fulminante that 'if [he] would tell the truth, he could be protected,' adds little if anything to the substance of the parties' stipulation. The decision of the Supreme Court of Arizona rests on an assumption that is squarely contrary to this stipulation, and one that is not supported by any testimony of Fulminante.

"The facts of record in the present case are quite different from those present in cases where we have found confessions to be coerced and involuntary. Since Fulminante was unaware that Sarivola was an FBI informant, there existed none of 'the danger of coercion result[ing] from the interaction of custody and official interrogation.' *Illinois v. Perkins* [p. 528]. [The] conversations between Sarivola and Fulminante were not lengthy, and the defendant was free at all times to leave Sarivola's company. Sarivola at no time threatened him or demanded that he confess; he simply requested that he speak the truth about the matter. Fulminante was an experienced habitue of prisons, and presumably able to fend for himself. In concluding on these facts that Fulminante's confession was involuntary, the Court today embraces a more expansive definition of that term than is warranted by any of our decided cases."

B. *COLORADO V. CONNELLY*: DID THE COURT DECLINE TO EXPAND THE "VOLUNTARINESS" TEST OR DID IT REVISE THE TEST SIGNIFICANTLY?

In COLORADO v. CONNELLY, 479 U.S. 157, 107 S.Ct. 515, 93 L.Ed.2d 473 (1986) (also discussed at pp. 451–52, fns. b and c), the Court held, per REHNQUIST, C.J., that "coercive police activity is a necessary predicate to the finding that a confession is not 'voluntary' within the meaning of the Due Process Clause"; "[a]bsent police conduct causally related to the confession, there is simply no basis for concluding that any state action has deprived a criminal defendant of due process of law." The case arose as follows:

Respondent, a mentally ill person flew from Boston to Denver, approached a uniformed police officer on a downtown Denver street and, without any prompting, told the officer that "he had killed someone" and wanted to talk to the officer about it. Respondent was then handcuffed and informed of his *Miranda* rights. After stating that he understood his rights, respondent elaborated further on the initial statement. A homicide detective soon arrived on the scene. He readvised respondent of his rights, and asked him "what he had on his mind." Respondent then stated that he had come all the way from Boston because he wanted to confess to murdering a young girl, a crime he had committed in Denver nine months earlier. He then gave the detective the name of the victim. Next, respondent was taken to police headquarters, where records revealed that an unidentified female body had been discovered in the area respondent described. Connelly then made more incriminating statements and took the police to the place where he said the murder had occurred.

Respondent was initially found incompetent to stand trial. But he achieved competency after six months of hospitalization and treatment with antipsychotic and sedative medication. A psychiatrist, previously appointed to conduct a competency examination of respondent, testified for the defense that Connelly's statements to the police had resulted from "command auditory hallucinations," a symptom of his mental disorder. The "voice of God" had told Connelly to return to Denver to confess his crime. When he returned, the same voice became stronger and told him either to confess to the killing or to commit suicide. At that point, reluctantly following the voice's command, Connelly approached the first officer he could find and confessed. Because people suffering from command hallucinations feel they must do whatever the voice tells them, the psychiatrist was of the opinion that Connelly was unable to make a free and intelligent decision about whether to speak with, and to confess to, the police.

The trial court suppressed Connelly's statements because they were "involuntary"; respondent had not exercised "free will" in choosing to speak to the police, but had been "compelled" by his illness to confess. In upholding the trial court on this issue, the Colorado Supreme Court observed that "[o]ne's capacity for rational judgment and free choice may be overborne as much by certain forms of severe illness as by external pressure." The U.S. Supreme Court reversed:

"[The confession cases] considered by this Court over the 50 years since *Brown v. Mississippi* have focused upon the crucial element of police overreaching. [A]ll have contained a substantial element of coercive police conduct. Absent police conduct causally related to the confession, there is simply no basis for concluding that any state actor has deprived a criminal defendant of due process of law. * * *

"Respondent relies on *Blackburn v. Alabama,* 361 U.S. 199, 80 S.Ct. 274, 4 L.Ed.2d 242 (1960), and *Townsend v. Sain* [discussed briefly at p. 452, fn. c, a case some commentators had read as barring the use of confessions obtained from a person whose volitional power is seriously impaired, whatever the reason]. But respondent's reading of *Blackburn* and *Townsend* ignores the integral element of police overreaching present in both cases. In *Blackburn,* the Court found that [defendant] was probably insane at the time of his confession and the police learned during the interrogation that he had a history of mental problems.

"The police exploited this weakness with coercive tactics [and these] tactics supported a finding that the confession was involuntary. * * * *Townsend* presented a similar instance of police wrongdoing. In that case, a police physician had given Townsend a drug with truth-serum properties. The subsequent confession, obtained by officers who knew that Townsend had been given drugs, was held involuntary. These two cases demonstrate that while mental condition is surely relevant to an individual's susceptibility to police coercion, mere examination of the confessant's state of mind can never conclude the due process inquiry.

"[The] difficulty with the approach of the Supreme Court of Colorado is that it fails to recognize the essential link between coercive activity of the State, on the one hand, and a resulting confession by a defendant, on the other. The flaw in respondent's constitutional argument is that it would expand our previous line of 'voluntariness' cases into a far-ranging requirement that courts must divine a defendant's motivation for speaking or acting as he did even though there be no claim that governmental conduct coerced his decision.

"The most outrageous behavior by a private party seeking to secure evidence against a defendant does not make that evidence inadmissible under the Due Process Clause. * * * [S]uppressing respondent's statements would serve absolutely no purpose in enforcing constitutional guarantees. The purpose of excluding confessions seized in violation of the Constitution is to substantially deter future violations of the Constitution. Only if we were to establish a brand new constitutional right—the right of a criminal defendant to confess to his crime only when totally rational and properly motivated—could respondent's present claim be sustained.

"We have previously cautioned against expanding 'currently applicable exclusionary rules by erecting additional barriers to placing truthful and probative evidence before state juries * * *.' *Lego v. Twomey* (1972) [p. 833]. We abide by that counsel now. [Respondent] would now have us require sweeping inquiries into the state of mind of a criminal defendant who has confessed, inquiries quite divorced from any coercion brought to bear on the defendant by the State. We think the Constitution rightly leaves this sort of inquiry to be resolved by state laws governing the admission of evidence and erects no standard of its own in this area. A statement rendered by one in the condition of respondent might be proved to be quite unreliable, but this is a matter to be governed by the evidentiary laws of the forum and not by the Due Process Clause * * *."

Dissenting Justice BRENNAN, joined by Marshall, J., recalled that the *Blackburn* Court had observed: "Surely in the present stage of our civilization a most basic sense of justice is affronted by the spectacle of incarcerating a human being upon the basis of a statement he made while insane * * *." "[T]he use of a mentally ill person's involuntary confession," maintained Justice Brennan, "is antithetical to the notion of fundamental fairness embodied in the Due Process Clause." He argued that "[the] holding that involuntary confessions are only those procured through police misconduct [is] inconsistent with the Court's historical insistence that only confessions reflecting an exercise of free will be admitted into evidence" and that "[u]ntil today, we have never upheld the admission of a confession that does not reflect the exercise of free will."[a] He continued:

"Since the Court redefines voluntary confessions to include confessions by mentally ill individuals, the reliability of these confessions becomes a central concern. A concern for reliability is inherent in our criminal justice system, which relies upon accusatorial rather than inquisitorial practices. * * *

"Because the admission of a confession so strongly tips the balance against the defendant in the adversarial process, we must be especially careful about a confession's reliability. We have to date not required a finding of reliability for involuntary confessions only because all such confessions have been excluded upon a finding of involuntariness, regardless of reliability. The Court's adoption today of a restrictive definition of an 'involuntary' confession will require heightened scrutiny of a confessions' reliability.

"The instant case starkly highlights the danger of admitting a confession by a person with a severe mental illness. The trial court made no findings concerning the reliability of Mr. Connelly's involuntary confession, since it believed that the confession was excludable on the basis of involuntariness. However, the overwhelming evidence in the record points to the unreliability of Mr. Connelly's delusional mind. * * *

"Moreover, the record is barren of any corroboration of the mentally ill defendant's confession. No physical evidence links the defendant to the alleged crime. Police did not identify the alleged victim's body as the woman named by the defendant. Mr. Connelly identified the alleged scene of the crime, but it has not been verified that the unidentified body was found there or that a crime actually occurred there. There is not a shred of competent evidence in this record linking the defendant to the charged homicide. There is only Mr. Connelly's confession.

"Minimum standards of due process should require that the trial court find substantial indicia of reliability, on the basis of evidence extrinsic to the confes-

---

a. The dissenters took sharp exception to the majority's reading of *Townsend* : "[Although the majority maintains that the confession in that case was obtained by officers who knew that a police doctor had given defendant a drug with truth-serum properties], in fact [as the *Townsend* Court pointed out], 'the police * * * did not know what [medications] the doctor had given [the defendant].' And the *Townsend* Court expressly states that police wrongdoing was not an essential factor:

" 'It is not significant that the drug may have been administered and the questions asked by persons unfamiliar with [the drug's] properties as a" truth serum," if these properties exist. Any questioning by police officers which *in fact* produces a confession which is not the product of a free intellect renders that confession inadmissible. The Court has usually so stated the test.' (Emphasis in original.)"

sion itself, before admitting the confession of a mentally ill person into evidence. I would require the trial court to make such a finding on remand. To hold otherwise allows the State to imprison and possibly to execute a mentally ill defendant based solely upon an inherently unreliable confession."

Notes and Questions

1. *Is "the (exclusionary) tail wagging the (due process) dog"?* Consider Laurence Benner, *Requiem for Miranda: The Rehnquist Court's Voluntariness Doctrine in Historical Perspective,* 67 Wash.U.L.Q. 59, 136–37 (1989):

"[The *Connelly* Court] concluded that in the absence of coercive police misconduct 'suppressing [Connelly's] statements would serve absolutely no purpose in enforcing constitutional guarantees.' From this narrow premise, the Court then leaped to the broad conclusion that the use of Connelly's deranged statements as evidence against him did not violate the due process clause.

"But surely this is the (exclusionary) tail wagging the (due process) dog, for the upshot of the Court's position is that unless exclusion will deter someone in an official capacity, there can be no due process violation no matter how unjust the result. By allowing the deterrence rationale for the exclusionary rule to control the nature of the due process inquiry, the Court thus permits the logic of deterrence to shape the actual content of due process itself. Under this formula any concern for justice is excluded from the equation. Indeed, any attempt to develop a coherent theory of justice under the due process clause is precluded."

2. *Confessions vs. guilty pleas.* The *Connelly* Court balked at requiring "sweeping inquiries into the state of mind of a criminal defendant who has confessed, inquiries quite divorced from any [police] coercion brought to bear on the defendant." Would such inquiries be any more burdensome than constitutionally required inquiries into a defendant's competency to stand trial, to waive her right to counsel, or to be executed? See Benner, *supra,* at 137. Connelly, recalls Professor Benner, "was found incompetent to stand trial immediately following the making of his custodial confession. Does it not therefore appear incongruous that Connelly could not have pled guilty in open court, on the same day he sealed his fate with a confession obtained within the precincts of the Denver police headquarters?"

3. *Should the admissibility of a confession turn on whether in fact it is the product of a "free will" or whether in fact it is voluntary?* What is the *Connelly* dissenters' argument? That a confession by a mentally ill (or drugged) person is inherently unreliable or at least highly suspect? Or that the use of a mentally ill (or drugged) person's confession violates due process *regardless* of how impressively corroborated or otherwise reliable the confession turns out to be? Or both? If a confession is not the product of police overreaching and doubts about its reliability have been dispelled, why should it matter whether it was *in fact* involuntarily made?

(a) *Changing the facts of the Townsend case.* In *Townsend,* the defendant was suffering from severe heroin withdrawal symptoms. A police doctor was called in to treat this condition and injected the suspect with a drug that, unknown to the doctor or the police who subsequently questioned him (according to the record), had the properties of a "truth serum." About an hour later, defendant confessed.

Suppose that Townsend's sister had visited him in his cell and given him pills to relieve his suffering and that, unknown to her, these pills had the properties of a "truth serum." Suppose further that after taking these pills Townsend had told a guard that he wanted to confess and then had proceeded to do so. Would (should) such a confession be excluded? Why (not)?

Is the confession in the hypothetical *Townsend* case any more an exercise of "free will" or any less involuntary in fact than the confession in the actual *Townsend* case? If there is a distinction, is it that in the actual case the police doctor or the police who subsequently questioned Townsend were negligent? That even if the "truth serum" were not the result of police *wrong*doing, it was still the result of *their doing?*

(b) *Changing the facts of the Connelly case.* Suppose that Connelly had never returned to Denver, but had phoned a Denver police officer from Boston and—with the "voice of God" ringing in his ears—had made a detailed confession over the phone. Or suppose Connelly had stayed in Boston and—with the "voice of God" doing the dictation—had written out a detailed confession and mailed it to the Denver police department. Would (should) such confessions be admissible? What would Justices Brennan and Marshall say? How, if at all, are the confessions in the hypotheticals different from the statements Connelly made in the actual case?

(c) A court should care whether a confession is the product of police wrongdoing or whether it is reliable, but why should it care whether it is voluntary or involuntary *in fact?* If a confession is neither the product of impermissible police methods nor untrustworthy (i.e. if doubts about its reliability have been removed), why should the confession's voluntariness be a relevant constitutional question?

(d) Was the question presented in *Connelly* whether the Court should adopt a new rule or whether it should rid itself of the terminology of the old one? Would *Connelly* have been an appropriate occasion to scrap the "voluntariness" terminology altogether and to consider directly the "complex of values" underlying, but long masked by, the rhetoric? See Albert W. Alschuler, *Constraint and Confession,* 74 Denv.U.L.Rev. 957, 959 (1997).

4. *Does the Connelly case mark the decline and fall of the "reliability" element?* As we have seen (pp. 451–55), the reliability of a confession does not necessarily make it admissible. But should the *unreliability* of a confession (or the absence of substantial indicia of reliability) render a confession *inadmissible* as a matter of federal constitutional law? Compare George Dix, *Federal Constitutional Confession Law: The 1986 and 1987 Supreme Court Terms,* 67 Tex.L.Rev. 231, 272–76 (1988) with Albert Alschuler, Note 4 (d) supra, at 959–60.

Professor Dix finds "the rejection of reliability as a relevant consideration in federal constitutional law" "the most surprising aspect" of *Connelly.* The opinion, comments Dix, "misleadingly represents that the Court's prior decisions definitively settled the matter, when in fact, until *Connelly,* reliability played an important role in traditional confession law analysis." Dix concludes that "at least in the absence of more thorough consideration than *Connelly* demonstrates, a total deconstitutionalization of traditionally important reliability issues is unjustified."

"Just as the Constitution does not mandate the exclusion of unreliable eyewitness testimony," maintains Professor Alschuler, "it does not mandate the exclusion of unreliable confessions. [The] Constitution requires the exclusion of unreliable eyewitness testimony only when improper governmental conduct—for example, an impermissibly suggestive police line-up—has produced it. The rule should be no different for unreliable confessions. Unless improper governmental conduct has generated a confession, the Constitution should give the defendant only a right to present evidence of the confession's unreliability to the jury."

5. *Can (should) Connelly Be Read Very Narrowly?* Consider Welsh S. White, *What Is an Involuntary Confession Now?*, 50 Rutgers L.Rev. 2001, 2018–20 (1998):

"The *Connelly* case was unusual [in] at least two respects. First, the police exerted no pressure whatsoever on the suspect to confess. The interrogating detective merely asked him 'what he had on his mind.' After that, the suspect gave an unsolicited confession. Under these circumstances, the Court could properly conclude that the suspect's confession was not the product of police conduct.

"Moreover, the police who dealt with the *Connelly* suspect had no reason to be aware that he was suffering from a serious mental disability at the time he confessed. [Under] these circumstances, the Court could properly distinguish *Connelly* from cases in which interrogating officers exploited a suspect's known weaknesses.

"On its face, the *Connelly* majority's refusal to consider a confession's lack of reliability does seem inconsistent with dicta in pre-*Miranda* decisions stating that excluding unreliable confessions was one of the goals of the voluntariness test. A distinction should be drawn, however, between assessing the reliability of a particular confession and determining whether an interrogation method is likely to produce an unreliable confession. [Although] the pre-*Miranda* Due Process test was designed to discourage interrogation methods likely to produce untrustworthy confessions, the pre-*Miranda* cases applying this test never assessed the actual trustworthiness of particular confessions. Thus, *Connelly*'s dicta is consistent with these cases. Although a confession's lack of trustworthiness will not tend to establish that it is involuntary, an interrogation method that is likely to induce an untrustworthy statement should still be impermissible under the Due Process clause.

"Indeed, the post-*Miranda* Due Process cases offer no reason whatsoever to believe that this principle has been discarded. In *Fulminante*, a case in which the undercover agent employed an interrogation method that was likely to elicit an untrustworthy statement, the confession was held involuntary. Moreover, both *Fulminante* and *Connelly* purported to apply the same totality of circumstances test that was applied in pre-*Miranda* cases."

SECTION 5. *MASSIAH* REVISITED; *MASSIAH* AND *MIRANDA* COMPARED AND CONTRASTED

A. THE REVIVIFICATION OF *MASSIAH*

"Until the Christian burial speech case [*Brewer v. Williams*, set forth below] * * * lasting fame had eluded *Massiah v. United States* [p. 460]. It was apparently lost in the shuffle of fast-moving events that reshaped constitutional-criminal procedure in the 1960s. [In] constitutional-criminal procedure circles, 1964 was the year of *Escobedo v. Illinois* [p. 462], and *Massiah* was understandably neglected in the hue and cry raised over the Illinois case. To the extent that *Massiah* was remembered at all, it was [only as a] stepping stone to *Escobedo* * * *.

"*Escobedo* may have seized the spotlight from *Massiah*, but *Esobedo* was soon shoved offstage by that blockbuster, *Miranda*, [a case that] '[did] not [enlarge]

Escobedo as much as [it] *displaced* it.' Assuming that *Escobedo* had not already done so, did *Miranda* also displace *Massiah?* After *Miranda,* was the institution of judicial proceedings, by way of indictment or otherwise, no more constitutionally relevant than whether the investigation had 'begun to focus on a particular suspect'? [If] one searches the *Miranda* opinion for answers to these questions, [one] discovers that *Massiah* is never mentioned—not once in Chief Justice Warren's sixty-page opinion for the Court, nor in any of the three dissenting opinions, which total another forty-six pages. Yet *very little else* even remotely bearing on the general subject is left out."

—Kamisar, *Police Interrogation and Confessions* 160–64 (1980).

BREWER v. WILLIAMS (WILLIAMS I)

430 U.S. 387, 97 S.Ct. 1232, 51 L.Ed.2d 424 (1977).

Justice STEWART delivered the opinion of the Court. * * *

On the afternoon of December 24, 1968, a 10–year-old girl named Pamela Powers went with her family to the YMCA in Des Moines, Iowa. [When] she failed to return from a trip to the washroom, a search for her began. The search was unsuccessful.

Robert Williams, who had recently escaped from a mental hospital, was a resident of the YMCA. Soon after the girl's disappearance Williams was seen in the YMCA lobby carrying some clothing and a large bundle wrapped in a blanket. He obtained help from a 14–year-old boy in opening the street door of the YMCA and the door to his automobile parked outside. When Williams placed the bundle in the front seat of his car the boy "saw two legs in it and they were skinny and white." Before anyone could see what was in the bundle Williams drove away. His abandoned car was found the following day in Davenport, Iowa, roughly 160 miles east of Des Moines. A warrant was then issued in Des Moines for his arrest on a charge of abduction.

On the morning of December 26, a Des Moines lawyer named Henry McKnight went to the Des Moines police station and informed the officers present that he had just received a long distance call from Williams, and that he had advised Williams to turn himself in to the Davenport police. Williams did surrender that morning to the police in Davenport, and they booked him on the charge specified in the arrest warrant and gave him the [*Miranda* warnings]. The Davenport police then telephoned their counterparts in Des Moines to inform them that Williams had surrendered. McKnight, the lawyer, was still at the Des Moines police headquarters, and Williams conversed with McKnight on the telephone. In the presence of the Des Moines Chief of Police and a Police Detective named Leaming [a captain and 20–year veteran of the Des Moines police department], McKnight advised Williams that Des Moines police officers would be driving to Davenport to pick him up, that the officers would not interrogate him or mistreat him, and that Williams was not to talk to the officers about Pamela Powers until after consulting with McKnight upon his return to Des Moines. As a result of these conversations, it was agreed between McKnight and the Des Moines police officials that Detective Leaming and a fellow officer would drive to Davenport to pick up Williams, that they would bring him directly back to Des Moines, and that they would not question him during the trip.

In the meantime Williams was arraigned before a judge in Davenport on the outstanding arrest warrant. The judge advised him of his *Miranda* rights and committed him to jail. Before leaving the courtroom, Williams conferred with a lawyer named Kelly, who advised him not to make any statements until consulting with McKnight back in Des Moines.

Detective Leaming and his fellow officer arrived in Davenport about noon to pick up Williams and return him to Des Moines. Soon after their arrival they met with Williams and Kelly, who, they understood, was acting as Williams' lawyer. Detective Leaming repeated the *Miranda* warnings, and told Williams:

> " * * * we both know that you're being represented here by Mr. Kelly and you're being represented by Mr. McKnight in Des Moines, [and] I want you to remember this because we'll be visiting between here and Des Moines."

Williams then conferred again with Kelly alone, and after this conference Kelly reiterated to Detective Leaming that Williams was not to be questioned about the disappearance of Pamela Powers until after he had consulted with McKnight back in Des Moines. When Leaming expressed some reservations, Kelly firmly stated that the agreement with McKnight was to be carried out—that there was to be no interrogation of Williams during the automobile journey to Des Moines. Kelly was denied permission to ride in the police car back to Des Moines with Williams and the two officers.

The two Detectives, with Williams in their charge, then set out on the 160–mile drive. At no time during the trip did Williams express a willingness to be interrogated in the absence of an attorney. Instead, he stated several times that "[w]hen I get to Des Moines and see Mr. McKnight, I am going to tell you the whole story." Detective Leaming knew that Williams was a former mental patient, and knew also that he was deeply religious.

The Detective and his prisoner soon embarked on a wide-ranging conversation covering a variety of topics, including the subject of religion. Then, not long after leaving Davenport and reaching the interstate highway, Detective Leaming delivered what has been referred to [as] the "Christian burial speech." Addressing Williams as "Reverend," the Detective said:

> "I want to give you something to think about while we're traveling down the road. * * * Number one, I want you to observe the weather conditions, it's raining, it's sleeting, it's freezing, driving is very treacherous, visibility is poor, it's going to be dark early this evening. They are predicting several inches of snow for tonight, and I feel that you yourself are the only person that knows where this little girl's body is, that you yourself have only been there once, and if you get a snow on top of it you yourself may be unable to find it. And, since we will be going right past the area on the way into Des Moines, I feel that we could stop and locate the body, that the parents of this little girl should be entitled to a Christian burial for the little girl who was snatched away from them on Christmas Eve and murdered. And I feel we should stop and locate it on the way in rather than waiting until morning and trying to come back out after a snow storm and possibly not being able to find it at all."[a]

a. Although no member of the Supreme Court discussed, or even noted, this point, Captain Leaming offered two different versions of the "Christian burial speech." The captain's first version was given at a pretrial hearing to suppress evidence; his second version, the only one quoted and discussed by the Supreme Court and lower federal courts, was given four weeks later at the trial. See Kamisar, *Foreword: Brewer v. Williams—A Hard Look at a Discomfiting Record*, 66 Geo.L.J. 209, 215–18

Williams asked Detective Leaming why he thought their route to Des Moines would be taking them past the girl's body, and Leaming responded that he knew the body [was near] Mitchellville—a town they would be passing on the way to Des Moines.[1] Leaming then stated: "I do not want you to answer me. I don't want to discuss it further. Just think about it as we're riding down the road."

As the car approached Grinell, a town approximately 100 miles west of Davenport, Williams asked whether the police had found the victim's shoes. When Detective Leaming replied that he was unsure, Williams directed the officers to a service station where he said he had left the shoes; a search for them proved unsuccessful. As they continued towards Des Moines, Williams asked whether the police had found the blanket, and directed the officers to a rest area where he said he had disposed of the blanket. Nothing was found. The car continued towards Des Moines, and as it approached Mitchellville, Williams said that he would show the officers where the body was. He then directed the police to the body of Pamela Powers.

[The trial judge admitted all evidence relating to or resulting from statements Williams made in the car ride. He found that "an agreement" had been made between defense counsel and the police that Williams would not be questioned on the return trip to Des Moines, but ruled that Williams had waived his rights before giving such information.] [On federal habeas corpus, the] District Court made findings of fact as summarized above, and concluded as a matter of law that the evidence in question had been wrongly admitted at Williams' trial. This conclusion was based on three alternative and independent grounds: (1) that Williams had been denied his constitutional right to the assistance of counsel; (2) that he had been denied [his *Miranda* rights]; and (3) that in any event, [his] statements [had] been involuntarily made. [The] Court of Appeals appears to have affirmed the judgment on [the first two] grounds. We have concluded that only one of them need be considered here.

Specifically, there is no need to review the [*Miranda* doctrine] [or the] ruling of the District Court that Williams' self-incriminating statements were, indeed, involuntarily made. For it is clear that the judgment before us must in any event be affirmed upon the ground that Williams was deprived of a different constitutional right—the right to the assistance of counsel.

* * * Whatever else it may mean, the right to counsel * * * means at least that a person is entitled to the help of a lawyer at or after the time that judicial proceedings have been initiated against him—"whether by way of formal charge, preliminary hearing, indictment, information, or arraignment." *Kirby v. Illinois* [p. 655].

There can be no doubt in the present case that judicial proceedings had been initiated against Williams before the start of the automobile ride from Davenport to Des Moines. A warrant had been issued for his arrest, he had been arraigned on

(1977). For the view that these two versions are significantly different, see id. at 218–33.

Justice Stewart notes that the captain addressed Williams as "Reverend," and then gives the captain's *second* version of the speech and related testimony *in its entirety*. But Captain Leaming did not testify that he addressed Williams as "Reverend" in the second version, only in the first. Justice Stewart may have called attention to the "Reverend" address be-

cause the Attorney General of Iowa was sufficiently troubled by it to go outside the record to explain in his brief why Captain Leaming employed it. See Kamisar, supra, at 223. For a discussion of the significance of the " 'Reverend' ploy," see id. at 221–23.

1. The fact of the matter, of course, was that Detective Leaming possessed no such knowledge.

that warrant before a judge in a Davenport courtroom, and he had been committed by the court to confinement in jail. The State does not contend otherwise.

There can be no serious doubt, either, that Detective Leaming deliberately and designedly set out to elicit information from Williams just as surely as—and perhaps more effectively than—if he had formally interrogated him. Detective Leaming was fully aware before departing for Des Moines that Williams was being represented in Davenport by Kelly and in Des Moines by McKnight. Yet he purposely sought during Williams' isolation from his lawyers to obtain as much incriminating information as possible. Indeed, Detective Leaming conceded as much when he testified at Williams' trial:

> "Q. In fact, Captain, whether he was a mental patient or not, you were trying to get all the information you could before he got to his lawyer, weren't you?

> "A. I was sure hoping to find out where that little girl was, yes, sir.

> "Q. Well, I'll put it this way: You [were] hoping to get all the information you could before Williams got back to McKnight, weren't you?

> "A. Yes, sir."[6]

The state courts clearly proceeded upon the hypothesis that Detective Leaming's "Christian burial speech" had been tantamount to interrogation. Both courts recognized that Williams had been entitled to the assistance of counsel at the time he made the incriminating statements. Yet no such constitutional protection would have come into play if there had been no interrogation.

The circumstances of this case are thus constitutionally indistinguishable from those presented in *Massiah*. [That] the incriminating statements were elicited surreptitiously in [*Massiah*], and otherwise here, is constitutionally irrelevant. Rather, the clear rule of *Massiah* is that once adversary proceedings have commenced against an individual, he has a right to legal representation when the government interrogates him.[b] It thus requires no wooden or technical application of the *Massiah* doctrine to conclude that Williams was entitled to the assistance of counsel guaranteed to him by the Sixth and Fourteenth Amendments.

The Iowa courts recognized that Williams had been denied the constitutional right to the assistance of counsel. They held, however, that he had waived that right during the course of the automobile trip from Davenport to Des Moines. The state trial court explained its determination of waiver as follows:

> "The time element involved on the trip, the general circumstances of it, and more importantly the absence on the Defendant's part of any assertion of his right or desire not to give information absent the presence of his attorney, are the main foundations for the Court's conclusion that he voluntarily waived such right."

[The] District Court and the Court of Appeals were correct in the view that the question of waiver was not a question of historical fact, but one [that] requires "application of constitutional principles to the facts as found." The [lower federal

---

6. Counsel for the State, in the course of oral argument in this Court, acknowledged that the "Christian burial speech" was tantamount to interrogation * * *.

b. Isn't the clear rule of *Massiah* that once adversary proceedings have commenced against an individual, he has a right to counsel when the government *deliberately elicits* in-criminating information from him (whether or not the government's efforts to obtain information constitute "interrogation" within the meaning of *Miranda*'s Fifth Amendment rights)? Did Justice Stewart, in effect, correct himself three years later in fn. 4 to his opinion in *Rhode Island v. Innis* (p. 521)?

courts] were also correct in their understanding of the proper standard to be applied in determining the question of waiver as a matter of federal constitutional law—that it was incumbent upon the State to prove "an intentional relinquishment or abandonment of a known right or privilege." *Johnson v. Zerbst.* [That] strict standard applies equally to an alleged waiver of the right to counsel whether at trial or at a critical stage of pretrial proceedings.

We conclude, finally that the Court of Appeals was correct in holding that, judged by these standards, the record in this case falls far short of sustaining the State's burden. It is true that Williams had been informed of and appeared to understand his right to counsel. But waiver requires not merely comprehension but relinquishment, and Williams' consistent reliance upon the advice of counsel in dealing with the authorities refutes any suggestion that he waived that right. [His] statements while in the car that he would tell the whole story *after* seeing McKnight in Des Moines were the clearest expressions [that] he desired the presence of an attorney before any interrogation took place. But even before making these statements, Williams had effectively asserted his right to counsel by having secured attorneys at both ends of the automobile trip, both of whom, acting as his agents, had made clear to the police that no interrogation was to occur during the journey. Williams knew of that agreement and, particularly in view of his consistent reliance on counsel, there is no basis for concluding that he disavowed it.

Despite Williams' express and implicit assertions of his right to counsel, Detective Leaming proceeded to elicit incriminating statements from Williams. Leaming did not preface this effort by telling Williams that he had a right to the presence of a lawyer, and made no effort at all to ascertain whether Williams wished to relinquish that right. The circumstances of record in this case thus provide no reasonable basis for finding that Williams waived his right to the assistance of counsel.

The Court of Appeals did not hold, nor do we, that under the circumstances of this case Williams *could not,* without notice to counsel, have waived his rights under the Sixth and Fourteenth Amendments. It only held, as do we, that he did not.

* * * Although we do not lightly affirm the issuance of a writ of habeas corpus in this case, so clear a violation of the Sixth and Fourteenth Amendments as here occurred cannot be condoned.

[The] judgment of the Court of Appeals is affirmed.[12]

Justice MARSHALL, concurring.

12. The District Court stated that its decision "does not touch upon the issue of what evidence, if any, beyond the incriminating statements themselves must be excluded as 'fruit of the poisonous tree.'" We too have no occasion to address this issue, and in the present posture of the case there is no basis for the view of our dissenting Brethren [that] any attempt to retry the respondent would probably be futile. While neither Williams' incriminating statements themselves nor any testimony describing his having led the police to the victim's body can constitutionally be admitted into evidence, evidence of where the body was found and of its condition might well be admissible on the theory that the body would have been discovered in any event, even had incriminating statements not been elicited from Williams. In the event that a retrial is instituted, it will be for the state courts in the first instance to determine whether particular items of evidence may be admitted.

[On retrial, the state court ruled that the body of Pamela Powers "would have been found in any event" and Williams was again convicted of murder. The U.S. Supreme Court upheld the state court's use of the "inevitable discovery" exception. See *Williams II*, p. 797.]

I concur wholeheartedly in my Brother Stewart's opinion for the Court, but add these words in light of the dissenting opinions filed today. The dissenters have, I believe, lost sight of the fundamental constitutional backbone of our criminal law. They seem to think that Detective Leaming's actions were perfectly proper, indeed laudable, examples of "good police work." In my view, good police work is something far different from catching the criminal at any price. It is equally important that the police, as guardians of the law, fulfill their responsibility to obey its commands scrupulously.

[In] this case, there can be no doubt that Detective Leaming consciously and knowingly set out to violate Williams' Sixth Amendment right to counsel and his Fifth Amendment privilege against self-incrimination, as Leaming himself understood those rights. * * * Leaming surely understood, because he had overheard McKnight tell Williams as much, that the location of the body would be revealed to police. Undoubtedly Leaming realized the way in which that information would be conveyed to the police: McKnight would learn it from his client and then he would lead police to the body. Williams would thereby be protected by the attorney-client privilege from incriminating himself by directly demonstrating his knowledge of the body's location, and the unfortunate Powers child could be given a "Christian burial."

Of course, this scenario would accomplish all that Leaming sought from his investigation except that it would not produce incriminating statements or actions from Williams. Accordingly, Leaming undertook his charade to pry such evidence from Williams.

[If] Williams is to go free—and given the ingenuity of Iowa prosecutors on retrial or in a civil commitment proceeding, I doubt very much that there is any chance a dangerous criminal will be loosed on the streets, the blood-curdling cries of the dissents notwithstanding—it will hardly be because he deserves it. It will be because [Leaming] intentionally denied Williams the right of *every* American under the Sixth Amendment to have the protective shield of a lawyer between himself and the awesome power of the State. * * *

Justice POWELL, concurring. * * *

Prior to the automobile trip from Davenport to Des Moines, Williams had been arrested, booked, and carefully given *Miranda* warnings. It is settled constitutional doctrine that he then had the right to the assistance of counsel. His exercise of this right was evidenced uniquely in this case. * * * Significantly, the recognition by the police of the status of counsel was evidenced by the *express agreement* between McKnight and the appropriate police officials that the officers who would drive Williams to Des Moines would not interrogate him in the absence of counsel.

[The] dissent of the Chief Justice concludes that prior to [making his incriminating statements], Williams had "made a valid waiver" of his right to have counsel present. This view disregards the record evidence clearly indicating that the police engaged in interrogation of Williams. [The Chief Justice also maintains] that the Court's holding today "conclusively presumes a suspect is legally incompetent to change his mind and tell the truth until an attorney is present." I find no justification for this view. On the contrary, the opinion of the Court is explicitly clear that the right to assistance of counsel may be waived, after it has attached, without notice to or consultation with counsel. We would have such a case here if the State had proved that the police officers refrained from coercion and interrogation, as they had agreed, and that Williams freely on his own initiative had confessed the crime. * * *[c]

Chief Justice BURGER, dissenting.

The result in this case ought to be intolerable in any society which purports to call itself an organized society. It continues the Court—by the narrowest margin—on the much-criticized course of punishing the public for the mistakes and misdeeds of law enforcement officers, instead of punishing the officer directly, if in fact he is guilty of wrongdoing. It mechanically and blindly keeps reliable evidence from juries whether the claimed constitutional violation involves gross police misconduct or honest human error.

Williams is guilty of the savage murder of a small child; no member of the Court contends he is not. While in custody, and after no fewer than *five* warnings of his rights to silence and to counsel, he led police to the concealed body of his victim. The Court concedes Williams was not threatened or coerced and that he spoke and acted voluntarily and with full awareness of his constitutional rights. In the face of all this, the Court now holds that because Williams was prompted by the detective's statement—not interrogation but a statement—the jury must not be told how the police found the body.

[The] evidence is uncontradicted that Williams had abundant knowledge of his right to have counsel present and of his right to silence. Since the Court does not question his mental competence, it boggles the mind to suggest that Williams could not understand that leading police to the child's body would have other than the most serious consequences. * * *

One plausible but unarticulated basis for the result reached is that once a suspect has asserted his right not to talk without the presence of an attorney, it becomes legally impossible for him to waive that right until he has seen an attorney. But constitutional rights are *personal,* and an otherwise valid waiver should not be brushed aside by judges simply because an attorney was not present.

[Even] if there was no waiver, and assuming a technical violation occurred, the Court errs gravely in mechanically applying the exclusionary rule without considering whether that draconian judicial doctrine should be invoked in these circumstances, or indeed whether any of its conceivable goals will be furthered by its application here.

* * * Today's holding interrupts what has been a more rational perception of the constitutional and social utility of excluding reliable evidence from the truth-seeking process. In its Fourth Amendment context, we have now recognized that the exclusionary rule is in no sense a *personal* constitutional right, but a judicially conceived remedial device designed to safeguard and effectuate guaranteed legal rights generally [referring to *Stone v. Powell,* p. 130; *United States v. Janis,* p. 130; and *United States v. Calandra,* p. 146]. We have repeatedly emphasized that deterrence of unconstitutional or otherwise unlawful police conduct is the only valid justification for excluding reliable and probative evidence from the criminal factfinding process.

Accordingly, unlawfully obtained evidence is not automatically excluded from the factfinding process in all circumstances. In a variety of contexts we inquire

c. Stevens, J., joined the opinion of the Court, but also added a brief comment concluding: "If, in the long run, we are seriously concerned about the individual's effective representation by counsel, the State cannot be permitted to dishonor its promise to this lawyer."

whether application of the rule will promote its objectives sufficiently to justify the enormous cost it imposes on society. * * *

Against this background, it is striking that the Court fails even to consider whether the benefits secured by application of the exclusionary rule in this case outweigh its obvious social costs. Perhaps the failure is due to the fact that this case arises not under the Fourth Amendment, but under *Miranda,* and the Sixth Amendment right to counsel. The Court apparently perceives the function of the exclusionary rule to be so different in these varying contexts that it must be mechanically and uncritically applied in all cases arising outside the Fourth Amendment. * * *

Justice WHITE, with whom Justice BLACKMUN and Justice REHNQUIST join, dissenting.

[The] issue in this case is whether respondent—who was entitled not to make any statements to the police without consultation with and/or presence of counsel[1] —validly waived those rights.

[I disagree with the majority's finding that no waiver was proved in this case.] That respondent knew of his right not to say anything to the officers without advice and presence of counsel is established on this record to a moral certainty. He was advised of the right by three officials of the State—telling at least one that he understood the right—and by two lawyers.[4] Finally, he further demonstrated his knowledge of the right by informing the police that he would tell them the story in the presence of McKnight when they arrived in Des Moines. The issue in this case, then, is whether respondent relinquished that right intentionally.

Respondent relinquished his right not to talk to the police about his crime when the car approached the place where he had hidden the victim's clothes. Men usually intend to do what they do and there is nothing in the record to support the proposition that respondent's decision to talk was anything but an exercise of his own free will. Apparently, without any prodding from the officers, respondent—who had earlier said that he would tell the whole story when he arrived in Des Moines—spontaneously changed his mind about the timing of his disclosures when the car approached the places where he had hidden the evidence. However, even if his statements were influenced by Detective Leaming's above-quoted statement, respondent's decision to talk in the absence of counsel can hardly be viewed as the product of an overborne will. The statement by Leaming was not coercive; it was accompanied by a request that respondent not respond to it; and it was delivered hours before respondent decided to make any statement. Respondent's waiver was thus knowing and intentional.

The majority's contrary conclusion seems to rest on the fact that respondent "asserted" his right to counsel by retaining and consulting with one lawyer and by consulting with another. How this supports the conclusion that respondent's later relinquishment of his right not to talk in the absence of counsel was unintentional is a mystery. The fact that respondent consulted with counsel on the question whether he should talk to the police in counsel's absence makes his

1. It does not matter whether the right not to make statements in the absence of counsel stems from *Massiah,* or *Miranda.* In either case the question is one of waiver. Waiver was not addressed in *Massiah* because there the statements were being made to an informant and the defendant had no way of knowing that he had a right not to talk to him without counsel.

4. Moreover, he in fact received advice of counsel on at least two occasions on the question whether he should talk to the police on the trip to Des Moines.

later decision to talk in counsel's absence *better* informed and, if anything, more intelligent.

The majority recognizes that even after this "assertion" of his right to counsel, it would have found that respondent waived his right not to talk in counsel's absence if his waiver had been express—i.e., if the officers had asked him in the car whether he would be willing to answer questions in counsel's absence and if he had answered "yes." But waiver is not a formalistic concept. Waiver is shown whenever the facts establish that an accused knew of a right and intended to relinquish it. Such waiver, even if not express, was plainly shown here. The only other conceivable basis for the majority's holding is the implicit suggestion that the right involved in *Massiah,* as distinguished from the right involved in *Miranda,* is a right not to be *asked* any questions in counsel's absence rather than a right not to *answer* any questions in counsel's absence, and that the right not to be *asked* questions must be waived *before* the questions are asked. Such wafer thin distinctions cannot determine whether a guilty murderer should go free.[d] The only conceivable purpose for the presence of counsel during questioning is to protect an accused from making incriminating *answers.* Questions, unanswered, have no significance at all. Absent coercion—no matter how the right involved is defined—an accused is amply protected by a rule requiring waiver before or simultaneously with the giving by him of an answer or the making by him of a statement.

* * *

Justice BLACKMUN, with whom Justice WHITE and Justice REHNQUIST join, dissenting. * * *

The Court rules that the Sixth Amendment was violated because Detective Leaming "purposely sought during Williams' isolation from his lawyers to obtain as much incriminating information as possible." I cannot regard that as unconstitutional *per se.*

First, the police did not deliberately seek to isolate Williams from his lawyers so as to deprive him of the assistance of counsel. Cf. *Escobedo.* The isolation in this case was a necessary incident of transporting Williams to the county where the crime was committed.

Second, Leaming's purpose was not solely to obtain incriminating evidence. The victim had been missing for only two days, and the police could not be certain that she was dead. Leaming, of course, and in accord with his duty, was "hoping to find out where that little girl was," but such motivation does not equate with an intention to evade the Sixth Amendment.[e] * * *

---

d. But see Joseph D. Grano, *Rhode Island v. Innis: A Need to Reconsider the Constitutional Premises Underlying the Law of Confessions,* 17 Am.Crim.L.Rev. 1, 34 (1979): "Justice White could not be more wrong in his criticism. The whole point of *Massiah* is the prevention of the state from taking advantage of an uncounseled defendant once Sixth Amendment rights attach. The Christian burial speech case was an attempt to take advantage of Williams. The attempt itself is what *Massiah* prohibits. The attempt itself violates the constitutional mandate that the system proceed, after some point, only in an accusatorial manner."

e. But see Kamisar, *Police Interrogation and Confessions* 146–47 (1980), maintaining that although at one point Leaming did testify that he was "hoping to find out where that little *girl* was," in light of the entire record he apparently meant the girl's *body.* Leaming testified that he heard Williams' lawyer say to him over the phone that he would have to tell the police "where *the body* is" when he got back. Leaming also testified that before he drove to Davenport to pick up Williams, Williams' lawyer told him that the girl "was dead when [Williams] left the YMCA with her."

Third, not every attempt to elicit information should be regarded as "tantamount to interrogation." I am not persuaded that Leaming's observations and comments, made as the police car traversed the snowy and slippery miles between Davenport and Des Moines that winter afternoon, were an interrogation, direct or subtle, of Williams. Williams, after all, was counseled by lawyers, and warned by the arraigning judge in Davenport and by the police, and yet it was he who started the travel conversations and brought up the subject of the criminal investigation.

[In] summary, it seems to me that the Court is holding that *Massiah* is violated whenever police engage in any conduct, in the absence of counsel, with the subjective desire to obtain information from a suspect after arraignment. Such a rule is far too broad. Persons in custody frequently volunteer statements in response to stimuli other than interrogation. * * *

Notes and Questions

1. **Was it constitutionally irrelevant whether the "Christian burial speech" constituted "interrogation"?** Did the Court deem it necessary (or at least important) to classify Leaming's speech as a "form of interrogation" or "tantamount to interrogation"? If so, why? Once the Court chose the "Sixth Amendment-*Massiah*" route over a "Fifth Amendment-*Miranda*" approach, did the question whether Leaming engaged in "interrogation" become, or should it have become, constitutionally irrelevant? Did the secret government agent engage in "interrogation" in *Massiah?*

2. **Even if Brewer v. Williams were deemed a "Miranda case," would whether Leaming engaged in "interrogation" still be the wrong question?** Since Williams had asserted both his right to remain silent and his right to counsel *several times* before he was driven back to Des Moines, should the relevant question have been whether Leaming "fully respected" or "scrupulously honored" Williams' *Miranda* rights? Cf. *Michigan v. Mosley,* p. 547. How could it be said that Leaming did, when he "deliberately and designedly set out to elicit information" from *Williams?*

Brewer v. Williams was decided four years before *Edwards v. Arizona,* p. 548. Looking back at *Williams* in light of *Edwards,* if *Williams* were a "*Miranda* case," should the relevant question have been whether, after expressing his unwillingness to talk to the police without his lawyer, Williams changed his mind on his own initiative or whether Leaming "persuaded" or "prompted" him to change his mind?

3. **What constitutes a valid waiver of the "Sixth Amendment–Massiah" right?** PATTERSON v. ILLINOIS, 487 U.S. 285, 108 S.Ct. 2389, 101 L.Ed.2d 261 (1988), per WHITE, J., rejected "petitioner's argument, which has some acceptance from courts and commentators, that since 'the sixth amendment right [to counsel] is far superior to that of the fifth amendment right' and since '[t]he greater the right the greater the loss from a waiver of that right,' waiver of an accused's Sixth Amendment right to counsel should be 'more difficult' to effectuate than waiver of a suspect's Fifth Amendment rights." The Court ruled instead that "[a]s a general matter [an] accused who is [given the *Miranda* warnings] has been sufficiently apprised of the nature of the Sixth Amendment rights, and of the consequences of abandoning those rights, so that his waiver on this basis will be considered a knowing and intelligent one."

The case arose as follows: Patterson and other members of a street gang were arrested in the course of investigating the murder of Jackson. Patterson was advised of his *Miranda* rights and agreed to answer questions, but denied knowing anything about Jackson's death. He was held in custody while the investigation continued. Two days later, Patterson and two other gang members were indicted for the murder of Jackson. The same officer who had questioned him earlier told him that because he had been indicted he was being transferred from the lockup, where he was being held, to the county jail. Patterson asked the officer which of the gang members had been indicted for Jackson's murder, and upon learning that one particular gang member had not been indicted, responded: "[W]hy wasn't he indicted, he did everything."

Patterson then began to explain that a witness would support his account of the crime. At this point, the officer handed Patterson a *Miranda* waiver form and read the warnings aloud. Patterson initialed each of the warnings, signed the form and made a lengthy incriminating statement. He subsequently made additional statements. He was found guilty of murder, but maintained that the warnings he received, although they protected his *Miranda* rights, did not adequately inform him of his Sixth Amendment right to counsel during postindictment questioning. A 5–4 majority disagreed:

"[The] key inquiry in a case such as this one must be: Was the accused, who waived his Sixth Amendment rights during postindictment questioning, made sufficiently aware of his right to have counsel present during the questioning, and of the possible consequences of a decision to forgo the aid of counsel? In this case, we are convinced that by admonishing petitioner with the *Miranda* warnings, [the State] has met this burden and that petitioner's waiver of his right to counsel at questioning was valid. * * *

"Our conclusion is supported by petitioner's inability, in the proceedings before this Court, to articulate with precision what additional information should have been provided to him before he would have been competent to waive his right to counsel. * * *[8]

"As a general matter, then, an accused who is admonished with the [*Miranda* warnings] has been sufficiently apprised of the nature of his Sixth Amendment rights, and of the consequences of abandoning these rights, so that his waiver on this basis will be considered a knowing and intelligent one.[9]

8. [Some courts have suggested] that, in addition to the *Miranda* warnings, an accused should be informed that he has been indicted before a postindictment waiver is sought. Because, in this case, petitioner concedes that he was so informed, we do not address [this issue].

Beyond this, only one Court of Appeals—the Second Circuit—has adopted substantive or procedural requirements (in addition to *Miranda*) that must be completed before a Sixth Amendment waiver can be effectuated for postindictment questioning. See *United States v. Mohabir*, 624 F.2d 1140 (1980). [Stressing that the "strict standard" governing waiver of counsel at trial should apply to an alleged waiver of the *Massiah* right to counsel as well, the *Mohabir* court exercised its supervisory power over federal criminal justice to hold that a valid waiver of the "Sixth Amendment— *Massiah*" right "must be preceded by a federal judicial officer's explanation of the content and significance of this right."] As have a majority of the Court of Appeals, we reject *Mohabir's* holding that some "additional" warnings or

discussions with an accused are required in this situation or that any waiver in this context can only properly be made before a "neutral * * * judicial officer."

9. This does not mean, of course, that all Sixth Amendment challenges to the conduct of postindictment questioning will fail whenever the challenged practice would pass constitutional muster under *Miranda*. For example, we have permitted a *Miranda* waiver to stand where a suspect was not told that his lawyer was trying to reach him during questioning; in the Sixth Amendment context, this waiver would not be valid. See *Moran v. Burbine* * * *.

Thus, because the Sixth Amendment's protection of the attorney-client relationship— "the right to rely on counsel as a 'medium' between [the accused] and the State"—extends beyond *Miranda's* protection of the Fifth Amendment right to counsel, there will be cases where a waiver which would be valid under *Miranda* will not suffice for Sixth Amendment purposes.

"[While] our cases have recognized a 'difference' between the Fifth Amendment and Sixth Amendment rights to counsel, and the 'policies' behind these Constitutional guarantees, we have never suggested that one right is 'superior' or 'greater' than the other, nor is there any support in our cases for the notion that because a Sixth Amendment right may be involved, it is more difficult to waive than the Fifth Amendment counterpart.

"[W]e require a more searching or formal inquiry before permitting an accused to waive his right to counsel at trial than we require for a Sixth Amendment waiver during postindictment questioning—*not* because postindictment questioning is 'less important' than a trial [but] because the full 'dangers and disadvantages of self-representation,' *Faretta,* during questioning are less substantial and more obvious to an accused than they are at trial. Because the role of counsel at questioning is relatively simple and limited, we see no problem in having a waiver procedure at that stage which is likewise simple and limited. So long as the accused is made aware of the 'dangers and disadvantages of self-representation' during postindictment questioning, by use of the *Miranda* warnings, his waiver of his Sixth Amendment right to counsel at such questioning is 'knowing and intelligent.' "

Justice STEVENS, joined by Brennan and Marshall, JJ., dissented:

"The Court should not condone unethical forms of trial preparation by prosecutors or their investigators. In civil litigation it is improper for a lawyer to communicate with his or her adversary's client without either notice to opposing counsel or the permission of the court [referring to Disciplinary Rule 7–104 of the ABA Model Code of Professional Responsibility (1982)]. An attempt to obtain evidence for use at trial by going behind the back of one's adversary would be not only a serious breach of professional ethics but also a manifestly unfair form of trial practice. In the criminal context, the same ethical rules apply and, in my opinion, notions of fairness that are at least as demanding should also be enforced.

" * * * Given the significance of the initiation of formal proceedings and the concomitant shift in the relationship between the state and the accused, I think it quite wrong to suggest that *Miranda* warnings—or for that matter, any warnings offered by an adverse party—provide a sufficient basis for permitting the undoubtedly prejudicial—and, in my view, unfair—practice of permitting trained law enforcement personnel and prosecuting attorneys to communicate with as-of-yet unrepresented criminal defendants.

"[The] majority premises its conclusions that *Miranda* warnings lay a sufficient basis for accepting a waiver of the right to counsel on the assumption that those warnings make clear to an accused 'what a lawyer could "do for him" during the postindictment questioning: namely, advise [him] to refrain from making any [incriminating] statements.' Yet, this is surely a gross understatement of the disadvantage of proceeding without a lawyer and an understatement of what a defendant must understand to make a knowing waiver. The *Miranda* warnings do not, for example, inform the accused that a lawyer might examine the indictment for legal sufficiency before submitting his or her client to interrogation or that a lawyer is likely to be considerably more skillful at negotiating a plea bargain and that such negotiations may be most fruitful if initiated prior to any interrogation. Rather, the warnings do not even go so far as to explain to the accused the nature of the charges pending against him—advice that a court would insist upon before allowing a defendant to enter a guilty plea with or without the presence of an attorney.

"[Once] it is conceded that certain advice is required and that after indictment the adversary relationship between the state and the accused has solidified, it inescapably follows that a prosecutor may not conduct private interviews with a charged defendant. [N]either the prosecutor nor his or her agents can ethically provide the unrepresented defendant with the kind of advice that should precede an evidence-gathering interview after formal proceedings have been commenced. Indeed, in my opinion even the *Miranda* warnings themselves are a species of legal advice that is improper when given by the prosecutor after indictment. * * * "a

Notes and Questions

(a) In addition to his principal contention, Patterson also argued (unsuccessfully) that someone in his situation should be equated with a preindictment suspect who asserts his right to counsel, thereby triggering *Edwards*. Even if this is so, didn't Patterson, when being transferred to the county jail, "initiate" further communication with the police within the meaning of *Edwards?*

(b) Reconsider fn. 9 to the majority opinion in *Patterson.* Is the Court saying that even if a postindictment interrogatee were unaware that a friend or relative had retained a lawyer on his behalf, a waiver of his Sixth Amendment right to counsel would not be valid unless the police informed him that he had a lawyer and that that lawyer was trying to reach him? If so, why? Does this view make the Sixth Amendment right to counsel "superior" to the Fifth when somebody happens to retain a lawyer for the defendant, but not when the defendant is too unlucky or friendless for this to occur? Should the test for waiver of the Sixth Amendment right to counsel vary at different times "depending on the fortuity of whether [the suspect's family] happens to have retained counsel [for him] prior to interrogation"? Cf. *Moran v. Burbine.*

5. The "no-contact" rule: Should prosecutors be bound by the ethical rule prohibiting a lawyer from communicating with an opposing party represented by counsel without the consent of the other lawyer? The "no-contact" or "anti-contact" ethical rule discussed by Justice Stevens in his *Patterson* dissent has a long history in legal ethics: The rule is designed to protect laypersons from overreaching by those who have superior legal skills and knowledge and to protect the attorney-client relationship. The most common version of the ethical rule is Rule 4.2 of the ABA Model Rules of Professional Conduct, which provides: "In representing a client, a lawyer shall not communicate about the subject of the representation with a party the lawyer knows to be represented by another lawyer in the matter, unless the lawyer has the consent of the other lawyer or is authorized by law to do so." Disciplinary Rule 7–104 (A) (1) of the Model Code of Professional Responsibility is a virtually identical provision. Every state and the District of Columbia has adopted a version of the Model Code or Model Rules to govern the conduct of lawyers admitted to practice in that jurisdiction.

Should this rule apply in criminal, as well as civil, proceedings or should communications between a prosecutor and a suspect or defendant be judged by the special body of law developed by *Massiah* and its progeny? Do disciplinary rules such as Rule 4.2 take into account the full range of interests governing the balance between effective law enforcement and defendants' rights? Are the inter-

---

a. Blackmun, J., wrote a separate dissent, "agree[ing] with most of what Justice Stevens said." He would equate someone in Patterson's situation with a suspect who asserted his Fifth Amendment right to counsel, thus invoking the protection of *Edwards.*

ests protected by Rule 4.2 adequately protected in the criminal context by the Sixth Amendment and the Federal Rules of Criminal Procedure? See Roger Cramton & Lisa Udel, *State Ethics Rules and Federal Prosecutors,* 53 U.Pitt.L.Rev. 291, 332–33 (1992); F. Dennis Saylor & J. Douglas Wilson, *Putting a Square Peg in a Round Hole: The Application of Model Rule 4.2 to Federal Prosecutors,* 53 U.Pitt.L.Rev. 459, 464–65 (1992).

Most cases hold that the anti-contact rule applies generally to prosecutors, but if the prosecutor's conduct satisfies Sixth Amendment standards "there is a strong tendency in the decisions to reject a claim that the ethics rule has been violated." Cramton & Udel, supra, at 327–28. However, *United States v. Hammad,* 858 F.2d 834 (2d Cir.1988), took the position that an undercover agent's contact, at a federal prosecutor's direction, with a represented suspect during the pre-indictment stage violated the anti-contact rule and that the exclusionary rule is available to enforce violations of the rule. But much of *Hammad*'s sting was reduced by the court's view that the "authorized by law" language of the rule permitted some government contacts with represented persons. Subsequently, then-Attorney General Richard Thornburgh issued a memorandum setting forth the Department of Justice's long-held view that the no-contact ethical rule did not prohibit Department Attorneys and their agents from making legitimate investigatory and prosecutive contacts with represented parties. The defense bar responded by charging that the Attorney General was seeking to exempt Department Attorneys from all ethical rules and the ABA passed a resolution condemning the Department's policy. See Saylor & Wilson, supra, at 485.

United States v. Lopez, 765 F.Supp. 1433 (N.D.Cal.1991), marked the first time a court dismissed a federal criminal charge because, relying on Justice Department practice, a federal prosecutor had talked to an indicted defendant without the consent or presence of the defendant's lawyer. Lopez had retained a prominent lawyer whose representation was conditioned upon Lopez not cooperating with the government. Incarcerated pending trial, and wanting to cooperate with the prosecution if that would lead to his release, Lopez used his co-defendant's lawyer to initiate discussion with the prosecutor. Relying on the Attorney General's memorandum, the prosecutor spoke to Lopez several times outside the presence of his lawyer. Even assuming that the prosecutor acted unethically, the Court of Appeals failed to see how the government's conduct substantially prejudiced the defendant. In the absence of such a showing, it deemed "lesser sanctions" adequate to discipline government attorneys. Thus, it vacated the district court order dismissing the indictment. 4 F.3d 1455 (9th Cir.1993).

In 1994, Attorney General Janet Reno promulgated a rule (codified at 28 C.F.R. pt. 77 and set forth in 53 Crim.L.Rep. 2269 (Aug. 10, 1994)) purporting to exempt federal government lawyers from state ethical rules prohibiting ex parte communications with persons represented by counsel if the communication occurred prior to the initiation of formal proceedings against the person. This rule was struck down in part in *United States ex rel. O'Keefe v. McDonnell Douglas Corp.,* 132 F.3d 1252 (8th Cir.1998). The particular regulation at issue, 28 C.F.R. § 77.10(a), dealt with employees of organizations represented by counsel, but the Eighth Circuit opinion seems to apply to the entire set of regulations of which § 77.10(a) is a part.

Because Missouri Supreme Court rules based on Model Rule 4.2 (and adopted by the U.S. District Court for the Eastern district of Missouri) barred such ex parte contracts, the federal district court issued a protective order preventing federal government attorneys from engaging in ex parte communications with employees of defendant corporation without the consent of the corporation's counsel. The government argued that the protective order was unwarranted because its lawyers' conduct was authorized by 28 C.F.R. § 77.10(a).

The Eighth Circuit, per Hansen, J., disagreed. It concluded that neither the "Housekeeping Statute," 5 U.S.C. § 301 (which provides that the head of an executive agency may prescribe regulations for the governance of his or her department and the conduct of department employees) nor various provisions of Title 28 relating to the powers and duties of the Attorney General and the role of U.S. Attorneys provide a basis for the regulation promulgated by the Attorney General.

Among the questions raised by the Department of Justice's resistance to the "no-contact" rule and the promulgation of its own version of the rule are whether the no-contact rule should apply to criminal prosecutors only after formal charges have been lodged against a suspect (*i.e.*, should exist coextensively with the Sixth Amendment right to counsel); whether, and to what extent, the rule should govern the activities of non-attorney "alter egos" of the prosecution (*i.e.*, government agents whose communications with suspects occur with the knowledge of, or at the direction of, a prosecutor); and what the appropriate remedy should be for a violation of the rule. For example, should an indictment be dismissed for a violation, at least if it is egregious and has caused substantial prejudice to the defendant? Should evidence obtained as a result of a violation of the rule be suppressed or is suppression only appropriate when the defendant's constitutional rights have been violated? The Department of Justice provides that enforcement of its version of the no-contact rule is exclusively within the authority of the Attorney General and Justice's Office of Professional Responsibility. Is such enforcement bound to be inadequate? Should enforcement be the business of the state bar associations and the courts? Is this, too, likely to be inadequate? Should a special commission be established to address the problems of ethical violations by prosecutors? See generally Jeanette Stull, *The Department of Justice's No–Contact Rule: A Proposal for a Modified Rule*, 34 Crim.L.Bull. 411, 420–47 (1998).

6. *If the government obtains incriminating statements from a defendant after her right to counsel has attached, but the government does so for* legitimate reasons unrelated *to the gathering of evidence concerning charges to which the right to counsel has attached (e.g. to investigate a report that defendant plans to harm a witness), are the statements admissible at the trial of the crimes for which formal charges had already been filed?* No, answered the Court, per BRENNAN, J., in MAINE v. MOULTON, 474 U.S. 159, 106 S.Ct. 477, 88 L.Ed.2d 481 (1985):

"In *Massiah,* the Government also contended that incriminating statements obtained as a result of its deliberate efforts should not be excluded because law enforcement agents had 'the right, if not indeed the duty, to continue their investigation of [Massiah] and his alleged criminal associates.' [We] rejected this argument, and held:

" 'We do not question [that] it was entirely proper to continue an investigation of the suspected criminal activities of the defendant and his alleged confederates, even though the defendant had already been indicted. [But] the defendant's own incriminating statements, obtained by federal agents under the circumstances here disclosed, could not constitutionally be used by the prosecution as evidence against him at his trial.' (Emphasis omitted.)

"We reaffirm this holding, which states a sensible solution to a difficult problem. The police have an interest in the thorough investigation of crimes for which formal charges have already been filed. They also have an interest in investigating new or additional crimes. Investigations of either type of crime may require surveillance of individuals already under indictment. Moreover, law enforcement officials investigating an individual suspected of committing one crime and formally charged with having committed another crime obviously seek to discover evidence useful at a trial of either crime. In seeking evidence pertaining to pending charges, however, the Government's investigative powers are limited by the Sixth Amendment rights of the accused. To allow the admission of evidence obtained from the accused in violation of his Sixth Amendment rights whenever the police assert an alternative, legitimate reason for their surveillance [in this case, to insure the safety of their secret agent and to gather information concerning a report that defendant was planning to kill a witness] invites abuse by law enforcement personnel in the form of fabricated investigations and risks the evisceration of the Sixth Amendment right recognized in *Massiah*. On the other hand, to exclude evidence pertaining to charges as to which the Sixth Amendment right to counsel had not attached at the time the evidence was obtained, simply because other charges were pending at that time, would unnecessarily frustrate the public's interest in the investigation of criminal activities. Consequently, incriminating statements pertaining to pending charges are inadmissible at the trial of those charges, notwithstanding the fact that the police were also investigating other crimes, if, in obtaining this evidence, the State violated the Sixth Amendment by knowingly circumventing the accused's right to the assistance of counsel."

Chief Justice BURGER, joined by White, Rehnquist and O'Connor, JJ., dissented, maintaining that "application of the exclusionary rule here makes little sense."

"We have explained, [that] 'the deterrent purpose of the exclusionary rule necessarily assumes that the police have engaged in willful, or at the very least negligent, conduct which has deprived the defendant of some right.' Here the trial court found that the State obtained statements from respondent 'for legitimate purposes not related to the gathering of evidence concerning the crime for which [respondent] had been indicted.' Since the State was not trying to build its theft case against respondent in obtaining the evidence, excluding the evidence from the theft trial will not affect police behavior at all. The exclusion of evidence 'cannot be expected, and should not be applied, to deter objectively reasonable law enforcement activity.' *Leon*. Indeed, [it] is impossible to identify any police 'misconduct' to deter in this case. In fact, if anything, actions by the police of the type at issue here should be encouraged. The diligent investigation of the police in this case may have saved the lives of several potential witnesses and certainly led to the prosecution and conviction of respondent for additional serious crimes."

B. "Passive" vs. "Active" Secret Agents

The *Massiah* doctrine probably reached its high point in UNITED STATES v. HENRY, 447 U.S. 264, 100 S.Ct. 2183, 65 L.Ed.2d 115 (1980), which applied the doctrine to a situation where the FBI had instructed its paid government informant, ostensibly defendant's "cellmate," not to question defendant about the crime, and there had been no showing that he had. Nevertheless, a 6–3 majority, per BURGER, C.J., rejected the argument that the incriminating statements were not the result of any "affirmative conduct" on the part of the government agent to solicit evidence. The informant "was not a passive listener; rather he had 'some conversations with Mr. Henry' while he was in jail and Henry's incriminating statements were 'the product of this conversation.' "Moreover, and more generally—

"[Even if we accept the FBI agent's statement that] he did not intend that [the informant] would take affirmative steps to secure incriminating information, he must have known that such propinquity likely would lead to that result. [By] intentionally creating a situation likely to induce Henry to make incriminating statements without the assistance of counsel [after Henry had been indicted and counsel had been appointed for him], the government violated [his] Sixth Amendment right to counsel."

This broad language would seem to prohibit the government from "planting" even a completely "passive" secret agent in a person's cell once adversary proceedings have commenced against him. But the *Henry* Court cautioned that it was not "called upon to pass on the situation where an informant is placed in [close] proximity [to a prisoner] but makes no effort to stimulate conversations about the crime charged."

Moreover, concurring Justice POWELL made it plain that he could not join the majority opinion if it held that "the mere presence or incidental conversation of an informant in a jail cell would violate *Massiah*." The *Massiah* doctrine, emphasized Powell, "does not prohibit the introduction of spontaneous statements that are not elicited by governmental action. Thus, the Sixth Amendment is not violated when a passive listening device collects, but does not induce, incriminating comments."[a]

———

As the most recent "jail plant" case, *Kuhlmann v. Wilson* (set forth below), well illustrates, the line between "active" and "passive" secret agents—between *"stimulating"* conversations with a defendant in order to "elicit" incriminating statements and taking no action "beyond *merely listening*"—is an exceedingly difficult one to draw.

KUHLMANN v. WILSON
477 U.S. 436, 106 S.Ct. 2616, 91 L.Ed.2d 364 (1986).

Justice POWELL delivered the opinion of the Court.

[Respondent Wilson and two confederates robbed a garage and fatally shot the night dispatcher. Four days later, respondent turned himself in. He admitted that he had witnessed the robbery and murder, but denied any involvement in them, claiming that he had fled because he was afraid of being blamed for the crimes. He gave the police a description of the robbers, but denied knowing them.

[After his arraignment, Wilson was placed in a cell with a prisoner named Benny Lee. Unknown to Wilson, Lee had agreed to act as a police informant. Since

a. Dissenting Justice Blackmun, joined by White, J., contended that "the Court not only missteps in forging a new *Massiah* test; it proceeds to misapply the very test it has created. The new test requires a showing that the agent created a situation 'likely to induce' the production of incriminating remarks, and that the informant in fact 'prompted' the defendant. Even accepting the most capacious reading of both this language and the facts, I believe that neither prong of the Court's test is satisfied."

In a separate dissent, Justice Rehnquist maintained "that *Massiah* constitutes such a substantial departure from the traditional concerns that underlie the Sixth Amendment guarantee that its language, if not its actual holding, should be re-examined."

the police had positive evidence of Wilson's involvement, the purpose of placing Lee in the cell was to determine the identities of the other perpetrators. According to his arrangement with Detective Cullen, Lee was not to ask Wilson any questions, but simply to "keep his ears open" for the names of Wilson's confederates. Wilson first spoke to Lee about the crimes after looking out the cellblock window at the garage, where the crime had occurred. He told Lee the same story he had given the police. Lee advised Wilson that his story "didn't sound too good" and that "things didn't look too good for him," but Wilson did not alter his story at that time. However, several days later, after a visit from his brother, who mentioned that members of the family were upset because they believed he had killed the dispatcher, Wilson changed his story. He admitted to Lee that he and two other men had planned and carried out the robbery and killed the dispatcher. Lee reported these incriminating statements to Detective Cullen.

[The trial court denied Wilson's motion to suppress the incriminating statements, finding that Lee had obeyed police instructions only to listen to Wilson for the purpose of identifying his confederates, but not to question him about the crime. The trial court also found that Wilson's statements were "spontaneous" and "unsolicited." After he was convicted of murder and the conviction was affirmed, Wilson sought federal habeas corpus relief. After considering *Massiah*, the district court denied relief, finding "no interrogation whatsoever" by Lee and "only spontaneous statements" from Wilson. A divided U.S. Court of Appeals affirmed.

[Following the decision in *Henry*, Wilson decided to relitigate his Sixth Amendment claim. After his motion to vacate his conviction was denied, Wilson again sought federal habeas corpus relief. The district court concluded that the trial court's findings were "fatal" to Wilson's claim under *Henry* since they showed that the informant made "no affirmative effort" of any kind to elicit information from him. A divided Court of Appeals reversed, finding the circumstances indistinguishable from the facts of *Henry*.]

[In] *Henry*, the Court applied the *Massiah* test to incriminating statements made to a jailhouse informant * * * holding that the Court of Appeals reasonably concluded that the government informant "deliberately used his position to secure incriminating information from [the defendant] when counsel was not present." Although the informant had not questioned the defendant, the informant had "stimulated" conversations with the defendant in order to "elicit" incriminating information. The Court emphasized that those facts, like the facts of *Massiah*, amounted to " 'indirect and surreptitious interrogatio[n]' "of the defendant.

[Since] "the Sixth Amendment is not violated whenever—by luck or happenstance—the State obtains incriminating statements from the accused after the right to counsel has attached," *Moulton,* a defendant does not make out a violation of that right simply by showing that an informant, [reported] his incriminating statements to the police. Rather, the defendant must demonstrate that the police and their informant took some action, beyond merely listening, that was designed deliberately to elicit incriminating remarks.

It is thus apparent that the Court of Appeals erred in concluding that respondent's right to counsel was violated under the circumstances of this case. [It failed] to accord to the state trial court's factual findings the presumption of correctness expressly required by 28 U.S.C. § 2254(d).

The state court found that Officer Cullen had instructed Lee only to listen to respondent for the purpose of determining the identities of the other participants in the robbery and murder. [The] court further found that Lee followed those instructions, that he "at no time asked any questions" of respondent concerning the pending charges, and that he "only listened" to respondent's "spontaneous" and "unsolicited" statements. The only remark made by Lee that has any support in this record was his comment that respondent's initial version of his participation in the crimes "didn't sound too good." Without holding that any of the state court's findings were not entitled to the presumption of correctness under § 2254(d), the Court of Appeals focused on that one remark and gave a description of Lee's interaction with respondent that is completely at odds with the facts found by the trial court. [After] thus revising some of the trial court's findings, and ignoring other more relevant findings, the Court of Appeals concluded that the police "deliberately elicited" respondent's incriminating statements. This conclusion conflicts with the decision of every other state and federal judge who reviewed this record, and is clear error in light of the provisions and intent of § 2254(d).[b]

Justice BRENNAN, with whom Justice MARSHALL joins, dissenting.

[The] Court concludes [that] the Court of Appeals failed to recognize that this case presents the question, reserved in *Henry*, whether the Sixth Amendment forbids the admission into evidence of an accused's statements to a jailhouse informant who was "placed in close proximity but [made] no effort to stimulate conversations about the crime charged." I disagree with the Court's characterization of the Court of Appeals' treatment of the state court's findings and, consequently, I disagree with the Court that the instant case presents the "listening post" question.

The state trial court simply found that Lee did not ask respondent any direct questions about the crime for which respondent was incarcerated. The trial court considered the significance of this fact only under State precedents, which the court interpreted to require affirmative "interrogation" by the informant as a prerequisite to a constitutional violation. The court did not indicate whether it referred to a Fifth Amendment or to a Sixth Amendment violation in identifying "interrogation" as a precondition to a violation.

[The]   Court of Appeals did not disregard the state court's finding that Lee asked respondent no direct questions regarding the crime. Rather, [it] *expressly accepted* that finding, but concluded that, as a matter of law, the deliberate elicitation standard of *Henry* and *Massiah*, encompasses other, more subtle forms of stimulating incriminating admissions than overt questioning. [The court] observed that, while Lee asked respondent no questions, Lee nonetheless stimulated conversation concerning respondents' role in [the] robbery and murder by remarking that respondent's exculpatory story did not " 'sound too good' "and that he had better come up with a better one. Thus,[it] concluded that the respondent's case did not present the situation reserved in *Henry*, [but was] virtually indistinguishable from *Henry*.

[In] *Henry*, [we] rejected the Government's argument that because Henry initiated the discussion of his crime, no Sixth Amendment violation had occurred. We pointed out that under *Massiah*, it is irrelevant whether the informant asks pointed questions about the crime or "merely engage[s] in general conversation about it."

[In]   the instant case, as in *Henry*, the accused was incarcerated and therefore was "susceptible to the ploys of undercover Government agents." Like

b. Chief Justice Burger, the author of *Henry*, joined the opinion of the Court, but also wrote a brief concurring opinion noting "a vast difference between placing an 'ear' in the suspect's cell and placing a voice in the cell to encourage conversation for the 'ear' to record."

Nichols, [the informant in *Henry*], Lee was a secret informant, usually received consideration for the services he rendered the police, and therefore had an incentive to produce the information which he knew the police hoped to obtain. Just as Nichols had done, Lee obeyed instructions not to question respondent and to report to the police any statements made by the respondent in Lee's presence about the crime in question. And, like Nichols, Lee encouraged respondent to talk about his crime by conversing with him on the subject over the course of several days and by telling respondent that his exculpatory story would not convince anyone without more work. However, unlike the situation in *Henry,* a disturbing visit from respondent's brother, rather than a conversation with the informant, seems to have been the immediate catalyst for respondent's confession to Lee. While it might appear from this sequence of events that Lee's comment regarding respondent's story and his general willingness to converse with respondent about the crime were not the *immediate* causes of respondent's admission, I think that the deliberate elicitation standard requires consideration of the entire course of government behavior.

The State intentionally created a situation in which it was foreseeable that respondent would make incriminating statements without the assistance of counsel, *Henry*— it assigned respondent to a cell overlooking the scene of the crime and designated a secret informant to be respondent's cellmate. The informant, while avoiding direct questions, nonetheless developed a relationship of cellmate camaraderie with respondent and encouraged him to talk about his crime. While the *coup de grace* was delivered by respondent's brother, the groundwork for respondent's confession was laid by the State. Clearly the State's actions had a sufficient nexus with respondent's admission of guilt to constitute deliberate elicitation within the meaning of *Henry.*[c]

Notes and Questions

1. *The distinction between placing an "ear" in the defendant's cell and placing a "voice" there to encourage conversations.* As a practical matter, is there any difference, let alone "a vast difference" (see fn. b, supra), between placing an "ear" in the cell and placing a "voice" there? Doesn't the "voice" go with the "ear"?

Is a defendant likely to make incriminating statements to a "cellmate" unless the latter has developed a relationship of trust and confidence with the defendant? Doesn't a police informant have to exchange remarks with the defendant if only to avoid "alerting" the defendant that something is amiss? If two people share the same cell for days or even weeks, don't they *both* talk—and talk back and forth? How likely is it that the flow of conversation and the progression of various conversations can be accurately reconstructed? How much incentive does the informant have to do so? Once formal proceedings have been initiated, is the only effective way to prevent police interference with the attorney-client relationship to prohibit any government agent from *approaching* a defendant in the absence of counsel? See the remarks of Professor Kamisar in Choper, Kamisar & Tribe, *The Supreme Court: Trends and Development,* 1979–80 (1981) at 107–08.

2. *Are the courts asking the wrong questions in cases like Henry and Wilson? Is the true issue in these cases "privacy"?* Yes, maintains H. Richard Uviller,

c. Stevens, J., filed a separate dissent, agreeing with Justice Brennan's analysis of the   merits of respondent's habeas petition.

Evidence from the Mind of the Criminal Suspect, 87 Colum.L.Rev. 1137, 1191, 1195 (1987):

"The fourth amendment is the guardian of privacy and the questions the courts should be asking are: Did the defendant enjoy a protected expectation of privacy in the circumstances, and if so did the state have a properly predicated warrant to encroach, or some good basis for the lack of it? * * *

"[W]hile a defendant may be required to bear the risk of ordinary disloyalty among trusted associates, it does not follow that he must also bear the risk that the government is engaging in surreptitious invasions. The fact that informers are commonplace in the councils of criminals does not deprive the criminals of reasonable expectations of privacy for fourth amendment purposes any more than the frequency of wiretaps in Mafia investigations excuses the government from the duty to take its case to a judge for advance authorization of an electronic surveillance. [The *Hoffa* Court, see p. 388] should have regarded Partin as the human bug he was and treated his intrusion as a search and seizure (unless, of course, the government was right in the claim that they had not 'placed' him in Hoffa's company).

"Thus, Stewart [, who wrote the opinion of the Court in both *Hoffa* and *Massiah,*] unnaturally distorted the sixth amendment's promise of a skilled advocate in order to narrow the interval in which the suspect's mind could be probed and unwisely shortened the reach of the fourth amendment's guarantee of security by permitting the government deliberately to insert a human spy into the suspect's private space to report on declarations and behavior that might betray a guilty mind."

3.   But consider James Tomkovicz, *An Adversary System Defense of the Right to Counsel Against Informants: Truth, Fair Play, and the Massiah Doctrine,* 22 U.C.Davis L.Rev. 1, 36–38 (1988):

"[If the fourth amendment] were the real basis for protection against government informants, the resulting doctrine would have to be considerably different than the current *Massiah* doctrine. For example, fourth amendment protection would not depend either on the initiation of adversarial proceedings or on active elicitation.

"More important, *Massiah's* substantive sixth amendment protection is radically different than the substance of prospective fourth amendment shelter. The prohibition against 'unreasonable' searches would provide a *limited* safeguard *against the informant surveillance itself.* The *Massiah* right, on the other hand, raises an *absolute* barrier not to the surveillance, but *to the use of its products at trial.* Consequently, one cannot rationalize the current *Massiah* entitlement upon a fourth amendment foundation. Both the doctrine and the right belie any fourth amendment roots.[175]"

175. This statement is not meant to imply that the Court's unease with its repeated refusals to accord any fourth amendment protection against informant surveillance [has] not contributed to the birth and perpetuation of the *Massiah* doctrine. Although not a principled basis, the Court's discomfort cannot be discounted entirely as an actual influence upon the law in this area.

In addition, the textual discussion is not meant to imply that the fourth amendment should not have a role in informant contexts. [Rather,] the point [is] that the *Massiah* doctrine is not fourth amendment law in disguise.

Chapter 9

LINEUPS, SHOWUPS AND OTHER PRE–TRIAL IDENTIFICATION PROCEDURES

SECTION 1. *WADE* AND *GILBERT*: CONSTITUTIONAL CONCERN ABOUT THE DANGERS INVOLVED IN EYEWITNESS IDENTIFICATIONS

UNITED STATES v. WADE*
388 U.S. 218, 87 S.Ct. 1926, 18 L.Ed.2d 1149 (1967).

Justice BRENNAN delivered the opinion of the Court.

The question here is whether courtroom identifications of an accused at trial are to be excluded from evidence because the accused was exhibited to the witnesses before trial at a post-indictment lineup conducted for identification purposes without notice to and in the absence of the accused's appointed counsel.

The federally insured bank in Eustace, Texas, was robbed on September 21, 1964. A man with a small strip of tape on each side of his face entered the bank, pointed a pistol at the female cashier and the vice president, the only persons in the bank at the time, and forced them to fill a pillowcase with the bank's money. The man then drove away with an accomplice who had been waiting in a stolen car outside the bank. On March 23, 1965, an indictment was returned against respondent, Wade, and two others for conspiring to rob the bank, and against Wade and the accomplice for the robbery itself. Wade was arrested on April 2, and counsel was appointed to represent him on April 26. Fifteen days later [after counsel was appointed] an FBI agent, without notice to Wade's lawyer, arranged to have the two bank employees observe a lineup made up of Wade and five or six other prisoners and conducted in a courtroom of the local county courthouse. Each person in the line wore strips of tape such as allegedly worn by the robber and upon direction each said something like "put the money in the bag," the words allegedly uttered by the robber. Both bank employees identified Wade in the lineup as the bank robber.

At trial the two employees, when asked on direct examination if the robber was in the courtroom, pointed to Wade. The prior lineup identification was then elicited from both employees on cross-examination.

[The] fact that the lineup involved no violation of Wade's privilege against self-incrimination[a] does not [dispose] of his contention that the courtroom identifi-

---

* The Court decided two other pretrial identification cases the same day: *Gilbert v. California*, 388 U.S. 263, 87 S.Ct. 1951, 18 L.Ed.2d 1178 (1967) and *Stovall v. Denno*, 388 U.S.

293, 87 S.Ct. 1967, 18 L.Ed.2d 1199 (1967), both discussed infra.

a. On this issue, relying on *Schmerber v. California* (p. 42,) a 5–4 majority ruled that cations should have been excluded because the lineup was conducted without notice to and in the absence of his counsel. [In] this case it is urged that the assistance of counsel at the lineup was indispensable to protect Wade's most basic right as a criminal defendant—his right to a fair trial at which the witnesses against him might be meaningfully cross-examined.

[T]he principle of *Powell v. Alabama* and succeeding cases requires that we scrutinize *any* pretrial confrontation of the accused to determine whether the presence of his counsel is necessary to preserve the defendant's basic right to a fair trial as affected by his right meaningfully to cross-examine the witnesses against him and to have effective assistance of counsel at the trial itself. It calls upon us to analyze whether potential substantial prejudice to defendant's rights inheres in the particular confrontation and the ability of counsel to help avoid that prejudice.

The Government characterizes the lineup as a mere preparatory step in the gathering of the prosecution's evidence, not different—for Sixth Amendment purposes—from various other preparatory steps, such as systematized or scientific analyzing of the accused's fingerprints, blood sample, clothing, hair, and the like. We think there are differences which preclude such stages being characterized as critical stages at which the accused has the right to the presence of his counsel. Knowledge of the techniques of science and technology is sufficiently available, and the variables in techniques few enough, that the accused has the opportunity for a meaningful confrontation of the Government's case at trial through the ordinary processes of cross-examination of the Government's expert witnesses and the presentation of the evidence of his own experts. The denial of a right to have his counsel present at such analyses does not therefore violate the Sixth Amendment; they are not critical stages since there is minimal risk that his counsel's absence at such stages might derogate from his right to a fair trial.[b]

But the confrontation compelled by the State between the accused and the victim or witnesses to a crime to elicit identification evidence is peculiarly riddled with innumerable dangers and variable factors which might seriously, even crucially, derogate from a fair trial. The vagaries of eyewitness identification are well-known; the annals of criminal law are rife with instances of mistaken identification. [A] major factor contributing to the high incidence of miscarriage of justice from mistaken identification has been the degree of suggestion inherent in the manner in which the prosecution presents the suspect to witnesses for pretrial identification. A commentator has observed that "[t]he influence of improper suggestion upon identifying witnesses probably accounts for more miscarriages of

neither requiring a person to appear in a lineup and to speak for identification (*Wade*) nor requiring a person to provide handwriting exemplars (*Gilbert*) violated the privilege. *Schmerber*, which involved the taking of a blood sample, over his objection, from a person arrested for drunken driving, rejected the contention that the defendant had been "compelled [to] be a witness against himself" in violation of the Fifth Amendment. The self-incrimination clause, observed the Court, "protects an accused only from being compelled to testify against himself, or otherwise provide the State with evidence of a testimonial or communicative nature." See also the discussion of these rulings in *Doe v. United States*, p. 733, and fn. b at p. 734.

b. Consider, too, the companion case of *Gilbert*, where the Court held, 5–4 on this issue, that the taking of handwriting exemplars from petitioner "was not a 'critical' stage of the criminal proceedings entitling petitioner to the assistance of counsel" for "there is minimal risk that the absence of counsel might derogate from his right to a fair trial. [If,] for some reason, an unrepresentative exemplar is taken, this can be brought out and corrected through the adversary process at trial since the accused can make an unlimited number of additional exemplars for analysis and comparison by government and defense handwriting experts."

justice than any other single factor—perhaps it is responsible for more such errors than all other factors combined." Wall, *Eye-Witness Identification in Criminal Cases* 26 [1965]. Suggestion can be created intentionally or unintentionally in many subtle ways. And the dangers for the suspect are particularly grave when the witness' opportunity for observation was insubstantial, and thus his susceptibility to suggestion the greatest.

Moreover, "[i]t is a matter of common experience that, once a witness has picked out the accused at the line-up, he is not likely to go back on his word later on, so that in practice the issue of identity may (in the absence of other relevant evidence) for all practical purposes be determined there and then, before the trial."

The pretrial confrontation for purpose of identification may take the form of a lineup, also known as an "identification parade" or "showup," as in the present case, or presentation of the suspect alone to the witness, as in *Stovall v. Denno*.[c] It is obvious that risks of suggestion attend either form of confrontation and increase the dangers inhering in eyewitness identification. But as is the case with secret interrogations, there is serious difficulty in depicting what transpires at lineups and other forms of identification confrontations. [For] the same reasons, the defense can seldom reconstruct the manner and mode of lineup identification for judge or jury at trial. [The] impediments to an objective observation are increased when the victim is the witness. Lineups are prevalent in rape and robbery prosecutions and present a particular hazard that a victim's understandable outrage may excite vengeful or spiteful motives. In any event, neither witnesses nor lineup participants are apt to be alert for conditions prejudicial to the suspect. And if they were, it would likely be of scant benefit to the suspect since neither witnesses nor lineup participants are likely to be schooled in the detection of suggestive influences.[13] Improper influences may go undetected by a suspect, guilty or not, who experiences the emotional tension which we might expect in one being confronted with potential accusers. Even when he does observe abuse, if he has a criminal record he may be reluctant to take the stand and open up the admission of prior convictions. Moreover any protestations by the suspect of the fairness of the lineup made at trial are likely to be in vain; the jury's choice is between the accused's unsupported version and that of the police officers present. In short, the accused's inability effectively to reconstruct at trial any unfairness that occurred at the lineup may deprive him of his only opportunity meaningfully to attack the credibility of the witness' courtroom identification.

[The] potential for improper influence is illustrated by the circumstances, insofar as they appear, surrounding the prior identifications in the three cases we decide today. In the present case, the testimony of the identifying witnesses elicited on cross-examination revealed that those witnesses were taken to the courthouse and seated in the courtroom to await assembly of the lineup. The courtroom faced on a hallway observable to the witnesses through an open door. The cashier testified that she saw Wade "standing in the hall" within sight of an FBI agent. Five or six other prisoners later appeared in the hall. The vice president testified that he saw a person in the hall in the custody of the agent who "resembled the person that we identified as the one that had entered the bank."

---

c. See pp. 654 and 664.

13. An additional impediment to the detection of such influences by participants, including the suspect, is the physical conditions often surrounding the conduct of the lineup. In many, lights shine on the stage in such a way that the suspect cannot see the witness. [In] some a one-way mirror is used and what is said on the witness' side cannot be heard. * * *

The lineup in *Gilbert* was conducted in an auditorium in which some 100 witnesses to several alleged state and federal robberies charged to Gilbert made wholesale identifications of Gilbert as the robber in each other's presence, a procedure said to be fraught with dangers of suggestion. And the vice of suggestion created by the identification in *Stovall* was the presentation to the witness of the suspect alone handcuffed to police officers. It is hard to imagine a situation more clearly conveying the suggestion to the witness that the one presented is believed guilty by the police.

The few cases that have surfaced therefore reveal the existence of a process attended with hazards of serious unfairness to the criminal accused and strongly suggest the plight of the more numerous defendants who are unable to ferret out suggestive influences in the secrecy of the confrontation. We do not assume that these risks are the result of police procedures intentionally designed to prejudice an accused. Rather we assume they derive from the dangers inherent in eyewitness identification and the suggestibility inherent in the context of the pretrial identification. Williams & Hammelmann, in one of the most comprehensive studies of such forms of identification, said, "[T]he fact that the police themselves have, in a given case, little or no doubt that the man put up for identification has committed the offense, and that their chief pre-occupation is with the problem of getting sufficient proof, because he has not 'come clean,' involves a danger that this persuasion may communicate itself even in a doubtful case to the witness in some way * * *." *Identification Parades, Part I,* [1963] Crim.L.Rev. 479, 483.

Insofar as the accused's conviction may rest on a courtroom identification in fact the fruit of a suspect pretrial identification which the accused is helpless to subject to effective scrutiny at trial, the accused is deprived of that right of cross-examination which is an essential safeguard to his right to confront the witnesses against him. And even though cross-examination is a precious safeguard to a fair trial, it cannot be viewed as an absolute assurance of accuracy and reliability. Thus in the present context, where so many variables and pitfalls exist, the first line of defense must be the prevention of unfairness and the lessening of the hazards of eyewitness identification at the lineup itself. The trial which might determine the accused's fate may well not be that in the courtroom but that at the pretrial confrontation, with the State aligned against the accused, the witness the sole jury, and the accused unprotected against the overreaching, intentional or unintentional, and with little or no effective appeal from the judgment there rendered by the witness—"that's the man."

Since it appears that there is grave potential for prejudice, intentional or not, in the pretrial lineup, which may not be capable of reconstruction at trial, and since presence of counsel itself can often avert prejudice and assure a meaningful confrontation at trial,[d] there can be little doubt that for Wade the post-indictment lineup was a critical stage of the prosecution at which he was "as much entitled to such aid [of counsel as] at the trial itself." *Powell v. Alabama.* Thus both Wade and his counsel should have been notified of the impending lineup, and counsel's presence should have been a requisite to conduct of the lineup, absent an "intelligent waiver." No substantial countervailing policy considerations have been advanced against the requirement of the presence of counsel. Concern is expressed that the requirement will forestall prompt identifications and result in obstruction of the confrontations. As for the first, we note that in the two cases in which the right to counsel is today held to apply, counsel had already been

---

d. At this point, the Court refers to and describes a model statute proposed in Daniel E. Murray, *The Criminal Lineup at Home and Abroad,* 1966 Utah L.Rev. 610, 627–28, a statute providing not only for counsel, but other safeguards as well.

appointed and no argument is made in either case that notice to counsel would have prejudicially delayed the confrontations. Moreover, we leave open the question whether the presence of substitute counsel might not suffice where notification and presence of the suspect's own counsel would result in prejudicial delay.[27] And to refuse to recognize the right to counsel for fear that counsel will obstruct the course of justice is contrary to the basic assumptions upon which this Court has operated in Sixth Amendment cases. We rejected similar logic in *Miranda*, concerning presence of counsel during custodial interrogation.

[In] our view counsel can hardly impede legitimate law enforcement; on the contrary, for the reasons expressed, law enforcement may be assisted by preventing the infiltration of taint in the prosecution's identification evidence. That result cannot help the guilty avoid conviction but can only help assure that the right man has been brought to justice.[29]

Legislative or other regulations, such as those of local police departments, which eliminate the risks of abuse and unintentional suggestion at lineup proceedings and the impediments to meaningful confrontation at trial may also remove the basis for regarding the stage as "critical." But neither Congress nor the federal authorities have seen fit to provide a solution. What we hold today "in no way creates a constitutional strait-jacket which will handicap sound efforts at reform, nor is it intended to have this effect." *Miranda*.

We come now to the question whether the denial of Wade's motion to strike the courtroom identification by the bank witnesses at trial because of the absence of his counsel at the lineup required, as the Court of Appeals held, the grant of a new trial at which such evidence is to be excluded. We do not think this disposition can be justified without first giving the Government the opportunity to establish by clear and convincing evidence that the in-court identifications were based upon observations of the suspect other than the lineup identification. * * * Where, as here, the admissibility of evidence of the lineup identification itself is not involved, a *per se* rule of exclusion of courtroom identification would be unjustified.[e] [A] rule limited solely to the exclusion of testimony concerning identification at the lineup itself, without regard to admissibility of the courtroom identification, would render the right to counsel an empty one. The lineup is most often used, as in the present case, to crystallize the witnesses' identification of the defendant for future reference. We have already noted that the lineup identification will have that effect. The State may then rest upon the witnesses' unequivocal courtroom identification, and not mention the pretrial identification as part of the State's case at trial. Counsel is then in the predicament in which Wade's counsel found himself—realizing that possible unfairness at the lineup may be the sole means of attack upon the unequivocal courtroom identification, and having to probe in the dark in an attempt to discover and reveal unfairness, while bolstering

27. Although the right to counsel usually means a right to the suspect's own counsel, provision for substitute counsel may be justified on the ground that the substitute counsel's presence may eliminate the hazards which render the lineup a critical stage for the presence of the suspect's *own* counsel.

29. Many other nations surround the lineup with safeguards against prejudice to the suspect. In England the suspect must be allowed the presence of his solicitor or a friend; Germany requires the presence of retained counsel; France forbids the confrontation of the suspect in the absence of his counsel; Spain, Mexico, and Italy provide detailed procedures prescribing the conditions under which confrontation must occur under the supervision of a judicial officer who sees to it that the proceedings are officially recorded to assure adequate scrutiny at trial. Murray, [fn. d supra, at 621–627].

e. In *Gilbert*, however, the Court did apply a *per se* exclusionary rule to the testimony of various prosecution witnesses that they had also identified petitioner at a pretrial lineup. See fn. f infra.

the government witness' courtroom identification by bringing out and dwelling upon his prior identification. Since counsel's presence at the lineup would equip him to attack not only the lineup identification but the courtroom identification as well, limiting the impact of violation of the right to counsel to exclusion of evidence only of identification at the lineup itself disregards a critical element of that right.

We think it follows that the proper test to be applied in these situations is that quoted in *Wong Sun v. United States* [p. 786], " '[W]hether, granting establishment of the primary illegality the evidence to which instant objection is made has been come at by exploitation of that illegality or instead by means sufficiently distinguishable to be purged of the primary taint.' Maguire, *Evidence of Guilt* 221 (1959)." Application of this test in the present context requires consideration of various factors; for example, the prior opportunity to observe the alleged criminal act, the existence of any discrepancy between any pre-lineup description and the defendant's actual description, any identification prior to lineup of another person, the identification by picture of the defendant prior to the lineup, failure to identify the defendant on a prior occasion, and the lapse of time between the alleged act and the lineup identification. It is also relevant to consider those facts which, despite the absence of counsel, are disclosed concerning the conduct of the lineup.[33]

On the record now before us we cannot make the determination whether the in-court identifications had an independent origin. [T]he appropriate procedure to be followed is to vacate the conviction pending a hearing to determine whether the in-court identifications had an independent source, or whether, in any event, the introduction of the evidence was harmless error, *Chapman v. California* [Ch. 27, § 5], and for the District Court to reinstate the conviction or order a new trial, as may be proper.[f] * * *

Judgment of Court of Appeals vacated and case remanded with direction.

Justice BLACK, dissenting in part and concurring in part. * * *

I would reverse Wade's conviction without further ado had the prosecution at trial made use of his lineup identification either in place of courtroom identification or [as it did in *Gilbert*] to bolster in a harmful manner crucial courtroom

---

33. Thus it is not the case that "[i]t matters not how well the witness knows the suspect, whether the witness is the suspect's mother, brother, or long-time associate, and no matter how long or well the witness observed the perpetrator at the scene of the crime" [quoting from Justice White's opinion in *Wade*]. Such factors will have an important bearing upon the true basis of the witness' in-court identification. Moreover, the State's inability to bolster the witness' courtroom identification by introduction of the lineup identification itself, see *Gilbert*, will become less significant the more the evidence of other opportunities of the witness to observe the defendant. Thus where the witness is a "kidnap victim who has lived for days with his abductor" [again quoting from Justice White] the value to the State of admission of the lineup identification is indeed marginal, and such identification would be a mere formality.

f. Compare *Gilbert*, where various witnesses who identified petitioner in the courtroom also testified, on direct examination by the prosecution, that they had identified petitioner at a prior lineup. "That [pretrial lineup] testimony," ruled the Court, "is the direct result of the illegal lineup 'come at by exploitation of [the primary] illegality.' *Wong Sun*. The State is therefore not entitled to an opportunity to show that that testimony had an independent source. Only a *per se* exclusionary rule as to such testimony can be an effective sanction to assure that law enforcement authorities will respect the accused's constitutional right to the presence of his counsel at the critical lineup. [That] conclusion is buttressed by the consideration that the witness' testimony of his lineup identification will enhance the impact of his in-court identification on the jury and seriously aggravate whatever derogation exists of the accused's right to a fair trial. Therefore, unless the [state supreme court] is 'able to declare a belief that it was harmless beyond a reasonable doubt,' *Chapman*, Gilbert will be entitled on remand to a new trial * * *."

identification. But the prosecution here did neither of these things. After prosecution witnesses under oath identified Wade in the courtroom, it was the defense, and not the prosecution, which brought out the prior lineup identification. While stating that "a *per se* rule of exclusion of courtroom identification would be unjustified," the Court, nevertheless remands this case for "a hearing to determine whether the in-court identifications had an independent source," or were the tainted fruits of the invalidly conducted lineup. From this holding I dissent.

In the first place, even if this Court has power to establish such a rule of evidence, I think the rule fashioned by the Court is unsound. The "tainted fruit" determination required by the Court involves more than considerable difficulty. I think it is practically impossible. How is a witness capable of probing the recesses of his mind to draw a sharp line between a courtroom identification due exclusively to an earlier lineup and a courtroom identification due to memory not based on the lineup? [In] my view, the Fifth and Sixth Amendments are satisfied if the prosecution is precluded from using lineup identification as either an alternative to or corroboration of courtroom identification. If the prosecution does neither and its witnesses under oath identify the defendant in the courtroom, then I can find no justification for stopping the trial in midstream to hold a lengthy "tainted fruit" hearing. * * *

Justice WHITE whom Justice HARLAN and Justice STEWART join, dissenting in part and concurring in part.

The Court has again propounded a broad constitutional rule barring the use of a wide spectrum of relevant and probative evidence, solely because a step in its ascertainment or discovery occurs outside the presence of defense counsel.

[The] Court's opinion is far-reaching. It proceeds first by creating a new *per se* rule of constitutional law: a criminal suspect cannot be subjected to a pretrial identification process in the absence of his counsel without violating the Sixth Amendment. If he is, the State may not buttress a later courtroom identification of the witness by any reference to the previous identification. Furthermore, the courtroom identification is not admissible at all unless the State can establish by clear and convincing proof that the testimony is not the fruit of the earlier identification made in the absence of defendant's counsel—admittedly a heavy burden for the State and probably an impossible one. To all intents and purposes, courtroom identifications are barred if pretrial identifications have occurred without counsel being present.

The rule applies to any lineup, to any other techniques employed to produce an identification and *a fortiori* to a face-to-face encounter between the witness and the suspect alone, regardless of when the identification occurs, in time or place, and whether before or after indictment or information. It matters not how well the witness knows the suspect, whether the witness is the suspect's mother, brother, or long-time associate, and no matter how long or well the witness observed the perpetrator at the scene of the crime. The kidnap victim who has lived for days with his abductor is in the same category as the witness who has had only a fleeting glimpse of the criminal. Neither may identify the suspect without defendant's counsel being present. The same strictures apply regardless of the number of other witnesses who positively identify the defendant and regardless of the corroborative evidence showing that it was the defendant who had committed the crime.

The premise for the Court's rule is not the general unreliability of eyewitness identifications nor the difficulties inherent in observation, recall, and recognition. The Court assumes a narrower evil as the basis for its rule—improper police suggestion which contributes to erroneous identifications. The Court apparently believes that improper police procedures are so widespread that a broad prophylactic rule must be laid down, requiring the presence of counsel at all pretrial identifications, in order to detect recurring instances of police misconduct.[1] I do not share this pervasive distrust of all official investigations. None of the materials the Court relies upon supports it. Certainly, I would bow to solid fact, but the Court quite obviously does not have before it any reliable, comprehensive survey of current police practices on which to base its new rule. Until it does, the Court should avoid excluding relevant evidence from state criminal trials.

[There] are several striking aspects to the Court's holding. First, the rule does not bar courtroom identifications where there have been no previous identifications in the presence of the police, although when identified in the courtroom, the defendant is known to be in custody and charged with the commission of a crime.[g] Second, the Court seems to say that if suitable legislative standards were adopted for the conduct of pretrial identifications, thereby lessening the hazards in such confrontations, it would not insist on the presence of counsel. But if this is true, why does not the Court simply fashion what it deems to be constitutionally acceptable procedures for the authorities to follow? Certainly the Court is correct in suggesting that the new rule will be wholly inapplicable where police departments themselves have established suitable safeguards.

Third, courtroom identification may be barred, absent counsel at a prior identification, regardless of the extent of counsel's information concerning the circumstances of the previous confrontation between witness and defendant—apparently even if there were recordings or sound-movies of the events as they occurred. But if the rule is premised on the defendant's right to have his counsel know, there seems little basis for not accepting other means to inform. A disinterested observer, recordings, photographs—any one of them would seem adequate to furnish the basis for a meaningful cross-examination of the eyewitness who identifies the defendant in the courtroom. * * *

Finally, I think the Court's new rule is vulnerable in terms of its own unimpeachable purpose of increasing the reliability of identification testimony.

Law enforcement officers have the obligation to convict the guilty and to make sure they do not convict the innocent. They must be dedicated to making the criminal trial a procedure for the ascertainment of the true facts surrounding the commission of the crime. To this extent, our so-called adversary system is not adversary at all; nor should it be. But defense counsel has no comparable obligation to ascertain or present the truth. Our system assigns him a different mission. He must be and is interested in preventing the conviction of the innocent, but, absent a voluntary plea of guilty, we also insist that he defend his client whether he is innocent or guilty. The State has the obligation to present the evidence. Defense counsel need present nothing, even if he knows what the truth

---

1. Yet in *Stovall v. Denno* [p. 654] the Court recognizes that improper police conduct in the identification process has not been so widespread as to justify full retroactivity for its new rule.

g. Consider Joseph D. Grano, *Kirby, Biggers, and Ash: Do Any Constitutional Safeguards Remain Against the Danger of Convicting the Innocent?*, 72 Mich.L.Rev. 717, 785 (1974): "[A]n identification more unreliable than the witness's familiar selection of the conspicuous defendant, frequently after scan-

ning the courtroom for dramatic effect, is difficult to imagine. In effect, [these identifications are] one-man showups, albeit in the courtroom." Consider, too, H. Richard Uviller, *The Role of the Defense Lawyer at a Lineup in Light of the Wade, Gilbert and Stovall Decisions*, 4 Crim.L.Bull. 273, 284 (1968).

How can defense counsel avoid or minimize the impact of a suggestive confrontation between a witness and defendant in the courtroom? See Note 6 following this case.

is. [If] he can confuse a witness, even a truthful one, or make him appear at a disadvantage, unsure or indecisive, that will be his normal course. * * *

I would not extend this system, at least as it presently operates, to police investigations and would not require counsel's presence at pretrial identification procedures. Counsel's interest is in not having his client placed at the scene of the crime, regardless of his whereabouts. Some counsel may advise their clients to refuse to make any movements or to speak any words in a lineup or even to appear in one. [Others] will hover over witnesses and begin their cross-examination then, menacing truthful factfinding as thoroughly as the Court fears the police now do. Certainly there is an implicit invitation to counsel to suggest rules for the lineup and to manage and produce it as best he can.[h] I therefore doubt that the Court's new rule, at least absent some clearly defined limits on counsel's role, will measurably contribute to more reliable pretrial identifications. My fears are that it will have precisely the opposite result. * * *

ON THE MEANING OF THE LINEUP DECISIONS

1. Waiver. If *Wade* seeks to protect the reliability of the identification process and to make available testimony about the conditions under which such process is carried out, why should the right to counsel at the lineup be subject to waiver? Permitting waiver of *Miranda* rights may be defended on the ground that an important, legitimate object is served by permitting suspects to bear witness to the truth under conditions which safeguard the exercise of responsible choice, but what comparable value is served by allowing suspects to waive counsel at the identification process?

2. The role of counsel. What is the role of defense counsel at the lineup? Consider Commentary to the *Model Pre–Arraignment Code* at 429–33:

"The two extreme positions might be stated thus:

"(1) Counsel is to be present merely as an observer to assure against abuse and bad faith by law enforcement officers, and to provide the basis for any attack he might wish to make on the identification at trial.

"(2) The lineup procedure is to be a fully adversary proceeding in which the counsel for the suspect may make objections and proposals, which if they are proper or even reasonable must be respected.

"The cases and commentaries, as well as the practice since *Wade* would indicate that the first interpretation of the counsel's role comes closer to describing the general interpretation of the constitutional requirement and to describing the practice under it. The major difficulty with this interpretation is that by forcing counsel into the role of a merely passive observer it gives him a job which at best can be accomplished in a large variety of ways including video recording and at worst is uncomfortable or demeaning.

"[On] the other hand, any attempt to give counsel at identification a more active role is fraught with difficulties not only for the police but for counsel himself. For the police the difficulty is that a procedure which is often under the supervision not of lawyers but of police officers will be subject to manipulation and objection by a trained legal counsel for one side only.

"[The] assigning of a more active role to counsel has perils for counsel as well. If he is entitled to make objections at the lineup procedure, will he be held to have

---

h. But see Note 2 following this case.

waived these objections if he does not make them at the procedure and he wishes later to question the fairness or accuracy of the identification at trial? If such a possibility of waiver exists will he not almost be under an obligation to raise every conceivable objection? Moreover, this hard choice would be imposed on a lawyer at a very early stage of his contact with the case. Indeed the lawyer who did this work is often likely to be a junior member of the public defender's staff assigned on rotation to do 'lineup work,' and thus would not likely be the lawyer to handle the case at trial.

"[Thus, where] a lawyer is present he should not be obliged to make his objections or be deemed to have waived them. Similarly, there does not appear to be any reason to require the police to abide by any objections or suggestions that the lawyer makes. All the Code would require is that any objections that the lawyer might have be made part of the record of the identification procedure. In this way if something has taken place to which defense counsel objects and which the record might not otherwise clearly show, the fact of the lawyer's objection will make this issue prominently available for use at the trial. At the same time, the police in hearing the objection would have the opportunity to remedy the situation if they chose. To be sure, the absence of any objection might possibly carry some factual implication that the defendant and his counsel acquiesced in an identification procedure to which they then find themselves subsequently objecting at trial. This possibility may be thought to provide just the right degree of incentive for defense counsel to make reasonable objections which the police might heed, rather than sitting back and hoping to trap the police in error."

3. *Refusals to cooperate; obstructionist efforts.* Since the lineup or the taking of exemplars is not protected by the privilege against self-incrimination, the prosecution may comment on the suspect's refusal to cooperate. The refusal is considered circumstantial evidence of consciousness of guilt. On occasion, courts have utilized civil or criminal contempt to coerce or punish the suspect who refuses to comply with a court order to participate in some identification proceeding. Still another possibility is for the police to proceed to conduct the identification proceeding over the suspect's objection. See LaFave & Israel, § 7.2(c).

What may be done in response to a suspect's drastic alteration of his appearance between the time of arrest (or the occurrence of the crime) and his appearance in a lineup?[a] One possibility is to bring this alteration to the attention of the jury for consideration as evidence of defendant's consciousness of guilt. Another possibility is to conduct the identification procedure in such a way as to simulate the defendant's prior appearance. See LaFave & Israel, § 7.2(d).

4. *Invalid pre-trial identification procedures and the "independent origin" of in-court identifications.* Reconsider Justice Black's complaint in *Wade* about the difficulties involved in determining whether or not an in-court identification is the "tainted fruit" of an improperly conducted lineup. Does it follow, as Justice Black maintained, that therefore *every* courtroom identification made subsequent to an illegal police lineup (so long as not supplemented or corroborated by the earlier lineup) should be admitted? Or do the very reasons advanced by Justice Black—the great difficulties, if not impossibility of ascertaining the "taint" or lack of it—suggest that *no* courtroom identification preceded by an illegal police lineup should be allowed?[b]

---

a. What ethical questions, if any, are raised by a defense lawyer who encourages his client to "disguise himself" prior to a lineup?

b. The difficulties of determining whether there is an "independent source" for in-court identifications following invalid pre-trial lineups are illustrated by *Clemons v. United*

Is the requirement that the prosecution establish by clear and convincing proof that the courtroom testimony is untainted by the earlier illegal identification a "heavy" and "probably an impossible" burden, as Justice White maintained in *Wade*? If pre-trial identifications are held in violation of the suspect's right to counsel, does the *Wade-Gilbert* rule, as Justice White claimed, bar all courtroom identifications "to all intents and purposes"? Consider the remarks of A.J. Davis, *The Role of the Defense Lawyer at a Lineup in Light of the Wade, Gilbert and Stovall Decisions,* 4 Crim.L.Bull. 273, 294–95 (1968) (panel discussion), a year after the lineup cases were decided:

"How [is the defense lawyer] going to prove that the in-court identification that the victim is about to make is the fruit of [the invalid police lineup]? The Supreme Court may say the burden of proof is on the prosecution, but you know and I know that the attitude of the trial judge is going to be that the burden of proof is on [the defense lawyer] as a practical matter to convince that judge. He is not going to be terribly sympathetic to these cases.

"What is the prosecution going to do? The prosecution is going to put the victim on the stand and the victim is going to say, 'When this robber came to me and put that gun in my face, I looked at him and I formed a mental picture. [Then,] I had this lineup and I compared this portrait in my mind with the people in the lineup and I picked out that defendant. Now I am in court and what am I doing? I am not paying any attention to the lineup. I am again conjuring up that [mental picture] which I evolved in my mind at the time of the robbery, and I am taking that [picture] and putting it next to this defendant at the counsel table and I am saying that they are precisely the same,' and the judge is going to say, 'Whoopie, there's an independent origin,' and you can attempt to prove from today to tomorrow that the pre-trial identification was unfair, but the trial court has a finding of fact to make here, and nine times out of ten, unless you have a very exceptional trial court, he is going to find against you on this issue."

Mr. Davis has turned out to be a better prognosticator than Justice White. The cases support the conclusions of commentators that when confronted with invalid pre-trial identifications the lower courts have "easily found an 'independent source' for an in-court identification," Note, 55 Minn.L.Rev. 779, 818 (1971), and have "readily avoided reversing convictions by stretching, often beyond reason and logic, the doctrines of independent source and harmless error," Grano, p. 648, fn. g, at 722.

5. *Defendant's right to a lineup or other identification procedure.* Reconsider fn. g, p. 648. Should a defendant be allowed to sit among spectators or with nonsuspects at counsel table? Should he be entitled to an in-court lineup, or a pretrial lineup, before being required to confront witnesses in the courtroom?

Consider *Moore v. Illinois,* 434 U.S. 220, 98 S.Ct. 458, 54 L.Ed.2d 424 (1977) (also discussed at p. 658). In rejecting the contention that because the corporeal

---

States, 408 F.2d 1230 (D.C.Cir.1968) and explored in Robert Pitler, *"The Fruit of the Poisonous Tree" Revisited and Shepardized,* 56 Calif.L.Rev. 579, 636–41 (1968); Note 45 Wash.L.Rev. 202 (1970). See generally Felice J. Levine & June L. Tapp, *The Psychology of Criminal Identifications: The Gap from Wade to Kirby,* 121 U.Pa.L.Rev. 1079 (1973). The difficulties are compounded when a courtroom identification is preceded by a corporeal identification which, in turn, is preceded by a photographic identification. For the corporeal identification "may be based not upon the witness's recollection of the features of the guilty party, but upon his recollection of the photograph. Thus, although a witness who is asked to attempt a corporeal identification of a person whose photograph he has previously identified may say, 'That's the man that did it,' what he may actually mean is, 'That's the man whose photograph I identified.'" Patrick E. Wall, *Eye-Witness Identification in Criminal Cases* 68 (1965).

identification occurred "in the course of a judicial proceeding" (a preliminary hearing to determine whether petitioner should be bound over to the grand jury and to set bail) petitioner had no *Wade-Gilbert* right to counsel at the identification procedure, the Court, per Powell, J., pointed out that the identification, "a one-on-one confrontation," had been made under highly suggestive circumstances and that "[h]ad petitioner been represented by counsel, some or all of this suggestiveness could have been avoided." It then noted:

"For example, counsel could have requested that the hearing be postponed until a lineup could be arranged at which the victim would view petitioner in a less suggestive setting. Short of that, counsel could have asked that the victim be excused from the courtroom while the charges were read and the evidence against petitioner was recited, and that petitioner be seated with other people in the audience when the victim attempted an identification. * * * Because it is in the prosecution's interest as well as the accused's that witnesses' identifications remain untainted, we cannot assume that such requests would have been in vain. Such requests are usually addressed to the sound discretion of the court; we express no opinion as to whether the preliminary hearing court would have been required to grant any such requests."

Although such requests are occasionally granted, trial judges, in their discretion, often deny them. See generally LaFave & Israel, § 7.4(g). A leading case on this point is *Evans v. Superior Court,* 522 P.2d 681 (Cal.1974), holding that due process requires that in an appropriate case defendant should be afforded a pretrial lineup, but that such a right arises "only when eyewitness identification is shown to be in material issue and there exists a reasonable likelihood of a mistaken identification which a lineup would tend to resolve." See also *United States v. Archibald,* 734 F.2d 938 (2d Cir.1984), per Oakes, J., pointing out that defendant's request that he be seated away from the defense table and that other black men be seated in the courtroom "should not have been dismissed so quickly or so absolutely by the trial court. [While] it was not necessary for the court to conduct a true *Wade*-type lineup, these relatively minor steps were required to ensure that the identification was not unfair. The in-court identification procedure utilized here was so clearly suggestive as to be impermissible, however traditional it may be."[c]

Model Pre–Arraignment Code § 170.2 permits a person "arrested for or charged with an offense or a person who shows a reasonable basis for believing he may be so charged" to request a nontestimonial identification order requiring persons *other than himself* to appear (presumably to "clear" himself by shifting suspicion to another) or to request an identification procedure involving himself.[d]

6. *The use of "blank" lineups.* To guard against the danger that an eyewitness will assume that the suspect is present in the lineup and thus tend to identify the person who *most nearly resembles* his recollection of the perpetrator of

c. On petition for rehearing, 756 F.2d 223 (2d Cir.1984), *Archibald* was modified to make it clear that special in-court identification procedures are necessary "only when (1) identification is a contested issue; (2) the defendant has moved in a timely manner prior to trial for a lineup; and (3) despite that defense request, the witness has not had an opportunity to view a fair out-of-court lineup prior to his trial testimony."

d. Perhaps because trial judges frequently deny requests, to hold an in-court lineup or to seat the defendant in the courtroom audience before and during the testimony of the prosecution's identification witnesses, defense attorneys have sometimes resorted to "self-help," i.e., substituted another person for the defendant at counsel table without the court's permission or knowledge. This "has been viewed as a violation of ethical standards and an obstruction of justice punishable by criminal contempt." LaFave & Israel, § 7.5(g).

the crime, some commentators have urged the use of "blank" lineups. See Randolph N. Jonakait, *Reliable Identification; Could the Supreme Court Tell in Manson v. Brathwaite?*, 52 U.Colo.L.Rev. 511, 525 (1981); Gerald Lefcourt, *The Blank Lineup: An Aid to the Defense,* 14 Crim.L.Bull. 428 (1978). "The procedure of a blank lineup entails the viewing by the eyewitness of two separate line-ups. The witness should be told that the suspect may or may not appear in the room being viewed. Thereafter, the suspect is not in the first line-up but is presented in the second. Thus, if the witness is one who has a tendency to make an identification because of an assumption that the suspect is present, this tendency would be brought out during the course of the first line-up. On the other hand, if the witness [is] able to identify the suspect [in the second lineup], that identification will carry even greater weight, as it should." Lefcourt, supra, at 430.

7. *On the use of cautionary instructions.* Edith Greene, *Eyewitness Testimony and the Use of Cautionary Instructions,* 8 U.Bridgeport L.Rev. 15 (1987), casts serious doubt about the effectiveness of the most widely used cautionary instruction on eyewitness testimony. Jurors given this instruction seem to be no better informed about the governing legal standards and the factors that affect the reliability of eyewitness testimony than jurors who received no cautionary instruction. Thus, concludes Greene, the many judges who refuse to admit expert testimony about the factors that influence witness reliability because they believe a cautionary instruction will be effective at conveying the information to jurors are acting on an unwarranted assumption. This is not surprising, since other research shows that most jurors fail to understand most of the instructions they receive. See R. Charrow & V. Charrow, *Making Legal Language Understandable: A Psycholinguistic Study of Jury Instructions,* 79 Colum.L.Rev. 1306 (1979).

8. *The use of expert psychological testimony.* Increasingly, defendants are attempting to use experts to explain to the jury the frailty and fallibility of eyewitness testimony. But the admissibility of expert testimony is largely a matter of trial court discretion. And in the main the judicial response to such defense efforts has been very cool. For a discussion—and strong criticism—of the arguments against the use of expert testimony on eyewitness identification, see James Murphy, *An Evaluation of the Arguments Against the Use of Expert Testimony on Eyewitness Identification,* 8 U.Bridgeport L.Rev. 21 (1987). Professor Murphy maintains that "eyewitness testimony, not sufficiently understood by the jury is dangerous evidence which may easily result in miscarriages of justice," and that trial court discretion "is not a license for a court to shut its eyes to advancements in knowledge in other fields."

9. *Despite its unreliability, is eyewitness identification the source of only a relatively small number of wrongful convictions?* Yes, suggests Samuel Gross, *Loss of Innocence: Eyewitness Identification and Proof of Guilt,* 16 J.Legal Studies 395 (1987). "[W]hile convictions based on eyewitness errors may be more frequent than are other types of erroneous convictions," observes Professor Gross, id. at 396, "in absolute terms they are rare. And that presents a paradox: eyewitness identification is (1) a notoriously unreliable type of evidence, (2) the basis of numerous guilty verdicts, and yet (3) the source of only a small number of wrongful convictions. Why?"

According to Gross, "eyewitness testimony is frequently less important to the determination of the identity of a criminal than it appears to be because the eyewitness evidence is corroborated by other information that is often undervalued or inadmissible at trial." Gross examines an extensive set of criminal prosecutions ultimately proven to have been based on misidentifications. He "focuses on the informal mechanisms that are used to sort criminal cases before trial," id., in particular the various types of information that lead the police to suspect the defendant in the first place, and the process by which the prosecutor decides to dismiss some charges and press others.

"If [juries] return few erroneous convictions," maintains Gross, "it is because they are given few opportunities to judge innocent defendants." Id. at 432. Therefore, the best way to reduce the number of convictions based on misidentifications "is to improve the quality of pretrial determination of identity and to tighten the standards for prosecution in cases in which identity is in dispute. Some reforms in trial procedure might be useful, but primarily those designed to force the police and prosecutors to improve their investigations rather than those armed at improving the accuracy of courtroom judgments. The major impetus for change, however, must come from the law enforcement community itself." Id. at 448.

THE DUE PROCESS "BACK–UP" TEST

STOVALL v. DENNO, 388 U.S. 293, 87 S.Ct. 1967, 18 L.Ed.2d 1199 (1967) (a federal habeas corpus proceeding collaterally attacking a state criminal conviction) (discussed more extensively in § 3, infra), held that the newly announced *Wade-Gilbert* principles would not be applied retroactively but would affect only those identification procedures conducted in the absence of counsel after the date the *Wade* and *Gilbert* decisions were handed down.[a] The court did consider, however, whether "the confrontation conducted in this case was so unnecessarily suggestive and conducive to irreparable mistaken identification" that petitioner was denied due process of law—"a recognized ground of attack upon a conviction independent of any right to counsel claim," but one that must be evaluated in light of the totality of surrounding circumstances. Since the record revealed that the showing of petitioner to a victim of the assault "in an immediate hospital confrontation was imperative," the due process claim was denied. As *Stovall* illustrates, and as the Court later articulated the due process test when it applied it to a pretrial identification by photograph, the question is whether the identification procedure "was so *impermissibly* suggestive as to give rise to a very substantial likelihood of irreparable misidentification." *Simmons v. United States*, 390 U.S. 377, 88 S.Ct. 967, 19 L.Ed.2d 1247 (1968). (Emphasis added.)

THE EYE–WITNESS TESTIMONY PROVISIONS
OF THE 1968 CRIME CONTROL ACT

Consider the constitutionality of Title II of the Omnibus Crime Control and Safe Streets Act of 1968, 18 U.S.C. § 3502, designed to "repeal" the *Wade-Gilbert* rule in federal prosecutions: "The testimony of a witness that he saw the accused commit or participate in the commission of the crime for which the accused is being tried shall be admissible in evidence in a criminal prosecution in any trial court ordained and established under article III of the Constitution of the United States."

Consider Judge Carl McGowan, *Constitutional Interpretation and Criminal Identification,* 12 Wm. & Mary L.Rev. 235, 249–50 (1970): "As a practical matter,

a. For a general discussion of the retroactive effect of a new constitutional decision in   the criminal procedure field, see pp. 45–50.

the Congressional [response to *Wade-Gilbert–Stovall*] has proved to be meaningless. The inferior federal courts have considered themselves bound by the Supreme Court's reading of the Constitution rather than that of the Congress and have appeared to ignore the new statute. [Congress] appeared to overlook completely the threat to the conviction rate inherent in the impatience of juries with prosecution cases limited to in-court identification. It showed no awareness of the values that may reside, for the prosecution as well as the defense, in tightening up pretrial identification procedures so that impressively credible identification evidence can be adduced." See also Commentary to *Model Pre–Arraignment Code* at 427 & n. 15.

In light of its sparse legislative history, may § 3502 be read as excepting from its language lineups conducted in violation of due process, which *Stovall* recognized as a basis for attacking identification testimony independent of any right to counsel claim?

SECTION 2. THE COURT RETREATS: *KIRBY* AND *ASH*

KIRBY v. ILLINOIS
406 U.S. 682, 92 S.Ct. 1877, 32 L.Ed.2d 411 (1972).

Justice STEWART announced the judgment of the Court in an opinion in which The Chief Justice, Justice BLACKMUN, and Justice REHNQUIST join.

[In] the present case we are asked to extend the *Wade-Gilbert* per se exclusionary rule to identification testimony based upon a police station show-up that took place *before* the defendant had been indicted or otherwise formally charged with any criminal offense.

On February 21, 1968, [one] Willie Shard reported to the Chicago police that the previous day two men had robbed him on a Chicago street of a wallet containing, among other things, travellers checks and a Social Security card. On February 22, two police officers [investigating an unrelated crime] stopped petitioner and a companion, [Bean], [on a Chicago street]. When asked for identification, the petitioner produced a wallet that contained three travellers checks and a Social Security card, all bearing the name of Willie Shard. * * *

Only after arriving at the police station, and checking the records there, did the arresting officers learn of the Shard robbery. [The police] picked up Shard and brought him to the police station. Immediately upon entering the room [where petitioner and Bean were seated], Shard positively identified them as [his robbers].[a] No lawyer was present [and neither suspect had asked for] or been advised of any right to the presence of counsel. [At the trial Shard] described his identification of the two men at the police station [and] identified them again in the courtroom as the men who had robbed him.

[In] a line of constitutional cases in this Court stemming back to the Court's landmark opinion in *Powell v. Alabama,* it has been firmly established that a person's Sixth and Fourteenth Amendment right to counsel attaches only at or after the time that adversary judicial proceedings have been initiated against him.

---

a. According to dissenting Justice Brennan, Shard testified that he identified petitioner and Bean only after the officers who brought him to the room asked him if they were the robbers.

This is not to say that a defendant in a criminal case has a constitutional right to counsel only at the trial itself. [But] the point is [that] *all* of [the right to counsel cases] have involved points of time at or after the initiation of adversary judicial criminal proceedings—whether by way of formal charge, preliminary hearing, indictment, information, or arraignment.

The only seeming deviation from this long line of constitutional decisions was *Escobedo* [which] is not apposite here for two distinct reasons. First, the Court in retrospect perceived that the "prime purpose" of *Escobedo* was not to vindicate the constitutional right to counsel as such, but, like *Miranda*, "to guarantee full effectuation of the privilege against self-incrimination. * * * "*Johnson v. New Jersey* [p. 46]. Secondly, and perhaps even more important for purely practical purposes, the Court has limited the holding of *Escobedo* to its own facts, and those facts are not remotely akin to the facts of the case before us.

The initiation of judicial criminal proceedings is far from a mere formalism. It is the starting point of our whole system of adversary criminal justice. For it is only then that the Government has committed itself to prosecute, and only then that the adverse positions of Government and defendant have solidified. It is then that a defendant finds himself faced with the prosecutorial forces of organized society, and immersed in the intricacies of substantive and procedural criminal law. It is this point, therefore, that marks the commencement of the "criminal prosecutions" to which alone the explicit guarantees of the Sixth Amendment are applicable.

In this case we are asked to import into a routine police investigation an absolute constitutional guarantee historically and rationally applicable only after the onset of formal prosecutorial proceedings. We decline to do so. We decline to [impose] a *per se* exclusionary rule upon testimony concerning an identification that took place long before the commencement of any prosecution whatever.

What has been said is not to suggest that there may not be occasions during the course of a criminal investigation when the police do abuse identification procedures. Such abuses are not beyond the reach of the Constitution. [The] Due Process Clause of the Fifth and Fourteenth Amendments forbids a lineup that is unnecessarily suggestive and conducive to irreparable mistaken identification.[8] When a person has not been formally charged with a criminal offense, *Stovall* strikes the appropriate constitutional balance between the right of a suspect to be protected from prejudicial procedures and the interest of society in the prompt and purposeful investigation of an unsolved crime.

The judgment is affirmed.[b]

Justice BRENNAN, with whom Justice DOUGLAS and Justice MARSHALL join, dissenting. * * *

While it should go without saying, it appears necessary, in view of the plurality opinion today, to re-emphasize that *Wade* did not require the presence of counsel at pretrial confrontations for identification purposes simply on the basis of an abstract consideration of the words "criminal prosecutions" in the Sixth

---

8. In view of our limited grant of certiorari, we do not consider whether there might have been a deprivation of due process in the particularized circumstances of this case. That question remains open for inquiry in a federal habeas corpus proceeding.

[Following the U.S. Supreme Court's decision, the denial of Kirby's petition for federal habeas corpus relief was affirmed by the Seventh Circuit in *United States ex rel. Kirby v. Sturges*, 510 F.2d 397 (1975).]

b. As he "would not extend the *Wade-Gilbert* exclusionary rule," Powell, J., concurred in the result.

Amendment, [but] in order to safeguard the accused's constitutional rights to confrontation and the effective assistance of counsel at his trial.

In view of *Wade,* it is plain, and the plurality today does not attempt to dispute it, that there inhere in a confrontation for identification conducted after arrest[5] the identical hazards to a fair trial that inhere in such a confrontation conducted "after the onset of formal prosecutorial proceedings." The plurality apparently considers an arrest, which for present purposes we must assume to be based upon probable cause, to be nothing more than part of "a routine police investigation," and thus not "the starting point of our whole system of adversary criminal justice." [The] plurality offers no reason, and I can think of none, for concluding that a post-arrest confrontation for identification, unlike a post-charge confrontation, is not among those "critical confrontations of the accused by the prosecution at pretrial proceedings where the results might well settle the accused's fate and reduce the trial itself to a mere formality."

The highly suggestive form of confrontation employed in this case underscores the point. This showup was particularly fraught with the peril of mistaken identification. In the setting of a police station squad room where all present except petitioner and Bean were police officers, the danger was quite real that Shard's understandable resentment might lead him too readily to agree with the police that the pair under arrest, and the only persons exhibited to him, were indeed the robbers. [On] direct examination, Shard identified petitioner and Bean not as the alleged robbers on trial in the courtroom, but as the pair he saw at the police station. * * *

Wade and *Gilbert,* of course, happened to involve post-indictment confrontations. Yet even a cursory perusal of the opinions in those cases reveals that nothing at all turned upon that particular circumstance. In short, it is fair to conclude that rather than "declin[ing] to depart from [the] rationale" of *Wade* and *Gilbert,* the plurality today, albeit purporting to be engaged in "principled constitutional adjudication," refuses even to recognize that "rationale." * * *

Justice WHITE, dissenting.

Wade and *Gilbert* govern this case and compel reversal of the judgment below.

Notes and Questions

1. *Wade and Escobedo.* Does the "reinterpretation" of *Escobedo* (as designed not to vindicate the right to counsel as such but to effectuate the privilege against self-incrimination) support Justice Stewart's holding in *Kirby?* Consider Grano at 728: "*Wade,* like *Escobedo* in its new guise, did not vindicate the right to counsel as such, but rather vindicated the rights of cross-examination, confrontation, and fair trial. *Escobedo* still suggests that counsel must be provided at *any* pretrial stage when necessary to protect other constitutional rights."

2. *Wade and Powell.* Did the early right to counsel precedents, as Justice Stewart indicates, mandate the result in *Kirby?* Consider Grano at 727: "*Powell v. Alabama* [and its pre-*Gideon* progeny] relied on the fourteenth amendment due process clause rather than on the sixth amendment. Since the protections under the fourteenth amendment are not limited to any particular stage of a criminal proceeding, the fact that the defendants in these cases had already been charged is irrelevant."

---

5. This case does not require me to consider confrontations that take place before custody, nor accidental confrontations not arranged by the police, nor on-the-scene encounters shortly after the crime.

3. *"Custody" vs. "the initiation of adversary judicial criminal proceedings."* Is it sound to view (as does Justice Stewart for the plurality in *Kirby*) the "initiation of judicial criminal proceedings [as] the starting point of our whole system of adversary criminal justice"? Is it realistic to say, (as Justice Stewart does for the *Kirby* plurality) that "it is only then [that] the adverse positions of Government and defendant have solidified"? Is the postcustody police attitude supposed to be "neutral" or merely "investigative" rather than "accusatory"? Didn't the Court explicitly recognize in *Miranda* that the accusatory function begins very soon after the defendant is taken into custody? Again, see Grano at 726–27. Recall the statement in *Escobedo*—over Justice Stewart's strong dissent— that "it would exalt form over substance to make the right to counsel, under these circumstances, depend on whether at the time of the interrogation the authorities had secured a formal indictment. Petitioner had, for all practical purposes, already been charged * * *."

But consider Israel, *Criminal Procedure, the Burger Court, and the Legacy of the Warren Court,* 75 Mich.L.Rev. 1320, 1368 n. 224 (1977): "[A]ccepting the premise that the need for counsel is often equivalent in the post-indictment and pre-indictment lineup, it does not necessarily follow that appointment of counsel is constitutionally required in both situations. The sixth amendment, it can be argued, does not provide for counsel at every stage in which counsel's assistance is helpful. Rather, by its history, language, and function, the amendment sought to draw a starting point after which counsel's assistance is generally required as an element of our adversary system. That point, Justice Stewart argues, is the initiation of judicial criminal proceedings. Before that point, counsel may be constitutionally required only if essential to the protection of some other constitutional right, as in *Miranda. Kirby* obviously concluded that it was not so essential as to be required to implement the right of confronting the eyewitness at trial."

4. *Alley confrontations.* To what extent did *Kirby* reject the "custody" approach because such an approach would pose a serious threat to the common police practice of conducting "alley confrontations," i.e., prompt confrontations with the victim or an eyewitness at the scene of the crime? See Grano at 731. Prior to *Kirby* most courts exempted these identifications from the right to counsel requirement. See, e.g., *Russell v. United States,* 408 F.2d 1280 (D.C.Cir. 1969) (Bazelon, C.J.).

For the view that all the psychological assumptions on which *Russell* and similar cases are premised—(a) the victim or witness to a crime can be counted on to form an accurate mental image of the offender; (b) this image will be more accurate on the scene immediately after the crime than at the police station some hours later; and (c) the suggestion inherent in one-man confrontations is insignificant in light of the other factors—are speculative and questionable, see Grano at 734–38.

5. *When are adversary judicial criminal proceedings "initiated"?* In MOORE v. ILLINOIS, 434 U.S. 220, 98 S.Ct. 458, 54 L.Ed.2d 424 (1977), a police officer accompanied the victim to a courtroom where petitioner, a rape suspect, was to appear for his preliminary hearing to determine whether he should be bound over to the grand jury and to set bail. Petitioner was not represented by counsel at this hearing, nor offered appointed counsel. After petitioner's name was called and he was led before the bench, and after the prosecutor had recited evidence believed to implicate petitioner, the victim was asked by the prosecutor where she saw her assailant in the courtroom and she pointed at petitioner. At trial, the victim testified on direct that she had identified petitioner at the preliminary hearing. In reversing the judgment of the federal court of appeals denying habeas corpus relief, the Court, per POWELL, J., rejected, inter alia, the contention that evidence of a corporeal identification conducted in the absence of defense counsel must be excluded only if the identification is made after the defendant is indicted:

"The prosecution in this case was commenced under Illinois law when the victim's complaint was filed in court. The purpose of the preliminary hearing was to determine whether there was probable cause to bind petitioner over to the grand jury and to set bail. Petitioner had the right to oppose the prosecution at that hearing by moving to dismiss the charges and to suppress the evidence against him. He faced counsel for the State * * *. It is plain that '[t]he government ha[d] committed itself to prosecute,' and that petitioner found 'himself faced with the prosecutorial forces of organized society, and immersed in the intricacies of substantive and procedural criminal law.' *Kirby.* The State candidly concedes that the preliminary hearing marked the 'initiation of adversary judicial criminal proceedings' against petitioner, and it hardly could contend otherwise."[a]

Section 160.3(2) of the *Model Code* "codifies" *Kirby* by granting a suspect a right to counsel at corporeal identification procedures "if a complaint has been filed charging a person with crime, or a person has been indicted for crime." Rule 403 of the *Model Rules* reads *Kirby* as giving a suspect "the right to a lawyer for any lineup connected with an arrest for which he was arrested or charged—and to have a lawyer appointed for this purpose if he cannot afford one—if the lineup is held following the start of criminal proceedings against him" (emphasis in the original) and provides further: "Criminal proceedings may be begun by any one of the following: a formal charge (sworn complaint); a preliminary hearing; an indictment; an arraignment; an initial appearance for a magistrate." See also Grano at 788–89.

Consider Israel, Note 3 supra, at 1368–69 n. 226: "Most defendants are arrested without warrants and are placed in lineups prior to their appearance before a magistrate—i.e., before a formal charge or a complaint has been filed against them. Where the individual has been arrested pursuant to a warrant, the complaint will have been filed before his arrest, but the lineup still is likely to be held prior to his first appearance before a magistrate. Arguably, *Wade* also would not apply in that situation. Even though a complaint has been filed in the process of obtaining a warrant, adversary judicial criminal proceedings may be viewed as being initiated only after the accused is brought before a magistrate on that complaint. [This] starting point would make sense from an administrative standpoint because counsel for the indigent ordinarily would not be appointed until the defendant has appeared before the magistrate."[b]

---

a. The Court also rejected the view that petitioner had no right to counsel at this identification procedure because "it was conducted in the course of a judicial proceeding": "The reasons supporting *Wade's* holding that a corporeal identification is a critical stage of a criminal prosecution for Sixth Amendment purposes apply with equal force to this identification. It is difficult to imagine a more suggestive manner in which to present a suspect to a witness for their critical first confrontation than was employed in this case. * * * Had petitioner been represented by counsel, some or all of this suggestiveness could have been avoided."

b. Professor Israel adds: "The English apparently use a similar starting point with respect to counsel at lineups. The Parade Rules provide that the 'suspect should be informed that if he so desires he may have his solicitor or friend present at the identification parade.' *Home Office Circular on Identification Parades* '10, reprinted in Report to the Secretary of State for the Home Department of the Departmental Committee on Evidence of Identification in Criminal Cases 158, 159 (1976) [hereinafter cited as the Devlin Report (for the committee chairman, Lord Devlin)]. [The] Devlin Report states, however, that, for the overwhelming majority of suspects, the solici-

6. *Do adversary judicial proceedings commence at the same time for Massiah and Kirby purposes?* Consider Kamisar, *Brewer v. Williams, Massiah, and Miranda: What is "Interrogation"? When Does it Matter?*, 67 Geo.L.J., 86 n. 503 (1978): "Although the Supreme Court and courts generally seem to have treated the question of when judicial proceedings commence within the meaning of (1) *Massiah* and (2) *Kirby* as the same question, the different procedural contexts may have at least a strong subliminal impact on some courts. As a policy matter, it seems considerably more difficult to resist the presence of counsel at a lineup than in the interrogation room. When he can do so, a defense lawyer will usually prevent all police questioning, but he is unlikely—indeed, not empowered?—to disrupt pretrial identification proceedings. Moreover, unlike the Warren Court 'confession' cases, which arguably 'furthered societal values not usually related to guilt or innocence,' the Warren Court pretrial identification cases 'explicitly sought to protect the innocent from wrongful conviction.' (Grano at 722.)"

UNITED STATES v. ASH
413 U.S. 300, 93 S.Ct. 2568, 37 L.Ed.2d 619 (1973).

Justice BLACKMUN delivered the opinion of the Court.

[Shortly before trial, almost three years after the crime, and long after defendant had been incarcerated and appointed counsel, the government conducted a photographic display without notifying counsel. The prosecutor showed five color photographs to four witnesses who previously had tentatively identified the black and white photograph of defendant. Three witnesses selected defendant's photo, but one was unable to make any selection. The U.S. Court of Appeals for the D.C. Circuit ruled that defendant's right to counsel had been violated when his attorney was not afforded the opportunity to be present at the photographic display. The Supreme Court reversed.]

"[Although the right to counsel guarantee has been expanded beyond the formal trial itself], the function of the lawyer has remained essentially the same as his function at trial. In all cases considered by the Court, counsel has continued to act as a spokesman for, or advisor to, the accused. The accused's right to the "Assistance of Counsel" has meant just that, namely, the right of the accused to have counsel acting as his assistant. [In] *Massiah* counsel could have advised his client on the benefits of the Fifth Amendment and could have sheltered him from the overreaching of the prosecution.

[The] function of counsel in rendering "Assistance" continued at the lineup under consideration in *Wade* and its companion cases. Although the accused was not confronted there with legal questions, the lineup offered opportunities for prosecuting authorities to take advantage of the accused.

[A] substantial departure from the historical test would be necessary if the Sixth Amendment were interpreted to give Ash a right to counsel at the photographic identification in this case. Since the accused himself is not present at the time of the photographic display, and asserts no right to be present, no possibility arises that the accused might be misled by his lack of familiarity with the law or

tor has to be provided by legal aid, and if the 'parade' is arranged 'before a suspect is brought before the magistrates,' legal aid assistance most often is unavailable. Devlin Report at ¶ 5.39. Accordingly, solicitors are not provided for many lineups conducted before the defendant's first appearance, notwithstanding the Parade Rules. The Devlin Report considered but rejected requiring counsel in all such cases."

overpowered by his professional adversary. Similarly, the counsel guarantee would not be used to produce equality in a trial-like adversary confrontation. Rather, the guarantee was used by the Court of Appeals to produce confrontation at an event that previously was not analogous to an adversary trial.

Even if we were willing to view the counsel guarantee in broad terms as a generalized protection of the adversary process, we would be unwilling to go so far as to extend the right to a portion of the prosecutor's trial-preparation interviews with witnesses. Although photography is relatively new, the interviewing of witnesses before trial is a procedure that predates the Sixth Amendment. [The] traditional counterbalance in the American adversary system for these interviews arises from the equal ability of defense counsel to seek and interview witnesses himself.

That adversary mechanism remains as effective for a photographic display as for other parts of pretrial interviews. No greater limitations are placed on defense counsel in constructing displays, seeking witnesses, and conducting photographic identifications than those applicable to the prosecution. Selection of the picture of a person other than the accused, or the inability of a witness to make any selection, will be useful to the defense in precisely the same manner that the selection of a picture of the defendant would be useful to the prosecution.

[Pretrial] photographic identifications, [are] hardly unique in offering possibilities for the actions of the prosecutor unfairly to prejudice the accused. Evidence favorable to the accused may be withheld; testimony of witnesses may be manipulated; the results of laboratory tests may be contrived. In many ways the prosecutor, by accident or by design, may improperly subvert the trial. The primary safeguard against abuses of this kind is the ethical responsibility of the prosecutor, who, as so often has been said, may "strike hard blows" but not "foul ones." If that safeguard fails, review remains available under due process standards. These same safeguards apply to misuse of photographs. * * *

We are not persuaded that the risks inherent in the use of photographic displays are so pernicious that an extraordinary system of safeguards is required. * * *

Reversed and remanded.

Justice STEWART, concurring in the judgment. * * *

[The *Wade* Court held] that counsel was required at a lineup, primarily as an observer, to ensure that defense counsel could effectively confront the prosecution's evidence at trial. Attuned to the possibilities of suggestive influences, a lawyer could see any unfairness at a lineup, question the witnesses about it at trial, and effectively reconstruct what had gone on for the benefit of the jury or trial judge.*

A photographic identification is quite different from a lineup, for there are substantially fewer possibilities of impermissible suggestion when photographs are used, and those unfair influences can be readily reconstructed at trial. It is true that the defendant's photograph may be markedly different from the others displayed, but this unfairness can be demonstrated at trial from an actual

---

* I do not read *Wade* as requiring counsel because a lineup is a "trial-type" situation, nor do I understand that the Court required the presence of an attorney because of the advice or assistance he could give to his client at the lineup itself. Rather, I had thought the reason-

ing of *Wade* was that the right to counsel is essentially a protection for the defendant at trial, and that counsel is necessary at a lineup in order to ensure a meaningful confrontation and the effective assistance of counsel at trial.

comparison of the photographs used or from the witness' description of the display. Similarly, it is possible that the photographs could be arranged in a suggestive manner, or that by comment or gesture the prosecuting authorities might single out the defendant's picture. But these are the kinds of overt influence that a witness can easily recount and that would serve to impeach the identification testimony. In short, there are few possibilities for unfair suggestiveness—and those rather blatant and easily reconstructed. Accordingly, an accused would not be foreclosed from an effective cross-examination of an identification witness simply because his counsel was not present at the photographic display. For this reason, a photographic display cannot fairly be considered a "critical stage" of the prosecution.[a]* * *

Justice BRENNAN, with whom Justice DOUGLAS and Justice MARSHALL join, dissenting.

[T]oday's decision marks simply another step towards the complete evisceration of the fundamental constitutional principles established by this Court, only six years ago, in *Wade, Gilbert* and *Stovall*.

[To] the extent that misidentification may be attributable to a witness' faulty memory or perception, or inadequate opportunity for detailed observation during the crime, the risks are obviously as great at a photographic display as at a lineup. But "[b]ecause of the inherent limitations of photography, which presents its subject in two dimensions rather than the three dimensions of reality, [a] photographic identification, even when properly obtained, is clearly inferior to a properly obtained corporeal identification." P. Wall, *Eye-Witness Identification in Criminal Cases* 70 (1965). * * *

Moreover, as in the lineup situation, the possibilities for impermissible suggestion in the context of a photographic display are manifold.

[A]s with lineups, the defense can "seldom reconstruct" at trial the mode and manner of photographic identification. It is true, of course, that the photographs used at the pretrial display might be preserved for examination at trial. But "it may also be said that a photograph can preserve the record of a lineup; yet this does not justify a lineup without counsel."[b] Indeed, in reality, preservation of the photographs affords little protection to the unrepresented accused. [For] retention of the photographs [cannot] in any sense reveal to defense counsel the more subtle, and therefore more dangerous, suggestiveness that might derive from the manner in which the photographs were displayed or any accompanying comments or gestures.

[The] fundamental premise underlying *all* of this Court's decisions holding the right to counsel applicable at "critical" pretrial proceedings, is that a "stage" of the prosecution must be deemed "critical" for the purposes of the Sixth

a. Is a post-indictment corporeal lineup recorded on video tape and played for the trial court at the suppression hearing a "critical stage" within the meaning of *Wade?*

b. Doesn't it, at least after *Ash?* Suppose defense counsel was not notified of or in attendance at either a post-indictment lineup viewed by witness A or at the subsequent exhibition of a photograph of the lineup viewed by witness B. Would *Wade* prevent witness A from testifying that he had identified the accused at the uncounselled lineup or would the fact that the lineup was photographed and thus "preserved" for the trial court mean that it was not a "critical stage"? Assuming arguendo that *Wade* would bar witness A from testifying that he had identified the accused at the uncounselled lineup, wouldn't *Ash* allow witness B to testify that he had identified the accused at the subsequent showing of the photograph of the lineup?

See *United States v. Barker*, 988 F. 2d 77 (9th Cir.1993) holding that when the defendant is identified in a photograph of a lineup *Ash* applies, not *Wade* because, inter alia, the defendant's absence at the time the photo of the lineup is shown means that he cannot be "misled" or "overpowered."

Amendment if it is one at which the presence of counsel is necessary "to protect the fairness of *the trial itself.*" *Schneckloth v. Bustamonte* (emphasis added). [This] established conception of the Sixth Amendment guarantee is, of course, in no sense dependent upon the physical "presence of the accused," at a "trial-like confrontation" with the Government, at which the accused requires the "guiding hand of counsel." * * *

[C]ontrary to the suggestion of the Court, the conclusion in *Wade* that a pretrial lineup is a "critical stage" of the prosecution did not in any sense turn on the fact that a lineup involves the physical "presence of the accused" at a "trial-like confrontation" with the Government. And that conclusion most certainly did not turn on the notion that presence of counsel was necessary so that counsel could offer legal advice or "guidance" to the accused at the lineup. On the contrary, *Wade* envisioned counsel's function at the lineup to be primarily that of a trained observer, able to detect the existence of any suggestive influences and capable of understanding the legal implications of the events that transpire. Having witnessed the proceedings, counsel would then be in a position effectively to reconstruct at trial any unfairness that occurred at the lineup, thereby preserving the accused's fundamental right to a fair trial on the issue of identification.

There is something ironic about the Court's conclusion today that a pretrial lineup identification is a "critical stage" of the prosecution because counsel's presence can help to compensate for the accused's deficiencies as an observer, but that a pretrial photographic identification is not a "critical stage" of the prosecution because the accused is not able to observe at all. * * *

Notes and Questions

1. *Wade, Kirby and Ash.* The *Ash* majority, per Blackmun, J., looks back on *Wade* as concluding that "the lineup constituted a trial-like confrontation" requiring counsel in order "to render 'Assistance' [to a suspect] in counterbalancing any 'overreaching' by the prosecution," implying that counsel is to be an active adversary at this stage. Was the *Ash* majority compelled to so interpret *Wade* because its historical analysis led it to the conclusion that the lawyer's assistance is limited to the *immediate* aid he can give his client? See Note, 64 J.Crim.L.C. & P.S. 428 (1973). Does concurring Justice Stewart disclaim this reading of *Wade?* If so, which interpretation is more consistent with the cases, commentaries and practice since *Wade?* Reconsider Note 2, p. 649. Consider, too, 64 J.Crim.L.C. & P.S. at 433 & n. 40.

2. *Massiah and Ash.* According to the *Ash* majority, "in *Massiah* counsel could have advised his client on the benefits of the Fifth Amendment and could have sheltered him from the overreaching of the prosecution." Was the defendant in *Massiah* entitled to Fifth Amendment protection? Was he compelled to speak? How would the presence of counsel in *Massiah* have provided "assistance" at the "confrontation" unless counsel were aware the meeting was a confrontation? And if counsel were so aware, wouldn't he have *prevented* the confrontation from occurring? See Grano at 762 & n. 285.

3. *The significance of defendant's right to be personally present.* As noted by the Court, the defendant in *Ash* did not claim the right to be personally present at the photographic display. But does the right to counsel *only* exist when the defendant is entitled to be personally present? Voluntary absence or contumacious conduct (see *Illinois v. Allen,* Ch. 25, § 3) may cause a defendant to lose his right to be present at trial, but does it follow that he also loses his right to counsel?

Defendants on appeal have the right to counsel, but do they have the right to be personally present? See generally Grano at 764–67.

4. *Justice Stewart's concurring opinion.* All of the distinctions Justice Stewart made between photographic displays and lineups—photographic displays are less vulnerable to improper suggestion, are easier to reconstruct at trial and are less indelible in their effect upon a witness—are sharply challenged in Grano at 767–70.

5. *Photographic displays and other pretrial interviews of prospective witnesses.* Both the majority and concurring opinions in *Ash* indicated concern that granting a right to counsel at photographic displays might lead to the extension of the right to counsel to all pretrial interviews of prospective witnesses. But consider Note, 26 Stan.L.Rev. 399, 416–17 (1974): "[The] basis for extending the right to counsel to the identification context was that identifications by eyewitnesses—like confessions—are such damning evidence that they may completely decide the guilt or innocence of the accused. Photographic identifications can be just as critical to the future outcome of a trial as can corporeal identifications. Routine interviews between the prosecutor and his witnesses, on the other hand, do not have the potential for such damaging results, at least assuming good faith on the part of the prosecutor."

SECTION 3. DUE PROCESS AND OTHER LIMITATIONS

As already pointed out, see p. 654 supra, one unable to make a *Wade-Gilbert* right to counsel argument may still establish that the identification procedure conducted in his case "was so unnecessarily suggestive and conducive to irreparable mistaken identification that he was denied due process of law." STOVALL v. DENNO, 388 U.S. 293, 87 S.Ct. 1967, 18 L.Ed.2d 1199 (1967). In this case, the stabbing victim (Mrs. Behrendt), was hospitalized for major surgery. Without affording petitioner time to retain counsel (an arraignment had been promptly held but then postponed until petitioner could retain counsel), the police, with the cooperation of the victim's surgeon, arranged a confrontation between petitioner and the victim in her hospital room. Petitioner was handcuffed to one of the seven law enforcement officials who brought him to the hospital room. He was the only black person in the room. After being asked by an officer whether petitioner "was the man," the victim identified him from her hospital bed. Both Mrs. Behrendt and the police then testified at the trial to her identification in the hospital. Despite the suggestiveness of the confrontation, the Court, per BRENNAN, J., affirmed the Second Circuit's denial of federal habeas corpus relief, observing:

"The practice of showing suspects singly to persons for the purpose of identification, and not as part of a lineup has been widely condemned. However, a claimed violation of due process of law in the conduct of a confrontation depends on the totality of the circumstances surrounding it, and the record in the present case reveals that the showing of Stovall to Mrs. Behrendt in an immediate hospital confrontation was imperative. The Court of Appeals en banc, stated [355 F.2d 731, 735 (2d Cir.1966) (per Moore, J.)]:

"'Here was the only person in the world who could possibly exonerate Stovall. Her words, and only her words, "He is not the man" could have resulted in freedom for Stovall. The hospital was not far distant from the courthouse and jail. No one knew how long Mrs. Behrendt might live. Faced with the responsibility of identifying the attacker, with the need for immediate action and with the knowledge that Mrs. Behrendt could not visit the jail, the police followed the only feasible procedure and took Stovall to the hospital room. Under these circumstances, the usual police station line-up, which Stovall now argues he should have had, was out of the question.' "[a]

MANSON v. BRATHWAITE
432 U.S. 98, 97 S.Ct. 2243, 53 L.Ed.2d 140 (1977).

Justice BLACKMUN delivered the opinion of the Court. * * *

[Several minutes before sunset, Glover, a black undercover police officer, purchased heroin from a seller through the open doorway of an apartment while standing for two or three minutes within two feet of the seller in a hallway illuminated by natural light. A few minutes later, Glover described the seller to a back-up officer, D'Onofrio, as being "a colored man, approximately five feet eleven inches tall, dark complexion, black hair, short Afro style, and having high cheekbones, and of heavy build. He was wearing at the time blue pants and a plaid shirt."

[On the basis of the description, D'Onofrio thought that respondent might be the heroin seller. He obtained a single photograph of respondent from police files and left it at Glover's office. Two days later, while alone, Glover viewed the photograph and identified it as that of the seller. At respondent's trial, Glover testified that there was "no doubt whatsoever" that the person shown in the photograph was respondent. Glover also made a positive in-court identification. No explanation was offered by the prosecution for the failure to utilize a photographic array or to conduct a lineup.

[After the Connecticut Supreme Court affirmed respondent's conviction, he sought federal habeas corpus relief. The Second Circuit, per Friendly, J., held that because the showing of the single photograph was "suggestive" and concededly "unnecessarily so," evidence pertaining to it was subject to a *per se* rule of exclusion.]

Neil v. Biggers, 409 U.S. 188, 93 S.Ct. 375, 34 L.Ed.2d 401 (1972), concerned a respondent who had been convicted [of] rape, on evidence consisting in part of the victim's visual and voice identification of Biggers at a [one-person] station-house showup seven months after the crime. [The] Court expressed concern about

---

a. But consider Judge Friendly, joined by Waterman, J., dissenting below, 355 F.2d at 744–45:

"[The argument that law enforcement officials were confronted with an emergency] ignores the huge amount of circumstantial identification the excellent police investigation had produced; moreover, if the state officials were motivated [by] solicitude [for Stovall], the natural course would have been to ask Stovall whether he wanted to go. The emergency argument fails both on the facts and on the law. [If] Mrs. Behrendt's condition had been as serious as my brothers suppose, nothing prevented the prosecutor from informing the state district judge at the preliminary hearing that Stovall had to be taken immediately before her, and suggesting that counsel be assigned forthwith for the limited purpose of advising him in that regard—rather than standing silent when Stovall told the judge of his desire to have counsel and then carting him off to a confrontation by the victim which counsel might have done something to mitigate."

Lower courts have not only followed *Stovall* in similar cases of serious injury to the victim or a witness but have applied it to situations where the *suspect* is seriously injured. See Commentary to '160.5 of the *Model Pre–Arraignment Code* at 451–52. Is a "showup" in such cases necessary? Could a photographic array be utilized? If the suspect is hospitalized for an extended period, could the witness be taken to several hospital rooms? See *Model Code* at 452.

the lapse of seven months between the crime and the confrontation, [but pointed out that the] "central question" [was] "whether under the 'totality of the circumstances' the identification was reliable even though the confrontation procedure was suggestive." Applying that test, the Court found "no substantial likelihood of misidentification. The evidence was properly allowed to go to the jury."[a]

Biggers well might be seen to provide an unambiguous answer to the question before us: The admission of testimony concerning a suggestive and unnecessary identification procedure does not violate due process so long as the identification possesses sufficient aspects of reliability.[9] In one passage, however, the Court observed that the challenged procedure occurred pre-*Stovall* and that a strict rule would make little sense with regard to a confrontation that preceded the Court's first indication that a suggestive procedure might lead to the exclusion of evidence. One perhaps might argue that, by implication, the Court suggested that a different rule could apply post-*Stovall*. The question before us, then, is simply whether the *Biggers* analysis applies to post-*Stovall* confrontations as well to those pre-*Stovall*. * * *

Petitioner at the outset acknowledges that "the procedure in the instant case was suggestive [because only one photograph was used] and unnecessary" [because there was no emergency or exigent circumstance]. The respondent, in agreement with the Court of Appeals, proposes a *per se* rule of exclusion that he claims is dictated by the demands of the Fourteenth Amendment's guarantee of due process. He rightly observes that this is the first case in which this Court has had occasion to rule upon strictly post-*Stovall* out-of-court identification evidence of the challenged kind.

Since the decision in *Biggers,* the Courts of Appeals appear to have developed at least two approaches to such evidence. See Pulaski, *Neil v. Biggers: The*

---

a. The *Biggers* Court, per Powell, J., observed:

"The victim spent a considerable period of time with her assailant, up to half an hour. She was with him under adequate artificial light in her house and under a full moon outdoors, and at least twice, once in the house and later in the woods, faced him directly and intimately. [Her] description to the police, which included the assailant's approximate age, height, weight, complexion, skin texture, build, and voice [was] more than ordinarily thorough. She had 'no doubt' that respondent was the person who raped her. [The] victim here, a practical nurse by profession, had an unusual opportunity to observe and identify her assailant. She testified at the habeas corpus hearing that there was something about his face 'I don't think I could ever forget.'

"There was, to be sure, a lapse of seven months between the rape and the confrontation. This would be a seriously negative factor in most cases. Here, however, the testimony is undisputed that the victim made no previous identification at any of the showups, lineups, or photographic showings. Her record for reliability was thus a good one, as she had previously resisted whatever suggestiveness inheres in a showup. Weighing all the factors, we find no substantial likelihood of misidentification."

9. Justice Marshall argues in dissent that our cases have "established two different due process tests for two very different situations." Pretrial identifications are to be covered by *Stovall*, which is said to require exclusion of evidence concerning unnecessarily suggestive pretrial identifications without regard to reliability. In-court identifications, on the other hand, are to be governed by *Simmons [v. United States*, 390 U.S. 377, 88 S.Ct. 967, 19 L.Ed.2d 1247 (1968)] and admissibility turns on reliability. The Court's cases are sorted into one category or the other. *Biggers,* which clearly adopts the reliability of the identification as the guiding factor in the admissibility of both pre-trial and in-court identifications, is condemned for mixing the two lines and for adopting a uniform rule.

[Our cases] hardly suggest the formal structure the dissent would impose on them. If our cases truly established two different rules, one might expect at some point at least passing reference to the fact. There is none. And if *Biggers* departed so grievously from the past cases, it is surprising that there was not at least some mention of the point in Justice Brennan's dissent. * * * *Biggers* is not properly seen as a departure from the past cases, but as a synthesis of them.

Supreme Court Dismantles the Wade Trilogy's Due Process Protection, 26 Stan. L.Rev. 1097, 1111–1114 (1974). The first, or *per se* approach, employed by the Second Circuit in the present case, focuses on the procedures employed and requires exclusion of the out-of-court identification evidence, without regard to reliability, whenever it has been obtained through unnecessarily suggested confrontation procedures.[10] The justifications advanced are the elimination of evidence of uncertain reliability, deterrence of the police and prosecutors, and the stated "fair assurance against the awful risks of misidentification."

The second, or more lenient, approach is one that continues to rely on the totality of the circumstances. It permits the admission of the confrontation evidence if, despite the suggestive aspect, the out-of-court identification possesses certain features of reliability. This second approach, in contrast to the other, is ad hoc and serves to limit the societal costs imposed by a sanction that excludes relevant evidence from consideration and evaluation by the trier of fact. * * *

There are, of course, several interests to be considered and taken into account. The driving force behind [*Wade, Gilbert* and *Stovall*] was the Court's concern with the problems of eyewitness identification. Usually the witness must testify about an encounter with a total stranger under circumstances of emergency or emotional stress. The witness' recollection of the stranger can be distorted easily by the circumstances or by later actions of the police. Thus, *Wade* and its companion cases reflect the concern that the jury not hear eyewitness testimony unless that evidence has aspects of reliability. It must be observed that both approaches before us are responsive to this concern. The *per se* rule, however, goes too far since its application automatically and peremptorily, and without consideration of alleviating factors, keeps evidence from the jury that is reliable and relevant.

The second factor is deterrence. Although the *per se* approach has the more significant deterrent effect, the totality approach also has an influence on police behavior. The police will guard against unnecessarily suggestive procedures under the totality rule, as well as the *per se* one, for fear that their actions will lead to the exclusion of identifications as unreliable.

The third factor is the effect on the administration of justice. Here the *per se* approach suffers serious drawbacks. Since it denies the trier reliable evidence, it may result, on occasion, in the guilty going free. Also, because of its rigidity, the *per se* approach may make error by the trial judge more likely than the totality approach. And in those cases in which the admission of identification evidence is error under the *per se* approach but not under the totality approach—cases in which the identification is reliable despite an unnecessarily suggestive identification procedure—reversal is a Draconian sanction. Certainly, inflexible rules of exclusion that may frustrate rather than promote justice have not been viewed recently by this Court with unlimited enthusiasm. * * *

We therefore conclude that reliability is the linchpin in determining the admissibility of identification testimony for both pre-and post-*Stovall* confrontations. The factors to be considered are set out in *Biggers*. These include the opportunity of the witness to view the criminal at the time of the crime, the

---

10. Although the *per se* approach demands the exclusion of testimony concerning unnecessarily suggestive identifications, it does permit the admission of testimony concerning a subsequent identification, including an in-court identification, if the subsequent identification is determined to be reliable. The totality approach, in contrast, is simpler: if the challenged identification is reliable, then testimony as to it and any identification in its wake is admissible.

witness' degree of attention, the accuracy of his prior description of the criminal, the level of certainty demonstrated at the confrontation, and the time between the crime and the confrontation. Against these factors is to be weighed the corrupting effect of the suggestive identification itself.

We turn, then, to the facts of this case and apply the analysis:

1. The opportunity to view. Glover testified that for two to three minutes he stood at the apartment door, within two feet of the respondent. The door opened twice, and each time the man stood at the door. * * * Natural light from outside entered the hallway through a window. There was natural light, as well, from inside the apartment.

2. The degree of attention. Glover was not a casual or passing observer, [but] a trained police officer on duty—and specialized and dangerous duty—when he [made the heroin purchase]. Glover himself was a Negro and unlikely to perceive only general features of [black males].

3. The accuracy of the description. Glover's description was given to D'Onofrio within minutes after the transaction. It included the vendor's race, his height, his build, the color and style of his hair, and the high cheekbone facial feature. It also included clothing the vendor wore. No claim has been made that respondent did not possess the physical characteristics so described. * * *

4. The witness' level of certainty. There is no dispute that the photograph in question was that of respondent. Glover, in response to a question whether the photograph was that of the person from whom he made the purchase, testified: "There is no question whatsoever." This positive assurance was repeated.

5. The time between the crime and the confrontation. Glover's description of his vendor was given to D'Onofrio within minutes of the crime. The photographic identification took place only two days later. We do not have here the passage of weeks or months between the crime and the viewing of the photograph.

These indicators of Glover's ability to make an accurate identification are hardly outweighed by the corrupting effect of the challenged identification itself. Although identifications arising from single-photograph displays may be viewed in general with suspicion, we find in the instant case little pressure on the witness to acquiesce in the suggestion that such a display entails. D'Onofrio had left the photograph at Glover's office and was not present when Glover first viewed it two days after the event. There thus was little urgency and Glover could view the photograph at his leisure. And since Glover examined the photograph alone, there was no coercive pressure to make an identification arising from the presence of another. The identification was made in circumstances allowing care and reflection. * * *

Surely, we cannot say that under all the circumstances of this case there is "a very substantial likelihood of irreparable misidentification." Short of that point, such evidence is for the jury to weigh. We are content to rely upon the good sense and judgment of American juries, for evidence with some element of untrustworthiness is customary grist for the jury mill. Juries are not so susceptible that they cannot measure intelligently the weight of identification testimony that has some questionable feature.

Of course, it would have been better had D'Onofrio presented Glover with a photographic array. [But] we are not disposed to view D'Onofrio's failure as one of constitutional dimension to be enforced by a rigorous and unbending exclusionary rule. The defect, if there be one, goes to weight and not to substance.

We conclude that the criteria laid down in *Biggers* are to be applied in determining the admissibility of evidence offered by the prosecution concerning a post-*Stovall* identification, and that those criteria are satisfactorily met and complied with here.

[Reversed].[b]

Justice MARSHALL, with whom Justice BRENNAN joins, dissenting.

Today's decision can come as no surprise to those who have been watching the Court dismantle the protections against mistaken eyewitness testimony erected a decade ago in [*Wade, Gilbert* and *Stovall*]. But it is still distressing to see the Court virtually ignore the teaching of experience embodied in those decisions and blindly uphold the conviction of a defendant who may well be innocent.

[In] determining the admissibility of the *post-Stovall* identification in this case, the Court considers two alternatives, a *per se* exclusionary rule and a totality-of-the-circumstances approach. The Court weighs three factors in deciding that the totality approach, which is essentially the test used in *Biggers,* should be applied. In my view, the Court wrongly evaluates the impact of these factors.

First, the Court acknowledges that one of the factors, deterrence of police use of unnecessarily suggestive identification procedures, favors the *per se* rule. Indeed, it does so heavily, for such a rule would make it unquestionably clear to the police they must never use a suggestive procedure when a fairer alternative is available. I have no doubt that conduct would quickly conform to the rule.

Second, the Court gives passing consideration to the dangers of eyewitness identification recognized in the *Wade* trilogy. It concludes, however, that the grave risk of error does not justify adoption of the *per se* approach because that would too often result in exclusion of relevant evidence. In my view, this conclusion totally ignores the lessons of *Wade.* The dangers of mistaken identification are, as *Stovall* held, simply too great to permit unnecessarily suggestive identifications. * * *

Finally, the Court errs in its assessment of the relative impact of the two approaches on the administration of justice. The Court relies most heavily on this factor, finding that "reversal is a Draconian sanction" in cases where the identification is reliable despite an unnecessarily suggestive procedure used to obtain it. Relying on little more than a strong distaste for "inflexible rules of exclusion," the Court rejects the *per se* test. In so doing, the Court disregards two significant distinctions between the *per se* rule advocated in this case and the exclusionary remedies for certain other constitutional violations.

First, the *per se* rule here is not "inflexible." Where evidence is suppressed, for example, as the fruit of an unlawful search, it may well be forever lost to the prosecution. Identification evidence, however, can by its very nature be readily and effectively reproduced. The in-court identification, permitted under *Wade* [if] it has a source independent of an uncounseled or suggestive procedure, is one example. Similarly, when a prosecuting attorney learns that there has been a suggestive confrontation, he can easily arrange another lineup conducted under scrupulously fair conditions. * * *

b. Stevens, J., concurring, joined the Court's opinion, but emphasized that although "the arguments in favor of fashioning new rules to minimize the danger of convicting the innocent on the basis of unreliable eyewitness testimony carry substantial force, [this] rule-making function can be performed 'more effectively by the legislative process than by somewhat clumsy judicial fiat,' and that the Federal Constitution does not foreclose experimentation by the States in the development of such rules."

Second, other exclusionary rules have been criticized for preventing jury consideration of relevant and usually reliable evidence in order to serve interest unrelated to guilt or innocence, such as discouraging illegal searches or denial of counsel. Suggestively obtained eyewitness testimony is excluded, in contrast, precisely because of its unreliability and concomitant irrelevance. Its exclusion both protects the integrity of the truth-seeking function of the trial and discourages police use of needlessly inaccurate and ineffective investigatory methods.

[For] these reasons, I conclude that adoption of the *per se* rule would enhance, rather than detract from, the effective administration of justice. In my view, the Court's totality test will allow seriously unreliable and misleading evidence to be put before juries. Equally important, it will allow dangerous criminals to remain on the streets while citizens assume that police action has given them protection. According to my calculus, all three of the factors upon which the Court relies point to acceptance of the *per se* approach.

Even more disturbing than the Court's reliance on the totality test, however, is the analysis it uses, which suggests a reinterpretation of the concept of due process of law in criminal cases. The decision suggests that due process violations in identification procedures may not be measured by whether the government employed procedures violating standards of fundamental fairness. By relying on the probable accuracy of a challenged identification, instead of the necessity for its use, the Court seems to be ascertaining whether the defendant was probably guilty. * * *

Despite my strong disagreement with the Court over the proper standards to be applied in this case, I am pleased that its application of the totality test does recognize the continuing vitality of *Stovall*. In assessing the reliability of the identification, the Court mandates weighing "the corrupting effect of the suggestive identification itself" against the "indicators of [a witness'] ability to make an accurate identification." The Court holds, as *Biggers* failed to, that a due process identification inquiry must take account of the suggestiveness of a confrontation and the likelihood that it led to mis-identification, as recognized in *Stovall* and *Wade*. Thus, even if a witness did have an otherwise adequate opportunity to view a criminal, the later use of a highly suggestive identification procedure can render his testimony inadmissible. Indeed, it is my view that, assuming applicability of the totality test enunciated by the Court, the facts of the present case require that result.

I consider first the opportunity that Officer Glover had to view the suspect. Careful review of the record shows that he could see the heroin seller only for the time it took to speak three sentences of four or five short words, to hand over some money, and later after the door reopened, to receive the drugs in return. The entire face-to-face transaction could have taken as little as 15 or 20 seconds. But during this time, Glover's attention was not focused exclusively on the seller's face. He observed that the door was opened 12 to 18 inches, that there was a window in the room behind the door, and, most importantly, that there was a woman standing behind the man. Glover was, of course, also concentrating on the details of the transaction—he must have looked away from the seller's face to hand him the money and receive the drugs. The observation during the conversation thus may have been as brief as 5 or 10 seconds.

As the Court notes, Glover was a police officer trained in and attentive to the need for making accurate identifications. [But] the mere fact that he has been so trained is no guarantee that he is correct in a specific case. * * * Moreover, "identifications made by policemen in highly competitive activities, such as undercover narcotic [work], should be scrutinized with special care." P. Wall, *Eye-Witness Identification in Criminal Cases* 14 (1965). Yet it is just such a searching inquiry that the Court fails to make here.

Another factor on which the Court relies—the witness' degree of certainty in making the identification—is worthless as an indicator that he is correct.[10] Even if Glover had been unsure initially about his identification of respondent's picture, by the time he was called at trial to present a key piece of evidence for the State that paid his salary, it is impossible to imagine his responding negatively to such questions as "is there any doubt in your mind whatsoever" that the identification was correct. * * *

Next, the Court finds that because the identification procedure took place two days after the crime, its reliability is enhanced. While such temporal proximity makes the identification more reliable than one occurring months later, the fact is that the greatest memory loss occurs within hours after an event. After that, the dropoff continues much more slowly.[11] * * *

Finally, the Court makes much of the fact that Glover gave a description of the seller to D'Onofrio shortly after the incident. [But the description was only] a general summary of the seller's appearance. We may discount entirely the seller's clothing, for that was of no significance later in the proceeding. Indeed, to the extent that Glover noticed clothes, his attention was diverted from the seller's face. * * * Conspicuously absent is any indication that the seller was a native of the West Indies, certainly something which a member of the black community could immediately recognize from both appearance and accent.[12]

From all of this, I must conclude that the evidence of Glover's ability to make an accurate identification is far weaker than the Court finds it. In contrast, the procedure used to identify respondent was both extraordinarily suggestive and strongly conducive to error. In dismissing "the corrupting effect of the suggestive identification" procedure here, the Court virtually grants the police license to convict the innocent. By displaying a single photograph of respondent to the witness Glover under the circumstances in this record almost everything that could have been done wrong was done wrong.

[The] use of a single picture (or the display of a single live suspect, for that matter) is a grave error, of course, because it dramatically suggests to the witness that the person shown must be the culprit. Why else would the police choose the person? And it is deeply ingrained in human nature to agree with the expressed opinions of others—particularly others who should be more knowledgeable—when making a difficult decision. In this case, moreover, the pressure was not limited to that inherent in the display of a single photograph. Glover, the identifying witness, was a state police officer on special assignment. He knew that D'Onofrio, an [experienced] narcotics detective, presumably familiar with local drug operations, believed respondent to be the seller. There was at work, then, both loyalty to another police officer and deference to a better-informed colleague. * * *

I must conclude that this record presents compelling evidence that there was "a very substantial likelihood of misidentification" of respondent Brathwaite. The

---

10. See, e.g., P. Wall, supra, at 15–16 * * *.

11. See, e.g., Levine & Tapp, *The Psychology of Criminal Identification: The Gap From Wade to Kirby,* 12 U.Pa.L.Rev. 1079, 1100–01 (1973) * * *.

12. Brathwaite had come to the United States from his native Barbados as an adult. It is also noteworthy that the informant who witnessed the transaction and was described by Glover as "trustworthy," disagreed with Glover's recollection of the event. The informant testified that it was a woman in the apartment who took the money from Glover and gave him the drugs in return.

suggestive display of respondent's photograph to the witness Glover likely erased any independent memory that Glover had retained of the seller from his barely adequate opportunity to observe the criminal. * * *

Notes and Questions

1. *Deterrence.* Will the *Manson* approach significantly deter the use of suggestive identification procedures? Consider Randolph Jonakait, *Reliable Identification: Could the Supreme Court Tell in Manson v. Brathwaite?*, 52 U.Colo. L.Rev. 511, 515 n. 15 (1981): "[R]egardless of how specifically opinions define what is unnecessarily suggestive, a police officer can never know whether he is violating a suspect's constitutional rights when he is conducting an identification procedure. That can be determined only when the indicia of reliability are examined. These factors may not be known to the officer and certainly cannot be controlled by him. The Court's approach leaves the officer without any firm rules as to what conduct violates the Constitution. If the officer has no way of knowing what actions are forbidden, he can hardly be deterred from those actions."

See also Steven Grossman, *Suggestive Identifications: The Supreme Court's Due Process Test Fails to Meet Its Own Criteria,* 11 Balt.L.Rev. 53, 59–60 (1981) (rather than deterring show-ups and the showing of single photographs, "the effect of *Biggers* and *Manson* has been to provide the police with a fairly clear signal that absent extremely aggravating circumstances, the one-on-one presentation of suspects to witnesses will result in no suppression"); Wallace Sherwood, *The Erosion of Constitutional Safeguards in the Area of Eyewitness Identification,* 30 How.L.J. 731, 770 (1987) (the "totality of circumstances" test, "which places a premium on the probable guilt of the accused, will not serve as a deterrent to police use of suggestive procedures but will have the opposite result").

2. *"The other side of the scale": suggestiveness.* Although the *Manson* Court offered guidelines to determine reliability, "it failed," comments Grossman, supra, at 80, 96–97, "to articulate such criteria in evaluating the other side of the scale, suggestiveness. Police and lower courts were not given examples of what types of identification procedures were objectionable and, perhaps more important in a weighing process, what forms of suggestive behavior were more likely than others to result in an unreliable identification. [As] a result, many courts have come to regard suggestion as a monolithic concept devoid of gradations or merely as a prerequisite to be met prior to analyzing the [*Biggers-Manson*] reliability factors. * * * [The] Supreme Court can [provide guidance] by indicating what types of suggestive conduct are more likely to result in unreliable identification testimony. As to these extreme forms of suggestive procedures [e.g., informing a witness that the suspect has confessed, having several witnesses view a display at the same time, presenting the suspect with a distinguishing trait or item also possessed by the perpetrator], a higher degree of reliability need be shown than that necessary to overcome nominal or less severe types of suggestive practices."

3. *Do the assumptions of the Manson majority find support in psychological research?* Drawing upon studies by Elizabeth Loftus and others, Jonakait, Note 1 supra, at 519–22, maintains that many of the assumptions made by the *Manson* majority are unwarranted. E.g., "studies do not support the idea that police make more reliable witnesses than civilians or that their training in any way improves their ability to make identifications"; dangerous police work generates great stress and, although the Court may think that danger heightens awareness, "psychologists have known for some time that stress does not aid perception and learning, but inhibits them"; research indicates no relationship between the expressed

confidence of an eyewitness and the accuracy of his or her identification. See also Grossman, supra, at 72–79.

DETENTION FOR IDENTIFICATION PROCEDURES IN THE ABSENCE OF PROBABLE CAUSE

In *Davis v. Mississippi* (1969) (p. 336, petitioner and 24 other black youths were detained for questioning and fingerprinting in connection with a rape for which the only leads were a general description given by the victim and a set of fingerprints around the window through which the assailant entered. Petitioner's prints were found to match those at the scene of the crime, and this evidence was admitted at his trial. The Court, per Brennan, J., held that the prints should have been excluded as the fruits of a seizure of petitioner in violation of the Fourth Amendment, but intimated that a detention for such a purpose might sometimes be permissible on evidence falling short of the traditional probable cause needed for an arrest.

See also *Hayes v. Florida*, 470 U.S. 811, 105 S.Ct. 1643, 84 L.Ed.2d 705 (1985). Although the Court, per White, J., held that *transporting a suspect to the police station* without probable cause or prior judicial authorization violated his Fourth Amendment right, it reserved the possibility, as it had in *Davis*, that "a brief detention *in the field* for the purpose of fingerprinting, where there is only reasonable suspicion not amounting to probable cause" (emphasis added), might pass constitutional muster. *Hayes* also left open the possibility that "under circumscribed procedures, the Fourth Amendment might permit *the judiciary to authorize* the seizure of a person on less than probable cause and his removal to the police station for the purpose of fingerprinting." (Emphasis added.)

As noted in Charles H. Whitebread & Christopher Slobogin, *Criminal Procedure* 447 (3d ed. 1993), "the reasoning of the dictum in *Hayes* would also justify seizures from the home for the purpose of a lineup or showup, based solely on a judicial finding of reasonable suspicion. Further, again assuming reasonable suspicion, *Hayes* would allow police to act on their own in arranging on-the-scene lineups or showups. On the other hand, suspicionless or random seizures of a person for such identification procedures would be impermissible."

On the basis of the *Davis* dictum, Art. 170 of the *Model Pre-Arraignment Code* delineates a court order procedure for detaining persons for nontestimonial identification purposes on less than "probable cause" and a number of states have passed similar legislation. See Commentary to Art. 170 at 475–77; LaFave, § 9.7(b); Note, 45 Fordham L.Rev. (1976) (hereafter referred to as "Fordham Note"). The Model Code article covers many "identification procedures," e.g., procedures to obtain identification by fingerprints, footprints, dental impressions, specimens or samples of blood, urine or hair, and procedures to obtain witness identification through lineups and handwriting exemplars. To what extent should the requisite basis for the detention vary with the kind of identification involved? For example, since eyewitness identifications are a less reliable form of evidence than fingerprints, should Fourth Amendment requirements for detentions for lineup purposes be significantly more stringent? Or should the basis for detention for lineup purposes be the same, but the suspect afforded the right to counsel at the lineup? See Fordham Note at 128–29.

Although the most serious Fourth Amendment question would seem to be whether, when the police lack "probable cause" to arrest a person *for any offense*, they may detain him for identification purposes (with or without a court order),

Fourth Amendment problems also arise in other contexts. Courts have generally found no Fourth Amendment violation when a person *lawfully in custody for one crime* is ordered into a lineup for other crimes for which there is no probable cause to arrest him. But some courts have indicated that even under these circumstances there must be a "reasonable suspicion" that the person committed the crimes. See generally Fordham Note at 125–32. However, why should *the viewing* of suspects by witnesses—as opposed to *the basis for detaining* them in order to permit the viewing—raise any Fourth Amendment problems? Cf. *United States v. Dionisio* (1973) (p. 695).

When a defendant has been released on bail, he is generally subject to the control of the court, which is empowered to order his appearance. A number of courts have exercised this power to order defendants to appear in a lineup for an unrelated crime, but again it is unclear whether this may be done indiscriminately or only when there is at least "reasonable suspicion" that the defendant has committed the unrelated crime under investigation. See Fordham Note at 127.

Chapter 10

GRAND JURY INVESTIGATIONS

SECTION 1. THE ROLE OF THE INVESTIGATIVE GRAND JURY[aa]

A.   THE INVESTIGATIVE AUTHORITY OF THE GRAND JURY

1. *Dual functions.* The grand jury is often described as constituting both "the shield" and "the sword" of the criminal justice process. It is said to provide a "shield" against mistaken and vindictive prosecutions in deciding whether or not to issue an indictment. In making that determination, the grand jury's role is to "screen" the prosecution's decision to charge, issuing indictments only where the available evidence is sufficient to justify a prosecution. On the other side, the grand jury is said to act as a "sword," combating crime, in the use of its investigative authority. Here, the grand jury's role is to uncover evidence not previously available to the government and thereby secure convictions that might otherwise not be obtained. The shielding function of the grand jury will be discussed in Chapter Fifteen.[b] In this Chapter we will concentrate upon the operation of the grand jury in its investigatory role. It should be kept in mind, however, that the two functions of the grand jury commonly are performed by the same grand jury. In particular, once a grand jury investigation is complete, the same group of grand jurors ordinarily will then be called upon to determine whether the evidence produced is sufficient to issue an indictment.

2. *Historical development.* The English origins of the grand jury are traced to the Assize of Clarendon, created in 1166 during the reign of Henry II. The Assize established juries of 12 persons, selected from each community, who were directed to accuse those persons in the community believed to have committed crimes. It was assumed initially that the jurors would accuse based on their own knowledge, but they soon sought out information from others. The Assize was designed not to protect against improper prosecutions by the Crown, but rather to lend assistance to government officials in the apprehension of criminals. The jurors were familiar with the local scene and could present charges that otherwise might not be known by the Crown's representatives. Any hesitancy the jurors

---

aa. For citations to relevant source materials, as well as a more detailed discussion of the subject, See S. Beale, W. Bryson, J. Felman, M. Elsion, *Grand Jury Law and Practice* (2d Ed. 1998) (hereafter cited as Beale et al.) S. Bronner and G. Lockhart, *Federal Grand Jury* (1996) (hereafter cited as Brenner and Lockhart); LaFave, Israel, and King, *Criminal Procedure Treatise*, ch. 8 (2nd ed., forthcoming) (hereafter cited as LaFave, Israel and King).

b. The organization and operation of the grand jury are described briefly in Chapter 1, at p. 27. Various aspects of the grand jury's procedure and structure relate both to its screening and investigatory functions. Those aspects that have a major impact upon its investigatory performance (e.g., grand jury secrecy) are discussed in this Chapter. Others that have a less significant bearing on investigations are discussed in Chapter 15. The composition of the grand jury, because it arguably has a greater impact on the screening function, is discussed in Chapter 15.

might have in bringing accusations against their neighbors would be overcome by the substantial fines the jurors faced for failing to bring forward any known offense.

By the end of the fourteenth century the English had turned to trial by jury rather than by ordeal and the original jury had been divided into two separate juries. The trial of guilt was before a 12 person petit jury, and the accusatory jury was expanded to a 23 person group, chosen from the entire county, which became known as *"le graunde inquest."* At this point, the grand jury remained essentially a body designed to assist the Crown in ferreting out criminals. Accusations were either initiated by the jurors themselves, acting on the basis of community knowledge, or were initiated by a representative of the Crown, typically a justice of the peace, who produced witnesses to testify before the grand jury in support of a particular charge. When the accusation was initiated by the jury itself, its formal charge was described as a "presentment." When the accusation stemmed from a case placed before the jury by the Crown's representative, the grand jury's charging document was described as an "indictment."

Over the next few centuries, the grand jury began to assume a significant degree of independence, as evidenced by its occasional refusal to issue indictments sought by the Crown's representative. In the late seventeenth century, it established its reputation as a "bulwark against the oppression and despotism of the Crown" when it refused to indict various supporters of the Protestant cause (including, most notably, Stephen Colledge and the Earl of Shaftesbury). During the same period, the grand jury also achieved some prominence in fighting governmental corruption, as various presentments were issued based upon grand jury inquiries into the misconduct of minor officials in matters of local administration.

In this country, the colonial grand juries expanded upon the use of grand jury inquiries and issued not only presentments but also reports criticizing actions of local officials that fell short of criminal misconduct. The colonial grand juries achieved even greater prestige, however, when they refused to issue indictments requested by Crown officials. Thus, the infamous prosecution of John Peter Zenger for seditious libel was brought by a prosecutor's information because colonial grand juries twice refused to issue requested indictments. In light of such actions, it was not surprising that the constitutions of the original states generally required that all felony prosecutions be brought by grand jury indictment or presentment, and once it was decided to add a Bill of Rights to the federal constitution, the inclusion of a similar provision in the Fifth Amendment was accepted without controversy.

During the period before the Civil War, grand juries, particularly in the western states, actively reviewed a wide range of grievances presented by citizens, and often conducted "searching investigations into corruption in government or widespread evasion of the laws." While grand juries thus achieved a considerable reputation as a "public watchdog," the value and cost of grand jury screening of cases developed by local prosecutors came under sharp attack. In 1859, Michigan became the first state to grant prosecutors the option of proceeding either by grand jury indictment or by a prosecutor's information. It is noteworthy that neither Michigan nor the many other states that adopted similar option provisions abolished the grand jury, as the English eventually did. The grand jury was still viewed as a valuable instrument for occasional cases requiring the use of its investigatory authority.

Over the period between the Civil War and the mid–1900s, a majority of the states moved to allow prosecution by information. At the same time, however, grand juries remained active in both those "information" states and in the remaining "indictment" states in the investigation of corruption in local government. In several instances, the resulting indictments were so widespread as to unseat entire municipal administrations. As might be expected, local prosecutors were sometimes less than enthusiastic in cooperating with such investigations. Grand juries responded by seeking outside help (usually through court appointment of a special prosecutor) or by simply pushing forward against the wishes of a reluctant prosecutor. The most famous of these "runaway" grand jury investigations was the mid–1930s New York investigation of "racketeering" offenses, which led to the appointment of special prosecutor Thomas E. Dewey. The exploits of Dewey and his "racket busters" inspired a series of runaway grand jury investigations throughout the country and established the reputation of the grand jury as the nation's "number one instrument of discovery against organized crime."

3. *Current status.* While it was the shielding function that was responsible for the constitutional recognition of the grand jury in the indictment clause of the Fifth Amendment and in similar provisions in the early state constitutions, the grand jury's investigatory role has proven to have the greater staying power in the approximately two-thirds of our states which no longer require prosecution by indictment. The practice in these states is to bring the vast majority of prosecutions by information rather than indictment. Grand juries are still used, however, to conduct investigations where the police investigatory authority is thought to be less helpful, and that use explains most of those cases in the information states that are prosecuted by indictment. In the states that still require prosecution by indictment, the vast majority of grand juries are engaged simply in screening cases that the prosecution presents to the grand jury as fully investigated and ready for indictment. However, in a small percentage of the cases presented to grand juries in indictment states, extensive use is made of the grand jury's investigatory authority. The federal system, because of the nature of the crimes it prosecutes, makes the most extensive use of the grand jury's investigatory authority. But as in other indictment jurisdictions, the vast majority of the cases presented to federal grand juries require only screening.

The grand jury's investigative authority continues to be recognized as a major tool in uncovering organized crime and government corruption. Over the last few decades, federal grand jury investigations of white collar crime have added further luster to the grand jury's reputation as an investigative force. On the other hand, the grand jury's reputation has been sullied, at least in some quarters, by investigations that might suggest that its investigative authority was there used for partisan political ends. Some highly publicized investigations of public figures have produced damaging accusations that were clearly lacking in evidentiary support at trial, and investigations of the alleged criminal activities of "radical" groups (primarily during the Nixon administration) seemed to some observers to be directed more toward harassment than producing supportable indictments. See Deutsch, *The Improper Uses of the Federal Grand Jury: An Instrument for the Internment of Political Activists,* 75 J.Crim.L. & Criminology 1159 (1984). Notwithstanding various legislative proposals aimed at restricting the investigative authority of federal grand juries and expanding the rights of grand jury witnesses, see e.g., A.B.A. Grand Jury Policy (1982), Congress has largely left regulation of federal grand juries to the courts. Various states, on the other hand, have adopted legislation that expands the rights of grand jury witnesses and imposes additional prerequisites for use of the grand jury's investigative authority. See Note 6, p 727; LaFave, Israel, and King § 8.6.

B. Investigative Advantages

Compared to police investigations, grand jury investigations are expensive, time consuming, and logistically cumbersome. Accordingly, the grand jury ordinarily is used to investigate only when it has a distinct investigative advantage over the police. It usually has such an advantage where investigators must unravel a complex criminal structure, deal with victims reluctant to cooperate, obtain information contained in extensive business records, or keep a continuing investigative effort from the public gaze. Criminal activities presenting such investigative problems include public corruption (e.g., bribery), misuse of economic power (e.g., price-fixing), and widespread distribution of illegal services and goods (e.g., gambling or narcotics distribution), and most grand jury investigations are directed at such activities. The grand jury's advantages in investigating this type of criminal activity stem primarily from five elements of its investigatory processes—(1) the use of subpoena authority, (2) the psychological pressure imposed by the grand jury setting, (3) the use of immunity grants, (4) grand jury secrecy requirements, and (5) public confidence attributable to lay participation.

1. *Subpoena authority.* The basic investigative advantage of the grand jury stems from its ability to use the subpoena authority of the court that impaneled it. The grand jury may utilize the subpoena duces tecum to obtain tangible evidence and the subpoena ad testificandum to obtain testimony. Both subpoenas are supported by the court's authority to hold in contempt any person who willfully refuses, without legal justification, to comply with a subpoena's directive.[a]

The contempt sanction makes the grand jury subpoena particularly useful in obtaining statements from persons who will not voluntarily furnish information to the police. While those persons have the right to refuse to cooperate with the police, their refusal to comply with a grand jury subpoena invokes the threat of a possible jail sentence. Faced with that threat, a recalcitrant witness often will have a change of heart and will give to the grand jury information that he previously refused to give to the police. Of course, if the information sought could be incriminating, the witness (unless granted immunity) may still refuse to cooperate by relying on his privilege against self-incrimination. However, many persons unwilling to furnish information to the police, will willingly testify before the grand jury without regard to whether the self-incrimination privilege might offer an avenue for refusing to do so. Thus, the victim of a fraudulent gambling operation or a loansharking operation may be either too embarrassed or too fearful to voluntarily furnish information to the police, yet be willing to furnish that information to the grand jury when faced with the threat of contempt. Similarly, an employee may wish to avoid the appearance of voluntarily assisting officials investigating his employer, yet testify freely under the compulsion of a subpoena.

a. The contemnor may be held in either civil or criminal contempt. Civil contempt is used to coerce the contemnor into complying with the subpoena. The contemnor is sentenced to imprisonment or to a fine (which may increase daily), but he may purge himself of the sentence by complying with the subpoena. As courts have frequently noted, he "carries the keys to the prison in his pocket." The civil contemnor who refuses to purge himself will remain under sentence until the grand jury completes its term and is discharged. Moreover, if the information the contemnor possesses is still needed, he may be subpoenaed by a successor grand jury and held in contempt again if he continues to refuse to supply that information.

The grand jury subpoena ad testificandum also has the advantage of requiring witnesses to testify under oath. If a witness fails to tell the truth, he may be prosecuted for perjury. Generally, a person who gives false information to a police officer will not have committed a crime (though there is such a crime as to federal officials). Accordingly, where a witness might be willing to talk to the police, but also is likely to "shade his story," requiring him to testify before a grand jury may produce more complete and truthful statements. Even where a witness is willing to give an entirely truthful statement to the police, there may be value in requiring him to testify before the grand jury. Arguably, a person who has testified under oath before the grand jury will be somewhat more hesitant to "change his story" when he testifies at trial. Also, if the witness does change his story and his prior statement is used to impeach him, the petit jurors may give greater weight to his prior grand jury testimony than they would to a prior statement he made to the police.

Finally, the grand jury subpoena duces tecum offers certain advantages over the primary device available to the police for obtaining records and physical evidence—the search pursuant to a warrant. Unlike the search warrant, the subpoena duces tecum can issue without a showing of probable cause. See *United States v. Dionisio,* § 2 infra. Moreover, even where probable cause could be established, there are times when the subpoena will be more appropriate. For example, there may be a need to seize so many records from various locations that a search would be impractical. At other times, there may be a need to obtain records from uninvolved third parties (e.g., a bank) and a subpoena will be preferred because it is far less disruptive to the third party's operations. Cf. *Zurcher v. Stanford Daily,* p. 177.

2. *Psychological pressure.* In addition to the compulsion of the subpoena, the psychological pressure of grand jury interrogation also is cited as a factor that frequently enables the grand jury to obtain statements from witnesses unwilling to cooperate with the police. Proponents of grand jury investigations claim that this pressure stems from the moral force exerted by the grand jury. Thus, two prosecuting attorneys note:

> "Most witnesses before grand juries feel a moral compulsion to be honest and forthright in discharging their duties as citizens, because their peers, the members of the grand jury, have also been taken away from their jobs, businesses, and private pursuits, and have accepted the inconvenience of becoming involved. The grand jurors manifest a serious purpose and are persons with whom witnesses can identify. Thus, even though their associates may be determined not to cooperate, certain witnesses may be ashamed to engage or persist in deceitful or obstreperous conduct to deny the grand jury the information it needs." John Keeney and Paul Walsh, *The American Bar Association's Grand Jury Principles: A Critique From A Federal Criminal Justice Perspective,* 14 Idaho L.Rev. 545, 579 (1978).

On the other side, critics of grand jury investigations claim that the psychological pressure stems primarily from what they describe as the "star chamber setting" of grand jury interrogation. "In all of the United States legal system," they note, "no person stands more alone than a witness before a grand jury; in a secret hearing he faces an often hostile prosecutor and 23 strangers with no judge present to guard his rights, no lawyer present to counsel him, and sometimes no indication of why he is being questioned."

3. *Immunity grants.* An immunity grant is a court order granting a witness sufficient immunity from future prosecution to supplant the witness' self-incrimi-

nation privilege. Once the recalcitrant witness has been granted immunity, he may no longer rely upon the privilege. Since immunity grants are tied to the exercise of the privilege by a person under a legal obligation to testify, they are not available to persons who simply refuse to give a statement to the police. At the investigatory stage, almost the only way the prosecution can make use of an immunity grant is in conjunction with a subpoena directing the uncooperative witness to testify before the grand jury. The immunity grant may be needed to gain information from various types of recalcitrant witnesses. For example, immunity quite frequently is given to a lower-level participant in organized crime in order to obtain testimony against higher-level participants. It also often is used to force testimony from witnesses who are not themselves involved in criminal activities, but desire not to give testimony that may hurt others. Although the privilege is not available simply to protect others (see Note 4, p. 717), witnesses who do not actually fear personal incrimination have been known to falsely claim that they do in order to avoid testifying against their friends. Since such claims are difficult to dispute, the prosecutor may simply prefer to grant the witness immunity.

4. *Secrecy.* Grand jury secrecy requirements vary among jurisdictions, but it generally is agreed that even the weakest of those requirements adds to the grand jury's effectiveness as an investigative agency. All jurisdictions prohibit the prosecutor, the prosecutor's staff (including investigative agents), the grand jurors, and the grand jury stenographer from disclosing grand jury testimony except when authorized by court order. A substantial majority of jurisdictions, however, do not impose an obligation of secrecy upon grand jury witnesses.[b] A witness may disclose, publicly or privately, both his own testimony and whatever information was revealed to him in the course of his examination before the grand jury. Where the witness desires not to disclose, however, his decision, combined with the obligations of secrecy imposed upon the other participants, usually keeps his testimony secret—at least until an indictment is issued.[c]

b. In roughly a dozen states, witnesses are subjected to a requirement of secrecy as to their testimony, disclosure generally being allowed only to counsel in the course of seeking legal advice. See Beale et al., § 5.5. While such witness-secrecy provisions by their terms tend to go beyond the life of the grand jury, the Supreme Court in *Butterworth v. Smith*, 494 U.S. 624, 110 S.Ct. 1376, 108 L.Ed.2d 572 (1990), held that a law "prohibiting a grand jury witness from disclosing [the 'content, gist, or import' of] his own testimony after the term of the grand jury has ended * * * violates the First Amendment."

c. During the pendency of the investigation, every effort is made to assist the witness who wants to keep his testimony secret. Thus jurisdictions commonly provide that the names of persons to whom subpoenas have been issued shall be kept under seal. So too, a hearing relating to the investigation may be closed to the public where necessary to prevent disclosure of grand jury matters. See Fed.R.Crim.P. 6(e)(5) (noting, however, that such power is "subject to any right to an open hearing in contempt proceedings"). Of course, even during the pendency of the investigation, the court has authority, upon a special showing of need,

to order disclosure to a third party (e.g., a civil litigant who is familiar with the general subject matter of the investigation and believes that the grand jury testimony is critical to his presenting a defense in a related civil case). However, courts are extremely reluctant to exercise that authority while the investigation is ongoing. See *Douglas Oil Co. v. Petrol Stops Northwest*, 441 U.S. 211, 99 S.Ct. 1667, 60 L.Ed.2d 156 (1979).

Once the investigation has ended, there is a somewhat greater likelihood of court-ordered disclosure to a litigant in a related civil case, but the court here still will give considerable weight to the grand jury witness' interest in keeping his testimony secret. Consider, e.g., *Douglas Oil,* supra, where the Court (in discussing the "particularized need" standard that must be met by the civil litigant to gain disclosure) noted: "[I]n considering the effects of disclosure on grand jury proceedings, the courts must consider not only the immediate effects upon a particular grand jury, but also the possible effect upon the functioning of future grand juries. Persons called upon to testify will consider the likelihood that their testimony may one day be disclosed to outside parties. Fear of future retribution or social

In *United States v. Procter & Gamble Co.,* 356 U.S. 677, 78 S.Ct. 983, 2 L.Ed.2d 1077 (1958), the Supreme Court noted five objectives of grand jury secrecy requirements:

"(1) to prevent the escape of those whose indictment may be contemplated; (2) to insure the utmost freedom to the grand jury in its deliberations, and to prevent persons subject to indictment or their friends from importuning the grand jurors; (3) to prevent subornation of perjury or tampering with the witnesses who may testify before grand jury and later appear at the trial of those indicted by it; (4) to encourage free and untrammeled disclosures by persons who have information with respect to the commission of crimes; (5) to protect the innocent accused who is exonerated from disclosure of the fact that he has been under investigation, and from the expense of standing trial where there was no probability of guilt."

While the second objective cited by the Court relates primarily to the screening function of the grand jury, the remaining four promote the grand jury's effectiveness as an investigative agency. The first objective—preventing the flight of the person being investigated—depends, of course, upon the cooperation of the grand jury witnesses. Since they are not sworn to secrecy, they may lawfully warn the target of the investigation. However, if the witnesses cooperate, grand jury secrecy requirements generally should deter the leaks that accompany most other types of investigation. If the target is kept unaware of the investigation until after the indictment is issued, the third objective cited by the Court also is served. When the witnesses against him have already testified, it is too late for the target to try to influence their grand jury testimony and it will be more difficult for him to successfully influence their trial testimony.

The fourth objective noted in *Procter & Gamble* probably is the most significant for investigatory success. Witnesses often are much more willing to testify if they know that their identity will be kept from the target of the investigation. Of course, if an indictment is issued, and the witness testifies at trial, the target (now the defendant) eventually will learn that the particular person furnished evidence against him (see fn. c supra). However, the witness may not necessarily be called to testify at trial. Grand jury witnesses often are subpoenaed simply to obtain leads to more crucial evidence. Moreover, if the witness can be assured that his identity will be revealed only if an indictment is issued, he may have fewer qualms about cooperating. He may be less wary of being criticized as an "informer" if he knows that his role will be revealed only after a grand jury has supported his judgment and veracity by issuing an indictment.

The fifth objective noted in *Procter & Gamble* can be of special significance in the decision to institute an investigation. Where the person being investigated occupies a position of public prominence, public disclosure of the investigation may cause irreparable damage to the person's career even though the investigation eventually reveals no basis for a prosecution. Accordingly, a prosecutor may

stigma may act as powerful deterrents to those who would come forward and aid the grand jury in the performance of its duties. Concern as to the future consequences of frank and full testimony is heightened where the witness is an employee of a company under investigation. Thus, the interests in grand jury secrecy, although reduced, are not eliminated merely because the grand jury has ended its activities."

By far the greatest likelihood of court ordered disclosure occurs where the investigation ends in an indictment and the defendant seeks to examine the grand jury testimony. Where the grand jury witness will also be a trial witness, most jurisdictions grant automatic disclosure of the witness' grand jury testimony, either pretrial or after the witness testifies at trial. Indeed, in some jurisdictions, defendants may gain pretrial disclosure of all grand jury testimony, including that of grand jury witnesses who will not testify at trial.

hesitate to initiate a police investigation unless the currently available evidence makes it most likely that the investigation will result in a prosecution. On the other hand, if grand jury secrecy requirements can provide reasonable assurance that the investigation will be kept secret if an indictment is not issued, the prosecutor may feel less reluctant to initiate a grand jury investigation. In particular, when he has a strong suspicion that rumors of illegal activities might be well founded, he may be willing to pursue the investigation of a public figure even though the evidence currently available is fairly flimsy.[d]

5. *Maintaining public confidence.* Where the subject to be investigated is a matter of public knowledge (as in the case of investigations into matters already given considerable media coverage), grand jury participation often helps in maintaining community confidence in the integrity of the investigatory process. This is especially important where the person under investigation is a public official. The community tends to be suspicious of partisan influences in such investigations, especially where the investigation results in a decision not to prosecute. As one court noted: "Where corruption is charged, it is desirable to have someone outside the administration [i.e., the grand jury] act, so that the image, as well as the fact of impartiality in the investigation can be preserved and allegations of cover-up or white-wash can be avoided." *Losavio v. Kikel,* 529 P.2d 306 (Colo.1974). The prosecutor may also look to the grand jury to help allay other public concerns, as in cases in which investigated parties are almost certain to claim police and prosecutor harassment.

6. *Grand jury reports.* Another potential investigative advantage, also relating to maintaining public confidence, lies in the grand jury's authority to issue reports in those situations in which an investigation reveals transactions that are of questionable propriety, though not criminal. A substantial number of jurisdictions permit a grand jury to issue a report summarizing the evidence found on non-indictable activities thought to merit public attention. Where such reports are critical of specific individuals, the law authorizing reports commonly will include certain procedural safeguards for those individuals (e.g., judicial review to ensure that the report's claims have evidentiary support, and a right of the individual to include a response). See Barry Stern, *Revealing Misconduct by Public Officials Through Grand Jury Reports,* 136 U.Pa.L.Rev. 73 (1987). Though obviously of less significance to the prosecutor than those grand jury powers that facilitate development of a successful prosecution, the alternative of issuing a report, if a crime is not found, may be helpful in maintaining the image of the prosecutor's office as an effective "public watchdog."

7. *Alternative investigative agencies.* A small number of states have adopted statutes providing for criminal investigations through the use of the subpoena power by an authority other than the grand jury. The object of these provisions is to grant to the particular authority at least some of the investigative advantages of the grand jury through a process that is "less cumbersome" than a grand jury investigation. These investigative alternatives include the "one-man grand jury"

d. Of course, secrecy provisions do not work to perfection and consideration must be given to the possibility of "leaks" to the press. Federal courts have authority under Federal Rule 6 to hold in contempt persons who have violated grand jury secrecy provisions. However, even where the nature of the information reported in the press clearly indicates that the source was a secrecy violation (rather than a disclosure by a witness), it will often be impossible to identify the violator, as reporters will refuse to identify their sources, even if that means being held in contempt. Still, the supervising court may require the prosecution to make an extensive in camera showing that its staff is not responsible for the leaks, and court may impose safeguards to insure against future leaks. See *In re Sealed Case No. 98–3077,* 151 F.3d 1059 (D.C.Cir.1998).

(a judge acting, in effect, as a grand jury, assisted by a specially appointed prosecutor), the "John Doe" proceeding (a prosecutorial inquiry into the commission of specified criminal activity, conducted before a judge), and direct grant of the subpoena power to the prosecutor (in some jurisdictions only with the prior approval of the court). Many elements of the law governing these proceedings are identical to those governing grand jury proceedings. Thus, most of the issues discussed in section three of this chapter with respect to the privilege against self-incrimination are also presented in these alternative investigative proceedings. However, certain witness challenges and witness rights typically not recognized in the grand jury setting (e.g., relevancy objections, and the presence of counsel) are commonly available in such proceedings.

C. JUDICIAL REGULATION: SOME DIFFERING PERSPECTIVES

1. *LaFave, Israel, and King, § 8.2(c) ("The Relevance of History"):*

"The grand jury investigation is frequently described as introducing an 'inquisitorial element' into a criminal justice system that is basically accusatorial. Critics argue that the grand jury's investigative authority should therefore be viewed as an anomaly and kept within narrow confines by close judicial supervision. They recognize that this position faces difficulties if history reveals that the grand jury inquest was accepted from the outset as an institution that coexisted with the accusatorial elements of the Anglo–American criminal justice process. The critics argue, however, that a careful reading of the history of the grand jury reveals no such accommodation. First, they note, the early grand juries did not frequently exercise the basic element of its modern investigative authority—its power to compel testimony—but instead relied primarily upon information known to the jurors or the voluntary testimony of aggrieved persons. Secondly, they argue, the investigative role of the grand jury was not critical to its initial acceptance in this country. It was the shielding role of the grand jury that earned it a place in the Bill of Rights and the early state constitutions. The grand jury's investigatory role was then viewed as entirely secondary and not necessarily distinct from its screening role. Today, it is argued, the significance of the two roles has been reversed.

"Supporters of the grand jury respond that the early history of the grand jury clearly establishes the legitimacy of its extensive investigative authority. The power of the grand jury to compel testimony was recognized well before the adoption of the Constitution and was used in some of the most notable grand jury inquests. At the time of the Constitution's adoption, the grand jury was a revered institution not simply because it served as a buffer between the state and the individual, but equally for its service as a watchdog against public corruption and its capacity to ferret out criminal activity that local officials either chose to ignore or were unable to investigate. The importance of this investigative authority was implicitly recognized, it is argued, in constitutional and statutory provisions authorizing the institution of prosecution by presentment as well as indictment.

"With few exceptions, American courts have accepted the position that the history of the grand jury provides a solid foundation for its broad investigative authority. The Supreme Court's discussion of that authority in *Blair v. United States* [see Note 2 infra] is typical. The Court there noted that the grand jury's authority to resort to compulsory process had been recognized in England as early as 1612, and the inquisitorial function of the grand jury was well established at the time of the Constitution's adoption. Both the Fifth Amendment and the earliest federal statutes recognized an investigative authority of the grand jury that included the 'same powers that pertained to its British prototype.' The Supreme Court would not view that authority with suspicion and subject it to new limitations. * * *

"Critics of the grand jury also contend that even if a broad investigative authority is sanctioned by history, the same historical sources also indicate that authority was tied to an assumption of substantial grand jury independence. * * * Today, the critics argue, the sweeping powers of the grand jury are exercised in reality by the prosecutor alone. Working with the police, the prosecutor determines what witnesses will be called and when they will appear. He examines the witnesses and advises the grand jury on the validity of any legal objections the witnesses might present. If a witness refuses to comply with a subpoena, it is the prosecutor who seeks a contempt citation. If a witness refuses to testify on grounds of self-incrimination, it is the prosecutor who determines whether an immunity grant will be obtained. The grand jury must, almost of necessity, rely upon the prosecutor's leadership. Few investigations can succeed without the investigative work, skillful interrogation, legal advice, and even the secretarial assistance, provided by the prosecutor and his staff. So too, grand jurors are neophytes in the field of criminal investigation and are participating only on a part-time basis; it is only natural that they are disposed to rely upon the prosecutor—the 'professional' who commands the expertise necessary to their venture.

"Critics argue that this change in the nature of the investigative grand jury, which [they say] has converted it into the 'prosecutor's puppet,' requires a corresponding change in judicial attitudes. The courts should not, they argue, feel bound by precedent that was developed during an era when grand juries were independent bodies. Instead, they should 'pull back the veil of history and view the investigating grand jury as one would view any other investigatory instrument of government.' The power of the grand jury should be subject to the same kinds of limitations as are imposed upon other weapons in the prosecutor's investigative arsenal.

"Supporters of the grand jury readily acknowledge that the prosecutor plays a substantial role in directing today's grand jury investigations. They suggest that this is a beneficial development that makes the investigatory authority more effective and helps to ensure that it is not misused. Moreover, it is noted, this development dates back over one hundred years, preceding many of the decisions that speak most eloquently of the necessary breadth of the grand jury's investigative authority. The key to the historical grant of that authority, they argue, was a legal structure that rendered the government's use of the grand jury's investigative powers subject to the veto of the jurors, who sat as community representatives. That structure has not been substantially altered, and its very presence, the argument continues, serves to hold the prosecutor in check and to distinguish grand jury investigations from investigatory tools granted directly to the prosecutor or the police.[a] The fact that the grand jury only occasionally exercises its

---

a. See e.g., Justice Black's oft-quoted dissent in *In re Groban*, 352 U.S. 330, 77 S.Ct. 510, 1 L.Ed.2d 376 (1957). Commenting on the distinction between a grand jury proceeding (where Justice Black agreed that "a witness cannot insist, as a matter of constitutional right, on being represented by counsel") and a fire marshall's closed inquiry (where Justice Black, disagreeing with the *Groban* majority,

argued that the witness had a constitutional right to be accompanied by counsel), Justice Black emphasized the special role of the grand jurors: "They bring into the grand jury room the experience, knowledge and viewpoint of all sections of the community. They have no axes to grind and are not charged personally with the administration of the law. No one of them is a prosecuting attorney or law-enforcement power to override the prosecutor does not detract from the significance of that power. The prosecutor must respect the existence of that power and act in a way that he knows, from past experience, will be acceptable to the jurors."

2. BLAIR v. UNITED STATES, 250 U.S. 273, 39 S.Ct. 468, 63 L.Ed. 979 (1919). Responding to a grand jury witness' challenge to a subpoena on the ground that the federal government lacked constitutional authority to regulate, and the federal grand jury therefore lacked jurisdiction to investigate, the campaign practices of a candidate in a state primary election for U.S. Senator, Pitney, J., speaking for a unanimous Court, noted:

"[T]he giving of testimony and the attendance upon court or grand jury in order to testify are public duties which every person within the jurisdiction of the Government is bound to perform upon being properly summoned, and for performance of which he is entitled to no further compensation than that which the statutes provide. The personal sacrifice involved is a part of the necessary contribution of the individual to the welfare of the public. The duty, so onerous at times, yet so necessary to the administration of justice according to the forms and modes established in our system of government is subject to mitigation in exceptional circumstances; there is a constitutional exemption from being compelled in any criminal case to be a witness against oneself, entitling the witness to be excused from answering anything that will tend to incriminate him; some confidential matters are shielded from considerations of policy, and perhaps in other cases for special reasons a witness may be excused from telling all that he knows.

"But, aside from exceptions and qualifications—and none such is asserted in the present case—the witness is bound not only to attend but to tell what he knows in answer to questions framed for the purpose of bringing out the truth of the matter under inquiry. He is not entitled to urge objections of incompetency or irrelevancy, such as a party might raise, for this is no concern of his. On familiar principles, he is not entitled to challenge the authority of the court or of the grand jury, provided they have a *de facto* existence and organization. He is not entitled to set limits to the investigation that the grand jury may conduct. * * * It is a grand inquest, a body with powers of investigation and inquisition, the scope of whose inquiries is not to be limited narrowly by questions of propriety or forecasts of the probable result of the investigation, or by doubts whether any particular individual will be found properly subject to an accusation of crime."

3. IN RE GRAND JURY PROCEEDINGS (SCHOFIELD I), 486 F.2d 85 (3d Cir.1973). Rejecting the government's claim that a grand jury witness should be held in contempt for failing to respond to a grand jury subpoena with no more showing as to the grounding of the subpoena than "what appears on the face of the subpoena", the Third Circuit (per GIBBONS, J.) noted:

"[I]t is well to start with some fundamental propositions. First, although federal grand juries are called into existence by order of the district court, Fed.R.Crim.P. 6(a), they are 'basically . . . a law enforcement agency.' They are for all practical purposes an investigative and prosecutorial arm of the executive branch of government. Second, although like all federal court subpoenas grand jury subpoenas are issued in the name of the district court over the signature of the clerk, they are issued pro forma and in blank to anyone requesting them.

officer ferreting out crime. It would be very difficult for officers of the state seriously to abuse or deceive a witness in the presence of the grand jury. Similarly the presence of the jurors offers a substantial safeguard against the officers' misrepresentation, unintentional or otherwise, of the witness statements and conduct before the grand jury.''

Fed.R.Crim.P. 17(a). The court exercises no prior control whatsoever upon their use. Third, although grand jury subpoenas are occasionally discussed as if they were the instrumentalities of the grand jury, they are in fact almost universally instrumentalities of the United States Attorney's office or of some other investigative or prosecutorial department of the executive branch. Grand jury subpoenas then, when they are brought before the federal courts for enforcement, for all practical purposes are exactly analogous to subpoenas issued by a federal administrative agency on the authority of a statute * * *. [A] court's determination under 28 U.S.C. § 1826(a) [the civil contempt enforcement provision] of the existence or nonexistence of just cause for refusing to obey a subpoena entails the same full judicial consideration as in the administrative subpoena cases."

4. UNITED STATES v. WILLIAMS, 504 U.S. 36, 112 S.Ct. 1735, 118 L.Ed.2d 352 (1992). The *Williams* majority opinion held that a federal court could not on its own initiative impose a duty on the government to present to the grand jury material exculpatory evidence within its possession, and the court accordingly could not dismiss an indictment because the prosecutor failed to present such evidence, even when the grand jury otherwise might not have approved the indictment. Explaining the limited authority of federal courts to mandate grand jury procedures beyond those "specifically required by the Constitution or Congress," SCALIA, J., noted:

" '[R]ooted in long centuries of Anglo–American history,' the grand jury is mentioned in the Bill of Rights, but not in the body of the Constitution. It has not been textually assigned, therefore, to any of the branches described in the first three Articles. It 'is a constitutional fixture in its own right.' In fact the whole theory of its function is that it belongs to no branch of the institutional government, serving as a kind of buffer or referee between the Government and the people. * * * Although the grand jury normally operates, of course, in the courthouse and under judicial auspices, its institutional relationship with the judicial branch has traditionally been, so to speak, at arm's length. Judges' direct involvement in the functioning of the grand jury has generally been confined to the constitutive one of calling the grand jurors together and administering their oaths of office. * * * The grand jury requires no authorization from its constituting court to initiate an investigation, nor does the prosecutor require leave of court to seek a grand jury indictment. And in its day-to-day functioning, the grand jury generally operates without the interference of a presiding judge. It swears in its own witnesses, Fed.Rule 6(c), and deliberates in total secrecy.

"True, the grand jury cannot compel the appearance of witnesses and the production of evidence, and must appeal to the court when such compulsion is required. And the court will refuse to lend its assistance when the compulsion the grand jury seeks would override rights accorded by the Constitution * * *. Even in this setting, however, we have insisted that the grand jury remain 'free to pursue its investigations unhindered by external influence or supervision so long as it does not trench upon the legitimate rights of any witness called before it.' *United States v. Dionisio* [p. 695]. Recognizing this tradition of independence, we have said that the Fifth Amendment's 'constitutional guarantee *presupposes* an investigative body "acting independently of either prosecuting attorney *or judge*" . . . .' *Dionisio.*

"Given the grand jury's operational separateness from its constituting court, it should come as no surprise that we have been reluctant to invoke the judicial supervisory power as a basis for prescribing modes of grand jury procedure. Over the years, we have received many requests to exercise supervision over the grand jury's evidence-taking process, but we have refused them all, including some more appealing than the one presented today. [Citing *Calandra*, Note 3, p. 716]. * * * These authorities suggest that any power federal courts may have to fashion, on their own initiative, rules of grand jury procedure is a very limited one, not remotely comparable to the power they maintain over their own proceedings."

SECTION 2. FOURTH AMENDMENT CHALLENGES TO THE INVESTIGATION

BOYD v. UNITED STATES
116 U.S. 616, 6 S.Ct. 524, 29 L.Ed. 746 (1886).

[Customs officials seized 35 cases of glass, imported by the partnership of Boyd and Sons, and instituted a forfeiture proceeding. That proceeding was brought under a statute providing that any importer who defrauded the government and thereby avoided payment of customs revenue was subject to fine, incarceration, and forfeiture of the imported merchandise. Utilizing an 1874 statute, the government's attorney obtained a court "notice" directing Boyd to produce an invoice covering 29 of the cases of glass. That statute authorized the trial judge, on motion of the prosecutor describing a particular document and indicating what it might prove, to issue a notice directing the importer to produce the document. The importer could refuse to produce without being held in contempt (which distinguished the "notice" from a subpoena), but the consequence of a failure to produce was that the allegation of the prosecutor as to what the document stated was "taken as confessed." The defendants produced the invoice in compliance with the notice, but objected to the validity of the court's order, and objected again when the invoice was offered as evidence. The jury subsequently found for the United States, and a judgment of forfeiture against the 35 cases was granted.]

BRADLEY, J.

* * * [I]n regard to Fourth Amendment, it is contended that * * * [the Act of 1874], under which the order in the present case was made, is free from constitutional objection, because it does not authorize the search and seizure of books and papers, but only requires the defendant or claimant to produce them. That is so; but it declares that if he does not produce them, the allegations which it is affirmed they will prove shall be taken as confessed. This is tantamount to compelling their production; for the prosecuting attorney will always be sure to state the evidence expected to be derived from them as strongly as the case will admit of. It is true that certain aggravating incidents of actual search and seizure, such as forcible entry into a man's house and searching amongst his papers, are wanting, and to this extent the proceeding under the act of 1874 is a mitigation of that which was authorized by the former acts; but it accomplishes the substantial object of those acts in forcing from a party evidence against himself. It is our opinion, therefore, that a compulsory production of a man's private papers to establish a criminal charge against him, or to forfeit his property, is within the scope of the Fourth Amendment to the Constitution, in all cases in which a search and seizure would be; because it is a material ingredient, and effects the sole object and purpose of search and seizure.

The principal question, however, remains to be considered. Is a search and seizure, or, what is equivalent thereto, a compulsory production of a man's private papers, to be used in evidence against him in a proceeding to forfeit his property for alleged fraud against the revenue laws—is such a proceeding for such a purpose an "*unreasonable* search and seizure" within the meaning of the Fourth Amendment of the Constitution? or, is it a legitimate proceeding? * * *

As before stated, the [predecessor] act of 1863 was the first act in this country, and, we might say, either in this country or in England, so far as we have been able to ascertain, which authorized the search and seizure of a man's private papers, or the compulsory production of them, for the purpose of using them in evidence against him in a criminal case, or in a proceeding to enforce the forfeiture of his property. Even the act under which the obnoxious writs of assistance were issued did not go as far as this, but only authorized the examination of ships and vessels, and persons found therein, for the purpose of finding goods prohibited to be imported or exported, or on which the duties were not paid, and to enter into and search any suspected vaults, cellars, or warehouses for such goods. The search for and seizure of stolen or forfeited goods, or goods liable to duties and concealed to avoid the payment thereof, are totally different things from a search for and seizure of a man's private books and papers for the purpose of obtaining information therein contained, or of using them as evidence against him. The two things differ toto coelo. In the one case, the government is entitled to the possession of the property; in the other it is not. * * *

In order to ascertain the nature of the proceedings intended by the Fourth Amendment to the Constitution under the terms "unreasonable searches and seizures," it is only necessary to recall the contemporary or then recent history of the controversies on the subject, both in this country and in England. * * * Prominent and principal among these was the practice of issuing general warrants by the Secretary of State, for searching private houses for the discovery and seizure of books and papers that might be used to convict their owner of the charge of libel. * * * The case [which] will always be celebrated as being the occasion of Lord Camden's memorable discussion of the subject, was that of *Entick v. Carrington and Three Other King's Messengers,* reported at length in 19 Howell's State Trials, 1029. The action was trespass for entering the plaintiff's dwelling-house in November, 1762, and breaking open his desks, boxes, & c., and searching and examining his papers. The jury rendered a special verdict, and the case was twice solemnly argued at the bar. Lord Camden pronounced the judgment of the court in Michaelmas Term, 1765, and the law as expounded by him has been regarded as settled from that time to this, and his great judgment on that occasion is considered as one of the landmarks of English liberty. It was welcomed and applauded by the lovers of liberty in the colonies as well as in the mother country. It is regarded as one of the permanent monuments of the British Constitution, and is quoted as such by the English authorities on that subject down to the present time. As every American statesmen, during our revolutionary and formative period as a nation, was undoubtedly familiar with this monument of English freedom, and considered it as the true and ultimate expression of constitutional law, it may be confidently asserted that its propositions were in the minds of those who framed the Fourth Amendment to the Constitution, and were considered as sufficiently explanatory of what was meant by unreasonable searches and seizures. * * *

After describing the power claimed by the Secretary of State for issuing general search warrants, and the manner in which they were executed, Lord Camden says [in *Entick*]:

> * * * Papers are the owner's goods and chattels; they are his dearest property; and are so far from enduring a seizure, that they will hardly bear an

inspection; and though the eye cannot by the laws of England be guilty of a trespass, yet where private papers are removed and carried away the secret nature of those goods will be an aggravation of the trespass, and demand more considerable damages in that respect. Where is the written law that gives any magistrate such a power? I can safely answer, there is none; and therefore, it is too much for us, without such authority, to pronounce a practice legal which would be subversive of all the comforts of society. * * *

Lastly, it is urged as an argument of utility, that such a search is a means of detecting offenders by discovering evidence. I wish some cases had been shown, where the law forceth evidence out of the owner's custody by process. There is no process against papers in civil causes. It has been often tried, but never prevailed. Nay, where the adversary has by force or fraud got possession of your own proper evidence, there is no way to get it back but by action. In the criminal law such a proceeding was never heard of; and yet there are some crimes, such, for instance, as murder, rape, robbery, and house-breaking, to say nothing of forgery and perjury, that are more atrocious than libelling. But our law has provided no paper-search in these cases to help forward the conviction. Whether this proceedeth from the gentleness of the law towards criminals, or from a consideration that such a power would be more pernicious to the innocent than useful to the public, I will not say. It is very certain that the law obligeth no man to accuse himself; because the necessary means of compelling self-accusation, falling upon the innocent as well as the guilty, would be both cruel and unjust; and it would seem, that search for evidence is disallowed upon the same principle. Then, too, the innocent would be confounded with the guilty.

* * * The principles laid down in this opinion affect the very essence of constitutional liberty and security. They reach farther than the concrete form of the case then before the court, with its adventitious circumstances; they apply to all invasions on the part of the government and its employees of the sanctity of a man's home and the privacies of life. It is not the breaking of his doors, and the rummaging of his drawers, that constitutes the essence of the offence; but it is the invasion of his indefeasible right of personal security, personal liberty and private property, where that right has never been forfeited by his conviction of some public offence,—it is the invasion of this sacred right which underlies and constitutes the essence of Lord Camden's judgment. Breaking into a house and opening boxes and drawers are circumstances of aggravation; but any forcible and compulsory extortion of a man's own testimony or of his private papers to be used as evidence to convict him of crime or to forfeit his goods, is within the condemnation of that judgment. In this regard the Fourth and Fifth Amendments run almost into each other. * * *

Reverting then to the peculiar phraseology of this act, and to the information in the present case, which is founded on it, we have to deal with an act which expressly excludes criminal proceedings from its operation (though embracing civil suits for penalties and forfeitures), and with an information not technically a criminal proceeding, and neither, therefore, within the literal terms of the Fifth Amendment to the Constitution any more than it is within the literal terms of the Fourth. Does this relieve the proceedings or the law from being obnoxious to the prohibitions of either? We think not; we think they are within the spirit of both.

We have already noticed the intimate relation between the two amendments. They throw great light on each other. For the "unreasonable searches and seizures" condemned in the Fourth Amendment are almost always made for the purpose of compelling a man to give evidence against himself, which in criminal cases is condemned in the Fifth Amendment; and compelling a man "in a criminal case to be a witness against himself," which is condemned in the Fifth Amendment, throws light on the question as to what is an "unreasonable search and seizure" within the meaning of the Fourth Amendment. And we have been unable to perceive that the seizure of a man's private books and papers to be used in evidence against him is substantially different from compelling him to be a witness against himself. * * * We are also clearly of opinion that proceedings instituted for the purpose of declaring the forfeiture of a man's property by reason of offences committed by him, though they may be civil in form, are in their nature criminal. In this very case, the ground of forfeiture * * * consists of certain acts of fraud committed against the public revenue in relation to imported merchandise, which are made criminal by the statute * * *. As, therefore, suits for penalties and forfeitures incurred by the commission of offences against the law, are of this quasi-criminal nature, we think that they are within the reason of criminal proceedings for all the purposes of the Fourth Amendment of the Constitution, and of that portion of the Fifth Amendment which declares that no person shall be compelled in any criminal case to be a witness against himself; and we are further of opinion that a compulsory production of the private books and papers of the owner of goods sought to be forfeited in such a suit is compelling him to be a witness against himself, within the meaning of the Fifth Amendment to the Constitution, and is the equivalent of a search and seizure—and an unreasonable search and seizure—within the meaning of the Fourth Amendment.

Though the proceeding in question is divested of many of the aggravating incidents of actual search and seizure, yet, as before said, it contains their substance and essence, and effects their substantial purpose. It may be that it is the obnoxious thing in its mildest and least repulsive form; but illegitimate and unconstitutional practices get their first footing in that way, namely, by silent approaches and slight deviations from legal modes of procedure. This can only be obviated by adhering to the rule that constitutional provisions for the security of person and property should be liberally construed. A close and literal construction deprives them of half their efficacy, and leads to gradual depreciation of the right, as if it consisted more in sound than in substance. It is the duty of courts to be watchful for the constitutional rights of the citizen, and against any stealthy encroachments thereon. Their motto should be *obsta principiis*. * * *

Justice MILLER, with whom was The Chief Justice concurring:

I concur in the judgment of the court * * * and in so much of the opinion of this court as holds the 5th section of the act of 1874 void as applicable to the present case. * * * The order of the court under the statute is in effect a subpoena duces tecum, and, though the penalty for the witness's failure to appear in court with the criminating papers is not fine and imprisonment, it is one which may be made more severe, namely, to have charges against him of a criminal nature, taken for confessed, and made the foundation of the judgment of the court. That this is within the protection which the Constitution intended against compelling a person to be a witness against himself, is, I think, quite clear.

But this being so, there is no reason why this court should assume that the action of the court below, in requiring a party to produce certain papers as evidence on the trial, authorizes an unreasonable search or seizure of the house, papers, or effects of that party. There is in fact no search and no seizure authorized by the statute. No order can be made by the court under it which

requires or permits anything more than service of notice on a party to the suit.
* * *

Nothing in the nature of a search is here hinted at. Nor is there any seizure, because the party is not required at any time to part with the custody of the papers. They are to be produced in court, and, when produced, the United States attorney is permitted, under the direction of the court, to make examination in presence of the claimant, and may offer in evidence such entries in the books, invoices, or papers as relate to the issue. The act is careful to say that "the owner of said books and papers, his agent or attorney, shall have, subject to the order of the court, the custody of them, except pending their examination in court as aforesaid." . . .

The things . . . forbidden [by the Fourth Amendment] are two—search and seizure. * * * But what search does this statute authorize? If the mere service of a notice to produce a paper to be used as evidence, which the party can obey or not as he chooses is a search, then a change has taken place in the meaning of words, which has not come within my reading, and which I think was unknown at the time the Constitution was made. The searches meant by the Constitution were such as led to seizure when the search was successful. But the statute in this case uses language carefully framed to forbid any seizure under it, as I have already pointed out. * * *

Notes and Questions

1. *The significance of Boyd. Boyd* was subsequently praised by commentators and courts as the landmark civil liberties case of its era, and its statement on the need for liberal construction of constitutional safeguards [see the last paragraph of the majority's opinion] has been quoted with approval in numerous Supreme Court opinions. Nonetheless, *Boyd*'s precise holding was soon subjected to question, and would be viewed today as clearly inconsistent with applicable precedent (see e.g., the *Bellis* ruling, discussed at p. 760, and Note 4 infra). Moreover, much of its underlying analysis of the Fourth Amendment, the Fifth Amendment, and the relationship between the two, has been rejected. While that analysis reflects what might be described as a "false start," the Court has struggled with that start ever since. See e.g., *Fisher v. United States*, p. 746. Consider also Note, 76 Mich.L.Rev. 212 (1977) ("*Boyd* is dead," but a case which Justice Brandeis described as one "that will be remembered as long as civil liberty lives in the United States" deserves the "decent burial" that the Court has never given it).

2. *Boyd* has been described as a product of "nineteenth century legal formalism" that was founded on "the view that adjudication proceeds by deduction from virtually absolute legal principles rooted in natural law and enshrined in both the common law and the Constitution." Note, 90 Harv.L.Rev. 943 (1977). It is said to have rested on "two fundamental principles which formed an impenetrable boundary around the individual's sphere of privacy as defined by his common law property rights and his privilege against self-incrimination. The Fourth Amendment prohibited the government from seizing and using as evidence the defendant's personal books and papers because they are articles of personal property; the Fifth Amendment added a second layer of protection for books and papers which might tend to incriminate the owner." Id. at 955. As suggested by the same author, the jurisprudential approach of *Boyd* contrasts with the "more pragmatic and relativist vision of the law" associated with constitutional developments since the 1930s. Do the Court's subsequent decisions (discussed below as to the Fourth Amendment and in section 4 as to the Fifth Amendment) simply

reflect this difference in approach or do they suggest a more basic disagreement with the substantive values that *Boyd* sought to protect? See also Note 1, p. ____.

3. *Hale v. Henkel (the introduction of the overbreadth doctrine).* Insofar as *Boyd* suggested that the Fourth Amendment prohibited searches for property the defendant was entitled to possess (i.e., property other than the fruits or instrumentalities of crime), that aspect of *Boyd* was flatly rejected in *Warden v. Hayden* [p. 174] decided in 1967. Insofar as *Boyd* read the Fourth Amendment as prohibiting a search for documents, that interpretation was overturned in *Andresen v. Maryland* [p. 174] decided in 1976. But long before these developments, the Court had restructured *Boyd*'s view of the bearing of the Fourth Amendment upon a subpoena duces tecum. In HALE v. HENKEL, 201 U.S. 43, 26 S.Ct. 370, 50 L.Ed. 652 (1906), the Court had before it a challenge to a subpoena directing the petitioner to produce before a grand jury (which was conducting an investigation into possible violations of the antitrust laws) various corporate documents. Petitioner's challenge was based on the combined impact of the Fourth and Fifth Amendments, but the Court initially separated those claims. Cases subsequent to *Boyd,* it noted, had "treated the Fourth and Fifth Amendments as quite distinct, having different histories, and performing separate functions." Turning first to the petitioner's self-incrimination claim, the Court found that claim clearly unsupportable since the statute authorizing the subpoena granted petitioner immunity from prosecution (see p. 743) and the corporation itself had no self-incrimination privilege (see p. 774). The petitioner's Fourth Amendment claim did have merit, but for reasons other than what might have been assumed from *Boyd*. Speaking for the Court, BROWN, J., noted:

"Although * * * we are of the opinion that an officer of a corporation * * * cannot refuse to produce the books and papers of such corporation, we do not wish to be understood as holding that a corporation is not entitled to immunity, under the Fourth Amendment, against *unreasonable* searches and seizures. A corporation is, after all, but an association of individuals under an assumed name and with a distinct legal entity. In organizing itself as a collective body it waives no constitutional immunities appropriate to such body. * * * We are also of opinion that an order for the production of books and papers may constitute an unreasonable search and seizure within the Fourth Amendment. While a search ordinarily implies a quest by an officer of the law, and a seizure contemplates a forcible dispossession of the owner, still, as was held in the *Boyd* case, the substance of the offense is the compulsory production of private papers, whether under a search warrant or a subpoena duces tecum, against which the person, be he individual or corporation, is entitled to protection. Applying the test of reasonableness to the present case, we think the subpoena duces tecum is far too sweeping in its terms to be regarded as reasonable. It does not require the production of a single contract, or of contracts with a particular corporation, or a limited number of documents, but all understandings, contracts, or correspondence between the MacAndrews & Forbes Company, and no less than six different companies, as well as all reports made, and accounts rendered by such companies from the date of the organization of the MacAndrews & Forbes Company, as well as all letters received by that company since its organization from more than a dozen different companies, situated in seven different States in the Union.

"If the writ had required the production of all the books, papers and documents found in the office of the MacAndrews & Forbes Company, it would scarcely be more universal in its operation, or more completely put a stop to the business of that company. Indeed, it is difficult to say how its business could be carried on after it had been denuded of this mass of material, which is not shown to be necessary in the prosecution of this case, and is clearly in violation of the general principle of law with regard to the particularity required in the description of documents necessary to a search warrant or subpoena. Doubtless many, if not all, of these documents may ultimately be required, but some necessity should be shown, either from an examination of the witnesses orally, or from the known transactions of these companies with the other companies implicated, or some evidence of their materiality produced, to justify an order for the production of such a mass of papers. A general subpoena of this description is equally indefensible as a search warrant would be if couched in similar terms."

McKENNA, J., concurring separately in *Hale,* questioned the Court's Fourth Amendment analysis: "It is said 'a search implies a quest by an officer of the law; a seizure contemplates a forcible dispossession of the owner.' Nothing can be more direct and plain; nothing more expressive to distinguish a subpoena from a search warrant. Can a subpoena lose this essential distinction from a search warrant by the generality or speciality of its terms? I think not. The distinction is based upon what is authorized or directed to be done—not upon the form of words by which the authority or command is given. 'The quest of an officer' acts upon the things themselves—may be secret, intrusive, accompanied by force. The service of a subpoena is but the delivery of a paper to a party—is open and aboveboard. There is no element of trespass or force in it. It does not disturb the possession of property. It cannot be finally enforced except after challenge, and a judgment of the court upon the challenge. This is a safeguard against abuse the same as it is of other processes of the law, and it is all that can be allowed without serious embarrassment to the administration of justice."

4. *Explaining the overbreadth doctrine.* As Judge Friendly noted in *In re Horowitz,* 482 F.2d 72 (2d Cir.1973), "the Fourth Amendment portion of the *Boyd* decision was surely not based on the overbreadth of the Government's demand; the Government [there] sought only a single invoice of unquestionable relevance." Although relying on *Boyd, Hale v. Henkel*

> left the applicability of the Fourth Amendment to subpoena duces tecum in a most confusing state. None of the Justices seemed to think that such a subpoena could be issued only "upon probable cause, supported by oath or affirmation," as would be required for a search warrant. Nevertheless, except for Mr. Justice McKenna, all were of the view that an overbroad subpoena duces tecum against an individual would be an unreasonable search and seizure.

Judge Friendly suggested in *Horowitz* that the overbreadth doctrine of *Hale* might find firmer support in the due process clause than in the Fourth Amendment. Although a due process grounding for the doctrine is suggested in *Oklahoma Press Publishing Co. v. Walling,* 327 U.S. 186, 66 S.Ct. 494, 90 L.Ed. 614 (1946) (a leading case on the application of the overbreadth doctrine to administrative agency subpoena[a]), later cases have referred to the doctrine as based on the Fourth Amendment. See e.g., *United States v. Dionisio,* p. 695.

---

a. Speaking to petitioner's claim that enforcement of the subpoena duces tecum would violate rights secured by the Fourth Amendment, Justice Rutledge noted that the "short answer" to this contention was that "these cases present no question of actual search and seizure" as they involved no attempt by government officials "to enter petitioners' premises against their will, to search them, or to seize or examine their books." He later added: "The primary source of misconception concerning the Fourth Amendment's function lies perhaps in the identification of cases involving so-called 'figurative' or 'constructive' search with cases of actual search and seizure. Only in this analogical sense can any question related to search and seizure be thought to arise in situations which, like the present ones, involve only the validity of authorized judicial orders."

Accepting the Court's premise that the Fourth Amendment does apply to the subpoena duces tecum, why should the overbreadth doctrine be the sole Fourth Amendment limitation as to the subpoena duces tecum? Does *Hale* reflect a determination that the requirements of the Fourth Amendment's warrant clause were inapplicable in light of the long history of subpoenas issued without regard to probable cause (particularly in the trial context, see Fed.R.Crim.P. 17) and the lesser intrusion upon privacy (as compared to the traditional search), thereby leaving applicable only the Fourth Amendment's general mandate of reasonableness? See Wayne LaFave, *Search and Seizure* § 4.13(e) (3d ed. 1996). If so, *Hale* would be the forerunner of the various regulatory search cases that have eliminated the probable cause requirement for such searches. See Ch. 5, § 9. Consider also the suggestion that "the Court may have viewed a subpoena as falling within the Fourth Amendment only when it was clearly overbroad and thereby had the effect of a physical search in allowing the government to sift through a mass of documents while looking for the few that might be relevant." LaFave, Israel, and King, § 8.7(a).

5. *Applying the overbreadth doctrine.* Lower courts applying the overbreadth doctrine in the grand jury setting frequently note that the doctrine requires a fact-specific judgment, with each ruling tied to the circumstances of the individual case. At the same time, they have sought to develop some general criteria to guide their judgment. Initially, the subpoena carries with it a presumption of regularity that will be called into question only if the subpoena has "sufficient breadth to suggest either that compliance will be burdensome or that the subpoena's scope may not have been shaped to the purposes of the inquiry." LaFave, Israel, and King, § 8.7(c). If it has such breadth, the courts will then examine its scope in light of three criteria: (1) whether it "commands only the production of documents relevant to the investigation being pursued"; (2) whether the specification of the documents is made with "reasonable particularity" (measured in terms of both the subpoenaed party's ability to identify what "he is being asked to produce" and any "unreasonable business detriment" flowing from the quantity and range of the documents requested); and (3) whether the documents to be produced cover "only a reasonable period of time." Ibid. Applying these criteria, courts have upheld subpoenas requiring production of as much as 50 tons of documents. See *Petition of Borden*, 75 F.Supp. 857 (N.D.Ill.1948); yet they also have rejected requests for records that presumably could have occupied no more than a single filing cabinet, see *In re Certain Chinese Family Benevolent Assoc.*, 19 F.R.D. 97 (N.D.Cal.1956) (rejecting subpoenas requiring various Chinese family associations to produce available membership lists, income records, and membership photographs, dating back to the association's origin, for use in an investigation of immigration fraud). Much depends upon the nature of the investigation, as courts recognize that certain types of investigations, such as antitrust, necessarily demand a broader range of documents since the violation may be reflected in many aspects of a company's business. See also *In re Corrado Brothers*, 367 F.Supp. 1126 (D.Del.1973) (where the grand jury was investigating a kickback scheme involving the government highway department, all financial records were relevant since "cash for kickbacks can be readily generated by padding the * * * accounting records relating to a totally unrelated party"). Courts recognize also that "some exploration or fishing necessarily is inherent" since the grand jury will not ordinarily have a "catalogue of what books or papers exist nor any basis for knowing what their character or contents immediately are." *Schwimmer v. United States*, 232 F.2d 855 (8th Cir.1956). Although the overbreadth doctrine is a

separate ground for challenging a subpoena duces tecum, as to the federal courts, it may largely overlap with the Rule 17(c) objection discussed in *R. Enterprises* (p. 703).

6. *The subpoena ad testificandum.* The overbreadth doctrine is generally viewed as limited to a subpoena duces tecum requiring the production of documents. No Fourth Amendment objection is available to persons subpoenaed to testify or to provide an identification exemplar. Why not? Consider *United States v. Dionisio*, infra.

UNITED STATES v. DIONISIO
410 U.S. 1, 93 S.Ct. 764, 35 L.Ed.2d 67 (1973).

Justice STEWART delivered the opinion of the Court.

A special grand jury was convened in the Northern District of Illinois in February 1971, to investigate possible violations of federal criminal statutes relating to gambling. In the course of its investigation the grand jury received in evidence certain voice recordings that had been obtained pursuant to court orders. The grand jury subpoenaed approximately 20 persons, including the respondent Dionisio, seeking to obtain from them voice exemplars for comparison with the recorded conversations that had been received in evidence. Each witness was advised that he was a potential defendant in a criminal prosecution. Each was asked to examine a transcript of an intercepted conversation, and to go to a nearby office of the United States Attorney to read the transcript into a recording device. The witnesses were advised that they would be allowed to have their attorneys present when they read the transcripts. Dionisio and other witnesses refused to furnish the voice exemplars, asserting that these disclosures would violate their rights under the Fourth and Fifth Amendments. The Government then filed separate petitions in the District Court to compel Dionisio and the other witnesses to furnish the voice exemplars to the grand jury. * * * Following a hearing, the district judge rejected the witnesses' constitutional arguments and ordered them to comply with the grand jury's request. * * * When Dionisio persisted in his refusal to respond to the grand jury's directive, the District Court adjudged him in civil contempt and ordered him committed to custody. * * *

The Court of Appeals for the Seventh Circuit reversed. * * * The court found that the Fourth Amendment applied to the grand jury process * * *. Equating the procedures followed by the grand jury in the present case to the fingerprint detentions in *Davis v. Mississippi* [p. 336], the Court of Appeals reasoned that "[t]he dragnet effect here, where approximately 30 persons were subpoenaed for purposes of identification, has the same invidious effect on fourth amendment rights as the practice condemned in *Davis.*" The Court of Appeals held that the Fourth Amendment required a preliminary showing of reasonableness before a grand jury witness could be compelled to furnish a voice exemplar, and that in this case the proposed "seizures" of the voice exemplars would be unreasonable because of the large number of witnesses summoned by the grand jury and directed to produce such exemplars. We disagree. * * *

As [this] Court made clear in *Schmerber v. California* [p. 42], the obtaining of physical evidence from a person involves a potential Fourth Amendment violation at two different levels—the "seizure" of the "person" necessary to bring him into contact with government agents, see *Davis v. Mississippi,* and the subsequent search for and seizure of the evidence. * * * The constitutionality of the compulsory production of exemplars from a grand jury witness necessarily turns on the same dual inquiry—whether either the initial compulsion of the person to appear before the grand jury, or the subsequent directive to make a voice recording is an unreasonable "seizure" within the meaning of the Fourth Amendment.

It is clear that a subpoena to appear before a grand jury is not a "seizure" in the Fourth Amendment sense, even though that summons may be inconvenient or burdensome. Last Term we again acknowledged what has long been recognized, that "[c]itizens generally are not constitutionally immune from grand jury subpoenas...." *Branzburg v. Hayes* [p. 710]. * * * [*Branzburg* and other decisions] are recent reaffirmations of the historically grounded obligations of every person to appear and give his evidence before the grand jury. "The personal sacrifice involved is a part of the necessary contribution of the individual to the welfare of the public." *Blair v. United States* [Note 2, p. 685].

The compulsion exerted by a grand jury subpoena differs from the seizure effected by an arrest or even an investigative "stop" in more than civic obligation. For, as Judge Friendly wrote for the Court of Appeals for the Second Circuit:

> "The latter is abrupt, is effected with force or the threat of it and often in demeaning circumstances, and, in the case of arrest, results in a record involving social stigma. A subpoena is served in the same manner as other legal process; it involves no stigma whatever; if the time for appearance is inconvenient, this can generally be altered; and it remains at all times under the control and supervision of a court."

Thus, the Court of Appeals for the Seventh Circuit correctly recognized in a case subsequent to the one now before us, that a "grand jury subpoena to testify is not that kind of governmental intrusion on privacy against which the Fourth Amendment affords protection, once the Fifth Amendment is satisfied." * * *

This case is thus quite different from *Davis v. Mississippi*, on which the Court of Appeals primarily relied. For in *Davis* it was the initial seizure—the lawless dragnet detention—that violated the Fourth and Fourteenth Amendments—not the taking of the fingerprints. * * * *Davis* is plainly inapposite to a case where the initial restraint does not itself infringe the Fourth Amendment.

This is not to say that a grand jury subpoena is some talisman that dissolves all constitutional protections. The grand jury cannot require a witness to testify against himself. It cannot require the production by a person of private books and records that would incriminate him. See *Boyd v. United States*. The Fourth Amendment provides protection against a grand jury subpoena *duces tecum* too sweeping in its terms "to be regarded as reasonable." *Hale v. Henkel*. And last Term, in the context of a First Amendment claim, we indicated that the Constitution could not tolerate the transformation of the grand jury into an instrument of oppression: "Official harassment of the press undertaken not for purposes of law enforcement but to disrupt a reporter's relationship with his news sources would have no justification. Grand juries are subject to judicial control and subpoenas to motions to quash. We do not expect courts will forget that grand juries must operate within the limits of the First Amendment as well as the Fifth." *Branzburg v. Hayes*.

But we are here faced with no such constitutional infirmities in the subpoena to appear before the grand jury or in the order to make the voice recordings. There is * * * no valid Fifth Amendment claim. There was no order to produce private books and papers, and no sweeping subpoena *duces tecum*. And even if *Branzburg* be extended beyond its First Amendment moorings and tied to a more generalized due process concept, there is still no indication in this case of the kind of harassment that was of concern there.

The Court of Appeals found critical significance in the fact that the grand jury had summoned approximately 20 witnesses to furnish voice exemplars. We think that fact is basically irrelevant to the constitutional issues here. The grand jury may have been attempting to identify a number of voices on the tapes in evidence, or it might have summoned the 20 witnesses in an effort to identify one voice. But whatever the case, "[a] grand jury's investigation is not fully carried out until every available clue has been run down and all witnesses examined in every proper way to find if a crime has been committed." * * * The grand jury may well find it desirable to call numerous witnesses in the course of an investigation. It does not follow that each witness may resist a subpoena on the ground that too many witnesses have been called. Neither the order to Dionisio to appear, nor the order to make a voice recording was rendered unreasonable by the fact that many others were subjected to the same compulsion.

But the conclusion that Dionisio's compulsory appearance before the grand jury was not an unreasonable "seizure" is the answer to only the first part of the Fourth Amendment inquiry here. Dionisio argues that the grand jury's subsequent directive to make the voice recording was itself an infringement of his rights under the Fourth Amendment. We cannot accept that argument. In *Katz v. United States* [p. 155], we said that the Fourth Amendment provides no protection for what "a person knowingly exposes to the public, even in his home or office...." The physical characteristics of a person's voice, its tone and manner, as opposed to the content of a specific conversation, are constantly exposed to the public. Like a man's facial characteristics, or handwriting, his voice is repeatedly produced for others to hear. No person can have a reasonable expectation that others will not know the sound of his voice, any more than he can reasonably expect that his face will be a mystery to the world. * * *

Since neither the summons to appear before the grand jury, nor its directive to make a voice recording infringed upon any interest protected by the Fourth Amendment, there was no justification for requiring the grand jury to satisfy even the minimal requirement of "reasonableness" imposed by the Court of Appeals. A grand jury has broad investigative powers to determine whether a crime has been committed and who has committed it. The jurors may act on tips, rumors, evidence offered by the prosecutor, or their own personal knowledge. *Branzburg v. Hayes.* No grand jury witness is "entitled to set limits to the investigation that the grand jury may conduct." *Blair v. United States.* And a sufficient basis for an indictment may only emerge at the end of the investigation when all the evidence has been received. * * * Since Dionisio raised no valid Fourth Amendment claim, there is no more reason to require a preliminary showing of reasonableness here than there would be in the case of any witness who, despite the lack of any constitutional or statutory privilege, declined to answer a question or comply with a grand jury request. Neither the Constitution nor our prior cases justify any such interference with grand jury proceedings.[14]

---

14. Mr. Justice Marshall in dissent suggests that a preliminary showing of "reasonableness" is required where the grand jury subpoenas a witness to appear and produce handwriting or voice exemplars, but not when it subpoenas him to appear and testify. Such a distinction finds no support in the Constitution. The dissent argues that there is a poten- tial Fourth Amendment violation in the case of a subpoenaed grand jury witness because of the asserted intrusiveness of the initial subpoena to appear—the possible stigma from a grand jury appearance and the inconvenience of the official restraint. But the initial directive to appear is as intrusive if the witness is called

The Fifth Amendment guarantees that no civilian may be brought to trial for an infamous crime "unless on a presentment or indictment of a Grand Jury." This constitutional guarantee presupposes an investigative body "acting independently of either prosecuting attorney or judge," whose mission is to clear the innocent, no less than to bring to trial those who may be guilty. Any holding that would saddle a grand jury with minitrials and preliminary showing would assuredly impede its investigation and frustrate the public's interest in the fair and expeditious administration of the criminal laws. The grand jury may not always serve its historic role as a protective bulwark standing solidly between the ordinary citizen and an overzealous prosecutor, but if it is even to approach the proper performance of its constitutional mission, it must be free to pursue its investigations unhindered by external influence or supervision so long as it does not trench upon the legitimate rights of any witness called before it. * * *

Justice MARSHALL, dissenting.[a]

* * * There can be no question that investigatory seizures effected by the police are subject to the constraints of the Fourth and Fourteenth Amendments. *Davis v. Mississippi.* * * * Like *Davis,* the present cases involve official investigatory seizures which interfere with personal liberty. The Court considers dispositive, however, the fact that the seizures were effected by the grand jury, rather than the police. I cannot agree. * * * [I]n *Hale v. Henkel,* the Court held that a subpoena *duces tecum* ordering "the production of books and papers [before a grand jury] may constitute an unreasonable search and seizure within the Fourth Amendment," and on the particular facts of the case, it concluded that the subpoena was "far too sweeping in its terms to be regarded as reasonable." Considered alone, *Hale* would certainly seem to carry a strong implication that a subpoena compelling an individual's personal appearance before a grand jury, like a subpoena ordering the production of private papers, is subject to the Fourth Amendment standard of reasonableness. The protection of the Fourth Amendment is not, after all, limited to personal "papers," but extends also to "persons," "houses," and "effects." It would seem a strange hierarchy of constitutional values that would afford papers more protection from arbitrary governmental intrusion than people.

The Court, however, offers two interrelated justifications for excepting grand jury subpoenas directed at "persons," rather than "papers," from the constraints of the Fourth Amendment. These are an "historically grounded obligation of every person to appear and give his evidence before the grand jury" [p. 696], and the relative unintrusiveness of the grand jury subpoena on an individual's liberty.

In my view, the Court makes more of history than is justified. The Court treats the "historically grounded obligation" which it now discerns as extending to all "evidence," whatever its character. Yet, so far as I am aware, the obligation "to appear and give evidence" has heretofore been applied by this Court only in the context of testimonial evidence, either oral or documentary. * * * In the present case, * * * it was not testimony that the grand jury sought from respondents, but physical evidence. * * *

simply to testify as it is if he is summoned to produce physical evidence.

a. In the companion case of *United States v. Mara,* 410 U.S. 19, 93 S.Ct. 774, 35 L.Ed.2d 99 (1973), the Court applied *Dionisio* to reject a lower court ruling that a preliminary showing of reasonableness was needed to justify a grand jury subpoena directing a witness to produce handwriting exemplars for the purpose of determining whether he was the author of certain writings. Justice Marshall's dissent was to both rulings. The separate dissents of Justices Douglas and Brennan are omitted.

The Court seems to reason that the exception to the Fourth Amendment for grand jury subpoenas directed at persons is justified by the relative unintrusiveness of the grand jury process on an individual's liberty. * * * It may be that service of a grand jury subpoena does not involve the same potential for momentary embarrassment as does an arrest or investigatory "stop." But this difference seems inconsequential in comparison to the substantial stigma which—contrary to the Court's assertion—may result from a grand jury appearance as well as from an arrest or investigatory seizure. Public knowledge that a man has been summoned by a federal grand jury investigating, for instance, organized criminal activity can mean loss of friends, irreparable injury to business, and tremendous pressures on one's family life. Whatever nice legal distinctions may be drawn between police and prosecutor, on the one hand, and the grand jury, on the other, the public often treats an appearance before a grand jury as tantamount to a visit to the station house. Indeed, the former is frequently more damaging than the latter, for a grand jury appearance has an air of far greater gravity than a brief visit "downtown" for a "talk." The Fourth Amendment was placed in our Bill of Rights to protect the individual citizen from such potentially disruptive governmental intrusion into his private life unless conducted reasonably and with sufficient cause.

Nor do I believe that the constitutional problems inherent in such governmental interference with an individual's person are substantially alleviated because one may seek to appear at a "convenient time." In *Davis v. Mississippi,* it was recognized that an investigatory detention effected by the police "need not come unexpectedly or at an inconvenient time." But this fact did not suggest to the Court that the Fourth Amendment was inapplicable * * *. No matter how considerate a grand jury may be in arranging for an individual's appearance, the basic fact remains that his liberty has been officially restrained for some period of time. In terms of its effect on the individual, this restraint does not differ meaningfully from the restraint imposed on a suspect compelled to visit the police station house. Thus, the nature of the intrusion on personal liberty caused by a grand jury subpoena cannot, without more, be considered sufficient basis for denying respondents the protection of the Fourth Amendment.

Of course, the Fourth Amendment does not bar all official seizures of the person, but only those that are unreasonable and are without sufficient cause. With this in mind, it is possible at least to explain, if not justify, the failure to apply the protection of the Fourth Amendment to grand jury subpoenas requiring individuals to appear and *testify.* Thus, while it is true that we have traditionally given the grand jury broad investigatory powers, particularly in terms of compelling the appearance of persons before it, *Blair v. United States,* it must be understood that we have done so in heavy reliance on certain essential assumptions.

Certainly the most celebrated function of the grand jury is to stand between the Government and the citizen and thus to protect the latter from harassment and unfounded prosecution. The grand jury does not shed those characteristics which give it insulating qualities when it acts in its investigative capacity. Properly functioning, the grand jury is to be the servant of neither the Government nor the courts, but of the people. As such, we assume that it comes to its task without bias or self-interest. Unlike the prosecutor or policeman, it has no election to win or executive appointment to keep. The anticipated neutrality of the grand jury, even when acting in its investigative capacity, may perhaps be relied upon to prevent unwarranted interference with the lives of private citizens and to ensure that the grand jury's subpoena powers over the person are exercised in only a reasonable fashion. Under such circumstances, it may be justifiable to give the grand jury broad personal subpoena powers that are outside the purview of the Fourth Amendment, for—in contrast to the police—it is not likely that it will abuse those powers.

Whatever the present day validity of the historical assumption of neutrality which underlies the grand jury process, it must at least be recognized that if a grand jury is deprived of the independence essential to the assumption of neutrality—if it effectively surrenders that independence to a prosecutor—the dangers of excessive and unreasonable official interference with personal liberty are exactly those which the Fourth Amendment was intended to prevent. So long as the grand jury carries on its investigatory activities only through the mechanism of testimonial inquiries, the danger of such official usurpation of the grand jury process may not be unreasonably great. Individuals called to testify before the grand jury will have available their Fifth Amendment privilege against self-incrimination. Thus, at least insofar as incriminating information is sought directly from a particular criminal suspect, the grand jury process would not appear to offer law enforcement officials a substantial advantage over ordinary investigative techniques.

But when we move beyond the realm of grand jury investigations limited to testimonial inquiries, as the Court does today, the danger increases that law enforcement officials may seek to usurp the grand jury process for the purpose of securing incriminating evidence from a particular suspect through the simple expedient of a subpoena. * * * Thus, if the grand jury may summon criminal suspects [to obtain handwriting and voice exemplars] without complying with the Fourth Amendment, it will obviously present an attractive investigative tool to prosecutor and police. For what law enforcement officers could not accomplish directly themselves after our decision in *Davis v. Mississippi,* they may now accomplish indirectly through the grand jury process.

Thus, the Court's decisions today can serve only to encourage prosecutorial exploitation of the grand jury process, at the expense of both individual liberty and the traditional neutrality of the grand jury. * * * [B]y holding that the grand jury's power to subpoena these respondents for the purpose of obtaining exemplars is completely outside the purview of the Fourth Amendment, the Court fails to appreciate the essential difference between real and testimonial evidence in the context of these cases, and thereby hastens the reduction of the grand jury into simply another investigative device of law enforcement officials. By contrast, the Court of Appeals, in proper recognition of these dangers, imposed narrow limitations on the subpoena power of the grand jury which are necessary to guard against unreasonable official interference with individual liberty but which would not impair significantly the traditional investigatory powers of that body. * * *

Notes and Questions

1. *Subpoenas and "seizures."* Are there any circumstances under which a grand jury subpoena might be viewed as producing "a 'seizure' in the Fourth Amendment sense" (see *Dionisio* at p. 696)? What if the subpoena calls for "forthwith" compliance, i.e., the immediate production of evidence for presentation to the grand jury or the immediate appearance of the witness before the grand jury? See Beale et al., § 6.14: "The use of forthwith subpoenas also raises Fourth Amendment issues. Because the subpoena's process lacks the safeguards of a probable cause requirement and the prior approval of a neutral magistrate which apply to the process of obtaining a warrant, the courts are agreed that a forthwith subpoena cannot be used to substitute for a search or arrest warrant.

Accordingly, several courts have held that a forthwith subpoena does not give government agents the right to seize the person or items subpoenaed in the face of a refusal to comply with the subpoena's terms. If the persons who serve the subpoena seize the subpoenaed materials without consent, the seizure violates the Fourth Amendment. Whether consent was given turns on whether the subpoenaed party's compliance was voluntary or occurred in response to the compelling presence of government agents. "[b]

2. *Other identification procedures.* Does the reasoning of *Dionisio* extend to a grand jury subpoena directing the subpoenaed party to appear in a lineup? Several courts have held that it does, although some (to preclude the use of such orders simply to assist a police investigation, see Note 1, p. 713) have required that such a subpoena be approved by the grand jury itself. See *In re Melvin,* 546 F.2d 1 (1st Cir.1976). Considering, however, *In re Kelley,* 433 A.2d 704 (D.C.App. 1981) (en banc). The court there had earlier held that police could obtain a court order directing a non-arrested suspect to appear in a lineup upon a *Terry v. Ohio* (p. 304) showing of reasonable suspicion [see Note 4, at pp. 673–74]. However, the government here "candidly acknowledged" that it had put that procedure "in mothballs," and relying on *Dionisio,* had utilized a "grand jury pass-through"— i.e., the "government now passes such police requests through the grand jury and thereby obtains grand jury lineup directives." The court initially rejected the government's reliance on *Dionisio,* noting that *Dionisio*'s Fourth Amendment ruling dealt only with a summons to present evidence such as a voice sample or handwriting exemplar. A lineup, it noted, was a substantially different process: "A lineup appearance is not simply showing one's face to the public. It involves considerable social stigma and personal risk. It entails the humiliation of standing on a stage under floodlights, removed from counsel, subject to being compelled to speak certain words and perform actions directed by the police, all at considerably more risk of mistake and misidentification that the more scientifically grounded fingerprinting and, to some extent, voiceprinting techniques involved in *Dionisio* and *Mara.*"

The *Kelley* court concluded, however, that there was no need to decide whether *Dionisio*'s rejection of a Fourth Amendment restraint should apply as well to lineups. This was an appropriate setting for use of its supervisory power to avoid "the appearance of, or potential for, abuse of the grand jury system" inherent in the government's pass-through procedure. Accordingly, in the exercise of that power, it would hold that "a prosecutor seeking judicial enforcement of a grand jury directive to appear in a lineup must, by affidavit of law enforcement officer or * * * [prosecutor], make a minimal factual showing sufficient to permit the judge to conclude that there is a reason for the lineup which is consistent with the legitimate function of the grand jury." Consider also, *In re May 1991 Will County Grand Jury,* 604 N.E.2d 929 (Ill.1992) (with state constitutional counterpart of Fourth Amendment providing "greater protection than *Dionisio,*" grand jury subpoena for physical evidence of a "noninvasive nature, such as in-person appearance in a lineup or fingerprinting," requires some showing of individualized

---

b. "Because of the potential for abuse and the unfairness that can result from requiring an immediate response from a witness, a Department of Justice internal policy limits the use of forthwith subpoenas. The policy requires prosecutors to consider the following in deciding if a forthwith subpoena is warranted: (I) the risk of flight; (ii) the risk that evidence will be destroyed or fabricated; (iii) the need for the orderly presentation of evidence to the grand jury; and (iv) the degree of inconvenience to the witness. A forthwith subpoena must be approved in advance by the U.S. Attorney. Like other Department of Justice policies, this policy does not create any rights that can be enforced against the government." Brenner and Lockhart, § 14.5

suspicion as well as relevance to the investigation; *Dionisio* must be read in light of cases like *Winston v. Lee* (p. 250) and *Schmerber* (pp. 42, 250), so a grand jury subpoena for pubic hair samples requires a showing of probable cause under both Fourth Amendment and state constitution). Courts have divided as to the showing needed for a grand jury subpoena for a blood sample. See *Woolverton v. Multi–County Grand Jury*, 859 P.2d 1112(Okla.Cr.App.1993) (probable cause); *Henry v. Ryan*, 775 F.Supp. 247 (N.D.Ill.1991) ("individualized suspicion").

3. *Underlying Fourth Amendment violations.* In UNITED STATES v. CALANDRA, 414 U.S. 338, 94 S.Ct. 613, 38 L.Ed.2d 561 (1974), grand jury witness Calandra was asked questions about certain records (evidencing "loan-sharking" activities) that had been seized by federal agents in connection with a search of Calandra's office. Calandra initially invoked his privilege against self-incrimination, but subsequently was granted immunity. He then requested and received a postponement of the grand jury proceedings so that he could present a pre-charge motion for return and suppression of the seized evidence under Federal Rule 41(e). The district court granted the motion, holding that the search had been unconstitutional. The district court also held that "Calandra need not answer any of the grand jury's questions based on suppressed evidence," since such questions constituted the fruit of the poisonous tree. A divided Supreme Court (6–3), per POWELL, J., reversed.

"In deciding whether to extend the exclusionary rule to grand jury proceedings, we must weigh the potential injury to the historic role and functions of the grand jury against the potential benefits of the rule as applied in this context. It is evident that this extension of the exclusionary rule would seriously impede the grand jury. Because the grand jury does not finally adjudicate guilt or innocence, it has traditionally been allowed to pursue its investigative and accusatorial functions unimpeded by the evidentiary and procedural restrictions applicable to a criminal trial. Permitting witnesses to invoke the exclusionary rule before a grand jury would precipitate adjudication of issues hitherto reserved for the trial on the merits and would delay and disrupt grand jury proceedings. Suppression hearings would halt the orderly progress of an investigation and might necessitate extended litigation of issues only tangentially related to the grand jury's primary objective. The probable result would be 'protracted interruptions of grand jury proceedings,' effectively transforming them into preliminary trials on the merits. In some cases the delay might be fatal to the enforcement of the criminal law. Just last Term we reaffirmed our disinclination to allow litigious interference with grand jury proceedings. *United States v. Dionisio*.

"Against this potential damage to the role and functions of the grand jury, we must weigh the benefits to be derived from this proposed extension of the exclusionary rule. * * * [The Court here considered the "incremental deterrent effect which might be achieved by extending the exclusionary rule to grand jury proceedings," and for reasons discussed in Note 1, p. 146, found "unrealistic" the assumption that such an extension would significantly further deterrence of illegal searches.] We decline to embrace a view that would achieve a speculative and undoubtedly minimal advance in the deterrence of police misconduct at the expense of substantially impeding the role of the grand jury."[a]

a. In *Gelbard v. United States*, 408 U.S. 41, 92 S.Ct. 2357, 33 L.Ed.2d 179 (1972), the Court held that the broad exclusionary remedy of the Omnibus Crime Control Act (see fn. f, p. 369) gave grand jury witnesses the right to object to the grand jury's use of information derived from illegal electronic surveillance.

SECTION 3. OTHER OBJECTIONS TO THE INVESTIGATION

UNITED STATES v. R. ENTERPRISES, INC.

498 U.S. 292, 111 S.Ct. 722, 112 L.Ed.2d 795 (1991).

Justice O'CONNOR delivered the opinion of the Court.

This case requires the Court to decide what standards apply when a party seeks to avoid compliance with a subpoena *duces tecum* issued in connection with a grand jury investigation.

Since 1986, a federal grand jury sitting in the Eastern District of Virginia has been investigating allegations of interstate transportation of obscene materials. In early 1988, the grand jury issued a series of subpoenas to three companies—Model Magazine Distributors, Inc. (Model), R. Enterprises, Inc., and MFR Court Street Books, Inc. (MFR). Model is a New York distributor of sexually oriented paperback books, magazines, and videotapes. R. Enterprises, which distributes adult materials, and MFR, which sells books, magazines, and videotapes, are also based in New York. All three companies are wholly owned by Martin Rothstein. The grand jury subpoenas sought a variety of corporate books and records and, in Model's case, copies of 193 videotapes that Model had shipped to retailers in the Eastern District of Virginia. All three companies moved to quash the subpoenas, arguing that the subpoenas called for production of materials irrelevant to the grand jury's investigation and that the enforcement of the subpoenas would likely infringe their First Amendment rights.

The District Court, after extensive hearings, denied the motions to quash. As to Model, the court found that the subpoenas for business records were sufficiently specific and that production of the videotapes would not constitute a prior restraint. As to R. Enterprises, the court found a "sufficient connection with Virginia for further investigation by the grand jury." The court relied in large part on the statement attributed to Rothstein that the three companies were "all the same thing, I'm president of all three." Additionally, the court explained in denying MFR's motion to quash that it was "inclined to agree" with "the majority of the jurisdictions," which do not require the Government to make a "threshold showing" before a grand jury subpoena will be enforced. Even assuming that a preliminary showing of relevance was required, the court determined that the Government had made such a showing. It found sufficient evidence that the companies were "related entities," at least one of which "certainly did ship sexually explicit material into the Commonwealth of Virginia." * * * Notwithstanding these findings, the companies refused to comply with the subpoenas. The District Court found each in contempt and fined them $500 per day, but stayed imposition of the fine pending appeal.

The Court of Appeals for the Fourth Circuit upheld the business records subpoenas issued to Model, but remanded the motion to quash the subpoena for Model's videotapes. Of particular relevance here, the Court of Appeals quashed the business records subpoenas issued to R. Enterprises and MFR. In doing so, it applied the standards set out by this Court in *United States v. Nixon,* 418 U.S. 683, 94 S.Ct. 3090, 41 L.Ed.2d 1039 (1974). The court recognized that *Nixon* dealt with a trial subpoena, not a grand jury subpoena, but determined that the rule was "equally applicable" in the grand jury context. Accordingly, it required the Government to clear the three hurdles that *Nixon* established in the trial context—relevancy, admissibility, and specificity—in order to enforce the grand jury subpoenas. The court concluded that the challenged subpoenas did not satisfy the *Nixon* standards, finding no evidence in the record that either company had ever shipped materials into, or otherwise conducted business in, the Eastern District of Virginia. The Court of Appeals specifically criticized the District Court for drawing an inference that, because Rothstein owned all three businesses and one of them had undoubtedly shipped sexually explicit materials into the Eastern District of Virginia, there might be some link between the Eastern District of Virginia and R. Enterprises or MFR. It then noted that "any evidence concerning Mr. Rothstein's alleged business activities outside of Virginia, or his ownership of companies which distribute allegedly obscene materials outside of Virginia, would most likely be inadmissible on relevancy grounds at any trial that might occur," and that the subpoenas therefore failed "to meet the requirements [*sic*] that any documents subpoenaed under [Federal] Rule [of Criminal Procedure] 17(c) must be admissible as evidence at trial," citing *Nixon*. The Court of Appeals did not consider whether enforcement of the subpoenas *duces tecum* issued to respondents implicated the First Amendment.

We granted certiorari to determine whether the Court of Appeals applied the proper standard in evaluating the grand jury subpoenas issued to respondents. We now reverse.

The grand jury occupies a unique role in our criminal justice system. * * * [It] "can investigate merely on suspicion that the law is being violated, or even just because it wants assurance that it is not." * * * As a necessary consequence of its investigatory function, the grand jury paints with a broad brush. * * * A grand jury subpoena is thus much different from a subpoena issued in the context of a prospective criminal trial, where a specific offense has been identified and a particular defendant charged. * * *

This Court has emphasized on numerous occasions that many of the rules and restrictions that apply at a trial do not apply in grand jury proceedings. This is especially true of evidentiary restrictions. The same rules that, in an adversary hearing on the merits may increase the likelihood of accurate determinations of guilt or innocence do not necessarily advance the mission of a grand jury, whose task is to conduct an *ex parte* investigation to determine whether or not there is probable cause to prosecute a particular defendant. * * * The teaching of the Court's decisions is clear: A grand jury "may compel the production of evidence or the testimony of witnesses as it considers appropriate, and its operation generally is unrestrained by the technical procedural and evidentiary rules governing the conduct of criminal trials." *United States v. Calandra.*

This guiding principle renders suspect the Court of Appeals' holding that the standards announced in *Nixon* as to subpoenas issued in anticipation of trial apply equally in the grand jury context. The multifactor test announced in *Nixon* would invite procedural delays and detours while courts evaluate the relevancy and admissibility of documents sought by a particular subpoena. We have expressly stated that grand jury proceedings should be free of such delays. * * * *United States v. Dionisio.* Additionally, application of the *Nixon* test in this context ignores that grand jury proceedings are subject to strict secrecy requirements. See Fed.Rule Crim.Proc. 6(e). Requiring the Government to explain in too much detail the particular reasons underlying a subpoena threatens to compromise "the indispensable secrecy of grand jury proceedings." Broad disclosure also affords the targets of investigation far more information about the grand jury's internal workings than the Federal Rules of Criminal Procedure appear to contemplate.

The investigatory powers of the grand jury are nevertheless not unlimited. Grand juries are not licensed to engage in arbitrary fishing expeditions, nor may they select targets of investigation out of malice or an intent to harass. In this case, the focus of our inquiry is the limit imposed on a grand jury by Federal Rule of Criminal Procedure 17(c), which governs the issuance of subpoenas *duces tecum* in federal criminal proceedings. The Rule provides that "the court on motion made promptly may quash or modify the subpoena if compliance would be unreasonable or oppressive."

This standard is not self-explanatory. As we have observed, "what is reasonable depends on the context." In *Nixon,* this Court defined what is reasonable in the context of a jury trial. We determined that, in order to require production of information prior to trial, a party must make a reasonably specific request for information that would be both relevant and admissible at trial. But, for the reasons we have explained above, the *Nixon* standard does not apply in the context of grand jury proceedings. In the grand jury context, the decision as to what offense will be charged is routinely not made until after the grand jury has concluded its investigation. One simply cannot know in advance whether information sought during the investigation will be relevant and admissible in a prosecution for a particular offense.

To the extent that Rule 17(c) imposes some reasonableness limitation on grand jury subpoenas, however, our task is to define it. In doing so, we recognize that a party to whom a grand jury subpoena is issued faces a difficult situation. As a rule, grand juries do not announce publicly the subjects of their investigations. A party who desires to challenge a grand jury subpoena thus may have no conception of the Government's purpose in seeking production of the requested information. Indeed, the party will often not know whether he or she is a primary target of the investigation or merely a peripheral witness. Absent even minimal information, the subpoena recipient is likely to find it exceedingly difficult to persuade a court that "compliance would be unreasonable." As one pair of commentators has summarized it, the challenging party's "unenviable task is to seek to persuade the court that the subpoena that has been served on [him or her] could not possibly serve any investigative purpose that the grand jury could legitimately be pursuing." S. Beale & W. Bryson, Grand Jury Law and Practice § 6:28 (1986).

Our task is to fashion an appropriate standard of reasonableness, one that gives due weight to the difficult position of subpoena recipients but does not impair the strong governmental interests in affording grand juries wide latitude, avoiding minitrials on peripheral matters, and preserving a necessary level of secrecy. We begin by reiterating that the law presumes, absent a strong showing to the contrary, that a grand jury acts within the legitimate scope of its authority. * * * Consequently, a grand jury subpoena issued through normal channels is presumed to be reasonable, and the burden of showing unreasonableness must be on the recipient who seeks to avoid compliance. Indeed, this result is indicated by the language of Rule 17(c), which permits a subpoena to be quashed only "on motion" and "if *compliance* would be unreasonable" (emphasis added). To the extent that the Court of Appeals placed an initial burden on the Government, it committed error. Drawing on the principles articulated above, we conclude that where, as here, a subpoena is challenged on relevancy grounds, the motion to quash must be denied unless the district court determines that there is no reasonable possibility that the category of materials the Government seeks will produce information relevant to the general subject of the grand jury's investigation. Respondents did not challenge the subpoenas as being too indefinite nor did they claim that compliance would be overly burdensome. The Court of Appeals accordingly did not consider these aspects of the subpoenas, nor do we.

It seems unlikely, of course, that a challenging party who does not know the general subject matter of the grand jury's investigation, no matter how valid that party's claim, will be able to make the necessary showing that compliance would be unreasonable. After all, a subpoena recipient "cannot put his whole life before the court in order to show that there is no crime to be investigated." Consequently, a court may be justified in a case where unreasonableness is alleged in requiring the Government to reveal the general subject of the grand jury's investigation before requiring the challenging party to carry its burden of persuasion.[a] We need not resolve this question in the present case, however, as there is no doubt that respondents knew the subject of the grand jury investigation pursuant to which the business records subpoenas were issued. In cases where the recipient of the subpoena does not know the nature of the investigation, we are confident that district courts will be able to craft appropriate procedures that balance the interests of the subpoena recipient against the strong governmental interests in maintaining secrecy, preserving investigatory flexibility, and avoiding procedural delays. For example, to ensure that subpoenas are not routinely challenged as a form of discovery, a district court may require that the Government reveal the subject of the investigation to the trial court *in camera*, so that the court may determine whether the motion to quash has a reasonable prospect for success before it discloses the subject matter to the challenging party.[b]

Applying these principles in this case demonstrates that the District Court correctly denied respondents' motions to quash. It is undisputed that all three companies—Model, R. Enterprises, and MFR—are owned by the same person, that all do business in the same area, and that one of the three, Model, has shipped sexually explicit materials into the Eastern District of Virginia. The District Court could have concluded from these facts that there was a reasonable possibility that the business records of R. Enterprises and MFR would produce information relevant to the grand jury's investigation into the interstate transportation of obscene materials. Respondents' blanket denial of any connection to Virginia did not suffice to render the District Court's conclusion invalid. A grand jury need not accept on faith the self-serving assertions of those who may have committed criminal acts. Rather, it is entitled to determine for itself whether a crime has been committed.

Both in the District Court and in the Court of Appeals, respondents contended that these subpoenas sought records relating to First Amendment activities, and that this required the Government to demonstrate that the records were particularly relevant to its investigation. The Court of Appeals determined that the subpoenas did not satisfy Rule 17(c) and thus did not pass on the First Amendment issue. We express no view on this issue and leave it to be resolved by the Court of Appeals. * * *

Justice STEVENS, with whom Justices MARSHALL and BLACKMUN join, concurring in part and concurring in the judgment.

a. The United States Attorneys' Manual directs that subpoenas contain an "advice of rights" statement (see Note 2, p. 725), which includes the following: "The grand jury is conducting an investigation of possible violations of federal criminal laws involving: (State here the general subject matter of inquiry, e.g., the conducting of an illegal gambling business in violation of 18 U.S.C. § 1955)." U.S.A.M. 9–11.150.

b. Justice Scalia did not join this paragraph of the Court's opinion.

Federal Rule of Criminal Procedure 17(c) * * * requires the district court to balance the burden of compliance, on the one hand, against the governmental interest in obtaining the documents on the other. A more burdensome subpoena should be justified by a somewhat higher degree of probable relevance than a subpoena that imposes a minimal or nonexistent burden. Against the procedural history of this case, the Court has attempted to define the term "reasonable" in the abstract, looking only at the relevance side of the balance. Because I believe that this truncated approach to the Rule will neither provide adequate guidance to the district court nor place any meaningful constraint on the overzealous prosecutor, I add these comments. * * *

The moving party has the initial task of demonstrating to the Court that he has some valid objection to compliance. This showing might be made in various ways. Depending on the volume and location of the requested materials, the mere cost in terms of time, money, and effort of responding to a dragnet subpoena could satisfy the initial hurdle. Similarly, if a witness showed that compliance with the subpoena would intrude significantly on his privacy interests, or call for the disclosure of trade secrets or other confidential information, further inquiry would be required. Or, as in this case, the movant might demonstrate that compliance would have First Amendment implications.

The trial court need inquire into the relevance of subpoenaed materials only after the moving party has made this initial showing. And, as is true in the parallel context of pretrial civil discovery, a matter also committed to the sound discretion of the trial judge, the degree of need sufficient to justify denial of the motion to quash will vary to some extent with the burden of producing the requested information. For the reasons stated by the Court, in the grand jury context the law enforcement interest will almost always prevail, and the documents must be produced. I stress, however, that the Court's opinion should not be read to suggest that the deferential relevance standard the Court has formulated will govern decision in every case, no matter how intrusive or burdensome the request. * * *

Notes and Questions

1. *The Schofield Approach.* In IN RE GRAND JURY PROCEEDINGS (*Schofield*), 486 F.2d 85 (3d Cir.1973), a pre-*R. Enterprises* ruling, the Third Circuit adopted an approach to relevancy objections that was distinctive among the federal circuits. The petitioner there had refused to comply with a subpoena directing her to provide handwriting samples, photographs, and fingerprints to the grand jury, and the government had sought to have her held in civil contempt. The Third Circuit concluded that the petitioner could not be found in contempt since the government had failed to show that the items sought were "relevant to the grand jury's investigation of an offense falling within its jurisdiction." The Court (per GIBBONS, J.) reasoned:

"In view of the fact that information which would justify obtaining the handwriting exemplars, fingerprints, and a mug shot, is in the Government's sole possession, we think it reasonable that the Government be required to make some preliminary showing by affidavit that each item is at least relevant to an investigation being conducted by the grand jury and properly within its jurisdiction, and is not sought primarily for another purpose. We impose this requirement both pursuant to the federal courts' supervisory power over grand juries and pursuant to our supervisory power over civil [contempt] proceedings brought in the district court pursuant to 28 U.S.C. § 1826(a). We do not rule out the possibility that the Government's affidavit may be presented to the court *in* *camera,* but we do hold that Rule 6(e) does not require *in camera* presentation. * * * [U]nless extraordinary circumstances appear, the nature of which we cannot anticipate, the Government's supporting affidavit should be disclosed to the witness in the enforcement proceeding. If after such disclosure the witness makes application to the district court for additional discovery in the enforcement proceeding, the court must in deciding that request weigh the quite limited scope of an inquiry into abuse of the subpoena process, and the potential for delay, against any need for additional information which might cast doubt upon the accuracy of the Government's representations."

As noted in Beale et al., § 6.21, the Third Circuit has "generally deferred to the district courts' judgments about the sufficiency of particular '*Schofield* affidavits' in the circumstances of each case," and it accordingly has affirmed rulings holding "adequate even 'scanty' affidavits which describe the relevance of the subpoenaed material and the purpose of the grand jury material in only general terms." See e.g., *In re Grand Jury, Schmidt,* 619 F.2d 1022 (3d Cir.1980) (affidavit identified particular manufacturing practice under investigation, noted possible statutes violated, and identified witnesses as employees likely to be familiar with the practice and the whereabouts of relevant records). Even so interpreted, is the *Schofield* requirement consistent with the discussion in *R. Enterprises* of the applicable standard of reasonableness and the district court's authority in crafting appropriate procedures for relevancy challenges? Does *R. Enterprises* recognize that Rule 17 (c) restrictions go beyond Fourth Amendment requirements (as assumed in *Schofield*)?

2. *Schofield* was subsequently applied to witness refusals to testify as well as refusals to comply with a subpoena *duces tecum.* However, where the witness cited for contempt had refused to give testimony, *Schofield's* relevancy element was held to require a showing of relevancy only as to the general subject matter of the total group of questions rather than as to specific questions. See *In re Grand Jury Investigation (Bruno),* 545 F.2d 385 (3d Cir.1976). Since *R. Enterprises* was based on Rule 17(c), which refers only to a subpoena *duces tecum,* does it allow for application of a similar standard of relevancy (either as to a general group of questions or as to specific questions) with respect to witness testimony? Consider also the statement of *Blair,* Note 2, p. 685, as to witness objections to relevancy. Compare *Ex parte Jennings,* 240 S.W. 942 (Tex.Cr.App.1922) (to establish contempt, prosecutor must establish compliance with the statutory requirement that he first announced the "subject matter under investigation" and then asked "pertinent questions relative to the transaction in general terms").

3. *Subject matter challenges.* After commenting generally upon the scope of the grand jury's investigative authority and the corresponding obligations and rights of grand jury witnesses [see Note 2, p. 685], the Court in *Blair v. United States,* 250 U.S. 273, 39 S.Ct. 468, 63 L.Ed. 979 (1919), quickly disposed of the petitioners' claim that their refusal to testify was justified because the subject under investigation (possible violations of the Federal Corrupt Practices Act in the course of a primary election) was beyond the regulatory authority of the federal government. Justice Pitney noted for the Court: "And for the same reasons, witnesses are not entitled to take exception to the jurisdiction of the grand jury or the court over the particular subject-matter that is under investigation. In truth it is in the ordinary case no concern of one summoned as a witness whether the offense is within the jurisdiction of the court or not. At least, the court and grand jury have authority and jurisdiction to investigate the facts in order to determine the question whether the facts show a case within their jurisdiction. The present cases are not exceptional, and for the reasons that have been outlined we are of

opinion that appellants were not entitled to raise any question about the constitutionality of the statutes under which the grand jury's investigation was conducted."

Prior to *R. Enterprises,* lower courts had divided as to whether *Blair* precluded consideration of a witness' objection that a grand jury inquiry concerns alleged criminal activity having no bearing upon the district in which the grand jury sits (and therefore activity for which the grand jury may not indict). Does *R. Enterprises* now make that a cognizable objection (albeit one difficult to sustain)? What of the challenge raised in *In re Sealed Case,* 827 F.2d 776 (D.C.Cir.1987)— that the grand jury subpoena was issued upon application of the office Independent Counsel and "that office violated constitutional principles of separation of powers"? In *Morrison v. Olson,* 487 U.S. 654, 108 S.Ct. 2597, 101 L.Ed.2d 569 (1988), the Court reached the merits of that claim (and rejected it), but noted that the Independent Counsel had failed to object in the district court to consideration of the merits of the challenge to her office, and such an objection, "is not 'jurisdictional' in the sense that it cannot be waived by failing to raise it at the proper time and place." As discussed in Notes 1–4 at pp. 713–14, federal courts have long held cognizable challenges to alleged prosecutorial misuse of grand jury subpoenas.

NOTES ON SPECIAL–BURDEN OBJECTIONS

1. *First Amendment challenges.* On remand in *R. Enterprises,* the Fourth Circuit rejected the First Amendment claim that has not been considered by the Supreme Court. See IN RE GRAND JURY 87–3 SUBPOENA DUCES TECUM, 955 F.2d 229 (4th Cir.1992). The court (per ERVIN, J.) refused to adopt the "substantial relationship" test that had been urged by the petitioners. Under that test, once the recipient of a subpoena "makes a prima facie showing of arguable First Amendment infringement," the prosecution has "the burden of establishing that the subpoena serves a compelling governmental interest and the requested evidence substantially relates to the investigation." Judge Ervin acknowledged that such a standard had been adopted by the Ninth Circuit in *Bursey v. United States,* 466 F.2d 1059 (9th Cir.1972), but refused to follow that ruling. *Bursey* had involved a grand jury's demand that two witnesses, employees of a newspaper published by a radical organization (the Black Panthers), furnish it with information about the identity and activities of persons who worked on the paper and who were members of the Black Panthers. The information was sought in connection with a grand jury investigation of threats against the president and incitements to insubordination of the armed forces, including reported speeches of a Black Panther leader. Relying on Supreme Court cases involving governmental demands for membership information in other settings, e.g., *Gibson v. Florida Legislative Investigation Committee,* 372 U.S. 539, 83 S.Ct. 889, 9 L.Ed.2d 929 (1963) (legislative investigation), the *Bursey* court had concluded that such a demand could only be sustained upon a governmental showing "that its interests [in the information] are legitimate and compelling and that the incidental infringement upon First Amendment rights is no greater than is essential to vindicating its subordinating interests." In the grand jury context, this would require a showing (not present in *Bursey*) "that there is a substantial possibility that the information sought will expose criminal activities within the compelling subject matter of the investigation."

The Fourth Circuit in *In re Grand Jury 87–3* initially noted that the case before it arguably could be distinguished from *Bursey.* While that case involved "a crackdown on political dissidents," the government contended that the subpoenas here involved only "typical business records." However, it added: "[T]o refer to the grand jury's subpoenas here as business records subpoenas may be something of a euphemism. It appears that the government may really be after R. Enterprises' customer lists. In such a case, all the government need do is threaten this sort of subpoena, and, if word of it leaked, the business of any enterprise would dry up. Therefore, a business records subpoena can potentially have a very chilling effect."

The Fourth Circuit found the more compelling reason for rejecting the substantial relationship test to be Supreme Court precedent. It relied in particular on *Branzburg v. Hayes,* 408 U.S. 665, 92 S.Ct. 2646, 33 L.Ed.2d 626 (1972), which had also involved a grand jury setting. *Branzburg* considered the claims of newspaper reporters that they should not be compelled to testify before the grand jury as to the identity of confidential sources, or relevant facts obtained from those sources, unless the grand jury established a "compelling need" to obtain that information. Rejecting that claim, the *Branzburg* majority noted that even if requiring reporters to testify as to such information might have a negative impact upon newsgathering by deterring future confidential sources, that impact did not outweigh the interest of the public in the grand jury's investigation of crime. The majority noted (and Justice Powell's concurring opinion stressed in particular) that judicial control of the grand jury process was always available to provide an appropriate remedy if the grand jury process was used to harass the press.

The Fourth Circuit found particularly influential the concurring opinion in *Branzburg* of Justice Powell, who provided the majority's fifth vote. Justice Powell had stated that the majority's recognition of a "bad faith objection" would allow for "striking * * * a proper balance between freedom of the press and the obligation of all citizens to give relevant testimony with respect to criminal conduct," but that balance would be struck on a case-by-case analysis of the facts, not through a threshold imposition of "constitutional preconditions." In light of that statement, the Fourth Circuit noted, though it declined to impose a substantial relationship test, First Amendment interests would not be unprotected. The court stated:

"Under Justice Powell's analysis in *Branzburg,* the district court should balance the possible constitutional infringement and the government's need for documents when it rules on the motion to quash, on a case-by-case basis and without putting any special burden on the government. The district court below satisfied that standard in finding that the subpoenas were properly 'tailored' and that the documents were relevant. Indeed, the Supreme Court discussed the documents' relevancy at length, noting especially that the same individual owned Model, MFR, and R. Enterprises, and that Model had shipped materials into the Eastern District of Virginia in the past. *United States v. R. Enterprises* [p. 703]. With courts both below and above finding the government needs these documents, we are bound to agree. * * * Although we [therefore] affirm the district court's denial of the motion to quash on these facts, we also must note that we are not prepared to rubber-stamp every subpoena of business records of a commercial enterprise that distributes material in a presumptively protected medium. There would be a serious danger of prosecutorial abuse if a grand jury could subpoena the business records of any enterprise in the country on the flimsiest of connections to the judicial district in which the prosecutor operates. Such an unchecked subpoena power would allow any prosecutor to target the affairs of a business with whose expressive activities that prosecutor disagrees or when that prosecutor senses the prospect of political profit in so targeting. To prevent the chilling effect such prosecutorial abuse would cause, we caution district courts to apply with special sensitivity, where values of expression are potentially implicated, the traditional rule that '[g]rand juries are not licensed to engage in arbitrary fishing expeditions, nor may they select targets of investigation out of malice or an intent to harass.' *R. Enterprises* [p. 705]."

Other courts have adopted a similar approach in rejecting First Amendment objections to grand jury subpoenas, although not always without dissent. See *In re Grand Jury Matter (Gronowicz)*, 764 F.2d 983 (3d Cir.1985) (en banc) (where grand jury was investigating author's possible fraud in representing to the publisher that the book was based on interviews with high church officials, and it subpoenaed materials concerning the alleged interviews, no special First Amendment limitations would be imposed even though grand jury inquiry necessarily would be examining the truthfulness of the book in its description of those interviews; two dissenters argued that the government lacked a sufficiently compelling interest for such an investigation, which would undermine First Amendment values, and it therefore could not justify the subpoena); *In re Grand Jury Subpoenas for Locals 17, 135, 257 and 608*, 528 N.E.2d 1195 (N.Y.1988) (where grand jury was investigating union corruption, possibly extending to rank and file members as well as officials, subpoena requesting names, addresses, telephone numbers and social security numbers of all 10,000 members is supported by a "legitimate and compelling" need as it will enable the grand jury to locate and identify potential witnesses "without unduly burdening or delaying the search and without having to proceed through the traditional channels of first notifying the union leaders and exposing witnesses to possible intimidation"; dissent concluded that disclosure would infringe "on associational and privacy rights by chilling members' participation in the full range of union activities," particularly with fear of newspaper leaks regarding the investigation, and the grand jury therefore should be required to show the inadequacy of seemingly viable alternatives, such as disclosure of a percentage of the membership, or protecting against the union learning of the key target groups by having it deliver the complete list to a neutral third party, with the government then obtaining from that custodian the needed information as to those groups). The Second Circuit has held that to sustain a subpoena that implicates the witness's First Amendment right to freedom of association, the government must show a "compelling interest" (met by the investigation of a crime), a "substantial relationship" of the information sought to the compelling interest, and the absence of overbreadth (met where the grand jury was not asking irrelevant or unnecessarily broad questions). Moreover, an otherwise proper investigation can be curtailed if particularized harm, such as reprisals, might result from disclosure of organizational relations. See *In re Grand Jury Proceedings*, 776 F.2d 1099 (2d Cir.1985) (sustaining contempt charge against member of Hell's Angels Motorcycle Club who refused to answer questions about the Club's membership, funding, and organizational structure).

2. *Attorney subpoenas.* Assume that a grand jury subpoenas the attorney representing one of several targets in an organized crime investigation and asks that attorney for information of possible relevancy to the investigation that is not protected by the attorney-client privilege (e.g., whether that target arranged for the legal representation of certain persons thought to be a member of the same organized crime "family"). Should a special showing of need, similar to that imposed in *Bursey*, Note 1 supra, be required to overcome the "chilling impact" that such questioning may have upon the lawyer-client relationship? The several circuit courts considering the issue have all refused to impose such a requirement

as a general rule (although some dissenting judges would have done so). See LaFave, Israel, and King, § 8.8. They have noted that: (1) the target has no constitutional right to counsel with respect to the grand jury proceeding (see Note 4, p. 726); (2) the attorney-client privilege provides adequate protection of the attorney-client relationship; (3) it is at most a "speculative" and "abstract possibility" that the attorney's testimony before the grand jury will lead to his or her disqualification as defense counsel should the target eventually be indicted; (4) the target is asking, in effect, for the "same kind of preliminary showing which the Supreme Court had disapproved [in *Dionisio* and *Branzburg*] as causing indeterminate delays in grand jury investigations." At the same time, the district court has been held to have authority to quash such a subpoena under "compelling circumstances". See *In re Grand Jury Matters*, 751 F.2d 13 (1st Cir.1984) (attorneys were currently representing same client in a state criminal proceeding).

In 1990, the ABA amended Rule 3.8 of the Model Rules of Professional Responsibility to deal specifically with attorney subpoenas. Subsection (f) provided that a "prosecutor in a criminal case * * * shall not subpoena a lawyer in a grand jury or other criminal proceeding to present evidence about a past or current client unless (1) the prosecutor reasonably believes: (i) the information sought is not protected from disclosure by any applicable privilege; (ii) the evidence sought is essential to the successful completion of an ongoing investigation or prosecution; (iii) there is no other feasible alternative to obtain the information; and (2) the prosecutor obtains prior judicial approval after an opportunity for an adversarial proceeding."

In 1995, the subparagraph (2) requirement of prior judicial approval was deleted from Rule 3.8 (f). However several states had already adopted Rule 3.8 with that provision. When federal district courts sought to make those ethical rules applicable to United States Attorneys, two circuits divided on whether they had the authority to do so. See *United States v. Colorado Supreme Court*, 87 F.3d 1161 (10th Cir.1996) (collecting citations and also recognizing the standing of the U.S. Attorney to challenge the state high court's application of those rules to lawyers in that office). Then, in 1998, Congress adopted the Citizen Protection Act, 28 U.S.C.A § 530B, which provides that an "attorney for 'the Government' shall be subject to State laws and rules and local Federal court rules governing attorneys * * * to the same extent and in the same manner as other attorneys in that State." Where states have adopted the original version of Rule 3.8 (f), does the Citizens Protection Act create federal district court jurisdiction to review under the standards of Rule 3.8 (f) all grand jury subpoenas directed to attorneys? As noted in *United States v. Colorado Supreme Court,* supra, the 3.8 (f) standards differ from the internal regulations of the U.S. Attorneys' Manual 9–2.161(a). Those regulations authorize use of attorney subpoenas (upon approval of an Assistant Attorney General) where (i) there exists "reasonable grounds to believe that a crime has been or is being committed and that the information sought is reasonably needed for the successful completion of the investigation or prosecution," (ii) "all reasonable attempts to obtain the information from alternative sources shall have proved to be unsuccessful," (iii) the information is not "protected by a valid claim of privilege," and is not "peripheral or speculative," and (iv) the "reasonable need for the information * * * outweigh[s] the potential adverse effects upon the attorney-client relationship" (in particular, "the risk that the attorney will be disqualified from representation of the client as a result of having to testify against the client").

3. *Other burdens.* In *In re Grand Jury Proceedings (Danbom)*, 827 F.2d 301 (8th Cir.1987), the court acknowledged that a subpoena seeking records of all wire

transfers of $1,000 or more over a 2 year period from Western Union's major Kansas City office met relevancy requirements for a grand jury investigating drug trafficking, but concluded that, under Rule 17(c)'s reasonableness requirement, consideration could be given to Western Union's concern that the publicity resulting from its production of the records of many innocent persons would lead such persons to stop transmitting funds through Western Union.

NOTES ON MISUSE OBJECTIONS

1. Both federal and state courts traditionally have recognized witness objections to alleged prosecutorial misuse of the grand jury process for purposes other than furthering the grand jury's investigation. Such instances of misuse include: (1) employment of the grand jury process "primarily" to elicit evidence for use in a pending or future civil action; (2) employment of the grand jury process "for the sole or dominating purpose of preparing an already pending indictment for trial"; (3) employment of the grand jury process to further independent investigations by police or prosecutor rather than to produce evidence for grand jury use; and (4) calling a witness for the purpose of "harassment," with "harassment" described as encompassing various objectives other than producing relevant evidence, such as burdening the witness with repeated appearances or seeking to punish the witness by forcing him into a situation where he will refuse to answer (or lie) and be held for contempt (or perjury). See LaFave, Israel, and King § 8.8. While misuse objections commonly are raised by witnesses, courts have recognized the right of other persons who are the targets of the misuse to seek a protective order restricting the grand jury investigation. See e.g., *United States v. Doe (Ellsberg)*, 455 F.2d 1270 (1st Cir.1972) (indicted defendant could seek protective order to bar the prosecution's use of grand jury to further prepare its case against him). Consider also Anne Bowen Poulin, *Supervising the Grand Jury*, 68 Wash.U.L.Q. 885 (1990) (in light of limitations placed upon challenges to indictments based upon alleged prosecutorial misconduct before the grand jury, courts should be more willing to consider target requests for judicial intervention to stop ongoing grand jury abuse).

2. As noted in LaFave, Israel, and King, § 8.8, a common thread running through the judicial treatment of misuse objections is that "a presumption of regularity" attaches to the grand jury proceeding and the objecting party bears a substantial burden in seeking to overcome that presumption. It clearly is not sufficient simply to show that the use of the process has (or will) benefit the government with respect to civil discovery, criminal discovery on a pending indictment, or some other alleged improper purpose. Courts have stressed that misuse exists only if the "sole or dominant" prosecutorial purpose is improper, and that the prosecutor will not be enjoined from carrying forward a legitimate grand jury investigation simply because one byproduct may be the production of evidence useful in other proceedings in which the government has some interest. To gain an evidentiary hearing on a claim of alleged misuse, the objecting party ordinarily must at least point to surrounding circumstances "highly suggestive" of improper purpose.

What should constitute such a showing? Where a grand jury investigation was instituted shortly after the target's legal challenges stymied a civil investigation, does that suggest misuse notwithstanding a substantial overlap in the applicable civil and criminal law governing the activities in question? Cf. *In re Grand Jury Subpoenas, April, 1978*, 581 F.2d 1103 (4th Cir.1978). Where a grand jury is investigating the same basic activities that led to indictment of the objecting party, and that party alleges that some of the witnesses to be called before grand jury may be defense witnesses, does that establish a sufficient grounding for an evidentiary hearing notwithstanding a government response that the grand jury investigation is aimed at determining whether others had been involved in the offense? Cf. *United States v. Doe (Ellsberg)*, supra.

3. Even where the surrounding circumstances strongly suggest improper use to obtain civil discovery or discovery on a pending criminal indictment, courts have expressed a reluctance to judge the dominant purpose of the investigation while it is still ongoing. The objecting party, it is noted, should not be allowed to "break up the play before it was started and then claim the government was offsides." *United States v. Doe (Ellsberg)*, supra. A preferable remedy, courts note, is to allow the investigation to continue to its completion and then judge its purpose if the government should attempt to utilize the fruits of its alleged misuse in another proceeding. Where the alleged improper purpose is the development of evidence for a civil proceeding, the Rule 6(e) motion needed to disclose the grand jury material to civil attorneys (see fn. c, p. 680) ordinarily will provide the objecting party with an opportunity to challenge the purpose of the investigation after it has been completed. See *In re Grand Jury Subpoenas, April, 1978*, supra. Where the alleged improper purpose is gaining additional information for use in the trial on a pending indictment, the judge presiding at that trial can determine whether to require an inquiry into the dominant purpose of the post-indictment grand jury investigation when (and if) the government makes use in its prosecution of the fruits of that allegedly tainted investigation. See *United States v. Doe (Ellsberg)*. Does this approach simply "invite" the prosecution to ensure that the challenged investigation results in an indictment, thereby establishing its claim to legitimacy?

4. Claims that the grand jury process was used to further independent police investigations commonly are presented where the individual subpoenaed to appear before the grand jury was offered the opportunity to avoid the grand jury appearance by giving a statement to the police or prosecutor. Although noting that it is improper to use the grand jury subpoena "as a ploy to secure the attendance of a witness at the prosecutor's office," courts have held that offering the witness the option of presenting information informally is not misuse where the prosecutor intends (after screening) to present that information to the grand jury. LaFave, Israel, and King, § 8.8. So too, where the witness was first approached by the police and refused to provide information, the prosecutor may convert the investigation into a grand jury inquiry and seek the same information by subpoena. Ibid.

SECTION 4. APPLICATION OF THE PRIVILEGE AGAINST SELF–INCRIMINATION

A. GRAND JURY TESTIMONY[a]

1. *Application of the privilege. Counselman v. Hitchcock*, 142 U.S. 547, 12 S.Ct. 195, 35 L.Ed. 1110 (1892), put to rest any doubts as to whether the privilege

---

a. The grand jury witness may also utilize any other testimonial privilege recognized in the particular jurisdiction. Thus, the privileges applicable before federal grand juries are those generally recognized in federal courts. See Fed. R.Evid. 1101(d)(2), 501. We have focused here on the privilege against self-incrimination because it provides "what is undoubtedly [the witness'] most significant safeguard in responding to a subpoena ad testificandum." La-Fave, Israel, and King, § 8.10(a).

against self-incrimination was available to a grand jury witness. The Court there rejected the contention that the privilege did not apply because the grand jury witness was not being compelled to incriminate himself "in a criminal case." The reference in the Fifth Amendment to compelled testimony "in a criminal case," the Court noted, was to the eventual use of testimony and not to the nature of the proceeding in which the testimony was compelled. The Fifth Amendment, it concluded, applies to a witness "in any proceeding" who is being compelled to give testimony that might be incriminating in a subsequent criminal prosecution. In support of this interpretation, the Court noted that "the privilege must have a broad construction in favor of the right it was intended to secure," and that its objective was to "insure that a person should not be compelled, when acting as a witness in any investigation, to give testimony which might tend to show that he himself had committed a crime." Does this reasoning, as the *Counselman* Court suggested, find "support" in "the ruling of [the] Court in *Boyd v. United States*"? Does it "miss the boat" in recognizing a witness self-incrimination right to refuse to testify in the grand jury proceeding, rather than simply a right to preclude use of that testimony in any subsequent criminal trial in which he might be a defendant? Consider fn. a at p. 728.

2. *The nature of "incriminating" testimony.* As *Counselman* noted, the privilege only applies to testimony which is "incriminating"—i.e., to testimony which may "tend to show" that the witness himself "had committed a crime." What standard is applied in determining whether particular testimony has that tendency and who makes that determination? The leading case on both questions is HOFFMAN v. UNITED STATES, 341 U.S. 479, 71 S.Ct. 814, 95 L.Ed. 1118 (1951). In that case, a witness subpoenaed before a federal grand jury relied on the privilege in refusing to answer questions as to his current occupation and his contacts with a fugitive witness. The district court found that there was "no real and substantial danger of incrimination" and the privilege therefore was inapplicable. When the witness persisted in his claim, he was held in contempt. In reversing that conviction, the Supreme Court (per CLARK, J.) set forth the following guidelines for the district courts:

"The privilege afforded not only extends to answers that would in themselves support a conviction under a federal criminal statute but likewise embraces those which would furnish a link in the chain of evidence needed to prosecute the claimant for a federal crime. But this protection must be confined to instances where the witness has reasonable cause to apprehend danger from a direct answer. The witness is not exonerated from answering merely because he declares that in so doing he would incriminate himself—his say-so does not of itself establish the hazard of incrimination. It is for the court to say whether his silence is justified, and to require him to answer if 'it clearly appears to the court that he is mistaken.' However, if the witness, upon interposing his claim, were required to prove the hazard in the sense in which a claim is usually required to be established in court, he would be compelled to surrender the very protection which the privilege is designed to guarantee. To sustain the privilege, it need only be evident from the implications of the question, in the setting in which it is asked, that a responsive answer to the question or an explanation of why it cannot be answered might be dangerous because injurious disclosure could result."

It has been suggested that under the *Hoffman* guidelines, it will be a "rare case" in which a court can reject a witness' assertion of the privilege. See LaFave, Israel, and King, § 8.10(a). Consider in this connection the *Hoffman* case itself, where the Court had no difficulty in concluding that the district court erred in denying petitioner's claim of the privilege. The Court reasoned that, since the district court was aware that the grand jury was investigating racketeering, it should have recognized that questions concerning Hoffman's current occupation might require answers relating to violations of federal gambling laws. It also should have recognized that information concerning Hoffman's contacts with the fugitive witness might tie him to efforts to hide that witness. See also *Malloy v. Hogan,* 378 U.S. 1, 84 S.Ct. 1489, 12 L.Ed.2d 653 (1964) (lower court erred in refusing to recognize self-incrimination claim by witness who had pled guilty to a gambling charge and was asked about the circumstances surrounding his arrest and plea; the questions were designed to determine the identity of the witness' employer in the gambling operation, and "if this person were still engaged in unlawful activity, disclosure of his name might furnish a link in a chain of evidence sufficient to connect the petitioner with a more recent crime for which he might still be prosecuted").

3. *Incrimination under the laws of another sovereign.* For many years, American courts took the position that the privilege protected only against incrimination under the laws of the sovereign which was attempting to compel the incriminating testimony. However, in *Murphy v. Waterfront Comm.,* 378 U.S. 52, 84 S.Ct. 1594, 12 L.Ed.2d 678 (1964), the Supreme Court rejected this "separate sovereign" limitation as applied to state and federal inquiries. Noting that a "separate sovereign" limitation would permit a witness to be "whipsawed into incriminating himself under both state and federal law," the Court concluded that the "policies and purposes" of the Fifth Amendment required that the privilege protect "a state witness against incrimination under federal as well as state law and a federal witness against incrimination under state as well as federal law." Does it follow from *Murphy* that the privilege should be available where the witness' testimony would be incriminating only in a foreign country?

In UNITED STATES v. BALSYS, 524 U.S. 666, 118 S.Ct. 2218, 141 L.Ed.2d 575 (1998), the Court majority (7–2) held that the separate sovereign doctrine continued to apply as to incrimination under the laws of a foreign country. Thus, respondent Balsys, a resident alien subpoenaed to testify about his possible participation in Nazi persecution during World War II, could not utilize the privilege to refuse to provide answers which could subject him to a "real and substantial danger of prosecution of Lithuania and Israel." (The only consequence of his testimony in this country was deportation, long established as having a 'civil character'). The Court majority (per SOUTER, J.) acknowledged that *Murphy* included reasoning that supported a complete rejection of the separate sovereign limitation. Thus, the two dissenting justices (Ginsberg, J. and Breyer, J.), relied in part on *Murphy's* reading of the legal history of the privilege (including the English common law), and on *Murphy's* analysis of the purposes of the privilege as inconsistent with a separate sovereign limitation. As to legal history, the *Balsys* majority rejected *Murphy's* conclusion that pre-*Murphy* Supreme Court precedent had misread the English common law precedent as to its recognition of a separate sovereign limitation. As to policy, the Court noted that, while Murphy catalogued multiple "aspirations" of the self-incrimination clause (see p. 735), some of which might support the privilege's extension to the fear of foreign prosecution, *Murphy* had failed "to weigh the host of competing policy concerns that would be raised in a legitimate reconsideration of the Clause's scope."[b] Those costs included the loss of evidence in domestic law enforcement, due to the government's inability to grant immunity that would extend to foreign prosecution.

b. Justices Scalia and Thomas did not join Part IV of the opinion for the Court, which considered relevant (and discussed) *Murphy's* discussion of self-incrimination policies and competing policy concerns not considered in *Murphy.*

The Balsys majority concluded that *Murphy* is better read as resting on an "alternative rationale," which tied its rejection of the separate sovereign limitation to the applicability of the self-incrimination privilege to both the federal and state governments. The Court explained: "[M]urphy was undoubtedly correct, given the decision rendered that very day in *Malloy v. Hogan* [fn. a., p. 34], which applied that doctrine of the Fourteenth Amendment due process incorporation to the Self–Incrimination Clause, so as to bind the States as well as the National Government to recognize the privilege. * * * As the Court immediately thereafter said in *Murphy, Malloy* 'necessitate[d] a reconsideration' of the unqualified *Murdock* rule that a witness subject to testimonial compulsion in one jurisdiction, state or federal, could not plead fear of prosecution in the other. After *Malloy*, the Fifth Amendment limitation could no longer be seen as framed for one jurisdiction alone, each jurisdiction having instead become subject to the same claim of privilege flowing from the one limitation. Since fear of prosecution in the one jurisdiction bound by the Clause now implicated the very privilege binding upon the other, the *Murphy* opinion sensibly recognized that if a witness could not assert the privilege in such circumstances, the witness could be 'whipsawed into incriminating himself under both state and federal law even though the constitutional privilege against self-incrimination is applicable to each.' The whipsawing was possible owing to a feature unique to the guarantee against self-incrimination among the several Fifth Amendment privileges. In the absence of waiver, the other such guarantees are purely and simply binding on the government. But under the Self–Incrimination Clause, the government has an option to exchange the stated privilege for an immunity to prosecutorial use of any compelled inculpatory testimony. *Kastigar v. United States* [p. 730]. The only condition on the government when it decides to offer immunity in place of the privilege to stay silent is the requirement to provide an immunity as broad as the privilege itself. After *Malloy* had held the privilege binding on the state jurisdictions as well as the National Government, it would therefore have been intolerable to allow a prosecutor in one or the other jurisdiction to eliminate the privilege by offering immunity less complete than the privilege's dual jurisdictional reach. *Murphy* accordingly held that a federal court could not receive testimony compelled by a State in the absence of a statute effectively providing for federal immunity, and it did this by imposing an exclusionary rule prohibiting the National Government 'from making any such use of compelled testimony and its fruits.' "

4. *Waiver.* Once a grand jury witness begins to provide incriminating information on a particular subject, does that action bar raising the privilege as to subsequent questions dealing with the same subject? If the answer might be incriminating as to a different offense, the privilege clearly is available, but that may not be the case where the only potential for incrimination is to the same offense suggested by the earlier testimony. Here the applicable standard is that set forth in *Rogers v. United States*, 340 U.S. 367, 71 S.Ct. 438, 95 L.Ed. 344 (1951). The Court there noted that "disclosure of [an incriminating] fact waives the privilege as to details" as the further disclosure does not then present "a reasonable danger of further incrimination in light of all the circumstances, including [the] previous disclosures." To allow a claim of the privilege as to details "would [only] open the way to distortion of facts by permitting a witness to select any stopping point in the testimony."

Application of the *Rogers* standard is not always easy, as the division of the Court in *Rogers* itself suggests. In that case, a grand jury was seeking various records of the Communist Party branch in Denver. The witness Rogers admitted that she had been treasurer of the branch, but stated that she had turned the records over to another person. When asked to name that person, she initially refused to do so on the ground that she would not subject other persons to "the same thing that I'm going through." After consulting with counsel, she shifted to reliance on her privilege against self-incrimination. A divided Supreme Court (5–3) rejected that claim (described by the Court majority as a "pure afterthought"). The majority noted that the privilege was "purely personal" and could not be utilized to protect others. Rogers had already incriminated herself by admitting her party membership and her prior possession and transfer of the records; the "mere disclosure of the name of the recipient of the books" presented no more than an "imaginary possibility" of "increasing the danger of her prosecution" for a possible conspiracy to violate the Smith Act. While it was true that "at least two persons are required to constitute a conspiracy, * * * the identity of the other members [is] not needed inasmuch as one person can be convicted of conspiring with persons whose names are unknown." The dissenters saw the matter quite differently. There was a clear potential for additional incrimination, they noted, since petitioner's conviction could well "depend on testimony of the witnesses she was * * * asked to identify." The Court's analysis, they contended, made the "protection [of the privilege] dependent on timing that was so refined that lawyers, let alone laymen, will have difficulty in knowing when to claim it."

UNITED STATES v. MANDUJANO
425 U.S. 564, 96 S.Ct. 1768, 48 L.Ed.2d 212 (1976).

Chief Justice BURGER announced the judgment of the Court in an opinion in which Justice WHITE, Justice POWELL, and Justice REHNQUIST join.

This case presents the question whether the warnings called for by *Miranda v. Arizona* [p. 477] must be given to a grand jury witness who is called to testify about criminal activities in which he may have been personally involved; and, whether absent such warnings, false statements made to the grand jury must be suppressed in a prosecution for perjury based on those statements.

[In March 1973, an undercover agent received information that Mandujano was dealing in narcotics. Keeping his identity secret, the agent met Mandujano and arranged for the purchase of heroin. Mandujano received $650.00 for the purchase, but returned the same night without the heroin and refunded the money. After Mandujano failed to keep a subsequent appointment, the agent closed the investigative file and reported his contact with Mandujano to federal prosecutors. Six weeks later Mandujano was subpoenaed to testify before a special grand jury investigating the drug traffic in the local area. Before testifying, the prosecutor informed Mandujano of his general duty to answer, his right not to answer incriminatory questions, and of possible perjury liability for false answers. Mandujano was also told that he could have a lawyer outside the room with whom he could consult. When asked if he had a lawyer, Mandujano responded: "I don't have one. I don't have the money to get one."]

[During the grand jury questioning, Mandujano admitted that he had purchased heroin as recently as five months ago, but denied knowledge of the identity of any dealers, except for one street-corner source. He maintained this position notwithstanding the prosecutor's suggestion that "our information is that you can tell us more * * * than you have today." Mandujano "steadfastly denied either selling or attempting to sell heroin since the time of his conviction 15 years before." He "specifically disclaimed having discussed the sale of heroin with anyone during the preceding year and stated that he would not even try to purchase an ounce of heroin for $650.00."]

[Mandujano subsequently was indicted for attempting to distribute heroin and for willfully and knowingly making a false material declaration to the grand jury. The prosecution sought to introduce the grand jury testimony as the basis for the false declaration charge. Mandujano argued that his grand jury testimony should be suppressed since he was not given full *Miranda* warnings prior to his testimony. The District Court sustained the motion on the ground that a "putative" or "virtual" defendant was entitled to *Miranda* warnings. The Court of Appeals affirmed.]

* * * The very availability of the Fifth Amendment privilege to grand jury witnesses suggests that occasions will often arise when potentially incriminating questions will be asked in the ordinary course of the jury's investigation. * * * It is in keeping with the grand jury's historic function as a shield against arbitrary accusations to call before it persons suspected of criminal activity, so that the investigation can be complete. This is true whether the grand jury embarks upon an inquiry focused upon individuals suspected of wrongdoing, or is directed at persons suspected of no misconduct but who may be able to provide links in a chain of evidence relating to criminal conduct of others, or is centered upon broader problems of concern to society. It is entirely appropriate—indeed imperative—to summon individuals who may be able to illuminate the shadowy precincts of corruption and crime. Since the subject matter of the inquiry is crime, and often organized, systematic crime—as is true with drug traffic—it is unrealistic to assume that all of the witnesses capable of providing useful information will be pristine pillars of the community untainted by criminality. * * *

Accordingly, the witness, though possibly engaged in some criminal enterprise, can be required to answer before a grand jury, so long as there is no compulsion to answer questions that are self-incriminating * * *. The witness must invoke the privilege, however, as the "Constitution does not forbid the asking of criminative questions." *United States v. Monia,* 317 U.S., at 433, 63 S.Ct. at 413 (1943) (Frankfurter, J., dissenting).

> "The [Fifth] Amendment speaks of compulsion. It does not preclude a witness from testifying voluntarily in matters which may incriminate him. If, therefore, he desires the protection of the privilege, he must claim it or he will not be considered to have been 'compelled' within the meaning of the Amendment." Id.

Absent a claim of the privilege, the duty to give testimony remains absolute.

The stage is therefore set when the question is asked. If the witness interposes his privilege, the grand jury has two choices. If the desired testimony is of marginal value, the grand jury can pursue other avenues of inquiry; if the testimony is thought sufficiently important, the grand jury can seek a judicial determination as to the bona fides of the witness' Fifth Amendment claim, in which case the witness must satisfy the presiding judge that the claim of privilege is not a subterfuge. If in fact "there is reasonable ground to apprehend danger to the witness from his being compelled to answer," the prosecutor must then determine whether the answer is of such overriding importance as to justify a grant of immunity to the witness. If immunity is sought by the prosecutor and granted by the presiding judge, the witness can then be compelled to answer, on pain of contempt, even though the testimony would implicate the witness in criminal activity. * * *

In this constitutional process of securing a witness' testimony, perjury simply has no place whatever. Perjured testimony is an obvious and flagrant affront to the basic concepts of judicial proceedings. Effective restraints against this type of egregious offense are therefore imperative. * * * [O]ur cases have consistently—indeed without exception—allowed sanctions for false statements or perjury; they have done so even in instances where the perjurer complained that the Government exceeded its constitutional powers in making the inquiry. See e.g., *Bryson v. United States,* 396 U.S. 64, 90 S.Ct. 355, 24 L.Ed.2d 264 (1969). * * *

* * * In this case, the Court of Appeals required the suppression of perjured testimony given by respondent, as a witness under oath, lawfully summoned before an investigative grand jury and questioned about matters directly related to the grand jury's inquiry. The court reached this result because the prosecutor failed to give *Miranda* warnings at the outset of Mandujano's interrogation. Those warnings were required, in the Court of Appeals' view, because Mandujano was a "virtual" or "putative" defendant—that is, the prosecutor had specific information concerning Mandujano's participation in an attempted sale of heroin, and the focus of the grand jury interrogation, as evidenced by the prosecutor's questions, centered on Mandujano's involvement in narcotics traffic. * * *

The court's analysis, premised upon the prosecutor's failure to give *Miranda* warnings, erroneously applied the standards fashioned by this Court in *Miranda.* Those warnings were aimed at the evils seen by the Court as endemic to police interrogation of a person in custody. *Miranda* addressed extra-judicial confessions or admissions procured in a hostile, unfamiliar environment which lacked procedural safeguards. The decision expressly rested on the privilege against compulsory self-incrimination; the prescribed warnings sought to negate the "compulsion" thought to be inherent in police station interrogation. But the *Miranda* Court simply did not perceive judicial inquiries and custodial interrogation as equivalents: " * * * the compulsion to speak in the isolated setting of the police station may well be greater than in courts or other official investigations, where there are often impartial observers to guard against intimidation or trickery."

The Court thus recognized that many official investigations, such as grand jury questioning, take place in a setting wholly different from custodial police interrogation. Indeed, the Court's opinion in *Miranda* reveals a focus on what was seen by the Court as police "coercion" derived from "factual studies [relating to] police violence and the 'third degree' * * * physical brutality—beating, hanging, whipping—and to sustained and protracted questioning incommunicado in order to extort confessions. * * * " To extend these concepts to questioning before a grand jury inquiring into criminal activity under the guidance of a judge is an extravagant expansion never remotely contemplated by this Court in *Miranda;* the dynamics of constitutional interpretation do not compel constant extension of every doctrine announced by the Court. * * *

The warnings volunteered by the prosecutor to respondent in this case were more than sufficient to inform him of his rights—and his responsibilities—and particularly of the consequences of perjury.[a] To extend the concepts of *Miranda,* as contemplated by the Court of Appeals, would require that the witness be told that there was an absolute right to silence, and obviously any such warning would be incorrect, for there is no such right before a grand jury. Under *Miranda,* a person in police custody has, of course, an absolute right to decline to answer any question, incriminating or innocuous, whereas a grand jury witness, on the

---

a. At a subsequent point in the opinion, Chief Justice Burger added in a footnote [note 7] the following: "The fact that warnings were provided in this case to advise respondent of his Fifth Amendment privilege makes it unnecessary to consider whether any warning is re-quired, as the Government asks us to determine. In addition to the warning implicit in the oath, federal prosecutors apparently make it a practice to inform a witness of the privilege before questioning begins."

contrary, has an absolute duty to answer all questions, subject only to a valid Fifth Amendment claim. And even when the grand jury witness asserts the privilege, questioning need not cease, except as to the particular subject to which the privilege has been addressed. Other lines of inquiry may properly be pursued.

Respondent was also informed that if he desired he could have the assistance of counsel, but that counsel could not be inside the grand jury room. That statement was plainly a correct recital of the law. No criminal proceedings had been instituted against respondent, hence the Sixth Amendment right to counsel had not come into play. *Kirby v. Illinois* [p. 655].[6] A witness "before a grand jury cannot insist, as a matter of constitutional right, on being represented by his counsel.... " *In re Groban,* 352 U.S. 330, 77 S. Ct. 510, 1 L. Ed. 2d 376 (1957). Under settled principles the witness may not insist upon the presence of his attorney in the grand jury room. Fed.Rule Crim.Proc. 6(d).

* * * Respondent was free at every stage to interpose his constitutional privilege against self-incrimination, but perjury was not a permissible option. * * * The judgment of the Court of Appeals is therefore reversed.

Justice STEVENS took no part in the consideration or decision of this case.

Justice BRENNAN, with whom Justice MARSHALL joins, concurring in the judgment.

I concur in the result reached by the Court, for "even when the privilege against self-incrimination permits an individual to refuse to answer questions asked by the Government, if false answers are given the individual may be prosecuted for making false statements." *Mackey v. United States,* 401 U.S. 667, 91 S.Ct. 1160, 28 L.Ed.2d 404 (1971) (Brennan, J., concurring). * * *. "Our legal system provides methods for challenging the Government's right to ask questions—lying is not one of them." *Bryson v. United States.* Further, the record satisfies me that the respondent's false answers were not induced by governmental tactics or procedures so inherently unfair under all the circumstances as to constitute a prosecution for perjury a violation of the Due Process Clause of the Fifth Amendment.

However, two aspects of the plurality opinion for the Court suggests a denigration of the privilege against self-incrimination and the right to the assistance of counsel with which I do not agree. The plurality opinion mechanically quotes *United States v. Monia,* for the proposition that

> "[t]he [Fifth] Amendment speaks of compulsion. It does not preclude a witness from testifying voluntarily in matters which may incriminate him. If, therefore, he desires the protection of the privilege, he must claim it or he will not be considered to have been 'compelled' within the meaning of the Amendment." * * *

In my view, the conception of the Fifth Amendment privilege expressed in the *Monia* dictum is explainable only by reference to the facts and circumstances of the only case cited in support by *Monia*—[a case, Justice Brennan explained, in which the potential for incrimination could not be evaluated without a claim by the witness because that potential was not readily apparent from the context of the question]. * * * It is only in a context where this "lack of notice on the part of the government" rationale has significance that we can possibly justify the *Monia* dictum that a witness testifying under judicial compulsion—that classic form of

---

6. The right to counsel mandated by *Miranda* was fashioned to secure the suspect's Fifth Amendment privilege in a setting thought inherently coercive. The Sixth Amendment was not implicated.

compulsion to which the Fifth Amendment is centrally addressed—must claim the privilege or else, without any further analysis, "he will not be considered to have been 'compelled' within the meaning of the Amendment." * * *

* * * Indeed, in the situation where a prior claim is excused and a knowing and completely voluntary waiver of the privilege is required—the situation of the *Miranda*-type custodial interrogation—the reason is that "the inquiring government is *acutely aware* of the potentially incriminating nature of the disclosures sought." * * * I submit that this more discriminating analysis is also required in the situation in which a putative or *de facto* defendant is called to testify under judicial compulsion before a grand jury; otherwise we countenance a serious erosion of fundamental guarantees of the Constitution.

* * * [T]he use by prosecutors of the tactic of calling a putative defendant before a grand jury and interrogating him regarding the transactions and events for which he is about to be indicted is, in the absence of an "intentional relinquishment or abandonment" of his "known" privilege against compulsory self-incrimination, a blatant subversion of the fundamental adversary principle—that the State "establish its case, not by interrogation of the accused even under judicial safeguards, but by evidence independently secured through skillful investigation." * * * Such tactics by prosecutors are exemplars of the very evils sought to be prevented by the enshrinement of the Fifth Amendment privilege in the Constitution. * * *

Thus, I would hold that, in the absence of an intentional and intelligent waiver by the individual of his known right to be free from compulsory self-incrimination, the Government may not call before a grand jury one whom it has probable cause—as measured by an objective standard[15]—to suspect committed a crime, and by use of judicial compulsion compel him to testify with regard to that crime. In the absence of such a waiver, the Fifth Amendment requires that any testimony obtained in this fashion be unavailable to the Government for use at trial. Such a waiver could readily be demonstrated by proof that the individual was warned prior to questioning that he is currently subject to possible criminal prosecution for the commission of a stated crime, that he has a constitutional right to refuse to answer any and all questions that may tend to incriminate him, and by record evidence that the individual understood the nature of his situation and privilege prior to giving testimony. * * *

A second and also disturbing facet of the plurality opinion today is its statement that "[n]o criminal proceedings had been instituted against respondent, hence, the Sixth Amendment right to counsel had not come into play." It will not do simply to cite, as does the plurality opinion, *Kirby v. Illinois,* for this proposition. *Kirby's* premise, so fundamental that it was "note[d] at the outset," was that "the constitutional privilege against compulsory self-incrimination is in no way implicated here." In sharp contrast, the privilege against compulsory self-incrimination is inextricably involved in this case since a putative defendant is called and interrogated before a grand jury. Clearly in such a case a defendant is

---

15. Others have argued for a rule which would combine objective elements with the prosecutor's subjective intent subsequently to charge the individual by indictment. But this subjective intent requirement may pose grave administrative difficulties, whereas the purely objective standard is easily manageable both for the prosecutor at the point of decision to call an individual suspect before the grand jury, and for the reviewing court. Clearly it costs the prosecutor nothing in terms of constitutionally permissible criteria to resolve any doubts in favor of warning the witness. I would at present leave open the proper answer to the case of a witness called to testify in the absence of probable cause, but whose testimony thereafter develops a case of probable cause.

"faced with the prosecutorial forces of organized society, and immersed in the intricacies of substantive and procedural criminal law."

It is true that dictum in *In re Groban,* denied there is any constitutional right of a witness to be represented by counsel when testifying before a grand jury. But neither *Groban* nor any other case in this Court has squarely presented the question. Moreover, more recent decisions, e.g., *Miranda v. Arizona,* and *Escobedo v. Illinois,* recognizing the "substantive affinity" and therefore the "coextensive[ness]" in certain circumstances of the right to counsel and the privilege against compulsory self-incrimination, have led many to question the continuing vitality of such older dicta.

* * * Given the inherent danger of subversion of the adversary system in the case of a putative defendant called to testify before a grand jury, and the peculiarly critical role of the Fifth Amendment privilege as the bulwark against such abuse, it is plainly obvious that some guidance by counsel is required. * * * It may be that a putative defendant's Fifth Amendment privilege will be adequately preserved by a procedure whereby, in addition to warnings, he is told that he has a right to consult with an attorney prior to questioning, that if he cannot afford an attorney one will be appointed for him, that during the questioning he may have that attorney wait outside the grand jury room, and that he may at any and all times during questioning consult with the attorney prior to answering any question posed.[22] At least if such minimal protections were present, a putative defendant would be able to consult with counsel prior to answering any question that he might in any way suspect may incriminate him. * * *

It is of course unnecessary in this case to define the exact dimensions of the right to counsel since the testimony obtained by the grand jury interrogation was not introduced as evidence at respondent's trial on the charge concerning which he was questioned. I write only to make plain my disagreement with the implication in the plurality opinion that constitutional rights to counsel are not involved in a grand jury proceeding, and my disagreement with the further implication that there is a right to have counsel present for consultation outside the grand jury room but that it is not constitutionally derived and therefore may be enjoyed only by those wealthy enough to hire a lawyer. I cannot accede to a return to the regime of "squalid discrimination," where the justice "a man gets depends on the amount of money he has." *Griffin v. Illinois* [p. 78]. * * * If indeed there is, as the plurality opinion says, a right to have counsel present outside the door to the grand jury room, it is most assuredly in my view everyone's right, regardless of economic circumstance. * * *

Justice STEWART, with whom Justice BLACKMUN joins, concurring in the judgment.

The Fifth Amendment privilege against compulsory self-incrimination provides no protection for the commission of perjury. * * * *Bryson v. United States.* The respondent's grand jury testimony is relevant only to his prosecution for perjury and was not introduced in the prosecution for attempting to distribute heroin. Since this is not a case where it could plausibly be argued that the perjury prosecution must be barred because of prosecutorial conduct amounting to a

---

22. [Justice Brennan here noted that several commentators had argued that more was needed, "that the presence of counsel inside the grand jury room is required." He then added: "Certainly there is no viable argument that allowing counsel to be present in the grand jury room for purposes of consultation regarding testimonial privileges would subvert the nature or functioning of the grand jury proceeding. Such a procedure is sanctioned by statute in several states."]

denial of due process, I would reverse the judgment without reaching the other issues explored in The Chief Justice's opinion and by Mr. Justice Brennan in his separate opinion.

Notes and Questions

1. *Exercise of the privilege by the target.* The self-incrimination privilege has long been held to prohibit the prosecution from forcing a defendant to appear as a witness at his own trial. Should the prosecutor similarly be prohibited from forcing the target of an investigation who desires to exercise the privilege to appear before the grand jury, or is the Fifth Amendment satisfied by simply allowing the target-witness, like any other witness, to refuse to respond to individual questions where his answer might be incriminating? A few state courts have argued that the target of an investigation is, in effect, a "putative" or "de facto" defendant, and he therefore should be allowed to exercise his privilege in much the same manner as a "de jure defendant" at trial. They suggest that, unless the target expressly waives his self-incrimination privilege, the prosecution cannot use the grand jury's subpoena authority to force him to appear. See LaFave, Israel, and King, § 8.10(c). On the other side, the federal courts, as reflected in *Mandujano,* and most state courts have taken the position that the Fifth Amendment, as to the target as well as any other grand jury witness, presents only an "option of refusal and not a prohibition of inquiry." *O'Connell v. United States,* 40 F.2d 201 (2d Cir.1930). The "obligation to appear," the Supreme Court noted in *Dionisio,* is "no different for a person who may himself be the subject of the grand jury inquiry." See p. 695.

What justifies the different treatment of the trial defendant and the grand jury target, even when that target is so close to indictment that a court will refer to him as a "putative" defendant? Consider the following arguments: (1) the defendant's right of silence grew out of the early common law rule on the incompetency of parties to testify, which had a bearing only on the trial; (2) the defendant's right not to take the stand at trial is aimed, in part, at protecting the defendant from being placed in a position where he may be forced to refuse to answer questions on self-incrimination grounds in the presence of the jury (who may conclude that he therefore has something to hide), but that protective feature has less significance in the grand jury setting since that body does no more than charge and its proceedings therefore need not be conducted "with the assiduous regard for the preservation of procedural safeguards which normally attends the ultimate trial of the issues"; (3) the grand jury, having an obligation to "run down every clue," cannot ignore the possibility that the target's testimony may lead to the identification of others who also participated in the criminal enterprise;[a] (4) the grand jury, having an obligation to "shield the innocent," must be able to seek the target's own testimony to determine whether it might not "explain away" the

a. Internal Justice Department guidelines provide that, because of the possible "appearance of unfairness," where the target's testimony might be helpful, an effort should first be made to secure the voluntary appearance of the target. However, the grand jury and U.S. Attorney may jointly agree to subpoena the target in exceptional cases. In making that determination, the grand jury and U.S. Attorney are directed to give "careful attention" to the importance of the testimony sought from the target, whether the substance of that testimony could be provided by other witnesses, and whether the "questions the prosecutor and the grand jurors intend to ask * * * would be protected by a valid claim of the privilege." U.S. Attorneys' Manual 9–11.150. Should the subpoenaed "target and his or her attorney state in writing, signed by both, that the 'target' will refuse to testify in Fifth Amendment grounds, the witness ordinarily should be excused," but the "grand jury and United States Attorney [may] agree to assist on appearance" based on the considerations "which justified the subpoena in the first place." U.S.A.M. 9–11.154.

evidence against him; and (5) determining whether a witness is a "target" is not easy under any standard for establishing that status, so that a prohibition against compelling a target to appear invariably would lead to after-the-fact disputes as to whether a later-indicted witness actually had been a target.[b]

2. *Self-incrimination warnings.* It generally is agreed that the Fifth Amendment does not demand that a non-target witness be advised of his privilege against self-incrimination. Relying on the *Mandujano* plurality opinion, the lower federal courts generally have assumed that such "warnings" also are not constitutionally mandated even as to targets.[c] Several state courts, however, adopting a rationale similar to that of Justice Brennan, have held that self-incrimination warnings for target witnesses are constitutionally required. See LaFave, Israel, and King, § 8.10(d). In the federal system, internal prosecutorial guidelines require that both subpoenaed "targets" and "subjects" (see fn. b) be informed of the self-incrimination privilege, both by an "advice of rights" statement appended to the subpoena and a statement of the prosecutor on record when the witness appears before the grand jury. The prescribed statement includes notification to the subpoenaed witness that "you may refuse to answer any question if a truthful answer to the question would tend to incriminate you" and that "anything that you do say may be used against you by the grand jury or in a subsequent legal proceeding." United States Attorneys' Manual 9–11.151. Warnings on the record also are common in state practice, at least as to targets, and are required by statute in roughly 10 jurisdictions. See Beale et al., § 6.24.

3. *Target warnings.* In UNITED STATES v. WASHINGTON, 431 U.S. 181, 97 S.Ct. 1814, 52 L.Ed.2d 238 (1977), the Court answered one of the issues left open in *Mandujano:* a witness need not be warned that he is a target of the grand jury investigation. Noted the Court (per BURGER, C.J.):

"After being sworn, respondent was explicitly advised that he had a right to remain silent and that any statements he did make could be used to convict him of crime. It is inconceivable that such a warning would fail to alert him to his right to refuse to answer any questions which might incriminate him. * * * Even in the presumed psychologically coercive atmosphere of police custodial interrogation, *Miranda* does not require that any additional warnings be given simply because

---

b.   The United States Attorneys' Manual, in connection with its provisions on target subpoenas (see fn. a) and target notification (see Note 3), uses the following definition of a target: "[A] person as to whom the prosecutor or the grand jury has substantial evidence linking him/her to the commission of a crime and who, in the judgment of the prosecutor, is a putative defendant." The target is distinguished from a "subject of an investigation," who is "a person whose conduct is within the scope of the grand jury's investigation." U.S.A.M. 9–11.151. Compare Ind.Code § 35–34–2–1 (target is a person "who is a subject of a grand jury investigation"). See also Arnold Enker and Sheldon Elson, *Counsel for the Suspect,* 49 Minn.L.Rev. 47, 74 (1964) (critical of a solely objective standard that asks only whether probable cause existed, as prosecutors, "having not yet analyzed the complete record of the investigation, or hav[ing] done so only tentatively or hastily, or hav[ing] made an error—as happens in any large human enterprise—may not realize that probable cause exists" as to witnesses they do

not view as targets). As noted in Beale et al., § 6.23, "most of the court decisions and statutes addressing grand jury procedures do not address [the definitional] issue, but simply use terms such as 'suspect,' 'target,' 'subject' and 'prospective defendant' interchangeably."

c.   In *Minnesota v. Murphy,* fn. b, p. 517, the Supreme Court drew an analogy to the grand jury setting in holding that a probationer questioned by his probation officer was not entitled to *Miranda* warnings. The interview setting in *Murphy,* the Court noted, subjected the probationer to "less intimidating pressure than is imposed upon a grand jury witness." Accordingly, since the Court had "never held that [warnings] must be given to the grand jury witness," it would "decline to require them here." Lower courts have looked to *Murphy* as reaffirming the strong suggestion of *Mandujano,* but the lower court cases have involved target/witnesses who received some form of notification of rights. See *United States v. Myers,* 123 F.3d 350 (6th Cir.1997) the suspect is a potential defendant; indeed, such suspects are potential defendants more often than not. Respondent points out that unlike one subject to custodial interrogation, whose arrest should inform him only too clearly that he is a potential criminal defendant, a grand jury witness may well be unaware that he is targeted for possible prosecution. While this may be so in some situations, it is an overdrawn generalization. In any case, events here [which included prior questioning by the prosecutor] clearly put respondent on notice that he was a suspect in the motorcycle theft. * * *

"However, all of this is largely irrelevant, since we do not understand what constitutional disadvantage a failure to give potential defendant warnings could possibly inflict on a grand jury witness, whether or not he has received other warnings. * * * Because target witness status neither enlarges nor diminishes the constitutional protection against compelled self-incrimination, potential defendant warnings add nothing of value to protection of Fifth Amendment rights."

Justice Brennan, joined by Justice Marshall, dissented, relying in substantial part on his discussion of the need for warnings in *Mandujano*. Several state courts, relying on a state statute or state constitutional provision, have held that target witnesses must be warned of their target status. United States Attorneys' Manual 9–11.151 states that the prosecutor should "advise witnesses who are known 'targets' that their conduct is being investigated for possible violation of federal criminal law." As to targets who are not witnesses, prosecutors are encouraged to provide notification of target status in "appropriate cases" (not the "ordinary clear case" or the case presenting a potential for flight or evidence tampering) in order to permit that person to request the opportunity to testify voluntarily. U.S.A.M. 9–11. 153

4. *Constitutional right to counsel.* The *Mandujano* plurality opinion, generally is viewed as having put to rest any possible Sixth Amendment grounding for a constitutional right to counsel. See also Pt. B, p. 75. Several lower courts, following an analysis similar to that advanced by Justice Brennan, have suggested a Fifth Amendment grounding for the right to counsel. Beale, et al. § 6.26, suggest that this grounding has "broad implications that some courts may be hesitant to accept"—such as applicability to witnesses in other settings (e.g., administrative and civil proceedings relating to transactions that could conceivably involve criminality), recognizing a right to appointed counsel as well as a right to retained counsel, and limiting the right to consult with counsel to instances in which the witness could conceivably rely upon the self-incrimination privilege. A due process grounding for a right to counsel has also been suggested. Here, the right would flow from a general liberty interest of the individual to expend his resources to seek counsel's assistance whenever that assistance would not disrupt or alter the basic character of the proceeding involved. See Beale et al., § 6.26 (noting the statement in *Powell v. Alabama,* p. 64, that an "arbitrary" denial of a right to be represented by retained counsel even in a civil case would be viewed as a "denial of a hearing" and therefore a due process violation). Cf. Note 3, p. 67; fn. 6 at p. 95. In treating the issues discussed in Notes 5 and 7 below, several courts appear to have assumed such a due process right to retain and consult with counsel.

5. *Availability of counsel.* Pursuant to internal guidelines, all federal grand jury witnesses are advised that they may retain counsel (who may be located in the anteroom) and "that the grand jury will permit you a reasonable opportunity to step outside the grand jury room to consult with counsel if you so desire." U.S. Attorney's Manual, § 9–11.151. Where the witness requests the assistance of

counsel, but notes that he is indigent, that request is often conveyed to the federal district judge, who may then request that the federal defender or private counsel (in districts without defenders) assume representation. However, the Criminal Justice Act does not provide for appointment of counsel for grand jury witnesses. See 18 U.S.C. § 3006A(a)(1).

Lawyers representing federal grand jury witnesses commonly urge their clients to take full advantage of the opportunity to leave the grand jury room and consult with counsel. Indeed, some lawyers insist that their clients consult after each question, which allows the lawyer to construct a complete record of the questions asked. Although federal prosecutors contend that this practice demands more than a "reasonable opportunity" to consult, it usually has not been contested. A few federal courts have stated that, at least where the witness has been granted immunity (and therefore does not need self-incrimination advice), the witness can be limited to consultations on a less regular basis (e.g., after every few questions). See National Lawyer's Guild, *Representation of Witnesses Before Federal Grand Juries* § 6.5(c) (3d ed. 1985).

Most states follow a practice similar to the federal practice as to notification of the right to consult with retained counsel and providing through an informal arrangement public defender assistance for the indigent witness who requests counsel (although several states provide by statute for the appointment of counsel for indigent witnesses). State courts may be somewhat less liberal, however, in allowing the witness to leave the grand jury for consultations. Those states that are less liberal commonly justify that position on two grounds—avoidance of "undue delay" and restricting counsel to his proper role. If witnesses are allowed to consult after each question, no matter what its nature, they may, it is argued, simply "wear down the grand jury." Moreover, if the attorney's advice properly is limited to counseling the witnesses on the exercise of testimonial privileges, there simply is no reason to allow consultation when the question clearly poses no such difficulty. See e.g., *People v. Ianniello,* 235 N.E.2d 439 (N.Y.1968) (where witness had been immunized and had previous opportunity to consult with counsel on the same line of questioning, grand jury appropriately refused to allow him to leave for the obvious purpose of obtaining "strategic advice" rather than counseling as to any legal right that would allow him to refuse to answer).

6. *The location of counsel.* Twenty states now have statutes permitting at least certain witnesses to be assisted by counsel located within the grand jury room. See Beale et al., § 6.27. Most of these provisions apply to all witnesses, but several are limited to targets or to witnesses who have not been immunized. The statutes commonly contain provisions limiting the role of counsel while before the grand jury. Several state that the lawyer may "advise the witness," but "may not otherwise take any part in the proceeding." One jurisdiction also allows counsel to "interpose objections on behalf of the witness." See Kan.Stat.Ann. § 22–3009 (2).

Proponents of such statutes argue that they are needed to adequately protect the rights of the grand jury witness. They contend that even the most liberal right to leave the grand jury room to consult with counsel imposes substantial burdens upon the client's access to counsel and counsel's ability to advise the client. Those opposing the presence of counsel in the grand jury room acknowledge that the location of counsel outside the grand jury room poses certain difficulties for the witness and counsel, but claim that those difficulties are not so great as to undermine the witness' ability to exercise his rights, particularly as to the privilege against self-incrimination. They see any additional protection of witness rights as clearly outweighed by the detrimental effect that counsel's presence would have upon the grand jury's capacity to conduct effective investigations. They argue that, notwithstanding statutory prohibitions, counsel accompanying witnesses would find techniques, such as stage whispers and objections presented through the witness, for challenging the prosecutor's questions, and conveying their arguments to the jurors. With no judge present to put an immediate stop to such tactics, the end result would be disruption and delay of the investigation. They further argue that with counsel at the witness' side, more witnesses will reply to questions by merely parroting responses formulated by counsel—responses that too often furnish as little information as possible or are purposely ambiguous so as to avoid potential perjury charges. The critics draw an analogy to the trial, where the defendant, once taking the stand, is not allowed to interrupt his testimony for further discussions with counsel. Finally, it is noted that, in some instances, the witness may not be entirely trustful of counsel and therefore prefer not to have counsel present. The witness may be forced to accept counsel provided by others (e.g., his employer) and fear retaliation if the full scope of his testimony is carried back to such persons. Once the law permits counsel to be present, the witness will be under pressure to allow counsel to accompany him, and will lose the capacity to be selective in the disclosure of his testimony to counsel.

B. Immunity Grants

1. *Constitutionality.* The use of an immunity grant to preclude reliance upon the self-incrimination privilege dates back to the English practice known as providing "indemnity" against prosecution. See *Kastigar v. United States,* Note 2 infra (also noting the use of immunity grants in the American Colonies). Immunity grants were first upheld under the federal constitution in *Brown v. Walker,* 161 U.S. 591, 16 S.Ct. 644, 40 L.Ed. 819 (1896). A divided Court there concluded that the Fifth Amendment could not be "construed literally as authorizing the witness to refuse to disclose any fact which might tend to incriminate, disgrace, or expose him to unfavorable comments." The history of the Amendment, the majority noted, indicated that its object was only to "secure the witness against criminal prosecution." Thus, the self-incrimination privilege had been held inapplicable where the witness' compelled testimony would relate only to an offense as to which he had been pardoned or as to which the statute of limitations had run. So too, the privilege did not apply where the witness' response might tend to "disgrace him or bring him into disrepute" but would furnish no information relating to a criminal offense. The majority reasoned that once it was accepted that the object of the privilege was limited to protecting the witness against criminal prosecution, the constitutionality of the immunity grant necessarily followed. Since the grant removed the danger against which the privilege protected the witness, the witness could no longer rely upon the privilege.

2. *Scope of the Immunity. Counselman v. Hitchcock,* 142 U.S. 547, 12 S.Ct. 195, 35 L.Ed. 1110 (1892), struck down a federal immunity statute that granted the witness protection only against the use of his immunized testimony as evidence in any subsequent prosecution. The Supreme Court concluded that such limited protection immunity was not sufficient to replace the Fifth Amendment privilege. The Court stressed that there was no protection against derivative use of the witness' testimony. Thus, the statute "could not, and would not, prevent the use of his testimony to search out other testimony to be used in evidence against him."[a] At the conclusion of its opinion, however, the Court spoke in terms

---

a. Akhil Amar and Renee Letow, *Fifth Amendment First Principles: The Self–Incrimi-*   *nation Clause,* 93 Mich. L. Rev. 857 (1995), argue that *Counselman* erred in allowing a of even broader protection. "To be valid," it noted, an immunity grant "must afford absolute immunity against future prosecution for the offense to which the question relates." This statement was read as indicating that the immunity grant must absolutely bar prosecution for any transaction noted in the witness' testimony. Accordingly, Congress adopted a new immunity statute providing for "transactional immunity." It provided that a witness directed to testify or produce documentary evidence pursuant to an immunity order could not be prosecuted "for or on account of any transaction, matter, or thing concerning which he may testify or produce evidence." The constitutionality of this provision was upheld in *Brown v. Walker,* supra, and subsequent state and federal immunity statutes were largely patterned upon the *Brown* statute.

Subsequent decisions—and the language of later statutes—recognized two limitations on the scope of transactional immunity. First, transactional immunity does not preclude a prosecution for perjury based on the immunized testimony. Second, transactional immunity does not extend to an event described in an answer totally unresponsive to the question asked. Thus, the witness cannot gain immunity from prosecution for all previous criminal acts by simply including a reference to those acts in his testimony without regard to the subject on which he was asked to testify.

In *Murphy v. Waterfront Commission,* Note 3, p. 716, the Court first upheld immunity that was not as broad in scope as the traditional transactional immunity. After rejecting the separate sovereign doctrine as a limitation on the privilege's availability in either federal or state proceedings, *Murphy* turned to the scope of the immunity that must be granted to supplant the privilege as it related to prosecution in another jurisdiction. It concluded that the immunity granted in one jurisdiction (federal or state) need not absolutely bar prosecution in the other; it was sufficient to bar both use and derivative use of the witness' testimony in the other jurisdiction.

Following *Murphy,* Congress adopted a general immunity provision that granted federal witnesses protection only against use and derivative use as to federal as well as state prosecution. The statute provided that "no testimony or other information compelled under the [immunity] order (or any information

person to refuse to testify on self-incrimination grounds in a grand jury proceeding (or other proceeding outside of the person's criminal trial) and in insisting that immunity extend to evidentiary fruits. The privilege should have been read simply to prohibit later prosecution use at the criminal trial of the testimony compelled at the grand jury. The authors note: "The textual argument [for this position] is remarkably clean. A defendant cannot be forced to be a 'witness against himself'—to testify with his own words introduced against him—at trial *in* [his own] *criminal case. Witness* here is used in its natural sense, meaning someone whose testimony, or utterances, are introduced at trial. Witnesses are those who take the stand and testify, or whose out-of-court depositions or affidavits are introduced at trial in front of the jury. Indeed, this is exactly how the word *witness* seems to be used in the companion Sixth Amendment and in the Treason Clause of Article III. Physical evidence, on the other hand, can be introduced at trial whatever its source—even if that source is a compelled pretrial utterance. A witness testifies but physical evidence does not. A thing is not a witness. Although our suspect has indeed been forced to testify pretrial, that testimony occurred outside his own criminal case, beyond the earshot of the jury. Unless these words are introduced at trial, a suspect is not a *witness* against himself in a criminal case.

"This clean reading makes sense of all the words of the Self–Incrimination Clause and shows how they fit together (and with kindred words of the Sixth Amendment), but it also does much more than that. It flushes out the heretofore elusive rationale of the Self–Incrimination Clause, as best read: reliability. Compelled testimony may be partly or wholly misleading and unreliable; even an innocent person may say seemingly inculpatory things under pressure and suspicion and when flustered by trained inquisitors. But physical fruit is far more sturdy and reliable evidence, so it should be brought before the jury."

directly or indirectly derived from such testimony or other information) may be used against the witness in any criminal case, except a prosecution for perjury, giving a false statement, or otherwise failing to comply with the order." 18 U.S.C. § 6002. In KASTIGAR v. UNITED STATES, 406 U.S. 441, 92 S.Ct. 1653, 32 L.Ed.2d 212 (1972), a divided Court (5–2) upheld the new federal provision.

Justice POWELL's opinion for the *Kastigar* majority discounted the "broad language in *Counselman*," which suggested the need for transactional immunity, as inconsistent with the "conceptual basis" of the *Counselman* ruling. The crucial question, as *Counselman* noted, was whether the immunity granted was "coextensive with the scope of the privilege against self-incrimination." Both *Murphy* and the cases applying the exclusionary rule to confessions obtained through Fifth Amendment violations indicated that the constitutional privilege required no more than a prohibition against use and derivative use. The new federal statute clearly met that standard: "The statute provides a sweeping proscription of any use, direct or indirect, of the compelled testimony and any information derived therefrom. This total prohibition on use provides a comprehensive safeguard, barring the use of compelled testimony as an 'investigatory lead,' and also barring the use of any evidence obtained by focusing investigation on a witness as a result of his compelled disclosures."

The *Kastigar* majority rejected the argument, relied on by the dissenters, that the bar against derivative use could not be enforced effectively. Appropriate procedures for "taint hearings" could ensure that derivative use was not made of immunized testimony. Those procedural safeguards were described as follows: "As stated in *Murphy*: 'Once a defendant demonstrates that he has testified, under a state grant of immunity to matters related to the federal prosecution, the federal authorities have the burden of showing that their evidence is not tainted by establishing that they had an independent, legitimate source for the disputed evidence.' This burden of proof, which we reaffirm as appropriate, is not limited to a negation of taint; rather, it imposes on the prosecution the affirmative duty to prove that the evidence it proposes to use is derived from a legitimate source wholly independent of the compelled testimony. This is very substantial protection, commensurate with that resulting from invoking the privilege itself. * * * [Indeed], a defendant against whom incriminating evidence has been obtained through a grant of immunity may be in a stronger position at trial than a defendant who asserts a Fifth Amendment coerced-confession claim. One raising a claim under this statute need only show that he testified under a grant of immunity in order to shift to the government the heavy burden of proving that all of the evidence it proposes to use was derived from legitimate independent sources. On the other hand, a defendant raising a coerced-confession claim under the Fifth Amendment must first prevail in a voluntariness hearing before his confession and evidence derived from it become inadmissible."

3. In a companion case to *Kastigar*, *Zicarelli v. New Jersey State Comm. of Investigation*, 406 U.S. 472, 92 S.Ct. 1670, 32 L.Ed.2d 234 (1972), the Court upheld a state immunity statute providing for use/derivative-use immunity. Since *Zicarelli* was decided, a substantial number of states have moved from transactional to use/derivative-use immunity. The A.B.A. and N.C.C.U.S.L. have urged retention of transactional immunity, however, and roughly twenty states continue to provide the broader immunity, see Beale et al., § 7.8. Those opposing a shift to use/derivative use immunity have argued that the opportunity it offers to prosecute based on independently obtained evidence is too insignificant as a practical matter to offset the risk that derivative use will not be detected by a taint hearing. Those supporting use/derivative use immunity contend that taint hearings are

effective and that instances allowing permissible prosecutions of immunized witnesses, though small in number, should not be cut off where that is not constitutionally required. They also argue, however, that use/derivative use immunity affords substantial advantages apart from the possibility of a subsequent prosecution. They maintain that such immunity encourages the immunized witness to provide as much detail as possible so as to make it more difficult for the government to survive a taint hearing should it subsequently decide to prosecute. They also contend that the absence of an absolute protection against subsequent prosecution makes the immunized witness' testimony more credible to the jury.

4. *Subsequent prosecutions and the problem of taint.* While use/derivative use immunity leaves open the possibility of prosecuting an immunized witness, the prosecution must meet the prerequisite of establishing that its evidence is independently derived, as described in *Kastigar*. Lower courts have read *Kastigar* to be satisfied by application of a preponderance of the evidence standard to this burden. See LaFave, Israel, and King, § 8.11. Also, some courts have been willing to hold the *Kastigar* taint hearing after trial, thereby allowing the government to proceed to trial without providing the broad pretrial disclosure that is inherent in a pretrial taint hearing. Ibid. Nonetheless, prosecuting an immunized witness is not lightly undertaken, and commonly requires advance planning at the time the witness gives the immunized testimony.

The *Kastigar* burden is most likely to be met when the prosecution has completed or substantially completed its investigation before the witness is immunized. In some instances, the prosecution has sufficient evidence to prosecute, and intends to prosecute, but has an immediate need for use of the witness' testimony in a prosecution against another participant in the same general criminal enterprise. In others, the prosecution is well on its way to obtaining an indictment when another governmental agency (a prosecutor in another jurisdiction or a legislative body) grants immunity. The preferred practice in such cases is for the prosecutor to make a record of all of the evidence collected prior to the grant of immunity, to file that record with the court, and then at the taint hearing, note its intent to utilize only that previously acquired evidence and further evidence directly acquired from that evidence. See Beale et al., § 7.20. That procedure may not be foolproof, however.

In *United States v. North,* 910 F.2d 843 (D.C.Cir.1990), the Independent Counsel conducting a grand jury investigation of the Iran–Contra affair followed such a procedure when Congress proceeded to hold public hearings and grant witness immunity to the target. Although the government's criminal prosecution rested on the testimony of witnesses who had previously testified before the grand jury, and Independent Counsel had established a "Chinese Wall" to ensure that its staff was not exposed to the immunized testimony at the Congressional hearings, that was held insufficient to met the *Kastigar* burden. The district court had found that the "witnesses had their memories refreshed with immunized testimony by 'hearing the testimony, reading about it, being questioned about aspects of it before the Select Committees and, to some extent, by exposure to it in the course of responding to inquiries within their respective agencies.' "Insofar as the testimony of the witnesses was shaped by their memories having been refreshed, the government was making "use" of the immunized testimony contrary to *Kastigar*. Accordingly the case was remanded for further proceedings to see if "it is possible * * * to separate the wheat of the witness' unspoiled memory from the chaff of North's immunized testimony."[b]

b. The lower court was directed to engage in a "line-by-line" inquiry into "the content as well as the sources" of each witness' testimony. On the denial of an application for rehear-

Assuming the prosecution can establish that the evidence it will use at trial is independently derived, some courts have found that mere prosecutorial familiarity with the immunized testimony poses difficulties because of the possibility of "nonevidentiary use." Indeed, *United States v. McDaniel,* 482 F.2d 305 (8th Cir.1973), characterized as "insurmountable" the government's burden in such a case, as the court could not "escape the conclusion that the testimony could not be wholly obliterated from the prosecutor's mind in his preparation and trial of the case." The *McDaniel* court reasoned that "if the immunity protection is to be coextensive with the Fifth Amendment privilege, as it must to be constitutionally sufficient, then it must forbid all prosecutorial use of the testimony, not merely that which results in the presentation of evidence before the jury." Other courts have disagreed, arguing that the Fifth Amendment privilege is concerned only with direct and indirect use of evidence and not such matters as "deciding to initiate prosecution, refusing to plea bargain, interpreting evidence, planning cross-examination, and otherwise generally planning trial strategy." *United States v. Serrano,* 870 F.2d 1 (1st Cir.1989).

5. *Prosecutorial discretion.* Although immunity statutes commonly require that the immunity order be issued by the court, the judge's role in ruling on a request for such an order often is limited to ensuring that the procedural requirements of the statute are met (e.g., under the federal statute, that the application was approved by one of the statutorily designated higher echelon Justice Department officials and that the order properly states the scope of the immunity[c]). Under such provisions, the judge may not refuse to grant the order because it disagrees with the prosecutor's judgment that a grant of immunity is in the public interest. United States Attorneys' Manual 9–23.21 directs the appropriate Justice Department official, in making that judgment, to consider a wide range of factors, including the following: (1) the importance of the investigation; (2) the

ing, the Court of Appeals rejected the Independent Counsel's argument that *Kastigar* did not apply because its own activities were free from taint. The Court noted: *"Kastigar* is * * * violated whenever the prosecution puts on a witness whose testimony is shaped, directly or indirectly, by compelled testimony, regardless of *how or by whom* he was exposed to that compelled testimony." 920 F.2d 940 (D.C.Cir. 1990). The government subsequently was unable to meet its burden, the target's conviction was reversed and the charges against him dismissed.

In *United States v. Helmsley,* 941 F.2d 71 (2d Cir.1991), the prosecution successfully argued that it was not using what *Kastigar* described as "investigative leads" furnished by the immunized testimony. There, a newspaper article, reporting on the defendant's immunized state testimony regarding her alleged participation in a scheme to avoid state sales taxes, led a reporter to reopen his own investigation of the possibility that the defendant had misused corporate funds for personal purchases. His subsequent article, in turn, contributed to a federal grand jury investigation and prosecution for tax evasion relating to that misuse of funds. The court concluded that the connection to the immunized testimony was far more at-

tenuated than in *North,* with the newspaper report of the immunized testimony merely "sparking the curiosity" of a "private party" and leading to his investigation of matters "factually and legally unrelated to the immunized testimony."

c. Does it follow from the legislative authorization of immunity grants under specific procedures that the prosecutor should not be allowed to employ informal grants of immunity (i.e., an agreement not to exercise prosecutorial authority in exchange for the witness' testimony)? Very often, the informal grants not only will bypass the statutory procedures for immunity grants, but also will contain prosecutorial promises that are substantially narrower than the immunity provided by statute. While such informal grants are dependent upon witness acceptance (i.e., the court will not force a witness to testify in response to such a nonstatutory promise), if the witness does accept and does testify, the court will require the prosecution to live up to its promise. See Hughes, *Agreements for Cooperation in Criminal Cases,* 45 Vand.L.Rev. 1 (1992). Federal prosecutors regularly utilize such informal grants as simply another exercise of the prosecutor's discretion over the decision to charge. See United States Attorneys' Manual 9–27.00, Beale et al., § 7.12.

value of the person's testimony; (3) the likelihood of prompt and full compliance, and the effectiveness of available sanctions if there is no compliance; (4) the person's relative culpability; (5) the possibility of successfully prosecuting the person prior to compelling testimony through immunization; and (6) the likelihood of adverse collateral consequences to the person if compelled to testify.

C. THE SUBPOENA DUCES TECUM

DOE v. UNITED STATES[a]
487 U.S. 201, 108 S.Ct. 2341, 101 L.Ed.2d 184 (1988).

Justice BLACKMUN delivered the opinion of the Court.

This case presents the question whether a court order compelling a target of a grand jury investigation to authorize foreign banks to disclose records of his accounts, without identifying those documents or acknowledging their existence, violates the target's Fifth Amendment privilege against self-incrimination. * * *

[Petitioner, John Doe, was the target of a federal grand jury investigation of suspected fraudulent manipulation of oil cargoes and receipt of unreported income. Appearing before the grand jury pursuant to subpoena directing him to produce records of transactions in accounts at three named banks in the Cayman Islands and Bermuda, petitioner produced some of the records and testified that no additional records were within his possession. When questioned about the existence of additional records, he invoked the Fifth Amendment privilege against self-incrimination. Grand jury subpoenas then were issued to United States branches of each of the banks, but the banks refused to comply because their governments' laws prohibited disclosure of account records without the customer's consent. The prosecution then filed a motion with the district court requesting that petitioner be ordered to sign forms stating that he was "directing any bank * * * at which I may have a bank account of any kind or at which a corporation has a bank account of any kind upon which I am authorized to draw" to deliver records of those accounts to the grand jury. The form specifically noted that petitioner's directive was being made pursuant to court order, and that the directive was intended to provide compliance with the bank secrecy laws of the Cayman Islands and Bermuda. Petitioner refused to sign the consent directive on self-incrimination grounds, and after being held in contempt, sought appellate review. The Court of Appeals affirmed the contempt order.]

* * * Petitioner's sole claim is that his execution of the consent forms directing the banks to release records as to which the banks believe he has the right of withdrawal has independent testimonial significance that will incriminate him, and that the Fifth Amendment prohibits governmental compulsion of that act. * * * The execution of the consent directive at issue in this case obviously would be compelled, and we may assume that its execution would have an incriminating effect. The question on which this case turns is whether the act of executing the form is a "testimonial communication." The parties disagree about both the meaning of "testimonial" and whether the consent directive fits the proposed definitions.

Petitioner contends that a compelled statement is testimonial if the Government could use the content of the speech or writing, as opposed to its physical

a. To avoid confusion with *United States v.* *Doe*, reprinted infra at p. 751, this case is commonly cited as *Doe II*.

characteristics, to further a criminal investigation of the witness. The second half of petitioner's "testimonial" test is that the statement must be incriminating, which is, of course, already a separate requirement for invoking the privilege. Thus, Doe contends, in essence, that every written and oral statement significant for its content is necessarily testimonial for purposes of the Fifth Amendment. Under this view, the consent directive is testimonial because it is a declarative statement of consent made by Doe to the foreign banks, a statement that the Government will use to persuade the banks to produce potentially incriminating account records that would otherwise be unavailable to the grand jury.

The Government, on the other hand, suggests that a compelled statement is not testimonial for purposes of the privilege, unless it implicitly or explicitly relates a factual assertion or otherwise conveys information to the Government. It argues that, under this view, the consent directive is not testimonial because neither the directive itself nor Doe's execution of the form discloses or communicates facts or information. Petitioner disagrees.

The Government's view of the privilege * * * is derived largely from this Court's decisions in *Fisher* [p. 743] and *Doe I* [p. 751]. The issue presented in those cases was whether the act of producing subpoenaed documents, not itself the making of a statement, might nonetheless have some protected testimonial aspects. The Court concluded that the act of production could constitute protected testimonial communication because it might entail implicit statements of fact: by producing documents in compliance with a subpoena, the witness would admit that the papers existed, were in his possession or control, and were authentic. Thus, the Court made clear that the Fifth Amendment privilege against self-incrimination applies to acts that imply assertions of fact.

We reject petitioner's argument that this test does not control the determination as to when the privilege applies to oral or written statements. While the Court in *Fisher* and *Doe* did not purport to announce a universal test for determining the scope of the privilege, it also did not purport to establish a more narrow boundary applicable to acts alone. To the contrary, the Court applied basic Fifth Amendment principles. An examination of the Court's application of these principles in other cases indicates the Court's recognition that, in order to be testimonial, an accused's communication must itself, explicitly or implicitly, relate a factual assertion or disclose information.[9] Only then is a person compelled to be a "witness" against himself.

This understanding is perhaps most clearly revealed in those cases in which the Court has held that certain acts, though incriminating, are not within the privilege. Thus, a suspect may be compelled to furnish a blood sample, to provide a handwriting exemplar or a voice exemplar, to stand in a lineup, and to wear particular clothing. * * * These decisions are grounded on the proposition that "the privilege protects an accused only from being compelled to testify against himself, or otherwise provide the State with evidence of a testimonial or communicative nature." *Schmerber v. California.*[b] * * * It is the "extortion of information

---

9. We do not disagree with the dissent that "[t]he expression of the contents of an individual's mind" is testimonial communication for purposes of the Fifth Amendment. We simply disagree with the dissent's conclusion that the execution of the consent directive at issue here forced petitioner to express the contents of his mind. In our view, such compulsion is more like "be[ing] forced to surrender a key to a strong box containing incriminating documents," than it is like "be[ing] compelled to reveal the combination to [petitioner's] wall safe."

b. In *Schmerber*, as discussed in fn. 9 at p. 641, the Court rejected the contention that the compelled extraction of a blood sample from defendant's body constituted a violation of his self-incrimination privilege. "History and a from the accused," the attempt to force him "to disclose the contents of his own mind," that implicates the Self–Incrimination Clause. * * * "Unless some attempt is made to secure a communication—written, oral or otherwise—upon which reliance is to be placed as involving [the accused's] consciousness of the facts and the operations of his mind in expressing it, the demand made upon him is not a testimonial one." 8 J. Wigmore, Evidence § 2265 (McNaughton rev. 1961).

It is consistent with the history of and the policies underlying the Self–Incrimination Clause to hold that the privilege may be asserted only to resist compelled explicit or implicit disclosures of incriminating information. Historically, the privilege was intended to prevent the use of legal compulsion to extract from the accused a sworn communication of facts which would incriminate him. Such was the process of the ecclesiastical courts and the Star Chamber—the inquisitorial method of putting the accused upon his oath and compelling him to answer questions designed to uncover uncharged offenses, without evidence from another source. The major thrust of the policies undergirding the privilege is to prevent such compulsion. * * * The Court in *Murphy v. Waterfront Comm'n* [Note 3, p. 716] explained that the privilege is founded on

"[1] our unwillingness to subject those suspected of crime to the cruel trilemma of self-accusation, perjury or contempt; [2] our preference for an accusatorial rather than an inquisitorial system of criminal justice; [3] our fear that self-incriminating statements will be elicited by inhumane treatment and abuses; [4] our sense of fair play which dictates 'a fair state-individual balance by requiring the government to leave the individual alone until good cause is shown for disturbing him and by requiring the government in its contest with the individual to shoulder the entire load,' . . .; [5] our respect for the inviolability of the human personality and of the right of each individual 'to a private enclave where he may lead a private life,' . . .; [6] our distrust of self-deprecatory statements; and [7] our realization that the privilege, while sometimes 'a shelter to the guilty,' is often 'a protection to the innocent.' "

These policies are served when the privilege is asserted to spare the accused from having to reveal, directly or indirectly, his knowledge of facts relating him to the offense or from having to share his thoughts and beliefs with the Government.[11]

---

long line of authorities in lower courts," the Court noted, had "consistently limited" the privilege to the compelled production of an accused's " 'communications' or 'testimony.' "Although the protection of the privilege went beyond statements coming from a "persons own lips" and extended to "communications * * * [in] whatever form they may take," this did not encompass "compulsion which makes a suspect or accused the source of 'real or physical' evidence," as illustrated by *Holt v. United States*, 218 U.S. 245, 31 S.Ct. 2, 54 L.Ed. 1021 (1910). There, a unanimous Court, rejecting a challenge to the admission of evidence that the "accused * * * over his protest put on a blouse that fitted him," had held that the privilege, as a prohibition against the use of compulsion to "extort communications," did not require the "exclusion of * * * [the] body as evidence."

In *United States v. Wade* (p. 641), where defendant had been required to speak in a lineup, the Court rejected the contention that such required participation in a "volitional act" would constitute a communication within the framework of the privilege. See fn. a at p. 641. Justice Fortas, in dissent, argued that *Schmerber* was distinguishable because "the forced extraction of blood from the veins did not compel the person actively to cooperative"; here, in contrast, the defendant was required "to accuse himself by a volitional act which differs only in degree from compelling him to act out the crime." The majority responded that there was no basis for distinguishing one identification procedure from another, that the privilege offered no protection "against compulsion to submit to fingerprinting, photography, or measurement, to write or speak for identification, to appear in court, to stand, to assume a stance, to walk, or make a particular gesture." Compelling the defendant to speak the words purportedly spoken by the robber "was not compulsion to utter statements of a 'testimonial' nature; he was required to use his voice as an identifying physical characteristic, not to speak his guilt."

We are not persuaded by petitioner's arguments that our articulation of the privilege fundamentally alters the power of the Government to compel an accused to assist in his prosecution. There are very few instances in which a verbal statement, either oral or written, will not convey information or assert facts. The vast majority of verbal statements thus will be testimonial and, to that extent at least, will fall within the privilege. Furthermore, it should be remembered that there are many restrictions on the Government's prosecutorial practices in addition to the Self–Incrimination Clause. Indeed, there are other protections against governmental efforts to compel an unwilling suspect to cooperate in an investigation, including efforts to obtain information from him.[13] We are confident that these provisions, together with the Self–Incrimination Clause, will continue to prevent abusive investigative techniques.

* * * We turn, then, to consider whether Doe's execution of the consent directive at issue here would have testimonial significance. We agree with the Court of Appeals that it would not, because neither the form, nor its execution, communicates any factual assertions, implicit or explicit, or conveys any information to the Government.

The consent directive itself is not "testimonial." It is carefully drafted not to make reference to a specific account, but only to speak in the hypothetical. Thus, the form does not acknowledge that an account in a foreign financial institution is in existence or that it is controlled by petitioner. Nor does the form indicate whether documents or any other information relating to petitioner are present at the foreign bank, assuming that such an account does exist. The form does not even identify the relevant bank. Although the executed form allows the Government access to a potential source of evidence, the directive itself does not point the Government toward hidden accounts or otherwise provide information that will assist the prosecution in uncovering evidence. The Government must locate that evidence "by the independent labor of its officers." As in *Fisher,* the Government is not relying upon the " 'truthtelling' " of Doe's directive to show the existence of, or his control over, foreign bank account records.

---

11. Petitioner argues that at least some of these policies would be undermined unless the Government is required to obtain evidence against an accused from sources other than his compelled statements, whether or not the statements make a factual assertion or convey information. Petitioner accordingly maintains that the policy of striking an appropriate balance between the power of the Government and the sovereignty of the individual precludes the Government from compelling an individual to utter or write words that lead to incriminating evidence. Even if some of the policies underlying the privilege might support petitioner's interpretation of the privilege, "it is clear that the scope of the privilege does not coincide with the complex of values it helps to protect. Despite the impact upon the inviolability of the human personality, and upon our belief in an adversary system of criminal justice in which the Government must produce the evidence against an accused through its own independent labors, the prosecution is allowed to obtain and use ... evidence which although compelled is generally speaking not 'testimonial,' *Schmerber v. California.*" *Grosso v. United States,* 390 U.S. 62, 88 S.Ct. 709, 19 L.Ed.2d 906 (1968) (Brennan, J., concurring). If the societal interests in privacy, fairness, and restraint of governmental power are not unconstitutionally offended by compelling the accused to have his body serve as evidence that leads to the development of highly incriminating testimony, as *Schmerber* and its progeny make clear, it is difficult to understand how compelling a suspect to make a nonfactual statement that facilitates the production of evidence by someone else offends the privilege.

13. For example, the Fourth Amendment generally prevents the Government from compelling a suspect to consent to a search of his home; the attorney-client privilege prevents the Government from compelling a suspect to direct his attorney to disclose confidential communications; and the Due Process Clause imposes limitations on the Government's ability to coerce individuals into participating in criminal prosecutions, see generally *Rochin v. California* [p. 38].

Given the consent directive's phraseology, petitioner's compelled act of executing the form has no testimonial significance either. By signing the form, Doe makes no statement, explicit or implicit, regarding the existence of a foreign bank account or his control over any such account. Nor would his execution of the form admit the authenticity of any records produced by the bank. Not only does the directive express no view on the issue, but because petitioner did not prepare the document, any statement by Doe to the effect that it is authentic would not establish that the records are genuine. Authentication evidence would have to be provided by bank officials.

Finally, we cannot agree with petitioner's contention that his execution of the directive admits or asserts Doe's consent. The form does not state that Doe "consents" to the release of bank records. Instead, it states that the directive "shall be construed as consent" with respect to Cayman Islands and Bermuda bank-secrecy laws. Because the directive explicitly indicates that it was signed pursuant to a court order, Doe's compelled execution of the form sheds no light on his actual intent or state of mind. The form does "direct" the bank to disclose account information and release any records that "may" exist and for which Doe "may" be a relevant principal. But directing the recipient of a communication to do something is not an assertion of fact or, at least in this context, a disclosure of information. In its testimonial significance, the execution of such a directive is analogous to the production of a handwriting sample or voice exemplar: it is a nontestimonial act. In neither case is the suspect's action compelled to obtain "any knowledge he might have."[15]

We read the directive as equivalent to a statement by Doe that, although he expresses no opinion about the existence of, or his control over, any such account, he is authorizing the bank to disclose information relating to accounts over which, in the bank's opinion, Doe can exercise the right of withdrawal. * * * When forwarded to the bank along with a subpoena, the executed directive, if effective under local law,[16] will simply make it possible for the recipient bank to comply with the Government's request to produce such records. As a result, if the Government obtains bank records after Doe signs the directive, the only factual statement made by anyone will be the *bank's* implicit declaration, by its act of production in response to the subpoena, that *it* believes the accounts to be petitioner's. Cf. *Fisher*. The fact that the bank's customer has directed the disclosure of his records "would say nothing about the correctness of the bank's

---

15. * * * [T]he acknowledgment that Doe directed the bank to disclose any records the bank thinks are Doe's—an acknowledgment implicit in Doe's placing his signature on the consent directive—is not sufficiently testimonial for purposes of the privilege. The dissent apparently disagrees with us on this point, although the basis for its disagreement is unclear. Surely, the fact that the executed form creates "a new piece of evidence that may be used against petitioner" is not relevant to whether the execution has testimonial significance, for the same could be said about the voice and writing exemplars the Court found were not testimonial in nature. Similarly irrelevant to the issue presented here is the dissent's invocation of the First Circuit's hypothetical of how the Government might use the directive to link petitioner to whatever documents the banks produce. That hypothetical * * * goes only to showing that the directive

may be *incriminating,* an issue not presented in this case. It has no bearing on whether the compelled execution of the directive is *testimonial.*

16. The Government of the Cayman Islands maintains that a compelled consent, such as the one at issue in this case, is not sufficient to authorize the release of confidential financial records protected by Cayman law. * * * Respondent argues * * * that Cayman law on the point has not been definitely settled. The effectiveness of the directive under foreign law has no bearing on the constitutional issue in this case. Nevertheless, we are not unaware of the international comity questions implicated by the Government's attempts to overcome protections afforded by the laws of another nation. We are not called upon to address those questions here.

representations." Brief for United States. Indeed, the Second and Eleventh Circuits have concluded that consent directives virtually identical to the one here are inadmissible as an admission by the signator of either control or existence. * * *

Justice STEVENS, dissenting.

A defendant can be compelled to produce material evidence that is incriminating. Fingerprints, blood samples, voice exemplars, handwriting specimens or other items of physical evidence may be extracted from a defendant against his will. But can he be compelled to use his mind to assist the prosecution in convicting him of a crime? I think not. He may in some cases be forced to surrender a key to a strong box containing incriminating documents, but I do not believe he can be compelled to reveal the combination to his wall safe—by word or deed.

The document the Government seeks to extract from John Doe purports to order third parties to take action that will lead to the discovery of incriminating evidence. The directive itself may not betray any knowledge petitioner may have about the circumstances of the offenses being investigated by the Grand Jury, but it nevertheless purports to evidence a reasoned decision by Doe to authorize action by others. The forced execution of this document differs from the forced production of physical evidence just as human beings differ from other animals.

If John Doe can be compelled to use his mind to assist the Government in developing its case, I think he will be forced "to be a witness against himself." The fundamental purpose of the Fifth Amendment was to mark the line between the kind of inquisition conducted by the Star Chamber and what we proudly describe as our accusatorial system of justice. It reflects "our respect for the inviolability of the human personality," *Murphy v. Waterfront Comm'n.* * * * In my opinion that protection gives John Doe the right to refuse to sign the directive authorizing access to the records of any bank account that he may control. Accordingly, I respectfully dissent.

Notes and Questions

1. *"Value analysis."* In determining the appropriate scope of the self-incrimination privilege, the Court has often turned to an analysis of the values underlying the privilege, citing most frequently Justice Goldberg's listing of those values in *Murphy v. Waterfront Comm'n.* See e.g., *Miranda v. Arizona* at p. 179. While the *Doe II* majority also refers to those values, it acknowledges in footnote 11 that the case before it may present one of those instances where "the scope of the privilege does not coincide with the complex of values it helps to protect." What justifies adopting a more limited view of the privilege than a logical extension of those values might suggest, particularly in light of the admonition of *Counselman v. Hitchcock* (Note 2, p. 728) that the privilege be construed "as broad as the mischief against which it seeks to guard"? Does the answer lie in the language of the Fifth Amendment, particularly in its limitation to compelling a person to be a "witness" against himself? See Charles Geyh, *The Testimonial Component of the Right Against Self–Incrimination,* 36 Catholic U.L.Rev. 611 (1987) (rulings such as *Schmerber,* fn-b supra, have rejected broad readings of "witness" as encompassing either anyone who is the "source of evidence" or who "assist[s] in the disclosure of evidence"); Amar and Lettow, quoted in fn. a, p. 728.

Does the answer lie in the history of the self-incrimination clause, particularly in the early common law development of the privilege as a response to the *ex-officio* oath procedure utilized in both the ecclesiastical courts and the Star

Chamber?[c] Commentators have suggested that a construction of the privilege tied to that history would have resulted in limiting its scope to formal testimony, in contrast to the conclusion in *Schmerber* that "the privilege reaches an accused's communications, whatever form they may take." Moreover, while the Court has expressed agreement with Justice Frankfurter's comment that the "privilege * * * is a specific provision of which it is particularly true that 'a page of history is worth a volume of logic,' "it also has noted, in explaining its acceptance of a privacy rationale for the privilege (see Note 5 infra), that " 'a noble principle often transcends its origins.' " See *Miranda* at p. 479 (quoting in part from an observation by Judge Frank: "The critics of the Supreme Court * * *, in their over-emphasis on the history of the Fifth Amendment privilege, overlook the fact that a noble privilege often transcends its origins, that creative misunderstandings account for some of our most cherished values and institutions").

The distinction drawn in *Schmerber* and other identification-procedure cases between compelled communicative and non-communicative acts has been characterized as producing an interpretation of the privilege that "cannot be reconciled with the purposes served by the right against self-incrimination," but which finds its justification in "a pragmatic compromise." That compromise, it is said, seeks to preserve the "individual's right to resist more egregious forms of self-incrimination" while recognizing the "government interest in unrestricted access to relevant evidence" by allowing it to obtain "vital nontestimonial physical evidence" from the suspect. Geyh, supra. Cf. Harlan, J., dissenting in *Spevack v. Klein*, 385 U.S. 511, 87 S.Ct. 625, 17 L.Ed.2d 574 (1967) (the Court "has chiefly derived its [Fifth Amendment] standards from consideration of two factors: the history and purposes of the privilege and the character and urgency of the other public interests involved"). Does *Doe II*'s ruling as to what constitutes a communicative or testimonial statement reflect a similar compromise?

2. The "complex of values" underlying the Fifth Amendment have been the subject of extensive commentary, and the commentators are virtually unanimous in concluding that at least some of the values cited in *Murphy* simply do not assist in explaining the privilege. See David Dolinko, *Is There a Rationale for the Privilege Against Self–Incrimination?*, 33 U.C.L.A.L.Rev. 1063 (1986).[d] The commentators have noted that while the privilege may incidentally serve the various values cited in *Murphy*, certain of those values (and for some commentators, all of those values) fail to provide a logical conceptual foundation for the existence of the privilege. Does the *Doe II* Court, in effect, take a similar position? Cf. Peter Arenella, *Schmerber and the Privilege Against Self–Incrimination: A Reappraisal*, 20 Am.Crim.L.Rev. 31 (1982) (the Court has obviously concluded, in several pre– *Doe II* cases, that "some Fifth Amendment purposes are more important than

---

c. As to that history, see the essays collected in R. H. Hemholz, Charles Gray, John Langbein, Eben Moglen, Henry Smith, and Albert Alschuler, *The Privilege Against Self–Incrimination. It's Origins and Developments* (1997); Leonard Levy, *The Origins of the Fifth Amendment: The Right Against Self–Incrimination* (2d ed. 1986); Helen Silving, *The Oath*, 68 Yale L.J. 1329, 1527 (1959).

d. The questioning of the conceptual foundation of the privilege dates back at least Jeremy Bentham's classic critique of the privilege in 1827. See Jeremy Bentham, *A Rationale of Judicial Evidence* (1827). Professor Dolinko's article contains an excellent summary and

analysis of the more recent commentary. See also Akhil Amar, *The Constitution and Criminal Procedure, First Principles,* ch. 2 (1997); Amar and Lettow, fn. a, p. 728; Donald Dripps, *Against Police Interrogation—And the Privilege Against Self–Incrimination,* 78 J.Crim.L. & Criminology 699 (1998); William Stuntz, *Self-Incriminations and Excuse,* 88 Colum.L.Rev. 1277 (1988); Donald Dripps, *Self-Incrimination and Self–Preservation: A Skeptical View,* 1991 Ill.L.Rev. 329; Stephen Schulhofer, *Some Kind Words for the Privilege against Self–Incrimination,* 26 Val. U. L. Rev. 311 (1991); and the sources cited in fn. c. supra.

others" and not all "justify restrictions on the state's capacity to promote valid societal interests").

3. *Systemic rationales.* Commentators have most frequently discounted those values listed in *Murphy* that provide a "systemic rationale" for the privilege—i.e., the values that see the privilege as designed to further distinct procedural objectives of the criminal justice process, rather than as an end in itself, directed at safeguarding "human dignity and individuality". See Dolinko, supra. Among these, the values most frequently cited as failing to explain the privilege are the 3rd, 6th, and 7th values cited in *Murphy*.

Murphy's third listed value sees the privilege as a prophylactic measure that withdraws the inducement for officials to seek statements through "inhumane treatment and abuses." Although some have argued that the privilege was designed historically to prevent such abuses, especially torture, that claim is highly questionable. See Dolinko, supra (noting that torture had become a rarely used procedure long before the common law development of the privilege). Moreover, the commentators note, such a justification fails to explain why the privilege was available at trial (where openness precluded physical abuse). Indeed, it has been argued that "precisely because the privilege bars humane interrogation under legal supervision, subterranean interrogation has known tolerance and even encouragement." Dripps, fn. a supra.

Murphy's sixth listed value sees the privilege as a reflection of the concern that incriminatory admissions are inherently unreliable. That concern, however, would hardly justify an absolute prohibition against the use of compelled incriminatory admissions, failing to take account of corroborating evidence suggesting the reliability of a particular admission and excluding undoubtedly reliable physical evidence derived from a compelled admission. Admittedly, such an absolute prohibition would have a historical counterpart in the common law rule that excluded all testimony by parties to a case because their inherent self-interest might lead them to lie. But to view the privilege as playing a similar role would be to render it no more than a rigid and outmoded common law evidentiary standard (and some would argue, inconsistent as well with the common law's ready acceptance of guilty pleas).

Murphy's seventh value—protecting the innocent—is seen by many as primarily related to the previously mentioned concern as to the reliability of self-deprecatory statements. Some commentators have suggested, however, that the privilege may also protect the innocent where an innocent accused, if forced to testify, would leave the jury with a false impression as to his guilt (due to poor demeanor on the stand or an extensive criminal record used by the prosecution to impeach his credibility). See Schulhofer, fn. a supra. But this would explain only one aspect of the privilege (the defendant's right to refuse to testify), not the privilege as a whole. Moreover, the Supreme Court itself has noted that "the basic purposes that lie behind the privilege against self-incrimination do not relate to protecting the innocent from conviction." *Tehan v. United States ex rel. Shott,* 382 U.S. 406, 86 S.Ct. 459, 15 L.Ed.2d 453 (1966).

The second and fourth values cited in *Murphy* have garnered the most commentator support among the systemic justifications for the privilege, but they too have fallen short for many commentators. In part, these two values simply state in different terms the same basic objective of the process. The second value notes a preference for an "accusatorial process," but as the Court has noted in several opinions, an accusatorial process is basically one in which the government "shoulders the entire load" (part of *Murphy*'s fourth value). The imposition of this "entire load" obligation upon the prosecution may be seen as an aspect of neutralizing certain basic resource advantages of the state so as to achieve a "fair state-individual balance" (disparaged by Bentham as the "fox hunters' reason," designed to give the defendant a "sporting chance"), or it may be viewed as simply an additional safeguard to ensure against the conviction of the innocent. The end requirement, however, remains the same—that the state bear the full responsibility for establishing guilt, as contrasted to a system in which the defendant must establish his innocence.

Though accepting that requirement, commentators contend that it hardly follows from its logic that the state also must be prohibited from compelling a defendant to furnish incriminating evidence. While the "accusatorial process" or "entire load" obligation is often described as mandating that the state establish its case through its "own independent labors," see *Miranda v. Arizona*, p. 479, that requirement has never been seen as barring use of the subpoena to compel other non-cooperative witnesses to testify or produce physical evidence. Evidence compelled from a suspect or defendant, the commentators note, is no less a product of the prosecution's "independent labors," unless there is an added prohibition against using the suspect or defendant as a source of evidence. That an accusatorial process does not impose such an additional prohibition is evidenced by the state's ability to use statements made voluntarily by the defendant and to seize evidence in the defendants' possession (including his own words). Thus, the commentators conclude, though the privilege certainly affects the structure of the state-individual balance in prohibiting state use of incriminatory communications compelled from the defendant, it does not do so out of any principle inherent in the preference for an accusatorial process.[e]

Murphy's fourth listed value also refers to requiring the "government to leave the individual alone until good cause is shown for disturbing him." The privilege obviously assists in this regard by restricting what the state can expect to gain through a prosecution that is a mere fishing expedition. It cannot "charge first" and then hope to make its case by forcing the defendant to explain his actions. Also, while the privilege does not bar prosecutorial attempts to harass political opponents and other targets by subjecting them to questioning under oath without any substantial basis for believing they are guilty of wrongdoing, it places in the hands of the potential victims of such harassment a means of limiting their disclosures in response to such questioning. However, objectives hardly explain the availability of the privilege even though the prosecution has substantial

e. *Murphy*'s description of the accusatorial process as one contrasted with an "inquisitorial process" might also be seen as seeking primarily to distinguish the non-adversarial aspect of an inquisitorial process. Under this view, the privilege is characterized as a natural attribute of the adversarial element of the criminal justice process. See Abe Fortas, *The Fifth Amendment: Nemo Tenetur Prodere Seipsum*, 25 Cleve.B.A.J. 95 (1954): "[T]he principle that man is not obliged to furnish the state with ammunition to use against him is basic to this conception. Equals meeting in battle, owe no duty to one another, regardless of the obligations they may be under prior to battle." Here too, however, critics have responded that, in light of the state's capacity to use the defendant as a source of evidence in other ways, the restriction imposed by the privilege can no more be said to flow from the basic tenets of an adversarial system than from the basic tenets of an accusatorial system. The adversary process does not have as its objective the structuring of a "battle between equally meritorious combatants to see which of two inconsistent but equally weighty goals" will prevail, but rather the achievement of "accurate determinations" that "clear the innocent and convict the guilty." Kent Greenawalt, *Silence as a Moral and Constitutional Right*, 23 Wm. & Mary L.Rev. 15, 38–39 (1981). Thus, as evidenced by the prosecutor's obligation to disclose exculpatory evidence, it is not inconsistent with an adversary process to impose upon the litigants an obligation to produce evidence that contributes to an accurate fact-finding determination (just as it is appropriate to bar litigant concealment or destruction of relevant evidence), though that obligation obviously is contrary to their interests as adversaries.

independent evidence that justifies the charge or inquiry. In an early stage of its evolution, the privilege was designed to protect against persons being forced to submit to the oath without any properly supported accusation, but the self-incrimination privilege adopted in the Fifth Amendment had long since been extended to proceedings (e.g., the trial) that followed a formal independent determination by the grand jury that there existed sufficient evidence to charge the individual.

4. *The cruel trilemma.* Although many commentators quarrel with the underlying moral judgment, almost all acknowledge that the privilege arose originally from a belief that it was uniquely cruel and inhumane to subject a person to what *Murphy* described as the "the cruel trilemma of self-accusation, perjury, or contempt."[f] Assuming that historical function, there remains the difficult task of determining the needed scope of the privilege to avoid the "cruel trilemma". Can that function justify, for example, the distinction drawn in *Doe II* between compelled statements that convey information and those that do not? Is the compulsion of a statement that does not "convey information or assert facts" less cruel because it does not present as one of the forced alternatives the possibility of lying under oath, an act considered historically to be an "unpardonable and cardinal sin * * * simply not an option for a religious man." Levy, fn c. Compare Erwin Griswold, *The Fifth Amendment Today* 7 (1955) (drawing a parallel between compelled self-incrimination and requiring a condemned murderer to "sign his own death warrant or dig his grave"). In determining what forces a "cruel trilemma", should it matter whether a required directive that the individual is compelled to sign indicates on its face that it was drafted by the government and signed under compulsion? See *Doe II* at fn. 14. Should it matter whether the directive contains allegations of fact if those allegations were dictated by the government and will not be used at trial as expressing the thoughts of the person compelled to sign?

5. *Protection of privacy.* The fifth value cited in *Murphy*—"respect for the inviolability of the human personality" and the need for a "private enclave"—has commonly been characterized as the "privacy" justification for the privilege. Both critics and supporters of this rationale acknowledge that it remains unpersuasive unless there exists a satisfactory answer to a critical question—why the particular element of privacy that falls within the privilege is given absolute protection, as compared to the relative protection given other privacy interests under the Fourth and First Amendments. The answer usually offered is that the privilege protects the most significant element of individual privacy, the privacy "of the mind"; it "respects a private inner sanctum of individual feeling and thought." *Couch v. United States* (p. 744). But this response only raises the further question as to why the privilege, if it is designed to protect mental privacy from state intrusion, affords such protection only as to thoughts, feelings, and beliefs that would furnish a link in the chain of evidence needed to establish criminal liability. See

---

f. The assumption that forcing such a choice upon a defendant is uniquely cruel was challenged by Bentham, supra fn. c (who characterized it as the "old woman's reason" for the privilege) and modern critics have built upon his analysis. They argue that the choice imposed here is no more cruel than that imposed in other settings (e.g., where a parent is forced to testify against a child), that it assumes a moral justification in refusing to confess to criminality that is contrary to commonly accepted moral and social standards in most other settings, and that it is justified by a legitimate state objective (determining the truth) no less significant than other interests thought to justify requiring a person to act against his natural instinct of self-preservation. Some argue that by the time the privilege became firmly established in this country, its grounding had shifted away from this policy. See Amar and Lettow, fn. a, p. 728. (stressing concerns relating to the reliability of compelled statements).

United States v. Balsys, Note 3, p. 716.[g] One explanation for this limitation is that privilege seeks to protect only a "particular corner of the private enclave" that is especially significant in the development of "moral autonomy"—the "integrity of conscience." See Robert Gerstein, *The Demise of Boyd: Self–Incrimination and Private Papers in the Burger Court*, 27 U.C.L.A.L.Rev. 343 (1979). The critical element of the privilege, from this perspective, is that it preserves to the individual alone the essential right of determining whether and when to acknowledge responsibility for his actions. See Fortas, fn. e supra ("*Mea culpa* belongs to a man and his God. It is a plea that cannot be extracted from free men by human authority.") Accepting this view, should the privilege be even narrower than suggested in *Doe II?* Is there a sufficient element of compulsory "self-condemnation" present to render the privilege applicable when a person is required to furnish only factual information, especially where it is not incriminatory on its face (as in the compelled disclosure of the combination to one's safe)?

FISHER v. UNITED STATES
425 U.S. 391, 96 S.Ct. 1569, 48 L.Ed.2d 39 (1976).

Justice WHITE delivered the opinion of the Court.

In these two cases we are called upon to decide whether a summons directing an attorney to produce documents delivered to him by his client in connection with the attorney-client relationship is enforceable over claims that the documents were constitutionally immune from summons in the hands of the client and retained that immunity in the hands of the attorney. In each case, an Internal Revenue agent visited the taxpayer or taxpayers and interviewed them in connection with an investigation of possible civil or criminal liability under the federal income tax laws. Shortly after the interviews * * *, the taxpayers obtained from their respective accountants certain documents relating to the preparation by the accountant of their tax returns. Shortly after obtaining the documents * * *, the taxpayers transferred the documents to their lawyers—each of whom was retained to assist the taxpayer in connection with the investigation. Upon learning of the whereabouts of the documents, the Internal Revenue Service served summonses on the attorneys directing them to produce documents listed therein. [Those documents were accountants' work sheets, retained copies of income tax returns, and the accountants' copies of correspondence between the accounting firm and the taxpayer]. * * * In each case, the lawyer declined to comply with the summons directing production of the documents, and enforcement actions were commenced by the Government. * * *

---

g. The *Balsys* majority sharply questioned *Murphy's* suggestion that the self-incrimination' clause reflects the "the inviolability of the human personality and the right of each individual to a private enclave where he may lead a private life". It noted initially that" 'inviolability' is, after all, an uncompromising term, and we know as well from Fourth Amendment law * * * that breaches of privacy are complete at the moment of illicit intrusion, whatever use may or may not later be made of such fruits." "Inviolability", it pointed out, hardly describes a regime which allows the government to compel testimony provided it was will to pay the price of "use and derivative use immunity." The Court then added: "One might reply that the choice of the word 'inviolability' was just unfortunate; while testimonial integrity may not be inviolable, it is sufficiently served by requiring the Government to pay a price in the form of use (and derivative use) immunity before a refusal to testify will be overruled. But that answer overlooks the fact that when a witness's response will raise no fear of criminal penalty, there is no protection for testimonial privacy at all. Thus, what we find in practice is not the protection of personal testimonial inviolability, but a conditional protection of testimonial privacy subject to basic limits recognized before the framing and refined through immunity doctrine in the intervening years.

All of the parties in these cases and the Court of Appeals have concurred in the proposition that if the Fifth Amendment would have excused a *taxpayer* from turning over the accountant's papers had he possessed them, the *attorney* to whom they are delivered for the purpose of obtaining legal advice should also be immune from subpoena. Although we agree with this proposition for the reasons set forth * * * infra, we are convinced that, under our decision in *Couch v. United States,* 409 U.S. 322, 93 S.Ct. 611, 34 L.Ed.2d 548 (1973), it is not the taxpayer's Fifth Amendment privilege that would excuse the *attorney* from production.

The relevant part of that Amendment provides:

"No person ... shall be *compelled* in any criminal case to be a *witness against himself.*" (Emphasis added.)

The taxpayer's privilege under this Amendment is not violated by enforcement of the summonses involved in these cases because enforcement against a taxpayer's lawyer would not "compel" the taxpayer to do anything—and certainly would not compel him to be a "witness" against himself. The Court has held repeatedly that the Fifth Amendment is limited to prohibiting the use of "physical or moral compulsion" exerted on the person asserting the privilege. In *Couch v. United States,* supra, we recently ruled that the Fifth Amendment rights of a taxpayer were not violated by the enforcement of a documentary summons directed to her accountant and requiring production of the taxpayer's own records in the possession of the accountant. We did so on the ground that in such a case "the ingredient of personal compulsion against an accused is lacking." Here, the taxpayers are compelled to do no more than was the taxpayer in *Couch.* The taxpayers' Fifth Amendment privilege is therefore not violated by enforcement of the summonses directed toward their attorneys. This is true whether or not the Amendment would have barred a subpoena directing the taxpayer to produce the documents while they were in his hands.

The fact that the attorneys are agents of the taxpayers does not change this result. *Couch* held as much, since the accountant there was also the taxpayer's agent, and in this respect reflected a longstanding view. * * * "It is extortion of information from the accused which offends our sense of justice." *Couch v. United States.* Agent or no, the lawyer is not the taxpayer. The taxpayer is the "accused," and nothing is being extorted from him. Nor is this one of those situations, which *Couch* suggested might exist, where constructive possession is so clear or relinquishment of possession so temporary and insignificant as to leave the personal compulsion upon the taxpayer substantially intact. * * *

The Court of Appeals suggested that because legally and ethically the attorney was required to respect the confidences of his client, the latter had a reasonable expectation of privacy for the records in the hands of the attorney and therefore did not forfeit his Fifth Amendment privilege with respect to the records by transferring them in order to obtain legal advice. It is true that the Court has often stated that one of the several purposes served by the constitutional privilege against compelled testimonial self-incrimination is that of protecting personal privacy. See e.g., *Murphy v. Waterfront Comm'n* [p. 735]. But the Court has never suggested that every invasion of privacy violates the privilege. Within the limits imposed by the language of the Fifth Amendment, which we necessarily observe, the privilege truly serves privacy interests; but the Court has never on any ground, personal privacy included, applied the Fifth Amendment to prevent the otherwise proper acquisition or use of evidence which, in the Court's view, did not involve compelled testimonial self-incrimination of some sort.

The proposition that the Fifth Amendment protects private information obtained without compelling self-incriminating testimony is contrary to the clear statements of this Court that under appropriate safeguards private incriminating statements of an accused may be overheard and used in evidence, if they are not compelled at the time they were uttered, *Katz v. United States* [p. 155], and that disclosure of private information may be compelled if immunity removes the risk of incrimination. *Kastigar v. United States* [p. 730]. If the Fifth Amendment protected generally against the obtaining of private information from a man's mouth or pen or house, its protections would presumably not be lifted by probable cause and a warrant or by immunity. * * * We cannot cut the Fifth Amendment completely loose from the moorings of its language, and make it serve as a general protector of privacy—a word not mentioned in its text and a concept directly addressed in the Fourth Amendment. We adhere to the view that the Fifth Amendment protects against "compelled self-incrimination, not [the disclosure of] private information." * * * Insofar as private information not obtained through compelled self-incriminating testimony is legally protected, its protection stems from other sources—the Fourth Amendment's protection against seizures without warrant or probable cause and against subpoenas which suffer from "too much indefiniteness or breadth in the things required to be 'particularly described,'" "the First Amendment, or evidentiary privileges such as the attorney-client privilege.[7]

* * * [While the] taxpayers have erroneously relied on the Fifth Amendment without urging the attorney-client privilege in so many words, they have nevertheless invoked the relevant body of law and policies that govern the attorney-client privilege. In this posture of the case, we feel obliged to inquire whether the attorney-client privilege applies to documents in the hands of an attorney which would have been privileged in the hands of the client by reason of the Fifth Amendment. * * * This Court and the lower courts have * * * uniformly held that pre-existing documents which could have been obtained by court process from the client when he was in possession may also be obtained from the attorney by similar process following transfer by the client in order to obtain more informed legal advice. * * * It is otherwise if the documents are not obtainable by subpoena duces tecum or summons while in the exclusive possession of the client, for the client will then be reluctant to transfer possession to the lawyer unless the documents are also privileged in the latter's hands. Where the transfer is made for

---

7. The taxpayers and their attorneys have not raised arguments of a Fourth Amendment nature before this Court and could not be successful if they had. The summonses are narrowly drawn and seek only documents of unquestionable relevance to the tax investigation. Special problems of privacy which might be presented by subpoena of a personal diary, *United States v. Bennett*, 409 F.2d 888, 897 (C.A.2 1969) (Friendly, J.), are not involved here. First Amendment values are also plainly not implicated in these cases.

[In *Bennett*, the Court of Appeals upheld the seizure of a letter from a co-conspirator that had been discovered in the source of a search incident to defendant's arrest. Judge Friendly noted that "while the demise of the 'mere evidence rule' [see p. 174] may well require the development of some new restriction on allowable search and seizure in its place, we suggest with deference that an approach geared to the objective of the Fourth Amendment to secure privacy would seem more promising than one based on the testimonial character of what was seized." The key from this perspective, he added, was the "vice of the unlimited search," as illustrated in the case of the search of a diary. The *Bennett* opinion noted: "The reason why we shrink from allowing a personal diary to be the object of a search is that the entire diary must be read to discover whether there are incriminating entries; most of us would feel rather differently with respect to a 'diary' whose cover page bore the title 'Robberies I Have Performed.'" Consider also *Andresen v. Maryland*, p. 174, a post-*Fisher* decision, in which the Court upheld a search for specified business documents conducted pursuant to a warrant. While the Court there did cite *Bennett*, no reference was made to this portion of Judge Friendly's opinion in *Bennett*, even though execution of the search apparently required the examination of numerous documents to find those specified in the warrant.]

the purpose of obtaining legal advice, the purposes of the attorney-client privilege would be defeated unless the privilege is applicable. * * *

Since each taxpayer [here] transferred possession of the documents in question from himself to his attorney in order to obtain legal assistance in the tax investigations in question, the papers, if unobtainable by summons from the client, are unobtainable by summons directed to the attorney by reason of the attorney-client privilege. We accordingly proceed to the question whether the documents could have been obtained by summons addressed to the taxpayer while the documents were in his possession. The only bar to enforcement of such summons asserted by the parties or the courts below is the Fifth Amendment's privilege against self-incrimination. * * *

The proposition that the Fifth Amendment prevents compelled production of documents over objection that such production might incriminate stems from *Boyd v. United States* * * *.

Several of *Boyd's* express or implicit declarations have not stood the test of time. The application of the Fourth Amendment to subpoenas was limited by *Hale v. Henkel* [p. 692] and more recent cases. Purely evidentiary (but "nontestimonial") materials, as well as contraband and fruits and instrumentalities of crime, may now be searched for and seized under proper circumstances, *Warden v. Hayden* [p. 174]. Also, any notion that "testimonial" evidence may never be seized and used in evidence is inconsistent with [various cases] approving the seizure under appropriate circumstances of conversations of a person suspected of crime. See *Katz v. United States* [p. 155]. It is also clear that the Fifth Amendment does not independently proscribe the compelled production of every sort of incriminating evidence but applies only when the accused is compelled to make a *testimonial* communication that is incriminating. See *Schmerber v. California* [fn. a, p. 641]. * * * Furthermore, despite *Boyd*, neither a partnership nor the individual partners are shielded from compelled production of partnership records on self-incrimination grounds. *Bellis v. United States.* It would appear that under that case the precise claim sustained in *Boyd* would now be rejected for reasons not there considered.

The pronouncement in *Boyd* that a person may not be forced to produce his private papers has nonetheless often appeared as dictum in later opinions of this Court. * * * To the extent, however, that the rule against compelling production of private papers rested on the proposition that seizures of or subpoenas for "mere evidence," including documents, violated the Fourth Amendment and therefore also transgressed the Fifth, the foundations for the rule have been washed away. In consequence, the prohibition against forcing the production of private papers has long been a rule searching for a rationale consistent with the proscriptions of the Fifth Amendment against compelling a person to give "testimony" that incriminates him. Accordingly, we turn to the question of what, if any, incriminating testimony within the Fifth Amendment's protection, is compelled by a documentary summons.

A subpoena served on a taxpayer requiring him to produce an accountant's workpapers in his possession without doubt involves substantial compulsion. But it does not compel oral testimony; nor would it ordinarily compel the taxpayer to restate, repeat, or affirm the truth of the contents of the documents sought. Therefore, the Fifth Amendment would not be violated by the fact alone that the papers on their face might incriminate the taxpayer, for the privilege protects a person only against being incriminated by his own compelled testimonial communications. *Schmerber v. California*, supra. The accountant's workpapers are not the taxpayer's. They were not prepared by the taxpayer, and they contain no testimonial declarations by him. Furthermore, as far as this record demonstrates, the preparation of all of the papers sought in these cases was wholly voluntary, and they cannot be said to contain compelled testimonial evidence, either of the taxpayers or of anyone else. The taxpayer cannot avoid compliance with the subpoena merely by asserting that the item of evidence which he is required to produce contains incriminating writing, whether his own or that of someone else.

The act of producing evidence in response to a subpoena nevertheless has communicative aspects of its own, wholly aside from the contents of the papers produced. Compliance with the subpoena tacitly concedes the existence of the papers demanded and their possession or control by the taxpayer. It also would indicate the taxpayer's belief that the papers are those described in the subpoena. The elements of compulsion are clearly present, but the more difficult issues are whether the tacit averments of the taxpayer are both "testimonial" and "incriminating" for purposes of applying the Fifth Amendment. These questions perhaps do not lend themselves to categorical answers; their resolution may instead depend on the facts and circumstances of particular cases or classes thereof. In light of the records now before us, we are confident that however incriminating the contents of the accountant's workpapers might be, the act of producing them—the only thing which the taxpayer is compelled to do—would not itself involve testimonial self-incrimination.

It is doubtful that implicitly admitting the existence and possession of the papers rises to the level of testimony within the protection of the Fifth Amendment. The papers belong to the accountant, were prepared by him, and are the kind usually prepared by an accountant working on the tax returns of his client. Surely the Government is in no way relying on the "truthtelling" of the taxpayer to prove the existence of or his access to the documents. The existence and location of the papers are a foregone conclusion and the taxpayer adds little or nothing to the sum total of the Government's information by conceding that he in fact has the papers. Under these circumstances by enforcement of the summons "no constitutional rights are touched. The question is not of testimony but of surrender."

When an accused is required to submit a handwriting exemplar he admits his ability to write and impliedly asserts that the exemplar is his writing. But in common experience, the first would be a near truism and the latter self-evident. In any event, although the exemplar may be incriminating to the accused and although he is compelled to furnish it, his Fifth Amendment privilege is not violated because nothing he has said or done is deemed to be sufficiently testimonial for purposes of the privilege. This Court has also time and again allowed subpoenas against the custodian of corporate documents or those belonging to other collective entities such as unions and partnerships and those of bankrupt businesses over claims that the documents will incriminate the custodian despite the fact that producing the documents tacitly admits their existence and their location in the hands of their possessor. The existence and possession or control of the subpoenaed documents being no more in issue here than in the above cases, the summons is equally enforceable.

Moreover, assuming that these aspects of producing the accountant's papers have some minimal testimonial significance, surely it is not illegal to seek accounting help in connection with one's tax returns or for the accountant to prepare workpapers and deliver them to the taxpayer. At this juncture, we are quite unprepared to hold that either the fact of existence of the papers or of their possession by the taxpayer poses any realistic threat of incrimination to the taxpayer.

As for the possibility that responding to the subpoena would authenticate the workpapers, production would express nothing more than the taxpayer's belief that the papers are those described in the subpoena. The taxpayer would be no more competent to authenticate the accountant's workpapers or reports by producing them than he would be to authenticate them if testifying orally. The taxpayer did not prepare the papers and could not vouch for their accuracy. The documents would not be admissible in evidence against the taxpayer without authenticating testimony. Without more, responding to the subpoena in the circumstances before us would not appear to represent a substantial threat of self-incrimination. * * *

Whether the Fifth Amendment would shield the taxpayer from producing his own tax records in his possession is a question not involved here; for the papers demanded here are not his "private papers," see *Boyd v. United States, supra.* We do hold that compliance with a summons directing the taxpayer to produce the accountant's documents involved in this case would involve no incriminating testimony within the protection of the Fifth Amendment.

Justice STEVENS took no part in the consideration or disposition of these cases.

Justice BRENNAN, concurring in the judgment.

Given the prior access by accountants retained by the taxpayers to the papers involved in these cases and the wholly business rather than personal nature of the papers, I agree that the privilege against compelled self-incrimination did not in either of these cases protect the papers from production in response to the summonses. See *Couch v. United States.* I do not join the Court's opinion, however, because of the portent of much of what is said of a serious crippling of the protection secured by the privilege against compelled production of one's private books and papers. * * * [I]t is but another step in the denigration of privacy principles settled nearly 100 years ago in *Boyd v. United States.* * * *

Expressions are legion in opinions of this Court that the protection of personal privacy is a central purpose of the privilege against compelled self-incrimination. * * * The Court pays lip-service to this bedrock premise of privacy in the statement that "[w]ithin the limits imposed by the language of the Fifth Amendment, which we necessarily observe, the privilege truly serves privacy interests." But this only makes explicit what elsewhere highlights the opinion, namely, the view that protection of personal privacy is merely a byproduct and not, as our precedents and history teach, a factor controlling in part the determination of the scope of the privilege. This cart-before-the-horse approach is fundamentally at odds with the settled principle that the scope of the privilege is not constrained by the limits of the wording of the Fifth Amendment but has the reach necessary to protect the cherished value of privacy which it safeguards. * * * History and principle, not the mechanical application of its wording, have been the life of the amendment. * * *

History and principle teach that the privacy protected by the Fifth Amendment extends not just to the individual's immediate declarations, oral or written, but also to his testimonial materials in the form of books and papers. * * * The common-law and constitutional extension of the privilege to testimonial materials, such as books and papers, was inevitable. An individual's books and papers are generally little more than an extension of his person. They reveal no less than he could reveal upon being questioned directly. Many of the matters within an individual's knowledge may as easily be retained within his head as set down on a scrap of paper. I perceive no principle which does not permit compelling one to disclose the contents of one's mind but does permit compelling the disclosure of the contents of that scrap of paper by compelling its production. Under a contrary view, the constitutional protection would turn on fortuity, and persons would, at their peril, record their thoughts and the events of their lives. The ability to think private thoughts, facilitated as it is by pen and paper, and the ability to preserve intimate memories would be curtailed through fear that those thoughts or the events of those memories would become the subjects of criminal sanctions however invalidly imposed. Indeed, it was the very reality of those fears that helped provide the historical impetus for the privilege. * * *

The Court's treatment of the privilege falls far short of giving it the scope required by history and our precedents. * * * [The Court's] analysis is patently incomplete: the threshold inquiry is whether the taxpayer is compelled to produce incriminating papers. That inquiry is not answered in favor of production merely because the subpoena requires neither oral testimony from nor affirmation of the papers' contents by the taxpayer. To be sure, the Court correctly observes that "[t]he taxpayer cannot avoid compliance with the subpoena *merely* by asserting that the item of evidence which he is required to produce contains incriminating writing, whether his own or that of someone else." For it is not enough that the production of a writing, or books and papers, is compelled. Unless those materials are such as to come within the zone of privacy recognized by the Amendment, the privilege against compulsory self-incrimination does not protect against their production.

We are not without guideposts for determining what books, papers, and writings come within the zone of privacy recognized by the Amendment. * * * *Couch v. United States* expressly held that the Fifth Amendment protected against the compelled production of testimonial evidence only if the individual resisting production had a reasonable expectation of privacy with respect to the evidence. * * * Under *Couch,* therefore, one criterion is whether or not the information sought to be produced has been disclosed to or was within the knowledge of a third party. That is to say, one relevant consideration is the degree to which the paper holder has sought to keep private the contents of the papers he desires not to produce. * * *

A precise cataloguing of private papers within the ambit of the privacy protected by the privilege is probably impossible. Some papers, however, do lend themselves to classification. Production of documentary materials created or authenticated by a State or the Federal Government, such as automobile registrations or property deeds, would seem ordinarily to fall outside the protection of the privilege. They hardly reflect an extension of the person. Economic and business records may present difficulty in particular cases. The records of business entities generally fall without the scope of the privilege. But, as noted, the Court has recognized that the privilege extends to the business records of the sole proprietor or practitioner. Such records are at least an extension of an aspect of a person's activities, though concededly not the more intimate aspects of one's life. Where the privilege would have protected one's mental notes of his business affairs in a less complicated day and age, it would seem that that protection should not fall away because the complexities of another time compel one to keep business records.

Nonbusiness economic records in the possession of an individual, such as canceled checks or tax records, would also seem to be protected. They may provide clear insights into a person's total lifestyle. They are, however, like business records and the papers involved in these cases, frequently, though not always, disclosed to other parties; and disclosure, in proper cases, may foreclose reliance upon the privilege. Personal letters constitute an integral aspect of a person's private enclave. And while letters, being necessarily interpersonal, are not wholly private, their peculiarly private nature and the generally narrow extent of their disclosure would seem to render them within the scope of the privilege. Papers in the nature of a personal diary are *a fortiori* protected under the privilege.

The Court's treatment in the instant cases of the question whether the evidence involved here is within the protection of the privilege is, with all respect, most inadequate. The gaping hole is in the omission of any reference to the taxpayer's privacy interests and to whether the subpoenas impermissibly invade those interests. * * *[a] For the reasons I have stated at the outset, however, I do not believe that the evidence involved in these cases falls within the scope of privacy protected by the Fifth Amendment. * * *

Justice MARSHALL, concurring in the judgment.

* * * I would have preferred it had the Court found some room in its theory for recognition of the import of the contents of the documents themselves. * * * Nonetheless, I am hopeful that the Court's new theory, properly understood and applied, will provide substantially the same protection as our prior focus on the contents of the documents. * * * Indeed, there would appear to be a precise inverse relationship between the private nature of the document and the permissibility of assuming its existence. Therefore, under the Court's theory, the admission through production that one's diary, letters, prior tax returns, personally maintained financial records, or canceled checks exist would ordinarily provide substantial testimony. The incriminating nature of such an admission is clear, for while it may not be criminal to keep a diary, or write letters or checks, the admission that one does and that those documents are still available may quickly—or simultaneously—lead to incriminating evidence. If there is a "real danger" of such a result, that is enough under our cases to make such testimony subject to the claim of privilege. Thus, in practice, the Court's approach should still focus upon the private nature of the papers subpoenaed and protect those about which *Boyd* and its progeny were most concerned.

The Court's theory will also limit the prosecution's ability to use documents secured through a grant of immunity. If authentication that the document produced is the document demanded were the only testimony inherent in production, immunity would be a useful tool for obtaining written evidence. So long as a document obtained under an immunity grant could be authenticated through other sources, as would often be possible, reliance on the immunized testimony— the authentication—and its fruits would not be necessary, and the document could be introduced. The Court's recognition that the act of production also involves

---

a. Justice Brennan's opinion also added: "I also question the Court's treatment of the question whether the act of producing evidence is 'testimonial.' I agree that the act of production implicitly admits the existence of the evidence requested and possession or control of that evidence by the party producing it. It also implicitly authenticates the evidence as that identified in the order to compel. I disagree, however, that implicit admission of the exis-tence and possession or control of the papers in this case is not 'testimonial' merely because the Government could readily have otherwise proved existence and possession or control in these cases. I know of no Fifth Amendment principle which makes the testimonial nature of evidence and, therefore, one's protection against incriminating himself, turn on the strength of the Government's case against him."

testimony about the existence and possession of the subpoenaed documents mandates a different result. Under the Court's theory, if the document is to be obtained the immunity grant must extend to the testimony that the document is presently in existence. Such a grant will effectively shield the contents of the document, for the contents are a direct fruit of the immunized testimony—that the document exists—and cannot usually be obtained without reliance on that testimony. Accordingly, the Court's theory offers substantially the same protection against procurement of documents under grant of immunity that our prior cases afford.* * *

UNITED STATES v. DOE
465 U.S. 605, 104 S.Ct. 1237, 79 L.Ed.2d 552 (1984).

Justice POWELL delivered the opinion of the Court.

This case presents the issue whether, and to what extent, the Fifth Amendment privilege against compelled self-incrimination applies to the business records of a sole proprietorship. * * *

[Respondent, the owner of several sole proprietorships had objected to a series of five subpoenas directing him to produce a broad range of business records, including billings, ledgers, cancelled checks, telephone records, contracts, and paid bills. The district court sustained the respondent's Fifth Amendment challenge, noting that the act of producing the documents had "communicative aspects" which could prove incriminating since the respondent would thereby be required to "admit that the records exist, that they are in his possession, and that they are authentic." On appeal, the Third Circuit agreed with the district court, but also added another self-incrimination ground justifying the quashing of the subpoenas. Following *Fisher,* that circuit had held, relying on *Boyd,* that an individual's private papers, though created voluntarily, were still privileged under the self-incrimination clause. That analysis, the Third Circuit reasoned, was also applicable to the business records of a sole proprietor.]

We granted certiorari to resolve the apparent conflict between the Court of Appeals holding and the reasoning underlying this Court's holding in *Fisher.* We now affirm in part, reverse in part, and remand for further proceedings. * * *

The Court in *Fisher* expressly declined to reach the question whether the Fifth Amendment privilege protects the contents of an individual's tax records in his possession. The rationale underlying our holding in that case is, however, persuasive here. As we noted in *Fisher,* the Fifth Amendment only protects the person asserting the privilege only from *compelled* self-incrimination. Where the preparation of business records is voluntary, no compulsion is present. A subpoena that demands production of documents "does not compel oral testimony; nor would it ordinarily compel the taxpayer to restate, repeat, or affirm the truth of the contents of the documents sought." Id. * * * This reasoning applies with equal force here. Respondent does not contend that he prepared the documents involuntarily or that the subpoena would force him to restate, repeat, or affirm the truth of their contents. The fact that the records are in respondent's possession is irrelevant to the determination of whether the creation of the records was compelled. We therefore hold that the contents of those records are not privileged. * * *

Although the contents of a document may not be privileged, the act of producing the document may be. *Fisher v. United States.* A government subpoena compels the holder of the document to perform an act that may have testimonial aspects and an incriminating effect. * * * In *Fisher,* the Court explored the effect that the act of production would have on the taxpayer [there] and determined that the act of production would have only minimal testimonial value and would not operate to incriminate the taxpayer. Unlike the Court in *Fisher,* we have the explicit finding of the District Court that the act of producing the documents would involve testimonial self-incrimination.[11] The Court of Appeals agreed.[12] The District Court's finding essentially rests on its determination of factual issues. Therefore, we will not overturn that finding unless it has no support in the record. Traditionally, we also have been reluctant to disturb findings of fact in which two courts below have concurred. *Rogers v. Lodge,* 458 U.S. 613, 102 S.Ct. 3272, 73 L.Ed.2d 1012 (1982). We therefore decline to overturn the finding of the District Court in this regard, where, as here, it has been affirmed by the Court of Appeals.[13]

* * * The Government, as it concedes, could have compelled respondent to produce the documents listed in the subpoena. Sections 6002 and 6003 of Title 18 provide for the granting of use immunity with respect to the potentially incriminating evidence. The Court upheld the constitutionality of the use immunity statute in *Kastigar v. United States* [p. 730]. The Government did state several times before the District Court that it would not use respondent's act of production against him in any way. But counsel for the Government never made a statutory request to the District Court to grant respondent use immunity. We are urged to adopt a doctrine of constructive use immunity. Under this doctrine, the courts would impose a requirement on the Government not to use the incriminatory aspects of the act of production against the person claiming the privilege even though the statutory procedures have not been followed.

We decline to extend the jurisdiction of courts to include prospective grants of use immunity in the absence of the formal request that the statute requires. As

11. The District Court stated: "With few exceptions, enforcement of the subpoenas would compel [respondent] to admit that the records exist, that they are in his possession, and that they are authentic. These communications, if made under compulsion of a court decree, would violate [respondent's] Fifth Amendment rights.... The government argues that the existence, possession and authenticity of the documents can be proved without [respondent's] testimonial communication, but it cannot satisfy this court as to how that representation can be implemented to protect the witness in subsequent proceedings." 541 F.Supp., at 3.

12. The Court of Appeals stated: "In the matter sub judice, however, we find nothing in the record that would indicate that the United States knows, as a certainty, that each of the myriad documents demanded by the five subpoenas in fact is in the appellee's possession or subject to his control. The most plausible inference to be drawn from the broad-sweeping subpoenas is that the Government, unable to prove that the subpoenaed documents exist—or that the appellee even is somehow connected to the business entities under investigation—is attempting to compensate for its lack of knowledge by requiring the appellee to become, in effect, the primary informant against himself." 680 F.2d, at 335.

13. The Government concedes that the act of producing the subpoenaed documents might have had some testimonial aspects, but it argues that any incrimination would be so trivial that the Fifth Amendment is not implicated. * * * On the basis of the findings made in this case we think it clear that the risk of incrimination was "substantial and real" and not "trifling or imaginary." [See Note 2, p. 715]. Respondent did not concede in the District Court that the records listed in the subpoena actually existed or were in his possession. Respondent argued that by producing the records, he would tacitly admit their existence and his possession. Respondent also pointed out that if the Government obtained the documents from another source, it would have to authenticate them before they would be admissible at trial. See Fed.R.Evid. 901. By producing the documents, respondent would relieve the Government of the need for authentication. These allegations were sufficient to establish a valid claim of the privilege against self-incrimination. This is not to say that the Government was foreclosed from rebutting respondent's claim by producing evidence that possession, existence, and authentication were a "foregone conclusion." *Fisher.* In this case, however, the Government failed to make such a showing.

we stated in *Pillsbury Co. v. Conboy,* 459 U.S. 248, 103 S.Ct. 608, 74 L.Ed.2d 430 (1983), in passing the use immunity statute, "Congress gave certain officials in the Department of Justice exclusive authority to grant immunities." "Congress foresaw the courts as playing only a minor role in the immunizing process: . . ." Id. The decision to seek use immunity necessarily involves a balancing of the Government's interest in obtaining information against the risk that immunity will frustrate the Government's attempts to prosecute the subject of the investigation. Congress expressly left this decision exclusively to the Justice Department. If, on remand, the appropriate official concludes that it is desirable to compel respondent to produce his business records, the statutory procedure for requesting use immunity will be available.[17]

We conclude that the Court of Appeals erred in holding that the contents of the subpoenaed documents were privileged under the Fifth Amendment. The act of producing the documents at issue in this case is privileged and cannot be compelled without a statutory grant of use immunity pursuant to 18 U.S.C. §§ 6002 and 6003. The judgment of the Court of Appeals is, therefore, affirmed in part, reversed in part, and the case is remanded to the District Court for further proceedings in accordance with this decision.[a]

Justice O'CONNOR, concurring.

I concur in both the result and reasoning of Justice Powell's opinion for the Court. I write separately, however, just to make explicit what is implicit in the analysis of that opinion: that the Fifth Amendment provides absolutely no protection for the contents of private papers of any kind. The notion that the Fifth Amendment protects the privacy of papers originated in *Boyd v. United States,* but our decision in *Fisher v. United States,* sounded the death-knell for *Boyd.* "Several of Boyd's express or implicit declarations [had] not stood the test of time," *Fisher,* and its privacy of papers concept "had long been a rule searching for a rationale. . . ." Id. Today's decision puts a long-overdue end to that fruitless search.

Justice MARSHALL, with whom Justice BRENNAN joins, concurring in part and dissenting in part.

* * * Contrary to what Justice O'Connor contends, I do not view the Court's opinion in this case as having reconsidered whether the Fifth Amendment provides protection for the contents of "private papers of any kind." This case presented nothing remotely close to the question that Justice O'Connor eagerly poses and answers. First, as noted above, the issue whether the Fifth Amendment protects the contents of the documents was obviated by the Court of Appeals' rulings relating to the act of production and statutory use immunity. Second, the documents at stake here are business records which implicate a lesser degree of concern for privacy interests than, for example, personal diaries.

---

17. Respondent argues that any grant of use immunity must cover the contents of the documents as well as the act of production. We find this contention unfounded. To satisfy the requirements of the Fifth Amendment, a grant of immunity need be only as broad as the privilege against self-incrimination. *Murphy v. Waterfront Commission* [p. 744]. As discussed above, the privilege in this case extends only to the act of production. Therefore, any grant of use immunity need only protect respondent from the self-incrimination that might accompany the act of producing his business records.

a. Justice Stevens, in a separate opinion, argued that the judgment below should simply be affirmed. Since the Court agreed with the district court's reasoning, which was also accepted by the Court of Appeals, there was no reason to review any suggestion in the Third Circuit opinion as to the protection of the contents of the documents. Justice Marshall's separate opinion (see infra) also argued that there was no reason to consider that aspect of the Third Circuit's opinion.

Were it true that the Court's opinion stands for the proposition that "the Fifth Amendment provides absolutely no protection for the contents of private papers of any kind," (O'Connor, J.), I would assuredly dissent. I continue to believe that under the Fifth Amendment "there are certain documents no person ought to be compelled to produce at the Government's request." *Fisher v. United States* (Justice Marshall, concurring).

Notes and Questions

1. *The role of privacy.* Looking back to *Boyd,* can the ruling there be viewed (as suggested by Justices Brennan and Marshall) as resting upon a privacy rationale of the Fifth Amendment? The *Fisher* majority apparently subscribed to the view (held by most commentators) that the *Boyd* ruling rested on a subsequently discarded "property rights" rationale. *Boyd,* under this view, simply utilized the privilege to characterize as "unreasonable" all "searches" (which included required production) aimed at obtaining a person's personal property for possible use against him in a "criminal case" (which included a forfeiture proceeding). See Robert Heidt, *The Fifth Amendment Privilege and Documents— Cutting Fisher's Tangled Line,* 49 Mo.L.Rev. 440 (1984). See also Note 2, p. 691. Yet, *Boyd,* particularly because of its reliance on *Entick v. Carrington* and the characterization there of the individual's papers as his "dearest property" (see p. 688), has also been viewed as suggesting a broad personal privacy grounding for the self-incrimination privilege. *Entick,* it is suggested, regards a person as being "embodied" in his papers and *Boyd* recognized that it was therefore a violation of the privilege to make his papers "speak" against him. *Entick,* however, had in mind the individual's personal political writings, while *Boyd* had before it an invoice written by another firm. *Gerstein,* Note 5, p. 743. See also Heidt, supra (*Boyd's* inclusion of all documents can logically be extended to make the privilege applicable to any property that "contained communications," including "photographs, phonograph records, and old newspapers").[a]

Does the rationale of *Fisher* and *Doe* require, as suggested in Justice O'Connor's concurring opinion in *Doe,* that the "embodiment" concept be rejected even as to the most private papers? Might that concept still play a significant role in protecting those papers under other constitutional provisions? See footnote 7 of *Fisher.* Consider also Heidt, supra (noting that the protection of the most private documents from forced disclosure is more appropriately considered as a First Amendment issue, as procedural requirements applicable to Fifth Amendment

---

a. Compare, however, *Matter of Grand Jury Proceedings of Guarino,* 516 A.2d 1063 (N.J.1986), where the court relying on state law, rejected *Fisher* and *Doe* and retained the "*Boyd*" doctrine, described as holding that the "privilege against self-incrimination protects the individual's right 'to a private enclave where he may lead a private life.' "The Court added: "Nevertheless, * * * we agree with the result in *Fisher* and *Doe.* The subpoenaed documents [here] in issue are the business records of Guarino, doing business as Green Acres Estates, a real estate concern. The business records of a sole proprietor do not lie within that special zone of privacy that forms the core of the documents protected by *Boyd* and its progeny. * * * They do not contain the requisite element of privacy or confidentiality essential to be privileged. The purpose of business records is frequently to record transactions with second and third parties. In today's highly computerized, commercialized and regulated world, there is little expectation of privacy for such records that touch so little on the intimate aspects of one's personal life."

Dissenting in *Guarino,* Handler, J., also supported the retention of the *Boyd* doctrine, but rejected the majority's application of that doctrine. The dissent noted: "The majority * * * purports to do what the Supreme Court and other authorities have recognized to be impossible: to withdraw the privilege while retaining the privacy rationale supporting it. * * * The boundary between personal and public is so nebulous in the case of a sole proprietor that the privilege cannot be denied without abandoning the rationale supporting it."

claims, as prescribed in *Hoffman,* Note 2, p. 728, would restrict judicial inquiry into elements relevant to a privacy claim, such as whether the party actually authored the subpoenaed documents); Michael Mello and Paul Perkins, *Ted Kaczynski's Diary,* 22 Vt.L.Rev. 83 (1997) (*Boyd's* privacy analysis provides the "bridge" between the Fourth and Fifth Amendments needed to protect a personal diary against subpoena, and various lower courts have left open the possibility that enough of *Boyd* remains in effect to provide that protection, although others have held that *Fisher/Doe* rejects any such content-based grounding).

2. *Third-party production.* As noted in *Fisher,* (p. 744), *Couch* recognized that there may be situations in which "constructive possession is so clear or relinquishment of possession so temporary and insignificant as to leave the personal compulsion * * * [upon the owner of the subpoenaed record] substantially intact." Does that situation arise where a subpoena for records of a sole proprietor is directed to an office employee as custodian of the records and the sole proprietor seeks to assert his or her self-incrimination privilege? See *In re Grand Jury (Kent),* 646 F.2d 963 (5th Cir.1981) (yes, where proprietor actively participated in management of small office where records were held and employee was "never delegated the exclusive responsibility for the preparation and custody of the subpoenaed records"); *In re Grand Jury Investigation (Heller),* 921 F.2d 1184 (11th Cir.1991) (no, where legal secretary had intimate involvement in preparation and maintenance of subpoenaed trust account records of the attorney, although the attorney also was actively involved with records in his practice and maintained "a degree of control over them").

3. *The foregone conclusion doctrine.* As Justice Brennan notes in *Fisher* (see fn. a, p. 765), in determining whether a witness' testimony might be viewed as incriminatory under the *Hoffman* standard (see Note 2, p. 715), courts do not look to whether the facts conveyed in the witness' testimony might be established by the government through other sources. Does the *Fisher/Doe* ruling that the privilege does not apply when "possession, existence and authentication" are a "foregone conclusion" require precisely that inquiry in determining the communicative aspects of the act of production? If so, why this special treatment for that act? Consider in this connection, Robert Mosteller, *Simplifying Subpoena Law: Taking the Fifth Amendment Seriously,* 73 Va.L.Rev. 1, 32–33 (1987):

"More plausibly, the Court is suggesting [in its 'foregone conclusion' analysis] that when an implicit as opposed to an explicit communication is involved, it is necessary to consider whether the government is really asking a 'question' through the subpoena. Granted, the defendant's response to a documentary subpoena always reveals that the item does or does not exist; the government cannot eliminate the implicit question about the document's existence no matter how it phrases the subpoena's demand. But if the government already knows the answer to that question and is truly uninterested in the implicit answer provided by production, the witness' gratuitous communication of it should not violate the fifth amendment. In short, the *Fisher* decision suggests that constitutional rights are not violated by implicit communications that are inherent in a response to a documentary subpoena where those communications are unwanted because, though technically admissible, they are not substantially relevant to the prosecution's case given its other evidence."

4. What must be shown to establish that the existence and possession of the subpoenaed documents are a foregone conclusion. Is the key to the finding of a foregone conclusion in *Fisher* the fact that: (1) the papers subpoenaed were of a type normally used and possessed by a business taxpayer; (2) the papers had been

prepared by a third party who could readily testify as to their existence and transfer to the taxpayer; or (3) the attorneys, to raise the attorney-client privilege (and through it, the protection coextensive with the client's self-incrimination privilege), had to establish that the papers had been given to them by their clients? Why, in contrast, had the government failed to make a "foregone conclusion" showing under the facts of *Doe* (see fn. 13)? Was the key here the factors cited in footnote 12 of the Court's opinion? Consider the analysis offered in *United States v. Clark,* 847 F.2d 1467 (10th Cir.1988):

"[T]he records sought in *Doe* had always been (or for purposes of the opinion in *Doe* were presumed to have been) in the taxpayer's own possession. In contrast, the records in question here were either the accountant's workpapers [subpoenaed from the accountant] or the other records which had been delivered into the accountant's hands, and possessed by him for purposes of doing work in or from them [before returning them to the subpoenaed taxpayer]. * * * As to the taxpayer's records which the accountant had in his possession, their existence and possession are a 'foregone conclusion.' See *Fisher.* The accountant could be placed under oath and directed to identify each record which he had had in his possession, and the fact of his delivery of those records into the possession of another, specific party. In addition, logic dictates that the accountant's workpapers, which must be produced, will also show the existence of many if not all of the records subject to the [taxpayer] summonses, including such items as bank and brokerage accounts. * * * It simply strains credulity to theorize that records which had been delivered to the accountant for him to work on or from would not show up in some identifiable fashion in the accountant's own work. * * * This conclusion is quite unlike that arrived at by the court of appeals in *Doe.*"

5. *Authentication as a foregone conclusion.* See *Beale* et al., § 6.15 "In many cases, business records can be authenticated circumstantially, without any live witness testimony, or they can readily be authenticated by a third party other than the subpoenaed witness, such as the person who actually prepared the records or an office employee who worked with or maintained them.[b] If the government shows that it can authenticate the documents by such alternative means and represents that it does not intend to rely on the witness's production of the documents to authenticate them, is that sufficient to overcome the witness's claim that his implicit authentication of the documents in incriminating? The courts that have addressed this question have reached differing conclusions. Some courts have taken the position that if the subpoenaed witness prepared the documents in question, his production of the documents would always constitute an "implicit authentication" of them sufficient to trigger the Fifth Amendment protection * * * Other courts have taken a more lenient view of the matter and have suggested that the "implicit authentication" is not sufficiently incriminating to trigger the Fifth Amendment privilege as long as the documents 'could be authenticated through another witness'. * * *

The approach that seems most consistent with the Supreme Court's decisions in *Fisher* and *Doe* is for the court to try to determine whether, as a practical matter, authentication is a disputed issue. If the government can make a convincing

b. Fed R. Evid. 901 provides that authentication "is satisfied by evidence sufficient to support a finding that the matter in question is what its proponent claims." The Rule offers various illustrations of sufficient evidence, including (1) testimony of a witness with knowledge, (2) expert and nonexpert testimony as to the genuineness of handwriting, and (3) distinctive characteristics of the document as contained on its "appearance, contents, substance, internal patterns, or other distinctive characteristics, taken in conjunction with circumstances."

showing that authentication is simply not an issue, an issue, and that it would gain nothing from the implicit authentication of the documents by the witness's production of them, the Fifth Amendment claim should not upheld."

6. *Potential incrimination.* Assuming that the government does not establish that possession, authentication, and existence are a foregone conclusion, under what circumstances will the privilege nonetheless not be applicable because the likelihood of incrimination is not "substantial and real" (see *Doe* at fn. 13)? Note in this regard *Fisher's* comments on the incriminatory aspects of producing records that were authored by another and clearly could be lawfully possessed. What did the Court mean when it said that "at this juncture," it was unwilling to hold that either the existence of the papers or their possession posed a realistic threat of incrimination (see p. 747)? Assuming that the contents of the papers were incriminatory, wouldn't acknowledgment of their existence pose a realistic threat as found in *Doe?* Assuming that the contents were incriminatory, wouldn't possession suggest knowledge of that content and thereby pose a realistic threat? Is the answer that the Court in *Fisher* may not have been willing to conclude, on the record before it, that a realistic threat existed that the contents were incriminatory? See LaFave and Israel, § 8.12. Is the answer that the Court was saying that the threat of incrimination is to be judged without regard to the possible content of the record (i.e., simply by the nature of the record). If so, how could it then have accepted the lower court rulings in *Doe* as establishing a sufficient risk of incrimination?

7. *Act of production immunity.* Where the government contends that it could otherwise establish existence, possession, and authentication, why would it not simply grant act-of-production immunity and thereby avoid dispute as to the "foregone conclusion" issue? Heidt, Note 1 supra, argues that the government, if it granted such immunity, would face a difficult hurdle in later establishing that it had made no derivative use of the act of production. See also *Braswell,* p. 778 at fn. 10. Beale et al., § 6.15, suggest that prosecutors have been reluctant to grant "act of production immunity" because of concern that "the scope of the immunity grant will generate substantial litigation."

Where act of production immunity is given, what should constitute a derivative use? In particular, may the government simply look upon the documents as if they were found in the grand jury room with their source unknown, and proceed to use them in its investigation on that basis? See Kenneth Melilli, *Act-of-Production Immunity,* 52 Ohio St.L.J. 223 (1991) (exploring the ramifications of this analogy, which basically reflects the position urged by the Department of Justice). A synopsis of the limited judicial commentary on the subject is presented in Kevin Reitz, *Clients, Lawyers, and the Fifth Amendment Privilege: The Need For a Projected Privilege,* 41 Duke L.J. 572 (1991):

"One of the most enduring of *Fisher's* mysteries is the legal effect that will be given a grant of use immunity for the act of production. Fifteen years after *Fisher,* no reported decision has yet defined the scope of such immunity. * * * Justice Marshall, concurring in *Fisher,* argued that immunity for the act of producing evidence will normally foreclose any subsequent use of the evidence against the suspect, because such use would derive from the fact of its existence, which is one of the admissions included within the immunized testimony [provided by the act of production]. Thus, the contents of any document produced under immunity could not be used by the prosecution either in the courtroom or to develop leads, because 'the contents are a direct fruit of the immunized testimony—that the document exists.' At the opposite extreme, the Court of Appeals for the First

Circuit has, in dictum, taken a narrow view of the effect of use immunity in a *Fisher*-type case. Under the First Circuit theory, the contents of documents procured under a grand of act of production immunity can always be used against the person who produced them. This is because, under *Fisher,* the contents of voluntarily created records are not viewed as compelled communications, and therefore those contents must fall outside any immunity protection that is merely coextensive with the Fifth Amendment privilege. The Supreme Court gave the First Circuit view a powerful shot in the arm when it dropped a footnote in *Doe I* stating, in dictum, that it found the argument 'unfounded' that a grant of use immunity would cover the contents of documents as well as the act of production itself."

BRASWELL v. UNITED STATES
487 U.S. 99, 108 S.Ct. 2284, 101 L.Ed.2d 98 (1988).

Chief Justice REHNQUIST delivered the opinion of the Court.

This case presents the question whether the custodian of corporate records may resist a subpoena for such records on the ground that the act of production would incriminate him in violation of the Fifth Amendment. We conclude that he may not. * * *

[A federal grand jury issued a subpoena to petitioner Braswell, as the president of two corporations, requiring him to produce the books and records of the two corporations, Worldwide Machinery, Inc. and Worldwide Purchasing, Inc. Petitioner had funded Worldwide Purchasing with his 100 percent interest in Worldwide Machinery and was the sole shareholder of Worldwide Purchasing. While both corporations had three directors, petitioner, his wife, and his mother, only petitioner had authority over the business affairs of the corporations. The grand jury subpoena provided that petitioner could deliver the records to the grand jury agent serving the subpoena and did not require petitioner to testify. Petitioner moved to quash the subpoena, arguing that the act or producing the records would continue a violation of his Fifth Amendment privilege against self-incrimination. The district court denied the motion and the Fifth Circuit affirmed.]

There is no question but that the contents of the subpoenaed business records are not privileged. See *United States v. Doe* [*Doe*]; *Fisher v. United States.* Similarly, petitioner asserts no self-incrimination claim on behalf of the corporations; it is well established that such artificial entities are not protected by the Fifth Amendment. *Bellis v. United States,* 417 U.S. 85, 94 S.Ct. 2179, 40 L.Ed.2d 678 (1974). Petitioner instead relies solely upon the argument that his act of producing the documents has independent testimonial significance, which would incriminate him individually, and that the Fifth Amendment prohibits government compulsion of that act. The bases for this argument are extrapolated from the decisions of this Court in *Fisher* and *Doe.* * * *

Had petitioner conducted his business as a sole proprietorship, *Doe* would require that he be provided the opportunity to show that his act of production would entail testimonial self-incrimination. But petitioner has operated his business through the corporate form, and we have long recognized that for purposes of the Fifth Amendment, corporations and other collective entities are treated differently from individuals. This doctrine—known as the collective entity rule—has a lengthy and distinguished pedigree.

The rule was first articulated by the Court in the case of *Hale v. Henkel,* 201 U.S. 43, 26 S.Ct. 370, 50 L.Ed. 652 (1906). Hale, a corporate officer, had been served with a subpoena ordering him to produce corporate records and to testify concerning certain corporate transactions. Although Hale was protected by personal immunity, he sought to resist the demand for the records by interposing a Fifth Amendment privilege on behalf of the corporation. The Court rejected that argument: "[W]e are of the opinion that there is a clear distinction * * * between an individual and a corporation, and * * * the latter has no right to refuse to submit its books and papers for an examination at the suit of the State." The Court explained that the corporation "is a creature of the State," with powers limited by the State. As such, the State may, in the exercise of its right to oversee the corporation, demand the production of corporate records. * * *

Although *Hale* settled that a corporation has no Fifth Amendment privilege, the Court did not address whether a corporate officer could resist a subpoena for corporate records by invoking his personal privilege—Hale had been protected by immunity. In *Wilson v. United States,* 221 U.S. 361, 31 S.Ct. 538, 55 L.Ed. 771 (1911), the Court answered that question in the negative. * * * Wilson refused to produce [subpoenaed corporate] books, arguing that the Fifth Amendment prohibited compulsory production of personally incriminating books that he held and controlled. The Court rejected this argument, observing * * *:

"[Wilson] held the corporate books subject to the corporate duty. If the corporation were guilty of misconduct, he could not withhold its books to save it; and if he were implicated in the violations of law, he could not withhold the books to protect himself from the effect of their disclosures. The [State's] reserved power of visitation would seriously be embarrassed, if not wholly defeated in its effective exercise, if guilty officers could refuse inspection of the records and papers of the corporation. No personal privilege to which they are entitled requires such a conclusion. * * * "

In a companion case, *Dreier v. United States,* 221 U.S. 394, 31 S.Ct. 550, 55 L.Ed. 784 (1911), the Court applied the holding in *Wilson* to a Fifth Amendment attack on a subpoena addressed to the corporate custodian. Although the subpoena in *Wilson* had been addressed to the corporation, the Court found the distinction irrelevant: "Dreier was not entitled to refuse the production of the corporate records. By virtue of the fact that they were the documents of the corporation in his custody, and not his private papers, he was under the obligation to produce them when called for by proper process."

The next significant step in the development of the collective entity rule occurred in *United States v. White,* 322 U.S. 694, 64 S.Ct. 1248, 88 L.Ed. 1542 (1944), in which the Court held that a labor union is a collective entity unprotected by the Fifth Amendment. * * * [We reasoned] that the Fifth Amendment privilege applies only to natural individuals and protects only private papers. Representatives of a "collective group" act as agents "[a]nd the official records and documents of the organization that are held by them in a representative rather than in a personal capacity cannot be the subject of the personal privilege against self-incrimination, even though production of the papers might tend to incriminate them personally." With this principle in mind, the Court turned to whether a union is a collective group:

"The test * * * is whether one can fairly say under all the circumstances that a particular type of organization has a character so impersonal in the scope of its membership and activities that it cannot be said to embody or represent the purely private or personal interests of its constituents, but rather to embody their common or group interests only. If so, the privilege cannot be invoked on behalf of the organization or its representatives in their official capacity. Labor unions—national or local, incorporated or unincorporated—clearly meet that test."

In applying the collective entity rule to unincorporated associations such as unions, the Court jettisoned reliance on the visitatorial powers of the State over corporations owing their existence to the State—one of the bases for earlier decisions.

The frontiers of the collective entity rule were expanded even further in *Bellis v. United States,* 417 U.S. 85, 94 S.Ct. 2179, 40 L.Ed.2d 678 (1974), in which the Court ruled that a partner in a small partnership could not properly refuse to produce partnership records. * * * After rehearing prior precedent involving corporations and unincorporated associations, the Court examined the partnership form and observed that is had many of the incidents found relevant in prior collective entity decisions. The Court suggested that the test articulated in *White* for determining the applicability of the Fifth Amendment to organizations was "not particularly helpful in the broad range of cases." The Court rejected the notion that the "formulation in *White* can be reduced to a simple proposition based solely upon the size of the organization. It is well settled that no privilege can be claimed by the custodian of corporate records, regardless of how small the corporation may be." *Bellis* held the partnership's financial records in a "representative capacity" and therefore "his personal privilege against compulsory self-incrimination is inapplicable." Ibid.

The plain mandate of these decisions is that without regard to whether the subpoena is addressed to the corporation, or as here, to the individual in his capacity as a custodian, see *Dreier; Bellis,* a corporate custodian such as petitioner may not resist a subpoena for corporate records on Fifth Amendment grounds. Petitioner argues, however, that this rule falls in the wake of *Fisher* and *Doe.* In essence, petitioner's argument is as follows: In response to *Boyd v. United States,* with its privacy rationale shielding personal books and records, the Court developed the collective entity rule, which declares simply that corporate records are not private and therefore are not protected by the Fifth Amendment. The collective entity decisions were concerned with the contents of the documents subpoenaed, however, and not with the act of production. In *Fisher* and *Doe,* the Court moved away from the privacy based collective entity rule, replacing it with a compelled testimony standard under which the contents of business documents are never privileged but the act of producing the documents may be. Under this new regime, the act of production privilege is available without regard to the entity whose records are being sought. * * *

To be sure, the holding in *Fisher*—later reaffirmed in *Doe*—embarked upon a new course of Fifth Amendment analysis. We cannot agree, however, that it rendered the collective entity rule obsolete. The agency rationale undergirding the collective entity decisions, in which custodians asserted that production of entity records would incriminate them personally, survives. From *Wilson* forward, the Court has consistently recognized that the custodian of corporate or entity records holds those documents in a representative rather than a personal capacity. Artificial entities such as corporations may act only through their agents, and, a custodian's assumption of his representative capacity leads to certain obligations, including the duty to produce corporate records on proper demand by the Government. Under those circumstances, the custodian's act of production is not deemed a personal act, but rather an act of the corporation. Any claim of Fifth

Amendment privilege asserted by the agent would be tantamount to a claim of privilege by the corporation—which of course possesses no such privilege. * * *

Indeed, the opinion in *Fisher*—upon which petitioner places primary reliance—indicates that the custodian of corporate records may not interpose a Fifth Amendment objection to the compelled production of corporate records, even though the act of production may prove personally incriminating. The *Fisher* court cited the collective entity decisions with approval and offered those decisions to support the conclusion that the production of the accountant's workpapers would "not * * * involve testimonial self-incrimination." * * * In a footnote, the Court explained: "In these cases compliance with the subpoena is required even though the books have been kept by the person subpoenaed and his producing them would itself be sufficient authentication to permit their introduction against him." n. 14. The Court thus reaffirmed the obligation of a corporate custodian to comply with a subpoena addressed to him.

That point was reiterated by Justice Brennan in his concurrence in *Fisher*. Although Justice Brennan disagreed with the majority as to its use of the collective entity cases to support the proposition that the act of production is not testimonial, he nonetheless acknowledged that a custodian may not resist a subpoena on the ground that the act of production would be incriminating. * * * [For] "one in control of the records of an artificial organization undertakes an obligation with respect to those records foreclosing any exercise of his privilege." Thus, whether one concludes—as did the Court—that a custodian's production of corporate records is deemed not to constitute testimonial self-incrimination, or instead that a custodian waives the right to exercise the privilege, the lesson of *Fisher* is clear: A custodian may not resist a subpoena for corporate records on Fifth Amendment grounds.

Petitioner also attempts to extract support for his contention from *Curcio v. United States,* 354 U.S. 118, 77 S.Ct. 1145, 1 L.Ed.2d 1225 (1957). But rather than bolstering petitioner's argument, we think *Curcio* substantiates the Government's position. Curcio had been served with two subpoenas addressed to him in his capacity as secretary treasurer of a local union. One subpoena required that he produce union records, the other that he testify. Curcio appeared before the grand jury, stated that the books were not in his possession, and refused to answer any questions as to their whereabouts.

The *Curcio* Court made clear that with respect to a custodian of a collective entity's records, the line drawn was between oral testimony and other forms of incrimination. "A custodian, by assuming the duties of his office, undertakes the obligation to produce the books of which he is custodian in response to a rightful exercise of the State's visitorial [*sic*] powers. But he cannot lawfully be compelled, in the absence of a grant of adequate immunity from prosecution, to condemn himself by his own *oral testimony*. (Emphasis added). In distinguishing those cases in which a corporate officer was required to produce corporate records and merely identify them by oral testimony, the Court showed that it understood the testimonial nature of the act of production: "The custodian's act of producing books or records in response to a subpoena *duces tecum* is itself a representation that the documents produced are those demanded by the subpoena. Requiring the custodian to identify or authenticate the documents for admission in evidence merely makes explicit what is implicit in the production itself." In the face of this recognition, the Court nonetheless noted: "In this case petitioner might have been proceeded against for his failure to produce the records demanded by the subpoena *duces tecum*."

We note further that recognizing a Fifth Amendment privilege on behalf of the records custodians of collective entities would have a detrimental impact on the Government's efforts to prosecute "white-collar crime," one of the most serious problems confronting law enforcement authorities. "The greater portion of evidence of wrongdoing by an organization or its representatives is usually found in the official records and documents of that organization. Were the cloak of the privilege to be thrown around these impersonal records and documents, effective enforcement of many federal and state laws would be impossible." *White.* If custodians could assert a privilege, authorities would be stymied not only in their enforcement efforts against those individuals but also in their prosecutions or organizations. In *Bellis*, the Court observed: "In view of the inescapable fact that an artificial entity can only act to produce its records through its individual officers or agents recognition of the individual's claim of privilege with respect to the financial records of the organization would substantially undermine the unchallenged rule that the organization itself is not entitled to claim any Fifth Amendment privilege, and largely frustrate legitimate governmental regulation of such organizations."

Petitioner suggest, however, that these concerns can be minimized by the simple expedient of either granting the custodian statutory immunity as to the act of production, 18 U.S.C. §§ 6002–6003, or addressing the subpoena to the corporation and allowing it to choose an agent to produce the records who can do so without incriminating himself. We think neither proposal satisfactorily addresses these concerns. Taking the last first, it is no doubt true that if a subpeona is addressed to a corporation, the corporation "must find some means by which to comply because no Fifth Amendment defense is available to it." The means most commonly used to comply is the appointment of an alternate custodian. But petitioner insists he cannot be required to aid the appointed custodian in his search for the demanded records, for any statement to the surrogate would itself be testimonial and incriminating. If this is correct, then petitioner's "solution" is a chimera. In situations such as this—where the corporate custodian is likely the only person with knowledge about the demanded documents—the appointment of a surrogate will simply not ensure that the documents sought will ever reach the grand jury room; the appointed custodian will essentially be sent on an unguided search.

This problem is eliminated if the Government grants the subpoenaed custodian statutory immunity for the testimonial aspects of his act of production. But that "solution" also entails a significant drawback. All of the evidence obtained under a grant of immunity to the custodian may of course be used freely against the corporation, but if the Government has any thought of prosecuting the custodian, a grant of act of production immunity can have serious consequences. Testimony obtained pursuant to a grant of statutory use immunity may be used neither directly nor derivatively. 18 U.S.C. § 6002. And "[o]ne raising a claim under [the federal immunity] statute need only show that he testified under a grant of immunity in order to shift to the government the heavy burden of proving that all of the evidence it proposes to use was derived from legitimate independent sources." *Kastigar* [p. 730]. Even in cases where the Government does not employ the immunized testimony for any purpose—direct or derivative—against the witness, the Government's inability to meet the "heavy burden" it bears may result in the preclusion of crucial evidence that was obtained legitimately.[10]

---

10. The dissent asserts that recognition of an act of production privilege on behalf of corporate custodians will not seriously undermine law enforcement efforts directed against

Although a corporate custodian is not entitled to resist a subpoena on the ground that his act of production will be personally incriminating, we do think certain consequences flow from the fact that the custodian's act of production is one in his representative rather than personal capacity. Because the custodian acts as a representative, the act is deemed one of the corporation and not the individual. Therefore, the Government concedes, as it must, that it may make no evidentiary use of the "individual act" against the individual. For example, in a criminal prosecution against the custodian, the Government may not introduce into evidence before the jury the fact that the subpoena was served upon and the corporation's documents were delivered by one particular individual, the custodian. The Government has the right, however, to use the corporation's act of production against the custodian. The Government may offer testimony—for example, from the process server who delivered the subpoena and from the individual who received the records—establishing that the corporation produced the records subpoenaed. The jury may draw from the corporation's act of production the conclusion that the records in question are authentic corporate records, which the corporation possessed, and which it produced in response to the subpoena. And if the defendant held a prominent position within the corporation that produced the records, the jury may, just as it would had someone else produced the documents, reasonably infer that he had possession of the documents or knowledge of their contents. Because the jury is not told that the defendant produced the records, any nexus between the defendant and the documents results solely from the corporation's act of production and other evidence in the case.[11]

Consistent with our precedent, the United States Court of Appeals for the Fifth Circuit ruled that petitioner could not resist the subpoena for corporate documents on the ground that the act of production might tend to incriminate him. The judgment is therefore affirmed.

Justice KENNEDY, with whom Justice BRENNAN, Justice MARSHALL, and Justice SCALIA join, dissenting.

* * * The majority's apparent reasoning is that collective entities have no privilege and so their employees must have none either. The Court holds that a corporate agent must incriminate himself even when he is named in the subpoena and is a target of the investigation, and even when it is conceded that compliance requires compelled, personal, testimonial, incriminating assertions. I disagree with that conclusion; find no precedent for it; maintain that if there is a likelihood of personal self-incrimination the narrow use immunity permitted by statute can be granted without frustrating the investigation of collective entities; and submit that basic Fifth Amendment principles should not be avoided and manipulated, which is the necessary effect of this decision.

those custodians because only the custodian's act of production need be immunized. But the burden of proving an independent source that a grant of immunity places on the Government could, in our view, have just such a deleterious effect on law enforcement efforts.

11. We reject the suggestion that the limitation on the evidentiary use of the custodian's act of production is the equivalent of constructive use immunity barred under our decision in *Doe.* Rather, the limitation is a necessary concomitant of the notion that a corporate custodian acts as an agent and not an individual when he produces corporate records in response to a subpoena addressed to him in his representative capacity.

We leave open the question whether the agency rationale supports compelling a custodian to produce corporate records when the custodian is able to establish, by showing for example that he is the sole employee and officer of the corporation, that the jury would inevitably conclude that he produced the records.

* * * The majority does not challenge the assumption that compliance with the subpoena here would require acts of testimonial self-incrimination from Braswell; indeed, the Government itself made this assumption in submitting its argument. The question presented, therefore, is whether an individual may be compelled, simply by virtue of his status as a corporate custodian, to perform a testimonial act which will incriminate him personally. The majority relies entirely on the collective entity rule in holding that such compulsion is constitutional.

The collective entity rule provides no support for the majority's holding. * * * In none of the collective entity cases cited by the majority, and in none that I have found, were we presented with a claim that the custodian would be incriminated by the act of production, in contrast to the contents of the documents. The distinction is central. * * * Our decision in *Wilson,* and in later collective entity cases reflected, I believe, the Court's understandable unease with drawing too close a connection between an individual and an artificial entity. On a more practical level, the Court was also unwilling to draw too close a connection between the custodian and the contents of business documents over which he had temporary control but which belonged to his employer, often were prepared by others, and in all events were prepared voluntarily. This last factor became the focus of our analysis in *Fisher,* where we made clear that the applicability of the Fifth Amendment privilege depends on compulsion. *Fisher* put to rest the notion that a privilege may be claimed with respect to the contents of business records that were voluntarily prepared.

The act of producing documents stands on an altogether different footing. While a custodian has no necessary relation to the contents of documents within his control, the act of production is inescapably his own. Production is the precise act compelled by the subpoena, and obedience, in some cases, will require the custodian's own testimonial assertions. That was the basis of our recognition of the privilege in *United States v. Doe (Doe I).* The entity processing the documents in *Doe* was, as the majority points out, a sole proprietorship, not a corporation, partnership, or labor union. But the potential for self-incrimination inheres in the act demanded of the individual, and as a consequence the nature of the entity is irrelevant to determining whether there is ground for the privilege.

* * * Recognition of the privilege here would * * * avoid adoption of the majority's metaphysical progression, which, I respectfully submit, is flawed. Beginning from ordinary principles of agency, the majority proceeds to the conclusion that when a corporate employee, or an employee of a labor union or partnership, complies with a subpoena for production of documents, his act is necessarily and solely the act of the entity. * * * [But] the heart of the matter, as everyone knows, is that the Government does not see Braswell as a mere agent at all; and the majority's theory is difficult to square with what will often be the Government's actual practice. The subpoena in this case was not directed to Worldwide Machinery Sales, Inc., or Worldwide Purchasing, Inc. It was directed to "Randy Braswell, President, Worldwide Machinery Sales, Inc., Worldwide Purchasing, Inc." and informed him that "[y]ou are hereby commanded" to provide the specified documents. The Government explained at oral argument that it often chooses to designate an individual recipient, rather than the corporation generally, when it serves a subpoena because "[we] want the right to make that individual comply with the subpoena." This is not the language of agency. By issuing a subpoena which the Government insists is "directed to petitioner personally," it has forfeited any claim that it is simply making a demand on a corporation that, in turn, will have to find a physical agent to perform its duty. What the Government seeks instead is the right to choose any corporate agent as a target of its subpoena and compel that individual to disclose certain information by his own actions.

The majority gives the corporate agent fiction a weight it simply cannot bear. In a peculiar attempt to mitigate the force of its own holdings, it impinges upon its own analysis by concluding that, while the Government may compel a named individual to produce records, in any later proceeding against the person it cannot divulge that he performed the act. But if that is so, it is because the Fifth Amendment protects the person without regard to his status as a corporate employee; and once this be admitted, the necessary support for the majority's case has collapsed. * * *

The majority's abiding concern is that if a corporate officer who is the target of a subpoena is allowed to assert the privilege, it will impede the Government's power to investigate corporations, unions, and partnerships, to uncover and prosecute white collar crimes, and otherwise to enforce its visitatorial powers. There are at least two answers to this. The first, and most fundamental, is that the text of the Fifth Amendment does not authorize exceptions premised on such rationales. Second, even if it were proper to invent such exceptions, the dangers prophesied by the majority are overstated.

Recognition of the right to assert a privilege does not mean it will exist in many cases. In many instances, the production of documents may implicate no testimonial assertions at all. In *Fisher,* for example, we held that the specific acts required by the subpoena before us "would not itself involve testimonial self-incrimination" because, in that case, "the existence and location of the papers [were] a foregone conclusion and the taxpayer adds little or nothing to the sum total of the Government's information by conceding that he in fact has the papers." Whether a particular act is testimonial and self-incriminating is largely a factual issue to be decided in each case. In the case before us, the Government has made its submission on the assumption that the subpoena would result in incriminating testimony. The existence of a privilege in future cases, however, is not an automatic result.

Further, to the extent testimonial assertions are being compelled, use immunity can be granted without impeding the investigation. Where the privilege is applicable, immunity will be needed for only one individual, and solely with respect to evidence derived from the act of production itself. The Government would not be denied access to the records it seeks, it would be free to use the contents of the records against everyone, and it would be free to use any testimonial act implicit in production against all but the custodian it selects. In appropriate cases the Government will be able to establish authenticity, possession, and control by means other than compelling assertions about them from a suspect.

In one sense the case before us may not be a particularly sympathetic one. Braswell was the sole stockholder of the corporation and ran it himself. Perhaps that is why the Court suggests he waived his Fifth Amendment self-incrimination rights by using the corporate form. One does not always, however, have the choice of his or her employer, much less the choice of the business enterprise through which the employer conducts its business. Though the Court here hints at a waiver, nothing in Fifth Amendment jurisprudence indicates that the acceptance of employment should be deemed a waiver of a specific protection that is as basic a part of our constitutional heritage as is the privilege against self-incrimination.

The law is not captive to its own fictions. Yet, in the matter before us the Court employs the fiction that personal incrimination of the employee is neither sought by the Government nor cognizable by the law. That is a regrettable holding, for the conclusion is factually unsound, unnecessary for legitimate regulation, and a violation of the Self–Incrimination Clause of the Fifth Amendment of the Constitution. For these reasons, I dissent.

Notes and Questions

1. *The collective entity rule.* Although neither the majority nor dissent in *Braswell* question the collective entity doctrine itself (as distinguished from its bearing on the availability of the privilege to the custodian), that doctrine has been questioned by commentators. See e.g., Mosteller, Note 3, p. 755; Gerstein, Note 5, p. 743. First, it is noted that several of the systemic values cited in *Murphy* as supporting the privilege (e.g., the accusatorial process) are clearly applicable to the prosecution of entities as well as individuals.[a] Second, it is suggested that the difficulties that application of the privilege would present to "legitimate government regulation" (see p. 762) are also likely to be presented where a business is a sole proprietorship. Thus, the required records doctrine (see Note 5 infra), which also finds support in the state's regulatory authority, draws no distinction between collective entities and sole proprietors. Finally, the point is made that the doctrine applies to all entity records based in part on the suggestion that those records necessarily are accessible to others, but the entity may be so small or the records viewed as so secretive in content as to be accessible only to a single person.

2. *The "small family partnership."* Consider in light of *Braswell*, IN RE GRAND JURY SUBPOENA DUCES TECUM DATED NOVEMBER 13, 1984 (DOE), 605 F.Supp. 174 (E.D.N.Y.1985). The court there considered a self-incrimination objection of one of two partners in a New York consulting firm to a grand jury subpoena directing the production of various partnership records. The partnership consisted of petitioner and his wife, had no employees, and produced annual gross receipts of $85,000. The petitioner argued that the collective entity doctrine should not apply to such a partnership. He noted that while *Bellis* had held the doctrine applicable to a small partnership (a law partnership of 3 partners and six employees), the Court there had noted that "[t]his might be a different case if it involved a small family partnership, see *United States v. Slutsky,* 352 F.Supp. 1105 (S.D.N.Y.1972) * * * or, as the Solicitor General suggests, if there were some other pre-existing relationship of confidentiality among the partners." McLAUGHLIN, D.J., agreed that this case presented such an exception:

"[A] ritualistic, mechanical application of the *Bellis* test will almost invariably result in a holding that partnership records are never privileged. The reasons for this are clear. The rights and obligations of partners under New York law, discussed above, are enumerated in the Uniform Partnership Act. The Act is presently in effect in 48 States as well as the District of Columbia, and its provisions were discussed at length in *Bellis.* * * * Similarly, all partnerships, no matter their size, must file income tax returns *qua* partnership. * * * Finally, it is impossible to imagine a partner who will be able to demonstrate, under the *Bellis*

---

a. Consider also the availability (and unavailability) to the collective entity of other constitutional rights, such as Fourth Amendment protection against unreasonable searches (applicable), Fifth Amendment protection against being placed twice in jeopardy (assumed to apply), the Fifth Amendment right to prosecution by grand jury indictment (not applicable, according to the Ninth Circuit, Since potential punishment, lacking imprisonment, is not "infamous"), the Sixth Amendment right to a jury trial (applicable). See Peter Henning, *The Conundrum of Corporate Criminal Liability: Seeking A Consistent Approach to the Constitutional Rights of Corporations in Criminal Prosecutions,* 63 Tenn.L. Rev. 793, (1996).

test, that he holds subpoenaed records in a personal capacity. As discussed above, and as was emphasized in *Bellis*, partnership records are partnership property; access to them, and control over them, is regulated by state partnership law. This, coupled with an artfully drawn subpoena, effectively precludes any partner from claiming he holds subpoenaed records in a personal capacity. * * * Nonetheless, * * * [i]f, as *Bellis* suggests, there exists a partnership whose records are protected by the Fifth Amendment from compelled disclosure, petitioner's husband-wife consulting firm is it. The two criteria suggested in *Bellis* for the exception, a small family partnership, or one with a pre-existing relationship of confidentiality between partners, are both satisfied here. There are no employees, and no office outside the partners' home. * * * It seems clear that the *Bellis* Court contemplated that individual owners of the proverbial 'Mom and Pop' stores would continue to enjoy the protection of the Fifth Amendment even though they elected to conduct business as a partnership. If the *Bellis* Court intended to hold that no partners could ever invoke the Fifth Amendment with respect to partnership records, it would easily have said so."

Compare *In re September 1975 Special Grand Jury*, 435 F.Supp. 538 (N.D.Ind.1977) (holding the entity doctrine applicable to a husband and wife who operated a trailer park as co-owners under an enterprise name, shared profits, and filed a partnership tax return, although they did not have a written partnership agreement). Consider also Peter Henning, *Testing the Limits of Investigation and Prosecuting White Collar Crime*, 54 U. Pitt L.Rev. 406 (1992): "After *Braswell*, the production of the exact same types of records, such as invoices or ledgers, depends on whether the owner of the enterprise chose to incorporate the business, or maintain a sole proprietorship or small partnership arrangement. That decision can have momentous consequences, because if the business is not incorporated, the owner may be able to shield the records through the assertion of the Fifth Amendment privilege. It is even possible under *Braswell* for a person to own two businesses, one a corporation and the other a sole proprietorship, and be able to assert the privilege to resist production of one set of records yet be forced to produce the records for the other business. It is odd that the seemingly inconsequential choice of what organizational form to use for a business, which may have little if any effect of its operations, can determine the applicability of a constitutional right."

3. *Scope of the entity agent's obligation*. In *Curcio v. United States*, discussed in *Braswell* (p. 761), the Court held that the obligation of the entity agent did not extend to explaining the whereabouts of records no longer in his possession. *Curcio* noted that lower court rulings had held that "a corporate officer who has been required by subpoena to produce corporate records may also be required, by oral testimony, to identify them," but those cases were "distinguishable" and the Court had no need "to pass on their validity." Does *Braswell* necessarily affirm those rulings? See *In re Custodian of Records of Variety Distributing*, 927 F.2d 244 (6th Cir.1991). Looking to *Braswell*'s discussion of *Curcio*, the *Variety Distributing* court concluded that the custodian can be required to authenticate the documents for admission in evidence, as that "merely makes explicit what is implicit in the production itself (*Curcio*)." This duty existed even though the necessary statements (e.g., that the custodian is familiar with the company's recordkeeping and knows the company has kept the records in the course of regular business activity) may be potentially incriminating in some situations. However, "because the custodian of corporate records is acting in a representative rather than a personal capacity, he is protected against the future evidentiary use of the testimony." Consider, however, Peter Henning, *Finding What Was Lost: Sorting Out the*

Custodian's Privilege Against Self–Incrimination From the Compelled Production of Records, 77 Neb. L.Rev. 34 (1998) (*Variety Distributing* erred in reading *Curcio* as going beyond simply requiring the custodian "to testify before a grand jury only to make explicit to the grand jurors what was implicit in the production of records", and "compelling evidentiary testimony related solely to the trial phase").

4. *The prohibition against evidentiary use of the custodian's act of production.* What is the grounding of the evidentiary-use prohibition imposed by *Brasswell*? See Henning, supra Note 3, asking whether the Court here has established a "quasi-constitutional" prohibition or a standard based upon its "supervisory power" (see Note 4, p. 686). As to the significance of limiting the prohibition to evidentiary use, as opposed to granting immunity, consider the investigative value of determining that a particular person designated as custodian does have access to the records in question. See Henning, supra (discussing that potential investigative value in light of case law that refuses to allow the individual designated by the government to refuse to respond to the subpoena because the corporation has designated another person as its official custodian).

5. *Production by the "single-person" corporation.* What is the significance of the second paragraph of footnote 11 of *Braswell* ? In *In re Grand Jury 89–4 Subpoena Duces Tecum,* 727 F.Supp. 265 (E.D.Va.1989), suggested that the issue left open in that footnote could bear upon not only a one-person corporation, but also a small family corporation in which one member (Doe) was the dominant actor. The court noted that a two step inquiry was required: "(1) would a jury, told that the corporation produced the documents, nonetheless inevitably conclude that it was Doe who had possession of the documents and produced them, and if so (2) would this give rise to any incriminating inferences concerning a documents (i) existence, (ii) authenticity, or (iii) custody." Finding that an insufficient showing had been made as to the second step, the court found it unnecessary to consider the consequences if both inquiries produced affirmative responses. Would the court then hold the privilege applicable, or require the corporation to make production through a specially appointed agent, with the jury informed that it was the agent who produced the documents on behalf of the corporation? If the latter approach is taken, would that agent be barred from testifying to conversations with the dominant actor that enabled him to identify the records (and to provide authentication, where needed)?

6. *Personal documents.* Where the document subpoenaed is a desk calendar, pocket diary, or similar item, the claim is oftener made that, through kept by a corporate employee, it constitutes a "personal record" and therefore is not subject to the entity doctrine. In responding to such a claim, courts apply a "multifactor balancing approach" that attempts to identify "the essential nature" of the document "in light of the entire context of [its] ownership preparation, and use." *In re Grand Jury Proceedings,* 55 F.3d 1012 (5th Cir.1995) ("We agree with the Second Circuit that the following nonexhaustive list of criteria is relevant in the inquiry: who prepared the document; the nature of its contents; its purpose or use; who possessed it; who had access to it; whether the corporation required its preparation; and whether its existence was necessary to or in furtherance of corporate business").

7. *"Required records." Shapiro v. United States,* 335 U.S. 1, 68 S.Ct. 1375, 92 L.Ed. 1787 (1948), expanding upon some dictum in *Wilson,* held that the self-incrimination clause is not violated by requiring a person to keep records of certain business activities and to make those records available for government

inspection. Accordingly, a grand jury subpoena requiring the production of required records may not be successfully challenged on self-incrimination grounds even though the records are those of a business conducted as an individual proprietorship rather than an entity. See *Grand Jury Subpoena Duces Tecum (Underhill)*, 781 F.2d 64 (1986) (although act of production may be incriminating, *Fisher–Doe* do not apply to required records, as nothing in these opinions casts doubt as the "continuing validity of * * * *Shapiro* and its progeny"). Business records will not be classified as required records under *Shapiro* unless three prerequisites are met: (1) the governmental requirement that records be kept must be "essentially regulatory" in nature; (2) the records must be "of a kind which the regulated party has customarily kept," and (3) the records "must have assumed some 'public aspects' which render them at least analogous to public documents." *Grosso v. United States*, 390 U.S. 62, 88 S.Ct. 709, 19 L.Ed.2d 906 (1968). See also Stephen Saltzburg, *The Required Records Doctrine: Its Lessons for the Privilege Against Self–Incrimination*, 53 U.Chi.L.Rev. 6 (1986).[c]

8. The implications of the several doctrines discussed in this section were brought together in an unusual setting in *Baltimore City Department of Social Services v. Bouknight*, 493 U.S. 549, 110 S.Ct. 900, 107 L.Ed.2d 992 (1990). The Supreme Court there rejected a self-incrimination objection to a subpoena directing respondent Bouknight to produce her infant son, an abused child who had previously been declared a ward of the court. The Court noted that the respondent could not claim the privilege based upon "anything an examination of the [child] might reveal," as that would be a claim based upon "the contents or nature of the thing demanded." However, the mother could conceivably claim the privilege because "the act of production would amount to testimony regarding her control over and possession of [the child]." While the state could "readily introduce [other] evidence of Bouknight's continuing control over the child" (including the court order giving her limited custody and her previous statements reflecting control), her "implicit communication of control over [the child] at the moment of production might aid the state in prosecuting Bouknight [for child abuse]." The Court had no need to decide, however, whether "this limited testimonial assertion is sufficiently incriminating and sufficiently testimonial for purposes of the privilege." In receiving conditional custody from the juvenile court, the mother had "assumed custodial duties related to production" (analogous to that of an entity agent) and had done so as part of noncriminal regulatory scheme which included a production component (analogous to regulations sustained under the required records doctrine). The Court added that it had no need in the case before it "to define the precise limitations that may exist upon the State's ability to use the testimonial aspects of Bouknight's act of production in subsequent criminal proceedings," but the "imposition of such limitations," as done in *Braswell,* was not "foreclosed."

c. The Court has also upheld other statutes requiring disclosure of information in a regulatory setting notwithstanding that such information "could well be 'a link in the chain' of evidence leading to prosecution." *California v. Byers*, 402 U.S. 424, 91 S.Ct. 1535, 29 L.Ed.2d 9 (1971). *Byers* sustained a state "hit and run" statute which required the driver of a motor vehicle involved in an accident to stop at the scene and give his name and address. The Court noted that such statutes were regulatory measures, "not intended to facilitate criminal convictions," and were directed to all persons who drove automobiles. Also, there was no disclosure of inherently illegal activity as "most automobile accidents occur without creating criminal liability."

Chapter 11

THE SCOPE OF THE EXCLUSIONARY RULES*

SECTION 1. "STANDING" TO OBJECT TO THE ADMISSION OF EVIDENCE (OR "THE EXTENT OF A PARTICULAR DEFENDANT'S RIGHTS UNDER THE FOURTH AMENDMENT")**

A. HISTORICAL BACKGROUND AND OVERVIEW

1. *Must the person asserting a Fourth Amendment claim have been the victim of the challenged search or seizure?* Long before the Supreme Court authoritatively resolved the issue, the lower courts had developed the doctrine that a defendant lacked "standing" to challenge evidence seized in violation of a third party's constitutional rights. The early basis for this doctrine seems to have been "the joint foundation of the Fourth Amendment and the self-incrimination clause of the Fifth," Comment, 58 Yale L.J. 144, 156 (1948). The rule was also "based on the theory that the evidence is excluded to provide a remedy for a wrong done to the defendant, and that accordingly, if the defendant has not been wronged he is entitled to no remedy." *People v. Martin,* 290 P.2d 855, 857 (Cal.1955) (Traynor, J.).

Six years before *Mapp,* the California Supreme Court's emphasis on the deterrence rationale for the exclusionary rule led it to abolish the "standing" requirement. *People v. Martin, supra.* "Such a limitation," observed the California court, "virtually invites law enforcement officers to violate the rights of third parties and to trade the escape of a criminal whose rights are violated for the conviction of others by the use of the evidence illegally obtained against them." Id.[a]

---

* Harmless error is treated elsewhere; see Ch. 27, § 4.

** *Rakas v. Illinois* (1980) (discussed at p. 776).

a. *In re Lance W.,* 694 P.2d 744 (Cal.1985) (discussed at p. 57), held that Proposition 8, an initiative approved by California voters in 1982, had abolished *Martin's* "vicarious exclusionary rule."

The California Supreme Court had ruled earlier, *People v. Varnum,* 427 P.2d 772 (1967), that *Martin* did not apply to *Escobedo-Miranda* violations. The majority, per Traynor, J., reasoned: "Noncoercive questioning is not in itself unlawful [and the rights] protected by *Escobedo* [and] *Miranda* are violated only when evidence obtained without the required warnings and waiver is introduced against the person whose questioning produced the evidence. The basis for the [*Miranda* warnings] is the privilege against self-incrimination [which] is not violated when the information elicited from an unwarned suspect is not used against him. [Unlike unreasonable searches and seizures], there is nothing unlawful in questioning an unwarned suspect so long as the police refrain [from tactics] condemned by due process and do not use against the suspect any evidence obtained."

For criticism of *Varnum,* see Notes, 37 U.Cin.L.Rev. 234 (1968); 15 U.C.L.A.L.Rev. 1060 (1968).

California's abolition of the "standing" requirement was "enthusiastically endorsed by most commentators." LaFave, § 11.3(j) at 227 (citing thirteen commentators), and when, in *Linkletter v. Walker* (1965) (p. 45), the U.S. Supreme Court seemed to explain and to justify the Fourth Amendment exclusionary rule as "the only effective deterrent to lawless police action," there was reason to think that the High Court, too, might scrap the "standing" requirement. Thus, two years after *Linkletter* and two years before *Alderman* infra, one commentator pointed out that "a system of classification based on 'victimness' provides no deterrence" against "searches that turn up evidence against persons other than the victim" and concluded that "the standing requirement is inconsistent with the presently accepted general deterrence theory of the exclusionary rule." Note, 34 U.Chi.L.Rev. 342, 358 (1967).

However, in ALDERMAN v. UNITED STATES, 394 U.S. 165, 89 S.Ct. 961, 22 L.Ed.2d 176 (1969), the Court, per WHITE, J., reaffirmed "the established principle [that] suppression of the product of a Fourth Amendment violation can be successfully urged only by those whose rights were violated by the search itself, not by those who are aggrieved solely by the introduction of damaging evidence. Coconspirators and codefendants have been accorded no special standing."[b] The Court was unmoved by the ascendancy of the deterrence rationale: "[We] are not convinced that the additional benefits of extending the exclusionary rule to other defendants would justify further encroachment upon the public interest in prosecuting those accused of crime and having them acquitted or convicted on the basis of all the evidence which exposes the truth."

Concurring in part and dissenting in part, FORTAS, J., argued that there was much to be said for abolishing the "standing" requirement: "The Fourth Amendment, unlike the Fifth, is couched in terms of a guarantee that the Government will not engage in unreasonable searches and seizures. It is a general prohibition[,] * * * not merely a privilege accorded to him whose domain has been lawlessly invaded. [It] is an assurance to all that the Government will exercise its formidable powers to arrest and to investigate only subject to the rule of law."[c]

2. *Does Alderman represent a genuine effort to strike a balance between the costs of exclusion and the need for deterrence?* Daniel Meltzer, *Deterring Constitutional Violations by Law Enforcement Officials: Plaintiffs and Defendants as Private Attorneys General,* 88 Colum.L.Rev. 247, 275 (1988) finds it hard to so understand the Court's standing doctrine: "It is possible, of course, that an effort to strike a desirable balance would result in a standing doctrine limited to those whose rights were violated by the illegal search. But such a result would be extremely surprising, as there are factors more relevant to the need for and benefits of deterrent remedies. These include the seriousness of the harm

b. A quarter-century later, in *United States v. Padilla,* 508 U.S. 77, 113 S.Ct. 1936, 123 L.Ed.2d 635 (1993) (per curiam), a unanimous Court quoted this language from *Alderman* in rejecting a so-called "coconspirator exception" to the standing doctrine. Under this exception, developed by the U.S. Court of Appeals for the Ninth Circuit, a coconspirator obtained a legitimate expectation of privacy for Fourth Amendment purposes if she had either a supervisory role in the conspiracy or joint control over the place of property involved in the challenged search or seizure. Such an exception, observed the *Padilla* Court is "not only contrary to the holding of *Alderman,* but at odds with [the

expectation of privacy approach taken in *Rakas,* p. 776, that now] govern[s] the analysis of Fourth Amendment search and seizure claims. Participants in a criminal conspiracy may have [exceptions of privacy and property interests], but the conspiracy itself neither adds to or detracts from them."

c. Justice Fortas' view is supported in Donald Doernberg, *"The Right of the People": Reconciling Collective and Individual Interests under the Fourth Amendment,* 58 N.Y.U.L.Rev. 259 (1983); Richard B. Kuhns, *The Concept of Personal Aggrievement in Fourth Amendment Standing Cases,* 65 Iowa L.Rev. 493 (1980).

caused by the search; the likelihood of detection; the perception of the sanction's severity; whether the violation was obvious or intentional; how susceptible to deterrence the search is; and how easily the resulting rules can be administered. A truly deterrence-focused standing doctrine would at least consider such factors, rather than simply assume that the optimal result is reached when only those who were victims of the search are empowered to suppress evidence."

3.   *The tension between the standing requirement and the exclusionary rule*. Consider Joshua Dressler, *Understanding Criminal Procedure* 303 (2d ed.1997): "Professor Anthony Amsterdam once noted that there are two competing perspectives on the Fourth Amendment. One view, the 'atomistic' perspective, is that the Fourth Amendment is 'a collection of protections of atomistic spheres of interest of individual citizens.' That is, the Fourth Amendment protects isolated individuals ('atoms'), in the sense that the amendment 'safeguard[s] *my* person and *your* house and *her* papers and *his* effects against unreasonable searches and seizures.'[12] The second view, the 'regulatory' perspective, is that the Fourth Amendment functions 'as a regulation of governmental conduct.' In other words, the amendment is intended to safeguard the collective 'people,' as in 'we, the people,' from governmental overreaching.

"As Fourth Amendment jurisprudence has developed, standing—based as it is on the premise that a person may raise a Fourth Amendment challenge only if he *personally* was a victim of unreasonable police activity—is based on the atomistic philosophy. In contrast, the exclusionary rule is regulatory in nature, in that its purpose is to deter police misconduct, in order to safeguard society as a whole.

"Understood in this way, the standing requirement and the exclusionary rule act, at least in part, in opposition to each other. This is because evidence seized in violation of the Fourth Amendment is excluded at trial in order to deter police misconduct; but, the requirement of standing to raise a Fourth Amendment claim often undercuts this deterrence goal, as it limits the number of people ('atoms') who can bring the misconduct to the attention of the courts so that the exclusionary rule can be applied."

As an example, Professor Dressler cites the *Payner* case, discussed in the next Note.

4.   *The use of the federal courts' "supervisory power" to overcome the standing requirement*. If there has ever been a case that called for the exercise of the federal courts' supervisory power to break out of the standing restriction it was UNITED STATES v. PAYNER, 447 U.S. 727, 100 S.Ct. 2439, 65 L.Ed.2d 468 (1980) (also discussed at p. 52). Nevertheless, a 6–3 majority, per POWELL, J., was unmoved.

Payner arose as follows: An IRS investigation into the financial activities of American citizens in the Bahamas focused on a certain Bahamian bank. When an official of that bank visited the United States, IRS agents stole his briefcase for a time, removed hundreds of documents from the briefcase, and photographed them. As a result of this "briefcase caper," Payner—precisely the kind of offender the IRS agents were seeking when they violated the bank official's rights—was convicted of federal income tax violations. Hemmed in by the standing requirement, but outraged by the government's "purposefully" illegal tactics, the federal district court invoked its supervisory power to exclude the tainted evidence.

12. Anthony G. Amsterdam, *Perspectives*   349, 367 (1974).
on the Fourth Amendment, 58 Minn.L.Rev.

But the Supreme Court rejected the federal court's "substitution of individual judgment for the controlling decisions of this Court." "The values assigned to the competing interests do not change," pointed out Justice Powell, "because a court has elected to analyze the question under the supervisory power instead of the Fourth Amendment. In either case, the need to deter the underlying conduct and the detrimental impact of excluding the evidence remain precisely the same."[d]

The *Payner* Court cautioned that exclusion of evidence in every case of illegality must be "weighed against the considerable harm that would flow from *indiscriminate application* of an exclusionary rule" (emphasis added), and that "*unbending application* of the exclusionary sanction * * * would impede unacceptably the truthfinding functions of judge and jury" (emphasis added). But consider Kamisar, *Does (Did) (Should) the Exclusionary Rule Rest on a "Principled Basis" Rather than an "Empirical" "Proposition"*, 16 Creighton L.Rev. 565, 638 (1983):

"The relevant question in *Payner* [was] not whether the exclusionary rule should *always* be applied when police illegality is somewhere in the picture, but whether it should *ever* be applied—taking into account the seriousness or flagrancy of the illegality—when the defendant lacks 'standing.' The question was not whether the exclusionary rule should be given 'unbending application,' but whether *the 'standing' requirement* should be. By deciding that even in a case like *Payner* a federal court is *unable* to exercise its supervisory powers to bar the evidence—by holding that 'judicial impotency is *compelled* in the face of such scandalous conduct' [LaFave, § 11.3(h)]—the Court gave us its answer.

"[The] *Payner* Court seemed content [to rely on] the balance it had struck in the early standing cases. But because it grew out of special and outrageous circumstances, the interests to be balanced in *Payner* were different. The question presented was[:] When the government has *intentionally manipulated* the standing requirement of the fourth amendment—when it has *deliberately and patently* violated the constitutional rights of a third party in order to obtain evidence against its real targets, and defendant is one of those targets—does the interest in discouraging (or reducing) the incentive to make *such* searches justify the exclusion of tainted evidence at the instance of a party who was not the [direct] victim of the challenged practice? The *Payner* Court never really spoke to this issue because it never really asked this question."

5. *"Automatic" standing.* In *Jones v. United States,* 362 U.S. 257, 80 S.Ct. 725, 4 L.Ed.2d 697 (1960), the defendant was charged with selling and distributing narcotics and facilitating the concealment and sale of the same narcotics, which permitted conviction largely on proof of unexplained possession of narcotics. The lower court denied standing because defendant had failed either to assert a sufficient interest in the apartment where the search occurred[e] or to allege ownership or possession of the narcotics, although doing so would have "forced" him to allege facts that would tend to convict him. The Supreme Court reversed: The "same element in this prosecution which has caused a dilemma, i.e., that possession both convicts and confers standing, eliminates any necessity for a

---

d. "The Court's decision to engraft the standing limitations of the Fourth Amendment onto the exercise of supervisory powers," protested dissenting Justice Marshall, joined by Brennan and Blackmun, JJ., "appears to render the supervisory powers superfluous. In order to establish that suppression of evidence under the supervisory powers would be proper,

the Court would also require Payner to establish a violation of his [constitutional rights]. This approach is totally unfaithful to our prior supervisory power cases [see generally pp. 51–55], which, contrary to the Court's suggestion, are not constitutional cases in disguise."

e. For this aspect of *Jones,* see Note 6 infra.

preliminary showing of an interest in the premises searched or the property seized, which ordinarily is required when standing is challenged." To hold otherwise "would be to permit the Government to have the advantage of contradictory positions as a basis of conviction."

However, the Court subsequently held, in *Simmons v. United States,* 390 U.S. 377, 88 S.Ct. 967, 19 L.Ed.2d 1247 (1968), that testimony given by a defendant in order to establish his "standing" "may not thereafter be used against him at trial on the issue of guilt." Were it otherwise, "a defendant who wishes to establish standing must do so at the risk that the words which he utters may later be used to incriminate him."

On the basis of *Simmons,* the Court subsequently abolished the *Jones* "automatic standing" rule and held that "defendants charged with crimes of possession may only claim the benefits of the exclusionary rule if their own Fourth Amendment rights have in fact been violated." UNITED STATES v. SALVUCCI, 448 U.S. 83, 100 S.Ct. 2547, 65 L.Ed.2d 619 (1980). Observed the Court, per REHNQUIST, J.: "The 'dilemma' identified in *Jones* * * * was eliminated [by] *Simmons,* [which] not only extends protection against [the] risk of self-incrimination in all of the cases covered by *Jones,* but also grants a form of 'use' immunity to those defendants charged with nonpossessory crimes."[f]

As for the vice of prosecutorial contradiction, the Court stated it need not decide whether that "could alone support a rule countenancing the exclusion of probative evidence on the grounds that someone other than the defendant was denied a Fourth Amendment right," for at least after *Rakas* [p. 776] it is clear that "a prosecutor may simultaneously maintain that a defendant criminally possessed the seized good, but was not subject to a Fourth Amendment deprivation, without legal contradiction." For a "person in legal possession of a good seized during an illegal search has not necessarily been subject to a Fourth Amendment deprivation. * * * We simply decline to use possession of a seized good as a substitute for a factual finding that the owner of the good has a legitimate expectation of privacy in the area searched."[g]

6. *Residential premises.* It has long been true, and is still so under the current expectation-of-privacy approach discussed in the next subsection, that one with a present possessory interest in the premises searched, e.g., a member of the

f. Dissenting Justice Marshall, joined by Brennan, J., disagreed that "*Simmons* provides complete protection against the 'self-incriminating dilemma,'" for "the prosecutor may still be permitted to use the defendant's testimony [at the suppression hearing] to impeach him at trial." The *Salvucci* majority managed to sidestep this argument, but somewhat misleadingly it asserted that "the Court has held that 'the protective shield of *Simmons* is not to be converted into a license for false representations,'" quoting from *United States v. Kahan,* 415 U.S. 239, 94 S.Ct. 1179, 39 L.Ed.2d 297 (1974). But *Kahan* involved the impeachment use of false testimony given at a pretrial hearing to establish defendant's eligibility for appointed counsel and the *Kahan* Court pointed out: "We are not dealing, as was the Court in *Simmons,* with what was 'believed' by the claimant to be a 'valid' constitutional claim. Respondent was not, therefore, faced with the type of intolerable choice *Simmons* sought to relieve. The protective shield of

Simmons is not to be converted into a license for false representations *on the issue of indigency* free from the risk that the claimant will be held accountable for his falsehood." (Emphasis added.)

Consider LaFave & Israel, § 9.2(a): "The best analogy [is] *New Jersey v. Portash* [440 U.S. 450, 99 S.Ct. 1292, 59 L.Ed.2d 501 (1979)], holding that testimony given before a grand jury following a grant of use testimony could not be used for impeachment purposes at the subsequent criminal trial. [It] would seem that defendant's testimony at a suppression hearing [is] 'compelled' in the *Portash* sense, for, as *Simmons* teaches, the defendant is confronted with the choice 'either to give up what he believed, with advice of counsel, to be a valid Fourth Amendment claim or, in effect, to waive his Fifth Amendment privilege against self-incrimination.'"

g. See also *Rawlings v. Kentucky,* p. 777.

family regularly residing in a home, may challenge that search even though not present when the search was conducted. As the *Alderman* Court explained: "If the police make an unwarranted search of a house and seize tangible property belonging to third parties [the] home owner may object to its use against him, not because he had any interest in the seized items [but] because they were the fruits of an unauthorized search of his house, which is itself expressly protected by the Fourth Amendment." The *Alderman* majority thus concluded that a person should have standing to challenge the legality of electronically overheard conversations in which he participated "or *conversations occurring on his premises, whether or not he was present or participated in those conversations*" (emphasis added).[h]

In *Jones v. United States,* Note 5, the Court held that "anyone legitimately on premises where a search occurs may challenge its legality." The defendant not only had permission to use the apartment of his friend, but had a key to the apartment with which he admitted himself on the day of the search. He also kept some possessions in the apartment. In the more recent *Rakas* case (p. 776), the Court rejected the *Jones* "legitimately on premises" *formulation*—this phrase "creates too broad a gauge for measurement of Fourth Amendment rights"—but it did not question *the result* in that case. The *Jones* holding "can best be explained," observed the *Rakas* Court, "by the fact that Jones had a legitimate expectation of privacy in the premises he was using [even] though his 'interest' in those premises might not have been a recognized property interest at common law."

Thirty years after *Jones* was decided, the Court held in *Minnesota v. Olson* (1990) (also discussed at p. 272), that defendant's "status as an overnight guest" showed that he had "an expectation of privacy in the home that society is prepared to recognize as reasonable." Thus he had a sufficient interest in the home to challenge the legality of the warrantless entry there.

7. Business premises. In *Mancusi v. DeForte,* 392 U.S. 364, 88 S.Ct. 2120, 20 L.Ed.2d 1154 (1968), where state police seized records belonging to a union local from an office defendant shared with several other union officials, the Court viewed the "crucial issue" as "whether the area was one in which there was a reasonable expectation of freedom from governmental intrusion." The Court answered in the affirmative. Even though defendant shared an office with others, he "still could reasonably have expected that only those persons and [their guests] would ever enter the office, and that records would not be touched except with their permission or that of union higherups."

"Consistent with *Mancusi,* courts have held that a corporate or individual defendant in possession of the business premises searched has standing, and that an officer or employee of the business enterprise has standing if 'there was a demonstrated nexus between the area searched and the work space of the defendant.' Exclusive use would seem clearly to establish standing, but (as *Mancusi* teaches) there can be a justified expectation of privacy even absent exclusivity." LaFave & Israel, § 9.1(c).

---

h. Justice Harlan, joined by Stewart, J., argued that this should not be so when the eavesdropped occurred without physical penetration, for then the absent householder's property interest has not been disturbed, and he can claim no privacy interest in conversations in which he did not participate.

B.   The Current Approach

In RAKAS v. ILLINOIS, 439 U.S. 128, 99 S.Ct. 421, 58 L.Ed.2d 387 (1978), as Charles H. Whitebread & Christopher Slobogin, *Criminal Procedure* 123 (3d.ed. 1993), observe, "the Court explicitly recognized the connection between search and standing analysis. That is, the Court held that standing should depend on whether the police action sought to be challenged is a search (i.e., a violation of legitimate expectations of privacy) *with respect to the person challenging the intrusion.*"

In *Rakas*, in the course of affirming a ruling that when the police stopped and searched a car, which petitioners neither owned nor leased but were occupying as passengers, the police violated none of *their* rights,[a] REHNQUIST, J., speaking for a 5–4 majority, asked "whether it serves any useful analytical purpose to consider [the principle that Fourth Amendment rights are personal rights] a matter of standing, distinct from the merits of a defendant's Fourth Amendment claim." He answered that inquiry in the negative: "[W]e think the better analysis forthrightly focuses on the extent of a particular defendant's rights under the Fourth Amendment, rather than on any theoretically separate, but invariably intertwined concept of standing. * * * Analyzed in these terms, the question is whether the challenged search or seizure violated the Fourth Amendment rights of a criminal defendant who seeks to exclude the evidence obtained during it. That inquiry in turn requires a determination of whether the disputed search and seizure has infringed an interest of the defendant which the Fourth Amendment was designed to protect."

Is there still something to be said for treating "standing" and the issue whether a Fourth Amendment violation has occurred at all as distinct inquiries? Consider LaFave, § 11.3 at 121: "[It] is important to keep in mind that the question traditionally labeled as standing (did the police intrude upon *this*

---

a. Suspecting that the vehicle might have been the "getaway car" in a recent robbery, police stopped the car in which petitioners were riding. After the occupants of the car (petitioners and two female companions) were ordered out, the police searched the interior of the vehicle and discovered a sawed-off rifle under the front passenger seat and a box of rifle shells in the glove compartment (which had been locked). Because petitioners did not assert ownership of the rifle or the shells and because they conceded that they did not own the automobile, but were simply passengers (the owner of the vehicle had been driving it at the time of the search), the trial court ruled that they lacked "standing" to contest the search and seizure. Thus the judge denied their motions to suppress the evidence, without ever reaching the question whether the police conduct involved was lawful.

Applying its new approach to what had traditionally been called "standing" problems, the U.S. Supreme Court agreed that "petitioners' claims must fail": "They asserted neither a property nor a possessory interest in the automobile, nor an interest in the property seized. And [the] fact that they were "legitimately on [the] premises" in the sense that they were in the car with the permission of its owner is not determinative of whether they had a legitimate expectation of privacy in the particular areas of the automobile searched. It is unnecessary for us to decide here whether the same expectations of privacy are warranted in a car as would be justified in a dwelling place in analogous circumstances. [But] here petitioners' claim is one which would fail even in an analogous situation in a dwelling place, since they made no showing that they had any legitimate expectation of privacy in the glove compartment or area under the seat of the car in which they were merely passengers. Like the trunk of an automobile, these are areas in which a passenger *qua* passenger simply would not normally have a legitimate expectation of privacy.

"[*Jones v. United States* (1960)] involved significantly different factual circumstances. Jones not only had permission to use the apartment of his friend, but had a key to the apartment with which he admitted himself on the day of the search and kept possessions in the apartment. Except with respect to his friend, Jones had complete dominion and control over the apartment and could exclude others from it. [Jones] could legitimately expect privacy in the areas which were the subject of the search and seizure [he] sought to contest. No such showing was made by these petitioners with respect to those portions of the automobile which were searched and from which incriminating evidence was seized."

defendant's justified expectation of privacy?) is not identical to, for example, the question of whether any Fourth Amendment search has occurred (did the police intrude upon *anyone's* justified expectation of privacy?), and that therefore the [issues traditionally called "standing" issues] are still rather discrete and deserving of separate attention, no matter what label is put on them."[b]

In *Rakas*, it should be noted, Justice Rehnquist could "think of no decided cases of this Court that would have come out differently had we concluded, as we do now, that [the standing requirement] is more properly subsumed under substantive Fourth Amendment doctrine." He also told us that although he believed that the traditional standing requirement "belongs more properly under the heading of substantive Fourth Amendment doctrine," he was under no illusion that by dispensing with the rubric of standing * * * we have rendered any simpler the determination of whether the proponent of a motion to suppress is entitled to contest the legality of a search and seizure."

In *Rakas*, as pointed out earlier, neither passenger asserted ownership in the items taken from the car. The Court seemed to imply that if the passengers had done so, they could have challenged the police conduct. But RAWLINGS v. KENTUCKY, 448 U.S. 98, 100 S.Ct. 2556, 65 L.Ed.2d 633 (1980), rejected the argument that one could challenge a search of an area (in this instance another person's purse) simply because he claimed ownership of the property seized during the search. The case arose as follows:

On the day of the challenged police conduct, petitioner and Ms. Cox, who had been his companion for several days, were visitors at the house of one Marquess. Shortly before six police officers arrived, armed with a warrant for the arrest of Marquess, petitioner, who had been carrying a large quantity of illegal drugs, dumped them into the purse of Ms. Cox. Although there was a dispute about their discussion, petitioner testified that he had asked Ms. Cox "if she would carry this for me, and she said 'yes.'" (Although unclear, one plausible inference is that petitioner had put the contraband in the purse because he had seen police approaching the house.)

While unsuccessfully searching for Marquess in his house, the police came upon evidence of drug violations. Two of the officers then left to obtain a warrant to search the house, while the remaining officers detained the occupants, including petitioner and Cox, allowing them to leave only if they consented to a body search. Upon returning with the search warrant some 45 minutes later, the officers ordered Cox to empty her purse onto a table. As she poured out the contents of her purse, Cox told petitioner "to take what was his" and petitioner immediately claimed ownership of the drugs. Considering the "totality of the circumstances," including petitioner's admission at the suppression hearing that he did not believe that Cox's purse would be free from governmental intrusion, the state supreme court concluded that petitioner had no "standing" because he had failed to make "a sufficient showing that his legitimate or reasonable expectations of privacy were violated by the search of the purse." A 7–2 majority, again per REHNQUIST, J., found no reason to overturn that conclusion:

"[1] At the time petitioner dumped thousands of dollars worth of illegal drugs into Cox's purse, he had known her only a few days. [2] According to Cox's uncontested testimony, petitioner had never sought or received access to her purse prior to that sudden bailment. [3] Nor did petitioner have any right to exclude other persons access to Cox's purse. [4] In fact, [a third person] a longtime

---

b. See also Joshua Dressler, *Understanding Criminal Procedure* 302–03 (2d ed. 1997).

acquaintance and frequent companion of Cox's had free access to her purse. [5] [Moreover,] even assuming that petitioner's version of the bailment is correct [,the] precipitous nature of the transaction hardly supports a reasonable inference that petitioner took normal precautions to maintain his privacy. [6] [Finally] the record also contains a frank admission by petitioner that he had no subjective expectation that Cox's purse would remain free from governmental intrusion * * *.c

"Petitioner contends nevertheless that, because he claimed ownership of the drugs in Cox's purse, he should be entitled to challenge the search regardless of his expectation of privacy. We disagree. While petitioner's ownership of the drugs is undoubtedly one fact to be considered in this case, *Rakas* emphatically rejected the notion that 'arcane' concepts of property law ought to control the ability to claim the protections of the Fourth Amendment. Had petitioner placed his drugs in plain view, he would still have owned them, but he could not claim any legitimate expectation of privacy. Prior to *Rakas*, petitioner might have been given 'standing' in such a case to challenge a 'search' that netted those drugs but probably would have lost his claim on the merits. After *Rakas*, the two inquiries

---

c. According to LaFave § 11.3(c) at 154, none of the points made by Justice Rehnquist "can withstand close scrutiny." He then responds to Justice Rehnquist's points as follows (id. At 154–58):

(1) The fact that Rawlings had only known Ms. Cox for a few days "hardly establishes the absence of a justified expectation of privacy."

(2) Rawlings' expectation of privacy was not diminished because this was the first time he had used Ms. Cox's purse. Otherwise, "we would be left with the curious notion that a first-time bailment [would] not carry with it a justified expectation that one's goods are secure in the hands of the bailee."

As for (3), "while a 'right to exclude' may be an easy way to establish the requisite legitimate expectation of privacy, it hardly follows that it is the *only* way * * *. Reliance on this 'right to exclude' factor is also inconsistent with the later [holding] of *Minnesota v. Olson*, (1990) [p. 775], [that] an overnight guest had [a legitimate expectation of privacy in the premises] without regard to whether the guest 'had complete dominion and control over the apartment and could exclude others from it.' "

(4) The fact that a third party had access to Ms Cox's purse should not matter. The issue was not whether Rawlings "reasonably believed he was free from intrusion by *anyone*," but " 'whether the area [searched] was one in which there was a reasonable expectation of privacy from *governmental* intrusion.' "

As for (5), the argument that Rawlings did not take adequate precautions to maintain his privacy, "a container does not have to be locked to give rise to that especially strong expectation of privacy which makes the warrant clause of the Fourth Amendment applicable and thus it can hardly be said that an unlocked container carries with it no justified privacy expectation at all." Furthermore, if it

can be said that Rawlings did not take adequate precautions in putting his effects into a closed container with the owner's consent, "then surely Ms. Cox likewise had no justified expectation of privacy in the same purse because she did not better safeguard her effects in that purse."

(6) The "frank admission" by Rawlings that "he had no subjective expectation that Cox's purse would remain free from governmental intrusion" turns out to be a "No, sir" answer when asked at the suppression hearing whether he thought the purse would be free from police intrusion. Rawlings was being asked "what he thought was going to happen *after* the police were on the scene and *after* they told him and others that a warrant was being sought and they could leave prior to the warrant execution only by submitting to a personal search. [But] if one can be deprived of Fourth Amendment standing by being informed in advance by the police of the intrusion they intend to make, [then] Rawlings likewise had no standing with respect to his own person, which he also expected would be intruded upon by the police."

According to Professor LaFave, "*Rawlings* is best viewed as an unusual case in which the result is more attributable to certain undercurrents in the case than to the reasoning offered by the Court." LaFave notes at this point that although none of the lower courts specifically found that Ms. Cox had not consented to the bailment, "the trial court was somewhat 'skeptical about [Rawlings'] version of events' and seemed to think that [he] probably saw the police approaching the premises and then thrust the controlled substances onto Cox over her objection. The thrust of the majority opinion in *Rawlings* strongly suggests the Court was influenced by an assumption that this latter version was correct."

merge into one: whether governmental officials violated any legitimate expectation of privacy held by petitioner."

BLACKMUN, J., joined the Court's opinion, but also wrote separately. He agreed with the majority that determining (1) whether the defendant has a "legitimate expectation of privacy" that has been invaded by the police and (2) whether "applicable cause and warrant requirements have been properly observed" " 'merge into one' in the sense that both are to be addressed under the principles of Fourth Amendment analysis developed in *Katz* and its progeny." But he did not read *Rawlings*, or *Rakas*, "as holding that it is improper for lower courts to treat these inquiries as distinct components of a Fourth Amendment claim." "Indeed," he added, "I am convinced that it would invite confusion to hold otherwise. It remains possible for a defendant to prove that his legitimate interest of privacy was invaded, and yet fail to prove that the police acted illegally in doing so. And it is equally possible for a defendant to prove that the police acted illegally, and yet fail to prove that his own privacy interest was affected."

It is interesting to note that in the very recent case of *Minnesota v. Carter*, set forth immediately below, "the parties' briefs to the U.S. Supreme Court, as well as the state supreme court's opinion, analyze[d] the case in terms of the defendants' 'standing' to assert a Fourth Amendment violation." 64 Crim.L.Rep. 2033, 2037 (Oct. 14, 1998). At one point during the oral arguments before the U.S. Supreme Court, the lawyer for the state referred to the defendants' "standing" to raise a search and seizure claim. This led Justice Kennedy to point out that in *Rakas* the Court had "abandoned the idea of 'standing' in the Fourth Amendment context." Id. Nevertheless, "throughout the oral arguments, the idea of Fourth Amendment 'standing' continued to be employed by the parties and the justices to describe the concepts at issue." *Id*.

MINNESOTA v. CARTER
___ U.S. ___, 119 S.Ct. 469 , 142 L.Ed. 2d 373 (1998).

[A confidential informant told a Minnesota police officer (Thielen) that he had walked by the window of a ground-floor apartment and had seen people putting a white powder into bags. After looking in the same window through a gap in the closed blind and observing three men engaged in the bagging operation (respondents Carter and Johns and the apartment's lessee, Ms. Thompson), the officer notified headquarters, which began preparing affidavits for a search warrant. When respondents left the building in a previously identified vehicle, they were stopped and arrested. A later police search of the vehicle turned up cocaine. After seizing the vehicle, the police returned to the apartment and arrested the occupant, Ms. Thompson. A search of the apartment pursuant to a warrant revealed more evidence of cocaine.

[The police later learned that Carter and Johns had never been in Thompson's apartment before and were only in it for 2½ hours, and that they had come to the apartment for the sole purpose of packaging the cocaine. In return for the use of the apartment, Carter and Johns had given Thompson one-eighth of an ounce of the cocaine.

[Respondents were convicted of state drug offenses. The trial court held that (a) since they were only temporary out-of-state visitors, respondents could not challenge the legality of the government intrusion into Ms. Thompson's apartment; (b) Officer Thielen's observations through a gap in the closed blind was not a "search" within the meaning of the Fourth Amendment. The state supreme court reversed, holding that respondents did have "standing" because they had a " 'legitimate expectation of privacy in the invaded place' " (quoting *Rakas*). Even though "society does not recognize as valuable the task of bagging cocaine," observed the court, "society does recognize as valuable the rights of property owners or leaseholders to invite persons into the privacy of their homes to conduct a common task, be it legal or illegal activity." The court went on to hold that the officer's observation constituted an unreasonable "search" of the apartment. The U.S. Supreme Court reversed without reaching the question whether the officer's observation was a "search."]

The Minnesota courts analyzed whether respondents had a legitimate expectation of privacy under the rubric of "standing" doctrine, an analysis which this Court expressly rejected 20 years ago in *Rakas*. In that case, we held that automobile passengers could not assert the protection of the Fourth Amendment against the seizure of incriminating evidence from a vehicle where they owned neither the vehicle nor the evidence. Central to our analysis was the idea that in determining whether a defendant is able to show the violation of his (and not someone else's) Fourth Amendment rights, the "definition of those rights is more properly placed within the purview of substantive Fourth Amendment law than within that of standing." Thus, we held that in order to claim the protection of the Fourth Amendment, a defendant must demonstrate that he personally has an expectation of privacy in the place searched, and that his expectation is reasonable; *i.e.*, one which has a "source outside of the Fourth Amendment, either by reference to concepts of real or personal property law or to understandings that are recognized and permitted by society."

[The Fourth] Amendment protects persons against unreasonable searches of "their persons [and] houses" and thus indicates that the Fourth Amendment is a personal right that must be invoked by an individual. See *Katz*. ("[T]he Fourth Amendment protects people, not places"). But the extent to which the Fourth Amendment protects people may depend upon where those people are. We have held that "capacity to claim the protection of the Fourth Amendment depends [upon] whether the person who claims the protection of the Amendment has a legitimate expectation of privacy in the invaded place." *Rakas*.

The text of the Amendment suggests that its protections extend only to people in "their" houses. But we have held that in some circumstances a person may have a legitimate expectation of privacy in the house of someone else. In *Minnesota v. Olson* (1990), for example, we decided that an overnight guest in a house had the sort of expectation of privacy that the Fourth Amendment protects. We said:

> "To hold that an overnight guest has a legitimate expectation of privacy in his host's home merely recognizes the every day expectations of privacy that we all share. Staying overnight in another's home is a longstanding social custom that serves functions recognized as valuable by society. We stay in others' home when we travel to a strange city for business or pleasure, we visit our parents, children, or more distant relatives out of town, when we are in between jobs or homes, or when we house-sit for a friend.

> "[From] the overnight guest's perspective, he seeks shelter in another's home precisely because it provides him with privacy, a place where he and his

possessions will not be disturbed by anyone but his host and those his host allows inside. * * *''

In *Jones v. United States* (1960), the defendant seeking to exclude evidence resulting from a search of an apartment had been given the use of the apartment by a friend. He had clothing in the apartment, had slept there "maybe a night," and at the time was the sole occupant of the apartment. But while the holding of *Jones*—that a search of the apartment violated the defendant's Fourth Amendment rights—is still valid, its statement that "anyone legitimately on the premises where a search occurs may challenge its legality" was expressly repudiated in *Rakas*. Thus an overnight guest in a home may claim the protection of the Fourth Amendment, but one who is merely present with the consent of the householder may not.

Respondents here were obviously not overnight guests, but were essentially present for a business transaction and were only in the home a matter of hours. There is no suggestion that they had a previous relationship with Thompson, or that there was any other purpose to their visit. Nor was there anything similar to the overnight guest relationship in *Olson* to suggest a degree of acceptance into the household.[1] While the apartment was a dwelling place for Thompson, it was for these respondents simply a place to do business.

Property used for commercial purposes is treated differently for Fourth Amendment purposes than residential property. [And] while it was a "home" in which respondents were present, it was not their home. Similarly, the Court has held that in some circumstances a worker can claim Fourth Amendment protection over his own workplace. See, *e.g. O'Connor v. Ortega* [p. 163]. But there is no indication that respondents in this case had nearly as significant a connection to Thompson's apartment as the worker in *O'Connor* had to his own private office.

If we regard the overnight guest in *Minnesota v. Olson* as typifying those who may claim the protection of the Fourth Amendment in the home of another, and one merely "legitimately on the premises" as typifying those who may not do so, the present case is obviously somewhere in between. But the purely commercial nature of the transaction engaged in here, the relatively short period of time on the premises, and the lack of any previous connection between respondents and the householder, all lead us to conclude that respondents' situation is closer to that of one simply permitted on the premises. We therefore hold that any search which may have occurred did not violate their Fourth Amendment rights. [Thus] we need not decide whether the police officer's observation constituted a "search." * * *

JUSTICE SCALIA, with whom JUSTICE THOMAS joins, concurring.

I join the opinion of the Court because I believe it accurately applies our recent case law, including *Minnesota v. Olson*. I write separately to express my view that that case law—like the submissions of the parties in this case—gives short shrift to the text of the Fourth Amendment, and to the well and long understood meaning of that text. Specifically, it leaps to apply the fuzzy standard of "legitimate expectation of privacy"—a consideration that is often relevant to

1. Justice Ginsburg's dissent would render the operative language in *Minnesota v. Olson* almost entirely superfluous. There, we explained the justification for extending Fourth Amendment protection to the overnight visitor: "Staying overnight in another's home is a longstanding social custom that serves functions recognized as valuable by society . . . We are at our most vulnerable when we are asleep because we cannot monitor our own safety or the security of our belongings." If any short-term business visit by a stranger entitles the visitor to share the Fourth Amendment protection of the lease holder's home, the Court's explanation of its holding in *Olson* was quite unnecessary.

whether a search or seizure covered by the Fourth Amendment is "unreasonable"—to the threshold question whether a search or seizure covered by the Fourth Amendment *has occurred*. If that latter question is addressed first and analyzed under the text of the Constitution as traditionally understood, the present case is not remotely difficult.

The Fourth Amendment protects "[t]he right of the people to be secure in *their* persons, houses, papers, and effects, against unreasonable searches and seizures...." U.S. Const., Amdt. 4 (emphasis added). [The] obvious meaning of the provision is that *each* person has the right to be secure against unreasonable searches and seizures in *his own* person, house, papers, and effects.

The Founding-era materials that I have examined confirm that this was the understood meaning. [Justice Scalia then discusses various historical materials, including *Semayne's Case*, 77 Eng.Rep. 194 (K.B. 1604), the leading English case for the common-law maxim that "a man's home is *his* castle"; and the leading American case of *Oystead v. Shed*, 13 Mass. 520 (1816), which reasoned that the "inviolability of dwellinghouses" described by various leading commentators extends to "the occupier or any of his family" and to those "who have made the house *their* home," but not to one such as "a stranger, or perhaps a visitor."]

Thus, in deciding the question presented today we write upon a slate that is far from clean. The text of the Fourth Amendment, the common-law background against which it was adopted, and the understandings consistently displayed after its adoption make the answer clear. We were right to hold in *Chapman v. United States* [p. 357] that the Fourth Amendment protects an apartment tenant against an unreasonable search of his dwelling, even though he is only a leaseholder. And we were right to hold in *Bumper v. North Carolina* [p. 350] that an unreasonable search of a grandmother's house violated her resident grandson's Fourth Amendment rights because the area searched "was *his* home" (emphasis added). We went to the absolute limit of what text and tradition permit in *Minnesota v. Olson*, when we protected a mere overnight guest against an unreasonable search of his hosts' apartment. But whereas it is plausible to regard a person's overnight lodging as at least his "temporary" residence, it is entirely impossible to give that characterization to an apartment that he uses to package cocaine.

[The] dissent believes that "[o]ur obligation to produce coherent results" requires that we ignore this clear text and four-century-old tradition, and apply instead the notoriously unhelpful test adopted in a "benchmar[k]" decision that is 31 years old, citing *Katz*. In my view, the only thing the past three decades have established about the *Katz* test (which has come to mean the test enunciated by Justice Harlan's separate concurrence in *Katz*) is that, unsurprisingly, those "actual (subjective) expectation[s] of privacy" that society is prepared to recognize as 'reasonable' " bear an uncanny resemblance to those expectations of privacy that this Court considers reasonable. When that self-indulgent test is employed (as the dissent would employ it here) to determine whether a "search or seizure" within the meaning of the Constitution has *occurred* (as opposed to whether that "search or seizure" is an "unreasonable" one), it has no plausible foundation in the text of the Fourth Amendment. That provision did not guarantee some generalized "right of privacy" and leave it to this Court to determine which particular manifestations of the value of privacy "society is prepared to recognize as 'reasonable.' "

[The] dissent may be correct that a person invited into someone else's house to engage in a common business (even common monkey-business, so to speak) *ought* to be protected against government searches of the room in which that business is conducted; and that persons invited in to deliver milk or pizza (whom the dissent dismisses as "classroom hypotheticals," as opposed, presumably, to flesh-and-blood hypotheticals) ought *not* to be protected against government searches of the rooms that they occupy. I am not sure of the answer to those policy questions. But I am sure that the answer is not remotely contained in the Constitution, which means that it is left—as *many*, indeed *most*, important questions are left—to the judgment of state and federal legislators. * * *

JUSTICE KENNEDY, concurring.

I join the Court's opinion, for its reasoning is consistent with my view that almost all social guests have a legitimate expectation of privacy, and hence protection against unreasonable searches, in their host's home.

[The] homeowner's right to privacy is not an issue in this case. The Court does not reach the question whether the officer's unaided observations of Thompson's apartment constituted a search. If there was in fact a search, however, then Thompson had the right to object to the unlawful police surveillance of her apartment and the right to suppress any evidence disclosed by the search. [Our] cases establish, however, that respondents have no independent privacy right, the violation of which results in exclusion of evidence against them, unless they can establish a meaningful connection to Thompson's apartment.

[In] this case respondents have established nothing more than a fleeting and insubstantial connection with Thompson's home. For all that appears in the record, respondents used Thompson's house simply as a convenient processing station, their purpose involving nothing more than the mechanical act of chopping and packing a substance for distribution.

[If] respondents here had been visiting twenty homes, each for a minute or two, to drop off a bag of cocaine and were apprehended by a policeman wrongfully present in the nineteenth home; or if they had left the goods at a home where they were not staying and the police had seized the goods in their absence, we would have said that *Rakas* compels rejection of any privacy interest respondents might assert. So it does here, given that respondents have established no meaningful tie or connection to the owner, the owner's home, or the owner's expectation of privacy.

We cannot remain faithful to the underlying principle in *Rakas* without reversing in this case, and I am not persuaded that we need depart from it to protect the homeowner's own privacy interests. * * *

JUSTICE GINSBURG, with whom JUSTICE STEVENS and JUSTICE SOUTER join, dissenting.

The Court's decision undermines not only the security of short-term guests, but also the security of the home resident herself. In my view, when a homeowner or lessor personally invites a guest into her home to share in a common endeavor, whether it be for conversation, to engage in leisure activities, or for business purposes licit or illicit, that guest should share his host's shelter against unreasonable searches and seizures.

I do not here propose restoration of the "legitimately on the premises" criterion stated in *Jones*, for the Court rejected that formulation in *Rakas* * * *. First, the disposition I would reach in this case responds to the unique importance of the home—the most essential bastion of privacy recognized by the law. See *United States v. Karo*, [p. 171] ("Our cases have not deviated from this basic Fourth Amendment principle."); *Payton v. New York* [p. 266] ("The Fourth Amendment protects the individual's right to privacy in a variety of settings. In none is the zone of privacy more clearly defined than when bounded by the unambiguous physical dimensions of an individual's home.") Second, even within the home itself, the position to which I would adhere would not permit "a casual visitor who has never seen, or been permitted to visit, the basement of another's house to object to a search of the basement if the visitor happened to be in the kitchen of the house at the time of the search." *Rakas.* Further, I would here decide only the case of the homeowner who chooses to share the privacy of her home and her company with a guest, and would not reach classroom hypotheticals like the milkman or pizza deliverer.

My concern centers on an individual's choice to share her home and her associations there with persons she selects. Our decisions indicate that people have a reasonable expectation of privacy in their homes in part because they have the prerogative to exclude others. [The] power to exclude implies the power to include. See, e.g., Mary Irene Coombs, *Shared Privacy and the Fourth Amendment, or the Rights of Relationships*, 75 Calif.L.Rev. 1593, 1618 (1987); Albert W. Alschuler, *Interpersonal Privacy and the Fourth Amendment* 4 N.Ill.U.L.Rev. 1, 13 (1983). Our Fourth Amendment decisions should reflect those complementary prerogatives.

A home dweller places her own privacy at risk, the Court's approach indicates, when she opens her home to others, uncertain whether the duration of their stay, their purpose, and their "acceptance into the household" will earn protection. * * * Human frailty suggests that today's decision will tempt police to pry into private dwellings without warrant, to find evidence incriminating guests who do not rest there through the night. See Eulis Simien, *The Interrelationship of the Scope of the Fourth Amendment and Standing to Object to Unreasonable Searches*, 41 Ark.L.Rev. 487, 539 (1988) ("[I]f the police have no probable cause, they have everything to gain and nothing to lose if they search under circumstances where they know that at least one of the potential defendants will not have standing."). *Rakas* tolerates that temptation with respect to automobile searches. See Gerald D. Ashdown, *The Fourth Amendment and the "Legitimate Expectation of Privacy*," 34 Vand.L.Rev. 1289, 1321 (1981). * * * I see no impelling reason to extend this risk into the home.

[Through] the host's invitation, the guest gains a reasonable expectation of privacy in the home. *Minnesota v. Olson,* so held with respect to an overnight guest. The logic of that decision extends to shorter term guests as well. See 5 W. LaFave, *Search and Seizure: A Treatise on the Fourth Amendment* § 11.3(b), p. 137 (3d ed. 1996). [In] sum, when a homeowner chooses to share the privacy of her home and her company with a short-term guest, the twofold requirement "emerg[ing] from prior decisions" has been satisfied: Both host and guest "have exhibited an actual (subjective) expectation of privacy"; that "expectation [is] one [our] society is prepared to recognize as 'reasonable.'" *Katz* (Harlan, J., concurring).[2] * * *

2. In his concurring opinion, Justice Kennedy maintains that respondents here lacked "an expectation of privacy that society recognizes as reasonable" because they "established nothing more than a fleeting and insubstantial connection" with the host's home. As the Minnesota Supreme Court reported, however, the stipulated facts showed that respondents were inside the apartment with the host's permission, remained inside for at least 2 1/2 hours, and, during that time, engaged in concert with the host in a collaborative venture. These stipulated facts—which scarcely resemble a stop of a minute or two at the 19th of 20 homes to drop off a packet—securely demonstrate that the host intended to share her privacy with respondents, and that respondents, therefore, had entered into the homeland of Fourth Amendment protection. While I agree with the Minnesota Supreme Court that, under the rule settled since *Katz,* the reasonableness of the expectation of privacy controls,

Our leading decision in *Katz* is key to my view of this case. There, we ruled that the Government violated the petitioner's Fourth Amendment rights when it electronically recorded him transmitting wagering information while he was inside a public telephone booth. We were mindful that "the Fourth Amendment protects people, not places," and held that this electronic monitoring of a business call "violated the privacy upon which [the caller] justifiably relied while using the telephone booth." Our obligation to produce coherent results in this often visited area of the law requires us to inform our current expositions by benchmarks already established.

[The] Court's decision in this case veers sharply from the path marked in *Katz*. I do not agree that we have a more reasonable expectation of privacy when we place a business call to a person's home from a public telephone booth on the side of the street, see *Katz*, than when we actually enter that person's premises to engage in a common endeavor. * * * [a]

SECTION 2. THE "FRUIT OF THE POISONOUS TREE"

A. Historical Background and Overview

"In the simplest of exclusionary rule cases," observe LaFave & Israel, § 9.3(a), "the challenged evidence is quite clearly 'direct' or 'primary' in its relationship to the prior arrest, search, interrogation [or lineup] [e.g., a confession made in response to impermissible interrogation or physical evidence obtained by an illegal search]." Not infrequently, however, point out LaFave & Israel, "challenged evidence is 'secondary' or 'derivative' in character. This occurs when, for example, a confession is obtained after an illegal arrest[a] [or] physical evidence is located after an illegally obtained confession.[b] [In] these situations, it is necessary to determine whether the derivative evidence is 'tainted' by the prior constitutional or other violation. To use the phrase coined by Justice Frankfurter, it must be decided whether that evidence is 'the fruit of the poisonous tree.' "[c]

1. *Genesis of the rule; the doctrine of "attenuation."* (a) The genesis of the "taint" or "fruit of the poisonous tree" doctrine, as it came to be called, appears in *Silverthorne Lumber Co. v. United States,* 251 U.S. 385, 40 S.Ct. 182, 64 L.Ed. 319 (1920), where, in holding that the government could not use information obtained during an illegal search to subpoena the very documents illegally viewed, the Court, per Holmes, J., pointed out: "The essence of a provision forbidding the acquisition of evidence in a certain way is that not merely evidence so acquired shall not be used before the Court but that it shall not be used at all. Of course this does not mean that the facts thus obtained become sacred and inaccessible. If knowledge of them is gained from an independent source they may be proved like any others, but the knowledge gained by the Government's own wrong cannot be used by it in the way proposed."

not the visitor's status as social guest, invitee, licensee, or business partner, I think it noteworthy that five Members of the Court would place under the Fourth Amendment's shield, at least, "almost all social guests."

a. Although Justice Breyer concurred in the judgment because he did not believe that Officer Thielen's observation of the apartment,

"made from a public area outside the curtilage," constituted an "unreasonable" search," he "agree[d] with Justice Ginsburg that respondents can claim the Fourth Amendment's protection."

a. See, e.g., *Brown v. Illinois,* p. 787.

b. See, e.g., *New York v. Quarles,* p. 532.

c. *Nardone v. United States,* Note 1(b).

Did *Silverthorne* mean that illegally seized *evidence* may never be used by the government although the *facts* revealed by that evidence may be obtained from an independent source? See Robert M. Pitler, *"The Fruit of the Poisonous Tree" Revisited and Shepardized,* 56 Calif.L.Rev. 579, 589 (1968).

(b) In *Nardone v. United States,* 308 U.S. 338, 60 S.Ct. 266, 84 L.Ed. 307 (1939), which first used the phrase "fruit of the poisonous tree," the Court, per Frankfurter, J., refused to permit the prosecution to avoid an inquiry into its use of information gained by illegal wiretapping, observing that "to forbid the direct use of methods [but] to put no curb on their full indirect use would only invite the very methods deemed 'inconsistent with ethical standards and destructive of personal liberty.' "[a] The case also established the "attenuation" doctrine, being the first to authoritatively recognize that even where the challenged evidence did not have an "independent source" it might still be admissible: "Sophisticated argument may prove a causal connection between information obtained through illicit wire-tapping and the Government's proof. As a matter of good sense, however, such connection may have become so attenuated as to dissipate the taint."

2. Verbal evidence as the "fruit" of illegal search and seizure. In WONG SUN v. UNITED STATES, 371 U.S. 471, 83 S.Ct. 407, 9 L.Ed.2d 441 (1963) (other aspects of which are discussed at pp 206, 655), six federal narcotics agents illegally broke into Toy's laundry, chased him into the living quarters at the back of his shop, where Toy's wife and child were sleeping, and handcuffed him. Toy then told the agents that Yee had been selling narcotics. The agents immediately went to Yee, who surrendered heroin to them and implicated Toy and a third party, Wong Sun. A 5–4 majority, per BRENNAN, J., held that both Toy's declarations, upon being handcuffed in his bedroom, *and* "the narcotics taken from Yee, to which [Toy's] declarations led the police" had to be excluded as the "fruits" of the agents' unlawful entry into Toy's bedroom and the "bedroom arrest."

The Court recognized that "traditionally" the exclusionary rule had barred only "physical, tangible materials," but concluded that "verbal evidence which derives so immediately from an unlawful entry and an unauthorized arrest [as here] is no less the 'fruit' of official illegality than the more common tangible fruits of the unwarranted intrusion."[b] Not "all evidence is 'fruit of the poisonous tree' simply because it would not have come to light but for the illegal actions of the police. Rather, the more apt question in such a case is 'whether, granting establishment of the primary illegality [the evidence] has been come at by exploitation of that illegality or instead by means sufficiently distinguishable to be purged of the primary taint.' J. Maguire, *Evidence of Guilt* 221 (1959). We think it clear that the narcotics [taken from Yee] were 'come at by the exploitation of that illegality [the lawless search and seizure of Toy]' and hence that they may not be used against Toy."

On the other hand, although Wong Sun had also been unlawfully arrested, his confession was not the "fruit" of his illegal arrest. Since he had been released on his own recognizance after a lawful arraignment and had returned voluntarily

---

a. But cf. *United States v. Calandra,* p. 146, holding that a witness may not refuse to answer grand jury questions on the ground that they are based on evidence obtained from him in an earlier unlawful search.

b. The dissenters, Clark, J., joined by Harlan, Stewart and White, JJ., did not challenge the manner in which the Court applied the "fruits" doctrine, but maintained that Toy's arrest was lawful and thus provided "no 'poisonous tree' whose fruits we must evaluate."

several days later to make the statement, "the connection between [Wong Sun's] arrest and [his] statement had 'become so attenuated as to dissipate the taint.' "

Notes and Questions

(a) *The relevant question.* Does the *Wong Sun* Court's talk of "purging the primary taint" obfuscate the relevant question—whether the admission of the secondary evidence will significantly encourage police misconduct in the future? See Pitler, supra, at 588–89; Note, 115 U.Pa.L.Rev. 1136, 1147 (1967).

(b) *"Purging the taint" of Fourth Amendment violations.* Are there events short of release from custody (which occurred in *Wong Sun*) which operate to "purge the taint" of an illegal arrest or search? Can the mere passage of time suffice? Or would such a rule only "postpone the testing" of the fruit but "not diminish its temptation"? See *Collins v. Beto,* 348 F.2d 823, 828 (5th Cir.1965). Would *Miranda* warnings purge the taint of an illegal arrest? See *Brown v. Illinois,* below.

3. *"Independent source"; "inevitable discovery."* The *Wong Sun* Court quoted from *Silverthorne,* supra, the proposition that the exclusionary rule has no application when "the Government learned of the evidence 'from an independent source.' "This means that if not even a "but for" test can be satisfied, the challenged evidence is not a fruit of the prior violation—a violation of a person's rights should not put him beyond the law's reach if his guilt can be established by evidence unconnected with or "untainted" by the violation.

A variation of the "independent source" exception is the "inevitable discovery" or "hypothetical independent source" rule, a doctrine long utilized by many lower courts and recently accepted by the U.S. Supreme Court.[a] This doctrine differs from the "independent source" exception in that the question is not whether the police *actually* acquired certain evidence by reliance upon an untainted source, but whether evidence in fact obtained illegally would inevitably or eventually or probably have been discovered lawfully.

The doctrine is most palatable, and has been most frequently applied, when the police misconduct occurred "while an investigation was already in progress and resulted in the discovery of evidence that would have eventually have been obtained through routine police investigatory procedure. The illegalities in such cases, therefore, had the effect of simply accelerating the discovery." Note, 74 Colum.L.Rev. 88, 90 (1974).

Because mechanical application of the "inevitable discovery" doctrine would seem to encourage unconstitutional shortcuts, and one purpose of the exclusionary rule is to discourage such shortcuts, it has been argued that the doctrine should be permitted only when the police have not acted in "bad faith" to accelerate the discovery of the challenged evidence. See, e.g., LaFave, § 11.4(a) at 382. But the Court rejected such a limitation in the recent case of *Nix v. Williams,* p. 797.

4. *Confession as the "fruit" of an illegal arrest.* BROWN v. ILLINOIS, 422 U.S. 590, 95 S.Ct. 2254, 45 L.Ed.2d 416 (1975), arose as follows: Following his illegal arrest, petitioner, a murder suspect, was taken to a police station where, after being given the *Miranda* warnings and waiving his rights, he made incriminating statements within two hours of the arrest. The state supreme court affirmed the murder conviction, taking the view that "the *Miranda* warnings in and of themselves" purged the taint of the prior illegal arrest. The Court, per BLACKMUN, J., reversed:

a. See *Nix v. Williams,* p. 797.

"The exclusionary rule, [when] utilized to effectuate the Fourth Amendment, serves interests and policies that are distinct from those it serves under the Fifth. [E]xclusion of a confession made without *Miranda* warnings might be regarded as necessary to effectuate the Fifth Amendment, but it would not be sufficient fully to protect the Fourth. *Miranda* warnings, and the exclusion of a confession made without them, do not alone sufficiently deter a Fourth Amendment violation.

"[If] *Miranda* warnings, by themselves, were held to attenuate the taint of an unconstitutional arrest, regardless of how wanton and purposeful the Fourth Amendment violation, the effect of the exclusionary rule would be substantially diluted. [Illegal arrests] would be encouraged by the knowledge that evidence derived therefrom hopefully could be made admissible at trial by the simple expedient of giving *Miranda* warnings. Any incentive to avoid Fourth Amendment violations would be eviscerated by making the warnings, in effect, a 'cure-all' * * *."

Although the Court rejected the *per se* rule of the Illinois court whereunder the *Miranda* warnings were deemed to break the causal connection between the arrest and confession, it declined to adopt a *per se* or "but for" rule running in the other direction. It concluded instead that such taint issues "must be answered on the facts of each case. No single fact is dispositive. [The] *Miranda* warnings are an important factor, to be sure, in determining whether the confession is obtained by exploitation of an illegal arrest. But they are not the only factor to be considered. The temporal proximity of the arrest and the confession, the presence of intervening circumstances and, particularly, the purpose and flagrancy of the official misconduct, are all relevant. The voluntariness of the statement is a threshold requirement. And the burden of showing admissibility rests, of course, on the prosecution."

The Court then concluded that the prosecution had failed to sustain its burden: "[Petitioner's] first statement was separated from his illegal arrest by less than two hours, and there was no intervening event of significance whatsoever. * * * We could hold [petitioner's] first statement admissible only if we overrule *Wong Sun.* We decline to do so. [The] illegality here, moreover, had a quality of purposefulness. The impropriety of the arrest was obvious. [The] detectives embarked upon this expedition for evidence in the hope that something might turn up."

Justice WHITE expressed agreement with the Court insofar as it "holds (1) that despite *Miranda* warnings the Fourth and Fourteenth Amendments require the exclusion from evidence of statements obtained as the fruit of an arrest which the arresting officers *knew or should have known* was without probable cause and unconstitutional, and (2) that the statements obtained in this case were in this category" (emphasis added), and therefore concurred in the judgment.

Justice POWELL, joined by Rehnquist, J., joined the Court insofar as it rejected the Illinois courts' *per se* rule, but "would remand the case for reconsideration under the general standards articulated in the Court's opinion." In Justice Powell's view, "the flagrantly abusive violations of Fourth Amendment rights, on the one hand, and 'technical' Fourth Amendment violations, [on the other] call for significantly different judicial responses":

"I would require the clearest indication of attenuation in cases in which official conduct was flagrantly abusive of Fourth Amendment rights. [In such cases] I would consider the equalizing potential of *Miranda* warnings rarely sufficient to dissipate the taint. [At] the opposite end of the spectrum lie 'technical' violations of Fourth Amendment rights where, for example, officers in good faith arrest an individual in reliance on a warrant later invalidated or pursuant to a statute that subsequently is declared unconstitutional. [In such cases] the deterrence rationale of the exclusionary rule does not obtain, and I can see no legitimate justification for depriving the prosecution of reliable and probative evidence. Thus, with the exception of statements given in the immediate circumstances of the illegal arrest—a constraint I think is imposed by existing exclusionary rule law—I would not require more than proof that effective *Miranda* warnings were given and that the ensuing statement was voluntary in the Fifth Amendment sense."

In *Dunaway v. New York,* other aspects of which are discussed at p. 337, the Court, per Brennan, J., reaffirmed the view that *Miranda* warnings, by themselves, are insufficient to attenuate the taint of an unconstitutional arrest: "The situation in this case is virtually a replica of the situation in *Brown.* Petitioner was also admittedly seized without probable cause in the hope that something might turn up, and confessed without any intervening event of significance. [To] admit petitioner's confession in such a case would allow 'law enforcement officers to violate the Fourth Amendment with impunity, safe in the knowledge that they could wash their hands in the "procedural safeguards" of the Fifth' [Comment, 25 Emory L.J. 227, 238 (1976)]."

Justice Stevens joined the Court's opinion but added a comment on "the significance of two factors that may be considered when determining whether a confession has been obtained by exploitation of an illegal arrest":

"The temporal relationship between the arrest and the confession may be an ambiguous factor. If there are no relevant intervening circumstances, a prolonged detention may well be a more serious exploitation of an illegal arrest than a short one. Conversely, even an immediate confession may have been motivated by a prearrest event such as a visit with a minister. The flagrancy of the official misconduct is relevant, in my judgment, only insofar as it has a tendency to motivate the defendant. A midnight arrest with drawn guns will be equally frightening whether the police acted recklessly or in good faith. Conversely, a courteous command has the same effect on the arrestee whether the officer thinks he has probable cause or knows that he does not. In either event, if the Fourth Amendment is violated, the admissibility question will turn on the causal relationship between that violation and the defendant's subsequent confession."[a]

The *Brown-Dunaway* rule was applied (extended?) to a complicated set of facts in *Taylor v. Alabama,* 457 U.S. 687, 102 S.Ct. 2664, 73 L.Ed.2d 314 (1982). A 5–4 majority, per Marshall, J., held that petitioner's confession was the impermissible fruit of his illegal arrest even though (a) six hours had elapsed between the illegal arrest and the time petitioner confessed; (b) petitioner was advised of his rights three times; and (c) he was allowed to visit briefly with his girlfriend and his neighbor shortly before he confessed.

Dissenting Justice O'Connor joined by the Chief Justice, and Powell and Rehnquist, JJ., maintained that *Brown* and *Dunaway* required a contrary result. As the dissent saw it, "[t]he petitioner's confession was not proximately caused by

a. Rehnquist, J., joined by Burger, C.J., dissented, maintaining that the police had acted in "good faith and not in a flagrant manner" and that in such cases "no more [should be required] than that proper *Miranda* warnings [be] given and that the statement be voluntary within the meaning of the Fifth Amendment."

his illegal arrest, but was the product of a decision based both on knowledge of his constitutional rights and on the discussion with his friends."

———

Compare the *Brown-Dunaway–Taylor* line of cases with *Rawlings v. Kentucky* (1980), discussed at p. 777. Petitioner argued that his admission of the ownership of drugs which had been found in Ms. Cox's purse (after the contents of the purse had been emptied, pursuant to a police order) was the fruit of an illegal detention. The Court, per Rehnquist, J., disagreed. Assuming that Rawlings and others were illegally detained in a house while the police obtained a search warrant for the premises, the Court noted, inter alia, that the detention was in a "congenial atmosphere"; that petitioner's admissions were "apparently spontaneous reactions to the discovery of his drugs in Cox's purse" and not the product of the initial illegality, and the police action "does not rise to the level of conscious or flagrant misconduct requiring prophylactic exclusion of petitioner's statements. Contrast *Brown*."[b]

———

5.   *Identification of a person as a "fruit" of an illegal arrest.* *United States v. Crews*, 445 U.S. 463, 100 S.Ct. 1244, 63 L.Ed.2d 537 (1980), arose as follows: Immediately after being assaulted and robbed in a public restroom, the victim gave the police a full description of her assailant. Crews, who matched the suspect's description, was illegally taken into custody, photographed, and then released. Thereafter, when shown an array of eight photographs, the victim selected Crews' photograph as that of the man who had robbed her. At a court-ordered lineup, Crews was again positively identified. Finally, Crews was identified at the trial. Crews was convicted of robbery, but the District of Columbia Court of Appeals held the victim's in-court identification inadmissible, viewing it as obtained by official "exploitation" of the "primary illegality"—Crews' unlawful arrest.[a] The Court, per Brennan, J., disagreed:

A victim's in-court identification has "three distinct elements": "[1], the victim is present at trial to testify as to what transpired between her and the offender, and to identify the defendant as the culprit. [2], the victim possesses knowledge of and the ability to reconstruct the prior [crime] and to identify the defendant from her observations of him at the time of the crime. And [3], the defendant is also physically present in the courtroom, so that the victim can observe him and compare his appearance to that of the offender. In the present case, none of these three elements 'has been come at by exploitation' of the defendant's Fourth Amendment rights."

As for (1), the victim's presence and cooperation were "surely not the product of any police misconduct"; as for (3), because an "illegal arrest, without more, has never been viewed as a bar to subsequent prosecution," the defendant was "not himself a suppressible 'fruit,' and the illegality of his detention cannot deprive the

b. Dissenting Justice Marshall, joined by Brennan, J., maintained that "petitioner's admissions were obviously the fruit of the illegal detention."

a. The trial court had excluded both the photographic and lineup identifications as the "fruits" of Crews' illegal arrest and on appeal the government conceded that both were inadmissible. Why? Wasn't *the lineup identification* admissible for the same reasons the Supreme Court held that the in-court identification was?

Government of the opportunity to prove his guilt through the introduction of evidence wholly untainted by the police misconduct."

As for (2): "Nor did the illegal arrest infect the victim's ability to give accurate identification testimony. Based upon her observations at the time of the robbery, [she] constructed a mental image of her assailant. At trial, she retrieved this mnemonic representation, compared it [to] defendant, and positively identified him as the robber. No part of this process was affected by [the] illegal arrest."

Because it was clear that prior to his illegal arrest, the police both knew defendant's identity and had some reason to believe he was involved in the robbery, Justice Brennan would have reserved judgment as to whether a defendant's face could ever be considered a suppressible "fruit" of an illegal arrest.[b] But a majority of the Court, in two separate concurring opinions, explicitly rejected this possibility.

6. *Confession as the "fruit" of a Payton violation.* *Payton v. New York* (p. 266) holds that the Fourth Amendment prohibits the police from effecting a warrantless entry into a suspect's home in order to make a routine felony arrest. In NEW YORK v. HARRIS, 495 U.S. 14, 110 S.Ct. 1640, 109 L.Ed.2d 13 (1990), a 5–4 majority, per WHITE, J., held that where the police have probable cause to arrest a suspect, the exclusionary rule does not bar the use of a statement made by the suspect *outside* his home even though the statement is obtained after an *in-house* arrest in violation of *Payton.*

The police had probable cause to believe Harris had killed a woman. They went to his apartment to take him into custody, but did not first obtain an arrest warrant. After being advised of his *Miranda* rights and waiving them, Harris reportedly admitted that he had committed the homicide. He was then taken to the station house, where, after again being advised of his rights and again waiving them, he signed a written inculpatory statement. Since the state did not challenge the trial court's suppression of Harris' statement to the police while still inside his home, the sole issue was the admissibility of the statement he made at the station house. The New York Court of Appeals ruled that it was the inadmissible fruit of the *Payton* violation, but the Supreme Court reversed:

"[As] emphasized in earlier cases, 'we have declined to adopt a "*per se* or 'but for' rule" that would make inadmissible any evidence, whether tangible or live-witness testimony, which somehow came to light through a chain of causation that begins with an illegal arrest.' *United States v. Ceccolini* [p. 796]. Rather, in this context, we have stated that '[t]he penalties visited upon the Government, and in turn upon the public, because its officers have violated the law must bear some relation to the purposes which the law is to serve.' Id. In light of these principles, we decline to apply the exclusionary rule in this context because *Payton* was designed to protect the physical integrity of the home, [not] grant criminal suspects, like Harris, protection for statements made outside their premises where the police have probable cause to arrest the suspect. * * *

"Nothing in the reasoning of [*Payton*] suggests that an arrest in a home without a warrant but with probable cause somehow renders unlawful continued custody of the suspect once he is removed from the house. [Because] the officers had probable cause to arrest Harris for a crime, Harris was not unlawfully in custody when he was removed to the station house. [For] Fourth Amendment

---

b. As Justice Brennan noted, this part of his opinion was joined only by Stewart and   Stevens, JJ.

purposes, the legal issue is the same as it would be had the police arrested Harris on his door step, illegally entered his home to search for evidence, and later interrogated Harris at the station house. Similarly, if the police had made a warrantless entry into Harris' home, not found him there, but arrested him on the street when he returned, a later statement made by him after proper warnings would no doubt be admissible.

"[In *Brown, Dunaway* and *Taylor*], evidence obtained from a criminal defendant following arrest was suppressed because the police lacked probable cause. [These] cases stand for the familiar proposition that the indirect fruits of an illegal search or arrest should be suppressed when they bear a sufficiently close relationship to the underlying illegality. [But] attenuation analysis is only appropriate where, as a threshold matter, courts determine that 'the challenged evidence is in some sense the product of illegal governmental activity.' *Crews.* * * *

"Harris's statement taken at the police station was not the product of being in unlawful custody. Neither was it the fruit of having been arrested in the home rather than someplace else. The case is analogous to *Crews.* In that case, we refused to suppress a victim's in-court identification despite the defendant's illegal arrest. The Court found that the evidence was not 'come at by exploitation [of] the defendant's Fourth Amendment rights,' and that it was not necessary to inquire whether the 'taint' of the Fourth Amendment violation was sufficiently attenuated to permit the introduction of the evidence. Here, likewise, the police had a justification to question Harris prior to his arrest; therefore, his subsequent statement was not an exploitation of the illegal entry into Harris' home. * * *

"[S]uppressing the statement taken outside the house would not serve the purpose of the rule that made Harris's in-house arrest illegal. The warrant requirement for an arrest in the home is imposed to protect the home, and anything incriminating the police gathered from arresting Harris in his home, rather than elsewhere, has been excluded, as it should have been; the purpose of the rule has thereby been vindicated. [The] principal incentive to obey *Payton* still obtains: the police know that a warrantless entry will lead to the suppression of any evidence found or statements taken inside the home. If we did suppress statements like Harris', moreover, the incremental deterrent value would be minimal. Given that the police have probable cause to arrest a suspect in Harris' position, they need not violate *Payton* in order to interrogate the suspect. It is doubtful therefore that the desire to secure a statement from a criminal suspect would motivate the police to violate *Payton.* As a result, suppressing a station-house statement obtained after a *Payton* violation will have little effect on the officers' actions, one way or another."

Dissenting Justice MARSHALL, joined by Brennan, Blackmun and Stevens, JJ., deemed *Brown v. Illinois* controlling:

"An application of the *Brown* factors to this case compels the conclusion that Harris' statement at the station house must be suppressed. About an hour elapsed between the illegal arrest and Harris' confession, without any intervening factor other than the warnings required by *Miranda.* This Court has held, however, that '*Miranda* warnings, *alone* and *per se,* ... cannot assure in every case that the Fourth Amendment violation has not been unduly exploited.' *Brown.* Indeed, in *Brown,* we held that a statement made almost *two* hours after an illegal arrest, and after *Miranda* warnings had been given, was not sufficiently removed from the violation so as to dissipate the taint.

"[The] officers decided, apparently consistent with a 'departmental policy,' to violate Harris' Fourth Amendment rights so they could get evidence that they could not otherwise obtain. As the trial court held, 'No more clear violation of [*Payton*], in my view, could be established.' Where, as here, there is a particularly flagrant constitutional violation and little in the way of elapsed time or intervening circumstances, the statement in the police station must be suppressed.

"[The] majority's *per se* rule in this case fails to take account of our repeated holdings that violations of privacy in the home are especially invasive. Rather, its rule is necessarily premised on the proposition that the effect of a *Payton* violation magically vanishes once the suspect is dragged from his home. But the concerns that make a warrantless home arrest a violation of the Fourth Amendment are nothing so evanescent. A person who is forcibly separated from his family and home in the dark of night after uniformed officers have broken down his door, handcuffed him, and forced him at gunpoint to accompany them to a police station does not suddenly breathe a sigh of relief at the moment he is dragged across his doorstep. Rather, the suspect is likely to be so frightened and rattled that he will say something incriminating. These effects, of course, extend far beyond the moment the physical occupation of the home ends. The entire focus of the *Brown* factors is to fix the point at which those effects are sufficiently dissipated that deterrence is not meaningfully advanced by suppression. The majority's assertion, as though the proposition were axiomatic, that the effects of such an intrusion *must* end when the violation ends is both undefended and indefensible. * * *

"Perhaps the most alarming aspect of the Court's ruling is its practical consequences for the deterrence of *Payton* violations. Imagine a police officer who has probable cause to arrest a suspect but lacks a warrant. [The] officer knows that if he breaks into the house without a warrant and drags the suspect outside, the suspect, shaken by the enormous invasion of privacy he has just undergone, may say something incriminating. Before today's decision, the government would only be able to use that evidence if the Court found that the taint of the arrest had been attenuated; after the decision, the evidence will be admissible regardless of whether it was the product of the unconstitutional arrest.[5] Thus, the officer envisions the following best-case scenario if he chooses to violate the Constitution: he avoids a major expenditure of time and effort, ensures that the suspect will not escape, and procures the most damaging evidence of all, a confession. His worst-case scenario is that he will avoid a major expenditure of effort, ensure that the suspect will not escape, and will see evidence in the house (which would have remained unknown absent the constitutional violation) that cannot be used in the prosecution's case-in-chief. The Court thus creates powerful incentives for police officers to violate the Fourth Amendment. In the context of our constitutional rights and the sanctity of our homes, we cannot afford to presume that officers will be entirely impervious to those incentives."

7. A warrant search as the fruit of an illegal entry and occupation of the premises. SEGURA v. UNITED STATES (1984) (also discussed at p. 263) arose as follows: When Segura, a suspected narcotics violator, entered his apartment building one evening, he was immediately arrested and taken to his apartment. The agents entered the apartment without requesting or obtaining permission. Four other people were there. The agents told them that Segura was under arrest and that a search warrant for the premises was being obtained.

---

5. Indeed, if the officer, as here, works in New York State, the Court's assertion that "[i]t is doubtful therefore that the desire to secure a statement from a criminal suspect would motivate the police to violate *Payton*" takes on a singularly ironic cast. The court below found as a matter of fact that the officers in this case had intentionally violated *Payton* for *precisely* the reason the Court identifies as "doubtful."

The agents then conducted a limited security check of the apartment, in the process observing drug paraphernalia. They then took Segura and the other occupants of the apartment to headquarters. Two agents remained in the apartment awaiting the warrant. Because of "administrative delay," the search warrant was not issued until some 19 hours after the initial entry. When the agents executed the warrant they discovered narcotics and records of narcotics transactions.

Since the government did not dispute the rulings below that the initial entry and security search were unlawful, "the only issue" before the Court was whether items "not observed during the illegal entry and first discovered by the agents the day after the entry, under an admittedly valid search warrant, should have been suppressed."[a] A 5–4 majority, per BURGER, C.J., answered in the negative. The legality of the initial entry had no bearing on the admissibility of the challenged evidence "because there was an independent source for the warrant under which that evidence was seized": "No information obtained during the initial entry or occupation of the apartment was needed or used by the agents to secure the warrant. [The] valid warrant search was a 'means sufficiently distinguishable' to purge the evidence of any 'taint' arising from the entry."

Dissenting Justice STEVENS, joined by Brennan, Marshall and Blackmun, JJ., maintained that "the controlling question" was "whether the deterrent purposes of the exclusionary rule would be served or undermined by the suppression of this evidence." He thought the deterrence rationale "plainly applicable": "The agents impounded the apartment precisely because they wished to avoid risking a loss of access to the evidence within it. Thus, the unlawful benefit they [obtained] was exactly the benefit [that] motivated [them] in the case to violate the Constitution."

In MURRAY v. UNITED STATES, 487 U.S. 533, 108 S.Ct. 2529, 101 L.Ed.2d 472 (1988), the Court, by a 4–3 vote (Brennan and Kennedy, JJ., not participating), declined to read *Segura* narrowly and held that evidence observed by the police during an illegal entry of premises need not be excluded if such evidence is subsequently discovered during the execution of an otherwise valid search warrant sought and issued on the basis of information wholly unconnected to the prior entry. After receiving information that a warehouse was being used for illegal drug activities, federal agents forced their way into the warehouse and observed in plain view bales of marijuana. The agents then left without disturbing the bales and applied for a search warrant. In their application, they did not mention the prior entry or include any recitations of their observations during that entry. Upon issuance of the warrant, the agents reentered the warehouse and seized the bales and other evidence of crime. In upholding the admissibility of the evidence, the Court, per SCALIA, J., observed:

"Knowledge that the marijuana was in the warehouse was assuredly acquired at the time of the unlawful entry. But it was also acquired at the time of entry pursuant to the warrant, and if that later acquisition was not the result of the earlier entry there is no reason why the independent source doctrine should not apply. Invoking the exclusionary rule would put the police (and society) not in the *same* position they would have occupied if no violation occurred, but in a *worse* one. See *Nix v. Williams* [p. 797]. We think this is also true with respect to the

---

a. Such illegal entries, observed the Court, are sufficiently deterred by the officers' realization that "whatever evidence they discover as a direct result of the entry may be suppressed." The four dissenters found the suggested distinction a puzzling one: "If the execution of a valid warrant takes the poison out of the hidden fruit, I should think that it would also remove the taint from the fruit in plain view."

tangible evidence, the bales of marijuana. [S]o long as a later, lawful seizure is genuinely independent of an earlier, tainted one (which may well be difficult to establish where the seized goods are kept in the police's possession) there is no reason why the independent source doctrine should not apply.

"The ultimate question, therefore, is whether the search pursuant to warrant was in fact a genuinely independent source of the information and tangible evidence at issue here. This would not have been the case if the agents' decision to seek the warrant was prompted by what they had seen during the initial entry, or if information obtained during that entry was presented to the Magistrate and affected his decision to issue the warrant. [The] District Court found that the agents did not reveal their warrantless entry to the Magistrate and that they did not include in their application for a warrant any recitation of their observations in the warehouse. It did not, however, explicitly find that the agents would have sought a warrant if they had not earlier entered the warehouse. [Thus], we vacate the judgments and remand these cases [for] determination whether the warrant-authorized search of the warehouse was an independent source of the challenged evidence in the sense we have described."

Dissenting Justice MARSHALL, joined by Stevens and O'Connor, JJ., maintained that "the Court's decision, by failing to provide sufficient guarantees that the subsequent search was, in fact, independent of the illegal search, emasculates the Warrant Clause and undermines the deterrence function of the exclusionary rule":

"[When], as here, the same team of investigators is involved in both the first and second search, there is a significant danger that the 'independence' of the source will in fact be illusory, and that the initial search will have affected the decision to obtain a warrant notwithstanding the officers' subsequent assertions to the contrary. It is therefore crucial that the factual premise of the exception—complete independence—be clearly established before the exception can [apply]. I believe the Court's reliance on the intent of the law enforcement officers who conducted the warrantless search provides insufficient guarantees that the subsequent legal search was unaffected by the prior illegal search. * * *

"*Segura* is readily distinguished from the present case. The admission of evidence first discovered during a legal search does not significantly lessen the deterrence facing the law enforcement officers contemplating an illegal entry *so long as* the evidence that is seen is excluded. This was clearly the view of [the *Segura* majority]. [E]xtending *Segura* to cover evidence discovered during an initial illegal search will eradicate this remaining deterrence to illegal entry. Moreover, there is less reason to believe that an initial illegal entry was prompted by a desire to determine whether to bother to get a warrant in the first place, and thus was not wholly independent of the second search, if officers understand that evidence they discover during the illegal search will be excluded even if they subsequently return with a warrant."[a]

Consider Craig M. Bradley, *Murray v. United States: The Bell Tolls for the Search Warrant Requirement*, 64 Ind.L.J. 907, 920 (1989):

"While I agree with the dissent in *Murray* that the decision 'emasculates the Warrant Clause,' I don't necessarily disagree with the result. This is [because]

a. While Stevens, J., joined Justice Marshall's dissent, he noted in a separate dissent that he "remain[ed] convinced that the *Segura* decision itself was unacceptable" because it provided government agents with an "affirmative incentive" to conduct illegal searches.

nothing in the amendment itself or, apparently, in the minds of its framers, requires a warrant as a prerequisite for a reasonable search; it only requires probable cause as a prerequisite for a warrant. [I]nstead of claiming that there is a warrant requirement and then, as recently illustrated in *Murray*, repeatedly finding ways to ignore it, the Court ought to adopt one of two models of the fourth amendment * * *.

[Professor Bradley then discusses the 'no lines' or 'general reasonableness' model, under which obtaining a warrant is only one of a number of relevant factors; and the 'bright line' approach, under which a warrant is *always* required for *every* search and seizure when it is practicable to obtain one.] With *Murray*, the Court clearly shows its preference for [a] reasonableness approach to fourth amendment law. *Murray* reeks of 'reasonableness' analysis and cannot be reconciled with the proposition that a search warrant is, in any meaningful sense, required."

8. The "tainted" witness. UNITED STATES v. CECCOLINI, 435 U.S. 268, 98 S.Ct. 1054, 55 L.Ed.2d 268 (1978), grew out of the following facts: An officer in a flower shop on a social visit illegally picked up an envelope and found it to contain money and policy slips. He then learned from his friend, Ms. Hennessey, an employee of the shop (who did not notice his discovery), that the envelope belonged to the defendant, the owner of the shop. The information reached the FBI four months later. An agent questioned Hennessey about defendant, without specifically mentioning the illegally discovered policy slips. She said she was willing to help, and she testified against defendant both before the grand jury and at his trial for perjury.

A 6–2 majority of the Court (Blackmun, J., not participating) held Hennessey's testimony admissible. Although it declined to adopt a *per se* rule that the testimony of a live witness should always be admissible,[a] the Court, per REHNQUIST, J., pointed out that various factors indicate that "the exclusionary rule should be invoked with much greater reluctance where the claim is based on a causal relationship between a constitutional violation and the discovery of a live witness than when a similar claim is advanced to support suppression of an inanimate object":

"The greater the willingness of the witness to freely testify, the greater the likelihood that he or she will be discovered by legal means and, concomitantly, the smaller the incentive to conduct an illegal search to discover the witness. Witnesses are not like guns or documents which remain hidden from view until one turns over a sofa or opens a filing cabinet. Witnesses can, and often do, come forward and offer evidence entirely of their own volition. And evaluated properly, the degree of free will necessary to dissipate the taint will very likely be found more often in the case of live-witness testimony than other kinds of evidence."

"Moreover, exclusion of testimony" would perpetually disable a witness from testifying about relevant and material facts, regardless of how unrelated such testimony might be to the purpose of the originally illegal search or the evidence discovered thereby. [S]ince the cost of excluding live-witness testimony often will be greater, a closer, more direct link between the illegality and that kind of testimony is required."

Dissenting Justice MARSHALL, joined by Brennan, J., did not see how "the same tree, having its roots in an unconstitutional search or seizure, can bear two different kinds of fruit, with one kind less susceptible than the other to exclusion

a. Concurring Chief Justice Burger would adopt such a rule.

on Fourth Amendment grounds." The dissent charged the majority with "judicial 'double counting' ": "The majority allows a court to consider whether the witness came forward and then, if he did not, to consider that generally (but not in this case) witnesses come forward." As for the majority's argument that often the exclusion of live-witness testimony will be very costly to society, "at least as often the exclusion of physical evidence [will be equally] costly * * *."

B. THE "INEVITABLE DISCOVERY" DOCTRINE: THE SEQUEL TO *BREWER V. WILLIAMS*

NIX v. WILLIAMS (WILLIAMS II)
467 U.S. 431, 104 S.Ct. 2501, 81 L.Ed.2d 377 (1984).

Chief Justice BURGER delivered the opinion of the Court.

[At] Williams' second trial [the] prosecution did not offer Williams' statements into evidence, nor did it seek to show that Williams had directed the police to the child's body. However, evidence of the condition of her body as it was found, articles and photographs of her clothing, and the results of post mortem medical and chemical tests on the body were admitted. The trial court concluded that the State had proved by a preponderance of the evidence that, if the search had not been suspended and Williams had not led the police to the victim, her body would have been discovered *"within a short time"* in essentially the same condition as it was actually found. The trial court also ruled that if the police had not located the body, "the search would clearly have been taken up again where it left off, given the extreme circumstances of this case and the body would [have] been found *in short order*" (emphasis added).

In finding that the body would have been discovered in essentially the same condition as it was actually found, the court noted that freezing temperatures had prevailed and tissue deterioration would have been suspended. The challenged evidence was admitted and the jury again found Williams guilty of first-degree murder; he was sentenced to life in prison.

[Both the Supreme Court of Iowa, which affirmed the conviction, and the U.S. District Court, which denied habeas relief, adopted the "inevitable discovery" exception to the exclusionary rule and sustained the conviction on that basis. Both courts concluded that the body would have been discovered in any event and that the police had not acted in bad faith in obtaining the excluded statements from Williams. But the U.S. Court of Appeals for the Eighth Circuit reversed the District Court's denial of habeas relief because, assuming an inevitable discovery exception, such an exception requires proof that the police did not act in "bad faith" and the record could not support such a finding.]

[The] core rationale consistently advanced by this Court for extending the Exclusionary Rule to evidence that is the fruit of unlawful police conduct has been that this admittedly drastic and socially costly course is needed to deter police from violations of constitutional and statutory protections. [On] this rationale, the prosecution is not to be put in a better position than it would have been in if no illegality had transpired.

By contrast, the derivative evidence analysis ensures that the prosecution is not put in a *worse* position simply because of some earlier police error or misconduct. The independent source doctrine allows admission of evidence that has been discovered by means wholly independent of any constitutional violation. That doctrine, although closely related to the inevitable discovery doctrine, does not apply here; Williams' statements to Leaming indeed led police to the child's body, but that is not the whole story. The independent source doctrine teaches us that the interest of society in deterring unlawful police conduct and the public interest in having juries receive all probative evidence of a crime are properly balanced by putting the police in the same, not a *worse,* position than they would have been in if no police error or misconduct had occurred.[4] When the challenged evidence has an independent source, exclusion of such evidence would put the police in a worse position than they would have been in absent any error or violation. There is a functional similarity between these two doctrines in that exclusion of evidence that would inevitably have been discovered would also put the government in a worse position, because the police would have obtained that evidence if no misconduct had taken place. Thus, while the independent source exception would not justify admission of evidence in this case, its rationale is wholly consistent with and justifies our adoption of the ultimate or inevitable discovery exception to the Exclusionary Rule.

It is clear that the cases implementing the Exclusionary Rule "begin with the premise that the challenged evidence is *in some sense* the product of illegal governmental activity." *United States v. Crews* (emphasis added). Of course, this does not end the inquiry. If the prosecution can establish by a preponderance of the evidence that the information ultimately or inevitably would have been discovered by lawful means—here the volunteers' search—then the deterrence rationale has so little basis that the evidence should be received.[5] Anything less would reject logic, experience, and common sense.

The requirement that the prosecution must prove the absence of bad faith, [would] place courts in the position of withholding from juries relevant and undoubted truth that would have been available to police absent any unlawful police activity. Of course, that view would put the police in a *worse* position than they would have been in if no unlawful conduct had transpired. And, of equal importance, it wholly fails to take into account the enormous societal cost of excluding truth in the search for truth in the administration of justice. Nothing in

---

4. The ultimate or inevitable discovery exception to the Exclusionary Rule is closely related in purpose to the harmless-error rule of *Chapman.* The harmless-constitutional-error rule "serve[s] a very useful purpose insofar as [it] block[s] setting aside convictions for small errors or defects that have little, if any, likelihood of having changed the result of the trial." The purpose of the inevitable discovery rule is to block setting aside convictions that would have been obtained without police misconduct.

5. As to the quantum of proof, we have already established some relevant guidelines. In *United States v. Matlock* (1974) [p. 353] (emphasis added), we stated that "the controlling burden of proof at suppression hearings should impose *no greater burden* than proof by a preponderance of the evidence." In *Lego v. Twomey* (1972) [p. 833] we observed "from our experience [that] no substantial evidence has accumulated that federal rights have suffered from determining admissibility by a preponderance of the evidence" and held that the prosecution must prove by a preponderance of the evidence that a confession sought to be used at trial was voluntary. We are unwilling to impose added burdens on the already difficult task of proving guilt in criminal cases by enlarging the barrier to placing evidence of unquestioned truth before juries.

Williams argues that the preponderance-of-the-evidence standard used by the Iowa courts is inconsistent with *United States v. Wade* [p. 641]. In requiring clear and convincing evidence of an independent source for an in-court identification, the Court gave weight to the effect an uncounseled pre-trial identification has in "crystalliz[ing] the witnesses' identification of the defendant for the future reference." The Court noted as well that possible unfairness at the lineup "may be the sole means of attack upon the unequivocal courtroom identification," and recognized the difficulty of determining whether an in-court identification was based on independent recollection unaided by the lineup identification. By contrast, inevitable discovery involves no speculative elements but focuses on demonstrated historical facts capable of ready verification or impeachment and does not require a departure from the usual burden of proof at suppression hearings.

this Court's prior holdings supports any such formalistic, pointless, and punitive approach.

The Court of Appeals concluded, without analysis, that if an absence of bad faith requirement were not imposed, "the temptation to risk deliberate violations of the Sixth Amendment would be too great, and the deterrent effect of the Exclusionary Rule reduced too far." We reject that view. A police officer who is faced with the opportunity to obtain evidence illegally will rarely, if ever, be in a position to calculate whether the evidence sought would inevitably be discovered.

[On] the other hand, when an officer is aware that the evidence will inevitably be discovered, he will try to avoid engaging in any questionable practice. In that situation, there will be little to gain from taking any dubious "shortcuts" to obtain the evidence. Significant disincentives to obtaining evidence illegally— including the possibility of departmental discipline and civil liability—also lessen the likelihood that the ultimate or inevitable discovery exception will promote police misconduct. In these circumstances, the societal costs of the Exclusionary Rule far outweigh any possible benefits to deterrence that a good-faith requirement might produce.

[The] Court of Appeals did not find it necessary to consider whether the record fairly supported the finding that the volunteer search party would ultimately or inevitably have discovered the victim's body. However, three courts independently reviewing the evidence have found that the body of the child inevitably would have been found by the searchers.

[When this finding was challenged] the prosecution offered the testimony of Agent Ruxlow, [who] had organized and directed some 200 volunteers who were searching for the child's body. The searchers were instructed "to check all the roads, the ditches, any culverts * * *." Ruxlow testified that he marked off highway maps of Poweshiek and Jasper Counties in grid fashion, divided the volunteers into teams of four to six persons, and assigned each team to search specific grid areas. Ruxlow also testified that, if the search had not been suspended because of Williams' promised cooperation, it would have continued into Polk County, using the same grid system. Although he had previously marked off into grids only the highway maps of Poweshiek and Jasper Counties, Ruxlow had obtained a map of Polk County, which he said he would have marked off in the same manner had it been necessary for the search to continue.

[The] search was not resumed once it was learned that Williams had led the police to the body, which was found two and one-half miles from where the search had stopped in what would have been the easternmost grid to be searched in Polk County. There was testimony that it would have taken an additional three to five hours to discover the body if the search had continued; the body was found near a culvert, one of the kinds of places the teams had been specifically directed to search.

On this record it is clear that the search parties were approaching the actual location of the body and we are satisfied, along with three courts earlier, that the volunteer search teams would have resumed the search had Williams not earlier led the police to the body and the body inevitably would have been found. * * *

Justice WHITE, concurring.

I join fully in the opinion of the Court. I write separately only to point out that many of Justice Stevens' remarks are beside the point when it is recalled that *Brewer v. Williams* was a 5–4 decision and that four members of the Court, including myself, were of the view that Officer Leaming had done nothing wrong at all, let alone anything unconstitutional. * * *

Justice STEVENS, concurring in the judgment.

[It] was the majority in *Williams I* that recognized that "evidence of where the body was found and of its condition might well be admissible on the theory that the body would have been discovered in any event, even had incriminating statements not been elicited from Williams." It was the author of today's opinion of the Court who characterized this rule of law as a "remarkable" and "unlikely theory." (Burger, C.J., dissenting).

* * * *Williams I* held that Detective Leaming had violated "the clear rule of *Massiah*" by deliberately eliciting incriminating statements from respondent during the pendency of the adversarial process and outside of that process. [Thus] the now-familiar plaint that "[t]he criminal is to go free because the constable has blundered" is entirely beside the point.

[The] majority is correct to insist that any rule of exclusion not provide the authorities with an incentive to commit violations of the Constitution. If the inevitable discovery rule provided such an incentive [it] would undermine the constitutional guarantee itself, and therefore be inconsistent with the deterrent purposes of the Exclusionary Rule. But when the burden of proof on the inevitable discovery question is placed on the prosecution, *it* must bear the risk of error in the determination made necessary by its constitutional violation. The uncertainty as to whether the body would have been discovered can be resolved in its favor here only because, as the Court explains, petitioner adduced evidence demonstrating that at the time of the constitutional violation an investigation was already under way which, in the natural and probable course of events, would have soon discovered the body. This is not a case in which the prosecution can escape responsibility for a constitutional violation through speculation; to the extent uncertainty was created by the constitutional violation the prosecution was required to resolve that uncertainty through proof.[8]

[The] majority refers to the "societal cost" of excluding probative evidence. In my view, the more relevant cost is that imposed on society by police officers who decide to take procedural shortcuts instead of complying with the law. What is the consequence of the shortcut that Detective Leaming took when he decided to question Williams in this case and not to wait an hour or so until he arrived in Des Moines?[9] [Instead] of having a 1969 conviction affirmed in routine fashion, the case is still alive 15 years later. Thanks to Detective Leaming, the State of Iowa has expended vast sums of money and countless hours of professional labor in his defense. That expenditure surely provides an adequate deterrent to similar violations; the responsibility for that expenditure lies not with the Constitution, but rather with the constable. * * *

Justice BRENNAN, with whom Justice MARSHALL joins, dissenting. * * *

8. I agree with the majority's holding that the prosecution must prove that the evidence would have been inevitably discovered by a preponderance of the evidence rather than by clear and convincing evidence. An inevitable discovery finding is based on objective evidence concerning the scope of the ongoing investigation which can be objectively verified or impeached. Hence an extraordinary burden of proof is not needed in order to preserve the defendant's ability to subject the prosecution's case to the meaningful adversarial testing required by the Sixth Amendment.

9. In this connection, it is worth noting, as Justice Marshall did in *Williams I*, that in light of the assistance that respondent's attorney had provided to the Des Moines police, it seems apparent that the lawyer intended to learn the location of the body from his client and then reveal it to the police. Thus, the need for a shortcut was practically nonexistent.

[T]he Court concludes that unconstitutionally obtained evidence may be admitted at trial if it inevitably would have been discovered in the same condition by an independent line of investigation that was already being pursued when the constitutional violation occurred. As has every federal Court of Appeals previously addressing this issue, I agree * * *.

The inevitable discovery exception necessarily implicates a hypothetical finding that differs in kind from the factual finding that precedes application of the independent source rule. To ensure that this hypothetical finding is narrowly confined to circumstances that are functionally equivalent to an independent source, and to protect fully the fundamental rights served by the exclusionary rule, I would require clear and convincing evidence before concluding that the government had met its burden of proof on this issue. * * *a

Notes and Questions

1. *Must the independent line of investigation be underway?* In his dissent, Justice Brennan describes the *Williams II* majority as "conclud[ing] that unconstitutionally obtained evidence may be admitted at trial if it inevitably would have been discovered in the same condition by an independent line of investigation *that was already being pursued* when the constitutional violation occurred." (Emphasis added.) Consider also concurring Justice Stevens' observation that "[t]he uncertainty as to whether the body would have been discovered can be resolved in [the prosecution's] favor here *only because* [the prosecution demonstrated] that at the time of the constitutional violation an investigation *was already under way which, in the natural and probable course of events, would have soon discovered the body.*" (Emphasis added.) Is *Williams II* limited along the lines indicated by Justices Brennan and Stevens? Should it be? See *United States v. Larsen*, 127 F.3d 984 (10th Cir. 1997).

2. *Primary evidence vs. secondary evidence. Nix* applied the inevitable discovery exception to secondary or derivative evidence, but most federal courts of appeals have also applied the exception to primary evidence (evidence acquired during the course of the search itself). See Robert M. Bloom, *Inevitable Discovery: An Exception beyond the Fruits,* 20 Am.J.Crim.L. 79, 87 (1992). Should a distinction between primary and secondary evidence be drawn on the ground that application of the inevitable discovery rule to secondary evidence does not excuse the unlawful police action by admitting what was obtained as a direct result of the initial misconduct, but that application of the rule to primary evidence constitutes an after the fact purging of initial wrongful conduct? See id. at 87–94.

3. *The significance of Murray v. United States.* Recall that in *Murray,* an *independent source* case, bales of marijuana (primary evidence) were discovered as the result of an illegal entry. Nevertheless, the Court allowed for the introduction of the bales, provided that the subsequent lawful entry with a warrant was not based on information related to the initial illegal entry. Does *Murray* support the use of the *inevitable discovery exception* to avoid suppression of primary evidence? See Bloom, supra, at 92–94.

4. *Inevitable discovery and the warrant requirement.* If the police have probable cause to conduct a search, but do not bother to obtain a warrant,

a. For an in-depth analysis of the Supreme Court's opinion in *Williams II,* see Silas J. Wasserstrom & William J. Mertens, *The Exclusionary Rule on the Scaffold: But Was it a Fair Trial?* 22 Am.Crim.L.Rev. 85, 130–79 (1984). For an incisive treatment of the "fruit of the poisonous tree" problems raised by the second *Williams* case prior to the Supreme Court's decision in that case, see Phillip E. Johnson, *The Return of the "Christian Burial Speech" Case,* 32 Emory L.J. 349 (1983).

although they had plenty of time to do so, can (should) the inevitable discovery exception be used to avoid the need for a warrant?[a] Consider Bloom, supra, at 95:

"Because the *Nix* decision dealt with a Sixth Amendment violation, the Court probably was not focusing on the effect this exception would have on the Fourth Amendment warrant requirement. To the extent that the *Nix* Court concluded that there would be a limited deterrence effect by utilizing the inevitable discovery exception, its reasoning was flawed with regard to the warrant requirement.

"[The] existence of the inevitable discovery exception *will* provide the police with an incentive to avoid the warrant requirement. The police might seek the most expeditious method of obtaining the evidence without regard to its illegality, knowing that, as long as they could have obtained the evidence legally, their efforts will not result in its suppression. [For] example, if the police can demonstrate that they *could* have gotten a search warrant, what incentive will there be for them to go actively through the procedural hassle of actually obtaining one, since the effects of an illegal warrantless search could be nullified by the application of the inevitable discovery exception?"

See also *United States v. Griffin*, 502 F.2d 959 (6th Cir.1974): "[P]olice who believe they have probable cause to search cannot enter a house without a warrant merely because they plan subsequently to get one. The assertion by police (after an illegal entry and after finding evidence of crime) that the discovery was 'inevitable' because they planned to get a search warrant and had sent an officer on such a mission, would as a practical matter be beyond judicial review." See generally LaFave § 11.4(a) at 243–46 and cases discussed therein.

5. *The issue not reached in Wilson v. Arkansas*. In *Wilson*, the knock-and-announce case discussed at p. 213, the Court declined to reach an argument the state advanced as an alternative ground for affirming the denial of defendant's motion to suppress. Analogizing to the "independent source" doctrine applied in *Segura* and the "inevitable discovery" rule adopted in *Nix v. Williams*, the state argued that "any evidence seized after an unreasonable, unannounced entry is causally disconnected from the constitutional violation and that exclusion goes beyond the goal of precluding any benefit to the government flowing from the constitutional violation." Assuming that the Court had reached this issue, what (would) (should) the result be?

C.   IS A CONFESSION OBTAINED IN VIOLATION OF *MIRANDA* A "POISONOUS TREE"?

Because a majority of the Court held that there was no violation of *Miranda* in NEW YORK v. QUARLES, (1984), p. 532, it had no occasion to reach the question whether, even if Quarles' initial statement should have been suppressed, the gun was nevertheless admissible because it was "nontestimonial" evidence or because the police would inevitably have discovered it absent their questioning. But Justice O'CONNOR, concurring in part and dissenting in part, devoted much of her opinion to a discussion of why she believed that the gun itself was admissible even though the statement that led to its discovery was not:

" * * * Only the introduction of a defendant's own *testimony* is proscribed by the Fifth Amendment's mandate that no person 'shall be compelled in any

---

a. A similar question may be asked about illegal searches of vehicles which turn up items that would have been discovered through an inventory search. On this issue compare *United States v. Halls*, 40 F.3d 275 (8th Cir.1994) and *United States v. Mancera–Londono*, 912 F.2d 373 (9th Cir.1990) with *United States v. $639,558.00 in United States Currency*, 955 F.2d 712 (D.C.Cir.1992) and *United States v. Infante–Ruiz*, 13 F.3d 498 (1st Cir.1994).

criminal case to be a witness against himself.' That mandate does not protect an accused from being compelled to surrender *nontestimonial* evidence against himself. The distinction between testimonial and nontestimonial evidence was explored in some detail in *Schmerber v. California* [p. 42], a decision this Court handed down within a week of deciding *Miranda*. [The blood tests at issue in *Schmerber* were held] admissible because they were neither testimonial nor communicative in nature.

"[W]hatever case can be made for suppression evaporates when the statements themselves are not admitted, given the rationale of the *Schmerber* line of cases. Certainly interrogation which provides leads to other evidence does not offend the values underlying the Fifth Amendment privilege any more than the compulsory taking of blood samples, fingerprints, or voice exemplars, all of which may be compelled in an 'attempt to discover evidence that might be used to prosecute [a defendant] for a criminal offense.' *Schmerber*. Use of a suspect's answers 'merely to find other evidence establishing his connection with the crime [simply] differs only by a shade from the permitted use for that purpose of his body or his blood.' H. Friendly, *Benchmarks* 280 (1967). [When]the only evidence to be admitted is derivative evidence such as a gun—derived not from actual compulsion but from a statement taken in the absence of *Miranda* warnings—[the values underlying the privilege] simply cannot require suppression, at least no more so than they would for other such nontestimonial evidence.[4] * * * *a

Dissenting Justice MARSHALL, joined by Brennan and Stevens, JJ., considered Justice O'Connor's treatment of derivative evidence "a much more radical departure from precedent than that opinion acknowledges." Continued Justice Marshall:

"The gun was the direct product of a coercive custodial interrogation. In *Silverthorne* and *Wong Sun* this Court held that the Government may not introduce incriminating evidence derived from an illegally obtained source. [When] they ruled on the issue, the New York courts were entirely correct in deciding that Quarles' gun was the tainted fruit of a nonconsensual interrogation and therefore was inadmissible under our precedents.

"However, since the New York Court of Appeals issued its opinion, [this Court, in *Nix v. Williams,* has accepted the 'inevitable discovery' doctrine.] [The State] has argued that the 'inevitable-discovery' rule, if applied to this case, would permit the admission of Quarles' gun. [Under the circumstances] I believe that the proper disposition of the matter is to vacate the state court order suppressing Quarles' gun and remand the matter [for] further consideration in light of *Nix v. Williams.*"

OREGON v. ELSTAD

470 U.S. 298, 105 S.Ct. 1285, 84 L.Ed.2d 222 (1985).

Justice O'CONNOR delivered the opinion of the Court.

This case requires us to decide whether an initial failure of law enforcement officers to administer the warnings required by *Miranda,* without more, "taints"

---

4. In suggesting that *Wong Sun* requires exclusion of the gun, Justice Marshall fails to acknowledge this Court's holding in *Michigan v. Tucker* [p. 502]. In *Tucker,* the Court very clearly held that *Wong Sun* is inapplicable in cases involving mere departures from *Miranda.* *Wong Sun* and its "fruit of the poisonous tree" analysis lead to exclusion of derivative evidence only where the underlying police misconduct infringes a "core" constitutional right. Failure to administer *Miranda* warnings violates only a nonconstitutional prophylactic. * * *

a. Compare Justice O'Connor's opinion for the Court in *Oregon v. Elstad,* below.

subsequent admissions made after a suspect has been fully advised of and has waived his *Miranda* rights. [Respondent was convicted of burglary.] The Oregon Court of Appeals reversed, holding that respondent's signed confession, although voluntary, was rendered inadmissible by a prior remark made in response to questioning without benefit of *Miranda* warnings. [We] reverse.

[When the Gross home was burglarized, a witness contacted the sheriff's office, implicating respondent Elstad, an 18–year-old neighbor and friend of the Grosses' teenage son. Officers Burke and McAllister went to Elstad's home, with a warrant for his arrest for the aforementioned burglary. Elstad's mother led the officers to his room. The officers asked Elstad to get dressed and to accompany them to the living room. Officer Burke sat down with Elstad in the living room and, without telling him that the police had a warrant for his arrest, stated that he "felt" Elstad was involved in the Gross burglary. Elstad replied, "Yes, I was there."

[Elstad was then transported to sheriff headquarters and, approximately an hour later, Officer McAllister, in the presence of Officer Burke, advised Elstad of his *Miranda* rights for the first time. Elstad agreed to talk to the police and made a statement detailing his involvement in the burglary. The statement was typed, reviewed by Elstad, read back to him for correction and signed by him.

[The trial judge excluded the incriminating remark Elstad made in his living room, but admitted the statement made at the sheriff's office. Following his conviction of burglary, Elstad appealed. The state conceded that Elstad had been in custody when he replied, "Yes, I was there," and thus that this statement was obtained in violation of *Miranda*, but maintained that any conceivable "taint" had been dissipated prior to Elstad's written confession by Officer McAllister's careful administration of the *Miranda* warnings. The Oregon Court of Appeals disagreed.

[In reversing Elstad's conviction, the Oregon court identified the crucial constitutional inquiry as whether there was "a sufficient break in the stream of events" between the inadmissible statement in respondent's living room and the written confession in the sheriff's office "to insulate the latter statement from the effect of what went before." It concluded that, because of the brief period separating the two incidents, the "cat was sufficiently out of the bag to exert a coercive impact on [respondent's] later admissions."]

[The] Oregon court assumed and respondent here contends that a failure to administer *Miranda* warnings necessarily breeds the same consequences as police infringement of a constitutional right, so that evidence uncovered following an unwarned statement must be suppressed as "fruit of the poisonous tree." We believe this view misconstrues the nature of the protections afforded by *Miranda* warnings and therefore misreads the consequences of police failure to supply them.

[A]s we explained in *Quarles* and *Tucker,* a procedural *Miranda* violation differs in significant respects from violations of the Fourth Amendment, which have traditionally mandated a broad application of the "fruits" doctrine. The purpose of the Fourth Amendment exclusionary rule is to deter unreasonable searches, no matter how probative their fruits.

[The] *Miranda* exclusionary rule, however, serves the Fifth Amendment and sweeps more broadly than the Fifth Amendment itself. It may be triggered even in the absence of a Fifth Amendment violation.[1] The Fifth Amendment prohibits use

---

1. Justice Stevens expresses puzzlement at our statement that a simple failure to adminis- ter *Miranda* warnings is not in itself a viola- tion of the Fifth Amendment. Yet the Court so by the prosecution in its case in chief only of *compelled* testimony. Failure to administer *Miranda* warnings creates a presumption of compulsion.

[But] the *Miranda* presumption, though irrebuttable for purposes of the prosecution's case in chief, does not require that the statements and their fruits be discarded as inherently tainted [discussing *Harris v. New York,* (p. 812) (permitting the use of statements obtained in violation of *Miranda* for impeachment purposes) and *Tucker*]. Where an unwarned statement is preserved for use in situations that fall outside the sweep of the *Miranda* presumption, "the primary criterion of admissibility [remains] the 'old' due process voluntariness test." Schulhofer, *Confessions and the Court,* 79 Mich.L.Rev. 865, 877 (1981).

[In] deciding "how sweeping the judicially imposed consequences" of a failure to administer *Miranda* warnings should be, the *Tucker* Court noted that neither the general goal of deterring improper police conduct nor the Fifth Amendment goal of assuring trustworthy evidence would be served by suppression of the witness' testimony. The unwarned confession must, of course, be suppressed, but the Court ruled that introduction of the third-party witness' testimony did not violate Tucker's Fifth Amendment rights.

We believe that this reasoning applies with equal force when the alleged "fruit" of a noncoercive *Miranda* violation is neither a witness nor an article of evidence but the accused's own voluntary testimony. As in *Tucker,* the absence of any coercion or improper tactics undercuts the twin rationales—trustworthiness and deterrence—for a broader rule. Once warned, the suspect is free to exercise his own volition in deciding whether or not to make a statement to the authorities.

[If] errors are made by law enforcement officers in administering the prophylactic *Miranda* procedures, they should not breed the same irremediable consequences as police infringement of the Fifth Amendment itself. It is an unwarranted extension of *Miranda* to hold that a simple failure to administer the warnings, unaccompanied by any actual coercion or other circumstances calculated to undermine the suspect's ability to exercise his free will so taints the investigatory process that a subsequent voluntary and informed waiver is ineffective for some indeterminate period. Though *Miranda* requires that the unwarned admission must be suppressed, the admissibility of any subsequent statement should turn in these circumstances solely on whether it is knowingly and voluntarily made.

[There] is a vast difference between the direct consequences flowing from coercion of a confession by physical violence or other deliberate means calculated to break the suspect's will and the uncertain consequences of disclosure of a "guilty secret" freely given in response to an unwarned but noncoercive question, as in this case. Justice Brennan's contention that it is impossible to perceive any causal distinction between this case and one involving a confession that is coerced by torture is wholly unpersuasive.[3] Certainly, in respondent's case, the causal

---

held in *Quarles* and *Tucker*. The *Miranda* Court itself recognized this point when it disclaimed any intent to create a "constitutional straight-jacket" and invited Congress and the States to suggest "potential alternatives for protecting the privilege." A *Miranda* violation does not *constitute* coercion but rather affords a bright-line, legal presumption of coercion, requiring suppression of all unwarned statements. It has never been remotely suggested

that any statement taken from Mr. Elstad without benefit of *Miranda* warnings would be admissible.

3. Most of the 50 cases cited by Justice Brennan in his discussion of consecutive confessions concern an initial unwarned statement obtained through overtly or inherently coercive methods which raise serious Fifth Amendment and Due Process concerns [discussing many cases].

connection between any psychological disadvantage created by his admission and his ultimate decision to cooperate is speculative and attenuated at best. It is difficult to tell with certainty what motivates a suspect to speak. * * * We must conclude that, absent deliberately coercive or improper tactics in obtaining the initial statement, the mere fact that a suspect has made an unwarned admission does not warrant a presumption of compulsion. A subsequent administration of *Miranda* warnings to a suspect who has given a voluntary but unwarned statement ordinarily should suffice to remove the conditions that precluded admission of the earlier statement. In such circumstances, the finder of fact may reasonably conclude that the suspect made a rational and intelligent choice whether to waive or invoke his rights.

Though belated, the reading of respondent's rights was undeniably complete. [There] is no question that respondent knowingly and voluntarily waived his right to remain silent before he described his participation in the burglary. It is also beyond dispute that respondent's earlier remark was voluntary, within the meaning of the Fifth Amendment. Neither the environment nor the manner of either "interrogation" was coercive. The initial conversation took place at midday, in the living room area of respondent's own home, with his mother in the kitchen area, a few steps away.

[The] state has conceded the issue of custody and thus we must assume that Burke breached *Miranda* procedures in failing to administer *Miranda* warnings before initiating the discussion in the living room. [But] the incident had none of the earmarks of coercion. Nor did the officers exploit the unwarned admission to pressure respondent into waiving his right to remain silent.

Respondent, however, has argued that he was unable to give a fully *informed* waiver of his rights because he was unaware that his prior statement could not be used against him. Respondent suggests that Deputy McAllister, to cure this deficiency, should have added an additional warning to those given him at the Sheriff's office. Such a requirement is neither practicable nor constitutionally necessary. In many cases, a breach of *Miranda* procedures may not be identified as such until long after full *Miranda* warnings are administered and a valid confession obtained. The standard *Miranda* warnings explicitly inform the suspect of his right to consult a lawyer before speaking. Police officers are ill equipped to pinch-hit for counsel, construing the murky and difficult questions of when "custody" begins or whether a given unwarned statement will ultimately be held admissible.

[Where] the suspect's initial inculpatory statement, though technically in violation of *Miranda,* was voluntary, [the] relevant inquiry is whether, in fact, the second statement was also voluntarily made. [The] fact that a suspect chooses to speak after being informed of his rights is, of course, highly probative. We find that the dictates of *Miranda* and the goals of the Fifth Amendment proscription against use of compelled testimony are fully satisfied in the circumstances of this case by barring use of the unwarned statement in the case in chief. No further purpose is served by imputing "taint" to subsequent statements obtained pursuant to a voluntary and knowing waiver. We hold today that a suspect who has once responded to unwarned yet uncoercive questioning is not thereby disabled

Justice Brennan cannot seriously mean to equate such situations with the case at bar. Likewise inapposite are the cases the dissent cites concerning suspects whose invocation of their rights to remain silent and to have counsel present were flatly ignored while police subjected them to continued interrogation. * * *

from waiving his rights and confessing after he has been given the requisite *Miranda* warnings. * * *

Justice BRENNAN, with whom Justice MARSHALL joins, dissenting.

[Today's decision] delivers a potentially crippling blow to *Miranda* and the ability of courts to safeguard the rights of persons accused of crime. For at least with respect to successive confessions, the Court today appears to strip remedies for *Miranda* violations of the "fruit of the poisonous tree" doctrine prohibiting the use of evidence presumptively derived from official illegality.[2]

[The] threshold question is this: What effect should an admission or confession of guilt obtained in violation of an accused's *Miranda* rights be presumed to have upon the voluntariness of subsequent confessions that are preceded by *Miranda* warnings? [This] Court has had long experience with the problem of confessions obtained after an earlier confession has been illegally secured. Subsequent confessions in these circumstances are not *per se* inadmissible, but the prosecution must demonstrate facts "sufficient to insulate the [subsequent] statement from the effect of all that went before."

[Although] we have thus rejected a *per se* rule forbidding the introduction of subsequent statements in these circumstances, we have emphasized that the psychological impact of admissions and confessions of criminal guilt nevertheless can have a decisive impact in undermining the voluntariness of a suspect's responses to continued police interrogation and must be accounted for in determining their admissibility. * * *

Our precedents did not develop in a vacuum. They reflect an understanding of the realities of police interrogation * * *. Expert interrogators and experienced lower-court judges will be startled, to say the least, to learn that the connection between multiple confessions is "speculative" and that a subsequent rendition of *Miranda* warnings "ordinarily" enables the accused in these circumstances to exercise his "free will" and to make "a rational and intelligent choice whether to waive or invoke his rights."

[The] correct approach, administered for almost 20 years by most courts with no untoward results, is to presume that an admission or confession obtained in violation of *Miranda* taints a subsequent confession unless the prosecution can show that the taint is so attenuated as to justify admission of the subsequent confession. Although the Court warns against the "irremediable consequences" of this presumption, it is obvious that a subsequent confession, just like any other evidence that follows upon illegal action, does not become "sacred and inaccessible." As with any other evidence, the inquiry is whether the subsequent confession "has been come at by exploitation of [the] illegality or instead by means sufficiently distinguishable to be purged of the primary taint." *Wong Sun.*

Until today the Court has recognized that the dissipation inquiry requires the prosecution to demonstrate that the official illegality did not taint the challenged confession, and we have rejected the simplistic view that abstract notions of "free will" are alone sufficient to dissipate the challenged taint [quality from *Brown v. Illinois*]. Instead, we have instructed courts to consider carefully such factors as the strength of the causal connection between the illegal action and the challenged

---

2. The Court repeatedly casts its analysis in terms of the "fruits" of a *Miranda* violation, but its dicta nevertheless surely should not be read as necessarily foreclosing application of derivative-evidence rules where the *Miranda* violation produces evidence other than a subsequent confession by the accused. See n. 29, infra.

evidence, their proximity in time and place, the presence of intervening factors, and the "purpose and flagrancy of the official misconduct."

[Where] an accused believes that it is futile to resist because the authorities already have elicited an admission of guilt, the mere rendition of *Miranda* warnings does not convey the information most critical at that point to ensuring his informed and voluntary decision to speak again: that the earlier confession may not be admissible and thus that he need not speak out of any feeling that he already has sealed his fate. The Court therefore is flatly wrong in arguing, as it does repeatedly, that the mere provision of *Miranda* warnings prior to subsequent interrogation supplies the accused with "the relevant information" and ensures that a subsequent confession "ordinarily" will be the product of "a rational and intelligent choice" and "an act of free will."

[The] foundation of the derivative-evidence doctrine has always been that, where the authorities have acted illegally, *they* must bear the "ultimate burden" of proving that their misconduct did not "taint" subsequently obtained evidence. That is precisely the point of the derivative-evidence presumption. By rejecting this presumption in *Miranda* cases, the Court today appears to adopt a "go ahead and try to prove it" posture toward citizens whose Fifth Amendment *Miranda* rights have been violated, an attitude that marks a sharp break from the Court's traditional approach to official lawlessness. * * *

Not content merely to ignore the practical realities of police interrogation and the likely effects of its abolition of the derivative-evidence presumption, the Court goes on to assert that nothing in the Fifth Amendment or the general judicial policy of deterring illegal police conduct "ordinarily" requires the suppression of evidence derived proximately from a confession obtained in violation of *Miranda*. The Court does not limit its analysis to successive confessions, but recurrently refers generally to the "fruits" of the illegal confession. Thus the potential impact of the Court's reasoning might extend far beyond the "cat out of the bag" context to include the discovery of physical evidence and other derivative fruits of *Miranda* violations as well.[29] * * *

[The] Court today refuses to apply the derivative-evidence rule even to the extent necessary to deter objectively unreasonable failures by the authorities to honor a suspect's *Miranda* rights. Incredibly, faced with an obvious violation of *Miranda*, the Court asserts that it will not countenance suppression of a subsequent confession in such circumstances where the authorities have acted "legitimate[ly]" and have not used "improper tactics." One can only respond: whither went *Miranda*?

* * * How can the Court possibly expect the authorities to obey *Miranda* when they have every incentive now to interrogate suspects without warnings or an effective waiver, knowing that the fruits of such interrogations "ordinarily" will be admitted, that an admissible subsequent confession "ordinarily" can be obtained simply by reciting the *Miranda* warnings shortly after the first has been procured and asking the accused to repeat himself, and that unless the accused

---

29. Notwithstanding the sweep of the Court's language, today's opinion surely ought not be read as also foreclosing application of the traditional derivative-evidence presumption to physical evidence obtained as a proximate result of a *Miranda* violation. The Court relies heavily on individual "volition" as an insulating factor in successive-confession cases. Although the Court's reliance on this factor is clearly misplaced, the factor is altogether missing in the context of inanimate evidence.

As they have in successive-confession cases, most courts considering the issue have recognized that physical evidence proximately derived from a *Miranda* violation is presumptively inadmissible. * * *

can demonstrate otherwise his confession will be viewed as an "act of free will" in response to "legitimate law enforcement activity"? * * *

Justice STEVENS dissenting.

[In] my opinion, the Court's attempt to fashion a distinction between actual coercion "by physical violence or other deliberate means calculated to break the suspect's will" and irrebuttably presumed coercion cannot succeed. The presumption is only legitimate if it is assumed that there is always a coercive aspect to custodial interrogation that is not preceded by adequate advice of the constitutional right to remain silent. Although I would not support it, I could understand a rule that refused to apply the presumption unless the interrogation took place in an especially coercive setting—perhaps only in the police station itself—but if the presumption arises whenever the accused has been taken into custody or his freedom has been restrained in any significant way, it will surely be futile to try to develop subcategories of custodial interrogation. Indeed, a major purpose of treating the presumption of coercion as irrebuttable is to avoid the kind of fact-bound inquiry that today's decision will surely engender.

* * * [S]urely the fact that an earlier confession was obtained by unlawful methods should add force to the presumption of coercion that attaches to subsequent custodial interrogation and should require the prosecutor to shoulder a heavier burden of rebuttal than in a routine case. Simple logic, as well as the interest in not providing an affirmative incentive to police misconduct, requires that result. I see no reason why the violation of a rule that is as well recognized and easily administered as the duty to give *Miranda* warnings should not also impose an additional burden on the prosecutor.[13]

[For] me, the most disturbing aspect of the Court's opinion is its somewhat opaque characterization of the police misconduct in this case. The Court appears ambivalent on the question whether there was any constitutional violation. This ambivalence is either disingenuous or completely lawless. This Court's power to require state courts to exclude probative self-incriminatory statements rests entirely on the premise that the use of such evidence violates the Federal Constitution.[15] The same constitutional analysis applies whether the custodial interrogation is actually coercive or irrebuttably presumed to be coercive. If the Court does not accept that premise, it must regard the holding in the *Miranda* case itself, as well as all of the Federal jurisprudence that has evolved from that decision, as nothing more than an illegitimate exercise of raw judicial power. * * *

Notes and Questions

1. *The role of the police officer vs. the role of the defense lawyer.* During the oral argument in *Elstad,* one Justice suggested that it would not be unduly burdensome for the police to tell a suspect that they had treated him improperly at an earlier session and that therefore the incriminating statement(s) obtained at the earlier session would not be used against him. Such a requirement, responded

---

13. In view of the Court's holding, it is not necessary to consider how that additional burden should be discharged in all cases. In general, however, I should think that before the second session of custodial interrogation begins, the prisoner should be advised that his earlier statement is, or may be, inadmissible. I am not persuaded that the *Miranda* rule is so "murky" that the law-enforcement profession would be unable to identify the cases in which

a supplementary warning would be appropriate. * * *

15. At least that is my view. In response to this dissent, however, the Court has added a fn. 1, implying that whenever the Court commands exclusion of a presumptively coerced confession, it is standing—not on a constitutional predicate—but merely on its own shoulders.

the Attorney General of Oregon, "might do a great deal of mischief because it confuses the role of the police officer with that of the criminal defense attorney." Does this argument come pretty late in the day? Doesn't *Miranda* itself "confuse the role of the police officer with that of the criminal defense lawyer"?

Should the police at least be able to tell whether there is a *substantial question* about the admissibility of an earlier statement? Should they at least be required to give a supplementary warning that the earlier statement is or *may be* inadmissible? Or that it is *unclear* whether the earlier statement is admissible and that the suspect is entitled to the advise of counsel on this point? If the police are "ill equipped" to do even this much, then when they obtain a statement from a person without advising him of his rights and want to question him again, instead of asking or expecting them to "pinch-hit" for counsel, should we require them to let defense counsel "bat for himself"?

2. *Does Elstad compromise Miranda's promises* ? Consider Note, 99 Harv. L.Rev. 141, 146–47 (1985): "By dramatically multiplying the situations in which the Court will permit introduction of the fruits of improperly obtained statements into evidence, *Elstad* significantly increases the burden on courts to determine whether particular confessions were actually compelled. *Elstad* thus compromises *Miranda*'s promises to accommodate judicial competence and serve judicial economy. Collateral judicial inquiries into the voluntariness of confessions are both time-consuming and imprecise. Indeed, the perception that judicial findings of voluntariness are extraordinarily unreliable prompted the *Miranda* Court to attempt to extinguish such inquiries with a bright-line rule excluding both improperly obtained confessions and their derivative fruits. * * * *Elstad* sacrifices the precision of *Miranda* and promises once again to sink lower courts in a mire of inquiries into voluntariness."

3. *Physical evidence obtained as a result of a Miranda violation.* Would the Court deliver a "crippling blow" to *Miranda* if it permitted the prosecution to use the nontestimonial fruits of a *Miranda* violation? Consider David Wollin, *Policing the Police: Should Miranda Violations Bear Fruit?*, 53 Ohio St.L.J. 805, 845?46 (1992):

"[There] are many reported cases where the police have arrested suspects and interrogated them without the *Miranda* warnings in order to discover the existence or location of nontestimonial evidence. This should not come as a surprise to those knowledgeable about police practices. Expert interrogators have long recognized, and continue to instruct, that a confession is a primary source for determining the existence and whereabouts of the fruits of a crime, such as documents or weapons. * * *

"Suppression of a suspect's unwarned statements alone will not provide sufficient deterrence of police misconduct. Police officers seeking physical evidence are not likely to view the loss of an unwarned confession as particularly great when weighed against the opportunity to recover highly probative evidence, such as a murder weapon or narcotics. Recovery of such evidence might well convince a suspect to forego a trial and plead guilty, thereby preventing the *Miranda* issue from ever being raised."

4. *How broadly have the lower courts read Elstad?* Dissenting in *Elstad,* Justice Brennan maintained that the language and reasoning of the majority opinion should not be read as foreclosing application of the "fruit of the poisonous tree" doctrine to *physical evidence* derived from a *Miranda* violation. However, according to Wollin, Note 3 supra at 835–36, "[f]ollowing *Elstad,* federal and state courts have almost uniformly ruled that the prosecution can introduce nontesti-

monial fruits of a *Miranda* violation in a criminal trial. The poisonous tree doctrine will be applicable only if there is evidence of actual coercion or other circumstances designed to overbear the suspect's will."

5. *Edwards violations vs. "mere" Miranda violations.* For purposes of *Elstad,* should *Edwards* violations, i.e., violations of a suspect's invocation of her right to counsel, be treated differently than "mere" *Miranda* violations? *Correll v. Thompson,* 63 F.3d 1279, 1290 (4th Cir.1995), answers in the negative, observing that an *Edwards* violation "is also a technical violation of *Miranda,* not a Fifth Amendment violation." But see Note, 62 Ind.L.J. 1061, 1099–1100 (1987), maintaining that "the right to counsel, once invoked by suspect in a custodial interrogation, [is] more than a procedural device," and that the poisonous tree doctrine should apply with its full vigor to the fruits of its violation.

6. *The physical fruits of coerced confessions.* Should courts ever admit physical evidence derived from "involuntary" or coerced confessions? Is this a logical extension of the sharp distinction the Court drew in *Schmerber* (p. 42) between testimonial evidence and physical evidence? Did Justice O'Connor point the way in her *Quarles* concurring opinion? Could the same result be reached by expanding the "inevitable discovery" exception, i.e., by simply presuming that the fruits of a coerced confession could or would always have come to light anyway? *Compare* Akhil Reed Amar & Renée B. Lettow, *Fifth Amendment First Principles: The Self–Incrimination Clause,* 93 Mich.L.Rev. 857 (1995) (yes) *with* Kamisar, *On the Fruits of Miranda Violations, Coerced Confessions and Compelled Testimony,* 93 Mich.L.Rev. 929 (1995) (no).

SECTION 3. USE OF ILLEGALLY OBTAINED EVIDENCE FOR IMPEACHMENT PURPOSES

A. THE EXPANSION OF A ONCE-NARROW EXCEPTION

1. In *Walder v. United States,* 347 U.S. 62, 74 S.Ct. 354, 98 L.Ed. 503 (1954), defendant, charged with various illegal narcotics transactions, asserted early on his direct examination that he had never possessed any narcotics or sold or given any narcotics to anyone in his life. The Court held, per Frankfurter, J., that this assertion "opened the door," for purposes of attacking the defendant's credibility, to evidence of heroin seized from the defendant's home, in his presence, in an earlier, unrelated case. "Of his own accord," observed the Court, "the defendant went beyond a mere denial of complicity in the crimes of which he was charged and made the sweeping claim that he had never dealt in or possessed any narcotics. [A defendant] must be free to deny all the elements of the case against him without thereby giving leave to the Government to introduce by way of rebuttal evidence illegally secured by it, and thereby not available for its case in chief. Beyond that, however, there is hardly justification for letting the defendant affirmatively resort to perjurious testimony in reliance on the Government's disability to challenge his credibility."

The instant situation, emphasized the *Walder* Court, is to be "sharply contrasted" with that presented by *Agnello v. United States,* 269 U.S. 20, 46 S.Ct. 4, 70 L.Ed. 145 (1925). There, the government sought to "smuggle in" the tainted evidence on cross-examination by asking the defendant whether he had ever seen narcotics before, and eliciting the expected denial. In *Agnello,* the defendant "did nothing" to waive his constitutional protection or to justify cross-examination with respect to the illegally seized evidence.

2.   HARRIS v. NEW YORK, 401 U.S. 222, 91 S.Ct. 643, 28 L.Ed.2d 1 (1971), often called the first blow the Burger Court struck *Miranda,* arose as follows: Petitioner, charged with selling heroin to an undercover officer, took the stand in his own defense. He admitted knowing the officer, but denied making a sale of heroin. Statements made by petitioner immediately following his arrest which partially contradicted his direct trial testimony were used to impeach his credibility. According to the Court, petitioner made no claim that the statements were coerced or involuntary,[a] but they were preceded by defective *Miranda* warnings, and thus inadmissible to establish the prosecution's case in chief. A 5–4 majority, per BURGER, C.J., held that under the circumstances "petitioner's credibility was appropriately impeached by use of his earlier conflicting statements."

The Court noted that "[s]ome comments in the *Miranda* opinion can indeed be read as indicating a bar to use of [a statement obtained in violation of *Miranda*] for any purpose," but dismissed this discussion as "not at all necessary to the Court's holding" and not "controlling."[b] The Court noted, but also seemed untroubled by the fact, "that Walder was impeached as to collateral matters included in his direct examination, whereas petitioner here was impeached as to testimony bearing more directly on the crimes charged." The Court next observed:

"The impeachment process here undoubtedly provided valuable aid to the jury in assessing petitioner's credibility, and the benefits of this process should not be lost [because] of the speculative possibility that impermissible police conduct will be encouraged thereby. Assuming that the exclusionary rule has a deterrent effect * * * sufficient deterrence flows when the evidence in question is made unavailable to the prosecution in its case in chief.

"[The privilege to testify in one's defense] cannot be construed to include the right to commit perjury. [The] prosecution here did no more than utilize the traditional truth-testing devices of the adversary process. [The] shield provided by *Miranda* cannot be perverted into a license to use perjury by way of a defense, free from the risk of confrontation with prior inconsistent utterances."

Dissenting Justice BRENNAN, joined by Douglas and Marshall, JJ., criticized the majority for disregarding language in *Miranda* and for selectively quoting from *Walder.* The dissent emphasized that "*Walder* was not a case where tainted evidence was used to impeach an accused's direct testimony on matters directly related to the case against him," but only such testimony "on matters *collateral* to the crime charged." Continued the dissent:

"While *Walder* did not identify the constitutional specifics that guarantee 'a defendant the fullest opportunity to meet the accusation against him [and permit him to be free to deny all the elements of the case against him],' in my view *Miranda* identified the Fifth Amendment's privilege against self-incrimination as one of those specifics. [It] is fulfilled only when an accused is guaranteed the right

---

a.   According to Alan Dershowitz & John Hart Ely, *Harris v. New York: Some Anxious Observations on the Candor and Logic of the Emerging Nixon Majority,* 80 Yale L.J. 1198, 1201 (1971), "the record is clear" that he did.

b.   But consider Geoffrey Stone, *The Miranda Doctrine in the Burger Court,* 1977 Sup. Ct.Rev. 99, 107–08: "Rightly or wrongly, *Miranda* was deliberately structured to canvass a wide range of problems, many of which were not directly raised by the cases before the Court. This approach was thought necessary in order to 'give concrete constitutional guidelines for law enforcement agencies and courts to follow.' Thus, a technical reading of *Miranda,* such as that employed in *Harris,* would enable the Court to label many critical aspects of the decision mere dictum and therefore not 'controlling.' "

'to remain silent unless he chooses to speak in the *unfettered* exercise of his own will' (emphasis added). The choice of whether to testify in one's own defense must therefore be 'unfettered' * * *. [But] the accused is denied an 'unfettered' choice when the decision whether to take the stand is burdened by the risk that an illegally obtained prior statement may be introduced to impeach his direct testimony denying complicity in the crime charged against him.'"[c]

3. *The Fourth Amendment vs. the Fifth.* Should the Court have considered the significance of *Miranda's* Fifth Amendment underpinning before applying (or extending) the Fourth Amendment *Walder* case to *Harris?* Is impeachment by means of evidence obtained in violation of the Fourth Amendment more defensible than such use of evidence obtained in violation of the Self–Incrimination Clause of the Fifth because the Fourth's "exclusionary rule" is a court-created device designed to deter the police and as the link between police illegality and subsequent evidence becomes more attenuated it becomes less likely that exclusion would affect future police conduct? On the other hand, is the essence of the constitutional wrong under the Fifth the *use* against him of a defendant's compelled testimony, not the mere act of compelling him to speak (otherwise no immunity statute would be constitutional)? Doesn't the Self–Incrimination Clause by its own terms seem to prohibit the use of statements obtained in violation of its command? See Dershowitz & Ely, fn. a supra, at 1214–15; Stone, fn. b supra, at 110–111.

4. The Court went a step beyond *Harris* in *Oregon v. Hass,* 420 U.S. 714, 95 S.Ct. 1215, 43 L.Ed.2d 570 (1975). In *Hass,* after being advised of his rights, the defendant *asserted* them—he asked for a lawyer. But the police refused to honor his request and continued to question him. A 6–2 majority, per Blackmun, J., ruled that here, too, the resulting statements could be used for impeachment purposes. "One might concede," wrote the Court, "that when proper *Miranda* warnings have been given, and the officer then continues his interrogation after the suspect asks for an attorney, the officer may be said to have little to lose and perhaps something to gain by way of possibly uncovering impeachment material. This speculative possibility, however, is even greater where the warnings are defective and the defect is not known to the officers. In any event, the balance was struck in *Harris,* and we are not disposed to change it now."

But wasn't a *different* balance struck in *Hass?* Dissenting Justice Brennan, joined by Marshall, J., thought so: "Even after *Harris,* police had some incentive for following *Miranda* by warning an accused of his [rights]. If the warnings were given, the accused might still make a statement which could be used in the prosecution's case-in-chief. Under today's holding, however, once the warnings are given, police have almost no incentive for following *Miranda's* requirement that '[i]f the individual states that he wants an attorney, the interrogation must cease until an attorney is present.' If the requirement is followed there will almost surely be no statement since the attorney will advise the accused to remain silent. If, however, the requirement is disobeyed, the police may obtain a statement which can be used for impeachment if the accused has the temerity to testify in his own defense."

5. *Does the Harris–Hass exception apply even when a police officer deliberately fails to honor a suspect's request for counsel for the very purpose of obtaining evidence for impeachment purposes? Even when an officer fails to honor a suspect's request for counsel pursuant to a police department policy to violate Miranda in order to obtain evidence for impeachment purposes?* In PEOPLE v. PEEVY, 953

c. Black, J., also dissented, without opin-   ion.

P.2d 1212 (1998), the California Supreme Court, per GEORGE, J., answered the first question in the affirmative. However, it did not reach the second question because the issue had not been timely raised below. As for the first question, the court rejected the defendant's argument that the *Harris-Hass* rule was based upon the assumption that a *purposeful or deliberate* violation of *Miranda* and *Edwards* would not occur:

"Language in *Hass* and subsequent cases [demonstrates the U.S. Supreme Court's belief] that the *Harris* rule sufficiently deters individual police misconduct, *whether the misconduct occurred as the result of negligence or design*. In *Hass*, there is some indication that the violation of the suspect's rights was deliberate. [In] *Michigan v. Harvey* [p. 821], it is even more apparent that the interrogating police officer's failure to honor the defendant's Sixth Amendment right to counsel was deliberate.

"[Moreover,] it would be anomalous to hold that the applicability of the *Harris* rule depends upon the subjective intent of the interrogating police officer, when other applications of the *Miranda* rule generally do not turn upon the individual officer's state of mind, but rather upon the accused's perception of his or her circumstances. [Evidence] of deliberation on the part of the police and—as apparent in this case—of a purpose to violate the suspect's rights in order to secure evidence [may] call into question the accuracy of the high court's conclusion in *Harris* that police misconduct will be deterred adequately by excluding improperly obtained evidence from the prosecution's case-in-chief, but such evidence does not render the *Harris* rule inapplicable."

Although concurring Justice MOSK concurred in the result, he made clear his belief that if a statement secured in violation of a suspect's right to counsel had been obtained by a member of a law enforcement agency pursuant to that agency's policy to violate *Miranda*[a] the statement could not be used for impeachment purposes:

"Any policy of a law enforcement agency to obtain statements from criminal suspects in violation of *Miranda* would strike through the suspect's 'prophylactic' rights towards his substantive Fifth Amendment privilege against self-incrimination itself. [Moreover,] any policy of a law enforcement agency to obtain statements from criminal suspects in violation of *Miranda* would necessarily constitute proof that 'sufficient deterrence' of [police misconduct] does not, in fact, 'flow from exclusion of such statements from the prosecution's case-in-chief' [quoting from *Harris*]. It would rather present itself as an actual fact.

"[It] may indeed be true, as stated in *Michigan v. Tucker*, that '[where] official action [is] pursued in complete good faith [the] deterrence rationale loses much of its force.' But if so, it must also be true that, where official action is pursued in utter bad faith, as in accordance with the type of policy in question, the deterrence rationale retains its force without any diminution whatsoever."

6. In UNITED STATES v. HAVENS, 446 U.S. 620, 100 S.Ct. 1912, 64 L.Ed.2d 559 (1980), what had "started out in *Walder* as a narrow and reasonable exception" to the exclusionary rule took on "awesome proportions," LaFave &

---

a. Recent litigation has uncovered California training materials teaching police officers that it is permissible to continue to question suspects who have invoked their right to counsel or their right to remain silent in order to obtain statements that may be used for impeachment purposes or to discover other evidence. The police commonly refer to this technique as questioning "outside *Miranda*." See Charles D. Weisselberg, *Saving Miranda*, 84 Cornell L.Rev. 109, 132–62 (1998). For more extensive discussion of questioning "outside *Miranda*," see p. 826.

Israel, § 9.6(a) at 772. On direct examination, defendant denied being involved with his codefendant in the transportation of cocaine and on cross-examination denied being involved in sewing a pocket (in which drugs were found) into his codefendant's clothing or having in his own suitcase cloth from which the swatch was cut to make the pocket. Defendant's testimony was impeached by admitting the illegally seized cloth, but the Fifth Circuit reversed, maintaining that illegally seized evidence could be used for impeachment only if it contradicts a defendant's direct testimony. A 5–4 majority, per WHITE, J., disagreed:

"[The] policies of the exclusionary rule no more bar impeachment here than they did in *Walder, Harris,* and *Hass.* [The] incremental furthering of [the ends of the exclusionary rules] by forbidding impeachment of the defendant who testifies was deemed insufficient to permit or require that false testimony go unchallenged, with the resulting impairment of the integrity of the fact-finding goals of the criminal trial. We reaffirm this assessment of the competing interests, and hold that a defendant's statements made in response to proper cross-examination reasonably suggested by the defendant's direct examination are subject to otherwise proper impeachment by the government, albeit by evidence that has been illegally obtained."

Dissenting Justice BRENNAN, joined by Stewart, Marshall and Stevens, JJ., on this point, protested: "The identical issue was confronted in *Agnello,* which determined—contrary to the instant decision—that it was constitutionally impermissible to admit evidence obtained in violation of the Fourth Amendment to rebut a defendant's response to a matter first raised during the Government's cross-examination. [The] exclusionary rule exception established by *Harris* and *Hass* may be fairly easily cabined by defense counsel's unwillingness to forego certain areas of questioning. But [today's holding] passes control of the exception to the Government, since the prosecutor can lay the predicate for admitting otherwise suppressible evidence with his own questioning."

Justice Brennan (joined only by Marshall, J., on this point) then voiced "a more fundamental difference with the Court's holding here, which culminates the approach taken in *Harris* and *Hass*":

"[T]he Court has undertaken to strike a 'balance' between the 'policies' it finds in the Bill of Rights and the 'competing interest' in accurate trial determinations. This balancing effort is completely freewheeling. Far from applying criteria intrinsic to the Fourth and Fifth Amendments, the Court resolves succeeding cases simply by declaring that so much exclusion is enough to deter police misconduct. That hardly conforms to the disciplined analytical method described as 'legal reasoning,' through which judges endeavor to formulate or derive principles of decision that can be applied consistently and predictably.[a] [More] disturbingly, by treating Fourth and Fifth Amendment privileges as mere incentive schemes, the Court denigrates their unique status as *constitutional* protections."

7. *The Court refuses to extend the impeachment exception to defense witnesses other than the defendant.* In JAMES v. ILLINOIS, 493 U.S. 307, 110 S.Ct. 648, 107 L.Ed.2d 676 (1990), the Court halted nearly forty years of the impeachment exception's expansion. A 5–4 majority, per BRENNAN, J., refused to expand the "impeachment exception" to the exclusionary rule to permit the prosecution to impeach the testimony of *all* defense witnesses with illegally obtained evidence. According to the majority, expanding the impeachment exception to such an

---

a. Support for this criticism may be found in James Kainen, *The Impeachment Exception* *to the Exclusionary Rules: Policies, Principles and Politics,* 44 Stan.L.Rev. 1301 (1992).

extent "would not further the truthseeking value with equal force but would appreciably undermine the deterrent effect of the exclusionary rule."

The case arose as follows: A day after a murder occurred, the police took James, a suspect, into custody. He was found at his mother's beauty salon sitting under a hair dryer; when he emerged, his hair was black and curly. When the police questioned James about his prior hair color, he told them it had been reddish-brown, long, and combed straight back. When questioned later at the police station, James stated that he had his hair dyed black and curled at the beauty parlor in order to change his appearance. Because the police lacked probable cause for James' arrest, both statements regarding his hair were suppressed.

At the trial, five eye witnesses testified that the person responsible for the murder had long, "reddish" hair, worn in a slicked-back style and that they had seen James several weeks earlier, at which time he had the aforementioned hair color and style. James did not testify in his own defense. He called as a witness Jewel Henderson, a family friend. She testified that on the day of the shooting James' hair had been black. The state then impeached Henderson's testimony by reporting James' prior admissions that he had reddish hair at the time of the shooting and had dyed and curled his hair the next day in order to change his appearance. James ultimately was convicted of murder. The Illinois Supreme Court concluded, that, in order to deter "perjury by proxy," the impeachment exception ought to allow the state to impeach the testimony of defense witnesses other than the defendant himself. The U.S. Supreme Court reversed:

"Expanding the class of impeachable witnesses from the defendant alone to all defense witnesses would create different incentives affecting the behavior of both defendants and law enforcement officers. As a result, this expansion would not promote the truthseeking function to the same extent as did creation of the original exception, and yet it would significantly undermine the deterrent effect of the general exclusionary rule. Hence, we believe that this proposed expansion would frustrate rather than further the purposes underlying the exclusionary rule.

"The previously recognized exception penalizes defendants for committing perjury by allowing the prosecution to expose their perjury through impeachment using illegally obtained evidence. [But] the exception leaves defendants free to testify truthfully on their own behalf; they can offer probative and exculpatory evidence to the jury without opening the door to impeachment by carefully avoiding any statements that directly contradict the suppressed evidence. The exception thus generally discourages perjured testimony without discouraging truthful testimony.

"In contrast, expanding the impeachment exception to encompass the testimony of all defense witnesses would not have the same beneficial effects. First, the mere threat of a subsequent criminal prosecution for perjury is far more likely to deter a witness from intentionally lying on a defendant's behalf than to deter a defendant, already facing conviction for the underlying offense, from lying on his own behalf. Hence the Illinois Supreme Court's underlying premise that a defendant frustrated by our previous impeachment exception can easily find a witness to engage in 'perjury by proxy' is suspect.

"More significantly, expanding the impeachment exception to encompass the testimony of all defense witnesses likely would chill some defendants from presenting their best defense—and sometimes any defense at all—through the testimony of others. Whenever police obtained evidence illegally, defendants would have to assess prior to trial the likelihood that the evidence would be admitted to impeach the otherwise favorable testimony of any witness they call. Defendants might reasonably fear that one or more of their witnesses, in a position to offer truthful and favorable testimony, would also make some statement in sufficient tension with the tainted evidence to allow the prosecutor to introduce that evidence for impeachment. [As] a result, an expanded impeachment exception likely would chill some defendants from calling witnesses who would otherwise offer probative evidence.[6]

"This realization alters the balance of values underlying the current impeachment exception governing defendants' testimony. * * * Given the potential chill created by expanding the impeachment exception, the conceded gains to the truthseeking process from discouraging or disclosing perjured testimony would be offset to some extent by the concomitant loss of probative witness testimony. Thus, the truthseeking rationale supporting the impeachment of defendants in *Walder* and its progeny does not apply to other witnesses with equal force.

"Moreover, the proposed expansion of the current impeachment exception would significantly weaken the exclusionary rule's deterrent effect on police misconduct. This Court has characterized as a mere 'speculative possibility,' *Harris v. New York,* the likelihood that permitting prosecutors to impeach defendants with illegally obtained evidence would encourage police misconduct. Law enforcement officers will think it unlikely that the defendant will first decide to testify at trial and will also open the door inadvertently to admission of any illegally obtained evidence. Hence, the officers' incentive to acquire evidence through illegal means is quite weak.

"In contrast, expanding the impeachment exception to *all* defense witnesses would significantly enhance the expected value to the prosecution of illegally obtained evidence. First, this expansion would vastly increase the number of occasions on which such evidence could be used. Defense witnesses easily outnumber testifying defendants, both because many defendants do not testify themselves and because many if not most defendants call multiple witnesses on their behalf. Moreover, due to the chilling effect identified above, illegally obtained evidence holds even greater value to the prosecution for each individual witness than for each defendant. The prosecutor's access to impeachment evidence would not just deter perjury; it would also deter defendants from calling witnesses in the first place, thereby keeping from the jury much probative exculpatory evidence. For both of these reasons, police officers and their superiors would recognize that obtaining evidence through illegal means stacks the deck heavily in the prosecution's favor. It is thus far more than a 'speculative possibility' that police misconduct will be encouraged by permitting such use of illegally obtained evidence.

"The United States argues that this result is constitutionally acceptable because excluding illegally obtained evidence solely from the prosecution's case in chief would still provide a quantum of deterrence sufficient to protect the privacy interests underlying the exclusionary rule. We disagree. [Much] if not most of the time, police officers confront opportunities to obtain evidence illegally after they have already legally obtained (or know that they have other means of legally

---

6. * * * [The] dissent embraces the Illinois Supreme Court's suggestion that prosecutors could be allowed to impeach witnesses only when their testimony is in "direct conflict" with the illegally seized evidence. [But] the result of [an] inquiry distinguishing between "direct" and "indirect" evidentiary conflicts is far from predictable. [The] uncertainty whether a court might find a witness' testimony to pose a "direct" conflict and therefore trigger the impeachment exception likely will chill defendant's presentation of potential witnesses in many cases.

obtaining) sufficient evidence to sustain a prima facie case. In these situations, a rule requiring exclusion of illegally obtained evidence from only the government's case in chief would leave officers with little to lose and much to gain by overstepping constitutional limits on evidence gathering.[8] Narrowing the exclusionary rule in this manner, therefore, would significantly undermine the rule's ability 'to compel respect for the constitutional guaranty in the only effectively available way—by removing the incentive to disregard it.' So long as we are committed to protecting the people from the disregard of their constitutional rights during the course of criminal investigations, inadmissibility of illegally obtained evidence must remain the rule, not the exception."[a]

Dissenting Justice KENNEDY, joined by Rehnquist, C.J., and O'Connor and Scalia, JJ., maintained that the majority had given the exclusionary rule excessive protection but had afforded the truth-seeking function of the criminal trial inadequate weight:

"[The] line drawn by today's opinion grants the defense side in a criminal case broad immunity to introduce whatever false testimony it can produce from the mouth of a friendly witness. [A] more cautious course is available, one that retains Fourth Amendment protections and yet safeguards the truth-seeking function of the criminal trial.

"[The] interest in protecting the truth-seeking function of the criminal trial is every bit as strong in this case as in our earlier cases that allowed rebuttal with evidence that was inadmissible as part of the prosecution's case in chief. [To] deprive the jurors of knowledge that statements of the defendant himself revealed the witness' testimony to be false would result in a decision by triers of fact who were not just kept in the dark as to excluded evidence, but positively misled. The potential for harm to the truth-seeking process resulting from the majority's new rule in fact will be greater than if the defendant himself had testified. It is natural for jurors to be skeptical of self-serving testimony by the defendant. Testimony by a witness said to be independent has the greater potential to deceive. And if a defense witness can present false testimony with impunity, the jurors may find the rest of the prosecution's case suspect, for ineffective and artificial cross-examination will be viewed as a real weakness in the State's case. Jurors will assume that if the prosecution had any proof the statement was false, it would make the proof known. The majority does more than deprive the prosecution of evidence. The State must also suffer the introduction of false testimony and appear to bolster the falsehood by its own silence.

"The majority's fear that allowing the jury to know the whole truth will chill defendants from putting on any defense seems to me far too speculative to justify the rule here announced. No restriction on the defense results if rebuttal of testimony by witnesses other than the defendant is confined to the introduction of excludable evidence that is in direct contradiction of the testimony. [In] this context rebuttal can and should be confined to [such] situations. * * *

"[The] suggestion that the threat of a perjury prosecution will provide sufficient deterrence to prevent false testimony is not realistic. A heightened proof requirement applies in Illinois and other States, making perjury convictions

---

8. Indeed, the detectives who unlawfully detained James and elicited his incriminating statements already knew that there were several eyewitnesses to the shooting. Because the detectives likely believed that the exclusion of any statement they obtained from James probably would not have precluded the prosecution from making a prima facie case, an exclusionary rule applicable only to the prosecution's case in chief likely would have provided little deterrent effect in this case.

a. Stevens, J., who joined the opinion of the Court, also wrote a separate opinion.

difficult to sustain. Where testimony presented on behalf of a friend or family member is involved, the threat that a future jury will convict the witness may be an idle one.

"[The] majority's concerns may carry greater weight where contradicting testimony is elicited from a defense witness on cross-examination. In that situation there might be a concern that the prosecution would attempt to produce such testimony as the foundation to put excluded evidence before the jury. We have found that possibility insufficient to justify immunity for a defendant's own false testimony on cross-examination. *Havens.* As to cross-examination of other witnesses, perhaps a different rule could be justified. * * *

"It is unrealistic to say that the decision to make an illegal search turns on a precise calculation of the possibilities of rebuttal at some future trial. There is no reason to believe a police officer, unschooled in the law, will assess whether evidence already in his possession would suffice to survive a motion for acquittal following the case in chief. The officer may or may not even know the identity of the ultimate defendant.[3] He certainly will not know anything about potential defense witnesses, much less what the content of their testimony might be. What he will know for certain is that evidence from an illegal search or arrest (which may well be crucial to securing a conviction) will be lost to the case in chief.

"[Where] the jury is misled by false testimony, otherwise subject to flat contradiction by evidence illegally seized, the protection of the exclusionary rule is 'perverted into a license to use perjury by way of a defense, free from the risk of confrontation with prior inconsistent utterances.' *Havens.* The perversion is the same where the perjury is by proxy."

Notes and Questions

(a) *The "Pinocchio defense witness" (a defense witness other than the defendant who lies at trial to benefit the defendant).* Consider Note, 1990 U.Ill.L.F. 375, 473: "Although Pinocchio is deterred from lying by the threat of perjury prosecution, cases abound where defense witnesses nevertheless commit perjury. [Meanwhile, the defendant, Stromboli (in the Pinocchio story the puppeteer who caused Pinocchio to become a liar)], benefits from the lies by receiving an acquittal. To further the truthfinding function of the criminal justice system, the goal of judicial integrity, and the policy against perjury, Stromboli also must be deterred from resorting to Pinocchio's perjurious testimony. * * * If perjurious testimony is an affront to the legal system, it does not matter whether the perjury comes from the defendant's own lips or the lips of the Pinocchio defense witness."

(b) *The dissent's selective assumptions.* The *James* dissent, notes James Spira, *James v. Illinois: A Halt to the Expansion of the Impeachment Exception,* 15 So.Ill.U.L.J. 27, 51 (1990), "is willing to assume that a defense witness, unschooled and unfamiliar with the law, will be well versed in the quantum of proof necessary for a perjury conviction, but is unwilling to assume that police, who are in and out of court constantly, will not realize that the discovery of illegally

---

3. In this case, contrary to the impression conveyed by the majority, n. 8, the arresting officers knew almost nothing of the state of a future prosecution case. The officers did know there were several eyewitnesses to the shooting. But these eyewitnesses had made no identification of any suspect. The officers did not know petitioner's real name or his true appearance, but had sought him out at the beauty parlor on an anonymous tip. They could not know what physical evidence, such as the murder weapon, they might find on petitioner, or might lose, to the case in chief as a result of illegal conduct. The suggestion that the officers' calculated assessment of a future trial allowed them to ignore the exclusionary rule finds no support in the record and, in fact, is pure speculation.

obtained evidence will aid a conviction in light of an expanded impeachment exception."

(c) *Why should the impeachment of defense witnesses be restricted more severely than impeachment of defendants?* Consider James Kainen, *The Impeachment Exception to the Exclusionary Rules: Policies, Principles, and Politics,* 44 Stan.L.Rev. 1301, 1322–23 (1992):

"Although he argued that limitations on the impeachment of defense witnesses were necessary to confine the incentive to gather proof illegally to an acceptable level, Justice Kennedy was unable to explain why identical restrictions should not also be applied to the impeachment of defendants. Alternatively, if the impeachment of defendants should not be restricted, then such restrictions are similarly unnecessary to protect defense witnesses. As a result, Justice Kennedy could not demonstrate that extending the exception as he proposed would effect net gains, just as the majority could not demonstrate that its result would effect net losses when both truth-seeking and deterrence costs were tallied.

"Justice Kennedy's argument that restrictions were uniquely necessary to the impeachment of defense witnesses must have conceded that no such restrictions applied to the impeachment of defendants. [He] thus must have recognized that the *Havens* Court, by permitting impeachment of any cross-examination 'reasonably suggested' by direct testimony, effectively eliminated any requirement of a direct contradiction between the defendant's testimony and the prosecution's suppressed proof. Recognizing that the exception already permitted the impeachment of defendants' testimony with illegally obtained evidence merely in tension with that testimony, Justice Kennedy had to explain why this lenient approach should not also apply to defense witnesses. However, neither his truth-seeking nor his deterrence arguments supported more restrictive rules for impeaching defense witnesses; if anything, they argued for more leniency.

"Justice Kennedy's truth-seeking analysis contended that contradiction of defense witness testimony is particularly important because juries are more likely to believe such testimony. [If so,] witness testimony should be more readily impeached than that of defendants."

(d) *Are the impeachment exception cases based on a faulty premise?* Do *James* and other cases dealing with the impeachment exception rest on the premise that it is possible to accommodate both rules of evidence and principles of constitutional criminal procedure within a neutral framework? Is this premise sound? Are the contradictory values reflected in constitutional criminal procedure principles and evidentiary concepts susceptible to neutral accommodation? Should any analysis of the scope of the exclusionary rules be recast exclusively as an issue of constitutional procedure, rather than as a compromise between those rules and the rules of evidence? See Kainen, supra, at 1304–05, 1326–27, 1362–72.

B. WHAT KINDS OF CONSTITUTIONAL OR OTHER VIOLATIONS ARE ENCOMPASSED WITHIN THE IMPEACHMENT EXCEPTION?

1. *New Jersey v. Portash,* 440 U.S. 450, 99 S.Ct. 1292, 59 L.Ed.2d 501 (1979) held, per Stewart, J. that testimony given by a person in response to a grant of legislative immunity could not be used to impeach him at his subsequent trial for extortion and misconduct in office. "Central to the decisions" in *Harris* and *Hass,* emphasized the Court, was the fact that the defendant made no claim that the statements were coerced. But testimony before a grand jury in response to a grant of use immunity "is the essence of coerced testimony." Balancing of interests was

thought to be necessary in *Harris* and *Hass* "when the attempt to deter unlawful police conduct collided with the need to prevent perjury. Here, by contrast, we deal with the constitutional privilege against compulsory self-incrimination in its most pristine form. Balancing, therefore, is not simply unnecessary. It is impermissible."

2. In *Mincey v. Arizona* (1978), p. 456, the Court also distinguished *Harris* and *Hass* and made clear that the use of an "involuntary" or "coerced" statement even for impeachment purposes would constitute "a denial of due process of law." But the Court's discussion seemed to overlook the possibility that an "involuntary" statement may be trustworthy in a particular case.

3. *Use of statements obtained in violation of the Sixth Amendment Jackson rule.* In MICHIGAN v. HARVEY, 494 U.S. 344, 110 S.Ct. 1176, 108 L.Ed.2d 293 (1990), a 5–4 majority, per REHNQUIST, C.J., held that statements obtained in violation of the rule established in *Michigan v. Jackson,* may be used to impeach a defendant's false or inconsistent testimony:

"*Michigan v. Jackson* is based on the Sixth Amendment, but its roots lie in this Court's decisions in *Miranda* and succeeding cases. [*Edwards*] added a second layer of protection [to] *Miranda,* [establishing a] prophylactic rule designed to prevent police from badgering a defendant into waiving his previously asserted *Miranda* rights.

"*Jackson* simply superimposed the Fifth Amendment analysis of *Edwards* onto the Sixth Amendment. Reasoning that 'the Sixth Amendment right to counsel at a postarraignment interrogation requires at least as much protection as the Fifth Amendment right to counsel at any custodial interrogation,' [the *Jackson* Court] concluded that the *Edwards* protections should apply when a suspect charged with a crime requests counsel outside the context of interrogation. This rule, like *Edwards,* is based on the supposition that suspects who assert their right to counsel are unlikely to waive that right voluntarily in subsequent interrogations.

"We have already decided [that] statements taken in violation [of] the prophylactic *Miranda* rules [are] admissible to impeach conflicting testimony by the defendant. *Harris v. New York; Oregon v. Hass.* [There] is no reason for a different result in a *Jackson* case, where the prophylactic rule is designed to ensure voluntary, knowing, and intelligent waivers of the Sixth Amendment right to counsel rather than the Fifth Amendment privilege against self-incrimination or 'right to counsel.' [We] have never prevented use by the prosecution of relevant voluntary statements by a defendant, particularly when the violations alleged by a defendant relate only to procedural safeguards that are 'not themselves rights protected by the Constitution.' [In] such cases, we have decided that the 'search for truth in a criminal case' outweighs the 'speculative possibility' that exclusion of evidence might deter future violations of rules not compelled directly by the Constitution in the first place. *Hass.* [The *Hass* case] was decided 15 years ago, and no new information has come to our attention which should lead us to think otherwise now."

Dissenting Justice STEVENS (author of the Court's opinion in *Jackson*), joined by Brennan, Marshall and Blackmun, JJ., maintained that the Court had made it clear that "the constitutional rule recognized in *Jackson* is based on the Sixth Amendment interest in preserving 'the integrity of an accused's choice to communicate with police only through counsel,'" and that "the Court should acknowledge as much and hold that the Sixth Amendment is violated when the fruits of the State's impermissible encounter with the represented defendant are used for impeachment just as it is when the fruits are used in the prosecutor's case in chief ":

"[Unlike the situation when evidence is seized in violation of the Fourth Amendment or a statement is obtained in violation of *Miranda,* the] exclusion of statements made by a represented and indicted defendant outside the presence of counsel follows not as a remedy for a violation that has preceded trial but as a necessary incident of the constitutional right itself.[7] '[T]he Sixth Amendment right to counsel exists, and is needed, in order to protect the fundamental right to a fair trial.' It is not implicated, as a general matter, in the absence of some effect of the challenged conduct on the trial process itself. It is thus the use of the evidence for trial, not the method of its collection prior to trial, that is the gravamen of the Sixth Amendment claim."

4. *Use of statements obtained in violation of the Massiah right to counsel.* In *Harvey* the Court left open the question whether statements obtained in violation of *Massiah*—sometimes called the "core" Sixth Amendment protection, other times called the "pure" right to counsel—may be used to impeach a defendant. When the Court does address the issue, how should it decide it? How significant is it that unlike the *Jackson* rule, which the Court characterized as "prophylactic" in nature because based on *Edwards v. Arizona,* the *Massiah* doctrine is a constitutional rule (or is it)? How significant is it that the great bulk of statements obtained in violation of *Massiah* are voluntary statements? How significant is it that in *Patterson v. Illinois* (p. 629), the Court rejected the view that the *Massiah* right is "superior" to or "greater" than the *Miranda* right?

C. USE OF DEFENDANT'S PRIOR SILENCE FOR IMPEACHMENT PURPOSES

1. After being arrested for selling marijuana to an informant, defendants were given the *Miranda* warnings and chose to remain silent. At trial, each defendant claimed that he had been "framed" by narcotics agents. In an effort to undercut their testimony, the prosecution was allowed to ask each defendant why he had not told this story to the arresting officer. In *Doyle v. Ohio,* 426 U.S. 610, 96 S.Ct. 2240, 49 L.Ed.2d 91 (1976), a 6–3 majority, per Powell, J., held such use of a defendant's post-arrest silence, after receiving the *Miranda* warnings, impermissible. Not only is "every post-arrest silence * * * insolubly ambiguous because of what the State is required to advise the person arrested," but use of the silence to impeach would be "fundamentally unfair" given the fact that the *Miranda* warnings contain the "implicit" "assurance" that "silence will carry no penalty."[a] But *Doyle* has been distinguished in three subsequent impeachment cases.

---

7. As Professor Schulhofer has commented:

"[T]he *Massiah* 'exclusionary rule' is not merely a prophylactic device; it is not designed to reduce the *risk* of actual constitutional violations and is not intended to deter any pretrial behavior whatsoever. Rather, *Massiah* explicitly permits government efforts to obtain information from an indicted suspect, so long as that information is not used 'as evidence against *him* at his trial.' The failure to exclude evidence, therefore, cannot be considered *collateral* to some more fundamental violation. Instead, it is the admission at trial that in itself denies the constitutional right." Stephen Schulhofer, *Confessions and the Court,* 79 Mich.L.Rev. 865, 889 (1981). * * *

a. But cf. *South Dakota v. Neville* (1983) (also discussed at p. 521, fn. a), upholding a statute permitting a person suspected of driving while intoxicated to refuse to submit to a blood-alcohol test, but authorizing revocation of the driver's license of a person so refusing the test and also allowing such refusal to be used against him at trial. Although the defendant in *Neville* had not been told of the latter possibility, the Court thought it "unrealistic to say that the warnings given here implicitly assure a suspect that no consequences other than those mentioned will occur. Importantly, the warning that he could lose his driver's license made it clear that refusing the test was

2. *What constitutes "the use" of post-warnings silence for impeachment purposes?* Consider *Greer v. Miller*, 483 U.S. 756, 107 S.Ct. 3102, 97 L.Ed.2d 618 (1987), which arose as follows: At his trial for kidnapping and murder, respondent (who had received *Miranda* warnings at the time of his arrest and remained silent at the time) testified on direct examination that he had taken no part in the crimes, but that his co-defendants had subsequently sought his advice. On cross-examination, the prosecutor asked: "Why didn't you tell that story to anybody when you got arrested?"

The judge immediately sustained respondent's objection and instructed the jury to ignore the question. The prosecutor did not pursue the issue further, nor mention it during closing argument. After his conviction, respondent obtained federal habeas corpus relief in the Court of Appeals on the ground that the prosecutor's question had violated his right to a fair trial and that the error was not harmless beyond a reasonable doubt.

The Supreme Court, per Powell, J., reversed, concluding that under the circumstances no *Doyle* violation had occurred because "the trial court in this case did not permit the inquiry that *Doyle* forbids." The state supreme court, noted the Court, found the prosecutor's question harmless beyond a reasonable doubt. "We thus are convinced that it would find no due process violation under the facts of this case. [The] sequence of events * * * clearly indicates that the prosecutor's improper question did not violate [respondent's] due process rights."[b]

Dissenting Justice Brennan, joined by Marshall and Blackmun, JJ., charged that "today's decision saps *Doyle* of much of its vitality" and that the Court had reached its conclusion "only by confusing the question whether a *Doyle* violation occurred with the question whether that violation was harmless beyond a reasonable doubt."

3. *Impeachment by prior inconsistent statements after receiving Miranda warnings.* After being arrested while driving a stolen car and given the *Miranda* warnings, defendant agreed to talk to the police. But he gave a different version of the auto theft than he subsequently did when he testified in his own defense. On cross-examination, he was asked why he gave a different story at the time of his arrest. *Anderson v. Charles,* 447 U.S. 404, 100 S.Ct. 2180, 65 L.Ed.2d 222 (1980) (per curiam), had little difficulty in permitting such cross-examination: "[*Doyle*] does not apply to cross-examination that merely inquires into prior inconsistent statements. Such questioning makes no unfair use of silence, because a defendant who voluntarily speaks after receiving *Miranda* warnings has not been induced to remain silent."

4. *Use of defendant's prearrest silence for impeachment purposes.* In *Jenkins v. Anderson,* 447 U.S. 231, 100 S.Ct. 2124, 65 L.Ed.2d 86 (1980), where at his murder trial petitioner claimed self-defense, the prosecutor was allowed to question him about the fact that he had not surrendered to the authorities until two weeks after the killing. In closing argument, the prosecutor again referred to petitioner's prearrest silence, noting that he had "waited" at least two weeks before "reporting" the stabbing to anyone, suggesting that he would have spoken out if he had truly killed in self-defense. The Court, per Powell, J., held (1),

---

not a 'safe harbor' free of adverse consequences."

b. Concurring Justice Stevens would have overturned the conviction if the case were on direct appeal, for in such a procedural setting "a *Doyle* error should give rise to reversal of the conviction unless the State can prove that the error was harmless beyond a reasonable doubt." He concurred in the judgment, however, because he believed that a different standard in reviewing *Doyle* errors applied in a habeas corpus action. For more on Justice Stevens' approach, see Ch. 28, § 2.

relying heavily on *Raffel v. United States,* 271 U.S. 494, 46 S.Ct. 566, 70 L.Ed. 1054 (1926), that the Self–Incrimination Clause is not violated by the use of prearrest silence to impeach a defendant's credibility;[a] and (2) *Doyle* presents no obstacle for "no governmental action induced petitioner to remain silent before arrest. The failure to speak occurred before petitioner was taken into custody and given *Miranda* warnings."[b]

Dissenting Justice Marshall, joined by Brennan, J., contended that the Court's holding "has three patent—and in my view, fatal—defects": (1) Considering the various possible explanations for silence (e.g., Jenkins' story would have implicated him in the homicide), "the mere fact of prearrest silence is so unlikely to be probative of the falsity of the defendant's trial strategy that its use for impeachment is contrary to [due process]." (2) "[T]he drawing of an adverse inference from the failure to volunteer incriminating statements impermissibly infringes the privilege against self-incrimination." (3) "[T]he availability of the inference for impeachment purposes impermissibly burdens the decision to exercise the constitutional right to testify in one's own defense."

5. *Use of defendant's post-arrest silence for impeachment purposes.* When arrested, Weir, a murder suspect, said nothing, but the "significant difference" between this case and *Doyle* is that Weir did not receive any *Miranda* warnings during the period in which remained silent immediately after his arrest. When Weir testified at his trial that he had acted in self-defense, the prosecutor cross-examined him as to why, when arrested, he had not offered this exculpatory explanation. *Fletcher v. Weir,* 455 U.S. 603, 102 S.Ct. 1309, 71 L.Ed.2d 490 (1982) (per curiam), held that "in the absence of the sort of affirmative assurances embodied in the *Miranda* warnings" a state may permit cross-examination about post-arrest silence when a defendant chooses to take the stand. The Court rejected the argument that an arrest, by itself, is "governmental action which implicitly induces a defendant to remain silent," deeming such "broadening of *Doyle* * * * unsupported by the reasoning of that case and contrary to our post-*Doyle* decisions."

Notes and Questions

(a) Suppose, when arrested, Weir had said, "I believe I have a perfectly valid defense, but I don't think I should talk to you until I first have a chance to talk to my lawyer." Could that statement and/or the subsequent post-arrest silence be used for impeachment purposes?

(b) Suppose, when being driven to the station house, a suspect asks the arresting officer, "Do I have a right to remain silent?" Or, "Do I have a right to discuss my situation with a lawyer before saying anything about it to a police officer?" How should the officer respond?

(c) Suppose, when being driven to the station house, a suspect asks the arresting officer whether he has a right to remain silent or whether his silence can be used against him at the trial and the officer meets such questions with a stony

---

a. For strong criticism of this portion of the opinion, see Stephen A. Saltzburg, *Foreword: The Flow and Ebb of Constitutional Criminal Procedure in the Warren and Burger Courts,* 69 Geo. L.J. 151, 204–05 (1980).

b. But see Craig M. Bradley, *Havens, Jenkins, and Salvucci, and the Defendant's "Right" to Testify,* 18 Am.Crim.L.Rev. 419, 434–35 (1981), maintaining that the silence in *Jenkins* was just as equivocal as that in *Doyle*

for "an individual's reluctance to hand himself over to the police and admit a stabbing, in self-defense or otherwise," is not probative of guilt. "Anyone who believes that volunteering information to police is 'natural' for a resident of Detroit's inner-city has an unusually optimistic view of human nature." See also Note, 94 Harv.L.Rev. 77, 84–85 (1980).

silence? What result if the suspect then says nothing during the rest of the drive? What result if the suspect then starts talking and makes incriminating statements?

D. USE OF POST-MIRANDA WARNINGS SILENCE OR ASSERTION OF RIGHTS TO REBUT DEFENSE OF INSANITY

May a defendant's post-Miranda warnings silence or request for counsel be offered not to impeach but as substantive evidence to rebut defendant's defense of insanity at the time of the offense? No, answers Wainwright v. Greenfield, 474 U.S. 284, 106 S.Ct. 634, 88 L.Ed.2d 623 (1986). On three occasions shortly after his arrest in Florida for sexual battery, Greenfield was given the Miranda warnings. Each time he exercised his right to remain silent and stated that he wished to speak with an attorney before answering any questions. Greenfield later pled guilty by reason of insanity. At his trial two police officers described the occasions on which Greenfield had exercised his right to remain silent and had expressed a desire to consult with counsel. In his closing argument, the prosecutor reviewed this police testimony and suggested that Greenfield's responses to the warnings demonstrated a degree of comprehension inconsistent with his claim of insanity. Greenfield was convicted and sentenced to life imprisonment. The Court, per Stevens, J., overturned his conviction, holding that Doyle applied to his case:

"The point of [Doyle] is that it is fundamentally unfair to promise an arrested person that his silence will not be used against him and thereafter to breach that promise by using the silence to impeach his trial testimony. It is equally unfair to breach that promise by using silence to overcome a defendant's plea of insanity. In both situations [the State] implicitly promises that any exercise of these rights will not be penalized."[a]

E. HOW MUCH LEEWAY DO THE "IMPEACHMENT" CASES AND "FRUIT OF THE POISONOUS TREE" CASES GIVE A "BAD MAN OF THE LAW"?

"Ten years ago, Albert Alschuler hypothesized about the advice that 'Justice Holmes' "bad man of the law"' might offer in a [police] training manual.[134] Alschuler thought that a bad officer, one who cared only about the material consequences of and not the reason for his conduct, might author a manual advising police to continue to interrogate a suspect who asked for counsel or wished to remain silent. Alschuler's writing proved prescient. In deciding [such cases as *Harris, Hass, Tucker* and *Elstad*] the Court could not have intended to give police grounds to disobey this portion of *Miranda* deliberately, but this disregard is the natural consequence of these decisions. [These cases] provide an unfortunate opening for the quintessential 'bad man of the law.' "

—Charles D. Weisselberg, *Saving Miranda* 84 Cornell L.Rev. 109, 132 (1998).

a. Rehnquist, J., joined by the Chief Justice, concurred in the result because one of the prosecutor's remarks was "an improper comment on respondent's silence." But he maintained that "a request for a lawyer may be highly relevant where the plea is based on insanity"—"there is no 'insoluble ambiguity' in the request; it is a perfectly straightforward statement tending to show that an individual is able to understand his rights and is not incoherent or obviously confused or unbalanced"—and he did not read the warnings "as containing any promise, express or implied, that the words used in responding to notice of the right to a lawyer will not be used by the State to rebut a claim of insanity."

134. Albert W. Alschuler, *Failed Pragmatism: Reflections on the Burger Court*, 100 Harv.L.Rev. 1436, 1442 (1987) (quoting O. W. Holmes, *The Path of the Law*, 10 Harv.L.Rev. 457, 459 (1897).

Pointing to police training materials uncovered in the course of litigation seeking to stop officers in two California police departments from questioning custodial suspects after they have asserted their *Miranda* rights, Professor Weisselberg, supra, reports that "[in] California and, to a certain extent in other states, police have developed the tactics of questioning 'outside *Miranda*,' meaning questioning over the direct and unambiguous assertion of Fifth Amendment rights." Set forth below are extracts from the remarks of Devallis Rutledge in a California police training videotape. Mr. Rutledge is an Orange County Deputy District Attorney and a member of the California Commission on Peace Officer Standards and Training. The full transcript of the videotape is reprinted in the Appendix to Weisselberg's article.

CALIFORNIA POLICE TRAINING VIDEOTAPE–QUESTIONING "OUTSIDE *MIRANDA*" (1990)

This has to do with questioning "outside *Miranda*." * * *

What if you've got a guy [in custody] that you've only got one shot at? This is it, it's now or never because you're gonna lose him—he's gonna bail out or a lawyer's on the way down there, or you're gonna have to take him over to some other officials—you're never gonna have another chance at this guy, this is it. And you Mirandize him and he invokes [his rights]. What you can do—legally do—in that instance in go "outside *Miranda*" and continue to talk to him because you've got other legitimate purposes in talking to him other than obtaining an admission of guilt that can be used in his trial. And that's what *Miranda* protects him against—you compelling him to make a statement that is later used in trial to convict him of the charge.

But you may want to go "outside *Miranda*" and get information to help you clear cases. [Or,] maybe it will help you recover a dead body or missing person. * * * You may be able to recover stolen property. He tells you where the property is ditched, his statement will not be admissible against him in trial if you go "outside *Miranda*," but you'll get the property back and the owner will get the property back. That's a legitimate function. Maybe his statement "outside *Miranda*" will reveal methods—his methods of operation. How he was able to obtain these credit cards and how he was able to pull of his scam or whatever. * * *

Or his statements might reveal the existence and the location of physical evidence. You've got him, but you'd kinda like to have the gun that he used or the knife that he used or whatever else it was. But he ditched it somewhere and you can't find it. And so you've arrested him, he's invoked *Miranda* and you say, "Well I'd still like to find the evidence in the case." So you go "outside *Miranda*," and if he talks "outside *Miranda*"—if the only thing that was shutting him up was the chance of it being used against him in court—and then you go "outside *Miranda*" and take a statement and then he tells you where the stuff is, we can go and get all that evidence.

And it forces the defendant to commit to a statement that will prevent him from pulling out some defense and using it at trial—that he's cooked up with some defense lawyer—that wasn't true. So if you get a statement "outside *Miranda*" and he tells you that he did it and how he did it or if he gives you a denial of some sort, he's tied to that, he is married to that, because the U.S.

Supreme Court [and] the California Supreme Court [have] told us that we can use statements "outside *Miranda*" to impeach or to rebut. We can't use them for our case-in-chief. The D.A. can't trot them out to the jury before he says, "I rest," but if the defendant then gets up there and gets on the stand and lies and says something different, we can use his "outside *Miranda*" statements to impeach him. We can use it to rebut his case.

* * * The *Miranda* exclusionary rule is limited to the defendant's own statement out of his mouth. That is all that is excluded under *Miranda*. It doesn't have a fruits of the poisonous tree theory attached to it the way constitutional violations do. When you violate *Miranda*, you're not violating the Constitution. *Miranda* is not in the Constitution. It's a court-created decision that affects the admissibility of testimonial evidence and that's all it is. [There's] no law says you can't question people "outside *Miranda*." You don't violate the Constitution. The Constitution doesn't say you have to do that. It's a court decision. So all you're violating is a court decision controlling admissibility of evidence. So you're not doing anything unlawful, you're not doing anything illegal, you're not violating anybody's civil rights, you're not doing nothing improper. [When we question someone who has invoked his *Miranda* rights] [all] we lose is the statement taken in violation of *Miranda*. We do not lose physical evidence that resulted from that. We do not lose the testimony of other witnesses that we learned about only by violating his *Miranda* invocation.

––––––

Consider Weisselberg, supra, at 184–85, 188:

"If the Court's pronouncement in *Miranda* is to receive the respect of law enforcement, it needs a legitimate foundation. Until the Court restores *Miranda*'s link to the Fifth Amendment, *Miranda* cannot escape the attack and evasion of those who claim that it describes merely optional procedures. [In] addition to excluding *Miranda*-violative statements from the prosecution's case-in-chief, [the] Court must adopt a rule of exclusion that deters officers from deliberately breaching *Miranda*. * * *

"This rule of exclusion should prove relatively simple to administer. The standard is objective, not subjective. Courts have clarified *Miranda*'s parameters during the last thirty years, so that a suspect must unequivocally assert Fifth Amendment rights for protection during a custodial interrogation. Consequently, courts should not experience any difficulty determining when an officer has acted in objective good or bad faith. Thus, when a court finds a genuine dispute whether the suspect was truly in custody or whether an officer's conduct amounted to interrogation, the prosecution may use the statement for impeachment, and the court may admit its fruits. But if an officer continues to question a suspect over the unambiguous invocation of Fifth Amendment rights, the court should not admit the statement or its fruits for any purpose.

"* * * Although the Court in the past has considered it a 'speculative' possibility that officers might violate *Miranda* deliberately, the evidence now shows that many receive training to do just that. [If] the Court allows [the tactic of questioning 'outside *Miranda*' to continue], the practice signifies the end of *Miranda*, or at least the original version of *Miranda*. [When] courts are unwilling to act in the face of open and direct defiance of a principle of law, that principle cannot survive."

SECTION 4. ALLOCATION OF THE BURDENS OF PROOF

PEOPLE v. BERRIOS
270 N.E.2d 709 (N.Y.1971).

SCILEPPI, Judge.

In each of [these] appeals, the defendants have been charged with possession of heroin and arresting officers have testified that glassine envelopes containing narcotics were dropped on the ground as the defendants were approached by the police.[a] We have been called upon to decide whether, in these "dropsy" cases, or for that matter whenever a warrantless search is presented, it is the People who must bear the burden of proving the legality of the search and seizure. [In each of the cases before the court, an officer testified that as he made a movement toward the defendant—leaving his car in one case, instructing the defendant to stop in another—the defendant dropped a glassine envelope containing narcotics. The officer was undercover in one case and in uniform in another.]

Simply stated, [defendants] have contended that the police testimony in these cases is inherently untrustworthy and the product of fabrication; hence, the argument is advanced that we should require that the People bear the burden of proving admissibility and depart from our present rule which places the burden of showing inadmissibility on the defendant. No argument is proffered that this departure is required by either the State or Federal Constitutions; rather, it is asserted that the change in burden of proof is necessary to alleviate the possibility of perjured police testimony. It is noted by this court that the District Attorney of New York County has joined defense counsel in [one] case in suggesting the change in burden of proof. This concession does not, however, relieve us from the performance of our judicial function and does not require us to adopt the proposal urged upon us. [W]e are not persuaded that a change in burden of proof is indicated.

Thus far, we have made it clear that where a defendant challenges the admissibility of physical evidence or makes a motion to suppress, he bears the ultimate burden of proving that the evidence should not be used against him. Indeed the very words employed by the Legislature in fashioning the motion to suppress suggest no other rational conclusion. Section 813–c of the Code of Criminal Procedure provides that "[a] *person claiming to be aggrieved* by an

---

a. In New York, as in most jurisdictions, challenges to the admissibility of evidence on the ground that it was illegally obtained must be presented by a pretrial motion to suppress. The motion must set forth the objection with sufficient particularity, which usually requires that the defense specify the nature of the alleged illegality in the acquisition of evidence (e.g., that a statement was obtained in violation of *Miranda,* or that the search in question was incident to an arrest not supported by probable cause). See LaFave and Israel, § 10.1(b). Assuming the form of the motion is correct, the trial judge will then hold a pretrial hearing at which both sides can offer its testimony regarding the acquisition of the evidence and cross-examine the other side's witnesses.

Denial of the pretrial motion does not allow an immediate appeal by the defense, but the prosecution often can appeal the granting of the motion. See Ch. 27, § 3.

In those jurisdictions that do not require a pretrial motion, an objection may be made at trial, contemporaneously with the introduction of the evidence. An objection at this point ordinarily requires the trial court to recess the trial in order to conduct a hearing on the suppression objection. Whether a state requires a pretrial motion or a contemporaneous objection, failure to make a timely objection can result in the procedural forfeiture of the objection. See *Wainwright v. Sykes,* Ch. 28, § 2; and LaFave and Israel, § 10.2(a).

unlawful search and seizure and having reasonable grounds to believe that the property * * * *claimed to have been unlawfully obtained* may be used as evidence against him [may] move for the return [or] suppression of its use as evidence." (Emphasis supplied). Since such a person makes the claim because he contends that he is aggrieved and requests the court to give redress to an alleged wrong, it is most reasonable to require him to bear the burden of proof of that wrong. The People must, of course, always show that police conduct was reasonable. Thus, though a defendant who challenges the legality of a search and seizure has the burden of proving illegality, the People are nevertheless put to "the burden of *going forward* to show the legality of the police conduct in the first instance". *People v. Baldwin*, 250 N.E.2d 62 (N.Y.1969). These considerations require that the People show that the search was made pursuant to a valid warrant, consent, incident to a lawful arrest or, in cases such as those here, that no search at all occurred because the evidence was dropped by the defendant in the presence of the police officer.

* * * We have been told that with the advent of *Mapp v. Ohio,* there has been a great incidence of "dropsy" testimony by police officers. Hence, this court has been asked to infer that the police are systematically evading the mandate of *Mapp* by fabricating their testimony. We cannot embrace this *post hoc ergo propter hoc* reasoning for, as the then Judge Warren Burger observed in *Bush v. United States,* 375 F.2d 602, 604 (D.C.Cir.1967), "[i]t would be a dismal reflection on society to say that when the guardians of its security are called to testify in court under oath, their testimony must be viewed with suspicion." Thus, we reject this frontal attack on the integrity of our entire law enforcement system. * * * Some police officers, as well as some in other callings may be tempted to tamper with the truth. But there is no valid proof that all members of law enforcement agencies or that all other citizens who testify are perjurers. Therefore, all policemen should not be singled out as suspect as a matter of law.

The fact that some witnesses may lie does not require a change in the burden of proof for it is our view that the proposal made in this appeal is no more effective in preventing perjury than the present burden of proof. Under both the suggested change and the present system, the defendant must still refute the testimony of the police officer. Thus, even where the officer testifies that glassine envelopes were dropped by the defendant or to facts which would sustain a warrantless search, the court would still be faced with the same credibility question. Since a change in the burden of proof would be ineffective to combat the alleged evil about which the defendants herein complain, principles of *stare decisis* do not allow a departure from our present rule of burden of proof.

[Where] the Judge at the suppression hearing determines that the testimony of the police officer is unworthy of belief, he should conclude that the People have not met their burden of coming forward with sufficient evidence and grant the motion to suppress. Similarly, appellate courts by a careful exercise of their jurisdiction, in reviewing the evidence, can effectively curtail the alleged abuses.

Additionally, there are more appropriate methods of dealing with the abuses about which the defendants complain. For example, as the District Attorney of Bronx County has suggested, a possible solution to the problem of some police fabrication can be found within the several police departments of this State. They can effectively formulate internal procedures and policies within the department to eliminate any such abuses. This should at the very least take the form of training and official action to prevent fabrication. Lastly, the district attorneys of this State should evaluate the testimony of police officers, as they do the testimony of all witnesses, in determining what proof will be offered in the prosecution of a case. * * *

FULD, Chief Judge (dissenting).

[The] District Attorney of New York County informs us [that]: "For the last ten years participants in the system of justice—judges, prosecutors, defense attorneys and police officials—have privately and publicly expressed the belief that in some substantial but indeterminable percentage of dropsy cases, the testimony [that a defendant dropped narcotics or gambling slips to the ground as a police officer approached him] is tailored to meet the requirements of search-and-seizure rulings" and "it is very difficult in many [such] cases to distinguish between fact and fiction." When so able and dedicated a prosecutor as District Attorney Frank Hogan believes that there is basis for questioning the truthfulness of the testimony in a "substantial * * * percentage of dropsy cases," the conclusion seems to me inescapable [that] the integrity of the judicial process demands that there be a reallocation of the burden of proof. * * *

Underlying the Fourth and Fourteenth Amendments is the basic proposition that "no man is to be convicted on unconstitutional evidence." In light of the situation as it today exists, the present rule—which imposes upon the accused the burden of proving the illegality of a seizure on a motion to suppress—subverts this principle by making it possible for some defendants to be convicted on evidence obtained in violation of constitutional guarantees. This follows from the fact that a trial judge who is unsure whether the prosecution's account of the seizure is credible must, nevertheless, resolve his doubt in favor of the People and admit the evidence. To thus increase the likelihood of a conviction on proof of dubious constitutionality must be stamped as highly unreasonable and unfair. A change in the rule will help assure that a defendant's constitutional rights will not be violated since, by placing the burden on the People, the judge will be permitted to suppress evidence in cases where, for instance, he finds the testimony of each side evenly balanced on the scales of credibility and is unable to make up his mind as to who is telling the truth.

[It] is noteworthy that commentators and judges—in addition to the New York County District Attorney—have noted the existence of possible fabrication, and the studies which have been made, based on research into arrest files and interviews with law enforcement officials, persuasively negate the court's charge that this conclusion is based on "post hoc ergo propter hoc reasoning." Those who recognize the problem and favor a change in the burden of proof rule do not, contrary to the majority's assertion, intend an "attack on the integrity of our entire law enforcement system." Rather, their concern is solely to promote adherence to the principles articulated in *Mapp v. Ohio*.

[In] point of fact, the suggested modification of the rule is not without support in the decisions. Thus, Federal courts and the courts of California hold that the prosecution should bear the burden of justifying a warrantless seizure of evidence. And, indeed, our court has already engrafted one exception on the present rule; "[w]hen a search and seizure is based upon consent," we declared, "the burden of proof rests heavily upon the People to establish the voluntariness of that waiver of a constitutional right." *People v. Whitehurst;* see, to same effect, *Bumper v. North Carolina* [p. 350].

In short, reason and the imperative of judicial integrity, as well as substantial authority, dictate that the burden of proving the lawfulness of a search or seizure should be cast on the People in all narcotics and gambling cases when the search or seizure has been effected without a warrant. To do less, to shift the burden of proof to the People only in the classic dropsy situation, seems to me, as it does to the New York County District Attorney, "unrealistic." This is so, as he observes, not only because an "untruthful officer fearing rejection of tailored dropsy testimony could easily shift to the other scenarios which are familiar in narcotics and gambling cases in the lower courts" but also because "it is the experience of many prosecutors and judges that the problems of credibility and fact-finding raised [are] not limited to literal dropsy cases [but] appear in all types of possessory narcotics and gambling cases."

BURKE, JASEN and GIBSON, JJ., concur with SCILEPPI, J. FULD, C.J., dissents and votes to reverse in a separate opinion in which BERGAN and BREITEL, JJ., concur.

Notes and Questions

1. *How common is police "falsification"*? As pointed out in Gabriel J. Chin & Scott C. Wells, *"The Blue Wall of Silence" As Evidence of Bias and Motive to Lie: A New Approach to Police Perjury*, 59 U.Pitt.L.Rev. 233, 234 (1998), in 1994 the Mollen Commission, established to investigate police misconduct in New York, "reported that police 'falsification'—which includes 'testimonial perjury, * * * documentary perjury, [and] falsification of police records'—is one of the most common forms of police corruption facing the nation's criminal justice system. In fact, the Mollen Commission indicated that in New York, 'the practice of police falsification [is] so common in certain precincts that it has spawned its own word: "testilying." ' " See also Morgan Cloud, *Judges, "Testilying," and the Constitution*, 69 S.Cal.L.Rev. 1341 (1996); Donald A. Dripps, *Police, Plus Perjury, Equals Polygraphy*, 86 J.Crim.L. & C. 693 (1996); Christopher Slobogin, *Testilying: Police Perjury and What to Do About It*, 67 U.Colo.L.Rev. 1037 (1996).

2. *Was there police perjury in the O.J. Simpson case*? Detective Mark Fuhrman tried to defend the warrantless search of Simpson's residential property shortly after the murder of his former wife by testifying that at the time of the search the police did not know "if we have a murder-suicide, a kidnapping, another victim" and "we had to find out if there's anybody in the residence that's injured, to save their life, to save other people's lives." Despite the incredulous public response to the claim, two judges denied Simpson's suppression motions. For a discussion of why the police testimony about the purpose of the search of Simpson's residence "raised the specter of perjury designed to shield the fruits of an illegal search," see Morgan Cloud, supra, at 1357–61.

3. *State variations*. Aside from the justification of a search on the basis of consent—where the burden universally is placed on the prosecution—states vary considerably in the allocation of both the burden of going forward and the ultimate burden of proof (the burden of persuasion) on Fourth Amendment claims. Ignoring minor variations, the state's position on these burdens usually will fall within one of four general categories:

(a) Under the New York approach, as noted in *Berrios,* the prosecution has the burden of going forward—i.e., introducing evidence that, if accepted, would establish the legality of the search. Thus, in a case involving a search incident to arrest, the prosecution would initially introduce the testimony of an officer showing that probable cause for the arrest existed and that the search was within the scope permitted incident to an arrest. The burden of persuasion would then be on the defendant to rebut this evidence and prove that the search was invalid.

(b) Several states place *both* burdens of proof on the defendant. This position has been justified on several grounds: "(a) the burden should be upon the moving party, (b) there is a presumption of regularity attending the actions of law enforcement officials, (c) relevant evidence is generally admissible and thus exceptions must be justified by those claiming the exception, and (d) [this allocation] will deter spurious allegations wasteful of court time." LaFave, § 11.2(b) at 40.

(c) A majority of the states follow the pattern of allocation adopted in the federal courts—if the search was pursuant to a warrant, the defendant has the burden of proof, but if the police acted without a warrant, the burden is on the prosecution. The burden of going forward follows the burden of proof. Where there was a search without a warrant, the defendant must make a prima facie showing of that fact before the prosecution is put to its burdens. Very often, however, the parties will agree as to how the evidence was obtained and an allegation of seizure without a warrant will be sufficient.

As noted in LaFave, § 11.2(b) at 38–39, the federal pattern's "warrant-no-warrant dichotomy is typically explained on the ground that when the police have acted with a warrant 'an independent determination on the issue of probable cause has already been made by a magistrate, thereby giving rise to a presumption of legality,' while when they have acted without a warrant 'the evidence comprising probable cause is particularly within the knowledge and control of the arresting agencies.' Moreover, it is said that '[w]ithout such a rule there would be little reason for law enforcement agencies to bother with the formality of a warrant.' "

(d) In some jurisdictions, the prosecution has both burdens of proof on all Fourth Amendment objections. The reason commonly given as noted in LaFave, § 11.2(b) at 39, is that "the state is the party which seeks to use the evidence and thus ought to bear the burden of establishing that it was lawfully come by."

4. *Practical consequences of the allocation.* Of what practical significance is the allocation of the ultimate burden of proof on Fourth Amendment claims? Compare the views of the majority and dissent in *Berrios* on the relation of the burden of proof to judicial treatment of police testimony in "dropsy" cases. Assuming one shared the objective of the dissent, would a better solution have been a direction to the lower courts to subject such testimony to "close scrutiny," in much the same way that a jury is directed that testimony of an accomplice or paid informer should be "scrutinized and received with care"? See Comment, 60 Geo.L.J. 507, 519–20 (1971).

Comments of defense counsel suggest that the allocation of the burden of going forward, and even the specificity required in the motion to suppress, may be more significant than the allocation of the ultimate burden of proof. Thus, Anthony Amsterdam, *Trial Manual for the Defense of Criminal Cases* § 252 (5th ed.1988), notes that a basic tactical objective of the defense is to avoid first disclosing its factual theories, lest the police "conform their testimony" to evade those theories. If defendant is required to go forward with the evidence, he often must, as a practical matter, first take the stand to tell "his side of the story." Although the officers, as prospective witnesses, usually may be excluded from the courtroom while this testimony is given, the defendant still is not in as good a position to rebut their testimony as he would be if he testified last. The defense bearing the burden of production may seek to satisfy it without using the defendant's testimony by calling the officers as its own witnesses. However, this tactic may backfire if the court is unwilling to treat the officers as "adverse" witnesses subject to impeachment. Id. at § 253.

5. *Constitutional requirements*. Why was it that the defendants in *Berrios* failed to argue that the federal constitution required the prosecution to bear the burden of proof? *Bumper v. North Carolina*, p. 350, held, as a matter of constitutional law, that when a prosecutor relies upon consent "he has the burden of proving that the consent was, in fact, freely and voluntarily given." If the Fourth Amendment requires that the prosecution bear the burden on this issue, why not on others? The Supreme Court has stated in various opinions that the Fourth Amendment generally requires a search warrant, and "the burden is on those seeking [an] exemption from [that] requirement to show the need for it." See, e.g., *Chimel v. California*, p. 253. Do such statements imply that, where a search is conducted without a warrant, the prosecution must bear the burden of proving facts that justify the search under one of the recognized exceptions to the warrant requirement, or do the statements refer only to the state's burden in appellate argument of justifying any request that the Supreme Court recognize a new or expanded exception to the warrant requirement? See LaFave, § 11.2(b) (the former interpretation seems closer to the mark).

6. *Confessions*. *Miranda* clearly places the burden on the prosecution to respond to a *Miranda* objection by showing that the "defendant knowingly and intelligently waived his privilege against self-incrimination and his right to retained or appointed counsel" (p. 483). Most jurisdictions also place upon the prosecution the burdens of production and persuasion in responding to a claim that a confession was involuntary. A few states, however, place the burden of proving involuntariness on the defendant. *Lego v. Twomey*, discussed at Note 10, raises serious doubts as to the constitutionality of this practice. Though concerned primarily with the applicable standard of proof, *Lego* indicated that it was the constitutional obligation of the prosecution to meet that standard of proof.

7. *Identification testimony*. *United States v. Wade*, p. 641, indicates that, once the Sixth Amendment is shown to be applicable, the prosecution carries the burden of establishing that defendant intelligently waived his right to counsel at a lineup. But what is the proper allocation of the burden on an objection that a lineup or other identification procedure was so unfairly conducted as to violate due process? Several courts have assumed, without extensive discussion, that the defendant, as the moving party, bears the burden of establishing the due process violation. LaFave and Israel, § 10.4(d). But compare *People v. Young*, 176 N.W.2d 420 (Mich.App.1970), holding that the prosecution bears the burdens of production and persuasion whenever the identification procedure was conducted "out of the presence of defendant's attorney." Does *Young* constitute an open invitation to defense "fishing expeditions," that will be "automatically available in all lineup-cases"? See *State v. Bishop*, 183 N.W.2d 536 (Minn.1971).

8. *Entrapment*. Reconsider Note 4 at p. 413.

9. *Exclusionary rule limitations*. Once a constitutional violation is established, does the burden of proof necessarily lie with the prosecution to establish that its evidence is not the fruit of the poisonous tree? See e.g., *Wade*, p. 786 (as to proof that the in-court identification was not tainted by the unconstitutional lineup); *Nardone*, p. ___ (once illegal wiretap established, government must convince the trial court that its proof had an independent origin). Consider also *Nix v. Williams*, p. 797, as to the government's burden in establishing that the same evidence would have inevitably been discovered by lawful means.

10. *Standards of proof*. Assuming that the prosecution bears the burden of persuasion on a particular exclusionary rule objection, what standard of proof should apply? In LEGO v. TWOMEY, 404 U.S. 477, 92 S.Ct. 619, 30 L.Ed.2d 618

(1972), the Court rejected the contention that the voluntariness of a confession must be established by proof beyond a reasonable doubt and accepted a preponderance of the evidence standard. Justice WHITE's opinion for the Court reasoned that *In re Winship,* 397 U.S. 358, 90 S.Ct. 1068, 25 L.Ed.2d 368 (1970), requiring proof beyond a reasonable doubt at trial, was not controlling: "Since the purpose that a voluntariness hearing is designed to serve has nothing whatever to do with improving the reliability of jury verdicts, we cannot accept the charge that judging the admissibility of a confession by a preponderance of the evidence undermines the mandate of *In re Winship.* * * * *Winship* [only] confirm[ed] the fundamental right that protects 'the accused against conviction except upon proof beyond a reasonable doubt of every fact necessary to constitute the crime with which he is charged.' A high standard of proof is necessary, we said, to ensure against unjust convictions by giving substance to the presumption of innocence. A guilty verdict is not rendered less reliable or less consonant with *Winship* simply because the admissibility of a confession is determined by a less stringent standard."

Lego also rejected the contention that application of a reasonable doubt standard was necessary "to give adequate protection to those values that the exclusionary rules are designed to serve": "Evidence obtained in violation of the Fourth Amendment has been excluded from federal criminal trials for many years. The same is true of coerced confessions offered in either federal or state trials. [But] no substantial evidence has accumulated that federal rights have suffered from determining admissibility by a preponderance of the evidence. Petitioner offers nothing to suggest [otherwise]. Without good cause, we are unwilling to expand currently applicable exclusionary rules by erecting additional barriers to placing truthful and probative evidence before state juries and by revising the standards applicable in collateral proceedings. [The] exclusionary rules are very much aimed at deterring lawless conduct by police and prosecution and it is very doubtful that escalating the prosecution's burden of proof in Fourth and Fifth Amendment suppression hearings would be sufficiently productive in this respect to outweigh the public interest in placing probative evidence before juries for the purpose of arriving at truthful decisions about guilt or innocence."[a]

11. Is *Lego* inconsistent with the philosophy underlying *Chapman v. California* (Ch. 27, § 4)? Cf. Note, 7 Harv.C.R.-C.L.L.Rev. 651 (1972), suggesting that the reasoning that led the Lego majority to conclude that implementation of a constitutional right did not require proof beyond a reasonable doubt could just as readily have led the Court in Chapman to conclude that there was no need to require the especially stringent harmless error standard imposed there. The dissent in Lego (see fn. a supra) also argued that the majority's position there was inconsistent with "the rule that automatically reverses a conviction when an involuntary confession was admitted at trial." Cf. Stephen A. Saltzburg, Standards of Proof and Preliminary Questions of Fact, 27 Stan.L.Rev. 271 (1975), arguing that a reasonable doubt standard should have been required in Lego because, inter alia, the test of involuntariness (as opposed to other exclusionary rule standards) is designed to exclude unreliable evidence and the admission of unreliable confessions is especially dangerous because juries give such evidence great weight.

a. Powell and Rehnquist, JJ., did not participate in the *Lego* decision. Dissenting Justice Brennan, joined by Justice Douglas and Marshall, argued that "the preponderance standard does not provide sufficient protection against the danger that involuntary confessions will be employed at trial." The preponderance standard, noted the dissent, was accepted in civil cases on the assumption that it was no more serious an error to have an erroneous decision in favor of one party or another, but the same could not be said for errors relating to the admission of confessions."

12. The Supreme Court noted in Lego that, while due process was satisfied by application of the preponderance standard, the states were always "free, pursuant to their own law, to adopt a higher standard." Several states have done exactly that. See LaFave and Israel, § 10.4. On the other hand, the states uniformly have held that the standard of proof applicable to Fourth Amendment claims, except on the issue of consent, will be the preponderance standard. Id. In a jurisdiction that has adopted the reasonable doubt standard for the determination of the voluntariness of confession, why shouldn't the same standard apply to search and seizure claims? See Saltzburg, supra.

13. Waiver of Miranda rights. In COLORADO v. CONNELLY, 479 U.S. 157, 107 S.Ct. 515, 93 L.Ed.2d 473 (1986), also discussed at p. 614, the Court held that the state need only prove a waiver of Miranda rights by the preponderance of the evidence. The majority, per REHNQUIST, C.J., reasoned:

"[The state supreme court] held that the State must bear its burden of proving waiver [by] 'clear and convincing evidence.' Although we have stated in passing that the State bears a 'heavy' burden in proving waiver Miranda,[b] we have never held that the 'clear and convincing evidence' standard is the appropriate one. [In] *Lego v. Twomey,* [we] upheld a procedure in which the State established the voluntariness of a confession by no more than a preponderance of the evidence [for] two reasons. First, the voluntariness determination has nothing to do with the reliability of jury verdicts; rather, it is designed to determine the presence of police coercion. [Second,] we rejected Lego's assertion that a high burden of proof was required to serve the values protected by the exclusionary rule.

"[If,] as we held in *Lego* [a case the Court reaffirmed in *Connelly*], the voluntariness of a confession need be established only by a preponderance of the evidence, then a waiver of the auxiliary protections established in *Miranda* should require no higher burden of proof. * * *"[c]

Does *Connelly* make *Miranda* "a much less prophylactic rule and a substantially more direct application of the fifth amendment compulsion standard"? Does *Connelly* "fuse" the fifth amendment compulsion standard with *Miranda?* See Mark Berger, *Compromise and Continuity: Miranda Waivers, Confession Admissibility, and the Retention of Interrogation Protections,* 49 U.Pitt.L.Rev. 1007, 1040–41 (1988). What follows from the fact that *Miranda* establishes special prophylactic rules governing custodial police interrogation? That special procedural requirements regulating the waiver process are also called for? Or that further protections governing the waiver process are unnecessary and undesirable, because likely to interfere unduly with appropriate police questioning? See id. at 1062.

14. *The trier of fact.* The factfinder on the constitutionality of a search has traditionally been the judge, but prior to *Jackson v. Denno,* 378 U.S. 368, 84 S.Ct.

b. In dissent, Justice Brennan, joined by Marshall, J. argued that the Court's ruling ignored both "the explicit command of *Miranda*" in describing the state's burden as "heavy" and the implications of *Wade,* which specifically referred to the "clear and convincing" standard in describing the prosecution's burden of establishing that an in-court-identification was not tainted by an unconstitutional identification.

c. In dissent, Justice Brennan argued that *Lego* was distinguishable because it involved a situation in which the defendant was not in custody. The special setting of custodial interrogation, because it poses an increased danger of police overriding, justified "plac[ing] a higher burden of proof on the government in establishing a waiver of *Miranda* rights."

1774, 12 L.Ed.2d 908 (1964), many states followed one of two procedures that give factfinding responsibility to the jury in judging the voluntariness of a confession. In states following the "Massachusetts rule," the trial court initially ruled on the admissibility of the confession. If the judge found the confession involuntary, that ruling was final. However, if the judge found the confession voluntary, it was then admitted subject to the jury's independent determination of voluntariness. In states following the "New York rule," the determination of voluntariness was left primarily to the jury. The judge would make an initial determination as to whether reasonable persons could differ on the issue of voluntariness. Unless there were "no circumstances" under which the confession could be voluntary, the issue went to the jury. The jury was instructed on the voluntariness standard and told to consider the confession only if it found it to be voluntary.

Jackson overruled an 11 year old precedent and held the New York procedure unconstitutional. The crux of *Jackson*'s reasoning was subsequently summarized in *Lego:* "We concluded that the New York procedure was constitutionally defective because at no point along the way did a criminal defendant receive a clear-cut determination that the confession used against him was in fact voluntary. The trial judge was not entitled to exclude a confession merely because he himself would have found it involuntary, and, while we recognized that the jury was empowered to perform that function, we doubted it could do so reliably. Precisely because confessions of guilt, whether coerced or freely given, may be truthful and potent evidence, we did not believe a jury [could] ignore the probative value of a truthful but coerced confession; it was also likely, we thought, that in judging voluntariness itself the jury would be influenced by the reliability of a confession it considered an accurate account of the facts. * * * "

15. As the Court noted in Lego, Jackson "cast no doubt upon" the Massachusetts procedure,[d] and many states continue to use that procedure (although most follow the "orthodox" procedure of having voluntariness determined initially and finally by the judge). Why should a defendant be given a "second crack" at the voluntariness issue, before the jury, where no such opportunity is given as to Fourth Amendment or other constitutional violations?

Of course, even under the orthodox procedure, the defendant may bring to the jury's attention the circumstances surrounding the confession for the purpose of challenging its credibility. Indeed, in *Crane v. Kentucky,* 476 U.S. 683, 106 S.Ct. 2142, 90 L.Ed.2d 636 (1986), a unanimous Court held that a trial court's foreclosure of a defendant's attempt to introduce testimony about the "physical and psychological environment" in which the confession was obtained deprived defendant of his "fundamental constitutional right to a fair opportunity to present a defense." As the Court there noted, "The [*Jackson*] requirement that the [trial] court make a pretrial *voluntariness* determination does not undercut the defendant's traditional prerogative to challenge the confession's *reliability* during the course of the same trial."

16. Does it follow from *Lego* that it would be improper for a trial court to hear testimony on a constitutional challenge to the admissibility of evidence

d. In distinguishing the Massachusetts procedure, the Court stressed that the judge there "himself resolves evidentiary conflicts and gives his own answer to the coercion issue" and the jury therefore only considers those confessions the judge believes to be voluntary. The dissenters responded that the acceptance of the Massachusetts rule revealed the "hollowness" of the Court's holding. They argued that the distinction between the New York and Massachusetts rule was more theoretical than real. They suggested, in particular, that in "cases of doubt," a judge operating under the Massachusetts rule was likely to "resolve the doubt in favor of admissibility, relying on the final determination by the jury."

without first excluding the jury? Consider WATKINS v. SOWDERS, 449 U.S. 341, 101 S.Ct. 654, 66 L.Ed.2d 549 (1981). *Watkins* involved two state cases in which hearings on the admissibility of identification testimony were held in the presence of the jury. In each case, in challenging an in-court identification, the defense sought to establish that the identification was based on a pretrial identification procedure that was so suggestive as to violate due process. Over defense objection, the challenge was heard in the presence of the jury, and was rejected by the trial judge. The Supreme Court found no constitutional error. It recognized that various lower courts had emphasized the prudence of holding a suppression hearing outside the presence of the jury, but stressed that it was concerned only with whether that practice was constitutionally required. On this issue, STEWART, J., noted for the Court:

"The Court in *Jackson* did reject the usual presumption that a jury can be relied upon to determine issues according to the trial judge's instructions, [but only] because of the peculiar problems the issue of the voluntariness of a confession presents. [Where] identification evidence is at issue, however, no such special considerations [apply]. It is the reliability of identification evidence that primarily determines its admissibility. *Manson v. Brathwaite* [p. 665]. And the proper evaluation of evidence under the instructions of the trial judge is the very task our system must assume juries can perform.

"[The] petitioners argue, however, [that] the presence of the jury deterred their lawyers from cross-examining the witnesses vigorously and fully as to the possible improprieties of the pretrial identifications in these cases. [They] point to no specific instances [when] their counsel were thus deterred, and the record reveals that the cross-examination on the identity issues was, if not always effective, both active and extended. Nonetheless, the petitioners rely on a passage from *Wade* [p. 641], which referred to, 'the predicament in which Wade's counsel found himself—realizing that possible unfairness at the lineup may be the sole means of attack upon the unequivocal courtroom identification, and having to probe in the dark in an attempt to discover and reveal unfairness, while bolstering the government witness' courtroom identification by bringing out and dwelling upon his prior identification.' [But the] 'predicament' described in *Wade* was no more than part of the Court's demonstration that, if identification stemming from an improperly conducted lineup was to be excluded, a courtroom identification based on such a lineup logically had to be excluded as well. A 'predicament,' if one chooses to call it that, is always presented when a lawyer decides on cross-examination to ask a question that may produce an answer unfavorable to his client. * * * We decline [to] hold that [due process] inevitably requires the abandonment of the time-honored process of cross-examination as the device best suited to determine the trustworthiness of testimonial evidence.

"A judicial determination outside the presence of the jury of the admissibility of identification evidence may often be advisable. In some circumstances, not presented here, such a determination may be constitutionally necessary. But it does not follow that the Constitution requires a *per se* rule compelling such a procedure in every case."[e]

e. The dissenting justices (Brennan, J., joined by Marshall, J.) argued that "the powerful impact that such eyewitness identification evidence has on juries, regardless of its reliability, virtually mandates that, when such evidence is inadmissible, the jury should know nothing about the evidence."

Index

References are to Pages

SECRECY

SECRET AGENTS

SEIZURE OF THE PERSON